Network Administrator

NetWare® 4.1

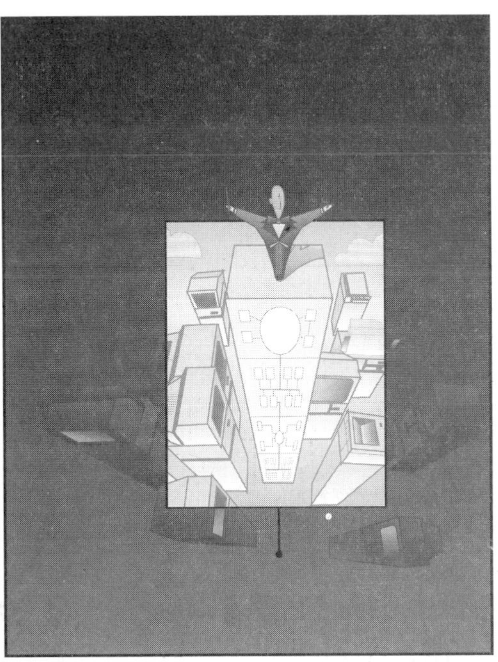

Ted L. Simpson
David Auer
Mark Ciampa

COURSE TECHNOLOGY

ONE MAIN STREET, CAMBRIDGE, MA 02142

an International Thomson Publishing company ITP®

Cambridge • Albany • Bonn • Boston • Cincinnati • London • Madrid • Melbourne • Mexico City
New York • Paris • San Francisco • Singapore • Tokyo • Toronto • Washington

Network Administrator: NetWare 4.1 is published by Course Technology.

Managing Editor:	Wendy Welch Gordon
Product Managers:	Richard Keaveny/Susan Roche
Production Editor:	Roxanne Alexander
Marketing Manager:	Tracy Wells
Manufacturing Supervisor:	Elizabeth Martinez
Development Editor:	Marta Partington
Copy Editor:	Karen Wise
Composition House:	GEX, Inc.
Cover Designer:	Doug Goodman
Text Designer:	David Reed

© 1997 by Course Technology—I(T)P®

For more information contact:
Course Technology
One Main Street
Cambridge, MA 02142

International Thomson Editores
Campos Eliseos 385, Piso 7
Col. Polanco
11560 Mexico D.F. Mexico

International Thomson Publishing Europe
Berkshire House 168-173
High Holborn
London WCIV 7AA
England

International Thomson Publishing GmbH
Königswinterer Strasse 418
53227 Bonn
Germany

Thomas Nelson Australia
102 Dodds Street
South Melbourne, 3205
Victoria, Australia

International Thomson Publishing Asia
211 Henderson Road
#05-10 Henderson Building
Singapore 0315

Nelson Canada
1120 Birchmount Road
Scarborough, Ontario
Canada M1K 5G4

International Thomson Publishing
Hirakawacho Kyowa Building, 3F
2-2-1 Hirakawacho
Chiyoda-ku, Tokyo 102 Japan

All rights reserved. This publication is protected by federal copyright law. No part of this publication may be reproduced, stored in a retrieval system, or transmitted in any form or by any means, electronic, mechanical, photocopying, recording, or otherwise, or be used to make a derivative work (such as translation or adaptation), without prior permission in writing from Course Technology.

Trademarks

Course Technology and the open book logo are registered trademarks of Course Technology.
I(T)P® The ITP logo is a registered trademark of International Thomson Publishing, Inc.
Some of the product names and company names used in this book have been used for identification purposes only and may be trademarks or registered trademarks of their respective manufacturers and sellers.

Disclaimer

Course Technology reserves the right to revise this publication and make changes from time to time in its content without notice.

0-7600-3299-8

Printed in the United States of America

10 9 8 7 6

Related Titles in the Networking Series

Networking Concepts

Guide to Networking, Second Edition, by Alan M. Cohen

Introductory Network Management, by Richard Burke *(forthcoming)*

Advanced Networking Concepts, by Michael J. Palmer

Windows NT

Hands-On Microsoft Windows NT 4.0 Server with Projects by Michael J. Palmer

Hands-On Microsoft Windows NT 4.0 Workstation for Server and Network Administrators, by Michael J. Palmer

Microsoft Windows NT 4.0: Network Administrator, by Michael J. Palmer *(forthcoming)*

Novell

Hands-On NetWare: A Guide to Novell NetWare 3.11/3.12 with Projects, by Ted L. Simpson

NetWare 3.11/3.12: Network Administrator, by Ted L. Simpson

Hands-On NetWare: A Guide to NetWare 4.1 with Projects, by Ted L. Simpson

Local Area Networks with Novell, by H. Rene Baca, Christopher M. Zager, Margaret A. Zinky

Local Area Networking With Novell Software, 2nd, by Alvin L. Rains, Michael J. Palmer

TEXT AND GRAPHIC CONVENTIONS

Whenever appropriate, additional information and exercises have been added to this book to help students better understand what is discussed within the chapter. Students are made aware of additional material and types of exercises through the use of icons. The icons used in this text are discussed below

Located at the end of each chapter is a continuous running case project (Northwestern Technical College.)

Located at the end of each chapter are case study problems that are indicated by the Case Study icon.

Located at the end of each chapter are exercises that enable you to use NetWare commands and utilities discussed in the text. These exercises are indicated by the Hands-On icon.

The Note icon is used to present additional helpful material related to the subject being discussed.

The Factoid icon is used to present material that provides you additional insight into the development of certain concepts or commands.

The Trend icon is used to present material that provides you with material relevant to the future of the computer industry. Trends can help you to see the current and future value of the concepts and techniques you are learning.

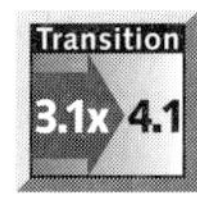

The NetWare 3.1x to NetWare 4.1 Transition icon is used to present material that describes the differences between NetWare 3.1x and NetWare 4.1. If you are familiar with NetWare 3.1x, this material can help you understand how the NetWare 3.1x technique, tool, or command is implemented in NetWare 4.1.

The NetWare 4.11 Preview icon identifies sections that describe the differences between NetWare 4.1 and NetWare 4.11.

DS STANDARD NDS MANAGER

One of main features of NetWare 4.1 is Novell Directory Services (NDS), which provides extensive network administration features for NetWare networks. To help you learn about NDS, this text includes a preview version of Cheyenne Software's DS Standard NDS Manager 3.0, a Windows-based NDS management tool shown here (DS Standard was originally created by Preferred Systems, Inc. Preferred Systems was acquired by Cheyenne Software Inc., a division of Computer Associates International Inc., and now functions as Cheyenne's Directory Management Group).

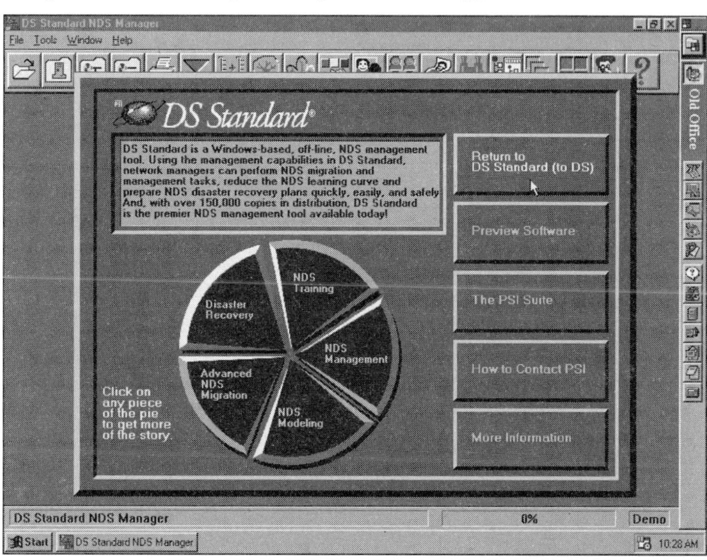

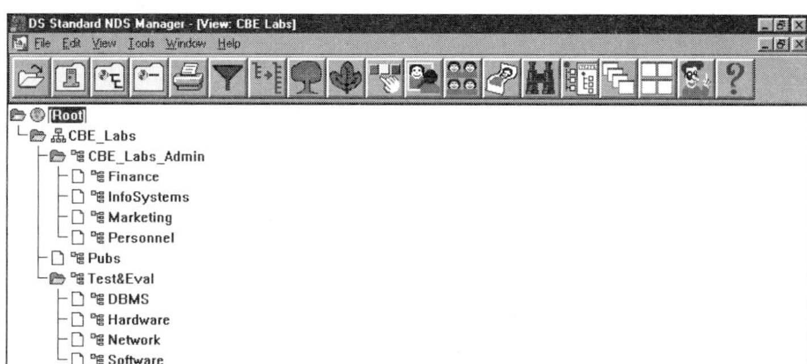

DS Standard NDS Manager is designed to be used by network administrators and network managers to help them plan, implement and manage the NDS environment. Its extensive NDS management capabilities include the following:

- Off line NDS planning and modeling without modifying the actual NDS data.
- Implements changes made in the DS Standard copy to the existing network NDS data with out interfering with the real-time operation of the network.
- Backs up network NDS data as files.
- Allows the network administrator to reuse NDS designs to develop alternate models during the NDS planning process.
- Discovers existing data on NetWare 3.1x servers which can be used for planning NetWare 4.1 conversions.

The preview edition of DS Standard NDS Manager 3.0 included in this book is a limited version of the software. It provides you with the ability to create NDS models, but does not enable you to create complete reports. A full discussion of DS Standards capabilities and the limitations of the preview version is in Chapter 4.

Supplements

All of the supplements for this text can be found in the **Instructor's Resource Kit**, which includes the following items:

Instructor's Manual

The Instructor's Manual is written by the authors and is quality-assurance tested. It includes:

- Additional instructional material to help for class preparation including suggestions for lecture topics and suggested lab activities
- Solutions to all end of chapter materials
- Transparency Masters

CD-ROM including:

Electronic Instructor's Manual

The Instructor's Manual is provided in electronic format so that the instructor can view and print sections of the manual online.

NetWare Server Setup

The NetWare Server Setup Disk is used to create the network file system directory structure needed in the exercises. The setup program also copies the contents of the Student Work Disk to the NetWare server. One of the students' first assignments is to copy the contents of the Student Work disk onto a blank disk for use in the exercises.

Student Work Disk

The Student Work Disk contains sample files and applications which will be used in the Northwestern Technical College project. Adopters of this text are granted permission to distribute these files to any student who purchases a copy of this text.

Solution Files

The solution files for end-of-chapter exercises and projects are provided.

Course Test Manager Version 1.1 Engine and Test Bank

Course Test Manager (CTM) is a cutting-edge Windows-based testing software program, developed exclusively for Course Technology, that helps instructors design and administer examinations and practice tests. This full-featured program allows students to generate practice tests randomly that provide immediate on-screen feedback and detailed study guides for questions incorrectly answered. Instructors can also use Course Test Manager to create printed and online tests. You can create, preview, and administer a test on any or all chapters of this textbook entirely over a local area network. Course Test Manager can grade the tests students take automatically at the computer and can generate statistical information on individual as well as group performance. A CTM test bank has been written to accompany your text and is included on the CD-ROM. The test bank includes multiple-choice, true/false, short answer, and essay questions.

Front Matter/3208 Page viii 3/25/97

Acknowledgments

Creating a book of this magnitude is an incredibly complex process with many people involved in the writing, editing, and production of the final product. This book, together with its predecessor, NetWare 3.11/3.12: Network Administrator, has required many, many hours of research, discussion, coordination and writing. Although the following is only a partial list of those who have contributed to this book, the authors wish to thank Wendy Welch Gordon for her support and encouragement, Richard Keaveny, Susan Roche, and Marta Partington for their editorial direction and contributions, our reviewers, Behrouz Forouzan (De Anza College), Melvin Heide (Western Washington University), Joyce Koerfer (College of DuPage), David Bass (Volunteer State Community College), and Nathan Hubbard. Doug Goodman for his contributions to the cover design, Roxanne Alexander, Karen Wise, Chris Smith, Natalie Bergeron, and Seth Andrews for their contributions to the production of this book, Greg Bigelow for his expert testing and validation of the contents of this book, and Angel Thibeault and everyone else at GEX who contributed to the composition of this book.

Ted Simpson would like to thank his wife Mary whose loving and patient help enabled him to complete this project. In addition, any success this book achieves is ultimately due to his parents, William and Rosemarie, who have made many sacrifices to provide a stable and motivating environment for learning and growing. He would also like to acknowledge Jan Brill, Bert Richard, Tom Lemler, and Lois Eichman at Wisconsin Indianhead Technical College for maintaining our school as a leader in the area of Novell Education. He is proud to have been a part of the development team and has really enjoyed the opportunity to work with authors like David and Mark who have worked so hard to upgrade this book to NetWare 4.1.

David Auer would like to acknowledge and thank his wife Donna Auer for her unfailing support and encouragement. He would also like to thank the College of Business and Economics at Western Washington University (the real CBE) for its support of this project, especially Dean Dennis Murphy.

Mark Ciampa would like to acknowledge and thank the Administration and Staff at Volunteer State Community College for their support in this project, especially Dr. Charles Lea, Vice President of Academic Affairs. A special round of applause goes to the people in Academic Computing—Roger, David, Clarence, Sharon, and Bob—for their assistance. And as always, Mark especially thanks his family, Brian, Grogory, and Susan, for without their encouragement, patience, and love, he never would have completed a single chapter.

TABLE OF CONTENTS

Network Administrator: NetWare 4.1

READ THIS BEFORE YOU BEGIN

To The Student

To use this book, you must have two data disks: a Student Work Disk for use with the NetWare 4.1 network, and a DS Standard Data Disk for use with the DS Standard NDS Manager software included with this book. See the inside front or back cover for instructions on how to obtain copies of these disks. Many of the hands-on exercises in the text require access to a NetWare 4.1 network, and in order to do them your workstation will need to be connected to a NetWare 4.1 network. Your instructor will provide you with a valid login name for your network. The DS Standard NDS Manager does not need to be connected to a network, and you may install the software on your own PC. Your instructor will provide you with DS Standard installation instructions.

To The Instructor

Setting Up the NetWare 4.1 Network. Many of the hands-on exercises in the text require access to a NetWare 4.1 network, and in order for your students to do them they will need access to a classroom NetWare 4.1 network with at least one NetWare 4.1 server. Providing student access to the network involves creating user accounts, an NDS Directory tree structure and a network file system structure that includes sample files. To help you set up your NetWare 4.1 network, Course Technology has provided a special NetWare 4.1 Network Setup located on the Instructor's Resource Kit CD-ROM. See the inside front or back cover for instructions on how to obtain a copy of this CD-ROM and alternate means of obtaining the needed files. Follow the instructions on the provided README file. Complete NetWare 4.1 network setup instructions are also included in your Instructor's Manual.

Setting Up the DS Standard NDS Manager. Many of the exercises in the text use the DS Standard NDS Manager to provide off-line NDS modeling capabilities. In order for your students to do these exercises, they will need access to a copy of DS Standard installed either in your classroom or on their own PC. To help you set up DS Standard, Course Technology has provided installation instructions on the Instructor's Resource Kit CD-ROM. See the inside front or back cover for instructions on how to obtain a copy of this CD-ROM and alternate means of obtaining the needed files. Follow the instructions on the provided DSREADME file. Complete DS Standard installation instructions are also included in your Instructor's Manual.

System Requirements

The minimum requirements for each network lab computer depend on whether Windows 3.1x or Windows 95 is being used on the computer. This text uses Windows 95 in discussions of network workstations, but the exercises can also be done on workstations running Windows 3.1x.

Windows 3.1x workstations require:

- a 386 processor (a 486 DX2/66 or higher is recommended for best performance)
- a 3.5 inch 1.44 MB floppy drive
- a mouse
- a VGA or higher monitor (SVGA at 800 × 600, 72 MHz or higher vertical refresh is recommended)
- 8 MB of RAM, 16 MB recommended
- a minimum of 55 MB of hard disk space for a full installation of DS Standard
- DOS 5.0 or higher (DOS 6.22 recommended)
- that the following command is included in the CONFIG.SYS file: FILES = 40 (NOTE: 40 is a minimum)
- NetWare client software (Novell's NetWare Client 32 is recommended, but the NetWare DOS Requester (VLMs) may also be used. DS Standard requires NetWare DLL files, and instructions about these files are in the DSREADME file.)

Windows 95 workstations require:

- a 486 DX 33 processor (a Pentium 75 or higher is recommended for best performance)
- a 3.5 inch 1.44 MB floppy drive
- a mouse
- a VGA or higher monitor (SVGA at 800 × 600, 72 MHz or higher vertical refresh is recommended)
- 16 MB of RAM is strongly recommended
- a minimum of 55 MB of hard disk space for a full installation of DS Standard
- that the following command is included in the CONFIG.SYS file: FILES = 40 (NOTE: 40 is a minimum)
- NetWare client software (Novell's NetWare Client 32 is strongly recommended, but the NetWare DOS Requester (VLMs) may also be used. DS Standard requires NetWare DLL files, and instructions about these files are in the DSREADME file.)

NetWare 4.1 servers require:

- a 486 processor (a 486 DX/2 66 or higher is recommended for best performance)
- a VGA or higher monitor
- RAM requirements vary depending upon the size of the hard drive(s) used (16 MB is the minimum)
- a minimum of 100 MB on the SYS volume for NetWare files, sample files and print queues
- at least 5 MB free for each student's directories and files

C H A P T E R   O N E

NETWORKING BASICS

The decade of the 1980s brought about a major change in the way data was processed in organizations. Traditional centralized data processing on minicomputers and mainframe computers gave way to decentralized or distributed personalized applications and productivity tools running on desktop and notebook-sized microcomputers. Along with the rapid development of microcomputer hardware and application software, the ability to connect these devices and applications for communications and resource sharing has developed. This rapid pace of development continues today, as the Internet ties local systems into a global network. In this chapter you will learn about the advantages of computer networks and how to select the appropriate network type for a given situation. You will learn how the NetWare network operating system can be used to meet the requirements and challenges of integrating microcomputers into a network that can facilitate communications, share resources, and exchange data. You will also examine the role that you will play as a network administrator and learn about the Certified Novell Administrator (CNA) program.

AFTER READING THIS CHAPTER AND COMPLETING THE EXERCISES YOU WILL BE ABLE TO:

- EXPLAIN THE ADVANTAGES OF A LOCAL AREA NETWORK.
- IDENTIFY AND DESCRIBE THE HARDWARE AND SOFTWARE COMPONENTS THAT MAKE UP A LOCAL AREA NETWORK.
- DEVELOP A RECOMMENDATION FOR THE IMPLEMENTATION OF A LOCAL AREA NETWORK SYSTEM.
- DESCRIBE THE RESPONSIBILITIES OF A CERTIFIED NOVELL ADMINISTRATOR.

COMPUTER NETWORKS

When two or more computers are connected so that they can communicate with each other, a **computer network** is created. A computer network that exists in one location is called a **local area network (LAN)**. If two or more LANs in different geographic locations are tied together, a **wide area network (WAN)** is created. Although this text focuses on LANs, the material covered is applicable to WANs as well. Figure 1-1 illustrates LANs and WANs.

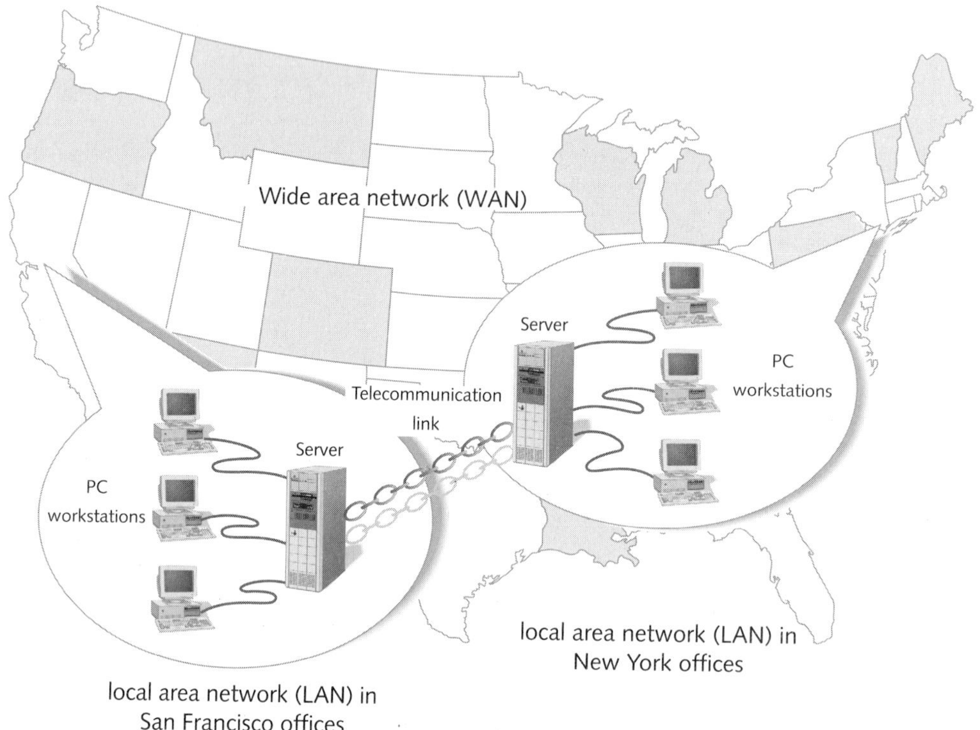

Figure 1-1 Local area networks and wide area networks

The **network administrator** is the person responsible for the network. The job of network administrator is one of the most exciting, challenging, and important jobs in an organization's information systems department. However, it can also be one of the most frustrating jobs because of the rapid changes in the field and the need for involvement with many different responsibilities. These responsibilities range from hardware (i.e., computers and cables) to software (i.e., operating systems and applications) to working with people (i.e., users and vendors). Therefore, in order to prepare to be a successful network administrator, you will need to build a strong understanding of the basic components that make up the network system. This background will act as a foundation upon which you can build the skills you will need as a network administrator to perform your job responsibilities. In this section you will learn about the basic components that make up a LAN. You will also learn about some of the different options you will need to consider when deciding how to put a LAN together.

We can more completely define a LAN as a high-speed communication system consisting of cables and cards (hardware) along with instructions (software) that provides a means for different types of computers and peripherals to communicate and share resources over short distances, such as within a building or room. LANs are significantly different from older mainframe computers and minicomputers. With a **mainframe computer** or

minicomputer system, all the processing is done by the mainframe computer or minicomputer running the programs. The user workstations are **terminals**, used simply as input and output devices for entering data and displaying results, without any computing power of their own. This type of processing is called **centralized processing** because all the processing is done by the computer connected to the terminals.

A LAN uses **microcomputers** (also called personal computers or **PCs**) as workstations, each of which has its own computing ability. The processing is done at the microcomputer workstations instead of at the central computer, and the LAN ties the microcomputer workstations together as a high-speed communication system. The LAN is used primarily to give the workstations access to shared data files and other hardware devices such as printers. This type of processing is called **distributed processing** because the processing is distributed to each of the workstations. In addition to the workstations, LANs also use servers. A **server** is a specialized computer that provides network resources for workstations. Several types of servers may be found on a network. Most common is a **file server**, which provides shared data and application storage for users. A **print server** allows users to share printers. An **application server** is used with **client/server applications**, such as database systems, which split the processing between the server and the workstations. In this situation, the application server runs the server portion of the application, while the client portion runs on the users' workstations. A server that uses NetWare can perform all these functions and is called a **NetWare server**. Figure 1-2 shows the differences between centralized processing and distributed processing.

Figure 1-2

Centralized processing and distributed processing

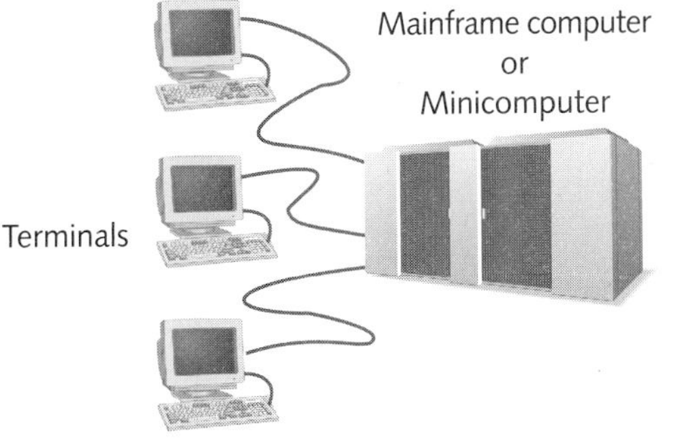

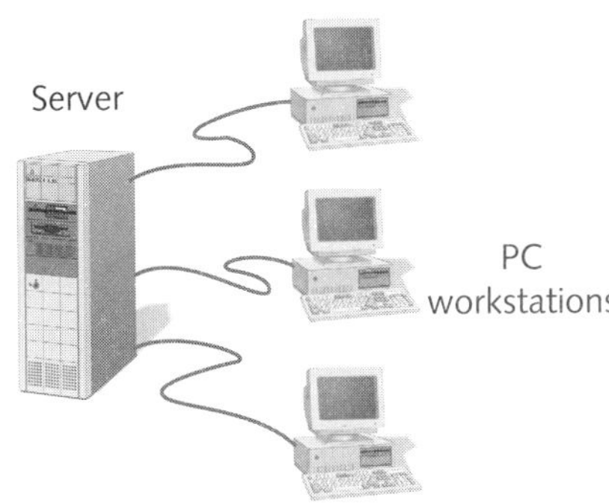

Centralized processing
- Terminals have no processing capability
- All processing done on Mainframe computer or minicomputer

Distributed processing
- PC workstations have their own processing capability
- Processing done on PC workstations

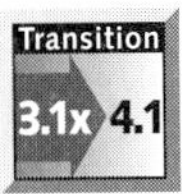

The term NetWare file server was used in NetWare 3.1x documentation. In NetWare 4.1, the term used is NetWare server.

LOCAL AREA NETWORK ADVANTAGES

While distributed processing can be performed by stand-alone computers not connected by a network, a LAN offers many advantages by sharing resources and improving communications. These advantages make distributed processing a strong competitor of traditional centralized minicomputer and mainframe computer systems, the traditional means of sharing resources and communicating between users. As a network administrator, you need to be aware of the following LAN advantages in order to help you prepare a recommendation for a network system.

Cost Savings

One important benefit of a LAN is cost savings, and management is always happy to hear how you can save money for the organization. The most direct cost savings a LAN provides come from sharing expensive computer hardware such as disk drives, CD-ROMs, printers, and communication devices (i.e., modems and fax equipment). For example, assume that your company needs to install an application package that requires 100 MB of disk space along with access to a high-resolution laser printer on ten different computers. The simple calculations in Figure 1-3 compare the cost of implementing this system on stand-alone computers versus sharing the application software package and laser printer on a network server.

Figure 1-3
Network cost savings

Stand-alone Computers			
Component	Quantity	Cost	Value
Disk space	10 × 100 MB	$0.20 per MB	$200
Printers	10	$1,500	$15,000
Total			$15,200
Network Server			
Component	Quantity	Cost	Value
Disk space	1 × 100 MB	$0.20 per MB	$20
Printers	1	$1,500	$1,500
Total			$1,500

Time Savings

A less tangible but perhaps even more important advantage of networks is the time saved by providing users with access to shared data and communication capability. Without a LAN, users have to resort to what is commonly called "sneaker net," where shared files are copied onto a floppy disk and physically transferred to another user's computer workstation by being carried on foot and copied to another hard drive.

Another time savings advantage of LANs is that they allow the network administrator to install and maintain a software package on a file server, a computer dedicated to storing commonly used program and data files, where it is accessible to all users. This is often preferable to installing the package on each user's workstation and then having to spend additional time going to each workstation in order to configure that software or install an upgraded version of it.

Centralized Data

Without a network, certain critical and often-used data files, such as customer and inventory files, might need to be duplicated on several workstations, resulting in redundant data storage and the inherent difficulty of keeping all files current. Storing database files on the network file server enables the information to be kept current while also giving many users access to it. This ability to have shared access to centralized database files makes the LAN a competitive alternative to centralized processing.

In addition to providing shared access to centralized data files, a network file server used for centralized data storage makes regular backups of data easier. This helps to establish a disaster recovery system for the organization. Data stored on users' workstations is rarely backed up, making it very difficult to recover lost data in the event of a workstation crash or physical damage to the building or equipment. On the other hand, keeping all of an organization's critical data on the network file server allows you to make a backup each night to protect data. Each week a backup tape is then stored offsite to provide recovery in the event of damage to the building. If a disaster occurs, you can restore the software and data onto a new file server and get the organization up and running again very quickly. In contrast, the alternative requires you to back up the data on each workstation and restore the individual workstation's software and data after a disaster.

Security

At first glance, centralizing company data on a network file server might appear to cause more security problems than it solves because more users have potential access to the data. In the case of NetWare servers, however, data can be made more secure on the server than data stored on local workstations. The reason is that NetWare provides many security features such as requiring passwords to gain access to the network and restricting user access to network files. In addition, user accounts can be limited to specific times, such as normal working hours, and to specific workstations, making it difficult for an intruder to gain access to the system by logging in with a user's name and password after normal office hours. Compare those security advantages to the alternative of storing data on a local workstation. With data on the workstation, anyone with a little knowledge of PC operating systems and physical access to the office can sit down at the computer and access the applications and data.

Fault Tolerance

When data is stored on individual workstations there is an increased probability of data loss due to operator error, software bugs, computer viruses, or hardware failure on the workstation. Data stored on the network file servers can be placed on microcomputers that are specially designed and configured to provide protection against loss of data due to software or hardware problems. This is called **fault tolerance**. For example, with a NetWare server, the data stored on a disk drive can be protected through a process called mirroring. **Mirroring** uses two identical disk drives that are linked so that all files on one disk drive are automatically duplicated on the second disk drive. If one drive fails, the data is still accessible on the second drive.

Communication

The high-speed communication between network computers provided by a LAN creates opportunities for major changes in office management. For example, workgroup-oriented applications such as electronic mail and scheduling are commonly used on LANs. **Electronic mail (e-mail) applications** enable users to send messages and files directly to other users on the LAN. Many users feel that e-mail is quicker and more effective than voice mail, particularly when faced with playing "phone tag" with hard-to-reach people. **Scheduling applications** enable individuals and groups to store their schedules on the server, where other users (with appropriate permission) can access them. This can save time by allowing managers to check the schedules of people and facilities quickly in order to find a free time in which to schedule meetings.

Network communication systems are rapidly incorporating support for new applications that utilize both video and voice data. Video conferencing and the integration of computers with telephone systems are just beginning to become popular in office environments and could see widespread use in the near future. This will enable members of a conference to see data being presented as well as the reactions of other conference members.

Additional advantages and conveniences of LANs are too numerous to include in this chapter. Examining the major advantages, however, makes it clear why the use of LANs has been growing at such a fast pace.

Types of Network Operating Systems

The **network operating system (NOS)** is the software that controls network services. Depending upon their design, NOSs can be defined as either peer-to-peer or client-server. **Peer-to-peer** NOSs enable workstations to communicate and share data with each other without the need for a dedicated file server computer. **Client-server** NOSs use one computer as a dedicated file server, which acts as a central storage unit for client workstations. NetWare is a client-server operating system because its operation depends upon the existence of a dedicated NetWare server. Peer-to-peer and client-server networks are illustrated in Figure 1-4. In this section you will learn about the features found in both client-server and peer-to-peer NOSs and how they compare to the NetWare operating system.

Figure 1-4 Peer-to-peer and client-server networks

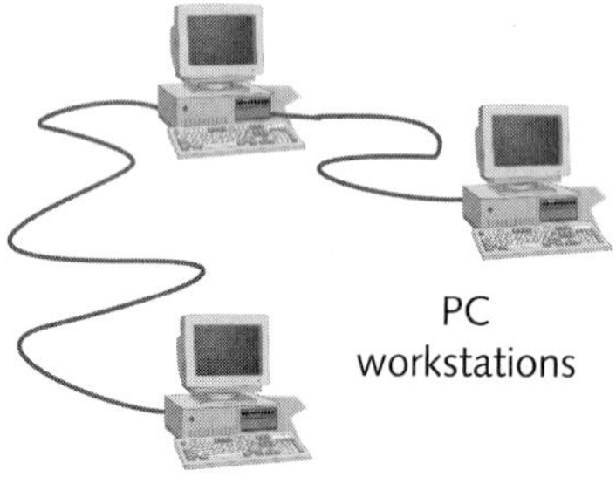

Peer-to-peer network
- Data stored on PC workstations
- PC workstations *can* access data on other PC workstations

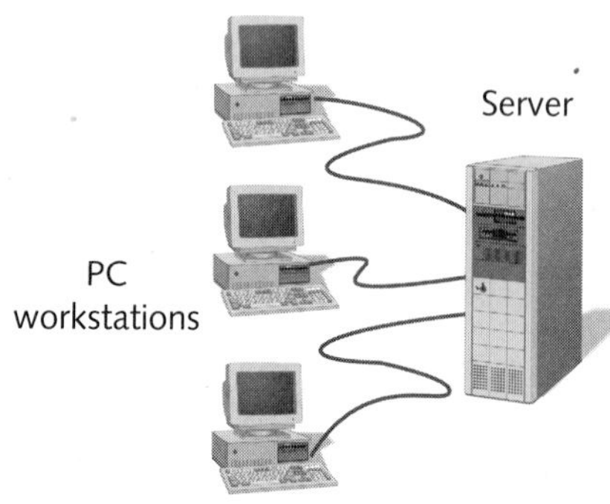

Client-server network
- Data stored on server
- PC workstations *cannot* access data on other PC workstations

Peer-to-Peer Networks

In peer-to-peer networks, each computer can be both a file server and a client workstation, allowing any computer to share its files with other users on the network. Each computer can also function as a print server, enabling other users to share its printer. The main advantage of peer-to-peer NOSs is the ability to implement low-cost networks by saving the expense of dedicating a computer as a file server. In addition, peer-to-peer systems allow users in workgroups to share data files and to communicate easily with each other. In theory this reduces the burden on the network administrator by placing more responsibility for data sharing in the hands of the users. However, large peer-to-peer networks can be very difficult to administer because shared data can exist in several locations, making it more difficult to retrieve, secure, and back up. For example, if a workstation containing data needed by other users fails to boot its system or shuts down unexpectedly, other users can lose data or will not be able to access the information they need. In this section you will learn about several peer-to-peer NOSs as well as their advantages and disadvantages when compared to Novell NetWare.

LANtastic

LANtastic is a peer-to-peer NOS that is produced by Artisoft Corporation. DOS-based and now rewritten for the Windows 95 environment, LANtastic is a great network system for sharing files and communicating among DOS-based computers and is very popular for small networks in which all computers are attached to the same cable system. The primary advantages of LANtastic are its low cost and ease of installation, making it an ideal choice for networks consisting of fewer than 10 workstations. Unfortunately, the major drawback of LANtastic as a peer-to-peer NOS is that it is built upon DOS, thereby reducing the performance of the workstations because of the memory limitations of the DOS operating system, which was not designed to support high-demand, peer-to-peer network workstations.

Windows for Workgroups and Windows 95

Microsoft added peer-to-peer networking capabilities to its Windows software to create Windows for Workgroups and has enhanced these networking capabilities in Windows 95. With the acceptance of the Windows environment, Windows for Workgroups became a widely used peer-to-peer NOS. Windows 95 has since become the most rapidly growing peer-to-peer NOS. Using Windows 95 to share files and printers eliminates the need to obtain and integrate another NOS into the network. Windows 95 also provides each workstation with e-mail (through the Windows Exchange client), and a scheduling client (Schedule+) is included with Microsoft's Office for Windows 95 software suite. Windows 95 also integrates easily into NetWare networks by allowing Windows users to access NetWare servers in addition to shared resources on other Windows workstations. The major disadvantage of Windows 95 as a peer-to-peer NOS is the need to have computers with a minimum of 16 MB of RAM (the realistic minimum, despite an advertised minimum of 8 MB) and at least 80486 processors in order to provide satisfactory performance.

Windows NT Workstation

Windows NT represents a more powerful "big brother" of the Windows family of operating systems. Windows NT Workstation is a leading-edge operating system designed to support the advanced capabilities of Pentium- and multiprocessor-based computers and is a completely different operating system from Windows. Developed simultaneously with other Microsoft Windows products, Windows NT was written to take advantage of the 32-bit instruction set offered by Intel 80386 and later processors. Windows, on the other hand, is based on the 16-bit instruction set of earlier Intel processors, and even Windows 95 retains some of the 16-bit heritage. Windows NT Workstation also provides additional levels of reliability, protection, and security not available in the Windows products. When used in peer-to-peer networks, the Windows NT Workstation operating system is intended to be used on very powerful workstations with at least 16 MB of RAM. They usually require the advanced features of Windows NT in order to support complex applications for technical, engineering, and scientific users.

Many observers of the computing field expect the Windows and Windows NT Workstation operating systems to merge in the future, although Microsoft claims that they won't. Microsoft is, however, recommending Windows NT Workstation as the operating system for businesses and Windows 95 as the operating system for home computing.

Client-Server

In a client-server network, file servers running specialized software are used to provide services to client workstation computers instead of having the workstations share data among themselves. As a result, client-server networks, such as those using NetWare, provide the advantages of centralized data storage, reliability, and high performance that are not currently attainable with peer-to-peer networks. One reason for the increased performance and reliability of client-server networks such as NetWare is that a file server's hardware can be specialized to perform the function of file sharing by providing multiple high-speed disk channels along with a large memory capacity for file caching. In Chapter 2 you will learn about many of the hardware options available that enable you to increase the performance and reliability of your file servers. The rest of this section compares the client-server NOSs currently available.

NetWare 3.12

Although NetWare 4.1x family is now Novell's flagship NOS, Novell continues to sell and support NetWare 3.12. NetWare 3.12 is a widely installed and highly stable network platform that network administrators depend upon for consistent and stable performance. The NetWare 3.1x series introduced many advances to the NetWare product line. One of the most significant was the use of **NetWare Loadable Modules (NLMs)**, which gave network administrators the ability to load and unload parts of the NOS, including hardware drivers and specialized network programs such as virus protection and backup services, without disrupting the users on the network.

NetWare 4.1

NetWare 4.1x is Novell's latest version of the NetWare 4.x NOS. It is a 32-bit dedicated NOS that is highly specialized to provide a variety of services to client workstations. NetWare 4.1x retains NetWare 3.1x's ability to load and unload NLMs.

NetWare 4.11 is the current Novell NOS. It replaces NetWare 4.1 in Novell's product line. In this book we will discuss NetWare 4.1 and preview NetWare 4.11. The term NetWare 4.1x refers to both products, while the terms NetWare 4.1 and Netware 4.11 will be used when a specific product is being referenced.

The biggest change from the NetWare 3.1x to the NetWare 4.x environment was the switch to a network-centric, rather than server-centric, environment. NetWare 3.1x was **server-centric**, which means that the network was managed by each server individually. NetWare 4.x is **network-centric**, which means that the network as a whole is managed through a centralized administration tool. The administration tool is **Novell Directory Services (NDS)**, which uses a database to store information about the various network resources. NetWare has a set of NDS administration utilities to let the network administrator manage the resources in the NDS database.

One example of the difference in the two approaches can be seen when adding a new user to a network with three servers. Using NetWare 3.1x, the network administrator has to create three accounts for the new user—one on each server. Using NetWare 4.x and NDS, only one account is created—in the NDS database. This is illustrated in Figure 1-5. You will learn about NDS in Chapter 4, and you'll work with it in many other chapters as you add resources to the network.

Figure 1-5
Server-centric and network-centric networks

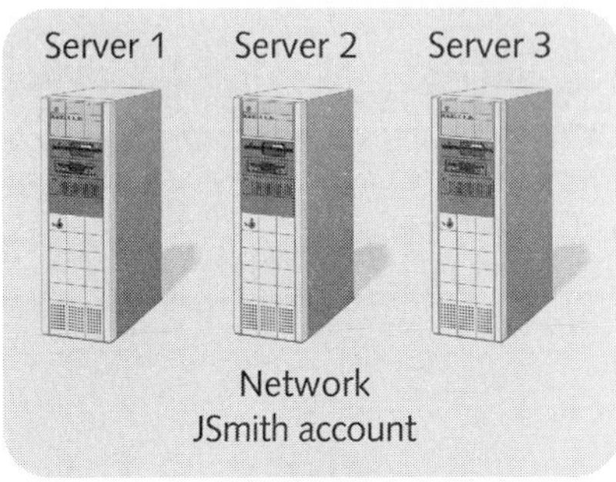

- NetWare 4.1x continues the use of NDS, with each version adding its own NDS enhancements, better graphical utilities, and improved file and printing services. NetWare 4.1 is a powerful and stable NOS that is readily adaptable by large firms that need to support multiple servers in multiple locations.

The many improvements added to NetWare 4.1, its acknowledged stability, and the increased need for large multiserver networks in industry cause many organizations to upgrade their NetWare 3.1x servers to NetWare 4.1. The added features of NetWare 4.11 should increase the number of companies upgrading from Netware 3.1x.

NetWare 4.11 incorporates enhancements to NetWare 4.1 released by Novell since the introduction of NetWare 4.1, and adds previously unavailable features.

Previously released enhancements include:

- The NetWare Client 32 workstation client software
- NetWare Application Manager (NAM) and NetWare Application Launcher (NAL) network application management software
- Enhanced printer support for printers attached to workstations
- Various network operating system patches and updates

Features that are being introduced with NetWare 4.11 include:

- Enhanced installation procedures, including a utility to plan the 4.11 network
- Major enhancements of the NetWare Administrator utility, which is the network administrator's main utility for managing the network; the enhancements include a Windows 95 version, a configurable toolbar, and the ability to simultaneously manage multiple networks
- Support for multiple microprocessors in the NetWare server
- Software licensing management capabilities
- Improved long filename support
- Directory entry volume capacity increased from 2 million to 16 million
- Integrated support for NetWare IP, Novell's version of the Internet (IP) Protocol
- Enhanced backup abilities
- Novell's new network printing system, NetWare Distributed Print Services (NDPS)
- Enhanced security

Some previously distributed enhancements, such as the NetWare Client 32 workstation client, have already become a standard feature of the NetWare 4.1x family. Discussion of these features is integrated into the main text of this book. Selected new features, such as the NetWare Administrator enhancements, are covered in more detail in the NetWare 4.11 preview sections of a relevant chapter. Together, this coverage will introduce you to NetWare 4.11 and provide a basis for upgrading your network to it.

The scope of the changes between these two versions of NetWare requires training and planning on the part of the network administrator before the conversion process from an existing NetWare 3.1x network to NetWare 4.1x can take place.

Banyan VINES

One of the major strengths of the Banyan VINES network is its "StreetTalk" protocol, which allows users to log in once to a multiserver network and then be able to access any file server to which they have been granted access rights. This is the same network-centric approach found in NetWare 4.1x. However, NetWare 4.1x follows the industry X.500 standard, implementing a network global database, whereas VINES does not. Despite this disadvantage, the VINES NOS, which was in existence several years prior to the release of NetWare 4.1, has obtained a respectable share of the client-server NOS market. This is because it offered several of the advantages only recently introduced in NetWare 4.1x. In many ways, Banyan forced Novell to move to a network-based file server environment or face losing many of its large multiserver customers.

Windows NT Server

The Windows NT Server client-server operating system provides client workstations with centralized and highly fault-tolerant high-speed access to data. The advantages of Windows NT are that it provides centralized management of multiple servers through the familiar Windows environment and that it supports access to TCP/IP and NetWare servers as well as mainframe computers. A final advantage is its usefulness as an application server, a server that runs the server portion of client/server applications. Many vendors offer client/server applications designed to run on the Windows NT server.

Many network administrators are using NetWare as their main network operating system for file and print services while using Windows NT Server for application servers.

NETWORK COMPONENTS

As defined previously, a LAN is basically a system that enables computers of different types to communicate and share data. As a network administrator, you need to understand the hardware and software components that make up the network so that you can select and maintain a network system that will meet the communication needs of your organization. This chapter introduces you to a network system's hardware and software components and explains why NetWare is the most prevalent NOS in use today. Chapters 2 and 3 will give you an in-depth view of the microcomputer hardware components and network cable system as well as the options you will need to know about in order to select and maintain computers on the network.

Hardware Components

Hardware components are the most obvious parts of a network system to identify because they can be easily seen. The hardware components of a typical network are shown in Figure 1-6.

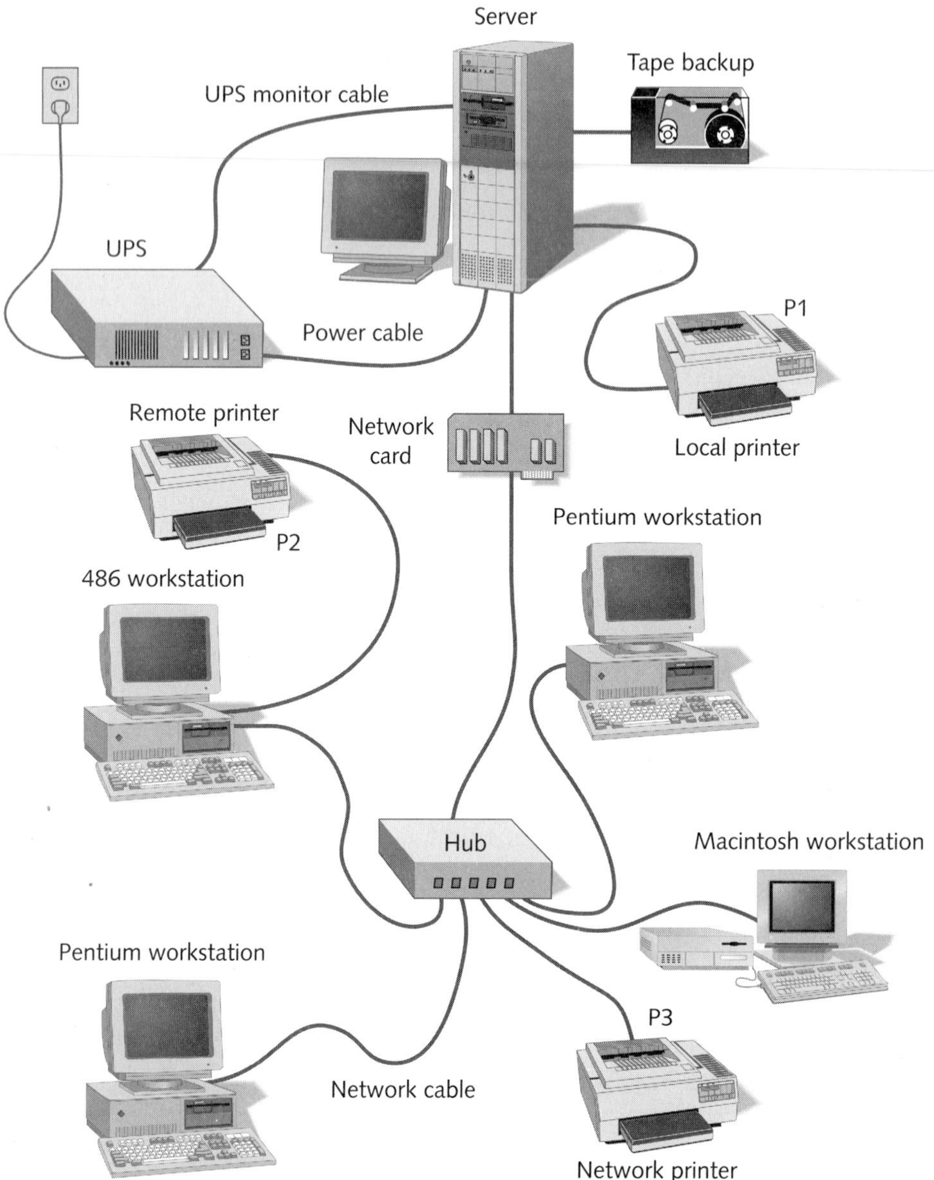

Figure 1-6 Sample network hardware components

The Server

The first stop on our tour of the network is the computer that is the network server, called a NetWare server in NetWare 4.1x networks. Many who are familiar with minicomputers and mainframe computers tend to think of the server in terms of network control. In a LAN, however, a file server is actually a servant of the network, responding to the requests of workstations for access to the files and software stored on the server's disk system. With the exception of its disk system and typically large memory capacity, a server is similar to the client workstation computers on the network. Some servers are **nondedicated**, meaning that they can function as a user's workstation in addition to providing access to shared areas of the disk system. The server in Figure 1-6 is **dedicated**, meaning that it cannot be used as a workstation, in order to provide better performance and eliminate the possibility of a user shutting down or rebooting the file server while other users are still accessing it.

Most network administrators keep servers in a separate room that can be secured in order to prevent unauthorized access to the server's hardware and software.

The server shown in Figure 1-6 is a PC specifically designed to be a server (many vendors offer PCs designed for use as servers); it has an Intel 133-MHz Pentium processor with 96 MB of memory and two high-capacity 4.2-GB disk drives. The two disk drives are automatically synchronized (mirrored) so that if one drive fails, the file server can continue to provide information services by using the data from the other drive.

The Client Workstation

Generally, each computer that is attached to the network for the purpose of running user applications is referred to as a **client workstation**. The client workstation is where the actual processing of user software applications occurs. Placing more memory or a faster processor on the server does not directly affect the speed of programs run on client workstations; to increase user application performance you must upgrade the client workstation. The processing power of the client workstation often equals or exceeds the speed of the file server computer. For example, in the sample network the file server contains a 133-Mhz Pentium processor with lots of memory and disk space and a low-resolution color monitor. The Windows-based workstations contain 200-MHz Pentium processors with 16 MB of memory, 1.2 GB of disk storage, and high-resolution color monitors. Because most of the files and software will be kept on the network file server, the client workstations can focus on processing speed and graphics resolution rather than high-capacity disk storage.

On networks needing file and print services, the server will be specialized to provide high-speed disk access, whereas the client workstations will require fast processors and high-resolution graphics. On networks using client/server applications, the server will need to run the server portion of the application and thus must be specialized to handle the application processing.

Network Interface Card

A **network interface card (NIC)** is installed in each computer attached to the network, including the servers. The NIC allows the computer to be attached to the network cable system and is responsible for the transmission and reception of data packets on the network. A **packet** consists of 500 to 4,200 bytes of formatted data that is framed with control bits identifying the address of the computer it is being sent to. Each NIC is assigned a unique address or serial number when it is manufactured. The NIC listens to the network and accepts any packets that contain its address. It then notifies the computer that a packet has been received, and if no errors are detected in the packet, it is sent to the operating system software for processing. When transmitting data, the network operating system will send a block of data to the NIC, which then waits for the network cable to become available. When no other computers are using the cable system, the NIC transmits the packet bit by bit.

The Cable System

A network's cable system is the highway through which information travels from one computer to another. A **cable system** consists of the wiring that connects the computers in the network. Just as getting onto a highway requires obeying certain traffic laws, so sending information through the network requires each computer to follow a set of access rules. And in the same way that gridlock can slow down or stop traffic on a highway, a network can also experience bottlenecks when the amount of information on the network exceeds the transmission capacity of the cable system. One of the responsibilities you will have as a network administrator is monitoring the network cable system for errors or performance bottlenecks. The cable system in the sample network consists of twisted-pair cable similar to the cable that connects your telephone's handset to its base unit. In Chapter 3 you will learn about the different types of cable systems and access methods that are commonly used in LANs, along with some of the advantages and disadvantages of each system. In the sample network, the twisted-pair cable runs from each computer in the network to a central connection box called a **hub** or **concentrator**, giving all computers equal access to the network system.

Uninterruptible Power Supply

The box next to the server in Figure 1-6 is the **uninterruptible power supply (UPS)**. The UPS contains batteries that will be used to supply temporary power to the server if the local power system fails. The UPS is a very important piece of equipment for the server computer because it will prevent the loss of data on the server in the event of a power outage or brownout.

Because a power outage that occurs while many users are accessing the server is likely to result in lost data, you should not consider running a server computer without first obtaining a UPS. Power interruptions occurring when a UPS unit is not attached to the server can even necessitate restoring data from a backup tape in order to restart the server.

The UPS in Figure 1-6 contains an optional monitor cable that connects to a port on the server. This connection enables the server to know when the UPS is using battery power. This connection is also an important feature in the event of a longer power outage because it allows the server to close all files and take itself off line automatically before the power stored in the UPS batteries is exhausted.

Tape Backup

The tape backup system in the network shown in Figure 1-6 consists of a Digital Audio Tape (DAT) cartridge tape drive and uses Novell's Storage Management System (SMS) software to back up all data on the server automatically every night. At 1:00 A.M. each weekday morning the tape software starts up and copies all data to the tape cartridge. The network administrator then places this tape in the organization's fireproof vault for safe storage. A rotation system utilizing several tapes allows each backup to be kept for at least one week, and one day's backup tape (for example, the tape made on Fridays) is then stored off site in case of a disaster that wipes out the entire site. In Chapter 17 you will learn more about developing a backup and recovery system for your server environment.

Network Printers

Sharing printers on the network is often an important advantage of implementing a LAN. Each client workstation can send output to any printer by first directing the printed output to the server to be stored in a special directory called a **print queue**. After a workstation has completed its printing, the server will direct the printout to the selected printer by using special print server software. Printers can be attached and shared on the network in three different ways: as local printers, as remote printers, and as directly attached printers.

Notice that printer P1 in the network shown in Figure 1-6 is attached to the server. This makes it a **local printer** because it is attached to the server's local printer port. Local printers have the advantage of being high-speed and reducing network traffic but have the disadvantage of limiting the locations in which the printers can be placed.

Printer P2 is attached to a user's workstation. It is controlled by the print server software, which allows users on any client workstation to send output through the server to printer P2. Printer P2 is referred to as a **remote printer** because it is not directly attached to a printer port of the server. Remote printers have the advantage of being located anywhere on the network where there is a workstation. However, performance problems, as well as software conflicts for the workstation's user, can occur when large print jobs are processed.

The third network printer shown in Figure 1-6, P3, is a **directly attached printer**, which has its own network card and is connected directly to the network cable system. This direct connection offers the benefits of independence from a workstation with no loss of speed associated with a remote printer. Today most network administrators attach their high-speed printers directly to the network cable system to obtain the highest possible level of performance.

Software Components

The software components of the network are perhaps the most difficult to understand because they are not physical objects. In the network configuration shown in Figure 1-6, the network software components can be divided into four major categories: card drivers, protocol stacks, the network operating system, and client support. Figure 1-7 shows how these software components are combined to allow workstations and servers to communicate on the network. In this section you will learn what role each of these software components plays in implementing a local area network.

Network Interface Card Drivers

Each server and client workstation must have a network interface card to attach it to the cable system and to communicate on the network. A **network interface card driver** is software that contains the instructions that allow the processor on the computer to control card functions and interface with the application software. Periodically, new versions of driver software are released by card manufacturers in order to fix bugs or provide compatibility with new applications. As a result, one of the responsibilities of a network administrator involves updating application and system software. In a later chapter you will learn how you can make this task more efficient by implementing the automatic software update utilities built into the NetWare operating system. In the sample network configuration, the workstations use MicroDyne NE2000 NICs, and an NE2000 driver program is used to control the network interface cards and provide an interface with the workstation operating system software.

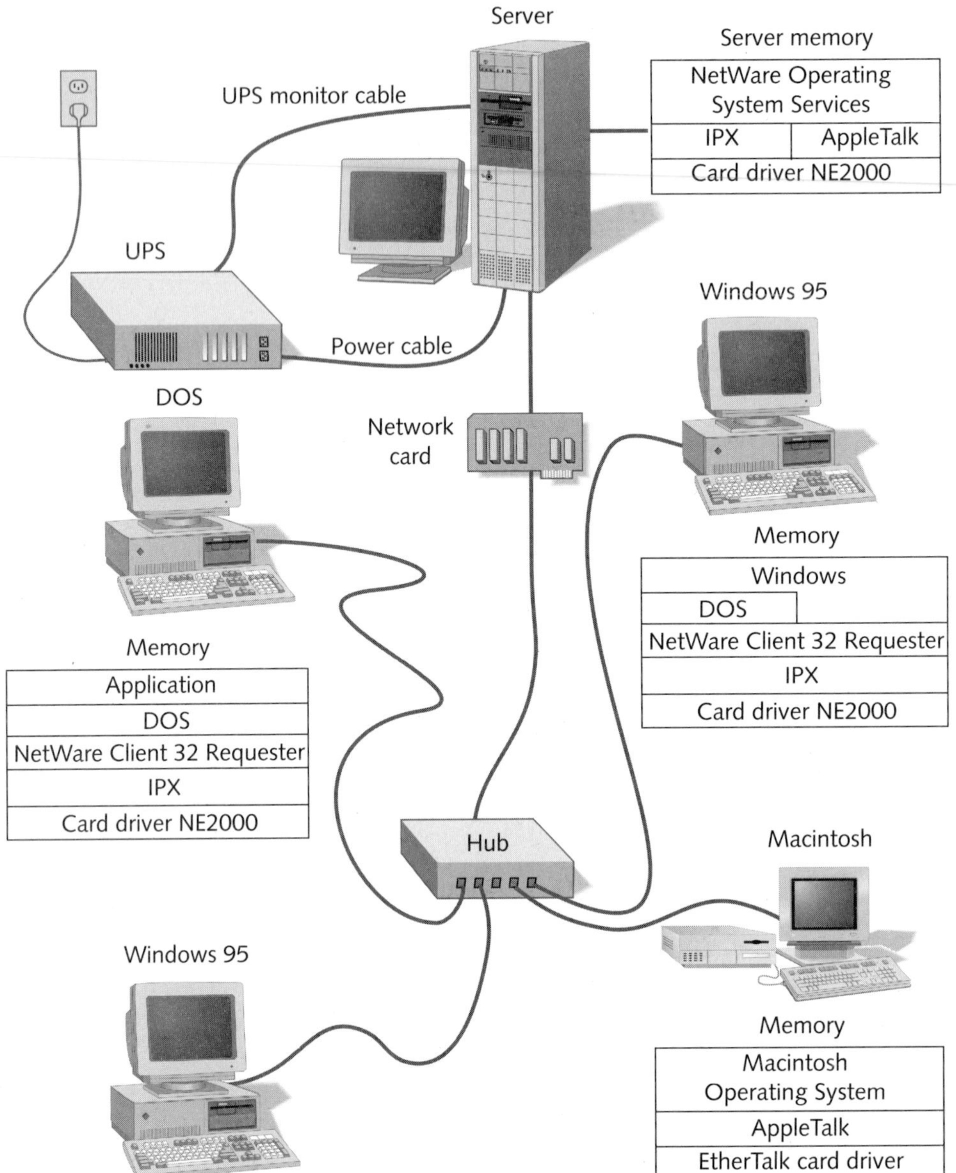

Figure 1-7 Network software components

Protocol Stacks

The **protocol stack** is the software used to format the requests and information packets that are transmitted on the network. The protocol you use will depend upon your server and client workstations. One of the most common protocols on NetWare networks is the Internetwork Packet eXchange (IPX) protocol because it is the default system used with the NetWare operating system. However, NetWare networks will support other protocols, such as the LocalTalk protocol used with Macintosh computers or the TCP/IP (Transmission Control Protocol/Internet Protocol) commonly used with the UNIX operating system.

The IPX protocol used by NetWare was first developed by the Xerox company in the late 1970s and later adopted by Novell for use in its networking products.

Network Operating System

As discussed before, the network operating system is the system software that provides network services. In a client-server network such as NetWare, the network operating system controls the server to provide services to the client workstations. While most of the NetWare operating system resides on the server computer, the client workstations also require a requester program, such as the Client 32 requester shown in Figure 1-7, to format and direct requests for network services to the server for processing. In Chapter 6 you will learn the steps for installing NetWare on both the server and client workstations.

The NetWare network operating system was specifically designed to directly control the server hardware as well as provide a server environment to support file sharing and other network services. This makes NetWare an efficient network operating system because it enables a NetWare server to provide faster support with fewer hardware requirements. There have been several versions of the NetWare operating system prior to NetWare 4.1x. Earlier versions include ELS NetWare, NetWare 2.1x and 2.2, NetWare 3.1x, and NetWare 4.0x. ELS NetWare was a very limited version of NetWare intended for small networks consisting of fewer than 10 users. It ran in nondedicated mode, which enabled the server computer to function as a user workstation as well. The NetWare 2.2 operating system was a much more powerful system that could be run either dedicated or nondedicated and could support up to 100 workstations. NetWare 3.1x is a 32-bit dedicated NOS that introduced the ability to load and unload programs called NetWare Loadable Modules (NLMs). This enabled network administrators to add or delete hardware drivers and additional network services without shutting down the server. NetWare 4.0x was an earlier version of NetWare 4.1x that contained many of the same features, including NDS, but was not widely implemented because of the scope of the changes it introduced combined with some problems that were finally fixed in NetWare 4.1.

The server in the network shown in Figure 1-7 runs NetWare 4.1 as its network operating system. It uses two protocols:

1. The IPX protocol to communicate with the DOS and Windows workstations.
2. The AppleTalk protocol to communicate with Apple Macintosh computers.

This enables both DOS/Windows and Macintosh computers to access the NetWare server and share data and other resources.

The ability to provide faster support for workstations will become even more important as servers are increasingly used to store large documents, images, and multimedia files. Similarly, the increasing use of application servers to run the server portion of client/server applications is requiring more processing power from the server itself.

Client Software

Client workstations require the following components:

1. Their own operating systems such as DOS, OS/2, Windows, Windows 95 Windows NT, or Macintosh System 7 to control local devices and run application software
2. Client workstations driver software to control the network interface card
3. Requester and protocol software programs to format and send requests for network file and print services to the server; the requester program works closely with DOS to provide access to network services

The network in Figure 1-7 illustrates DOS computers using NetWare Client 32 requesters to send IPX-formatted requests via the NE2000 driver through the cable system to the NetWare server. The Macintosh computer shown has an EtherTalk driver so that it can simultaneously use the same cable to send requests to the server by using the AppleTalk protocol. The ability to support different types of client operating systems is one of the strengths of the NetWare server.

The NetWare Server

As explained earlier in this chapter, the main function of a server is to provide file and printer services to client workstations. As a result, the server can be enhanced with specialized hardware and software to improve performance, security, and reliability beyond what can be expected from a peer-to-peer network operating system. Although Microsoft Windows NT and Banyan VINES offer client-server network operating systems, NetWare still has the largest share of the client-server network operating system market for Intel processors. NetWare offers server-based software that is designed from the ground up to make the maximum use of the server's hardware. It does this by including performance, fault tolerance, security, and client support features.

Performance

The performance of a server is determined by how fast it can respond to requests for data from client workstations. Therefore, the major factors that affect the server's performance are its ability to keep frequently used information in memory, the speed of its disk system, and, if the first two are adequate, the speed of its processor unit. Some of the performance features of NetWare are discussed in Chapter 2.

Fault Tolerance

Fault Tolerance can be defined as the ability of a system to continue to operate satisfactorily in the event of errors or other problems. The NetWare server environment was designed with different levels of fault tolerance in its disk system in order to continue server operations in the event of physical errors on the disk drives or controller cards. NetWare's fault tolerance system is discussed in Chapter 2.

Security preventing unauthorized access to information on the server is one of the most important responsibilities of a network administrator. To help you in this area the NetWare server provides security features that can be used to create an environment that will meet the security needs of your organization's users and data.

Login security requires all users of the server to provide a valid user name and optional password before being given access to the network. As a network administrator you can assign user names and passwords for each of your network users, thereby controlling use of the network. To provide additional protection for passwords, NetWare allows you to require users to have passwords of at least five characters and to force users to change their passwords within a specified time limit. In addition, the optional intruder protection system will lock out a user's account if someone exceeds the number of login attempts you have set. You will work with user accounts and login security in Chapter 9.

Trustee assignments enable you to assign privileges, called **trustee rights**, to NetWare users in order to allow them to perform certain functions on the network. Trustee assignments form the basis for **Novell Directory Services security**, which controls access to Novell Directory Services (NDS). NDS is Novell's system for managing network resources such as printers and servers. Trustee assignments are also the basis for **file system security**, which controls access to the network file system (the directory structure of the hard drive and the files in that directory structure). A newly created user has no rights to access any data stored on a NetWare server until you provide that user with rights to use certain parts of a file system on a NetWare server in your network. Trustee assignments, NDS security, and file system security are discussed in detail in Chapter 10.

Finally, NetWare provides **system console security** features. The **system console** is the keyboard and monitor connected to a NetWare server, which are used for many NetWare server and network-related tasks. NetWare enables you to set the system console so that only authorized individuals can use it. You will work with the system console in Chapter 16.

Client Support

Because a NetWare server runs its own network operating system, it is not dependent on a specific type of client environment (unlike peer-to-peer networks) and can support many types of workstations. As a result, implementing a NetWare server can allow you to integrate diverse computing environments, making it possible for Apple Macintosh users to share files with DOS- and Windows-based computers. In some organizations, NetWare has provided a means for engineering departments operating UNIX-based computers for computer aided design (CAD) software (used by engineers to draw plans and diagrams) to make the design files available to DOS-based computers that control the machines that actually cut out the parts that were engineered. Client support is discussed in Chapter 6.

SELECTING A NETWORK

Selecting a network system for an organization involves three steps:

1. Deciding on the type of network operating system to use
2. Determining the cable system that will best support the needs of the network
3. Specifying any computer hardware that will be needed to implement servers and attach workstations to the network

In this section you will learn about the criteria you should consider when developing a recommendation for a network operating system. In Chapters 2 and 3 you will learn about computer hardware options and cable configurations that you will need to know when recommending and implementing a new network or maintaining an existing system.

Defining Network Needs

Before recommending or justifying a network operating system, you first need to analyze the processing needs of the organization and determine how they will be supported by the network. The processing needs of an organization that affect the type of network operating system to be selected include number of users, diversity of workstations, type of applications to be supported, and the need for centralized data.

Network Size

An important consideration in determining whether to use a peer-to-peer or client-server network operating system is the number of workstations that will be attached to the network. As a general rule, the fewer users, the more likely a peer-to-peer network will meet the needs of the organization. In addition to the size of the current network, you also need to look at the future growth of the organization and how this will affect the network system. If you think that the organization will expand in the next few years to include more users requiring heavy-duty file and printer sharing in order to support such applications as desktop publishing and CAD, you might want to recommend a client-server network operating system.

Client Workstations

The types of client workstations that will be attached to the network are another factor to consider in determining the type of network operating system to be selected. Peer-to-peer networks are best used in networks in which all the attached clients are running the same type of operating system. For example, if all workstations will run Windows, the Windows 95 system could be an attractive alternative, provided it meets the other processing needs of the network. If the client workstations are running a combination of DOS and Windows, then LANtastic or a client-server operating system such as NetWare 4.1 might be the best choice, depending upon the organization's other processing needs.

Network Use

Certain common uses of networks, such as printer sharing and e-mail routing, have small disk storage needs and can run nicely on peer-to-peer networks. For example, if an organization plans to use its network to support workgroup-oriented software such as e-mail and scheduling with some sharing of files and printers within small workgroups, a peer-to-peer operating system that supports its workstation operating systems might be the best choice.

If an organization will be running applications that require fast access to large network data files such as desktop publishing, document imaging, and multimedia presentation packages, a client-server network such as NetWare should be selected in order to provide reliable, high-speed access to large disk systems consisting of gigabytes of data storage.

If the network is using a client/server application, then a client-server network with an applications server is necessary. The Windows NT Server environment provides a good platform for serving applications because the operating system is designed to support application development.

Database software such as Microsoft's SQL Server 6.5 and Oracle Corporation's Oracle are designed to run on an application server in order to perform certain database functions for the workstations, thereby reducing the load on the network and workstation. Clients will become an increasingly important function of LANs in the future.

Centralized Storage

Another important consideration in selecting a network operating system is the need for the network to contain centralized storage for files and documents. If an organization's employees use word processors and spreadsheet programs to access common documents and files, a client-server network system will provide them with consistent and reliable shared storage areas that can be routinely backed up in order to provide for disaster recovery.

Client-server environments are also the best choice when users in an organization need access to large centralized databases containing inventory and customer information. These database files should be placed on a dedicated file server or application server in order to take advantage of the speed associated with file caching and the assurance of high reliability and fault tolerance that can be gained by mirroring or duplexing the disk drives.

Selecting a Network Operating System

The flowchart shown in Figure 1-8 illustrates how to analyze the network processing needs of an organization to help select a network operating system.

As shown in the flowchart, the number of user workstations to be attached to the network is the first consideration. If there are fewer than 15 workstations, a peer-to-peer system will probably be the best network alternative. However, if several of these workstations will be working with large files that need to be shared on the network, such as those used by departments running computer aided design applications, a client-server network operating system is preferable. The choice of the peer-to-peer network operating system will also depend on the type of operating systems used by client workstations.

When the number of users exceeds 15, the need for centralized data typically becomes an important factor in choosing between a client-server and peer-to-peer system. If the network will be used mostly for sharing printers and personal communication, you will need to consider the operating systems that the client workstations will be running. If client workstations will be running different types of operating systems, NetWare is usually the best operating system choice because it can be configured to support communications and file sharing between different client operating environments.

When centralized data storage is a major function of the network, a client-server system such as NetWare or Windows NT Server is the best choice because it provides a secure and efficient platform that helps ensure that data will be available at all times. When large database or multimedia files that are critical to an organization's operation need to be accessed from a centralized server, NetWare 4.1x is generally the best choice, depending upon the number of servers. In most situations in which performance, security, and reliability are a must, NetWare is probably the best choice because it has been used extensively for many years and its performance and compatibility with many applications are well established. Other client-server environments, such as Windows NT Server, are newer to the marketplace and should be considered and researched carefully to determine their performance and compatibility in the proposed network environment.

Figure 1-8 Selecting a network operating system

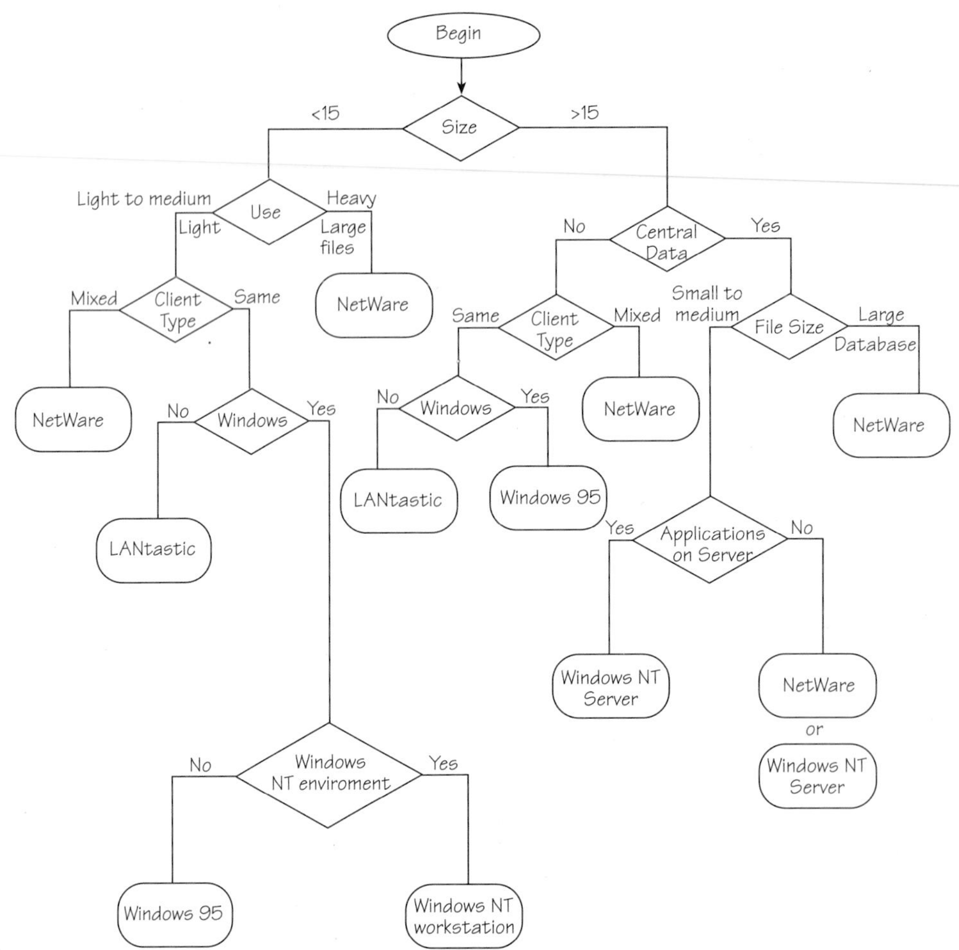

Today many network administrators are gaining the best of both peer-to-peer and client-server networks by implementing networks consisting of combinations of network operating systems. For example, a NetWare client-server network can include clients running Windows 95, while Windows NT Server is used to provide access to certain Windows NT–based client/server applications. As these operating systems gain popularity, network administrators will be increasingly called upon to implement network systems, using a combination of compatible products in order to provide the services needed by the organization's LAN users.

Cunningham, Burns, and Evans Laboratories

Let's consider how what we've learned about networks can be used to select a new network for an organization. The organization we'll work with is Cunningham, Burns, and Evans Laboratories (CBE Labs).

The Organization

Located in Portland, Oregon, CBE Labs is a small, independent consulting firm specializing in testing and reporting on computer hardware and software. The firm's highly respected industry newsletter, *The C/B/E Networker*, has a reputation for impartial and detailed evaluations, and information system specialists often refer to it when deciding which hardware or software to purchase. *The C/B/E Networker* is subscribed to by most, if not all, of the Fortune 500 companies and by all major firms in the computer industry.

CBE Labs is organized into three departments: administration, laboratories, and publications. An organization chart for CBE Labs is shown in Figure 1-9.

Figure 1-9

CBE Labs organization chart

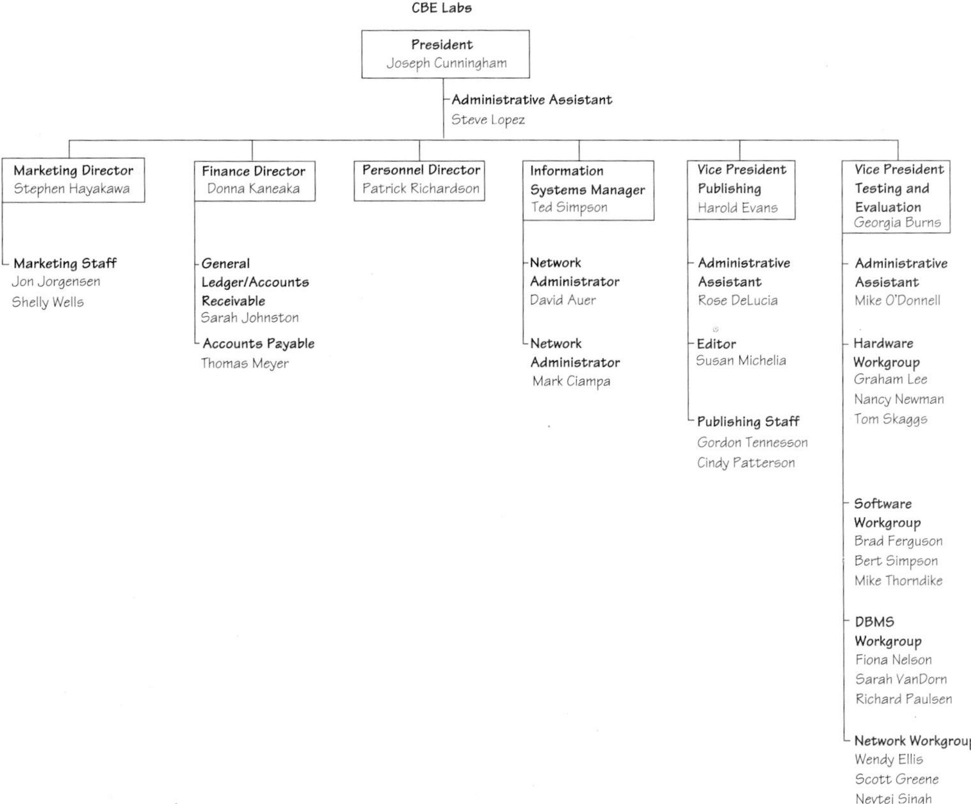

Administration of CBE is overseen by President Joseph Cunningham and an administration assistant. Administration includes marketing, finance, personnel, and information systems. There are three people in marketing, three in finance, one in personnel, and three in information systems.

The CBE Labs testing labs are organized around four technology workgroups: hardware (workstation PCs and their components), software (workstation operating systems and application programs), database management systems (DBMS), and networking (network server PCs and their components, network operating systems, and network applications). CBE Labs has three employees in each workgroup, along with Vice President for Testing and Evaluation Georgia Burns, and one administrative assistant. Hardware and software being tested is not considered part of CBE Labs' own equipment.

CBE Labs does use its own equipment to store the data resulting from testing and evaluations, to create *The C/B/E Networker*, and to run the business applications necessary to manage the organization. The publishing workgroup is managed by Vice President for Publishing Harold Evans, who oversees a staff of three plus one administrative assistant.

CBE Labs needs to update the company's LAN. Although CBE Labs could simply upgrade their existing software to newer versions, they have decided that they do not want to be locked into software simply because they already own a version of it. The purchasing decision will be a "zero-based" decision, in which all network operating systems will be evaluated.

The company expects to use three servers in the new network: one for lab data and reports, one for publishing *The C/B/E Networker*, and one for company administration. The company needs e-mail, fax capability, and Internet access in the network. All workstations will run Windows 95 and need to access large databases stored on the servers. Some applications will be run from the servers, but most standardized user applications (word processing, spreadsheet, and presentation graphics software) will be loaded on the users' workstations. Finally, the company's existing network is a client-server network using a single-server NetWare 3.12. Management wouldn't mind if the new network could accommodate the existing server and NetWare license, but this is not a requirement.

Choosing the New Network

Let's apply the flowchart in Figure 1-8 to determine which network operating system CBE Labs should use. The number of users is greater than 15, so we initially branch to the right at the Size decision point. The organization will be storing centralized data on the servers, so we branch to the right at the Central Data decision point. At the File Size decision point, we have to consider whether large database files will be kept on the servers. The answer is yes, so we branch to the right and choose NetWare as the network operating system. This path through the flowchart is shown in Figure 1-10.

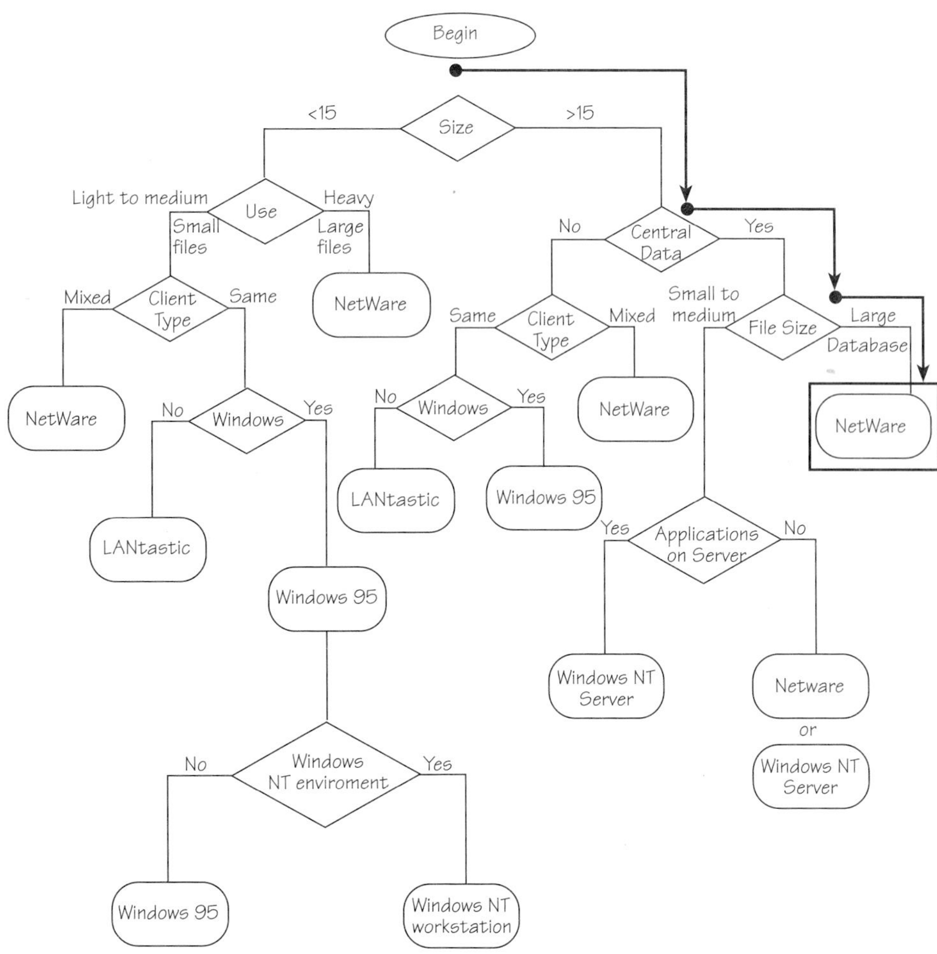

Figure 1-10 Selecting a NetWare operating system for CBE Labs

However, CBE Labs may also be using client/server applications. Windows NT Server is considered a better applications server NOS than NetWare. This doesn't mean that NetWare doesn't perform well as an applications server, only that Windows NT Server performs better. We can still run client/server applications if necessary, so NetWare is our choice for the network operating system.

What about the existing NetWare 3.12 server? Although it's a bit old, it still functions. NetWare 3.1x servers can exist in NetWare 4.1x networks. In fact, NetWare includes a NETSYNC utility to allow the network administrator to manage NetWare 3.1x servers from the NetWare 4.1 management utilities, so we'll be able to keep and use the existing server in the new network.

THE CERTIFIED NOVELL ADMINISTRATOR (CNA)

The microcomputer networking field is an exciting arena with new developments occurring on an almost daily basis. The rapid growth of this field has created the need for network professionals, trained individuals who can be trusted with the responsibilities of creating and maintaining LANs and WANs. Novell has created a means for a network administrator to demonstrate his or her competency at NetWare administration by passing a qualifying exam. Passing the exam earns the network administrator the designation of Certified Novell Administrator. A **Certified Novell Administrator (CNA)** is considered qualified to be the network administrator of an installed NetWare system. Originally called the Certified NetWare Administrator program, the CNA program was developed by Novell in 1992 to help define the role of network administrators in a NetWare environment by providing a standard of knowledge and performance that organizations can use to help ensure the quality of network administration and support.

Although it is not a required prerequisite to take the CNA exam, Novell expects that all CNAs understand DOS and can use DOS commands. This is even true for the Windows 95 environment because the DOS prompt is still available and DOS commands can still be run.

Notice that by Novell's definition, the CNA is ready to take care of an *already installed* network. The installation itself would be done by a Certified Novell Engineer. The **Certified Novell Engineer (CNE)** designation is awarded to individuals who earn 19 Novell credits by passing a series of exams about NetWare. (The CNA exam is actually one of the tests for CNE and is worth 4 CNE credits.) However, because of the importance to you as a network manager of understanding NetWare installation and creating the NDS and file system for the network, this text includes material on these topics.

CNA and CNE tests are available for a variety of Novell products, and the actual certification you receive depends on which test(s) you take. To be a CNA for NetWare 4.1x, you have to take Novell's Certified NetWare 4 Administrator exam. Tests are also available for certification on two earlier versions of NetWare and three products in Novell's GroupWare product line.

Current information on the CNA and CNE programs can be found on Novell Education's World Wide Web site at http://education.novell.com. A current list of test objectives for the CNA exam, as well as other CNA- and CNE-related information, can be obtained from Novell Education's FaxBack service at 1-800-233-EDUC. Since the content of these programs and exams changes periodically, it's a good idea to get the latest information from Novell before taking the CNA exam.

CNA was originally Certified *NetWare* Administrator, and CNE was Certified *NetWare* Engineer. Similarly, NDS was originally *NetWare* Directory Services. The name changes reflect a broadening of Novell's outlook and its product line. You can be certified on Novell products other than NetWare, and NDS is being developed to work with other network operating systems such as UNIX and Windows NT.

As a CNA your job will be to direct your organization's networking services and support in order to meet the workgroup-oriented processing needs of microcomputer users. To develop the CNA program, Novell researched the job duties of thousands of NetWare network administrators around the world in order to determine the common tasks that needed to be performed by network administrators on a regular basis. The sections that follow summarize Novell's research. They will help you understand the typical duties of a network administrator as well as give you an overview of the NetWare knowledge and skills you will need in order to become a CNA.

Understanding NetWare Components and Commands

One of the fundamentals a NetWare administrator needs is a solid foundation in the components that make up a NetWare network and how they interoperate. When a problem—such as the message "File server not found"—occurs on a workstation attached to the network, the network administrator must be able to troubleshoot the network and isolate the cause of the error by drawing upon his or her knowledge of the network components.

Just as a mechanic must learn how to use the tools necessary to maintain and repair an automobile, a CNA needs to know how to use the many NetWare commands and utilities to be able to perform network maintenance and repair tasks such as creating users, granting access rights, listing directory information, and working with printers. Starting with this chapter and continuing throughout the book, you will be learning how to use the commands and utilities that are the essential tools of CNAs.

Supporting Client Workstation Environments

The majority of computers attached to NetWare networks today run either the DOS or Windows operating system, and therefore, as a CNA, you will need to know how to install and configure the client software used to attach DOS or Windows workstations to the network and establish communications. With the rapid advances in microcomputer technology that require organizations to add new computers and replace existing ones each year, one of your main CNA tasks will be to install and update client software regularly.

In addition to the DOS and Windows workstations, your organization might also need to provide network support for Apple Macintosh and UNIX-based computers. While Novell does not currently require a CNA to install client software on Macintosh and UNIX operating systems, you will need to be able to identify how the NetWare software components allow UNIX and Macintosh computers to attach to a NetWare network.

Managing Novell Directory Services

One of the most important features in NetWare 4.1 is Novell Directory Services (NDS). On a NetWare 4.1x network, a user connects to the network itself rather than to a server (or group of servers) as shown in Figure 1-5. This requires a comprehensive, logical network design, as well as tools for administering the resources (such as disk space and printers) for the entire network. Novell Directory Services (NDS) is the tool that you as a CNA will use to create, maintain, and administer the network design and resources. The logical network design is called the **NDS Directory tree**. NDS is actually a database of information about the network and is based on the X.500 standard for implementing a network global database. You will learn about NDS in detail in Chapter 4 and create an NDS Directory tree in Chapter 8.

Novell Directory Services is proving to be a useful network design and administration tool, and Novell is licensing NDS to other companies, such as Hewlett-Packard and SCO, for use in their network operating systems and software products. Novell also has plans to develop NDS to run on the Windows NT Server NOS. These developments will make NDS a tool for managing a network with servers running a variety of network operating systems.

MANAGING THE NETWORK FILE SYSTEM

A network file system uses a directory structure to define the way in which the data storage of your server(s) is organized. You might already be aware of how a good directory structure on your workstation's local hard disk makes it easier to run applications and access files. On a server, a good directory structure becomes even more important because many users share the same storage device. As a result, one of the most important tasks a CNA must undertake when installing a new server is planning and implementing an efficient directory structure to support the processing needs of the users. In this book you will learn the essential NetWare file system components as well as the design techniques that will help you create and maintain a workable network directory structure.

ESTABLISHING AND MAINTAINING NETWORK USERS AND SECURITY

NetWare has a very sophisticated security system that enables the network administrator to provide users with access to information while at the same time protecting special information from unauthorized access. To implement this security system, as a CNA you will need to create a user account for each person who will access the network and then assign the appropriate security restrictions such as passwords and other limitations that you feel are necessary to protect user accounts from unauthorized access. In addition, in order to access files on the network, users need to be given access rights to NDS objects and the directories and files they will be using. As a CNA, you will assign these rights. In Chapters 9 and 10, you will learn how to use NetWare utilities and commands to create users as well as assign the necessary rights to access NDS objects and the network file system. Because organizational structures continually change, an ongoing task you will have as a CNA is to add and delete users as well as modify the rights assigned to users and groups.

SETTING UP AND MAINTAINING NETWORK PRINTING

Perhaps one of the most complex and demanding tasks of a network administrator is creating and maintaining the network printing environment. Network printing has become an increasingly important issue on networks with sophisticated applications such as desktop publishing and WYSIWYG (what you see is what you get) word processors and spreadsheets. These applications require expensive laser and ink-jet printers that are often shared in order to justify their cost. As a CNA, you will find that you need to continually upgrade your network printing environment in order to support faster and more sophisticated printers and applications as they become available. In this book you will learn how to use the NetWare printing components and tools that allow you to install and maintain a network printing environment that will meet the needs of your users.

Loading and Updating Application Software

An ongoing and important job of the network administrator is installing and upgrading application software packages that run on the client workstations. Whenever possible you will want to install applications on the server so they can be shared and centrally maintained. However, some applications will not run from a server, or will run much more efficiently when installed on the workstation's local hard drive. As a CNA, you will need to be familiar with installing and configuring many different application software packages and know how to support these packages on either the server or local workstations. An ongoing job of the CNA is to obtain and install software upgrades, as well as respond to user questions and problems. As a result, CNAs often find that they need to have the strong interpersonal skills sometimes required to work with frustrated or angry users.

Another responsibility of the network administrator is policing copyright licenses of application software to be sure your organization always has enough licenses to cover the number of users that are running the applications. This task is very important because your company can be exposed to a lawsuit and fined if it is found in violation of copyright laws. To make the CNA's responsibility easier, some companies produce software that will count the number of users who are currently using a software package and not allow more users than the number you have identified according to your software licenses.

Creating an Automated User Environment

Before the Windows environment became popular, users had to use DOS commands to log into the network or run software programs. Providing users with an easy-to-use system that prompted them to log in and then presented them with a simple menu containing their applications was another important task of the network administrator in that environment. The Windows—and particularly Windows 95—environment has eliminated most of the need for menu systems. However, there might still be instances of older DOS applications that need a menu system. In order for CNAs to set up and maintain an easy-to-use network environment, Novell requires them to know how to use NetWare utilities to create and maintain NetWare menus and login script files. The login script files are necessary even if you don't use the NetWare menu system. In Chapters 14 and 15 you will learn how to use NetWare login scripts and menus to create a user-friendly network environment that will allow users on your network to log into their assigned server easily and immediately bring up menus that allow them to select and run their software applications.

Developing and Implementing a Backup and Recovery System

Information is the lifeblood of an organization, and as a CNA you will be the guardian of the information stored on the local area network system. One of the worst nightmares a CNA can have is a server crashing with the loss of all the network information stored on its hard drives. To prevent this catastrophe and allow you to sleep more easily, you will need to be sure your server environment is as reliable as possible. You will also need a good backup system to restore all the programs and data on your server in the event of a major system failure. In Chapter 2 you will learn about the fail-safe measures that can be implemented on

NetWare servers and how you can develop system specifications that will provide a reliable and fault-tolerant system. No matter how reliable or fault-tolerant a system is, however, you still need to be prepared for a worst case scenario, such as your building being destroyed or the equipment being damaged by an electrical failure or lightning. In Chapter 16 you will learn how to plan for disasters by implementing a backup and recovery system by using the NetWare Storage Management System and utilities.

Managing the Server and Monitoring Network Performance

A NetWare server has its own operating system and console commands that enable a network administrator to control the server environment as well as run special software called NetWare Loadable Modules (NLMs) in order to perform certain tasks or add new services. As a result, a CNA will need to spend some time each week at the server console using console commands and utilities to monitor server activity as well as adding new services and modifying or configuring existing ones.

Network performance can sometimes falter with the addition of users to the network, large printing loads, and the ever-increasing demands by the high-speed workstations for graphics applications. As a CNA, you will regularly need to monitor your network system as well as the server in order to detect performance bottlenecks or problems and then determine if additional hardware or configuration changes are necessary. In Chapter 16 you will learn about several common network problems that are caused by insufficient hardware, as well as how to configure your server and workstations to help improve performance and avoid problems.

Supporting Network Communications

In addition to allowing users to share resources on a server, an important use of a LAN is communication among users, as well as access to a minicomputer or mainframe computer. One of the most common LAN communication applications is e-mail. As a CNA, you will be expected to help implement, maintain, and administer an e-mail application in your organization. Novell has provided NetWare with a built-in message delivery system called the Message Handling Services (MHS).

Chapter Summary

A computer network is formed when two or more computers are connected so that they can communicate electronically with each other. Local Area Networks (LANs) are located in one location, while Wide Area Networks (WANs) connect two or more LANs. The network administrator is responsible for running the network. Networks use servers, which are specialized computers that provide network services. Examples of servers are file servers, print servers, and application servers.

Networks are becoming widespread in many organizations because they provide cost savings by enabling users to share expensive hardware and software, time savings by making it easier for users to work together, shared access to database and document files, a more secure environment to protect sensitive data from unauthorized access, a more reliable storage system to prevent loss of data and time, and a communication system that can be used for electronic mail and scheduling applications, as well as providing access to minicomputer and mainframe computer systems.

Network operating systems (NOSs) can be classified into two types: peer-to-peer and client-server. Peer-to-peer operating systems do not require a dedicated server but instead are able to share data among the client workstations. Generally, peer-to-peer operating systems such as LANtastic, Windows 95, and Windows NT Workstation are best implemented for smaller workgroups that do not require frequent access to centralized data files. Because client-server operating systems such as NetWare and Windows NT Server have dedicated servers, they can be more efficient and reliable platforms for storage of centralized files.

When selecting an operating system for your network, you need to consider such factors as the number of users and workstations, the type of operating systems and applications that will be used by the client workstations, and the need for high-speed centralized data storage. In most cases in which a client-server network is needed, NetWare equals or exceeds the capabilities of other systems such as Windows NT Server and Banyan VINES. Because each type of operating system has certain strengths, however, many organizations must be able to integrate combinations of network operating systems and workstations in order to meet their network processing needs. Windows NT Server is often chosen as the operating system for an application server.

In order to succeed as a network administrator, you will need a good understanding of the hardware and software components that make up a network system and how they interoperate. The basic hardware components of a network consist of the server, cable system, network cards, uninterruptible power supply (UPS), client workstations, and shared printers. Printers can be added to the network by attaching them to a local printer port on the server, attaching them remotely to a client workstation, or attaching them directly to the network cable. The software components of a network consist of the card driver program, which is responsible for directly controlling the network interface card (NIC); the protocol stack, which performs the formatting of the data transmitted between computers; the DOS requester program, which provides an interface between applications and the network; and the network operating system, which runs on the server computer and provides the shared network services.

Network administration is an exciting field with a great future, and a Certified Novell Administrator (CNA) will be in a position to grow with the industry. As a CNA, your responsibilities will include such activities as supporting client workstation applications, creating and maintaining the network directory structures, creating and maintaining the Novell Directory Services (NDS) database and Directory tree, establishing network users and security, setting up and maintaining the network printing environment, managing the server console, maintaining a user-friendly environment, implementing a fail-safe backup and recovery system, and supporting network communications.

Key Terms

application server
cable system
centralized processing
Certified Novell Administrator (CNA)
Certified Novell Engineer (CNE)
client-server
client/server applications
client-service network operating system
client workstation
computer aided design (CAD)
computer network
concentrator
dedicated
directly attached printer
distributed processing
electronic mail (e-mail) applications
fault tolerance
file server
file system security
hub
local area network (LAN)
local printer
login security
mainframe computer
microcomputer
minicomputer
mirroring
NDS Directory tree
NetWare file server
NetWare Loadable Module (NLM)
NetWare server
NDS security
network administrator
network-centric
network interface card (NIC)
network interface card driver
network operating system (NOS)
nondedicated
Novell Directory Services (NDS)
packet
peer-to-peer
personal computer (PC)
protocol stack
print queue
print server
remote printer
scheduling applications
server
server-centric
system console
system console security
terminals
trustee assignments
trustee rights
uninterruptible power supply (UPS)
wide area network (WAN)

Review Questions

1. Two or more computers connected so that they can communicate electronically with each other are known as ____________________.
2. Computer networks that exist in one location are called ____________________; computer networks that exist in two or more geographic locations are called ____________________.
3. The LAN supports ____________________ processing by allowing microcomputers to access centralized data and resources.
4. Define the following types of servers:

   File server: ____________________

   Print server: ____________________

   Application server: ____________________
5. List two advantages of using a LAN for centralized data storage:

   ____

   ____

6. Identify two areas in which a LAN can be used to save personnel time:

   ____

   ____

7. In many networks, sharing ______________ will provide the most direct cost savings.

8. A network operating system that allows client computers to share files among themselves is called a ______________.

9. A ______________ network operating system requires a server.

10. List two advantages of peer-to-peer network operating systems:

    ____

    ____

11. List two advantages of client-server network operating systems:

    ____

    ____

12. A network in which a new user's account must be created on every server is ______________; a network where the account must be created only once is ______________.

13. List the seven network hardware components:

    ____

    ____

    ____

    ____

    ____

    ____

    ____

14. If a server can also be used as a client workstation, then it is a ______________ server.

15. List three ways a printer can be attached to a network:

    ____

    ____

    ____

16. The ______________ software component controls communications on the network cable.

17. The ______________ software component formats the information being transmitted between computers.

18. The ______________ software component provides access to shared files and other resources.

19. The ______________ software component interfaces the network to DOS.

20. List four types of NetWare security:

21. Identify the CNA responsibility under which each of the following tasks belongs.

a. Deciding where to place the quality-control database in order to allow shared access by several users throughout an organization:

b. Making a new printer available to the users in the sales department:

c. Making it possible for the users in the sales department to select the new sales printer easily from their menu:

d. Determining why certain workstations cannot log in to the new server:

e. Providing computers in the sales department with the ability to run the new PowerPoint presentation software:

f. Determining how much memory the server computer is using for file caching:

g. Getting a good night's sleep:

h. Adding users to the e-mail system:

i. Modifying the logical network design to accommodate the addition of a new server purchased for the use of the sales group:

Hands-On

EXERCISES

EXERCISE 1-1: RECORDING NETWORK INFORMATION

1. So that you can perform the exercises and project assignments in this book, your instructor has created a user account for you on the network. Your instructor will provide you with information about your user account. Record the information provided in the space below (you may not need to use all the lines provided):

NOS Directory tree name: __________

Username: __________

Last name: __________

Full name: __________

Student reference number: ______________________________

Context: ______________________________

Home directory location: ______________________________

Volume name: ______________________________

Home directory path and name: ______________________________

2. Your instructor will take your class on a tour of your local area network. Use information presented during the tour to fill in the following information in the tables in Figure 1-11.

Figure 1-11 Network information

NetWare Server Information

Name	Operating system	Memory (MB)	Disk capacity (MB)	NIC & Protocol	UPS

Network Printer Information

Printer name	Type	Location	Attachment method

Your Client Workstation

Name (if any)	Operating system	Memory (MB)	Disk capacity (MB)	NIC & Protocol

Exercise 1-2: Logging in to the Network

In this exercise you will learn how to log in to your network.

1. Your instructor will explain how to log in to your network. Record the steps in the area below:

____
____
____
____
____
____
____
____

2. Using the instructions given by your instructor, log in to the network.

Exercise 1-3: Setting Your Password

You can assign a password to provide more security for your user name. Be sure to assign a password you can remember or you will suffer the embarrassment of having to ask your instructor or lab supervisor to reassign a new password for you. To assign a password for your user name, you use the SETPASS command. The NetWare SETPASS command line utility will ask you to enter your password but will not display it on the screen. After you enter your password, the system will ask you to verify it by entering it a second time.

1. If necessary, log in to the network by using your assigned user name.
2. In Windows 95, click the Start button, select Programs, and then select MS-DOS prompt to switch to the DOS prompt.
3. Type the command SETPASS and press [Enter]. At the prompt. enter your new password and then press [Enter]. At the next prompt, reenter your new password and then press [Enter].
4. After you have changed your password, type EXIT and then press [Enter] to close the DOS prompt and return to Windows 95.

Exercise 1-4: Creating Your Student Work Disk

In this assignment you will copy your student work files and chapter study system from the server onto a formatted high-density disk. You will use this disk to do assignments in later chapters.

1. If necessary, log in to the network using your assigned user name.
2. In Windows 95, click the Start button, then select Programs, and then select MS-DOS prompt to switch to the DOS prompt.
3. Your instructor will tell you the drive letter of the drive that contains the files for you student work disk. Type d:, where d is the drive letter given you by your instructor, and then press [Enter] to change to that drive.
4. Type CD \NWTC\SOFTWARE.NTC\WORKDISK and then press [Enter].
5. Insert a formatted disk into drive A: (or another floppy disk drive as directed by your instructor).

The NetWare NCOPY command is similar in function and syntax to the DOS XCOPY command. For copying files between network directories, however, the NCOPY is more efficient and reliable. In this step you will practice using the NCOPY command to copy all files and subdirectories from the NWTC\SOFTWARE.NTC\WORKDISK directory onto your student work disk. To copy all files with one NCOPY command, type the command as shown below. The /S option is used to copy all subdirectories, and the /V option verifies that the files have been copied correctly.

6. Type NCOPY *.* A:\ /S /V and then press [Enter]. (If your formatted disk is in drive B:, type: NCOPY *.* B:\ /S /V and then press [Enter].)
7. After the files are copied, type EXIT and then press [Enter] to close the DOS prompt and return to Windows 95.
8. Remove your disk and label it "NetWare 4.1 Student Work Disk."

Exercise 1-5: Logging Out of the Network

In this exercise you will learn how to log out of your network.

1. Your instructor will explain how to log out of your network. Record the steps in the area below:

   ____

   ____

   ____

   ____

   ____

   ____

   ____

   ____

2. Using the instructions given by your instructor, log out of your network.

Exercises

Case 1-1: Selecting a Network Operating System for the J. Q. Adams Corporation

The J. Q. Adams Corporation manufactures office equipment and supplies and then sells these products to companies that retail them. J. Q. Adams does not sell directly to the end user of their products. J. Q. Adams is a medium-sized company with more than 15 employees.

The company is planning to downsize its quality-control system from a minicomputer to a LAN. Part of this system involves collecting information such as quantities produced and inspection results from the shop floor and saving them in a central database. Product defects from returned goods will also be coded and stored in a separate database. These database files are expected to become quite large, and it is critical that the collection process not be interrupted during daily operations. Other computers in the office will then have access to this data to be used in spreadsheet and database software in order to produce reports and analyze production problems.

Along with this reorganization of the quality control system, the information systems manager at J. Q. Adams has decided to expand the LAN to include administrative operations. He plans to use two servers, one for administration and one for production, connected by the LAN. Administration users will use word processing, spreadsheet, database, and accounting software.

Given the above information, use the flowchart in Figure 1-8 to help select the best network operating system for the J. Q. Adams Corporation. Write a memo to your instructor documenting your decision. In the memo, explain your decision by diagramming your path through the flowchart and writing a brief paragraph justifying your selection.

Case 1-2: Selecting a Network Operating System for the Jefferson County Courthouse

Jefferson County is getting ready to install a network in the Jefferson County Courthouse. The network will connect 12 users in the social services department. The network will allow them to implement e-mail and group scheduling applications while sharing access to two laser printers. The 12 users include program administrator Janet Hinds, her assistant Tom Norihama, receptionist Lisa Walsh, department secretary Terry Smith, and eight social workers. Terry Smith is familiar with advanced features of the word processing package and often does final editing of the documents created by the social workers. As a result, social workers will need to pass documents periodically to Terry's computer so she can finalize them for printing.

1. Given the above information, use the flowchart in Figure 1-8 to help select the best network operating system for the Jefferson County Courthouse social services department. Write a memo to your instructor documenting your decision. In the memo, explain your decision by diagramming your path through the flowchart and writing a brief paragraph justifying your selection.

The Jefferson County Courthouse also houses the county's courtroom facilities. There are three courtrooms that support the operations of four judges, four bailiffs, six court reporters and 12 administrative staff. Each judge has his or her own office. The bailiffs share an office, but each has a separate desk. A similar situation applies to the court reporters. The administrative staff is in four offices, and each has a desk. If a network was installed, each employee would have a client workstation on his or her desk. Additionally, the administration personnel would require four more workstations set up at windows where they deal with the public. A database of legal documents would be created and stored on the network, and this database is expected to grow very large over time. It is not clear whether a client-server database application would be used.

2. How would your decision change if Jefferson County also included the county court system in the network? What difference does it make if a client/server application is used for the database? Use the flowchart in Figure 1-8 to help select the best network operating system for the Jefferson County Courthouse with each database option. Write a memo to your instructor documenting your decision for each option. In the memo, explain your decision for each option by diagramming your path through the flowchart and writing a brief paragraph justifying your selection.

Northwestern Technical College

Congratulations! You have just been hired by Northwestern Technical College (NWTC) as a computer lab technician and network administrator for its main campus. The college campus where you are located contains administrative offices, faculty offices, classrooms, and computer labs. Your job is to implement and manage the microcomputer network at the campus as well as to help students and faculty with computer problems. Dave Johnson, whose office is in the administration building, is the head of Computer Information Systems for the college. He will be your direct supervisor in implementing the campus network. An organizational chart for Northwestern Technical College is shown in Figure 1-12.

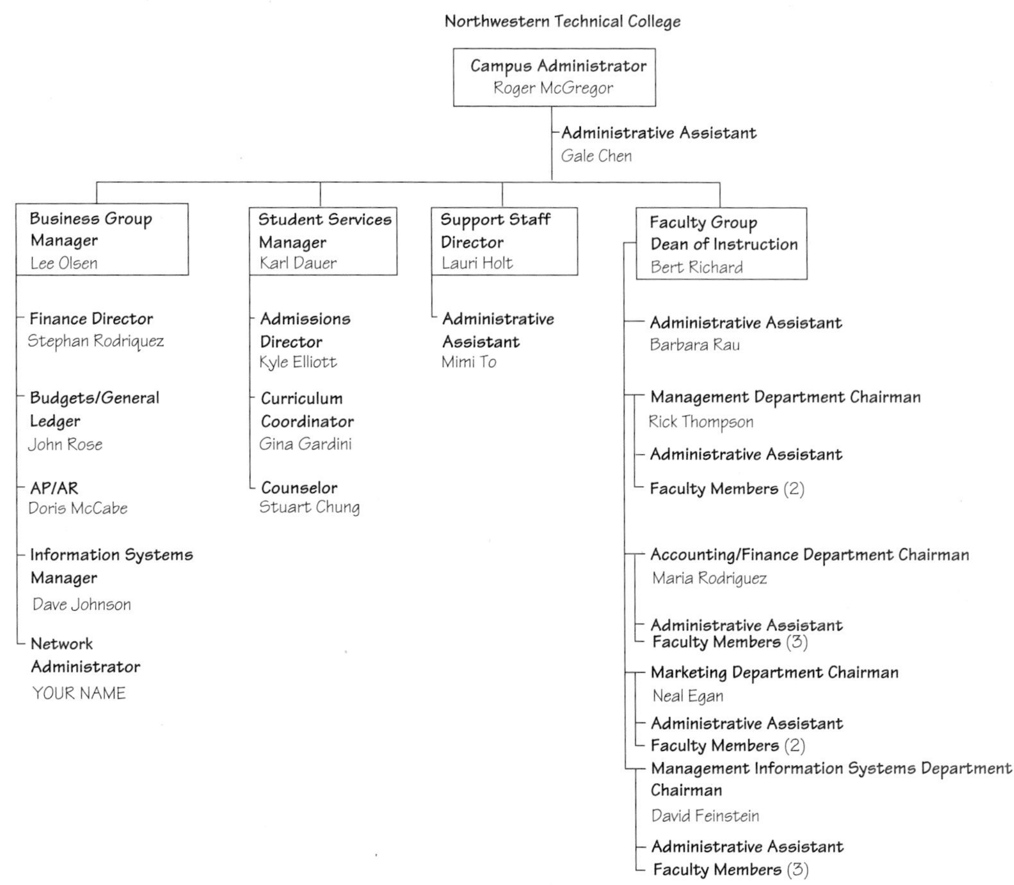

Figure 1-12 Organization chart for Northwestern Technical College

In your first meeting after being hired, Dave explained his plan for the campus network. The network at the campus will be used by students in both the computer labs and by the administration and faculty in their offices. There will be:

- Twenty-five computers in each computer lab for student use
- One computer in each of four classrooms
- One computer for each person on the organizational chart

Dave wants you to take security measures to ensure that students cannot access or damage the administrative or faculty data. In addition, Dave wants administrative and faculty data to be backed up daily, with weekly backups of student files and software. To meet the printing needs of the campus, Dave would like five laser printers to be placed on the network. Each of the two computer labs is to have one shared laser printer. In addition, one shared laser printer is to be used by the faculty, one for student service use, and one for faculty secretaries.

Dave explained that word processing, database, and spreadsheet software is currently installed separately on each computer in the lab. This software has become quite a problem to maintain due to students' changing the configurations and frequent software updates. The faculty have pointed out that it is very important for student learning that software configurations remain the same on all computers. The faculty want to have their computers on the network so they can access the laser printers, work with the same software the students use, and enable the students to access files they create without having to copy them to floppy disks. Dave also wants to implement e-mail for everyone.

Dave explained that the student services department has recently obtained a network version of a recruitment system. This system will allow student service staff to keep track of students who have inquired about programs being offered at the college and follow up on their registration status. Faculty members have also expressed an interest in being able to access this recruitment data to help follow up on potential students for their programs. This program, although it will be installed on the network, is not a client/server application. In addition to the recruitment system, the student services department uses a word processing program to draft letters and memos and has an aptitude testing program that it uses to help students select a career path. Currently, the testing software is on a stand-alone computer. However, this computer is sometimes in use and the student services department would like students to be able to take the tests on any machine in the student labs.

Finally, administrative assistants are responsible for preparing reports and typing for faculty. Currently the faculty members often bring disks to the administrative assistants with rough drafts of their documents to be formatted and printed. Dave hopes this process can be improved with the network system. Because of busy schedules, it is often difficult for faculty members to respond to requests made by other staff. Dave would like you to consider whether a network could be used to help with this communication problem.

The college needs e-mail, fax capability, and Internet access in the network. All workstations will run Windows 95 and need to access large databases stored on the servers. Some applications will be run from the servers, but most standardized user applications (word processing, spreadsheet, and presentation graphics software) will be loaded on the users' workstations.

PROJECT 1-1: COMPARING NETWORK OPERATING SYSTEMS

Dave Johnson would like you to write a memo to him listing the benefits that can be derived from implementing a network at the NWTC campus. This memo should list benefits in the following categories: hardware, sharing data, software, and communications. In addition, Dave would like you to compare and contrast the advantages and disadvantages of using client-server versus peer-to-peer network operating systems and make a recommendation as to which type of system you think would be most suitable. Dave said he would carefully consider your recommendation in making his purchasing decision.

CHAPTER TWO

MICROCOMPUTER HARDWARE

In the previous chapter you learned about networks and the basic components of a LAN. LANs support distributed processing on a variety of computer systems, so a network administrator must have a solid background in the fundamentals of microcomputer hardware and software components. Each new generation of software applications seems to demand more processing power, and microcomputer systems are based on complex and evolving technologies. Components from many manufacturers are combined to build a microcomputer. In order to help you make sense of the many concepts and terms that are used in today's computer environments, this chapter provides a basic background in microcomputer terminology and concepts to help you keep abreast of developments in microcomputer hardware and software. This knowledge will enable you to develop specifications for the purchase of PC workstations and NetWare servers. In addition, the information in this chapter provides a basis for configuring Network Interface Cards (NICs) and evaluating NetWare server performance, topics that are discussed in future chapters.

AFTER READING THIS CHAPTER AND COMPLETING THE EXERCISES YOU WILL BE ABLE TO:

- IDENTIFY THE HARDWARE COMPONENTS THAT MAKE UP A MICROCOMPUTER SYSTEM.
- COMPARE AND CONTRAST MICROPROCESSORS USED ON WORKSTATIONS AND NETWARE SERVERS.
- DESCRIBE THE PURPOSE OF AND USE OF EXPANSION BUSES, I/O PORTS, AND INTERRUPTS IN A MICROCOMPUTER SYSTEM.
- COMPARE AND CONTRAST STORAGE SYSTEMS USED ON NETWARE SERVERS.
- APPLY KNOWLEDGE OF COMPUTER HARDWARE COMPONENTS TO DEVELOPING NETWARE SERVER SPECIFICATIONS.

Computer Basics

A microcomputer operates on the same basic internal principles as its larger siblings, minicomputers and mainframe computers. All computers, regardless of their size or capacity, need to perform input, processing, storage, and output operations. The hardware that allows these processes to take place on a microcomputer system is shown in Figure 2-1.

Figure 2-1

The computing model

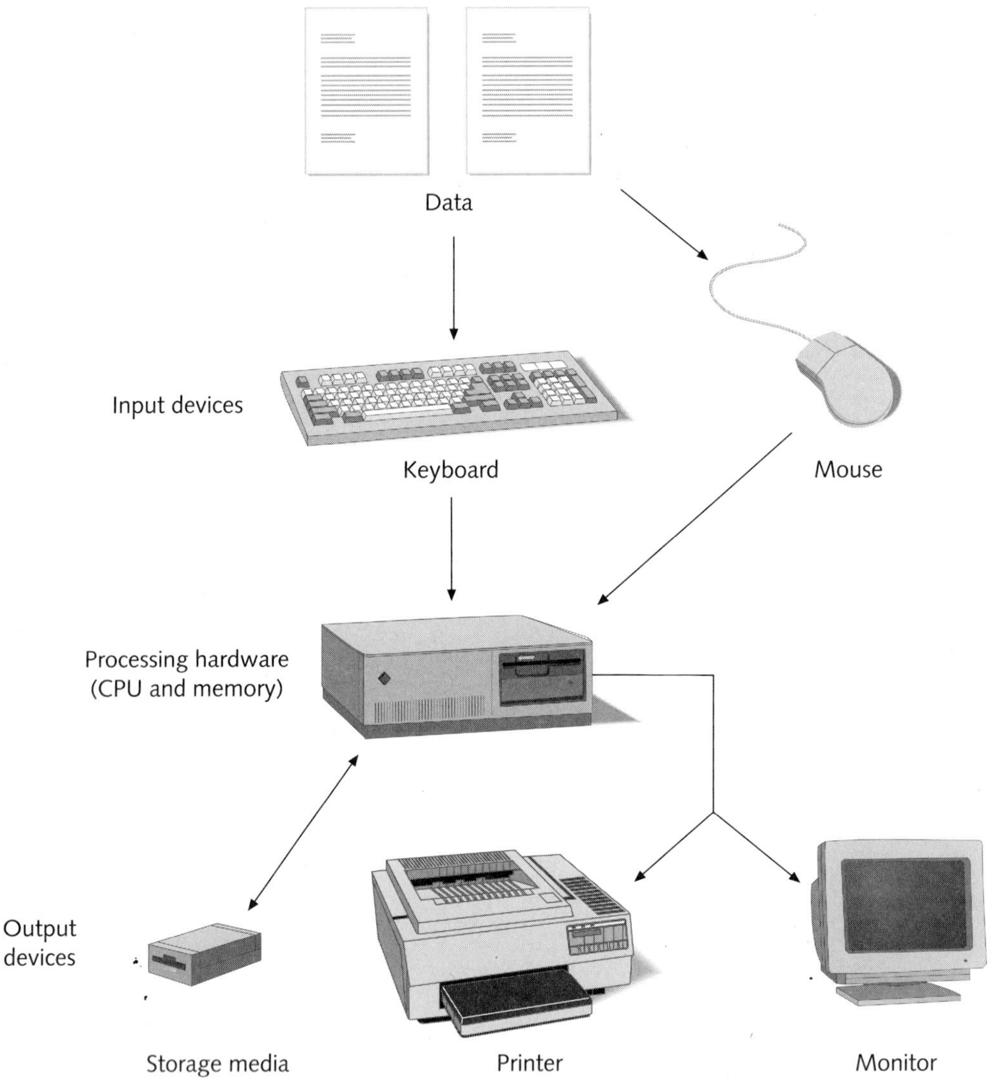

Input→Process→Output

The input units include such devices as keyboards, scanners, and the mouse, which convert data into electronic on/off signals that computer circuits can transmit and store. The processing hardware houses the computer circuits that are responsible for processing the data. As bits of data arrive at the system unit, they are stored in electronic circuits called **memory buffers**. A memory buffer is like a receiving room where the data bits wait until the computer is ready to process them. The **central processing unit (CPU)**, also called a **microprocessor** on a microcomputer, contains the electronic circuits that interpret the program instructions stored in memory and then perform the specified operations on the data, including input, arithmetic functions, decision making, and output.

A major component of the processing hardware is the primary memory, also called **random-access memory** or **RAM**. The primary memory stores program instructions and data in a form that is directly accessible to the CPU. Data storage in RAM is temporary because the RAM contents are lost when the computer is turned off or rebooted. In order to store software and data for later use, it is necessary to record the information from RAM into a storage system. The storage system of the computer consists of magnetic disks that allow the computer system to store and access software and data files. Some data, such as that needed to initially start the computer is stored in **read only-memory** or **ROM**. This data can be read into the computer's memory for processing, but the computer cannot write information back.

Output units consist primarily of video monitors, printers, and storage devices. The video card of your computer plays a very important role in how fast your computer performs and what software you can run by providing compatibility with several video standards in use today.

The hardware components found in all microcomputers can be divided into six major categories: microprocessors, memory, system boards, storage systems, video monitors, and power systems. This chapter covers the material a network administrator needs to know about the basic computer concepts and components that make up each of these major hardware categories and how they can be applied to supporting the distributed processing needs of a network system.

BITS, BYTES; BINARY AND HEXADECIMAL

The network administrator needs to be familiar with the basics of the binary and hexadecimal number systems in order to better understand and configure computer hardware. **Binary** refers to a number system with only two values: 0 and 1 (mathematicians refer to this as Base 2). It's like a light switch—either the switch is off (0 - the light is off) or the switch is on (1 - the light is lit). The 0 and 1 are called **binary digits**, and *all* data and instructions in a computer are stored as binary digits. A single binary digit is called a **bit** (short for **b**inary dig**it**). Since one bit by itself cannot convey much information, eight bits are grouped together to form a **byte**. The possible values of the bit positions in a byte are based on powers of 2, with the right-most bit position having the value 1, the next bit position to the left having the value 2, the next 4, then 8, and so on, increasing by a power of two, giving the left-most bit the position in the byte that has the value 128. This is shown in Figure 2-2.

Figure 2-2
Interpreting the byte

Power of 2	2^7	2^6	2^5	2^4	2^3	2^2	2^1	2^0
Value	128	64	32	16	8	4	2	1
Bit	0	1	1	0	0	1	0	1

In Figure 2-2, the byte is 01100101. The decimal value of this byte is

$$(0 \times 128) + (1 \times 64) + (1 \times 32) + (0 \times 16) + (0 \times 8) + (1 \times 4) + (0 \times 2) + (1 \times 1)$$
$$= 0 + 64 + 32 + 0 + 0 + 4 + 0 + 1$$
$$= 101$$

The maximum value that can be stored in a byte (11111111) is equal to 255 (128 + 64 + 32 + 16 + 8 + 4 + 2 + 1). The number of different values that can be stored in a byte is 256: the numbers from 1 (00000001) to 255 (11111111) plus 0 (00000000).

To represent characters, a coding system is used so that a byte represents one character of data. The most common coding system used on microcomputers is the **American Standard Code for Information Interchange (ASCII)** developed by the **American National Standards Institute (ANSI)**. Figure 2-3 contains a partial ASCII chart.

Figure 2-3

Partial ASCII code table

Character	Decimal number	Hexadecimal number	Character	Decimal number	Hexadecimal number
A	65	41	a	97	61
B	66	42	b	98	62
C	67	43	c	99	63
D	68	44	d	100	64
E	69	45	e	101	65
F	70	46	f	102	66
G	71	47	g	103	67
H	72	48	h	104	68
I	73	49	i	105	69
J	74	4A	j	106	6A
K	75	4B	k	107	6B
L	76	4C	l	108	6C
M	77	4D	m	109	6D
N	78	4E	n	110	6E
O	79	4F	o	111	6F
P	80	50	p	112	70
Q	81	51	q	113	71
R	82	52	r	114	72
S	83	53	s	115	73
T	84	54	t	116	74
U	85	55	u	117	75
V	86	56	v	118	76
W	87	57	w	119	77
X	88	58	x	120	78
Y	89	59	y	121	79
Z	90	5A	z	122	7A

Reading and writing eight-bit strings of binary numbers can cause errors because of the chance of transposition of numbers or omission of bits. One solution to this problem is to convert each byte to a decimal number. For example, the ASCII code for the letter "N" (01001110) would have the decimal value of 78 (0 + 64 + 0 + 0 + 8 + 4 + 2 + 0).

Another solution is to use the hexadecimal number system to make binary numbers and ASCII codes more manageable. The hexadecimal system is based on powers of 16 (mathematicians refer to this as Base 16), and uses 16 different values. You are already familiar with the symbols for the first 10 of these values (0–9); the other six values are represented by the first six letters of the alphabet (A–F), where the letter A represents ten, B represents eleven, C twelve, D thirteen, E fourteen, and F fifteen. The advantage of using the hexadecimal system is that when you divide a byte into two 4-bit sections, called **nybbles**, each nybble has a range from zero (0000) through 15 (1111). This means that each nybble can easily be represented by one hexadecimal digit (0–F), as shown in Figure 2-4.

Figure 2-4 Nybbles and hexadecimal notation

Nybble	Hexadecimal equivalent	Nybble	Hexadecimal equivalent
0000	0	1000	8
0001	1	1001	9
0010	2	1010	A
0011	3	1011	B
0100	4	1100	C
0101	5	1101	D
0110	6	1110	E
0111	7	1111	F

Hexadecimal numbers are often written with the letter "h" after the number to indicate that characters are hexadecimal numbers. For example, the hexadecimal number 4E would be written as 4Eh.

Figure 2-5 shows the word NOVELL translated from characters into binary. This is done by first finding the decimal and hexadecimal codes for each letter in the ASCII coding system using Figure 2-3. The hexadecimal nybbles are then converted to binary using Figure 2-4. The letter N is the 78th character in the *complete* ASCII table, so it has a decimal number of 78 in the partial ASCII table shown. The hexadecimal equivalent of 78 is 4E. Now we have the two nybbles needed to translate the character to binary, and using Figure 2-4, hexadecimal 4E = 0100 1110 = 01001110. Thus, the letter N is represented in binary as 01001110. After you become familiar with the hexadecimal number system, you can quickly convert "hex" values to their binary codes.

Figure 2-5 Characters represented in decimal, hexadecimal, and binary

Character	N	O	V	E	L	L
Decimal	78	79	86	69	76	76
Hexadecimal	4E	4F	56	45	4C	4C
Binary	01001110	01001111	01010110	01000101	01001100	01001100

THE MICROCOMPUTER

The microcomputer is commonly called a **personal computer** or **PC.** The people who use them to get the job done are referred to as **end users** or just **users**. PCs used by users are often referred to as **PC workstations** or just **workstations**.

The term *workstation* is sometimes used to refer to microcomputers that are more powerful than the normal PC. These workstations generally run the UNIX operating system and are often used for graphics-intensive work such as the engineering drawings produced by Computer Aided Design (CAD) systems.

THE SYSTEM BOARD

The **system board** (also called the **motherboard**) is the most important component of a microcomputer because it links all the individual system components. The design of the system board directly affects the performance of a computer system. Figure 2-6 illustrates a system board and its major components. In this section we'll discuss how the system board components are linked by using buses, and the following sections will discuss the components themselves.

Figure 2-6

System board components

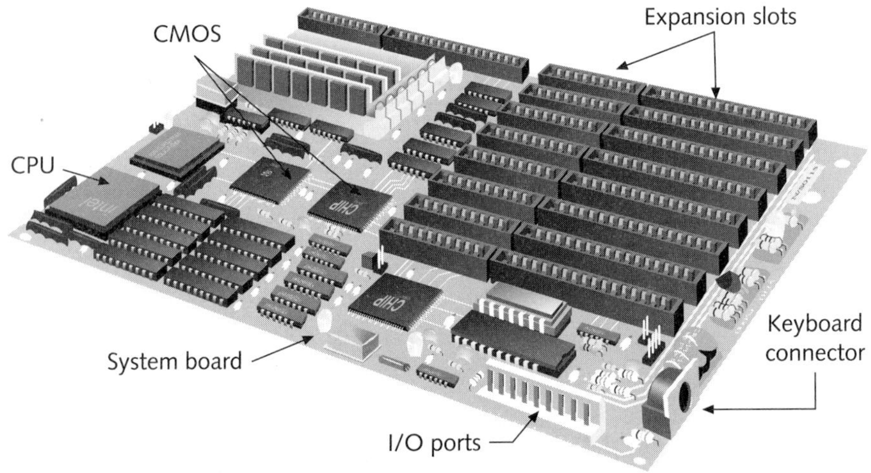

The System Board Buses

The system board circuits that connect components are called **buses**. Buses are the pathways for electronic communication between parts of the computer. They can be visualized as a set of wires running together (in "parallel") from component to component. In actuality, circuits etched into the system board are used instead of wires, but the idea is the same. Buses vary in size (number of "wires") and speed, and are usually referred to by names that reflect their purpose. In this section we'll discuss the data bus, the address bus, the expansion bus, and the local bus. A typical bus structure is shown in Figure 2-7.

Figure 2-7

System board bus structure

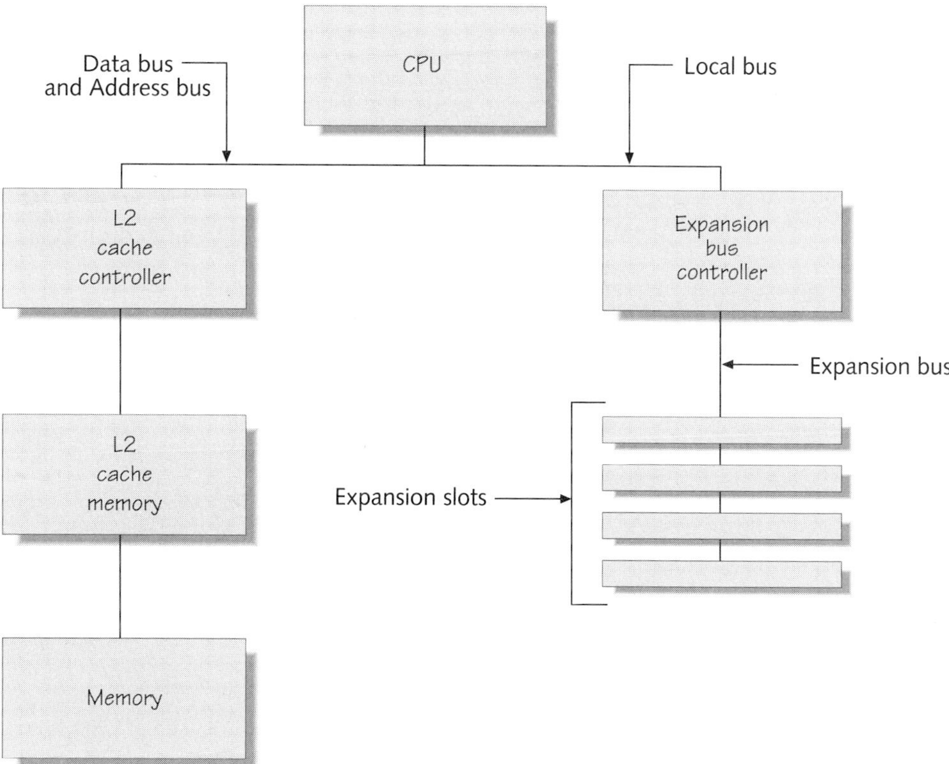

The Local Bus

The system board circuits that connect the CPU to memory and other system board components are referred to as the **local bus** of the computer. The local bus is closely associated with the functions of the microprocessor chip and is designed to support the data and address bus of a specific microprocessor.

The Data Bus

As shown in Figure 2-8, the **data bus** is the highway that transfers data bits to and from the microprocessor registers where the microprocessor stores the data it uses. Just as the number of lanes on a highway determines the amount of traffic that can flow, the size of the data bus determines the number of bits that can be transferred into the microprocessor at one time. Transferring information between the memory unit and the processor is called **fetching**. For example, an 80386SX microprocessor, which has a 16-bit data bus, requires two fetches from memory in order to load one register. An 80386DX microprocessor, which has a 32-bit data bus, can load a register with just one fetch.

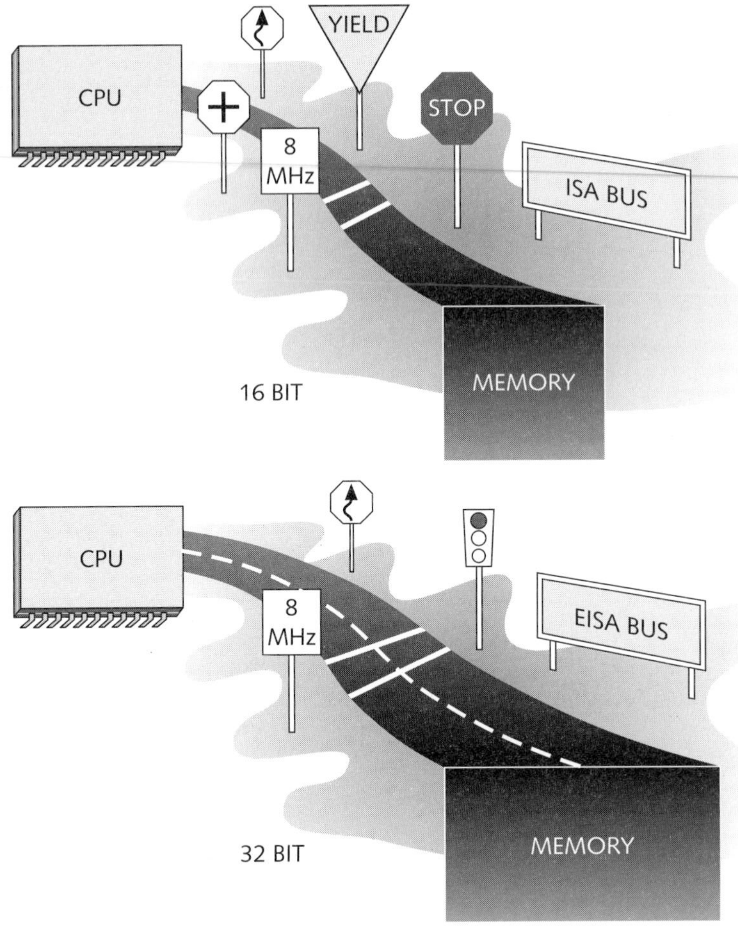

Figure 2-8
The data bus

The Address Bus

Just as each box in a post office is given a unique number to identify it, each byte in the computer's memory is identified by a binary number called an **address**. The microprocessor uses an address to identify the memory byte to or from which it is transferring data. The **address bus** carries the address of the memory byte from the microprocessor to the memory unit. When the memory unit receives the address along with a signal to read, it responds by placing the contents of that memory byte on the data bus. The number of bits in the address bus determines the maximum amount of memory the microprocessor can access directly. If an address bus consists of only two wires, for example, its maximum binary number is 11. A computer with this address bus is limited to a maximum of four byte addresses: 00, 01, 10, and 11. In the binary system, each additional bit on the address bus doubles the amount of memory capacity, so a three-bit address bus has a maximum of eight byte addresses: 000, 001, 010, 011, 100, 101, 110, and 111. The 16-bit address bus commonly found on microprocessors before 1980 could access only 64 KB of RAM; the 20-bit address bus found on the 8088 can access up to 1 MB; the 24-bit address bus on the 80286 and 80386SX can access up to 16 MB; and the 32-bit address bus on the 80386DX, 80486, Pentium, and Pentium Pro can access up to 4 GB.

The Expansion Bus

Some microcomputer components, such as video display controllers and network interface controllers, are not usually built into the system board. Instead these components are built on separate cards, called **expansion cards**, that can be attached to the system board by inserting them into an **expansion slot** on the system board. For example, network connections are commonly made using the Network Interface Card (NIC) described in Chapter 1. The NIC is inserted into one of the expansion slots. The **expansion bus** is the bus that connects the expansion card slots to the components of the system board. The expansion bus connection is made through a specialized chip set on the system board that controls the operation of the expansion bus and the expansion cards attached to it. There are several types of expansion buses, which are discussed in the section on expansion slots later in this chapter.

Direct Memory Access

A **direct memory access (DMA) channel** is the part of the local bus that is used to automate the transfer of data between the computer's memory and external devices such as disk drives and NICs. DMA channels are assigned to specific devices. This means that when you are configuring a device such as a NIC, you need to be sure to assign an unused DMA channel number.

Because local buses are designed to support a specific microprocessor, it is impossible to upgrade the microprocessor chip on the system board in older microcomputers. For example, if you want to upgrade a system from an Intel 80386SX to an Intel 80486 processor, you need to replace the system board. Newer system boards are designed for microprocessor upgrading. However, these system boards still have the original local bus built into them, which will limit the performance of the upgraded system. For example, Intel now sells a Pentium microprocessor to replace 80486 processors on properly designed system boards. But these boards were designed with a 32-bit data bus, whereas the Pentium is designed to work with a 64-bit data bus.

The Central Processing Unit (CPU)

The CPU, also referred to as a microprocessor, is the brain of the microcomputer system. Built into the silicon of modern microprocessors are more than 1 million transistors that make up circuits to interpret and control the execution of program instructions and perform arithmetic and logical operations.

Experts say that etching all the circuit paths onto a microprocessor chip is comparable to mapping all the highways and streets of Los Angeles onto the head of a pin.

This section describes the different types of microprocessor chips and explains the limitations and capabilities of each. In order to compare microprocessors, you first need to understand the parameters that determine the performance and functionality of microprocessors: clock speed, word size, instruction set, data bus size, and address bus size.

Clock Speed

If the microprocessor is the brain of the computer, then the clock is the heartbeat of the system unit, and its beats synchronize all the operations of the internal components. The microprocessor's **clock** is used to provide precisely timed signal pulses called **cycles**. Each clock cycle consists of an electronic pulse that is transmitted to each component of the system unit to trigger and synchronize processing within the computer system. Each clock pulse received by the microprocessor causes its circuits to perform part or all of an instruction.

Clock speed is measured in millions of cycles per second, called **megahertz (MHz)**. **Wait states** are clock cycles during which the processor does not perform any operations; they are necessary to slow down high-speed processor chips and allow them to work with slower devices. In general, higher clock rates mean faster processing speeds. The processing speed, when combined with the speed of a computer's disk storage and video card, determines its throughput performance.

Word Size

A microprocessor chip holds instructions and data temporarily in storage areas called **registers**. Each processor chip has several registers for various purposes. A microprocessor's **word size** is the number of bits each register can hold. A larger word size enables a microprocessor to work on more data per clock cycle. Older processor chips, such as Intel's 8088 and 80286, have 16-bit registers. Newer processors, such as the Pentium and Pentium Pro, have 32-bit registers.

Instruction Set

The **instruction set**, also called the **machine language**, is the group of commands that the microprocessor chip has been designed to process. All software must be converted to the microprocessor's machine language before it can be run. This is often accomplished with the aid of a special program called a **compiler**, which converts English-like commands to the binary language of the processor chip. DOS machine language programs use the filename extension .COM or .EXE. On a NetWare server, machine language programs have the extension .NLM.

A machine language program can be run only on the processor for which it was designed. Intel and Motorola processors, for example, have very different instruction sets, making it impossible for the Motorola chip to run a machine language program written for an Intel chip. The NetWare 3.12 and 4.1 operating systems were written for the instruction set of an Intel 80386 microprocessor and therefore cannot be run on earlier Intel processors or on Apple computers, which all use Motorola processor chips.

Computers with Intel and most Motorola chips are classified as **complex instruction set computers (CISC)** because their instructions have a wide range of formats and because one instruction can require many clock cycles. The resultant speed of the microprocessor is often expressed in **millions of instructions per second (MIPS)**.

Companies such as Cyrix and Advanced Micro Devices produce Intel-compatible processor chips that are used in some IBM-compatible systems.

To maximize speed, many engineering workstations running CAD applications (such as SUN workstations) are based on processors called **reduced instruction set computers (RISC)**. RISC processors are very fast and efficient because their instructions are all the same length, and each instruction performs a very specific process. The disadvantage of RISC processors is that the software development is more complex and requires sophisticated compilers to convert programs to the machine language format.

The biggest advantage of RISC- over CISC-based computers is the increased speed of floating-point math calculations. This speed advantage is the reason RISC-based processors are often used in workstations running engineering, CAD, or scientific applications.

A **math coprocessor** is an extension of a chip's basic instruction set that allows the microprocessor to perform more complex arithmetic operations such as square root and trigonometric functions. Math coprocessors are built into the 80486DX, Pentium, and Pentium Pro processors. Math coprocessors can greatly increase the speed of spreadsheet programs and applications used for engineering and CAD, which typically perform many square root and trigonometric calculations.

Intel Microprocessors

The Intel family of microprocessor chips is probably the best known because of the wide acceptance of IBM-compatible computers based on this processor design. You need to know the basic features of Intel processor chips and how they relate to the capabilities of the computer systems you are likely to encounter. Knowing the capabilities and limitations of the processors can help you make the best use of existing systems on a network as well as select the correct processor chip when a new system needs to be purchased.

Intel family history. The Intel 8088 processor chip, included in the IBM PC, which was introduced in 1981, started the IBM PC-compatible industry. The 8088 has a 4-MHz clock speed, a 20-bit address bus that can access up to 1 MB of RAM, and a 16-bit register system. It allowed designers to create everything a PC user would need in the then-foreseeable future. Running the instruction set that comes with the original Intel 8088 microprocessor is referred to as operating in **real mode**. Real mode instructions use 16-bit data registers and can directly access only 1 million bytes of memory. The DOS operating system—and the thousands of DOS software applications still in use—were designed specifically for the original 8088 microprocessor. This means that even if you have the latest and fastest Intel processor chip, your workstation computer is limited to 640 KB of RAM and 16-bit instructions when it runs DOS-based software in real mode.

The need for more powerful processor chips led to the development of the 80286 processor, which provided up to seven times the performance of the 8088 processor while providing compatibility for real mode programs. Included in the IBM AT, which was introduced in 1984, the 80286 microprocessor added three new capabilities:

- The address bus was increased to 24 bits to allow for up to 16 MB of system RAM.
- The clock speed was increased to between 8 and 20 MHz.
- It can switch between real mode and protected mode.

Real mode operation allows the microprocessor to act like a very fast 8088; **protected mode** allows it to run multiple programs more reliably by preventing one program from affecting the operation of another. For example, if you are using real mode to run a new program in your computer and the program attempts to write data into memory cells used by DOS, the computer can crash and interrupt all other applications. When the new program is run in protected mode, however, its attempt to write the data will be recognized as invalid and will be terminated while other programs continue to operate normally.

With more than 375,000 transistors, the 80386 chip represents a significant advancement over earlier chips while still retaining compatibility with software written for the older processors. Although the design is now dated, it was popular, and you will probably encounter a number of workstation computers based on the 80386 processor chip. Although the 80386 is capable of 32-bit processing (because of its 32-bit internal registers and data paths), most PC add-on boards and software were designed for older 8- or 16-bit processors and are therefore unable to make optimum use of the 80386's 32-bit capability. Because of this, Intel introduced a less expensive version of the 80386 chip, the 80386SX, and named the original chip the 80386DX. The main difference between the SX and DX versions is that the 80386SX has the same 16-bit external data bus and 24-bit address bus as the 80286 processor. It is therefore limited to a maximum of 16 MB of system RAM and generally runs at a slower speed. In addition to providing 32-bit processing, the 80386DX incorporated the following new features:

- It can directly access up to 4 GB of system RAM.
- It has the ability to switch between real and protected modes without the need to reset the processor.
- The use of **virtual memory** enables the 80386 processor to use hard disk space to simulate a large amount of internal RAM. Although the use of virtual memory slows down the computer's throughput, it also allows you to run large programs that would not otherwise fit in the existing RAM.
- The addition of **virtual real mode** enables multiple real mode programs to run simultaneously.
- It can run at a variety of clock speeds ranging from 16 to 40 MHz.

Beginning with NetWare 3.1x, the NetWare server requires an 80836 or later processor because the network operating system (NOS) was written for the virtual real mode instruction set. This requirement is the reason that you cannot use a computer based on the Intel 8088 or 80286 processor chips as a NetWare server.

Current Intel microprocessors. Although you will still encounter workstations and older NetWare servers based on earlier versions of the Intel processors, these early members of the Intel microprocessor family are no longer being produced, and all new Intel-based workstations and NetWare servers you install will be based on either 80486, Pentium, or Pentium Pro microprocessors. The 80486, Pentium, and Pentium Pro microprocessors all provide compatibility with software written for earlier processors and the computing power needed for high-speed graphics-based software. They can also support the powerful NetWare servers that accommodate multiple high-speed workstations.

80486. The 80486 chip is a supercharged version of the 80386 chip that incorporates more than 1 million transistor components. Many workstations you are likely to encounter as a network administrator will contain this processor. The 80486 includes the following features:

- Clock speeds are higher, ranging from 33 to 100 MHz.
- An 8-KB high-speed memory cache (L1 cache) allows the processor to access commonly used memory locations without going through the slower external data bus.
- A math coprocessor is built in.

There are two main versions of the 80486 chip. The 80486DX chip contains all the features just described. The 80486SX is a less expensive version of the 80486DX chip and does not include the math coprocessor. (Interestingly, the 80486SX actually has the math coprocessor, but it has been disabled to allow Intel to market the chip at a lower price.) A modified 80486DX chip, called the 80486DX2, uses a clock-doubling technique that doubles the processing throughput of the chip. An 80486DX at 33 MHz becomes an 80486DX2 at 66 MHz.

Yet another version of the 80486 chip, called the 80486DX4, can triple (not quadruple) clock speeds. Thus an 80486DX at 33 MHz becomes an 80486DX4 at 100 MHz.

Pentium. Intel's Pentium chip represents a major leap ahead of earlier Intel chips by incorporating two 80486-type microprocessors on a single chip that can process two instructions simultaneously. The Pentium chip can operate at least 200 MHz with 64-bit registers and more than 3 million transistors. The Pentium math coprocessor has been redesigned to achieve a 300% improvement in geometric computations over 80486 chips, allowing graphics-intensive applications to operate at much faster speeds.

Initial versions of Pentium processor chips have a known problem with the math coprocessor circuits, which produce incorrect results when performing calculations with large floating point numbers, and Intel has agreed to replace any of these chips with a corrected processor. However, because a NetWare server is not required to perform floating point arithmetic, this problem should not affect Pentium-based NetWare server computers that haven't had the processor replaced.

Pentium MMX. Intel has usually tried to move users to each new microprocessor as quickly as possible. With the Pentium, however, Intel has continued developing the chip to extend its useful life span. The result is the Pentium MMX microprocessor, a version of the Pentium released in late 1996 that has been enhanced to speed up multimedia functions. For example, one enhancement allows the Pentium MMX to perform an ADD instruction on eight bytes of data in the time formerly required for just one byte of data. This will result in significantly faster multimedia software processing but will not have as much of an effect on standard spreadsheet or word-processing software. The need for multimedia processing is increasing as more software products are delivered on CD-ROM and as Internet content includes more audio, video, and 3D components. Speeds may include a 200-MHz version, and these enhancements will keep the Pentium chip a viable choice for PC workstations.

Pentium Pro. The Intel Pentium Pro processor was designed for optimal performance with 32-bit software while maintaining compatibility with previous Intel processors. It still uses a 32-bit word, but its design includes 5.5 million transistors in the chip, and it operates at speeds up to 200 MHz. The Pentium Pro chip also includes a 256-KB L2 cache to accelerate data input. One of the Pentium Pro's main features is called Dynamic Execution. **Dynamic Execution** combines three processing techniques: multiple branch prediction, dataflow analysis, and speculative execution. In multiple branch prediction, the Pentium Pro looks several programming steps ahead in the program and predicts which steps will be processed next. Dataflow analysis is then used to set up an optimized schedule for performing the program steps, which leads to speculative execution, which performs the steps as scheduled by the dataflow analysis. Figure 2-9 lists the basic specifications of the Intel family of microprocessors for easy comparison.

Figure 2-9
Microprocessor specifications

Microprocessor	Word size	Data bus	Address bus	Maximum clock speed	Math coprocessor	Millions of instructions per second (MIPS)
8088	16	8	20	10 MHz	No	.33
80286	16	16	24	20 MHz	No	3
80386SX	32	16	24	33 MHz	No	5
80386DX	32	32	32	33 MHz	No	11
80486SX	32	32	32	33 MHz	No	41
80486DX	32	32	32	100 MHz (DX4)	Yes	80
Pentium	32	64	32	200 MHz	Yes	>100
Pentium MMX	32	64	32	200 MHz	Yes	>100
Pentium Pro	32	64 (+ 8 ECC)	36	200 MHz	Yes	>100

The Pentium Pro runs best with a true 32-bit operating system such as Windows NT Workstation or OS/2. Performance suffers if Windows 95 is used as the operating system. A Pentium system running Windows 95 can actually outperform the Pentium Pro system when using typical user applications such as word processing.

Other Microprocessors

Some workstations you will encounter as a network administrator are not based on Intel or Intel-compatible microprocessors. Apple Macintosh computers are based on the Motorola 68000 line of microprocessors; Apple PowerMac computers are based on the PowerPC microprocessor.

Motorola processors. The Motorola MC68000 chip was used on earlier Macintosh computers and is similar to the Intel 8088 microprocessor. The MC68020 chip was used in various Macintosh II machines and is comparable to the Intel 80386DX or 80486SX processors. The MC68030 represents the first attempt to do multiprocessing within a microprocessor chip and offers an internal memory cache, a math coprocessor, and clock speeds of up to 40 MHz. The MC68030 is used in the Macintosh SE and various Macintosh II computers. The MC68040 is comparable to the Pentium in that it offers 64-bit communication and higher clock speeds.

PowerPC. Intel's microprocessors are Complex Instruction Set Computer (CISC) processors. The **PowerPC processor**, developed cooperatively by Motorola, IBM, and Apple, is a member of the Reduced Instruction Set Computer (RISC) family of microprocessors. Because it is based on the RISC architecture, the PowerPC achieves much higher processing speeds than the existing CISC-type Motorola processors in the 68X family and competes well with Intel's microprocessors. Both Apple and IBM are using special versions of PowerPC processors to produce high-speed computers that can support both existing software and newer PowerPC-specific software. They do this with special emulator software that resides in ROM and automatically translates 68000-based instructions into PowerPC instructions. Although emulation slows down the effective speed of the systems, it provides functionality in the initial phase of the new product's release when there are few programs written for it.

The Apple Power Macintosh uses the first PowerPC chip, the PowerPC 601, which runs at between 60 and 80 MHz. Microsoft has a PowerPC version of the powerful Windows NT operating system that is intended to make the PowerPC chips more widely used on networked workstations. Newer versions of the PowerPC chip, such as the 603, 604, and 620, will provide lower power usage, higher clock speeds, and a larger word size. The PowerPC 620 is scheduled to have 64-bit registers along with a 64-bit external data bus to provide extremely high-speed processing required by such applications as speech recognition. As a network administrator you will need to keep abreast of the developments and products that become available for the PowerPC family of processor chips and how they will affect the processing needs of your network system.

Interrupts and I/O Ports

In order to provide for input from and output to the computer system, you need to be able to attach such devices as keyboards, printers, monitors, network cards, and the mouse. These devices are commonly known as **peripherals** because they are added on to the system board. Each peripheral device attached to the system board—from the hard disk to the keyboard—must be controlled and monitored by the microprocessor. This monitoring is accomplished by interrupts and input/output (I/O) ports. You need to know how interrupts and I/O ports work in order to configure adapter cards correctly. (Chapter 5 tells you how to configure network adapter cards and software when you install NetWare on both server and workstation computers.)

Common Interrupts

An **interrupt request (IRQ)** is a signal that a device or controller card sends to the processor to inform it that the device or controller needs attention. Your telephone is a good example of how an interrupt request works in a computer. When the phone rings, it means that someone is trying to contact you, and you normally try to answer it as soon as possible before you lose the opportunity to speak with the caller. On a network, when a packet arrives at the network card of the NetWare server, it signals the server by "ringing" its interrupt. When the NetWare server detects the interrupt signal of a packet arrival, it temporarily stops its work and spends a few microseconds putting the data packet from the network card into memory before returning to its work.

Each device in a computer system needs to have its own unique interrupt so that the processor will not misinterpret the source of the interrupt signal. If your doorbell is wired so that it also causes your telephone to ring, you cannot be sure which to answer when you hear them. A wrong guess results in the loss of information. In a similar way, two devices using the same interrupt number in a computer system cannot interact correctly with the processor, and your system performance will be sporadic at best.

Because of the limited number of system interrupt numbers, it is impossible to assign unique numbers to every category of computer peripheral. There are some general usage guidelines for system interrupts, however. Figure 2-10 shows interrupt numbers used on several of the most common system devices. Each manufacturer allows you to adjust the interrupt setting of its peripheral device, so you can choose an interrupt setting that does not conflict with other system devices.

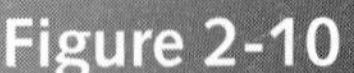

Figure 2-10

Common interrupt usage

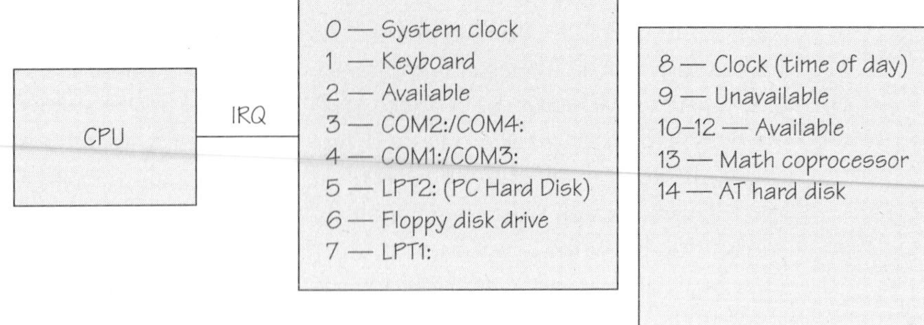

Input/Output Ports

An **input/output (I/O) port** is a memory location that the processor uses to send control commands to a peripheral device and read back status information. To communicate with each device separately, each peripheral attached to the computer system needs a unique I/O port address range. Figure 2-11 lists I/O port addresses for several common peripherals. To avoid conflicts with other devices in a computer, each peripheral controller card manufacturer provides a number of different I/O port address options. The network administrator's job includes assigning unique I/O port settings for network cards.

Figure 2-11

Common device configurations

Device	Interrupt	I/O Address
COM1	4	3F8–3FF
COM2	3	2F8–2FF
LPT1	7 (if used)	3BC–3BE
LPT2	5 (if used)	378–37A
LPT3	none	278–27A
IDE disk controller	14	IF0–IF8 170–177
XT disk controller	5	320–32F
IBM token ring (primary)	2	A20–A23
IBM token ring (secondary)	3	A24–A27

Parallel ports. The parallel port connects the computer to a parallel cable, which transfers data from the computer to a peripheral device eight bits at a time on parallel wires. The parallel port is commonly referred to as the printer port because almost all printers use a standard parallel port interface. This makes it easy to plug almost any printer into the parallel port of a computer. The use of the parallel port for printers was standardized by the Centronics printer company, and the parallel cable attaches to a 25-pin connector on the back of the computer and a larger 36-pin card edge connector on the printer. As a result of the early popularity of the Centronics standard, all IBM-compatible computer and printer manufacturers today include the Centronics parallel port on their systems.

Serial ports. In contrast to parallel ports, which transmit an entire byte at one time, the serial port on IBM-compatible computers sends only one bit of data at a time. One advantage of the serial port is its ability to send information between devices over long distances by using only a few wires in a twisted-pair cable. In addition, serial ports allow the attachment of devices, such as modems, that can translate bits into an analog signal compatible with telephone systems, thereby allowing a worldwide range of computer communications.

Timing is very important in serial communications in order for the receiving device to correctly interpret the signals coming from the transmitter. To understand the principle of serial communication, imagine sending the letter "C" to a friend by using a flashlight. In your code, on represents a one and off represents a zero. First you need to convert the letter "C" to its ASCII equivalent, 01000011. Next you need to agree on a timing interval—say one second—for each bit, so your friend can determine how many ones or zeros are being sent. You turn the light on or off for each second of the transmission. For the letter "C" (01000011), the light is off during the first second, on during the second second, off during the next four seconds, and then on again for the final two seconds. The correct timing is critical for your friend to receive the proper signal. If you flash the light on and off in two-second intervals, your friend will get completely different results.

The speed of the serial signal is the **baud rate**. In the example just described, the baud rate is one, indicating one signal change per second. Standard serial port baud rates on a computer range from 300 to 19,200 baud. For digital signals, such as those from the flashlight, the baud rate is equal to the number of bits per second (bps). When a modem sends analog frequencies over the telephone, the bit pattern is represented by a change in frequency, which allows several bits to be transmitted for each baud. In this case, the rate of bits per second is often much faster than the baud rate.

Serial communication can be either synchronous or asynchronous. **Synchronous communication**, commonly used with LAN cards to send packets consisting of 1,500 or more bytes between computers, takes place at very high speeds ranging from 4 to more than 100 Mbps (megabits per second). Synchronous ports are generally quite expensive because they require special control and timing circuitry. **Asynchronous communication** is much simpler, sending only one character at a time. Asynchronous communication is often used by modems to transmit information between microcomputers, or between a microcomputer and an on-line information service provider such as America Online, CompuServe, or Prodigy.

In asynchronous communication, each character is transmitted separately and is encapsulated with a start and stop bit and an optional **parity bit** for error checking (see Figure 2-12). The parity bit is set to either odd (off) or even (on). Even parity means that the total number of one bits, including the parity bit transmitted in the data frame, is even. In the case of the letter "C," the parity bit is turned on by the transmitter to indicate an even number of one bits. If one of the bits is accidentally changed during transmission by a bad cable or a noise on the line, the receiving computer detects the occurrence of an error because the number of one bits is no longer even. Parity works well for single-bit errors, but its reliability falls off when more than one bit is changed.

Figure 2-12

Asynchronous data frame

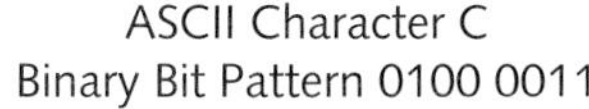

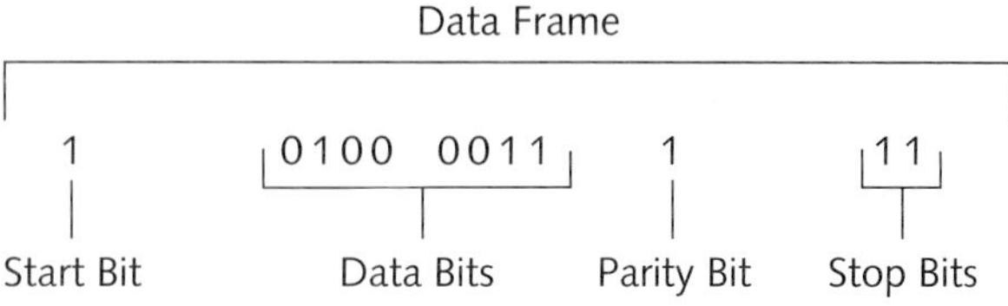

Most system board manufacturers build one or more asynchronous ports into their IBM-compatible systems. These ports are generally referred to as COM1 through COM4, have either 25-pin or 9-pin connectors, and are located on the back of the computer. Two types of serial port connectors, known as **RS232** connectors, were standardized by the Electronic Industry Association (EIA) in the early days of computing. **Data terminal equipment (DTE)** connectors are used on computers, and **data communications equipment (DCE)** connectors are used on modems. This means that a simple connector-to-connector cable can connect a computer to a modem, as shown in Figure 2-13. Most of the 25–pin connections on the RS232 cable are not used by standard PC serial communications, allowing a 9-pin connector to consist of only the required pin connections. A special type of RS232 cable called a **null modem cable** is used to connect two DTE computers without the use of a modem. Note that the null modem cable pictured at the bottom of Figure 2-13 has certain wires crossed in order to allow the signals from the sending computer to go to the correct connectors on the receiving computer.

Figure 2-13

RS232 Serial cables

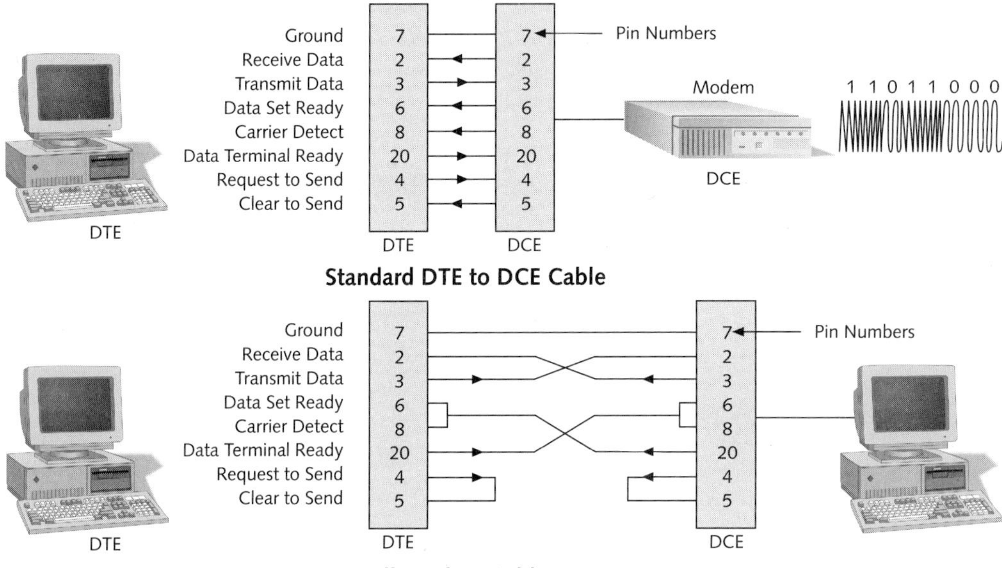

The Expansion Slots

As you learned earlier in this chapter, the expansion slots connect add-in cards, such as video cards and NICs, to the system board. They are connected to other components by the expansion bus. As the capabilities of microprocessors have improved, the demands placed on the expansion bus have grown. The architecture of the expansion bus has changed and improved over time. Part of the change in the expansion bus has been changes in the connectors used in the expansion slot. This is illustrated in Figure 2-14, which contrasts 8-bit ISA, 16-bit ISA, EISA, PCI, and Micro Channel connectors. Notice that an expansion card designed for one expansion bus system cannot be used in another because of the differences in the design of the expansion slot connectors.

Figure 2-14

ISA vs Microchannel Bus Types

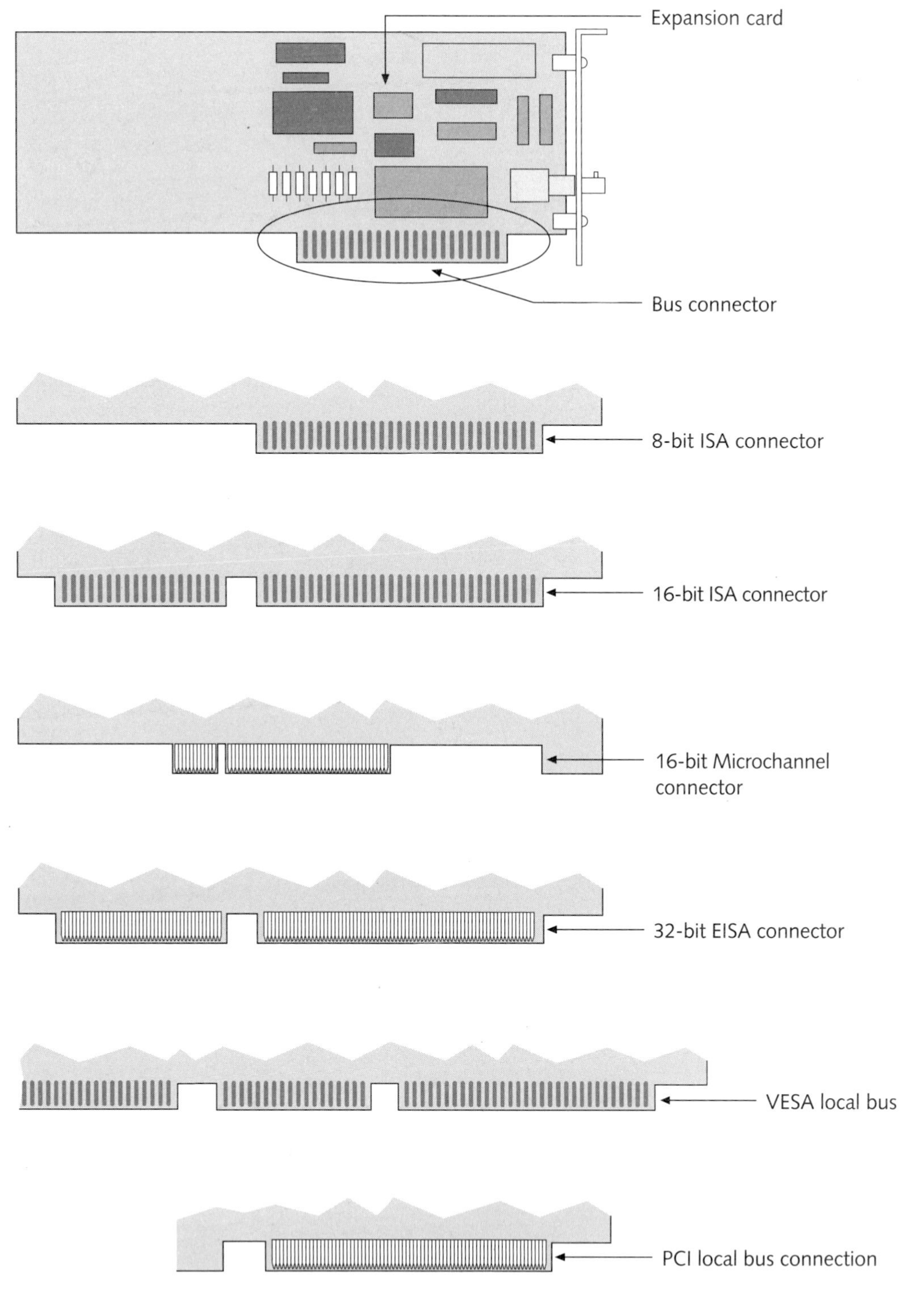

ISA Bus

The **industry standard architecture (ISA) bus** was introduced in 1984 with the IBM AT computer. It was originally designed for the 80286 microprocessor, and its expansion slots support 16-bit data and 24-bit address buses running at 8 MHz. The system board also contains a local bus that can support up to 32-bit data and address paths at high clock speeds (such as 33 MHz) between the microprocessor and memory. Many lower-cost personal computers use the ISA bus because it provides satisfactory performance for many applications and low-end NetWare servers. The main disadvantage of the ISA bus can be seen in graphics applications that require high-speed video processing. Because a video card placed in an ISA expansion slot is limited to a 16-bit data bus and an 8-MHz clock speed, Windows or graphics-based applications run slowly even on an 80486-based computer. To determine if a system has an ISA bus, you can check the system's manual or examine the system board. ISA slots on the system board have 16-bit card slots composed of two sockets placed together, one containing 31 pins and the other containing 18 pins.

Micro Channel Bus

The **Micro Channel bus** architecture is owned by IBM and can support 32-bit expansion slots running at high clock speeds (such as 33 MHz). It was developed for IBM's PS/2 line, but lack of success with that line and with licensing the architecture forced IBM to discontinue using Micro Channel in its PCs. IBM now uses Intel's PCI bus in its products. A major advantage of the Micro Channel architecture is that it keeps card configuration information in **CMOS (complementary metal oxide semiconductor) memory** on the system board, allowing software setting of card options and configurations. Because CMOS memory is backed up by a small battery, the settings are preserved when the computer is turned off. IBM owns this architecture, so a royalty must be paid by companies that make products based on it. Because the expansion slots are different, cards designed for the ISA bus cannot be used on a Micro Channel computer.

IBM developed the Micro Channel bus in the late 1980s to provide an expansion path for the 32-bit high-speed 80386DX-based processors. Because manufacturers of IBM-compatible computers were outselling IBM with their lower prices, IBM wanted to build the new systems with a proprietary bus and expansion card architecture. This would force clone manufacturers to pay royalties for use of the new bus and allow IBM to exert control over the market for personal computers. Although Micro Channel was used by IBM for its PS/2 line of computers, it never was adopted by the industry in general, and IBM returned to using the ISA bus for many of its less-expensive models before finally switching to the Intel PCI bus.

EISA Bus

When IBM introduced its proprietary Micro Channel bus, other PC manufacturers who wanted to sell systems with the increased performance of IBM's 32-bit bus slots were required to pay IBM royalties and redesign their systems. Because the Micro Channel bus does not accept the older ISA cards, users must purchase the more expensive Micro Channel cards even for slower devices such as modems and printers. In reaction to this, a number of IBM-compatible computer manufacturers cooperated on the design of an enhanced version of the ISA bus that would support 32-bit expansion cards and higher clock speeds. The result is the **extended industry standard architecture (EISA) bus**, which supports 32-bit data and address expansion slots that can support adapter cards at 8-MHz clock speeds. Because the EISA bus is an extension of the ISA bus, it includes 16-bit expansion slots that accept older ISA cards. Of course, ISA cards placed in these slots still use the limited ISA address and data bus sizes. Because this architecture is not owned by a single company, royalty fees for its use are not required. EISA bus computers became popular for higher-speed NetWare server applications. For example, a 32-bit disk interface card placed in an EISA bus slot provides better disk access times than a 16-bit card in an ISA-compatible slot. A typical EISA system board includes two 32-bit slots and six 16-bit ISA slots.

Bus mastering, a technique built into EISA and Micro Channel bus systems, enables adapter cards to off-load such tasks as moving information into memory in order to improve overall system performance. Bus mastering is an important option to consider when selecting a NetWare server computer. Much of a NetWare server's processing involves moving information to and from memory. The use of bus mastering can greatly improve the performance of a NetWare server by making the system's CPU available more frequently.

Although servers that use the Pentium or Pentium Pro microprocessor use the PCI bus, these same servers are often also equipped with EISA buses. Before the PCI bus became common, systems based on the EISA bus were good choices for medium- to large-capacity NetWare servers that supported more than 50 users, used more than 500 MB of disk storage, had multiple network cards, and contained additional peripheral devices.

VESA Bus

Not long after the 80486 chip was introduced, IBM-compatible system board manufacturers struggled to provide systems that would enable the video and hard-drive peripherals to match the increased speed of the latest microprocessors. The Video Electronics Standards Association (VESA) cooperated with Intel to design a new system bus architecture that would allow peripheral cards such as the video adapter to have direct access to the local bus of the system board at the same clock speed as the system board. With the advent of the Pentium chip, Intel's PCI bus became the commonly used expansion bus. You might encounter the VESA bus in PC workstations and NetWare servers that have an 80486 microprocessor. The **VESA bus** consists of an extension to the 16-bit ISA slot, enabling the slot to be used for either a VESA-compatible device or a 16-bit adapter. This extension allows a card placed in a VESA slot to become part of the local bus of the system board and achieve much better data transmission speeds. According to some industry experts, VESA cards can yield performances that are up to 10 times better than the standard ISA bus cards. VESA slots can be included on 80486 system boards that have both ISA or EISA expansion slots. On PC workstations using graphics-intensive applications, a system's VESA slot is best used for the video card, as this will greatly increase the performance of graphics-based applications, which need to send millions of bits per second to the screen. On NetWare servers, which must be able to move many large blocks of data to and from the disk and the network cards, the VESA slot is often used for high-speed disk controllers and NICs.

PCI Bus

The latest local bus designed by Intel is called the **Peripheral Component Interconnect (PCI) bus**. The PCI bus improves on the older VESA bus design by avoiding the standard input/output bus and using the system bus to take full advantage of the Pentium chip's 64-bit data path. In addition, the PCI bus runs at the 60- or 66-MHz speed of the processor (compared with the 33-MHz maximum speed of the VESA bus) and, as a result, is being used on many new system boards designed around the Pentium processors. Another advantage offered by the PCI bus is hardware compatibility between Intel-based computers and Apple PowerPC–based machines, due to the use of PCI slots in Apple Macintosh computers. The biggest limitation of the PCI bus is that it will support only three to four slots on a system board. However, new systems are being designed that will provide multiple PCI buses on the same system board in order to provide eight or more PCI slots.

Intel will continue to develop the PCI bus, and it will be used as a standard expansion bus in new workstations and servers. The PCI bus is the dominant bus on Pentium and Pentium Pro workstations and can also be found on later 80486 workstations. The VESA bus is found on older 486 workstations. Combination buses will be the normal configuration, as the PCI bus is usually combined with an ISA bus (on PC workstations) or the EISA bus (on servers).

NuBus

The Apple NuBus was originally developed by Texas Instruments and was then adopted by Apple for use on its Macintosh line of computers. The **NuBus** offers a 32-bit address and data bus running at 10 MHz and is similar to Micro Channel in that it supports self-configuring boards. With self-configuring boards, a computer's system will automatically identify and configure each peripheral added to the system, eliminating the need to configure them manually by using DIP switches or jumpers.

Memory

The purpose of the computer's primary memory unit is to store software and data in a manner that allows the microprocessor unit to access each storage cell directly. Memory is composed of millions of tiny switches built into silicon memory modules that can be turned on or off to represent a binary one or zero. The memory switches are arranged in groups of eight to form memory cells called bytes. Every byte is assigned a unique number or address that distinguishes it from other memory bytes. Each memory byte can then be used to store one character of data or part of an instruction. The microprocessor can access memory by sending the address number of the desired byte on the address bus and then receiving the contents of the memory cell(s) on the data bus. On a 32-bit data bus, four sequential memory bytes can be sent to or from the microprocessor with one memory access.

Memory Types

There are four primary types of memory used in microcomputer systems: RAM, ROM, CMOS, and high-speed cache. Each of these memory types has a specific function in the processing of information in a computer system. In this section you will learn about each type of memory and its role in the operation of a computer system.

RAM. Random-access memory (RAM) is considered a volatile form of memory because it depends on constant power; when power is turned off, the contents of the RAM are erased. A computer's RAM is its primary workspace where programs and data are stored during processing. More RAM in workstations allows the use of larger and more complex software applications. In a NetWare server computer, additional RAM is used for file and directory caching (file caching is the process of storing often-used disk information in memory and is discussed in detail later in this chapter). Because memory is more than 100 times faster than disk access time, the amount of memory available for file caching directly affects the performance of a NetWare server computer.

The latest development in RAM is **extended data out (EDO) RAM**. This type of RAM is faster than older RAM and is now the standard RAM used in Pentium and Pentium Pro microcomputers.

A special type of RAM, Video RAM or VRAM, is used on graphics cards.

When adding RAM to a microcomputer, be sure you add the correct type of RAM for that microcomputer. Check the specifications in the User's Guide that came with the PC.

ROM. Read-only memory (ROM), as its name suggests, cannot be changed. On most microcomputer systems, ROM is used to store boot instructions and control such basic hardware functions as the inputting of data from the keyboard or access to the disk drive. Because they cannot be changed, instructions stored in ROM are referred to as firmware. Because ROM is slower than RAM, most 80386 and later microprocessors allow moving the contents of ROM into RAM during booting, a process known as **RAM shadowing**. RAM shadowing can significantly increase the speed of such hardware-oriented operations as accessing the screen and keyboard.

CMOS. The original IBM PC bus contained switches that were used to set configuration options such as memory capacity, disk drives, and video. Today's system boards contain a built-in setup program that is used to store this configuration information in a special memory type called CMOS. **CMOS (complementary metal oxide semiconductor) memory** uses very little power, and its contents can be maintained with a small on-board battery when the computer's power is off. The CMOS battery is recharged whenever the system is powered. If you add a new disk drive or more memory, you will need to run a setup program to update your computer's CMOS configuration. Many CMOS setup programs are built into the ROM of the system board and can be executed by pressing a special key sequence (such as the Escape key) while the computer system is initially booting. Some computers need to be booted with a special disk in order to change the CMOS configuration settings.

Be aware that the CMOS battery can completely discharge when a computer is turned off for an extended period of time, causing loss of configuration information.

Cache. Cache memory is very high-speed memory made of chips called **SRAM (static RAM)**. Most RAM consists of relatively inexpensive chips called **DRAM (dynamic RAM)**. Although inexpensive, DRAM bears a hidden cost; it needs a special clock cycle to maintain its memory contents. Because of this extra refresh cycle, DRAM is slower than SRAM because it requires wait states when used with processors running at speeds above 20 MHz. SRAM's speed advantage over DRAM makes it more suitable for caching the most recently used memory locations. It increases the speed of processing by allowing the processor to access data or instructions without using wait states. High-speed (33 MHz and above) computers typically need and use 128-256 KB of cache memory to improve their performance. Intel 80486, Pentium, and Pentium Pro microprocessors use built-in cache. The 80486 has 8 or 16 KB of cache memory, the Pentium has 16 KB, and the Pentium Pro has 16 KB built in to the microprocessor chip. This is known as the level 1 (L1) cache (primary cache). Additional cache, known as the level 2 (L2) cache (secondary cache), can often be installed on the system board to increase system performance. Typically, 128-256 KB of L2 cache is used with the 80486 and Pentium. The Pentium Pro uses a built-in L2 cache of 256-512 KB.

Single In-Line Memory Modules

Most RAM is currently provided on small memory cards called **single in-line memory modules (SIMMs)**, shown in Figure 2-15. SIMMs are arranged on the system board in banks. A bank can contain from one to four SIMM sockets, and a computer's system board contains several memory banks. Memory is added in banks by filling all SIMM sockets in the bank with the same type of SIMM chip. The number of SIMM banks determines the maximum amount of memory that can be placed on the system board as well as the ease of memory expansion. If a memory board does not contain enough SIMM banks, you can replace existing SIMMs with SIMMs of higher capacity in order to expand the computer's memory.

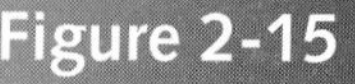
Figure 2-15

Single in-line memory module

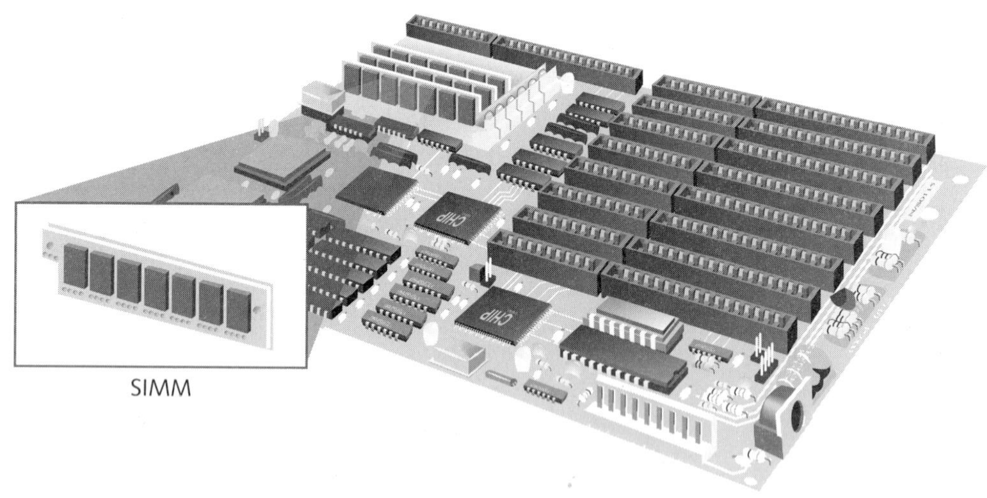

SIMMs contain 1, 4, 8, 16, or 32 MB of RAM and are supplied in either 30-pin or 72-pin models; 30-pin SIMMs supply 8 bits to the data bus per module; and 72-pin SIMMs supply 32 bits per module. When 30-pin SIMMs are used with an 80386SX processor, each bank must contain two SIMMs (8 bits × 2 SIMMs = 16-bit data bus width). If 30-pin SIMMs are used in an 80486 system that has a 32-bit data bus, each bank must contain four SIMMs (8 bits × 4 SIMMs = 32-bit data bus width). Make sure to choose system boards that use 72-pin SIMMs when you purchase computers based on 80486, Pentium, or Pentium Pro processors.

As mentioned previously, each memory bank must be filled with the same type of SIMM, because SIMMs of different capacities cannot be mixed within a bank. Assume, for example, you are using an 80386SX processor that has a 16-bit data bus with two SIMM slots per bank and that your computer currently has four 1-MB SIMMs in bank one for a total of 4 MB of RAM. You want to add more memory, so you will need to install SIMMs in matching pairs. You need to install at least two more 1-MB SIMMs, giving you a total of 6 MB. You could not place one 1-MB SIMM in bank two for a total capacity of 5 MB. The next step up would be to add two 4-MB SIMMs in bank two for a total capacity of 10 MB.

In addition to obtaining the correct capacity for the SIMMs, you need to make sure that the SIMMs are fast enough to keep up with the clock speed used for the memory banks. SIMMs that are too slow will cause the computer to crash. The speed of the memory chips is measured in nanoseconds (billionths of a second). The speed of most SIMMs ranges between 60 and 80 nanoseconds. When adding SIMMs to a computer, you should check the system's manual to verify the appropriate chip speeds.

Finally, you need to match the type of RAM used in the PC. If the PC was purchased with EDO RAM, you should use EDO RAM when you add memory.

The Pentium Pro also supports dual in-line memory modules (DIMMs). This is a combination of two SIMMs, which are read alternatively in memory access cycles. This results in an effective data bus of 128 bits over the Pentium Pro's 64-bit data bus.

Memory Usage

Windows 95 automates memory management that you previously had to specify by statements in the CONFIG.SYS and AUTOEXEC.BAT files. The same memory models and terms, however, still apply, because Windows 95 must still support old DOS applications. DOS was designed to run on an 8088 processor in real mode and therefore is limited to managing 1 MB (1,024 KB) of RAM. As shown in Figure 2-16, the first 640 KB of this 1-MB memory area is referred to as **conventional memory** and is used by DOS to run software applications. The memory between 640 KB and 1 MB is called **upper memory** and is reserved for hardware use. For example, part of upper memory is used by your video card to store data displayed on the screen. The network administrator might need to use this memory area when configuring certain NICs. The memory above 1 MB is called **extended memory** and is available to microprocessors running in either protected or virtual mode. Because DOS was not designed to use extended memory, it requires special driver software, called the extended memory system (XMS), to access this memory. An example of an XMS memory manager is the HIMEM.SYS driver, which provides access to the extended memory necessary to load the DOS operating system. Operating systems that do not rely on DOS—Windows NT workstation, UNIX, OS/2, and NetWare—can access extended memory directly, without the need for special drivers.

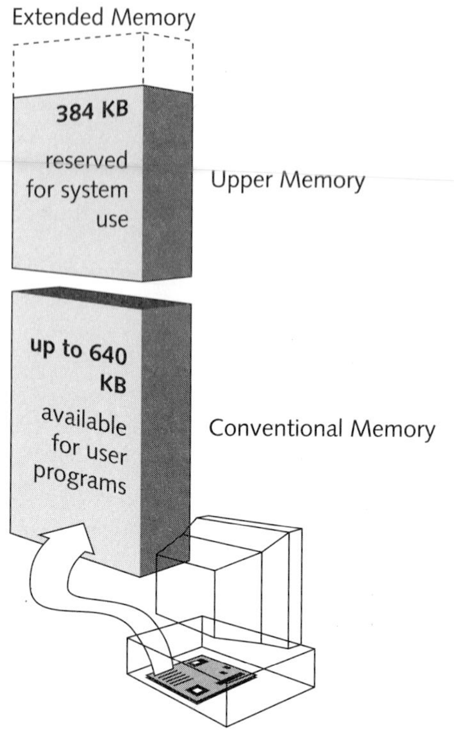

Figure 2-16
Memory map

You might hear the term **expanded memory** in connection with IBM-compatible computers. Expanded memory is an older technology that places RAM chips on a separate expansion card that is then added to the IBM-compatible system. Expanded memory was originally designed as a combined effort by Lotus, Microsoft, and Intel to provide a method for running large programs and worksheets with DOS on 8088-based computer systems. Because expanded memory is placed on a separate expansion card, it requires special software called an **expanded memory system (EMS)** to swap information or program instructions stored on the card into page frames located within the upper memory area. This swapping process causes computers using expanded memory to run more slowly than computers using extended memory. MS-DOS includes a special EMM386.EXE memory driver that can be used to make extended memory act like an expanded memory card in order to support applications written to use expanded memory. Today, application and system software is designed to use extended rather than expanded memory. You might still encounter IBM-compatible computers that are configured to use expanded memory in order to support older applications.

STORAGE SYSTEMS

Advances in disk storage systems have been as important to the development of microcomputer systems as the improvements made to processors and memory. Instructions and data need to be retrieved from disks and placed in RAM before the processor chip can act on them. Therefore, both the speed and the capacity of disk storage are critical to the performance of a computer system. Consider a NetWare server's primary purpose for a moment. Its major function involves the shared use of its hard disk drives. The NetWare operating system is specifically designed to maximize the performance and reliability of its disk storage system. In this section you will learn about the basic terminology and concepts needed to understand and configure disk systems.

Magnetic Disk Drives

The magnetic disk drive is the component of the disk storage system in which data is stored by means of magnetic fields representing ones and zeros. The recording surface of the disk is coated with a metal oxide that retains magnetic fields. The polarity of each magnetic field is used to represent either a one or a zero. To perform record and playback functions on the disk surfaces, recording heads containing electronic magnets are attached to a device called an **access arm** that allows the recording heads to move back and forth across the disk surface, as shown in Figure 2-17.

Figure 2-17

Disk drive components

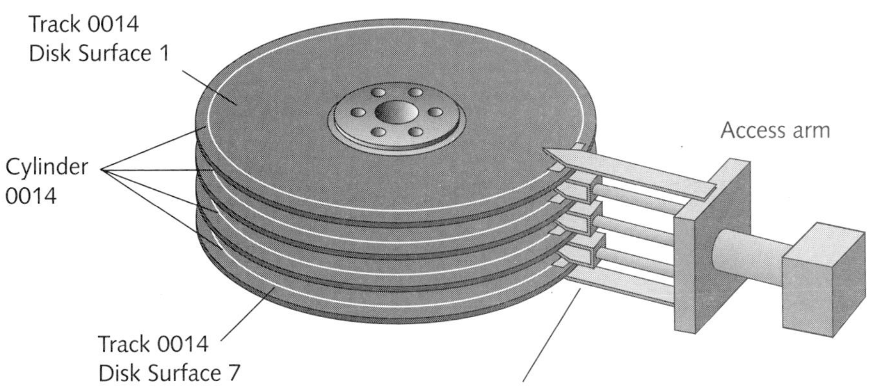

The disk surface is divided into concentric circles called **recording tracks**. The set of recording tracks that can be accessed by the recording heads without the access arm being repositioned is referred to as a **cylinder**. A track, which can contain a large amount of data, is divided into smaller recording areas called **sectors**, as shown in Figure 2-18. Reading or recording information in sectors, which are small, specific areas, allows efficient access to the information.

Figure 2-18

Tracks and sectors

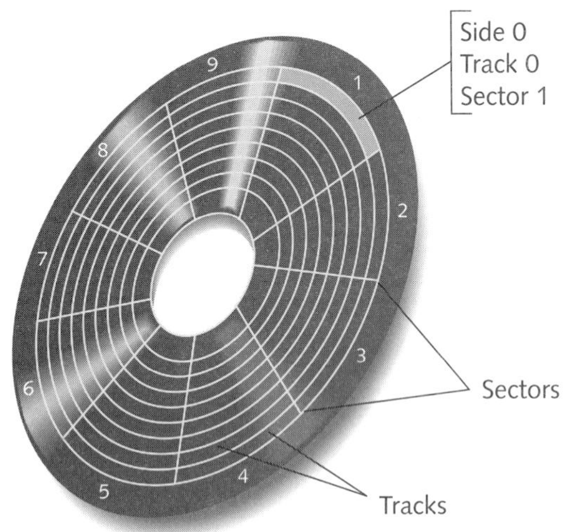

Floppy Disk Drives

Microcomputer floppy disks are available in two sizes: 5¼" or 3½". Although the 5¼" disks are nearly obsolete, be familiar with their proper use and handling in the event some of your older NetWare server or workstation computers contain 5¼" disk drives. The 3½" floppy disk provides higher densities, better reliability, and easier storage than the older 5¼" disk. Figure 2-19 compares the storage capacities of 5¼" and 3½" floppy disks. Although the 3½" drives have all but replaced the 5¼" floppy disk drives, if at least one computer in your network contains both types of drives, you can always access data on the older disks. Because the primary purpose of the floppy disk drive in a NetWare server computer is software installation and upgrades, a NetWare server computer should always have at least one high-density floppy disk drive for this purpose.

Figure 2-19

Floppy disk capacity chart

Size	Density	Number of tracks	Number of sectors	Capacity
5¼"	double	40	9	360 KB
5¼"	high	80	15	1,200 KB or 1.2 MB
3½"	double	80	9	720 KB
3½"	high	80	18	1,400 KB or 1.4 MB

Hard Disk Drives

A hard drive gets its name because it contains one or more rigid aluminum platters coated with a metal oxide that holds magnetic fields. Each platter has a read/write head positioned above and below each disk surface. Rotating the disk surface at high speeds causes the read/write head to fly just above the disk surface. Because the recording head on hard drives does not touch the disk surface, hard drives do not wear out like floppy disks and can last for several years.

You cannot assume that your data will always be safe even on a hard disk. Component failure, software bugs, and operator errors can and will eventually cause data loss, so it is critical that you establish a regular backup plan for data stored on hard disks.

For information to be recorded or retrieved on the hard disk, the recording head must first be positioned on the proper track. The time it takes to perform this operation is called the **seek time**. After it is positioned over the correct track, the read head begins looking for the requested sector. The time it takes for the sector to come into position is called the **rotational delay**. When the requested sector comes under the read head, it is read into a computer memory buffer. This is called the **transfer time**. The seek time plus the rotational delay plus the transfer time yields the **access time**. On hard disk drives, the access time is measured in milliseconds (ms). Most current hard disk drive access times range between 12 and 30 ms. The access time for floppy disks is close to 300 ms, making hard disk drives 10 to 25 times faster.

Once installed, a new hard disk needs to be partitioned for use by the operating system. With the exception of Windows, which uses a DOS partition, each operating system requires its own separate hard disk partition. **Partitioning** establishes boundaries within which an operating system formats and stores information on a hard disk. Several different operating system partitions can exist on the same hard disk. When you install NetWare on the NetWare server computer, for example, you need to create one partition for DOS and another for NetWare. Generally the DOS partition is very small—about 5 MB—because it is needed only to boot the computer and then load the NetWare operating system. The NetWare partition contains the storage areas used to store the data and software that will be available to the network. After the partition areas are established, each operating system needs to format its partition for its own use. In DOS this is done by the FORMAT program. The NetWare INSTALL utility allows you to partition and format the disk drive for the NetWare server.

The directory area of the disk partition contains the names and locations of files and other information about each file stored in the partition. Storing an entire file can require many sectors scattered throughout the partition. DOS 6.22 and earlier used a **file allocation table (FAT)** to link all the sectors belonging to one file. Windows 95 (and the included DOS 7.0) uses a 32-bit **virtual file allocation table (VFAT)**, which is backward-compatible with the older FAT.

When you add information to an existing file, the new sectors can be located anywhere in the disk partition. The FAT or VFAT allows the computer to find all sectors for a file. When you load a file from the disk, the computer first reads the directory to determine the location of the first sector. It then reads each sector of the file as specified by the FAT or VFAT. The NetWare network operating system also uses a FAT, and the NetWare server keeps the entire FAT and the most frequently accessed directory sectors in memory.

Disk Interfaces

Disk interfaces, or **controller cards**, enable a system's microprocessor to control the hard and floppy disk drives in a computer and provide a path for data to be transferred between the disk and memory. The disk controller card plugs into one of the expansion bus slots in a computer's system board or may be built into the circuits of the system board. There are several types of disk controller cards. This section describes the most common ones, including the early ST506 controllers used in older computers, the IDE controllers found in most workstations today, and the SCSI controller cards often used in NetWare servers and high-end workstations. A network administrator must be able to distinguish among different controller cards in order to configure the NetWare operating system correctly.

ST506 interface

The ST506 controller was developed by the Shugart company in the early 1980s. Although ST506 controllers are no longer installed in new computers, you might encounter this type of controller in older workstations and NetWare servers.

Enhanced Small Device Interface (ESDI)

The **enhanced small device interface (ESDI)** controller, an updated version of the ST506 controller, was developed by a consortium of disk drive manufacturers. ESDI supports a 1.25 MB/sec data transfer rate and is accepted as a reliable technology for midsized drives (up to 400 MB). Because of higher cost and the tendency for ESDI to break down in heavy load environments due to design flaws, most manufacturers have replaced ESDI controllers with the more efficient and reliable IDE controllers.

IDE Interface

Today there are two major types of **Integrated Drive Electronics (IDE)** hard disk controller cards on the market: IDE and enhanced IDE. IDE controller cards, often referred to as paddle cards, are smaller and cost less than the older ST506 disk controllers, which they have replaced because most of the control electronics are built in to the disk drive itself. Because few circuits are required for the IDE disk controller, most IDE controller cards come with a floppy disk controller as well as serial, parallel, and game ports.

Standard IDE controllers can control up to two hard disk drives and support drive capacities between 40 and 528 MB along with transfer speeds of 3.3 MB/sec and data access speeds of less than 18 ms. As a result of their low cost and high performance, IDE controllers are very popular and are used on most desktop computers today. Although IDE controllers and drives are appropriate for small- to medium-sized NetWare servers having a total disk capacity of less than 528 MB, most NetWare servers use either SCSI or enhanced IDE controller cards.

Enhanced IDE interface

Enhanced IDE controllers and drives offer **Logical Block Address (LBA)**, which allows them to provide up to 8.4 GB (billion bytes), well above the standard IDE limit of 528 MB. In addition, enhanced IDE offers transfer rates of up to 13.3 MB/sec and access times of 8.5 ms. The enhanced IDE speed improvements are achieved by increasing the disk drive rotational speed from 3,000 rpm to more than 5,000 rpm, by employing better read/write heads, and by using an advanced technology that allows the access arm to move from track to track in one-tenth the time required by standard IDE drives. In order to take advantage of the increased transfer speed, the enhanced IDE card must be installed in a PCI or VESA expansion slot. In addition to increased capacity and drive speed, enhanced IDE also provides for up to four devices, including nondisk peripherals such as CD-ROM or tape drives. The increased speed and capacity of the enhanced IDE disk system, combined with the ability to connect up to four devices, make it a good choice for many NetWare server environments.

SCSI

The **small computer system interface (SCSI)** is a general-purpose interface card that can control hard disks, tape backup systems, CD ROM drives, and floppy disks. As shown in Figure 2-20, up to seven SCSI devices can be chained together and attached to a single SCSI control card with the last device in each chain having a terminator enabled in order to properly end the cable segment. Multiple SCSI controllers can coexist in the same computer. Each device on the SCSI bus must be given a unique address between zero and six. Because the higher device addresses are given a higher priority, for optimal performance devices such as hard drives should be given the highest numbers, and devices such as tape and CD-ROM drives should be given lower numbers.

Figure 2-20

SCSI drive interface

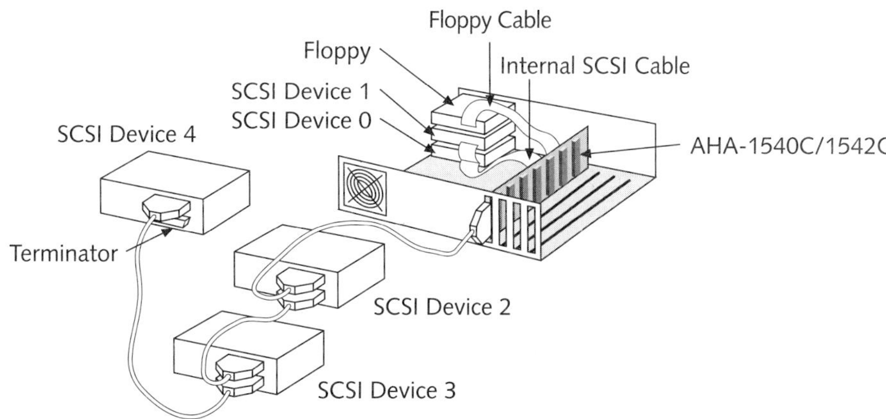

SCSI hard disk capacities normally range from 100 MB to 10 GB or more. Because they are more complex, SCSI controller cards and drives are generally more expensive. SCSI controllers use a parallel form of communication, sending eight or more bits to a drive at one time. This provides for higher transfer rates to and from the drive. Other controllers use serial communication, transferring only one bit at a time.

SCSI-2

SCSI-2 is an upgrade to the original SCSI specifications that provided a more standard command set along with additional commands to access CD-ROM drives, tape drives, optical drives, and several other peripherals. A feature of SCSI-2 called **command queuing** allows a device to accept multiple commands and execute them in the order the device deems most efficient. This feature is particularly important for NetWare servers that could have several workstations making requests for information from the disk system at the same time. Another feature of the SCSI-2 controller is a high-speed transfer option called FAST SCSI-2, which, at 40 Mbps, is nearly twice as fast as previous SCSI transfer speeds. In addition to the FAST SCSI-2 option, the SCSI-2 controller can further increase transfer speeds by using a 16-bit data bus between the SCSI-2 controller card and devices called WIDE SCSI-2. This 16-bit data bus allows for twice as much data to be transferred between the controller and disk drive as could be transferred using the original 8-bit data bus found on standard SCSI controllers.

Because SCSI-2 controller cards accommodate more devices and provide larger storage capacities, they are often the choice for NetWare server computers on medium to large networks requiring more than 1 GB of hard disk, along with support for CD-ROM drives and tape drives. SCSI-2 drives have the following advantages over enhanced IDE drives for use in a NetWare server:

- SCSI-2 supports as many as seven devices chained to a single adapter; enhanced IDE supports a maximum of four devices attached to two controller cards.
- SCSI-2 provides multitasking via command queuing, which results in better performance when multiple disk requests are pending.
- The variety of SCSI-2 storage peripherals is far greater than that afforded by enhanced IDE, especially regarding special devices such as magneto-optical drives that are sometimes used for data archiving.

The forthcoming SCSI-3 interface will provide the ability to transfer data at a rate of 100 Mbps over a six-wire cable as compared to the 40 Mbps maximum of FAST WIDE SCSI-2 over a 128-wire cable.

RAID Systems

A network administrator is concerned with data integrity because network downtime can result in significant losses of revenues for an organization. As a result, the NetWare server computer must be as reliable as possible. A popular way to increase the reliability of the NetWare server disk system is to use a **redundant array of inexpensive disks (RAID)**. RAID provides protection from loss of data due to a bad disk drive. There are three levels of RAID systems in general use: 1, 3, and 5. RAID level 1 is the most common; it uses multiple disk drives and controls along with software to provide basic disk mirroring and duplexing available with NetWare (these concepts are discussed later in the chapter). RAID level 3 is a hardware solution that takes each byte of data off several drives; one drive is used for parity checking and error correcting. If a drive fails in a level-3 RAID system, the parity drive can be used to reconstruct each data byte on the replacement drive.

A level-5 RAID system is more sophisticated. It takes data off the drives by sector. The parity information is embedded in the sectors, eliminating the use of a dedicated parity drive. Many RAID systems also support **hot-swapping**, which allows a drive to be replaced while the computer is running. With hot-swapping, the network administrator can replace a malfunctioning disk drive and have the system resynchronize the drive without interrupting network services. The hot-swapping feature can be well worth its extra cost when your NetWare server needs to support mission-critical applications that cannot be interrupted.

CD-ROM Drives

Compact disk-read-only memory (CD-ROM) technology is different from that of magnetic disk drives in that it uses light from low-intensity laser beams to read binary ones and zeros from the disk platter rather than sensing magnetic fields contained on hard and floppy disk surfaces. Data is permanently recorded on a CD-ROM at the factory and, as the name suggests, the data recorded on the CD-ROM cannot be changed by your computer system. The main benefit of a CD-ROM is its storage capacity. A standard CD-ROM can store more than 680 MB of data, the equivalent of more than 600 floppy disks' worth of information. This makes CD-ROMs a very good way to distribute and access large software applications, collections of programs, or other data-intensive files such as sound, graphic images, and video.

CD-ROMs store bits of information by using a laser beam to read microscopic "pits" arranged in a single spiral track that winds continuously from the outside to the inside of the disk, much like the tracks on phonograph records. There are about 2.8 billion pits on a single CD-ROM spiral track. When a CD-ROM is accessed, the drive uses a laser beam to measure the reflections off the pits in the spiral track. These reflections vary in intensity as the light reflects off the pits. The fluctuations in the reflected light are then converted into digital ones and zeros.

The formatting of the data frames or sectors on a CD-ROM is controlled by a standard developed in 1985 by a group of industry leaders that met in the High Sierra Casino and Hotel in Lake Tahoe, California. In this highly motivating setting, the group developed what came to be known as the High Sierra CD-ROM standard. This standard was later adopted by the International Standards Organization as ISO 9660. The ISO 9660 standard ensures that any CD-ROM disk will be accessible in any CD-ROM drive used with IBM PCs, Apple Macintosh, and UNIX-based computers.

Because of the large amounts and many types of data available in standard format on CD-ROMs, many users need access to CD-ROMs on their workstation computers. This can be accomplished by installing CD-ROM drives on each workstation, by sharing CD-ROM drives from the network NetWare server, or by a combination of both strategies. CD-ROM drives are attached to a computer through either an SCSI or a bus interface controller card. Some manufacturers sell their CD-ROM drives with their own proprietary bus-interfaced controllers, designed by the manufacturers to work only with the drives they sell. Although less expensive than SCSI-2 drives, proprietary bus interfaces do not always provide for multiple drive connections and can limit your choice of products to only those of the company that supplied the CD-ROM drive.

Although it supports floppy and hard disks, the MS-DOS operating system does not have built-in support for devices such as CD-ROM drives. Two software items are needed to control a CD-ROM drive on a DOS workstation: the device driver and Microsoft CD Extensions. A **device driver** is a program that supplies instructions the computer needs to control a specific device such as the CD-ROM drive. Windows 95 includes device drivers to handle most hardware devices, including CD-ROM controllers, and integrates the Microsoft Extensions in the operation system. Earlier versions of DOS and Windows used device drivers supplied with the CD-ROM controller card (for example, TOSHIBA.SYS or HITACHI.SYS) and added the Microsoft Extensions in a program named MSCDEX.EXE. MSCDEX.EXE allows MS-DOS to access the appropriate CD-ROM ISO 9660 data format.

If you accidentally try to store information on a CD-ROM, you will receive a Write Protected error message because the device is read-only.

The main advantage of attaching a CD-ROM drive to a NetWare server rather than attaching separate CD-ROM drives to each workstation is that it reduces the cost per workstation, eliminating the cost of multiple CD-ROM device drivers and extension software. When the CD-ROM drive is attached to the NetWare server, NetWare assigns a drive pointer to it. This allows the information to be accessed and shared across the network, just like any other data on the NetWare server's hard disks. Another reason for installing a CD-ROM drive on your NetWare server is that NetWare 4.1 is normally provided on a set of CD-ROMs (one CD-ROM actually contains NetWare 4.1 and the other contains the documentation). NetWare installation is completed much faster and more reliably with a CD-ROM than with a large number of floppy disks.

When purchasing a CD-ROM drive for a NetWare server computer, make sure to obtain SCSI-2 compatible drives that will work with the standard software drives available with NetWare. Before you purchase a CD-ROM drive, it's a good idea to check with the manufacturer to be sure that the drive and the controller card are certified by Novell and that proper NetWare driver software is available.

The digital video disk (DVD) is the successor to the CD-ROM. DVD uses the same disk size as the CD-ROM, but can store full-length motion pictures. DVD drives will become common in microcomputers, and because they can read the old CD-ROM format as well, they will eventually replace CD-ROM drives.

Video Monitors

A network administrator can be called on to make decisions regarding the types of monitors and adapter cards to be used in workstation computers. This section provides an overview of the video system information that you will need to know in order to meet the requirements of Novell's network administrator exam.

The ability of a computer to display graphics depends on the video adapter and type of monitor connected. A **pixel** (or picture element) is a point on the screen that can be turned on or off. It is composed of three very small dots—one red, one green, and one blue. The dots are adjusted and combined to create the color and intensity of the pixel. The **resolution** of a video adapter is measured by the number of pixels on each line and on the number of lines. For example, a resolution of 320 × 200 indicates 320 pixels per line with 200 lines, for a total of 64,000 pixels.

Dot pitch is a measurement of how close together the dots that make up each pixel are placed. A smaller dot pitch results in a clearer and crisper display screen. A dot pitch of 0.28 or less is generally desirable for a video monitor.

Noninterlaced monitors are preferable to interlaced monitors. An interlaced monitor scans every other line on the screen, causing more eye strain. Noninterlaced monitors have a faster scanning system that scans each line from top to bottom to create a smoother screen image.

Early Video Standards

The original PC computer with an 8088 microprocessor had a choice of either a TTL monochrome monitor or a color monitor. The color monitor used a special **Color Graphics Adapter (CGA)** to provide up to 16 colors (four at a time) by using the RGB (red, green, blue) digital interface and a resolution of 320 × 200 pixels. In addition, CGA could support composite monochrome monitors along with text, graphics, and color modes. The main drawback to CGA is the resolution, which is poor in text mode and makes viewing of word processing and spreadsheet applications difficult.

Monochrome monitors display only one color. They are the least expensive monitors and are usually satisfactory for use on NetWare server computers. Monochrome monitors fall into three basic categories: TTL, composite, and VGA. The first two are discussed in this section, and monochrome VGA is discussed in the section on VGA.

Transistor-to-Transistor Logic (TTL) monitors were the original green monochrome displays offered by IBM on the first IBM PCs. These monitors provided a good display, but the original IBM monochrome display adapter did not have graphics ability. The Hercules company, seeing an opportunity, created a version of the monochrome display adapter with graphics capability. The result, the Hercules card, became the most widely used monochrome graphics solution for many years.

Composite monochrome monitors provide the lowest resolution of all monochrome monitors, providing the same resolution as CGA monitors only without the color. Composite monitors are the least expensive and can be plugged into any CGA or compatible adapter.

When IBM's AT computer, using the Intel 80286 microprocessor, was introduced, so was a new graphics standard: the **Enhanced Graphics Adapter (EGA)**. Similar to CGA, EGA also used an enhanced version of the RGB digital signal and, as a result, the EGA cards work with either CGA or EGA monitors. When working with an EGA monitor, the EGA card provides 640 × 350 resolution with 64 different colors.

VGA

Currently the **Video Graphics Array (VGA)** adapter and monitor have all but replaced the earlier CGA and EGA systems. VGA supports all previous video modes and both monochrome and color monitors. A monochrome monitor is often the best choice for an inexpensive monitor for use on a NetWare server computer because it can be plugged directly into a standard VGA interface card and provides a good-quality text display. One big difference between VGA and previous video adapters is its use of analog signals rather than the digital RGB interface. The more expensive analog signal provides many more color variations over the same number of wires. The VGA monitor has the following advantages over EGA and CGA monitors:

- Displays up to 256 colors with 320 × 200 resolution
- Displays 16 colors at 640 × 480 resolution
- Provides emulation for all earlier display modes

Super VGA (SVGA)

The **Super VGA (SVGA)** adapter is an enhanced version of the VGA adapter that allows better resolution and more color combinations. Additional memory is usually required on VGA adapters in order to provide the enhanced capabilities. Super VGA adapters can display 256 colors with a resolution of 800 × 600, or up to 1,024 × 768 when used with 16 colors.

Graphics Accelerators

Because of the graphics demands of programs such as Microsoft Windows, video card manufacturers started building video adapters with a microprocessor called a **graphics accelerator** to speed up graphics operations. Accelerators are now found on most graphics cards and are often built in to the system board. Graphics adapters based on accelerators feature resolutions of 1,024 × 768, 1,280 × 1,024, and 1,600 × 1,200, with up to 16.7 million colors.

Power System

All system components depend on electricity to operate, so the last but most important part of any computer system is its power system. Power problems can often cause intermittent computer crashes and losses of data that cannot be tolerated on a NetWare server computer. A network administrator needs to be familiar with the components that make up a NetWare server's power system. In this section you will learn about the major power components and how you can use them to provide reliable power to a NetWare server.

Power Supply

A power supply that does not have enough amps or that does not filter out power irregularities can cause system errors or crashes. Because a NetWare server often has multiple high-capacity hard drives along with many other peripherals such as CD-ROM drives, tape drives, and NICs, the power supply must be able to support the amperage needed by all these devices. A NetWare server should have a switching power supply of at least 300 watts. A **switching power supply** will cease functioning if there is a serious component failure or short in the system. A built-in surge suppressor and a power filter are both good features that will help protect system components from damage resulting from voltage spikes during electrical storms or if your computer is running on the same power line as other high-power electrical equipment such as motors and copy machines.

Power Line

The first rule in providing good power to a NetWare server computer is to have an electrician provide a separate power line from the main fuse box to the server room. This power line should have no other equipment or computers attached to it. You should especially avoid attaching laser printers or copy machines to the same power line used by the NetWare server because these devices can create power fluctuations and electrical noise that adversely affect the system.

Power Filters

The second line of defense in the power system is a good power filter that will remove any noise or power surges from the incoming line. It is a good idea to have your local power company or an electrician use a voltage monitor on your incoming power over a period of several days in order to determine the extent of any electrical noise or power surges experienced in the NetWare server room. You can then use the voltage monitor information to buy the correct power filter to protect your server from unwanted electrical noise and surges.

Uninterruptible Power Supply

In addition to a high-quality power supply and filter, each NetWare server should be protected from brownouts and blackouts by an **Uninterruptible Power Supply (UPS)**. A UPS contains a battery that automatically provides power in the event of a commercial power failure. Depending on the capacity of its battery, a UPS unit can provide power to the server for up to 30 minutes after commercial power has failed. The capacity of most UPS systems is measured in volt-amps (VA). Volt-amps are calculated by multiplying the number of amps needed times the voltage. To determine the correct size of the UPS needed for a server, first make a list of each piece of equipment to be protected (CPU, monitor, external drives, and so on). Include its nameplate-rated wattage or VA. Then total all wattage and VA to obtain the total wattage and total volt-amps necessary—this total must be less than or equal to the recommended output of the UPS.

Another important feature of a UPS is its ability to send a signal to the computer informing it that the system has switched to battery backup power. NetWare has a UPS monitoring feature that allows the NetWare server to determine how much time the UPS battery will last and shut itself down before all power is drained from the UPS battery. Because a NetWare server keeps much information in RAM cache buffers, if a system's power is turned off prior to the NetWare server being shut down, important information can easily be lost. In many cases the NetWare server will not be able to mount its disk volumes after an unexpected crash, requiring the network administrator to take the extra step of performing a volume fix.

The Workstation

Now that we've discussed microcomputers in general, let's consider the user's workstation. Each user's workstation should provide that user with the ability to handle any job responsibilities and provide network connectivity. Although many operating systems exist that may be used on workstations—DOS, OS/2, Windows for Workgroups, Windows 95, Windows NT Workstation, Macintosh System 7.5—we'll focus on Windows 95 in this discussion. Windows 95 is the current version of the widely used Windows environment. Windows 95 also incorporates the current version of DOS, DOS 7.0, but generally keeps it hidden from the user.

Windows 95 Microprocessor Requirements

Windows 95 requires at least an Intel 80386 DX microprocessor, but the practical minimum is commonly considered to be at least an 80486 chip. As of mid-1996, most new PCs being sold have at least a 75-MHz Pentium CPU, so this minimum is easily met for new PC purchases. Network administrators typically purchase (or recommend for purchase if they don't have purchasing authority) an entry-level PC for most employees. An **entry-level PC** is the PC that a company commonly purchases as its standard microcomputer. The exact specifications of an entry-level PC differ from company to company, and they change over time as new hardware components push down the price of older components. For example, in late 1995 a typical entry-level PC used at least a 75-MHz Pentium CPU, but by mid-1996 at least a 133-MHz Pentium CPU was the standard.

A good general rule is to set the price you want to pay for the workstation and then buy the hardware configuration that is closest to that amount. As prices of existing components fall, you'll get faster CPUs for the same purchase price.

Windows 95 Memory Requirements

Windows 95 requires at least 8 MB of RAM, but it runs slowly with only 8 MB. A more practical minimum is 16 MB, especially when application programs are considered. For example, Microsoft Access 7.0 has a stated minimum of 12 MB of RAM.

Workstation Storage Requirements

The size of the hard drive needed in a workstation is determined by the number and size of applications programs and data files that will be stored on the workstation. As of mid-1996, most new PCs were being shipped with at least 850-MB hard drives, and many had hard drives with a capacity of 1.2 GB or more. These hard drives give you plenty of room to install Windows 95 and application software and still have sufficient disk space for most users' current storage needs.

THE NETWARE SERVER

As explained in Chapter 1, the main function of a NetWare server computer in a client server NOS such as NetWare 4.1 is to provide network resources such as file and print services to client workstations. As a result, the NetWare server can be enhanced with specialized hardware and software to improve performance, security, and reliability over what can be expected from a peer-to-peer NOS. NetWare offers server-based software that is designed from the ground up to make the maximum use of the NetWare server's hardware.

Microcomputer manufacturers often offer microcomputers designed as LAN servers. These microcomputers offer features not found in microcomputers designed as user workstations, and should be purchased for NetWare servers whenever possible.

NETWARE SERVER MICROPROCESSOR REQUIREMENTS

A NetWare 4.1 server requires at least an 80386 microprocessor. However, performance will be slow, and a faster CPU is desirable. A NetWare server typically is used more for input and output operations (reading and writing files) than for computations. Therefore, server performance can often be better enhanced by adding more memory or a faster NIC than by using the fastest processor. There are, however, some applications that run on the server. For example, a client/server database such as Oracle will run part of the program (the server portion) on the NetWare server and other parts of the program (the client) on the user workstations. In this case, a faster processor may be important for reasonable application performance.

A good general rule is that when you are purchasing a new NetWare server, you should buy one with a microprocessor at least equivalent to the microprocessor in the standard PCs you are buying for your users. For example, if the standard PCs you buy use a Pentium 133-MHz CPU, then your NetWare server should have at least a Pentium 133-MHz chip. Because your network depends upon the server, don't skimp on the processor in the server.

NETWARE SERVER MEMORY REQUIREMENTS

The NetWare server uses extended memory to run the NOS, to run the utility modules called NetWare Loadable Modules (NLMs), and to keep available in RAM information frequently accessed from the hard disk. Adding more memory to a NetWare server generally increases NetWare server performance because it allows more disk information to be kept in RAM, thereby reducing read and transmission time. Adding memory to a NetWare server will not enhance the performance of applications stored and used on the individual workstations, however, because each workstation's memory is managed by its own local operating system—the NetWare server provides only data and communication services.

In order to run NetWare 4.1, the NetWare server should contain at least 8 MB of RAM. This is an absolute minimum, and normally the NetWare Server will require more RAM than that. To calculate the approximate memory requirements for a NetWare server you can use the simplified equation shown in Figure 2-21.

The equation for calculating server memory requirements has four variables: operating system requirements, volume-related requirements, disk caching, and NLM requirements. You need to allow 7 MB for the operating system, and some large NLMs that are commonly used may require another 2 MB. For each hard disk volume, multiply the volume size by 0.008. Add a minimum of 4 MB for disk caching (you can add more if you want, and the additional RAM will improve caching performance).

Figure 2-21

Calculating NetWare server memory requirements

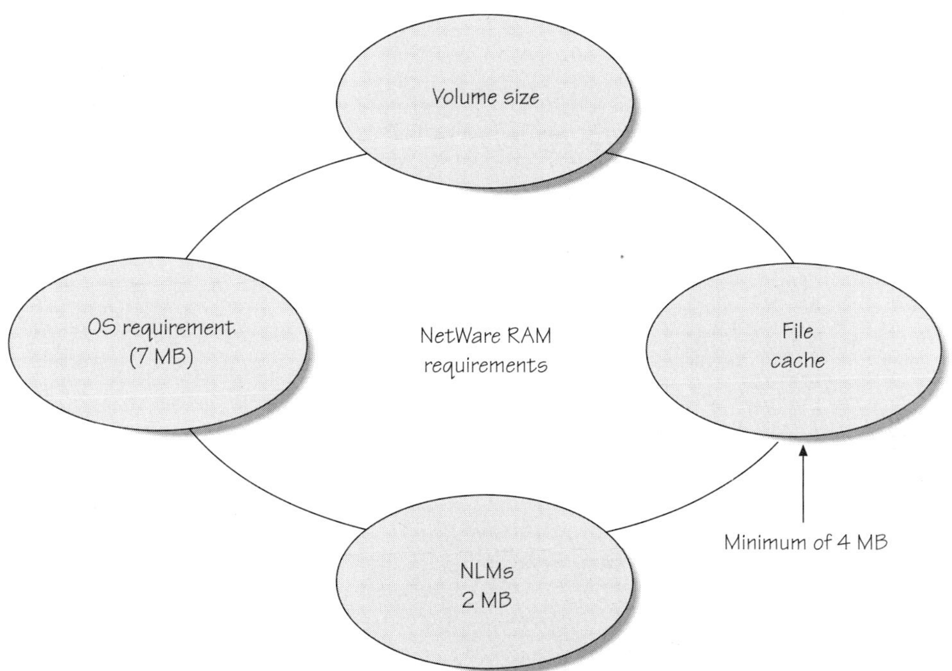

A sample calculation follows. If a NetWare server has a 1-GB disk capacity, the memory requirement is calculated as 7 MB for the operating system, plus 0.008 × 1,000 = 8 MB for disk space, plus 4 MB for file caching, plus 2 MB for NLMs. Thus the memory requirement for this NetWare server is 21 MB of RAM. You can round this up to 24 MB, and use three 8-MB SIMMs or, if your server requires that you install SIMMS in pairs, two 8-MB SIMMs and two 4-MB SIMMs.

Microcomputers designed as LAN servers are often available with a kind of RAM called **error checking and correcting (ECC) memory**. ECC memory employs algorithms that increase a server's ability to continue operating, despite a single-bit memory error, by actually correcting minor memory errors. If a company's NetWare server controls a mission-critical application, ECC memory can be worth its expense. A **mission-critical application** is one that an organization depends upon for the day-to-day operation of its business. In a mail-order business, for example, the order entry system is considered mission-critical because a system failure directly influences the company's profits.

The Pentium Pro microprocessor's data bus supports ECC by adding 8 bits of ECC circuits beyond the 64 bits used for the data itself to support ECC.

NETWARE SERVER STORAGE REQUIREMENTS

When selecting a hard disk system for your NetWare server, you first need to determine the storage capacity required for your server. Allow at least 80 MB for the NetWare 4.1 operating system files and print queues. Next, determine which software packages you want to store on the NetWare server and record how much storage space is required by each package. To determine how much data storage is required, identify each application and estimate the current storage requirement and future growth over the next three years. Determine how much space each user will be allowed for his or her personal data storage needs along with any shared document storage areas and add these to obtain the estimated total data requirements. After the storage requirements have been estimated, add at least 25% for expansion and overhead to obtain the total hard disk capacity needed.

PERFORMANCE FEATURES

The performance of a NetWare server is determined by how fast it can respond to requests for data from client workstations. Therefore the major factors that affect the server's performance are its ability to keep frequently used information in memory, the speed of its disk system, and, if the first two are adequate, the speed of its processor unit. NetWare is the best-performing network operating system in the industry because it was designed to be a NetWare server and therefore does not contain some of the additional overhead associated with general-purpose operating systems such as DOS, UNIX, or Windows NT. Some of the performance features of NetWare include file caching, directory caching, and elevator seeking.

File Caching

File caching is the process by which NetWare increases the speed of response to requests for disk information. It does this by keeping the most frequently accessed disk blocks in memory. Because the computer's memory is approximately 100 times faster than the disk system, retrieving a block of data from the file cache greatly improves the performance of the server. As a general rule, at least 50% of the computer's memory should be allocated to file caching, resulting in more than 70% of the data requests being handled from the computer's memory rather than read directly from the disk.

Directory Caching

Directory caching is the process of keeping the directory entry table and file allocation table (FAT) for each disk volume in the memory of the computer. Like file caching, directory caching greatly increases the performance of the server by allowing it to find filenames 100 times faster than when the directory information is read directly from disk. In addition to directory caching, NetWare also uses a process called **directory hashing** to create a binary index system that improves file lookup time by as much as 30%. Figure 2-22 illustrates how requests from two different workstations to run the WP.EXE program would be handled by NetWare's caching system. In step 1, the server initially loads the directory cache and FATs with directory information from the disk volume and then builds the hash table. In step 2, the first request arrives from workstation A for the file WP.EXE. The server looks up the WP.EXE file in the hash table and then uses the directory table and FAT to identify the necessary disk blocks. Because the cache buffers are empty, the server reads the necessary disk blocks into the cache and then sends the WP.EXE file to workstation A. In step 3, a second request, from workstation B, is received for the WP.EXE program file. This time, after looking up the filename in the hash table, the server finds that the needed disk blocks are contained in the cache buffers. The server then immediately responds to the request by sending the data directly to workstation B from the file cache, thereby saving the time required to read the WP.EXE file from disk.

Figure 2-22 Cache memory

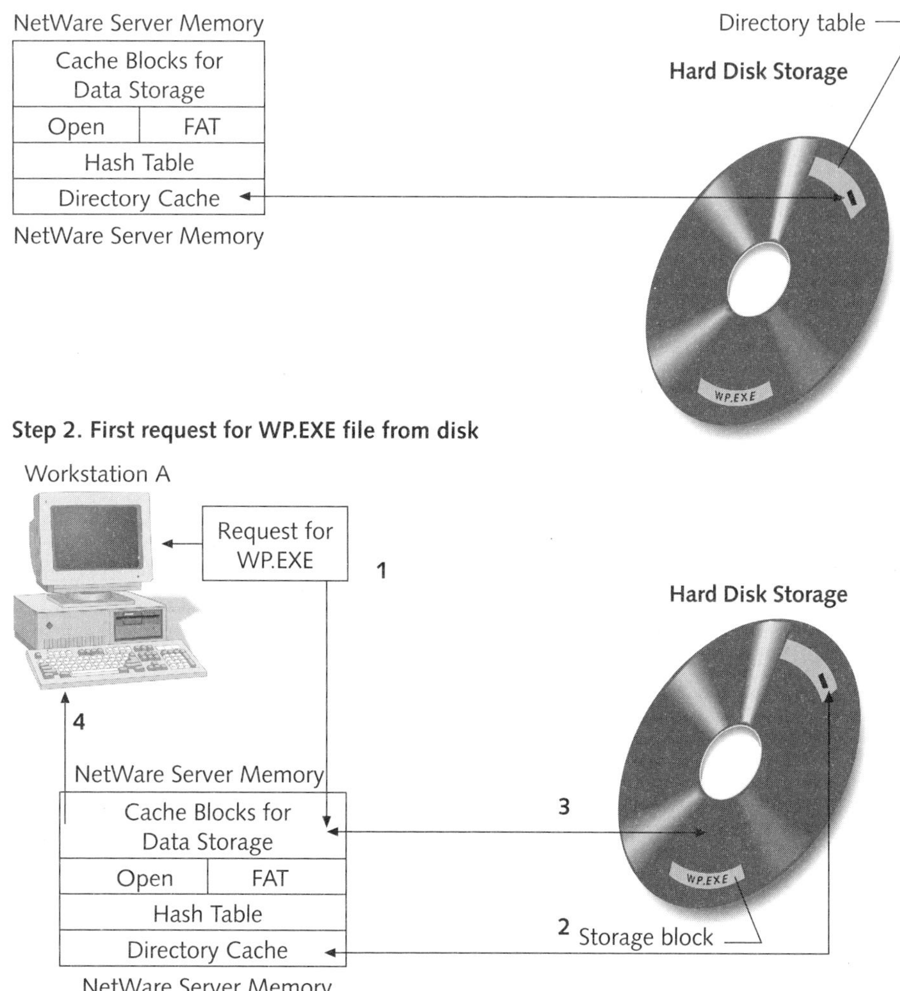

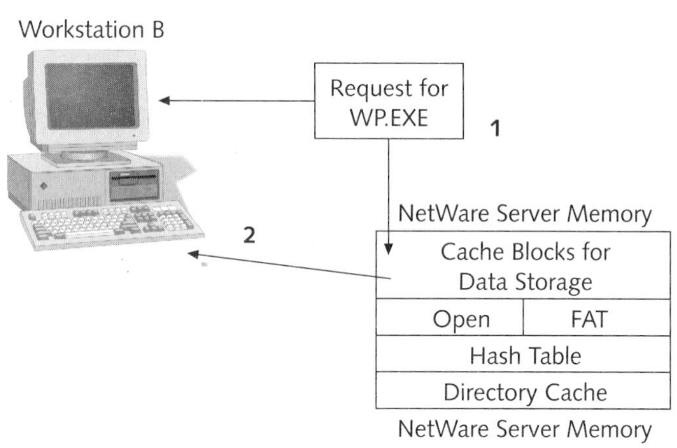

Elevator Seeking

Because the NetWare server environment is multitasking, at any given time it might be responding to several data requests from different client workstations. **Elevator seeking** is the process of minimizing the amount of disk drive head movement by accessing the information in the sequence of the head movement rather than in the order in which the requests were received. Elevator seeking gets its name from the way an elevator works when picking up people on different floors. Imagine that an elevator is at the top of a 10-story building when someone on floor 2 pushes the down button. As the elevator passes the eighth floor, another person on floor 5 also pushes the down button. The elevator will stop at floor 5 first and then floor 2 even though the person on floor 2 pushed the down button first. After picking up the person on floor 5, the elevator will finally move to floor 2 and pick up the person there.

Fault Tolerance

Fault tolerance can be defined as the ability of a system to continue to operate satisfactorily in the event of errors or other problems. In NetWare 4.1 the NetWare server environment was designed with four levels of fault tolerance in its disk system in order to continue server operations in the event of physical errors on the disk drives or controller cards.

A hard disk's directory information is extremely important in enabling the server to locate information on the disk system. Because of this, NetWare's first level of fault tolerance is provided by second copies of the directory entry table and FAT on different locations of the disk drive. If a storage block in one of the tables is damaged, NetWare automatically switches to the duplicate table to retrieve the requested directory information. The faulty sector is then listed in the disk's bad block table, and the data contained in the bad sector is stored in another disk location.

As a disk drive ages, certain recording sectors of the disk's surface can become unreliable. To make sure that data written to the disk is stored in a good storage sector, NetWare implements a read-after-write verification process. If data cannot be reliably written to a disk sector after three attempts, NetWare implements the second level of fault tolerance, referred to as "hot fix." **Hot fix** involves redirecting bad and unreliable disk storage sectors to a redirection area location elsewhere on the disk surface. When a new disk drive is first formatted by NetWare, a certain percentage of the disk capacity (2% by default) is reserved for the hot fix redirection area, allowing the disk drive to continue normal operation despite bad sectors that might develop on the disk surface. Step 1 in Figure 2-23 illustrates the NetWare server attempting to write a data buffer to disk block 201 and receiving a disk error when the data is read back by using the read-after-write verification process. In step 2, the data in the cache memory buffer is written to the redirection area and block 201 of the disk is remapped by the NetWare server to point to the block in the redirection area. As mentioned in Chapter 1, one of the responsibilities of a network administrator is to monitor the NetWare server in order to determine how many blocks have been redirected and thereby help determine when the disk drive should be replaced. In Chapter 17, you will learn how to use the NetWare MONITOR utility to track the condition of the redirection area and determine when a disk drive should be replaced.

Figure 2-23
NetWare's hot fix

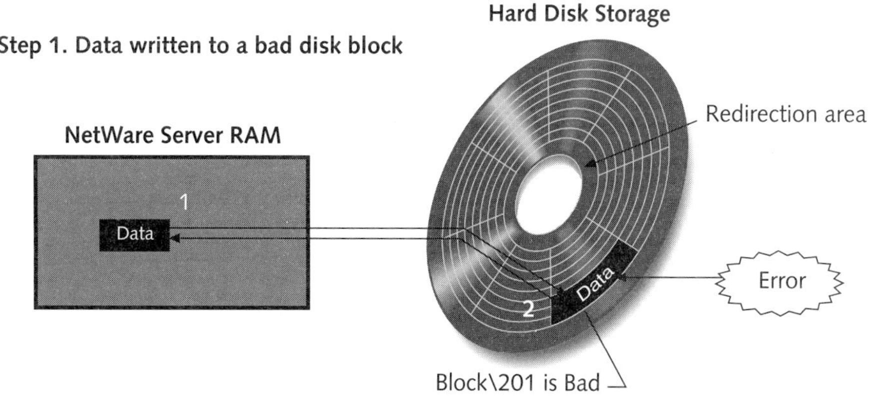

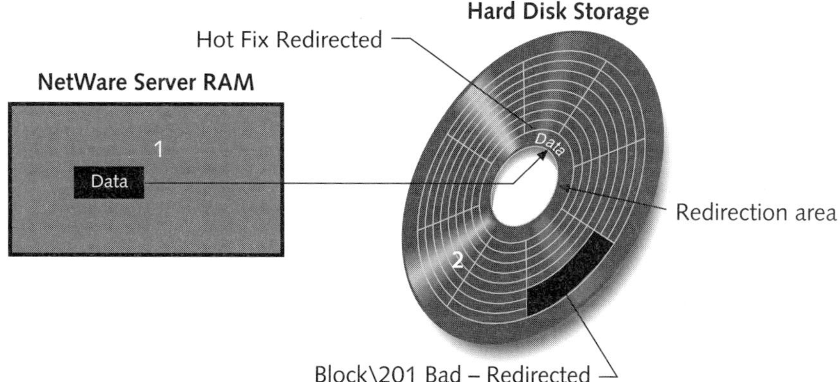

The third level of fault tolerance is the continued operation of the NetWare server in spite of a complete failure of the disk system. NetWare provides two methods to protect a NetWare server from major failures of the disk storage system. The first method, called **mirroring**, involves attaching two drives to the same disk controller card and then mirroring the drives in order to synchronize the data on both disks. After the disks have been mirrored, NetWare automatically keeps the information updated on both drives so that in the event of a failure of one of the disk drives, the server will be able to continue normal operation by using the second drive. The network administrator can then replace the defective drive at a time that is convenient, and NetWare will resynchronize the data on the new drive without requiring the network administrator to restore any information from the backup tape. Figure 2-24 illustrates the use of disk mirroring to protect your server against failure of a disk drive. Disk mirroring works well, but requires each block to be written twice by the controller card, which can decrease the performance of the NetWare server. In addition, with disk mirroring, a failure of the controller card will make data on both drives unusable.

Figure 2-24
Disk mirroring

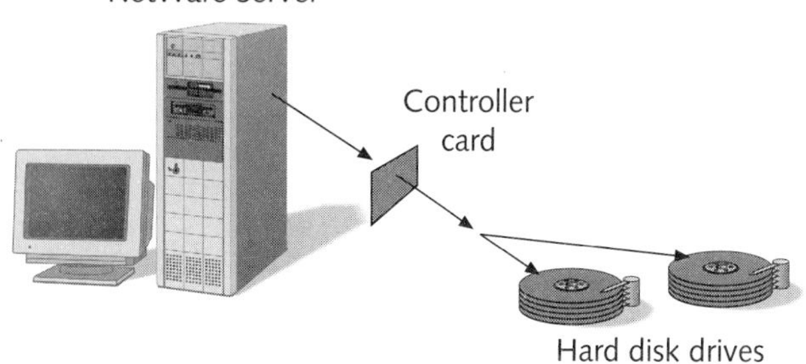

The second method is called **disk duplexing**, and with it Novell has provided a way for NetWare to provide fault tolerance for both the disk drive and controller card. Disk duplexing uses two disk drives and two controller cards, as illustrated in Figure 2-25.

Disk duplexing also increases performance over disk mirroring in that one disk write operation can be used to write data to both disk drives. An additional advantage of disk duplexing over a single disk drive is that it actually increases a NetWare server's performance. Both controllers are requested to find data, and then the information from whichever drive is closest to the data location is read first. In a sense, implementing disk duplexing is like doubling the number of disk heads and thereby increasing disk-read performance.

Figure 2-25
Disk duplexing

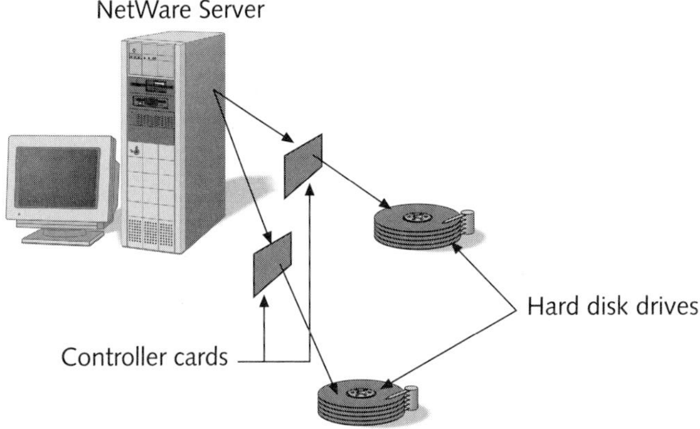

The fourth level of fault tolerance in NetWare 4.1 is **server duplexing**, which allows two NetWare servers on the network to be duplicated. This prevents a crash of one NetWare server from affecting the operation of the network. This feature is important in implementing mission-critical applications on LANs and thus appeals to organizations that cannot afford any interruption in network services.

File Compression

NetWare server disk storage capacity is always limited, no matter how much capacity you have. NetWare 4.1 provides a **file compression** capability so that infrequently used files can be compressed to a smaller size. You as the network manager can control how long a file is inactive before it is compressed, and it will be automatically uncompressed whenever a user opens it again. The compression can be scheduled to take place during server low-use hours. The file compression feature helps conserve disk space on the NetWare server so that you use your disk space more effectively.

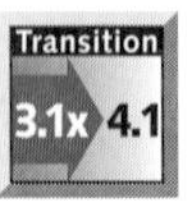

File compression is a new feature in NetWare 4.1.

Block Suballocation

NetWare 4.1 also helps conserve hard disk space by using block suballocation. On a hard disk, files are stored in blocks, where each block holds a set number of bytes. In NetWare 3.12, for example, the default block size was 4 KB. This means a file must be stored in 4-KB blocks, which leads to a problem with small files: a file with only one character in it (1 byte) would have to take up one block of 4 KB of storage—a waste of a lot of disk space. The problem gets worse with larger block sizes, and NetWare 4.1 uses different default block sizes depending on volume size, as shown in Figure 2-26.

Figure 2-26
Default block sizes

Volume Size	Default Block Size
1–31 MB	4 KB
32–149 MB	16 KB
150–499 MB	32 KB
500 or more MB	64 KB

NetWare 4.1 solves this problem with **block suballocation**, which allows large block sizes to be divided into 4-KB sub-blocks when necessary. For example, if the block size is 64 KB, and a file contains 65 KB, then the file will be stored in one 64-KB block and one 4-KB sub-block (a total of 68 KB) instead of in two 64-KB blocks (a total of 128 KB).

Although the problem of wasted disk space because of large block sizes also existed in NetWare 3.1x, there were no tools to fix it. NetWare 4.1 adds block suballocation to the network administrator's tools and provides a solution to the problem.

Chapter Summary

Microcomputer systems are similar to those of any other computer. They perform four basic processes: input, processing, storage, and output. Input devices take information and commands from the outside world and convert them into the binary one and zero system used in digital computers. The system unit of the computer, comprising several components, enables the computer to process the input data and produce information. The system board of the computer ties all the system unit components together.

The most important component on the system board is the brain of the system unit, the microprocessor chip, also known as the central processor unit (CPU). The CPU fetches instructions and data from memory and then performs the requested function. IBM-compatible computers are based on the Intel line of microprocessors, and Apple Macintosh computers use processor chips made by Motorola. Programs written for the Intel chips will not run on Motorola processors.

The power of a microprocessor chip is based on several factors including clock speed, word size, instruction set, and bus size. Most IBM-compatible computers today use the 80486, Pentium, or Pentium Pro microprocessor. The Pentium Pro features a Dynamic Execution feature that improves its performance.

The system board components are tied together by a bus structure. The local bus supports the data and address buses, and the expansion bus supports the expansion slots, which attach peripheral controller cards. The ISA expansion bus was designed for the 80286 computer with 16-bit data and 24-bit address buses running at 8 MHz. The EISA bus is an enhanced version of the ISA bus that allows 32-bit buses and higher clock speeds. IBM has used a proprietary bus, called the Micro Channel, that also provides 32-bit bus access at high clock speeds and an automatic configuration utility that makes it much easier to install cards. VESA and PCI are called local bus slots because they provide direct access to the CPU and memory at much higher speeds than either EISA or Micro Channel. You should use the

VESA or PCI bus slots for devices—such as video and disk controller cards—that require very high access speeds.

The system board uses I/O ports and interrupts to communicate with peripheral devices such as keyboards, video monitors, modems, disk drives, and network cards. Parallel ports are most frequently used to connect printers, while serial ports provide longer-distance communication. When a device is added with an expansion card, it is attached to a controller card that must be assigned a unique interrupt and I/O port address. This is done by changing settings on the cards or using a setup program. After the cards have been installed, the card driver software must be configured to use the selected interrupt and I/O address settings.

Memory is the primary storage area for the microcomputer system. All instructions and data must be stored in memory before they can be processed by the CPU. RAM is the computer's work area and is used primarily to contain instructions and data that are currently being processed. Workstations using just DOS can get by with only 1 or 2 MB of RAM. If you are using Windows 95 on a workstation, you should have at least 8 and preferably 16 MB of RAM to provide adequate performance.

Hard disk storage consists of the controller card and drive. Older computers used the ST506 controller card to operate slower drives of relatively low capacity. Modern hard drives are based on either IDE or SCSI controller cards. IDE is a very popular controller for DOS and Windows workstations and small- to medium-sized NetWare servers. The new enhanced IDE controllers provide higher speed and increased storage capacity (up to 8.5 GB) and support up to four devices. SCSI-2 controller cards can be used to attach up to seven different types of devices, including disk drives, CD-ROM drives, and tape drives. They allow for higher capacity and faster drives than IDE and are used for larger NetWare servers requiring multiple devices and more than 1 GB of disk space.

CD-ROMs represent an important new development in storage systems, allowing 680 MB to be stored permanently on a removable disk. CD-ROMs are used to store a variety of data including sound, text, fielded data, graphics, and video. Because of the amount of material available on CD-ROMs, sharing them on a network has become an important function controlled by the network administrator. If the CD-ROM drives are attached to a NetWare server, special NetWare modules are used to make the information on the CD-ROM available to all networked workstations.

The power system of the computer is critical to proper operation. Problems with computers locking up or giving parity error messages can be caused by insufficient or faulty power supplies. You need to be sure that the wattage of your computer's power supply provides the necessary amps for all attached devices. A UPS (uninterruptible power supply) uses a battery to provide continuous power to the computer for a short period of time after a commercial power failure. This gives the network administrator or the NetWare server computer time to save the contents of the computer's memory and properly shut itself down prior to loss of power. All NetWare server computers need to be protected by a UPS and proper power filters.

User workstations using Windows 95 need at least an 80486 CPU and 16 MB of RAM. Hard drive storage of at least 850 MB is preferred if applications and data will be stored on the PC.

Novell designed the NetWare network operating system specifically as a LAN server operating system, with performance features such as high-volume file caching, directory caching and hashing, and elevator seeking. In addition to its high performance, NetWare includes such fault-tolerant features as hot fix, disk mirroring, disk duplexing, and server duplexing. NetWare also provides automatic file compression and block suballocation to conserve disk space.

Although NetWare can run on an 80386 CPU, you should use at least an 80486. A NetWare server working as an applications server will need at least a Pentium processor. The NetWare server uses its RAM to run the operating system and cache information from the hard disk for faster access. While a NetWare server with a small disk drive can run with as little as 8 MB of RAM, this is an absolute minimum and you will normally need more RAM. A large server using multiple protocols may need up to 2 GB of RAM. Although placing additional RAM in a NetWare server does not directly affect what applications can be run on the workstation, it does provide for network performance. A shortage of memory in a NetWare server computer can cause it to crash or lock up the network.

KEY TERMS

access arm

access time

address

address bus

American National Standards Institute (ANSI)

American Standard Code for Information Interchange (ASCII)

asynchronous communication

baud rate

binary

binary digit

bit

block suballocation

bus

bus mastering

byte

cache memory

central processing unit (CPU)

clock

color graphics adapter (CGA)

command queuing

compact disk read-only memory (CD-ROM)

compiler

complementary metal oxide semiconductor (CMOS) memory

complex instruction set computer (CISC)

composite monochrome monitor

controller card

conventional memory

cycle

cylinder

data bus

data communications equipment (DCE)

data terminal equipment (DTE)

dataflow analysis

device driver

direct memory access (DMA) channel

directory caching

directory hashing

disk duplexing

dot pitch

Dynamic Execution

dynamic RAM (DRAM)

elevator seeking

end user

enhanced graphics adapter (EGA)

enhanced IDE

extended industry standard architecture (EISA) bus

entry-level PC

error checking and correcting (ECC) memory

expanded memory

expanded memory system (EMS)

expansion bus

expansion card

expansion slot

extended data out (EDO) RAM

extended memory

fault tolerance
fetching
file allocation table (FAT)
file caching
file compression
graphics accelerator
hot fix
hot-swapping
industry standard architecture (ISA) bus
input/output (I/O) port
instruction set
integrated drive electronics (IDE)
interrupt request (IRQ)
local bus
logical block address (LBA)
machine language
math coprocessor
megahertz (MHz)
memory buffers
Micro Channel bus
microprocessor
millions of instructions per second (MIPS)
mirroring
mission-critical application
monochrome monitor
multiple branch prediction
NuBus
null modem cable
nybble
parallel port
parity bit
partitioning
PC workstation
peripheral component interconnect (PCI) bus
peripherals
personal computer (PC)
pixel
PowerPC processor
protected mode
RAM shadowing
random-access memory (RAM)
read-only memory (ROM)
real mode
recording tracks
reduced instruction set computer (RISC)
redundant array of inexpensive disks (RAID)
register
resolution
rotational delay
RS232
sector
seek time
serial port
server duplexing
single in-line memory module (SIMM)
small computer system interface (SCSI)
speculative execution
static RAM (SRAM)
super VGA (SVGA)
switching power supply
synchronous communication
system board
transfer time
Transistor-to-Transistor Logic (TTL) monitor
uninterruptible power supply (UPS)
upper memory
users
VESA bus
video graphics array (VGA)
virtual file allocation table (VFAT)
virtual memory
virtual real mode
wait state
word size
workstation

REVIEW QUESTIONS

1. A(n) ______________________ is the amount of storage capacity needed to record one character of data in the computer's memory.
2. Using the data in Figures 2-3 and 2-4, complete the following table to illustrate how the word "NetWare" would be expressed in binary notation.

Character	N	e	t	W	a	r	e
Decimal							
Hexadecimal							
Binary							

3. Using the data in Figures 2-3 and 2-4, complete the following table to illustrate how the word "Server" would be expressed in binary notation.

Character	S	e	r	v	e	r
Decimal						
Hexadecimal						
Binary						

4. List the components found on the system board of a microcomputer system:
   ____
   ____
   ____
   ____
5. The ______________________ is the brain of a microcomputer system.
6. The ______________________ is used to provide precisely timed signals that synchronize the internal working of the system unit.
7. A microprocessor's word size is a measurement of the number of bits that can be stored in each ______________________.
8. The ______________________ is the part of the CPU that is responsible for performing calculations.
9. In addition to real and protected modes, the 80386 microprocessor adds ______________________.
10. Which processing mode is used by 8088 microprocessor chips?
    ____
11. Which processing mode allows access to extended memory?
    ____
12. The ______________________ is the highway that transfers bits to and from the memory chips.

13. The size of the ________________________________ limits the amount of memory the microprocessor can directly access.
14. Briefly explain a difference between the 80386SX and 80386DX microprocessors: ________________________________
15. Briefly explain a difference between the 80486SX and 80486DX microprocessors: ________________________________
16. Briefly explain a difference between the Pentium and Pentium P55C microprocessors: ________________________________
17. Briefly explain a difference between the Pentium and Pentium Pro microprocessors: ________________________________
18. The Apple Macintosh computers use the ________________________________ family of processor chips.
19. When DOS is used, application programs are limited to running in the ________________________________ memory area.
20. ________________________________ is a very high-speed form of memory that does not require refresh clock cycles.
21. The ________________________________ memory area is used by NetWare and other workstation operating systems such as Windows NT Workstation and OS/2.
22. The ________________________________ memory area is used by video cards, ROM, and expansion cards.
23. The ________________________________ expansion bus provides 32-bit buses and is owned by IBM.
24. The ____________________ and ____________________ are two local bus specifications used with expansion slots that provide high-speed direct access to the CPU and memory.
25. The ____________________ bus provides the best high-speed direct access to a Pentium processor.
26. The ____________________ bus provides compatibility with older expansion cards while providing 32-bit slots running at 8 MHz for use with disk controllers and network cards.
27. The ____________________ Apple bus most closely resembles EISA.
28. ________________________________ memory is used to store configuration information on the system board and is backed up by battery power.
29. What is the minimum amount of memory needed by a NetWare server that has 700 MB of disk space? (Write your calculations in the space provided.)

30. To increase the performance of 80486 and Pentium processors, from 64 to 256 KB of ____________________ memory is used because it does not require wait states and provides very high-speed memory access, being composed of expensive SRAM chips.

31. After low-level formatting, a drive needs to be ______________ for use by an operating system.

32. The ______________ is used to link all disk sectors belonging to one file.

33. If mirrored 600-MB disks are used on a small- to medium-sized network, what type of disk controller would you recommend for the NetWare server computer?

____

34. List three types of data that can be stored on CD-ROMs:

____

____

____

35. ______________ is measured by the number of pixels.

36. ______________ is the measurement of the distance between pixels.

37. Which provides the higher quality image, a monitor with 0.28-dot pitch or one with 0.35-dot pitch?

____

38. List two things to consider when you are purchasing a UPS for a NetWare server computer:

____

____

39. The ______________ is used by a device to send a signal to the CPU.

40. Each device must have a unique ______________ that is used to receive commands from the CPU.

41. A NetWare server uses

____

______________ to keep the most frequently accessed blocks of data in memory.

42. A NetWare server uses ______________ to keep the directory entry table and the FAT in memory.

43. List the four types of fault tolerance available in NetWare 4.1:

____

____

____

____

44. A NetWare server uses ______________ to make more efficient use of hard disk space.

45. List the *minimum* requirements for a Windows 95 workstation:

Processor: ______________
RAM: ______________MB

46. List the *minimum* requirements for a NetWare 4.1 server:

Processor: ______________
RAM: ______________MB
Hard Drive storage: ______________MB

47. One option in installing the NetWare 4.1 NOS is to put on-line documentation on the server. The on-line system uses the Dyna-Text viewer and requires 60 MB of disk space for the viewer and documentation files. List the *minimum* requirements for a NetWare 4.1 server with on-line documentation installed:

    Processor: ______________________

    RAM: ______________________ MB

    Hard drive storage: ______________________ MB

EXERCISES

EXERCISE 2-1: DETERMINING WORKSTATION HARDWARE CONFIGURATION

Your instructor will explain how to use MS-DOS commands and utilities or other hardware-documenting programs (supplied by your instructor) to determine information about the hardware environment of your PC workstation. Fill out the following worksheet to document that workstation environment.

Computer Worksheet

Specification developed by: ______________________

SYSTEM INFORMATION

Computer make/model: ______________________

CPU: __________ **Clock speed:** __________ **Bus:** __________

Memory capacity: __________

DISK INFORMATION

Disk controller

Type: __________

Manufacturer/model :__________

Drive address	Type	Manufacturer	Cyl/Hd/Sec	Speed/Capacity	DOS Partition size
________	____	________	__/__/__	________	________

DEVICE INFORMATION

Device name	IRQ	I/O port
________	________	________
________	________	________
________	________	________

Exercises

Case 2-1: Calculating NetWare Server Memory Requirements for J. Q. Adams

The J. Q. Adams Corporation is planning to obtain a dedicated NetWare server computer to support a 25-user network with a 1,000 MB (1 GB) hard disk drive. Using the memory formula in this chapter, calculate the amount of RAM that you would recommend for this NetWare server. Write a memo to your instructor with your recommendations. Show your calculations.

Case 2-2: Developing Workstation Specifications for J. Q. Adams

1. The J. Q. Adams Corporation wants to develop a specification for an entry-level PC workstation for the company. As the network administrator for this company, you have been asked to develop this specification.

   New workstations will run the Microsoft Windows 95 operating system and will need to be able to run word processing applications and do basic spreadsheet calculations. The workstations will require about 850 MB of local disk storage for software and work files plus access to the network.

   Write a memo to your instructor containing the specification. Attach a copy of the following worksheet.
2. Some new workstations are intended to be used for word processing and desktop publishing applications that need high-resolution graphics and a more powerful microprocessor. These workstations will require about 1.6 GB of local disk storage for software and work files. They will have access to the network so they can share data files and access network printers.

   Write a memo to your instructor containing the specification. Attach a copy of the following worksheet.

Bid Specification Form

Specification developed by: ____________________

SYSTEM INFORMATION

Computer make/model: ____________________

CPU: __________ **Clock speed:** __________ **Bus:** __________

Memory capacity: __________

Estimated cost: __________

DISK INFORMATION

Disk controller

Type: __________

Manufacturer/model :__________

Drive address	Type	Manufacturer	Cyl/Hd/Sec	Speed/Capacity	DOS Partition size
______	___	______	__/__/__	______	______

NETWORK CARD INFORMATION

Network type	Manufacturer ID	I/O port	Interrupt
______	______	______	______

NON-NETWORK DEVICE INFORMATION

Device name	IRQ	I/O port
______	______	______
______	______	______
______	______	______
______	______	______

CASE 2-3: DETERMINING NETWARE SERVER DISK REQUIREMENTS FOR J. Q. ADAMS

The J. Q. Adams Corporation wants to store catalog information on a NetWare server in order to give all computers access to the information. Currently the catalog comes on a CD-ROM, and copying it to the server's hard disk will require about 500 MB of disk storage. The company also wants to move a customer database, which currently takes up 50 MB of disk space, to the NetWare server, along with a word processing program.

1. What type of disk controller and disk system would you recommend for this application? Justify your choice. Write a memo to your instructor containing the specification. Discuss your decision in the memo by describing why you made the choices you did.
2. Given the NetWare server disk requirements you recorded above, calculate the amount of RAM that the J. Q. Adams NetWare server that stores this data will require. Write a memo to your instructor stating the requirements. Justify your decision in the memo by showing your calculations.

Case 2-4: Developing NetWare Server Specifications for J. Q. Adams

The J. Q. Adams Corporation wants to purchase a new NetWare server in order to replace its existing NetWare server and has budgeted $10,000 for the new computer. Its current NetWare server is an 80486DX computer with 16 MB of RAM and a 500-MB hard disk drive. The company's system is running out of storage space, and the NetWare server runs slowly when it performs network printing. In addition, the company recently experienced some disk errors on the NetWare server that required an employee to restore data from backups and then re-enter a day's worth of transactions. If possible, the company wants to avoid disk errors causing this type of problem in the future. As the company's network administrator, you have been asked to select a computer system that will meet these needs within the requested budget.

The new system will need to support at least 4 GB of usable hard drive space. Write a memo to your instructor containing the specification. Attach a copy of the following worksheet.

If you think that you need to spend more than $10,000 for the new server, develop two specifications: one for the system you think is necessary and one that stays within $10,000. In your memo, explain why the better system is needed and why the system that stays within budget is inadequate.

Netware Server Worksheet

Specification developed by: ____________________

SYSTEM INFORMATION

Computer make/model: ____________________

CPU: __________ **Clock speed:** __________ **Bus:** __________

Memory capacity: __________

Estimated cost: __________

DISK INFORMATION

Disk controller

Type: __________

Manufacturer/model : __________

Drive address	Type	Manufacturer	Cyl/Hd/Sec	Speed/Capacity	DOS Partition Size	NetWare	Mirrored with Controller Drive
______	___	______	__/__/__	______	____	____	______

NETWORK CARD INFORMATION

Network type	**Manufacturer ID**	**I/O port**	**Interrupt**
________	__________	______	______

NON-NETWORK DEVICE INFORMATION

Device name	IRQ	I/O port
________	________	________
________	________	________
________	________	________

NORTHWESTERN TECHNICAL COLLEGE

Dave Johnson is ready to purchase two NetWare servers for use at the Northwest Technical College campus. He would like to hear your ideas for the server specifications. One server will need to store the administrative applications and be available for faculty use. The other server will handle the academic computer lab. Dave would like you to write him a memo stating your specification for the servers. You are to fill out a storage requirements worksheet that lists requirements for each area along with estimated total disk space needed for the next two years. In addition, you are to complete a requisition worksheet containing the hardware specifications for the NetWare server you feel will best meet the requirements of all three areas. These should be attached to your memo. If possible, Dave would like the cost of each NetWare server to be kept under $10,000. The following paragraphs detail the three areas' needs.

Administration/Faculty. Each of the four departments shown on the Technical College organization chart in Chapter 1 will need approximately 250 MB for storing shared files along with at least 50 MB reserved for each user's personal files and work areas. The major application software packages used by the administrative department include the placement system, which requires about 50 MB, and the testing system, which requires approximately 20 MB for data files and software.

Computer lab. The major use of the server for the computer lab is storage of the software used by the students in the lab, along with a 20 MB area for faculty members to place files that they want their students to have access to. Along with these storage needs, each workstation in the lab will require a 5 MB work area on the server to store temporary files and configuration settings. Approximate software package storage needs are as follows:

Menus	3 MB
E-mail	20 MB
Windows 95	80 MB
Word processing	20 MB
Spreadsheet	25 MB
Database	35 MB
Presentation graphics	35 MB
Languages	20 MB

Storage Requirements

Northwestern Technical College

Prepared by: ______________________________

NetWare operating system requirements: __80 MB__

Administration:

____	__________
____	__________
____	__________
____	__________
Subtotal:	__________

Faculty:

____	__________
____	__________
____	__________
____	__________
Subtotal:	__________

Computer lab:

____	__________
____	__________
____	__________
____	__________
Subtotal:	__________
Total:	__________

Netware Server Worksheet

Specification developed by: ________________________________

SYSTEM INFORMATION

Computer make/model: ________________________________

CPU: __________ **Clock speed:** __________

Memory capacity: __________ **Bus type:** __________

DISK INFORMATION

Disk controller

Type: __________

Manufacturer/model :__________

Drive address	Type	Manufacturer	Cyl/Hd/Sec	Speed/Capacity	DOS Partition Size NetWare		Mirrored with Controller Drive
______	__	______	__/__/__	_______	___	___	_______

DISK CONTROLLER

Type: __________

Manufacturer/model :__________

Drive address	Type	Manufacturer	Cyl/Hd/Sec	Speed/Capacity	Partition Size DOS NetWare		Mirrored with Controller Drive
______	__	______	__/__/__	_______	___	___	_______

NETWORK CARD INFORMATION

Network type	**Manufacturer ID**	**I/O port**	**Interrupt**
________	__________	______	______

NON-NETWORK DEVICE INFORMATION

Device name	IRQ	I/O port
________	________	________

CHAPTER THREE

DESIGNING THE NETWORK

As a network administrator, you must understand the hardware and software components that make up a local area network. This knowledge will enable you to recommend and implement network systems. It will also help you troubleshoot problems on the network. In Chapter 1 you were introduced to the hardware and software components that make up a LAN. You also learned criteria for selecting a network operating system (NOS). In Chapter 2, you learned about the microcomputer hardware used in PC workstations and NetWare servers. In this chapter, you will learn about how data is transmitted between computers. You will increase your understanding of LANs by studying network cabling systems, network topologies, and protocols. As a network administrator, you will probably be the main source of network information for your organization. You will be asked to help make important decisions about which hardware and software to purchase when the LAN is implemented or expanded. Therefore, you will need a good background in how computers use LANs to communicate, as well as the options and standards currently available to accomplish this communication.

AFTER READING THIS CHAPTER AND COMPLETING THE EXERCISES YOU WILL BE ABLE TO:

- DESCRIBE THE PROCESS OF TRANSMITTING DATA ON A NETWARE LAN.
- IDENTIFY AND DESCRIBE THE HARDWARE AND SOFTWARE THAT CONNECT COMPUTERS TO THE NETWARE LAN.
- APPLY YOUR KNOWLEDGE OF LAN SYSTEMS TO DEVELOP A RECOMMENDATION FOR A NETWORK SYSTEM.

LAN Communications

Computers communicate over LANs by sending blocks of data called **packets**. Each packet contains the information to be transmitted, along with control information used by the receiving computer to identify and process the data contained in the packet. The reliable transmission of data packets over a network is a complex and technical task performed by the hardware and software, but the concepts can be broken down into basic steps or modules that are reasonably easy to understand.

For LAN communication to occur, it is first necessary to have standards that will enable products from different manufacturers to be able to work together. The term **interoperability** refers to the capability of different computers and applications to communicate and share resources on a network. Today, several organizations help to set and control recognized standards that provide worldwide interoperability. Because many products you will need to implement your network system depend on standards developed by these organizations, you should be familiar with their basic functions. The two major organizations that play a role in LAN standards are the **International Standards Organization (ISO)**, which works on LAN communication software models, and the **Institute of Electrical and Electronic Engineers (IEEE)**, which works on physical cable and access method standards. In this chapter you will learn about the LAN standards maintained by these institutions and how they affect the network products you will be working with as a network administrator.

OSI Model

In order to recommend and implement a LAN successfully, you first need a good understanding of the components that make up a network system and how they function together. Just as breaking a complex program into separate modules helps you to write a computer program, breaking the LAN communication process into separate logical tasks or modules makes it easier to understand and work with. To help develop standardized network system implementations, the ISO introduced a seven-layer model in 1980 known as the **open systems interconnect (OSI) model**. This seven-layer model acts as a blueprint to help network designers and developers build reliable network systems that can interoperate. As a network administrator, you need to know the basic levels and functions of the OSI model in order to understand the LAN communication process and be better able to select and configure network hardware and software components. In addition to helping you implement and maintain network systems, a good understanding of the basic principles of network communication provided by the OSI model will be important to help you troubleshoot and identify network problems.

As shown in Figure 3-1, the seven layers of the OSI model start at the application software level and work down to the physical hardware. The layers allow network software to be implemented in structured modules, providing the network administrator with more flexibility in designing and configuring network systems.

Figure 3-1
The OSI model

OSI Layer	Action	Result
Application	Interaction with user	Application program executed
Presentation	Conversion of input to ASCII, data compression, and encryption	Syntax of input checked and message formatted. Message packet formed
Session	Make initial connection with receiving computer, maintain communication during session, and end session when complete. Control data flow by sequencing packets. Addition of packet sequence numbers	Packet sequence number added to message packet
Transport	Identification and acknowledgement fields added to the message	Segment package formed
Network	Determination of the best route to the destination computer and addition of network address to the packet	Datagram packet formed
Data link	Addition of the physical address of the destination computer	Ethernet frame formed
Physical	Transmission of packet one bit at a time	Electronic signals representing bits appear on the cable system.

There is a simple phrase to help you remember the OSI layers, from the application layer to the physical layer: "All people seem to need data processing."

The application layer is where a request for network services—such as a word processing program you want to use to access a shared document stored on the NetWare server—is initiated. Starting with the application layer, each layer is responsible for performing certain network processing and control operations and then passing the data packet on to the next lower layer. Each layer in the OSI model communicates with its peer layer on the receiving computer. For example, the transport layer on one computer will include control information in the network packet that can be used by the transport layer on the receiving computer to acknowledge receipt of the packet. At the bottom of the OSI model, the physical layer consists of the network cards and cables that actually carry the signals, representing ones and zeros, of the data packet from one machine to another.

Learning the purpose of each OSI level and how it is applied to the communication process is an important part of developing an understanding of network communication components that will help you design and maintain a network system. The OSI functions can be compared to the process of sending a letter via the postal system, which relates the functions of the OSI layers to a communication task with which you are familiar.

Application Layer

The **application layer** consists of software that interacts with the users and enables them to perform their tasks without being involved with the complexity of the computer or network systems. Examples of application software include word processors, spreadsheets, and other software products used in offices. The function of the application layer is analogous to using a word processor to compose and print a letter you want to send. The word processor represents the application program you use to format and type the letter.

Presentation Layer

The purpose of the **presentation layer** is to organize the data in machine-readable form. The desktop operating system of your computer is the software component that is directly involved in taking input from devices and converting it into a format the machine can process. The resulting block of information created by the presentation layer is referred to as a **message packet**. The information in the message packet is then transmitted to the presentation layer on the receiving computer for processing.

Presentation layer software can also be used to compress information in order to save space and transmission time. For increased security, the presentation layer can also be used to encrypt the data by using a password or key in order to make it difficult for an intruder to capture and access the information. Banking companies often use special encryption software to secure electronic fund transfers.

The presentation layer can be compared to the mechanics of the word processor that allow your keystrokes to be printed. The resulting piece of paper containing your formatted letter, which you next place in an in-box on your assistant's desk, is the equivalent of a message packet.

Session Layer

The purpose of the **session layer** is to initiate and maintain a communication session with the network system. The session layer enables you to log in to the NetWare server by providing the server with a valid user name and password. Upon successful completion of the login, you are granted access to certain resources of the server.

The job of the session layer can be compared to your company's mail delivery schedule that has been arranged with the local post office. In order to use the mail service, your organization initially contacts the post office and sets up an address along with a schedule for delivery and pickup services. This process corresponds to the session layer initiating a login session with a NetWare server.

Transport Layer

The primary function of the **transport layer** is the reliable delivery of information packets from the source to the destination. This is accomplished by the transport layer on the sending computer, which provides proper address information, and by the transport layer on the receiving computer, which sends an acknowledgment of each packet successfully received from the network. The transport layer creates a packet, called a **segment**, by surrounding the message packet with the necessary acknowledgment and identification fields. The segment packet is then sent to the network layer to complete its addressing requirements.

The transport layer on some multitasking computers can also be used to place parts of several message packets from different applications into each segment. The process of placing pieces of multiple message packets into one segment is called **multiplexing**. Multiplexing can save communication costs by allowing one cable connection to carry information from several applications simultaneously.

The function of the transport layer can be related to the task performed by your assistant removing the letter from the in-box, checking to be sure it contains all the necessary address information, and then determining the type of service needed for your letter. If this is a very urgent letter, your assistant will probably use an overnight delivery service. If the message contains information that you must be certain is received, the letter can be sent by registered mail, requiring the receiver to acknowledge delivery. After the type of service is determined, your assistant fills out any necessary forms and places the letter in the appropriate envelope.

Network Layer

The **network layer** provides the information necessary to route packets through the proper network paths in order to arrive at the destination address. In order to route packets to a destination computer efficiently, the network layer uses **network addresses**, which identify each group of computers on your network system. The network layer then creates a **datagram packet** by encapsulating the information in the segment packet with the necessary packet routing information. The datagram packet is then sent to the data link layer for delivery.

When designing a NetWare network system, you will need to establish a network address for each cable system used in your network.

In postal delivery, a ZIP code is necessary to route a letter through the system. The ZIP code identifies the destination post office location. In a similar way, the network address is used to identify the destination location in a network. The network layer's task is comparable to looking up the correct ZIP code for the destination city and then correctly placing the ZIP code on the envelope along with the name and street address of the receiver. After the ZIP code information has been added to the letter, the envelope can be taken to the post office for delivery.

Data Link Layer

The **data link layer** is the delivery system of the computer network and is responsible for using the destination address to send the packet through the requested network cable system. Using the information provided by the network layer, the data link layer creates a packet, called a **frame**, that encapsulates the datagram packet with control information including the source and destination physical addresses.

Physical addresses are unique NIC addresses that are permanently assigned to each NIC by the manufacturer. Each physical address is a hexadecimal number divided into two parts: the first part identifies the manufacturer, and the second part is a unique number to identify the card among all cards produced by that manufacturer. For example, if the NIC has the hexadecimal physical address 0B00AA123456, then 0B00AA is a code assigned to the manufacturer, and 123456 is the unique number assigned to the card by the manufacturer.

The data link layer then transmits the frame to the physical layer. In our example, after the letter is placed in the mailbox, it is up to the postal system to deliver the letter. A postal employee determines to which post office the letter gets sent, based on the ZIP code and address information. The letter is then placed in a delivery truck to be taken to that post office.

The IEEE 802 committee, which is the IEEE group that works on network standards, divides the data link layer into two sublayers: the **logical link control (LLC)** layer and the **media access control (MAC)** layer. The LLC layer interfaces with the network layer, while the MAC layer provides compatibility with the NIC used by the physical layer.

Physical Layer

The **physical layer** comprises the network cable system and connectors that are responsible for sending the data frame packet out as a series of bits. The bits appears as electrical signals on the network cable system. In the postal system example, the physical level consists of aircraft, trucks, and trains that physically deliver the letter to the designated post office.

SENDING A MESSAGE

Now that you have a better idea of the purpose and function of each OSI layer, you can apply that knowledge to understand how NetWare sends a message between two network users.

For example, Ted Simpson, the Information Systems Manager of Cunningham, Burns, and Evans Laboratories, wants to sent a message to another user on the network. To do this, he will use the NetWare SEND command. This command enables a user to send messages to other users from the DOS prompt. Let's follow the steps Ted takes to send his message.

To send the message:

1. Click the **Start** button on the Windows 95 Taskbar, click **Programs**, and then click **MS-DOS Prompt**.
2. At the DOS prompt, type **SEND "I need to see you as soon as possible" TO DAuer**. The command appears as shown in Figure 3-2.

Figure 3-2
Netware Send command

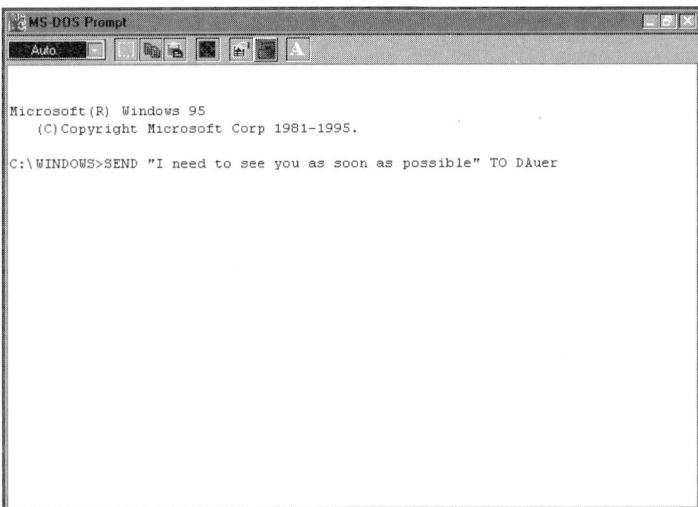
MS-DOS Prompt
Auto
Microsoft(R) Windows 95
(C)Copyright Microsoft Corp 1981-1995.
C:\WINDOWS>SEND "I need to see you as soon as possible" TO DAuer

Throughout this book, the MS-DOS Prompt window, such as seen in Figure 3-2, has been modified to display black text on a white background for clarity. The actual window displays white text on a black background on your screen.

3. Press **[Enter]** to send the message.
4. Type **Exit**, and then press **[Enter]** to return to the Windows 95 graphical user interface.

On a NetWare network, all messages are first received by the NetWare server and then distributed to the users. This is similar to the way the post office receives mail and then distributes it to individual mailboxes. The following steps, summarized in Figure 3-3, explain how the OSI model enables NetWare to send a message from one user to another.

Figure 3-3 Sending a message

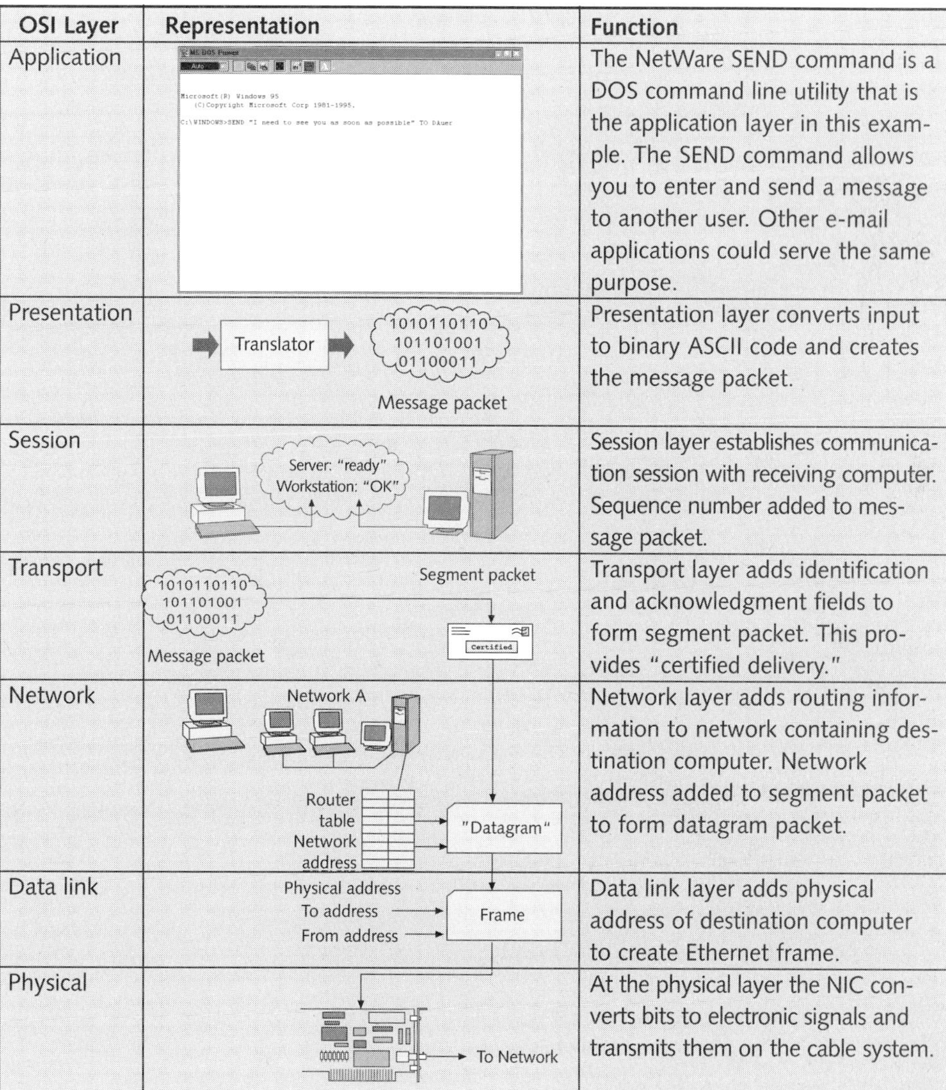

OSI Layer	Representation	Function
Application		The NetWare SEND command is a DOS command line utility that is the application layer in this example. The SEND command allows you to enter and send a message to another user. Other e-mail applications could serve the same purpose.
Presentation	Translator → 1010110110 101101001 01100011 Message packet	Presentation layer converts input to binary ASCII code and creates the message packet.
Session	Server: "ready" Workstation: "OK"	Session layer establishes communication session with receiving computer. Sequence number added to message packet.
Transport	1010110110 101101001 01100011 Message packet → Segment packet (Certified)	Transport layer adds identification and acknowledgment fields to form segment packet. This provides "certified delivery."
Network	Network A; Router table, Network address → "Datagram"	Network layer adds routing information to network containing destination computer. Network address added to segment packet to form datagram packet.
Data link	Physical address: To address, From address → Frame	Data link layer adds physical address of destination computer to create Ethernet frame.
Physical	→ To Network	At the physical layer the NIC converts bits to electronic signals and transmits them on the cable system.

The NetWare SEND command works with the presentation layer to convert the message to the proper ASCII format needed to form a message packet. The formatted message packet is then combined with the recipient's user name and passed to the session layer.

In a NetWare workstation, the session layer sets up and maintains a connection between Windows 95 and the NetWare operating system. A session is originally established when you boot your computer and run the NetWare software that attaches it to the NetWare server. When the session is established, the session layer maintains your workstation's connection to the network by responding to requests from the NetWare server. When the session layer receives the message packet, it checks the status of the network connection, adds any necessary control information needed by the NetWare software, and then sends the message to the transport layer.

One of the major functions of the transport layer is to guarantee the delivery of the message packet to the recipient's computer. It does this by placing control information in the packet in much the same way you would fill out identifying information if you were sending a registered letter through the postal system. The control information uniquely identifies the packet and tells the receiving computer how to return an acknowledgment. The new packet containing the transport control information is called a segment. The segment heading information will be processed by the transport layer on the recipient's computer in order to acknowledge that the segment packet has been received successfully. After adding its control information, the transport layer next passes the segment packet to the network layer.

The network layer in the computer is responsible for determining the correct route for sending the packet. In a NetWare network, each cable system is assigned a unique network address similar in purpose to the ZIP codes used by the postal system. The network address allows the packets to be routed quickly and efficiently to the cable system containing the destination computer. The network layer in each computer keeps a table—similar to a ZIP code reference book—that contains the correct network address of all NetWare servers. In this example, the network layer looks up the address of the recipient's NetWare server and then creates a datagram packet by encapsulating the segment information with control information including the network address of the recipient's NetWare server.

The data link layer is responsible for delivering the datagram by first creating a unique **data frame packet** for the network cable system. The data link layer encapsulates the datagram packet received from the network layer with heading information, including the addresses for the destination and source computers along with error-checking codes. The data link layer then sends the data frame to the network card for transmission, working closely with the network card to ensure the data frame is transmitted successfully. If an error occurs during transmission, the data frame is sent again. After several unsuccessful attempts, the data link layer will report an error back to the network layer, indicating that the packet could not be delivered.

The physical layer of a computer network consists of hardware devices such as NICs, connectors, and cable systems that are responsible for transmitting the message bit by bit across the network system. The task of transmitting the frame can be compared to the job of a telegraph operator. Just as the telegraph operator must wait for the line to become available and then translate the characters in a message into dots and dashes, so the physical layer must wait for the cable to be available and then use the network card to transmit the frame by encoding the binary digits into the correct electronic signals.

The standards controlling access on the physical network, as well as the electronic signals used, are controlled by the IEEE organization. The standards used on different network systems will be discussed later in this chapter.

Receiving a Message

A packet of data that is received from the network goes up the OSI stack, reversing the steps used in transmission, starting with the physical layer and proceeding to the application layer. The following steps describe the process.

The frame of information transmitted by the NIC is sent by the physical layer throughout the network—all network cards read the address contained in the data frame. Because all messages must be received and then retransmitted by a NetWare server, the frame is actually addressed to be initially received by a NetWare server. When the network card in the specified NetWare server recognizes its address, it reads the data frame and passes the bits of data to the data link layer. In the mail delivery example, this is comparable to unloading the letter at the destination post office.

The data link layer then uses the error-checking codes to perform a **cyclic redundancy check (CRC)**, in which a mathematical algorithm compares bits received to the CRC code contained in the frame packet. If the calculated CRC matches the CRC contained in the data frame, the frame is assumed to be valid and the datagram packet is unpacked and passed to the network layer. If the CRCs do not match, the frame is considered bad, which causes an error to be logged with the NetWare server.

Next, the network layer on the NetWare server checks the information contained in the datagram's heading. After confirming that the packet does not need to be sent to another server, it unpacks the segment packet and sends it to the transport layer. The transport layer then checks the control information contained in the segment packet heading, extracts the message packet, and, depending on the control information, creates and sends an acknowledgment packet segment to your computer. The analogy of this process is the recipient of a registered letter signing to confirm that the letter was received. The transport layer on the sending computer is then informed that the packet has been successfully delivered. The transport layer extracts the message information and passes it to the correct NetWare session layer.

The NetWare server presentation and application layers next process the message information and retransmit the message to the recipient's computer, where it is received and displayed in a dialog box on the screen. After reading the message, your friend can press the [Ctrl] [Enter] key combination to remove the message from the screen and continue with the current application.

NETWORK COMPONENTS

You can apply your knowledge of how information flows from one computer to another to understanding the components and product options available at each level of the OSI model. Knowledge of the common network components and product options will allow you to make good decisions in selecting, maintaining, and troubleshooting network systems. In this section you will learn about the network components that make up each layer of the OSI model, what product options are commonly used today, and some trends that might affect network products in the near future.

PHYSICAL LAYER COMPONENTS

The physical layer components of a network system consist of the hardware that sends electrical signals from computer to computer. A network administrator will not normally be required to install cables between computers. However, because you will probably be involved in network hardware selection decisions, you do need to be familiar with the different options available for connecting computers. Understanding the network cable system will also enable you to isolate network problems that result from a faulty cable component.

The two aspects of the physical network system are the **media**, the transmission systems used to send electronic signals, and the **topology**, the physical geometry of the network wiring. In this section you will learn about some common network media and topologies and their advantages and disadvantages.

Network Media

The **network media** consist of the communication systems that are used to transmit and receive bits of information. Most network media used today are in the form of cables or wires that run to each computer in the network. These types of media are often referred to as **bounded media** because the signals are contained in or "bounded" by a wire. Another medium type, which is much less common in LANs, involves beaming signals between computers with radio and light waves. These types of transmission media are referred to as **unbounded media**. Although unbounded media are generally used in **wide area network** (WAN) systems and involve satellite and microwave links over hundreds or thousands of miles, certain specialized types of unbounded media, such as infrared, are gaining acceptance for specialized **local area network** (LAN) applications.

You should consider three major factors when selecting a medium for your network system: bandwidth, resistance to electromagnetic interference, and cost. The **bandwidth** of a network medium is a measure of the medium's capacity in terms of the number of bits per second that can be transmitted. A general rule is that the higher the bandwidth, the more traffic and higher speed the network medium can support.

Electromagnetic interference (EMI) refers to the susceptibility of a medium to interference from outside electrical or magnetic fields. Networks that operate in the vicinity of high levels of electrical and magnetic fields, such as those given off by power plants or large pieces of electrical equipment, will need to install a medium with a high EMI resistance that can carry the network signals reliably without interference.

The cost of installation is another factor in selecting a medium. If more than one medium meets the bandwidth and EMI specifications of an organization, the final factor will depend on the cost of installing the system. Some media types—such as fiber optics—are relatively expensive to install and maintain when compared to other media types, so even though fiber has a very high bandwidth and virtually no EMI problems, it is not a common medium in most LANs.

The following sections describe some of the most common network medium options and compare these systems in terms of bandwidth, EMI, and cost to help you select the best medium for a network system.

Twisted-Pair Cable

Twisted-pair cable is probably the most common form of bounded medium in use on LANs today. **Twisted-pair cable** can be unshielded or shielded and consists of pairs of single-strand wire twisted together, as shown in Figure 3-4.

Figure 3-4

Twisted pair cable

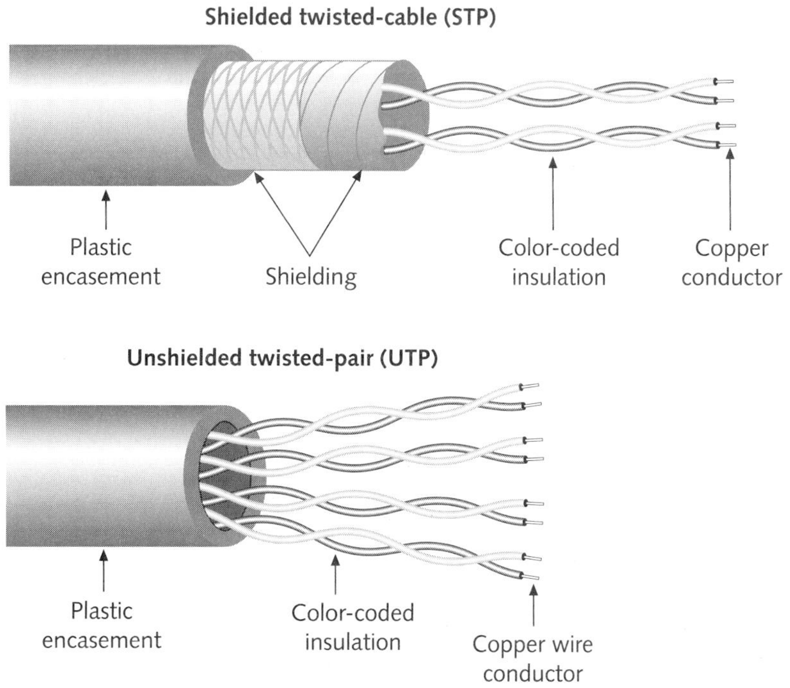

Twisting the wires together reduces the possibility of a signal in one wire affecting a signal in another wire. Normally if two wires run side by side, the electrical signal in one wire will create a magnetic field that can induce a small current in the nearby wire. This causes "noise" and results in errors on the network. Twisting the wires eliminates this noise by canceling out the magnetic field. Fifty or more pairs of twisted wire can be put together in one large cable, referred to as a **bundled pair**.

One problem of **unshielded twisted-pair (UTP) cable** is that external electrical voltages and magnetic fields can create noise inside the wire. The noise, or EMI, is unwanted current that can result when the twisted-pair cable lies close to a fluorescent light fixture or an electrical motor. To reduce EMI, **shielded twisted-pair (STP) cables** are surrounded by a metal foil that acts as a barrier to ground out the interference. For STP cable to work, it is important to connect the cable ground to the building's grounding system properly. Unfortunately, the shield of STP cable changes the electrical characteristics of the wire, reducing the distance and speed at which the network's signal can be transmitted.

Two types of connectors can be used on the ends of twisted-pair cable: RJ-45 plugs and IBM data connectors, shown in Figure 3-5. RJ-45 plugs are similar to the modular RJ-11 plugs commonly used to connect telephones to wall jacks and are generally preferred for unshielded cable because of their low cost and ease of installation. The data connector was engineered by IBM to be a universal connector for use with STP cables. Although the data connector is rather large and difficult to install, it provides a very reliable connection for high-speed signals and has the advantage of being able to connect cables without need for special cable connectors.

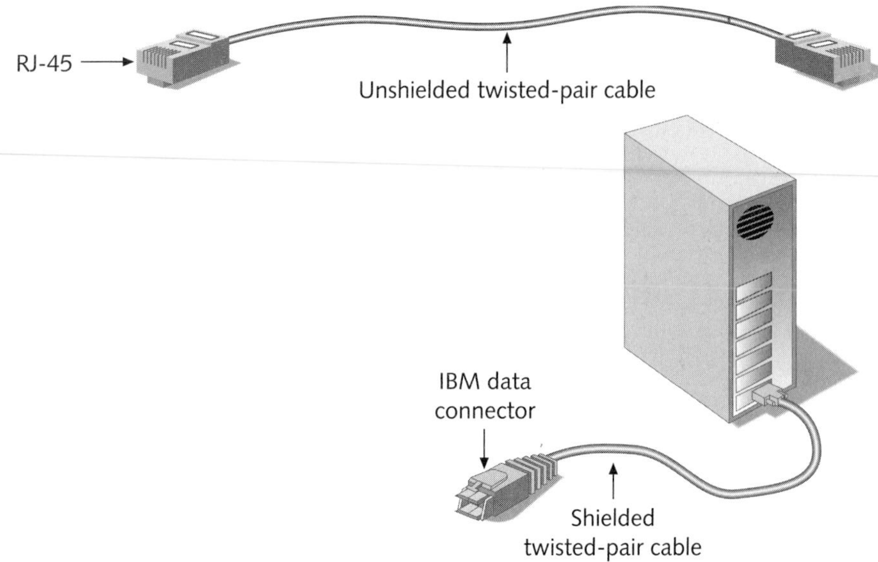

Figure 3-5 Connectors for twisted-pair cable

In general, UTP media are more common, less expensive, and more readily available than other bounded media. In addition to being shielded or unshielded, twisted-pair cable is available in different varieties that affect the speed at which signals can be sent over the cable. Signal speed is measured in millions of bits per second (Mbps). Figure 3-6 lists the common types of twisted-pair cable, their associated transmission speeds, and typical usage.

Figure 3-6 Twisted-pair cable specifications

Wire Type	Speed Range	Typical Use
1 and 2	Up to 4 Mbps	Voice and low-speed data
3	Up to 16 Mbps	Data
4	Up to 20 Mbps	Data
5	Up to 100 Mbps	High-speed data

Companies that install twisted-pair cable will normally provide you with the correct type of cable for your networking needs. If you are evaluating the existing wiring of a building for use in your network, however, you should first have the cable evaluated by a wire expert to determine if it will support the required network speeds.

The major disadvantages of twisted-pair cable, especially UTP, are its sensitivity to EMI and increased susceptibility to wiretapping by intruders. Wiretapping involves using special equipment, called a sniffer, to detect the signals on the cable by sensing the electrical fields. A wiretapper can also physically splice into the cable in order to access all network signals. You should consider using STP cable or some other medium that is more secure and less vulnerable to EMI if your organization is concerned about the possibility of security violations due to wiretapping or if it needs to run network cable in the vicinity of electrical motors or generators.

Coaxial Cable

Coaxial cable, commonly referred to as "coax," is made of two conductors, as shown in Figure 3-7. The name **coaxial** is derived from the fact that the two conductors in the cable share the same axis. At the center of the cable is a fairly stiff wire encased in insulating plastic. The plastic is surrounded by the second conductor, which is a wire mesh tube that also serves as a shield. A strong insulating plastic tube forms the cable's outer covering.

Figure 3-7
Coaxial cable

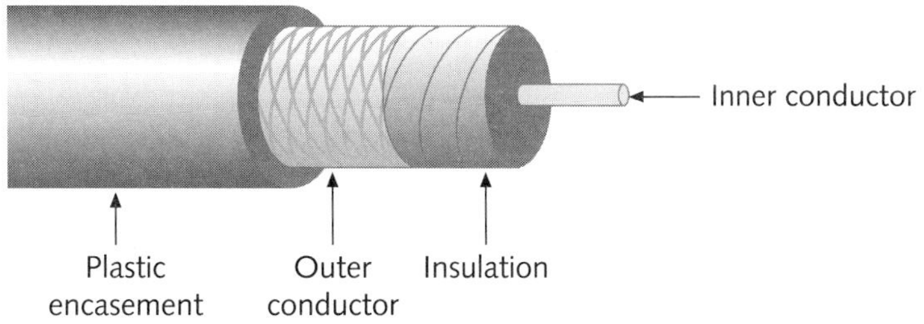

Coaxial cable is available in a variety of types and thicknesses for different purposes. Figure 3-8 lists the varieties of coaxial cables, their electrical resistance, and their typical use. Generally, thicker cable is used to carry signals longer distances but is more expensive and less flexible. When compared to twisted-pair, coaxial cable supports higher data rates and is less susceptible to EMI and wiretapping. On the other hand, coaxial cable is generally more expensive, harder to install, and more susceptible to damage due to linking. In the past, many networks were wired with coaxial cable. Improvements in twisted-pair cable's bandwidth, however, along with its flexibility and lower cost, are causing most organizations to select UTP as a medium over coaxial cable for new network installations.

Figure 3-8
Coaxial cable types

Cable Type	Resistance	Typical Usage
RG-8	50 ohms	Thick Ethernet networks
RG-58	50 ohms	Thin Ethernet networks
RG-59	75 ohms	Cable TV and IBM broadband networks
RG-62	93 ohms	ARCnet networks

Fiber Optic Cable

As shown in Figure 3-9, **fiber optic cable** looks similar to coaxial cable. It consists of light-conducting glass or plastic fibers at the center of a thick tube of protective cladding surrounded by a tough outer sheath. One or more fibers can be bounded in the center of the fiber optic cable. Pulses of light are transmitted through the cable by either lasers or light-emitting diodes (LEDs) and received by photo detectors at the far end. Fiber optic cables are much lighter and smaller than either coaxial or twisted-pair cables, and can support significantly higher data rates, from 100 million bits per second to more than 2 billion bits per second. Because light signals do not attenuate (lose strength) over distances as quickly as electrical signals, fiber optic cables can be used to carry high-speed signals over long distances. In addition, fiber optic transmission is not susceptible to EMI and is very difficult to tap. The principal disadvantages of fiber optic cable are its relatively high cost, lack of mature standards, and difficulty of locating trained technicians to install and troubleshoot it.

Figure 3-9
Fiber optic cable

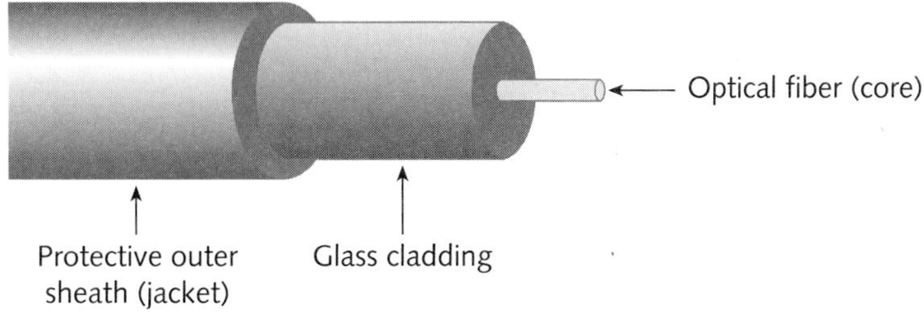

Fiber optic cable is used primarily to connect computers that require high-speed access to large data files or in situations where there is a need for maximum protection from EMI or wiretapping. One common use of fiber optic cable is in connecting several high-volume NetWare servers or minicomputers to form a backbone network, as shown in Figure 3-10. A **backbone network** is a cable system used primarily to connect a host computer to NetWare servers, each of which can have its own local network. Fiber makes a good backbone network because it allows the NetWare servers to be spread out over long distances and still provides a high-speed communication system that is safe from EMI or differences in grounding between buildings.

Figure 3-10
Backbone network

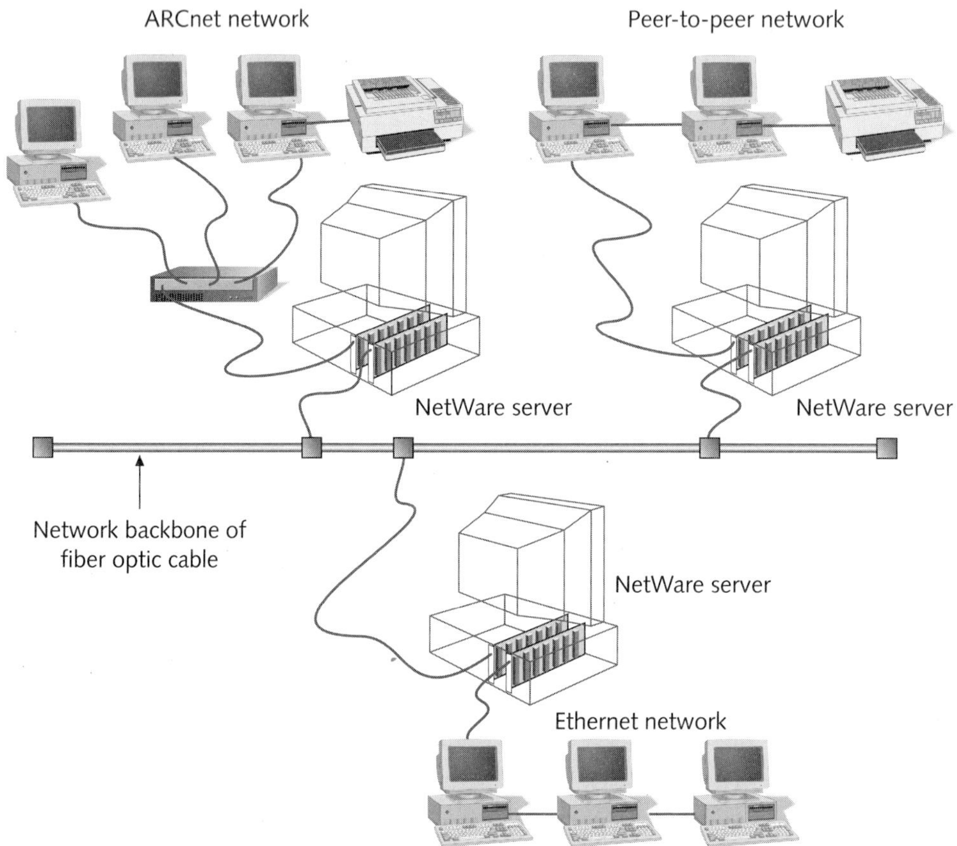

Infrared

Infrared is a wireless medium that is based on infrared light from LEDs. Infrared signals can be detected by direct line-of-sight receivers or by indirect receivers capturing signals reflected off walls or ceilings. Infrared signals, however, are not capable of penetrating walls or other opaque objects and are diluted by strong light sources. These limitations make infrared most useful for small, open, indoor environments such as a classroom or a small office area with cubicles.

Infrared transmission systems are very cost-efficient and capable of high bandwidths similar to those found in fiber optic cables. As a result, an infrared medium can be a good way of connecting wireless LANs when computers are all located within a single room or office. Infrared eliminates the need for cables and allows computers to be easily moved as long as they can always be pointed toward the infrared transmitter/receiver, normally located near the ceiling, as shown in Figure 3-11.

Figure 3-11

Infrared wireless network

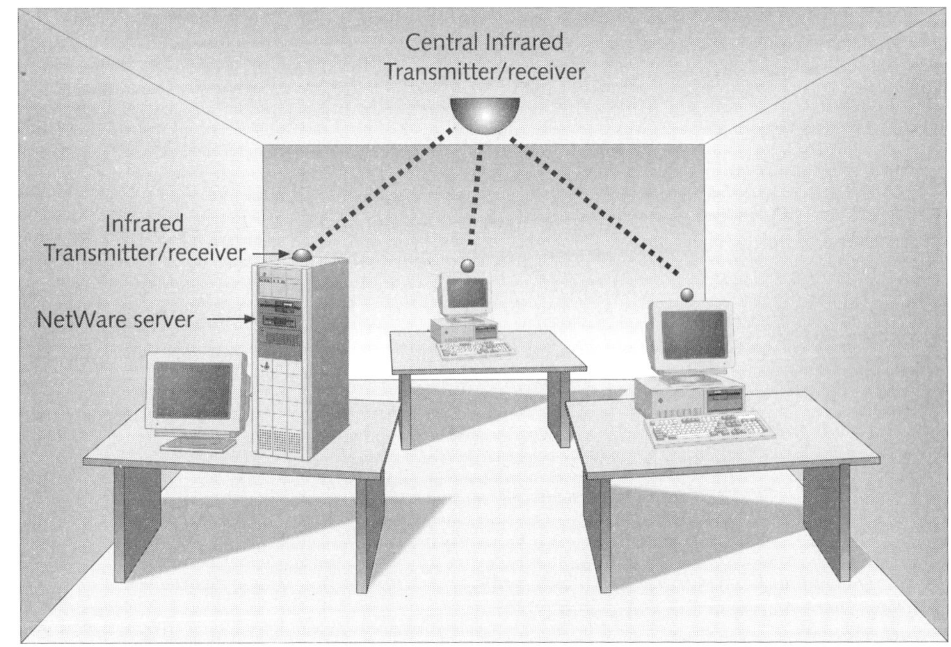

Although the high frequency of infrared waves can accommodate high data transfer rates, advances in infrared technology have been slow due primarily to its limitations in connecting computers separated by walls. Growth of infrared media is expected to accelerate as other radio frequencies become increasingly congested. A large pool of potential infrared installations exists in the networking of classroom computers and limited home or small business applications.

Comparing Network Media

Figure 3-12 summarizes the various network media in terms of cost, ease of installation, transmission capacity, and immunity to EMI and tapping. The cost comparisons are based on costs of media and other required hardware. The numbers given for maximum transmission capacity might be deceiving because they are based on the current use of the signaling technology and not on the media's raw bandwidth potential. In the case study exercises at the end of this chapter you will have an opportunity to apply this information to selecting cable systems.

Figure 3-12

Media summary

Medium	Cost	Installation	Capacity	Immunity from EMI and Tapping
Unshielded twisted-pair cable	Low	Simple	1–100 Mbps	Low
Shielded twisted-pair cable	Moderate	Simple to moderate	1–100 Mbps	Moderate
Coaxial cable	Moderate	Simple	10–1000 Mbps	Moderate
Fiberoptic cable	Moderate to high	Difficult	100–2000 Mbps	Very high
Infrared	Moderate	Simple	10–100 Mbps	Subject to interference from strong light sources

NETWORK TOPOLOGIES

An important aspect of a network system using bounded media is the method chosen to connect the networked computers. The physical geometry or cable layout used to connect computers in a LAN is called a **network topology**. As a network administrator, you will need to be familiar with the topology of your network in order to attach new computers or isolate network problems to a faulty segment of the cable. As shown in Figure 3-13, linear bus, ring, and star are the three major topologies used today to connect computers in a LAN. In this section you will learn about each of these topologies and how they affect network systems in terms of cost, reliability, and expandability.

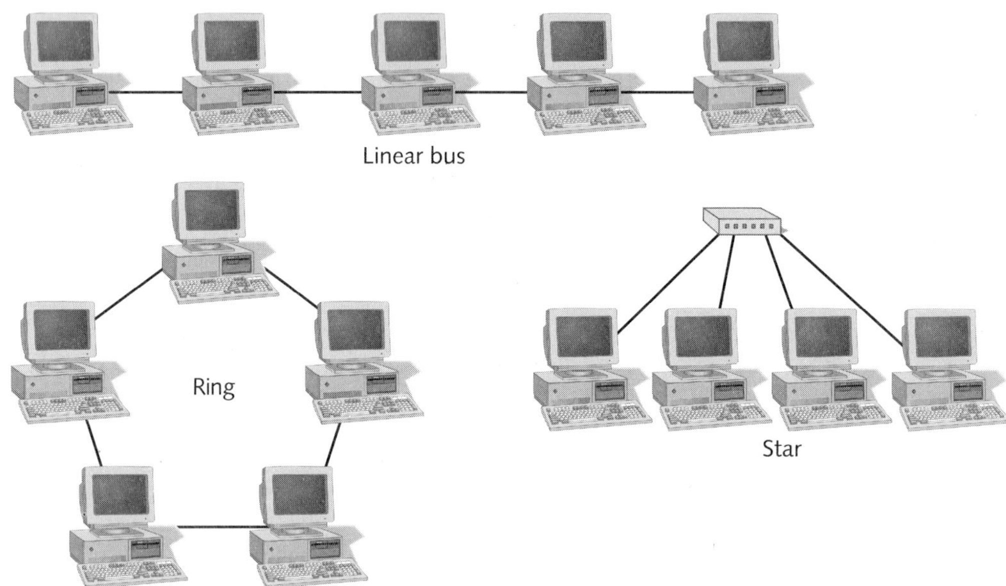

Figure 3-13 Topologies

Star Topology

The **star topology** derives its name from the fact that all cables on the network radiate from a central hub. The hub is a device that connects the network cables together and passes the signals from one cable to the next. The type of hub you need will depend on the access system used by the network cards (described in the section on data link components). Although star topologies entail higher costs due to the amount of wire needed, they are generally more reliable and easier to troubleshoot than other topologies. Because each cable in a star topology is a separate component, the failure of one cable does not affect the operation of the rest of the network. Troubleshooting for star topologies is easy because a network cable problem can be quickly isolated to the cable "run" on which a network device is experiencing errors. Another advantage of the star topology is the ease of adding or removing devices on the network without affecting the operation of other computers—by using unallocated access ports on the hub you simply plug or unplug cables.

The star topology is rapidly becoming the most popular way to wire computers together due to its exceptional flexibility and reliability.

Today star networks are usually wired with a **patch panel**, as shown in Figure 3-14. In a patch panel system, a wire runs from each potential computer location in the building through a drop cable to a central patch panel. A **patch cable** is then used to connect a device in any given location to the hub. A patch panel system makes it easy to move a computer to another location as well as to connect or disconnect computers from the network for troubleshooting purposes.

Figure 3-14

Patch panel system

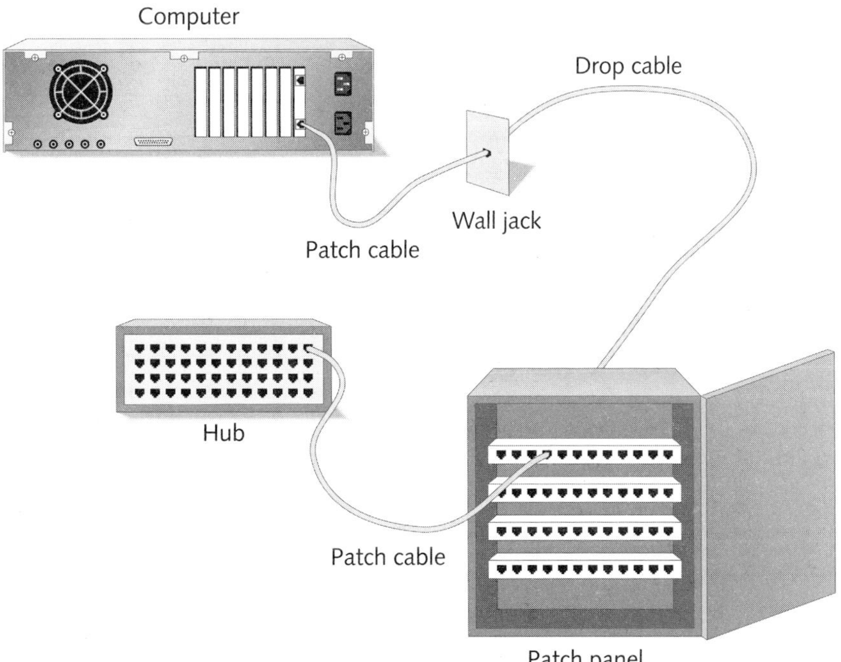

Star topologies are generally implemented with twisted-pair cable rather than coaxial cable because of lower cable cost combined with the increased flexibility and smaller size of twisted-pair cable. RJ-45 connectors on twisted-pair cable allow easy connection of computers to wall outlets and between hubs and patch panels.

Linear Bus Topology

The **linear bus topology** connects computers in series by running a cable from one computer to the next. The method of attaching the computers to the "bus" depends on the network card and cable system. When coaxial cable is used, each computer is usually attached to the bus cable by means of a T-connector, as shown in Figure 3-15. When twisted-pair cable is used, each network card usually contains two RJ-45 female connectors that allow twisted-pair cable to be run from one computer to the next.

Each end of a linear bus network requires some sort of terminator or "wire-wrap" plug in order to prevent echo signals from interfering with communication signals. The resistance and size of coaxial cable is an important factor and depends on the requirements of the network cards (described in the section on data link components).

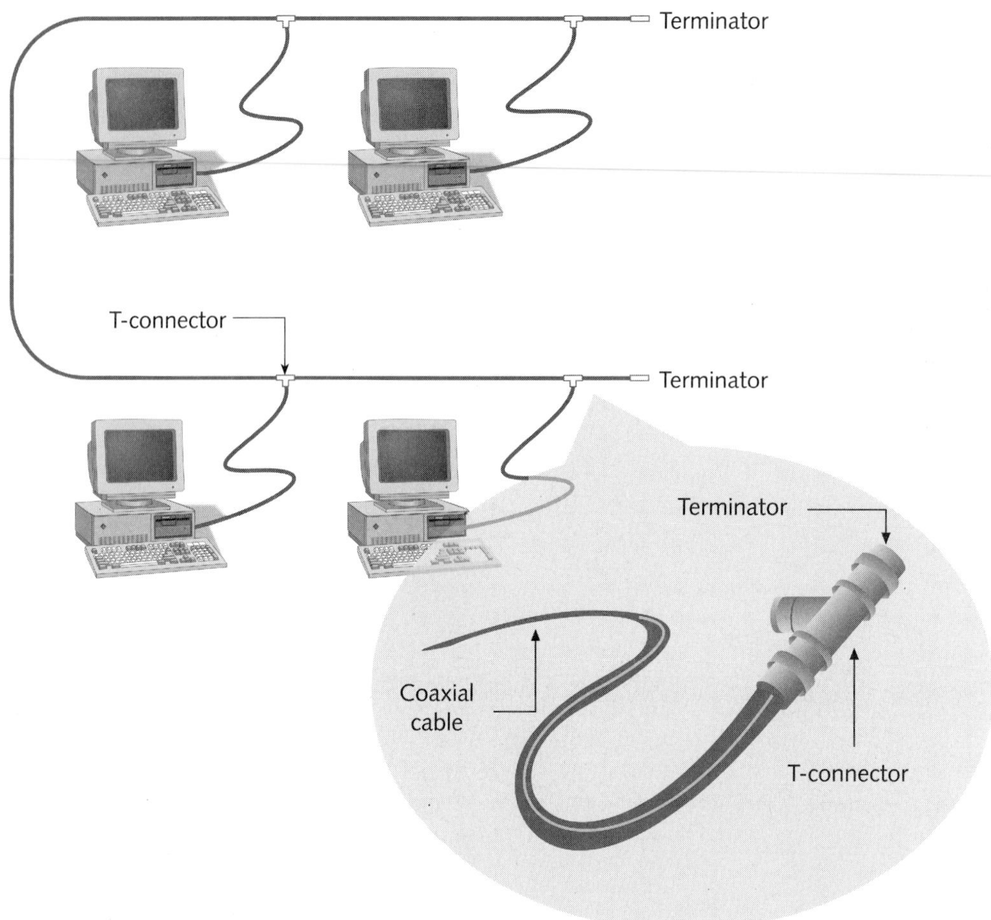

Figure 3-15 Coaxial cable network

The primary advantages of a linear bus topology are the reduced amount of cable needed and the ease of wiring computers that are clustered in locations such as a classroom or a computer lab. The two biggest disadvantages of a bus network are adding or removing computers and troubleshooting. Adding or removing a computer from a bus network often involves interrupting communication on the network segment. Troubleshooting the network is difficult because when the failure of a cable component causes a network error, it often disrupts communications on the entire network segment and requires the use of special test equipment to locate the faulty network component. Because of these disadvantages, linear bus networks are generally limited to smaller applications or are used in situations in which linking computers together is a particularly cost-effective solution.

Linear bus networks are gradually being replaced by star networks in many organizations because star networks are easier to troubleshoot. A broken wire in a star network configuration affects only one workstation. In a linear bus network, in contrast, all computers on the cable segment fail when the cable is disconnected or broken anywhere in the network.

Ring Topology

A **ring topology** is similar to a linear bus topology with the single difference being that the ends of the cable are connected instead of terminated. As a result, signals on the ring topology travel around the network in one direction until they return to the device from which they originated. In a ring topology, each computer in the ring receives signals and then retransmits them to the next computer in the ring. Because the signals are regenerated at each device along the network, a ring topology allows its network signals to traverse longer distances as long as there is another computer located within the distance limit of each network card's transmitter.

The disadvantage of a ring topology is the extra cable needed to complete the ring's circle when computers are spread out in a serial fashion. In addition, the ring has the same disadvantage as the linear bus in terms of interrupting network transmissions in order to add or remove workstations. An advantage of the ring topology over the linear bus topology is that rings are often easier to troubleshoot. Because each computer on the ring receives and then retransmits a signal, it is possible for the troubleshooter to use software that quickly determines which computer is not receiving the signal. The damaged cable component can then be isolated to the cable segment between the computer that does not receive the signal and its "upstream" neighbor.

Comparing Topologies

Figure 3-16 compares each of the three popular network topologies in terms of their wiring needs, ease of expansion, fault tolerance, and troubleshooting. The type of topology and cable system you select is closely linked to the types of network cards that will be supported on the network.

DATA LINK LAYER COMPONENTS

As mentioned in the previous section, the data link components actually control the way signals are transmitted and received on the network cable system. As a result, the components you select for the data link level of your network will determine what network topologies and cable types can be used on the network. Conversely, when you want to use an already existing cable system, you will want to select data link products that best support it. The data link layer components consist of the network interface cards and card driver programs.

Network Interface Card

The **network interface card (NIC)** is the component that acts as an interface between the network's data link and physical layers by converting the commands and data frames from the data link layer into the appropriate signals used by the connectors on the physical cable system.

Figure 3-16

Topology comparison

Topology	Wiring	Expansion	Fault Tolerance	Troubleshooting
Star	Requires the greatest amount of wire because a cable must be led from each computer to a central hub	Easy to expand by using a patch panel to plug new computers into the hub	Highly fault-tolerant because a bad cable or connector will affect only one computer	Easiest to trouble-shoot by removing suspect computers from the network
Linear bus	Usually requires the least amount of cable because the cable is con-nected from one computer to the next	Difficult to expand unless a connector exists at the location of the new computer	Poor fault toler-ance because a bad connector or cable will disrupt the entire network segment	The most difficult to troubleshoot because all computers can be affected by one problem
Ring	Wiring require-ments are more than those of a linear bus because of the need to connect the cable ends but are less than those of a star	Difficult to expand because of the need to break the ring in order to insert a new computer	Poor fault tolerance because a bad connector or cable will disrupt the entire network segment	Fairly easy to troubleshoot with proper software that can identify which computer cannot receive the signal

Driver software is needed to control the network card and provide an interface between the data link layer and the network layer software. In order to provide this software interface, Novell has developed a set of driver specifications, called the **open data interface (ODI)**. ODI-compatible drivers allow the network card to be shared by multiple programs running on the workstation or on the NetWare server. For example, ODI drivers enable the NetWare server to communicate with both Apple Macintosh and IBM PCs attached to the same network.

Microsoft networks, on the other hand, use a driver interface called **network driver interface specifications (NDIS)** to interface network card drivers to Microsoft's network operating system. NDIS-compatible drivers allow software developers to write programs for use on Windows 95 and Windows NT computers without requiring them to write instructions to control the network card—the NDIS drivers perform the hardware functions for them. Microsoft's approach results in fewer programming requirements for applications developers as well as more standardized and reliable networking functionality in those applications.

Because there are two types of driver interfaces, ODI and NDIS, you will need to be sure the network cards you obtain for your network contain the correct driver for the type of NOS you will be supporting. Novell provides ODI-compatible driver programs for many popular network cards with NetWare 4.1, but some cards are not supported. The manufacturer of an unsupported card should supply a disk with the ODI-compatible driver program that will interface its NIC to a NetWare server or workstation. In Chapter 6 you will learn about the standard card drivers that are included with NetWare and how to install them on the server or workstation computers.

Whenever possible, try to obtain NICs that work with the standard NetWare ODI drivers to make it easier to install and maintain your network system.

So that network cards and drivers from different manufacturers can communicate with each other, certain data link standards need to be followed. These standards are controlled by committees within the IEEE. The two major committees that affect LANs today are the IEEE 802.3 and IEEE 802.5 committees.

In addition to controlling types of signals, data link standards control how each computer accesses the network. Because only one signal can be sent on the network cable at any one time, a **channel access method** is necessary to control when computers transmit in order to reduce **collisions** that can occur when two or more computers attempt to transmit at the same time. Collisions cause network errors by distorting data signals, making them unreadable. Channel access methods used on today's LANs are either token passing or contention based.

The **token passing method** enables only one computer to transmit a message on the network at any given time. This access to the network is controlled by a **token**, which is a special packet passed from one computer to the next to determine which machine can use the network. When a computer needs to transmit data, it waits until it receives the token packet and then transmits its data frame packet on the network. After the transmission is complete, the transmitting computer releases the token. The next computer on the network can pick it up and then proceed to transmit. In its actual implementation, the token passing system is very complex, involving token priorities, early release of tokens, and network monitoring and error-detection functions. As a result, network cards based on the token passing method are generally more expensive.

The token passing technology was originally developed by IBM and has now been standardized by the IEEE 802.5 committee.

The **contention access method** allows a node to transmit a message whenever it detects that the channel is not in use. Think of the contention access method in terms of CB radio use. When no one is talking on a CB radio channel, you are free to transmit your message. When someone else is talking on the radio channel, however, you must wait for his or her transmission to end before you start your own transmission. The main problem with contention-based access arises when two or more computers sense an open channel and start transmitting at the same time. A collision results, and the colliding computers must wait a few microseconds before retransmitting their messages. On a computer network, this contention system is referred to as **carrier sense multiple access with collision detection (CSMA/CD)** and has been standardized by the IEEE 802.3 committee into several different product types, based on speed and cable type. The two most popular IEEE 802.3 committee standards, 10BaseT and 10Base2, will be described later.

A contention system works very well when network traffic is light, but its performance drops off quickly under heavy network transmission loads. Token-based systems perform better under heavy loads because the performance does not drop off as abruptly. The following sections describe the different types of NICs and data link standards in use today and compare the network topology, performance, and access methods of these products.

Token Ring Networks

IBM originally designed the token ring system for use in industrial environments that require reliable high-speed communications. Today, token ring is widely considered to be the best network system in terms of overall performance and reliability. A token ring network is shown in Figure 3-17.

Figure 3-17

Token ring network

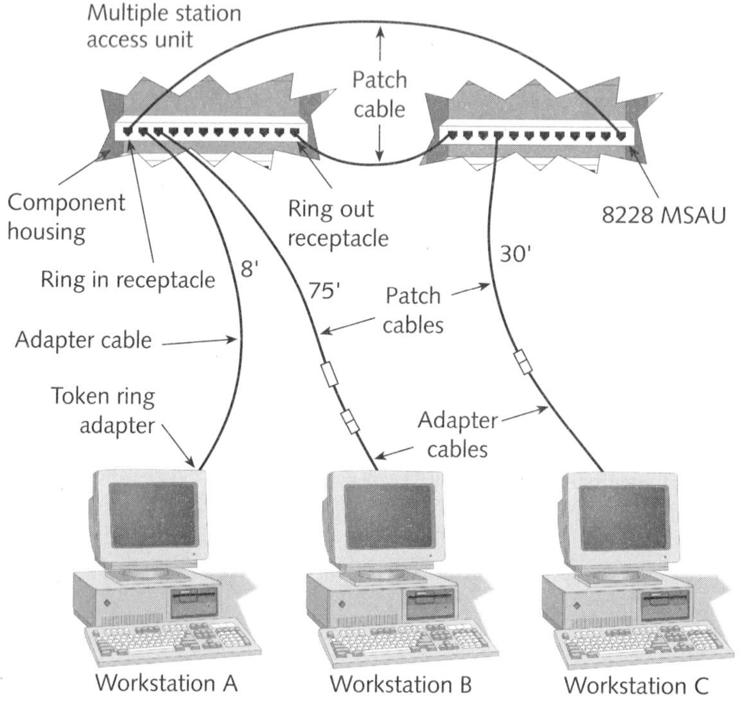

Standard token ring cards were originally transmitted at 4 Mbps. Today, however, most token ring cards use 16 Mbps transmission speeds. You cannot mix cards running at 4 Mbps with cards running at 16 Mbps on the same token ring network.

The token ring system shown in Figure 3-17 consists of workstations connected by twisted-pair cables to a central hub, called a **multiple station access unit (MSAU)**. Although this appears to be a star arrangement, the network signals actually travel in a ring, which is why it is often referred to as a star ring. A signal originating from workstation A in Figure 3-17, for example, is initially transmitted to the MSAU. The MSAU relays the signal to the cable for workstation B. After receiving the signal, workstation B retransmits the signal and returns it to the MSAU. The MSAU then relays the signal to workstation C, and workstation C transmits the signal back to the MSAU from whence it is relayed back to its source, workstation A. If the wire running from the MSAU to workstation B is broken or if workstation B is shut down, a relay in the MSAU will automatically pass the signal on to workstation C. In this manner, the token ring system is very resistant to breakdowns.

The IBM token ring network is often referred to as a star ring because it combines the physical topology of a star with the logical topology of a ring.

The advantages of token ring systems are speed, expandability, and fault tolerance. In addition, token ring systems are usually easy to troubleshoot because bad connections or cable runs can be quickly isolated. The disadvantages include the extra wiring required by the star topology and the higher cost of most token ring cards over other types of network cards. This, added to the cost of an MSAU for every eight computers on your network, makes token ring networks quite expensive.

Ethernet Networks

The term **Ethernet** originally applied to networks using a linear bus topology and CSMA/CD on coaxial cable. This system, discussed in detail below, is also known as 10Base2. However, several variants of the specification have been created, and now the term **Ethernet** is used as a general reference to the entire family of variations. The members of the Ethernet family discussed below are 10Base2, 10BaseT, 100BaseTX, and 100BaseFX.

10Base2 Networks

The 10Base2 system, shown in Figure 3-18, is based on the linear bus topology on coaxial cable and uses the CSMA/CD system standardized by the IEEE 802.3 committee. The term **10Base2** stands for 10-Mbps baseband using digital baseband signals over a maximum of two 100-meter coaxial cable segments. The term **baseband** describes a computer network that carries **digital signals**; a **broadband** system carries **analog signals**, like the signals used for television and radio transmissions. In 10Base2, thin RG-58 coaxial cable with T-connectors enables up to 30 machines to be attached to a single cable run, which is called a **segment**. According to the 10Base2 standards, a segment cannot exceed 607 feet in length, and no more than five segments can be joined by repeaters to form the entire network. Additionally, a maximum of three of the five segments can have workstations attached. Network professionals often refer to 10Base2 as **ThinNet** because of its thin coaxial cable.

10Base2 cards use the same CSMA/CD system and 10-Mbps speed as 10BaseT cards (discussed next). Some manufacturers supply cards that can be configured for either the twisted-pair 10BaseT system or the RG-58 cable bus. While both 10Base2 and 10BaseT provide excellent throughput under normal network loads, wiring 10Base2 is simpler and more cost-effective than 10BaseT in certain environments—those in which groups of computers are located in a small area, such as a computer lab, where one coaxial cable runs from machine to machine.

Thick coaxial cable is sometimes used instead of thin coaxial cables. Networks using thick coaxial cable are referred to as 10Base5, Thick Ethernet, or ThickNet.

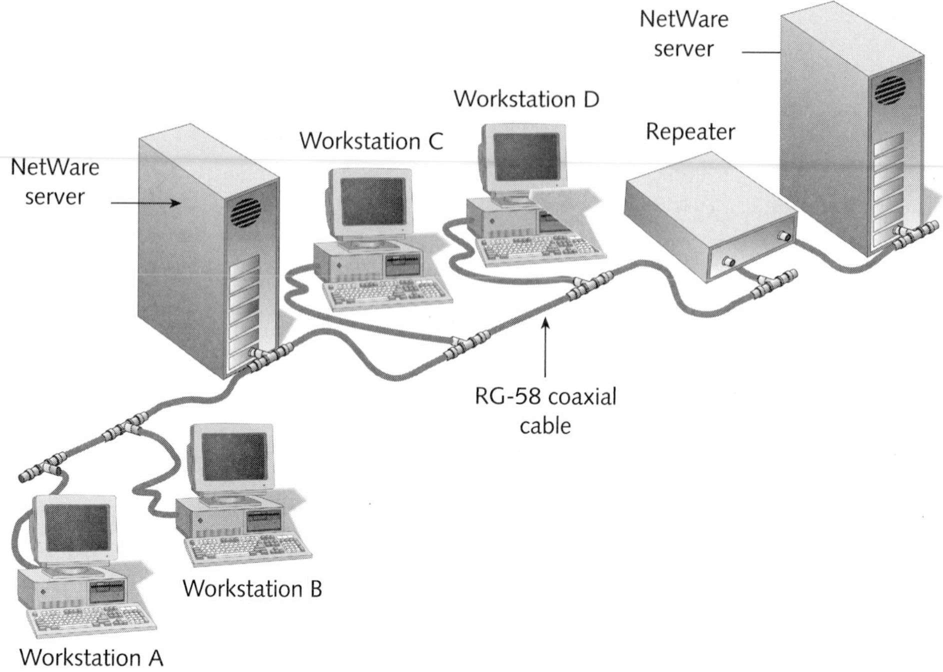

Figure 3-18
10Base2 network

10BaseT Networks

The 10BaseT network system is very popular in business offices today because it combines the flexibility of the star topology with the lower cost of the CSMA/CD channel access method. The IEEE 802.3 designation of **10BaseT** stands for 10-Mbps baseband network using twisted-pair cable. A 10BaseT network is shown in Figure 3-19.

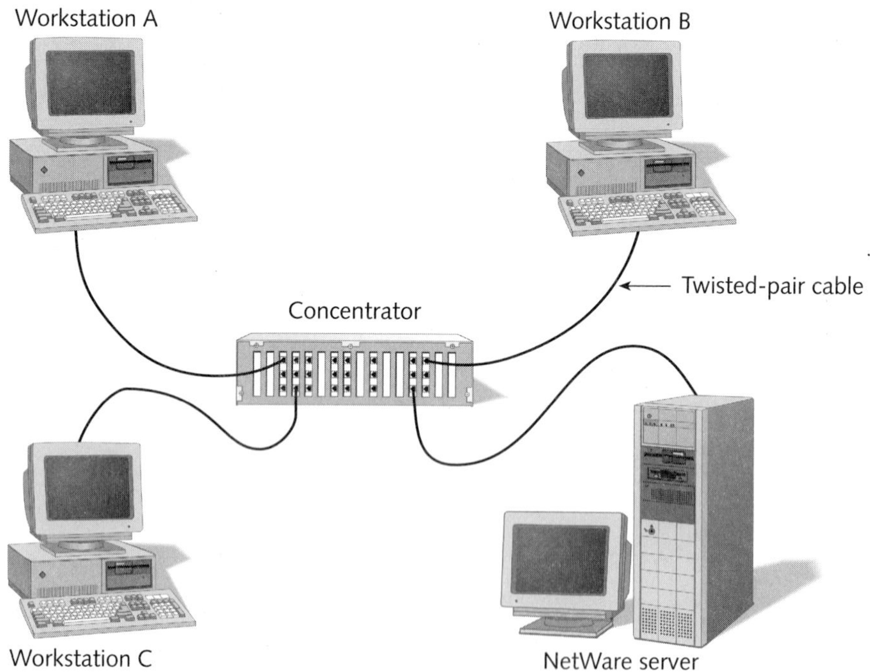

Figure 3-19
10BaseT network

A 10BaseT network uses a device called a **concentrator** as a hub to connect all machines in a star topology with twisted-pair cable. Although the 10BaseT network uses the same star topology as a token ring network, the 10BaseT signals are not sent from one station to the next as in token ring. They are broadcast to all stations simultaneously by using the CSMA/CD method standardized by the IEEE 802.3 committee. In many instances a cable system designed for token ring can easily be converted to support 10BaseT simply by replacing the MSAUs with concentrators. The concentrator acts as a repeater, receiving signals on one cable port and then retransmitting those signals on all other ports. When two or more network stations attempt to transmit at the same instant, a collision occurs, and the stations must retransmit after waiting a random period of time.

The advantages of 10BaseT include high performance under light to medium network loads and low costs for network cards due to the relative simplicity of the CSMA/CD system. Although 10BaseT performance can be faster than token ring under light loads, it is more easily slowed due to collisions when many stations are transmitting on the network. Another disadvantage of the 10BaseT system is additional cost both for concentrators and for the star topology wiring.

100BaseTX and 100BaseFX Networks

The 100BaseTX and 100BaseFX network systems are extensions of the 10BaseT system and are overseen by the IEEE 802.3 committee. They use the same star topology and the CSMA/CD channel access method. The designation of **100BaseTX** indicates a 100-Mbps baseband network using twisted-pair cable or IBM STP cable. The **100BaseFX** designation indicates the use of fiber optic cable. 100BaseTX and 100BaseFX networks appear identical to a 10BaseT network. A concentrator is used as the hub to connect all machines in a star topology. The concentrator still acts as a repeater.

The advantages of 100BaseTX and 100BaseFX include higher performance for networks needing fast data transmission, such as those using video. The disadvantages include shorter maximum cable run lengths in some cable systems, which is a tradeoff necessary to gain the extra speed, and a higher cost of hubs and NICs capable of handling the higher speed.

100VG-AnyLAN Networks

The 100VG-AnyLAN network system was originally developed by Hewlett-Packard and AT&T Microelectronics as the 100BaseVG Ethernet system. Hewlett-Packard then worked with IBM to create 100VG-AnyLAN, a 100-Mbps network solution to the emerging need for higher data transmission rates on the network, which is usable as an upgrade from either an Ethernet or token ring network. The standard is under the IEEE 802.12 committee, and designation of **100VG-AnyLAN** stands for a 100-Mbps baseband network using voice grade (category 3) twisted-pair cable, fiber optic cable, or IBM STP cable. It differs from other Ethernet systems and token ring by using a demand priority media access method instead of the CSMA/CD channel access method or token passing. A **demand priority** system enables only one workstation to broadcast at a time, so there are no collisions. Which workstation gets to broadcast is based on a priority system, so that more important network messages are broadcast first.

The term **AnyLAN** refers to the ability of a 100VG-AnyLAN system to use either Ethernet or token ring NICs. One network, however, must use one or the other—Ethernet and token ring cannot be combined in the same network. This ability makes 100VG-AnyLAN a potential upgrade path for both Ethernet and token ring networks. A 100VG-AnyLAN network appears identical to a 100BaseTX network, using a hub to connect all machines in a star topology.

The 100BaseFX specification has so far proved to be more popular than 100VG-AnyLAN. However, Hewlett-Packard and other vendors still support the technology and offer products to implement it.

ARCnet Networks

Despite its relatively slow speed (2 Mbps), **ARCnet** was popular for small networks because of its low cost and flexible topology. Today, the decreased cost of Ethernet systems combined with the lack of IEEE standards for ARCnet and its slower speed make it a poor choice for most networks. Because it has been popular in the past, however, you might encounter networks based on the ARCnet system. An ARCnet network is shown in Figure 3-20.

Figure 3-20

ARCnet network

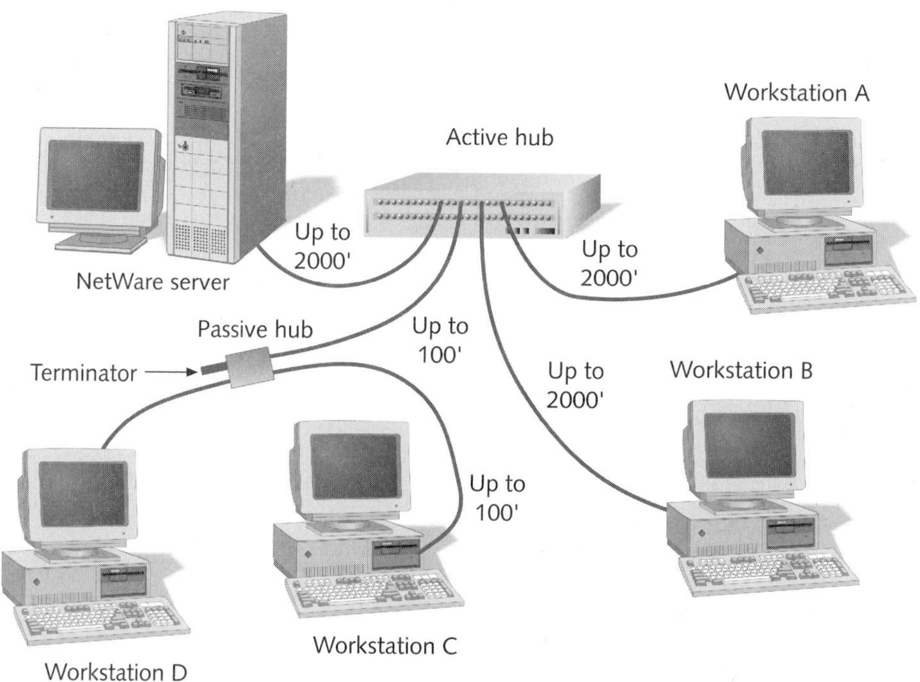

The ARCnet system has a star topology in which an **active hub** acts as a signal repeater, enabling cable runs of up to 2,000 feet from the active hub to the attached workstation computers. **Passive hubs** are simple signal splitters. They can be used at the end of a run to split the cable and allow up to three workstations to be attached to a single cable run. When a passive hub is used, wire length must be limited to 100 feet. Depending on the ARCnet cards used, either twisted-pair or RG-68 coaxial cable can connect computers. The advantages of ARCnet are low card cost and flexible wiring options. Its disadvantages are slow speed, higher cabling costs based on its star topology, and lack of standardization.

Comparing Network Systems

Selecting a network system is a complex task that depends on such variables as type and location of computers, existing wiring, and the amount of load expected on the network. In many organizations, multiple network systems are necessary to meet the needs of different departments. Such network systems can be connected with bridges and routers, described in the next section. Figure 3-21 contains a summary of the major network systems.

Figure 3-21
Network system comparison

Network System	Cable Types	Topology	Maximum Number of Nodes	IEEE Standard	Speed	Access Method	Distance
Token ring	UTP, STP, fiber	star	96	802.5	4–16 Mbps	token	150' per cable run
10Base2	coaxial	linear bus	30 per segment with maximum of 3 populated segments	802.3	10 Mbps	CSMA/CD	607' per segment
10BaseT	UTP	star	512	802.3	10 Mbps	CSMA/CD	100 meters per cable run on UTP Cat 3 & 4; 150 meters on UTP Cat 5
100BaseTX	UTP, STP	star	512	802.3	100 Mbps	CSMA/CD	100 meters per cable run on UTP Cat 3 & 4; 100 meters on UTP Cat 5; 100 meters on STP type 1
100BaseFX	fiber	star	512	802.3	100 Mbps	CSMA/CD	412 meters on fiber
100VG-AnyLAN	UTP, STP, fiber	star	240	802.12	100 Mbps	demand priority	100 meters per cable run on UTP Cat 3 & 4; 200 meters on UTP Cat 5; 100 meters on STP type 1; 2000 meters on fiber
ARCnet	RG-62 coaxial UTP	star	255	none	2 Mbps standard	token	2000' from active hub, 100' from passive hub

Be sure to obtain cable that meets your local building fire codes if you decide to install new cable above a ceiling or in walls.

REPEATERS, BRIDGES, AND ROUTERS

Each network system presented in this chapter has unique limitations. In some cases, you will want to take advantage of certain features found in two different products. For example, in a school environment you might want to implement the Ethernet system in computer labs to take advantage of the economical coaxial wiring arrangement. If other computers in the building are located many feet apart in completely separate areas, however, you will not want to connect them this way. You can solve this problem by creating two separate networks: Ethernet for the lab and token ring for the office. You then connect the networks so they share access to the same NetWare server. In other cases, it might be necessary to break a large network into two or more smaller networks to overcome performance problems or cabling distances, or to accommodate large numbers of users.

Within a network system, you use repeaters to maintain a strong, reliable signal throughout the network. To connect separate network systems you use bridges or routers, and the resulting connected networks are called an **internetwork**. Repeaters, bridges, and routers are shown in Figure 3-22.

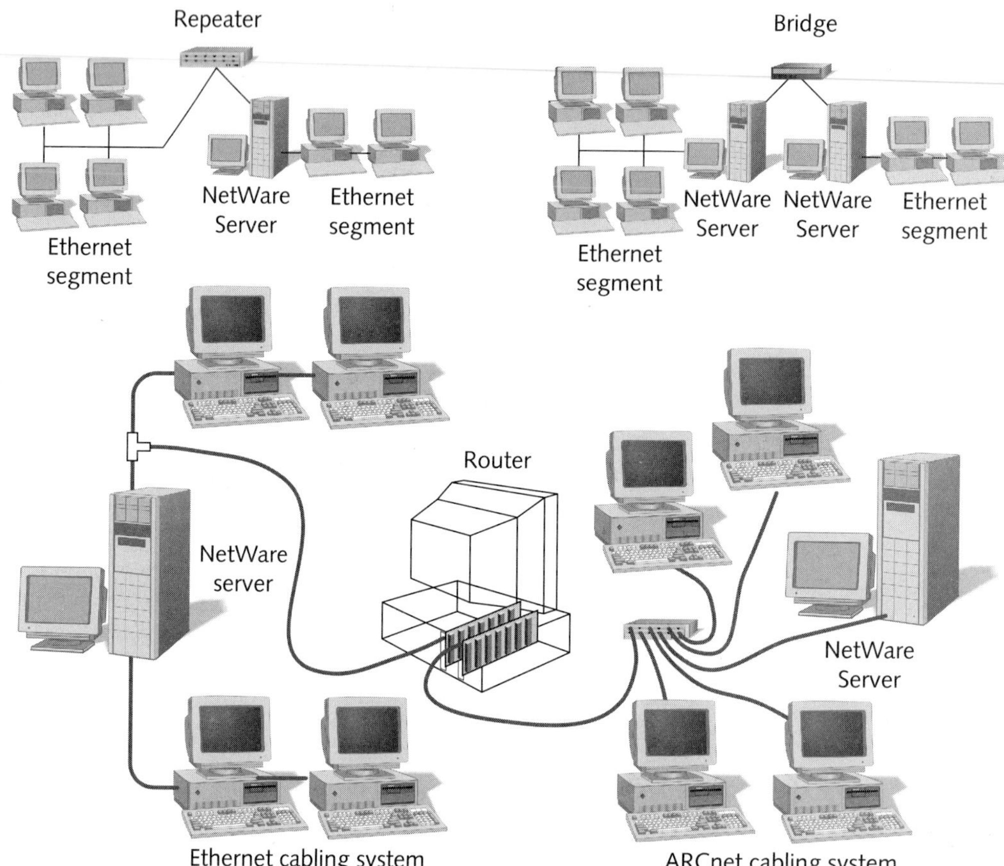

Figure 3-22 Repeaters, bridges, and routers

Repeaters

Network cable systems consist of one or more cable lengths, called segments, that have termination points on each end. **Repeaters** are hardware devices that allow you to link network segments together. Repeaters work at the physical layer of the OSI model. This means that the repeater simply receives signals from one network segment and then retransmits them to the next segments. The hub of a star network topology, for example, can act as a repeater, receiving a signal from one computer cable and broadcasting it on the other cables. Each computer in a ring topology acts as a repeater, receiving the signal from the "upstream" computer and retransmitting it to the next computer on the ring. Repeaters are also used to connect two linear bus segments, as shown in Figure 3-18. This use of repeaters increases the fault tolerance of a linear bus network because a bad connector or cable on one segment does not prevent computers on other segments from communicating. As a network administrator, you should be aware of the role of repeaters on your network for easy maintenance and troubleshooting of network problems.

Bridges

A **bridge** operates at the data link layer of the OSI model. This means that the bridge sees only the packet's frame information, which consists of the addresses of the sender and receiver along with error-checking information. During network operation, the bridge watches packets on both networks and builds a table of workstation node addresses for each network. When it sees a packet on one network that has a destination address for a machine on the other network, the bridge reads the packet, builds new frame information, and sends the packet out on the other network. Because bridges work at the data link level, they are used to connect networks of the same type. For example, a bridge can connect two different token ring networks and allow more than 100 users to access the same NetWare server. Another use for a bridge might be to break a heavily loaded Ethernet or 10BaseT network into two separate networks in order to reduce the number of collisions occurring on any one network system. A bridge is often contained in a separate black box but can also consist of specialized software running on a microcomputer that simply contains two network cards.

Routers

Routers are needed to create more complex internetworks. A **router** operates at the network layer of the OSI model and therefore has access to the datagram information containing the logical network address along with control information. When a router is used, each network must be given a separate network address. Remember that a network address is similar in function to a ZIP code. Just as each postal area has a unique ZIP code, each network system must have a unique network address. The router information contained in the datagram packet enables a router to find the correct path and, if necessary, break up a datagram for transmission on a different network system. Two disadvantages of routers are that they require a little more processing time than bridges and that network packets must use a datagram format that the router can interpret.

Generally, networks with different network topologies are connected with routers, whereas networks of the same topology are connected with bridges. Novell uses routers in its NetWare servers to allow up to eight different network cards to be installed in a single NetWare server computer. This enables you to use the NetWare server to connect networks of different types and topologies in order to form an internetwork.

Protocol Stacks

The network's **protocol stack** is responsible for formatting requests to access network services and transmit data. While the delivery of the data packets throughout a network system is the responsibility of its data link and physical layer components, the functions of the network, transport, and session layers are built in to a network operating system's protocol stack.

Novell's IPX/SPX protocol stack is commonly used to support DOS-based computers on NetWare networks, and a network administrator needs to know how to configure and maintain the IPX protocol. Because today's networks often need to support protocol stacks of computers running other operating systems as well, the network administrator should also be familiar with the common protocol stacks used by such operating systems as Macintosh, UNIX, and Windows.

In this section you will learn about protocol stacks and some of their advantages and disadvantages, which will enable you to make informed recommendations on which protocol stacks should be supported on a network.

IPX/SPX

The IPX/SPX protocol is Novell's proprietary system that implements the session, transport, and network OSI layers, as shown in Figure 3-23. Notice that IPX/SPX is not a true implementation of the OSI model because IPX and SPX functions overlap layers. This is true of many older protocol stacks that were developed before the OSI model was developed and standardized.

Figure 3-23

Novell IPX/SPX and NCP protocols

OSI Model Layers

	Physical	Data Link	Network	Transport	Session	Presentation	Application
NCP					X	X	
SPX				X	X		
IPX			X	X			
Ethernet	X	X					
Token ring	X	X					
ARCnet							
Others	X	X					

IPX (internetwork packet exchange) is the NetWare protocol that manages packet routing and formatting at the network layer. To function, IPX must be loaded on each network workstation and on the NetWare server. In addition to IPX, each workstation and NetWare server must have loaded a network card driver in order to transmit the frames containing the packets. IPX software and the network card driver are brought together during the network installation process, which will be described in Chapter 6. In addition to IPX, NetWare uses two protocols, SPX and NCP, to provide network services.

SPX (sequential packet exchange) operates at the OSI transport level and provides guaranteed delivery of packets by receiving an acknowledgment for each packet sent. **NCP (NetWare Core Protocol)** provides the session and presentation levels at the workstation through DOS requester workstation clients. The NetWare DOS Requester (VLMs) workstation client software is a 16-bit network client, while the NetWare Client 32 workstation client software is a full 32-bit client. Both requesters establish and maintain network sessions as well as direct information and requests from the workstation and format them for the NetWare server. On the NetWare server, NCP provides network services such as login, file sharing, printing, security, and administrative functions.

There is an older workstation client called NETX that was used with NetWare 3.1x. Although workstations using NETX can use a NetWare 4.1 server, they can do so only in bindery emulation mode, which provides access to only a limited subset of the resources available in NetWare 4.1. You should upgrade any workstations using NETX to the NetWare DOS Requester (VLMs) or, preferably, NetWare Client 32.

TCP/IP

As shown in Figure 3-24, **TCP/IP (transmission control protocol/internet protocol)** covers the network and transport OSI layers as does IPX/SPX. Unlike IPX/SPX, however, TCP and IP don't overlap in the transport layer.

Figure 3-24

TCP/IP protocol

OSI Model Layers

	Physical	Data Link	Network	Transport	Session	Presentation	Application
TCP				X			
IP			X				
Ethernet	X	X					
Token ring	X	X					
Others	X	X					

Like the IPX protocol, TCP/IP is responsible for formatting packets and then routing them between networks using IP (internet protocol). IP is more sophisticated than IPX in fragmenting packets and transmitting over wide area network links. When IP is used, each workstation is assigned a logical network and node address. IP allows packets to be sent out over different routers and then reassembled in the correct sequence at the receiving station. TCP (transport control protocol) operates at the transport level and provides the guaranteed delivery of packets by receiving acknowledgments. The acknowledgment system allows the sender and receiver to establish a window for the number of packets to be acknowledged. This allows for better performance over WANs because each packet does not need to be individually acknowledged before another packet is sent.

Today TCP/IP is commonly used on UNIX operating systems as well as the Internet. NetWare servers can use the TCP/IP protocol to communicate with UNIX-based computers, to provide Internet services, and to route TCP/IP packets between network cards.

The need to implement TCP/IP on a NetWare network is growing rapidly because of the exploding popularity of the Internet and the need for network administrators to provide more network support for UNIX-based workstations.

NetWare 4.1 provides a TCP/IP module that can be loaded on the NetWare Server. NetWare 4.1 also allows you to use TCP/IP as the NetWare protocol for the network in place of IPX. If you choose to use TCP/IP, IPX packets are placed *within* TCP/IP packets—the IPX structure is not totally eliminated.

NetBEUI

The **NetBEUI** protocol is Microsoft's own protocol stack and is integrated into Windows for Workgroups, Windows 95, and Windows NT products. Of the three protocols described in this section, NetBEUI is the smallest, fastest, and easiest to use. It has few features, however, and cannot be used in large internetwork environments because it does not support the network layer needed for routing packets between networks. As a result, the NetBEUI protocol is limited to communicating with other computers attached to the same network cable system. Another disadvantage of the NetBEUI protocol is that it was developed specifically to support peer-to-peer networking on small networks comprising 30 to 50 workstations.

Figure 3-25

NetBEUI protocol

OSI Model Layers

	Physical	Data Link	Network	Transport	Session	Presentation	Application
NetBIOS					X		
NBF or NBT			X	X			
Ethernet	X	X					
Token ring	X	X					
Others	X	X					

The NetBEUI protocol stack consists of **NetBIOS** and **service message blocks (SMBs)** at the session layer and **NetBIOS frames (NBF)** at the transport layer, as shown in Figure 3-25. SMBs and NetBIOS provide a well-defined standard method for servers and workstations to communicate with each other. Many peer-to-peer applications have been written to interface with NetBIOS, allowing an application to span multiple computers. Because NetBIOS-based applications are popular, Novell has provided a NetBIOS interface to work with its IPX/SPX protocol. This allows workstations to run peer-to-peer applications while still accessing services from NetWare servers. The LANtastic peer-to-peer network product also uses NetBIOS to establish communication among DOS-based computers.

Because NetBEUI's NBF does not maintain routing tables, it is extremely small and fast, making it ideal for networks ranging from 2 to 50 devices. Because the NBF does not support packet routing, however, the protocol is limited to communication among computers attached to a single network. The NetBEUI protocol allows for the replacement of NBF with **NBT (NetBIOS over TCP/IP)**, which allows the protocol stack to communicate directly over large TCP/IP-based networks.

AppleTalk

The **AppleTalk** protocol suite was originally developed to allow Macintosh computers to communicate in peer-to-peer networks. It currently provides connectivity for a variety of computer systems including IBM PCs running MS-DOS, IBM mainframes, and various UNIX-based computers. The AppleTalk protocol suite was developed after the OSI model was conceived and therefore can be mapped reasonably well to the OSI layers, as shown in Figure 3-26.

On the data link level, the **Apple Address Resolution Protocol (AARP)** connects the AppleTalk protocol stack to the Ethernet, 10BaseT, or token ring protocol. AppleTalk supports the routing of packets between networks by using the **Datagram Delivery Protocol (DDP)**. In addition, AppleTalk uses zones to organize the names of service providers logically on large internetworks. Zones limit the number of service providers that are presented at one time, which simplifies the user's choices.

Figure 3-26

AppleTalk protocol

OSI Model Layers

	Physical	Data Link	Network	Transport	Session	Presentation	Application
Apple Filing Protocol (AFP)						X	
Apple Session Protocol (ASP)					X		
Apple Transition Protocol (ATP)				X			
Datagram Delivery Protocol (DDP)			X				
AARP (Apple Address Resolution Protocol)	X	X					
Local Talk	X	X					
Ethertalk (Ethernet)	X	X					
Token Talk (token ring)	X	X					

Because of the popularity of the Macintosh and of the AppleTalk protocol, Novell has included AppleTalk support with NetWare 4.1. Loading the AppleTalk protocol on a NetWare server allows Macintosh or other computers using AppleTalk to see the NetWare server as another AppleTalk service provider.

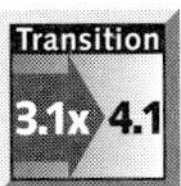

On NetWare 3.1x, the number of Macintosh clients on the network was limited. With NetWare 4.1, you can use any combination of PC and Macintosh clients. The total number of users who can simultaneously log in to the network is set by the NetWare license you purchase (for example, a 100-user NetWare license allows 100 simultaneous logins), but now it doesn't matter whether the workstation is a PC or a Macintosh.

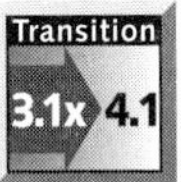

In the NetWare 4.1 environment, the Macintosh workstations can also log in to Novell Directory Services (NDS). However, the Mac workstations must load and run MacIPX, which allows the Macintoshes to use the IPX protocol. IPX is required in order for the Macintosh workstation to use NDS.

CHAPTER SUMMARY

Network communication depends on packets of information being passed from one computer to another. Understanding how information packets flow through a network system means knowing the functions of the seven layers of the open systems interconnect (OSI) model. The application layer software is responsible for interacting with the user and providing software tools to perform specific tasks. The presentation layer then translates the data from the application layer into the appropriate ASCII and binary codes. The session layer initiates and maintains a communication session with the NetWare server computer, providing an interface between the local DOS and the network operating system. The transport layer is responsible for the reliable delivery of data packets, called segments, and often requires the receiving computer to send acknowledgments confirming the receipt of the segment packets. The network layer places the segment packet in a datagram and handles routing of datagrams to the correct computer. The data link and physical layers act as the delivery system by placing the datagram packets in frames and sending them on the network cable system. Special committees of the Institute of Electronic and Electrical Engineers (IEEE) control the physical and data link standards for LAN network systems. The IEEE 802.3 committee controls the contention-based carrier sense multiple access with collision detection (CSMA/CD) system, and the IEEE 802.5 committee controls the token passing standard.

Cable types used with today's LANs include shielded and unshielded twisted-pair cable, coaxial cable, and fiber optic cable. Infrared is a special communication medium that uses light beams rather than cable to transmit information from each computer to a central device. The infrared system is a good alternative for a network in a single room where installing cable can be particularly difficult or expensive. The physical geometry of a bounded medium is called its topology. Major physical topologies include ring, linear bus, and star.

Regardless of the type of topology used, only one machine can transmit on a network at any given instant, and with some, a method of access control must be used to avoid data collisions. Network access control methods can be either contention-based or token-based. Ethernet 10Base2, 10BaseT, 100BaseTX, and 100BaseFX networks use a contention system, in which computers attempt to transmit whenever they sense an open period on the network. On busy networks, however, when two or more machines sense an open period and try to transmit at the same time, a collision occurs and the machines each wait a random time period before retrying their transmissions—this is CSMA/CD.

Token ring and ARCnet both use a deterministic system called token passing. A token is passed around the network when no data packet is being transmitted. A machine needing to transmit must wait for the token. When it receives the token, it can transmit its packet without any collisions. Collisions cause CSMA/CD systems to slow significantly under heavy network transmission loads, whereas token passing systems provide more uniform and predictable performance. 100VG-AnyLAN networks use a demand priority system, which allows the workstation claiming the highest priority the first opportunity to broadcast its message.

A repeater works at the physical layer, connecting network segments and passing signals between them. An internetwork consists of two or more network topologies connected by a bridge or router. Working at the data link layer, bridges are very efficient, but they are limited to moving frames between networks of similar design. Routers are more sophisticated because they work at the network layer and have access to the datagram control information. Because of this access, routers can select the most efficient path for a packet and fragment packets into the correct size to send over the selected network.

Protocols are the languages used to implement the OSI layers. Popular protocols you will probably encounter as a network administrator include Novell NetWare's IPX/SPX, the TCP/IP protocol used by UNIX and the Internet, NetBEUI used in Microsoft

Windows-based networks, and the AppleTalk protocol used for Macintosh computers. NetWare servers use Novell's IPX/SPX protocol by default, but can also be configured to handle TCP/IP and AppleTalk. TCP/IP is becoming a very popular protocol for use in UNIX environments and international WANs such as the Internet. Both IP and IPX are network layer protocols that control the routing and flow of packets in the network system. TCP and SPX are similar in that they are both transport protocols that provide guaranteed delivery of packets.

KEY TERMS

10Base2

10BaseT

100BaseFX

100BaseTX

100VG-AnyLAN

active hub

analog signals

Apple Address Resolution Protocol (AARP)

AppleTalk

application layer

ARCnet

backbone network

bandwidth

baseband

bounded media

bridge

broadband

bundled pair

carrier sense multiple access with collision detection (CSMA/CD)

channel access method

coaxial cable

collision

concentrator

contention access method

cyclic redundancy check (CRC)

data frame packet

data link layer

Datagram Delivery Prococol (DDP)

datagram packet

demand priority

digital signals

driver software

electromagnetic interference (EMI)

Ethernet

fiber optic cable

frame

infrared

Institute of Electrical and Electronic Engineers (IEEE)

International Standards Organization (ISO)

internetwork

internetwork packet exchange (IPX)

interoperability

linear bus topology

logical link control (LLC) layer

media

media access control (MAC) layer

message packet

multiple station access unit (MSAU)

multiplexing

NetBEUI

NetBIOS

NetBIOS frames (NBF)

NetBIOS over TCP/IP (NBT)

NetWare Core Protocol (NCP)

network address

network driver interface specifications (NDIS)

network layer

network media

network topology

open data interface (ODI)

open systems interconnect (OSI) model

packet

passive hub

patch cable

patch panel

physical address

physical layer

presentation layer

protocol stack

repeater

ring topology

router

segment

sequenced packet exchange (SPX)

service message block (SMB)

session layer

shielded twisted-pair (STP) cable

star topology

ThinNet

token

token passing method

topology

transport control protocol/internet protocol (TCP/IP)

transport layer

twisted-pair cable

unbounded media

unshielded twisted-pair (UTP) cable

REVIEW QUESTIONS

1. The ____________________ standards organization works on physical cable standards.
2. The ____________________ layer of the OSI model provides guaranteed delivery of segment packets.
3. The data link layer is responsible for ____________________.
4. Sequence the following OSI layers, starting from the hardware level, and match the packet types with the OSI layers that use them.

Sequence layer		Packet type	
______________	session	____________________	a. frame
______________	application	____________________	b. message
______________	presentation	____________________	c. segment
______________	data link	____________________	d. datagram
______________	physical	____________________	e. bits
______________	network		
______________	transport		

5. The ______________ unbounded medium would be well-suited for use in a classroom.
6. ______________ is the most common form of bounded medium.
7. ______________ network cable is similar to the wire used to connect your telephone to the phone system.
8. What can be done to reduce EMI in electrical cables?

____

____

____

9. In a(n) ______________ topology, a cable is run from each computer to a central device.
10. In a(n) ______________ network, all computers are attached to the same cable segment.
11. An MSAU is used on a(n) ______________ network system.
12. Under the ______________ access method, only one node is given permission to transmit a message on the network at any given time.
13. The ______________ access method performs best under heavy loads.
14. Match the IEEE standards to the appropriate products.

______________	10Base2	a. IEEE 802.3
______________	Token ring	b. IEEE 802.5
______________	10BaseT	c. IEEE 802.12
______________	ARCnet	d. no IEEE standard
______________	100BaseTX	
______________	100BaseFX	
______________	100VG-AnyLAN	

15. A concentrator is used on a(n) ______________ network system.
16. Identify which type of medium is commonly used by each of the following network systems.

10Base2	______________
10BaseT	______________
100BaseTX	______________
100BaseFX	______________
100VG-AnyLAN	______________
token ring	______________
ARCnet	______________

17. A(n) ______________ operates at the physical layer of the OSI model and relays messages from one segment to another.
18. A(n) ______________ operates at the network layer of the OSI model and can be used to connect networks of different topologies.
19. A(n) ______________ consists of two or more networks attached together by a bridge or router.

20. A(n) ______________________ is a method of implementing the network, transport, and session layers of the OSI model in a network system.
21. The ______________________ protocol is commonly used by the UNIX operating system.
22. The ______________________ protocol is commonly used with Windows NT and Windows 95 workstations.
23. The ______________________ is a proprietary protocol used in NetWare networks.
24. ______________________ is the protocol that provides NetWare network services.
25. TCP operates at the ______________________ layer of the OSI model.
26. IPX operates at the ______________________ layer of the OSI model.
27. List one advantage and one disadvantage of the NetBEUI protocol.

    ____

    ____

Exercises

In these exercises you will use the NetWare commands to demonstrate the OSI layers that attach your workstation to the network and access the NetWare server. You will then use NetWare commands on the server to view information about NetWare servers on your internetwork, log in to a selected NetWare server, view information about users attached to your NetWare server, send a message to another user, and log out from the network.

Each of the following exercises asks you to write a memo to your instructor discussing the results of each exercise. Depending on which of the exercises you complete, you may be able to combine these memos into one memo. Your instructor will tell you exactly how to report the results of your work.

Exercise 3-1: Attaching to the Network

You normally log in to the network from the Client 32 login dialog box in Windows 95. When you do so, you are using the NetWare Client 32 for Windows 95 software. This exercise demonstrates steps that the normal login automates. To demonstrate these steps, you will log in to the network for DOS, not Windows 95. This exercise also requires that the DOS client files be located in a separate directory from the Client 32 for Windows 95 directory (which is normally \NOVELL\CLIENT32). In the steps that follow, you may be using the NetWare VLM client or the NetWare Client 32 for DOS client. The steps that follow assume that the VLM client files are in a directory named NWCLIENT, and the Client 32 for DOS files are in a directory named C32DOS.

To do this exercise, your workstation must be booted in DOS (not Windows 95) but not attached to the NetWare server. Either the NetWare DOS Requester (VLMs) or NetWare Client 32 workstation client software may be used for this exercise, and there are many possible variations depending upon how your workstation is configured. Your instructor will provide you with specific instructions on how to prepare your workstation for this exercise, and on how to log in. Two possible sets of steps are listed below. Your instructor might tell you to use one of them as written, tell you a required modification for one of them, or give you an alternative set of steps. Record your instructor's comments and instructions below:

Exercise 3-1A: Attaching to the Network using the NetWare DOS Requester (VLMs)

When you are at the DOS prompt:

1. Type CD C:\NWCLIENT and then press [Enter] to make the NWCLIENT subdirectory the active directory.
2. Type LSL, and then press [Enter] to load the link support layer driver. Record the message obtained from loading LSL on the lines below:

   ____

   ____

   ____

3. Your instructor will tell you the name of your network interface card driver. Use this name in place of the name *NICdriver* in the following command.

   ____

   ____

   ____

   Type *NICdriver*, and then press [Enter] to load the network interface card driver. Record the message obtained from loading the NIC driver on the lines below:

   ____

   ____

   ____

4. Type IPXODI and then press [Enter] to load ODI IPX support. Record the message obtained from loading IPXODI on the lines below:

   ____

   ____

   ____

5. Type VLM and then press [Enter] to load the NetWare Virtual Loadable Modules (VLMs) for your network. Record the message obtained from loading VLM on the lines below:

   ____

   ____

   ____

   The session layer of the VLMs will attempt to make a connection with a NetWare server. If a preferred server is specified in a NetWare client configuration file named NET.CFG, the workstation attempts to attach to that NetWare server. If there is no preferred server, or if the preferred server is not available, the VLMs send out a special Get Nearest Server packet and the session is started with the first server to respond to this packet. Your instructor will tell you the name of your preferred server. Record that information below:

   Preferred server: ____

   After establishing a server connection, the VLMs map the first available network drive letter to the LOGIN directory of the attached NetWare server. The first available network drive is usually G:, but other drives may be used (the first network drive is also specified in the NET.CFG file). Your instructor will tell you which drive your workstation will use as the first network drive. Record that information below:

   First network drive: ____

   DOS then has access to load and run programs from the NetWare server by going through the first network drive. After VLMs are loaded in memory, they work with the DOS presentation layer to redirect any requests for network file or print services to the NetWare server.

6. Type the drive letter of your first network drive followed by a colon (for example, G:) and then press [Enter] to change to the NetWare server's LOGIN directory.
7. Type DIR and then press [Enter] to list the files in NetWare server's LOGIN directory.
8. Type DIR > PRN and then press [Enter] to print a copy of the files in the NetWare server's LOGIN directory.

Write a memo to your instructor discussing the process of attaching to the network. Include each command you used and the result of that command, and attach the printed copy of the results of the DIR command.

Exercise 3-1B: Attaching to the Network using NetWare Client 32 for DOS/Windows

When you are at the DOS prompt:

1. Type CD C:\C32DOS and then press [Enter] to make the C32DOS subdirectory the active directory.
2. Type SET NWLANGUAGE=ENGLISH, and then press [Enter]. Record any message obtained on the lines below:

   ____

   ____

   ____

3. Type NIOS.EXE, and then press [Enter] to load the network input-output system driver. Record the message obtained from loading NIOS on the lines below:

   ____

   ____

   ____

4. Type LOAD LSLC32.NLM, and then press [Enter] to load the 32-bit link support layer driver. Record the message obtained from loading LSLC32 on the lines below:

   ____

   ____

   ____

5. Your instructor will tell you the name of your NIC driver, as well as interrupt, port, and frame data. Use the driver name in place of the name *NICdriver* in the following command. Similarly, replace *INT#*, *PORT#,* and *FrameType* with the appropriate information.

   Type:

   LOAD *NICdriver* INT=*INT#* PORT=*PORT#* FRAME=*FrameType*

   and then press [Enter] to load the NIC driver. Record the message obtained from loading the NIC driver on the lines below:

   ____

   ____

   ____

6. Type IPX.NLM and then press [Enter] to load IPX support. Record the message obtained from loading IPX on the lines below:

   ____

   ____

   ____

7. Type CLIENT32.NLM and then press [Enter] to load the Client 32 module for your network. Record the message obtained from loading Client 32 on the lines below:

   ____

   ____

   ____

   The session layer of NetWare Client 32 will attempt to make a connection with a NetWare server. If a preferred server is specified in a NetWare client configuration file named NET.CFG, the workstation attempts to attach to that NetWare server. If there is no preferred server, or if the preferred server is not available, NetWare Client 32 sends out a special Get Nearest Server packet and the session is started with the first server to respond to this packet. Your instructor will tell you the name of your preferred server. Record that information below:

   Preferred server: ___________________________________

   After establishing a server connection, NetWare Client 32 maps the first available network drive letter to the LOGIN directory of the attached NetWare server. The first available network drive is usually G:, but other drives may be used (the first network drive is also specified in the NET.CFG file). Your instructor will tell you which drive your workstation will use as the first network drive. Record that information below:

First network drive: ______________________________

DOS then has access to load and run programs from the NetWare server by going through the first network drive. After NetWare Client 32 files are loaded in memory, they work with the DOS presentation layer to redirect any requests for network file or print services to the NetWare server.

8. Type the drive letter of your first network drive followed by a colon (for example, G:) and then press [Enter] to change to the NetWare server's LOGIN directory.
9. Type DIR and then press [Enter] to list the files in NetWare server's LOGIN directory.
10. Type DIR > PRN and then press [Enter] to print a copy of the files in the NetWare server's LOGIN directory.

Write a memo to your instructor discussing the process of attaching to the network. Include each command you used and the result of that command, and attach the printed copy of the results of the DIR command.

Exercise 3-2: Viewing Directory Tree Information

The NetWare command **NLIST** can be used to obtain network information about the network. You use the **/?** parameter to display information about the command and its parameters and options. The /? parameter is available with all NetWare command line commands.

1. Type NLIST /? and then press [Enter] to display information about the NLIST command.

An initial help screen which lists options for viewing other help screens is displayed. The ALL option displays all help screens, one after another, so that you can scroll through them.

2. Type NLIST /? ALL and then press [Enter] to display all help screens. After you have read each screen, press [Enter] to see the next screen.

You can use the NetWare command NLIST /TREE to display a list of directory trees on your internetwork.

3. Type NLIST /TREE and then press [Enter] to display a list of directory trees..
4. Type NLIST /TREE > PRN and then press [Enter] to print a copy of the list of servers.

Write a memo to your instructor discussing the NLIST command. In your discussion, include what you learned from using the help screens, describe the result of the NLIST /TREE command, and attach the printed copy of the results of the NLIST /TREE command.

Exercise 3-3: Logging in to a Specific NDS Directory Tree

The NetWare command **LOGIN** is used to log into your assigned directory tree. If you enter the command **LOGIN *fullusername***, the DOS requester will attempt to log in to the NDS tree. Your full user name is your user name preceded by a period (.), followed by your location in the directory tree. For example, .TSIMPSON.FACULTY.NWTC identifies the user Ted Simpson who is located in the FACULTY organizational unit of the organization NWTC. In most cases, the NDS tree that you try to log in to will be your assigned, or default, NDS tree. You can, however, specify the name of the directory tree when you enter the LOGIN command. This is done by specifying the name of the desired directory tree followed by a slash and then your full user name. For example, LOGIN NWTC/.TSIMPSON.FACULTY.NWTC could be used to log Ted Simpson into the NWTC directory tree. Your instructor will explain your login command. On the line below, write the command to log in to your directory tree regardless of the default directory tree.

Login command: ____

Test this command and record the results below:

Write a memo to your instructor discussing the result of the LOGIN command.

Exercise 3-4: Viewing User Information

The NetWare command **NLIST USER /R /S** can be used to obtain network information about each user on the network. You use the /R parameter to start the search at the "root" of the NDS directory tree and the /S parameter to include all branches of the tree below the starting context in the search.

1. Type NLIST USER /R /S and then press [Enter] to list users in your directory tree.
2. Type NLIST USER /R /S > PRN and then press [Enter] to print a copy of the list.

   Write a memo to your instructor discussing the NLIST command. In your memo, describe the result of the NLIST USER /R /S command and attach the printed copy of the results of the NLIST USER /R /S command.

Exercise 3-5: Sending a Message to Another User

In this exercise you will send a message to another user on the network.

The NetWare **NLIST USER /A /R /S** command can be used to create a list of users currently logged in to the network. You use the /A parameter to limit the search to currently logged in users, the /R parameter to start the search at the "root" of the NDS directory tree, and the /S parameter to include all branches of the tree below the starting context in the search.

The NetWare command **SEND *"message"* To *username*** is used to send a message to another user. You must provide the message and the username. Messages you receive are cleared by using the [Ctrl]+[Enter] key combination

1. Type NLIST USER /A /R /S and then press [Enter] to list the users currently logged in to the network. Select the name of a classmate in the lab with you and write it in the space below:

   Username: ______________________________

2. Type NLIST USER /A /R /S > PRN and then press [Enter] to print a copy of the list.
3. Create a message to send to your classmate. For example, you could use the message "Hello, username, this is a test message." Write the message, including quotation marks (" "), that you want to send in the space below:

   Message: ______________________________

4. Using the username you selected as *username* and the message you created as "message", type SEND "message" TO username and then press [Enter] to send the message.
5. When you receive a message, read it and then hold down the [Ctrl] key while pressing [Enter] to clear the message.

   Write a memo to your instructor discussing the use of the NLIST USER /A /R /S and SEND commands. In your memo, include the user name and message you used and attach the printed copy of the results of the NLIST USER /A /R /S command.

Exercise 3-6: Logging Out of the Network

To log out of the network from the DOS prompt, you use the NetWare command **LOGOUT**.

1. Type LOGOUT and then press [Enter]. Record the information provided by the logout process in the space below.

   ____

   ____

   ____

   ____

   ____

   ____

Write a memo to your instructor discussing the result of the LOGOUT command.

EXERCISES

CASE 3-1: THE J. Q. ADAMS NETWORK SYSTEM

As described in Chapter 1, the J. Q. Adams Corporation would like to update its network system in order to collect quality-control information from the shop floor and save it on the central NetWare server for processing by other computer users. J. Q. Adams currently has 12 computer workstations located in the business office, two data collection workstations in production and two data collection workstations in shipping/receiving. Two NetWare servers (one already owned by the company and one being purchased) are located in the wire and phone equipment room. One of the problems faced by the computers in the production shop is the increased level of electrical interference created by motors and other equipment. Your help is needed to recommend a topology and network system that will meet the needs of J. Q. Adams and then draw the necessary cable runs on the floor plan shown in Figure 3-27.

Figure 3-27

J. Q. Adams Corporation

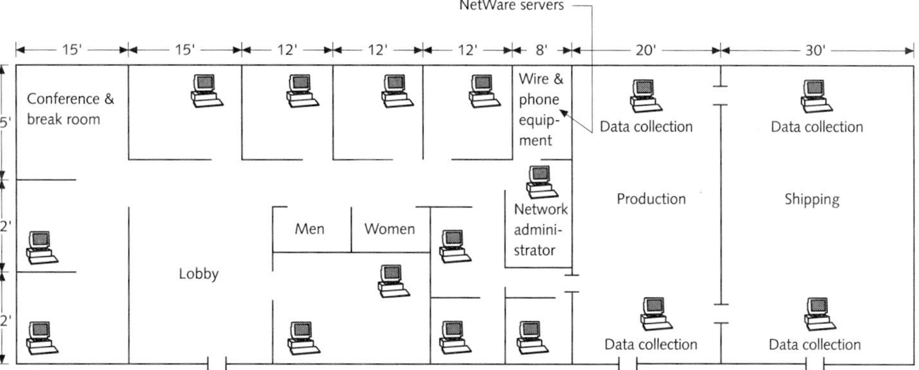

Select the topology and network system. Draw a proposed network cable system based on the building layout shown in Figure 3-27. Write a memo to your instructor recommending a topology and network system. Discuss your justification for this selection. Attach your proposed network cable system.

CASE 3-2: THE JEFFERSON COUNTY COURTHOUSE NETWORK

As described in Chapter 1, the social workers in the Jefferson County Courthouse are planning to implement a network system to allow 12 users to communicate and share files and printers. Plans are being developed to add additional users in other departments to the network so that the communication needs of the entire courthouse will be met. For this reason, the NetWare 4.1 network operating system has been chosen, and a new NetWare server has been ordered.

The floor plan for the first floor of the courthouse is shown in Figure 3-28. Based on this floor plan, recommend a topology and network system that will best meet the current needs of the social workers and provide for easy network expansion in the future.

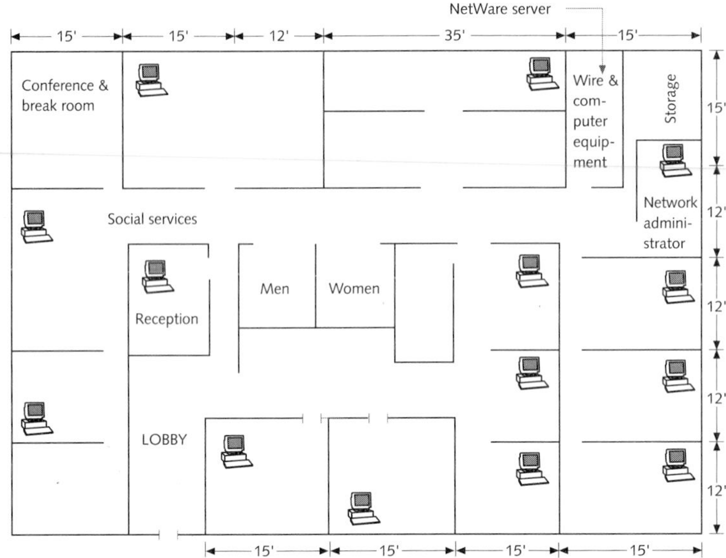

Figure 3-28

The Jefferson County Courthouse Network

Select the topology and network system. Draw a proposed network cable system based on the building layout shown in Figure 3-28. Write a memo to your instructor recommending a topology and network system. Discuss your justification for this selection. Attach your proposed network cable system.

NORTHWESTERN TECHNICAL COLLEGE

PROJECT 3-1: NETWORK DESIGN

Based on your recommendation, Dave Johnson has decided to proceed with the network project at Northwestern Technical College. He has decided to use two servers, one for faculty and administration and one for the computer labs.

To save wiring costs, Dave is exploring the option of using ThinNet (10Base2) in the computer lab. He plans on having the student lab NetWare server located in the computer room and connecting it to a repeater located in Lab A. The repeater will connect three 10Base2 segments: one for the server, one for the PCs in Lab A, and one for the PCs in Lab B. The two NetWare servers will be internetworked using a bridge or router located in the computer room. (Your instructor will tell you whether a bridge or router will be used, explain how it is set up, and provide the associated cost.)

Dave would like to use either a ring or star topology to connect the faculty and staff computers to the faculty/administration NetWare server. This server will be located in the computer room. Dave is unsure about which network system to use, and he wants you to investigate 10BaseT, 100BaseTX, 100VG-AnyLAN, and IBM token ring systems.

Dave would like you to document a network layout that shows the cabling necessary to implement a UTP star network for the administrative offices and classroom computers. Because 10BaseT, 100BaseTX, 100VG-AnyLAN, and IBM token ring can all use category 5 twisted-pair cable (with four pairs of wires), the same wiring plan should work for any of these networks. A linear bus network will be used for the computers in labs A and B. A floor plan for the first floor of Northwestern Technical College is shown in Figure 3-29.

Dave wants you to plan the wiring for only this floor at present. He will design the wiring for the faculty offices, which are on the second floor, at a later date.

Figure 3-29

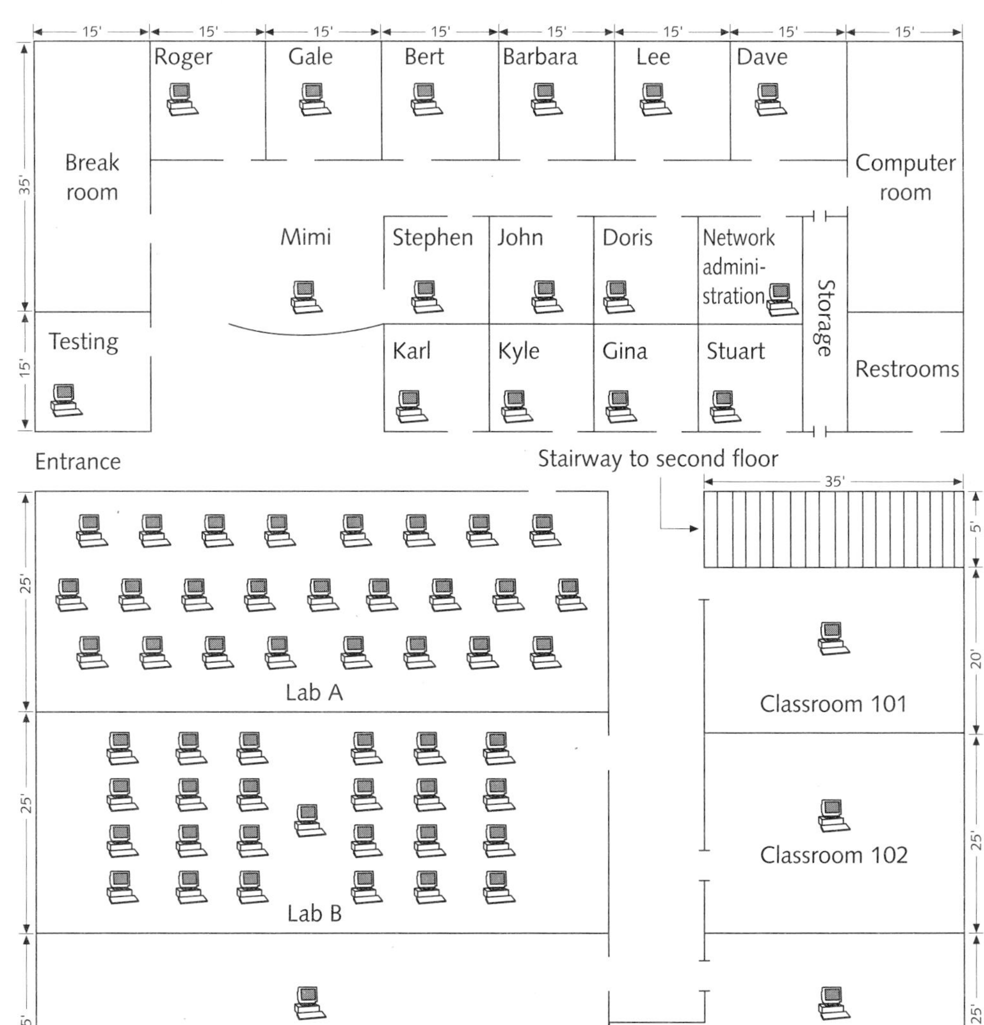

Draw a proposed network cable system based on the building layout shown in Figure 3-29. Write a memo to your instructor discussing your proposed network cable system and attach your drawing of the proposed network cable plan.

PROJECT 3-2: ESTIMATING NETWORK COSTS:

Since the star network you defined in Project 3-1 will support 10BaseT, 100BaseTX, 100VG-AnyLAN, and IBM token ring, Dave would like you to determine the cost differences between these network systems and recommend which network system you prefer. He then wants you to calculate the cost of the 10Base2 portion of the network, and finally calculate a total cost for the network.

1. In the table below, use current cost information as identified by your instructor to fill in the projected costs for Northwestern Technical College to implement the faculty and administration users and the computers in the classrooms on a 10BaseT network system.

10BaseT costs:

_______________ cards × $ _______________ each =$ _______________

_______________ hubs × $ _______________ each =$ _______________

Total =$ _______________

2. In the table below, use current cost information as identified by your instructor to fill in the projected costs for Northwestern Technical College to implement the faculty and administration users and the computers in the classrooms on a 100BaseX network system.

100BaseTX costs:

_______________ cards × $ _______________ each =$ _______________

_______________ hubs × $ _______________ each =$ _______________

Total =$ _______________

3. In the table below, use current cost information as identified by your instructor to fill in the projected costs for Northwestern Technical College to implement the faculty and administration users and the computers in the classrooms on a 100VG-AnyLAN network system.

100VG-AnyLAN costs:

_______________ cards × $ _______________ each =$ _______________

_______________ hubs × $ _______________ each =$ _______________

Total =$ _______________

4. In the table below, use current cost information as identified by your instructor to fill in the projected costs for Northwestern Technical College to implement the faculty and administration users and the computers in the classrooms on a token ring network system using 16-Mbps NICs.

Token ring costs:

_______________ cards × $ _______________ each =$ _______________

_______________ MSAUs × $ _______________ each =$ _______________

Total =$ _______________

5. In the table below, use current cost information as identified by your instructor to fill in the projected costs for Northwestern Technical College to implement the computer lab workstations on an Ethernet 10Base2 bus network system.

10Base2 costs:

_______________ cards × $ _______________ each =$ _______________

_______________ amount of cable × $ _______________ per foot =$ _______________

_______________ connectors × $ _______________ each =$ _______________

1 repeater × $ _______________ each =$ _______________

Total =$ _______________

6. Select the topology and network system for the administration and faculty. Record your choice below:

Recommended network system: ______________________________

7. Based on the network system you recommended in part 6 and the cost of the 10Base2 network system, calculate the total cost of Northwestern Technical College's network system:

Estimated costs (from 1, 2, 3, or 4): $______________________

Estimated 10Base2 costs (from 5): $______________________

Estimated cost of bridge or router: $______________________

Estimated total lab network cost: $______________________

8. Write a memo to the your instructor recommending a topology and network system. Discuss your justification for this selection, including copies of your calculations for steps 1, 2, 3, 4, 5, and 7. Discuss the reasons for your choice in the memo.

CHAPTER FOUR

PLANNING THE NOVELL DIRECTORY SERVICES (NDS) DIRECTORY TREE

In previous chapters, you studied the hardware and software components of a LAN. You learned how microcomputers, both NetWare servers and PC workstations, function. You studied the hardware that ties the microcomputers together into a LAN. You were also introduced to the operating systems software used by the servers and PC workstations, the network software protocols used for communication between microcomputers, and the software drivers used by the network interface cards to actually send messages across the network. Because as a network administrator you are specifically concerned with administering NetWare network operating systems, you need to go beyond a general knowledge of networks to a specific knowledge of NetWare.

AFTER READING THIS CHAPTER AND COMPLETING THE EXERCISES YOU WILL BE ABLE TO:

- Describe the components of Novell Directory Services (NDS).
- Explain the use of each object in an NDS Directory tree.
- Design an NDS Directory tree.
- Use DS Standard NDS Manager software.
- Plan the partitioning of an NDS Directory tree.

In this chapter you will start learning about the NetWare 4.1 NOS in detail. For a network administrator, the heart of NetWare 4.1 is Novell Directory Services (NDS). NDS provides the network administrator with the tools needed to manage network resources such as NetWare servers and printers from an organizational perspective. Although Novell made many other improvements in the NetWare 4.x series, the addition of NDS is arguably the most significant change. NDS forces the network administrator to redefine how he or she thinks about network resources and how they are linked together.

NOVELL DIRECTORY SERVICES (NDS)

Novell Directory Services (NDS) is a database that contains the data about all network resources, along with tools for using that data. The database is properly referred to as the Novell Directory database, but this is often shortened to Directory database or just Directory. All three terms refer to the same part of NDS, and in this book we'll consistently use the term Directory database.

The original name of NDS was NetWare Directory Services. Novell changed the name to Novell Directory Services in early 1996 to reflect the growing use of NDS on NOSs other than NetWare. You will still find references to NetWare Directory Services in many publications, including the Novell documentation that was provided with NetWare 4.1.

Novell's earlier versions of NetWare also had a database, called the **bindery**. The bindery, however, contained the data about the resources on only one server and was therefore described as **server-centric**. For example, each NetWare 3.1x server had its own bindery, and a network administrator could work with only one bindery at a time. NDS is **network-centric** and provides a central location for storing data about network resources such as users, printers, NetWare servers, and volumes. A network-centric system makes it easier for users to use the network and for network administrators to manage the network. For example, if you have three servers in your network, you can manage all three of them by using NDS, as shown in Figure 4-1.

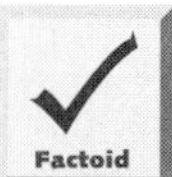

Both NetWare 3.1x and NetWare 4.1 use relational databases for storing network information. NetWare 3.1x used the Btrieve database program, which is a commercial product used by other software vendors with their products (for example, Cheyenne Software's ARCserve backup program uses the Btrieve program on a NetWare server to store information about data on tape backups). NetWare 4.1 uses a proprietary database program.

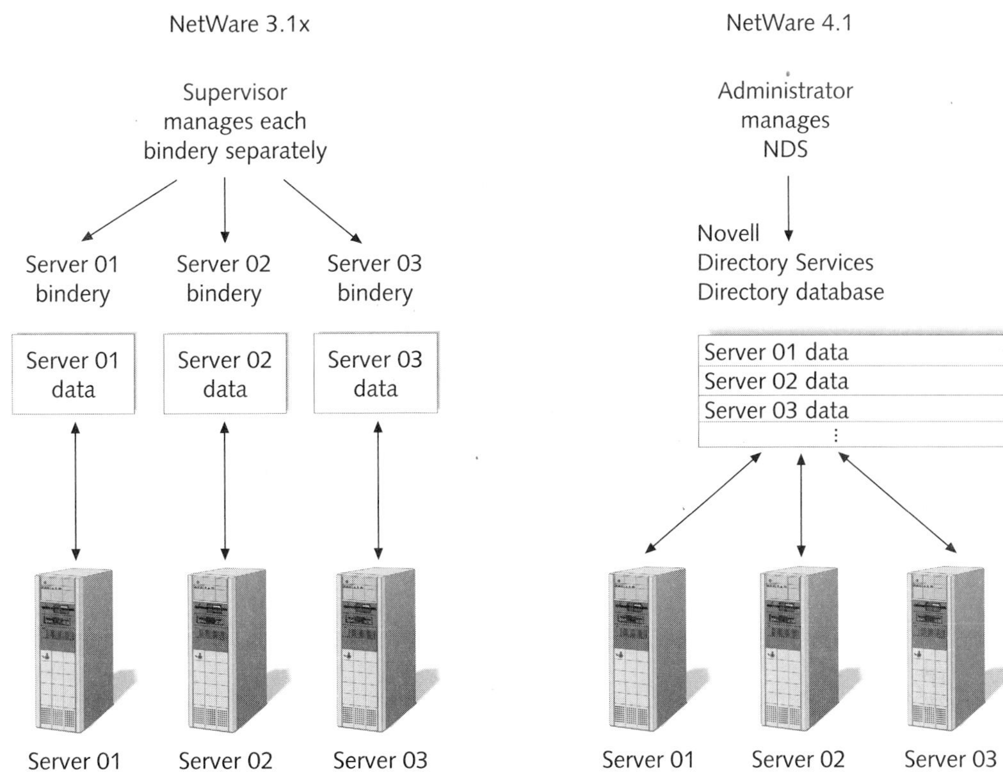

Figure 4-1 Managing binderies versus managing NDS

NDS has some other important features. The Directory database is divided into sections called **partitions**. The partitions are **distributed** among the servers in the network so that the loss of a single server doesn't mean the loss of the entire Directory database. Additionally, the partitions are **replicated**, which means that a copy of one partition, called a **replica**, is stored on one or more additional servers. This creates backup copies of the partitions so that the network data is safe even if the server containing the original copy of the partition stops working. These concepts are discussed in more detail later in this chapter.

Even though replicas are stored on other servers, you still need to make tape backup copies of your server's hard drives. The other files (programs and data) on the server are *not* replicated and must be backed up. The tape backup copies, of course, will also contain the NDS partition data.

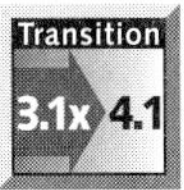

When you upgrade a NetWare 3.1x server to NetWare 4.1, most bindery data is automatically added to the Directory database. This saves you from having to recreate all the data about your users and groups, and makes upgrading a NetWare server a straightforward process.

LOGGING INTO THE NETWORK

As discussed in Chapter 1, the fact that NDS is network-centric means that when a user logs in, he or she logs into the *network*, not to an individual file server. In earlier versions of NetWare, each user initially logged into one specific server. As shown in Figure 4-2, the user would then use the NetWare ATTACH command to log into additional file servers and would have access to resources, such as files, on all those servers.

Figure 4-2

Logging into a server

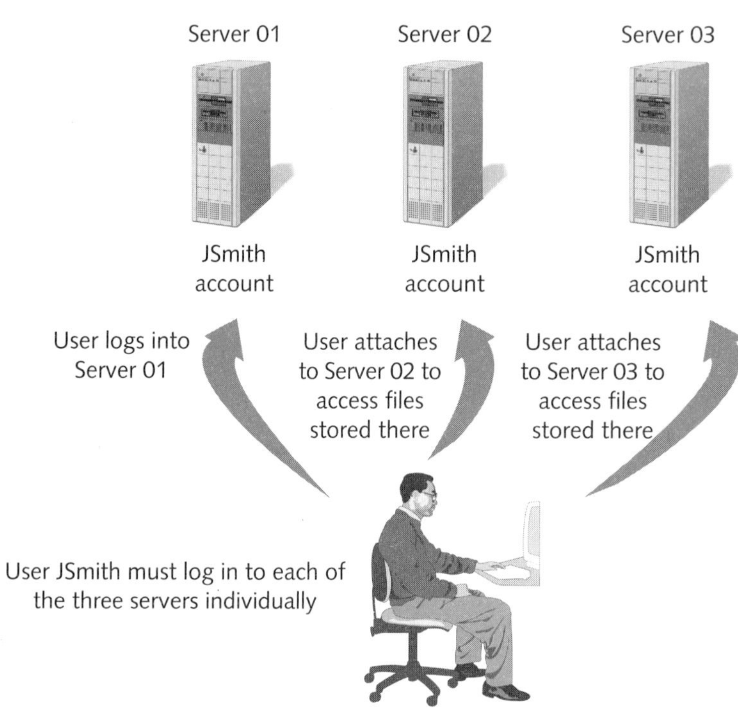
Server-Centric Network
Server 01
Server 02
Server 03
JSmith account
JSmith account
JSmith account
User logs into Server 01
User attaches to Server 02 to access files stored there
User attaches to Server 03 to access files stored there
User JSmith must log in to each of the three servers individually
User JSmith

In NetWare 4.1, the user logs into NDS and is then given access to whatever resources he or she has rights to. If those resources are files on three different file servers, then the user will have access to the servers where those resources are located, as shown in Figure 4-3.

Figure 4-3
Logging into the network

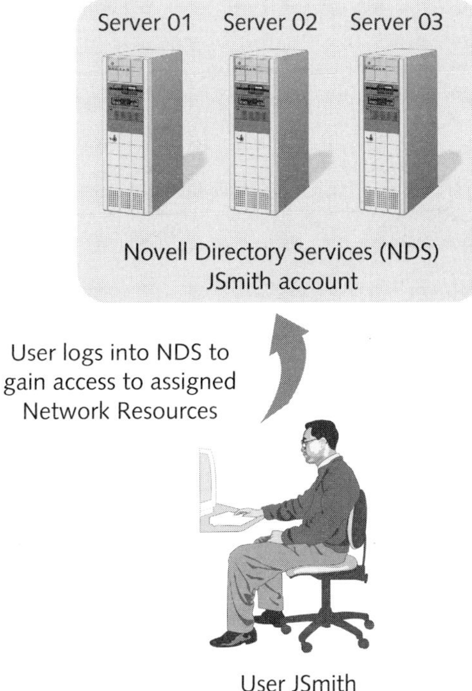
Server 01
Server 02
Server 03
Novell Directory Services (NDS)
JSmith account
User logs into NDS to
gain access to assigned
Network Resources
User JSmith
User JSmith logs into the network
with only one account

BENEFITS OF NDS

NDS provides the network administrator with several benefits beyond those found in NetWare 3.1x:

- **Administration.** With NDS, you can work with all your network resources at once, using one administration tool: the MS Windows-based NetWare Administrator utility or the DOS-based NETADMIN menu utility.
- **Security.** NDS uses the RSA encryption algorithm, which enables a secure, encrypted single login to the network.
- **Reliability.** Because the Directory database is distributed and replicated, NDS provides fault tolerance for the network. For example, because information about users will be stored on at least two servers, a single server going down doesn't prevent users from logging into the network and accessing those resources still available to them.
- **Scaleability.** Scaleability gives you the capability to work with systems of different sizes. NDS works just as well with small networks with only one server as with global networks with hundreds of servers. If your network expands, NDS can easily handle the expansion. No matter how large or small the network is, NDS can still be administered from one location.

NDS AND THE NETWORK FILE SYSTEM

As a network administrator, it is important that you understand that NDS is *not* a network file system. A **network file system** is used to organize file storage on the network. When you plan a network file system, you plan the set of volumes, directories, and subdirectories that will be created on the hard drives in your servers to store system, application, and data files. (You'll learn more about network file systems in Chapter 5.) When working with NDS, on the other hand, you create a logical design for administering network resources.

When Directory is spelled with a capital "D," the Directory database is being referenced; when directory is spelled with a lower case "d," part of the network file system is being referred to. The directories found in the network file system are discussed in Chapter 5.

NDS COMPONENTS

The logical design that you create to visualize the data in the Directory database is called the **Directory tree**. In computer terminology, the word *tree* refers to a **hierarchical structure** used for organizing data or information. A tree starts at a single point, called the **[Root]**, and branches out from there. The tree is usually drawn inverted, which means that, unlike a real tree, the [Root] is at the *top* of the diagram. A familiar example of a tree structure is a family tree, as shown in Figure 4-4.

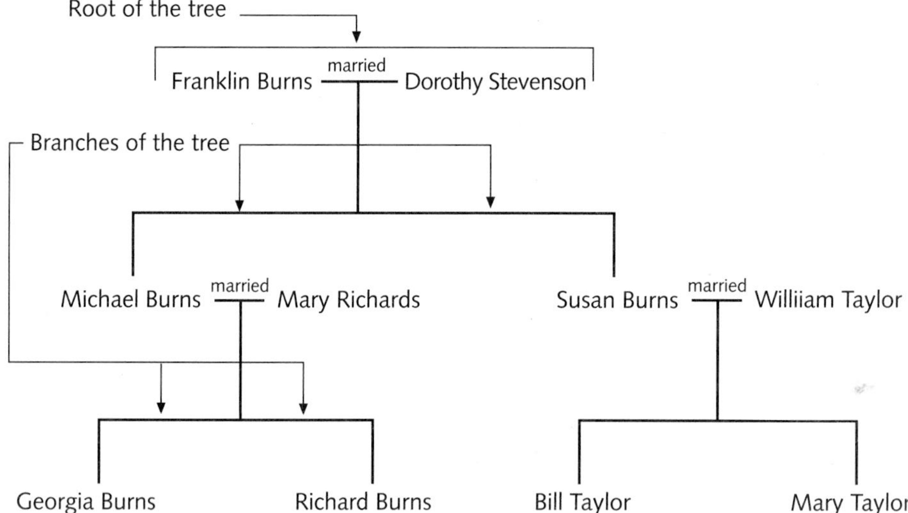

Figure 4-4 The Burns family tree

In the Burns family tree in Figure 4-4, the [Root] of the tree is the marriage of Franklin Burns and Dorothy Stevenson. Branches of the tree lead to their children, Michael and Susan. Additional branches lead to the children of Michael and his wife Mary Richards, and to the children of Susan and her husband, William Taylor. Because the [Root] of the tree is at the top of the diagram, this is an inverted tree.

NDS DIRECTORY TREES

The same inverted tree structure is seen in the Directory tree of F. D. Roosevelt Investments, Inc., as shown in Figure 4-5.

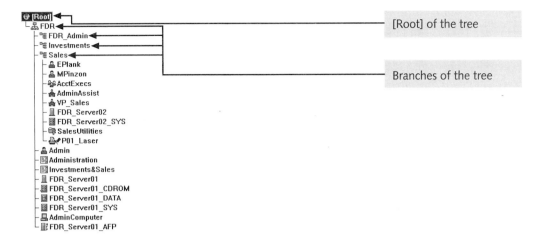

Figure 4-5 The Directory tree of F. D. Roosevelt Investments, Inc.

The Directory tree starts at the [Root] at the top of the diagram and branches down from there. The Directory tree's hierarchical structure makes it easy for the network administrator to create a graphical representation of his or her organization and the location of network resources within the organization. For example, in Figure 4-5, the Directory tree begins at the [Root], and then branches to an object named FDR, which represents the F. D. Roosevelt Investments organization. From FDR, the tree branches to the three organizational subdivisions of FDR: FDR_Admin (Administration), Investments, and Sales. Other branches from FDR lead to network resources: the user named Admin (the NetWare administrator), a NetWare server (FDR_Server01), and three volumes on the server (FDR_Server01_CDROM, FDR_Server01_DATA, and FDR_Server01_SYS). Branches from Sales lead to additional network resources.

The Directory tree links NDS objects into an organized and understandable structure; the term **object** is a general term, referring to any network resource in your network. An object is *not* the network resource itself; it is an NDS representation of the resource used to store data about the resource in the Directory database. Objects can be associated with:

- **Physical entities**—things that have a physical existence such as users, NetWare servers, and printers
- **Logical entities**—things that exist as a logical or mental creation, such as print queues, rather than a true physical entity. An important type of logical entity is the **organizational entity**, which represents a structural part of an organization, such as a group, an organizational unit, or the organization itself.

The term *object* comes from object-oriented programming languages, such as Smalltalk and C++. Many of the concepts developed for object-oriented programming languages have been carried into database management system development. A new type of database, the object-oriented database, is evolving based on these concepts. Other software, such as NDS, also uses the concept of objects, and you can expect to encounter objects in an increasing number of programs.

Objects are represented in the Directory tree by icons, symbols that help you visually recognize what an object represents. In Figure 4-5, object icons are included to represent the organization itself (FDR), subdivisions of the organization (FDR_Admin, Investments, and Sales), users (Admin, EPlank, and MPinzon), a group of users (AcctExecs), positions in the organization (VP_Sales and AdminAssist), a NetWare server used by FDR (FDR_Server01), and three volumes on the NetWare server (FDR_Server01_CDROM, FDR_Server01_DATA, and FDR_Server01_SYS).

The Directory tree is a graphical representation of the data in the Directory database. Data in the Directory database *must* be associated with an object in the Directory tree. In fact, you enter data into the Directory database by creating Directory tree objects and assigning the data to those objects. The Directory tree must be given a name, called the **Directory tree name**, when you first create the tree.

When you log in to NDS, you do so by logging into the Directory tree by name.

The NDS Directory tree was designed to be consistent with the CCITT X.500 specification (CCITT is the United Nations–chartered Comité Consultatif International Télégraphique et Téléphonique, which sets international telecommunications standards). The X.500 specification provides a basis for global directory services and is becoming an international standard. X.500 was developed to complement the CCITT X.400 e-mail specification, particularly to provide X.400-compatible name and address information to e-mail systems. The use of such standards becomes increasingly important as networks throughout the world communicate with one another.

NDS Objects, Properties, and Property Values

An NDS object always represents some definable network element, either physical or logical, for which you can record data. For example, for a user you can record login name, last name, first name, and so on. For a print queue, you can record the print queue name and the printers to which it sends print jobs. For a group, you can record the names of the members of the group.

The types of data that you use objects to collect are called **properties**. The data itself is called the **property value**. For example, the vice president for sales of FDR is Edgar Plank. Since Edgar is a network user, the Directory tree for FDR has a User object for Edgar named EPlank (which is Edgar's login name). One property of a User object is the user's Login Name, and for Edgar the property value for Login Name is EPlank. As shown in Figure 4-6, the Directory database stores the properties and property values for each object in the Directory tree.

Figure 4-6

Objects, properties, and property values

Object:	User
Property	**Property Value**
Login Name	EPlank
Last Name	Plank
Full Name	Edgar Plank

Object:	User
Property	**Property Value**
Login Name	MPinzon
Last Name	Pinzon
Full Name	Maria Pinzon

Object:	NetWare Server
Property	**Property Value**
Server Name	FDR_Server01
Network Address	080009 3D45F8

Object:	Printer
Property	**Property Value**
Printer Name	P1_LaserPrinter
Network Address	080009 12CF89

There are two types of NDS objects: container objects and leaf objects. **Container objects**, as the name implies, contain or hold other objects. **Leaf objects** cannot contain any other objects—they are the "leaves" at the ends of the "tree branches." Figure 4-7 shows the FDR Directory tree with container and leaf objects marked.

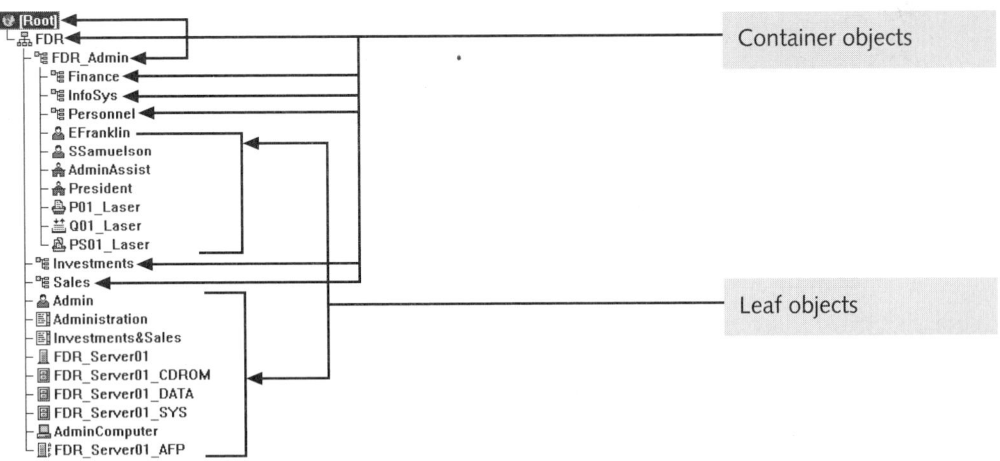

Figure 4-7

FDR Directory tree container and leaf objects

Container objects are used primarily to organize network resources (users, groups, NetWare servers, etc.), which are represented by the leaf objects. For example, in the FDR Directory tree, Sales is a container object that enables the resources of the FDR Sales group to be grouped together for ease of administration. In Figure 4-7, all employees in Sales (Edgar Plank and Maria Pinzon) have their associated user objects located in the Sales container. The network administrator can easily keep track of all Sales personnel this way, and the same concept applies to other container objects and the leaf objects they contain.

CONTAINER OBJECTS

There are four container objects that can be used in a Directory tree: [Root], Country, Organization, and Organizational Unit. The NDS container objects and their features are summarized in Figure 4-8.

Figure 4-8

NDS container objects

Object Icon	Object	Required/Optional	Can contain:
	[Root]	Required	Country Organization Alias (a leaf object)
	Country	Optional	Organization Alias (a leaf object)
	Organization	Required	Organizational Unit leaf objects
	Organizational Unit	Optional	Organizational Unit leaf objects

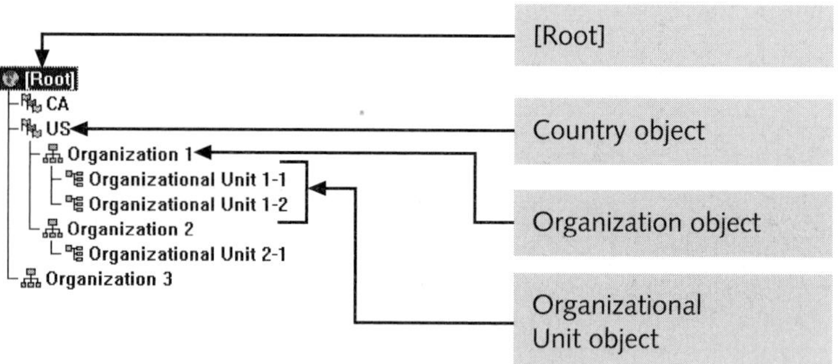

NDS actually has an unused fifth container object called Locality. The Locality object allows specification of geographical locations within a country. The Locality object is included in NDS for X.500 compliance but has not been implemented in NetWare 4.1. This means that although the object is coded into the operating system and discussed in the documentation, you cannot include it in a Directory tree at this time. Future versions of NetWare may implement the Locality object. If implemented, the Locality object would be optional, could be contained in [Root] and Organization objects, and could contain Organization and Organizational Unit objects. It could *not* contain leaf objects.

[Root]

The **[Root] object** is always the first object in the Directory tree, and there is only one [Root] object in each Directory tree. The [Root] object has no properties—its function is to be the highest access point in the Directory tree. When you first create a Directory tree during NetWare 4.1 installation, you assign the Directory tree name and create the [Root] object. The [Root] object is used by all other NetWare 4.1 servers added to the tree. There *must* be a [Root] object in a Directory tree, and you cannot modify or delete the [Root] object once it is created. For example, the [Root] object is the first object in the FDR Directory tree shown in Figure 4-7. The [Root] object can contain Country objects, Organization objects, and Alias objects (the Alias object is a leaf object described later in this chapter).

In network file systems, there is another root: the root directory. The root directory is the first directory on a hard disk or NetWare volume. For example, the root directory of the C: drive on a PC is C:\. Although both systems use the term *root*, they refer to two very different things.

Country

The **Country object** organizes the Directory tree for organizations that operate in more than one country. The Country object uses a unique two-letter code to designate each country. For example, in Figure 4-8, US is the United States. The Country object is optional, but if it is used, it must be used immediately after the [Root] object and before an Organization object. The Country object can contain Organization objects and Alias objects.

Although the Country object is included for X.500 compliance, it is generally not used. If you need to include countries in your Directory tree, you can use the Organization object or Organizational Unit object with a country name instead. This allows more flexibility, such as placing country designators *below* an Organization object. For example, you could have a Sales Organization unit that branches into two Organizational Unit objects named United States and Europe.

Organization

The **Organization object** is used to provide the first level of organizational structure to the Directory tree. You must use at least one Organization object in your Directory tree. There is usually only one Organization object in the Directory tree, representing the company or organization that built the network. For example, in Figure 4-5, there is only one Organization object, FDR. This, of course, represents the company F. D. Roosevelt Investments, the company that built and uses the network. You can, however, have more than one Organization object in your NDS tree if the organizational structure requires it. The Organization object can contain Organizational Unit objects and leaf objects.

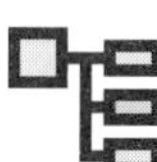

Organizational Unit

The **Organizational Unit object** subdivides the organizational structure of the Directory tree. Unlike the Organization object, you are not required to use any Organizational Unit objects. However, the Organizational Unit object is very useful for creating organizational structure in Directory trees. You will probably find yourself using this object frequently. For example, in Figure 4-5, the Directory tree for F. D. Roosevelt Investments uses three Organizational Unit objects to subdivide the company into administration (FDR_Admin), investments (Investments), and sales (Sales), for ease of network administration. The Organizational Unit object can contain Organizational Unit objects and leaf objects. In fact, the Organizational Unit object's ability to contain other Organizational Unit objects makes it the main "building block" of a Directory tree.

LEAF OBJECTS

Leaf objects represent network resources and are used to store data about those resources. Many types of leaf objects can be used in Directory trees. To understand the use of leaf objects, it is helpful to group them according to their purpose. As shown in Figure 4-9, Novell categorizes leaf objects as User-related, Server-related, Printer-related, Messaging-related, NetWare Application Manager-related, Informational, and Miscellaneous.

Figure 4-9 Leaf object groups

Leaf Object Group	Purpose
User-related	To manage network users
Server-related	To manage NetWare servers and their associated volumes
Printer-related	To manage printers and their associated queues and print servers
Messaging-related	To manage electronic messaging services on the network
NetWare Application Manager-related	To manage network applications used with the NetWare Application Manager
Informational	To store data about network resources that cannot be managed by NDS
Miscellaneous	Leaf objects that do not fit in the other groups

Leaf objects must be located in a container object, and they cannot contain any other objects. Before you create a leaf object, you select the container object that will hold it by clicking on that container object in the Directory tree. When a leaf object is created, it is always assigned to the active or selected container object.

NDS allows software companies to create additional leaf objects that are added into NDS when the new software is installed. The leaf objects listed here are the standard NetWare 4.1 objects, but as a network administrator you might have to become familiar with others associated with the software products you install.

User-Related Leaf Objects

User-related leaf objects have properties that enable you as a network administrator to manage the users on your network. User-related leaf objects include the User object, the Group object, the Organizational Role object, and the Profile object (see Figure 4-10).

Figure 4-10

User-related leaf objects

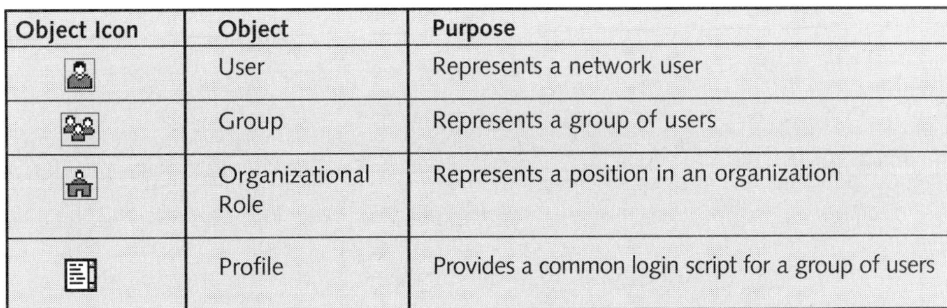

Object Icon	Object	Purpose
	User	Represents a network user
	Group	Represents a group of users
	Organizational Role	Represents a position in an organization
	Profile	Provides a common login script for a group of users

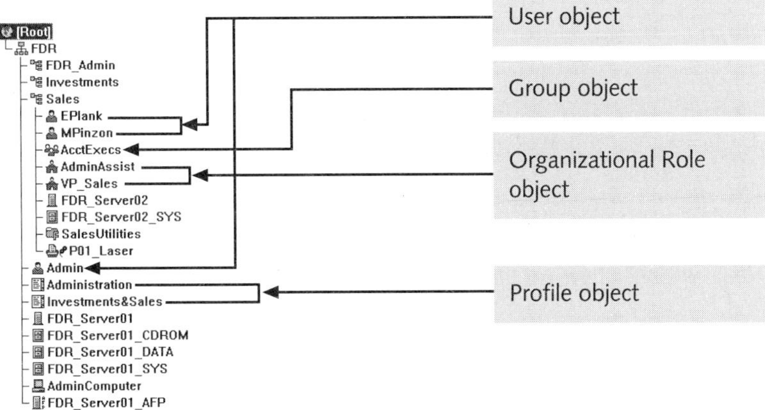

User

The **User object** represents each network user. As a network administrator, you use the User object to record and manage data about each of your users. There are about 67 properties associated with the User object. Two of these, Login Name and Last Name, are mandatory and must be specified when you create a user. As you create each user, a User object icon representing that user is added to the Directory tree.

In order to create users, you must be logged in to the network as a user. This requires that at least one user account be automatically created when NetWare 4.1 is installed. In fact, exactly one account is created for a user named Admin, and the Admin User object is added to the Directory tree. Admin is the network administrator and is assigned the necessary rights to create and manage the Directory tree and the network file structure. You will use the Admin user account in later chapters to create the objects in the Directory tree.

The network administrator account in NetWare 3.1x was named SUPERVISOR. Admin is the NetWare 4.1 equivalent of SUPERVISOR, although, as you will learn in Chapter 6, there are significant differences between these two user accounts. A related change is that although user (and group) names in NetWare 3.1x used only uppercase letters (for example, SUPERVISOR), object names in NetWare 4.1 can include both upper- and lowercase letters (for example, Admin).

The NetWare 3.1x installation process also created a user account for a user named GUEST. Since the GUEST account was created without a password requirement, anyone could log in to the server as GUEST. The GUEST account is *not* created by the NetWare 4.1 installation. This is because the GUEST account was too often a security loophole—anyone who knew about NetWare knew about the GUEST account. Normally, you should *not* create a GUEST account on a NetWare 4.1 network. If a GUEST account exists on any NetWare 3.1x server you administer, you should remove it.

User

The **Group object** represents groups of related network users and is used to record and manage data about each designated group on your network. The Group Name must be specified when you create a group. No groups are automatically created during the NetWare 4.1 installation process.

Groups are useful when you want to assign some network resource to several users. For example, the users who need to use a certain printer could be put into a group, and the group, rather than each individual user, is given the right to use the printer. Each group member then gets to use the printer because of his or her membership in the group, as shown in Figure 4-11.

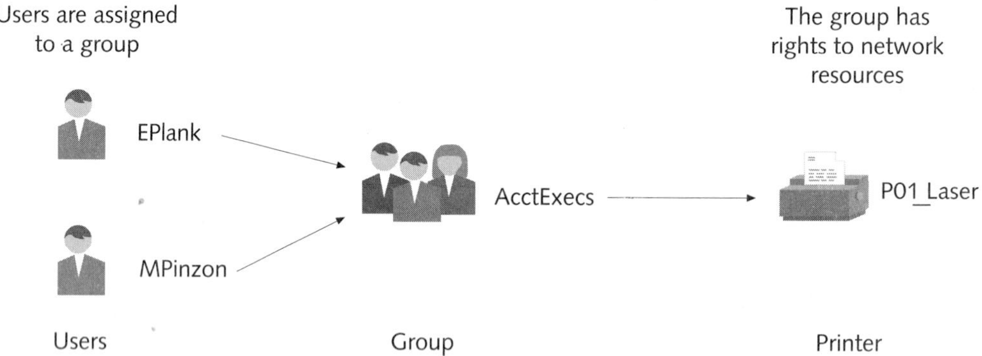

Figure 4-11 Using groups

During the NetWare 3.1x installation process a group named EVERYONE was created. Any user account that was created was automatically added to the EVERYONE group. The network administrator could easily handle assigning resources that needed to be shared by all users by assigning rights to the resource to the EVERYONE group. NetWare 4.1 does *not* create an EVERYONE group during installation. Instead, NetWare 4.1 uses the [Public] trustee to assign common rights to resources. The [Public] trustee is discussed briefly later in this chapter and in detail in Chapter 10.

Organizational Role

The **Organizational Role object** represents a position in an organizational structure such as president, chief financial officer (CFO), or sales manager. The Organizational Role object is used to record and manage data about each organizational role in your Directory tree. The Organizational Role name must be specified when you create the Organizational Role object. No organizational roles are automatically created during the NetWare 4.1 installation process.

Organizational roles are useful when a position in the organization has certain rights and resources available to it regardless of the person in that position. You can easily assign a user to an organizational role, and that user then automatically gets all the rights of that role. For example, Edgar Plank is the vice president of sales of FDR. Rather than assigning the rights of the vice president of sales to the User object EPlank, the FDR network administrator has created an Organizational Role object named VP-Sales and assigned the rights to that object. The network administrator then assigns the user EPlank to the role of vice president, so EPlank has the ability to do whatever the vice president can do. This is illustrated in Figure 4-12. If Martha Truman becomes vice president of FDR, the network administrator can remove EPlank from the role of vice president and assign MTruman to the role. Then she will automatically have the associated rights.

Figure 4-12

Using organizational roles

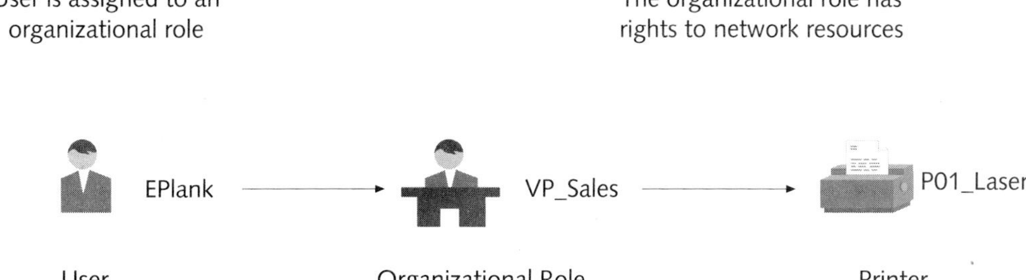

Profile

The **Profile object** is used to run login scripts and assign resources to groups of users. **Login scripts** are a series of NetWare commands that are automatically run when the user logs in to the network. Although you can create login scripts for Organization objects, Organizational Unit objects, and User objects, you cannot create a login script for a Group object. The Profile object provides the network administrator with a tool for creating login scripts for groups of users. You'll learn about login scripts in detail in Chapter 14. The Profile Name must be specified when you create a profile. No profiles are automatically created during the NetWare 4.1 installation process.

NetWare 4.1 creates a default login script that runs if no other login scripts have been created. The default login script provides access to the basic network resources that a user needs, and it is sufficient during the initial development of the network.

Although the Profile object provides the network administrator with a useful tool, you might find yourself initially confused between the use of the Group object and the use of the Profile object. They are conceptually similar because both are used with "groups" of users. To understand the differences between these two objects, remember that:

- Users are assigned to groups as members of the group, and groups are primarily used to give those members access to network resources.
- Profiles are assigned to users (not groups), and profiles are used primarily to give users a login script. Although a profile may be shared by many users, there is no formal "membership" in a profile.

For example, in FDR's Directory tree, the Investments&Sales Profile object is used as the source of the login script for users in both the Investments and Sales organizational units because all these users can use a common login script. However, each of these organizational units has a Group object that is used to grant access to department-specific network resources to the users in that department: the InvestMngrs Group object is Investments and the AcctExecs Group object is Sales. As shown in Figure 4-13, GSakharov and EPlank thus share a common login script through the Profile object but have their access to other network resources controlled by their departmental groups.

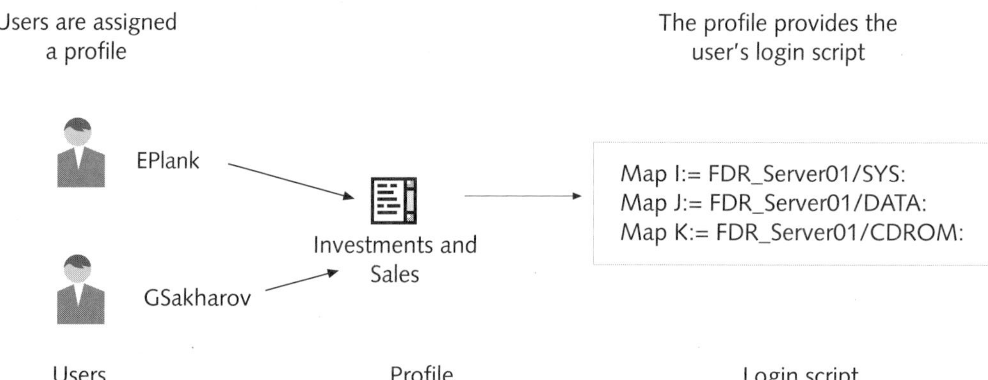

Figure 4-13 Using the Profile object

If Group objects could have login scripts, the same login requirements and resource assignments could have been provided by using just the InvestMngrs and AcctExecs groups. This would, of course, have required two separate copies of the same login script. But groups cannot have login scripts, so Profile objects are needed.

Login scripts assigned to organizations, organizational units, and profiles are new in NetWare 4.1. NetWare 3.1x had a system login script, which is similar to an organization or organizational unit login script. NetWare 3.1x also had a user login script and a default login script, which are identical to the user login script and the default login script in NetWare 4.1.

Server-Related Leaf Objects

Server-related leaf objects have properties that enable you to manage the NetWare servers on your network. Server-related leaf objects include the NetWare Server object, the Volume object, and the Directory Map object. These objects are shown in Figure 4-14.

Figure 4-14

Server-related leaf objects

Object Icon	Object	Purpose
	NetWare Server	Represents a network NetWare server
	Volume	Represents a hard disk volume on a server
	Directory Map	Represents a reference to a directory or sub-directory on a volume

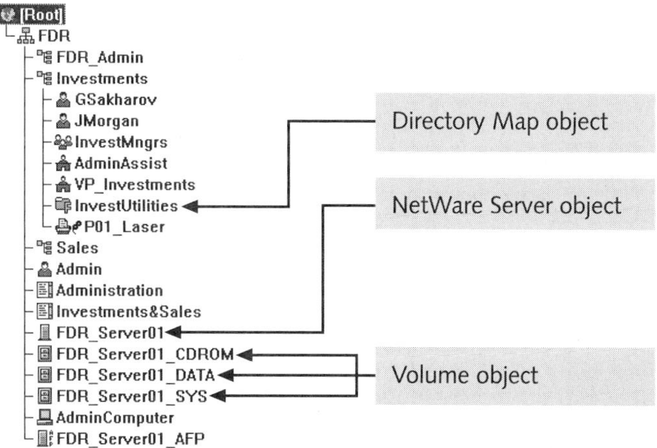

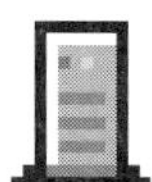

NetWare Server

The **NetWare Server object** represents each server on the network that is running a version of NetWare. This object is also referred to as an **NCP Server object**, where NCP stands for NetWare Core Protocol. The NetWare Server object must be created and placed in the Directory tree so that the server's volumes, directories, subdirectories, and files are available to users. The NetWare Server object is created for each NetWare 4.1 server during NetWare installation. For NetWare 3.1x servers, you must create the NetWare Server object yourself.

You must specify the NetWare server name whenever a NetWare Server object is created. For example, when FDR installs NetWare 4.1 on the NetWare server named FDR_Server01, the server name FDR_Server01 will be used to create a NetWare Server object named FDR_Server01. During the installation process, NetWare prompts you for the server's location in the Directory tree. In this case, the location of FDR_Server01 would be specified as the Organization object FDR, as shown in Figure 4-14.

Volume

Volumes, which you will study in detail in Chapter 5, are the physical hard disk storage spaces in NetWare servers. The **Volume object** represents a volume in the Directory tree. Volumes and their associated Volume objects are created during NetWare 4.1 installation. When they are created, you must specify a volume name, and this same name is used to create the Volume object name. The name of the Volume object will always be the server's name followed by an underscore character followed by the volume name:

```
ServerName_VolumeName
```

For example, NetWare requires that a volume named SYS (short for *system*) be created during installation. Therefore, when FDR installs NetWare 4.1 on FDR_Server01, a Volume object named FDR_Server01_SYS is created. The Volume object is placed in the same Directory tree location as the server, which in this case is the Organization object FDR, as shown in Figure 4-14. You will learn about planning network file systems in Chapter 5 and managing file systems in Chapter 7.

Directory Map

The **Directory Map object** is used to reference a single directory in the network file system. This object is a useful management tool for creating and managing login scripts, and you'll learn more about it when you study login scripts in Chapter 14. An example of a Directory Map object is shown in Figure 4-14, where the network manager for FDR has created the Directory Map object named InvestUtilities to refer to the location of some utility programs used by the investment managers in the Investments Organizational unit.

Printer-Related Leaf Objects

Printer-related leaf objects let you manage network printing. In order to understand these objects, you need to understand how NetWare handles network printing. This is illustrated in Figure 4-15.

Figure 4-15 Printing on a NetWare network

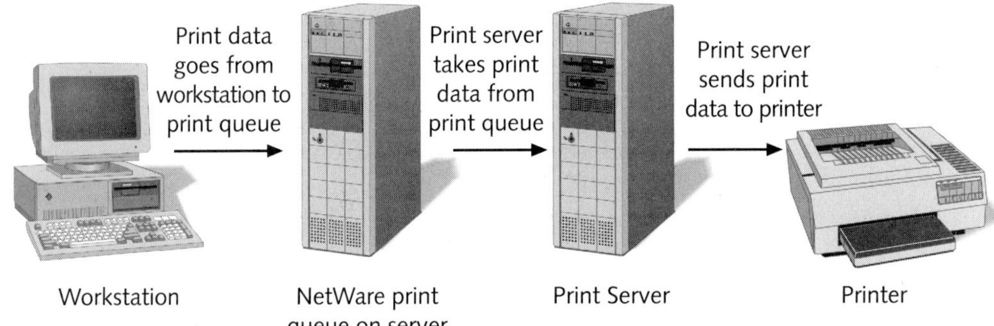

When a user wants to print a document or a spreadsheet on a network printer, the user begins the printing process by using the application's Print command. The application generates the **print data**, or the material to be printed. The print data is sent to a NetWare **print queue**, where it waits with other print jobs until its turn to be printed. Finally, the print data is taken from the print queue by a **print server**, which sends it to the printer.

The three key pieces of this system are the printer, the print queue, and the print server. Each of these is represented by a Printer-related leaf object, namely the Printer object, the Print Queue object, and the Print Server object. These objects are shown in Figure 4-16. NetWare printing is covered in detail in Chapters 12 and 13. The examples used in this chapter are intended to help you learn about Directory tree objects, not all the possible details of setting up printing on a NetWare network.

Figure 4-16 Printer-related leaf objects

Object Icon	Object	Purpose
	Printer	Represents a network printer
	Print Queue	Represents a print queue on a NetWare server
	Print Server	Represents a network print server

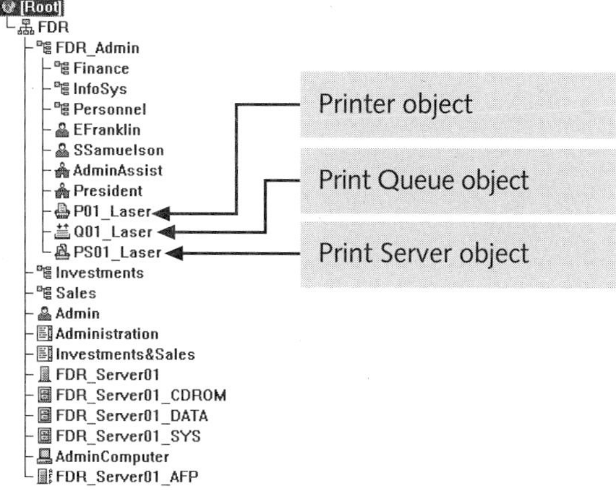

Printer

The **Printer object** is used to represent an actual printer. The Printer object must be created and placed in the Directory tree so that you can link a printer to print queues and print servers. You must name the printer when you create the Printer object.

For example, FDR has a laser printer used by the administration group that is referred to as P01_Laser (the "P" stands for printer, and "01" gives a number to the printer). Therefore, a Printer object named P01_Laser has been created and placed in the FDR_Admin organizational unit, as shown in Figure 4-16.

Print Queue

The **Print Queue object** is used to represent a NetWare print queue. The Print Queue object is necessary to link printers to the print queues and print servers. You must name the print queue and specify the volume where the print queue will store its print data when you create the Print Queue object.

For example, FDR needs a print queue for print jobs from the administration group that will be printed on the laser printer. A Print Queue object named Q01_Laser (the "Q" stands for queue, and "01" gives a number to the print queue) has been created. It is located in the FDR_Admin organizational unit, as shown in Figure 4-16, along with the P01_Laser Printer object.

Print Server

The **Print Server object** represents a NetWare print server. The Print Server object is necessary to link the print queues to printers. You must name the print server when you create the Print Queue object.

In the FDR example, a print server is needed to control print jobs for the administration group's laser printer. The FDR network administrator has created a Print Server object named PS01_Laser (the "PS" stands for print server, and "01" gives a number to the print server) in the FDR_Admin organizational unit, as shown in Figure 4-16.

Messaging-Related Leaf Objects

Messaging-related leaf objects, shown in Figure 4-17, have properties that enable you to manage the NetWare **Message Handling Service (MHS)** on your network. Novell includes a basic **e-mail** application named **FirstMail** with NetWare 4.1, and FirstMail uses the NetWare MHS to deliver mail to network users.

Figure 4-17 Messaging-related leaf objects

Object Icon	Object	Purpose
	Messaging Server	Represents an MHS server on the network
	Distribution List	Represents a group setup for message handling purposes
	Message Routing Group	Represents a group of MHS servers
	External Entity	Represents a user on a NetWare 3.1x server who is included in NetWare 4.1 MHS

NetWare Application Manager-Related Leaf Objects

When Novell released the NetWare Client 32 software in 1996, it included the NetWare Application Launcher software with the NetWare Client 32 files. The **NetWare Application Manager (NAM)** allows network managers to control which network users can use software applications that are stored on a NetWare server. The **NetWare Application Manager-related leaf objects**, shown in Figure 4-18, have properties that enable you to manage the application software control by the NAM. You'll study the NAM in Chapter 11, as well as the NetWare Application Manager-related leaf objects.

Figure 4-18

NetWare Application Manager-related leaf objects

Object Icon	Object	Purpose
	DOS Application	Represents a DOS application that will be run from a network NetWare server
	Windows 3.x Application	Represents a Windows 3.x application that will be run from a network NetWare server
	Windows 95 Application	Represents a Windows 95 application that will be run from a network NetWare server
	Windows NT Application	Represents a Windows NT application that will be run from a network NetWare server

The NetWare Application Manager and the associated NetWare Application Launcher client software are included as an integral part of NetWare 4.11. They were previously released as part of the NetWare Client 32 workstation client when NetWare Client 32 for Windows 95 was released. They have already been incorporated into many NetWare 4.1 networks.

Informational Leaf Objects

Informational leaf objects enable you to store data about network resources that would otherwise be unrepresented in the Directory tree. These objects are created only to provide a place for data storage—their creation has no effect on the operation of the network. The Informational leaf objects include the Computer object and the AFP Server object, shown in Figure 4-19. In order to be truly useful, the Directory database must be able to store all needed data about network resources, and these objects help provide that capability.

Figure 4-19

Informational leaf objects

Object Icon	Object	Purpose
	Computer	Represents a user's computer
	AFP Server	Represents a network AppleTalk File Protocol server

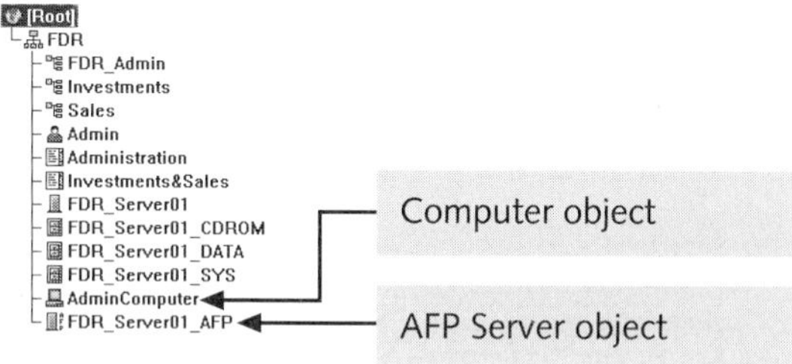

Computer

The **Computer object** represents any computer on the network that is not a server. You must specify a name for the Computer object when you create it. You can use it to store data such as the computer serial number and which user is using it. You can also add a description of the computer. Using a Computer object for each PC workstation on your network will provide you with a basic system for keeping an inventory of the PC workstations you manage. Alternatively, you can create a Computer object only for special-use PC workstations, such as Apple Macintosh workstations used in a PC workstation environment. For example, the FDR network manager has a Macintosh workstation that he uses to run graphics programs. A Computer object name AdminComputer has been created for this computer; it appears in Figure 4-19.

AFP Server

The **AFP Server object** is used to represent an **AppleTalk File Protocol (AFP) server**, a NetWare server that runs special modules that enable it to provide file and print services to Macintosh workstations. You can use this object to store data about the AFP server such as a description and network address. An AFP Server object in a Directory tree indicates that there are Apple Macintosh workstations attached to the network, and the AFP server acts as a router connecting the Macintoshes to the rest of the network. FDR is running the AFP modules on the FDR_Server01 NetWare server to connect the Macintosh computer named AdminComputer to the network. As shown in Figure 4-19, an AFP Server object named FDR_Server01_AFP has been created to store data about the configuration of the AFP server.

Miscellaneous Leaf Objects

As their name implies, **miscellaneous leaf objects** have various purposes. The Miscellaneous leaf objects include the Alias object, the Bindery object, the Bindery Queue object, and the Unknown object, shown in Figure 4-20.

Alias

The **Alias object** refers to another object in a different part of the Directory tree. The Alias object is useful because of how NetWare tracks a user's current location or context in the Directory tree (context is discussed later in this chapter). Referring to an object *not* in the same location can be a complex procedure, but using an Alias object in the same location can be helpful. The Alias object contains the location reference to the original object, so the user has to refer only to the Alias object to access the original object. For example, the Investments workgroup unit at FDR also needs to use the laser printer. To simplify how the users in the Investments workgroup specify the location of the laser printer, the network administrator has created an Alias object named P01_Laser in the Investments Organizational unit, as shown in Figure 4-20.

Object Icon	Object	Purpose
	Alias	Refers to another NDS object in another part of the Directory tree
	Bindery	Represents NetWare 3.1x bindery data unrecognized during an upgrade
	Bindery Queue	Represents a NetWare 3.1x queue unrecognized during an upgrade
	Unknown	Represents a corrupted object that cannot be recognized

Figure 4-20

Miscellaneous leaf objects

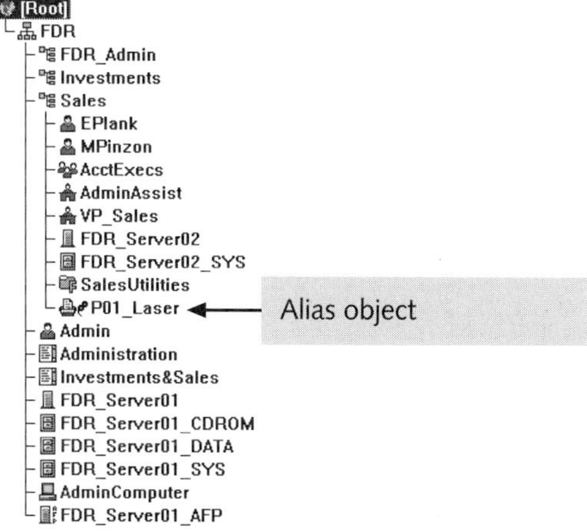

Bindery Object and Bindery Queue Object

When a NetWare 3.1x server is updated to NetWare 4.1, there might be objects or queues in the NetWare 3.1x bindery that NetWare 4.1 can't identify. Because there are network utilities that work with data stored in the bindery, a **Bindery object** or a **Bindery Queue object** will be created and placed in the Directory tree. This allows for backward compatibility with the network utilities that work with bindery data to use the NetWare 4.1 bindery emulation mode. **Bindery emulation mode** is a special connection feature that enables utilities designed to work with NetWare 3.1x's bindery database to operate in the NetWare 4.1 environment. The Bindery object and the Bindery Queue object exist only to support bindery emulation mode. They are automatically created during an upgrade if needed—you will never create them yourself. If these objects appear in your Directory tree, you should determine what they represent and, if possible, create a replacement NDS object.

Unknown

If an NDS object becomes corrupted so that NDS can't recognize it, NDS will rename it and identify it as an **Unknown object**. As the network administrator, you will need to reidentify the object, delete the Unknown object, and recreate the proper object for the network resource.

Unknown objects may occur during upgrades to NetWare 4.1 if NetWare cannot translate bindery data into an NDS object, a Bindery object, or a Bindery Queue object.

NDS is extendible, which means that new objects can be added to it by Novell and other vendors. For example, a software vendor could create objects that indicate that the software is installed on the network and provide software management capabilities. As a network administrator, you will need to be aware of any new objects that can be used in Directory trees.

NAMING NDS OBJECTS

Each object in a Directory tree has a name that uniquely identifies the object within the directory tree. In this section, you will learn about object names and the naming conventions that are used in NDS.

Common Names

NDS uses a set of **name types**, which are descriptions of the type of object being named, and each name type has an abbreviation The Country object, the Organization object, and the Organizational Unit object all have equivalent name types. The Country name type is abbreviated as C, the Organization name type is abbreviated as O, and the Organizational Unit name type is abbreviated as OU. There is no name type for the [Root] object, and all leaf objects are referred to by the **common name** name type, abbreviated as CN, because each leaf object is the object name that appears in the Directory tree. For example, the common name for the EFranklin User object is EFranklin.

Context

The position or location of an object in the Directory tree is called the object's **context**. Context is specified as the path from the [Root] to the object. For example, consider the context of the User object EFranklin in the FDR Directory tree shown in Figure 4-21.

Starting at EFranklin, we see that she is in the organizational unit FDR_Admin, which is in the organization FDR, which is directly below the [Root]. Her context is

```
.FDR_Admin.FDR
```

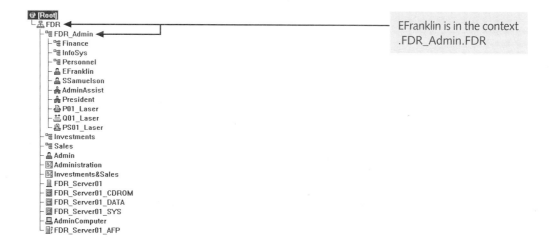

Figure 4-21 The context of User object EFranklin

The context of an object reads from left to right, starting at the lowest level of the tree, and works upward to the [Root]. Notice that [Root], however, is not included in the context. The **leading period** in the context, the period in front of FDR_Admin, indicates that the path begins at the [Root]. Periods are also used to separate object names. A period after an object name is called a **trailing period** and indicates a shift up one level in the Directory tree. For example, the FDR_Admin Organizational Unit object is one level lower down the Directory tree than the FDR Organization object; the period after FDR_Admin in the context shows the shift from one level to the next.

Although each object has a fixed context in the Directory tree, a network user will want to view different parts of the Directory tree while working on the network. The part of the Directory tree that the user is actively working with is called the user's **current context**. The context of an object never changes, but a user's current context does change as the user works with different parts of the Directory tree. This is why the leading period in a context is important—a context *with* a leading period is read starting at the [Root], regardless of the user's current context. A context *without* the leading period would be read starting at the user's current context.

Object Names

The complete name of any object is the object name plus the object's context. This is called the object's **distinguished name**, which specifies the path to the object starting at the [Root] object. As shown in Figure 4-22, EFranklin's distinguished name is

```
.EFranklin.FDR_Admin.FDR
```

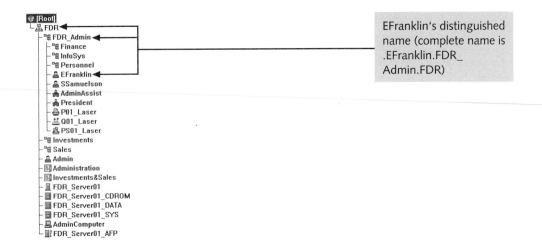

Figure 4-22 EFranklin's complete name

When the name is written with the name type initials, it's called a **typeful name**. Without the initials, the name is called a **typeless name**. Thus, **`.CN=EFranklin.OU=Admin.O=FDR`** is a typeful name, and **`.EFranklin.Admin.FDR`** is a typeless name.

Whereas a distinguished name shows the path to an object from the [Root], a **relative distinguished name** specifies the path to an object from another object. For example, if the current context is .FDR, the relative distinguished name for Eleanor Franklin is **`EFranklin.FDR_Admin`** without a leading period (not a path from the [Root]) or a trailing period (no need to move up a Directory tree level).

Object Names and Logging into the Network

Directory tree context and distinguished names have important uses in NetWare 4.1. When you log in to a NetWare 4.1 network, you log into an NDS Directory tree. In order for your login to succeed, you must use your **login name** (which is the same as the name of your User object in the tree) together with the correct context for your User object.

If Eleanor Franklin of F. D. Roosevelt Investments wants to log in to the FDR Directory tree from the DOS prompt, she would use her distinguished name. For example, she could use the following login command:

```
G:\LOGIN> Login .EFranklin.FDR_Admin.FDR
```

If Eleanor has access to more than one NetWare 4.1 Directory tree, she can also specify the name of the Directory tree that she wants to log into by preceding her distinguished name with the Directory tree name and a slash (/):

```
G:\LOGIN> Login FDR/.EFranklin.FDR_Admin.FDR
```

There are easy ways to designate the tree and context for login by modifying the user's NetWare Client 32 settings, which NetWare checks during the login process. You'll study NetWare Client 32 software settings in Chapter 6.

DESIGNING THE DIRECTORY TREE

One of the network administrator's main responsibilities when administrating a NetWare 4.1 network is designing the Directory tree. Now that you understand the components of Directory trees, you are ready to put these components together to create a Directory tree.

Although a Directory tree can be planned by using pen and paper, the DS Standard NDS Manager software package gives the network administrator the capability to design Directory trees on a PC workstation. A student version of DS Standard is included with this book. The figures used to illustrate Directory tree design principles in the following sections were created using DS Standard, and you will learn to use DS Standard later in this chapter. Figure 4-23 shows the F. D. Roosevelt Investments Directory tree drawn using DS Standard.

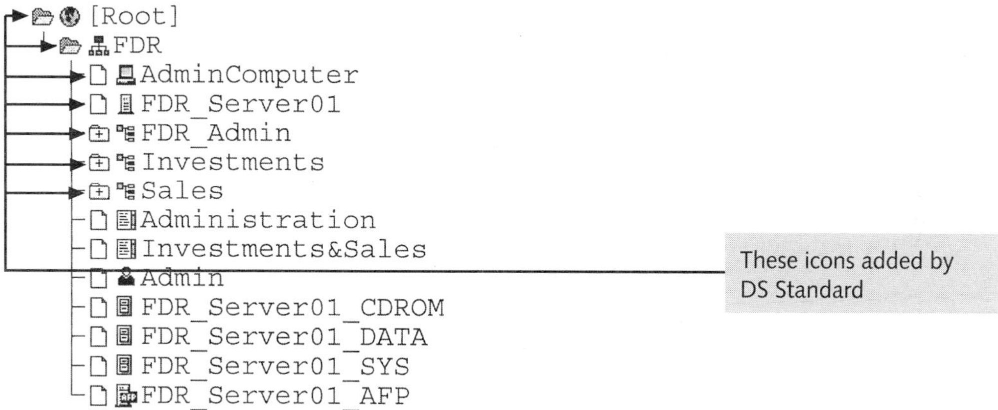

Figure 4-23 The FDR Directory tree drawn in DS Standard

Notice that in Figure 4-23, DS Standard uses the standard NDS Directory tree icons and also adds additional structural icons to the tree. These additional icons are the open folder, the closed folder, and the page, and they are used to indicate expanded, not expanded, and nonexpandable Directory tree branches, respectively. Except for the addition of these new icons, the Directory trees designed in DS Standard have the same appearance as Directory trees created with NetWare utilities.

There are three important design principles to keep in mind when designing a Directory tree:

- Use agreed-upon network standards such as naming conventions.
- Balance tree depth and tree width.
- Use a design approach that matches the Directory tree to the organization.

DEFINING NETWORK STANDARDS

As the size of the network increases, the use of network standards will minimize confusion as more servers are installed, more users are added, and new Directory tree objects appear in the Directory tree. **Network standards** are agreements about how to operate the network. For example, user names should be standardized. It's confusing if one network administrator creates user names based on the user's first initial and then last name, such as *EFranklin*, while another administrator creates user names based on the user's last name and then first initial, such *FranklinE*.

Naming Conventions

One of the most important areas for network standards is naming conventions. A consistent and meaningful way of assigning names to users, servers, printers, print queues, print servers, and other network resources can minimize confusion for the network administrator. Before discussing naming conventions, however, we need to know the rules for naming NDS objects.

First, because the complete or distinguished name of an object includes the context where the object is located, object names need be unique only in their container. For example, FDR could have two users named Eleanor Franklin with login EFrankin as long as they worked in different parts of the organization. An Eleanor Franklin in administration would be **.EFranklin.FDR_Admin.FDR**, while an Eleanor Franklin in Sales and would be **.EFranklin.Sales.FDR**. The problem, of course, is what happens if both of them end up in the same department? This would be a problem, so it's best to eliminate the potential problem by using *unique* object names for each object. For example, an Admin User object in the FDR Directory tree has the distinguished name **.Admin.FDR**. If the FDR administration Organizational Unit object was named simply **Admin** instead of **FDR_Admin**, then its distinguished name would also be **.Admin.FDR**, which would create two objects with the same distinguished name. Because each NDS distinguished name must be unique, the problem is resolved by naming the organizational unit **FDR_Admin**, creating the name **.FDR_Admin.FDR**, which is unique.

Second, you can use up to 64 characters in the object name. NDS names can use both uppercase and lowercase letters, but NDS names are not case-sensitive. For example, **EFRANKLIN** and **EFranklin** are identical as far as NDS is concerned.

Third, you can use any special character, spaces, and underscores. However, underscores are displayed as spaces, so "Eleanor_Franklin" and "Eleanor Franklin" are identical as far as NDS is concerned.

NetWare 3.1x allows only 47 characters in names. NetWare 4.1 allows some network clients, such as stand-alone print servers, to connect to the network in bindery emulation mode, which means that they behave as though they were attached to a NetWare 3.1x server. In this case, NetWare 4.1 object names longer than 47 characters are truncated to 47 characters.

Similarly, NetWare 3.1x does not allow spaces or the following characters in names:

/ (slash)
\ (backslash)
, (comma)
; (semicolon)
* (asterisk)
? (question mark)

For clients running in bindery emulation mode, spaces in names are converted to underscores. You should not use the other characters for client names that will connect to the NetWare server in bindery emulation mode.

If you use spaces in NetWare 4.1 object names, you have to enclose the name in quotation marks when using command line utilities. This may be reason enough for not using spaces in object names. Using the underscore instead eliminates this problem and helps ensure compatibility for bindery emulation clients.

When using these rules, you should develop consistent ways of naming NDS objects. One important consideration is length. Remember that the user, or for that matter you as network administrator, might have to use the names you create in distinguished names. Because of this, shorter names are better than longer names. For example, it is easier to write **`.EFranklin.FDR_Admin.FDR`** than it is to write **`.Eleanor_Franklin.FDR_Administration.FDRoosevelt_Investments`**.

User Name Considerations

User login names should always be created in the same way. It is easier to locate the user if user names are consistent. For example, if all user names start with the first letter of the user's first name, you know you need to look for E to find Eleanor Franklin. If there is no consistency, you will not be sure which letter to look for. There are various ways that this can be done:

- Use just the user's last name: Franklin
- Use the user's first initial and last name: EFranklin
- Use the user's first and last names: Eleanor_Franklin
- Use the first three characters of the user's first name and the first three characters of the user's last name: EleFra

How you choose to create user names will depend upon your and your users' preferences. It will also depend on how many users you are managing and how difficult it is to maintain uniqueness of the user name. For example, a small network may have only one John Smith but a larger organization could easily have two or more employees named John Smith. There are many ways to create user names that will work—the important consideration is consistency.

Print System Considerations

When working with some object types, it's a good idea to include a code in the name that identifies the object type. NetWare printing is a good example of this. If you start printer names with the code "P," print queue names with the code "Q," and print server names with the code "PS," you can easily identify the object type from the object name. You can also include a number, a location, or a type in the name.

For example, FDR can name a laser print P01_Laser, including a number and the type of printer. If this printer is going in room 201 and is a Hewlett-Packard LaserJet IV, the name could be P01_Rm201_HPLJIV. The same ideas work with print queues, print servers, and other NDS objects that have a physical existence on the network.

Directory Tree Name Considerations

It's possible to have more than one NetWare NDS Directory tree visible to network users in a WAN. For example, a corporation might not have implemented a corporatewide NetWare 4.1 network. Within the corporation, there might be two divisions that each have a NetWare 4.1 LAN. If these LANs are connected to a corporate backbone to form a WAN, NetWare users will see both NDS Directory trees and may log in to one or both LANs.

Directory tree names need to be unique if more than one exists on a WAN. The "shorter is better" idea also applies here—a user might need to specify the tree name during login. For example, FDR can use FDR as the tree name of their Directory tree.

Depth Versus Width

The term **depth** refers to the number of levels in a Directory tree. The term **width** refers to the number of branches at any level, but particularly at the first level of a Directory tree.

When designing a Directory tree, you need to be careful not to create more levels (depth) than are necessary, because each level adds another term to an object's distinguished name. If there are too many levels, the names become unwieldy. For example, what user wants a name of **`.JMartin.QualityControl.Prod.Ops.Plant16.Region2.DivisionIII.EastCoast.JKHCompany`**?

Novell considers five to eight levels reasonable but notes that NDS is capable of handling as many levels as necessary to reflect an organization's structure.

On the other hand, using too few levels will create a very flat Directory tree (width) that probably won't clearly capture the actual structure of most organizations. When designing a Directory tree, you're looking for a design that reflects the structure of the organization using the tree, while at the same time balancing the depth and width of the tree.

Approaches to Directory Tree Design

You can take a few approaches in designing the Directory tree. You can reflect the actual structure of the organization, you can build upon the geographic locations of the organization, or you can use a combination of the two.

Organizational Structure

Because resources within an organization are allocated and accounted for according to the organization's organization chart, the actual structure of an organization provides one approach to designing the Directory tree. Two possible organizational structures focus on functional areas and workgroups.

Functional

Most businesses can be organized around the classic functional areas of business: operations, marketing, finance, and personnel. Although this list doesn't include every possible organizational unit (for example, executive administration and support units such as information systems are not included), it does cover most of them. Other organizational units can be added and the four main units broken down into other organizational units as necessary. For example, marketing includes sales, advertising, and market research; and receiving, production, and shipping are part of operations. Figure 4-24 shows a Directory tree for Wilson Manufacturing, a company that manufactures home furniture. The Directory tree is based on a functional structure.

Figure 4-24 The Wilson Manufacturing Directory tree

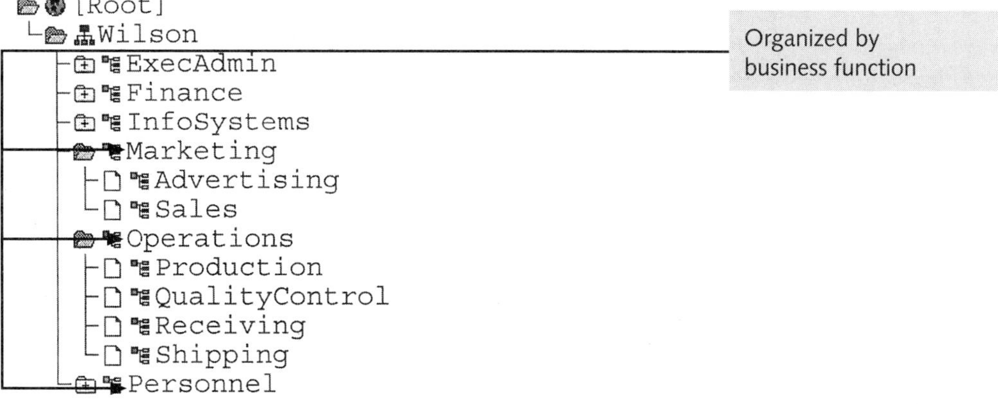

Workgroups

Some organizations prefer to focus on project workgroups composed of members from the functional areas. In this case, the Directory tree structure needs to show the resources assigned to each workgroup. Figure 4-25 shows a Directory tree for South Atlantic Coast Publishing, a book publisher that uses workgroups for different book topic areas. The Directory tree is based on a workgroup approach.

Figure 4-25 The South Atlantic Coast Publishing Directory tree

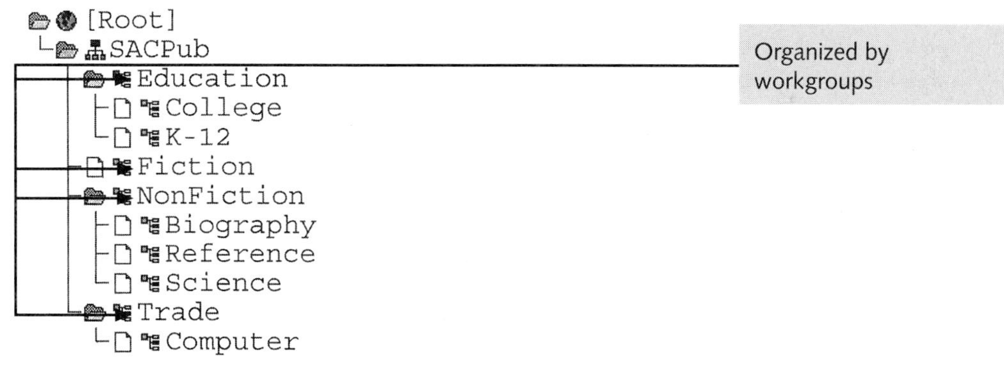

Geographical

Some organizations create their primary organizational structure based on geographic location. In each location, the Directory tree might then reflect a functional or workgroup structure. This is one situation in which you may want to use the Country object, although it is not absolutely necessary. Figures 4-26 and 4-27 show Directory trees for International Metals, a company that produces a variety of metal products in several countries. The Directory tree in Figure 4-26 uses the Country object, whereas the Directory tree in Figure 4-27 uses the Organization object to represent the countries. When using the Country object, you are limited to a standardized two-letter code for that country.

Figure 4-26 The International Metals Directory tree with Country objects

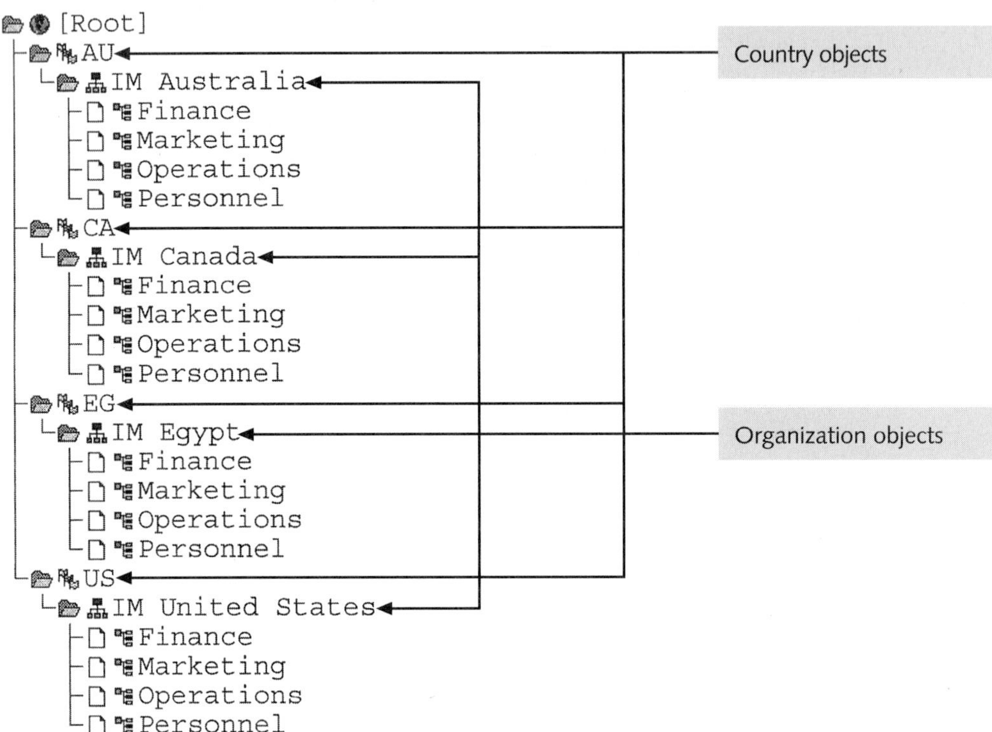

Combinations

In some situations, you might find yourself needing to combine the functional area, workgroup, and geographical approaches. A company organized along functional lines might still have some special workgroups or units in other geographical locations that need to be appropriately represented in the Directory tree. For example, Wilson Manufacturing recently bought a lumber mill in Canada to ensure a steady supply of wood to the company. Although now part of the company (*not* a separate organization), this operation is entirely different from Wilson's main business. The network administrator decided to show the network resources for the Canadian operation using a geographical extension to Wilson's Directory tree, as shown in Figure 4-28.

Figure 4-27
The International Metals Directory tree without Country objects

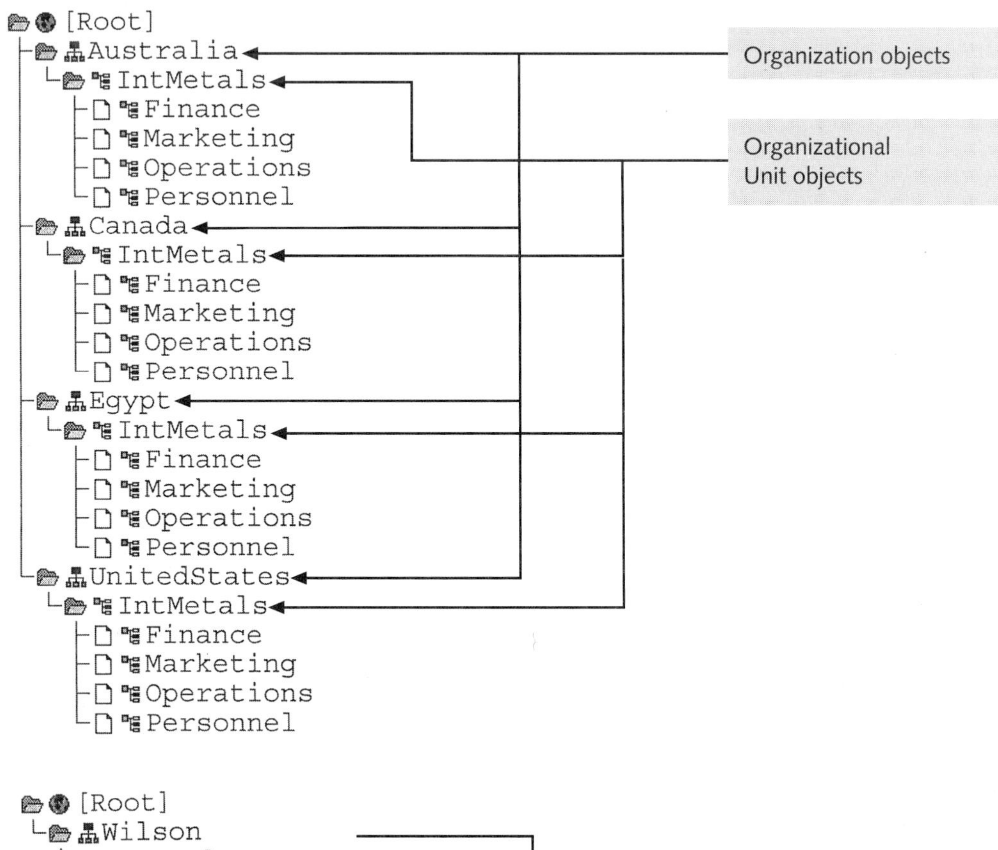

Figure 4-28
The extended Wilson Manufacturing Directory tree

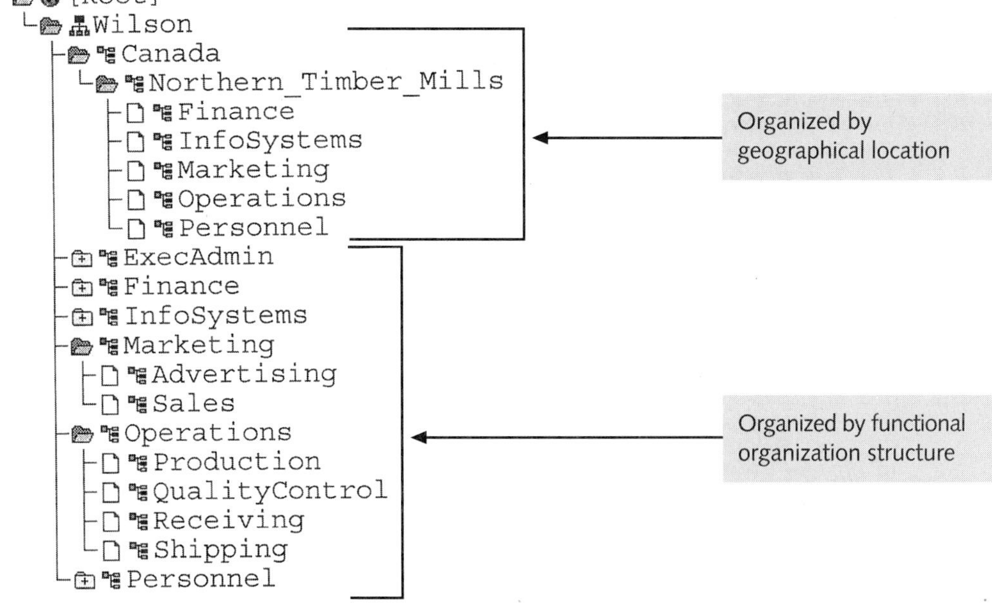

DS Standard NDS Manager

DS Standard NDS Manager 3.0 is a Windows-based NDS management tool designed to be used by network administrators and network managers to help them plan, implement, and manage the NDS environment. Offered by Cheyenne Software, the software package has extensive NDS management capabilities, including the following:

- Off-line Directory tree modeling. DS Standard can develop a model of a Directory tree without changing the existing network Directory tree. Alternatively, DS Standard can model Directory trees on a workstation not connected to the network.
- Discovering and documenting existing network Directory trees. DS Standard enables you to search an existing Directory tree on a network and to bring into DS Standard a copy of the Directory tree and its associated Directory database. Reports about the imported Directory tree can be printed as documentation of the Directory tree.
- Backing up network Directory trees. DS Standard saves all information about the Directory tree as files, which can be used as a backup copy of the Directory tree structure in case the Directory tree on the network becomes corrupted.
- Implementing changes in existing network Directory trees. DS Standard can send back to the network Directory tree modifications made in the DS Standard copy of the Directory tree. This enables changes to the network Directory tree to be made without interfering with the real-time operation of the network. After the changes have been approved, the network Directory tree can then be modified using the changes made in DS Standard.
- Reusing Directory tree designs. DS Standard enables you to export a DS Standard Directory tree structure to disk and to then import it as a new Directory tree with a new name. This renamed copy can then be modified as needed. This allows the network manager to develop alternate Directory tree models during the Directory tree planning process.
- Discovering existing bindery databases on NetWare 2.x and 3.x servers. DS Standard enables you to search an existing bindery database and to bring into DS Standard a copy of the bindery for use in Directory tree modeling. This is useful in planning conversions to NDS.
- Sharing data with Cheyenne Software's AuditWare for NDS software, which has extensive NDS report-generation capabilities. AuditWare is a separate product and is not included with DS Standard.

The Preview edition of DS Standard 3.0 included in this book is a limited version of the software. It provides you with the ability to create models of Directory trees, but does not enable you to create complete reports about your Directory trees. You also cannot use this version of DS Standard to discover all the information in the existing Directory trees or binderies. The Preview edition of DS Standard does give you the full range of DS Standard's Directory tree modeling tool, and you can print a diagram of the complete tree. You will use these modeling tools in the end of chapter case problem in many of the chapters of this book. Specifically, the discovery and object reporting components of the Preview version of DS Standard 3.0 are limited to:

- All alias objects
- 10 User objects
- 1 each of all other object types

Although AuditWare for NDS is a separate product, Cheyenne Software has incorporated part of its reporting capabilities into DS Standard to generate reports on NDS objects in the Directory tree. You will learn how to generate object reports later in this section.

Your instructor has a copy of the DS Standard system requirements and installation requirements. This chapter assumes that DS Standard has been installed on your workstation.

Starting the DS Standard NDS Manager

To illustrate the uses of DS Standard, we'll follow the process of designing a Directory tree model for Cunningham, Burns, and Evans Laboratories. Cunningham, Burns, and Evans Laboratories (CBE Labs) is a small, independent consulting firm that tests computer hardware and software and then reports the results in its publication, *The C/B/E Networker.* We observed CBE Lab's procedure for choosing a new NOS in Chapter 1, and more details about the company are discussed in that chapter. The organization chart for CBE Labs is shown in Figure 4-29.

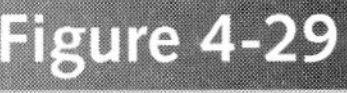

CBE Labs organization chart

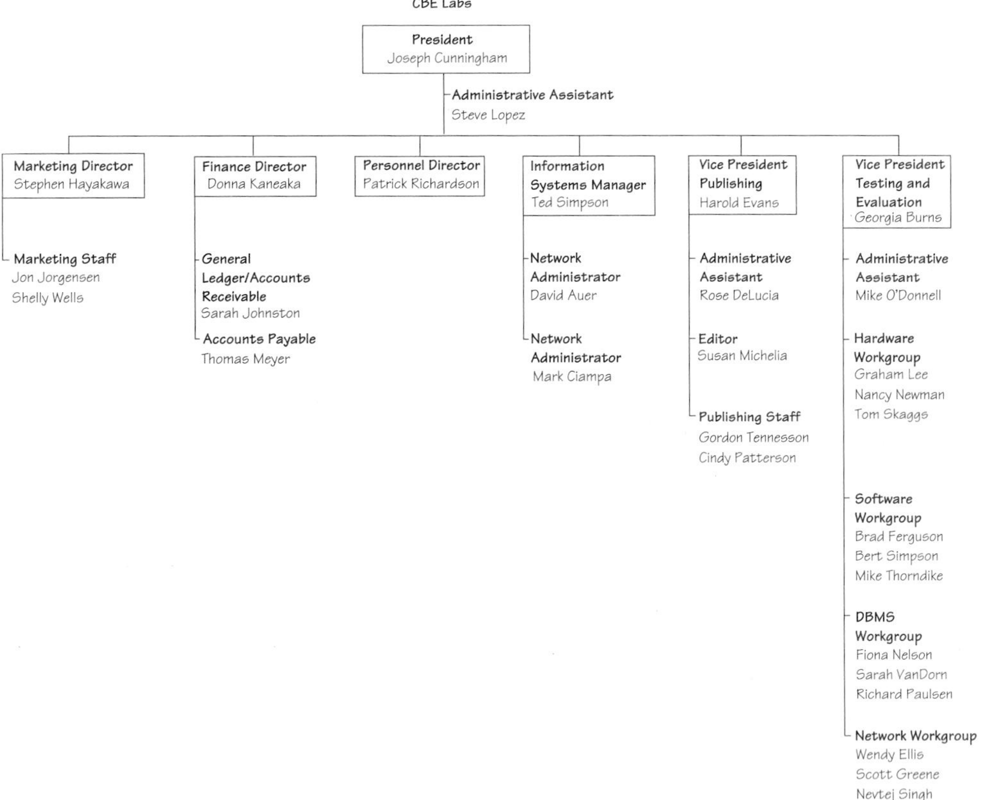

You start the DS Standard NDS Manager the same way you can start any Windows 95 application, by using the Windows 95 Start menu. Version 3.0 of the DS Standard NDS Manager is used in this book.

To start DS Standard:

1. If necessary, boot the PC workstation and launch Windows 95.
2. Click the **Start** button.
3. Click **Programs** to display the Programs menu, click **DS Standard NDS Manager v3** to display the DS Standard NDS Manager 3.0 menu, then click **DS Standard NDS Manager** to open the DS Standard NDS manager. A dialog containing a message that DS Standard is operating in preview mode is displayed.
4. Click **OK** to clear the preview mode warning. The DS Standard NDS Manager window appears as shown in Figure 4-30.

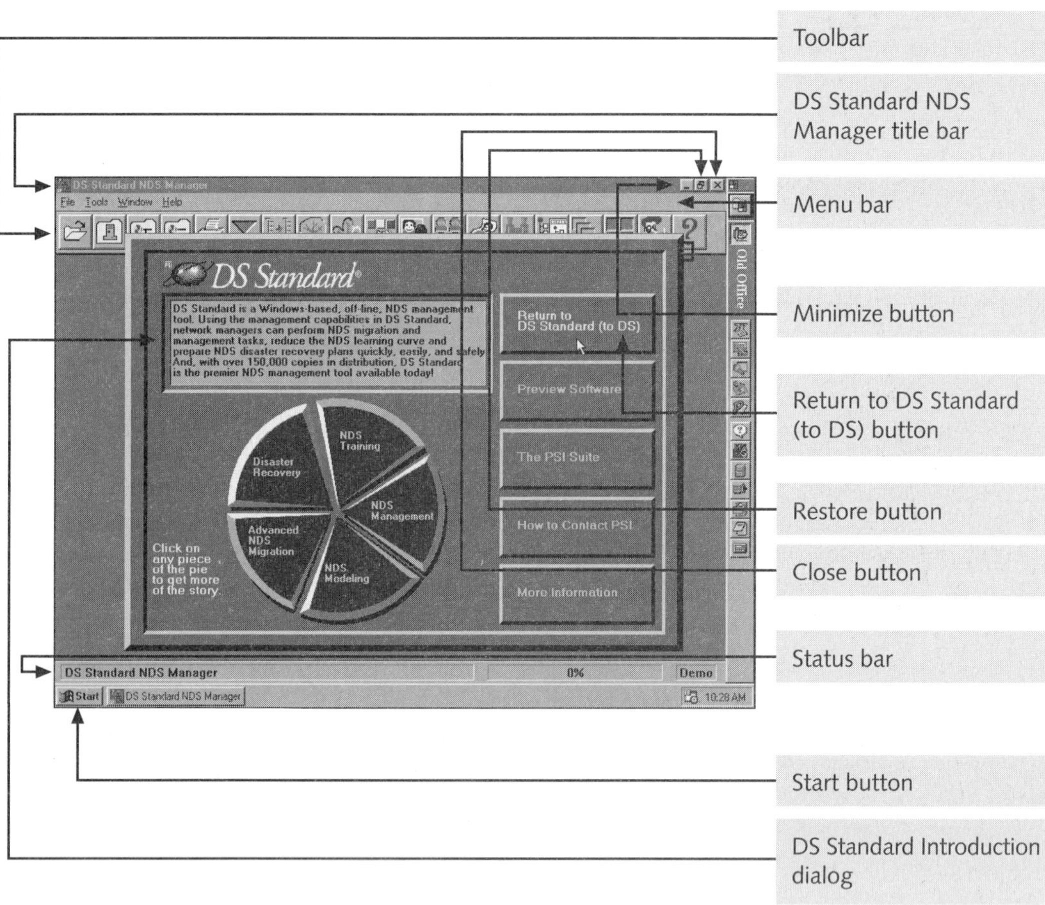

Figure 4-30 The DS Standard NDS Manager window

If your DS Standard application window is not maximized as shown in Figure 4-30, you can maximize it after closing the DS Standard introduction dialog.

The Preview Edition of DS Standard displays a DS Standard introduction dialog which is used to provide information about DS Standard. DS Standard itself displays a Tip of the day dialog each time the application is launched. This feature provides a convenient way for the user to learn about DS Standard features.

5. Click the **Return to DS Standard (to DS)** button to close the introduction dialog.
6. If necessary, click the **Maximize** button on the DS Standard NDS Manager title bar to maximize the DS Standard application window.

As shown in Figure 4-30, the DS Standard NDS Manager window has the common Windows applications components of a title bar, a menu bar, and a toolbar at the top of the window and a status bar at the bottom of the window. The title bar identifies the program and provides minimize, maximize, and close buttons. When the application window is maximized, a restore button replaces the maximize button—the restore button is shown in Figure 4-30 because the application window is maximized.

The menu bar provides a set of drop-down menus that contain various DS Standard commands. Many of these commands will be discussed later in this section. The menu items shown on the menu bar change depending upon what you are doing in DS Standard. Figure 4-30 shows the startup set of menu items, which include File, Tools, Window, and Help. Clicking any of these menu items displays a drop-down menu of DS Standard commands. Three other menu items are displayed on the menu bar:

- Edit: displayed whenever a View window is active
- View: displayed whenever a View window is active
- Project: displayed whenever a Project window is active

View and Project windows are discussed later in this section.

The toolbar gives you an easy way to execute many DS Standard commands; the buttons on the toolbar are discussed in the next section. The status bar displays information about DS Standard's operations. For example, when you point to a button on the toolbar, the function of the toolbar button is displayed on the left side of the status bar.

The DS Standard NDS Manager Toolbar

The DS Standard toolbar and a table listing the toolbar buttons and their functions are shown in Figure 4-31. You do not need to understand the use of each toolbar button—their use will be explained as needed in the following sections.

Figure 4-31
The DS Standard NDS Manager toolbar

Icon	Button	Function
	Open View	Open an existing view. The Select View dialog is displayed.
	Discover Bindery View	Discover a new bindery view. This feature is not available in the Student Edition of DS Standard NDS Manager.
	Discover NDS View	Discover a new NDS view. This feature is not available in the Student Edition of DS Standard NDS Manager.
	Create Empty View	Create a new empty view. The Enter New View Information dialog is displayed.
	Print Directory Tree	Print the Directory tree in the active view.
	Filter Directory Tree	Filter the objects displayed in the active view. The Filter View dialog is displayed.
	Expand Directory Tree	Expand the Directory tree in the active view. All objects in the Directory tree are displayed.
	Select All Objects	Select all objects in the Directory tree.
	Select Leaf Objects	Select all leaf objects in the Directory tree.
	Options	Display the Options dialog.
	Copy Object	Copy the selected object. The object dialog for the object is displayed with the Identification page active.
	Apply Object Template	Apply an object template. The Select Object dialog is displayed.
	Object Profile Report	Generate a report on the selected objects.
	Find and Replace	Find and replace property values for the selected objects. The Find and Replace dialog is displayed.
	Launch AuditWare	Launch AuditWare for NDS
	Cascade Windows	Cascade all open windows.
	Tile Windows	Tile all open windows.
	Assistant	Display the Assistant.
?	Help	Display online help.

DS Standard Views

The first four buttons on the toolbar work with DS Standard Directory tree views. A view is a window that displays a Directory tree. In the Student Edition of DS Standard, you can use the Open View button to open existing views and the Create Empty View button to create a new view. You cannot use the Discover Bindery View button or the Discover NDS View button to display bindery or NDS views—these features are not available in the Student Edition of DS Standard.

To open an existing DS Standard view:

1. Click the **Open View** button. The Open View dialog is displayed, as shown in Figure 4-32.

Figure 4-32 Open View dialog

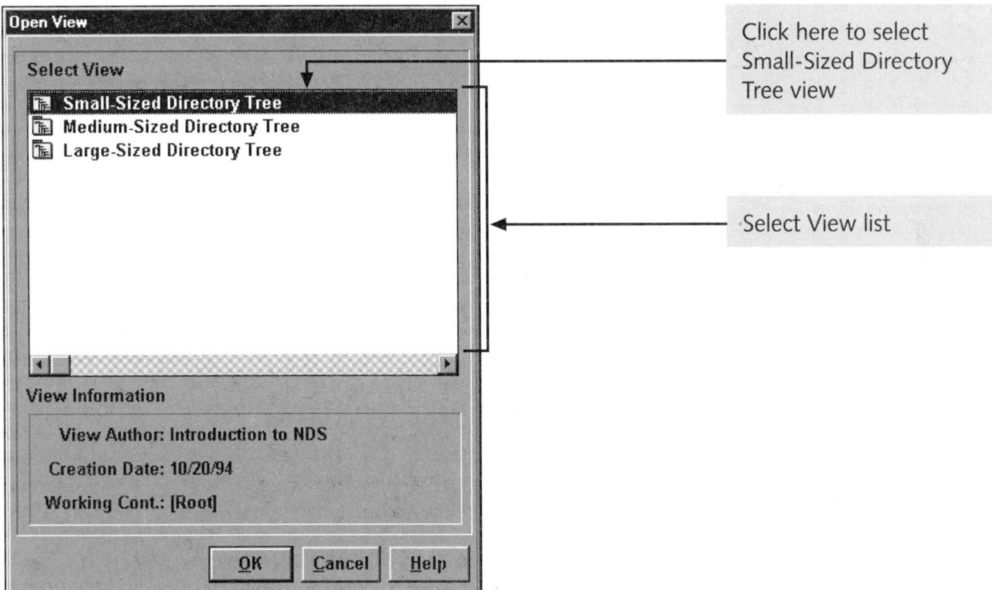

DS Standard provides views of three example Directory trees. The Open View dialog box lists those three views.

2. In the Select View list, click **Small-Sized Directory Tree**, and then click **OK**. The Small-Sized Directory Tree view is displayed with only the [Root] and an Organization object named HQ displayed. This is typical of NetWare Directory tree displays in NetWare utilities—only the first level of the Directory tree is initially shown.
3. Click the **Expand Directory tree** button to display the entire Directory tree, as shown in Figure 4-33.

Figure 4-33 The Small-Sized Directory Tree view

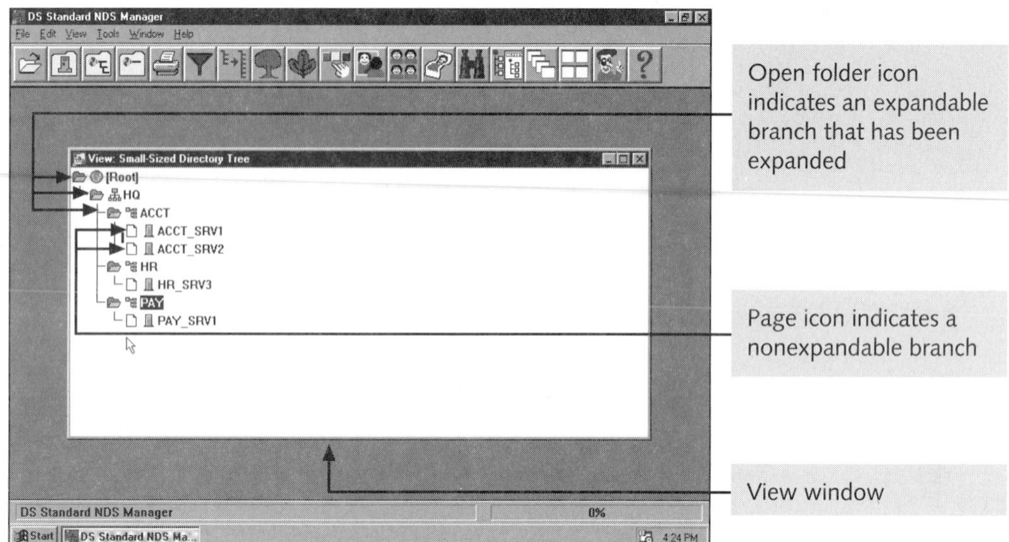

You should be familiar with the term *dialog box*, which refers to the screen displays Windows 95 uses to allow you to enter information for use by a program. Novell uses the term *dialog* as a short form of *dialog box* in NetWare documentation, and DS Standard follows the Novell convention. Thus, in step 1 above, the *Open View dialog* is displayed rather than the *Open View dialog box*. This book will also follow the Novell convention and use *dialog* instead of *dialog box*, but you should remember that the two terms refer to the same Windows 95 feature.

The Small-Sized Directory Tree view shows the elements of Directory trees as displayed by DS Standard. DS Standard Directory trees use the same icons as NetWare Directory trees to represent the NDS objects in Directory tree. For example, in Figure 4-33 the HQ Organization object, the ACCT Organizational Unit object, and the ACCT_SRV1 NetWare Server object are identifiable by their standard NDS icons. However, as explained early in this chapter, DS Standard adds a set of three icons not used to display NDS Directory trees in NetWare utilities: the open folder , which indicates an expanded branch, the closed folder , which indicates a branch that can be expanded, and the page , which indicates a nonexpandable branch.

Because the Small-Sized Directory Tree in Figure 4-33 is displayed with only open folder icons and page icons , all expandable branches are fully expanded. To collapse an expandable branch, you double-click on the open folder icon of the branch you want to collapse. Collapsing a branch hides all the objects on that branch. To expand a branch, you double-click on the closed folder icon of the branch you want to expand. You can use the Expand Directory Tree button on the toolbar to expand all expandable branches so that the entire Directory tree is displayed.

You can close an open view window by clicking the Windows 95 window Close button . You can also use the Close View command on the File menu. This command does not appear on the File menu unless a View window is open.

In order to model the CBE Labs Directory tree, a new view needs to be created. You do this by using the Create Empty View button on the toolbar.

To create a new DS Standard view for CBE Labs:

1. Click the **Create Empty View** button . The Enter New View Information dialog, shown in Figure 4-34, is displayed without the data in the text boxes.
2. In the View Name text box, type **CBE Labs**.
3. Click the **Author** text box to make it active, then type the user's name, which in this case is **David Auer**. The completed Enter New View Information dialog is shown in Figure 4-34.

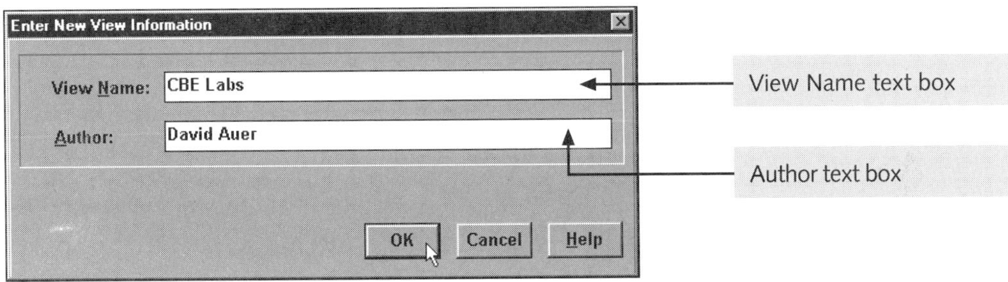

Figure 4-34 The Enter New View Information dialog

4. Click **OK**. The CBE Labs view is created and the View: CBE Labs window is displayed. As shown in Figure 4-35, the view is empty except for the [Root] object. Notice that the Edit and View menu items now appear on the Menu bar.

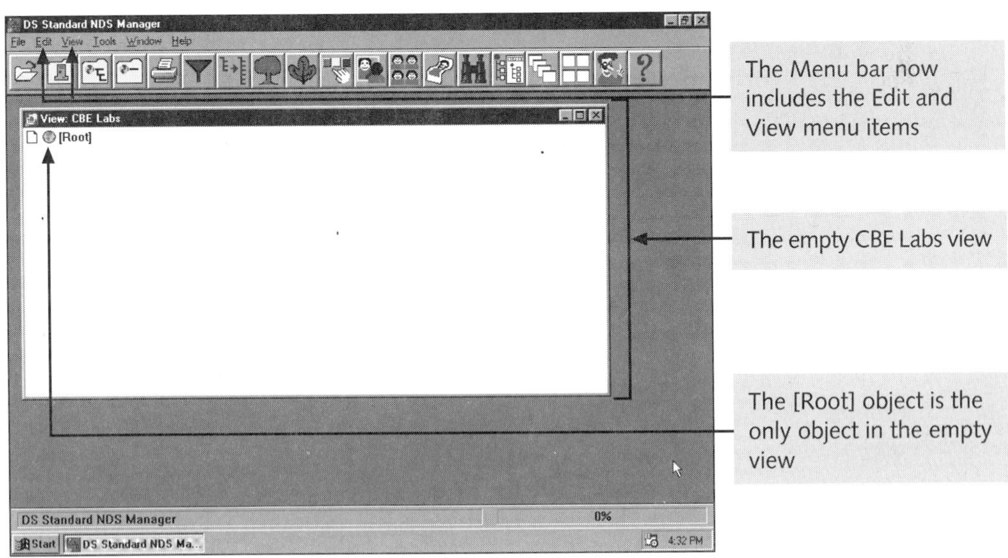

Figure 4-35 The View: CBE Labs window

5. Click the **Close** button on the CBE Labs view to close the view.

Views can be deleted by using the Delete View command on the File Menu. When you use this command, the Delete View dialog is displayed to allow you to specify which view will be deleted. After you select the view to be deleted and click OK to proceed, a Delete View dialog is used to confirm the deletion. A deleted view *cannot* be recovered.

DS Standard Projects

DS Standard uses projects to manage views. A project is a grouping of related views, together with identifying data and comments. You use commands on the File menu to create, open, and delete projects. There are no toolbar buttons to access projects. For example, the CBE Labs Directory tree that is being developed may have two or three alternative designs before the final structure is chosen. To allow for this, the CBE Labs network administrator has decided to create a DS Standard project named CBE Labs Directory Tree Model.

To create the CBE Labs Directory Tree Model project:

1. Click **File** and then click **New Project**. The Enter Project Information dialog, shown in Figure 4-36, is displayed without data in the text boxes.
2. In the Project Name text box, type **CBE Labs Directory Tree Models**.
3. Click the **Company Name** text box to make it active; then type **CBE Laboratories**.
4. Click the **Author** text box to make it active; then type the author's name, which in this case is **David Auer**.
5. Click the **Comment** text box to select it; then type **Alternative models for the CBE Labs Directory tree**. The completed Enter Project Information dialog is shown in Figure 4-36.

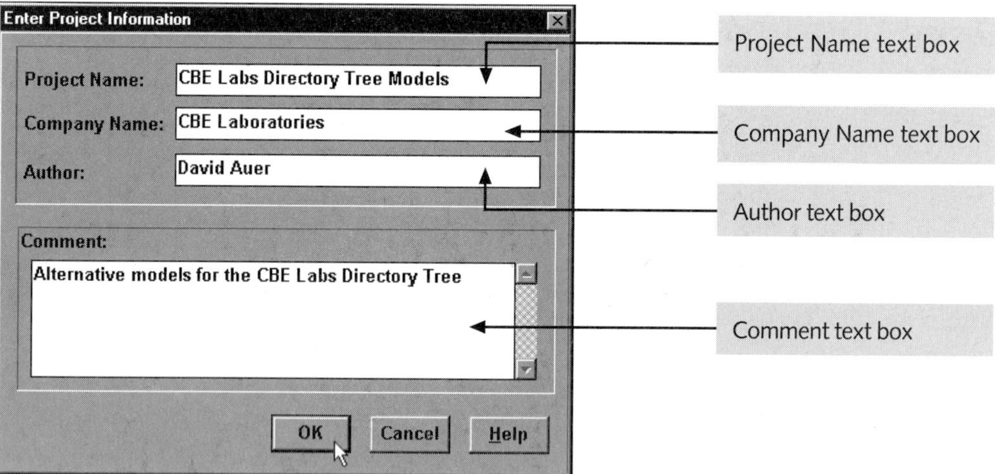

Figure 4-36 The Enter Project Information dialog

6. Click **OK**. The Project: CBE Labs Directory Tree Model window, shown in Figure 4-37, is displayed without any views in the View Name list. The Project menu item now appears on the Menu bar.

7. Press the **[Insert]** key (or click Project on the Menu bar and then click the AddView command). The AddView to Project dialog is displayed. In the Select View list, click **CBE Labs**, and then click **OK**. The CBE Labs view is added to the View Name list in the Project: CBE Labs Directory Tree Models window project dialog, as shown in Figure 4-37.

Figure 4-37 The CBE Labs Directory Tree Models project window

8. Click the **Close** button on the CBE Labs Directory Tree Model project dialog to close the dialog.

The CBE Labs view can now be easily accessed from the CBE Labs Directory Tree Model project.

DS Standard On-Line Help

DS Standard provides an extensive on-line help system, which can be opened by clicking the Help button on the toolbar. As shown in Figure 4-38, when the on-line help system is opened, both a standard Windows 95 Help window and a special browser called the Navigator are displayed. The Navigator can also be opened by clicking the Navigator button on the On-Line Help window toolbar if the Navigator window has been closed.

Figure 4-38 The DS Standard Online Help window

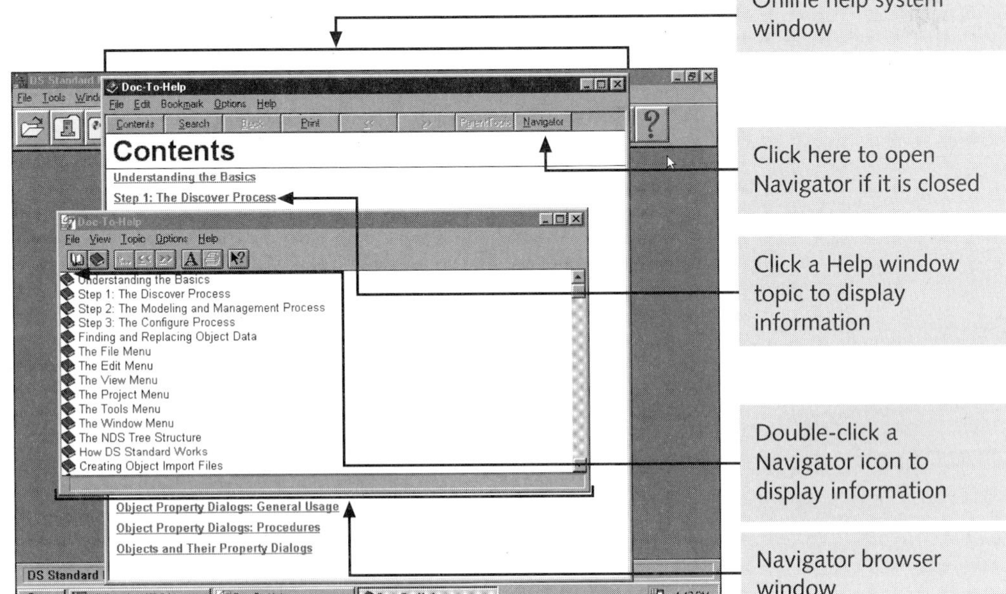

The Navigator displays the entire help system in an expanded outline format and is useful for quickly locating help topics. Selecting a topic in the Navigator results in the associated on-line help page being displayed in the On-Line help window. The Navigator is set to always stay on top of other windows, which can cause it to obscure material in the On-Line Help window. You will want to minimize the Navigator when you are not using it to locate a topic.

The on-line help system contains most of the material found in the DS Standard manual and is an excellent reference. It is well worth studying the on-line help material just as you would study any software manual. Screen shots are included, along with step-by-step directions on how to accomplish tasks in DS Standard.

The DS Standard Assistant

In addition to the on-line help system, DS Standard provides additional reference material in the Assistant. The Assistant contains material supplied by Novell, including an NDS Implementation Guide, articles from Novell's *Application Notes*, and other supplemental material.

Novell's *Application Notes* are published monthly. They contain articles about NetWare and are an excellent source for accurate and up-to-date information about NetWare. For example, an article in *Application Notes* discussed the Client 32 software before it was released to the public. A network administrator who had read the article had a good idea of how the software would operate when it was released and was therefore prepared to work with the software as soon as it became available. Information about *Application Notes* is available from Novell's World Wide Web site at http://www.novell.com.

The Assistant can be opened by clicking the Display the Assistant button on the toolbar. The Assistant is displayed in a standard Windows help window, and a Navigator window is also displayed. The Assistant contains material that discusses real-world implementations of NDS, as well as material from NetWare manuals. You will find much useful information in this material. You should, however, check which version of NetWare is being discussed in each source. For example, some of the NetWare manual material used in the Assistant comes from NetWare 4.02 manuals and should be verified before being used on a NetWare 4.1 network.

Setting DS Standard Options

DS Standard is preconfigured with many option settings when it is installed. Generally, these settings need no changing, but in some cases they do. You can change the option settings by clicking the Options button on the Toolbar or using the Options command on the Tools menu.

For example, DS Standard allows the user to set **tree metrics**, which include the following:

- The maximum common name length for each type of object (default = 15 characters)
- The maximum number of levels in a Directory tree (default = 6)

- The maximum number of container objects in a container object (default = 100)
- The maximum number of objects in a container object (default = 1000)
- The maximum distinguished name length (default = 127 characters)

You should set the metrics to be consistent with the network standards that you set for your network. For example, the CBE Labs Information Systems Manager set a maximum common name length standard of 47 characters for all objects in the CBE Labs Directory tree. This value needs to be set in DS Standard so that DS Standard will accept common names longer than 15 characters when the Directory tree is verified.

Another change needs to be made to the report settings. When CBE Labs prints reports, the network administrator wants to use the view name as the main title, called the report banner, instead of the DS Standard default of the name of the person who installed DS Standard.

To set the DS Standard options:

1. Click the **Options** button on the toolbar. The Options dialog is displayed.
2. Click the **Verify** button to display the Verify Settings page, as shown in Figure 4-39.

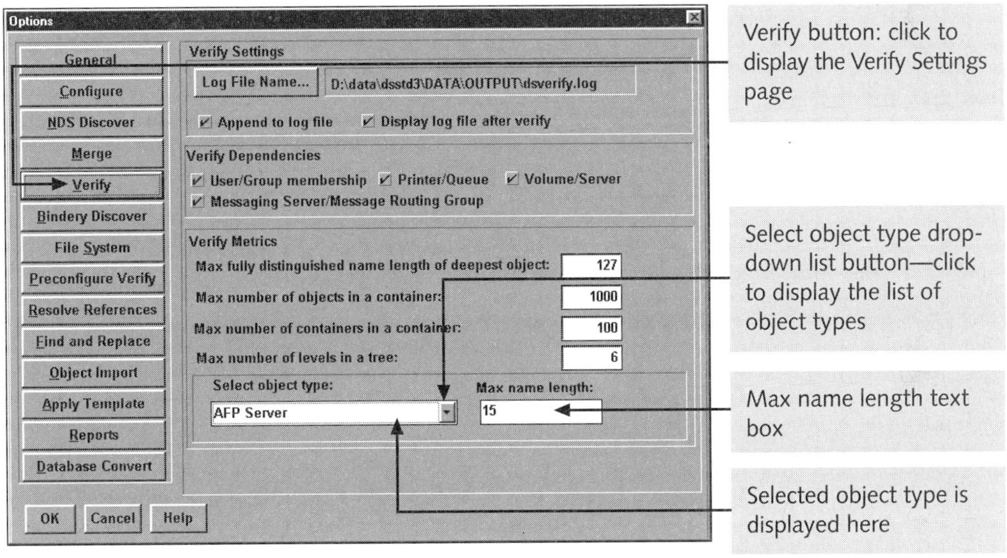

Figure 4-39 The Verify Settings page in the Options dialog

3. The AFP Server object is already selected in the Select object type drop-down list. Click the **Max name length** text box to activate it and then change the number from 15 to **47**.
4. Click the **Select object type** drop-down arrow to display the Select object type drop-down list. Click the next object type in the list, which is **Alias**, to select it. Click the **Max name length** text box to make it active and then change the number from 15 to **47**.
5. Repeat step 4 for each of the object types in the object type drop-down list.
6. Click the **Reports** button to display the Report Settings page.

7. Click the **Report Banner** drop-down list button and then click **@ViewName** to change the report banner heading to the view name, as shown in Figure 4-40.

Figure 4-40

The Report Settings page in the Options dialog

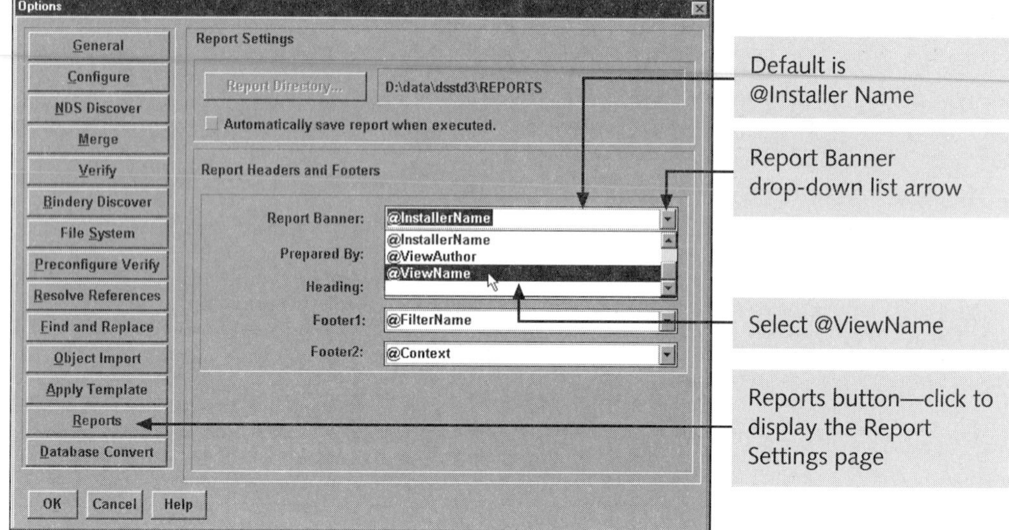

8. Click **OK** to close the Options dialog.

Although NDS does not use the Locality object in NetWare 4.1, DS Standard supports two variations of the Locality object: Locality and Locality State. Both these object types appear in the object type drop-down list in the Options dialog. You should set their maximum length to the same as the other object types for consistency.

BUILDING A DIRECTORY TREE MODEL

Now the CBE Labs Directory tree model can be created. After discussions between the CBE Labs information systems manager and the CBE Labs network administrators, a combination Directory tree structure has been selected for the CBE Labs Directory tree. The Directory tree will reflect the CBE Labs workgroup-oriented organization chart, while at the same time using traditional business function divisions within the administration workgroup. Using this structure, the CBE Labs' organization chart shown in Figure 4-29 should provide the basis for building the Directory tree model. DS Standard enables you to add objects through menu bar menu commands and shortcut menu commands. Both methods will be illustrated in the following examples.

Adding Container Objects

Construction of the Directory tree model begins with the creation of the container objects in the model. The container objects for CBE Labs are listed in Figure 4-41.

Figure 4-41

The CBE Labs Directory tree container objects

Object Type	Object Name	Branch Of
Organization	CBE_Labs	[Root]
Organizational Unit	CBE_Labs_Admin	CBE_Labs
Organizational Unit	Pubs	CBE_Labs
Organizational Unit	Test&Eval	CBE_Labs
Organizational Unit	Marketing	CBE_Labs_Admin
Organizational Unit	Finance	CBE_Labs_Admin
Organizational Unit	Personnel	CBE_Labs_Admin
Organizational Unit	InfoSystems	CBE_Labs_Admin
Organizational Unit	Hardware	Test&Eval
Organizational Unit	Software	Test&Eval
Organizational Unit	DBMS	Test&Eval
Organizational Unit	Network	Test&Eval

The first object to be added to the Directory tree will be the CBE_Labs Organization object.

To create the CBE Labs Organization object:

1. Click the **Open View** button. The Open View dialog is displayed.
2. In the Open View dialog, click **CBE Labs**, and then click **OK**. The View: CBE_Labs window is displayed.
3. Click the **Maximize** button in the View: CBE_Labs window title bar to maximize the view window.
4. Click the **[Root]** object to select it, click **Edit** on the menu bar, click **Add Object**, and then click **Organization**, as shown in Figure 4-42.

Figure 4-42

Adding a Directory tree object using the Edit menu

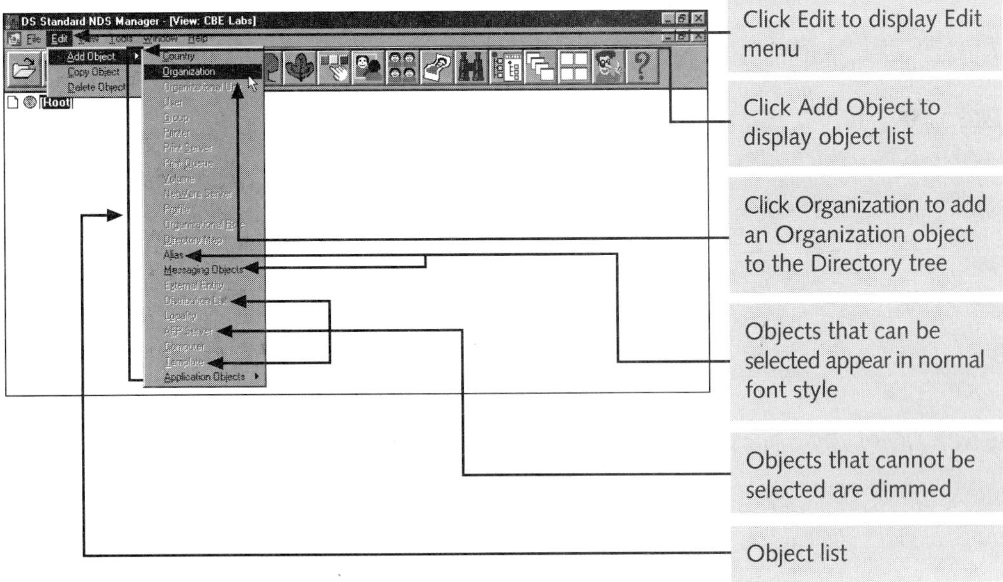
DS Standard NDS Manager - [View: CBE Labs]
Add Object
Copy Object
Delete Object
Country
Organization
Alias
Messaging Objects
Application Objects
[Root]
Click Edit to display Edit menu
Click Add Object to display object list
Click Organization to add an Organization object to the Directory tree
Objects that can be selected appear in normal font style
Objects that cannot be selected are dimmed
Object list

5. The Organization object dialog is displayed, as shown in Figure 4-43.

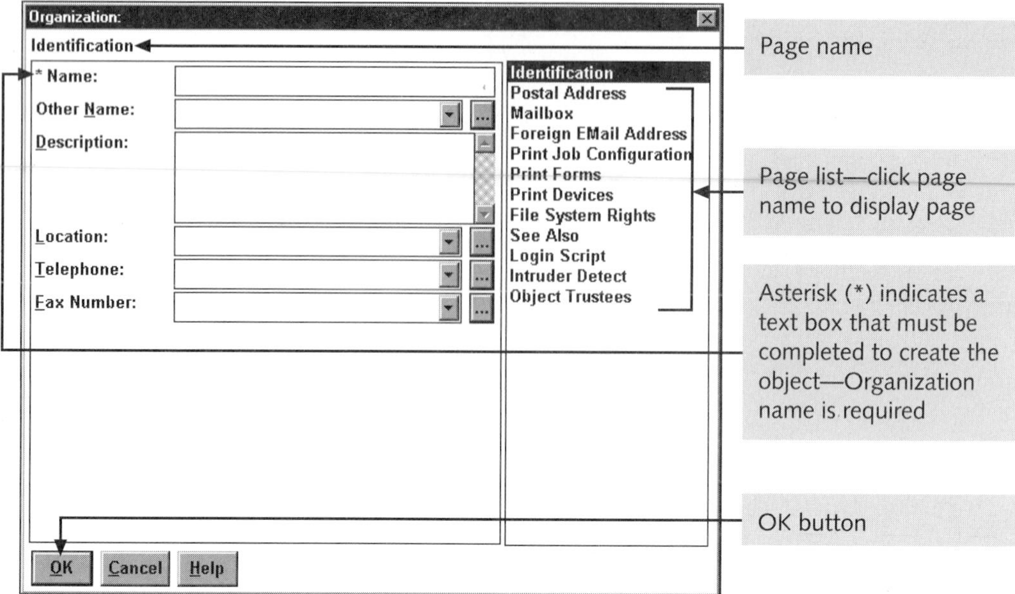

Figure 4-43 The Organization object dialog

6. Notice that the name text box has an asterisk (*) next to it. This indicates that you must enter a value into this text box in order to create the object. Type **CBE_Labs** in the text box.
7. Click **OK**. The CBE_Labs Organization object is added to the Directory tree.

Now the Organizational Unit objects can be added to the Directory tree. The next container object to be added to the Directory tree will be the CBE_Labs_Admin Organizational Unit object; then the rest of the Organizational Unit objects will be created.

To create the Organizational Unit objects:

1. Right-click the **CBE_Labs Organization object** to display the menu, click **Add Object**, and then click **Organizational Unit**, as shown in Figure 4-44.

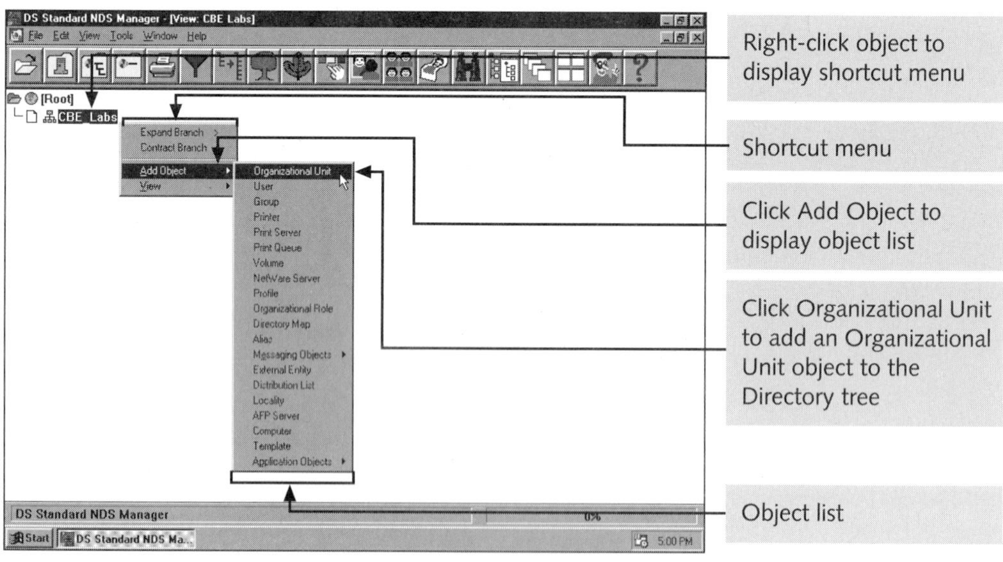

Figure 4-44 Adding a Directory tree object using the shortcut menu

2. The Organizational Unit object dialog, which has the same basic appearance as the Organization object dialog shown in Figure 4-43, is displayed.
3. Again, the name text box has an asterisk (*) next to it. You must enter a value into this text box in order to create the object. Type **CBE_Labs_Admin** in the text box.
4. Click **OK**. The CBE_Labs_Admin Organization object is added to the Directory tree.
5. Repeat steps 1 through 4, modifying them as necessary to create the other Organizational Unit objects for the CBE Labs Directory tree. When all the Organizational Units have been added, the Directory tree appears as shown in Figure 4-45.

Figure 4-45 The container objects in the CBE Labs Directory tree

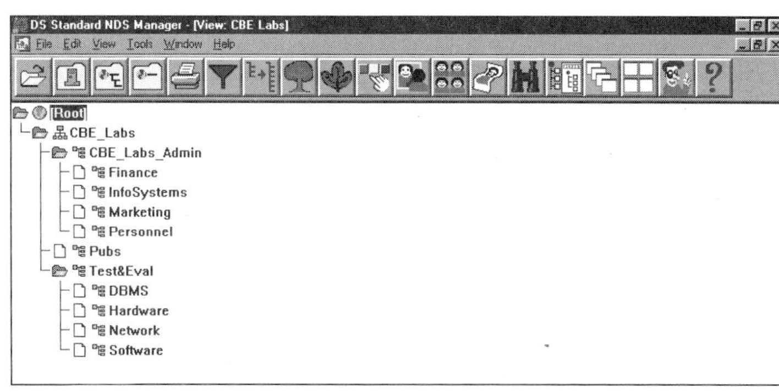

Adding Leaf Objects

Once the structure of the Directory tree is established by creating the container objects, the leaf objects must be added. However, DS Standard does not support all the NDS objects that NetWare supports—it does not support the Bindery, Bindery Queue, and Unknown objects. This selection makes sense because these objects cannot be created manually.

The process of creating the various leaf objects is similar to creating container objects. We will look at three examples of leaf object creation: creating a User object, a NetWare Server object, and a Volume object. Once you are familiar with these objects, you will have no trouble creating the other leaf objects yourself.

The first user to be added to the CBE Labs Directory tree will be the Admin user, representing the User object that NetWare 4.1 creates during the installation process. Although this User object can be placed anywhere in the Directory tree structure, the Admin User object is usually located near the [Root] of the tree. In this case, we will place the Admin object in the CBE_Labs Organization container.

To create the Admin User object:

1. Right-click the **CBE_Labs Organization object** to display the quick menu, click **Add Object**, and then click **User**. The User object dialog is displayed, as shown in Figure 4-46.

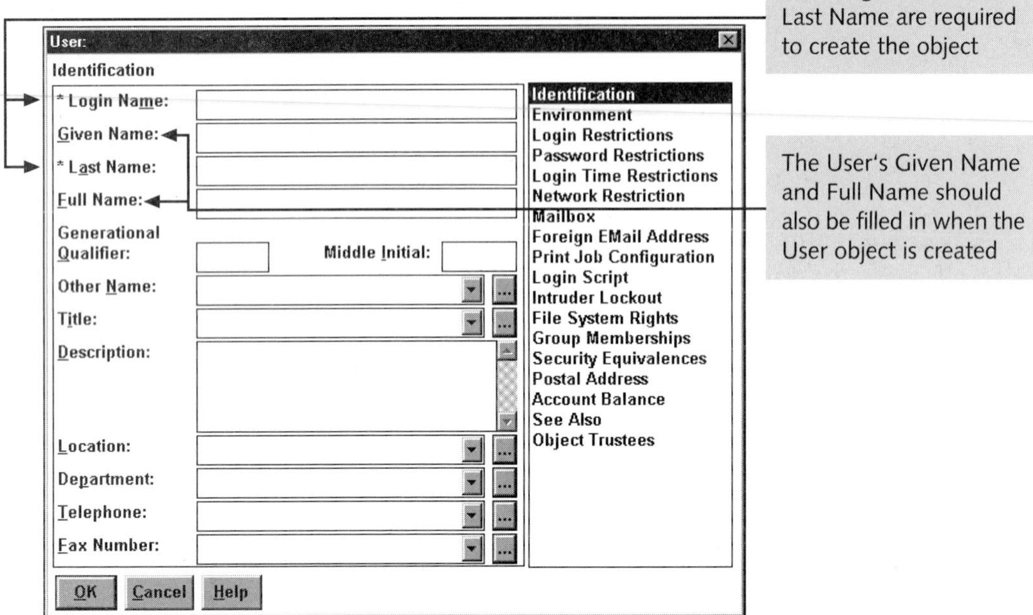

Figure 4-46 The User object dialog box

2. Notice that there are two text boxes that have an asterisk (*) next to them: Login Name and Last Name. You must enter a value in both these text boxes in order to create the object. Type **Admin** in the Login Name text box.
3. Click the **Last Name** text box to activate it. Type **Admin** in the Last Name text box.
4. Click **OK**. The Admin User object is added to the Directory tree.

CBE Labs will use three NetWare servers, named Server01, Server02, and Server03. The first two NetWare servers will use NetWare 4.1, and the third NetWare server will run NetWare 3.12. Server01 and Server02 each have three volumes—SYS, DATA, and CDROM—but Server03 has only a SYS volume.

The CBE Labs NetWare server named Server01 will be used by all the personnel at CBE Labs. For this reason, it is placed high in the Directory tree, in the CBE_Labs Organization object. The system volume for Server01, referred to as the SYS volume and with a common name of Server01_SYS, will also be accessed by all personnel. The Volume object for the volume Server01_SYS will be located with the Server01 object in the CBE_Labs Organization container.

To create the Server01 NetWare Server object:

1. Right-click the **CBE_Labs Organization object** to display the quick menu, then click **Add Object**, and then click **NetWare Server**. The NetWare Server object dialog is similar to the other object dialogs already discussed and requires only a name in the Name text box. Type **Server01** in the Name text box.
2. Click **OK**. The Server01 NetWare Server object is added to the Directory tree.

DS Standard often refers to NetWare servers as NCP servers. NCP stands for NetWare Core Protocol, which refers to the NetWare NOS running on the NetWare server. The two terms mean the same thing, and older Novell literature also uses the term NCP server.

Now the Volume object can be created.

To create the Server01_SYS Volume object:

1. Right-click the **CBE_Labs Organization** object to display the quick menu and then click **Volume.** The Volume object dialog, shown in Figure 4-48, is displayed without data in the text boxes.

   The Volume object dialog shows how an NDS object can have a required connection to anther NDS object. A volume must be linked to the NetWare Server that it is in. So in the Volume object dialog, you must enter a volume common name in the Name text box, the volume's short name in the Host Volume text box, and a NetWare Server name in the Host Server text box.

2. Type **Server01_SYS** in the Name text box.
3. Click the **Host Volume** text box to activate it; then type **SYS**.
4. To specify the host server, click the **More** button [...] to the right of the Host Server text box. The Select Object dialog is displayed with the Directory tree contracted.
5. Click the **Expand Children** button [>] to display the next level of the Directory tree, as shown in Figure 4-47.

Figure 4-47 The Select Object dialog

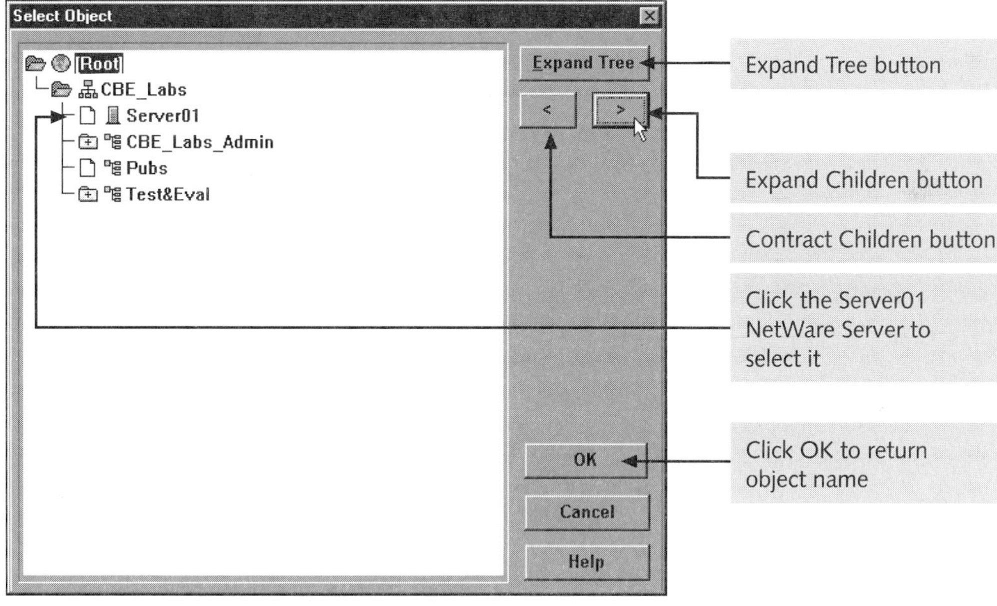

In a Directory tree, the container tree levels below a designated or selected container are called the **children** of that container, and the designated or selected container object is called the **parent**. These terms are relative—the container above a container is its parent and the container object below it are its children.

The Expand Children button [>] displays the next level of the Directory tree for the selected container. Each time it is used, another level of the Directory tree is displayed. The Contract Children button [<] has the opposite effect, hiding the lowest level of the Directory tree each time it is used. The Expand Tree button [Expand Tree] displays the entire tree. These buttons are useful for locating objects in the Directory tree that you want to select.

6. Click the **Server01 NetWare Server** object to select it and then click **OK**. The Volume object dialog is redisplayed with the typed name CN=Server01.O =CBE_Labs in the Host Server text box, as shown in Figure 4-48.

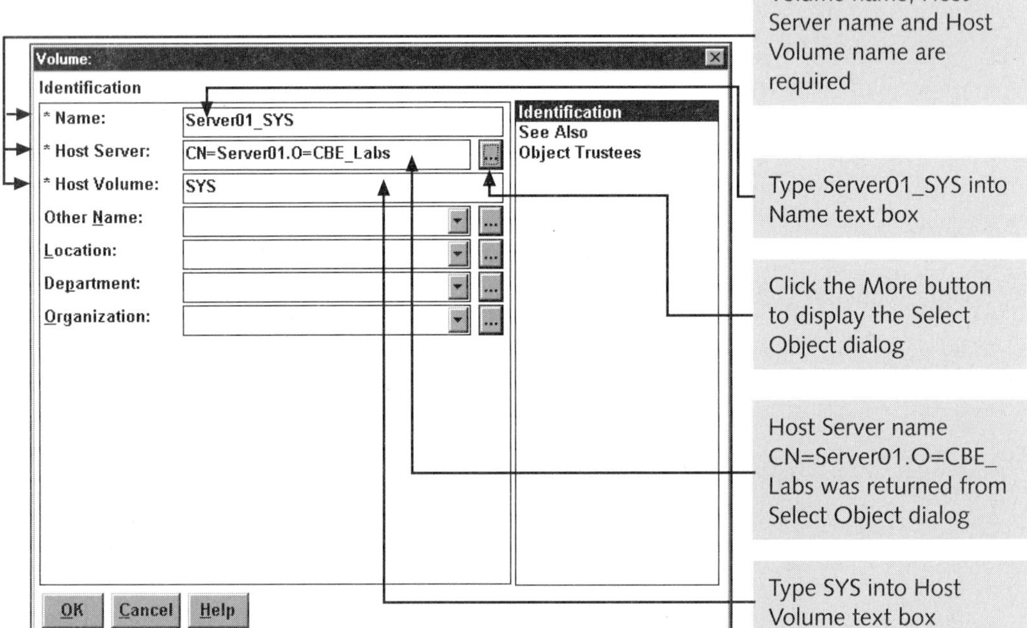
Volume:
Identification
* Name:
Server01_SYS
* Host Server:
CN=Server01.O=CBE_Labs
* Host Volume:
SYS
Other Name:
Location:
Department:
Organization:
Identification
See Also
Object Trustees
OK
Cancel
Help
Volume name, Host Server name and Host Volume name are required
Type Server01_SYS into Name text box
Click the More button to display the Select Object dialog
Host Server name CN=Server01.O=CBE_ Labs was returned from Select Object dialog
Type SYS into Host Volume text box

Figure 4-48 The Volume object dialog

7. Click **OK**. The Server01_SYS Volume object is added to the Directory tree.

Server01 has three volumes. In addition to the Server01_SYS volume, there is a DATA volume that will be represented by a Server01_DATA Volume object. There is also a CD-ROM drive, and a CD-ROM in that drive is treated as a volume on the NetWare server. A Server01_CDROM volume will be used in the CBE Labs Directory tree model to represent the CD-ROM drive. These Volume objects are now added to the Directory tree model, followed by the Volume objects for Server02 and Server03 (if you are working through this example on a computer, you should add these objects now).

Renaming Objects

When developing the structure of the Directory tree, it may become necessary to change the name of an object. This is not unusual during a creative process, when your ideas of what you want to create are modified by new insights or problems produced by early steps in the development process. It can also happen because of management decisions during the development of the Directory tree. For example, CBE Labs' president Joseph Cunningham served as an officer in the U.S. Navy and has requested that CBE Labs' NetWare servers be named after U.S. Navy aircraft carriers. Server01 is to be renamed CONSTELLATION after the

U.S.S. Constellation, Server02 is to become SARATOGA after the *U.S.S. Saratoga*, and Server03 is to be renamed RANGER after the *U.S.S. Ranger*. This will also require that the Volume objects associated with the servers be renamed.

To rename the NetWare Server object:

1. Double-click the **Server01 NetWare Server** object to display the NetWare Server object dialog.
2. In the **Name** text box, edit the current name to read **CONSTELLATION**.
3. Click **OK**. The Server01 NetWare Server object is renamed CONSTELLATION, and this name now appears in the Directory tree.

Changing the NetWare Server object name does not automatically change the Volume object names. So now the Volume objects will need to be renamed: Server01_SYS will become CONSTELLATION_SYS, Server01_DATA will become CONSTELLATION_DATA, and Server01_CDROM will become CONSTELLATION_CDROM. The other NetWare servers and their volumes will be similarly renamed (if you are working through this example on a computer, you should add these objects now).

After renaming the Volume objects, the CBE Labs network administrator will continue to build the CBE Labs Directory tree model by adding users, groups, organizational roles, profiles, printers, print queues, and print servers as necessary to complete the Directory tree design. A portion of the completed Directory tree is shown in Figure 4-49.

Deleting Projects, Views, and Objects

Developing a Directory tree is a process—you can expect that your initial ideas will change as you actually design the Directory tree. This may make it necessary to rename objects as discussed above or require you to delete an object, a view, or even a project. DS Standard allows you to delete projects, views, and objects as necessary, but you cannot recover them after they have been deleted. Deletion options are shown in Figure 4-49.

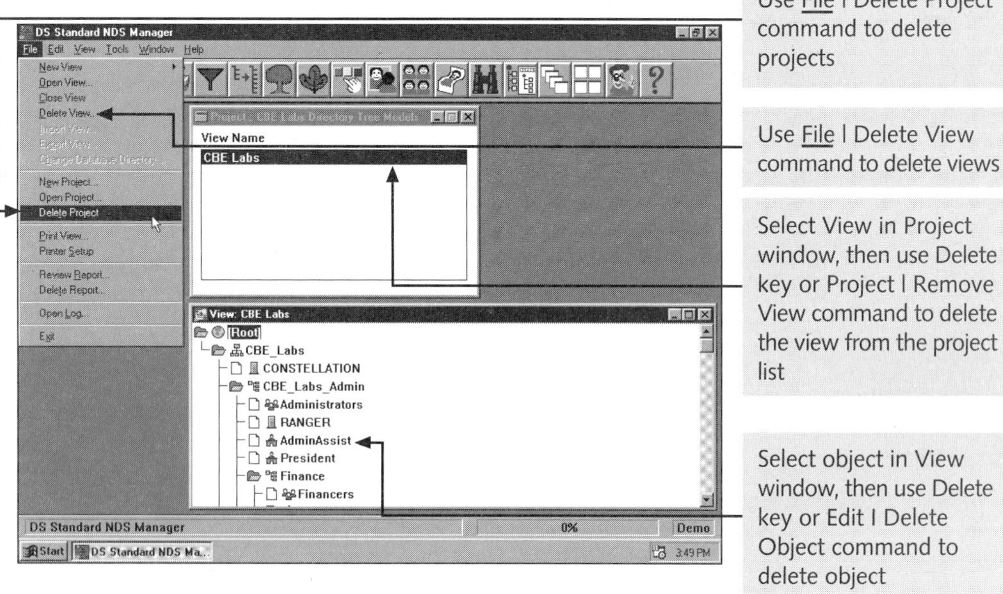

Figure 4-49 Deleting projects, views, and objects

To delete a project, you use the Delete Project command on the File menu. The project you want to delete cannot be open—only closed projects can be deleted. When you select this command, DS Standard displays the Delete Project dialog with a list of projects displayed. You then select the project you want to delete and click OK. A Delete View (not Delete *Project*) dialog is then displayed with the message "Are you sure you wish to delete project *ProjectName*? This operation cannot be undone later." Click the Yes button to confirm the deletion of the project. A Delete Project dialog with the message "Project *ProjectName* deleted" is displayed. Click OK to acknowledge the message. Deleting a project does not delete the views in the project—they remain in the DS Standard database.

Deleting a view is similar, except that you use the Delete | View command on the Edit menu. The view you want to delete cannot be open, and when you select this command, DS Standard displays the Delete View dialog with a list of views displayed. Select the view you want to delete and then click OK. A second, different Delete View dialog is then displayed with the message "Are you sure you wish to delete view *ViewName*? This operation cannot be undone later." Clicking the Yes button confirms the deletion of the view.

If you just want to remove a view from a project, click the view name to select it in the View list and then press the [Delete] key or use the Remove View command on the Project menu. The Project Information dialog is displayed with the message "Are you sure you wish to delete the view *ViewName* from the project list?" Click the Yes button to delete the view.

To delete an object, click the object in the Directory tree to select it and then press the [Delete] key (alternatively, you can select the Delete Object command on the Edit menu). An unnamed dialog is displayed with the message "Are you sure you wish to delete *ObjectType ObjectName*?" There is no warning that this operation cannot be undone. Clicking the Yes button confirms the deletion of the object, and the object is removed from the Directory tree. There is no message acknowledging that the object has been deleted—it is simply removed from the Directory tree.

Although the Student edition of DS Standard cannot interact with on-line NDS Directory trees, the commercial version can and does. It is important to understand that deleting an object in a DS Standard model does not delete the object in the corresponding on-line NDS Directory tree.

Resolving References for the Directory Tree

Once the Directory tree model is completed, you can have DS Standard test the object references and links to be sure that they are correct. An object reference or object link is a connection between two objects. For example, the CONSTELLATION_SYS Volume object contains a reference to the NetWare Server object CONSTELLATION because CONSTELLATION is the host server for the volume. You can see this reference illustrated in Figure 4-48 in the Host Server text box, which shows the reference when the NetWare Server object was still named Server01.

Checking for correct object references is an important step in verifying your Directory Tree design. It is especially important if you have made changes to your Directory tree, such as moving an object into a different container. For example, if the NetWare Server object CONSTELLATION had been moved into the CBE_Labs_Admin organizational unit, you should also have moved all the Volume objects associated with CONSTELLATION into the same container. If you didn't, the Volume object references to the host server will need to be corrected.

In the Preview edition of DS Standard 3.0 included in this book, this feature is limited to working with the reduced object set discussed earlier.

You can start the verification process by using the Resolve Reference for Selected Objects command on the View menu. A report is generated and displayed on screen in a report viewer. The report can be printed from the viewer and is also stored in a log file for later use.

To check object references for CBE Labs Directory tree:

1. Click the **Select All Objects** button on the toolbar. All objects in the Directory Tree are highlighted to show that they have been selected.
2. Click **View** on the menu bar and then click **Resolve References for Selected Objects**. The Confirm Resolve References dialog is displayed to confirm the verification process. Click **OK**.
3. A report is generated and displayed in the PSI viewer window. Scroll to the end of the report to see if any warnings or errors were found. As shown in Figure 4-50, no warnings or errors were found in the CBE Labs Directory tree.

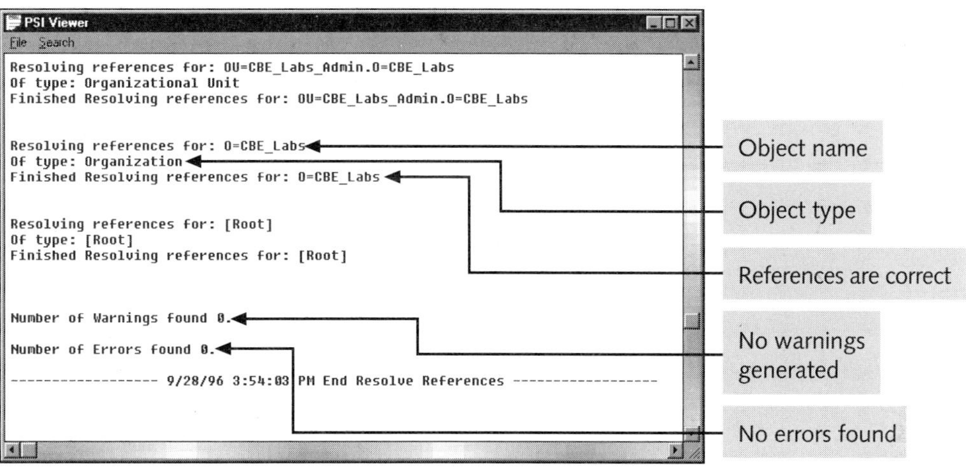

Figure 4-50 The Warnings and Errors in the CBE Labs Resolve References report

4. Click **File**, and then click **Print** to print the report. The PSI Viewer dialog is displayed to confirm printing. Click the **Yes** button. The report is printed.
5. Click the **PSI Viewer Close** button to close the PSI Viewer window.

Verifying Directory Tree Object Dependencies and Metrics

DS Standard has the ability to check a Directory tree design to ensure that the design is correct. DS Standard will check **object dependencies**, which are references between objects. For example, if user Georgia Burns has a login name of GBurns and is a member of a group named Administrators, then (1) the GBurns User object should list the Administrators group as one of the groups that Georgia is a member of and (2) the Administrators Group object should list GBurns as a member of the group. Both of these listings must be present for the Directory tree to be correct, and this is what DS Standard checks when it checks object dependencies.

DS Standard can also verify that the Directory tree conforms to the Directory tree metrics discussed earlier in this chapter. For example, DS Standard will warn you if any object names are longer than the 47 characters that were set earlier in this chapter, or if the distinguished name of an object is longer than 127 characters.

Although checking object dependencies and metrics are two separate steps, the results for both are recorded in the same report. It makes sense to run both checks sequentially and then print the report.

This feature is also limited to the reduced object set in the Preview edition of the DS Standard. You run the verification process by using the Verify Tree Metrics and Verify Object Dependencies commands on the View menu. A report is generated and displayed on screen in a report viewer after each step. After the second step, the report can be printed from the viewer. The report is also stored in a log file for later use.

To verify the CBE Labs Directory tree:

1. Click **View** on the menu bar and then click the **Verify Tree Metrics** command. The Confirm Verify Tree dialog is displayed to confirm the verification process. Click **OK**.
2. A report is generated and displayed in the PSI Viewer window. Click the **PSI Viewer Close** button Cancel to close the PSI Viewer.
3. Click **View** on the menu bar and then click the **Verify Object Dependencies** command. The Confirm Verify Object Dependencies dialog is displayed to confirm the verification process. Click **OK**.
4. A report is generated and displayed in the PSI Viewer window. Scroll to the end of the report to see if any metric errors or object dependency errors were found in the tree.
5. Click **File**, and then click **Print** to print the report. The PSI Viewer dialog is displayed to confirm printing. Click the **Yes** button. The report is printed.
6. Click the **PSI Viewer Close** button Cancel to close the PSI Viewer window.

Printing the Directory Tree

A Directory tree is often too complex to view on screen without scrolling. In order to get a view of the entire tree and to document the Directory tree design, you will often want to print out a copy of the Directory tree. You can print the Directory tree by clicking the Print Directory Tree button on the toolbar. This feature is *not* limited to the reduced object set in the Preview version of DS Standard 3.0—you can print the entire tree.

To print the CBE Labs Directory tree:

1. Click the **Print Directory Tree** button on the toolbar. The Print dialog is displayed to confirm printing the Directory tree. Click **OK**.
2. The Directory tree is printed. The output is shown for the complete CBE Labs Directory tree in Figure 4-51 (if you are following these steps on your computer, your output may look different from Figure 4-51 depending on the number of objects you created).

Figure 4-51

The printed Directory tree

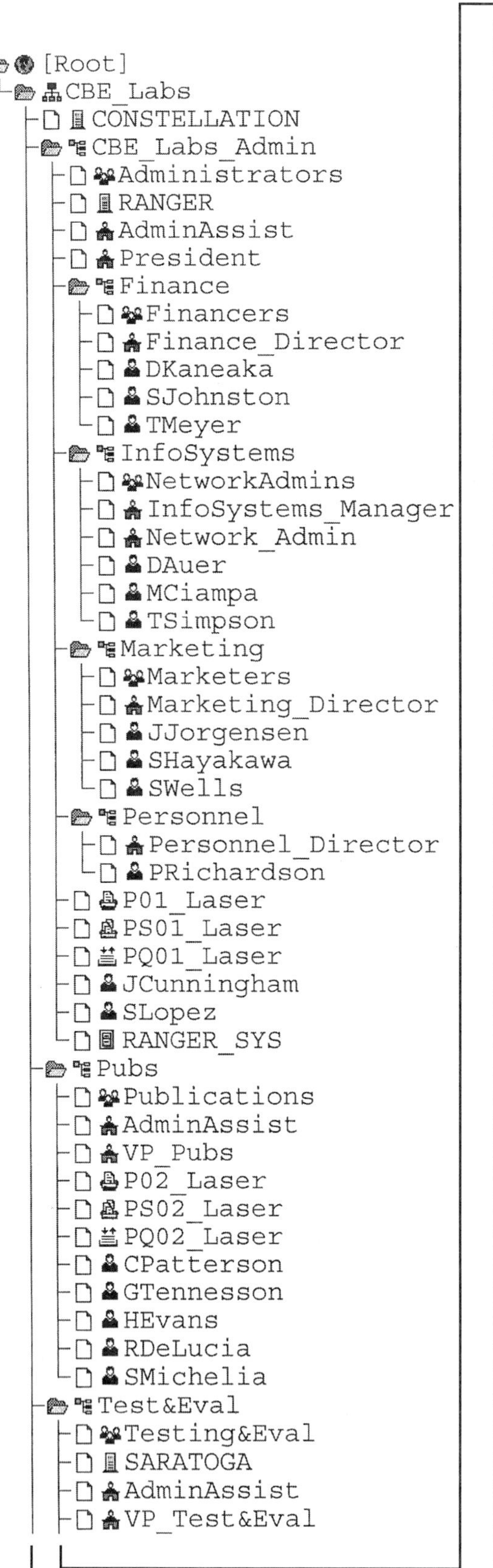

Printing Object Profile Reports

DS Standard can also create and print a report listing the details of the objects in the Directory tree. This report can be created for any set of selected objects in the Directory tree. To create a report on all objects in the Directory tree, you can select all Directory tree objects by clicking the Select All Objects button on the toolbar. You can also control which properties of each type of object are included in the report. To create the report, click the Object Profile Report button on the toolbar, or use the Object Profile command on the View menu.

The Object Profile report is not displayed in the PSI Viewer. Instead, Cheyenne Software uses its AuditWare report viewer to format and display the Object Profile report. The result is a more sophisticated report than the text reports seen in the PSI Viewer. The report can be

- Viewed in a print preview mode that shows what the printed report will look like.
- Printed directly without a print preview.
- Exported to one of many file formats for use by word processors and spreadsheets, including WordPerfect, Microsoft Word, Lotus 1-2-3, and Microsoft Excel, or to Microsoft Mail.
- Generated and stored in Cheyenne Software file format for later viewing and printing.

The reports generated by this process can quickly become very large. Each Directory tree object in the report starts on a new page and might require two or more pages to list all the data about the object. Even a small Directory tree can generate reports running into the hundreds of pages, so print this report with caution. This feature is limited to the reduced object set in the Preview version of DS Standard 3.0.

For example, the CBE Labs network administrator has decided to create an object profile report for the CBE Labs Directory tree that includes only the twelve container objects, and the Admin User object. This is a total of only thirteen objects.

To create an object profile report on selected objects in the CBE Labs Directory tree:

1. Click the **CBE_Lab** Object to select it.
2. Holding down the **[Ctrl]** key, click each of the other objects to be included in the report to add them to the selected set of objects.
3. Click the **Object Profile Report** button on the toolbar. The Object Profile Report dialog is displayed, as shown in Figure 4-52.

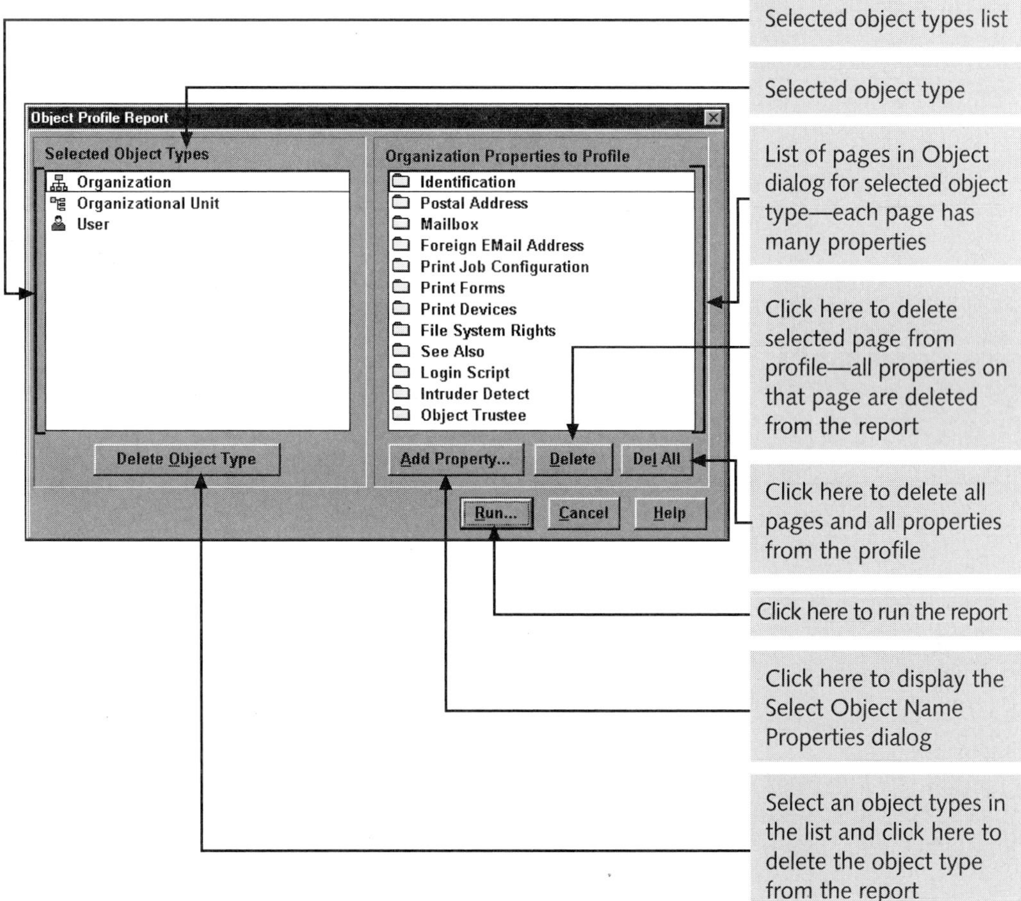
Object Profile Report
Selected Object Types
Organization
Organizational Unit
User
Delete Object Type
Organization Properties to Profile
Identification
Postal Address
Mailbox
Foreign EMail Address
Print Job Configuration
Print Forms
Print Devices
File System Rights
See Also
Login Script
Intruder Detect
Object Trustee
Add Property...
Delete
Del All
Run...
Cancel
Help
Selected object types list
Selected object type
List of pages in Object dialog for selected object type—each page has many properties
Click here to delete selected page from profile—all properties on that page are deleted from the report
Click here to delete all pages and all properties from the profile
Click here to run the report
Click here to display the Select Object Name Properties dialog
Select an object types in the list and click here to delete the object type from the report

Figure 4-52 The Object Profile Report dialog

The selected object types are listed in the Selected Object Types list. You can use the Delete Object Type button to remove a set of selected objects from the report, but you cannot add additional object types.

For each selected object type listed, you can control which properties are included in the report. By default, all properties are included. The *Object Type* Properties to Profile list actually shows a list of the pages in the object dialog for the selected object. You can delete one, some, or all of these pages and the properties they contain by using the Delete and Del All buttons. To add properties, you use the Add Property button, which displays the Select *ObjectName* Properties dialog shown in Figure 4-53 for the User object and with the Identification page properties expanded.

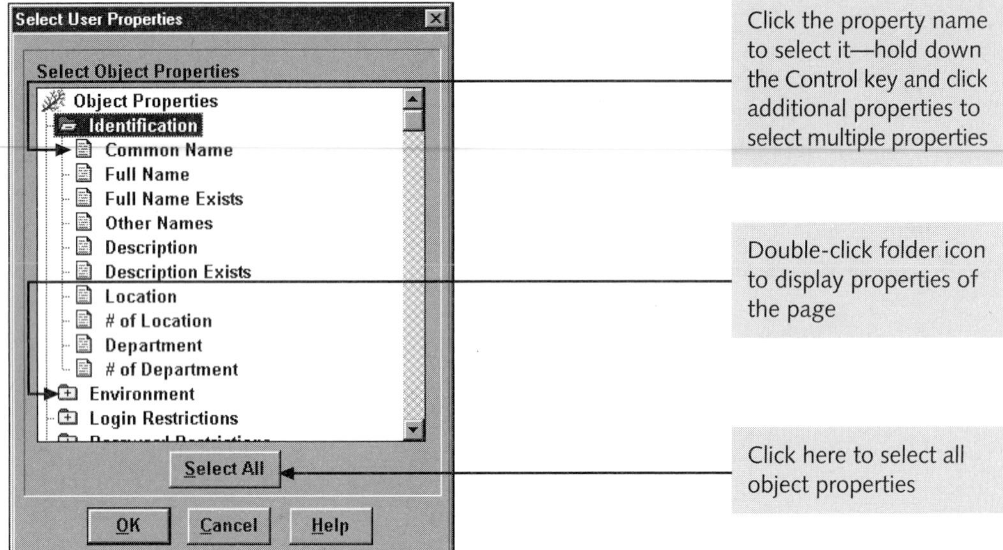

Figure 4-53 The Select ObjectName Properties dialog

Clicking a property selects it, and you can hold down the [Ctrl] key while clicking additional properties to add them to the set. Notice that you cannot delete selected properties on any page. You must delete the page and then add the properties you want back into the report set. For example, if you want to have only the user's Full Name included in the report, you have to delete the Identification page in the Object Profile Report dialog and then add the Full Name property itself back into the report using the Select User Properties dialog.

4. Because the CBE Labs report will include all properties for the included objects, click the **Run** button on the Object Profile Report dialog. The Run Report dialog, shown in Figure 4-54, is displayed.
5. Edit the report title in the Report Title text box to read **CBE Labs Directory Tree Object Profile**.
6. Click the **Include Title Page on Report** check box to add a title page to the report.

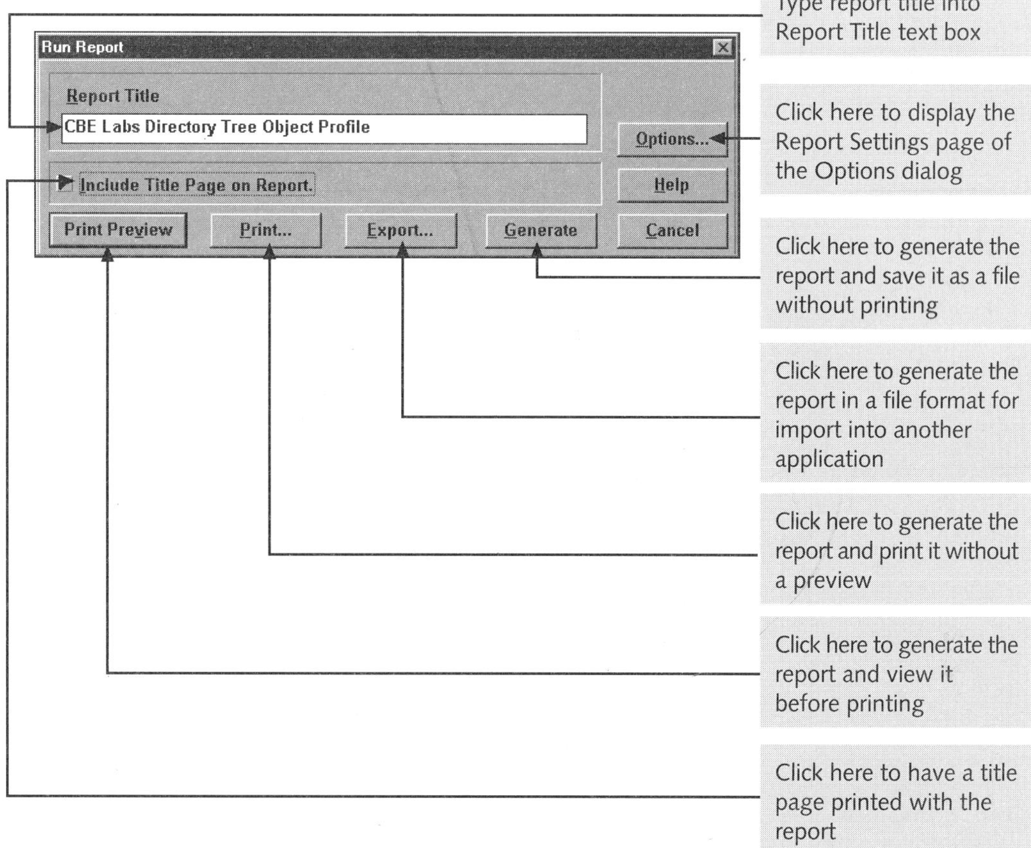
Run Report
Report Title
CBE Labs Directory Tree Object Profile
Options...
Include Title Page on Report.
Help
Print Preview
Print...
Export...
Generate
Cancel
Type report title into Report Title text box
Click here to display the Report Settings page of the Options dialog
Click here to generate the report and save it as a file without printing
Click here to generate the report in a file format for import into another application
Click here to generate the report and print it without a preview
Click here to generate the report and view it before printing
Click here to have a title page printed with the report

Figure 4-54 The Run Report dialog

The Print Preview, Print, Export, and Generate buttons run the four report options discussed above. The Options button displays the Report Settings page of the Options dialog, shown in Figure 4-40.

7. Click **Print Preview**. The report is generated and displayed in an AuditWare report window. Click the **Window Maximize** button ☐. The report title page is shown in Figure 4-55.

Figure 4-55

The object profile report window

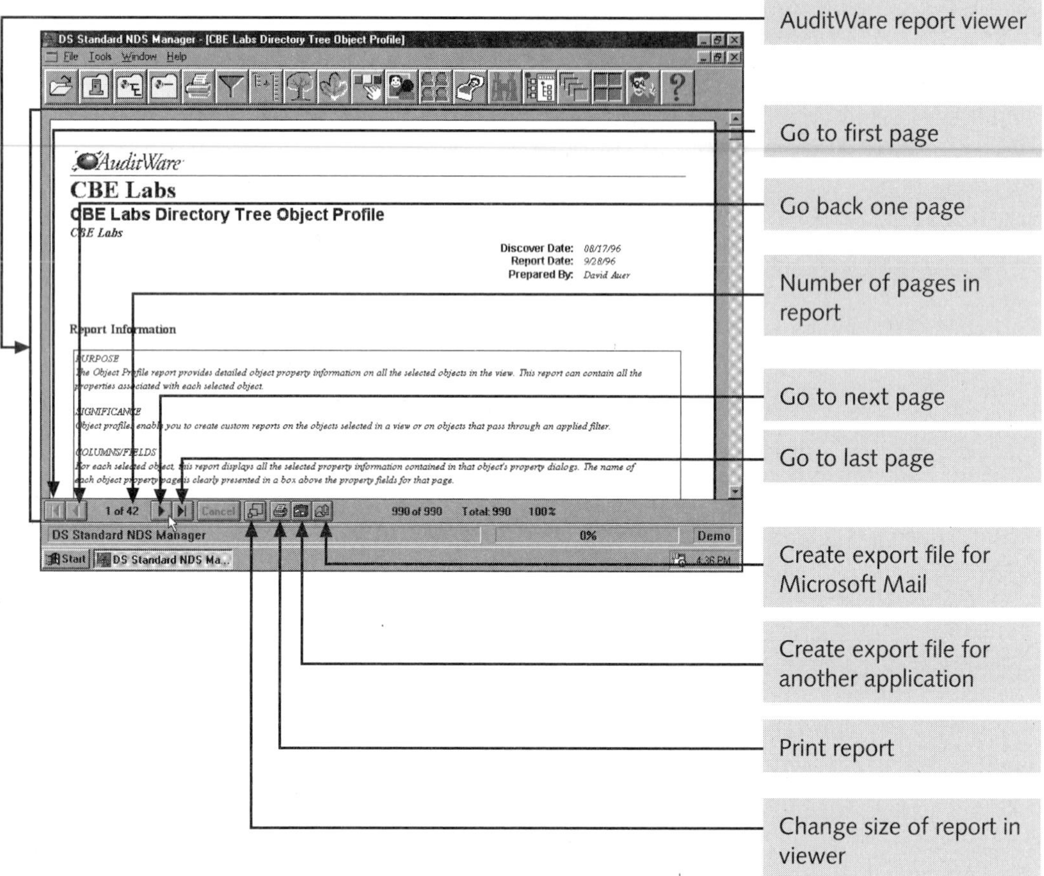

Notice that 13 objects generated a 42-page report. In this window, you can scroll through the report, print it, and export it to a file format for another software program or for Microsoft Mail.

8. If you want to print the object reports, click the **Print** button  to print the report. The PSI Viewer dialog is displayed to confirm printing. Click **OK**. The report is printed.

9. A *Object/Profile* dialog is displayed asking "Do you wish to save this report?" Click the **Yes** button.

4.11 Preview

NetWare 4.11 includes a version of DS Standard, which is named DS Migrate. DS Migrate is included with NetWare 4.11 to help users of NetWare 3.1x plan their transition to an NDS environment. It is based on version 2.1 of DS Standard: the DS Migrate toolbar is the older DS Standard toolbar with smaller buttons, and the NetWare Application Manager object icons are not included in the object icon set. The DS Migrate screen is shown in Figure 4-56.

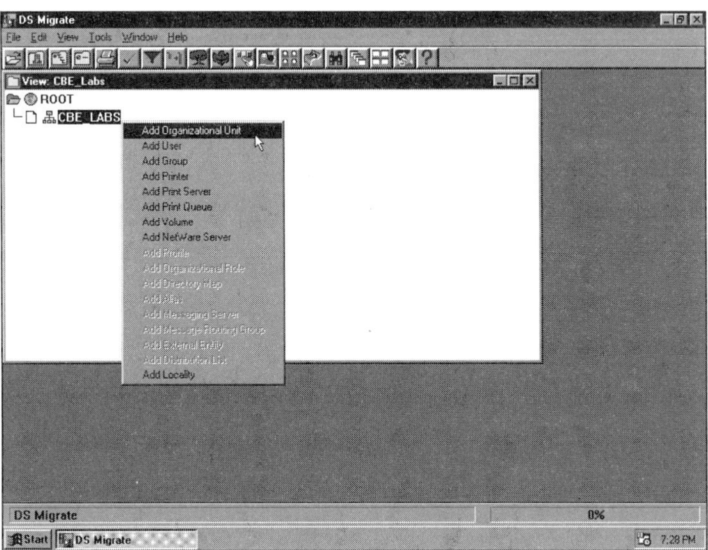

Figure 4-56 The DS Migrate screen

NDS AS A REPLICATED, DISTRIBUTED DATABASE

One of the main security concerns in the NetWare 4.1 environment is protecting the Directory database. Because the Directory database contains all the information necessary for users to log in to and use the network, the loss of this data would be catastrophic. Novell's solution assumes that there is more than one server in the network. With more than one NetWare server, the Directory database is broken into parts, and those parts are stored on different NetWare servers. For even better protection, copies of each part of Directory database are stored on additional NetWare servers. The parts of the database are called partitions, and the copies are called replicas. A database that is stored in sections on different computers is called a **distributed database**. The Directory database is a replicated, distributed database. To maintain current data in each of the replicas, NetWare 4.1 updates all replicas using a process called replica synchronization.

PARTITIONS

A **partition** is a logical division of the Directory database based on the Directory tree. A partition starts at some organization or organizational unit branch of the Directory tree and includes all leaf objects in that container plus all subsequent container and leaf objects in that branch of the tree. The data for each object is also included in the partition, but no data about the file system is included in a partition. Partitions cannot overlap, and an NDS object can be in only one partition. There should be at least one NetWare 4.1 server in each partition. For example, Figure 4-59 shows the partitioned Wilson Manufacturing Directory tree.

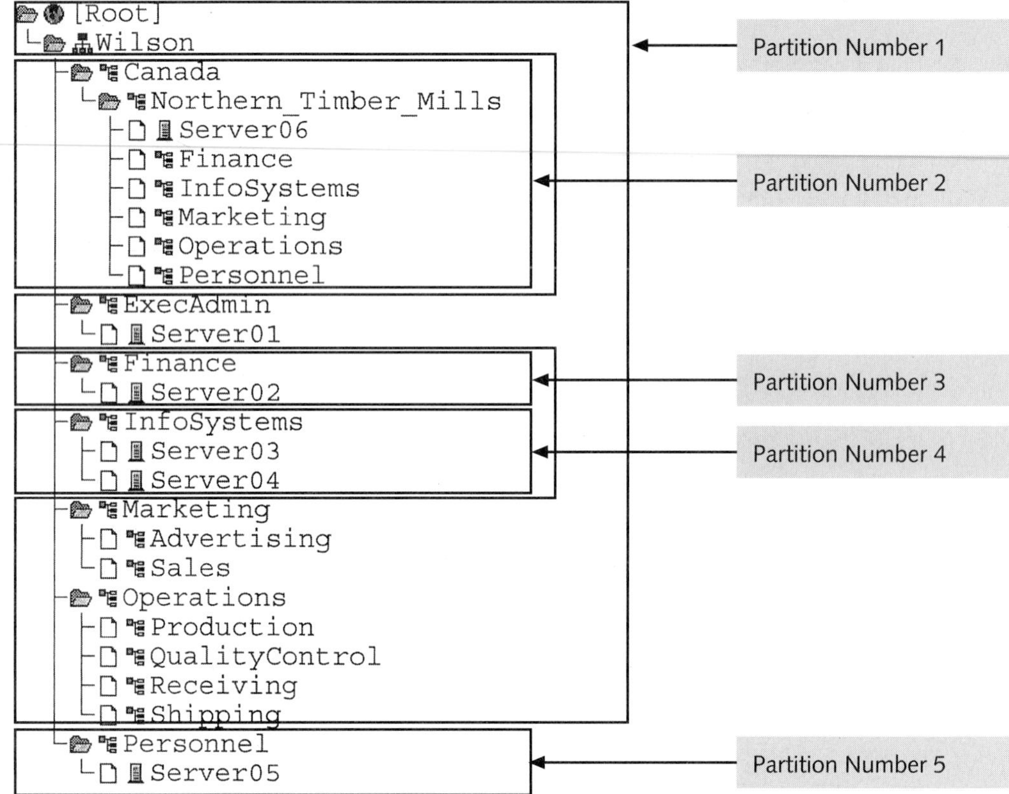

Figure 4-57 The partitioned Wilson Manufacturing Directory tree

There are five partitions in the Wilson Manufacturing Directory tree. The [Root] is included in the first partition, which is created when the first NetWare 4.1 server is installed. This partition is called the **[Root] partition**. Other partitions are given names based on the name of the container object in the partition closest to the [Root]. A partition is called a **child partition** if it is lower in the directory tree than another partition (**subordinate** to another partition), which is called the **parent partition**. In the Wilson Manufacturing Directory tree, the [Root] partition is the parent partition, and all the other partitions are child partitions.

We also use the term *partition* to mean a *physical subdivision of a hard drive*. Be careful not to confuse the two uses of the word *partition*.

REPLICAS

A **replica** is a copy of a partition. Replicas are stored on NetWare 4.1 servers to create NDS fault tolerance and faster access on a WAN. Fault tolerance is achieved because a user can log into the network even when the server containing the main copy of the user's data is not available. Faster access on a WAN is achieved when the main copy of a user's data is on a server physically close to the user. For example, if a WAN links offices in San Francisco and New York, a user in San Francisco will log into the network faster by accessing the replica on the San Francisco NetWare server. There are four types of replicas: master, read/write, read-only, and subordinate reference.

Master

The **master replica** is the main copy of the partition. There can be only one master replica for each partition. The master replica can be read from and written to and is also the place where other partition operations occur, including creating a partition, merging a partition, moving a partition, repairing a partition, creating a replica, and deleting a replica.

Read/Write

The **read/write replica** is a copy of the master replica that can be read from and modified. You can create as many read/write replicas as you want, but the actual number you create will be determined by the size of your network and the number of NetWare servers in the network. Read/write replicas can be used for user login authentication, so you must have enough replicas to permit users to log into the network if NetWare servers become inaccessible.

Read-only

The **read-only replica** is a copy of the master replica that can only be read from; however, read-only replicas cannot be used for user login. You can create as many read-only replicas as you want, but these copies are not as useful as read/write replicas. Servers that are running bindery services cannot have a read-only replica—they must have a master or read/write replica.

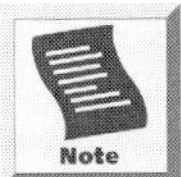

Because of the user login and bindery services limitations, it is usually more efficient to use a read/write replica than a read-only replica. Using the read/write replica allows users to authenticate logins and permits the setting up of bindery services later if the need arises.

Subordinate Reference

The subordinate reference replica is based on the parent partition/child partition system. If a parent partition has a master, read/write, or read-only replica on a NetWare server and a child partition does not have a replica on that NetWare server, NetWare 4.1 will automatically add a nonmodifiable replica of the child partition. This replica is called a **subordinate reference replica**. If you later put a read/write or read-only replica of the child partition on the server, NetWare 4.1 will automatically remove the subordinate reference replica. This is a safety measure built into NetWare 4.1 to make sure that there are sufficient replicas of all the partitions.

Replica Synchronization

Changes to the Directory database can be initially made in either the master replica or a read/write replica of a partition. When there is a change to an NDS object, a copy of the change is sent from the partition where the change was first recorded to all other replicas of the partition. This is necessary to ensure that the Directory database is **consistent**. However, because it takes some time to update all the replicas, the Directory database is said to be **loosely consistent** at any given moment. This updating procedure is called **replica synchronization.**

DESIGNING PARTITIONS AND REPLICA DISTRIBUTION

The purpose of partitioning the Directory database is to achieve fault tolerance and faster access on a WAN. The number of partitions that must be created depends on what it takes to achieve those goals, but you should have at least two read/write replicas for every master replica if possible.

NetWare 4.1 will automatically create some partitions and replicas for you. A new partition is created during NetWare 4.1 installation if (1) you create a new Organization object or Organizational Unit object during the installation and (2) the NetWare Server object corresponding to the new NetWare 4.1 server is a leaf object in the new branch. The new partition starts in the new container object and includes all branches of that container object. A master replica for this partition is created and stored on the NetWare server. For example, when you install your first NetWare 4.1 server, you have to create an Organization object. When you do so, NetWare creates a partition based on that Organization object and places a master replica on the server.

When you install NetWare 4.1 on a server whose corresponding Server object is a leaf in an Organization or Organizational Unit object that is already in a partition, NetWare 4.1 creates a read/write replica of that partition on the new server. However, NetWare creates only three replicas of a partition automatically. If you install more than three servers in a partition, replicas will only exist on the first three. You can, however, add more yourself if you want the added security of extra copies of the partition of additional NetWare servers.

The same rules for creating replicas apply if you're updating NetWare servers to NetWare 4.1. For example, suppose that you update three NetWare 3.1x servers to NetWare 4.1 and that all three NetWare servers are placed in the same container object. At the end of the upgrade process (1) there will be only one partition created (because all NetWare servers are in the same container), (2) the first NetWare server to be upgraded will have the master replica, and (3) the second and third NetWare servers to be upgraded will have read/write replicas of the partition.

In a small LAN, partitioning gains little access time, and a single partition can be sufficient. If you have at least three servers, you can have a master replica and two read/write replicas, which gives you the necessary fault tolerance.

In larger LANs and in WANs, partitioning improves user access. To accomplish this, the master replica containing the user's data should be stored on a server in the partition that contains the user's User object. Partitioning can also help create fault tolerance when read/write replicas are stored in partitions other than the partition containing the master replica.

The master replica of a partition doesn't have to be stored on a server in that partition. A large organization may place *all* master replicas on one server. A tape backup of this server then creates a backup of all the master replicas for the entire Directory database.

BINDERY SERVICES

Some network devices, such as stand-alone print servers, are not capable of logging into NDS but can log into a NetWare 3.1x bindery. If there are any client workstations on the network with older client software (NETX), they will also be unable to log into NDS. To accommodate these devices and users, NetWare 4.1 includes a bindery emulation mode called **bindery services**. Bindery services is automatically enabled during NetWare 4.1 installation, but you can disable it if you have no network devices that require it.

Bindery services allows access to a subset of the Directory tree. In its simplest form, the subset is based on the container object where the NetWare Server objects with bindery services enabled is located in the Directory tree—it consists of all the leaf objects in that container object. For example, in the CBE network, if Constellation has bindery services enabled, then all the leaf objects in the CBE Organization object are accessible to non-NDS devices and workstations. However, a user logging into bindery services logs into the Constellation NetWare server, *not* the network (see Figure 4-58).

Figure 4-58
Bindery services

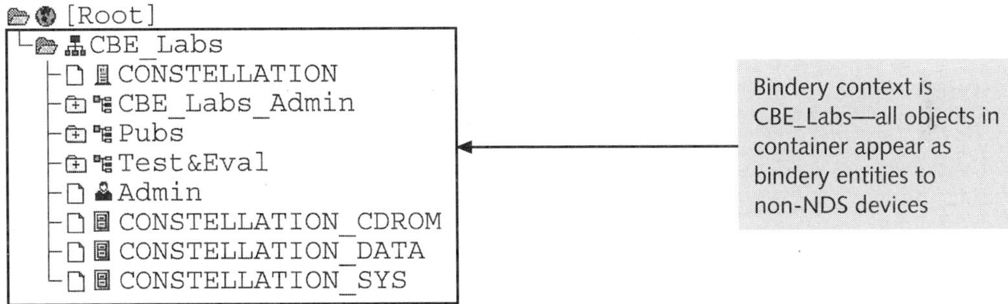

The name of the container object used for bindery services is called the **bindery context**. For example the bindery context for CBE is

```
BINDERY CONTEXT = .CBE_Labs
```

This is a simple, one-container bindery context. It is possible to use up to 16 containers in the bindery context supported by one server. It is not necessary for the NetWare server to be in any of the container objects in the bindery context, but a master or read/write replica of the partition that contains those container objects must be stored on the NetWare server. The container objects in the bindery context are separated by semicolons. For example, CBE could set the bindery context for Constellation as

```
BINDERY CONTEXT = .CBE_Labs_Admin.CBE_Labs;.Sales.CBE_Labs;
.Test&Eval.CBE_Labs;.CBE_Labs
```

Although the use of bindery services may be necessary for some network devices, there is no need for users to be logging into bindery services. You should update your users' client software to the NetWare Client 32 software so that they can make full use of NDS. Workstation installation of the NetWare Client 32 software is discussed in Chapter 6.

CHAPTER SUMMARY

Novell Directory Services (NDS) is the main administrative tool of NetWare 4.1. NDS consists of the Directory database and administrative tools to use the data in the Directory database. Earlier versions of NetWare used a database called the bindery.

NDS is network-centric—it deals with the entire network. Users log into the network, not to an individual server. The benefits of this include easier network administration, more network security, higher reliability, and scaleability (the ability to work with any size network).

The logical design of NDS is the Directory tree, which is a hierarchical tree structure containing objects that represent the organizational structure of the network and all network resources. The Directory tree, which is given a Directory tree name during NetWare 4.1 installation, consists of NDS objects. Objects represent physical, logical, or organizational entities. Objects have properties, which are the types of data associated with each object. Each property can have one or more property values stored in it.

The Directory tree consists of container objects and leaf objects. Container objects are used to provide organizational structure to the Directory tree. They can contain other container objects or leaf objects. Leaf objects represent network resources such as users and printers. They cannot contain other objects.

Container objects include the [Root] object, the Country object, the Organization object, and the Organizational Unit Object. These are abbreviated as [Root], C, O, and OU, respectively.

Leaf objects can be classified by function for easier understanding. User-related leaf objects have properties about users and include the User object, the Group object, the Organizational Role object, and the Profile object. Server-related leaf objects have properties about the NetWare servers on your network, and include the NetWare Server object, the Volume object, and the Directory Map object. Printer-related leaf objects represent network printing components and include the Printer object, the Print Queue object, and the Print Server object. Messaging-related leaf objects work with NetWare Message Handling Service (MHS) services on your network. Novell includes FirstMail, an e-mail program, with NetWare 4.1, and FirstMail uses the NetWare MHS during its operation. The NetWare Application Manager-related objects help the network administrator control access to software programs run from the NetWare servers. The Informational leaf objects include the Computer object and the AFP Server object. The Miscellaneous leaf objects include the Alias object, the Bindery object, the Bindery Queue object, and the Unknown object.

The location of an object in the Directory tree is called the object's context. Context is the path from the [Root] to the object. Context is combined with an object's name to create the distinguished name, which is the complete name of the object. If object type abbreviations are included in the name, it is called a typeful name. Names without abbreviations are called typeless names.

When designing a Directory tree, naming conventions should first be established to provide a uniform method of naming network objects. The depth of the Directory tree should be limited so that objects' distinguished names are not too long. The Directory tree can be designed based on functional or geographic principles, or on a combination of the two. Functional design principles include an organizational approach and a workgroup approach.

DS Standard NDS Manager is a software package that is used for off-line modeling and management of Directory trees. It gives you the ability to develop NDS Directory tree designs without endangering your on-line NDS Directory tree and Directory database.

The Directory database can be divided into sections called partitions. The partitions can and should be copied to other servers to provide fault tolerance and faster network response times on a WAN. The copies are called replicas. There are four types of replicas: master, read/write, read-only, and subordinate reference. Partitions and replicas are created automatically when NetWare 4.1 is installed, but they can and should be actively managed by the network administrator to ensure good network performance and security.

For network devices that can't work with NDS, NetWare 4.1 provides a bindery emulation mode called bindery services. A bindery context is established by specifying the container objects that make up the context. Leaf objects in those containers appear in the emulated bindery.

Key Terms

AFP Server object
Alias object
AppleTalk File Protocol (AFP) server
Bindery
bindery context
bindery emulation mode
Bindery object
Bindery Queue object
bindery services
child partition
children
common name (CN)
Computer object
consistent
container object
context
Country object
current context
depth
Directory database
Directory Map object
Directory tree
Directory tree name
distinguished name
distributed database
FirstMail
Group object
hierarchical structure
Informational leaf objects
leading period
leaf object
logical entity
login name
login scripts
loosely consistent
master replica
Message Handling Service (MHS)
Messaging-related leaf objects
Miscellaneous leaf objects
Name type
NCP Server object
NetWare Application Manager (NAM)
NetWare Applications Launcher-related objects
NetWare Server object
network-centric
network file system
network standards
Novell Directory Services (NDS)
object
object dependencies
organization object

organizational entity
Organizational Role object
Organizational Unit object
parent
parent partition
partition
physical entity
print data
print queue
Print Queue object
print server
print server object
Printer object
Printer-related leaf objects
Profile object
property
property value
read-only replica
read/write replica
relative distinguished name
replica
[Root]
[Root] object
[Root] partition
scaleability
server-centric
Server-related leaf objects
subordinate
subordinate reference replica
synchronization
trailing period
tree metric
typeful name
typeless name
Unknown object
User object
User-related leaf objects
Volume object
width

REVIEW QUESTIONS

1. ______________________ is a database about network resources, along with tools for using the data in the database.
2. The NetWare 4.1 NDS database is called the ______________________; the equivalent database in NetWare 3.1x is called the ______________________.
3. List four benefits of using NDS:

   ____

   ____

   ____

   ____

4. The logical design of NDS is called the ______________________.
5. The NDS database uses ______________________ to represent network resources. The types of data stored about each resource are called ______________________; the data itself is called the ______________________.
6. Briefly explain container objects:

7. Briefly explain leaf objects:

8. The container object created when the first NetWare 4.1 server is installed is the ________________. This object is assigned the name of the Directory tree.

9. List the names of the four container objects:

____

____

____

____

10. List the names of the four User-related leaf objects:

____

____

____

____

11. List the names of the three Server-related leaf objects:

____

____

____

12. For each of the objects in the Objects column, give the letter from the Object Groups column indicating which object group the object belongs to.

Objects	Object Groups
______ Printer object	A. Printer-related leaf object
______ Unknown object	B. Informational leaf object
______ Computer object	C. Miscellaneous leaf object
______ Print Queue object	
______ Print Server object	
______ Alias object	
______ Bindery object	
______ AFP Server object	
______ Bindery Queue object	

13. NetWare includes ________________________, which adds the capability of using electronic messaging and e-mail to the network.

14. The location of an object in a Directory tree is called its ________________.

15. For each object type listed below, list its associated abbreviation:

    Country ________________

    Organization ________________

    Organizational Unit ________________

    All leaf objects ________________

16. An object's complete name, which is the object's name together with its context, is called its ________________________.

17. The name *CN=GWashington.OU=WhiteHouse.O=USGovernment.C=US* is a(n) ________________________ name, whereas *GWashington.WhiteHouse.USGovernment.US* is a(n) ________________________ name.

18. For each of the following names, indicate whether it is an acceptable name in NetWare 4.1 and in bindery services (NetWare 3.1x naming conventions).

	NetWare 4.1	**Bindery services**
Joan Jones	________	________
Joan_Jones	________	________
Joan_with_a_very_very_very_very_very_very_very_long_name	________	________
Joan*Jones	________	________

19. The Directory database can be divided into sections called ________________. Copies of these are called ________________________ and can be stored on other servers to create fault tolerance in the network.

20. In order to accommodate devices that use the NetWare 3.1x bindery, but not NetWare 4.1 NDS, NetWare 4.1 includes ________________________.

21. Briefly describe the steps in planning an implementation of NDS:

22. Washington Management Services (WMS) is a consulting company specializing in consulting work with government organizations and agencies. The Directory tree for WMS is shown in Figure 4-59. In the Directory tree, identify and label

    - The [Root] object
    - All container objects by type
    - All leaf objects by type

Figure 4-59

Washington Management Services Directory tree

```
[Root]
└ WMS
  ├ Consulting
  │ ├ Consultants
  │ ├ VP_Consulting
  │ ├ Government
  │ ├ Industry
  │ └ GRoyce
  ├ ExecAdmin
  │ ├ President
  │ └ MDwyer
  ├ Fin&Acct
  │ ├ Finance&Accounting
  │ ├ VP_Fin&Acct
  │ ├ Accounting
  │ ├ Finance
  │ └ MMitchell
  ├ InfoSystems
  │ ├ WMS_Server01/SYS:Public
  │ ├ WMS_Server02/SYS:Public
  │ ├ WMS_Server01
  │ ├ WMS_Server02
  │ ├ P01_Laser
  │ ├ PS01_Laser
  │ ├ PQ01_Laser
  │ ├ WMS_Server01_SYS
  │ └ WMS_Server02_SYS
  └ Admin
```

EXERCISES

EXERCISE 4-1: USING THE DS STANDARD NDS MANAGER

In this exercise, you use the DS Standard NDS Manager to create an NDS Directory tree. You create a Directory tree for F. D. Roosevelt Investments, Inc. (FDR). A copy of the FDR organizational chart is shown in Figure 4-60. In these steps, you refer to the FDR Directory tree discussed in this chapter and recreate this tree using the DS Standard NDS Manager. When designing your own models, remember that a Directory tree is used for managing network resources and does not necessarily mirror a company's organizational chart.

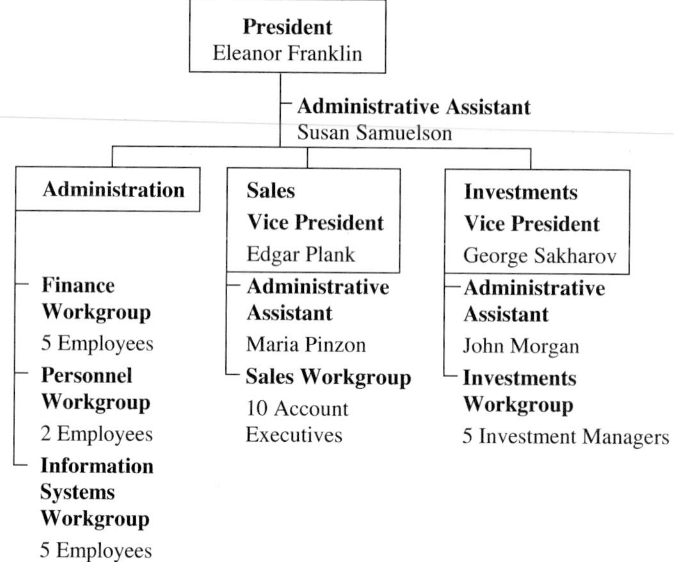

Figure 4-60 The FDR organization chart

1. Start DS Standard.
2. Create a DS Standard project named F. D. Roosevelt Investments.
3. Create an empty DS Standard view named FDR.
4. Add the FDR view to the F. D. Roosevelt Investments project.
5. Based on the organizational chart in Figure 4-60 and other figures showing the FDR Directory tree in this chapter, create the container objects for the FDR Directory tree.
6. Create a User object for each user in the FDR organization chart (do not create a User object unless the user is listed by name in the organization chart). Also create an Admin user object.
7. Create a set of Group objects for each workgroup at FDR.
8. Create Organizational Role objects for each position listed in the FDR organizational chart.
9. Based on the examples in the chapter, add NetWare Server and Volume objects to your Directory tree.
10. Based on the examples in the chapter, add Printer-related leaf objects to your Directory tree.
11. Check object references and links for the NDS container objects (including the root object) in your Directory tree. Print a copy of the report.
12. Verify the object dependencies and metrics for the NDS container objects (including the root object) in your Directory tree. Print a copy of the report.
13. Print out a copy of your Directory tree.
14. Create and print out an object profile report for the Admin user object in the FDR Directory tree.

15. Write a short memo to your instructor discussing an appropriate partitioning scheme for FDR.

16. Turn into your instructor (1) a copy of the memo you wrote in step 15, (2) copies of the reports you created in steps 11-14, and (3) a copy of your DS standard data disk.

EXERCISES

CASE 4-1: JEFFERSON COUNTY COURTHOUSE NETWORK

The Jefferson County Courthouse network is proceeding according to plan. The network proposal is still for just the twelve users in the Social Services section, including program administrator, Janet Hinds, her assistant, Tom Norihama, receptionist Lisa Walsh, department secretary, Terry Smith, and eight social workers. The group will use one NetWare server. Because the network may be expanded later to include other courthouse functions, NetWare 4.1 was selected as the NOS for its scaleability.

From discussions with Janet, the following decisions have been made:

1. The name of the Directory tree will be JCCH.
2. No Country or locality objects will be used, and there will be only one Organization object: JCCH.
3. Because of the use of stand-alone print servers, the NetWare 4.1 server will have to have bindery services enabled.

Create a proposed NDS Directory tree for the project. When designing your model, remember that a Directory tree is used for managing network resources and does not necessarily mirror a company's organizational chart. In your proposal discuss the following questions:

1. With only one server, there can be only one partition with a master replica. Because you don't have fault tolerance with read/write replicas on other servers, how will you protect the data in the Directory database?
2. What is the bindery context that will be used to provide bindery services?

Turn in the proposal to your instructor in memo form. Attach the following to the memo:

- A printout of your Directory tree
- A copy of a resolve references report for the NDS container objects in your Directory tree (include the root object)
- A copy of a verify object dependencies and tree metrics report for the NDS container objects in your Directory tree (include the root object)
- A copy of an object profile report for the Admin user object in your Directory tree
- A copy of your DS Standard data disk

Case 4-2: The J. Q. Adams Corporation Directory Tree

The J. Q. Adams Corporation is expanding its networking plans. Donna Hulbert, president of Adams, has decided to use two NetWare 4.1 servers in the network. One will be dedicated to administration tasks and the other to supporting production. After conferring with the appropriate people at J. Q. Adams, the following decisions have been made:

1. The name of the Directory tree will be ADAMS.
2. No Country or Locality objects will be used, and there will be only one Organization object: ADAMS.
3. There will be partitions of the Directory tree created for administration and production.
4. Because of the use of stand-alone print servers, both NetWare 4.1 servers will have to have bindery services enabled.

An organization chart for J. Q. Adams is shown in Figure 4-61.

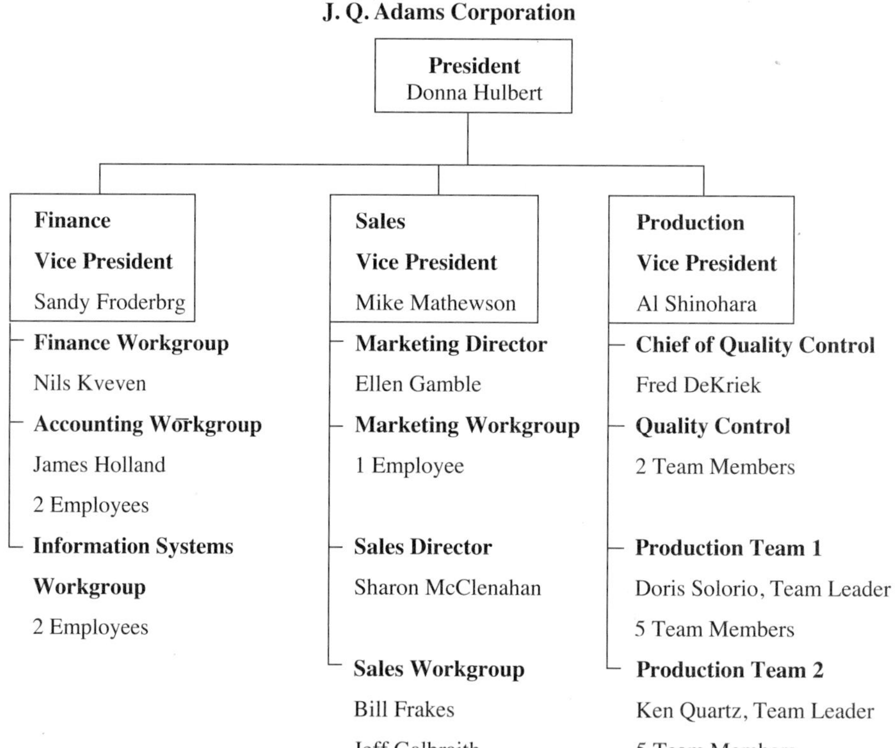

Figure 4-61 J. Q. Adams Corporation organization chart

Prepare your proposal for the NDS Directory tree. When designing your model, remember that a Directory tree is used for managing network resources and does not necessarily mirror a company's organizational chart. Include proposed partitions, replicas, and bindery contexts.

Turn in the proposal to your instructor in memo form. Attach the following to the memo:

- A printout of your Directory tree
- A copy of a resolve references report for the NDS container objects in your Directory tree (include the root object)
- A copy of a verify object dependencies and tree metrics report for the NDS container objects in your Directory tree (include the root object)
- A copy of an object profile report for the Admin user object in your Directory tree
- A copy of your DS Standard data disk

NORTHWESTERN TECHNICAL COLLEGE

PROJECT 4-1: NDS DIRECTORY TREE DESIGN

Dave Johnson has made his decision for the network implementation at Northwestern Technical College. He will use 10BaseT for the faculty/administration part of the network and 10Base2 for the student labs. Dave has purchased two new servers (your instructor will tell you the specifications of these servers as needed). He has also decided to use the NetWare 4.1 NOS on these machines and has purchased the software. Shortly after these purchases were made, NWTC received a donated server with the NetWare 3.12 NOS (your instructor will tell you the specifications of this server as needed). Dave's request for funds to upgrade this server to NetWare 4.1 were turned down on the basis that he already had the two servers he really needed. Dave has decided to use the third server as an additional administration server, to be used for administration data.

Dave wants you to create a proposed NDS Directory Tree for NWTC. He wants you to include the following points in your proposal:

1. The name of the Directory tree will be NWTC.
2. No Country or Locality objects will be used, and there will be only one Organization object: NWTC.
3. The first server to be installed with NetWare 4.1 will be the administration server.
4. There will be partitions of the Directory tree created for faculty/administration and students.
5. Because of the use of stand-alone print servers, both NetWare 4.1 servers will have to have bindery services enabled.

Prepare your proposal for the NDS Directory tree. When designing your model, remember that a Directory tree is used for managing network resources and does not necessarily mirror a company's organizational chart. Include proposed partitions, replicas, and bindery contexts.

Turn in the proposal to your instructor in memo form. Attach the following to the memo:

- A printout of your Directory tree
- A copy of a resolve references report for the NDS container object in your Directory tree (include the root object)
- A copy of a verify object dependencies and tree metrics report for the NDS container object in your Directory tree (include the root object)
- A copy of an object profile report for the Admin user object in your Directory tree
- A copy of your DS Standard data disk

CHAPTER FIVE

PLANNING THE NETWORK FILE SYSTEM

One of the network administrator's most important tasks is designing a network file system that will meet the special needs of the organization. The design needs to be completed prior to installing NetWare and setting up the network system. The structure of the network file system must be designed to allow a smooth workflow for network users. It must also prevent disruption of the information flow that existed before the network was implemented. The NetWare file system provides several advantages.

- Centralized management of data and backups ensures that duplicate copies of data are always automatically available for restoration of lost or damaged files.
- Improved security prevents users from modifying or accessing data they are not responsible for maintaining.
- Improved reliability and fault tolerance enable data to be backed up at regular intervals and provide a recovery process in the event of lost data or a down NetWare server.

AFTER READING THIS CHAPTER AND COMPLETING THE EXERCISES YOU WILL BE ABLE TO:

- DESCRIBE THE COMPONENTS OF THE NETWARE FILE SYSTEM.
- EXPLAIN THE PURPOSE OF EACH NETWARE-CREATED DIRECTORY AND NOVELL-SUGGESTED DIRECTORY.
- WRITE VALID PATH STATEMENTS TO IDENTIFY DIRECTORIES AND FILES.
- APPLY DIRECTORY DESIGN CONCEPTS TO DEVELOPING AND DOCUMENTING A DIRECTORY STRUCTURE FOR AN ORGANIZATION.
- USE NETWARE COMMANDS AND UTILITIES TO VIEW VOLUME AND DIRECTORY INFORMATION.

- Shared and private storage areas facilitate the creation of workgroups by enabling users to share files or to transfer files from one user to another without having to carry disks between machines. Private storage areas enable individuals to save their own work in a secure area of the NetWare server.
- Access to data by many different operating system platforms—NetWare supports Apple Macintosh, UNIX, and OS/2 file structures in addition to the standard DOS—saves money by eliminating the need for separate servers to handle each operating system. The NetWare file system can enable compatible applications running on Windows and Apple Macintosh platforms (for example Microsoft Word) to share data files. As networks grow, a network administrator's skill in integrating the file formats of different operating systems in the network file system is becoming increasingly important.

NetWare is frequently used by network administrators to integrate PC workstations using various desktop operating systems including DOS, Windows, Macintosh System 7.5, OS/2, and UNIX in order to enable people in an organization to communicate and exchange data easily.

NDS Components Versus Network File System Components

In Chapter 4, you learned about Novell Directory Services (NDS) and the Directory tree. The Directory tree is a logical organizational view of the entire network. The Directory tree allows a network administrator to manage and control network resources. A **network file system**, on the other hand, is a design for storing files on one or more hard disks in your NetWare servers. The term network file system refers to how file storage is structured across all NetWare servers in the network. The term *file system* refers to the file storage structure on an *individual* NetWare server. The network file system is the sum of all the NetWare server file systems.

The network file system enables a network administrator to manage and control system, application, and data files on the network. Each NetWare server file system is used to organize and secure the information stored on that server. A good file network file system design is necessary to facilitate the setup, use, and growth of a network.

Directory Tree Components

As you learned in Chapter 4, a Directory tree is composed of objects. Using container objects such as Organization objects and Organizational Unit objects, you can create the organizational structure of the Directory tree. Using leaf objects such as User objects and NetWare Server objects, you can represent network resources in the Directory tree.

Network File System Components

As shown in Figure 5-1, the four main components of the NetWare file system are the NetWare server, volumes, directories and subdirectories, and files.

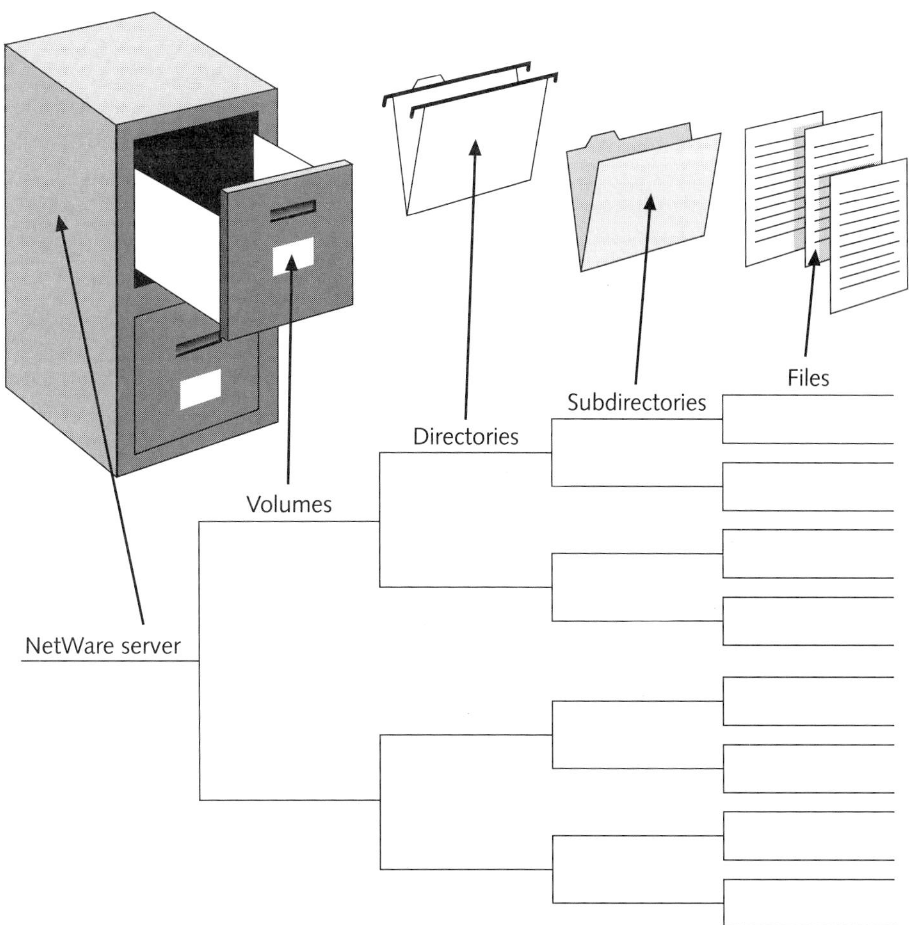

Figure 5-1
NetWare file system components

NetWare Server

The top level in the network file system structure is the NetWare server. As defined in Chapter 1, a NetWare server is a computer system dedicated to running the NetWare operating system. The function of a NetWare server in the network file system is similar to that of a file cabinet in an office because it contains applications and data for access by users on the network. Just as an office needs many file cabinets to organize all its data in an accessible and secure form, an organization's network file system often consists of multiple NetWare servers. In order to provide access to its unique data, each NetWare server is given a name consisting of 2 to 47 characters.

Server names cannot use any of the following special characters: = < > ? " * + , : ; \ / | [ ]

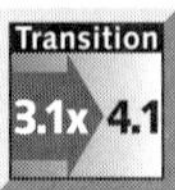

The name of a NetWare 3.1x NetWare server had a maximum of 45 characters, and a network user was limited to accessing files and print services on a maximum of 8 NetWare 3.1x servers at one time.

Volumes

Just as file cabinets have one or more drawers, the storage space on each NetWare server is divided into one or more volumes. **Volumes** are the major divisions of NetWare server storage; all files are accessed through volumes, and each volume is associated with a specific NetWare server. A NetWare volume is a physical amount of storage contained on one or more hard disk drives or other storage media, such as a CD-ROM. In DOS terms, a volume is equivalent to a partition of a hard disk drive on a local workstation. However, NetWare 4.1 volumes are more flexible than workstation hard disk drives because each volume can use or span multiple disk drives and occupy terabytes (TB) of data storage capacity. By allowing a volume to consist of up to 32 disk drives and a maximum capacity of 32 TB, NetWare provides for almost unlimited volume size. A NetWare 4.1 server can have a maximum of 64 volumes.

Each NetWare server is required to have at least one volume, and the volume is required to be named SYS: (for system). During installation, NetWare 4.1 creates and stores its operating system files and utility programs in directories it creates in the SYS: volume. In addition to the required SYS: volume, many network administrators create at least one additional volume in which to store the organization's data files separately from the NetWare operating system software. When multiple volumes are used, the SYS: volume is typically reserved for the operating system files, print queues, and general-purpose application software such as spreadsheets and word processors. One or more data volumes are then created to store the organization's files. Placing the organization's data files and special applications in separate volumes provides the following advantages:

- The administrator can ensure that free space is always available in the SYS: volume for NetWare's use.
- Security is enhanced because data can be stored off-line when it is not being used by dismounting the volume containing the sensitive data.
- Performance is improved when separate volumes hold other operating systems or large graphics and multimedia files. Placing these files in separate volumes enables the network administrator to increase the block size or add optional filename space support for other operating systems without decreasing the performance of DOS files stored on other volumes.
- Additional fault tolerance is provided because the server can continue to provide services even when a volume is taken off-line for repairs.

Network printing is one reason that additional free space in the SYS: volume is needed. When printed output is sent to a network printer, it is first stored on a NetWare server in directories called print queues. Although NetWare 4.1 allows you to place print queues on any volume, they are commonly placed on the SYS: volume. Consider, for example, the following situation. A company has a NetWare server with a SYS: volume that is almost full because of the many large data files stored there. If several users attempt to print rather large desktop publishing jobs on networked printers at the same time, the SYS: volume is inundated with the printed output stored in the print queue. If the SYS: volume runs out of space, the print jobs are canceled and error messages are sent to the users. The print jobs need to be resubmitted, or the network administrator must free up disk space. You can avoid problems like this by keeping data files in separate data volumes and allocating at least 100 MB for the NetWare 4.1 operating system files in the SYS: volume.

If you are going to install on-line documentation (DynaText viewer and NetWare 4.1 files) on the SYS: volume, you need to add another 60 MB.

If you do run out of space on a volume, you can increase the volume's size by adding another disk drive to the NetWare server and then directing NetWare to use empty space available on the new drive to expand the existing volume. This process is called **spanning** a volume.

When a volume spans more than one disk drive, you should mirror the disk drives, because a disk error on either drive makes the entire volume unavailable. Mirroring synchronizes the data on two disk drives so that an error on one drive will not prevent access to the volume's data.

When creating multiple volumes, you must use the following naming conventions:

- Each volume on a NetWare server must have a unique name.
- The volume name must be 2 to 15 characters long.
- Volume names cannot contain spaces or any of the following special characters: = < > ? " * + , : ; \ / | [ ]

Examples of valid volume names include: DATA, ICS_GRAPHIC16, CTS-ENGINEERING, MAC_ATTAC, and UNIX@WORLD.

The volume name must be followed by a colon when specified as part of a path, and it is a common convention to write volume names with the colon—for example, SYS:, DATA:, CTS-ENGINEERING:.

A backslash or forward slash must be used to separate the NetWare server name from the volume name. For example, the SYS: volume on Server01 would be written as Server01/SYS: (or Server01\SYS:) and the DATA: volume on Server02 would be written as Server02/DATA: (or Server02\DATA:).

A **block** is the amount of data that is read or written to the volume at one time. The block size of a volume is assigned when the volume is created during installation. By default, NetWare creates the block size based on the volume size, as shown in Figure 5-2.

Figure 5-2 Default NetWare volume block sizes

Volume Size	Default Block Size
1–32 MB	4 KB
32–150 MB	8 KB
150–500 MB	16 KB
500–2,000 MB	32 KB
2,000+ MB	64 KB

A larger block size can speed up access time when large files, such as bit-mapped graphics images and CAD applications, are used. However, larger block sizes use up more disk space, which makes them less efficient when a large number of small files need to be stored. NetWare 4.1 enables several files to share one block using a technique called block suballocation. As shown in Figure 5-3, block suballocation divides any partially used disk block into 512-byte suballocation blocks, enabling the unused space in that disk block to be allocated to another file rather than being left unused.

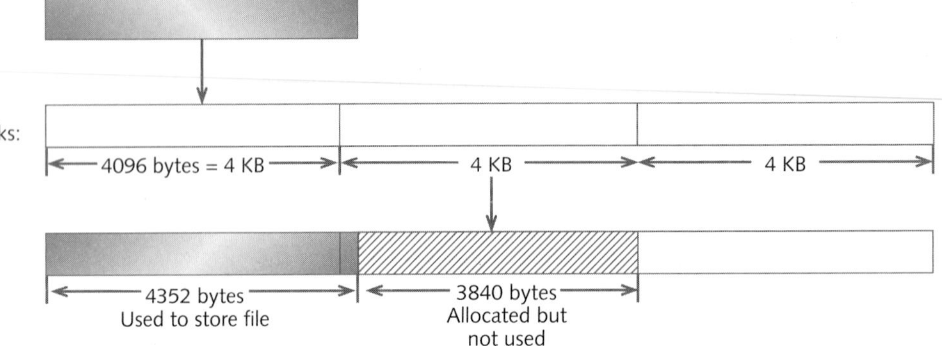

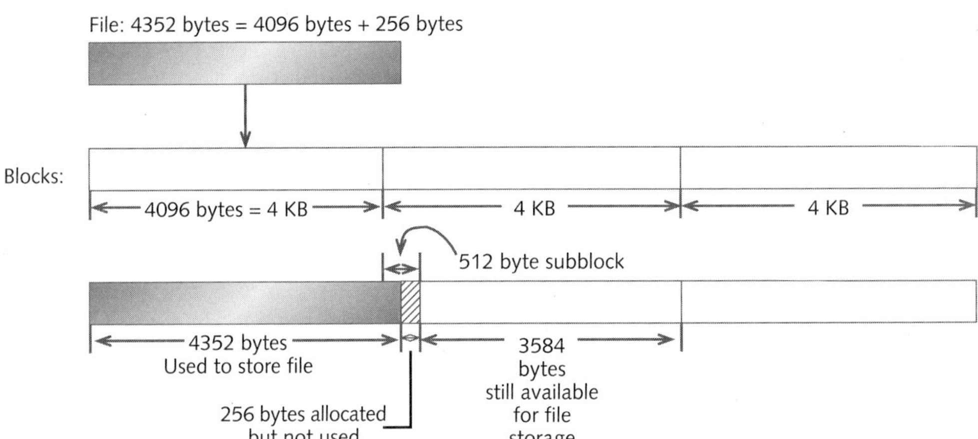

Figure 5-3 NetWare block suballocation

There is generally no need to change the default block size as long as block suballocation is enabled.

In addition to block suballocation, NetWare provides two other tools to manage volume space. **File compression** is a technique that reduces the size of a file by rewriting the file using a special coding technique. Although there are variations of this technique, the basic idea of file compression is to replace repeated characters or combinations of characters with a coded marker. For example, in the phrase "There the dog found the cat staring at the mouse" the combination of the three characters *the* is repeated four times. This combinations can be replaced with a code, for example *X*. Then the phrase can be stored as "Xre X dog found X cat staring at X mouse." When the file is used, it will be decompressed, which means that the codes will be replaced with the original characters. If you want to use file compression on a NetWare volume, it must be enabled for the volume. File compression enabled is the default setting for a NetWare volume.

NetWare also provides support for **data migration**, which enables files that have not been used for a long time to be moved to another type of storage medium, such as an optical disk. This frees up disk space on the NetWare volume. The filename, however, is still listed on the volume. If a user tries to open the file, it is then copied back from the optical disk to the volume before being opened. This technique enables little-used-files to be stored off the volume but to still be available to the user. Data migration requires special hardware and software, and the default setting for a NetWare volume is data migration disabled.

Directories and Subdirectories

The storage space in each NetWare volume can be organized into directories and subdirectories. A **directory** is a logical storage area on a volume. A **subdirectory** is a further division of a directory; we use the term subdirectory to refer to the directories within a directory. Directories are called **folders** in Windows 95. Creating directories within a NetWare volume is analogous to hanging folders in the drawer of a file cabinet. Directories and subdirectories enable you to keep files organized in a volume just as folders enable you to organize files in a file cabinet's drawer. An important network administrator responsibility is to design a directory structure for each volume that will separate software and data according to functionality and use. NetWare's SYS: volume contains several system-created directories that play important roles in the operation of the NetWare server. Novell also recommends an additional set of directories to help build a suitable directory structure to store software and data files. These directories are discussed in the following sections.

Required Directories

When you install NetWare 4.1, seven directories are created, as shown in Figure 5-4. The NetWare operating system stores its required system files and utilities in the SYS: volume by creating four main directories: Login, Public, System, and Mail. In Addition, NetWare creates the Deleted.Sav, Doc, and Etc directories. You need to understand how NetWare uses these required directories and where certain types of NetWare system files are stored. This section explains these directories and provides examples of their use by NetWare.

Figure 5-4

NetWare required directories

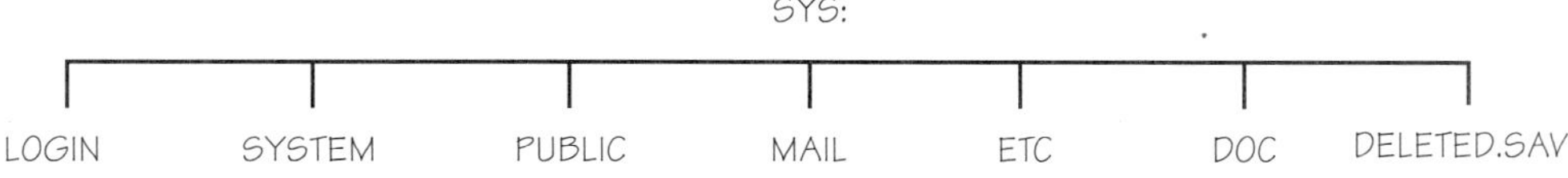

SYS:LOGIN. The SYS:LOGIN directory contains files and programs that can be accessed prior to logging in. You should think of this directory as NetWare's reception area. Just as you enter a reception area when you first go into a business office, a user is attached to the LOGIN directory of a NetWare server when he or she first connects to the network. When users complete this step and gain access to the LOGIN directory, they have limited access to any files and programs stored in that directory. Two important programs in the LOGIN directory that you worked on are NLIST.EXE and LOGIN.EXE.

When you visit an office building, you need to obtain permission from the receptionist before visiting someone's office. The NLIST.EXE program performs the receptionist's job of checking who is available to see you by listing the names of all NetWare servers on the network. Next the receptionist needs to identify you to the person you want to see. The LOGIN.EXE presents your user name and optional password to NDS and then provides you with access to network resources after you are identified as a valid user.

The LOGIN and NLIST programs can be copied from the LOGIN directory to a user's workstation and run from that workstation's local hard disk. This approach eliminates the need to change the active drive to a network drive in order to log in to the network. This option can be important when you are creating a DOS batch file and do not know what drive letter a workstation will be using for its network drive.

Many network administrators like to use the SYS:LOGIN directory to store common files and programs used by many workstations during the startup process. This technique allows you to update a new release of these programs simply by copying the new software into the LOGIN directory rather than copying it to each workstation's hard disk drive.

SYS:PUBLIC. The SYS:PUBLIC directory contains utility programs and files that are available to all network users after they have logged in. Many of these programs and files are necessary for users to be able to access and use network services. The NDIR.EXE, WHOAMI.EXE, NETUSER.EXE, and LOGOUT.EXE programs are all examples of NetWare utilities that are run from the PUBLIC directory. For a network administrator, the PUBLIC directory is like a toolbox containing many utilities you will need to perform such network tasks as creating new users, managing files, assigning access rights, and working with printers.

SYS:SYSTEM. The SYS:SYSTEM directory contains NetWare operating system files and utilities that are accessible only to users such as the Admin users who have been given supervisory privileges on the network. Novell uses the dollar symbol ($) in all filenames that contain system information. For example, the SYS$LOG.ERR file is the system error log.

Many of the NetWare system files are not accessible from the DOS DIR command; you need to use the NetWare NDIR command to display them when you work on the NetWare server. Only the network administrator should be given access rights to the SYSTEM directory to prevent users from erasing or modifying system files and using commands that affect the functioning of the NetWare server. Some network administrators will move certain program files that they do not want the user to run, such as the Windows client NetWare Administrator and the DOS client NETADMIN, from the PUBLIC directory to the SYSTEM directory.

SYS:MAIL. The SYS:MAIL directory is used in NetWare 4.1 by e-mail programs that use NetWare's Message Handling Service (MHS) to store data files. In earlier versions of NetWare, the MAIL directory of a server contained a subdirectory for each user, which is automatically created whenever a new user is added to the NetWare server. These subdirectories were used by e-mail software to pass electronic messages between users, but they were also needed by the NetWare operating system for storing user information such as personal login scripts. On a NetWare 4.1 server, personal user information such as login scripts are stored in the NDS Directory database instead of the SYS:MAIL directory. The SYS:MAIL is maintained to provide compatibility with network clients that access the NetWare server using bindery emulation mode.

Because the operating system uses these directories, you should not allow users to access the MAIL directories to store their personal files, because this is likely to cause critical

NetWare system files to be erased or changed. The network administrator needs to keep track of the MAIL directories in order to back up the NetWare server and perform maintenance tasks.

During an upgrade from NetWare 3.1x to NetWare 4.1 on an existing NetWare server, the user subdirectories of the SYS:MAIL subdirectory are maintained. Personal login script data is moved to the NDS Directory database. The name of each user's SYS:MAIL subdirectory is the same as his or her user ID, which is a hexadecimal number of from one to eight digits.

Other system directories. As shown in Figure 5-4, in addition to the four major system directories, you can also find ETC, DOC, and DELETED.SAV directories on the SYS: volume of a NetWare server. NetWare 4.1 automatically creates the SYS:ETC directory to store sample files to help the network administrator configure the server. The SYS:DOC directory is an optional directory for NetWare servers that NetWare creates when electronic versions of the NetWare manuals are installed.

To help users recover lost files, a network administrator should be aware of the purpose and use of the DELETED.SAV directory. The SYS:DELETED.SAV directory is automatically created on each NetWare volume and is the part of the NetWare file recovery system that allows the recovery of a file even after the directory that contained the file has been deleted. When files are deleted from a NetWare volume, the blocks on the hard disk that contained the file's information are not immediately reused (as would happen on your local DOS drive). Instead, as NetWare requires more disk space, it reuses disk blocks from the files that have been deleted the longest, allowing you to recover files even after they have been deleted for some time. Normally a file must be recovered in the directory from which it was deleted, but if that directory has been removed the file might still be found in the DELETED.SAV directory. In Chapter 7 you will have an opportunity to practice salvaging deleted files.

Suggested Directories

The seven required directories just described are automatically created for you during installation and provide the NetWare operating system with the storage areas it needs to perform its functions. In addition, an organization will probably require areas in the NetWare server disk volumes to meet its storage needs. The network administrator is responsible for planning, creating, and maintaining the directory structure necessary to store the organization's data and software on the NetWare server. There are four basic types of directories that Novell suggests should be part of an organization's file system: DOS directories, Application directories, user home directories, and shared directories. This section describes each of the suggested directories and explains how they can be applied to meet the storage needs of an organization.

DOS directories. Windows 3.1x required a version of DOS to be running before Windows 3.1x could be run. With the release of Windows 95, most of the functionality of DOS is found in Windows itself. However, there are still some DOS-based commands and utilities in Windows 95, such as the DISKCOPY command. As a network administrator, you will probably encounter a mix of workstations that run different versions of DOS and Windows. Because each DOS version and Windows 95 run external commands written for that version only, it is necessary to provide a separate directory for each DOS version. One solution is for each workstation's local hard disk drive to contain a directory with the DOS commands used by that workstation. However, this requires each workstation to have a hard drive containing the DOS commands as well as increasing the chance that the DOS commands are accidentally erased or damaged by a computer virus. To deal with this, it is a common practice among network administrators to create subdirectories in the PUBLIC directory for each version of the DOS operating system being used on the network. Each of the subdirectories contains only the DOS external commands (those not contained in COMMAND.COM), such as DISKCOPY, XCOPY, and FORMAT, that the administrator wants available on the network. This technique saves the administrator from having to keep DOS directories on each workstation's hard disk and updating all workstation hard drives when a newer version of DOS is installed.

The version of DOS built into Windows 95 is referred to as MS-DOS 7.0.

In addition to a subdirectory for the DOS component of Windows 95, the DOS structure shown in Figure 5-5 provides for different machine types and DOS environments by establishing a directory level for each machine type and then dividing the machine types into subdirectories corresponding to DOS versions. This structure is necessary because some PC manufacturers, such as Compaq and IBM, have modified Microsoft DOS to provide special features for their own brands of computers. For example, IBM provides a specialized version of DOS, so the IBM_PC directory is further divided into two subdirectories—one for IBM's DOS version and one for the standard Microsoft DOS versions. Each of the IBM_PC subdirectories can be further subdivided into additional subdirectories for each DOS version. Using the version number for the directory name, as shown in Figure 5-5, enables NetWare to locate the correct DOS directory automatically for the workstation to use when a user logs in.

Figure 5-5

Recommended DOS directory structure

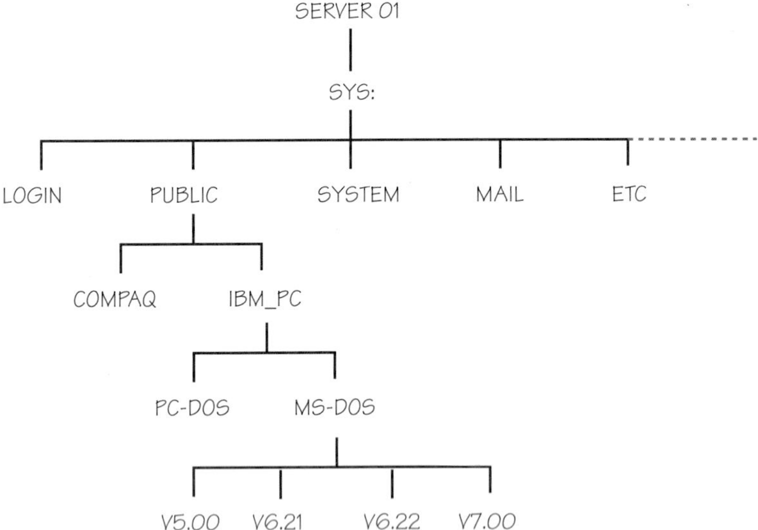

Application directories. In addition to creating the required NetWare directories, network administrators must create directories and subdirectories for the applications and data needed by network users. The first rule in organizing directories is to keep data and software separate whenever possible. This means you need to define a directory for each software application that will be stored in the NetWare server. Software applications fall into two basic categories: general-purpose packages, such as WordPerfect and Lotus 1-2-3, and special-purpose applications such as payroll or order-entry software. General-purpose software is often needed by multiple users throughout an organization, so these applications are often stored in directories in the server's SYS: volume. Special-purpose applications are often restricted to small groups of users or departments; they contain their own data directories and files and sometimes have large data storage needs. In order to provide restricted access or prevent the SYS: volume from filling up, some network administrators store special-purpose applications, such as payroll or inventory, in a separate data volume.

Home directories. In addition to having access to application directories, each user needs a private **home directory** in which to store files and documents. When planning your disk storage needs, you should anticipate space needed for users to store personal projects and files they use in their work. Generally, only the owner of a home directory has access rights to it; files that are needed by multiple users should be stored in shared directory areas. The location of user home directories depends on the design of the directory structure. If the server has only one volume (SYS:), they can be placed in a general-purpose directory named HOME or USERS (see Figure 5-6).

Figure 5-6 Novell suggested directories

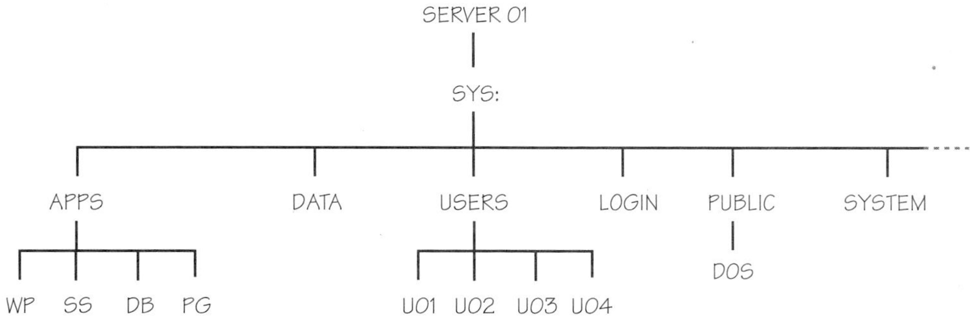

Alternatively, you can create a DATA directory and place HOME or USERS (and all other data subdirectories) in it, as shown in Figure 5-7. User home directories can also be separated by workgroup as described later in this chapter.

Figure 5-7 Using a DATA directory

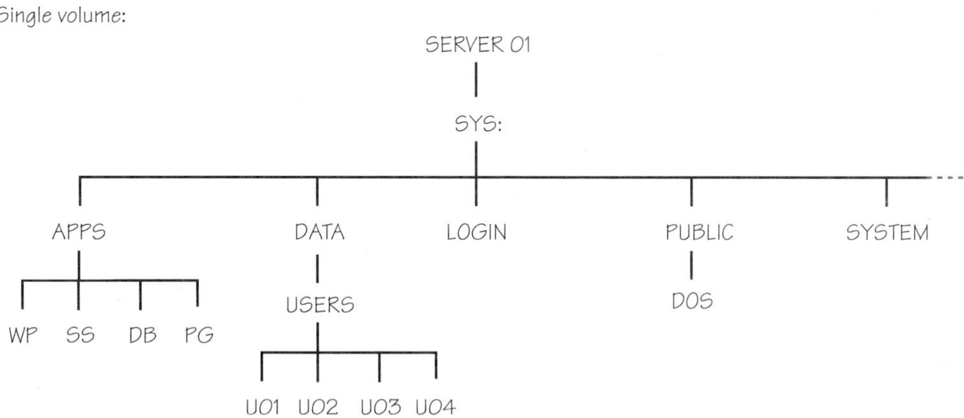

If the server has more than one volume, the additional volume(s) should be used for data storage, and the home directories can be located there (see Figure 5-8).

Figure 5-8
Using a DATA volume

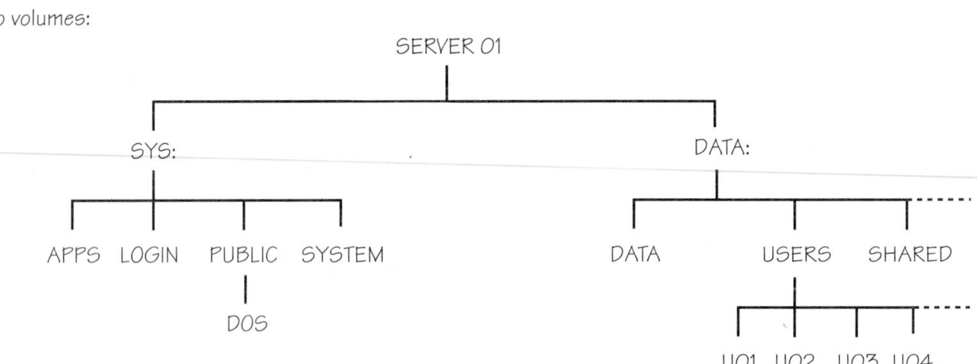

User home directories should be named with the user's login name. This enables the network administrator to assign a drive letter to the user's home directory when the user logs in. In Chapter 14, you will learn how to use NetWare login scripts to automate the process of mapping drives to user home directories.

Shared directories. One of the benefits of using a network is being able to share files. As a network administrator you will need to establish shared work directories that enable multiple users to work with common files and documents. Shared work directories enable one user to save a file and another user working on the same project to access it. Word processing documents and spreadsheet program worksheets stored in a shared directory are available to only one user at a time. Special software is needed to enable a file to be accessed by multiple users at the same time to prevent one user's changes from overwriting the changes made by another. Figure 5-8 shows a general-purpose shared directory named SHARED for use by all users. Later in the chapter you will learn how to create a departmental directory structure that includes shared directories for each workgroup.

Files

Files contain the actual blocks of data and software that can be loaded from the disk storage system into the computer's RAM. Every NetWare volume contains a **directory entry table (DET)** and a file allocation table (FAT) to keep track of each file's name and location on the disk volume. The DET also stores file attributes and access rights. **Access rights** control what operations a user can perform on a file or directory. **Attributes** are special flags that identify how the file is to be viewed or processed. Examples of common file attributes used in DOS are Read-Only, Hidden, and System. NetWare provides such additional attributes as Sharable and Delete-Inhibit. In Chapter 10 you will learn more about the file access rights and attributes available with NetWare.

NetWare supports DOS file naming conventions with filenames of up to eight characters and an optional three-character extension. The NetWare DET, however, is not limited to DOS filenames, because NetWare servers are often required to store files from workstations running other operating systems such as Windows 95, Windows NT, Apple Macintosh, OS/2, and UNIX. As a network administrator you will need to know how to set up and manage file storage from workstations running a variety of operating systems. Because non-DOS systems support longer filenames with special attributes, additional logic needs to be added to the NetWare server, and the DET needs to be expanded for the server volumes that will support files used by the non-DOS systems. Because of the importance of the DET and FAT in accessing files from a NetWare volume, a second copy of both tables is automatically maintained to enable recovery in the event of a disk error that damages the primary tables.

DIRECTORY PATHS

To access files, you need to specify the location of the directory or file within the NetWare file system. The **default drive** and **default directory** are the drive and directory you are currently using. A **directory path** is a list of file system components that identifies the location of the directory or file you want to access. A **complete directory path**, also called an **absolute directory path**, contains the NetWare server's name, volume name, directory, and all subdirectories leading to the target object. For example, the complete path to the U01 home directory, shown in Figure 5-5, is expressed as SERVER01/SYS:USERS\U01. A **partial directory path**, also called a **relative directory path**, lists only the locations leading from the default directory to the target object. Assume, for example, that your default directory is the SYS: volume. In this case, the partial directory path is specified as \USERS\U01. As a network administrator, you will often need to use both complete and partial paths when working with the NetWare file system.

Complete Path

When specifying the complete directory path to an object, you start with the NetWare server's name followed by a slash and then the name of the volume followed by a colon. Directories and subdirectories can then be specified by using either a forward slash (/) or a backslash (\) to separate the directory and subdirectory names. Although a slash can be added between the volume and directory names, some programs misinterpret the volume name as a directory name. Therefore it is best *not* to include a slash after the colon in a volume's name. To avoid confusion when you enter DOS paths, you should consistently use backslashes between directory and subdirectory names in NetWare paths because DOS does not accept forward slashes as part of directory paths on local disk drives.

Normally DOS commands do not accept NetWare complete directory paths because they contain unfamiliar objects, such as the NetWare server name and volume name. For example, the following command shows an attempt to use the DOS COPY command to copy files from drive A: to Eleanor Franklin's home directory, which is named EFRANKLN:

```
G:\> DIR USERS

Volume in drive G is SYS
Directory of G:\USERS

EFRANKLN      <DIR>          12-15-96    9:10a
SSAMLSN       <DIR>          12-15-96    9:10a
EPLANK        <DIR>          12-15-96    9:10a
MPINZON       <DIR>          12-15-96    9:10a
GSAKHARV      <DIR>          12-15-96    9:10a
JMORGAN       <DIR>          12-15-96    9:10a

G:\> COPY A:\*.* SYS:USERS\EFRANKLIN
Too many parameters
```

The result is an error message that says "Too many parameters." DOS cannot correctly interpret SYS: as a valid part of the directory path. You can, however, use volume names in the familiar DOS CD command to specify complete paths in the NetWare file system. For example, you can use the CD command with a complete path to change to the EFRANKLN home directory and then copy the desired file from drive A: as follows:

```
G:\> CD SYS:USERS\EFRANKLIN

G:\USERS\EFRANKLN> COPY A:\*.* G:
A:LETTER01.DOC
A:LETTER02.DOC
A:LETTER03.DOC
A:LETTER04.DOC
        4 file(s) copied
```

Partial Path

Entering a partial path is often much quicker than typing a complete path when the directory or file you want to identify is located within the same directory or volume as your default path. In most cases, therefore, you will specify the partial path to a directory or file. DOS commands can often be used with partial paths that do not include a volume name. For example, suppose your default directory path is SYS:USERS and you want to copy all files from the disk in drive A: into the EFRANKLN home directory. You could use either of these two partial paths:

```
G:\USERS> COPY A:*.* \USERS\EFRANKLN
G:\USERS> COPY A:*.* EFRANKLN
```

In the first copy command, the backslash at the beginning of the target path specifies that the path to the target directory starts at the beginning of the default volume, which in this case is the SYS: volume. In the second copy command, the backslash has been omitted. This tells DOS that the target path starts with the current directory and proceeds to the subdirectory named EFRANKLN. Placing a backslash before EFRANKLN would result in an "Invalid path" error message because DOS would look for a directory called EFRANKLN on the root of the volume.

File System NDS Objects

Two of the NDS objects that you studied in Chapter 4 represent parts of the file system—the NetWare Server object and the Volume object. Each NetWare Server in the network is represented by a NetWare Server object. For NetWare 4.1 servers, the NetWare Server object is automatically created and added to the Directory tree when NetWare 4.1 is installed on the server. The server must be named at the time NetWare 4.1 is installed, and this name is used as the name of the NetWare Server object. You will learn more about installing NetWare 4.1 in Chapter 6.

When a volume is created and named, NetWare also creates a Volume object and places it in the same context in the Directory tree as the NetWare Server object where the volume is physically located. The Volume object is named by combining the name of the

NetWare server and the name of the volume. For example, when the SYS: volume is created on Server01, a Volume object named Server01_SYS is placed in the same container holding the NetWare Server object Server01. You will learn about creating volumes in Chapter 6.

Although NDS does not allow you to create objects representing directories and files, it does read the directory structure of a volume, which can be displayed in the Directory tree. As shown in Figure 5-9, Volume objects can be expanded to show the directories in the volume and the files in a directory. You will work with NetWare utilities that manage directories and files in Chapter 7.

Figure 5-9

Directories and files in the NDS Directory tree

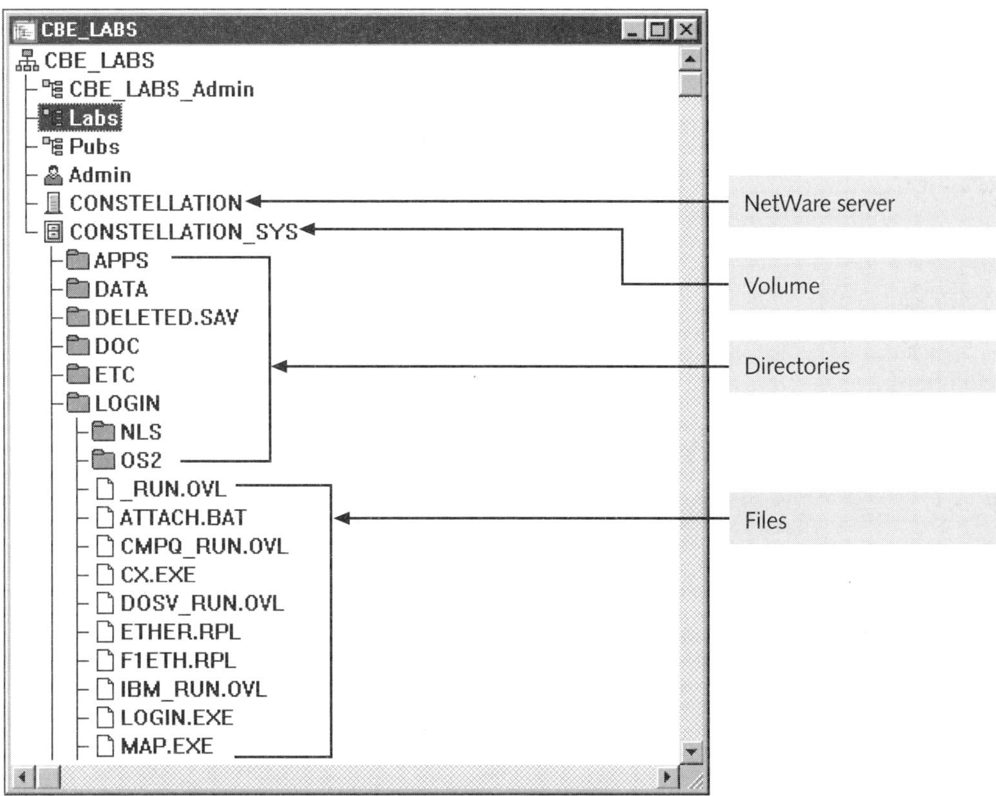

DIRECTORY STRUCTURE

Once you understand the components of a file system, you can design a directory structure that will meet the processing needs of an organization. Designing a directory structure can be compared to creating a blueprint for a building. Just as the blueprint enables the builder to determine the construction details and materials needed, the directory structure design enables the network administrator to allocate storage space and implement the file system on a network. Designing the directory structure involves two steps:

1. Defining the directories and subdirectories needed
2. Placing those directories in the file system structure

Before you design an organization's directory structure, however, you need to analyze the processing needs of the users in the organization to determine what directories will be needed. When creating the directory structure, you should be aware that there is no single best approach that all network administrators use. Instead, each network administrator develops his or her own unique style for defining and arranging directories. This section explains the concepts and techniques that will help you develop your own style for creating good directory structures.

DEFINE WORKGROUPS

The first step in designing a directory structure is to determine the storage required for the services the NetWare server will provide to the network users. To do this, we will work with the Information Systems personnel at Cunningham, Burns, and Evans Laboratories (CBE Labs), the same company we worked with in Chapters 1 and 4. The CBE Labs organizational chart is shown in Chapter 4 in Figure 4-29.

When determining storage needs, you start by examining an organizational chart in order to determine the computer users and any possible workgroups. From the CBE Labs organizational chart you can immediately see that the organization has three main workgroups: administration, publications, and testing and evaluation. In addition, administration can be divided into marketing, finance, personnel, and information systems, and testing and evaluation can be divided into hardware, software, database (DBMS stands for database management systems), and network.

DEFINE NETWARE SERVER USE

Although you may encounter small networks with only one NetWare server, a typical network will have two or more NetWare servers. When you have more than one NetWare server on the network, the use of each server needs to be defined. For example, Ted Simpson, the information systems manager at CBE Labs, has recommended that three NetWare servers be used in the network instead of the single NetWare 3.12 server that CBE Labs currently uses. Management has approved the purchase of two new servers that will run the NetWare 4.1 operating system. The old NetWare 3.12 server will be kept as a NetWare 3.12 server. Ted needs to decide how to use the three servers.

Considering that the purpose of CBE Labs is to test computer components and then report the results, the main server needs are for the testing and evaluation workgroup and for the publishing workgroup. Ted decides to initially allocate one NetWare 4.1 server to testing and evaluation and one NetWare 4.1 server to Publishing. This leaves administrative tasks and companywide requirements, such as e-mail, to be taken care of. Ted realizes that the testing and evaluation workgroup will need all the capacity of their NetWare server but that the publishing workgroup will use only.part of the capacity of their server. By allocating one NetWare 4.1 server as a combined administration/publishing server, many of the company's administration needs can be taken care of. However, the finance department needs resources for the company's accounting system. This system is an older, DOS-based system that is already running on the NetWare 3.12 server. Ted decides to leave that application where it is and to dedicate the NetWare 3.12 server to finance.

Many network administrators create naming schemes for the NetWare servers in their networks. Because CBE Labs president Joseph Cunningham served as an officer in the U.S. Navy, CBE Labs names servers after U.S. Navy aircraft carriers. The existing NetWare 3.12 server is named RANGER. The administration/publishing NetWare 4.1 server will be named CONSTELLATION, and the testing and evaluation NetWare 4.1 server will be named SARATOGA. The three servers, their proposed functions, and the volumes they will contain are shown in Figure 5-10.

Figure 5-10

CBE Labs NetWare Server Planning Form

NetWare Server Planning Form

Created By:	*Ted Simpson*	*Date:*	*9/15/97*
Organization:	*CBE Labs*		

NetWare Servers:

NetWare Server Name:	*CONSTELLATION*
NetWare Operating System:	*4.1*
Volumes:	**SYS**
	DATA
	CDROM
Purpose:	*CONSTELLATION is the main administration and publishing NetWare server.*
NetWare Server Name:	*SARATOGA*
NetWare Operating System:	*4.1*
Volumes:	**SYS**
	DATA
	CDROM
Purpose:	*SARATOGA is the main testing and evaluation labs NetWare server.*
NetWare Server Name:	*RANGER*
NetWare Operating System:	*3.12*
Volumes:	**SYS**
Purpose:	*RANGER is the secondary administration NetWare server and is used for accounting applications and data.*

Both of the new servers, CONSTELLATION and SARATOGA, have two hard drives, which will become a SYS: volume and a DATA: volume. They also each have a CD-ROM drive, and NetWare 4.1 will treat a CD-ROM in this drive as a volume. Each CD-ROM will have a separate volume name, but for planning purposes these volumes will be referred to as CDROM:. The existing NetWare server, RANGER, has only a SYS: volume. Instead of a DATA: volume, RANGER will use a DATA directory as part of the directory structure.

DEFINE DIRECTORIES

After you identify the network users and workgroups, you need to determine—through discussions with the users and department managers—what applications and data storage areas they will need. It is important to get users involved in the design of the network early in the directory design process to ensure that the result will adequately anticipate and serve their needs.

Directories can be divided into four general categories: general-purpose applications, vertical applications, shared data, and home directories. A **general-purpose application** is a software program—such as a word processor, spreadsheet, or CAD product—that is accessed by many different users to create and maintain their own files and documents. A **vertical application** is a software program that performs a specialized process such as payroll, order entry, or manufacturing requirements planning. Vertical applications are normally restricted to a department or a limited number of users and give multiple users access to shared database files within the application's directory structure.

Shared data areas enable users to exchange files by saving the files where multiple users can access them. In designing directory structures, a network administrator can include a **local shared directory**, which restricts access to shared files to the users of the workgroup concerned with them. The network administrator can also provide a **global shared directory** so that files can be shared among workgroups.

Let's follow this process for CBE Labs. Ted Simpson has discussed network usage with the CBE Labs staff and has gathered the following information:

- In finance, a DOS-based payroll application is used for weekly payroll processing. In addition, all users in finance use a spreadsheet package to work on budgets, and these budget spreadsheet files are shared only among the finance users.
- Each user in testing and evaluation has his or her own computer and uses it to access test results that are stored in a specialized SQL (Structured Query Language) database. Additionally, the testing and evaluation users periodically share word processing document files when working together on a report.
- Testing and evaluation has a specialized hardware analysis program that is used when evaluating hardware.
- The publishing personnel use word processing and desktop publishing software to work on shared documents such as the company's main publication, the *C/B/E Networker*. In addition, the publishing personnel work with the testing and evaluation personnel to help format and print special test reports being sent to customers.
- All staff members at CBE Labs need access to a word processing program to write their own correspondence and memos. To make work easier, everyone would like to share common word processing templates, forms, and customer lists.
- All staff members at CBE Labs need access to the company's e-mail program, a shared fax program, and Internet tools.
- CBE Labs has purchased a Windows 95-based software suite, WinOffice, which includes a word processor, an electronic spreadsheet, a presentation graphics program, and a database program. Enough licenses were purchased so that everyone at CBE Labs can use the suite.

Based on his discussions, Ted has filled out the Directory Planning Form shown in Figure 5-11. Ted must now allocate volume space for the applications and data storage needs. The general-purpose software directories for CBE Labs include the software suite application that is needed by all employees, the company's e-mail program, and the company's shared fax software. Vertical applications at CBE Labs include the payroll system used by administration, the SQL database used by testing and evaluation, the hardware analysis software used by testing and evaluation, and the desktop publishing application used by publishing. Ted decides to put application directories for the general-purpose software on the CONSTELLATION SYS: volume, along with the desktop publishing program used by publishing. He also decides to put the applications used by testing and evaluation on the SARATOGA SYS: volume and the accounting software on the RANGER SYS: volume. This arrangement puts each application on the NetWare server assigned to the workgroup using the software.

Ted plans to put data directories on the DATA volumes of CONSTELLATION and SARATOGA and in a DATA directory of RANGER. Data needs are shown in Figure 5-11. Shared directories include a SHARED directory for all users to contain common word processing forms, templates, and customer lists needed by all users; BUDGETS directories for general administration and finance; REPORTS directories for three administration workgroups, TESTDATA directories for each testing and evaluation workgroup to hold the results of the groups tests; and a REPORTS directory for testing and evaluation. There will also be 11 workgroup-shared work directories to hold each workgroup's working papers. Although it would be possible to have just one shared directory for the entire company, multiple directories will keep the files separate, making it easier for staff to locate and use only the files they need.

DESIGN THE DIRECTORY STRUCTURE

Once you have determined the directories that are needed, you are ready to design the layout and determine the location of the directories within the NetWare server's volumes. To design the directory structure for your NetWare server, you must first define the data and software directories needed by your users to perform their processing functions. Then you organize these directories into a logical and easy-to-use structure that will provide a foundation for your network's file system. In this section, you learn how to analyze the directory needs for an organization, as well as two major ways to organize a directory structure: department-oriented and application-oriented. In addition, this section provides you with forms and techniques that will help you design and document your directory structures.

The Volume Design Form and Directory Design Form

As shown in Figure 5-12, the Volume Design Form is used to document each volume's directory structure and all directories branching from the root of the volume. The Volume Design Form can also show subdirectory structures. For example, the PRODUCT directory is treated this way in Figure 5-12. In addition to laying out the directory structure, the Volume Design Form contains fields for specifying NetWare version, total volume capacity, block size, and whether block suballocation, file compression, and data migration are enabled on the volume. Notice that the planned block size is 64 KB. This is a change from NetWare default block size of 32 KB for a 1 GB volume. The larger block size is used with block suballocation to increase file storage efficiency on the volume.

Figure 5-11 CBE Labs Directory Planning Form

Directory Planning Form

Created By:	Ted Simpson	Date:	9/15/97
Organization:	CBE Labs		

Workgroups:

Workgroup Name:	Workgroup Members
Everyone	All CBE Labs users
Administration	13 Administration users
Publications	5 Publications users
Testing and evaluation	14 Testing and evaluation users
Marketing	3 Marketing users
Finance	3 Finance users
Personnel	1 Personnel user
Information systems	3 Information systems users
Hardware	3 Hardware users
Software	3 Software users
Database	3 Database users
Network	3 Network users

Directories:

Description	Type	Users	Estimated Size
WINOFFICE	general-purpose application	everyone	100 MB
e-Mail	general-purpose application	everyone	50 MB
Fax	general-purpose application	everyone	25 MB
Internet	general-purpose application	everyone	25 MB
Payroll	vertical application	finance	25 MB
SQL database	vertical application	testing & eval.	100 MB
Hardware analysis	vertical application	testing & eval.	50 MB
Desktop publishing	vertical application	publishing	25 MB
CBE shared	shared data	everyone	10 MB
Workgroup shared	shared data	11 workgroups	10 MB each
Test data	shared data	4 testing & eval. work-groups	100 MB
Reports	shared data	testing & eval.	100 MB
Payroll data	shared data	finance	250 MB
Desktop publishing documents	shared data	publishing	100 MB
Budgets	shared data	2 admin. workgroups	25 MB each
Reports	shared data	3 admin. workgroups	25 MB
Home directories for each user	private data	32 staff users	20 MB per user

Figure 5-12 Sample Volume Design Form

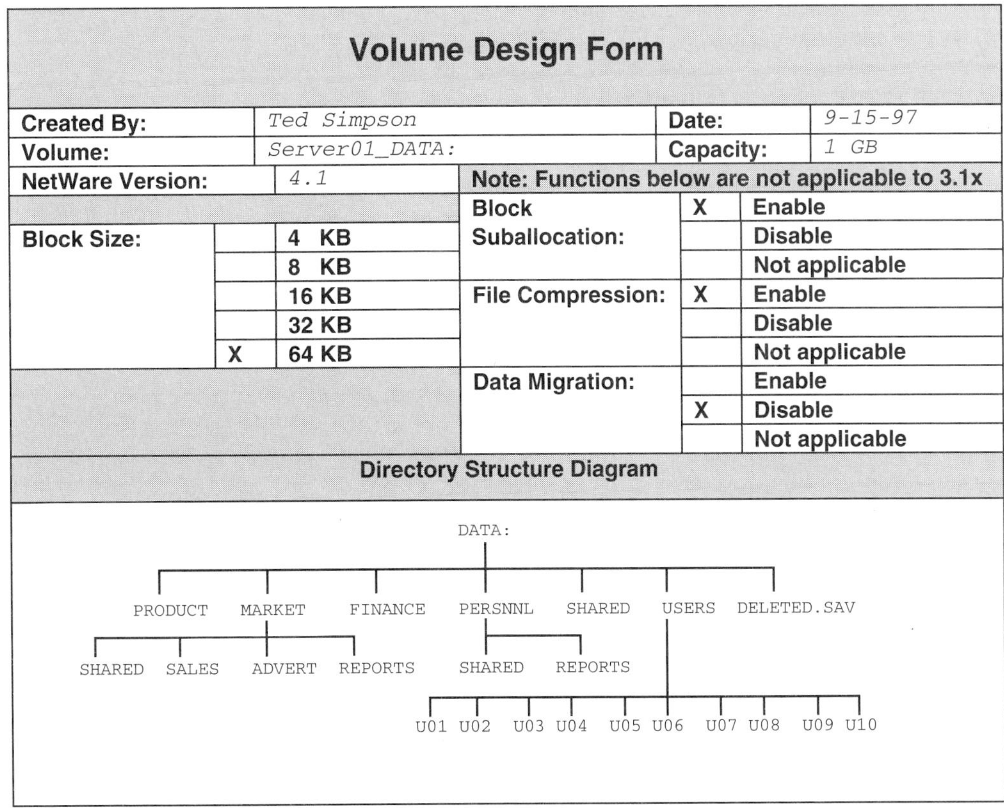

Volume Design Form

Created By:	*Ted Simpson*	Date:	*9-15-97*
Volume:	*Server01_DATA:*	Capacity:	*1 GB*
NetWare Version:	*4.1*	Note: Functions below are not applicable to 3.1x	

Block Size:			Block Suballocation:		
		4 KB		X	Enable
		8 KB			Disable
		16 KB			Not applicable
		32 KB	File Compression:	X	Enable
	X	64 KB			Disable
					Not applicable
			Data Migration:		Enable
				X	Disable
					Not applicable

Directory Structure Diagram

When diagramming a directory structure, however, you will find that it is often difficult to draw all directories and subdirectories for a volume on one sheet of paper. The volume design form does not provide enough space for you to diagram more complex directories. Having separate forms for subdirectories enables you to make alterations to a subdirectory without having to redraw an entire diagram. You should complete one Directory Design Form, shown in Figure 5-13, for each directory not fully documented on your volume design form.

Figure 5-13 Sample Directory Design Form

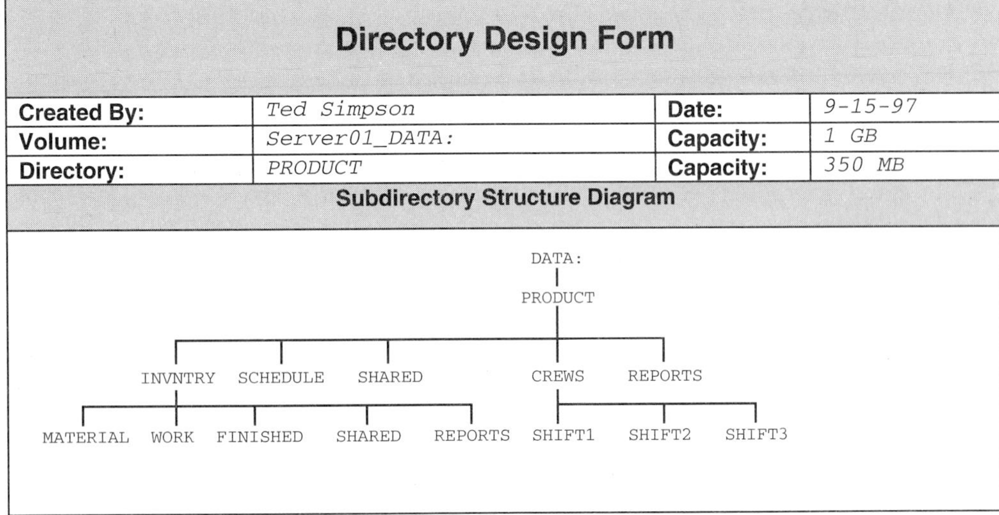

Directory Design Form

Created By:	*Ted Simpson*	Date:	*9-15-97*
Volume:	*Server01_DATA:*	Capacity:	*1 GB*
Directory:	*PRODUCT*	Capacity:	*350 MB*

Subdirectory Structure Diagram

Organizing the SYS: Volume

The simplest method for organizing the SYS: volume is to branch all directories from the root of the SYS: volume, as shown in Figure 5-14. The lack of hierarchy in this directory design, however, makes it inherently difficult to group directories by function or to manage and assign special trustee rights. In addition, storing all files in the SYS: volume can cause the NetWare server to crash if there is not enough disk space available for the operating system.

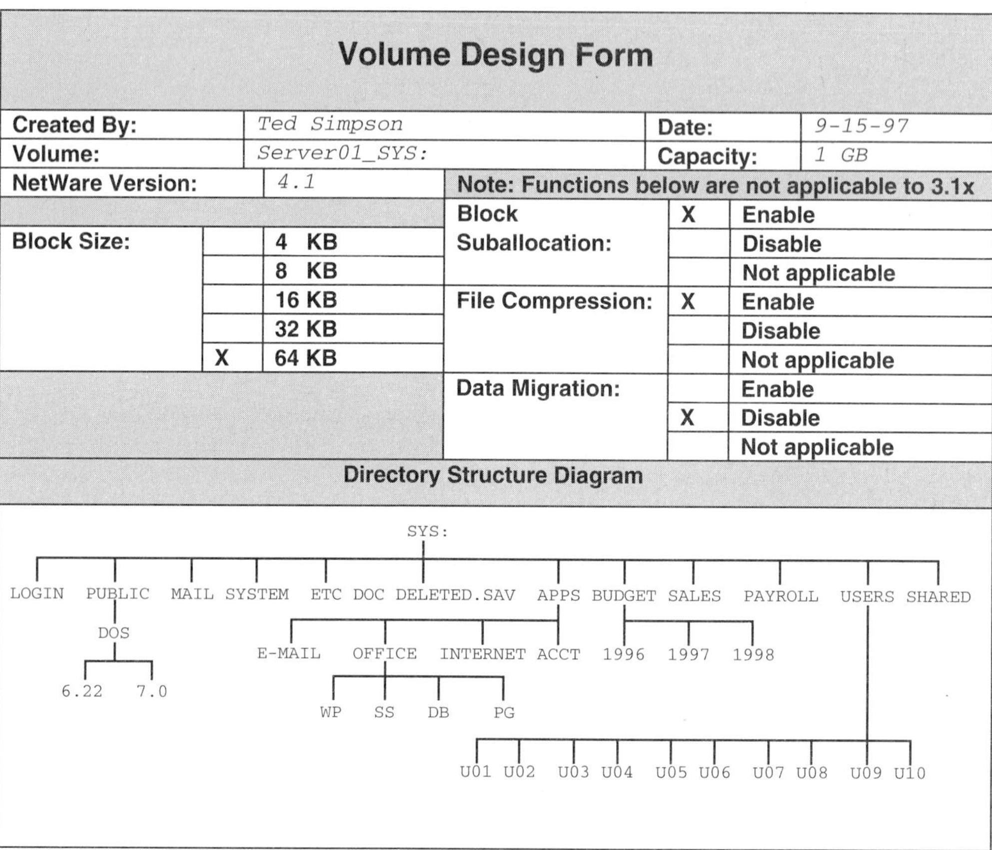

Volume Design Form

Created By:	Ted Simpson	Date:	9-15-97
Volume:	Server01_SYS:	Capacity:	1 GB
NetWare Version:	4.1		

Note: Functions below are not applicable to 3.1x

Block Size:			Block Suballocation:		
		4 KB		X	Enable
		8 KB			Disable
		16 KB			Not applicable
		32 KB	File Compression:	X	Enable
	X	64 KB			Disable
					Not applicable
			Data Migration:		Enable
				X	Disable
					Not applicable

Directory Structure Diagram

Figure 5-14 Simple SYS: volume directory design

To avoid these pitfalls, many network administrators separate the SYS: volume from data storage by using a DATA: volume. Not only does this method free up adequate space in the SYS: volume for system functions, but it also simplifies backup procedures and enables you to perform maintenance activities on the DATA: volume without taking the SYS: volume off line.

In a multiple-volume design, many network administrators place directories for the DOS operating system and general-purpose applications in the SYS: volume. Figure 5-15 illustrates this multiple-volume approach applied to the CBE Labs SYS: volume structure on the NetWare server CONSTELLATION. Notice that all the general-purpose application packages and special-purpose applications have been placed in separate subdirectories under the APPS directory. This will make it easy for the network administrator to assign access rights. The directories for CBE Labs' data will be located in a separate DATA: volume. Because over time the data directories will grow in size, placing them in a separate volume will enable the network administrator to monitor and maintain adequate storage space in the DATA: volume.

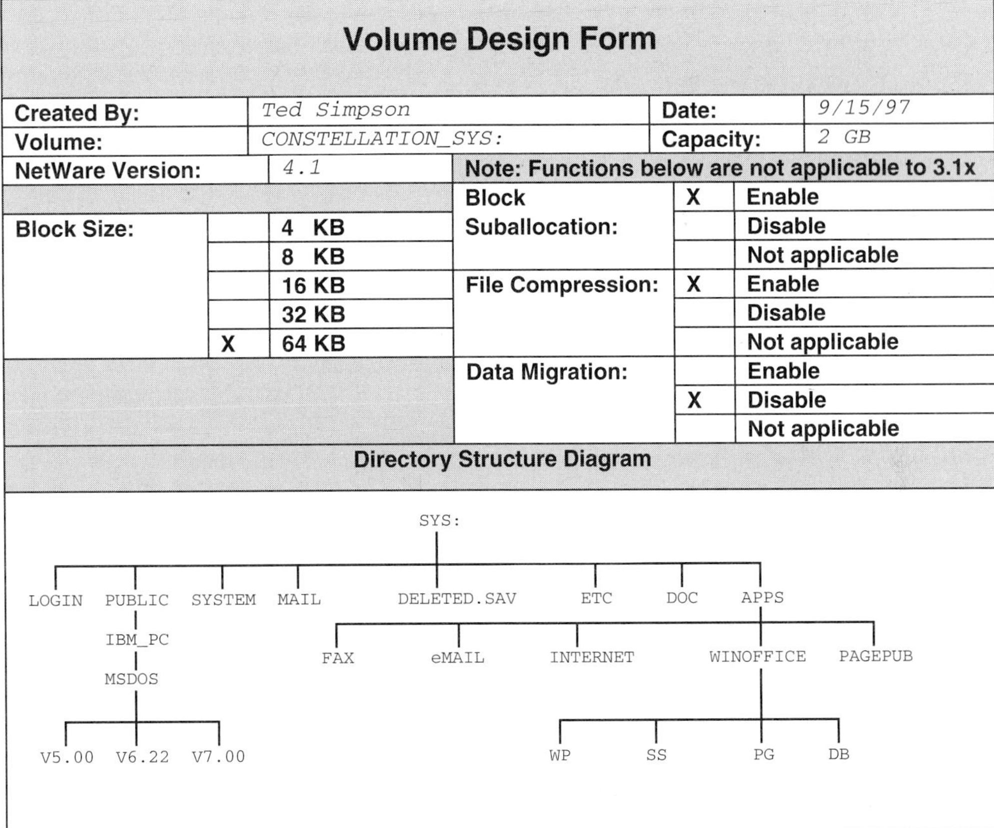

Volume Design Form

Created By:	*Ted Simpson*	Date:	*9/15/97*
Volume:	*CONSTELLATION_SYS:*	Capacity:	*2 GB*
NetWare Version:	*4.1*		

Block Size:		
		4 KB
		8 KB
		16 KB
		32 KB
	X	64 KB

Note: Functions below are not applicable to 3.1x		
Block Suballocation:	X	Enable
		Disable
		Not applicable
File Compression:	X	Enable
		Disable
		Not applicable
Data Migration:		Enable
	X	Disable
		Not applicable

Directory Structure Diagram

Figure 5-15 CBE Labs' CONSTELLATION SYS: volume

Organizing the DATA: Volume

Network administrators generally use two methods to organize directories in a DATA: volume: by application or by department or workgroup. The method you select will depend on your personal preference and on the size and type of processing performed by the organization. Generally, smaller network file systems can be organized by using an application-oriented structure that branches all directories from the root of the volume. This keeps the design simple and easy to manage. In larger file systems involving multiple workgroups and many data directories, it is often easier to maintain security and locate data when you use a departmental structure. This structure places data directories as subdirectories under workgroup directories. In some cases, a combination of both methods will work best for an organization.

Whatever design method you use for data directories, a good rule of thumb is not to exceed 6 subdirectory layers with no more than 16 subdirectories in any one directory. This way, you can always view all directories on a computer monitor at the same time.

Application-Oriented Structure

In an **application-oriented structure**, the directories are grouped by application rather than by department or workgroup. All user home directories, for example, can be placed in a common directory called USERS. The shared directories can then be grouped according to their use, and applications not placed on the SYS: volume can be placed in separate directories located on the root of the DATA: volume. Figure 5-16 shows the application-oriented method applied to the DATA volume.

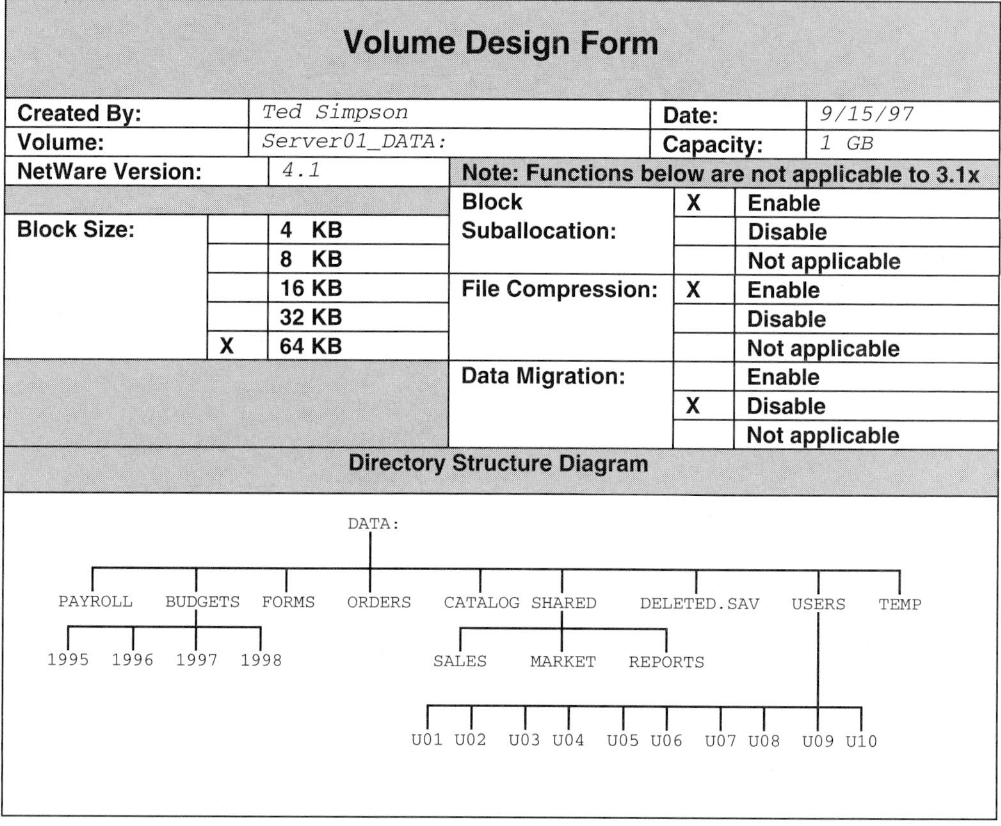

Volume Design Form

Created By:	Ted Simpson	Date:	9/15/97
Volume:	Server01_DATA:	Capacity:	1 GB
NetWare Version:	4.1	Note: Functions below are not applicable to 3.1x	

Block Size:					
	4 KB	Block Suballocation:	X	Enable
	8 KB			Disable
	16 KB			Not applicable
	32 KB	File Compression:	X	Enable
X	64 KB			Disable
				Not applicable
		Data Migration:		Enable
			X	Disable
				Not applicable

Directory Structure Diagram

Figure 5-16 The DATA: volume with an application-oriented structure

The advantage of an application-oriented structure is that it is fairly shallow, which makes it easier to locate files without going through multiple layers of directories. In large directory structures, however, the shallow nature of the application-oriented structure can actually be a disadvantage: it is difficult to know which directories are used by which departments. In an application-oriented structure, the network administrator will need to make more trustee assignments because rights will not automatically be granted for users to access the directories with the software applications they need.

Departmental Structure

In a **departmental structure**, user home directories, shared work directories, and applications are located within the workgroups and departments that control them. Directories that contain files available to all users are located at the root of the volume. Figure 5-17 illustrates organizing the directories for a DATA: volume using a departmental structure. A SHARED directory is located at the root of the DATA: volume to contain files that are used by the entire organization. The SHARED work directories located in each workgroup's directory structure provide separate shared file access for each department. A major difference between the departmental- and application-oriented structures is the location of the user home directories. Notice in Figure 5-17 that the user home directories are located under each department directory rather than placed all together under a general USERS directory.

Figure 5-17 The DATA: volume with a departmental structure

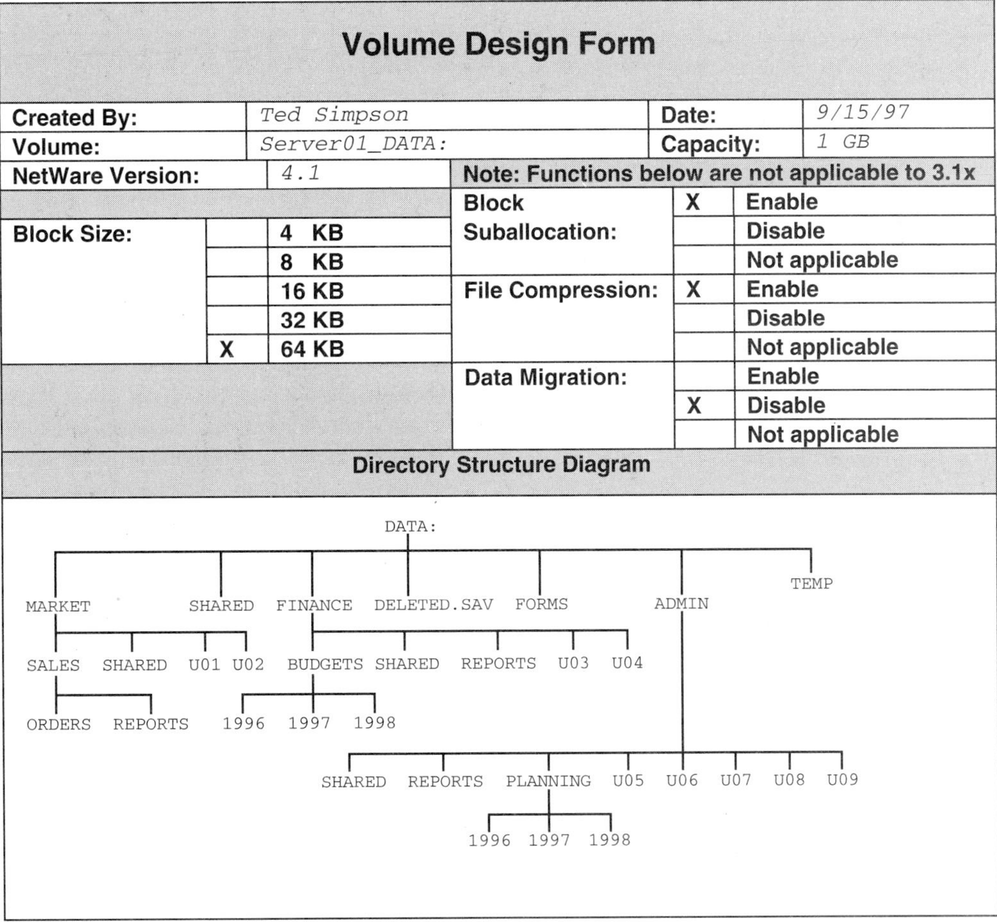

Volume Design Form

Created By:	*Ted Simpson*	Date:	*9/15/97*
Volume:	*Server01_DATA:*	Capacity:	*1 GB*
NetWare Version:	*4.1*	Note: Functions below are not applicable to 3.1x	

Block Size:					
			Block Suballocation:	X	Enable
Block Size:		4 KB			Disable
		8 KB			Not applicable
		16 KB	File Compression:	X	Enable
		32 KB			Disable
	X	64 KB			Not applicable
			Data Migration:		Enable
				X	Disable
					Not applicable

Directory Structure Diagram

Combined Structure

It is also possible to combine the two approaches. A common way of doing this is to use the departmental structure for most of the volume organization but to consolidate all user home directories in a common USER directory. This has the advantage of maintaining a logical structure for creating directories associated with departmental functions, while making user directories easier to manage by locating them in one place. This is the approach that CBE Labs will use for the CONSTELLATION DATA: volume and is shown in Figure 5-18.

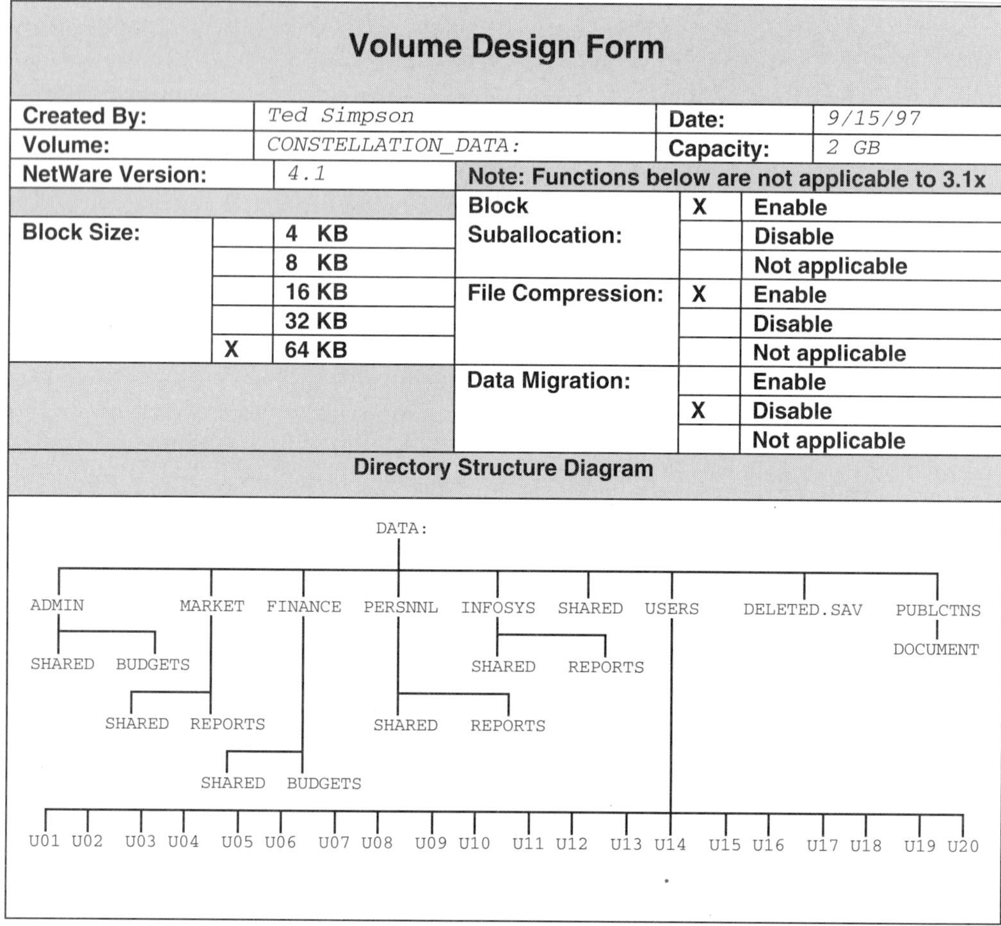

Volume Design Form

Created By:	*Ted Simpson*		**Date:**	*9/15/97*	
Volume:	*CONSTELLATION_DATA:*		**Capacity:**	*2 GB*	
NetWare Version:	*4.1*		**Note: Functions below are not applicable to 3.1x**		
			Block Suballocation:	X	**Enable**
Block Size:		**4 KB**			**Disable**
		8 KB			**Not applicable**
		16 KB	**File Compression:**	X	**Enable**
		32 KB			**Disable**
	X	**64 KB**			**Not applicable**
			Data Migration:		**Enable**
				X	**Disable**
					Not applicable

Directory Structure Diagram

Figure 5-18 The CONSTELLATION DATA: volume with a combined structure

The other CBE Labs volumes will be organized the same way, as shown in the directory structures of the SARATOGA SYS: and SARATOGA DATA: volumes in Figures 5-19 and 5-20. The RANGER SYS: volume follows the same guidelines but also includes a DATA directory, because RANGER has no DATA volume. The RANGER SYS: volume is shown in Figure 5-21.

Figure 5-19

The SARATOGA SYS: volume

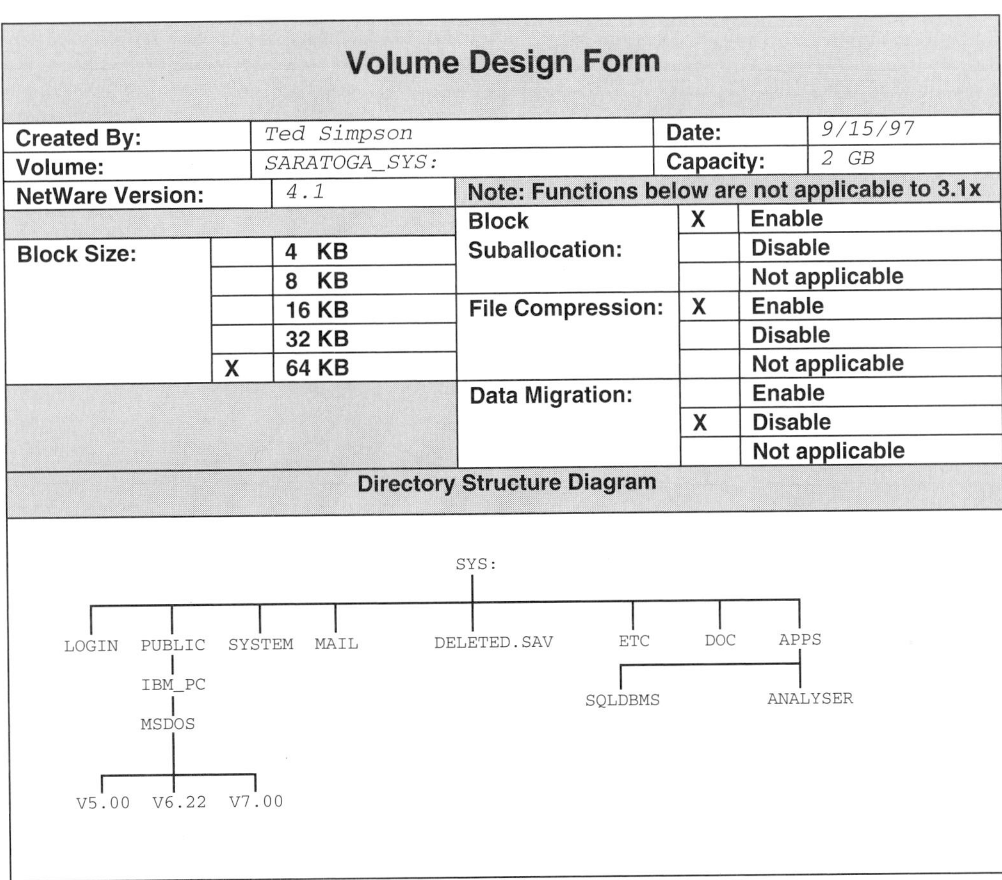

Volume Design Form

Created By:	Ted Simpson	Date:	9/15/97
Volume:	SARATOGA_SYS:	Capacity:	2 GB
NetWare Version:	4.1		

Block Size:		
		4 KB
		8 KB
		16 KB
		32 KB
	X	64 KB

Note: Functions below are not applicable to 3.1x		
Block Suballocation:	X	Enable
		Disable
		Not applicable
File Compression:	X	Enable
		Disable
		Not applicable
Data Migration:		Enable
	X	Disable
		Not applicable

Directory Structure Diagram

Figure 5-20

The SARATOGA DATA: volume

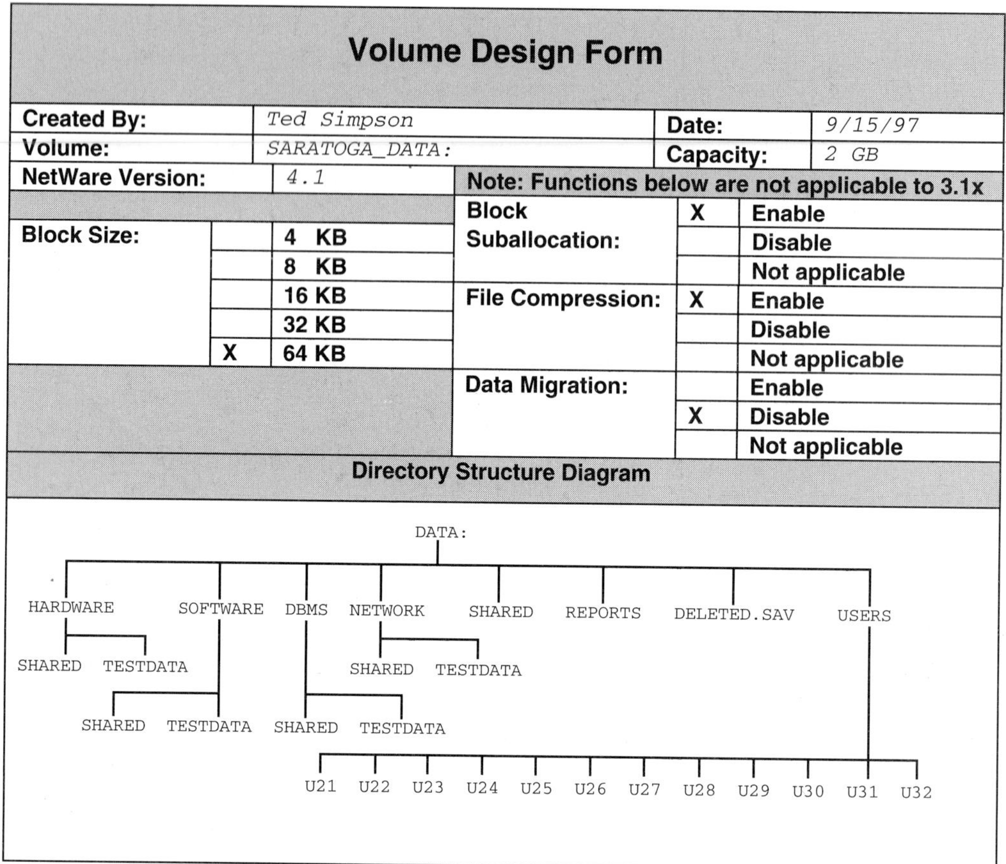

Volume Design Form

Created By:	*Ted Simpson*	**Date:**	*9/15/97*
Volume:	*SARATOGA_DATA:*	**Capacity:**	*2 GB*
NetWare Version:	*4.1*		

Note: Functions below are not applicable to 3.1x

Block Size:		
		4 KB
		8 KB
		16 KB
		32 KB
	X	64 KB

Block Suballocation:	X	Enable
		Disable
		Not applicable
File Compression:	X	Enable
		Disable
		Not applicable
Data Migration:		Enable
	X	Disable
		Not applicable

Directory Structure Diagram

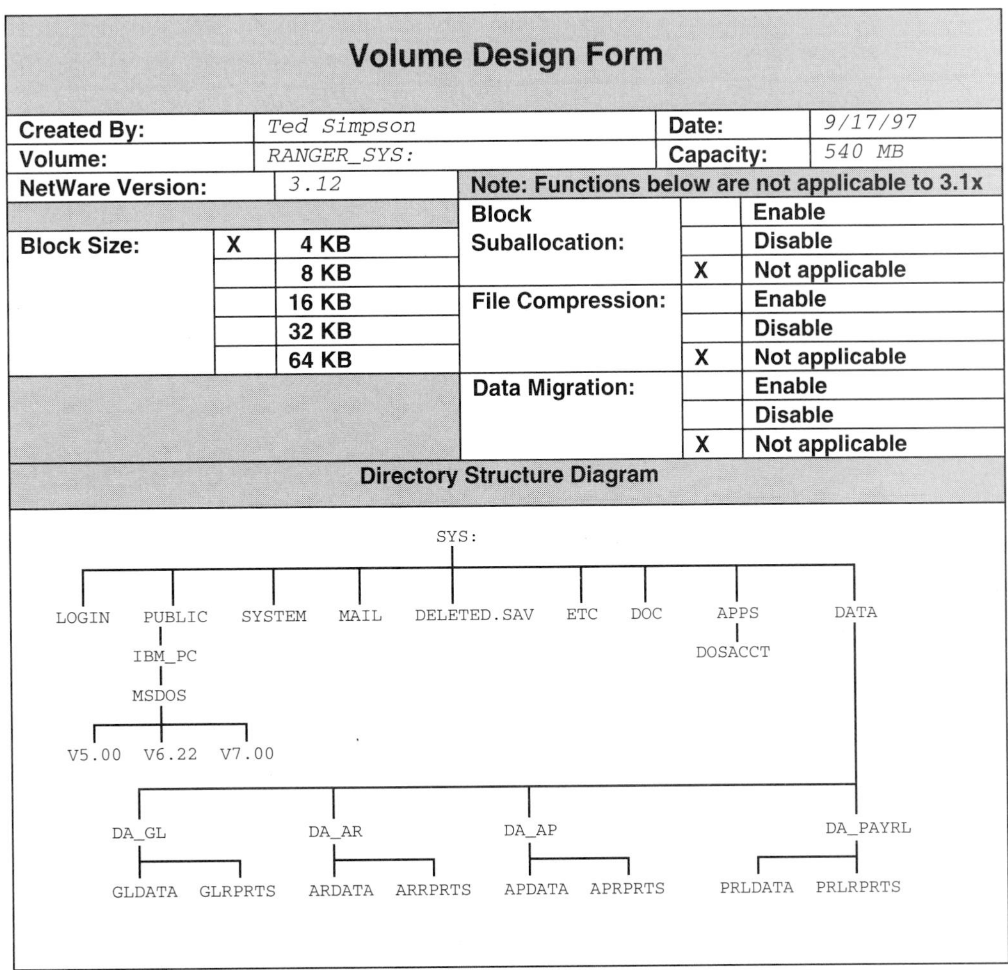

Volume Design Form

Created By:	Ted Simpson	Date:	9/17/97
Volume:	RANGER_SYS:	Capacity:	540 MB
NetWare Version:	3.12	Note: Functions below are not applicable to 3.1x	

Block Size:			Block Suballocation:		
	X	4 KB			Enable
		8 KB			Disable
				X	Not applicable
		16 KB	File Compression:		Enable
		32 KB			Disable
		64 KB		X	Not applicable
			Data Migration:		Enable
					Disable
				X	Not applicable

Directory Structure Diagram

SYS:
LOGIN PUBLIC SYSTEM MAIL DELETED.SAV ETC DOC APPS DATA
IBM_PC
MSDOS
V5.00 V6.22 V7.00
DOSACCT
DA_GL DA_AR DA_AP DA_PAYRL
GLDATA GLRPRTS ARDATA ARRPRTS APDATA APRPRTS PRLDATA PRLRPRTS

Figure 5-21 The RANGER SYS: volume

NETWARE COMMAND LINE UTILITIES

NetWare provides several command line utilities in the SYS:PUBLIC directory. **Command line utilities** are programs that you run by typing a command at the DOS prompt. This section describes the NetWare command line utilities that provide information about the volumes and directory structures on a NetWare server.

THE NDIR COMMAND

NetWare's NDIR command in NetWare 4.1 is similar to, but much more powerful than, the DOS DIR command. The NetWare 4.1 NDIR command has been enhanced from the NetWare 3.1x version of NDIR and has replaced several NetWare 3.1x commands including CHKVOL (Check Volume), CHKDIR (Check Directory), and LISTDIR (List Directory).

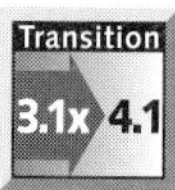

If you try to use a NetWare 3.1x command such as CHKVOL, NetWare 4.1 runs a batch file that triggers a message telling the user that the command is no longer available and giving the equivalent new command. For example, trying CHKVOL causes the CHKVOL.BAT file to be run. This generates the message "This utility is not supported with 4.x NetWare products. Use NDIR [path] /VOL."

The syntax of the NDIR command is

```
NDIR [path] [/options] [/?] [/VER]
```

As shown in the syntax, the NDIR command has several parameters that you can use with it. These are listed in Figure 5-22.

Figure 5-22

The NDIR command parameters

Parameter	Use this parameter to
path	See the directory path to the volume, directory, subdirectory, or file.
/?	Access help about NDIR. If this parameter is used, all others are ignored.
/VER	See the version number of the NDIR command. If this parameter is used, all others are ignored.

There are also several sets of options that you can use with the NDIR command, such as display options, formatting options, sorting options, attribute options, and restriction options. These are discussed in the examples below.

Volume and Space Restriction Information Using NDIR

The NDIR command has two very useful options to display volume information and space restriction information. These are shown in Figure 5-23.

Figure 5-23

The NDIR volume and space restrictions options

Option	Use this option to
/VOL	See volume information.
/SPA	See space information.

To obtain information about a volume using the NDIR command, you use the /VOL option. For example, to get information about the SYS: volume on the server SERVER01, you use this command:

```
G:\>NDIR SERVER01/SYS: /VOL
```

Use the NDIR [path] /VOL command instead of the NetWare 3.1x command CHKVOL.

This produces the following output:

```
G:\> NDIR SERVER01/SYS: /VOL
Statistics for fixed volume SERVER01/SYS:
Space statistics are in KB (1024 bytes).
```

```
Total volume space:                          908,096  100.00%
Space used by 3,504 entries:                 118,976   13.10%
Deleted space not yet purgeable:                   0    0.00%
                                         ----------- -------
Space remaining on volume:                   789,120   86.90%
Space available to AUER:                     789,120   86.90%

Maximum directory entries:                     8,704
Available directory entries:                   3,698   42.49%

Space used if files were not compressed:     244,556
Space used by compressed files:               80,704
                                          ----------
Space saved by compressing files:            163,852   67.00%

Uncompressed space used:                      38,272
```

This command provides detailed information about a specific volume. Information provided includes the volume size (908,096 KB or 908.096 MB) and the amount of space available on the volume (789,120 KB) and to the user (user AUER can still use 789,120 KB). This information can help a network administrator determine whether more disk space needs to be allocated for a user and whether space from deleted files is being properly reused by the operating system. It is important to remember that the space available to a user can be less than the total volume space if special disk space restrictions have been placed on the user by the network administrator.

The NDIR /VOL command also displays the amount of space used by both existing and deleted files (118,976 KB) and the amount of space used by deleted files that cannot be purged immediately (0 KB). By default, when a file is deleted, its data blocks are not immediately reused by NetWare but are held until needed. Blocks from the oldest deleted files are reused first. As long as NetWare has free space on the volume it will not use up the deleted file blocks, so they can be recovered by the network administrator if it turns out they are needed. You can easily determine how much unused space remains on a volume before NetWare begins to reuse the deleted file blocks. Subtract the space used by deleted files not yet purgeable (0 KB) from the space remaining on the volume (789,120 KB). In this example the result is 789,120 KB. This means that there are more than 789,000 KB of new space available in this volume that will need to be used before the system begins to recycle blocks from old deleted files. Use the NDIR /VOL command periodically to monitor how the disk space in NetWare volumes is being used and how it might affect volume capacity and server performance.

The output also shows the effect of the NetWare 4.1 file compression technology on volume space. In this example, 244,556 KB of data have been compressed into 80,704 KB, saving 163,852 KB of disk space (a 67% reduction of the space needed for these files).

You can also view volume information using the FILER utility, which you'll work with in Chapter 8.

To obtain information about disk space available on a volume using the NDIR command, you use the /SPA option. The NDIR /SPA command displays how much disk space is available in the volume and how much of that volume disk space is used by the specified directory. NetWare allows a size limit to be placed on a specific directory, and the command can be used to determine whether the directory is reaching its limit and whether the directory structure needs to have some of its files deleted or its size expanded. For example, to get information about the SYS: volume on the server SERVER01, you use this command:

```
G:\> NDIR SERVER01/SYS: /SPA
```

Use the NDIR [path] /SPA command instead of the NetWare 3.1x command CHKDIR.

This produces the following output:

```
G:\> NDIR SERVER01/SYS: /SPA

Restrictions = Physical or assigned space limitation in K bytes.
In Use       = Space in use at specified level.
Available    = Space available after restrictions applied.

User:   AUER
Server:   SERVER01
SYS
                            Restrictions       In Use     Available
Volume Size                      908,096      118,976       789,120
User volume restrictions:           None       33,028       789,120

Directory restrictions located at:
\                                             112,656       789,120
```

Notice the volume size for the SYS: volume under the Restrictions column. It shows the same amount displayed by the NDIR /VOL command. Under the In Use column, the NDIR /SPA command displays the amount of disk space in use for both the volume and the directory structure. Under the Available column, the command displays the amount of disk space available to both the volume and the directory structure (in line "Directory restrictions located at: \," where \ indicates the root of the volume). In this example, the amount of space available to the directory structure equals the amount of space on the volume. The amount available in the selected directory, however, is sometimes less than the amount available in the volume. This happens when a network administrator, using the NetWare Administrator or NETADMIN utility, has limited the amount of space used by a directory and its subdirectories. If a user receives a "disk full" error message from the NetWare server, the network administrator can determine whether there is additional space on the volume by using the NDIR /SPA command and then, using the NetWare Administrator or NETADMIN, increase the amount of space allocated to the directory structure.

Directory and File Information Using NDIR

The NDIR command has options for displaying and formatting displays of directory and file information. Display options are shown in Figure 5-24 and formatting options are shown in Figure 5-25.

Figure 5-24 The NDIR display options

Option	Use this option to
/DO	See a list of directories only.
/FO	See a list of files only.
/FI	See a list of every copy of the specified files in the current directory and the directories listed in the current PATH.
/SUB	Include all subdirectories below the specified directory.

Figure 5-25 The NDIR formatting options

Option	Use this option to
/DA	See date information.
/DE	See file detail information.
/R	See file attributes and user rights information.
/COMP	See file compression information
/LONG	See long filenames in name spaces that support long filenames.
/MAC	See Apple Macintosh files.

The default output for the NDIR command lists both directories and files. For example, to list the files and directories in the LOGIN directory, you use this command:

```
G:\> NDIR CONSTELLATION/SYS:LOGIN\*.*
```

This produces the following output:

```
G:\> NDIR CONSTELLATION/SYS:LOGIN\*.*

Files            = Files contained in this path
Size             = Number of bytes in the file
Last Update      = Date file was last updated
Owner            = ID of user who created or copied the file

CONSTELLATION/SYS:LOGIN\*.*
Files                       Size   Last Update          Owner
-------------------- ----------- -------------------- --------------
ATTACH.BAT                    27    9-24-92   11:48a    [Supervisor]
CMPQ_RUN.OVL               2,815    2-01-94    8:33a    [Supervisor]
CX.EXE                   214,059   10-20-94    3:27p    [Supervisor]
DOSV_RUN.OVL               3,568    4-09-93    8:39a    [Supervisor]
ETHER.RPL                 16,630   12-28-93    3:34p    [Supervisor]
F1ETH.RPL                 12,499   12-28-93    3:36p    [Supervisor]
IBM_RUN.OVL                2,815    2-01-94    8:33a    [Supervisor]
LOGIN.EXE                314,945   10-20-94    1:30p    [Supervisor]
MAP.EXE                  273,579   10-20-94    1:32p    [Supervisor]
MENU_X.BAT                   307   10-21-92    8:11p    [Supervisor]
NLIST.EXE                395,955   10-20-94    4:25p    [Supervisor]
PCN2L.RPL                 11,357   12-28-93    3:41p    [Supervisor]
RBOOT.RPL                  7,920   10-10-94    2:32p    [Supervisor]
SLIST.BAT                     26    9-24-92   11:48a    [Supervisor]
TEXTUTIL.IDX               9,170   12-10-90    1:37p    [Supervisor]
TOKEN.RPL                 18,253   10-10-94    2:47p    [Supervisor]
TYPEMSG.EXE               43,595   11-01-94   10:05a    [Supervisor]
_RUN.OVL                   2,815    2-01-94    8:33a    [Supervisor]

Directories      = Directories contained in this path
Filter           = Inherited Rights Filter
```

```
Rights          = Effective Rights
Created         = Date directory was created
Owner           = ID of user who created or copied the file

CONSTELLATION/SYS:LOGIN\*.*
Directories Filter     Rights      Created          Owner
--------------------- ----------  -------------- ------------
NLS          [SRWCEMFA] [SRWCEMFA]  2-17-95 11:48a [Supervisor]
OS2          [SRWCEMFA] [SRWCEMFA]  2-17-95 11:57a [Supervisor]

     1,330,335  bytes (1,335,808  bytes of disk space used)
            18  Files
             2  Directories
```

Notice that the filename, file size, date and time of the last file update, and the file owner are listed for each file. For each subdirectory of the current directory, the inherited rights filter, the user's effective rights in that subdirectory, the creation date and time, and the owner are displayed. In NetWare, directory rights and file rights control what a user can do in a directory or with a file. For example, the R read right, indicated by the letter R in the Filter and Rights output of the NDIR command, means that a user can only read file information from within a directory, but the user cannot change the file, delete it, or rename it. You will learn about directory and file rights, as well as effective rights and inherited rights filters, in Chapter 10. You will see several NDIR output listings containing rights information in this chapter. At this point, you should simply note that NDIR can be used to list some rights information.

To list only the subdirectories in the LOGIN directory, you use this command:

```
G:\> NDIR CONSTELLATION/SYS:LOGIN\*.* /DO
```

To list only the files in the LOGIN directory, you use this command:

```
G:\> NDIR CONSTELLATION/SYS:LOGIN\*.* /FO
```

To list information on the directory and all its subdirectories, you use the /SUB option. For example, to list all the subdirectories of the LOGIN directory without listing their files, you use this command:

```
G:\> NDIR CONSTELLATION/SYS:LOGIN\*.* /DO /SUB
```

This produces the following output:

```
G:\> NDIR CONSTELLATION/SYS:LOGIN\*.* /DO /SUB

Directories          = Directories contained in this path
Filter               = Inherited Rights Filter
Rights               = Effective Rights
Created              = Date directory was created
Owner                = ID of user who created or copied the file

CONSTELLATION/SYS:LOGIN\*.*
Directories Filter     Rights      Created          Owner
---------- ---------- ----------  -------------- ------------
NLS          [SRWCEMFA] [SRWCEMFA]  2-17-95 11:48a [Supervisor]
OS2          [SRWCEMFA] [SRWCEMFA]  2-17-95 11:57a [Supervisor]

     2  Directories
```

```
CONSTELLATION/SYS:LOGIN\NLS\*.*
Directories Filter     Rights      Created        Owner
----------- --------- ----------  -------------- ------------
ENGLISH     [SRWCEMFA] [SRWCEMFA]  2-17-95 11:58a [Supervisor]
      1  Directory


CONSTELLATION/SYS:LOGIN\OS2\*.*
Directories Filter     Rights      Created        Owner
---------- ---------- ----------  -------------- ------------
NLS         [SRWCEMFA] [SRWCEMFA]  2-17-95 11:57a [Supervisor]

      1  Directory


CONSTELLATION/SYS:LOGIN\OS2\NLS\*.*
Directories Filter     Rights      Created        Owner
----------- --------- ----------  -------------- ------------
ENGLISH     [SRWCEMFA] [SRWCEMFA]  2-17-95 11:58a [Supervisor]

       1  Directory
```

This indicates that the LOGIN directory has two subdirectories, NLS and OS2. The NLS subdirectory has one subdirectory, ENGLISH. The OS2 subdirectory has one subdirectory, NLS, which itself has one subdirectory, ENGLISH. Therefore, the subdirectory structure for LOGIN appears as shown in Figure 5-26.

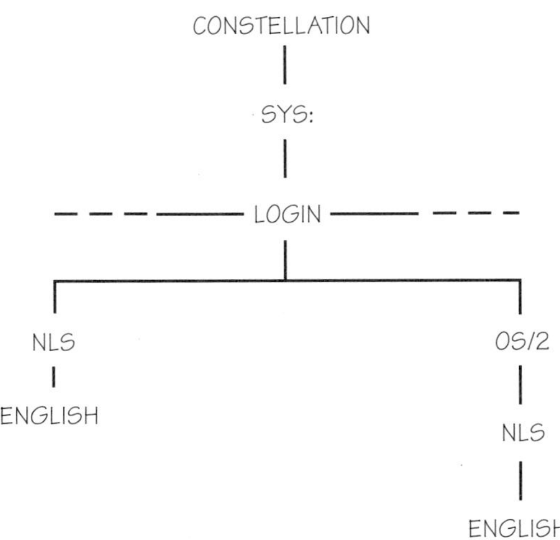

Figure 5-26 The LOGIN directory and its subdirectories

The NDIR command's /SUB option is useful if you are looking for a specific file in the directory structure and do not know what subdirectory the file is in. For example, to scan the entire DATA: volume looking for the file JAN93.WK1, you use this command:

```
F:\> NDIR CONSTELLATION/DATA:JAN93.WK1 /SUB
```

If the file is found, NDIR will display the file's information, including its home directory path.

Use the "NDIR /SUB" command instead of the NetWare 3.1x command LISTDIR.

When the /SUB option is used with files displayed, the total disk space used by all subdirectories and the files within them is displayed. You can use this information to determine how much space will be required to back up or move a directory structure to another location.

You can also control which details are listed by using the NDIR formatting options. To list date information about the files in the LOGIN directory, you use this command:

```
G:\> NDIR CONSTELLATION/SYS:LOGIN\*.* /DA
```

The output for this command shows the last update date, the archive date and status, the last access date, and the date and time the file was created or copied to the directory:

```
G:\> NDIR CONSTELLATION/SYS:LOGIN /DA


Files           = Files contained in this path
Last Update     = Date file was last updated
Archived        = Date file was last archived
Accessed        = Date file was last accessed
Created/Copied  = Date file was created or copied
* = Files marked A are flagged for archiving.

CONSTELLATION/SYS:LOGIN\*.*
Files           Last Update      Archived        * Accessed Created/Copied
------------ ---------------- --------------------------- ----------------
ATTACH.BAT     9-24-92  11:48a   0-00-00   0:00  -  2-17-95   2-17-95  11:57a
CMPQ_RUN.OVL   2-01-94   8:33a   0-00-00   0:00  -  2-17-95   2-17-95  11:52a
CX.EXE        10-20-94   3:27p   0-00-00   0:00  -  9-22-95   2-17-95  11:52a
DOSV_RUN.OVL   4-09-93   8:39a   0-00-00   0:00  -  2-17-95   2-17-95  11:52a
ETHER.RPL     12-28-93   3:34p   0-00-00   0:00  -  2-17-95   2-17-95  11:52a
F1ETH.RPL     12-28-93   3:36p   0-00-00   0:00  -  2-17-95   2-17-95  11:52a
IBM_RUN.OVL    2-01-94   8:33a   0-00-00   0:00  -  2-17-95   2-17-95  11:52a
LOGIN.EXE     10-20-94   1:30p   0-00-00   0:00  -  9-01-95   2-17-95  11:52a
MAP.EXE       10-20-94   1:32p   0-00-00   0:00  -  7-28-95   2-17-95  11:57a
MENU_X.BAT    10-21-92   8:11p   0-00-00   0:00  -  2-17-95   2-17-95  11:57a
NLIST.EXE     10-20-94   4:25p   0-00-00   0:00  -  2-17-95   2-17-95  11:52a
PCN2L.RPL     12-28-93   3:41p   0-00-00   0:00  -  2-17-95   2-17-95  11:52a
RBOOT.RPL     10-10-94   2:32p   0-00-00   0:00  -  2-17-95   2-17-95  11:52a
SLIST.BAT      9-24-92  11:48a   0-00-00   0:00  -  2-17-95   2-17-95  11:52a
TEXTUTIL.IDX  12-10-90   1:37p   0-00-00   0:00  -  2-17-95   2-17-95  11:52a
TOKEN.RPL     10-10-94   2:47p   0-00-00   0:00  -  2-17-95   2-17-95  11:52a
TYPEMSG.EXE   11-01-94  10:05a   0-00-00   0:00  -  2-17-95   2-17-95  11:52a
_RUN.OVL       2-01-94   8:33a   0-00-00   0:00  -  2-17-95   2-17-95  11:52a

Directories     = Directories contained in this path
Filter          = Inherited Rights Filter
Rights          = Effective Rights
Created         = Date directory was created
Owner           = ID of user who created or copied the file
```

```
CONSTELLATION/SYS:LOGIN\*.*
Directories Filter     Rights      Created          Owner
----------- ---------- ---------- --------------- ------------
NLS          [SRWCEMFA] [SRWCEMFA]  2-17-95 11:48a [Supervisor]
OS2          [SRWCEMFA] [SRWCEMFA]  2-17-95 11:57a [Supervisor]

      1,330,335  bytes (1,335,808  bytes of disk space used)
             18  Files
              2  Directories
```

To list detailed information about the files in a directory, you use the /DE option. This option produces very detailed information on each file listed. For example, to list the file details about the CX.EXE file in the LOGIN directory, you use this command:

```
>G:\> NDIR CONSTELLATION/SYS:LOGIN\CX.EXE /DE
```

The output for this command is

```
G:\> NDIR CONSTELLATION/SYS:LOGIN\CX.EXE /DE

-------------------------------------------------------------
CONSTELLATION/SYS:LOGIN\CX.EXE*
Files:
  DOS:  CX.EXE

Rights:
  DOS, OS/2:    Inherited: [SRWCEMFA]
                Effective: [--------]

Owner:  DOS, OS/2:     [Supervisor]

Owning namespace:      DOS

Miscellaneous NetWare information:
  Last update:        10-20-94  3:27p
  Last archived:       0-00-00  0:00
  Last accessed:       9-22-95
  Created/Copied:      2-17-95 11:52a
  Flags:               [Ro----]  [---Sh--DiRiDc----]  [---]
  File size:                 214,059

        214,059  bytes (1,335,808  bytes of disk space used)
              1  Files
```

In addition to providing rights information about the file (inherited rights and effective rights), this output also includes attributes for each file. You may already know about DOS file attributes, and you will learn about NetWare file attributes in detail in Chapter 10. The attribute information shows up in the Flags row on the output. It is divided into three sections—DOS attributes, NetWare attributes, and NetWare status flags—each contained in its own set of square brackets. For example, the CX.EXE file has the DOS attribute Ro, which stands for Read-Only, indicating that users can read but not change this file. Similarly, the file has the NetWare attributes Sharable [Sh], Delete Inhibit [Di], Rename Inhibit [Ri], and Don't Compress [Dc]. The attribute names are self-explanatory: the file can be shared by users (more than one user can use it at a time), a user cannot delete it, a user cannot rename it, and the file cannot be compressed by NetWare 4.1's compression utility. Finally, there are no flags in the third set of square brackets, which show NetWare status flags. An example of a status flag is Co, indicating that a compressable file has already been compressed. When you see NDIR output listings containing attributes information in this chapter, you simply need to note that NDIR can be used to list attribute information.

In fact, to specifically list information about rights and attributes for the files in a directory, you use the /R option. For example, to list the attributes and rights information for the files in the LOGIN directory, you use this command:

```
G:\> NDIR CONSTELLATION/SYS:LOGIN\*.* /R
```

The output for this command is

```
G:\> NDIR CONSTELLATION/SYS:LOGIN\*.* /R

Files                   = Files contained in this path
DOS Attr                = DOS file attributes
NetWare Attr            = NetWare file attributes
Status                  = Compression/Migration status
Filter                  = Inherited Rights Filter
Rights                  = Effective Rights
Owner                   = ID of user who created or copied the file

CONSTELLATION/SYS:LOGIN\*.*
Files            DOS Attr  NetWare Attr      Status Filter      Rights
-----------  ------------ ------------------ ---- ---------- -----------
ATTACH.BAT       [Ro—]     [--Sh--DiRiDc—]   [--] [SRWCEMFA] [SRWCEMFA]
CMPQ_RUN.OVL     [Ro—]     [--Sh--DiRiDc—]   [--] [SRWCEMFA] [SRWCEMFA]
CX.EXE           [Ro—]     [--Sh--DiRiDc—]   [--] [SRWCEMFA] [SRWCEMFA]
DOSV_RUN.OVL     [Ro—]     [--Sh--DiRiDc—]   [--] [SRWCEMFA] [SRWCEMFA]
ETHER.RPL        [Ro—]     [--Sh--DiRiDc—]   [--] [SRWCEMFA] [SRWCEMFA]
F1ETH.RPL        [Ro—]     [--Sh--DiRiDc—]   [--] [SRWCEMFA] [SRWCEMFA]
IBM_RUN.OVL      [Ro—]     [--Sh--DiRiDc—]   [--] [SRWCEMFA] [SRWCEMFA]
LOGIN.EXE        [Ro—]     [--Sh--DiRiDc—]   [--] [SRWCEMFA] [SRWCEMFA]
MAP.EXE          [Ro—]     [--Sh--DiRiDc—]   [--] [SRWCEMFA] [SRWCEMFA]
MENU_X.BAT       [Ro—]     [--Sh--DiRiDc—]   [--] [SRWCEMFA] [SRWCEMFA]
NLIST.EXE        [Ro—]     [--Sh--DiRiDc—]   [--] [SRWCEMFA] [SRWCEMFA]
PCN2L.RPL        [Ro—]     [--Sh--DiRiDc—]   [--] [SRWCEMFA] [SRWCEMFA]
RBOOT.RPL        [Ro—]     [--Sh--DiRiDc—]   [--] [SRWCEMFA] [SRWCEMFA]
SLIST.BAT        [Ro—]     [--Sh--DiRiDc—]   [--] [SRWCEMFA] [SRWCEMFA]
TEXTUTIL.IDX     [Ro—]     [--Sh--DiRiDc—]   [--] [SRWCEMFA] [SRWCEMFA]
TOKEN.RPL        [Ro—]     [--Sh--DiRiDc—]   [--] [SRWCEMFA] [SRWCEMFA]
TYPEMSG.EXE      [Ro—]     [--Sh--DiRiDc—]   [--] [SRWCEMFA] [SRWCEMFA]
_RUN.OVL         [Ro—]     [--Sh--DiRiDc—]   [--] [SRWCEMFA] [SRWCEMFA]

Directories          = Directories contained in this path
Attribute            = Directory attributes
Filter               = Inherited Rights Filter
Rights               = Effective Rights
Created              = Date directory was created
Owner                = ID of user who created or copied the file
```

```
CONSTELLATION/SYS:LOGIN\*.*
Directories   Attribute  Filter     Rights     Created          Owner
------------------ ------  ---------------  ---- ------------
NLS           [------]   [SRWCEMFA] [SRWCEMFA]  2-17-95 11:48a [Supervi
OS2           [------]   [SRWCEMFA] [SRWCEMFA]  2-17-95 11:57a [Supervi

      1,330,335  bytes (1,335,808  bytes of disk space used)
             18  Files
              2  Directories
```

There is an apparent bug in the NDIR /R option. Although the legend states that an owner will be listed for files, no owner name is shown in the printout. The owner name is also cut off in the listing of directories.

Notice the detailed NetWare rights and DOS and NetWare attributes information shown for each file.

Sorting File Information Using NDIR

The NDIR command has options for sorting the file information displayed. Sorting options are shown in Figure 5-27.

Figure 5-27

The NDIR sorting parameters

Option	**Use this option to**
/SORT [parameter]	Sort the list in ascending order (A to Z, earliest to latest, smallest to largest) according to the parameter(s) listed.
Parameter	**Use this parameter to**
UN	Display without sorting (stop sorting).
REV	Sort the list in descending order (Z to A, latest to earliest, largest to smallest).
AC	Sort the list by access date.
AR	Sort the list by archive date.
CR	Sort the list by creation or copy date.
OW	Sort the list by owner name.
SI	Sort the list by size.
UP	Sort the list by last update date.

For example, to display the files in the LOGIN directory sorted by size, you use this command:

```
G:\> NDIR CONSTELLATION/SYS:LOGIN\*.* /SORT SI
```

The result is

```
G:\> NDIR CONSTELLATION/SYS:LOGIN\*.* /SORT SI

Files           = Files contained in this path
Size            = Number of bytes in the file
Last Update     = Date file was last updated
Owner           = ID of user who created or copied the file

CONSTELLATION/SYS:LOGIN\*.*
Files                      Size     Last Update         Owner
----------------- ---------------- --------- --------- -------------
SLIST.BAT                       26    9-24-92    11:48a    [Supervisor]
ATTACH.BAT                      27    9-24-92    11:48a    [Supervisor]
MENU_X.BAT                     307   10-21-92     8:11p    [Supervisor]
_RUN.OVL                     2,815    2-01-94     8:33a    [Supervisor]
IBM_RUN.OVL                  2,815    2-01-94     8:33a    [Supervisor]
CMPQ_RUN.OVL                 2,815    2-01-94     8:33a    [Supervisor]
DOSV_RUN.OVL                 3,568    4-09-93     8:39a    [Supervisor]
RBOOT.RPL                    7,920   10-10-94     2:32p    [Supervisor]
TEXTUTIL.IDX                 9,170   12-10-90     1:37p    [Supervisor]
PCN2L.RPL                   11,357   12-28-93     3:41p    [Supervisor]
F1ETH.RPL                   12,499   12-28-93     3:36p    [Supervisor]
ETHER.RPL                   16,630   12-28-93     3:34p    [Supervisor]
TOKEN.RPL                   18,253   10-10-94     2:47p    [Supervisor]
TYPEMSG.EXE                 43,595   11-01-94    10:05a    [Supervisor]
CX.EXE                     214,059   10-20-94     3:27p    [Supervisor]
MAP.EXE                    273,579   10-20-94     1:32p    [Supervisor]
LOGIN.EXE                  314,945   10-20-94     1:30p    [Supervisor]
NLIST.EXE                  395,955   10-20-94     4:25p    [Supervisor]

Directories     = Directories contained in this path
Filter          = Inherited Rights Filter
Rights          = Effective Rights
Created         = Date directory was created
Owner           = ID of user who created or copied the file

CONSTELLATION/SYS:LOGIN\*.*
Directories Filter      Rights      Created         Owner
----------- --------- ----------  -------------- ------------
NLS         [SRWCEMFA] [SRWCEMFA]  2-17-95 11:48a [Supervisor]
OS2         [SRWCEMFA] [SRWCEMFA]  2-17-95 11:57a [Supervisor]

      1,330,335  bytes (1,335,808  bytes of disk space used)
             18  Files
              2  Directories
```

Notice that the smallest file (SLIST.BAT) is listed first, and the largest file (NLIST.EXE) is listed last.

The sorting options are used with the NDIR restriction options to select subsets of the files that meet certain criteria, such as "after a given date" or "greater than a given number of KB." Restriction options are shown in Figure 5-28.

Figure 5-28

The NDIR restriction options

Option	Use this option to
NOT	Show all files except those meeting the condition.
EQ	Show all files equal to the value or date.
LE	Show all files less than the value.
GR	Show all files greater than the value.
AFT	Show all files after the date.
BEF	Show all files before the date.

For example, to list the files in the LOGIN directory that were updated after January 1, 1994, you use this command:

```
G:\> NDIR CONSTELLATION/SYS:LOGIN\*.* /SORT UP UP GR 1/1/94
```

The output for this command is

```
G:\> NDIR CONSTELLATION/SYS:LOGIN\*.* /SORT UP UP GR 1/1/94

Files           = Files contained in this path
Size            = Number of bytes in the file
Last Update     = Date file was last updated
Owner           = ID of user who created or copied the file

CONSTELLATION/SYS:LOGIN\*.*
Files                         Size Last Update     Owner
---------------- ---------------- -------------- ----------
CMPQ_RUN.OVL              2,815  2-01-94  8:33a [Supervisor]
CX.EXE                  214,059 10-20-94  3:27p [Supervisor]
IBM_RUN.OVL               2,815  2-01-94  8:33a [Supervisor]
LOGIN.EXE               314,945 10-20-94  1:30p [Supervisor]
MAP.EXE                 273,579 10-20-94  1:32p [Supervisor]
NLIST.EXE               395,955 10-20-94  4:25p [Supervisor]
RBOOT.RPL                 7,920 10-10-94  2:32p [Supervisor]
TOKEN.RPL                18,253 10-10-94  2:47p [Supervisor]
TYPEMSG.EXE              43,595 11-01-94 10:05a [Supervisor]
_RUN.OVL                  2,815  2-01-94  8:33a [Supervisor]


     1,276,751  bytes (1,280,000  bytes of disk space used)
            10  Files
```

You could also sort by files that have not been accessed since a specified date. This will help you identify files that can be considered for deletion—just one example of how this kind of file information can greatly simplify a network administrator's job of managing network file systems.

THE NCOPY COMMAND

The syntax of the NCOPY command is very similar to that of the DOS XCOPY command. When creating or maintaining the directory structure, a network administrator often needs to copy files from a NetWare directory or local disk to another location in the network file system. One advantage of the NCOPY command is that you can specify a complete NetWare path, including NetWare server name and volume name. The XCOPY command works only with partial paths containing directory and subdirectory names; it does not accept NetWare complete paths because it does not know about NetWare servers and volumes.

Another advantage of the NCOPY command is that it is more efficient than the DOS COPY and XCOPY commands. Although the DOS COPY and XCOPY commands and the Windows File Manager can be used to copy files to and from NetWare drives, the NetWare NCOPY command is more efficient and powerful. This is due to the way the copy process is performed. When a DOS COPY command or File Manager is used to transfer files between two locations on the NetWare server, each block of the file is read from the source path and must therefore be transmitted to the workstation. The block is then written to the target directory, causing the data to be transmitted back to the NetWare server. NCOPY improves on COPY or File Manager by working directly with the NetWare server to transfer a file from one directory to another. The blocks do not need to be sent to the workstation and retransmitted back to the server. Instead, the transfer is performed internally at the NetWare server; only the status information is transmitted to the workstation that submitted the copy request. If your network cable system is busy, NCOPY can make a noticeable improvement in performance over the DOS copy commands or File Manager for transferring large files.

Another feature of the NCOPY command that makes it more powerful for copying NetWare files than the DOS commands or Windows File Manager is the way in which NetWare file attributes are handled. A file attribute is a flag, stored in the directory along with the file's name and location, that gives the file certain characteristics such as making it Read Only, Hidden, or Sharable. By default, the NCOPY command copies all the file attributes that are supported by the target server or local hard disk. The DOS copy command, in contrast, does not transfer NetWare file attributes.

The syntax of the NCOPY command is

```
NCOPY [source_ path] filename target_path [filename] [/option] [/?] [/VER]
```

Several parameters can be used with NCOPY. They are listed in Figure 5-29.

Figure 5-29 The NCOPY command parameters

Parameter	Use this parameter to
source_path	See the directory path to the file(s) to be copied.
filename	See the name(s) of the file(s) to be copied.
target_path	See the directory path to the new location for the file(s).
[filename]	See a new name for the file(s) if you want to rename them during the copy.
/?	Access help about NCOPY. If this parameter is used, all others are ignored.
/VER	See the version number of the NCOPY command. If this parameter is used, all others are ignored

There are also several options that can be used with NCOPY. Some of these are listed in Figure 5-30.

Figure 5-30

The NCOPY command parameters

Option	Use this option to
/S	Copy all subdirectories and their files.
/S /E	Copy all subdirectories including those that are empty.
/V	Verify that the copy is correct (works only on local DOS drives).

For example, to use the NCOPY command to transfer files from the FORMS directory of the SYS: volume of the NetWare server named CONSTELLATION to a floppy disk in drive A:, you use this command:

```
G:\>NCOPY CONSTELLATION/:SYS:NWTC\EXAMPLE\FORMS\*.FRM A:\*.*
```

The result of this command is

```
G:\>NCOPY CONSTELLATION/:SYS:NWTC\EXAMPLE\FORMS\*.FRM A:\*.*
  From CONSTELLATION\SYS:NWTC\EXAMPLE\FORMS\
  To   A:\
  ORDER.FRM          (1405)
  TIME.FRM           (5150)

2 files were copied.
```

THE RENDIR COMMAND

In managing directory structures, a network administrator sometimes needs to change the name of an existing directory or subdirectory in order to make it more meaningful or to avoid conflicts with other directory or filenames. In these situations, the RENDIR command can be used to change the name of any directory in the file system simply by specifying the current path followed by the new directory name. You do not need to specify the entire path a second time when specifying the new directory's name.

The syntax of the RENDIR command is

```
RENDIR path [TO] directory_name [/?] [/VER]
```

Several parameters can be used with RENDIR. They are listed in Figure 5-31.

Figure 5-31

The RENDIR command parameters

Parameter	Use this parameter to
path	See the directory path of the directory to be renamed.
directory_filename	See the new directory name.
/?	Access help about RENDIR. If this parameter is used, all others are ignored.
/VER	See the version number of the RENDIR command. If this parameter is used, all others are ignored.

For example, to change the name of the BUS directory in the SYS: volume to BUSINESS, you use this command:

```
G:\> RENDIR CONSTELLATION/SYS:NWTC\BUS BUSINESS
```

Notice that the new directory name does not need to be preceded by the path. The result is

```
G:\> RENDIR CONSTELLATION/SYS:\NWTC\BUS BUSINESS
```

The directory BUS has been renamed to BUSINESS.

The RENDIR command can also be used to rename directories on local DOS disk drives because many versions of DOS do not include a command to rename directories.

CHAPTER SUMMARY

Designing and maintaining a directory structure is one of the most important jobs of a network administrator because it is the foundation of the file system on a server. The NetWare file system consists of four parts: NetWare server, volumes, directories, and files. When fixing NetWare is installed on your NetWare servers, the seven required SYS: volume and system directories are created automatically. The NetWare required directories include LOGIN, PUBLIC, SYSTEM, MAIL, DOC, ETC, and DELETED.SAV. Each of these directories serves a specific purpose. The LOGIN directory contains files and programs that are available to a workstation before the user logs in. The PUBLIC directory contains NetWare commands and utilities that are available to all users after logging in. The SYSTEM directory is the responsibility of the NetWare server supervisor and contains operating system and supervisor utilities. The MAIL directory is used by electronic messaging programs. The DOC directory is used by on-line electronic documentation. The ETC directory is used for sample and example files. The DELETED.SAV directory holds deleted files when the directory or subdirectory containing them is also deleted.

In addition to the directories created by NetWare, the network administrator should create additional directories for Windows 95 and DOS, application software, shared data, and personal user home directories. There are two major methods of arranging these directories: by application and by department. Application-oriented structures are grouped around applications; departmental structures are grouped around workgroups. Application-oriented structures often work best in small and medium file systems; in large file systems with multiple workgroups and many directories and files, however, the departmental structure usually provides a better structure for directory organization.

A path is used to specify the location of a file or directory in the NetWare file system. A complete path contains all components of the directory structure leading to the specified file or directory. When specifying a complete path, you use a slash to separate the NetWare server's name from the volume name and a colon to separate the volume and directory names. A partial path consists of the directories and subdirectories leading from your current default directory to the desired file or directory location.

NetWare provides a number of commands that complement standard DOS commands and enable network administrators to view and manipulate the network file system more efficiently. The NDIR command is a network version of the DOS DIR command that allows you to select and sort files to obtain more useful information. The NDIR command can also display volume-specific information, as well as information about a specific directory structure. The NCOPY command provides an efficient means of copying network files and subdirectories. The RENDIR command enables you to rename network or local directories.

COMMAND SUMMARY

Command	Syntax	Definition
NCOPY	*NCOPY [source_path] filename target_path [filename] [/option] [/?] [/VER]*	Similar to the DOS XCOPY command except that it is able to use complete NetWare paths. Options include /S, which copies subdirectories with files; /E, which copies subdirectories without files; and /V, which verifies that the copy matches the original.
NDIR	*NDIR [path] [/options] [/?] [/VER]*	Displays network directory and file information including last date updated, size, and owner information. Display options include /VOL, which displays volume information including total free space, amount of space used, and amount of space available from deleted files; /SPA, which displays information about the selected directory structure including space used by all files and subdirectories along with space available to the directory; /DO (directories only); /FO (files only); and /SUB (include subdirectories). Format options include /DA (show date information), /DE (show file details), and /R (show rights information). Sort options include /SORT (sort files), which uses the parameters UN (unsorted), REV (descending sort), AC (access date), AR (archive date), CR (creation or copy date), OW (owner), SI (size), and UP (update date). Sorting can be controlled by restriction options, which include NOT (all files except), EQ (equals), LE (less than), GR (greater than), BEF (before), and AFT (after). These must be followed by a value or a date.
RENDIR	*RENDIR path [To] directory_name [/?] [/VER]*	Changes the name of a directory by specifying the name of the path and name of the original directory followed by the new directory name. It is not necessary to specify the complete path to the new directory.

KEY TERMS

absolute directory path
access rights
application-oriented structure
attributes
block
command line utilities
complete directory path
data migration
default directory
default drive
departmental structure
directory
directory entry table (DET)
directory path
file compression
folder
general-purpose application
global shared directory
home directory
local shared directory
network file system
partial directory path
relative directory path
spanning
subdirectory
vertical application
volume

REVIEW QUESTIONS

1. List three benefits of the NetWare file system:

   ____

   ____

   ____

2. List the file system components in sequence from major to minor:

   ____

   ____

   ____

   ____

3. A(n) ____________________ is a physical amount of storage contained on one or more hard disk drives or other storage media.
4. A volume can span up to ____________ disk drives.
5. What fault tolerance capability should you consider before spanning a volume over multiple disk drives?

   ____

6. The maximum length of a volume name is ____________ characters.

7. Identify each of the following as either a valid or invalid character in a volume name:

   $ ____________________

   # ____________________

   , ____________________

   (____________________

   + ____________________

   \ ____________________

   . ____________________

8. ____________________ is the name of the required NetWare volume.

9. ____________________ is the directory containing NetWare utilities that can be accessed by all users before they log in.

10. The ____________________ directory contains files and utilities available only to the supervisor.

11. When you compare a network file system to a file cabinet, which file system component corresponds to each of the following:

    cabinet: ____________________

    drawer: ____________________

    hanging folder: ____________________

    manila envelope: ____________________

12. The ____________________ directory contains the files that are used by all users after they log in.

13. The ____________________ directory is created in each volume to contain deleted files.

14. Briefly explain under what conditions files are placed in the DELETED.SAV directory.

15. List four types of Novell-suggested directories:

    ____

    ____

    ____

    ____

16. Given the directory structure shown in Figure 5-32, write a complete path to the JAN95.WK1 file.

    ____

Figure 5-32

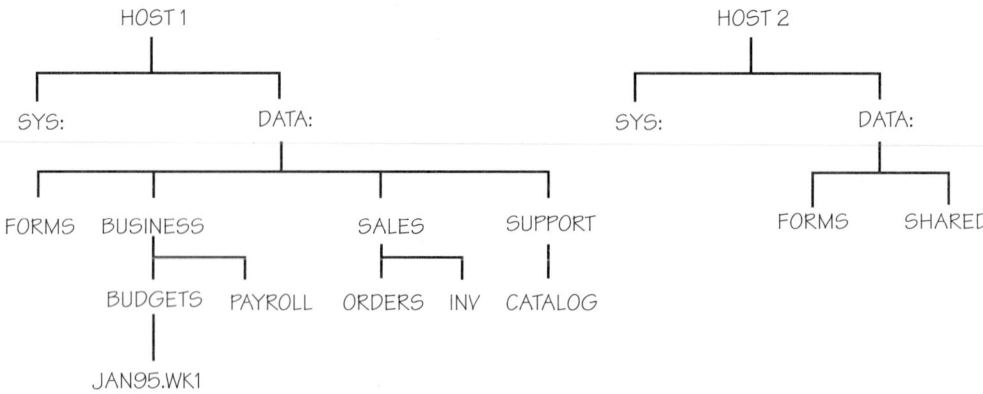

17. Use the directory structure shown in Figure 5-32 to write a CD command that uses a partial path to change your current directory from the FORMS directory of NetWare server HOST1 to the PAYROLL directory on HOST1.

____

18. In a(n) ________________ directory structure, the user home directories are located under a common directory called USERS.

19. What is the first step in designing a directory structure?

20. Briefly describe at least one disadvantage of storing data files in the SYS: volume.

21. Briefly explain two advantages of NDIR over the DOS DIR command.

22. Briefly explain an advantage of NCOPY over the DOS XCOPY command.

For questions 23 through 32, use the directory structure shown in Figure 5-32 and assume that your default directory is in the SYS: volume of a NetWare server named HOST1.

23. Write a command to list all directories on the DATA: volume along with your effective rights.

____

24. Write a command to find a file named BUDGET95.WK1 in the BUSINESS directory of the NetWare server HOST1.

____

25. What command would you use to determine the amount of space used by deleted files in the DATA: volume?

____

26. Write a command to determine how much space in the DATA: volume is occupied by the BUSINESS directory and all its subdirectories.

____

27. Write a command to copy all files with the .DOC extension from the FORMS directory of the HOST2 NetWare server to the FORMS directory on the DATA: volume of server HOST1.

____

28. Write the appropriate NetWare command to list all files in the DATA: volume that are larger than 1 MB.

____

29. Write the appropriate NetWare command to rename the INV subdirectory of SALES to INVENTORY.

____

30. Write a DOS command to change your default directory to the FORMS directory of the HOST2 NetWare server.

____

31. Write a command to list all the files in the ORDERS subdirectory on the DATA: volume sorted by size.

____

32. Write a command to list all the files in the CATALOG subdirectory that were updated after June 30, 1994.

____

EXERCISES

EXERCISE 5-1: CHECKING VOLUME INFORMATION

In this exercise you use the NDIR /VOL command to obtain volume information about a NetWare server on your network. As a network administrator, you need to know how to use the information this command provides to make such decisions as determining a location on the NetWare server in which there is room to install a new application.

1. Use the NDIR /VOL command to fill in a copy of the table given in Figure 5-33 for each of the volumes on your NetWare server.

   Command used: NDIR /VOL

Figure 5-33

	Bytes	Percent
Total volume space	716,800	100 %
Space used by entries	684,032	95.43 %
Deleted space not yet purgeable	0	0.00 %
Space remaining on volume	32,768	4.57 %

2. Use the NDIR /VOL command to determine the following information about the SYS: volume.

   Command used: __________

   Amount of space in use by compressed files: 0

   Amount of space saved by compressed files: 0

   Amount of space available in the volume: __________

3. Calculate the amount of unused disk space that is available without any deleted files being purged and record your work in the space below.

4. Use the information from step 3 to answer the following question: Will saving a 100-KB file on the SYS: volume require reclaiming space from deleted files? Briefly explain your reasoning.

5. Based on the information you recorded above, write a memo to your instructor describing the result of your work. Include the information you recorded above in your memo.

Exercise 5-2: Checking Directory Space

Use the NDIR /SPA command to determine the amount of disk space available at the root of your NetWare server's SYS: volume.

Command used: NDIR /SPA ______________________________

Enter in the information you found in Figure 5-34.

Figure 5-34

	Restrictions	In Use	Available
Volume	716,800	684,096	32,704
User volume restrictions	None	23,924	32,704
Directory restrictions at root	[illegible]	23,924	32,704

Turn in a copy of this form to your instructor.

Exercise 5-3: Checking Directory Information

Use the NDIR command to determine the amount of disk space used by each of the directories on the root of your NetWare server's SYS: volume.

Command used: ______________________________

Enter in the information you found in Figure 5-35.

Figure 5-35

Directory Name	Space Used
	KB
	KB
	KB
	KB
	KB
	KB
	KB
	KB

Turn in a copy of this form to your instructor.

Exercise 5-4: Checking Directory Structure

Use NetWare's NDIR command to list the directory structure of the NWTC\EXAMPLE directory. Use a copy of the Volume Design Form to document all subdirectories in the NWTC\EXAMPLE directory structure. Turn in a copy of this form to your instructor.

Command used: ______________________________

Exercise 5-5: Using the NDIR Command

1. Use NetWare commands to determine which volume contains the NWTC directory.

   Commands used: ______________________________

   ____

   ____

   Volume containing NWTC: ______________________________

2. Use NetWare's NDIR command to display all files with the filename extension .DOC that are located in the NWTC\EXAMPLE directory structure.

   Command used: ______________________________

   Use the same command followed by "> PRN" to redirect your output to a printer.

   (Your instructor will modify this if needed so that you can print output from this command.)

3. Use NetWare's NDIR command to display all files with the filename extension .DOC that are located in the NWTC\EXAMPLE directory structure, showing date information.

   Command used: ______________________________

   Use the same command followed by "> PRN" to redirect your output to a printer. (Your instructor will modify this if needed so that you can print output from this command.)

4. Use NetWare's NDIR command to display all files with the filename extension .DOC that are located in the NWTC\EXAMPLE directory structure, showing attributes and rights information.

   Command used: ______________________________

   Use the same command followed by "> PRN" to redirect your output to a printer. (Your instructor will modify this if needed so that you can print output from this command.)

5. Use NetWare's NDIR command to display all files with the filename extension .DOC that are located in the NWTC\EXAMPLE directory structure, showing detailed information for each file.

   Command used: ______________________________

   Use the same command followed by "> PRN" to redirect your output to a printer. (Your instructor will modify this if needed so that you can print output from this command.)

6. Use NetWare's NDIR command to display all files with the filename extension .DOC that are located in the NWTC\EXAMPLE directory structure, displaying files only.

   Command used: ______________________________

   Use the same command followed by "> PRN" to redirect your output to a printer. (Your instructor will modify this if needed so that you can print output from this command.)

7. Use NetWare's NDIR command to display all files with the filename extension .DOC that are located in the NWTC\EXAMPLE directory structure, sorted by size.

   Command used: ______________________________

   Use the same command followed by "> PRN" to redirect your output to a printer. (Your instructor will modify this if needed so that you can print output from this command.)

8. Use NetWare's NDIR command to display all files with the filename extension .DOC that are located in the NWTC\EXAMPLE directory structure and that were last updated after January 1, 1994.

   Command used: ______________________________

   Use the same command followed by "> PRN" to redirect your output to a printer. (Your instructor will modify this if needed so that you can print output from this command.)

9. Turn in copies of your printouts to your instructor.

EXERCISE 5-6: WORKING WITH NCOPY AND NDIR

In this exercise you will practice using the NCOPY and NDIR commands with full and partial NetWare paths to find files and then copy those files into the directories you have created. You will then use the NDIR command to verify that the files have been copied successfully into the specified directory locations.

1. Change to your ##ADMIN directory and create a subdirectory named LETTERS.
2. Suppose you need to copy all Microsoft Word document files from the SYS: volume into the LETTERS subdirectory you just created. Because Microsoft Word uses a .DOC extension, you can use the NDIR command to find and display all the Word filenames by entering the following command: NDIR SYS:*.DOC /SUB. Enter this command and record the path to the DOC files below:

   SERVER_01/SYS:\19ADMIN\LETTERS*.DOC

3. Use the NCOPY command to copy the .DOC files you recorded in step 2 into the LETTERS directory you created. Record the NCOPY command you used below: NCOPY SUPPORT\TEST1.DOC LETTERS\

   or NCOPY SUPPORT*.DOC LETTERS\

4. Use the RENDIR command to rename the directory LETTERS to DOCS. Record the command you used below:

   19ADMIN>RENDIR LETTERS DOC

5. Based on your work above, write a short memo to your instructor describing what you did, the commands you used, and the results of those commands:

EXERCISES

CASE 5-1: CREATING A NETWORK FILE STRUCTIRE FOR THE JEFFERSON COUNTY COURTHOUSE

The Jefferson County Courthouse network is proceeding according to plan. The network proposal is still for just the 12 users in the Social Services section. The twelve users include program administrator Janet Hinds, her assistant Tom Norihama, receptionist Lisa Walsh, department secretary Terry Smith, and 8 social workers. The group will use one NetWare 4.1 server.

From discussions with Janet, the following decisions have been made:

1. The NetWare server will have only one volume, a 2 GB SCSI drive.
2. The county is providing a license for a Windows-based suite of software that includes a word processor, an electronic spreadsheet, and a presentation graphics program. There is no personal database program included in this package. This program is named WinOffice, and the three programs are abbreviated as WP, SS, and PG.
3. The county has purchased a database management system named DBSys and has contracted for an application to be developed in DBSys that can be used to track the social services workers' cases. DBSys requires a directory named DBSys, and the application requires a subdirectory under that directory named Tracker. Additionally, a data directory named Trkrdata is required, and this directory must have three subdirectories named TForms, TTables, and TReports.
4. The staff needs a SHARED directory and a REPORTS directory that all members of the staff can access.
5. Each member of the staff requires a HOME directory that only they can access.

   Create a proposed network file system for the Jefferson County Courthouse. Document your proposal with a NetWare Server Planning Form, a Directory Planning Form, Volume Design Forms, and Directory Design Forms as needed. Turn in the proposal to your instructor in memo form, with copies of your work forms attached.

CASE 5-2: CREATING A NETWORK FILE STRUCTURE FOR J. Q. ADAMS CORPORATION

The J. Q. Adams network development is proceeding according to plan. The network will use two NetWare 4.1 servers. One will be dedicated to administration and one to production. The J. Q. Adams Corporation organization chart is shown in Figure 4-63.

From discussions with Donna Hulbert, the President of J. Q. Adams, the following decisions have been made:

1. Each NetWare server has two volumes: SYS: and DATA:.Each is a 2 GB SCSI drive.

2. The company has purchased a license for a Windows-based suite of software that includes a word processor, an electronic spreadsheet, and a presentation graphics program. There is no personal database program included in this package. This program is named WinOffice, and the three programs are abbreviated as WP, SS, and PG. This application will reside on the administration NetWare server.
3. The company has purchased an accounting system named AcctSys. This application and all its data will reside on the administration NetWare server. This application requires a program directory named AcctSys. It also requires a data directory named ASdata, and this directory must have subdirectories named AS_GL, AS_AP, AS_AR, and AS_PR.
4. The company has purchased an inventory tracking system that will reside on the production NetWare server. Named InvTrack, this application requires a program directory named InvTrack. Additionally, it requires a data directory named ITdata, and this directory must have subdirectories named ITForms, ITTables, and ITRprts.
5. The staff needs a SHARED directory and a REPORTS directory that all members of the staff can access on the administration server.
6. Each member of the staff requires a HOME directory on the administration server that only they can access.

Create a proposed network file system for the J. Q. Adams Corporation. Document your proposal with a NetWare Server Planning Form, a Directory Planning Form, Volume Design Forms, and Directory Design Forms as needed. Turn in the proposal to your instructor in memo form, with copies of your work forms attached.

NORTHWESTERN TECHNICAL COLLEGE

PROJECT 5-1: NETWORK FILE SYSTEM DESIGN

In Chapter 3, you identified the storage capacity requirements that were used to help develop the specifications for the NetWare servers that have recently been ordered by Dave Johnson. The new NetWare 4.1 servers are scheduled to arrive next week, and the donated NetWare 3.12 server will arrive the week after that.

While you wait for the NetWare servers to arrive, Dave Johnson would like you to develop a set of directory structures to meet Northwestern Technical College's processing needs. He has documented these processing needs in a memorandum. Read the memorandum below and then, using volume and directory design forms, document your network file system design.

NORTHWESTERN TECHNICAL COLLEGE
MEMORANDUM

DATE: 9/15/97

TO: Network Administrator

FROM: Dave Johnson, Data Processing Manager

SUBJECT: Directory Structure for the Superior Campus

I appreciate your prompt work in developing the specifications for the NetWare servers and want to inform you that the computers have been ordered and should arrive in about a week. The donated server will be here shortly after that. In the meantime, I would like you to develop a set of directory structures for the NetWare servers that will accommodate the processing needs that follow. I would like the directory structures to reflect the different needs of the computer lab environment versus the administrative and faculty usage.

Each of the new servers has two 2 GB drives, which I want you to use as separate SYS: and DATA: volumes. I've been informed that the donated server has a single 1 GB drive as a single SYS: volume.

Computer Lab:

The computer lab should have its own copies of the following software packages: word processing, spreadsheet, database, and presentation graphics. The configuration of these packages will need to be different from that of the administrative system. The computer lab area should contain a directory called CLASSES and subdirectories for all faculty members. This will allow the faculty to place files in their directories for students to access when they complete assignments. In addition, each workstation should have a subdirectory for temporary file storage and configuration information. This can be done by giving each workstation a login name and home directory. Finally, the computer lab should contain a directory called STUDENTS that can be used to contain home directories for students who are enrolled in advanced computer classes and are required to have individual access to the server in order to perform their work.

MEMO, Page 2

Administration:

The administration users will access applications on the new NetWare 4.1 server, but the donated NetWare 3.12 server will be used for administrative data storage. The administration and faculty need to have access to word processing, spreadsheet, database, and menu system applications. Recently the student services department acquired a student recruitment system, which you will need to install for them. In the future, the faculty want access to system information for advising purposes. The student services staff also wants to be able to put the aptitude testing software on the server so students can take these tests on any one of the department's computers. Each user in the administrative department will need his or her own directory to store personal work and configuration files. The administrative secretaries will need to have a shared directory to allow them to work jointly on projects as well as be able to pass files to and from faculty members. An additional directory should be set up to allow shared access to standardized forms that are used to print letters to students and businesses.

Faculty:

Faculty members are eager to be able to pass files directly to the secretaries and to the computer lab rather than carrying them around on a floppy disk. Make sure your structure provides shared directories that the faculty can use for these purposes. Also provide a separate shared directory that will allow faculty members to pass files among themselves. We are looking into a software package that handles grade records. If we obtain the software, it will require its own software directory. In your design, you should provide a directory for the future location of the system software.

Please fill out a NetWare Server Planning Form for our NetWare servers and a Directory Planning Form showing the storage requirements for each volume on each server. Use Volume Design Forms and Directory Design Forms as necessary to define the directory structures for each volume. Place all applications in the appropriate SYS: volume and all data directories in the DATA: volumes. I'll need a short memo from you outlining your plan, together with copies of your forms to support your ideas. Again, thanks for all your hard work. You're doing a great job and I look forward to working with you on the setup of the NetWare server directory structure. If you have any questions, be sure to give me a call.

CHAPTER SIX

INSTALLING NETWARE 4.1

Now that you have designed your NDS Directory tree and network file system, you are ready to get down to the business of working with NetWare and setting up your network. A network administrator must know the software components that make the network operate and be able to configure the NetWare operating system. In this chapter you will learn about loading and running NetWare 4.1 on a NetWare server and the NetWare Client 32 software on the attached workstations.

AFTER READING THIS CHAPTER AND COMPLETING THE EXERCISES YOU WILL BE ABLE TO:

- DESCRIBE THE STEPS INVOLVED IN INSTALLING NETWARE ON THE NETWARE SERVER.
- IDENTIFY AND LOAD COMMON DISK AND LAN DRIVERS.
- USE THE NETWARE INSTALL PROGRAM TO CREATE NETWARE DISK PARTITIONS AND VOLUMES.
- LOAD AND UNLOAD NETWARE LOADABLE MODULES.
- USE NETWARE CONSOLE COMMANDS TO CHECK YOUR SERVER INSTALLATION AND CONFIGURATION.
- INSTALL THE SOFTWARE COMPONENTS THAT ALLOW A DOS WORKSTATION TO ACCESS THE NETWARE SERVER.

NetWare installation can be divided into two major parts: NetWare server installation and workstation installation. NetWare server installation includes loading the NetWare operating system on the hard drive of the NetWare server computer, setting up the NetWare partitions on each drive, creating volumes, loading the necessary drivers to access the network interface cards (NICs), and doing the initial work with the NDS Directory tree. Workstation installation involves loading the software and drivers on the workstations to enable them to access the NetWare server computer and use the network.

Although a Certified Novell Engineer (CNE) is expected to be able to install the NetWare NOS on a NetWare server, a Certified Novell Administrator (CNA) is expected only to be able to administer the installation after it is done. Therefore, in this chapter we will explain what NetWare installation accomplishes, so that you can understand the results of the installation and how it affects the network. We will not, however, go through the steps of the installation in detail.

On the other hand, a CNA is expected to be able to install client software on the workstations. The current client is NetWare Client 32, which is available in versions for DOS, Windows 3.1x, and Windows 95. NetWare Client 32 is the successor to the NetWare DOS Requester (Virtual Loadable Module) client, which in turn succeeded the NETX client. It makes full use of the 32-bit computing power of current microprocessors, as well as using memory more effectively. In this chapter you will learn how to install and configure NetWare Client 32.

NETWARE NETWORK OPERATING SYSTEM INSTALLATION

There are eight main steps in installing NetWare 4.1 on a NetWare server:

1. Plan the network layout and complete a NetWare server information worksheet.
2. Install NetWare server hardware and configure the hardware.
3. Partition and install DOS on the bootable hard drive.
4. Complete the NetWare INSTALL program steps under DOS.
5. Complete the NetWare INSTALL program steps under the NetWare NOS.
   - Load disk and CD-ROM drivers.
   - Load LAN drivers and Protocols.
   - Create NetWare hard drive partitions and volumes.
6. Install Novell Directory Services.
7. Modify startup configuration files STARTUP.NCF and AUTOEXEC.NCF.
8. Choose Optional Installation Options.

In the following sections, we will discuss these steps and their effects on the NetWare server.

DOCUMENTING THE NETWARE SERVER ENVIRONMENT

Before you start the NetWare server installation, you must document the network system and hardware configuration of your NetWare server computer properly. The initial parts of the NetWare server installation plan, planning the NDS Directory tree, and preparation of the network file system volume and directory design forms were covered in Chapters 4 and 5. Now you need to complete the plan by documenting the network layout and NetWare server hardware configuration.

Defining the Network Layout

Defining the network layout requires understanding and documenting the network system in which the NetWare server computer will be installed. A network layout consists of the following components:

- The NetWare server's name and internal network number
- The network topology and network cards used
- The network address of each cable system where the NetWare server is to be connected
- The frame type to be used on each network cable system

To obtain this information, you need to look first at the network system. A good way to do this is to make a simple pencil sketch of the network system, which will include the network layout information. Figure 6-1 illustrates a network plan consisting of a NetWare server attached to a single ethernet cable system.

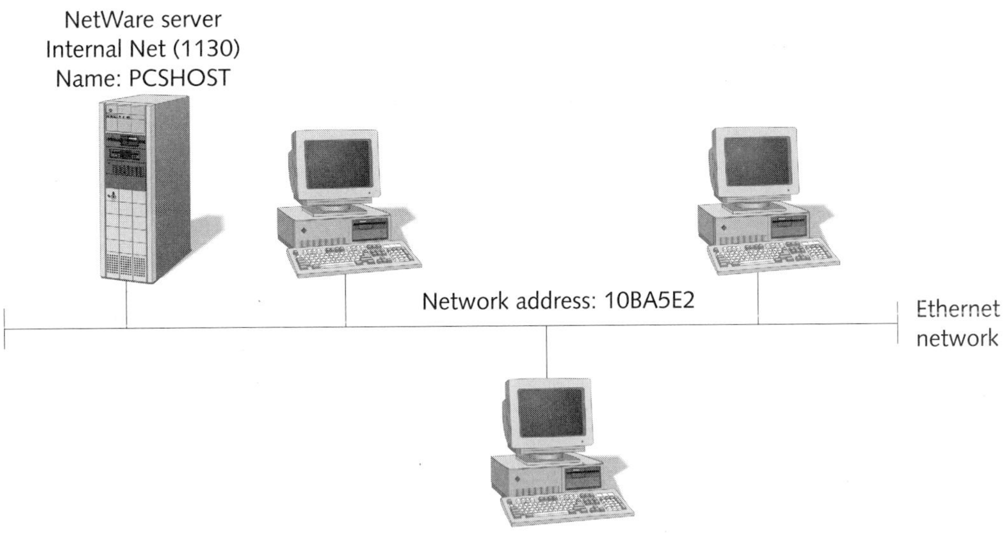

Figure 6-1 Network with a single NetWare server

NetWare server
Internal Net (1130)
Name: PCSHOST
Network address: 10BA5E2
Ethernet network

A **NetWare server name** is a unique identification of the server, distinguishing it from other machines on the network. It is important that each NetWare server be given a name that is both meaningful and unique. When assigning a NetWare server name, consider including the location and function of the NetWare server as part of its name. For example, the primary NetWare server at F. D. Roosevelt Investments could be named FDR_Server01. NetWare server names can be from 2 to 47 characters long and can include any alphanumeric character, hyphens, and underscores. You cannot use spaces in the server name. The following characters are also not allowed:

=<>?[ ]"*+,?|:;/\

Valid NetWare server names include FDR_Server01, CONSTELLATION, and FDR_NW-41_Server. However, the names FDR Server01 (using a space instead of an underscore), FDR+Server01 (using the + symbol), and FDR[Server01] (using square brackets) are not valid names.

Additionally, a NetWare server must be assigned a unique **internal network number**. This number is used by the NetWare operating system for communication among its device drivers. Although you can assign your own internal network number, most installations use the random server number suggested by the NetWare installation program. Some network administrators use the server program's serial number as the internal network number. This keeps the serial number handy for when you need to contact Novell for NetWare operating system software upgrades.

Both the NetWare server name and the internal network number are unique, so either is sufficient by itself to identify the NetWare server. However, they are used for different purposes: users refer to the NetWare server by name (while logging in, for example), whereas the network software uses the internal network number.

Chapter 3 defined a network address as a number assigned to each LAN system. The number is used to route packets between networks. With Novell IPX, a unique network address consisting of from one to eight hexadecimal digits must be assigned to each frame type used on each NIC. LAN addresses are necessary because several LANs may be connected to a common backbone to form an internetwork or joined together via telephone lines to form a WAN.

The network addresses you assign to your cable systems should help you identify a network when you see its address on a report or error message. As you learned in Chapter 2, hexadecimal digits are limited to the numbers 0 through 9 and the letters A through F. This might seem to limit your choices for names, but with a little imagination, you can create network addresses that are easy to remember. For example, the network address 10BA5E2 used in Figure 6-2 is the IEEE standard for a thin ethernet system. (Notice the use of the digit 5 in place of the letter S.

In addition to the network address, a network cable system must have one or more packet frame types assigned to it. As explained in Chapter 3, a frame type defines the formatting of the physical packet that is transmitted over the network. In order to communicate on the network, all machines must use the same frame type. There are several popular packet frame types in use. The two most common ethernet frame types used with NetWare are IEEE 802.3 and IEEE 802.2. IEEE 802.2 is the most up-to-date frame type and is the default for NetWare 4.1. If you are installing a NetWare server on an existing network with machines that use IEEE 802.3, you can convert all workstations and servers to IEEE 802.2 or you can load both frame types on your new server.

Note

Loading two frame types is a good temporary solution until you can get all machines converted to IEEE 802.2. This approach slows down performance, however, because each frame type must be treated as a separate logical network.

Adding a second NetWare server to an existing network creates what is known as a **multiple NetWare server network**, shown in Figure 6-2. Notice that although each NetWare server is given a unique name and internal network number, they both use the same network address and frame type for the LAN cable system on which they communicate.

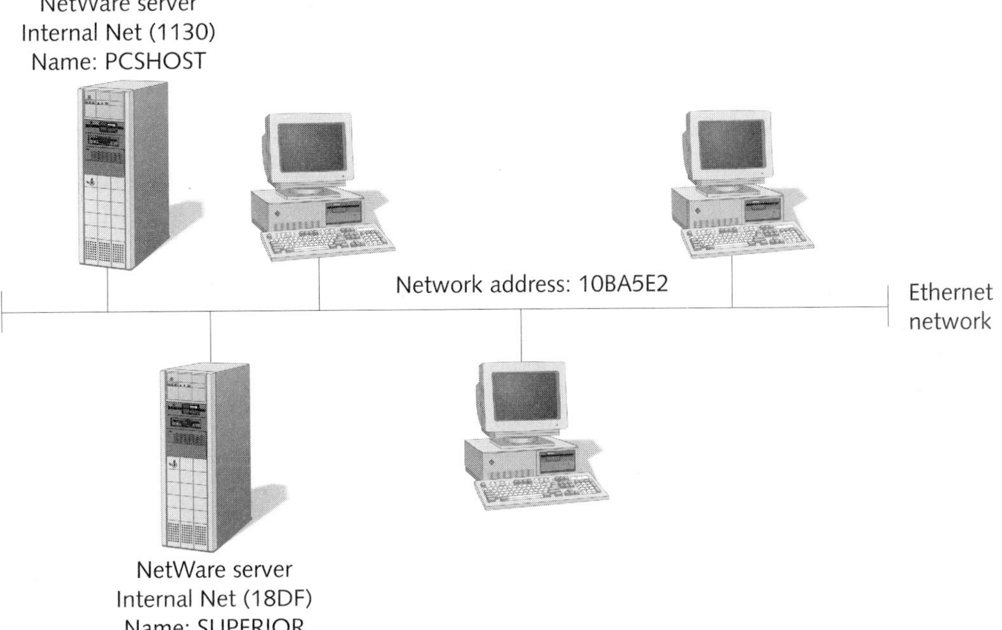

Figure 6-2 Network with multiple NetWare servers

Multiple networks can be connected to form an internetwork. As discussed in Chapter 3, an **internetwork** consists of networks connected together by bridges and routers. Figure 6-3 illustrates an internetwork created by adding a different network topology to the system. Notice that each network cable system in the internetwork is assigned a different network address. The NetWare server SUPERIOR is referred to as an internal router because it transfers packets between networks in addition to performing its NetWare server activities.

Completing the NetWare Server Worksheet

After the network system has been identified, you should record the NetWare server's name and internal network number along with the network address and frame type for each network card to be placed in the NetWare server. During the installation process you will also need the following NetWare server hardware information:

- Name of the disk driver program for each disk controller card
- Each disk controller card's settings, including interrupt and I/O port
- Capacity and configuration of each hard drive attached to a disk controller
- Name of the network card driver program to be used with each network card
- Each network card's settings, including interrupt, I/O port, and memory address range

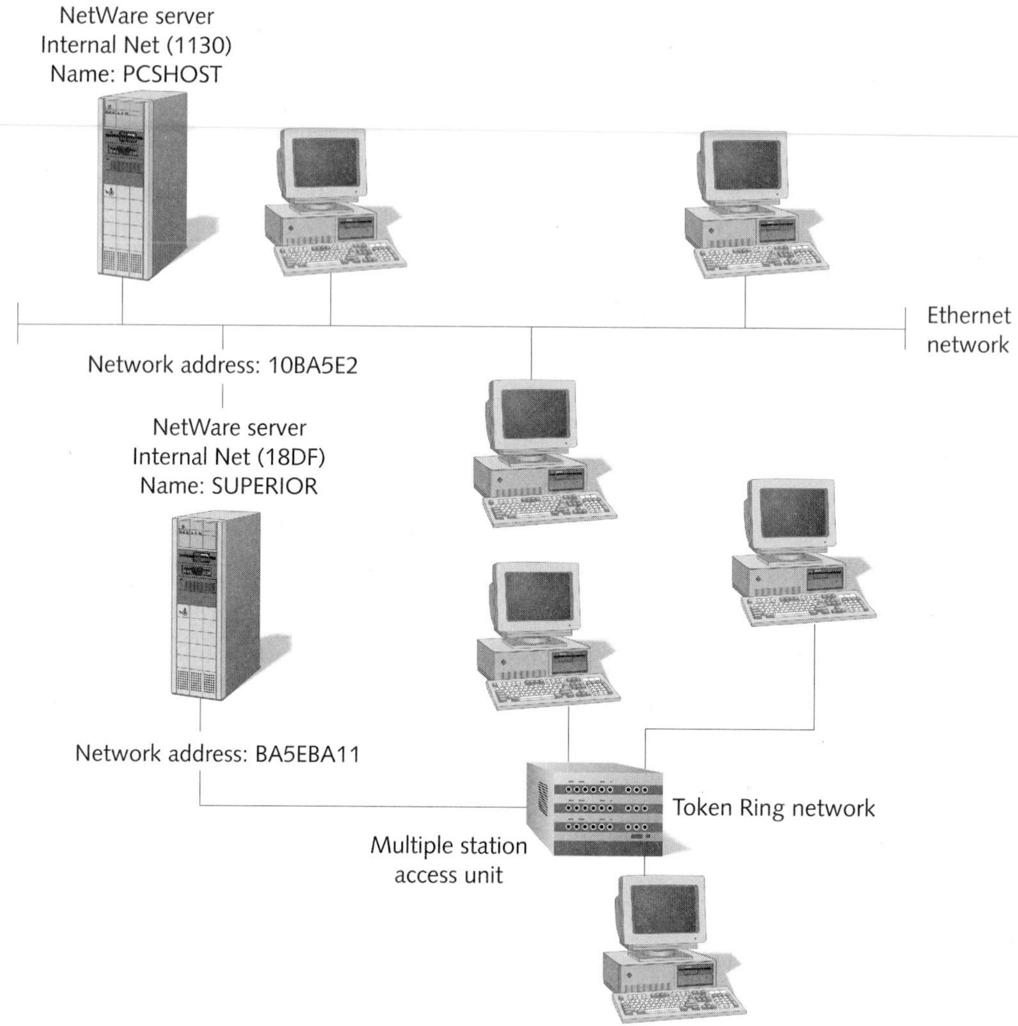

Figure 6-3 An internetwork

You can find this information in the documentation supplied with the NetWare server and network cards. If you cannot find it there, your hardware vendor can provide the necessary hardware settings. Documenting this information is best accomplished by completing a NetWare server worksheet similar to the one shown in Figure 6-4.

The NetWare server worksheet is divided into five main sections: identification, system information, disk information, network card information, and nonnetwork device information. In the identification section you record the installer's name, the name of the NetWare server, and the internal network number.

In the system information section you enter the make and model of the computer, the microprocessor type, clock speed, memory capacity, and types of expansion slots. Although you won't need this information during NetWare installation, you do need to know that your NetWare server computer meets or exceeds the minimum requirements for the NetWare version you are installing (you learned the minimum requirements for a NetWare 4.1 server in Chapter 2). This information is also useful after initial installation if you install additional server options or upgrade the NetWare server software.

Figure 6-4
NetWare server worksheet

NETWARE SERVER WORKSHEET

Installed by:	Ted Simpson		
NetWare Server Name:	CONSTELLATION	**Internal NetworkNumber:**	CBELAB01

SYSTEM INFORMATION

Computer Manufacturer:	HP	**Model:**	NetServer 5/133 LF		
CPU:	Pentium	**Clock Speed:**	133 MHz	**Bus:**	ISA/PCI
Memory Installed:	48 MB				

DISK INFORMATION

Disk Controller 1:

Type:	IDE	**Manufacturer:**		**Model**	
Interrupt:	14 (E hex)	**I/O Address**	1F0	**DMA Channel:**	None
Memory Address:					
Disk Driver Name:	IDE.DSK				

Drive Address	**Type**	**Manufacturer:**	**Cyl/Hd/Sec**	**Speed/ Capacity**	**Partitions Size**		**Mirrored with drive**
					DOS	**NetWare**	

Disk Controller 2:

Type:	SCSI	**Manufacturer:**	Adaptec	**Model**	2740
Interrupt:	5	**I/O Address**	340h	**DMA Channel:**	3
Memory Address:					
Disk Driver Name:	AIC7770.DSK				

Drive Address	**Type**	**Manufacturer:**	**Cyl/Hd/Sec**	**Speed/ Capacity**	**Partitions Size**		**Mirrored with drive**
					DOS	**NetWare**	
0	SCSI	HP		12ms/ 2.03 GB	100 MB	1933 MB	None
1	SCSI	HP		12ms/ 2.03 GB		2.03 GB	None

NETWORK CARD INFORMATION

Network Type	**Manufacturer**	**LAN Driver**	**I/O Port**	**Memory Address**	**IRQ/DMA**	**Frame Type**	**Network Address**
Ethernet	Intel	E100S.LAN	300	0D000	10/None	802.2/ 802.3	CBELAB01

NON-NETWORK DEVICE INFORMATION

Device Name	**IRQ**	**I/O Port**	**DMA**	**Memory Address**
COM1	4	3F8-3FF		

The disk information section of the NetWare server worksheet contains documentation for up to two disk controller cards in your NetWare server. You will need this information when you install the NetWare server. In addition, the capacity and partition size information for each disk drive is helpful in planning disk mirroring and duplexing. (Disk mirroring or duplexing requires that each mirrored NetWare partition be the same size.) The settings for the cylinder, head, and sector of IDE disk drives are stored in CMOS. You might need this information to reconfigure the CMOS after a battery or system failure.

The NetWare server described in Figure 6-4 contains both an IDE and a SCSI controller card. The IDE controller card manages the 3.5" floppy disk. The SCSI controller card manages a large capacity drive for the SYS: and DATA: volumes, a CD-ROM drive, and a tape backup system.

You need the controller card information to load the correct disk driver software during installation and to provide NetWare with the necessary configuration parameters. In addition, knowing the hardware configuration information, such as interrupt, I/O port, and DMA channel, will help you avoid hardware conflicts when you install other hardware, such as LAN cards.

One of the first steps in installing NetWare on a NetWare server computer is loading the correct disk driver program to give the NetWare operating system access to the server's hard drives. Because each type of controller requires a different disk driver, a network administrator needs to identify the name of the correct drive software before proceeding with the NetWare server installation. Figure 6-5 contains a list of common controllers and the disk driver software that is supplied with NetWare.

Figure 6-5

Common Netware disk drivers

Bus Architecture	Controller Type	Driver Name
ISA	AT-ST506	ISADISK.DSK
	ESDI	ISADISK.DSK
	IDE	IDE.DSK
	SCSI	See Vendor
EISA	ST506	ISADISK.DSK
	IDE	IDE.DSK
	SCSI	See Vendor
PCI	EIDE	IDE.DSK
	SCSI	See Vendor
Micro Channel	ESDI	PS2ESDI.DSK
	IBM SCSI	PS2SCSI.DSK

The IDE.DSK driver works with all standard IDE drives. SCSI controller cards, on the other hand, require special disk controllers for each card model or manufacturer. This difference makes installing an IDE drive a little easier than installing an SCSI drive. Notice that there are a number of similar drivers for certain computer models. You should check with your vendor to verify what driver you should use if you have one of these computer models.

It is often the network administrator's job to install network cards in the NetWare server and workstation computers. The network card information portion of the NetWare server worksheet contains important information identifying the network cards to be installed in the server along with their configurations. Your first concern is to obtain cards that are appropriate for the network system you are installing and to ensure that the network cards are certified by Novell to work with your version of NetWare. Next you will need to identify the correct network card driver to load during NetWare installation. This will enable NetWare to send and receive packets. To assist you in loading the correct driver, Novell has included network card drivers for many of the common network cards (see Figure 6-6). If you have one of the network cards listed or if the documentation that came with your card tells you to use a certain driver, record the name of the LAN driver on the NetWare server worksheet.

Figure 6-6
Common NetWare network interface card drivers

Cabling System	Network Interface Card	Driver Name
ARCNET	RX-Net RX-Net II RX-Net 2	TRXNET.LAN
Ethernet	Intel Ethernet Pro 10	EPRO.LAM
	MicroDyne NE/2 MicroDyne NE/2T	NE2.LAN
	MicroDyne NE2-32	NE2_32.LAN
	MicroDyne NE1000 (Assy 950-054401) MicroDyne NE1000 (Assy 810-160-001)	NE1000.LAN
	MicroDyne NE1500T	NE1500T.LAN
	MicroDyne NE2000 MicroDyne NE2000T	NE2000.LAN
	MicroDyne NE2100 (Assy 810-000209)	NE2100.LAN
	MicroDyne NE3200	NE3200.LAN
	MicroDyne NE32HUB	NE32HUB.LAN
	SMC 8100	SMC8100.LAN
	SMC 8232	SMC8232.LAN
	SMC 8332	SMC8332.LAN
	3COM 3C503	3C503.LAN
	3COM 3C509	3C5X9.LAN
	3COM 3C770	3C770.LAN
Token Ring	MicroDyne NTR2000	NTR2000.LAN
	IBM Token Ring	TOKEN.LAN

Each NIC installed in the NetWare server must be set to use a unique interrupt, I/O port, and memory address in order to avoid hardware conflicts with other devices in the computer. Because you might need to enter these hardware settings when first installing the card driver, it is useful to document the interrupt, I/O port, and memory address of each network card on the NetWare server worksheet.

The nonnetwork device information of the NetWare server worksheet enables you to document other devices and controller cards that are currently in the system. This information helps you avoid any current or future hardware interrupt conflicts.

NetWare Server Installation

After you have identified the network system and hardware specifications and filled out the NetWare server worksheet, you are ready to roll up your sleeves and start the NetWare installation process. The time spent planning and documenting the network and NetWare server environment will pay off by allowing you to avoid problems caused by loading the wrong drivers or entering incorrect card configurations. Before actually installing NetWare 4.1, however, you must make sure that the NetWare server is ready.

NetWare Server Preparation

Before installing the NetWare NOS, you must install all the necessary hardware. If your NetWare server is not shipped to you with all the hardware installed (such as disk drives, CD-ROMs, disk controller cards, and NICs), you will need to install and configure them. The manufacturer of the hardware will provide the necessary instructions and materials.

The NetWare 4.1 NOS also requires that DOS be running before the NetWare NOS can be started. This means that you will have to use a DOS setup disk to create a DOS partition on the primary hard disk and install DOS in this partition. Novell recommends a DOS partition of 15 MB. However, it is recommended that you create a larger DOS partition if you need space for other DOS-based programs. Remember that because you must boot DOS in order to boot the NetWare NOS, you can run DOS programs on the server itself before starting NetWare. Once NetWare is running, of course, you cannot use the DOS programs on the server.

Novell recommends that in order to facilitate troubleshooting of server problems, you add one megabyte to the DOS partition for every one megabyte of RAM in the NetWare server.

You should generally use the latest version of DOS available, such as Novell DOS 7. However, if you are using Microsoft DOS, the release of Windows 95 has created a problem. Prior to the introduction of Windows 95, DOS was a separate software product. Windows 3.1x ran as an application after DOS booted the workstation. When Windows 95 is started, however, the user sees no separation between DOS and Windows. Although you can exit the Windows 95 GUI to DOS 7.0, you cannot easily do this using AUTOEXEC.BAT. This makes it difficult to automatically boot a server. Therefore, you should install an earlier version of MS-DOS. MS-DOS 3.x, 4.x, 5.x, and 6.x are all compatible with NetWare 4.1.

Although DOS is initially used to boot the NetWare server, once NetWare is started it functions as a completely separate operating system that directly controls the computer hardware.

The final step in preparing the NetWare server is making sure that the date and time have been set accurately. NetWare 4.1 will use this information when the NOS takes control of the server.

NetWare Installation Methods

You can install NetWare 4.1 from a CD-ROM in a CD-ROM drive in the server or from a copy of NetWare 4.1 located on another server on the network (either from a CD-ROM in a CD-ROM drive or from files copied onto a server volume). If another NetWare server is available on the network, installing from files copied to a volume on that NetWare server is the fastest installation method. In this chapter, we assume that only one new NetWare server is available. Therefore, we will discuss using a CD-ROM in a CD-ROM drive for NetWare server installation. The CD-ROM drive has been installed and configured as part of the hardware installation of the NetWare server.

NetWare 4.1 can also be installed from floppy disks, but getting the disks requires a special order through the NetWare Fulfillment Center. Installing from disks is slow and tedious and should be used only if it is the only possible way to install NetWare. If you must use disks, be sure to make working copies and use those copies for the actual installation.

Simple Installation Versus Custom Installation

Novell provided two options for installing NetWare 4.1 on a new NetWare server: Simple Installation and Custom Installation. Simple Installation would normally be used on a small network. Custom Installation allows the network administrator more control of the installation process by enabling him or her to specifically name or set configuration options that NetWare automatically handles during a Simple Installation. In this chapter, we will discuss Custom Installation while noting when Simple Installation would provide a default parameter.

The First NetWare 4.1 Server in the NDS Directory Tree

Now that the NetWare server is ready, you can install the NetWare 4.1 NOS. If this is the first copy of NetWare 4.1 installed in your network, this installation will create Novell Directory Services (NDS) for the network. This includes the creation and naming of the NDS Directory tree and the NDS administrator. When additional NetWare 4.1 servers are installed into the network, they are added into the existing NDS Directory tree and are administered by the previously created network administrator.

The DOS Portion of the Installation

The first portion of the installation is controlled by the NetWare DOS program INSTALL.EXE. You begin the NetWare installation by running the INSTALL.EXE program from the DOS prompt. The INSTALL.EXE program is responsible for the following functions:

- Initiating a NetWare server installation
- Letting the user select a new Simple Installation, a new Custom Installation, or an upgrade of an existing NetWare NOS to NetWare 4.1
- Letting the user specify the NetWare server name
- Letting the user specify the NetWare server internal network number
- Copying NetWare DOS files to the DOS partition of the bootup hard drive of the NetWare server
- Letting the user specify a locale, language, and keyboard mapping for the NetWare server
- Letting the user specify whether to use the recommended DOS filename format or an alternative
- Creating the STARTUP.NCF file and letting the user add initial commands to it if desired
- Adding the ability to automatically start the NetWare server to the AUTOEXEC.BAT file

The first steps involve initiating the NetWare NOS installation and choosing the type of installation. In the Custom Installation process, you are asked for the NetWare server name and the internal network number, which you selected when you planned your NDS Directory tree and network environment. In a Simple Installation, NetWare chooses the internal network number.

After you have specified the NetWare server name and internal network number, the installation process copies NetWare DOS files to the DOS partition on the NetWare server. NetWare stores these files, which are needed by the NetWare server in order to boot the NetWare NOS, in a DOS directory. NetWare uses the default directory name C:\NW-SERVER. In a Custom Installation, you can change the directory name; there is no choice in a Simple Installation. As soon as the directory is selected, the files are copied.

In a Custom Installation, you are given a chance to choose the language and filename format that NetWare will use after the NetWare DOS directory is specified. The language configuration specifies the country, a code page to indicate the language to be displayed, and a keyboard mapping for keyboards other than standard United States English. Simple Installation accepts the defaults—Country Code 401 (United States), Code Page 437 (United States English), and standard U.S. keyboard—and does not display the options.

Custom Installation gives you two filename formats: DOS and NetWare. The NetWare filename format allows characters that may not be valid in DOS filenames, but there is usually no reason for choosing this option. Novell recommends using the DOS filename format. Simple Installation uses the DOS filename format and does not display this option. After the DOS files are copied, the NetWare Custom Installation gives you a chance to modify two files: the NetWare file STARTUP.NCF and the DOS file AUTOEXEC.BAT. Simple Installation does not give you the chance to modify these files.

When you start NetWare 4.1, it runs two special startup files: STARTUP.NCF and AUTOEXEC.NCF (the extension NCF stands for **NetWare Command File**. These files are similar to the DOS files CONFIG.SYS and AUTOEXEC.BAT. The installation program gives you a chance to add SET commands to STARTUP.NCF. **SET commands** are used to control NetWare performance parameters. STARTUP.NCF and AUTOEXEC.NCF are automatically created during installation, and the necessary commands are included in these files based on your actions during installation. You will have an opportunity to edit both files later in the installation. so there is no need to add special SET commands at this time.

You are also given a chance to modify the DOS AUTOEXEC.BAT file so that the NetWare 4.1 NOS is automatically started when the server is rebooted. This is done by adding the line

```
SERVER.EXE
```

to the AUTOEXEC.BAT file. Without this line, you have to type SERVER at the DOS prompt and press [Enter] to start the NetWare 4.1 NOS. Unless you have a reason to *not* automatically start NetWare, you should add the line to AUTOEXEC.BAT.

Installation decisions at this point are not critical—both files can be edited easily at a later time.

The NetWare 4.1 Portion of the Installation

A very significant point has been reached in the installation of the NetWare 4.1 server. Up to this point, the installation has been running as a DOS process. But now the **SERVER.EXE** program is automatically run, and the NetWare 4.1 NOS takes over. After SERVER.EXE is run, the INSTALL.NLM program is started to take control of the installation process. The extension NLM stands for NetWare Loadable Module, and NetWare Loadable Modules are programs that run on the NetWare server itself.

It is important to understand the difference between the INSTALL.EXE DOS program and the INSTALL.NLM NetWare NOS program. INSTALL.EXE runs under DOS and is used only for the initial installation of the NetWare NOS on the NetWare server. The INSTALL.NLM runs under the NetWare NOS. It is automatically loaded and used to complete the initial installations but can also be run using the LOAD INSTALL console command on the NetWare server to modify the installation after the initial installation is completed.

The core of the NetWare operating system is the SERVER.EXE program. When installing NetWare, you use DOS to boot the server computer and then load the NetWare operating system. After the SERVER.EXE program has been loaded into memory, it controls the computer, and DOS is no longer needed. After starting NetWare, you might actually want to remove DOS from memory to make more space (approximately 64 KB) available for NetWare file caching.

Although the SERVER.EXE program provides the core NetWare services, such as file and printer sharing, it uses other modules to access hardware devices such as disk drives and network cards or to provide additional services such as communications to a mainframe. These modules are shown in Figure 6-7. For this reason, Novell refers to the SERVER.EXE program as a software bus. NetWare 4.1 is a very flexible system that allows the network administrator to add and remove software drivers and services as required without needing to exit the server or reboot.

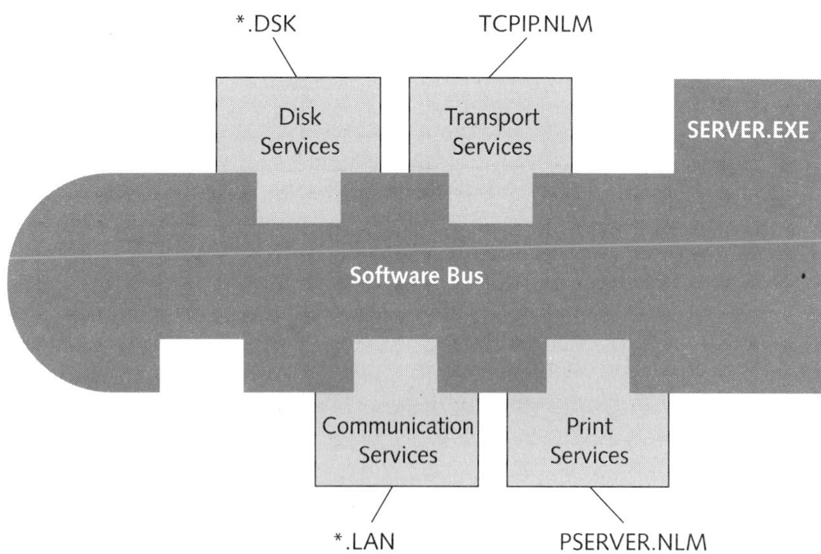

Figure 6-7 The SERVER.EXE software bus

In earlier versions of NetWare it was necessary to link disk and network card drivers into the operating system prior to starting the server. In order to make changes—such as the configuration or network address of a network card driver—you were required to stop the server, modify or relink the operating system, and then reboot the server computer. In NetWare 3.1x and NetWare 4.1, you can change the configuration of a LAN driver by simply unloading and loading it with the new parameters.

The final portion of the installation is controlled by the NetWare NOS INSTALL.NLM. The INSTALL.NLM portion of the installation is responsible for the following functions:

- Loading disk and CD-ROM drivers
- Loading LAN drivers and protocols
- Creating NetWare hard drive partitions
- Creating NetWare volumes
- Installing the NetWare license
- Creating the NetWare server SYS: volume directory structure
- Copying the NetWare server files to the NetWare directories on the SYS: volume
- Copying optional NetWare NOS files to the NetWare server

The STARTUP.NCF and AUTOEXEC.NCF Files

During this part of the installation process, the **STARTUP.NCF** and **AUTOEXEC.NCF** files will be created to record NetWare commands based on the options that are chosen during installation. The STARTUP.NCF and AUTOEXEC.NCF files are run automatically each time the NetWare NOS is started and are used to configure the NetWare operating environment. STARTUP.NCF is located (as is SERVER.EXE) in the NWSERVER directory on the DOS boot partition, whereas AUTOEXEC.NCF is located on the SYS: volume in the SYSTEM directory. This means that the NetWare commands in STARTUP.NCF can be read and executed by NetWare before the SYS: volume is mounted, but the commands in AUTOEXEC.NCF can be read only after the SYS: volume is mounted.

The STARTUP.NCF and AUTOEXEC.NCF files automate the server bootup process, and maintaining them is an important job of a network administrator. In the following sections we will discuss the impact of the installation steps upon these files and describe what commands are added to them during the installation process.

The STARTUP.NCF and AUTOEXEC.NCF files can be modified during installation, but, more importantly, they can be edited at any time after the installation is complete. This is done by reloading the INSTALL.NLM program using the command

```
LOAD INSTALL
```

This command is entered at the NetWare server console command line prompt. The **NetWare console** is the monitor and keyboard attached to the NetWare server. The console command line prompt is displayed on the monitor as the name of the NetWare server followed by a colon, as shown in Figure 6-8.

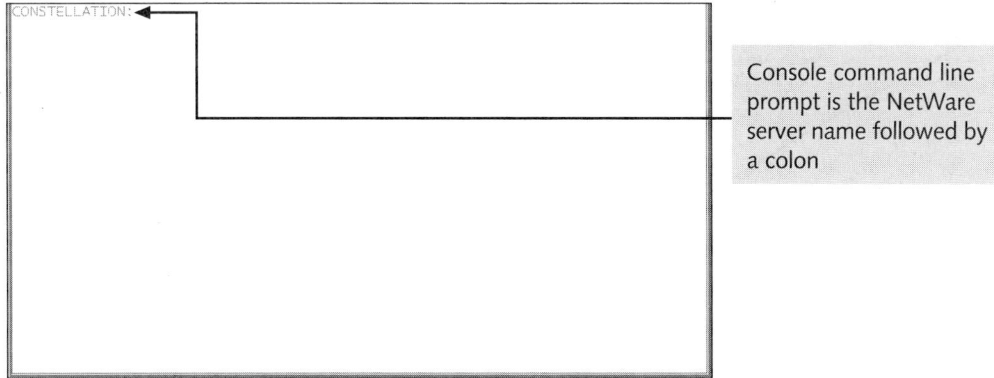

Figure 6-8 The NetWare server console command line prompt

The syntax of the LOAD command is

LOAD [path]loadable_module_name [module_parameters]

Loadable modules include four types:

1. Disk drivers (.DSK)
2. LAN drivers (.LAN, .HAM, .CDM)
3. NLM programs (.NLM)
4. Name space support modules (.NAM)

Several parameters can be used with the LOAD command; these parameters are listed in Figure 6-9.

Figure 6-9 The LOAD command parameters

Parameter	Use this parameter to
path	Specify the path to the loadable module you want to run
loadable_module_name	Specify the name of the loadable module you want to run
module_parameters	Specify parameters for the loadable module you want to run These vary from module to module

Loading Disk and CD-ROM Drivers

The next step in the installation process is to load disk and CD-ROM drivers. You documented the necessary disk drivers on the NetWare server worksheet. Now these drivers are copied to the NetWare server and then loaded into memory so that the NetWare NOS can access and use the drivers. As each driver is installed, the user also specifies any needed parameter values for that driver.

If a driver that is needed is not supplied by Novell on the NetWare 4.1 CD-ROM, you should have it on a floppy disk packaged with the controller card. During installation, put the disk in the A: drive, where the installation program locates the driver on the disk and loads it.

Because these drivers will need to be loaded each time the NetWare server is rebooted, a LOAD *DISKdriver* command is added to the NetWare STARTUP.NCF file for each driver. The LOAD driver command includes any module parameter values needed for the driver to be loaded correctly. Both disk drivers and LAN drivers use the shared set of module parameters listed in Figure 6-10 to specify information about a disk controller card or NIC installed in the NetWare server.

Figure 6-10

Disk driver and LAN module parameters

Module Parameter	Use this parameter to
DMA = number	Set the DMA (Direct Memory Access) channel
FRAME = FrameType	Set the frame type used with the board.
INT = number	Set the interrupt number (IRQ) used by the board
MEM = number	Set the memory address used by the board
NAME = name	Assign a name to this configuration of the board
PORT = number	Set the I/O (Input/Output) port used by the board
NODE = address	Set a node address for the board. Usually not needed since each board is encoded with a unique address
RETRIES = number	Set the number of retransmissions the board will make for frames that fail to reach their destination
SLOT = number	Specify the EISA, MCA, or PCI slot in which the board is installed on the system board

After the installation process is complete, you can modify the LOAD *DISKdriver* commands by editing the STARTUP.NCF file. An example of a STARTUP.NCF file with LOAD *DISKdriver* commands is shown in Figure 6-11.

Figure 6-11

LOAD DISKdriver commands in the STARTUP.NCF file

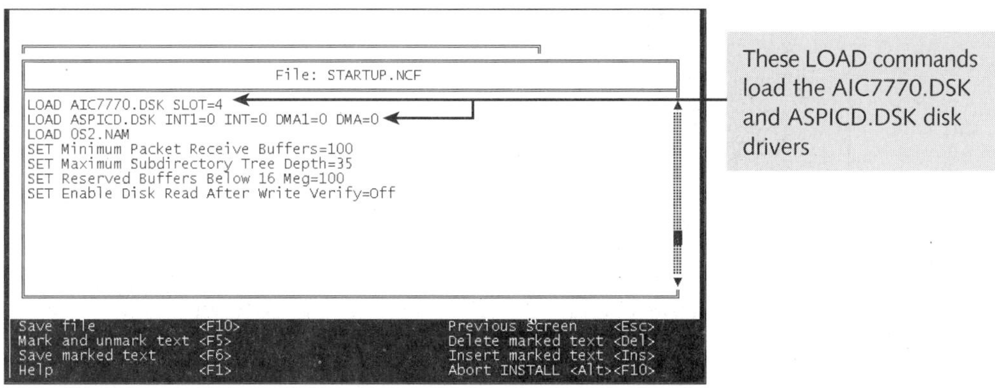

Until NetWare 4.1, NetWare had used single-file .DSK drivers. Known as monolithic drivers, these still exist in NetWare 4.1. But in NetWare 4.1 Novell has also added **Novell Peripheral Architecture (NPA)**, which breaks the monolithic drivers into two parts: the **Host Adapter Module (HAM)** and the **Custom Device Module (CDM)**. Novell provides both types of drivers for many devices; you can choose which you want to use. The monolithic drivers are stable and proven, whereas NPA is the architecture Novell will use in future releases of NetWare.

Loading LAN Drivers and Protocols

After the disk and CD-ROM drivers are loaded, the LAN drivers and protocols are loaded and configured. You also documented these on the NetWare server worksheet. At this time you also choose the frame types that will be used on the LAN. The choice of frame type is an important one. The Novell recommended frame type for NetWare 4.1 networks is 802.2. However, during installation, NetWare will load *all* the frame types that the network will support unless you manually select only the ones you want. The loading of all the frame types is not a problem, because during subsequent reboots of the server, NetWare will load only those that are actually used on your network. The optional manual selection is not usually necessary. Custom Installation gives you complete control of all LAN driver and protocol parameters. Simple Installation doesn't let you choose protocols.

The recommended frame type for NetWare 3.11 is 802.3. For NetWare 3.12, NetWare 4.0x, and NetWare 4.1, the recommended frame type is 802.2.

Each LAN driver that is loaded results in a LOAD *LANdriver* statement being created in the AUTOEXEC.NCF. The LOAD driver command includes any module parameter values needed for the LAN driver to be loaded correctly. LAN drivers use the set of module parameters listed in Figure 6-10 to specify information about NICs. You can modify the LOAD driver commands after the installation process is finished by editing the AUTOEXEC.NCF file. An example of an AUTOEXEC.NCF file with LOAD *LANdriver* commands is shown in Figure 6-12.

Figure 6-12 LOAD LANdriver commands in the AUTOEXEC.NCF file

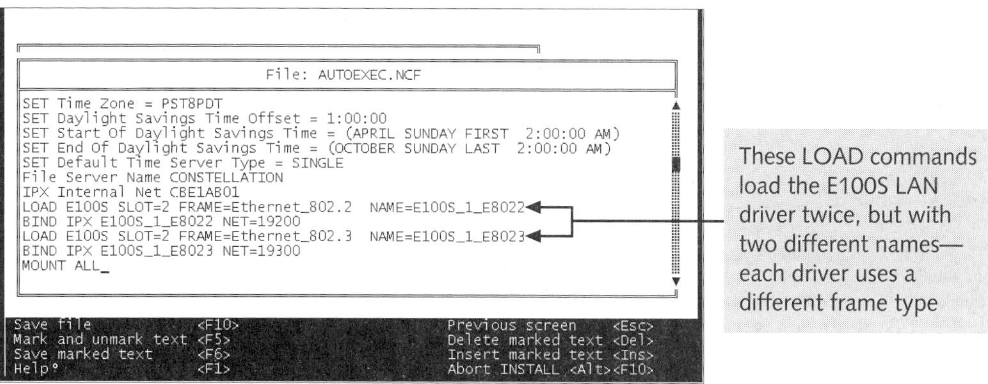

The LOAD *DISKdriver* commands are located in STARTUP.NCF; the LOAD *LANdriver* commands are located in AUTOEXEC.NCF.

After the LAN drivers are loaded and the protocols specified, it is necessary to link the protocols to the drivers. This is called **binding** a protocol, and each NIC must have at least one protocol bound to the card's LAN driver. NetWare automatically binds IPX to each frame type that has been selected during installation. For each frame type, there must be an IPX external network number associated with the frame type. For an existing network, NetWare will automatically detect the IPX external network associated with the frame type and then verify the binding. You may choose to *not* bind IPX to a particular frame type if there is some reason for doing so. If you manually selected frame types, however, you might be prompted to manually enter the IPX external network number for each frame type.

Each protocol that is bound to a LAN driver creates a BIND *protocol* statement in the AUTOEXEC.NCF. The syntax of the BIND command is

```
BIND protocol[TO] lan driver | board name [driver parameter...]
[protocol parameter...
```

The BIND *protocol* command includes any parameter values needed. Several parameters can be used with BIND (see Figure 6-13).

Figure 6-13

The BIND command parameters

Parameter	Use this parameter to
protocol	Specify the network protocol—for example, IPX
LAN driver I board name	Specify the LAN driver name or the name assigned to the NIC in a LOAD *LANdriver* statement
driver parameter	Specify LAN module parameters used to identify an NIC. The simplest to use is the NAME = name parameter
protocol parameter	Specify parameters necessary for the protocol. For the IPX protocol, the NET=IPX external network number parameter is required

You can modify the LOAD driver commands after the installation process is finished by editing the AUTOEXEC.NCF file. An example of an AUTOEXEC.NCF file with LOAD *LANdriver* commands is shown in Figure 6-14. Each frame type driver that is bound results in a BIND *frametype* statement being created in the AUTOEXEC.NCF.

Figure 6-14

BIND commands in the AUTOEXEC.NCF file

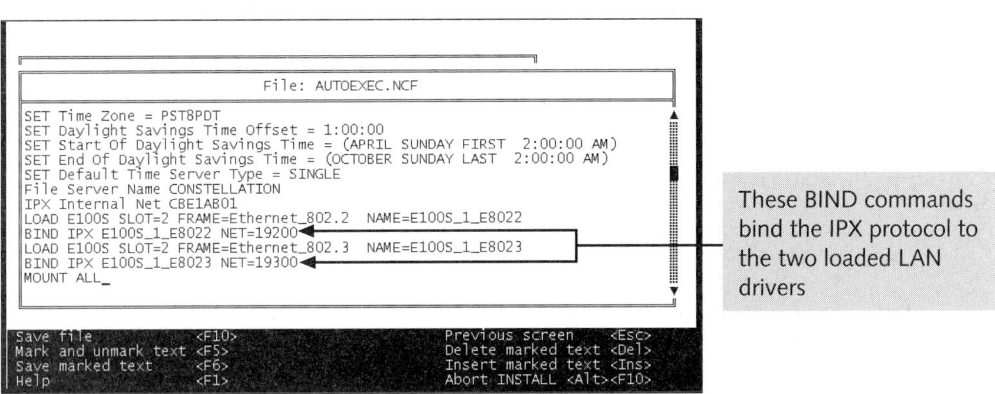

Creating NetWare Partitions

After the disk and LAN drivers are loaded, partitions are created on the hard disk and volumes are created. Custom Installation gives you a choice of automatic or manual creation of disk partitions. Simple Installation doesn't give you a choice—it automatically creates the disk partitions.

The automatic option uses all the space available on the disk as the partition (for a disk with a DOS partition, NetWare uses all the remaining available space) and then creates one volume within each partition. This means that by default you will have one large volume on each disk drive. The manual option enables you to set the size of the NetWare partition and then divide the space into one or more volumes. This capability is important in order to create mirrored or duplexed disk partitions on separate drives.

NetWare automatically assigns the **default volume name** SYS: to the first volume created. Subsequent volumes are given default volume names of VOL1, VOL2, VOL3, and so on. The name SYS: cannot be changed—this is the volume where NetWare will copy the NOS files—but you can change the names of the subsequent volumes.

Managing NetWare Volumes

After you create the disk partitions and volumes, NetWare 4.1 gives you a chance to modify the volume parameters. These parameters include the volume name, the block size, the use of file compression, the use of block suballocation, and the use of data migration.

A NetWare volume that is **mounted** is available for use by users; a **dismounted** (or not mounted) volume is not available for use by users. The volume must be dismounted when changes are made to volume parameters.

All volume names except SYS: can be modified at this point if you need to change a volume name. As discussed in Chapter 3, NetWare also uses a default block size based on volume size. You can change this, but there is really no need to as long as block suballocation is enabled. NetWare enables block suballocation by default, and there is no need to change this.

NetWare also enables file compression by default. File compression saves hard disk space, and normally you should leave it enabled. The NetWare file compression system uses a **data compression algorithm** to shrink the amount of disk space files need. Typically, data compression algorithms substitute codes for repeating sets of characters. For example, the phrase "here, there, and everywhere" can be compressed by using the substitution x = ere to "hx, thx, and everywhx," which saves the space of six characters. Because a header containing the coding information has to be added to the compressed file, this method is effective only on files that are larger than some minimum file size. NetWare 4.1 uses a minimum file size of 512 bytes and a default **minimum compression percentage gain** of 2% (the compressed file must be at least 2% smaller than the original). Also by default, NetWare 4.1 waits until a file has been unused for seven days before compressing it. Because file compression requires a lot of CPU utilization, file scans and compression are done between midnight and 6:00 a.m. by default. You can change the compression system defaults using SET commands.

NetWare **data migration** refers to the systematic moving of unused data to a storage device other than a volume. **Optical disks** are typically used for long-term storage because of their high capacities. Unlike file compression, which leaves the compressed file on the volume, data migration removes the file from the NetWare volume after copying it to the optical disk. Each NetWare volume has data migration disabled by default; you should leave it disabled unless you are working with data migration hardware.

Installing the Novell License

The NetWare 4.1 license for the NetWare server is on the LICENSE disk. NetWare now prompts you for the disk and then copies the license to the server.

NetWare 4.1 allows you to add users to your network by combining licenses on one server. For example, if you need a license for 35 users, you can combine a 25-user license and a 10-user license. Adding the additional license is done by running the INSTALL.NLM after the initial installation is complete.

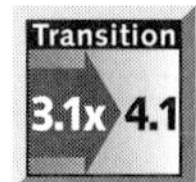

The NetWare 3.1x license was contained in the SERVER.EXE file, and the user count in this file could not be modified. To increase the number of users on a server, you had to buy a license for a larger number of users and copy the SERVER.EXE file from the new license to the server.

Installing Optional NetWare Files

NetWare now copies optional NetWare system files and utilities to the server. In Custom Installation, you select which files and utilities will be copied. Simple Installation doesn't give a choice; it just copies the default set.

Don't worry if you miss selecting a set of files at this point—you can add them later. Adding additional optional files is done by running the INSTALL.NLM after the initial installation is complete.

Installing Novell Directory Services

The initial setup of Novell Directory Services and the creation of the Directory tree occur during the first installation of NetWare 4.1 on a NetWare server. During a Custom Installation, this includes naming the Directory tree, setting time synchronization, creating enough of the Directory tree (Organization objects and Organizational Unit objects) to build the context for the NetWare Server object (the server's location in the Directory tree), and creating the network administrator's account and password. A Simple Installation reduces your choices. First, you can specify a time zone, but no other time synchronization options are available. Second, you are asked for your organization's name, which becomes the name of the Directory tree and an Organization object—no other Directory tree objects are created, and the server's context is the created Organization. Finally, you are prompted for only the administrator password—the administrator's User object will be named Admin.

By the end of this portion of the installation, the Novell Directory Services is operational and the Directory tree is established. After the installation is complete, you create the rest of the Directory tree and create objects representing network resources using the windows NetWare Administrator utility or the DOS NETADMIN utility.

Passwords should be several characters long and should not contain the user's name, account name, or numbers associated with the user. Using the first letters of the words in an easily remembered phrase is a good way to create passwords.

Modifying the NetWare Server Configuration Files

At this point in the Custom Installation process you are given a chance to edit the STARTUP.NCF and AUTO-EXEC.NCF files. Simple Installation omits this file editing. Both of these files have been created during the installation process and currently contain NetWare commands based on the options you have chosen so far during installation.

The commands in STARTUP.NCF are limited to those that can be executed with the resources on the DOS partition. This includes loading drivers, name space support, and a small group of SET commands, as shown in Figure 6-15.

Figure 6-15

SET commands that can be included in STARTUP.NCF

SET Command	Value Range	Default
SET Auto Register Memory Above 16 MB	ON, OFF	ON
SET Auto TTS Backout Flag	ON, OFF	ON
SET Maximum Physical Receive Packet Size	618 to 24682	4202
SET Maximum Subdirectory Tree Depth	10 to 100	25
SET Minimum Packet Receive Buffers	10 to 2000	50
SET Reserved Buffers Below 16 Meg	8 to 300	16

The Novell defaults for the SET commands are usually suitable. However, Novell recommends that if your NetWare server is using hardware devices that use an ASPI driver (for example ASPICD.DSK or ASPITRAN.DSK), you should increase the Reserved Buffers Below 16 MB to 200.

The STARTUP.NCF file (and the AUTOEXEC.NCF file) can be edited easily once installation is complete by using either the INSTALL or the SERVMAN utilities. You don't need to be concerned that any errors in choosing what to include or exclude at this point are final. In fact, you'll probably find yourself often editing these files as you add NLM programs (such as a backup utility) to your server.

The commands that can be used in AUTOEXEC.NCF are more extensive than those in STARTUP.NCF. Volumes can be mounted, and any NLM program can be run by loading the file. An extensive group of SET commands can be used to fine-tune server performance.

Before a volume is available on the network, it must be mounted on the server. When the disk driver for the hard drive containing the SYS: volume is loaded (usually while STARTUP.NCF is running), the SYS: volume is mounted automatically. All other volumes, however, must be mounted by name using a MOUNT command. The syntax of the MOUNT command is:

```
MOUNT volume_name | All
```

Individual volumes are mounted by using their volume name. For example, the SYS: volume is mounted using the command MOUNT SYS. NetWare provides the option of mounting all the remaining volumes by using the ALL parameter, so that the command becomes MOUNT ALL. Commands to load other volumes on your server should be added to AUTOEXEC.NCF at this point.

You might also have other NLM programs that you want to run on your server. Most network administrators run the MONITOR.NLM to display server information, and your server backup software will have NLMs that will have to be run as well. You should add the LOAD commands to run these modules to AUTOEXEC.NCF as well so that they are always started when the server is rebooted.

The changes you have made in the STARTUP.NCF and AUTOEXEC.NCF files do not take effect at this point. They will be acted upon the next time the server is rebooted.

Optional Installation Options

The final step in the installation process is choosing any optional installation options that you want to complete at this time. None of the options has to be done now; they can all be done whenever you want by running the INSTALL.NLM program on the server. Which options, if any, will be run will vary from network to network. The most useful may be (1) creating a registration disk to facilitate registering your copy of NetWare, (2) creating client installation disks if you are using the NetWare DOS Requester, and (3) installing online documentation.

Using NetWare Console Commands at the Server Command Prompt

You can execute NetWare console commands from the server command prompt. For example, the SEND "message text" console command can be used to broadcast messages to users. This is particularly useful for warning messages just before you shut down a NetWare server.

The SEND command replaces the NetWare 3.1x BROADCAST command.

A pair of useful console commands are DISABLE LOGIN and ENABLE LOGIN. The DISABLE LOGIN command allows the NetWare server to be on the network, but not available to users, when you're performing maintenance tasks for which you don't want any user on the server. ENABLE LOGIN reestablishes the users' ability to use the server's resources.

You can run NetWare NLMs by using the LOAD *filename* command. For example, although the command to start the MONITOR utility was added to the AUTOEXEC.NCF file, this command will not be executed until the server is rebooted. To start MONITOR now, you have to enter the command LOAD MONITOR yourself.

Adding Name Spaces to Support Long Filenames

In addition to DOS filenames, NetWare 4.1 supports other client operating system file naming conventions on a NetWare server through the use of NetWare **name spaces** modules. NetWare 4.1 includes name space support for Macintosh and OS/2 files, and support for UNIX files can be purchased from Novell. A .NAM extension is used for name space NLMs. The Macintosh name space (MAC.NAM) is important if you have Macintoshes connected to your network. The OS/2 name space (OS2.NAM) is obviously important for OS/2 workstations, but it is also used to support the long filenames used by Windows 95. You will want to load the OS/2 name space for that reason alone.

Adding a name space requires two steps:

1. Loading the name space .NAM module
2. Running the ADD NAME SPACE utility.

The **ADD NAME SPACE utility** needs to be run only once on each volume that will support long filenames. The name space .NAM module must be loaded each time the NetWare server is booted, and the .NAM module supports all volumes with added name spaces on the NetWare server. The syntax of the ADD NAME SPACE command is

```
ADD NAME SPACE [NAME [TO [VOLUME]] volume_name]
```

The ADD NAME SPACE command includes any parameter values needed. Several parameters can be used with ADD NAME SPACE; they are listed in Figure 6-16.

Figure 6-16

The ADD NAME SPACE command parameters

Parameter	Use this parameter to
no parameter	Display the name spaces that are currently loaded on the NetWare server
name	Specify the name space module. The possible names are OS/2, Macintosh, FTAM, and NFS
volume_name	Specify which volume the name space is being added to

In addition to the OS/2 name space, the NetWare Client 32 for Windows 95 workstation client files include two NLMs that need to be run on the NetWare server to support Windows 95 long filenames. The first is a NetWare 4.1 Patch Manager utility, PM410.NLM, which will control all patches added to the NetWare 4.1 NOS. A **patch** is a supplemental program written to correct a discovered problem in NetWare. Novell creates and issues patches to NetWare whenever necessary to fix problems. Novell also fixes problems by rewriting the module that they occur in and issuing an updated version of the module. Patches are separate from the module that the problem occurs in and are often issued as a temporary solution until the patch can be incorporated into the new version of the module. The second file included with the NetWare Client 32 for Windows 95 files is the patch itself, NSWILDFX.NLM.

To add the OS/2 name space to the SYS: volume, you use the following commands at the console command prompt:

1. At the prompt, type **LOAD PM410**, and then press **[Enter]**. The PM410.NLM patch manager is loaded on the NetWare server.
2. At the prompt, type **LOAD NSWILDFX**, and then press **[Enter]**. The NSWILDFX.NLM patch is loaded on the NetWare server.
3. At the prompt, type **LOAD OS/2.NAM**, and then press **[Enter]**. The OS/2.NAM name space support module is loaded on the NetWare server.
4. At the prompt, type **ADD NAME SPACE OS/2 TO VOLUME SYS**, and then press **[Enter]**. The OS/2 name space is added to the SYS: volume.

The first three commands need to be run every time the NetWare server is booted, so they should be added to the AUTOEXEC.NCF file. The ADD NAME SPACE command should be run for every volume on the server that will store Windows 95 files with long filenames.

Using MONITOR

The **MONITOR utility** provides essential information about NetWare server performance and workstation connection information. It's a good idea to always have MONITOR running on the server.

Because many network administrators keep MONITOR loaded for a continuous check on NetWare server status, the MONITOR program also provides a screen saver function. After several minutes of no keyboard activity, the MONITOR program displays a "worm" that moves randomly around the screen. The busier the NetWare server, the longer the worm. This is a quick way for you to see if your NetWare server computer is overloaded with network tasks. And because of the screen saver, the MONITOR screen is the safest image to have on your server's monitor screen!

To load the NetWare MONITOR utility, use the following commands:

1. At the prompt, type **LOAD MONITOR** and then press **[Enter]**. The MONITOR screen appears, as shown in Figure 6-17. This figure shows the contracted General Information window.

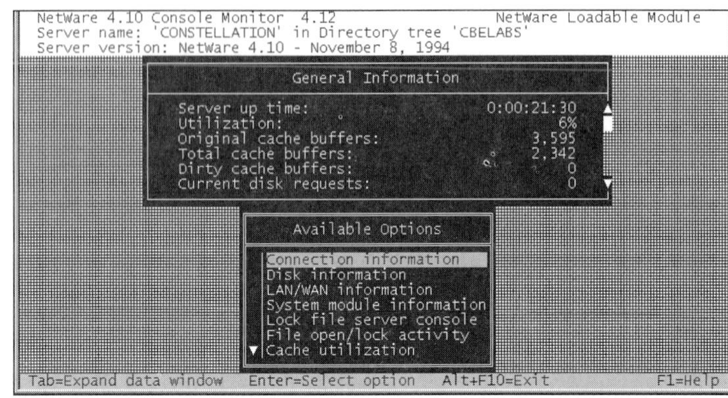

Figure 6-17 The MONITOR screen

2. Press **[Tab]** to expand the General Information window to see all the data in the window, as shown in Figure 6-18. You can press [Tab] a second time to toggle back to the compressed General Information window.

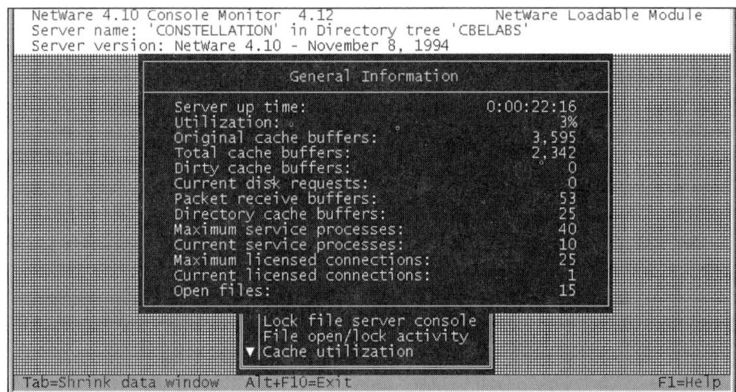

Figure 6-18 The expanded General Information window

Important MONITOR statistics to be aware of include the Utilization percentage and Total Cache Buffers figure. The Utilization percentage gives you a good idea of how busy the SERVER program is; normal utilization is in the 20%–60% range. Higher utilization numbers might mean that your NetWare server is overloaded and you should consider installing a faster processor, removing additional functions such as print servers, or increasing memory.

The cache buffer information displayed by MONITOR can be used to determine if more memory is needed. The Original Cache Buffers figure represents the amount of memory available for caching files after the SERVER.EXE program was loaded. Mounting volumes and running NLMs reduces the number of buffers originally available and results in the Total Cache Buffers figure, which represents the amount of space available. If the Total Cache Buffers is less than 50% of the Original Cache Buffers, you should consider increasing the amount of memory in the server. If the percentage falls below 20%, you have a critical situation and need to add more memory as soon as possible.

The Connection Information option on the Monitor Available Options menu can be used to view active connections on the server, the related user names, and files that are open on those connections. You can use this option before downing the NetWare server to view and clear active connections or send logout messages to individual users. Being able to clear a connection that does not have any files open eliminates the need to go to an active but unattended workstation to shut it down prior to downing the NetWare server.

You can use the [Alt]+[Esc] key combination to move between the MONITOR screen and the console command prompt (or the screen of any other NLM that's loaded).

Downing the NetWare Server

Once your NetWare server is operational, you should test the startup files to be sure the NetWare server will start correctly the next time you use it. Although it is not something a network administrator needs to do often, you need to know how to properly stop and restart the NetWare server computer when you maintain hardware or upgrade software.

Downing the NetWare server is the process of stopping the server program by logging off all users, taking the server off line so that it is no longer available to workstations, and dismounting all volumes to update the disk with any changes currently stored in the memory buffers. All these processes are accomplished by using NetWare's DOWN command.

Prior to using the DOWN command, you should issue the DISABLE LOGIN command to prevent users from logging into the NetWare server. Then use the SEND command to send a short message to any current users. Announce that the NetWare server will be shut down in several minutes and ask users to save their work and log out of the NetWare server.

If there are any users logged into the NetWare server when you issue the DOWN command, the NetWare server displays a warning on the console, asking if you want to proceed. Continuing with the DOWN command can cause data in files being processed to be lost. To determine if the current users have any files open, you can use the NetWare MONITOR utility to view existing connections and view any open files. You can then either send a message asking the user to log out or cancel the user's session if no files are open.

After the DOWN command is completed, the console prompt returns. At this time you can continue to use certain console commands and load NetWare modules to perform server maintenance or upgrade functions, or you can use the EXIT command to return to the NetWare server's DOS prompt.

Starting the NetWare Server

Starting the NetWare server involves booting the computer with DOS and then loading the SERVER.EXE program. The SERVER program starts by first loading the disk driver specified in the STARTUP.NCF file and then performing the commands in the AUTOEXEC.NCF file. These provide the server name, internal network number, and LAN drivers.

You can automate this server startup process by creating an AUTOEXEC.BAT file in the server's DOS partition that contains the following commands:

```
@ECHO OFF
CLS
CD\NWSERVER
PAUSE Use [Ctrl] [Break] keys to abort server startup
SERVER
```

The PAUSE command is optional. Issuing a PAUSE command in the server's AUTOEXEC.BAT file allows you to stop the computer in the DOS mode before starting the server program. This enables you to perform certain maintenance functions such as copying drivers and software upgrades to the NWSERVER directory before starting the NetWare server. However, the PAUSE command also requires that someone be present to respond to it. Some software that works with a UPS will down a server in the event of a power failure, followed by an automatic reboot when power is restored. The PAUSE command would prevent a complete unattended reboot.

THE DIRECTORY TREE AFTER INSTALLATION

After the first NetWare 4.1 server installation is complete, NDS is installed and the Directory tree has been created. At this point it consists of only the following:

- The [Root] has been created and named.
- The minimal set of Organization and Organizational Unit objects necessary to establish the NetWare server context have been created and named.
- The Admin User object has been created.
- The NetWare Server object for the NetWare server has been created.
- Volume objects for each volume on the NetWare server have been created.
- The [Public] trustee was created and given Browse rights at the [Root] object. This means that all users, as they are added, can browse the entire Directory tree.
- There are *no* groups created.

For example, Cunningham, Burns, and Evans Laboratories (CBE Labs) has installed their first NetWare 4.1 server. The server has an Intel 133-MHz Pentium CPU, 48 MB of RAM, one 3.5" floppy disk drive, two SCS I2-GB drives, and an SCSI CD-ROM drive. (The drivers for these controllers are IDE.DSK for the IDE controller and ASPITRAN.DSK, AIC7770.DSK, and ASPICD.DSK for the SCSI devices.) A 100-MB DOS partition has been created for MS-DOS 6.22.

CBE Labs decided to name their NetWare server CONSTELLATION and to use an internal network number of CBE1AB01. The number is coded: reading L instead of 1 between E and A, it reads CBELAB01. CONSTELLATION has an Intel Smart Pro/100 LAN adapter. This requires the E100S.LAN driver, which is not available in the standard driver set provided by Novell. The E100S.LAN driver is on a disk provided by Intel with the card. CBE Labs uses two protocols: 802.2 and 802.3. Both types were bound to the E100S during installation.

The two SCSI disk drives are partitioned as two volumes: SYS: and DATA:. Each partition uses all the available space on its hard drive. Neither partition will be mirrored or duplexed. Because CBE Labs needs to support Windows 95 long filenames, the OS/2 name space was added to both volumes. And because the CD-ROM in the server uses an ASPI driver, the Reserved Buffers Below 16 MB statement was added to the STARTUP.NCF file.

CBE Labs named their Directory tree with the tree name CBELABS and created the Organization object CBE_Labs. The context for the NetWare server CONSTELLATION is .CBE_Labs. The network administration account will use the standard User name Admin, and the password will be APSTNDP (the first letters of the seven layers of the OSI model). The context for the Admin User object is also .CBE_Labs. CBE_Labs is in the Pacific Coast time zone, and daylight-saving time is used. Since this is the first server on the network, it will be the time reference source for all other servers installed later. This is known as a **Single Reference time server**. Other types of time servers are discussed later in this chapter.

After the installation of NetWare 4.1, the CBE Labs Directory tree appears as shown in Figure 6-19. The [Public] trustee, although created, does not show up in the Directory tree because it is not a Directory tree object.

Figure 6-19

The CBE Labs Directory tree with the NetWare server CONSTELLATION

Installing Servers into an Established NDS Directory Tree

This discussion of installing NetWare 4.1 has focused on installing the NetWare NOS on the first NetWare 4.1 server. In this case, the Directory tree has to be created because it doesn't exist. Installing additional NetWare 4.1 servers follows the same steps except that the Directory tree exists and the server will be installed into it. The NetWare installation process will detect the existing Directory tree and present the options of installing in the existing tree or of creating a new tree. You should choose to install the server into the existing tree. During the installation you will have to specify the name context for the new NetWare server.

For example, CBE Labs has to install their second NetWare 4.1 server. The server is an Intel 133-MHz Pentium PC with a configuration identical to CONSTELLATION. CBE Labs decided to name this NetWare server SARATOGA and to use an internal network number of CBE1AB02. Two SCSI disk drives are partitioned as two volumes: SYS: and DATA:. Each partition uses all the available space on its hard drive. Neither partition will be mirrored or duplexed. Because CBE Labs needs to support Windows 95 long filenames, the OS/2 name space was added to both volumes.

During the installation, an Organizational Unit object named Test_Eval was created, and SARATOGA was installed into this organizational unit. The context for the SARATOGA is thus .Test_Eval.CBE_Labs. The CBE Labs network administrator wanted the organizational unit name to be Test&Eval. However, although the & is allowed in object names, it cannot be used for names created during an installation. The object name will be changed later to Test&Eval using a NetWare 4.1 utility. Because this is the second server on the network, it will obtain a time reference source from CONSTELLATION. This is known as a **Secondary time server**. After the installation of NetWare 4.1 on SARATOGA, the CBE Labs Directory tree appears as shown in Figure 6-20.

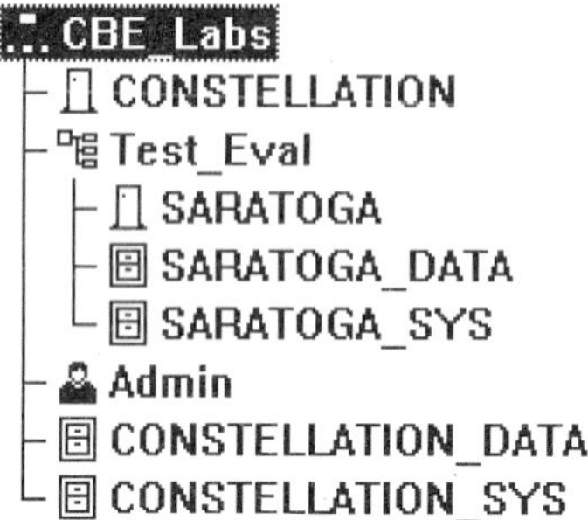

Figure 6-20
The CBE Labs Directory tree with the NetWare server SARATOGA

Network Time Synchronization: NetWare Time Servers

When there is only one NetWare server on the network, you don't need to worry about the different types of NetWare time servers. But with the addition of the second NetWare server on the network, the issue of time synchronization becomes important.

The goal is one common time used throughout the network. There are four types of NetWare time servers: Single Reference time server, Primary Time server, Reference time server, and Secondary Time server. As its name implies, a **Single Reference time server** is the only time reference on the network, and provides the time to all other servers and workstations on the network. The network administrator manually sets the time on an SRTS. A **Primary Time server**, on the other hand, synchronizes the official network time with other PTS NetWare servers and Reference time servers through a "voting" process. After the "official" time is established, all servers adjust their internal clocks to it. The time is also provided to all Secondary time servers and workstations. A **Reference time server** differs from a PTS by being able to synchronize with a time source (such as an atomic clock or radio clock) external to the network. Although Reference time server NetWare servers vote with PTS machines to determine the "official" network time, they don't adjust their clock to it. This has the effect of pulling the "official" network time, which is an averaged time, toward the time of the RTS. Over time, the RTS time will become the "official" network time. Again, the time is also provided to all Secondary time servers and workstations. **Secondary time servers (STS)** receive time information from Secondary Reference time server, Primary Time server, and Reference time server NetWare servers and set their clocks accordingly. They then send the time to workstations.

A Single Reference Time Server (SRTS) is most appropriate for small LANs. If an SRTS is used, no Primary Time servers or Reference Time servers can exist on the network. Primary Time servers and Reference Time servers must have at least one other Primary Time server or Reference Time server on the network to synchronize with. Using Primary Time servers and Reference Time servers NetWare servers is most appropriate in WANs, especially when portions of the WANs are in different geographic locations.

The NetWare 4.11 installation procedure is similar to the NetWare 4.1 installation. The Simple Installation and Custom Installation choices are still used, but automatic hardware recognition has been improved. The automatic hardware installation, however, is restricted to devices that use an advanced bus (including EISA, PCI, PNPISA, PCMCIA, and MCA) or devices based on current technology (IDE and SCSI). Older technology is not automatically recognized.

One major change is the name space support for long filenames. Instead of using the OS/2 name space, a new name space module, LONG.NAM, is used to support long filenames for Windows 95, Windows NT, and OS/2.

Workstation NetWare Client Software Installation

After NetWare has been installed on the NetWare server, the next task is setting up the workstations that will be attached to the network. Assuming the wiring is already in place and tested, setting up a workstation to use the network involves installing and configuring the NIC and then installing the client software. As a network administrator, you will need to be familiar with these processes in order to upgrade workstation software and install new workstations on the network.

Installing the Network Card

To connect a workstation to the network, you must first obtain the network cards appropriate for the topology and system you are using. NetWare is compatible with most network cards on the market, but it is a good idea to obtain cards that have been certified by Novell. They have gone through an extensive testing process in the Novell labs. Before you install the card, you need to determine the correct hardware settings—including interrupt number, I/O port, and memory address—in order to avoid conflicts with other devices in the workstation.

Network cards use either jumpers or software to store configuration settings. The software included on some network cards allows you to store the card's configuration settings in the CMOS memory contained on the network card. Network cards that are designed for the Micro Channel and EISA bus machines have an automatic configuration process that calculates the hardware settings for you and stores them in CMOS memory on the motherboard. The network driver program retrieves these configuration settings when it runs on the workstation. Using the software setup process allows driver programs to be self-configuring and means you don't need to modify the driver program parameters for different computer configurations.

Software Components

For a workstation connected to the network to communicate with a NetWare server, it needs three software components: a NIC driver, a protocol stack, and a network shell. These three components are shown in Figure 6-21.

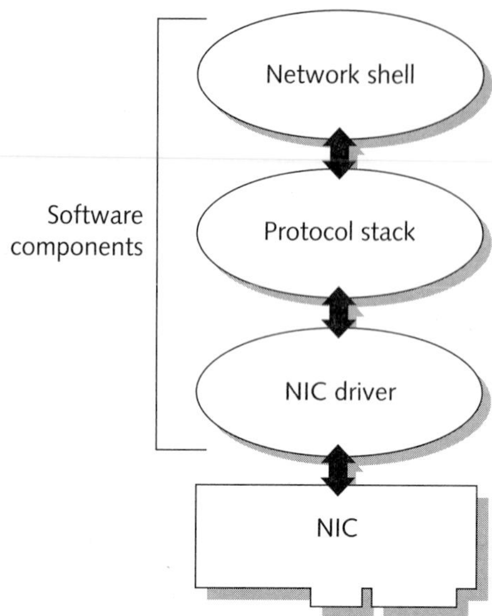

Figure 6-21 Workstation software components

The **NIC driver** software performs the data link process that controls the network adapter card so it can send and receive packets over the network cable system. Information on the correct driver program for use with NetWare should be included in the manual that comes with the network card. In some cases, the workstation driver software is contained on a disk included with the network card. Sometimes you will be instructed to use one of the many workstation driver programs included with the NetWare installation disks.

The second workstation component is the **protocol stack**, which includes the network and transport layers responsible for formatting the data within a network packet and routing that packet between networks. For example, NetWare servers use the default IPX/SPX protocol originally developed by Xerox. Another popular protocol stack often used with workstations running the UNIX operating system is TCP/IP.

Because of the increased need to support the UNIX operating system along with the rapidly growing use of the Internet, both of which use TCP/IP, most network administrators will probably need to support TCP/IP on NetWare networks.

The third workstation component is the **network shell**, which carries out the session and presentation layer functions by providing access to the network from the local operating system.

OVERVIEW OF ODI DRIVERS

To provide support for multiple protocols and to make it easier for network administrators to update card configurations and drivers, Novell developed the **open data interface (ODI)** software and driver specifications. The ODI driver specifications are standards for network card companies to use in developing drivers that are compatible with Novell's ODI software. In addition, the ODI client software allows the workstation to run multiple protocol stacks on the same network card. The ODI client software, for example, can communicate with a UNIX host (using TCP/IP) while also communicating with a NetWare server (using the IPX protocol). The connections to both servers will use the same network cable system. The ODI standard also supports more than one NIC in a workstation, so that, for example, a workstation could be connected to both an ethernet and a token ring network at the same time.

The ODI specification refers to an NIC driver as a **multiple link interface driver (MLID)**, reflecting ODI's ability to support multiple NICs in the workstation. In addition, ODI adds a fourth component to the three software components shown in Figure 6-21: the link support layer. The **link support layer (LSL)**, shown in Figure 6-22, is supplied by Novell to provide a connection within the data link layer between the protocol stack and the card driver so that more than one protocol stack can share the same network card. For example, as shown in Figure 6-22, the LSL allows you to run both TCP/IP and IPX/SPX simultaneously over the same network card by passing both TCP/IP packets and IPX packets to the NIC driver. Figure 6-22 also shows the use of two NICs in the workstation.

Figure 6-22 Workstation ODI components

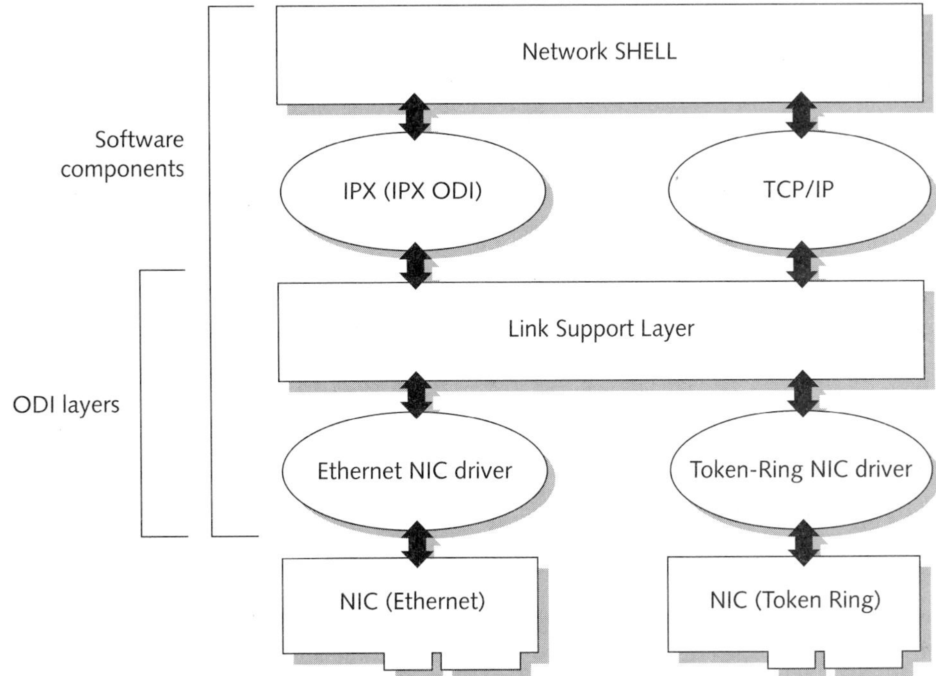

The IPX protocol stack used by ODI workstations is referred to as IPXODI. The IPXODI program is supplied by Novell and provides the SPX/IPX protocol normally used to communicate with the NetWare server. In terms of the OSI model described in Chapter 2, you can think of the IPXODI program as supplying the functions of the network and transport layers, and the LSL and MLID software as supplying the data link layer. The ODI NIC driver, the MLID software, is supplied either by Novell or by the network card's manufacturer and must be capable of working with the LSL according to Novell specifications.

Some older network cards do not have ODI-compatible drivers. You will need to obtain updated drivers from the manufacturer or replace the cards.

The Network Shell

The network shell, or just shell, is the software that allows the workstation's operating system to communicate with the network. A shell may be either a **redirector**—a program that checks workstation operations to see if the operation requires the workstation's resources or network resources—or a **requester**—a program called by the workstation's operating system when network resources are needed. Historically, there have been three

NetWare network shells: NETX, the NetWare DOS Requester, and NetWare Client 32. These are discussed in the following sections. In order to access NDS, a workstation must be using the NetWare DOS Requester, the Microsoft NDS client, or NetWare Client 32. NETX can access NetWare 4.1 servers only in bindery emulation mode.

NETX

Earlier versions of NetWare used the **NETX** redirector shell, which adapted itself to the version of DOS that was loaded and acted as a front end to DOS by intercepting all requests and routing them to either the NetWare server or local DOS. The earliest versions of the NETX shell (NET2.COM, NET3.COM, NET4.COM, and NET5.COM) were tailored to work with specific versions of DOS. To make things a little easier, Novell rewrote the shell program to eliminate the need to match the shell program to the DOS version and named it NETX.

The NetWare DOS Requester

In NetWare 3.12, the NETX shell was replaced by a requester shell named the **NetWare DOS Requester**. The NetWare DOS Requester is based on **Virtual Loadable Modules (VLMs)** and is sometimes referred to as VLMs. The NetWare DOS Requester works with DOS, allowing the requester and DOS to share drive table information, reducing memory requirements and providing better compatibility.

The NetWare DOS Requester software has several advantages over the older NETX shell program. Besides sharing DOS tables, providing better efficiency and DOS compatibility, the NetWare DOS Requester software also provides enhancements such as packet burst mode and better security. **Packet burst mode** provides faster communication to the NetWare server by allowing the workstation to receive a number of data packets at once before responding with an acknowledgment. Without packet burst mode, each data packet sent by the server must be acknowledged by the workstation before the next packet can be sent. Packet burst mode is especially effective on lightly used networks. When more workstations are accessing the network, large groups of packets can actually decrease performance for workstations that are waiting to use the network. For this reason, the packet burst mode is automatically adjusted by the NetWare DOS Requester shell and NetWare server based on the network load.

The enhanced security of the NetWare DOS Requester is provided by unique **packet signatures**, which ensure that packets are sent by authorized workstations. Before the packet signature system, it was possible for another workstation to "forge" a packet and make the NetWare server think it came from a workstation with higher privileges. Packet signatures prevent forged packets by requiring an encrypted code comprising the user's password and workstation connection number to verify that the workstation that originated the packet is authorized to do so.

ODI drivers must be loaded before the NetWare DOS Requester is initiated. The NetWare DOS requester consists of a manager, VLM.EXE, and other virtual loadable modules using the .VLM extension. A **NET.CFG** file contains a section named NetWare DOS Requester that specifies which VLMs will be loaded into the workstation memory. There is a default set of VLMs that will be loaded, but you can modify this in the NET.CFG file. The NET.CFG NetWare DOS Requester section is automatically created when you install the NetWare DOS Requester.

NetWare 4.1 includes a client installation program called INSTALL. This program can be found on NetWare's client installation disks, which were created during the server installation, or on the NetWare 4.1 CD-ROM in the \CLIENT\DOSWIN directory. To start the workstation installation process, change to the drive and directory containing the client installation program and enter the INSTALL command. NetWare copies all necessary files, including LSL.COM, IPXODI.COM, the correct driver program, and the VLMs to a directory named NWCLIENT on the workstation's hard drive.

The VLM files included on the NetWare 4.1 operating system CD-ROM are out of date. If you want to use the NetWare DOS Requester, you should download a set of current VLM files from Novell's Support Connection WWW site at http://support.novell.com.

NetWare Client 32

Novell's current network shell is **NetWare Client 32**. NetWare Client 32 is a requester that uses 32-bit code instead of the 16-bit code used in NETX and the NetWare DOS Requester. This means that a workstation must have an Intel 80386 or later microprocessor. NetWare Client 32 is composed of two parts:

- The NetWare Input/Output System (NIOS)
- Client NetWare Loadable Modules (NLMs)

The use of files named NetWare Loadable Modules with NetWare Client 32 is unfortunate, because it is no longer possible to determine files that can only run on a NetWare server by the file extension. Until NetWare Client 32 introduced NLMs for workstations, the extension .NLM always indicated a program file that would run only on a NetWare server.

The Link Support Layer (LSL) software has also been rewritten as 32-bit code, and 32-bit MLIDs can be used with NICs if they are available. NetWare Client 32 can also support older 16-bit NIC drivers and MLIDs. The Novell IPXODI protocol is replaced by the IPX 32-bit Protocol for NetWare Client 32.

NetWare Client 32 is available in versions for Windows 95 and DOS/Windows 3.1x. It is not supplied with NetWare 4.1, and to obtain a copy you must download the necessary files from Novell's Support Connection WWW site at http://support.novell.com.

You may be familiar with the Novell NetWire site as a source for update information and files. As of July 1996, the functions of the Novell NetWire site have been incorporated into the Novell Support Connection site. NetWire itself has been discontinued. This type of renaming and reorganizing is common in the computer and network industry. By the time you read this note, the Novell Support Connection may have changed into something else. However, regardless of the name, Novell will have a WWW location (and other sources, such as a CompuServe forum) where you will be able to find the update files.

If your network has workstations using Windows 3.1x, you must install the Microsoft Windows 32-bit extensions in order to use NetWare Client 32 for DOS/Windows. These extensions are available from Microsoft via the Internet and from CompuServe. This chapter will discuss the version of NetWare Client 32 for Windows 95.

The NetWare Client 32 for Windows 95 files are available in two forms. One form creates a set of seven 3.5" installation disks; the other is intended for installation of NetWare Client 32 over a network. In this chapter, the disk installation will be used. The network installation is similar and faster because there is no need to swap disks during the installation process.

NetWare Client 32 for Windows 95 provides a significantly changed user interface to NetWare tools. These include a graphic user interface (GUI) login and the NetWare Provider for Windows 95. The **NetWare Provider for Windows 95** adds NetWare tools to the Windows 95 Network Neighborhood and Explorer programs. These features will be discussed as needed in later chapters.

NetWare Client 32 has several enhancements over the NetWare DOS Requester, including better NDS support, simplified printing, autoreconnect, and enhanced packet burst support. NetWare Client 32 continues to support packet signatures, which were introduced with the NetWare DOS Requester.

INSTALLING THE NETWARE CLIENT 32 SOFTWARE

Novell provides an installation program with the NetWare Client 32 software that automates the installation of the NetWare Client 32 files. For example, the CBE Labs network administrator needs to install NetWare Client 32 on a workstation. Let's see how the installation works. A set of NetWare Client 32 installation disks were created after downloading the necessary files from Novell's support connection site, and these disks will be used for the client installation.

The workstation already has the NIC and Windows 95 installed, and the Microsoft Client for Windows Networks was installed as part of the Windows 95 installation procedure. The NIC is attached to a network cable connection. With the Microsoft client installed, the workstation is capable of logging into a NetWare server in bindery emulation mode, but not of logging into an NDS Directory tree.

NetWare Client 32 removes any existing NetWare network client when it is installed. Although you could remove an existing client manually, the NetWare Client 32 installation seems to have fewer problems when NetWare Client 32 is allowed to handle the removal.

NetWare Client 32 requires at least 6 MB of RAM. Because Windows 95 has a stated requirement of 8 MB, and runs much better with a minimum of 16 MB of RAM, a workstation that can run Windows 95 can run NetWare Client 32. NetWare Client 32 also requires 6 MB of hard drive storage. The NIC must be installed and attached to a network cable connection. During the installation of NetWare Client 32, the NetWare Client 32 installation disks and the Windows 95 CD-ROM will be needed.

To begin the installation of the NetWare Client 32 for Windows 95, use the following steps:

1. If the workstation is not running, start the workstation and let it boot Windows 95.
2. Insert the **NetWare Client 32 for Windows 95 Disk 1—Setup** into the A: drive.
3. Click the **Start** button, then click **Settings** and click the **Control Panel**. The Control Panel window is displayed.
4. Double-click the **Add/Remove Programs** icon. The Add/Remove Properties dialog box is displayed.

5. On the Install/Uninstall page, click the **Install** button. The Install program from Floppy Disk or CD-ROM dialog box is displayed.
6. Click the **Next** button. Windows 95 searches the A: drive and then the CD-ROM drive looking for a software installation program. It finds SETUP.EXE on the disk in drive A: and displays the Run Installation Program dialog box with A:\SETUP.EXE in the Command line for installation program: text box.
7. Click the **Finish** button. The Novell NetWare Client 32 Installation for Windows 95 window is displayed with the NetWare Client 32 License Agreement dialog box open. You can scroll through the license agreement to review it by using the vertical scroll bar on the dialog box.
8. Click the **Yes** button to accept the agreement and proceed. The NetWare Client 32 Installation dialog box is displayed, as shown in Figure 6-23.

Figure 6-23

The NetWare Client 32 Installation dialog box

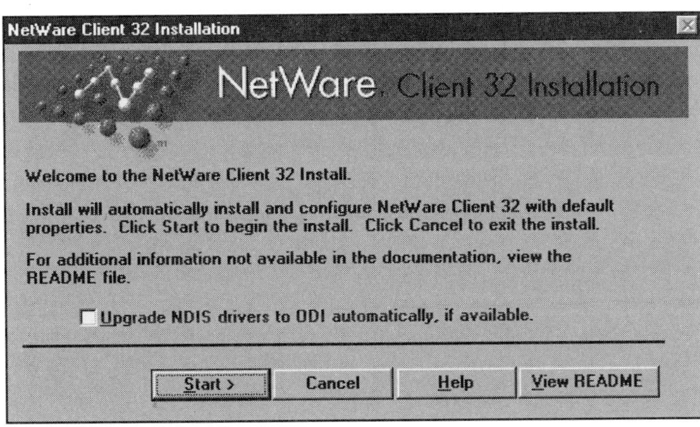

The README.TXT File

The NetWare Client 32 files include a README.TXT text file, which contains the latest release notes available when the NetWare Client 32 files were approved for distribution. The NetWare Client 32 installation program allows you to view the README file with a text editor. You can also print a copy for review. One important item in the NetWare Client 32 README.TXT file is that the primary documentation for NetWare Client 32 is the NetWare Client 32 Help file, which was copied to the workstation hard drive during installation. There is no separate printed documentation for NetWare Client 32.

You should always review the README file that comes with software packages for information that is not contained in the software manuals. README files contain the most recent configuration information and data about known problems with the software.

To view and print the NetWare Client 32 for Windows 95 README.TXT file, follow these steps:

1. Click the **View README** button on the NetWare Client 32 Installation dialog box. The README.TXT file is displayed in a text editor or word processor for viewing.
2. Use the **File | Print** command to print a copy of the README.TXT file; then click the **Windows 95 Close** button ☒ to close the text editor and return to the NetWare Client 32 Installation dialog box.

The NetWare Client 32 Software Installation

When the text editor displaying the README.TXT file is closed, the NetWare Client 32 Installation dialog box is displayed again. To begin the actual installation of the NetWare Client 32 software, click the **Start** button in the dialog box.)

The exact sequence of steps for installing NetWare Client 32 will vary depending upon the type of NIC installed in the workstation and the drivers already installed for the NIC. Possible variations include the following:

- Using the NetWare Client 32 LAN Drivers disk to install an NIC driver
- Using the Windows 95 CD to install Windows 95 files
- Being asked if you want to configure the NetWare Client 32 settings before disk 2 or at the end of the installation process.

The workstation installation shown in this chapter used a workstation with a 3COM 3C509B NIC. The Microsoft NetWare client had been installed as a part of the Windows 95 installation. During this installation, no additional LAN drivers or Windows 95 files were needed.

At this point, the NetWare Client 32 installation program removes the existing NetWare client installed on the workstation. The NetWare Client 32 installation program does a thorough and effective job of removing the installed client, so there is no need to remove a previously installed NetWare client before the installation of NetWare Client 32.

Windows 95 then records information into a Data Info Database, after which the NetWare Client 32 installation program copies files from the disk to the workstation's hard drive. These two processes alternate, and you will see message dialog boxes as each process runs. After each set of NetWare Client 32 files is copied, Windows 95 updates the Data Info Database. As the installation progresses, you are asked to swap disks so that the installation program can access the files on those disks. If the NetWare Client 32 installation program needs files from the Windows 95 CD-ROM, it will ask for the Windows 95 CD after it has copied files from the NetWare Client 32 disks.

The NetWare Client 32 installation program gives you a chance to specify NetWare Client 32 property settings. Although this can be done after the installation is complete, Novell recommends that at least a preferred NDS tree and default **name context**, the context of the user's User object, be set for a NetWare 4.1 network. For example, the CBE Labs network administrator takes this opportunity to set all the NetWare Client 32 property settings for each CBE workstation.

During the NetWare Client 32 installation, the Insert Disk dialog box contains the statement "This disk is provided by your computer manufacturer." This is obviously incorrect because you downloaded these files from the Novell Support Connection Web site. Novell may be planning on computer manufacturer distribution of NetWare Client 32 as a distribution channel in the future.

To install NetWare Client 32 for Windows 95, follow these steps:

1. Click the **Start** button on the NetWare Client 32 Installation dialog box. This button can be seen in Figure 6-23.
2. The NetWare Client 32 installation program copies files until it needs the files on the second disk.
3. Remove the **NetWare Client 32 for Windows 95 Disk 1—Setup** from the A: drive.
4. Insert the **NetWare Client 32 for Windows 95 Disk 2** into the A: drive; then click the **OK** button.
5. The NetWare Client 32 installation program continues copying files. When the NetWare Client 32 installation program prompts you for Disk 3, remove the **NetWare Client 32 for Windows 95 Disk 2** from the A: drive, insert the **NetWare Client 32 for Windows 95 Disk 3** into the A: drive, and then click the **OK** button.
6. The NetWare Client 32 installation program continues copying files. When the NetWare Client 32 installation program prompts you for Disk 4, remove the **NetWare Client 32 for Windows 95 Disk 3** from the A: drive, insert the **NetWare Client 32 for Windows 95 Disk 4** into the A: drive, and then click the **OK** button.
7. The NetWare Client 32 installation program continues copying files. If the NetWare Client 32 installation program needs files from the Windows 95 CD-ROM, it prompts you for the Windows 95 CD-ROM at this point. If needed, place the **Windows 95 CD-ROM** into the CD-ROM drive, and then click the **OK** button. The NetWare Client 32 installation program copies files from the Windows 95 CD-ROM.
8. After this is completed, the NetWare Client 32 installation process is complete. The NetWare Client 32 installation program displays the NetWare Client 32 Installation dialog box shown in Figure 6-24 to ask if you want to reboot the workstation so that the changes can take effect or customize the NetWare Client 32 settings.

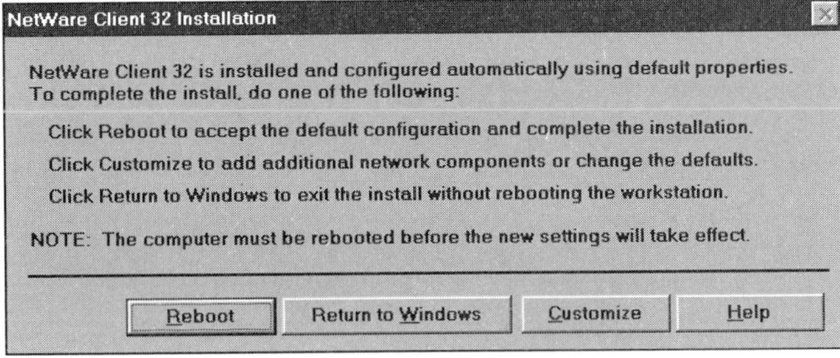

Figure 6-24 The NetWare Client 32 Installation dialog box after installation

9. Click the **Customize** button on the NetWare Client 32 Installation dialog box. The Windows 95 Network dialog box is displayed, as shown in Figure 6-25.

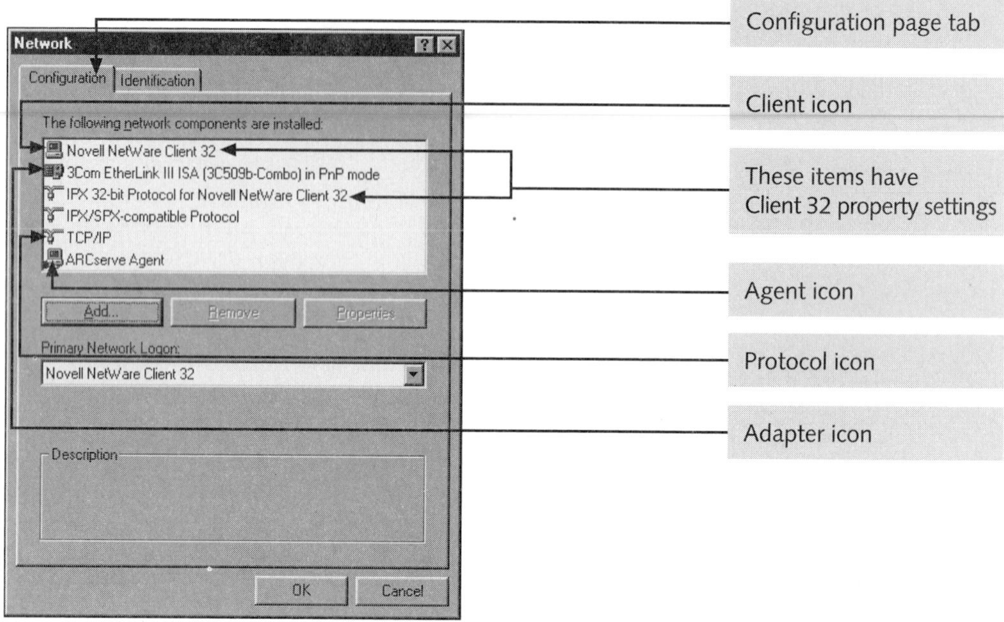

Figure 6-25

The Network dialog box

The Configuration page of the Network dialog box displays a list of installed network components. These components include clients, adapters, protocols, and agents. An **adapter** is a hardware component used to connect the workstation to the network. For example, in Figure 6-25, the workstation's 3Com Etherlink III NIC is an adapter. A **client** is the software that provides the network connectivity for the workstation, while a **protocol** (or **protocol stack**) is software that controls how the workstation communicates with the network and other workstations or NetWare servers on the network. In Figure 6-25, the client is Novell NetWare Client 32, and there are three protocols being used: Novell's IPX 32-bit protocol for Novell NetWare Client 32, the Microsoft IPX/SPX-compatible protocol, and the Microsoft TCP/IP protocol. Only the first of these is part of NetWare Client 32. Finally, an **agent** is client software that enables the workstation to use network services provided by server software on an applications server. In Figure 6-25, the ARCserve agent is client software that enables files on the workstation hard drives to be backed up to tape by ARCserve backup software residing and running on a NetWare server.

The Novell NetWare Client 32 client and the IPX 32-bit protocol for Novell NetWare Client 32 protocol are part of NetWare Client 32. You can access the settings for the NetWare Client 32 client and protocol by clicking them in the list of installed components and then clicking the Properties button.

To display the NetWare Client 32 Properties dialog, do the following:

1. Click the **NetWare Client 32 client** in the list of installed components in the Network dialog box.
2. Click the **Properties** button on the Network dialog box.

The Novell NetWare Client 32 Properties dialog box is displayed, as shown in Figure 6-26.

Novell NetWare Client 32 Properties Dialog Box Pages

The Novell NetWare Client 32 Properties dialog, shown in Figure 6-26, has four tabbed pages: the Client 32 page, the Login page, the Default Capture page, and the Advanced Settings page.

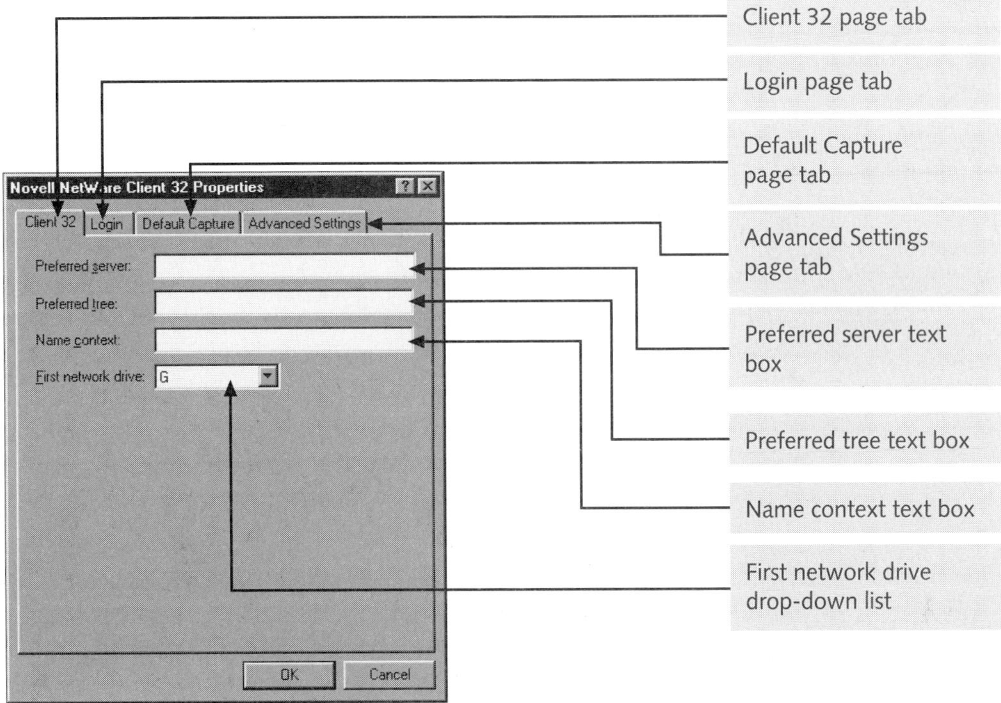

Figure 6-26
The Novell NetWare Client 32 Properties dialog box

The Client 32 page is initially displayed when the Novell NetWare Client 32 Properties dialog box is opened, and this page contains the preferred connection settings for the workstation. The settings on the Login page control the display of the Novell NetWare Login dialog box, including how many tabbed pages to display to the user and the default settings for those pages. The Default Capture page includes property settings to control printer output for printed output from the workstation. The Advanced Settings page enables the property settings for 45 parameters to be set, which enables the network administrator to fine-tune workstation connectivity to the network. These four pages are summarized in Figure 6-27.

Figure 6-27
The Novell Netware Client 32 Properties dialog box pages

Client 32 Properties Page	Purpose
Client 32	Set the workstation connection preferences
Login	Control the display of the Novell NetWare Login dialog box tabbed pages
Default Capture	Set the workstation preferences for printer output
Advanced Settings	Set property values of 45 Client 32 parameters

The Client 32 Page

As shown in Figure 6-26, the workstation connection settings include a server setting, a preferred tree setting, a user name context setting, and a first network drive setting. The values you set are property values and are stored in the Windows 95 registry. In fact, all settings you select for NetWare Client 32 are stored in the Windows 95 registry, which eliminates the need for a configuration file to store the property setting. The earlier workstation clients, NETX and the NetWare DOS Requester client software, used a configuration filename NET.CFG to store these property settings.

The preferred server setting specifies which server the workstation will attach to for login purposes if the workstation is attaching to a bindery-based NetWare 3.1x server or a NetWare 4.1 server in bindery mode. When connecting in bindery mode, the network shell functions by sending a request for the first available NetWare server as soon as it is loaded, then attaching to the first NetWare server that responds and making that server the default NetWare server. By specifying a preferred server, the network administrator can control which NetWare server the workstation attaches to.

When logging into an NDS Directory tree instead of a NetWare server, the preferred tree setting specifies which NDS Directory tree the workstation will use for login purposes. Thus, the preferred tree setting serves the same function for NDS that the preferred server setting does for bindery mode.

In an NDS Directory tree, the User object will be assigned a default server based on Directory tree partitioning. The preferred server setting can also be used to override the default server setting and thus enable the network administrator to control which NetWare 4.1 server is used to authenticate the user's login in an NDS environment.

A user must log into an NDS Directory tree in the proper context. This means that the context of the user's User object must be included in the login. The name context setting specifies the default context for users logging into the network using the workstation. For example, the CBE Labs Admin User object is in the context .CBE_Labs, as shown in Figure 6-28. The network administrator can set the name context for the workstation to .CBE_Labs. This context will automatically be used for logins from the workstation, and the network administrator can log into the network as the Admin user by simply entering the login name of Admin. Without the name context setting, the user would also have to enter the correct context of his or her User object when logging in.

After attaching to a NetWare server or an NDS Directory tree, the first available drive pointer is mapped to the SYS:LOGIN directory of the default NetWare server in bindery mode or the default NDS NetWare 4.1 server for the Directory tree. The first network drive setting allows the network administration to specify which drive letter will be mapped to the SYS:LOGIN directory. This mapping allows the user to access the NetWare LOGIN.EXE program for logging in.

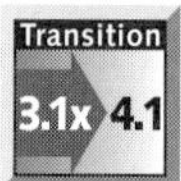

NETX client software used the last drive setting to delineate local and network drives instead of the first network drive setting. Starting with the NetWare DOS Requester, the last drive setting specifies the last drive letter available for either local or network use, with the first network drive setting controlling the switch from local to network drives.

The choice of the first network drive limits both the number of local drive letters available to the workstation and the number of drive letters available for network drive mappings. The F drive has often been designated as the first network drive. However, as workstations use more local drives, the G drive is often used as the first network drive.

Workstations are using more peripherals or hardware setups that require a local drive letter. Examples are CD-ROM drives, optical drives, and compressed hard disks that require a "host drive."

As part of the NetWare Client 32 installation, the CBE Labs network administrator now enters the settings he wants to use as the preferred and default login settings for users logging into the network from this workstation. The preferred tree is CBELABS, the name context is .CBE_Labs, and the first network drive will be G:. In addition, the network administrator will specify CONSTELLATION as the preferred server in case the user needs to log into the server in bindery mode.

To enter the Client 32 page preferred and default settings, follow these steps:

1. The Preferred server text box should be active. If it isn't, click it to activate it and then type **CONSTELLATION** to designate CONSTELLATION as the preferred NetWare server.
2. Click the **Preferred tree text** box to activate it. Type **CBELABS** to designate CBELABS as the preferred NDS Directory tree.
3. Click the **Name context tree text** box to activate it. Type **.CBE_Labs** to designate .CBE_Labs as the default context of the user's User object in the NDS Directory tree.
4. Check the First network drive text box to see if it is set to drive letter G:. If it isn't, then click the **First network drive** drop-down list arrow to display the drive letters in the drop-down list, then click **G** to set the G: drive as the first network drive. The completed Client 32 page settings are shown in Figure 6-28.

Figure 6-28 The Completed Client 32 page settings

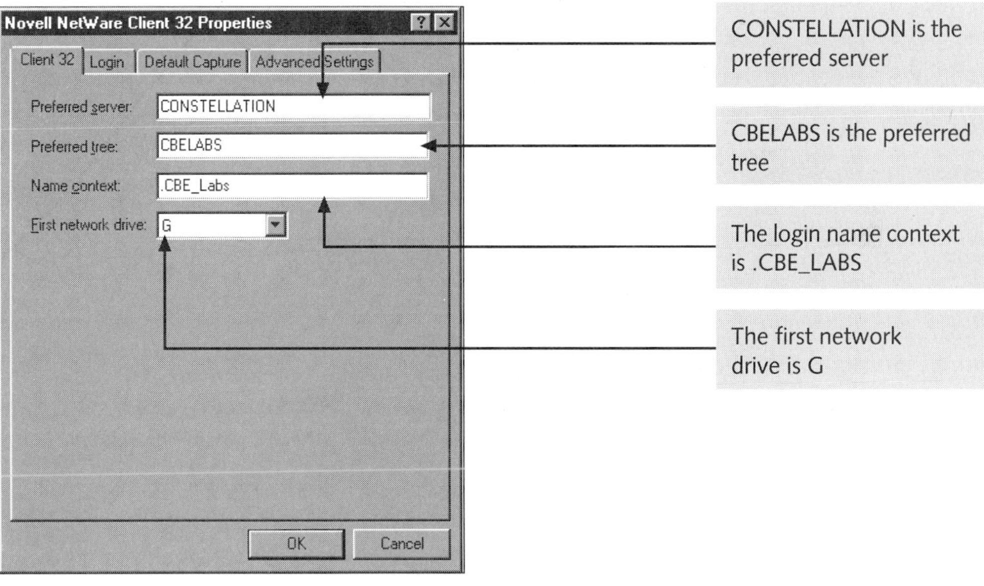

The Login Page

The Login page of the Novell NetWare Client 32 Property Settings dialog box controls how the user interacts with the Novell NetWare Login dialog box during login. The Novell NetWare Login dialog box is shown in Figure 6-29, where it has four tabbed pages: Login, Connection, Script, and Variables.

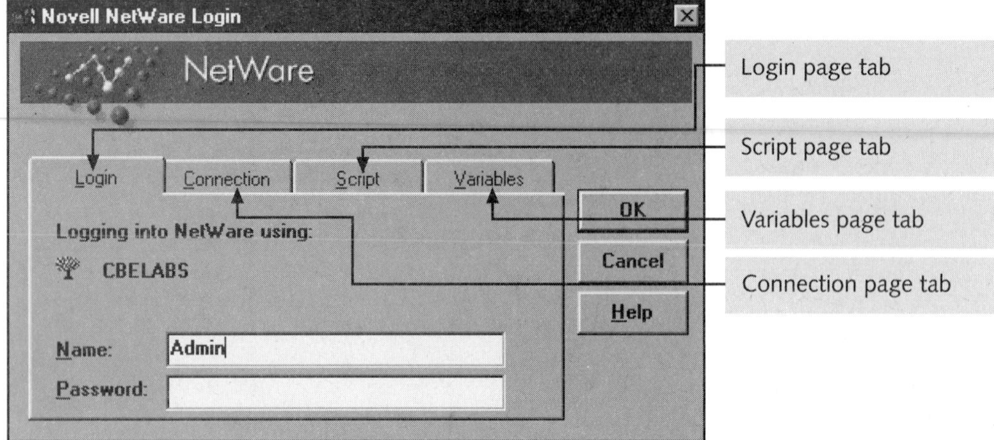

Figure 6-29 The Novell NetWare Login dialog box

The Login page of the Novell NetWare Login dialog box is always displayed. The preferences set on the Client 32 page of the Novell NetWare Client 32 Properties dialog box are used to determine the user's default network connection. In Figure 6-29, user Admin is logging into the NDS Directory Tree CBELABS. This connection is determined by the settings shown in Figure 6-28, where CBELABS is the name of the preferred NDS Directory tree.

The display of the Connection, Script, and Variable pages of the Novell NetWare Login dialog box is controlled by the Login page of the Novell NetWare Client 32 Properties dialog box. This page is shown in Figure 6-30.

Figure 6-30 The Login page of the Novell NetWare Client 32 Properties dialog box

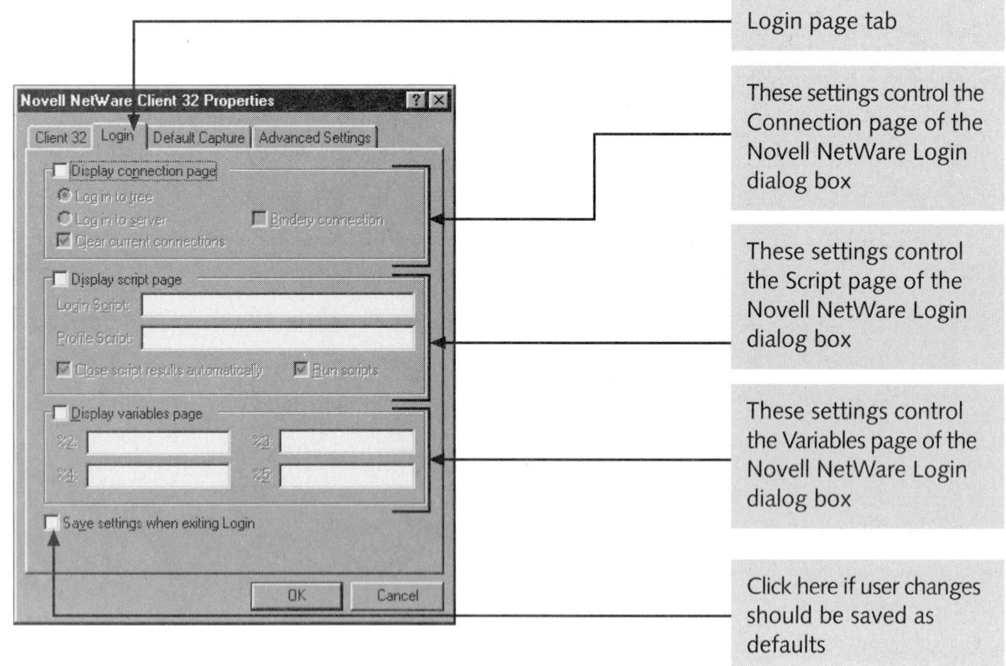

The Novell NetWare Client 32 Properties Login page in Figure 6-30 shows the default settings for the page. There are three important results of these settings. First, the Display connection page check box, the Display script page check box, and the Display variables check box are all unchecked, indicating that these pages will not be displayed in the Novell NetWare Login dialog box. This means that by default the only page displayed in the Novell NetWare Login dialog box is the Login page. Second, in the Connection page settings, the Log into tree and Clear current connections are enabled. This means that the default login will be to the preferred tree, which is why the CBELABS tree is the connection shown in Figure 6-29, and that any connections the user has to any Directory tree or NetWare server will be disconnected during the new login. Third, in the Script page settings, the Close script results automatically and Run scripts check boxes are checked. These settings will cause the user's login script to be run upon login and a window containing the results of the login script to be closed without user action.

You can use the settings on this page to control these features:

- Which pages of the Novell NetWare Login dialog box are displayed to the user
- The default type of connection for the workstation
- How login scripts are handled on the workstation
- The default values of variables needed by the login script
- Whether new settings specified by a user during login should be saved

You will choose which pages of the Novell NetWare Login dialog box to display to a user depending upon the user's needs. The Connection page is useful if the workstation is used to log into more than one network or NetWare server. If it is, then the user must be able to choose his or her login connection. On the other hand, if users of the workstation always log into the same network or NetWare server, there is no need to display this page. The need for the Script page is similar to that for the Connection page: if the defaults specified in the Client 32 Properties dialog box need to be changed or varied by the users of the workstation, the page should be displayed. If the defaults will always be used, there is no need for the users to see this page. Finally, the Variables page should be displayed only if users need to enter parameter values for their login script during login. If no variable values are needed (which is usually the case) or if the default parameter values are always used, there is no need to display the page.

The Save settings when exiting Login check box allows the default settings on this page to be updated by the user during login. If this check box is checked, the settings the user uses for his or her login will be saved as new defaults. For example, suppose that the Admin user logs into the CBELABS tree by default. However, the network administrator also needs to log into the NetWare server CONSTELLATION in bindery mode to check the bindery emulation. To do so, he logs in as SUPERVISOR instead of Admin, and he specifies a bindery login to CONSTELLATION on the Connection page of the Novell NetWare Login dialog box, as shown in Figure 6-31.

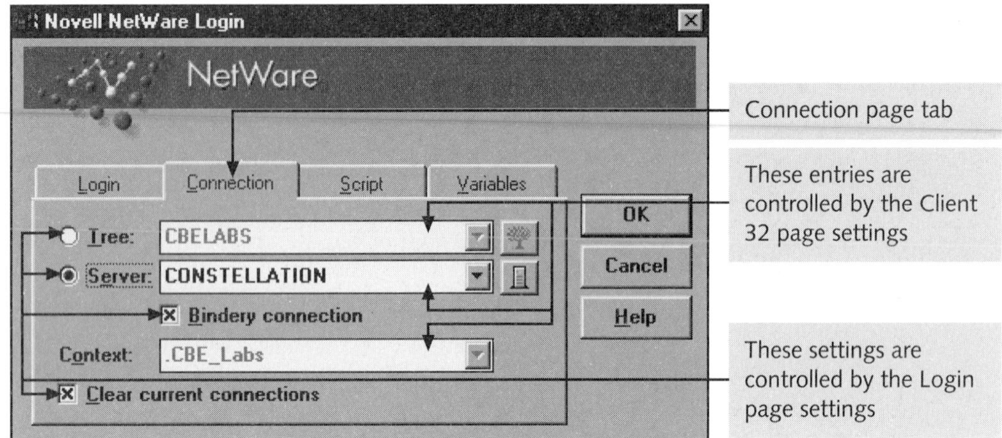

Figure 6-31 The Connection page of the Novell NetWare Login dialog box

When the Admin user is created during a NetWare 4.1 installation, a SUPERVISOR user is also created for administrative use in bindery mode. The SUPERVISOR user does not appear in the Directory tree. The SUPERVISOR user has the same initial password as the Admin user, and is equivalent to the NetWare 3.1x SUPERVISOR user.

If Save settings when exiting Login is enabled, then these settings will become the new defaults for the *workstation*, and the next user of the workstation will attempt to log into CONSTELLATION in bindery mode unless he or she changes the settings on the Connection page. There will usually be no need to enable users to change the default settings. However, you may encounter a situation where this feature is useful.

The workstation that the CBE Labs network administrator is working with will be used by the Information Systems workgroup at CBE Labs. Because workgroup members need to be able to specify their network connection, control login script display, and enter login script variables during login, the network administrator needs to modify the settings on the Login page of the Client 32 Properties dialog box. However, these will always be temporary changes, so there is no need to save the settings as new login defaults. Users of this workstation will normally log into the CBELABS Directory tree and clear previous connections, so there is no need to change these defaults. The user's User object property settings will determine which login script or profile script to use, so there is no need to specify a login script or profile script. Finally, login scripts and profiles scripts at CBE Labs normally don't need input values, so there is no need to set variables values.

To enter the Login settings, follow these steps:

1. Click the **Login page** tab of the Novell NetWare Client 32 Properties dialog box to display the Login page.
2. Click the **Display connection page** check box to select it.
3. Click the **Display script page** check box to select it.
4. Click the **Display variable page** check box to select it. The completed settings are shown in Figure 6-32.

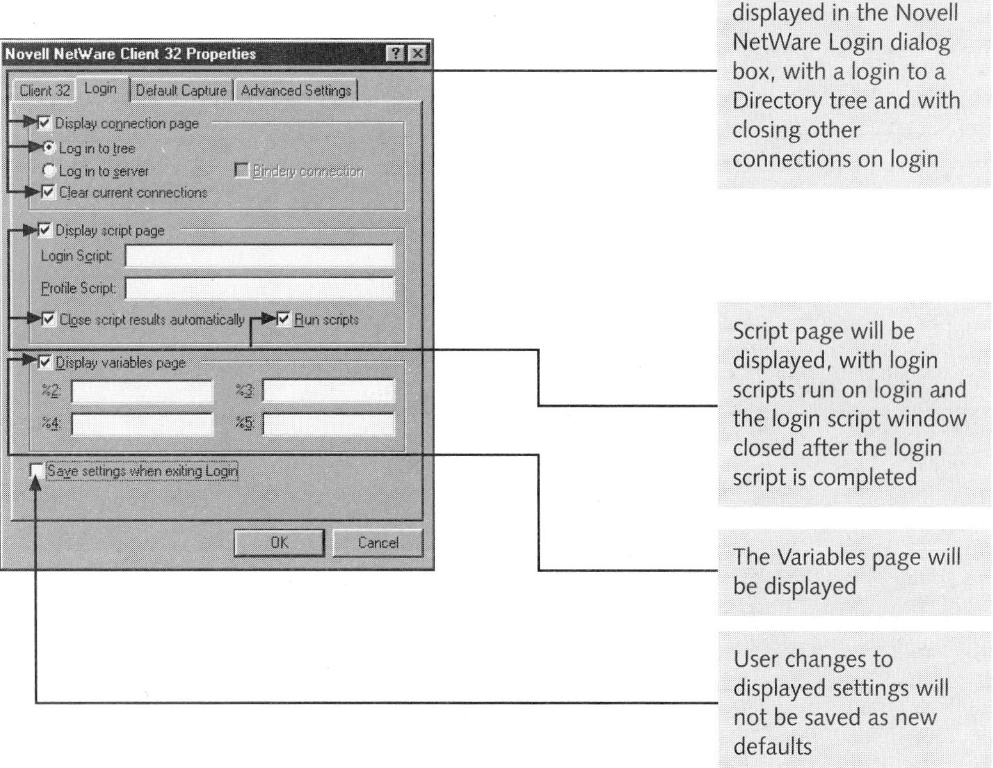

Figure 6-32

The completed Login page settings

The Default Capture Page

The Default Capture page of the Novell NetWare Client 32 Property Settings dialog box controls how print jobs are printed. This page is shown with default settings in Figure 6-33.

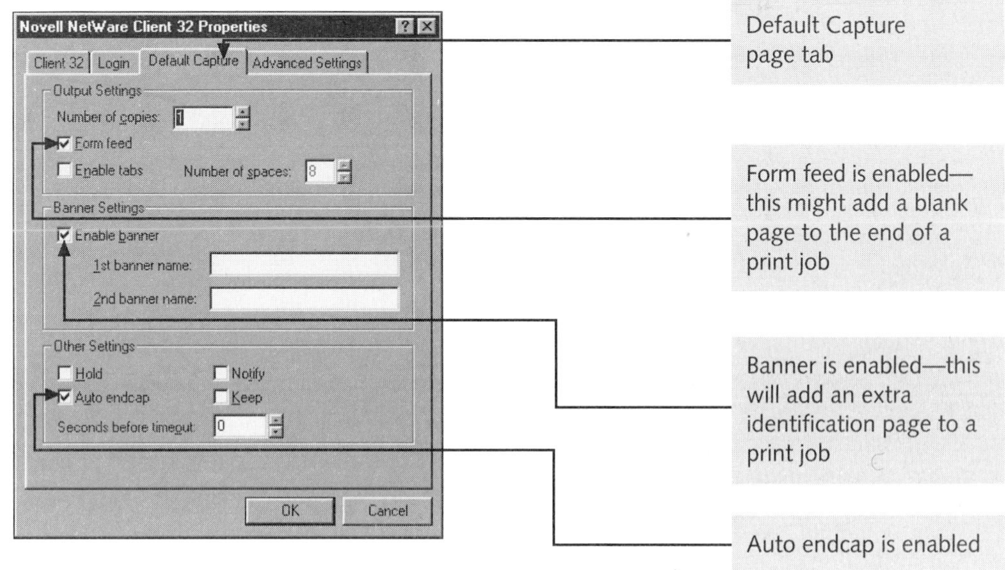

Figure 6-33

The Default Capture page of the Novell NetWare Client 32 Properties dialog box

NetWare printing is discussed in detail in Chapters 12 and 13; the discussion in this section does not cover printing in detail but includes only what you need to know for setting up NetWare Client 32. These settings are used with any printer port that is attached to a printer, which is referred to as a capture, within Windows 95. They do not apply to printer ports attached to printers in a login script or using the NetWare CAPTURE command at the DOS prompt. The important point to remember here is that the settings on this page are applied to every print job printed by Windows 95 in addition to any settings specified in Windows 95 printer setups. For example, Figure 6-33 shows a default settings of Form feed enabled in the Output Settings section. A form feed tells the printer that a printed page is complete and that the printer should move to the start of the next page. On a laser printer, this causes the page to be completed and run into the finished page tray. Although this is useful if the application program itself has not provided a form feed, it causes an extra, blank page to be "printed" if the application does provide a form feed. With the Form feed setting enabled, you will usually have a blank page added to every print job printed under Windows 95. This, of course, is a waste of paper, so the Form feed setting needs to be disabled.

But worse, the Form feed setting can also be independently controlled by the Windows 95 printer setup. If the NetWare Client 32 Form feed setting and the Windows 95 printer setup form feed setting both specify a form feed, you will see *two* extra blank pages printed after every page job!

Similarly, the Enable banner setting prints a banner (a page that identifies the user who printed the output) before every print job. This is often useful when users print to a shared printer because it allows users to easily identify their output. On the other hand, in a small workgroup users can often easily identify their output without the banner, in which case the banner is a wasted sheet of paper. Again, banners can also be enabled in the Windows 95 printer setup, which can result in a total of two banners being printed for each print job. In general, form feeds are not needed but banners may be useful. However, you must be careful where you enable the banner if you are going to use one—generally it is better to enable it in the printer settings rather than in the NetWare Client 32 properties.

Finally, the Auto endcap setting, which stands for automatic end capture, is enabled by default. The default value, auto endcap enabled, is usually preferred.

The CBE Labs network administrator prefers to control print settings for each individual printer available to the workstation rather than to set defaults on this page. Therefore he needs to disable the form feed and banner settings.

To enter the Default Capture settings, do the following:

1. Click the **Default Capture page** tab of the Novell NetWare Client 32 Properties dialog box to display the Default Capture page.
2. Click the **Form feed** check box to deselect it.
3. Click the **Enable banner** check box to deselect it. The completed settings are shown in Figure 6-34.

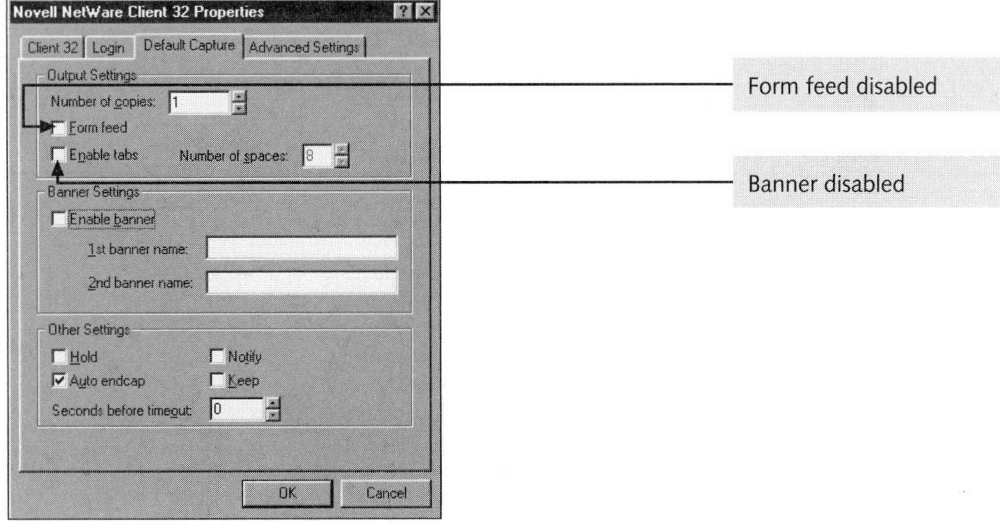

Figure 6-34

The completed Default Capture page settings

The Advanced Settings Page

The Advanced Settings page of the Novell NetWare Client 32 Property Settings dialog box allows you to set property values for 45 NetWare Client 32 parameters, grouped into eight parameter groups (or nine parameter groups if the All group is counted). The values that you set, like the values for the NetWare Client 32 property set for previous pages, are stored in the Windows 95 registry. In NETX and the NetWare DOS Requester, these property values (and the PREFERRED TREE, PREFERRED SERVER, NAME CONTEXT, and FIRST NETWORK DRIVE values set on the Login page) were specified in the NET.CFG file. This Advance Settings page is shown in Figure 6-35. The parameter groups used on the Advanced Settings page are detailed in Figure 6-36.

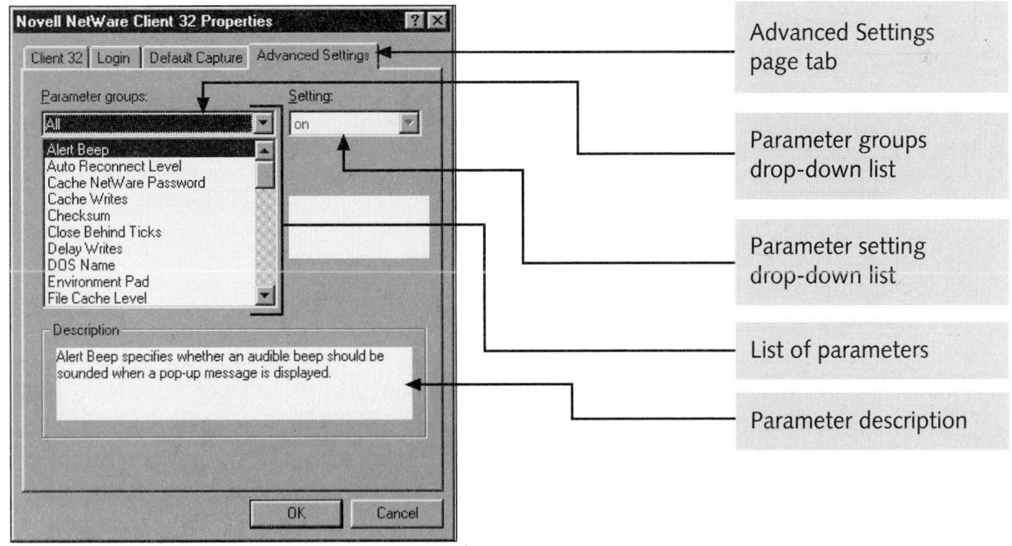

Figure 6-35

The Advanced Settings page of the Novell NetWare Client 32 Properties dialog box

The Novell NetWare Client 32 for DOS and Windows 3.1x still uses the NET.CFG file, which is where the NetWare Client 32 property values are set for the Novell NetWare Client 32 for DOS and Windows. Documentation on the NET.CFG file is in the Novell NetWare Client 32 for DOS and Windows Help File.

Figure 6-36
Client 32 Parameter Groups

Parameter Group	Used to Control
All	All parameter settings
Connection	Parameter settings for the user's LAN connection
Environment, NETX Compatibility	Parameter settings related to the user's workstation and ensuring backward compatibility with settings for the NETX shell
File System	Parameter settings for access to files stored in volumes on NetWare servers
Packet Management	Parameter settings related to the packets that the workstation sends and receives on the network
Cache Performance	Parameter settings for the workstation's interaction with file caching on NetWare servers
Printing	Parameter settings for network printing
Troubleshooting	Settings for parameters that can help determine problem sources
Wide Area Network (WAN)	Parameter settings for user's WAN connections

An example of a parameter set on the Advanced Settings page is the NetWare Protocol parameter in the Connection parameter group, as shown in Figure 6-37.

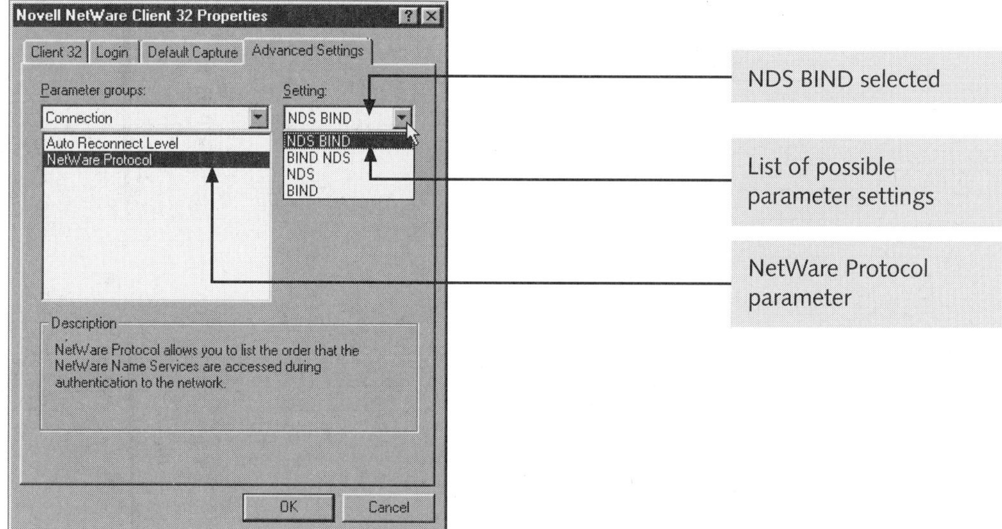

Figure 6-37
The NetWare Protocol parameter

The NetWare Protocol parameter is used to control which type of network connection is used by the workstation. There are two options: NDS for Novell Directory Services and BIND for bindery. This first protocol listed is the first one that NetWare Client 32 uses in connecting to the network. For example, in Figure 6-37, the NetWare protocol list is NDS BIND, which indicates that the workstation will first try to connect to an NDS Directory tree and then try to connect to a NetWare server in bindery mode if an NDS tree is not available. As shown in the drop-down list in Figure 6-37, there are four settings for the parameter. These settings are summarized in Figure 6-38.

Figure 6-38

Netware Client 32 Netware Protocol parameter settings

Parameter Setting	Comments
NDS BIND	Client 32 first attempts to connect to an NDS Directory tree; if that fails, attempts to connect to a NetWare server in bindery mode
BIND NDS	Client 32 first attempts to connect to a NetWare server in bindery mode; if that fails, attempts to connect to an NDS Directory tree
NDS	Client 32 attempts to connect to only an NDS Directory tree
BIND	Client 32 attempts to connect to only a NetWare server in bindery mode

You may develop standardized values for your NetWare Client 32 installations that differ from the defaults. If you do, then you will need to modify the NetWare Client 32 installation process to include setting the modified values.

The NetWare Client 32 installation process uses "Smart Default," which copies parameter settings from an existing NET.CFG file into the NetWare Client 32 property values. This means that if you are upgrading from the NetWare DOS Requester to NetWare Client 32, the values of the NetWare DOS Requester options also supported by NetWare Client 32 will be maintained.

The workstation default NetWare Client 32 properties have now been set, and the software installation can proceed.

Completing the NetWare Client 32 Software Installation

The installation is complete and the NetWare Client 32 parameters are set, but the workstation must be rebooted in order to allow the new settings to take effect.

To complete the NetWare Client 32 installation process, follow these steps:

1. Remove the **NetWare Client 32 for Windows 95 Disk 4** from the A: drive (and the **Windows 95 CD-ROM** from the CD-ROM drive if necessary).
2. Click the **OK** button on the Novell NetWare Client 32 Properties dialog.
3. Click the **OK** button on the Windows 95 Network dialog box.
4. The workstation must be rebooted for the settings to take effect. Windows 95 prompts you to reboot the workstation. Click the **OK** button and reboot the workstation with NetWare Client 32 as the NetWare client.

Updates to NetWare Client 32 Files

Novell updates NetWare files from time to time, sometimes to fix a known problem and sometimes to improve the functionality of the software. As a network administrator, you should regularly check for updates to NetWare files and implement these updates as they occur. Novell publishes a list of the current updates at the Novell Support Connection on its WWW site at http://support.novell.com. Individual update files are also available through this WWW site.

The NetWare Client 32 update file C3295D.EXE was released in August 1996. This book assumes that at least the update files from this file have been installed. If later updates have been released (they are identified by the letter x in the filename C3295x.EXE), you should also install those updates.

NETWARE CLIENT 32 DOCUMENTATION

The primary documentation for NetWare Client 32 is the Help system file that is installed during the NetWare Client 32 installation process. This help file can be accessed through the Windows 95 Start menu system.

To display the NetWare Client 32 documentation, follow these steps:

1. Click the **Start** button on the Windows 95 Taskbar, and then click Help. The Windows 95 Help Topic: Windows Help dialog box is displayed.
2. In the Contents page window, double-click **Novell NetWare Client 32** to display the table of contents for the NetWare Client 32 documentation. The table of contents is displayed, as shown in Figure 6-39. The table of contents can be expanded by double-clicking on the closed book icons. Double-clicking on page icons displays a help page on the topic.

Figure 6-39

The Novell Netware Client 32 table of contents

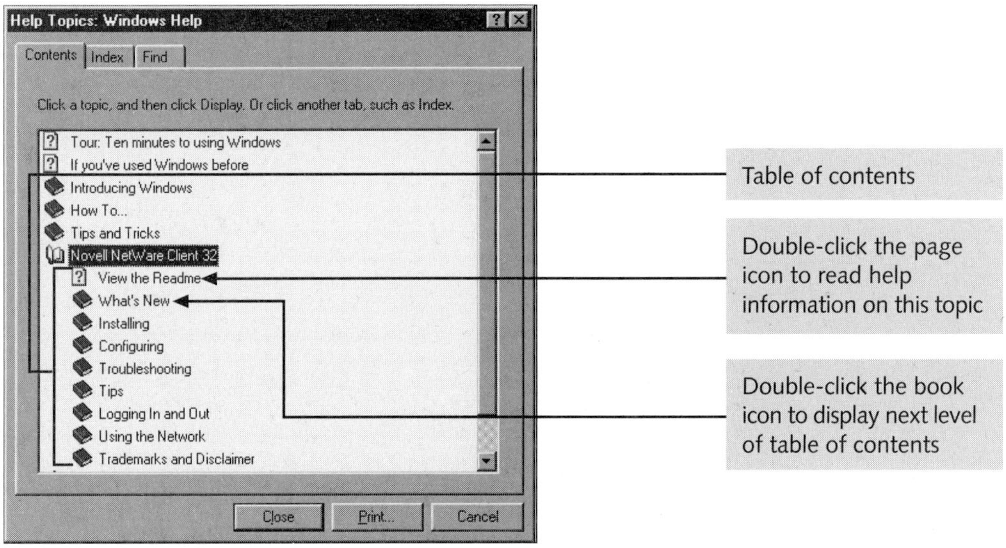

Table of contents

Double-click the page icon to read help information on this topic

Double-click the book icon to display next level of table of contents

3. To display a comparison of NetWare Client 32 and other NetWare workstation clients, double-click the **What's New** book icon, and then double-click **Comparing Client 32 with other NetWare Clients**. The Comparing Client 32 with Other NetWare Clients topic is displayed in the Windows Help window, as shown in Figure 6-40.

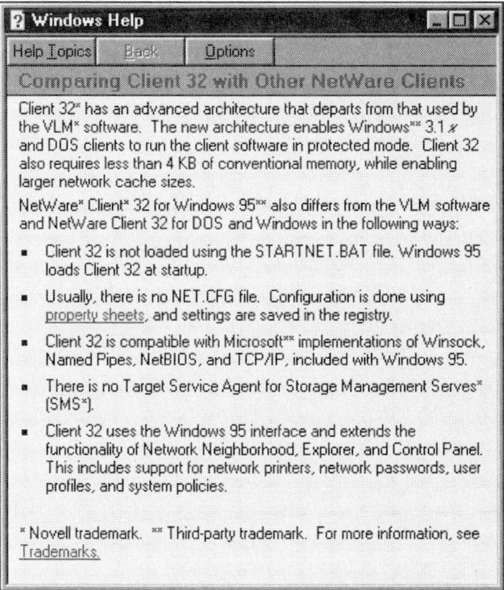

Figure 6-40 The Windows Help window

4. When you are finished reading the topic, click the **Close** button to close the Windows Help window.

NETWARE CLIENT 32 SETTINGS

After NetWare Client 32 is installed, the network administrator will still need access to NetWare Client 32 parameter settings in order to modify them. As discussed during the NetWare Client 32 installation procedure, the Novell NetWare Client 32 client and the IPX 32-bit protocol for Novell NetWare Client 32 protocol are part of NetWare Client 32. After installation is completed, you can access NetWare Client 32 settings through the Network folder in the Windows 95 Control Panel. Double-clicking the Network folder displays the Network dialog box, which was discussed above. The settings for NetWare Client 32 client and the IPX 32-bit protocol for Novell NetWare Client 32 protocol can be accessed from the Network dialog box. The NetWare Client 32 settings were discussed above as part of the installation process. The IPX 32-bit protocol for Novell NetWare Client 32 protocol settings are introduced in this section.

The Microsoft IPX/SPX-compatible protocol shown in Figure 6-25 is needed by the NetWare Client 32 components. It is installed as part of the NetWare Client 32 installation, and if you remove it the other NetWare Client 32 components will also be removed.

Clicking IPX 32-bit Protocol for Novell NetWare Client 32 in the installed components list of the Network dialog box and then clicking the Properties button displays the IPX 32-bit Protocol for Novell NetWare Client 32 Properties dialog box, as shown in Figure 6-41.

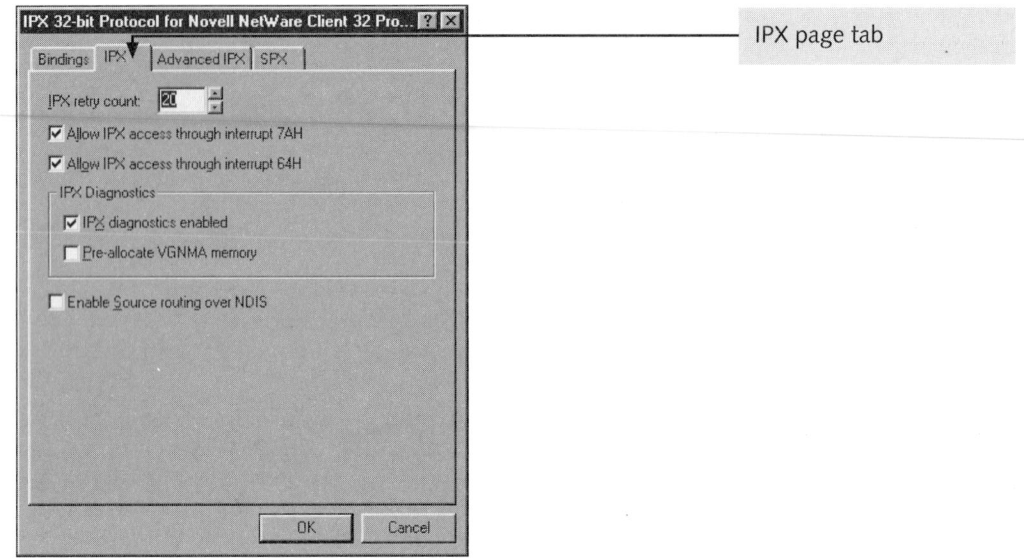

Figure 6-41 The IPX 32-bit Protocol for Novell NetWare Client 32 Properties dialog box

The IPX 32-bit Protocol for Novell NetWare Client 32 Properties dialog box has four pages: Bindings, IPX, Advanced IPX, and SPX. Notice that by default the IPX page is initially displayed. The IPX page contains the basic settings for Internetwork Packet Exchange (IPX) parameters, and the defaults initially set normally work well with most NetWare 4.1 networks. As its name implies, the Advanced IPX page, shown in Figure 6-42, contains other parameter settings for the protocol. This page is important because it allow the network administrator to select the frame types that will be used with the protocol. The default installation setting is to use all the frame types that are detected on the network. This, however, may not be efficient if, for example, there are several frame types in use on the network, but this workstation only needs to communicate with some of them. In this case, the network administrator can specify the frame types to be used, as shown in Figure 6-42.

The Advanced IPX page also allows the network administrator to specify whether the primary logical board is necessary. Each frame type that is used with an NIC is considered to be broadcast on a separate logical network, which is called a **subnetwork**. For example, in Figure 6-42, there are two frame types in use: ETHERNET_802.2 and ETHERNET_802.3. Therefore, there are two subnetworks operating in this LAN—they use the same cable and the same NICs, but they are in fact two different systems of communication. To understand this, think of a telephone connection between two houses, as shown in Figure 6-43.

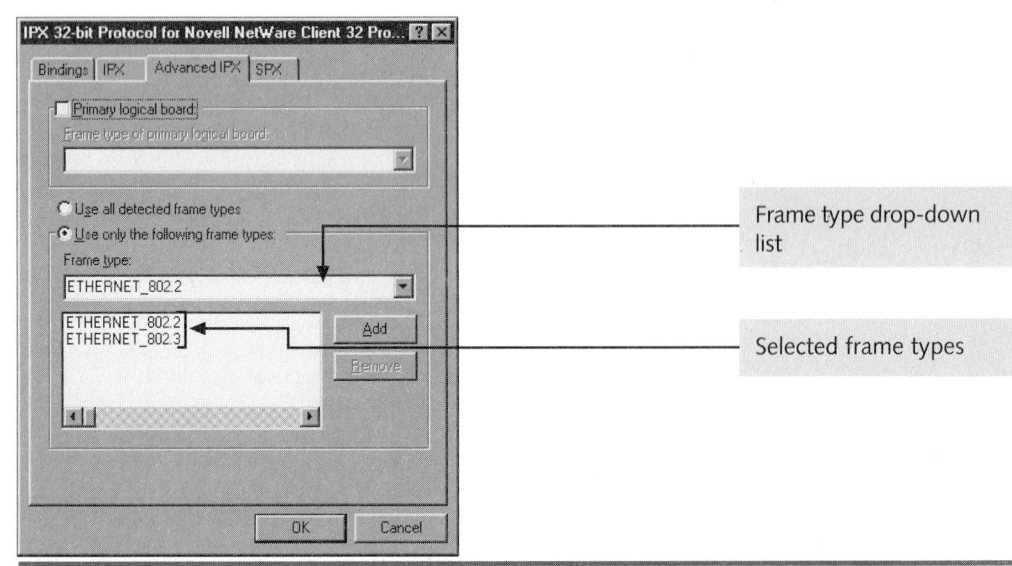

Figure 6-42 The Advanced IPX Page of the IPX 32-bit Protocol for Novell NetWare Client 32 Properties dialog box

Figure 6-43
Subnetworks

Both conversations travel on the same phone line at the same time
Each conversation is a subnetwork
"how are you?"
"how are you?"
"¿Como esta?"
"¿Como esta?"

In Figure 6-43, there are two people using the phone in each house, one of whom speaks only English and one of whom speaks only Spanish. The same phone line carries both the English conversation and the Spanish conversation, but only the English speakers understand the English communication and only the Spanish speakers understand the Spanish conversation. Similarly, the network components using ETHERNET_802.2 communicate only with each other, as do the network components using ETHERNET_802.3.

However, just as the English speakers and the Spanish speakers share one telephone in each household, the frame types can use the same NIC. One physical NIC becomes two logical NICs (also called logical boards)—one for each frame type. One of the logical NICs is designated the primary logical NIC or primary board. NetWare Client 32 usually selects the primary board itself, normally the logical board using ETHERNET_802.2, which is the default frame type for NetWare 4.1 when an ethernet NIC is used. However, if necessary, the network administrator can specify the primary board by checking the Primary logical board check box on the Advanced IPX page and then selecting the appropriate frame type. For example, in Figure 6-42, the Primary logical board check box is not checked, which indicates that the network administrator is using the NetWare Client 32 selected frame type instead of specifying a frame type himself.

Transition
3.1x 4.1

NetWare 3.12 servers also defaulted to the ETHERNET_802.2 frame type, but if your network contains older NetWare servers that you want to access from this workstation, you might be using the ETHERNET_802.3 frame type.

The SPX page contains the settings for the Sequenced Packet Exchange (SPX) protocol. The Bindings page, shown in Figure 6-44, shows which client software uses this protocol.

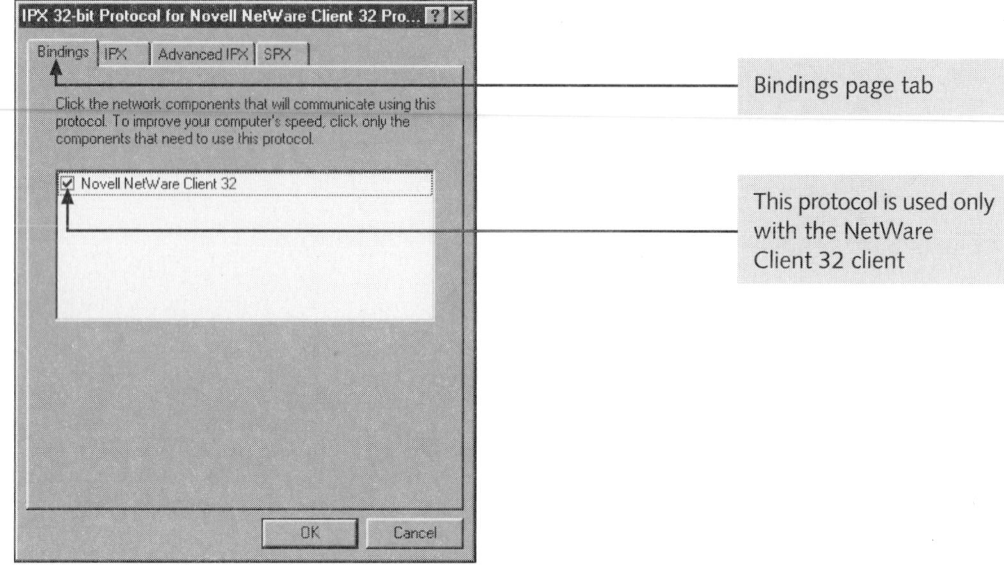

Figure 6-44 The Bindings Page of the IPX 32-bit Protocol for Novell NetWare Client 32 Properties dialog box

As you would expect, NetWare Client 32 is bound to the IPX 32-bit protocol for Novell NetWare Client 32, which means that the NetWare Client 32 requester passes data to this protocol for communication over the network.

The IPX 32-bit Protocol for Novell NetWare Client 32 dialog box can be closed by clicking the OK button or the Cancel button. If settings have been changed, you must click the OK button to save the changes. Clicking the Cancel Button closes the dialog box without making any changes.

Logging into the Network

When earlier network shells such as NETX and the NetWare DOS Requester were used, the user had to either enter a series of commands at the DOS prompt or include equivalent statements in a .BAT file in order to log into the network. For the NetWare DOS Requester, for example, these commands were normally included in a STARTNET.BAT file. With NetWare Client 32, however, the login steps become part of the Windows 95 bootup process, and there is no separate file that controls the NetWare Client 32 login. When Windows 95 starts, NetWare Client 32 is also started and the Novell NetWare Login dialog box, shown in Figure 6-45, is displayed.

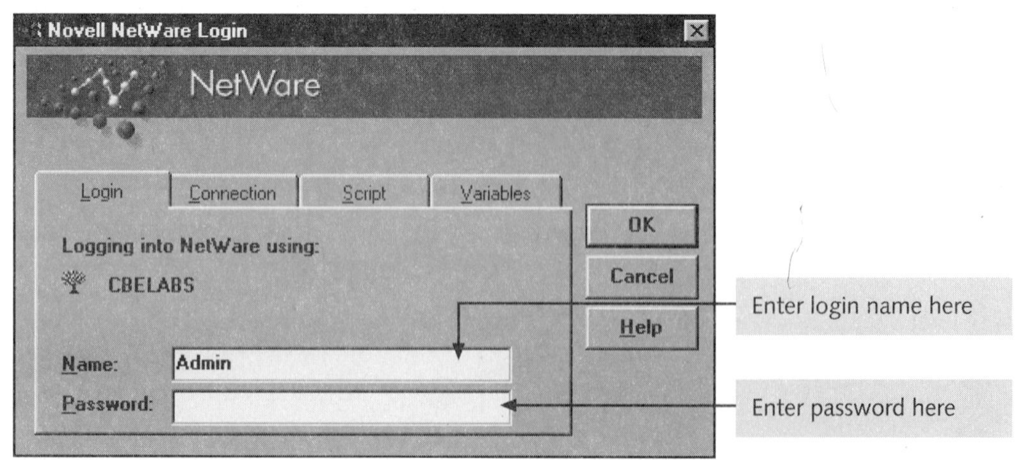

Figure 6-45 Logging into the network with the Novell NetWare Login dialog box

By specifying the required information, such as Name and Password, and then clicking the OK button, you are logged into the network. When the Novell NetWare dialog box is displayed, the name of the last user to log into the network is displayed. If the name is correct, you need to enter only the password, but if the name is incorrect, you must enter the correct user name. If the workstation has already started Windows 95 without making a network connection, the user can display the Novell NetWare Login dialog box by clicking the Start button, clicking Programs, clicking Novell, and then clicking NetWare Login.

The default settings for network connections, printer capture defaults, and scripts that were set during the NetWare Client 32 installation (or modified after the installation) in the Novell NetWare Client 32 Properties dialog box are used during the login. If the Connection, Script, and Variables pages of the Novell NetWare Login dialog box are displayed, the user can override the defaults during login by specifying values on these pages.

To log into the network, you can use the following steps:

- If the workstation is turned off, turn on the workstation.
- If the workstation is turned on, click the Start button, click Programs, click Novell, and then click NetWare Login.
- If necessary, click the Name text box to activate it and then type your user name.
- If necessary, click the Password text box to activate it and then type your password.
- If you need to change the default login settings, click the Connection, Script, or Variable page tabs to specify the new settings.
- Click the OK button.

For example, now that the NetWare Client 32 installation on the new workstation is complete, the CBE Labs network administrator will use this workstation to log into the network as the user Admin. The workstation is currently turned off, so starting the computer and Windows 95 will also display the Novell NetWare Login dialog box.

To log into the network using NetWare Client 32, you can use the following steps:

1. Turn on the workstation. Windows 95 loads, and the Novell NetWare Login dialog box is displayed, as shown in Figure 6-45.
2. Because the user name displayed in the Name text box, Admin, is correct, there is no need to change the user name.
3. The Password text box should be active. If it isn't, click the Password to activate it.
4. Type in the password, which will be displayed as a series of asterisks (********).
5. The workstation defaults are correct for user Admin, so there is no need to change them. Click the **OK** button. The workstation is logged into the network. During login, a script window will appear to display the login script. If printer port captures are done in the login script, DOS windows will be displayed during each capture because CAPTURE is a DOS command. After the login script is complete, all windows will automatically close themselves. The user is logged into the network.

LOGGING INTO ADDITIONAL NDS DIRECTORY TREES OR NETWARE SERVERS

NetWare Client 32 permits a user to log into more than one NDS Directory tree. It also allows the user to log into NetWare 3.1x servers that are not part of a tree or NetWare 4.1

servers that need to be attached in bindery mode. This can be done using the Novell NetWare Login dialog box, the Windows 95 Network Neighborhood program, or the Windows 95 Explorer.

To use the Novell NetWare Login dialog box, the user must be able to specify the connection on the Connection page of the Novell NetWare login dialog box. For example, Figure 6-46 shows the settings necessary for the CBE Labs network administrator to attach to the NetWare 3.12 server RANGER.

Figure 6-46

Logging in to additional Directory trees or NetWare servers with the Novell NetWare Login dialog box

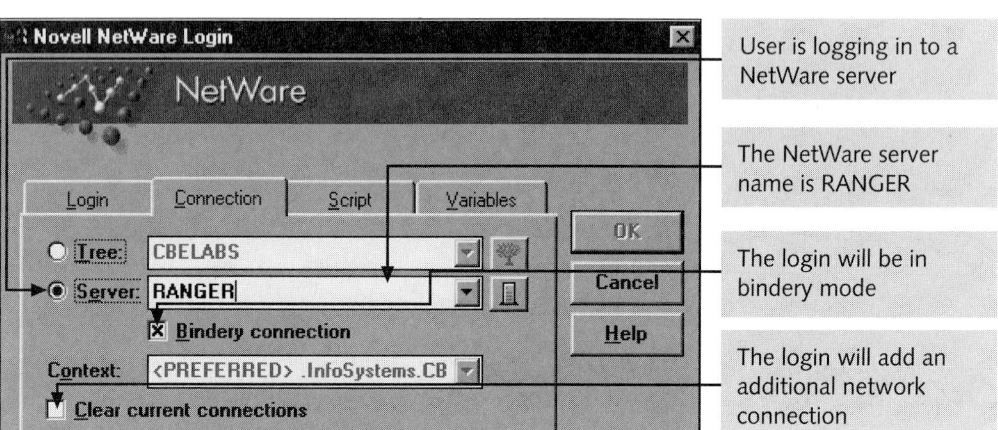

The Directory tree or NetWare server must be specified by clicking the appropriate radio button. In Figure 6-46, the Server radio button is selected, and the Bindery connection check box is checked to use the bindery of the NetWare 3.12 server. The Directory tree and NetWare server name can be entered by typing it in, or by selecting the name from a list. You can click the Search Directory Trees button to display a list of Directory trees, and you can click the Search NetWare Server button to display a list of NetWare servers. In Figure 6-46, the NetWare 3.12 server name RANGER has been typed into the Server text box. Finally, the Clear current connections check box has to be deselected. This is important—otherwise the existing connection to the CBELABS Directory tree would be cleared and only a connection to RANGER would exist. With these settings, the user will attach to the NetWare 3.12 server RANGER without losing his current connection to the CBELABS network. With these settings made, you would now switch back to the Login page and provide the user name and password. Clicking the OK button will complete the login.

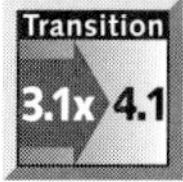

The NetWare DOS Requester client included a program named NetWare User Tools, which included the functions that the NetWare Client 32 NetWare Provider adds to the Windows 95 Network Neighborhood and Explorer. Although NetWare User Tools is disabled by default when NetWare Client 32 is installed—users trying to use it get an error message—you can use NetWare User Tools with NetWare Client 32. Instructions on how to do it are in the NetWare Client 32 Frequently Asked Questions (FAQ) at the Novell Support Connection WWW site (http://support.novell.com).

You can also attach to additional Directory trees and NetWare servers using the Windows 95 Network Neighborhood and Explorer programs through the features added to these programs by the NetWare Provider for Windows 95. Because the Network Neighborhood is accessible through Explorer, we'll look at Explorer. Figure 6-47 shows the Windows 95 Explorer program with the Network Neighborhood section expanded to show the available Novell Directory Services trees and NetWare Servers available on the entire network. You attach to an additional Directory Tree or NetWare server by authenticating on that NDS tree or NetWare server.

Figure 6-47

The Network Neighborhood resources displayed in Explorer

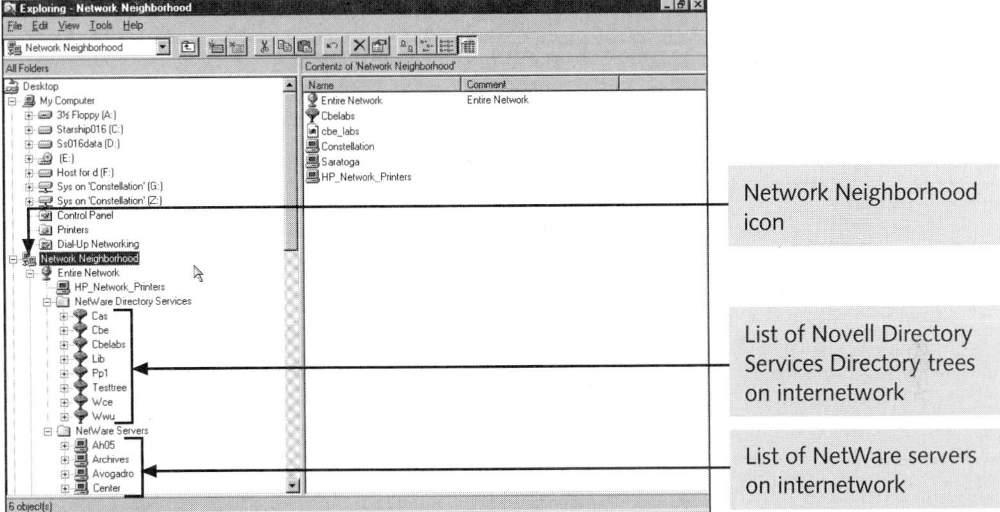

Authenticating is the process of sending your user name and password to the NDS Directory tree or NetWare server and having them checked and validated. This may be done automatically or by having you provide your user name and password. Automatic authentication occurs when the NetWare Client 32 Cache NetWare Password parameter is set to "On." The Cache NetWare Password parameter is one of the NetWare Client 32 parameters controlled on the Advanced Settings page of the Novel NetWare Client 32 Properties dialog box. The valid parameter values are "On" and "Off," and the default value is "On." When password caching is enabled, NetWare Client 32 stores or "caches" your user name and password in the memory of your workstation (*not* on the hard drive). When you attempt to use a network resource that requires you to attach to another NDS Directory tree or NetWare server, NetWare Client 32 automatically provides your user name and password and you are authenticated without any input from you. If, however, password caching is disabled, you will be prompted to provide your user name and password.

For Example, if CBE Labs network administrator Ted Simpson wants to attach to the NetWare 3.12 server RANGER, he would begin by locating RANGER in the list of NetWare servers in Explorer. He would then right-click the icon for RANGER, which would display the Shortcut Menu shown in Figure 6-48. He then clicks Authenticate to attach to RANGER.

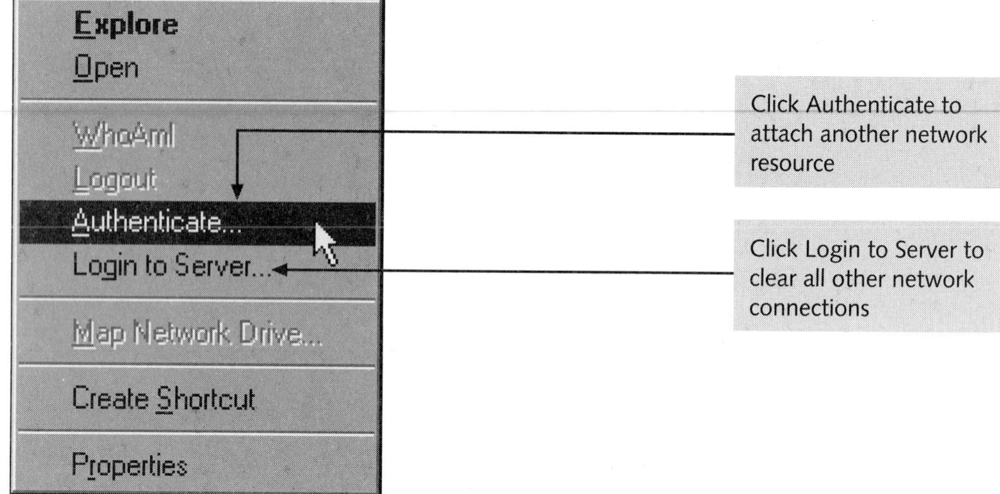

Figure 6-48

The NetWare server Shortcut Menu in Explorer

To attach to an additional NDS Directory tree or NetWare server, you can do the following:

- Click the Start button, click Programs, click Novell, and then click NetWare Login.
- Click the Connections page tab to switch to the Connections page, and then enter the necessary information.
- Click the Login page tab to switch to the Login page, and then enter the user name and password.
- Click the OK button.

or

- Launch Explorer; then expand the Network Neighborhood until the NDS Directory tree or NetWare server that you want to log in to is visible.
- Right-click the NDS Directory tree or NetWare server icon to display the Shortcut Menu,
- Click Authenticate. If NetWare password caching is enabled, your name and password will be automatically provided to the new resource. Otherwise, the Novell NetWare Login dialog box is displayed, and you must enter your login information and then click the OK button.

Viewing NetWare Resources

You can view a list of your NetWare connections using the extensions to Windows 95 Network Neighborhood and Explorer installed by NetWare Client 32. When you right-click the Network Neighborhood icon on the desktop or in Explorer, the Shortcut Menu shown in Figure 6-49 is displayed.

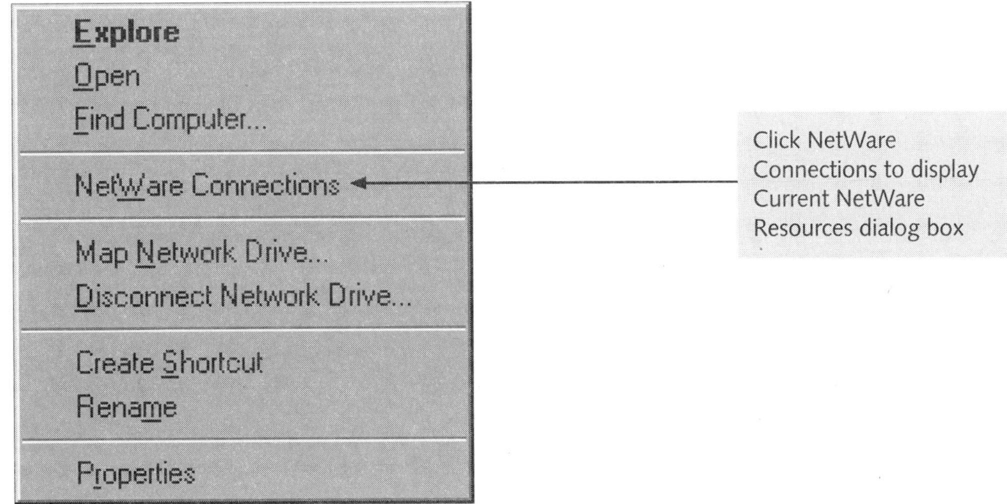

Figure 6-49 The Network Neighborhood Shortcut Menu

Clicking NetWare Connections displays the Current NetWare Resources dialog box shown in Figure 6-50. The user's current network connections are shown in this dialog box.

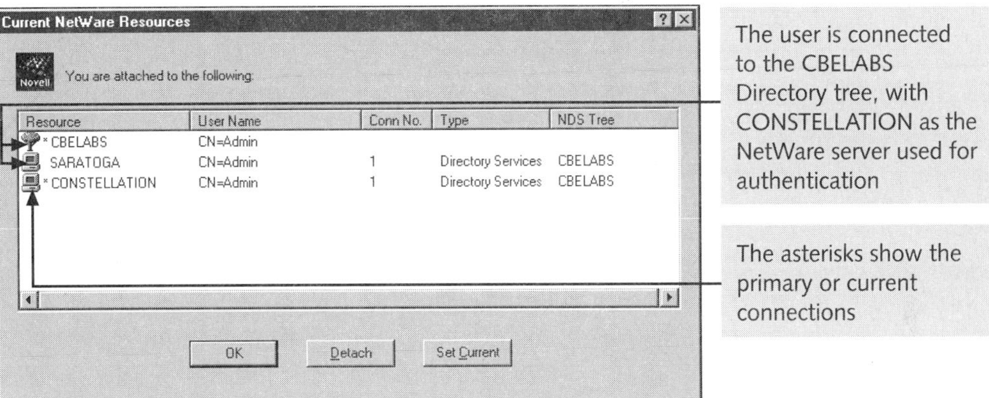

Figure 6-50 The Current NetWare Resources dialog box

Logging Out of the Network

The most secure way to log out of the network is to use the Windows 95 Shut Down command. This command is selected by clicking the Start button on the Windows 95 Taskbar and then clicking Shut Down. This displays the Shut Down Windows dialog box, which has several options. If you select the Shut down the computer? option, NetWare Client 32 will log you out of any NDS Directory trees and NetWare servers you are attached to as Windows 95 runs its shut down routine. If you select the close all programs and log on as a different user? option, NetWare Client 32 also closes all existing connections. In this case, however, the Novell NetWare Login dialog box is then displayed so that a new user can log in without rebooting the computer. In both cases, your user name and password are removed from memory if they were cached during your login.

To log out of the NDS Directory tree, you can do the following:

- Click the Start button, and then click Shut Down.
- In the Shut Down Windows dialog box, select the option you want.
- Click the OK button.

If you want to log out of an NDS Directory tree (or NetWare server) without shutting down the computer, you can use Network Neighborhood or Explorer. As usual, it's easier to use the Network Neighborhood portion of the Explorer display, as shown in Figure 6-51.

Figure 6-51

Logging out with the NDS Directory Tree shortcut menu

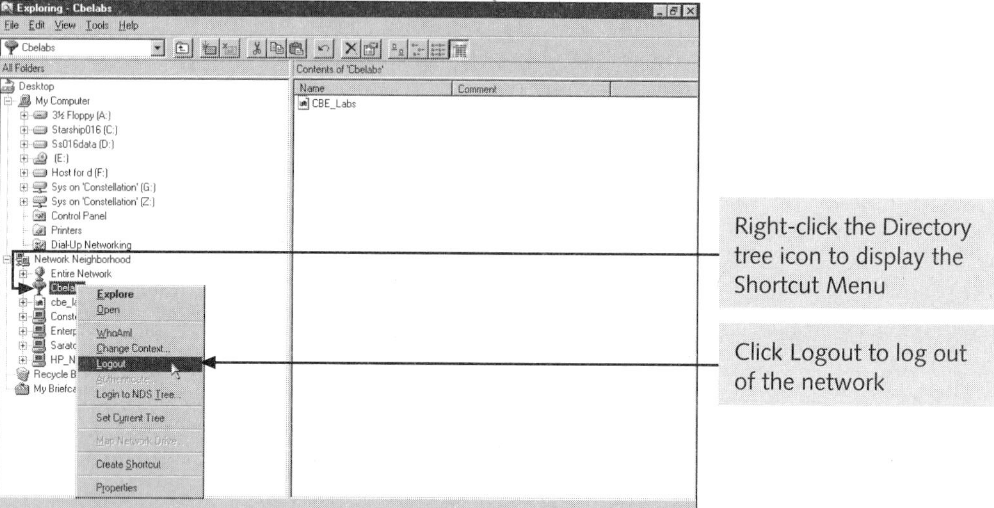

To log out of the NDS Directory tree, expand the Network Neighborhood tree until you can see the NDS Directory tree icon that you want to log out of. Right-click the icon to select it and display the Shortcut Menu shown in Figure 6-51. Click Logout on the Shortcut Menu to log out of the network. This is *not* a secure logout, because your user name and password remain cached in memory if NetWare password caching is enabled. You will continue to see network resources in Explorer and Network Neighborhood, and if you try to use a network resource you will be automatically logged in again so that you can access the resource.

VERIFYING THE INSTALLATION

After completion of the server and workstation installation, you should reboot your workstation to load the new parameters. If you see a "NetWare server not found" message, the most common causes are a defective cable, a faulty ethernet connector, an incorrect frame type, an interrupt being used by both the network card and some other device in either the server or the workstation, or the SPX/IPX protocol not being properly bound to the network card on the NetWare server.

Sometimes the reason for a problem can be so obvious that it escapes you. Take, for example, the case of a network administrator who spent some time looking for the cause of a "NetWare server not found" message only to discover that someone had broken into the NetWare server room and actually stolen the server. In this case the workstation was correct: the NetWare server could not be found.

Once you verify that the NetWare server and workstations are communicating correctly, you can continue the process of setting up the network by establishing the NetWare server's directory structure along with the user accounts and security as described in the following chapters. Installation is an ongoing process that involves expanding the network to incorporate additional workstations and enhancing the NetWare server. Chapters 17 and 18 provide the concepts and commands that allow a network administrator to monitor and improve NetWare server performance.

Officially, NetWare Client 32 for Windows 95 and NetWare Client 32 for DOS/Windows are part of NetWare 4.11. However, these workstation clients were released through Novell's Support Connection prior to the Release of NetWare 4.11, and they have already become part of a typical NetWare network installation. The NetWare Client 32 discussion in this chapter thoroughly covers what you need to know about NetWare Client 32 as part of NetWare 4.1 and NetWare 4.11. The main difference now is that the NetWare Client 32 files and documentation are provided with the NetWare 4.11 CDs and no longer need to be downloaded from Novell. Of course, there will be updates to NetWare Client 32 which will still have to be downloaded!

CHAPTER SUMMARY

The NetWare installation process is divided into two major operations: installing the NetWare server software and installing the workstation software. Installing NetWare on a NetWare server can be divided into eight main steps. Step 1 is to plan the network layout and complete a NetWare server worksheet to document the network environment and NetWare server hardware configuration. Step 2 is installing and configuring the NetWare server hardware. Step 3 includes partitioning the boot drive and installing DOS. In step 4 you complete the portion of the INSTALL program that runs under DOS. In step 5 you work with the main steps of the INSTALL program that runs under NetWare 4.1 itself. This includes loading the correct disk drivers, LAN drivers, and protocols, and creating drive partitions and volumes. In step 6 you install Novell Directory Services and create the NDS Directory tree. Step 7 is editing the STARTUP.NCF and AUTOEXEC.NCF startup files. Step 8 is choosing any installation options you want to use.

Disk drivers and NIC LAN drivers must be correctly loaded into the NetWare NOS for the NetWare server to connect to the network. Similarly, network protocols must be bound to the NICs. The commands to do this are stored in the STARTUP.NCF and the AUTOEXEC.NCF files so that they will be run automatically when the NetWare server is booted. The MONITOR NLM provides a useful tool for monitoring the NetWare server's performance.

The workstation computer requires three software components in order to access the NetWare server. The first component is the network card driver, which provides the data link process of transmitting and receiving packets over the network cable system. The second software component is the protocol stack, which is responsible for formatting the packets through the network, transport, and session layers of the OSI model. In NetWare, SPX/IPX is used as the default protocol. The third software component is the requester or shell that provides an interface from DOS to the NetWare server. NetWare Client 32 is the shell program that acts as a front end for DOS and directs all application and user requests for NetWare services to the network NetWare server. NetWare Client 32 software can improve network performance and security through the use of packet burst mode and packet signatures. NetWare 4.1 uses Novell's open data interface (ODI) drivers.

Novell has used three workstation shells: NETX, the NetWare DOS Requester, and NetWare Client 32. NetWare Client 32 is available in versions for DOS/Windows 3.1x and Windows 95 and Windows NT. The files must be obtained separately from the NetWare 4.1 files and are available free from Novell. Installation of NetWare Client 32 for Windows 95 is run under the Add/Remove Programs option of the Windows 95 Control Panel. During installation, you can configure NetWare Client 32 by setting parameters on pages of the Novell NetWare Client 32 Properties dialog box. These settings can be modified after installation through the Network icon in the Windows 95 Control Panel. The four NetWare Client 32 Properties pages are: the Client 32 page, which sets the connection preferences; the Login page, which controls the display of the Novell NetWare Login dialog box; the Default Capture page, which sets defaults for printed output; and the Advanced Settings page, which enables you to control the values of 45 parameters that affect NetWare Client 32. The parameter settings made in the Novell NetWare Client 32 Properties dialog box are stored in the Windows 95 registry; in previous workstation shells and in the version of NetWare Client 32 for DOS/Windows 3.1x, these settings are stored in the NET.CFG file.

Novell frequently issues updates and patch files to the NetWare 4.1 NOS and NetWare Client 32 files. After installation, you need to obtain and install any needed updates. After you have installed NetWare Client 32, you can access configuration settings through the Network icon in the Windows 95 Control Panel. You can access the Novell NetWare Properties for Client 32 dialog box through the listing for Novell NetWare Client 32 in the Network dialog box. You can also access IPX and SPX protocol settings through the Network dialog box.

The Novell NetWare Login dialog box provided with NetWare Client 32 allows you to log into NDS Directory trees and NetWare servers. You can log into more than one NDS Directory tree using NetWare Client 32. You can also log in through the extensions to Windows 95 added by the NetWare Provider for Windows 95. These same extensions enable you to view your current network connections through the Current NetWare Resources dialog box.

After installing the workstation software, you should reboot the computer and attempt to log into the NetWare server. NetWare Client 32 will attempt to attach to a Directory tree and a default NetWare server when it is first loaded. If the workstation does not receive a response from a NetWare server within a few moments, it returns a "NetWare server not found" error message. The most common causes of the "NetWare server not found" error message are a bad cable, incorrect frame type, overlapping interrupt assignments, or the IPX/SPX protocol not being properly bound to the network card on the NetWare server computer.

COMMAND SUMMARY

Command	Syntax	Definition
ADD NAME SPACE	*ADD NAME SPACE [name] [TO [VOLUME]] volume name*	Run once to create an additional name space on a volume. Needed to support the OS/2 name space, which is used to support Windows 95 long filenames.
BIND	*BIND protocol [TO] lan driver | board name [driver parameters...] [protocol parameters...]*	Allows NetWare to communicate with a LAN card by attaching a protocol stack to the card driver.
DISABLE LOGIN	*DISABLE LOGIN*	A NetWare console command that prevents users from logging in to the file server. Users currently logged in are not affected. Use this command before you shut down the NetWare server to prevent additional users from logging in after you have broadcast the warning message.
DISMOUNT	*DISMOUNT [ALL] [volume name]*	This console command takes the specified volume or all volumes off line, making them inaccessible to the network. It is usually used when you need to perform volume maintenance.
DOWN	*DOWN*	A NetWare console command that takes the server off line by stopping all network communication and dismounting all volumes. You receive a warning message if active connections to the server exist, and you can terminate the connections or cancel the command.
ENABLE LOGIN	*ENABLE LOGIN*	A NetWare console command that enables users to log into the NetWare server. Use this command to restore logins after you use the DISABLE LOGIN command.

EXIT	*EXIT*	A NetWare console command that is issued after the DOWN command, EXIT causes the SERVER.EXE program to end and returns the console to the DOS prompt. If DOS has been removed from memory, this command causes the file server computer to reboot.
INSTALL	*LOAD INSTALL*	A NetWare Loadable Module that is used to set up and maintain NetWare disk drives and volumes, as well as perform system operations such as copying system and public files and creating or modifying the startup files.
LOAD	*LOAD [path] Loadable_module_name* [module parameters]	Accesses and runs a NetWare Loadable Module in the NetWare server's RAM. By default, modules are loaded from the SYS:SYSTEM directory. Modules remain in RAM until unloaded. Because NetWare is a multitasking operating system, many modules can be loaded at one time. Examples of module names include the INSTALL and MONITOR modules described in this chapter.
MONITOR	*LOAD MONITOR*	A NetWare Loadable Module that displays information regarding the performance of a NetWare server.
MOUNT	*MOUNT [volume name] [ALL]*	This console command enables you to mount a specific volume or all volumes. Mounting a volume loads the file allocation table and directory entry table into RAM. A volume must be mounted before it can be accessed by the network.
SEND	*SEND "message"*	Send a message to all network users logged in to the network. You should issue this command to warn users that the NetWare server is going to be shut down.
UNLOAD	*UNLOAD module name*	Terminates execution of the specified module and removes it from memory.

KEY TERMS

adapter
Add Name Space utility
agent
authenticating
AUTOEXEC.NCF
binding
client
custom device module (CDM)
data compression algorithm
data migration
default volume name
dismounting a volume
DOWN command
host adapter module (HAM)
internal network number
internetwork
link support layer (LSL)
minimum compression percentage gain
MONITOR utility
mounting a volume
multiple link interface driver (MLID)
multiple NetWare server network
name context
name spaces
NET.CFG
NetWare Client 32
NetWare Command File
NetWare DOS Requester
NetWare Loadable Modules (NLMs)
NetWare Provider for Windows 95
NetWare server name
network layout
network shell
NETX
NIC driver
Novell Peripheral Architecture (NPA)
open data interface (ODI)
optical disks
packet burst mode
packet signature patch
primary time server (PTS)
protocol stack
redirector
reference time server (RTS)
requester
secondary time server (STS)
SERVER.EXE
SET commands
single reference time server (SRTS)
STARTUP.NCF
subnetwork
virtual loadable module (VLM)

REVIEW QUESTIONS

1. List the major steps for installing NetWare on a NetWare server computer.
2. A(n) ______________________ is used internally by the NetWare operating system to communicate with its device drivers.
3. A NetWare server's name can be from __ to __ characters in length.
4. All devices that communicate with each other over a network cable system must use the same ______________________.
5. A network containing two NetWare servers is referred to as a(n) ______________.
6. Multiple networks connected together by routers are called a(n) ______________.
7. A NetWare server that connects two networks is referred to as a(n) ______________.
8. Which of the following is an invalid network address?

   __ A __ 10BA5ET __ 1AB216A15 __ 1EEE8025
9. List three types of NetWare Loadable Modules and their corresponding extensions.

   ____

   ____

   ____

10. When it creates a partition and volumes, NetWare by default uses the volume names of:

____

____

____

and so on.

11. Describe the purpose of STARTUP.NCF and AUTOEXEC.NCF.

12. The ______ and ______ keys are used to switch the server console from one active module to another.

13. List the three workstation software components.

____

____

____

14. The Windows 95 ____________ contains configuration settings used by the ODI drivers. These settings were previously contained in the ____________________.

15. List the four pages in the Novell NetWare Client 32 Properties dialog box.

____

____

____

____

16. Describe how to install Client 32 when using Windows 95 as the operating system.

17. Where are updated Novell files and patches available?

18. Why do you need to add the OS/2 name space to a NetWare server supporting Windows 95?

19. List the four commands necessary to load the OS/2 name space support for Windows 95 for the first time.

____

____

____

____

20. List the two commands necessary to stop the NetWare NOS running on a NetWare server and return to the DOS prompt.

____

____

21. What command is used at the DOS prompt to start the NetWare NOS on a NetWare server?

EXERCISES

Exercise 6-1: Performing a Complete NetWare 4.1 Installation

In this exercise you install NetWare 4.1 from a CD-ROM drive. At the end of this exercise, you will also have configured a NetWare server that you can access from a workstation attached to the network. In order to perform this exercise, you will need the following components, which will be supplied by your instructor:

- Access to an 80386SX or later computer with at least 8 MB of RAM and a 120-MB hard disk
- An NIC and cable to connect to a network that has at least one other workstation attached to it
- A CD-ROM drive that can be attached to the NetWare server computer (or a CD-ROM drive that is shared on the network)
- A copy of a NetWare 4.1 Operating System CD-ROM
- A DOS boot disk containing the FDISK, FORMAT, and SYS commands

Once you have verified that your work area contains these components, use the following steps to install NetWare and initialize your NetWare server computer.

Step 1: Record NetWare server information

1. Sketch a diagram of the network system you are building, including all student NetWare servers and network topologies. Label the diagram with the following information:
   - Name of each NetWare server
   - Internal network number to be used for each server (Indicate RANDOM if you are going to let the installation process select a number for you.)
   - Network topology
   - Network card model and manufacturer
   - Ethernet frame type
2. Obtain a blank copy of the NetWare server worksheet illustrated in this chapter.
3. Fill in the identification section by supplying a valid name for your server.
4. Fill in the system information section by identifying the disk controller card type, drive information, and correct NetWare disk driver to be used. Your instructor will tell you where to obtain this information. You might need the documentation sheet included with the computer and system manuals.
5. Fill in the network card information section by reading the settings off the network card or using the network card handout provided by your instructor.
6. List any other equipment in the NetWare server in the nonnetwork device information section and check that no hardware interrupt conflicts exist.

Step 2: Install NetWare 4.1

In this step you use the CD-ROM drive to run the INSTALL program. Your instructor will provide instructions to supplement the description of the NetWare server installation given in this chapter. The following steps assume you have access to a CD-ROM drive as a drive letter on your computer:

1. Boot the computer with the DOS disk. This disk should contain the drivers that enable you to access a CD-ROM drive, either one attached to your computer or one shared on the network. Be sure the NetWare 4.1 CD-ROM is in the CD-ROM drive before you continue. If necessary, your instructor will give you directions for using the Fdisk, Format, and SYS commands.
2. Change to the drive letter containing the NetWare 4.1 CD-ROM.
3. Enter the command INSTALL. Follow the steps outlined in the chapter as supplemented by your instructor to complete the NetWare 4.1 installation. Your instructor will inform you of any special considerations that you need to be aware of during the installation.

Note on creating the server volumes: Make the SYS: volume size 80 MB and create a DATA: volume using all but 5 MB of the remaining disk space.

4. On the line below, record approximately how long this installation process took.

   ____

Step 3: Completing the installation

In the space below, briefly identify each of the processes you will need to perform to complete the NetWare server installation to the point where the server is available to the network and can be rebooted.

1. Use the hot-key sequence to return to the console prompt.
2. Record the contents of your STARTUP.NCF file below:
3. Record the contents of your AUTOEXE.NCF file below:
4. Where is the STARTUP.NCF file stored? ______________________
5. Where is the AUTOEXEC.NCF file stored? ______________________

Exercise 6-2: Testing the Installation

For this exercise you need access to a NetWare server console that you have recently installed or one that has been provided to you by your instructor. Figure 6-52 presents a set of console commands that were not discussed in the chapter. Try the commands on the console and record the results. Write a short memo to your instructor in which for each of the console commands you:

1. Briefly describe its purpose and why you might use it after performing an installation.
2. Report and interpret the results of the console command.

Figure 6-52

Selected Netware console commands

Command	Purpose
SPEED	Use this command to display the speed of the NetWare server's processor. This speed is a relative number. For example, an Intel 33 MHz 80386 DX processor will have a SPEED result in a range around 320.
MEMORY	Use this command to display the amount of installed memory.
MODULES	Use this command to display a list of the modules that are currently running on the NetWare server. The output includes the name, description, and version number (for .DSK, .LAN and .NLM modules).
VOLUMES	Use this command to display a list of the mounted volumes on the NetWare server. The output uses the following flags: Cp - File compression is enabled Sa - Block suballocation is enabled Mg - Data migration is enabled
DISPLAY SERVERS	Use this command to display a list of all NetWare servers and services that are broadcasting Service Advertising Protocol (SAP) packets. Services will include NetWare servers, NDS, print servers, Storage Management Services (SMS) devices, and Structured Query Language (SQL) servers. The output includes the network address of the server and the number of hops to the server, where a hop is defined as the number of routers the packer must pass through to get to the destination.
DISPLAY NETWORKS	Use this command to display a list of networks recognized by the NetWare server. The output includes the IPX external network number followed by the number of hops to the network and the time in tics (1/18th of a second) it takes for a packet to get to that address.

Exercise 6-3: Installing NetWare Client 32 for Windows 95 on a Workstation

In this exercise you install NetWare Client 32 for Windows 95 on a workstation to enable your workstation to access the network NetWare server. In order to complete this exercise, you will need the following components, which will be supplied by your instructor:

- A workstation computer with a LAN card and floppy disk drive
- A copy of the NetWare Client 32 for Windows 95 client disks
- A copy of the documentation that came with the card
- The diskette that was supplied with the network card (optional)
- The network card hardware settings (Your instructor might give you a copy of the network card manual with the card settings indicated and ask you to determine the hardware configuration given the jumper settings indicated in the diagram.)

1. Use the documentation supplied by your instructor to fill in the table in Figure 6-53 with the configuration of your network card.

Figure 6-53

Network Interface Card (NIC) specifications

Network Interface Card Make and Model	Other Novell cards emulated	ODI Driver	Interrupt	I/O Port	Memory Address

2. Install NetWare Client 32 for Windows 95 on your workstation, following the steps outlined in this chapter.
3. Reboot your workstation with your newly installed NetWare Client 32.
4. List two items you should check for if the workstation login cannot find the NetWare server on an ethernet network.

____

____

Exercise 6-4: Checking for Updated NetWare Client 32 Files

In this exercise you check the Novell Support Connection WWW site for the latest updates to NetWare Client 32. You download a copy of any update files and then update your NetWare Client 32 installation. In order to complete this exercise, you will need the following components, which will be supplied by your instructor:

- A workstation computer with a LAN card, a floppy disk drive, a hard drive, and Windows 95 installed
- NetWare Client 32 installed on the workstation
- Internet access at the workstation, and a WWW browser with FTP capabilities

1. Use the WWW browser to connect to the Novell Support Connection at http://support.novell.com.
2. Browse the site to see what information is available.
3. Download the most recent update file for NetWare Client 32 for Windows 95. Your instructor will provide additional information about where to store this file.
4. Your instructor will give you instructions on how to expand the contents of the file you downloaded and how to update the NetWare Client 32 for Windows 95 installation.

EXERCISES

Case 6-1: The Jefferson County Courthouse Network

The Jefferson County Courthouse is ready to install its NetWare 4.1 server.

Using the diagram of the Jefferson County Courthouse network you created in Chapter 3, label the diagram with the following information:

- Name of each NetWare server
- Internal network number to be used for each server (Indicate RANDOM if you are going to let the installation process select a number for you.)
- The network topology
- The network card model and manufacturer
- Ethernet frame type to be used

Case 6-2: The J. Q. Adams Corporation

The J. Q. Adams Corporation has installed its two NetWare 4.1 servers.

Using the diagram of the J.Q. Adams Corporation network you created in Chapter 3, label the diagram with the following information:

- Name of each NetWare server

- Internal network number to be used for each server (Indicate RANDOM if you are going to let the installation process select a number for you.)
- The network topology
- The network card model and manufacturer
- Ethernet frame type to be used

NORTHWESTERN TECHNICAL COLLEGE

The NetWare server computer that you helped develop specifications for in Chapter 2 has just been purchased and was installed by the vendor in the computer room. The vendor also installed NICs in all your computers and provided you with documentation showing the card type and configuration. In addition, the cabling company has completed installing the necessary wire and has tested all connections to ensure that they will work. In this exercise, you document the NetWare servers that are being used in your NWTC network.

Project 6-1: Documenting the NetWare servers

In this exercise you document the NetWare server installation for all NetWare servers you will actually be using in your implementation of the NWTC network. Your instructor will provide some of the information needed. Other information will be obtained from the servers themselves.

Yesterday, Jake Pence from the Computer Technology Services company delivered and tested the NetWare servers for the Northwestern Technical College campus. The NetWare 4.1 servers have been installed into the NWTC Directory tree. Your objective today is to document these NetWare 4.1 servers and the NDS Directory tree at this point.

1. Using the diagram of the Northwestern Technical College network you created in Chapter 3, label the diagram with the following information:
   - Name of each NetWare server
   - Internal network number to be used for each server (Indicate RANDOM if you are going to let the installation process select a number for you.)
   - The network topology
   - The network card model and manufacturer
   - Ethernet frame type to be used
2. Using a copy of the NetWare server worksheet used in the chapter, do the following:
   - Fill in the identification section of the NetWare server worksheet by supplying the name of your NetWare server and its Internal network number.
   - Fill in the system information section of the Worksheet by identifying the type of disk controller card, drive information, and correct NetWare disk drive being used. Your instructor will tell you where to obtain this information. You might need the documentation sheet included with the computer and system manuals.

- Fill in the network card information section by reading the settings off the network card or using the network card handout provided by your instructor.
- List any special NetWare server hardware in the nonnetwork device information section of the worksheet and check that no hardware interrupt conflicts exist.

Project 6-2: Using MONITOR

Dave Johnson would like you to record the new NetWare server's performance. Later, when the server starts to become more heavily used, the information can be used as a benchmark. Use the MONITOR utility to record the following statistics for each NetWare server in your NWTC network. Write a short memo to your instructor reporting the above for each server.

Percent utilization: ____________________

Original cache buffers: ____________________

Total cache buffers: ____________________

Percent of original cache buffers: ____________________

Packet receive buffers: ____________________

Directory cache buffers: ____________________

Service processes: ____________________

Project 6-3: Recording the STARTUP.NCF and the AUTOEXEC.NCF for Each Server

Dave Johnson would like you to record the STARTUP.NCF and AUTOEXEC.NCF for the new NetWare servers. Load the INSTALL utility and then use it to view (select the Edit option) the STARTUP.NCF and AUTOEXEC.NCF files for one of the NetWare servers on your NWTC network. Record the contents of each file. Write a short memo to your instructor reporting the above, adding comments on the purpose of each line in the files.

Project 6-4: Downing and Rebooting the NetWare server

Now that the server is running, you want to test your startup files to see if they can be restarted automatically. To down the server properly and return to the DOS prompt, follow the steps described in this chapter. Record each of the commands you use to down the server in the spaces provided. (Make sure to prevent new users from logging in and send a message to all users informing them that the server will be going down soon.)

____

____

____

____

____

Down and reboot the NetWare server. Write a short memo to your instructor, in which you describe the procedures you used and the results of restarting the server.

CHAPTER SEVEN

CREATING THE NDS DIRECTORY TREE STRUCTURE

Once the file server installation is complete, it's time to set up the NetWare Directory Services (NDS) Directory tree structure. You planned the NDS Directory tree in Chapter 4, and the first portions of the Directory tree were created during the NetWare 4.1 installation in Chapter 6. Now the organizational structure of the tree needs to be created and the network resources added in their proper organizational context.

To perform this important task, you need to understand the NetWare commands and utilities that are used to create and maintain the NDS Directory tree. In Chapter 4 you were introduced to DS Standard as an NDS directory planning tool. In this chapter you will acquire experience with NetWare 4.1 commands and utilities that are used to create, navigate, and display the actual Directory tree.

For example, the Cunningham, Burns, and Evans Laboratories (CBE Labs) network administrator has now installed the NetWare 4.1 servers on the CBE Labs network. Now the rest of the NDS Directory tree organizational structure for CBE Labs needs to be created. We'll need to use NetWare commands and utilities that work with NDS during this process.

AFTER READING THIS CHAPTER AND COMPLETING THE EXERCISES YOU WILL BE ABLE TO:

- USE NETWARE COMMANDS AND UTILITIES TO WORK WITH THE NETWARE DIRECTORY SERVICES (NDS) DIRECTORY TREE STRUCTURE.
- CREATE, MOVE, RENAME, AND DELETE CONTAINER OBJECTS.
- CREATE, MOVE, AND RENAME LEAF OBJECTS.
- MANAGE NDS PARTITIONS.
- RENAME AND MERGE DIRECTORY TREES.

NetWare Command and Utility Groups

There are six basic NetWare command and utility groups: command line utilities, menu utilities, graphical utilities, supervisor utilities, console commands, and NetWare Loadable Modules.

Command line utilities (CLUs) are NetWare commands that are executed from the DOS prompt. Prior to the popularization of the graphical Windows and OS/2 operating environments, CLUs were easier to use because of the constant availability of the DOS prompt. CLUs are still widely used and powerful tools that are easily customized by the use of parameters and options. To use a CLU, however, you need to know which NetWare command to use and what its proper syntax is. Every CLU has one or more help screens associated with it, and you always use the parameter /? after the command to display the help information. Examples of CLUs include CX, NDIR, and NCOPY.

Menu utilities are interactive programs that contain menus and help messages that allow you to perform more complex tasks. They can be slower to use than CLUs but don't require you to memorize command syntax. They use the Novell C-Worthy character user interface (CUI). This interface was an improvement on using CLUs at the command prompt but is not as flexible as the graphical user interface (GUI) used in Windows and OS/2. Examples of menu utilities are NETADMIN, FILER, and NETUSER.

All the NetWare menu utilities use certain keys that perform the same function in all utilities. It is important to learn the key functions shown in Figure 7-1.

Figure 7-1 NetWare menu utility keys

Key	Function
[Enter]	Selects an option or item and moves to the next menu level.
[Esc]	Returns back one level in the menu; often used to save the entry you have just completed.
[Ins]	Adds a new entry to a list.
[Del]	Removes an item from a list.
[F1]	Provides additional help information. Pressing the F1 key twice provides a list of keys and their functions.
[F3]	Used by most utilities. Allows you to change the highlighted item. When using the FILER utility, for example, you can use the F3 key to highlight and then change the name of a directory or file.
[F5]	Highlights multiple items in a list. Pressing [F5] a second time removes an item from the highlighted list. In the FILER utility, the F5 key can be used to delete several files from a directory; you mark each file and then press the Del key to delete all files at one time.
[Alt][F10]	This combination directly exits a menu utility without returning to the opening menu.

The NetWare menu utilities often present windows containing information such as a list of objects. If a window has a double-line border, it indicates that you can select, add, change, or delete objects in the window. If the window has a single-line border, you can view the objects, but you cannot change anything listed in the window. An example of a NetWare menu utility is the NETADMIN utility discussed later in this chapter.

Graphical utilities are interactive programs that use a GUI such as Windows or OS/2. These utilities take advantage of the GUI's menu, dialog box, and icon conventions to present choices, options, and tasks more visually. The utilities include help messages based on the Windows or OS/2 help system. These utilities are the most powerful in NetWare 4.1. An example of a NetWare graphical utility is the NetWare Administrator utility described later in this chapter.

Supervisor utilities are command line, menu, and graphical utilities that are stored in the SYS:SYSTEM directory. Supervisor utilities are used in system configuration and maintenance. In future chapters, you will learn how to use the supervisor utilities to perform such network management tasks as checking system security and fixing system problems.

Console commands are NetWare commands that are executed from the NetWare server console prompt. Console commands are built into the NetWare operating system. Examples are console commands such as LOAD, MOUNT, and BIND.

NetWare Loadable Modules (NLMs) are programs that run on the NetWare server. They are run by loading them at the console prompt. Functions such as network printing can be added to the NetWare server by running NLMs, and these programs often use Novell's C-Worthy interface to create a menu environment. Three different kinds of NLMs used during NetWare's installation are:

1. Disk drivers, such as IDE.DSK and ISADISK.DSK
2. LAN drivers, such as TOKEN.LAN and NE2000.LAN
3. Other NLMs, such as INSTALL and MONITOR

In other chapters you will work with the NetWare file server console commands and NLMs to perform additional tasks such as backing up the file system and configuring the server for improved performance.

NetWare 4.1 often provides an "equivalent" menu utility for each graphical utility. For example, NETADMIN is the menu equivalent of the NetWare Administrator (NWADMIN) graphical utility. NETUSER is the menu equivalent of the NetWare Tools graphical utility. However, not all of the same features are necessarily found in the two "equivalent" utilities.

Except for the user utility NetWare Tools, NetWare 3.1x lacked the graphical utilities now found in NetWare 4.1. The graphical utilities are one of the best features of NetWare 4.1 and make the network administrator's job much easier.

THE NETWARE COMMAND LINE UTILITY CX

The NetWare **CX command** is used to browse the Directory tree and change your context within it. You can also use it to view the leaf objects and container objects in the Directory tree. When you use the CX command by itself, you are told what your context is. For example, if Georgia Burns of CBE Labs uses the CX command to get her context, she might see the following output on her screen:

```
G:\LOGIN> CX
Test_Eval.CBE_LABS
```

The response of CX shows Georgia that her current context is the organizational unit container Test_Eval.

The CX command has several parameters that you can use with it. These are listed in Figure 7-2.

Figure 7-2
The CX command parameters

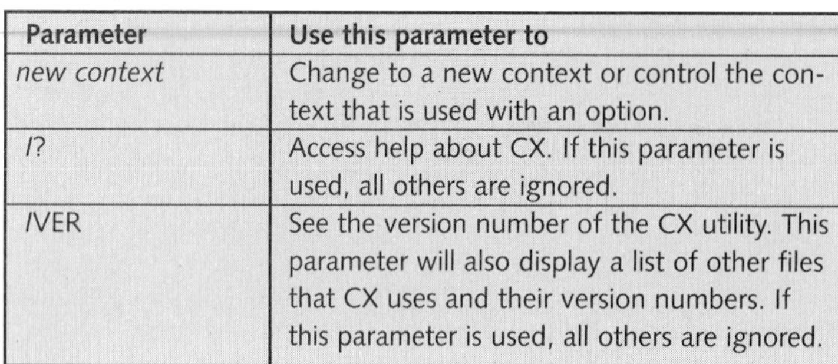

Parameter	Use this parameter to
new context	Change to a new context or control the context that is used with an option.
/?	Access help about CX. If this parameter is used, all others are ignored.
/VER	See the version number of the CX utility. This parameter will also display a list of other files that CX uses and their version numbers. If this parameter is used, all others are ignored.

There are also several options that you can use with the CX command. These are listed in Figure 7-3.

Figure 7-3
The CX command options

Option	Use this option to
/A	See a list of all objects at the current context or below. This option is used with the /CONT and /T options. Use this option to display the leaf objects in each container.
/C	Have the output scroll continuously.
/CONT	See an unstructured list of containers at the current context. You can use this option with the new context parameter to obtain a list of containers in another context.
/R	See a list of containers at the [Root] context. You can also use this option to change context relative to the [Root] rather than the current context.
/T	See a tree structure displaying containers below the current context. You can use this option with the new context parameter to obtain a tree structure of containers below another context.

Changing Current Context

The most common use of the CX command is to change the user's current context. For example, if Georgia wants to change context to an organizational unit named Network and it is contained in the Test_Eval organizational unit, she uses the CX command:

```
G:\LOGIN> CX .Network.Test_Eval.CBE_LABS
Network.Test_Eval.CBE_LABS
```

The Network organizational unit used in this example does not exist in the current CBE directory tree. It will be created later in this chapter.

The response of Network.Test_Eval.CBE_Labs shows Georgia that her context has changed to the organizational unit Network. In using this command, Georgia used the entire path from the [Root] to the organizational unit. Because she was already in the Test_Eval organizational unit container, she could also have used:

```
G:\LOGIN> CX Network
Network.Test_Eval.CBE_LABS
```

Notice that the first CX command used a leading period (.) before Network. The leading period tells NetWare to interpret the context from the [Root], and the full context from the [Root] is specified. The second command didn't use the leading period, and in this case NetWare added the new context onto the original context when the command was initiated. Since that context was .Test_Eval.CBE_Labs, NetWare moved to the context Network.Test_Eval.CBE_Labs.

If Georgia wants to return to the Test_Eval container, there are several ways she can do it. First, she can reference the [Root] by using the /R option:

```
G:\LOGIN> CX Test_Eval.CBE_LABS /R
Test_Eval.CBE_LABS
```

She could also have used this command:

```
G:\LOGIN> CX .
Test_Eval.CBE_LABS
```

A single period (.) moves you one level toward the [Root]. Because Georgia was in the context **Network.Test_Eval.CBE_Labs**, moving up one level took her to Test_Eval.CBE_Labs. You can use more than one period, and for every period you use, you'll be moved one level toward the [Root]. For example, if Georgia had used three periods (...) instead of one period, she would have moved up three levels to the [Root] itself:

```
G:\LOGIN> CX ...
[Root]
```

Notice that you *can* change context to the [Root]. Moving to the [Root] context can be helpful if there is more than one Organization object in the Directory tree.

In each of these examples, Georgia could have used typeful names in place of the typeless names. For example, to move from Test_Eval to Network, Georgia could have used this command:

```
G:\LOGIN> CX .OU=Network.OU=Test_Eval.O=CBE_LABS
Network.Test_Eval.CBE_LABS
```

Changing Context to Login

One use of the CX command is to change context to the container holding the user's User object before logging in. In this case, the user can log in using his or her login name. This is possible because the login name exists as a common name for an object in the current context. For example, Georgia can switch to the Test&Eval container and then simply log in as GBurns:

```
G:\LOGIN> CX .Test_Eval.CBE_LABS
Test_Eval.CBE_LABS
G:\LOGIN> Login GBurns
```

Displaying the Directory Tree Structure

The CX command is very useful for browsing and displaying the Directory tree. You can use the /R Option to display information starting at the [Root] without changing context to the [Root]. For example, to see the complete current CBE Directory tree displayed as a tree *without* leaf objects, Georgia would use the following command:

```
G:\LOGIN> CX /T /R

*** Directory Services Mapping ***

[Root]
   └─CBE_Labs
          └─Test_Eval
```

To see the complete current CBE Directory tree displayed as a tree *with* leaf objects, Georgia would use the following command:

```
G:\LOGIN> CX /T /R /A
*** Directory Services Mapping ***
[Root]
   └─CBE_Labs
          ├─Admin
          ├─CONSTELLATION
          ├─CONSTELLATION_SYS
          ├─CONSTELLATION_DATA
          └─Test_Eval
                 ├─SARATOGA
                 ├─SARATOGA_SYS
                 └─SARATOGA_DATA
```

THE NETWARE MENU UTILITY NETADMIN

The NetWare menu utility used with the NDS Directory tree is the **NETADMIN utility**. The NETADMIN utility is used to manage the Directory tree and NDS objects. You can use NETADMIN to browse the Directory tree and to change context within it. Unfortunately, you cannot use it to display the entire Directory tree structure at once.

The syntax of the command to start NETADMIN utility is

```
NETADMIN [/VER]
```

The /VER parameter is used to display the version number of the NETADMIN utility and a file list of supporting files—the utility is not run if the parameter is used.

When NETADMIN is used to browse the Directory tree, each browse screen will display a list of objects with an associated object class to identify each object. This is illustrated in Figure 7-4.

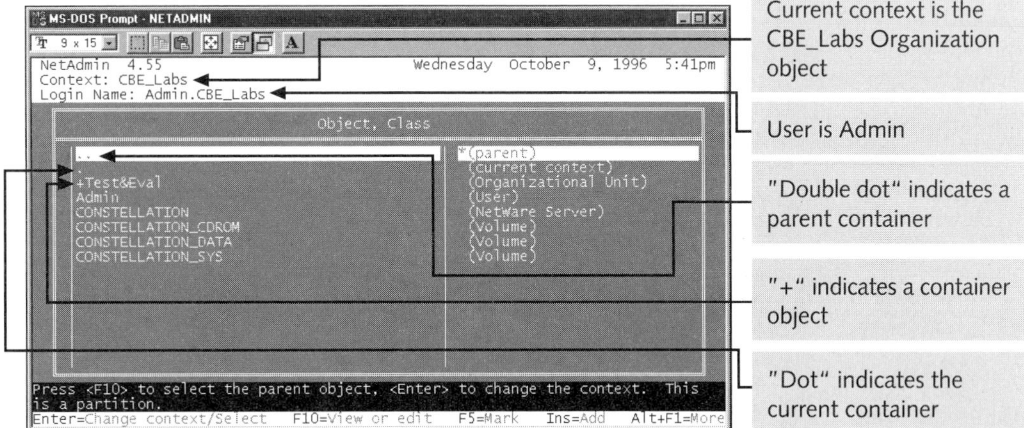

Figure 7-4 The NetAdmin Browse screen

The list of objects shows (1) the set of container objects immediately below the current context in the Directory tree, (2) the set of lead objects in the current container object, (3) "double dots"—two periods (..)—that indicate the *parent* container object in the Directory tree, and (4) "dot"—one period (.)—that indicates the *current* container object in the Directory tree. Container objects are indicated by a "+" (plus sign) in front of the object name, whereas leaf objects just show the object name. Selecting the "double dots" will change the context to the parent container object; selecting a container object's name will change the context to that container. Selecting a leaf object will display the properties for that object, and selecting the "dot" will display the properties for the current container object.

The NetWare 3.1x menu utility SYSCON is not used in NetWare 4.1. NETADMIN is the menu utility equivalent of SYSCON.

For example, the CBE Labs network administrator wants to browse the current structure of the CBELABS Directory tree. The current context for Admin is still [Root].

To browse the CBELABS Directory tree, follow these steps:

1. Launch the NETADMIN utility by clicking the **Start** button, then clicking **Programs**, and then clicking **NETADMIN**. The NETADMIN screen is displayed, as shown in Figure 7-5. The current utility version, context, and the user's login name are shown in the upper-left corner of the screen.

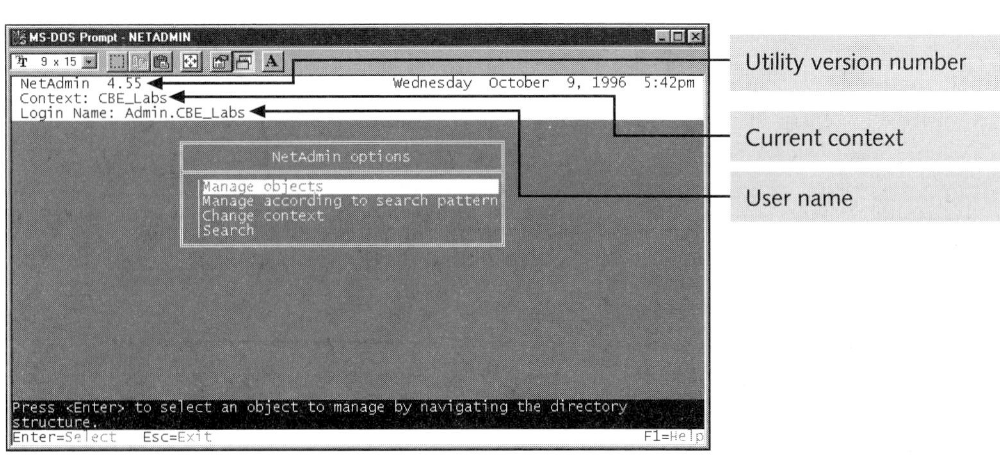

Figure 7-5 The NETADMIN screen

2. Highlight **Manage objects** and then press **[Enter]** to display the NETADMIN Browse screen, as shown in Figure 7-6.

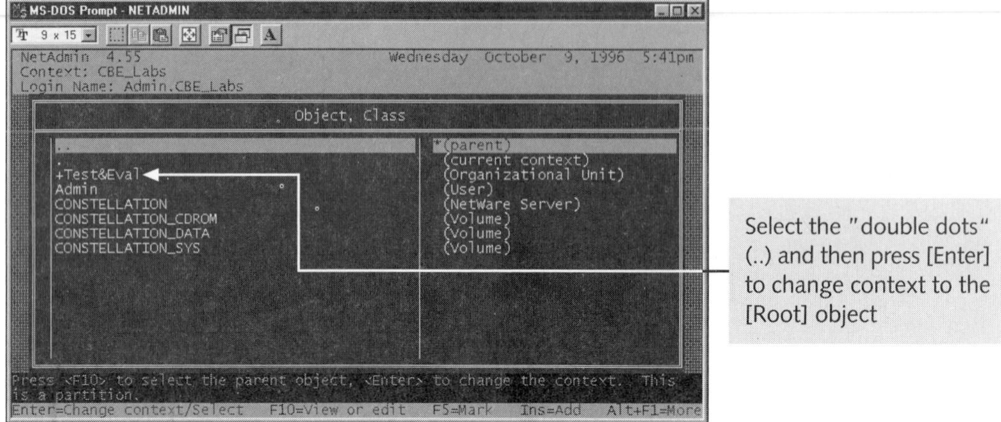

Figure 7-6
Using the NETADMIN Browse screen

3. Highlight the "double dots" (..) and then press [Enter] to switch context to the [Root] Container object.
4. Highlight **+CBE_Labs** and then press **[Enter]** to switch context to the CBE_LABS Organization container object.
5. Press **[Esc]**, Highlight **Yes**, and then press **[Enter]** to exit NETADMIN.

Although the NETADMIN utility enables the network administrator to access the Directory tree and NDS objects, it is not as powerful a tool as the NetWare graphical utility NetWare Administrator. We'll use NetWare Administrator later in this chapter and explore NETADMIN in the Hands-On Exercises at the end of the chapter.

THE NETWARE GRAPHICAL UTILITY NETWARE ADMINISTRATOR

The NetWare graphical utility **NetWare Administrator** is used to manage the NDS Directory tree. The NetWare Administrator is a Windows or OS/2 program that provides the centralized administration that makes the network easy to manage and administer.

NetWare Administrator 4.1 enables you to browse the NDS Directory tree, to create NDS container and leaf objects, and to manage the object properties. You can rename objects, move objects, and delete objects, within the Directory tree. You can manage NDS partitions and run a remote console session.

To use NetWare Administrator (or the NETADMIN menu utility) to create and manage objects in the Directory tree, you must have the needed trustee rights. The user Admin, who is the only user used in this chapter, has supervisor rights (which grant *all* trustee rights) and can therefore create and manage any objects anywhere in the Directory tree. Trustee rights and their assignment to users and groups will be discussed in detail in Chapter 10.

When NetWare Administrator is launched, the Directory tree is automatically displayed in a single browser window, as shown in Figure 7-7.

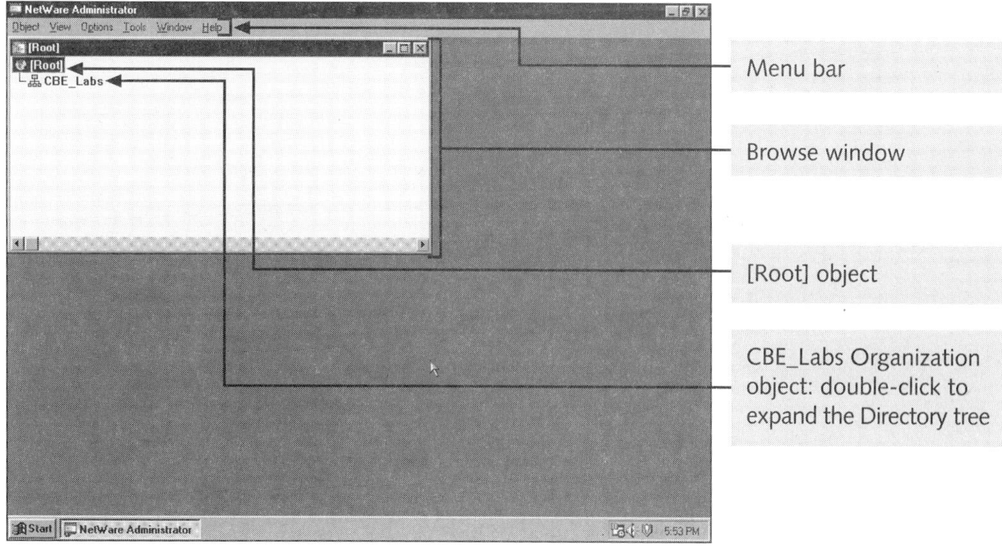

Figure 7-7 The NetWare Administrator opening screen

Notice that in Figure 7-7 the initial screen starts with only the [Root] and Organization objects displayed, and the Directory tree is *not* expanded beyond that.

To view the objects in a container object, you can follow these steps:

- Double-click the container object name or icon when the objects are *not* displayed.

or

- Click the container object, click View on the menu bar, and then click Expand.

To hide the objects in a container object, you can follow these steps:

- Double-click the container object or icon when the objects *are* displayed.

or

- Click the container object, click View on the menu bar, and then click Collapse.

To change context, you can follow these steps:

- Click View on the menu bar, click Set Context, and then type in new context.

or

- Click View on the menu bar, click Set Context, and then browse to new context.

You can open additional browser windows so that you can simultaneously view different sections of the Directory tree (NetWare Administrator supports a maximum of ten browser windows).

To open an additional browser window, you can follow these steps:

- Click Tools on the menu bar, and then click Browse.

To close a browser window, you can follow these steps:

- Click the browser window Close button.

For example, the CBE Labs network administrator wants to open a second Directory tree browser window that starts at the CBE_Labs context.

To create the CBE_Labs browser window, follow these steps:

1. If the NetWare Administrator is not open, launch it.
2. Click the **CBE_Labs Organization** object, and then click **Tools** in the menu bar. The Tools menu appears, as shown in Figure 7-8.

Figure 7-8 Opening a new browse window

3. Click **Browse** on the Tools menu. The CBE_Labs browse window appears as shown in Figure 7-9.

Figure 7-9 The CBE_Labs browse window

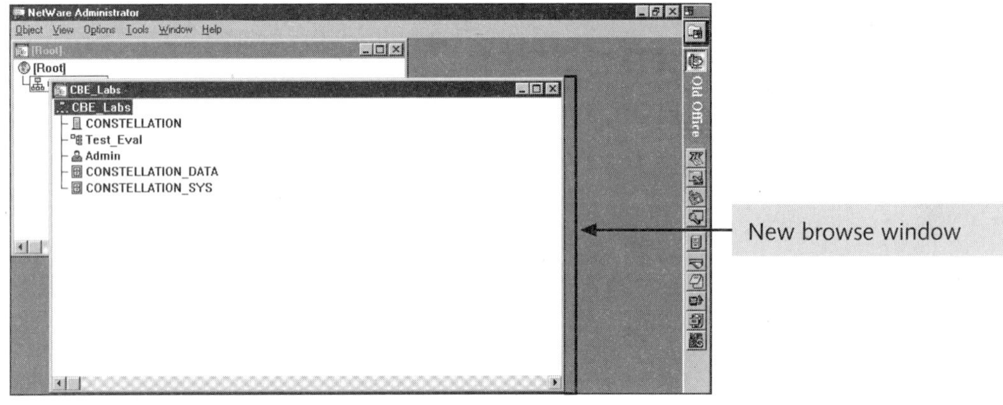

In NetWare 4.11, the NetWare Administrator utility, as shown in Figure 7-10, has some major improvements. Versions of NetWare Administrator are included for both the Windows 3.1x and Windows 95 environments.

Figure 7-10 The NetWare 4.11 NetWare Administrator opening screen

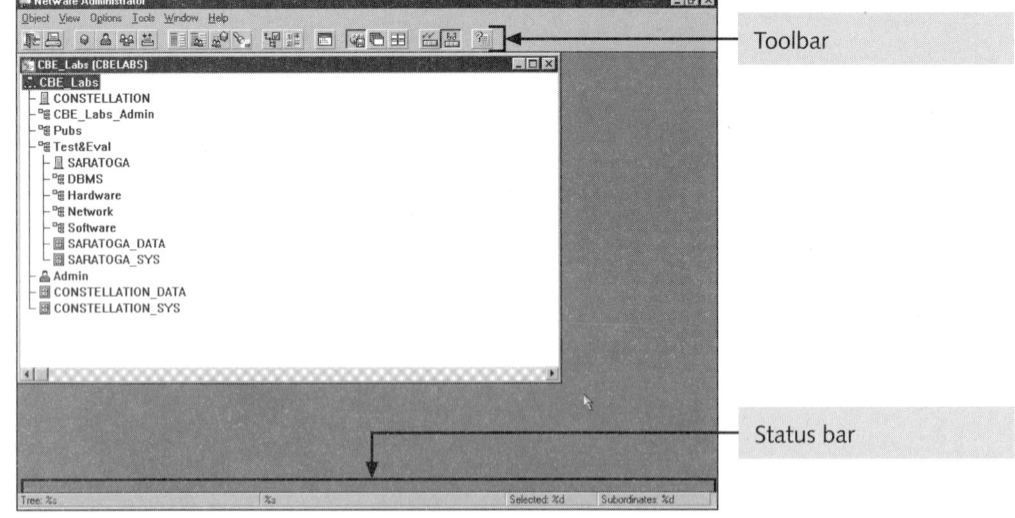

Visually the most obvious changes are the new Toolbar and Status bar. The Toolbar contains buttons to simplify many actions in NetWare Administrator. For example, clicking the Create user object button displays the dialog box to create a new user. The Status bar displays four status indicators: the current NDS Directory tree, the user login name, the number of objects selected, and the number of levels in the Directory tree that exist below (subordinate to) the level of the selected object.

The Toolbar and Status bar are configurable—you can choose whether or not to display them, and you can select the buttons displayed on the Toolbar and the status indicators on the Status bar.

Without the Toolbar and the Status bar displayed, the new NetWare Administrator is almost identical in appearance to the NetWare 4.1 version of NetWare Administrator discussed in this book. However, the NetWare 4.11 NetWare Administrator includes additional new functionality beyond the Toolbar and Status bar. With the new NetWare Administrator you can perform these functions:

- Work with more than one NDS Directory tree
- Select and work with multiple User objects
- Expedite print services setup
- Launch other utilities, including the DS Migrate NDS design and migration tool and the NDS Manager partition management tool
- Use the Internet to contact Novell support services (this feature requires the Windows 95 version of NetWare Administrator)

Completing the Organizational Structure in the Directory Tree

The NDS Directory tree is actually created during the installation process of the first NetWare 4.1 server in the Directory tree. This is necessary to specify the context of the NetWare server during installation of the NetWare 4.1 NOS on the server. When additional NetWare 4.1 servers are installed into the Directory tree, the context of each new NetWare server must be specified during its installation. This may require creating additional Organization or Organizational Unit objects in the Directory tree. You studied these aspects of Directory tree creation in Chapter 6, which covered installing NetWare 4.1.

When the installation of all NetWare 4.1 servers is complete, the NDS Directory tree contains the following:

- The [Root] object
- [Optional] One or more Country objects
- At least one Organization object
- [Optional] One or more Organizational Unit objects
- A NetWare Server object for each NetWare 4.1 server installed
- A SYS Volume object for each NetWare 4.1 server installed
- [Optional] A Volume object for each additional volume created during server installation

For example, after the CBE labs network administrator had installed NetWare 4.1 on the two CBE NetWare 4.1 servers, the CBE Labs directory tree appears, as shown in the CBE_LABS browser window in Figure 7-11.

Figure 7-11 The CBE LAB Directory tree after the installation process

CONSTELLATION was the first NetWare 4.1 server installed. During this installation, the [Root] object and the name of the Directory tree, CBELABS, were created. There were no Country objects created. The Organization object CBE_Labs, was created and CONSTELLATION is located in the context .CBE_Labs. CONSTELLATION has two volumes: SYS: DATA:. Volume objects for each of these volumes were created and placed in the same context as CONSTELLATION. The User object Admin was also created during this installation process.

Because SARATOGA was installed into the CBELABS Directory tree, there was no need to create a [Root] object or name the Directory tree. There were no Country or Organization objects created during the installation, but the Organizational Unit object Test_Eval was created. SARATOGA was installed in the context Test_Eval.CBE_Labs. SARATOGA has two volumes: SYS: DATA:. Volume objects for each of these volumes were created and placed in the same context as SARATOGA. Because the user Admin was already created, there was no need to create an administrator account.

The CBE Labs network administrator now needs to complete the organizational structure of the CBE Labs Directory tree by adding any necessary container objects to the Directory tree. The Directory tree needs to reflect the organization chart of CBE Labs, which is shown in Figure 7-12.

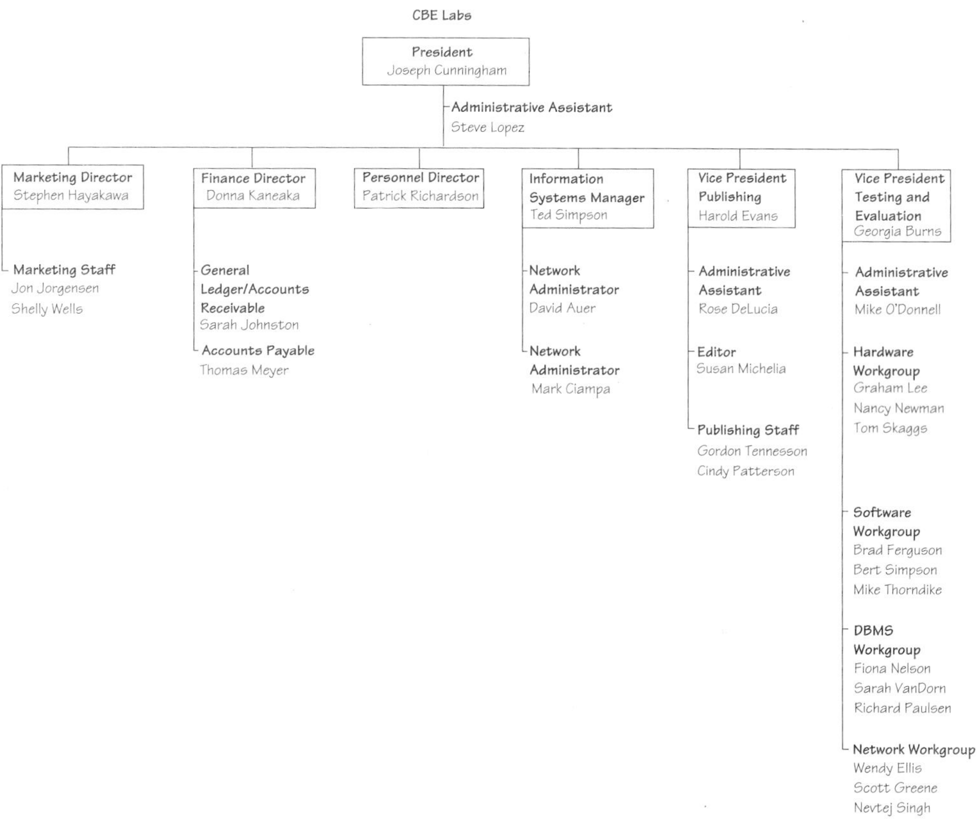

Figure 7-12

The CBE Labs organization chart

To administer a NetWare 4.1 server in bindery emulation mode or a NetWare 3.1x server in the network, you still use the SUPERVISOR account. Logging into a NetWare server in bindery emulation mode the first time uses the SUPERVISOR account with the Admin account password.

If any NetWare 3.1x servers were upgraded to NetWare 4.1 during the installation process, most bindery objects were converted to NDS objects during the conversion. This includes users and groups. An NDS Directory tree with upgraded NetWare 3.1x servers will therefore include additional NDS objects at this point in the Directory tree creation process.

CREATING NDS DIRECTORY TREE CONTAINER OBJECTS

Creating NDS Directory tree objects always uses the same basic procedure.

To create an object, you can follow these steps:

- Click the container object for the object, and then press [Insert].

or

- Click the container object for the object, click Object on the menu bar, and then click Create.

or

- Right-click the container object for the object, and then click Create on the QuickMenu.

then

- In the New Object dialog box, click the type of object in the Class of New Object list, and then click OK.

then

- In the Create ObjectType dialog box, enter the necessary property values, and then click the Create button.

The type of objects listed in the New Object dialog box's Class of New Object list will vary—only those types of objects that can be created will be displayed for you to choose from. When you choose an object type, the appropriate Create *ObjectType* dialog box for the object type will be displayed, where *ObjectType* is the name of object you choose in the Class of New Object list. For example, if you are creating an Organization Unit object, the Create Organizational Object dialog box will be displayed.

To finish creating an object, you must supply the property values required in the Create *ObjectType* dialog box. In this dialog box, you are also given the options of (1) defining additional property values for the object you are creating, (2) immediately creating another object of the same type in the same container object, or (3) other choices, depending upon which object is being created.

THE [ROOT] OBJECT

The [Root] Object is the only exception to the steps described above for creating a new Directory tree object. The [Root] object is created *only* during the installation of the first NetWare 4.1 server in the Directory tree. The name of the Directory tree is stored by the [Root] object. You cannot modify the [Root] object itself at this point.

The Directory tree can be renamed by using the DSMERGE utility, which is discussed later in this chapter.

THE COUNTRY OBJECT

Country objects can be added to the Directory tree. As discussed in Chapter 4, Country objects are optional, and network administrators often prefer to use Organization objects with geographical names instead of Country objects. The names of Country objects are limited to a standard two-letter identifier, some of which are shown in Figure 7-13. The codes shown are CCITT X.500 standard country codes. Notice that the code for the United Kingdom is GB not UK. Additional country codes are listed in Appendix B of the NetWare 4.1 Installation manual.

Figure 7-13

Examples of country codes

Country	Code
Australia	AU
Brazil	BR
Canada	CA
China	CN
Denmark	DK
Egypt	EG
France	FR
Germany	DE
India	IN
Japan	JP
Mexico	MX
New Zealand	NZ
Philippines	PH
Puerto Rico	PT
Russian Federation	RU
Saudi Arabia	SA
Spain	ES
Switzerland	CH
United Kingdom	GB
United States	US

Country objects can be created only immediately below the [Root] object. To add a Country object to a Directory tree, you select Country in the Class of New Object list, and you must specify a country name.

For example, CBE Labs has just created a European branch with an office in England. The CBE Labs network administrator wants to create a United Kingdom Country object in the tree.

To create the United Kingdom Country object, follow these steps:

1. If the NetWare Administrator is not open, launch it.
2. Click the **[Root]** object, click **Object** on the menu bar, and then click **Create**.
3. The New Object dialog box is displayed, as shown in Figure 7-14. Notice that the list of object types displayed in the Class of New Object window varies depending upon which types of new objects can be created within the container object. In this case, only an Alias object, a Country object, or an Organization object can be created.

Figure 7-14 The New Object dialog

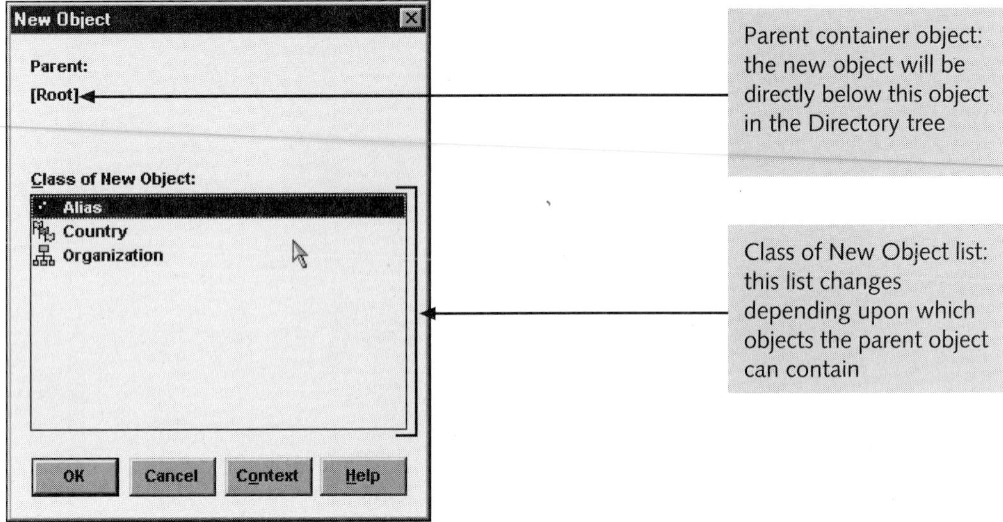

4. Click **Country**, and then click **OK**. The Create Country dialog box is displayed, as shown in Figure 7-15.

Figure 7-15 The Create Country dialog

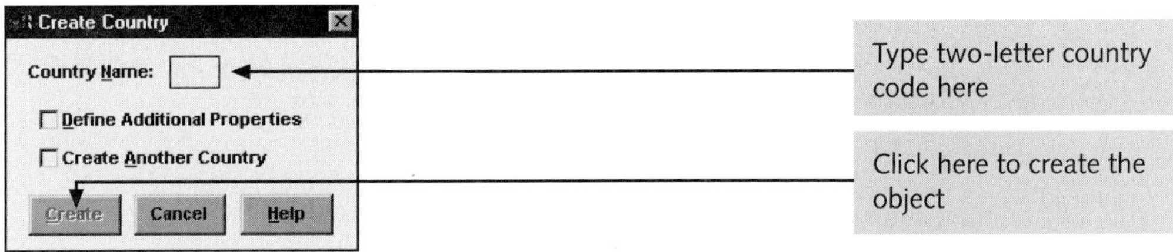

5. In the Country Name text box, type the country code for the United Kingdom, which is **GB**.
6. Click **Create**. The GB Country object is added to the Directory tree, as shown in Figure 7-16.

Figure 7-16 The GB Country object in the Directory tree

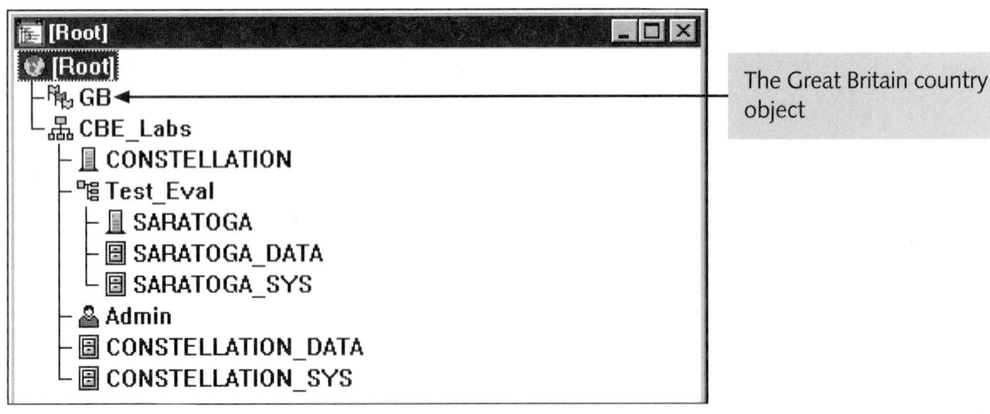

THE ORGANIZATION OBJECT

Organization objects can be added directly below the [Root] or below a Country object in the Directory tree. To add an Organization object to a Directory tree, you select Organization in the Class of New Object list, and you must specify a name for the organization.

For example, the CBE Labs network administrator needs to create the CBE_Labs_Europe Organization object below the GB Country object to show the existence of the new European operation.

To create the CBE_Labs_Europe Organization object, follow these steps:

1. Click the **GB** Country object, click **Object** on the menu bar, and then click **Create**.
2. The New Object dialog box is displayed. The Class of New Object list of available objects includes only the Alias object and the Organization object.
3. Click **Organization**, and then click **OK**. The Create Organization dialog box is displayed, as shown in Figure 7-17.

Figure 7-17 The Create Organization dialog box

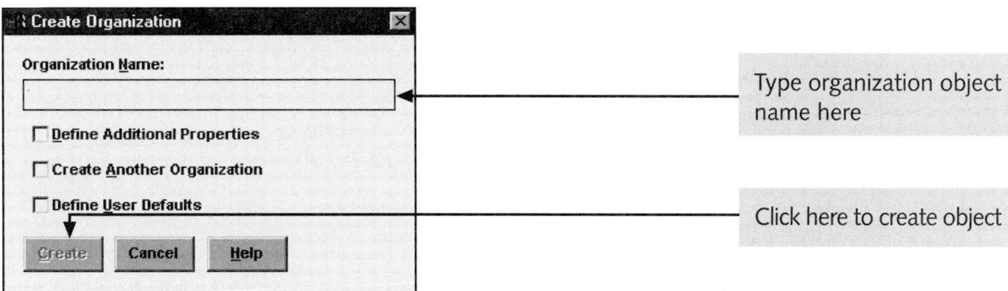
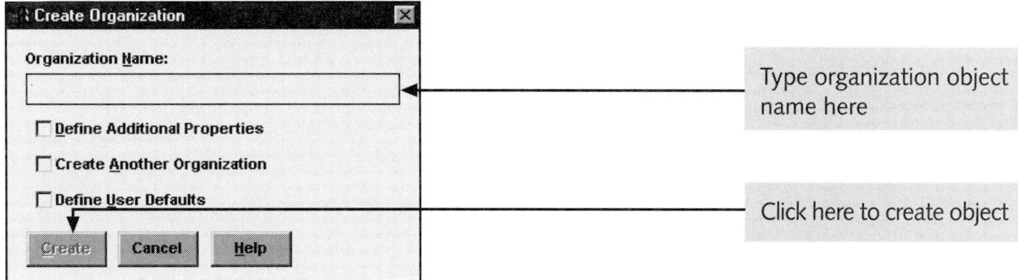

4. In the Organization Name text box, type **CBE_Labs_Europe**.
5. Click **OK**. The CBE_Labs_Europe object is added to the Directory tree, as shown in Figure 7-18.

Figure 7-18 The CBE_Labs_Europe object in the Directory tree

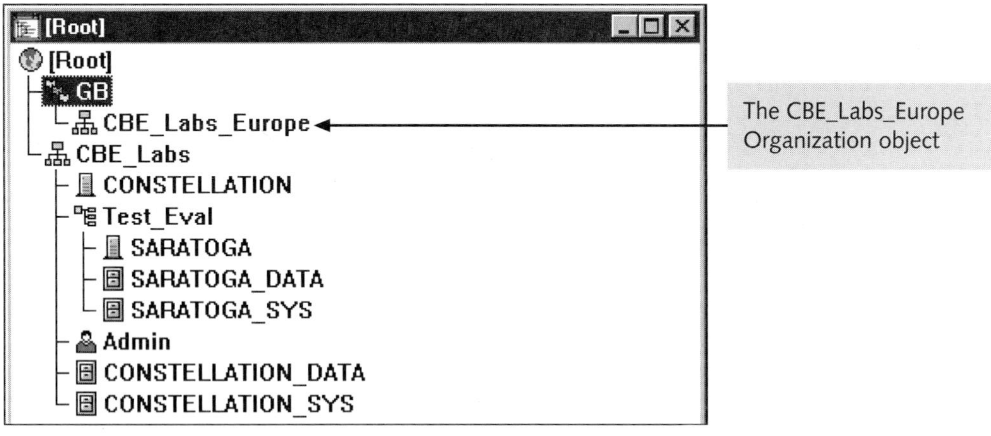

THE ORGANIZATIONAL UNIT OBJECT

Organizational Unit objects can be added directly below an Organization object or an Organizational Unit object in the Directory tree. To add an Organizational Unit object to a Directory tree, you select Organizational Unit in the Class of New Object list, and you must specify a name for the organizational unit.

The CBE Labs organizational chart, which was shown in Figure 7-12, shows that a number of Organizational Unit objects need to be added the CBE Labs Directory tree to complete the organizational structure of the tree:

- The Organizational Unit objects CBE_Labs_Admin and Pubs need to be created below the CBE_Labs Organization object.
- The Organizational Unit objects Finance, InfoSytems, Marketing, and Personnel need to be created below the CBE_Labs_Admin Organizational Unit object.
- The Organizational Unit objects Hardware, Software, DBMS, and Network need to be created below the Test&Eval Organizational object.

The network administrator starts with the Organizational Unit object for CBE_Labs_Admin.

To create the CBE_Labs_Admin Organizational Unit object, follow these steps:

1. Click the **CBE_Labs** Organization object, click **Object** on the menu bar, and then click **Create**.
2. The New Object dialog box is displayed. Click **Organizational Unit**, and then click **OK**. The Create Organizational Unit dialog is displayed, as shown in Figure 7-19.

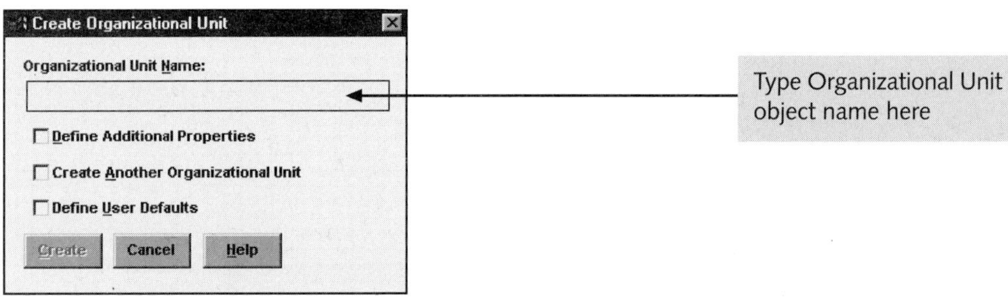

Figure 7-19 The Create Organizational Unit dialog box

3 In the Organizational Unit Name text box, type **CBE_Labs_Admin**.
4. Click **Create**. The CBE_Labs_Admin Organizational Unit object is added to the Directory tree.

The network administrator now creates the other Organizational Unit objects needed to complete the Directory tree. When these objects are completed, the organizational structure of the Directory tree is in place. All necessary container objects have been created, and the network administrator is ready to start adding leaf objects, such as User objects, in the containers. At this point, the CBE Labs Directory tree appears as shown in Figure 7-20.

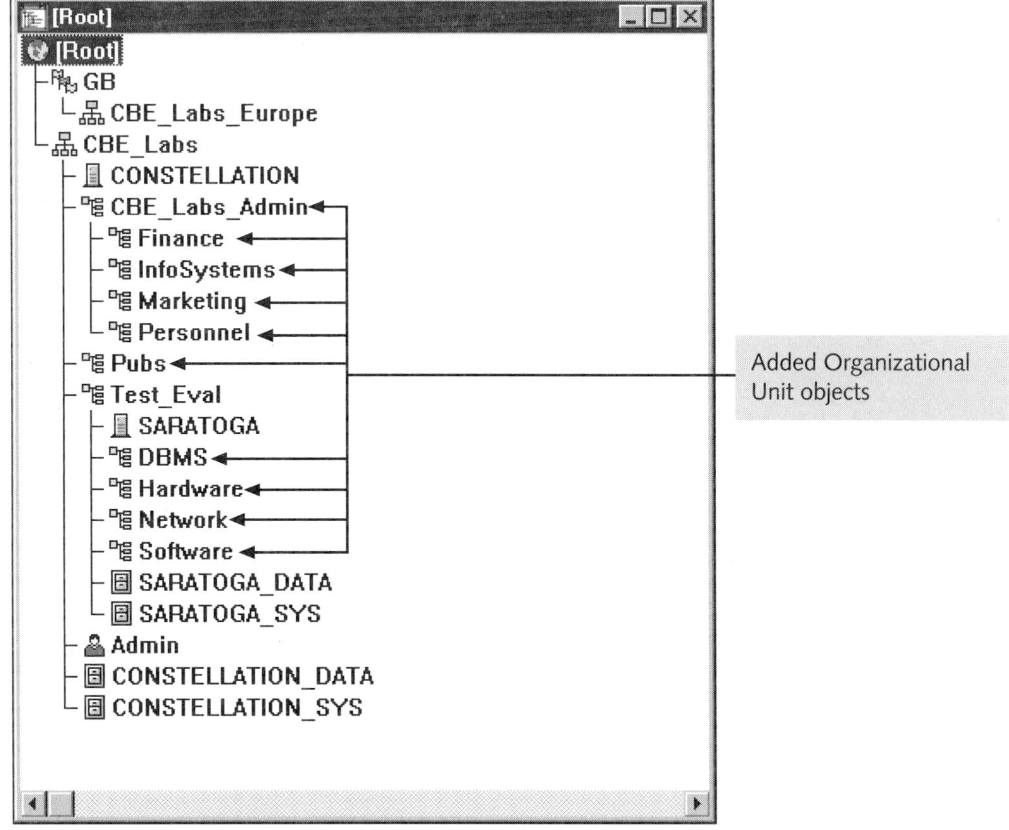

Figure 7-20 The CBE Labs Directory tree with all container objects in place

Viewing and Working with Container Object Properties

As you learned in Chapter 4, all Directory tree objects have properties, which are characteristics of the object that you can change. Each property stores one or more property values, which determine the characteristics of the objects. Properties are viewed using an **object dialog box** for the object, each of which contains one or more **pages** of property values related to the object.

To view a container object's properties you can follow these steps:

- Click the container object, and then press [Enter].

or

- Click the container object, click Object on the menu bar, and then click Details.

or

- Right-click the container object, and then click Details on the QuickMenu.

For example, the CBE Labs network administrator wants to enter some information about the CBE_Labs_Admin Organizational Unit object that was just created.

To view the CBE_Labs_Admin Organizational Unit object properties, follow these steps:

1. Right-click the **CBE_Labs_Admin** Organizational Unit object, and then click **Details**. The Organizational Unit: CBE_Labs_Admin object dialog box is displayed, as shown in Figure 7-21.

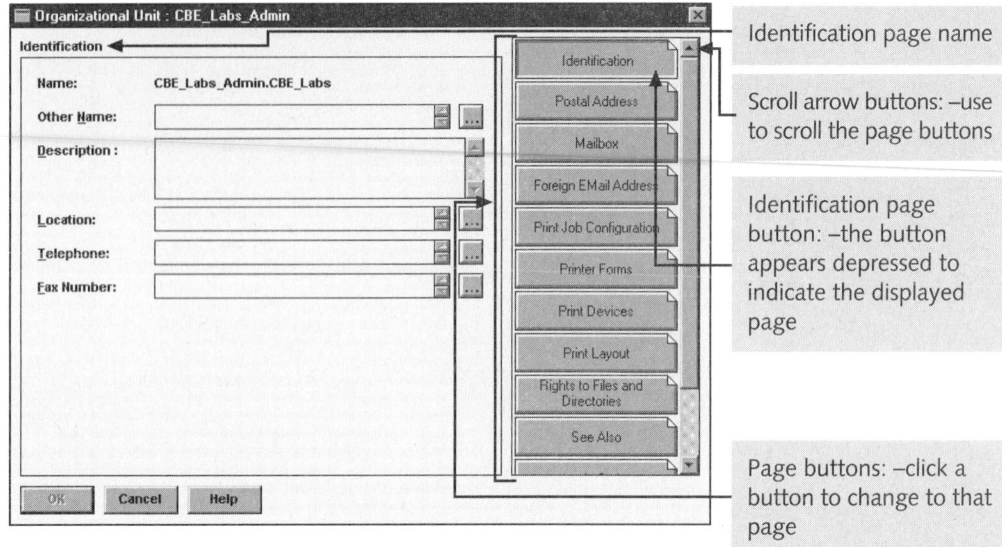

Figure 7-21 The Organizational Unit : CBE_Labs_Admin object dialog box

The object properties are grouped into pages that are (1) identified by a screen name in the upper-left corner of the screen and (2) accessed by clicking the associated button in the scrollable button bar on the right side of the dialog box. For example, as shown in Figure 7-21, the Identification page is displayed and the Identification button is shown as depressed (to indicate that it is selected) in the button bar. A group of Identification properties are shown on the Identification screen. You can change to another page by clicking the page's button. You can add, edit, or delete property values on a page by using the associated text box.

The CBE Labs network administrator needs to add the phone number and address for the marketing unit. The phone number is on the Identification page; the address information will go on the Postal Address page.

To add the CBE_Labs_Admin Organizational Unit's information, follow these steps:

1. Click the **Telephone** text box, and then type in the phone number **503-560-1548**. *Do not press [Enter].*
2. Click the **Postal Address** button in the button bar. The Postal Address page is displayed, as shown in Figure 7-22.

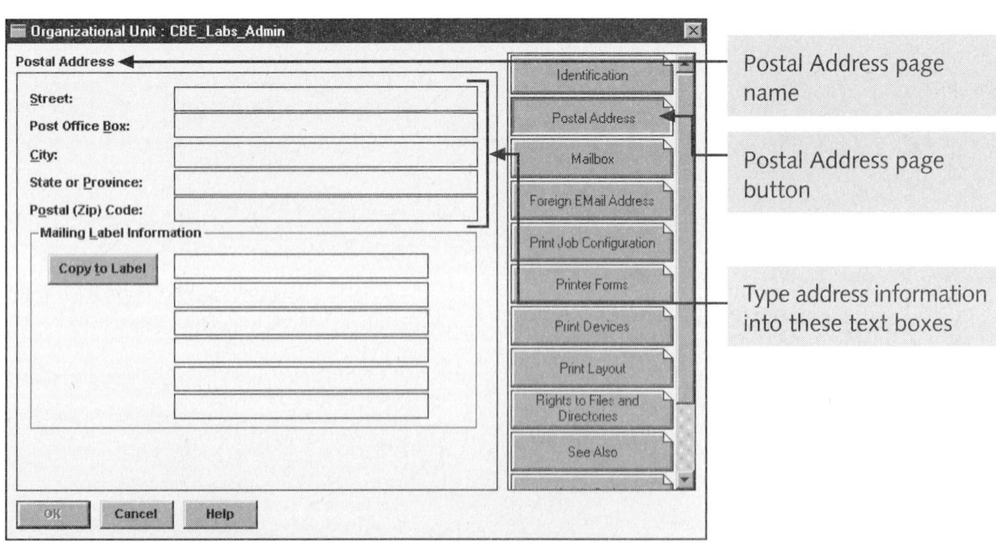

Figure 7-22 The Postal Address page

3. Click the **Street** text box and then type **539 Lincoln Avenue**.
4. Click the **City** text box and then type **Portland**.
5. Click the **State** text box and then type **OR**.
6. Click the **Postal (ZIP) Code** text box and then type **97205**.
7. Click **OK**.

WORKING WITH SERVER-RELATED LEAF OBJECTS

The first leaf objects added to the Directory tree are the User object Admin, NetWare Server objects for each NetWare 4.1 server installed into the Directory tree, and Volume objects for each volume created during the installation process. All these objects are created during the installation process. We'll work with User-related leaf objects in Chapter 9. In this chapter we'll work with Server-related leaf objects.

As discussed in Chapter 4, there are three Server-related leaf objects: NetWare Server objects, Volume objects, and Directory Map objects. Before discussing Directory Map objects, we need to understand the idea of mapping a network drive. Network drive mapping is discussed in Chapter 8, so we'll postpone our discussion of the Directory Map object until that chapter. In this chapter we'll work with NetWare server and Volume objects.

If the only NetWare servers used on the network are NetWare 4.1 servers, all necessary NetWare Server objects and Volume objects have already been created and placed in their proper context. If, however, there are any NetWare 3.1x servers on the network, the network administrator must create NetWare Server objects to represent each of them. Additionally, a Volume object must be created for each volume on the NetWare 3.1x servers so that the files on those volumes can be accessed on the network.

The CBE Labs network contains one NetWare 3.12 server. Named RANGER, the server is used for running an accounting system in administration. RANGER has one volume: SYS:. The CBE Labs network administrator needs to create the Directory tree objects for RANGER and the volume on RANGER.

THE NETWARE SERVER OBJECT

NetWare Server objects representing NetWare 4.1 servers are added directly into their context during installation, whereas NetWare Server objects representing NetWare 3.1x servers are added manually to the Directory tree. To add a NetWare Server object to a Directory tree, you select NetWare Server in the Class of New Object list, and you must specify a name for the server.

For example, the CBE Labs network administrator needs to create the RANGER NetWare Server in the CBE_Labs_Admin Unit container.

The NetWare 3.1x server must be running and on the network during the creation of the NetWare Server object that represents it.

1. To create the RANGER NetWare Server object, follow these steps:
2. Click the **CBE_Labs_Admin** Organizational Unit object, click **Object** on the menu bar, and then click **Create**.
3. The New Object dialog box is displayed. Click **NetWare Server** and then click **OK**. The Server login dialog box is displayed.

Figure 7-23 The Create NetWare Server dialog box

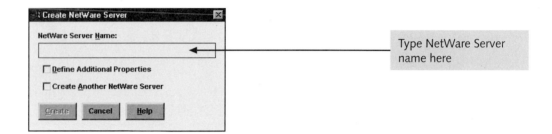

4. Log in as Supervisor. The Create NetWare Server dialog box is displayed, as shown in Figure 7-23.
5. Type **RANGER** in the Name text box, and then click the **Create** button. The RANGER NetWare Server object is added to the Directory.

THE VOLUME OBJECT

Like NetWare Server objects representing NetWare 4.1 servers, Volume objects for NetWare 4.1 servers are added directly into their context during installation. Volume objects representing volumes on NetWare 3.1x servers are added manually to the Directory tree. To add a Volume object to a Directory tree, you select Volume in the Class of New Object list, and you must specify a name for the volume.

For example, now that the CBE Labs network administrator has added the RANGER NetWare Server in the CBE_Labs_Admin Organizational Unit container, the Volume objects for the SYS: volume on RANGER must be created.

The NetWare 3.1x server must be running and on the network during the creation of the Volume objects that represent volumes on that server.

To create the SYS: volume object, follow these steps:

1. Click the **CBE_Labs_Admin** Organizational Unit object, click **Object** on the menu bar, and then click **Create**.
2. The New Object dialog box is displayed. Click **Volume**, and then click **OK**. The Create Volume dialog box is displayed, as shown in Figure 7-24.

Figure 7-24
The Create Volume dialog

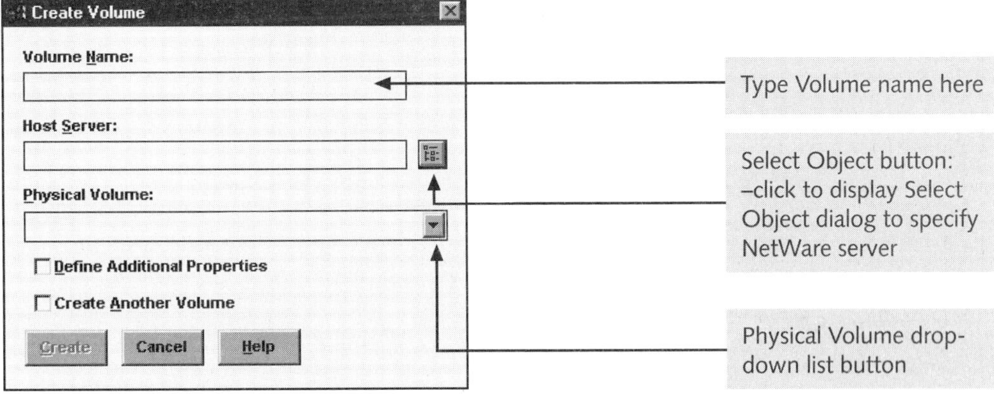

3. Type **RANGER_SYS** in the Name text box.
4. Click the **Select Object** button to the right of the Host Server text box. The Select Object dialog box is displayed, as shown in Figure 7-25.

Figure 7-25
The Select Object dialog

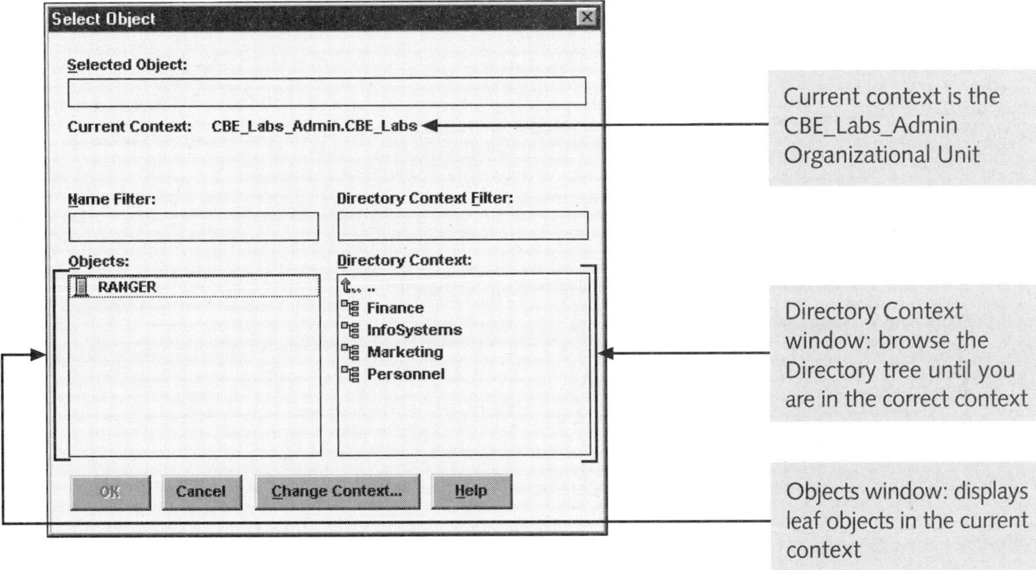

5. The Select Object dialog box is used to browse the Directory tree context to find an object. You browse the tree in the Directory Context window. In this case, the starting context is CBE_Labs_Admin.CBE_Labs. This is the correct context for the server RANGER that contains the SYS: volume, so there is no need to browse the tree. You select an object in the Objects window. In the Objects window, click the NetWare Server object RANGER. The name of the selected object is displayed in the Selected Object text box, as shown in Figure 7-26.

Figure 7-26

The selected object RANGER

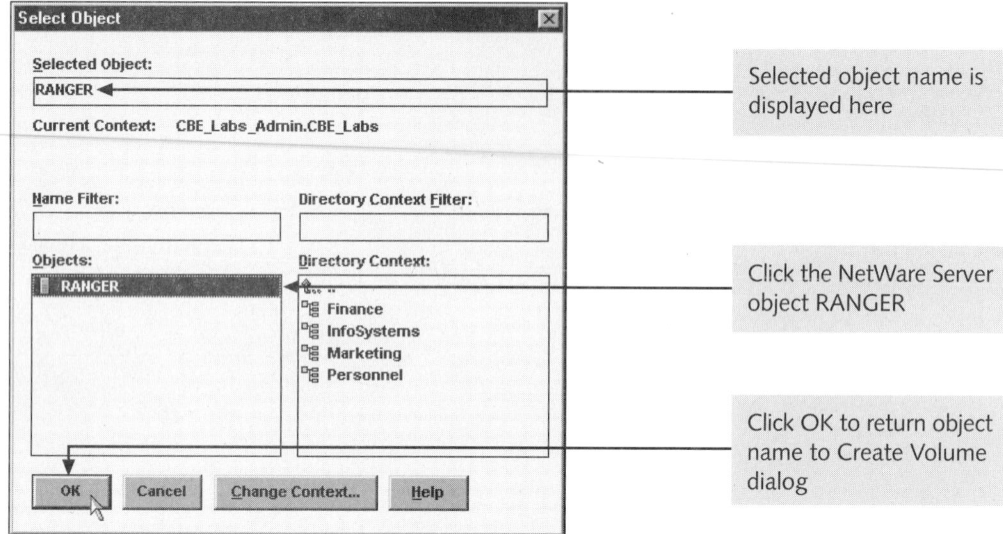

6. Click **OK**. The host server name RANGER.CBE_Labs_Admin.CBE_Labs is displayed in the Host Server text box of the Create Volume dialog box, as shown in Figure 7-27.

Figure 7-27

The Host Server name RANGER

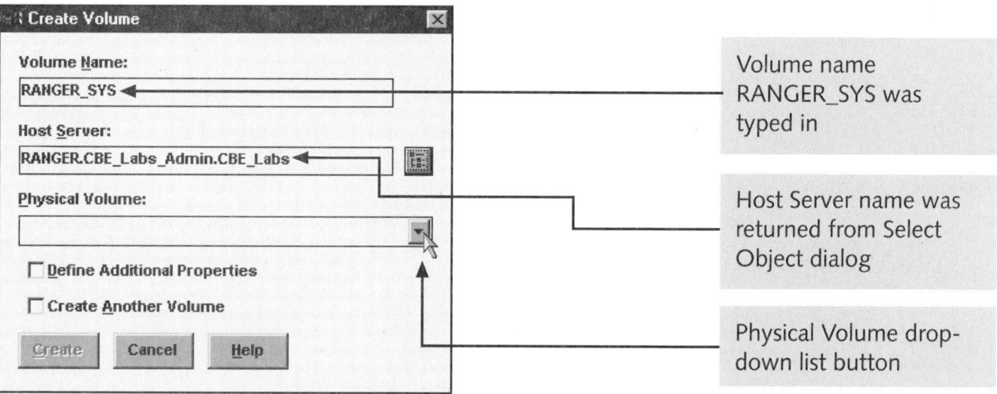

7. Click the **drop-down** list button to the right of the Physical Volume text box. The drop-down list of volumes on RANGER is displayed, as shown in Figure 7-28.

Figure 7-28

The volumes on RANGER

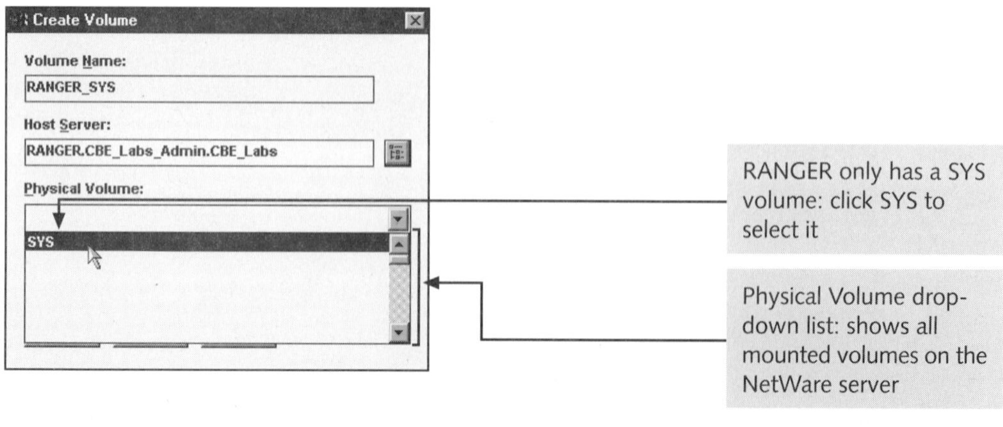

8. Click **SYS** to select the volume SYS:.
9. Click **Create**. The Volume object RANGER_SYS is created and added to the Directory tree. The CBE Labs Directory tree with the RANGER NetWare Server object and the RANGER_SYS volume is shown in Figure 7-29.

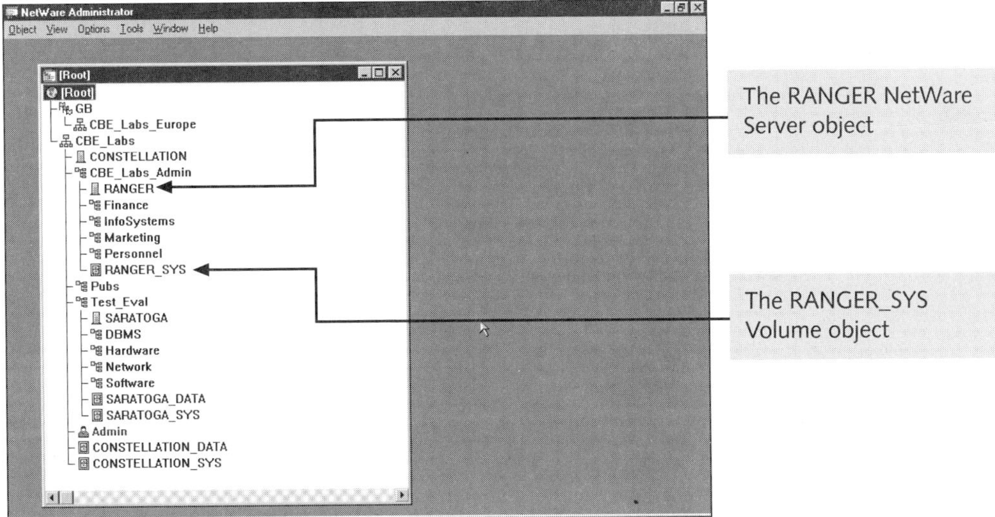

Figure 7-29 The Directory tree with the NetWare server RANGER and the RANGER_SYS volume

VIEWING AND WORKING WITH LEAF OBJECT PROPERTIES

Viewing and working with leaf object properties is similar to viewing and working with container object properties.

To view a leaf object's properties you can follow these steps:

- Click the leaf object and then press [Enter].

or

- Click the leaf object, click Object on the menu bar, and then click Details.

or

- Right-click the leaf object and then click Details on QuickMenu.

For example, the CBE Labs network administrator wants to see current volume statistics on the CONSTELLATION SYS: volume. This can be done by viewing the properties for the CONSTELLATION_SYS: volume.

To view the CONSTELLATION_SYS Volume object properties, follow these steps:

1. Right-click the **CONSTELLATION_SYS** Volume object and then click **Details**. The Volume: CONSTELLATION_SYS dialog box is displayed, as shown in Figure 7-30.

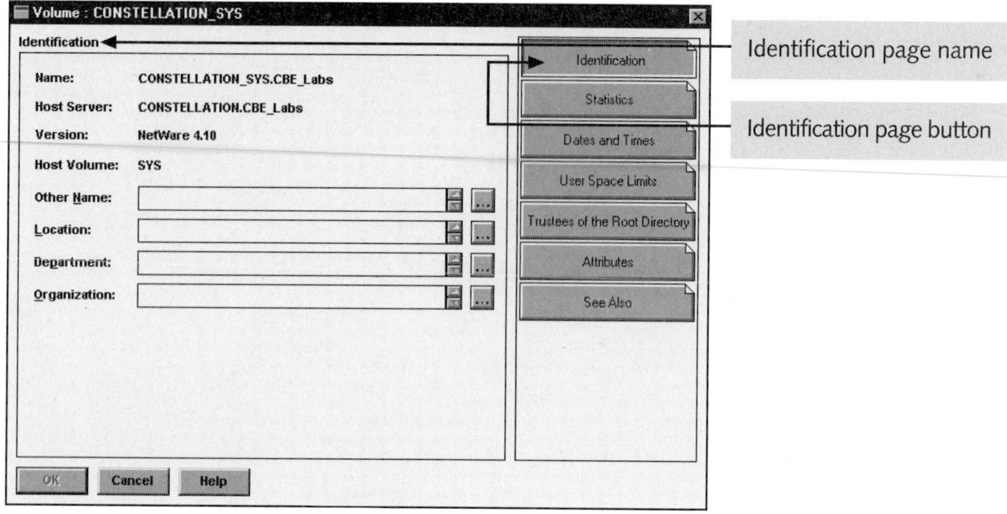

Figure 7-30 The CONSTELLATION _SYS Volume dialog

Just as in the container object property dialog boxes, the object properties are grouped into pages. The first page displayed is the Identification page. This page shows the volume name, the name of the host server, the version of NetWare running on the host server, and the volume name on the server. You can enter other information such as the location of the volume, which department it is associated with, and which organization it belongs to.

To view the volume statistics, you would click the Statistics button to see the Statistics page.

To view the CONSTELLATION_SYS volume statistics, follow these steps:

1. Click the **Statistics** button. The Statistics page for the CONSTELLATION_SYS volume is displayed, as shown in Figure 7-31.

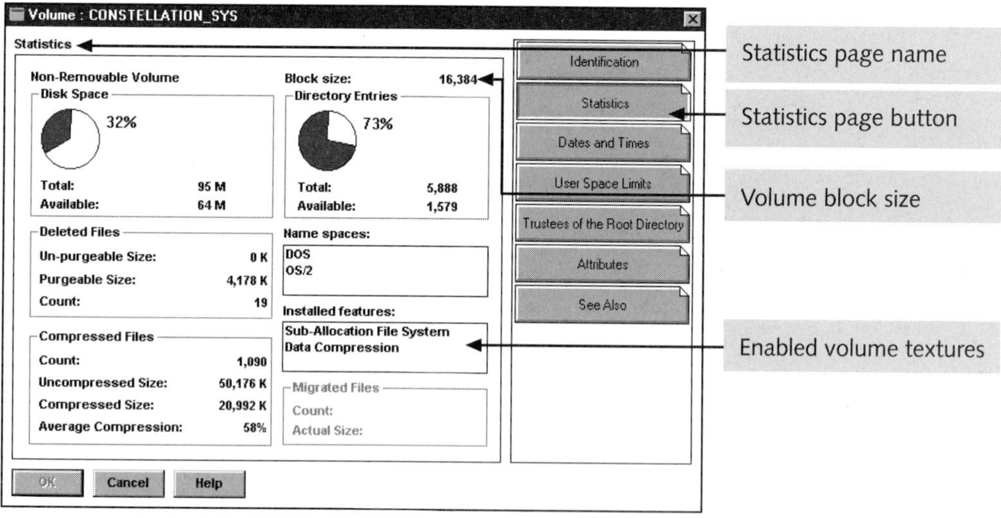

Figure 7-31 The CONSTELLATION _SYS volume statistics

2. When you are done reviewing the information, click **OK** if you have changed, added, or deleted any information or click the **Cancel** button if nothing has been changed.

The Statistics page contains a lot of useful information about each volume. For example, looking at the Statistics page in Figure 7-31, we can see that a 16-KB block size is being used along with block suballocation and data compression. There are 1,090 compressed files on the volume. The files have been compressed to 20,992 KB from their original 50,176 KB, which is an average compression of 58%. The volume has 32% of its disk space free, and 73% of the maximum number of directory entries are still available. Both the DOS and OS/2 name spaces are available on the volume.

WORKING WITH THE ALIAS LEAF OBJECT

The Alias object is one of the Miscellaneous leaf objects. As described in Chapter 4, the Alias object allows you to place a leaf object in one container object that references another leaf object in a different container. This is usually done for user convenience—it keeps the user from having to become familiar with complex complete names of objects in branches of the Directory tree. This is often done, for example, to enable a user to easily access printers, print queues, and print servers. In the end-of-chapter exercises in this chapter, you may need to use the Alias object to simulate NetWare servers and their volumes. Some of the exercises are based on networks with more than one NetWare server. If your network computer lab has only one NetWare server, you can use Alias objects to complete the exercises. For example, if you need to create a second NetWare server named Server02 in a network environment with only one NetWare server named Server01, you would create an Alias object named Server02 that references Server01. This allows the Directory tree to simulate two NetWare servers in the network.

MODIFYING AN NDS DIRECTORY TREE

As a network administrator, you will often need to modify an existing NDS Directory tree. Common modification tasks are renaming container and leaf objects, moving individual objects, moving sections of the Directory tree, deleting objects, renaming trees, and merging trees.

RENAMING OBJECTS

It is often necessary to rename an object; This is easily done; you can rename all objects except the [Root].

To rename an object, you can follow these steps:

- Click the object, click Object on the menu bar, and then click Rename.

then

- Type in the new name and then click OK.

For example,the Netware server SARATOGA should have been installed in the Test&Eval organizational unit, however, the limitations of the NetWare 4.1 installation process forced the CBE LABS network administrator to name the organizational unit Test_Eval. He can now rename it Test&Eval.

To rename the Test_Eval Organizational Unit object:

1. Click the **Test_Eval Organizational Unit** object to select it.
2. Click **Object** on the menu bar and then click the **Rename** commmand. The Rename dialog box appears.
3. Type **Test&Eval** in the New Name text box, as shown in Figure 7-32.
4. Click **OK**.

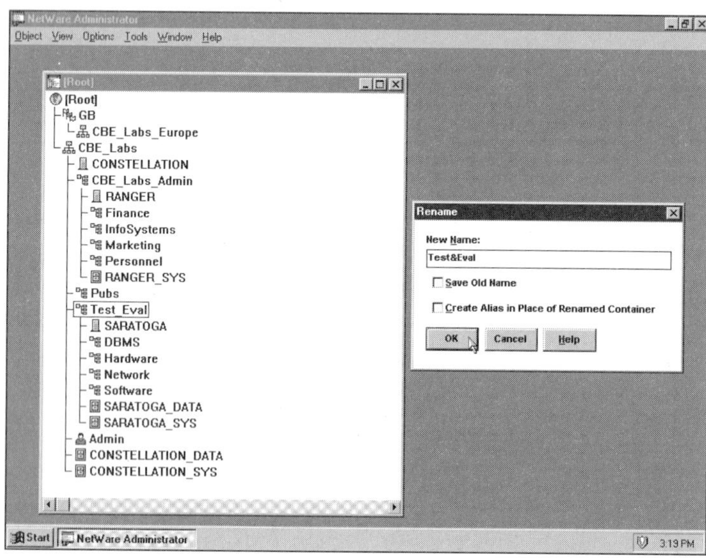

Figure 7-32

Renaming the Test_Eval Organizational Unit Object

MOVING LEAF OBJECTS

There will often be times when you need to move a leaf object, such as a User object or a Printer object, from one container to another. Doing this, of course, changes the object's context, but NDS will automatically make the necessary changes in the property values.

To move an object, you can follow these steps:

- Drag the object to its new context in the Directory tree.

or

- Click the object, then click Object on the menu bar, then click Move, then enter the new context and click OK.

or

- Click the object, click Object on the menu bar, click Move, and then browse to new context and click OK.

Deleting Objects

Managing and modifying the Directory tree will often require you to delete an object. Deleting most leaf objects, such as Users and Printers, presents no problem. Deleting a NetWare Server object, however, requires consideration of NDS partitions and replicas, which are discussed later in this chapter. Deleting a container object requires that you first delete or move all objects within that container object before you delete it.

To delete an object, you can follow these steps:

- Click the object and then press [Delete].

or

- Click the the object, click Object on the menu bar, and then click Delete.

or

- Right-click the container object for the object, and then click Delete on the QuickMenu.

Managing Partitions

As you learned in Chapter 4, NetWare 4.1 divides the NDS database into partitions, which are logical sections of the NDS database. The first partition that is created contains the [Root] object and the container objects that create the context for the first NetWare 4.1 server installed. As each additional NetWare 4.1 server is installed into the network, a new partition will be created if a new context is created during the server installation. Each partition contains subsidiary container objects and all leaf objects in the containers.

For example, when NetWare 4.1 was installed on the CBE Labs server CONSTELLATION, a first partition was created. This partition contained the [Root] object and all the container objects created during the installation process. After the installation was complete, a single partition existed, as shown in Figure 7-33. Note that this figure uses the new container name CBE_Labs.

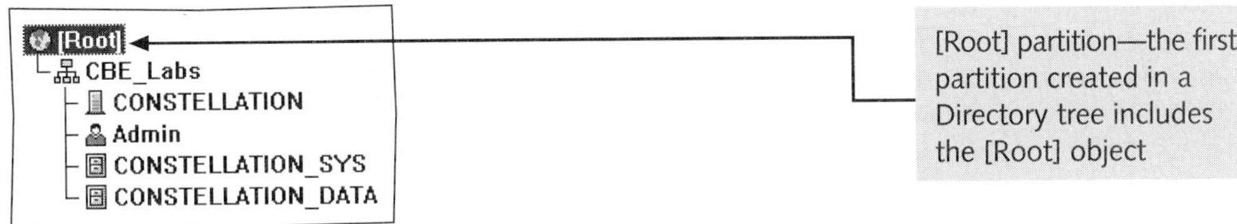

Figure 7-33 The first partition

Because there is only one partition, the word *partition* may seem a little strange—the NDS database still exists as a whole unit.

When NetWare 4.1 was installed on SARATOGA, a second partition was created. This partition starts at OU=Test&Eval.O=CBE_Labs, the context where SARATOGA was installed. After this installation, two partitions existed, as shown in Figure 7-34.

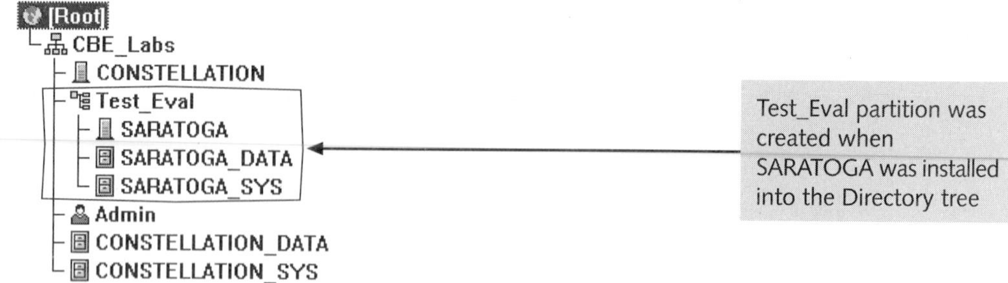

Figure 7-34 The second partition

As Organizational Unit objects were added under the containers CBE_Labs and Test&Eval, these objects were automatically included in their respective partitions. The Country object GB, its subsidiary Organization object CBE_Labs_Europe, and the Organizational Unit objects CBE_Labs_Admin and Pubs were included in the partition containing the [Root] object. The partitions in the CBE Labs Directory tree now appear as shown in Figure 7-35.

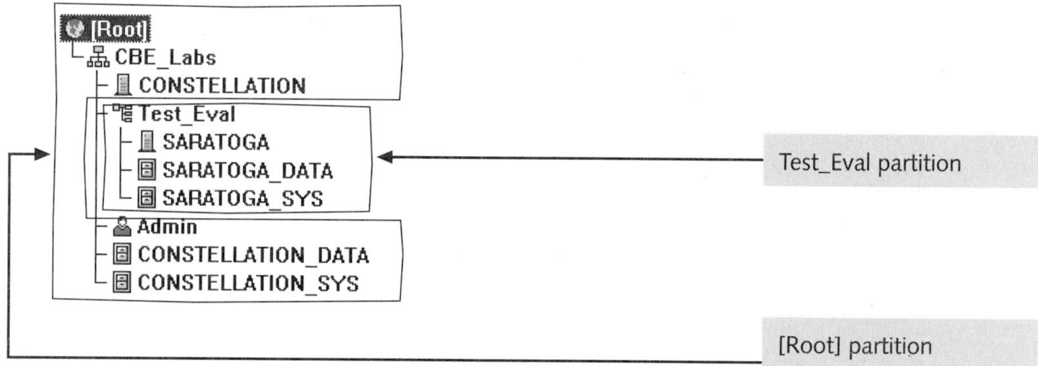

Figure 7-35 CBE Labs Directory tree partitions

Replicas, or copies, of each partition were automatically stored on each NetWare server within a partition. The master replica is stored on the first NetWare 4.1 server installed in the partition, and a read/write replica is stored on the other servers installed in that same partition. When the NetWare 4.1 server CONSTELLATION was added to the Directory tree, a master partition was created and stored on CONSTELLATION. When the NetWare 4.1 server SARATOGA was created in the Test&Eval Organizational unit, a master partition was created on SARATOGA. There are no copies of these partitions currently existing because the NetWare servers are in different partitions. Read/write replicas of both partitions need to be manually created. Because RANGER uses the NetWare 3.1x bindery database, there is no master NDS replica for RANGER created, nor are there other copies of the partitions on CONSTELLATION and SARATOGA stored on RANGER.

The partitions created by the NetWare 4.1 installation process may not give you the NDS database divisions that you want. You can control the partition structure by creating, moving, and merging partitions. Partition and replica information can be viewed and managed in NetWare Administrator and the NetWare menu utility PARTMGR. Although good for partition management, PARTMGR lacks the NetWare Administrator partition manager's ability to let you move container objects. In this chapter we'll work with NetWare Administrator.

Notice that "deleting partitions" is not listed as a function you can perform when managing partitions. Because the NDS database information is not deleted, you can't really delete a partition. To "delete" a partition, you *merge* it into another partition.

CREATING PARTITIONS

The partition creation logic built into NetWare 4.1 guarantees an appropriate division of partitions among servers. Because a partition is a portion of the NDS database and needs to be stored locally for easy login access, it makes sense that partitions be associated with installed servers and the context of those servers. There may still be occasions when you want to create another partition. This is necessary, for example, when you want to move a container object or subtree within a Directory tree. A **subtree** is a container object that contains leaf objects.

To create a partition, you can follow these steps:

- Click the [Root], Organization, or Organizational Unit object that contains the Country, Organization, or Organizational Unit object that will be the starting point for the partition.
- Click Tools, and then click Partition Manager.
- In the Partitions list, click the Country, Organization, or Organizational Unit object that will be the starting point for the partition.
- Click the Create as New Partition button.
- Click Yes in the Confirmation dialog box to confirm the creation of the new partition, then click OK in the Partition Manager message box.

To see the new partition, you must redisplay the container objects by double-clicking the up arrow symbol at the top of the Partitions list and then double-clicking the container object that contains the new partition.

For example, suppose that the network administrator at CBE Labs had originally created the Finance Organizational Unit immediately below the CBE_Labs Organization object instead of under the CBE_Labs_Admin Organizational Unit object. If he then decided to move the Finance Organizational Unit object into the CBE_Labs_Admin container, he would first have to create a new partition that starts at the Finance Organizational Unit object.

To create the Finance partition, follow these steps:

1. Click the **CBE_Labs Organization** object, because it contains the Finance Organizational Unit object.
2. Click **Tools**, and then click **Partition Manager**. The Partition Manager dialog box is displayed, as shown in Figure 7-36.

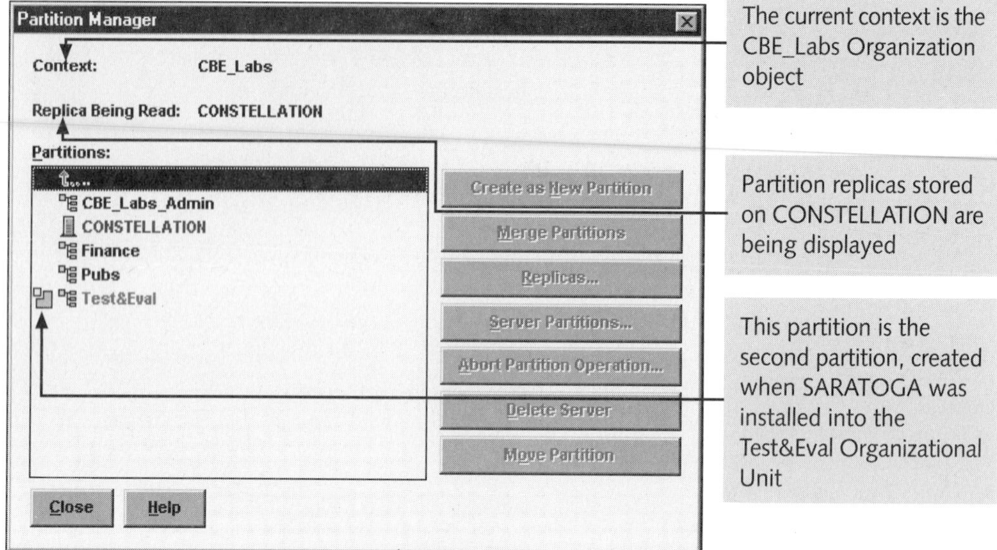

Figure 7-36 The Partition Manager dialog box

3. Click the **Finance Organizational Unit** object in the Partitions list.
4. Click the **Create as New Partition** button. A Confirmation dialog box is displayed, as shown in Figure 7-37.

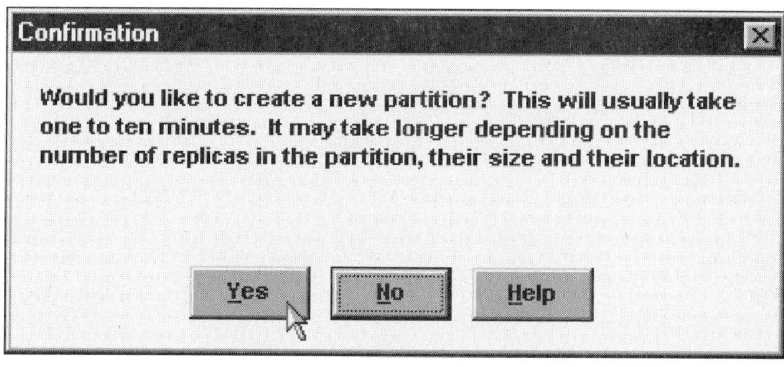

Figure 7-37 The Confirmation dialog box

5. Click the **Yes** button in the Confirmation dialog box. A Partition Manager message box is displayed, as shown in Figure 7-38.

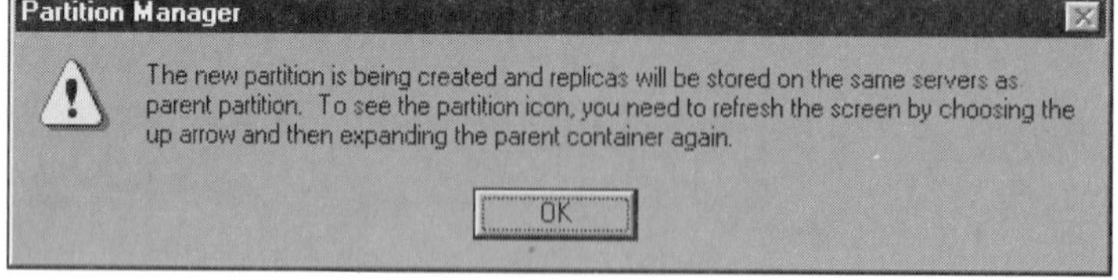

Figure 7-38 The Partition Manager message box

6. Click **OK**. The new partition is created. To see it, double-click the up arrow symbol and then double-click the CBE_Labs Organization object. The Partitions list is redisplayed with the new partition, as shown in Figure 7-39.

Figure 7-39

The new Finance partition

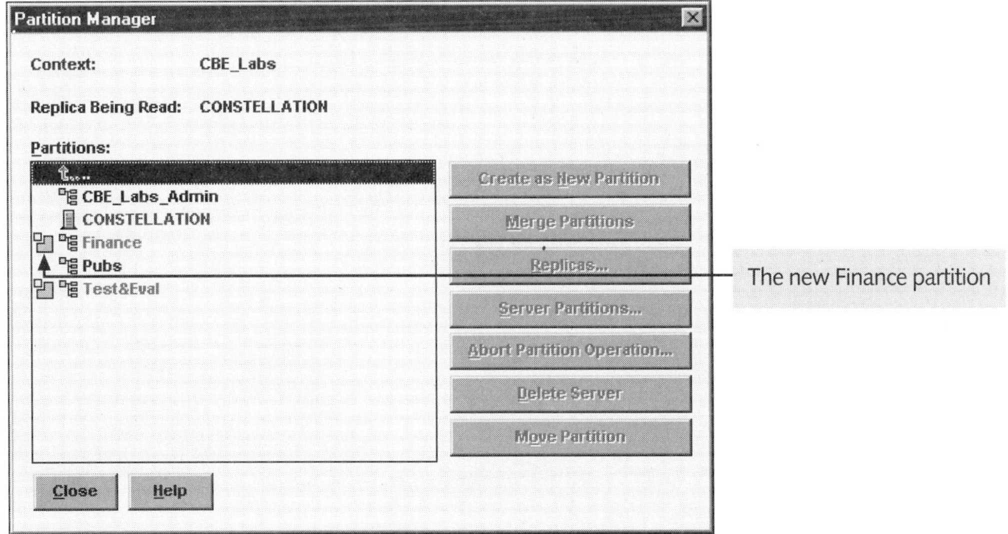

Moving Container Objects and Subtrees

Sometimes you'll want to rearrange the organizational structure of the Directory tree itself. This means moving a container object and every leaf object it contains to a new location in the Directory tree. You do this by creating a partition that starts at the container object you want to move and then moving the partition using Partition Manager. You do *not* need to create a partition to move a leaf object, such as a User object or a Printer object, from one container to another. Moving a leaf object, of course, changes the object's context, but NDS will automatically make the necessary changes in the property values.

To move a partition, you can follow these steps:

- Click the partition in the Partitions list in the Partition Manager.
- Click the Move Partition button.
- Click the Select Object button in the Move dialog box.
- Browse the Directory tree in the Select Object dialog box to locate the new context, and then click OK.
- Click OK in the Move dialog box.

For example, the CBE Labs network administrator needs to move the Finance partition into the CBE_Labs_Admin container object.

To move the Finance partition, follow these steps:

1. Click the **Finance** partition in the Partitions list in the Partition Manager, as shown in Figure 7-40.

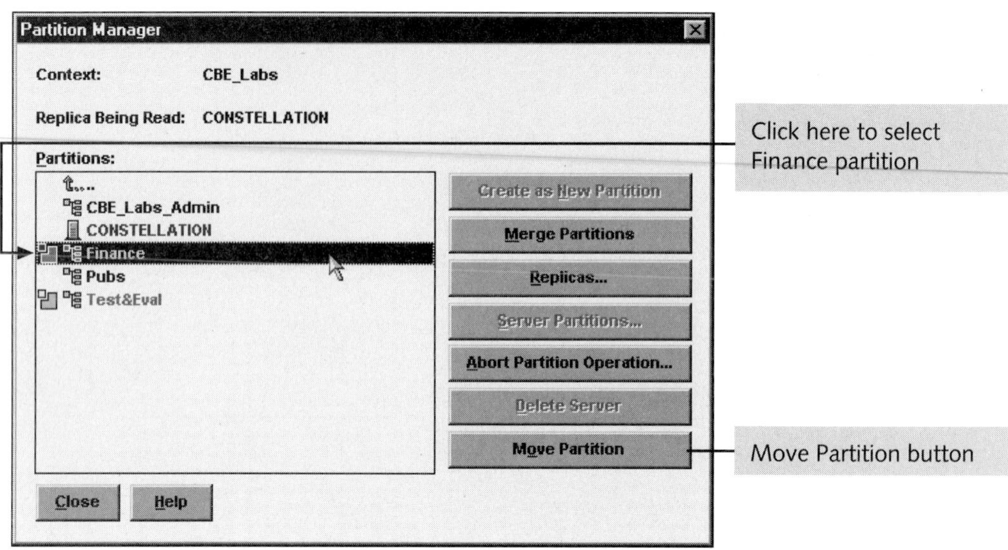

Figure 7-40 Moving the Finance partition

2. Click the **Move Partition** button. The Move dialog box appears, as shown in Figure 7-41.

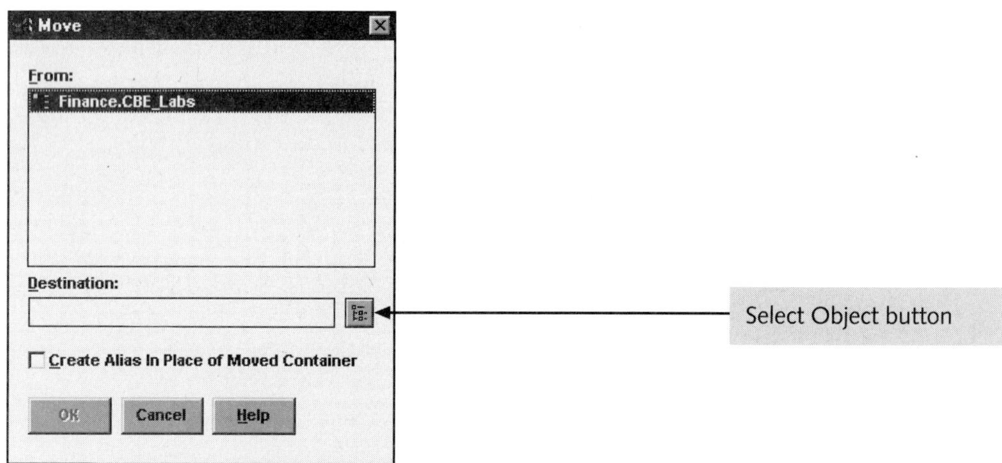

Figure 7-41 The Move dialog box

3. Click the **Select Object** button in the Move dialog box. The Select Object dialog box appears.

4. Click **CBE_Labs_Admin**, and then click **OK**.

5. Click **OK** in the Move dialog box. The Finance partition is moved into the CBE_Labs_Admin container. Double-click the CBE_Labs_Admin Organizational Unit object in the Partitions box. The Organizational Unit objects in the CBE_LABS_Admin Organizational unit object are displayed, including the Finance partition, as shown in Figure 7-42.

Figure 7-42

The Finance partition in its new context

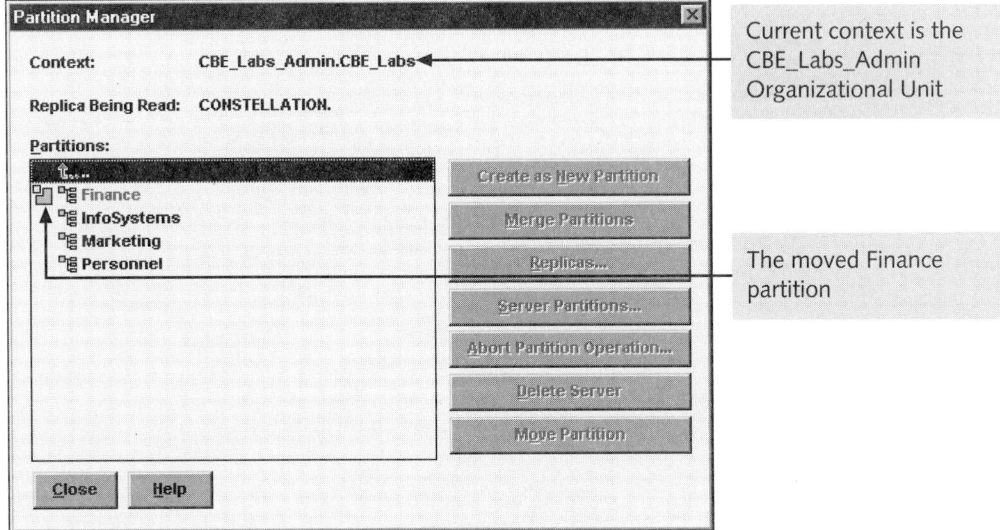

MERGING PARTITIONS

Sometimes you may need to join two partitions together. This is called merging partitions. This will happen, for example, when you have created a new partition in order to move a container object within a Directory tree. After moving the container object, you will need to eliminate the temporary partition you created. This is done by merging the partition into another partition.

To merge a partition, you can follow these steps:

- Click the partition in the Partitions list in the Partition Manager.
- Click the Merge Partitions button.
- Click the Yes button in the Confirmation dialog box.

To see the merged partition, you must redisplay the container objects by double-clicking the up arrow symbol at the top of the Partitions list and then double-clicking the container object that contains the merged partition.

For example, as the last step in moving the Finance Organizational Unit into the CBE_Labs_Admin container, the network administrator at CBE Labs needs to remove the Finance partition. To do this, the Finance partition must be merged back into the [Root] partition.

To merge the Finance partition into the [Root] partition, follow these steps:

1. The Partition Manager should still be open. If it isn't, click Tools, click Partition Manager, and then browse the Directory tree in the Partitions list until the context is CBE_Labs_Admin.CBE_Labs and the Partitions list shows the Organizational Units in the CBE_Labs_Admin container.

2. Click the **Finance** partition in the Partitions list. The partition is selected, as shown in Figure 7-43.

Figure 7-43 Merging partitions

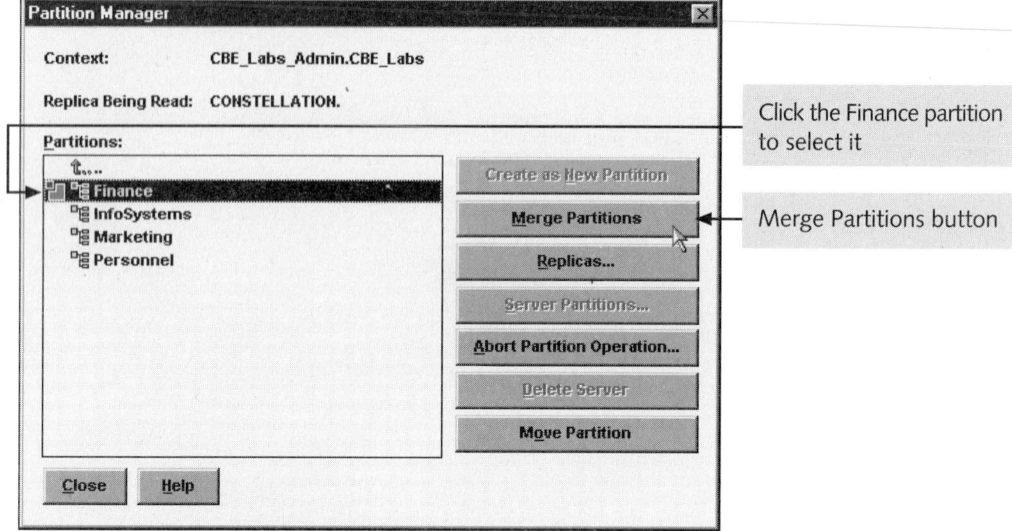

3. Click the **Merge Partitions** button. The Confirmation dialog box appears, as shown in Figure 7-44.

Figure 7-44 Confirming the partition merge

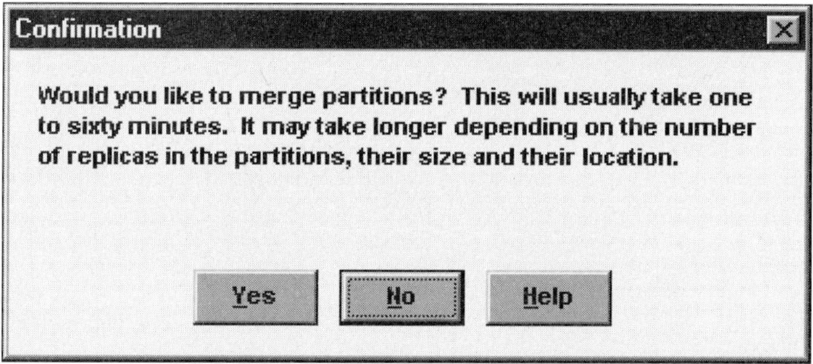

4. Click **Yes** in the Confirmation dialog box. The partitions are merged. To display the merged partition, double-click the up arrow symbol at the top of the Partitions list and then double-click the CBE_Labs_Admin object. The refreshed Partitions list is displayed, as shown in Figure 7-45.

Figure 7-45

The merged Finance partition

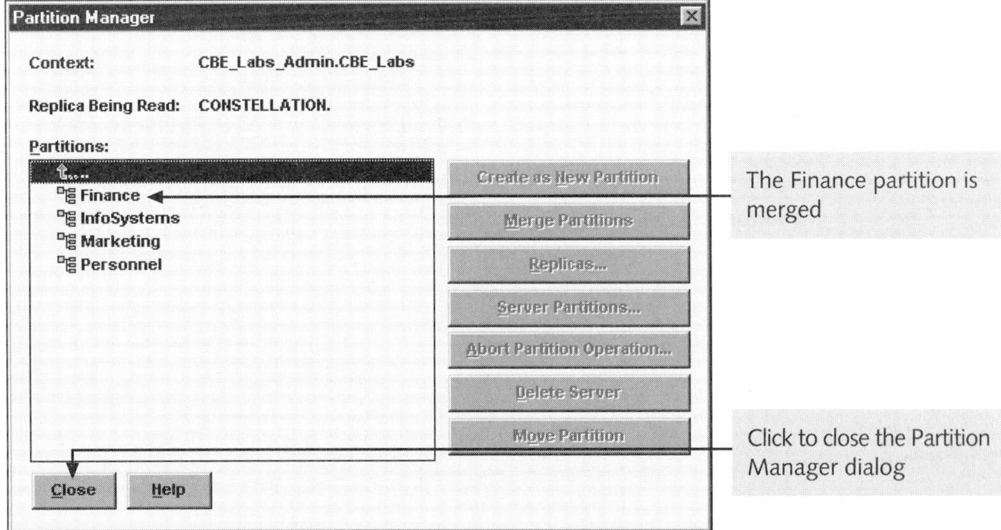

This completes the move of the Finance Organizational Unit object. As a network administrator, you will have to use the steps of creating, moving, and merging partitions whenever you move a container object within your Directory tree.

CREATING REPLICAS

Partition Manager can also be used to create replicas of partitions. This is necessary, for example, to store a replica of one partition in another partition. To create a new partition, you select the partition that you want to replicate in Partition Manager's Partitions list and then click the Replicas button. This displays a Partition Replicas dialog box, which enables you to manage the replicas. You can create replicas, change replica type, delete replicas, and update replica data using this dialog.

NetWare 4.11 introduces a Windows GUI utility named the NDS Manager for partition management. The NDS Manager screen is shown in Figure 7-45. The NDS Manager is much easier to work with than the partition manger built into the current NetWare Administrator utility or the PARTMGR menu utility. You can launch it from within the new version of NetWare Administrator or use it separately.

Figure 7-46

The NDS Manager screen

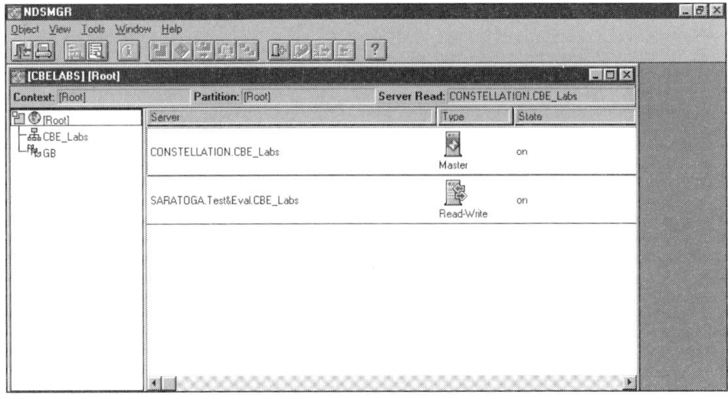

MANAGING DIRECTORY TREES

As a network administrator, you will occasionally need to work with the Directory tree as a whole, rather than with its component parts. This happens when you need to rename a Directory tree, or combine two Directory trees into one. For example, you may need to rename a Directory tree if the company name is changed. You may need to combine two Directory trees if there is more than one Directory tree on your internetwork, and it has been decided to consolidate the trees for easier management.

DSMERGE.NLM

The utility used to manage Directory trees is DSMERGE.NLM. DSMERGE.NLM is a NetWare Loadable Module that is run by loading it at the console prompt with the console command:

```
LOAD DSMERGE
```

When the module is loaded, it appears as shown in Figure 7-47.

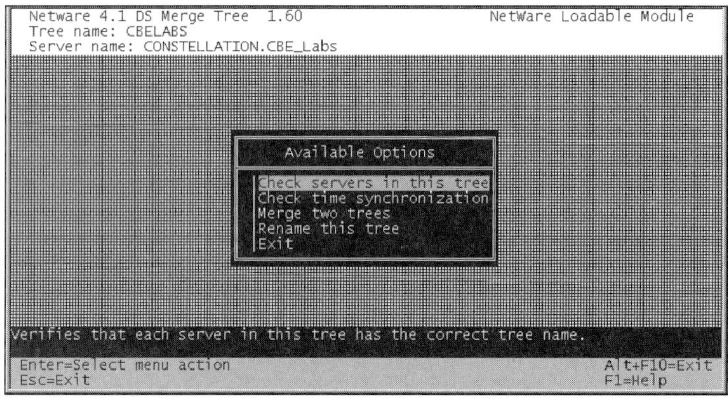

Figure 7-47 The DSMERGE screen

RENAMING A DIRECTORY TREE

You can rename a Directory tree by using the Rename this tree menu item. You must load DSMERGE on the NetWare server where the Master replica of the [Root] partition is stored. When you choose the Rename this tree menu item, you are required to log into the tree from the server as the Admin user and use the complete name of the Admin account (i.e., .Admin.CBE_Labs, not just Admin). You are then prompted for the name. When you are done, you press [F10] to complete renaming the tree.

MERGING TWO DIRECTORY TREES

You can merge two Directory trees by using the Merge two trees menu item. The two trees to be merged are called the source tree and the target tree. The **target tree** retains its name, whereas the **source tree** is merged into the target tree. When you merge two trees, you first need to make sure that (1) all NetWare servers in both Directory trees are up and running, (2) time is synchronized between the two Directory trees, and (3) the Directory trees have different names.

To check the conditions for merging two Directory trees, you can follow these steps:

- Load DSMERGE on the NetWare servers where the Master replica of the [Root] partitions of each of the two tree is stored.
- For each server, use the Check servers in this tree command to confirm that all servers in the trees are up and running.
- For each server, use the Check time synchronization to confirm that the servers in each tree are synchronized.
- If the two trees are not synchronized, reset the time in one Directory tree so that the times are the same within plus or minus two seconds.
- If necessary, rename one of the two Directory trees so that the names are unique.

When the trees are ready to be merged, make sure that no users are logged on to either network. Work at the server console for the NetWare server with the source Directory tree. Choose the Merge two trees menu item. You are required to log into the tree from the server as the Admin user and use the complete name of the Admin account (i.e., .Admin.CBE_Labs, not just Admin). You then choose the name of the target Directory tree. You are required to log into this tree as the Admin user and use the complete name of the Admin account. When you are done, you press [F10] to complete merging the Directory trees.

When you merge two Directory trees, you cannot have any leaf objects or aliases directly under the [Root] of either tree. You also need to make sure that you do not have similar object names that will result in duplicate object names when the Directory trees are merged. For example, you might want to name an administration Organizational Unit with the obvious shorter name for Administration, which is Admin. However, this can't be used if the User object Admin exists in the same container as the administration Organizational Unit. The typed name for the user Admin is CN=Admin.O=CBE_LABS. If Administration were shortened to Admin, the typed name would be OU=Admin.O=CBE_LABS. Both of these are Admin.CBE_LABS in untyped form, which creates a problem for NDS.

CHAPTER SUMMARY

NetWare network administrators must master the NetWare commands and utilities in order to set up and manage a network. This chapter described the six different types of NetWare tools available to the network administrator: command line utilities, menu utilities, graphical utilities, supervisor utilities, console commands, and NetWare Loadable Modules (NLMs). Console commands and NLMs are used from the file server's console; command line utilities, menu utilities, and graphical utilities run at the workstations. Command line utilities are similar to DOS commands in that you must know the command and its correct syntax in order to use it. Menu utilities are interactive and more user-friendly in that they enable you to select options and provide you with lists and input windows. They use the following set of special function keys:

- The Esc key is used to go back one menu level.
- The F1 key is used to obtain additional help information.
- The F3 key is used to change a highlighted entry in a window.
- The F5 key is used to mark items in a window.
- The Alt and F10 keys are used to exit the menu utility from any level.

Graphical utilities are similar to menu utilities, but they use the Windows or OS/2 GUI. The term *supervisor utilities* refers to any utility stored in the SYS:SYSTEM directory that is used by the network administrator for system administration. Console commands are NetWare commands that must be run from the NetWare server console prompt, not the DOS prompt on a workstation. NetWare Loadable Modules (NLMs) are programs and utilities that run on the NetWare server.

The CX command line utility is used for navigating and browsing the NDS Directory tree. You can use it to change context and display Directory tree information.

The NETADMIN menu utility is used to manage the NDS Directory tree and the objects in the Directory tree. You can use it to browse the Directory tree but not to display the entire tree at one time. Using NETADMIN, you can create, delete, and rename container and leaf objects, as well as manage their properties.

The NetWare Administrator graphical utility is the preferred tool for working with the NDS Directory tree. It enables you to do everything you can do using the CX command or the NETADMIN menu utility using an easy Windows or OS/2 interface. NetWare Administrator also includes a partition manager that is needed for moving container objects within the Directory tree.

You can use NetWare Administrator to display portions or all of a Directory tree. You can also open additional browser windows to display different sections of the Directory tree in separate browser windows. A maximum of ten browser windows can be open at one time.

The initial creation of the Directory tree is done during the installation of NetWare 4.1 servers. After all NetWare 4.1 servers in a network have been installed, the Directory tree contains the following elements:

- The [Root] object
- [Optional] One or more Country objects
- At least one Organization object
- [Optional] One or more Organizational Unit objects
- The User object Admin
- A NetWare Server object for each NetWare 4.1 server installed
- A SYS Volume object for each NetWare 4.1 server installed
- [Optional] A Volume object for each additional volume created during server installation

At this point, the network administrator needs to complete building the organizational structure of the Directory tree and add any NetWare 3.1x servers and their associated volumes into the tree.

To complete the organizational structure, container objects are added to the Directory tree. Container objects include the [Root], Country, Organization, and Organizational Unit objects. Using NetWare Administrator, you can create, rename, and delete container objects and manage their properties. You cannot, however, simply move a container object to another part of the tree. To do this, you must use the NDS partition manger.

You can use NetWare Administrator to create, rename, and delete leaf objects in container objects, as well as to manage their properties. In this chapter, the leaf objects that need to be added are the NetWare server objects for each 3.1x server in the network and Volume objects for each volume on a NetWare 3.1x server.

NetWare Administrator can also be used to move a leaf object from one container object to another. To move a container object, however, is a more complicated process. First, a new partition is created, if necessary, starting at the container object to be moved. Second, the new partition, which now includes the container object and all subsidiary container objects and leaf objects, is moved to a new location in the Directory tree. Finally, the partition is merged into a parent partition. You cannot delete partitions—only merge them into other partitions. The DSMERGE.NLM is used to rename Directory trees and to merge two Directory trees into one.

COMMAND SUMMARY

Command	Syntax	Definition
CX	*CX [new context] [/A /C /CONT /R /T] [/? | /VER]*	Changes the user's current context in the NDS Directory tree. Can also browse and display the Directory tree. Options include /A, which lists all objects at the current context and below in the Directory tree; /C, which scrolls the output continuously; /CONT, which displays a list of containers at the current context; /R, which displays results from [Root]; and /T, which displays a tree diagram of container objects at the current context and below. Options can be combined with the [new context] parameter to set the starting context for the option.
DSMERGE	*Load DSMERGE*	NLM utility that enables you to manage the NDS Directory tree. You can rename a Directory tree and merge two Directory trees into one. Menu options include: Check servers in this tree Check time synchronization Merge two trees Rename this tree
NETADMIN	*NETADMIN [/VER]*	Menu utility that enables you to create and manage objects in the NDS Directory tree. Main menu options include: Manage objects Manage according to search patterns Change context Search

NetWare Administrator		Windows or OS/2 graphical utility that enables you to create and manage objects in the NDS Directory tree. Includes a partition manager for working with NDS partitions and moving container objects in the Directory tree.
PARTMGR	*PARTMGR [/VER]*	Menu utility that enables you to create and manage NDS partitions. Main menu options include: Manage partitions Change context

KEY TERMS

command line utility (CLU)
console command
CX command
DSMERGE.NLM
graphical utility
menu utility
NETADMIN utility
NetWare Administrator utility
NetWare Loadable Module (NLM)
object dialog box
page
PARTMGR
source tree
subtree
supervisor utility
target tree

REVIEW QUESTIONS

1. Identify each of the following as being either a command line utility, menu utility, graphical utility, console command, or NetWare Loadable Module (NLM):

   CX ____________________

   NETADMIN ____________________

   NetWare Administrator ____________________

   PARTMGR ____________________

   DSMERGE ____________________

2. In the space below, briefly explain an advantage of a command line utility over a menu utility:

3. In the space below, briefly explain an advantage of a menu utility over a command line utility:

4. In the space below, briefly explain an advantage of a graphical utility over a menu utility:

5. Write a command line command to display the Directory tree starting at the [Root] and showing all subordinate container and leaf objects:

____

For questions 6 through 9, use the Directory tree for Washington Management Services shown in Figure 7-48 and assume that your initial context is [Root].

Figure 7-48

```
[Root]
└WMS
  ├Consulting
  │ ├Consultants
  │ ├VP_Consulting
  │ ├Government
  │ ├Industry
  │ └GRoyce
  ├ExecAdmin
  │ ├President
  │ └MDwyer
  ├Fin&Acct
  │ ├Finance&Accounting
  │ ├VP_Fin&Acct
  │ ├Accounting
  │ ├Finance
  │ └MMitchell
  ├InfoSystems
  │ ├WMS_Server01/SYS:Public
  │ ├WMS_Server02/SYS:Public
  │ ├WMS_Server01
  │ ├WMS_Server02
  │ ├P01_Laser
  │ ├PS01_Laser
  │ ├PQ01_Laser
  │ ├WMS_Server01_SYS
  │ └WMS_Server02_SYS
  └Admin
```

6. Write a command to change context to the Consulting organizational unit container.

____

____

7. Having changed context to the Consulting organizational unit container, write a command to change context to the WMS organization container.

____

8. Write a command to display the entire Directory tree *without* leaf objects in tree form regardless of the current context.

____

9. Write a command to display the entire Directory tree *with* leaf objects in tree form regardless of the current context.

____

10. The following symbols are used by the NETADMIN menu utility. Explain the meaning of each:

    . ("dot") ______________________________

    .. ("double dots") ______________________________

    + (plus sign) ______________________________

11. When using the NetWare Administrator, you can display or hide the objects in a con tainer object. In the space below, explain how to do this:

12. When using the NetWare Administrator, you can change context. In the space below, explain how to do this:

13. When using the NetWare Administrator, you can open an additional browser window or close an existing browser window. In the space below, explain how to do this:

14. For each of the objects listed below, state whether at least one of the objects must exist when the installation of all NetWare 4.1 servers in the network is complete:

    The [Root] object ______________________________

    The Country object ______________________________

    The Organization object ______________________________

    The Organizational Unit object ______________________________

    The NetWare Server object for a NetWare 4.1 server ______________________________

    The NetWare Server object for a NetWare 3.1x server ______________________________

    The Volume object for a NetWare 4.1 server ______________________________

    The Volume object for a NetWare 3.1x server ______________________________

    The User object ______________________________

    The Group object ______________________________

15. In the space below, explain how to create Directory tree objects when using the NetWare Administrator:

16. Match each of the country codes listed below with its corresponding country:

COUNTRY CODE		COUNTRY
AU	________________	a. Saudi Arabia
CA	________________	b. United States
JP	________________	c. Canada
SA	________________	d. Australia
US	________________	e. United Kingdom
GB	________________	f. Japan

17. An object's properties are managed using the ________________, which consists of one or more ________________ of property values.

18. Some dialog boxes used to create objects contain a Select Object button. In the space below, describe how to use the Select Object button to select an object.

19. In the space below, explain how to rename Directory tree objects when using the NetWare Administrator:

20. In the space below, explain how to move leaf objects when using the NetWare Administrator:

21. In the space below, explain how to delete leaf objects when using the NetWare Administrator:

22. When a new Directory tree is created during NetWare 4.1 installation, which partition is the [Root] object placed in?°

____

23. A subtree is a container object that contains ________________.

24. In the space below, describe the steps to move a container object or subtree to a new context in th Directory tree:

25. To rename a Directory tree, you must use the ______________________.
26. In the space below, list the five steps that must be completed before merging two Direcory trees:

    a.

    b.

    c.

    d.

    e.

EXERCISES

EXERCISE 7-1: USING THE CX COMMAND

Your instructor has created an NDS Directory tree for your network environment, including a section based on the Franklin D. Roosevelt Investments (FDR) Directory tree discussed in Chapter 4 of this text. In this exercise, you use the CX command to change your context within the NDS Directory tree and to view Directory tree information within the FDR section of the Directory tree.

1. Log into your network using your normal login procedure.
2. Open a DOS prompt window.
3. Change directories to the G: drive (or other network drive as specified by your instructor).
4. Use the CX command to view your current context.

   Command used: ______________________
5. Use the CX command to change your context to [Root].

   Command used: ______________________
6. Use the CX command to change your context to the FDR_Admin organizational unit of FDR.

   Command used: ______________________
7. Use the CX command to change context to the FDR organization unit using a "dot" shortcut.

   Command used: ______________________
8. Use the CX command to view the Directory tree from the [Root] down *without* leaf objects.

   Command used: ______________________
9. Use the CX command to view the Directory tree from the [Root] down *with* leaf objects.

   Command used: ______________________
10. Use the CX command to view the Directory tree from the FDR organization object down *without* leaf objects.

    Command used: ______________________
11. Using the same command you used in Step 10, add PRN to the end of the command to print the tree on a printer.

12. Use the CX command to view the Directory tree from the FDR organization object down *with* leaf objects.

    Command used: ____

13. Using the same command you used in Step 12, add PRN

    to the end of the command to print the tree on a printer.

14. Close the DOS prompt window and return to Windows 95.

Write a memo to your instructor listing the commands you used and describing the results of each command. Attach a copy of your printouts from steps 11 and 13.

Exercise 7-2: Creating a Directory Tree Structure with NETADMIN

In this exercise you use the NETADMIN menu utility to work with the Directory tree structure. Your instructor has created an NDS Directory tree for your network environment. To create a place for you to work with the Directory tree, your instructor has created Organizational Units named ##Admin, where ## is a two-digit number that identifies you or the group that you belong to. Your instructor will tell you your two-digit number.

1. Log into your network using your normal login procedure.
2. Open a DOS prompt window.
3. Change directories to the G: drive (or other network drive as specified by your instructor).
4. At the DOS prompt, type **NETADMIN** and then press [Enter] to start the NETADMIN menu utility.
5. Choose **Manage Objects** in the NETADMIN main menu. Use the browser window that is displayed to change context to the NWTC Organization, and then to the ##Admin Organizational Unit.
6. Press **[Insert]**, and then choose **Organizational Unit** from the list of object types (called classes). Name the Organizational Unit **NextLevelDown**, and then press **[Esc]**. When you are asked if you want to create another object, answer **No**.
7. Highlight the Organizational Unit **NextLevelDown**. Press **[F10]** to display the Actions menu.
    a. Choose **View or Edit Properties** to see the property values for the object. Press **[Esc]** to return to the Actions menu.
    b. Choose **Rename** to rename the object. Use the new name **OneLevelDown**. Do not save the old name. Press **[Esc]** to return to the Actions menu.
    c. Press **[Esc]** to return to the Main menu.
8. You can either use the Delete option on the Actions menu or simply press **[Delete]** to delete objects. To delete the OneLevelDown Organizational Unit object, highlight the object name and then press **[Delete]**. Answer **Yes** to confirm the deletion.
9. Press **[Esc]** to exit NETADMIN and then choose **Yes** to confirm the exiting.
10. Close the DOS prompt window and return to Windows 95.

Write a memo to your instructor describing your use of NETADMIN and the results you recorded above.

Exercise 7-3: Viewing Directory Tree Partitions with PARTMGR

In this exercise you use the PARTMGR menu utility to work with the NDS partitions.

1. Log into your network using your normal login procedure.
2. Open a DOS prompt window.
3. Change directories to the G: drive (or other network drive as specified by your instructor).
4. At the DOS prompt, type **PARTMGR** to start the PARTMGR menu utility.
5. Choose **Change Context** in the NETADMIN main menu. Use the browser to move to the **[Root]** level.

   List the name of each partition shown:

   Name of Partition

   ____

   ____

   ____

   ____

   ____

6. Highlight a partition, and then press **[F10]**. Choose **View/Edit replicas** in the Partition Management menu.

   List the name and type of each replica shown:

Name of Replica	Type

7. Highlight a partition, and then press **[F10]** to see the replica operations that are available to you. List the available options:

   Name of Option

   ____

   ____

   ____

   ____

   ____

8. Press **[Esc]** as many times as necessary to back out of the menus and exit PARTMGR. Answer **Yes** to confirm exiting PARTMGR.
9. Close the DOS prompt window and return to Windows 95.

Write a memo to your instructor describing your use of PARTMGR and the results you recorded above.

Exercise 7-4: Viewing Directory Tree Information with DSMERGE

This exercise requires access to a NetWare 4.1 server console.

In this exercise you use the DSMERGE NLM utility to work with the NDS Directory tree.

1. At the NetWare server console prompt, type **LOAD DSMERGE** and then press **[Enter]** to start the DSMERGE NLM utility.
2. Choose **Check servers in this tree** in the DSMERGE main menu.

   List the name of each server shown:

   Name of Server

   ____

   ____

   ____

   ____

3. Choose **Check time synchronization** in the DSMERGE main menu. In the space below, summarize the time synchronization in the network as described by DSMERGE.

4. Choose **Exit** in the DSMERGE main menu to unload the DSMERGE utility.

Write a memo to your instructor describing your use of DSMERGE and the results you recorded above.

Exercises

Case 7-1: Creating the Jefferson County Courthouse Directory Tree Organizational Structure

In Chapter 4, you designed an NDS Directory tree for the Jefferson County Courthouse. The network administrator has installed the NetWare 4.1 Server and is ready to finish creating the Directory tree. Your job is to put your Directory tree plan into practice.

Because you don't have the Jefferson County Courthouse network available, you'll use DS Standard to create the Jefferson County Courthouse Directory tree. After discussing your design with the Courthouse personnel, you agreed upon the Directory tree design shown in Figure 7-49.

Figure 7-49

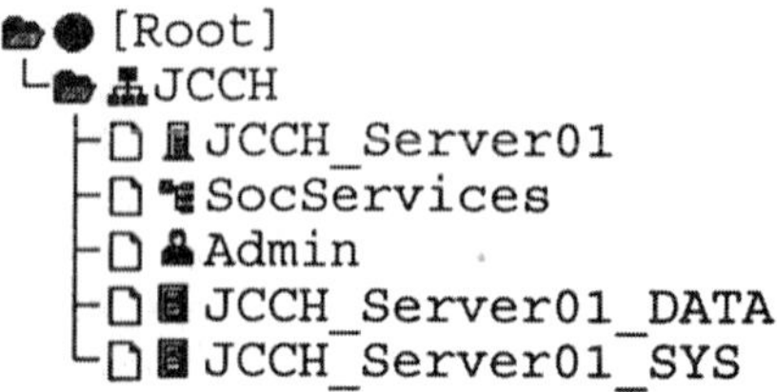

1. Launch DS Standard.
2. Open the Jefferson County Courthouse view. This view shows the courthouse network after installation of the NetWare 4.1 server. The objects that would normally be created during a NetWare 4.1 installation—the NetWare server, its associated volumes, and the Admin user—are included in the view.
3. Create the rest of the Jefferson County Courthouse Directory tree structure as shown in Figure 7-49.
4. Print a copy of your completed Directory tree.
5. Write a memo to your instructor stating that you have completed this assignment. Attach a copy of your printed Directory tree. Turn in your memo and a copy of your DS Standard data disk.

Case 7-2: Creating the J. Q. Adams Corporation Directory Tree Organizational Structure

In Chapter 4, you designed an NDS Directory tree for the J. Q. Adams Corporation. The network administrator has installed its two NetWare 4.1 Servers and is ready to finish creating the Directory tree. Your job is to put your Directory tree plan into practice.

Because you don't have the J. Q. Adams network available, you'll use DS Standard to create the J. Q. Adams Directory tree. After discussing your design with J. Q. Adams management personnel, you agreed upon the Directory tree design shown in Figure 7-50. Notice that Figure 7-50 shows a third NetWare server: JQA_Server03 is a NetWare 3.12 server that will be used in Production to help with quality control. It has two volumes: SYS: and DATA:. Because this is a NetWare 3.12 server, the JQA_Server03 NetWare Server object and the associated Volume objects do not exist in the current Directory tree structure and will need to be added.

1. Launch DS Standard.
2. Open the J. Q. Adams view. This view shows the J. Q. Adams network after installation of the NetWare 4.1 servers. The objects that would normally be created during a NetWare 4.1 installation—the NetWare servers, their associated volumes, and the Admin user—are included in the view.
3. Create the rest of the J. Q. Adams Directory tree structure as shown in Figure 7-50.
4. Print a copy of your completed Directory tree.

5. Write a memo to your instructor stating that you have completed this assignment. Attach a copy of your printed Directory tree. Turn in your memo and a copy of your DS Standard data disk.

Figure 7-50

```
[Root]
└JQAdams
  ├JQA_Server01
  ├FinServices
  │ ├Accting
  │ ├Finance
  │ └InfoSys
  ├JQA_Admin
  ├Production
  │ ├JQA_Server02
  │ ├JQA_Server03
  │ ├QC
  │ ├Team01
  │ ├Team02
  │ ├JQA_Server02_DATA
  │ ├JQA_Server02_SYS
  │ ├JQA_Server03_DATA
  │ └JQA_Server03_SYS
  ├Sales&Mrkting
  │ ├Mrkting
  │ └Sales
  ├Admin
  ├JQA_Server01_DATA
  └JQA_Server01_SYS
```

Project

NORTHWESTERN TECHNICAL COLLEGE

Now that Northwestern Technical College (NWTC) has completed the installation of NetWare 4.1 on the two new NetWare servers, Dave Johnson is ready to complete creating the NDS Directory tree organizational structure. He also needs to include the NetWare 3.12 Server and its SYS: volume in the Directory tree. The NWTC Directory tree currently appears as shown in Figure 7-51.

Figure 7-51

```
[Root]
└NWTC
  ├NWTC_Server01
  ├NWTC_CompLabs
  │ ├NWTC_Server02
  │ ├NWTC_Server02_DATA
  │ └NWTC_Server02_SYS
  ├Admin
  ├NWTC_Server01_DATA
  └NWTC_Server01_SYS
```

Although the NetWare Server object names of NWTC_Server01 and NWTC_Server02 are used in Figure 7-51 (the NetWare 3.12 server will be named NWTC_Server03), your instructor may have different names for these servers. In that case, your instructor will tell you what server names you will see in your Directory tree.

Notice that NWTC_Server01 and its associated volumes have been placed in the NWTC Organization container, along with the User object Admin. The NetWare server NWTC_Server02 and its associated volumes have been installed in the NWTC_CompLabs Organizational Unit, which represents the computer laboratories at NWTC.

If your computer lab setup is using only one NetWare 4.1 server, then all objects labeled as NWTC_Server02 in Figure 7-51 will appear in your tree as Alias objects, which are objects that appear as leaf objects in a container but actually point to or reference a leaf object in another container. (Similarly, the objects for the NetWare 3.12 server will have to be Alias objects in your Directory tree if your lab is not using a NetWare 3.12 server.) A version of the NWTC Directory tree using Alias objects is shown in Figure 7-52.

Figure 7-52

```
[Root]
└ NWTC
  ├ NWTC_Server01
  ├ NWTC_CompLabs
  │ ├ NWTC_Server02
  │ ├ NWTC_Server02_DATA
  │ └ NWTC_Server02_SYS
  ├ Admin
  ├ NWTC_Server01_DATA
  └ NWTC_Server01_SYS
```

Because these exercises require a shared NetWare server or servers, the NWTC Directory tree that has been created in your network computer lab differs from what you would expect to see in a standard network environment. To create a place for you to work with the Directory tree, your instructor has created Organization objects for each user or user group named ##NWTC and ##PRACTICE, where ## is a two-digit number that identifies you or the group that you belong to. Your instructor will tell you your two-digit number. Your instructor has also created a User object, ##Admin, that represents a network administrator, but your ability to administer the Directory tree is limited to your Organizational objects Unit ##NWTC and ##PRACTICE and container objects you create below them in the Directory tree. This means that you can create and manage a portion of the Directory tree, but only that portion. Your instructor retains full administrator rights to the entire Directory tree.

In the exercises that follow, you add container and leaf objects to your portion of the Directory tree.

Project 7-1: Simulating the Directory Tree After Installation

Now that NetWare has been installed on the campus file server and the user workstations are able to boot up and attach to the network, your next job is to create the Directory tree structure that can support the processing needs of the organization. To perform this task, you recently had a meeting with Dave Johnson and together you have finalized the Directory tree structure you were working on in Chapter 4. Although the final design shown in Figure 7-53 may not exactly match your original design, it has everyone's approval and will meet the processing needs of the campus. The design is organized by computer lab, faculty, and administration. Each department has an Organizational Unit to hold the associated leaf objects. Now Dave wants you to create the actual Directory tree structure in NDS.

Figure 7-53

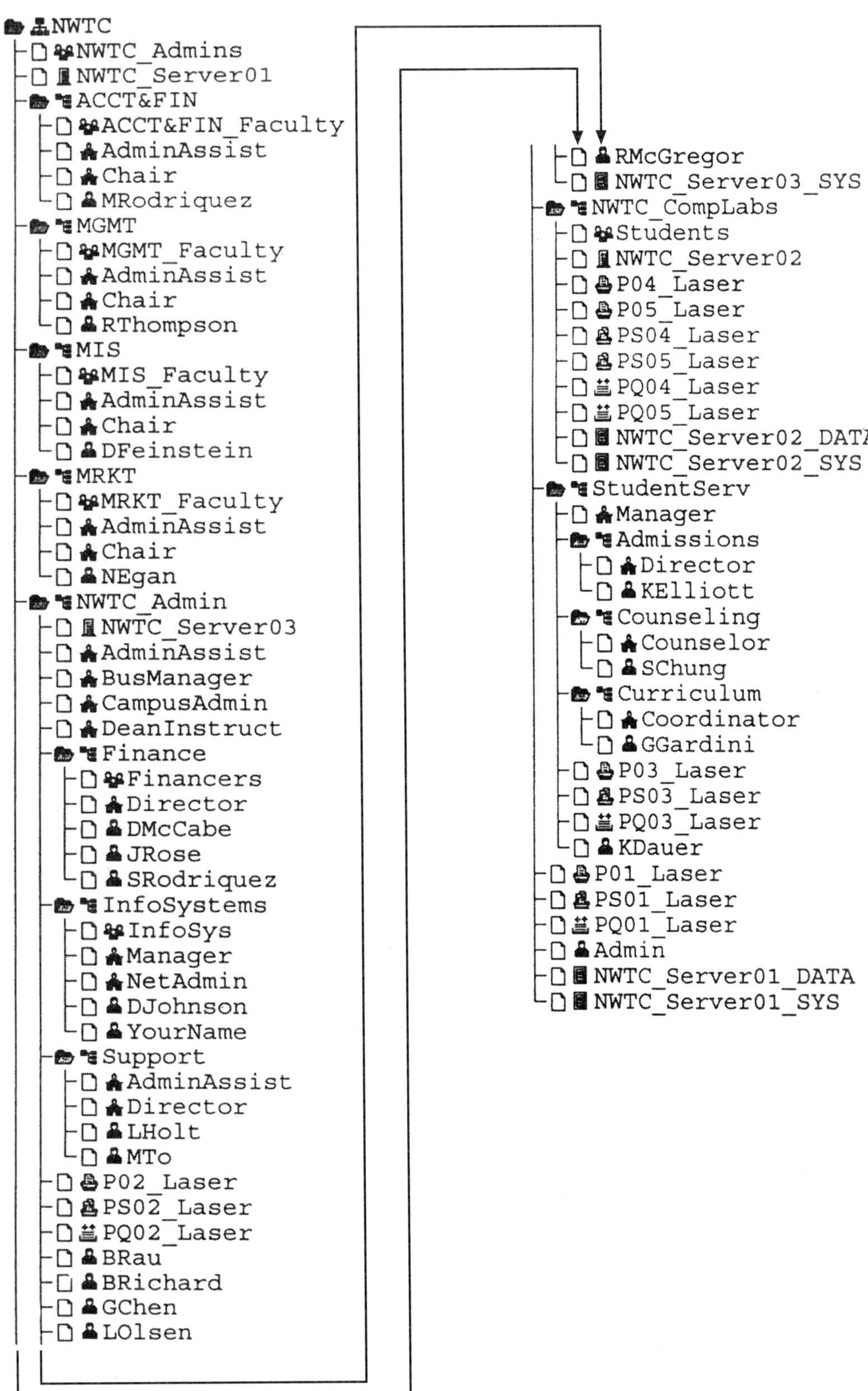
NWTC
NWTC_Admins
NWTC_Server01
ACCT&FIN
ACCT&FIN_Faculty
AdminAssist
Chair
MRodriquez
MGMT
MGMT_Faculty
AdminAssist
Chair
RThompson
MIS
MIS_Faculty
AdminAssist
Chair
DFeinstein
MRKT
MRKT_Faculty
AdminAssist
Chair
NEgan
NWTC_Admin
NWTC_Server03
AdminAssist
BusManager
CampusAdmin
DeanInstruct
Finance
Financers
Director
DMcCabe
JRose
SRodriquez
InfoSystems
InfoSys
Manager
NetAdmin
DJohnson
YourName
Support
AdminAssist
Director
LHolt
MTo
P02_Laser
PS02_Laser
PQ02_Laser
BRau
BRichard
GChen
LOlsen
RMcGregor
NWTC_Server03_SYS
NWTC_CompLabs
Students
NWTC_Server02
P04_Laser
P05_Laser
PS04_Laser
PS05_Laser
PQ04_Laser
PQ05_Laser
NWTC_Server02_DATA
NWTC_Server02_SYS
StudentServ
Manager
Admissions
Director
KElliott
Counseling
Counselor
SChung
Curriculum
Coordinator
GGardini
P03_Laser
PS03_Laser
PQ03_Laser
KDauer
P01_Laser
PS01_Laser
PQ01_Laser
Admin
NWTC_Server01_DATA
NWTC_Server01_SYS

First, create the portions of the Directory tree that would have been created in a normal NetWare 4.1 installation process:

1. In a normal NetWare installation, the container objects with NetWare 4.1 servers in them would be created. This means that the ##NWTC Organization object and the NWTC_CompLabs Organizational Unit object would have been created. Because your instructor has already created the ##NWTC Organizational Unit object, you need to create only an NWTC_CompLabs Organizational Unit object under it.
2. In a normal NetWare installation, the leaf objects for each NetWare 4.1 server and the volumes on the server would be created. This means that NetWare Server objects ##NWTC_Server01 and ##NWTC_Server02 and their associated Volume objects would have been created. Because these objects actually refer to NWTC_Server01 and NWTC_Server02 and their respective volumes, you need to use Alias objects to create your objects. To do this, choose the Alias object when you start to create the leaf object, and then choose the type of object you are referencing and complete the steps required by the dialog box. If you are working with only one NetWare 4.1 server, your ##NWTC_Server02 NetWare server object and its associated volumes should also be aliases of NWTC_Server01 and its volumes.

Using Alias objects, create the NetWare Server objects ##NWTC_Server01 and ##NWTC_Server02 and their associated Volume objects in the appropriate container objects.

Project 7-2: Completing the Directory Tree Organizational Structure

Now you are ready to create the remaining parts of the Directory tree structure shown in Figure 7-53.

1. Create an NWTC_Admin Organizational Unit object, and under it create Finance, InfoSystems, and Support Organizational Unit objects.
2. Create a StudentServ Organizational Unit object.
3. Create the Organizational Unit objects for the four academic departments: ACCT&FIN for the Accounting and Finance Department, MGMT for the Management Department, MIS for the Management Information Systems Department, and MRKT for the Marketing Department.

Project 7-3: Adding the NetWare 3.12 Server and Volumes

Now you are ready to add the NetWare 3.12 server ##NTWC_Server03 and its SYS: volume, shown in Figure 7-53, to the Directory tree. Because these objects actually refer to the NetWare 3.12 Server NWTC_Server03 and its volume, you again need to use Alias objects to create your objects. If there is no NetWare 3.12 server in your network, your aliases should reference NWTC_Server01 and the NWTC_Server01_SYS volume.

1. Using Alias objects, create the NetWare Server object ##NWTC_Server03 and the associated SYS:Volume object.

Project 7-4: Working with Properties

1. Add the following information about the Computer Lab into the property pages of the NWTC_CompLabs Organizational Unit object:

Phone number:	999-888-7777
Street Address:	123 Technical Way, Room CL01
City:	Portland
State:	OR
ZIP:	99999

2. Check the statistics of the SYS: volume on ##NWTC_Server01. Write a memo to your instructor reporting on this volume. In your memo include this information:

   Total disk space and amount available on volume
   Block size
   Whether or not block suballocation is in effect
   Whether or not data compression is in effect
   Number of compressed files, compressed size, and average compression ratio
   Which name spaces are loaded

Project 7-5: Working with Partitions

Create new partitions for your portion of the Directory tree to reflect the partitions that would have been created during a normal NetWare installation.

1. In a normal NetWare installation, a partition containing the [Root] would have been created when the NetWare server NWTC_Server01 was installed. Simulate this partition by creating a partition starting at the ##NWTC Organization object.
2. In a normal NetWare installation, a partition starting at the NWTC_CompLabs Organizational Unit would have been created when the NetWare server NWTC_Server02 was installed. Simulate this partition by creating a partition starting at your NWTC_CompLabs Organizational Unit object.

CHAPTER EIGHT

CREATING THE NETWORK FILE SYSTEM

Once the file server installation is complete, it's time to set up the network file system. To perform this important task, you need to understand the NetWare commands and utilities that are used to create and maintain the NetWare file system. In Chapter 5 you were introduced to several NetWare commands that affect the directory structure: NDIR, NCOPY, and RENDIR. In this chapter you will acquire experience with some additional NetWare commands and utilities. You learned about the six basic NetWare command groups: command line utilities, menu utilities, graphical utilities, supervisor utilities, console commands, and NetWare Loadable Modules (NLMs) in Chapter 7.

The information in this chapter is divided into three major sections: directory management, drive pointers, and file management. In the directory management section you will learn about applying certain DOS and Windows 95 commands that you are already familiar with to the NetWare file system to create the network directory structure. In the drive pointer section, you will learn about using the MAP command, the NETUSER utility, and the Windows 95 Explorer with the NetWare Provider for Windows 95 extensions (included in NetWare Client 32) with network drive pointers in order to facilitate information access in your file system. The drive pointers section also contains ideas on how to plan the drive pointer usage in your network system. In the file management section you will learn about NetWare command line utilities, menu utilities, and graphical utilities that help you manage the files on your NetWare servers.

AFTER READING THIS CHAPTER AND COMPLETING THE EXERCISES YOU WILL BE ABLE TO:

- CREATE A NETWORK FILE SYSTEM.
- DESCRIBE THE USE OF NETWORK AND SEARCH DRIVE POINTERS.
- ESTABLISH A DRIVE POINTER USAGE PLAN FOR YOUR NETWORK SYSTEM.
- USE THE MAP, AND NETUSER NETWARE UTILITIES AND THE WINDOWS 95 EXPLORER TO CREATE DRIVE POINTERS TO DIRECTORIES WITHIN A FILE SYSTEM.
- USE NETWARE ADMINISTRATOR TO CREATE A DIRECTORY MAP OBJECT.
- USE NETWARE UTILITIES TO WORK WITH FILES AND DIRECTORIES IN THE NETWARE FILE SYSTEM.
- SALVAGE AND PURGE DELETED FILES.

DIRECTORY MANAGEMENT

In Chapter 5, you learned how to design the server's file system using volumes, directories, and subdirectories. In this section you will learn how to apply DOS, NetWare, and Windows 95 commands when creating and maintaining directories and subdirectories for your server. Because setting up and maintaining the file system is one of the important jobs you need to perform as a network administrator, you need to be familiar with the NetWare commands and menu utilities that enable you to perform these functions.

In this chapter, we'll continue watching the network administrator for CBE Labs as he creates the new CBE Labs network. In Chapter 5, the directory structure for each volume in the CBE Labs network was planned. In this section, the directory structures will actually be created.

Recall that CBE Labs has two NetWare 4.1 servers, CONSTELLATION and SARATOGA, and one NetWare 3.12 server, RANGER. CONSTELLATION and SARATOGA each have a SYS: and DATA: volume, but RANGER has only a SYS: volume. Because CD-ROMs provide their own directory structures, the network administrator doesn't need to worry about CD-ROM directory structures, only those for volumes on hard disks.

At CBE Labs, CONSTELLATION is used by the administration and publishing workgroups. This results in the CONSTELLATION_SYS volume storing a major set of application software, including the company's e-mail, fax, and Internet software. Additionally, CONSTELLATION_SYS stores a shared copy of the company's Windows 95 compatible desktop publishing software, PagePublisher. CBE Labs also keeps a copy of the user workstations' software package WinOffice on the volume so that installation of the software onto the users' PCs can be done from the network instead of disks.

The CONSTELLATION_DATA volume is used to store administration and publishing data. A SHARED directory is maintained at the root level so that users can easily transfer files to each other, and SHARED subdirectories are maintained for each administration section for file sharing between the administration groups (the publishing workgroup has no access to these directories). Finally, private personal directories are maintained for each user in the administration and publishing workgroups under the USERS directory.

SARATOGA is used by the Lab workgroups. Therefore the SARATOGA_SYS volume stores the application software needed and shared by the Lab workgroups, including an SQL Database Management System program and a program named Analyzer that is used to evaluate hardware and software. The SARATOGA_DATA volume is used to store Lab workgroup test and evaluation data and reports. As on CONSTELLATION_DATA, a SHARED directory is maintained at the root level so that users can easily transfer files to each other, and SHARED subdirectories are maintained for each Lab workgroup for file sharing between the groups. Additionally, a REPORTS subdirectory holds the final Lab reports; this directory can be accessed by everyone at CBE Labs. For example, the publishing group picks up copies of reports from this directory for inclusion in *The C/B/E NetWorker.* And as on CONSTELLATION_DATA, private personal directories are maintained for each user in the Labs workgroups under a USERS directory.

RANGER, the NetWare 3.12 server, is used by the Finance department to run the legacy DOS-based accounting system. The RANGER_SYS volume contains the program files in the APPS\DOSACCT subdirectory, and the DATA directory holds the subdirectories for the data files for the program. There is no need for a SHARED directory or user directories on RANGER_SYS.

The Volume Design Forms for each volume in the CBE Labs network are shown in Figures 5-15 and 5-18 through 5-21. For reference the Volume Design Forms for the CONSTELLATION_SYS and CONSTELLATION_DATA volumes are shown in Figures 8-1 and 8-2.

Figure 8-1 The CONSTELLATION_SYS: volume

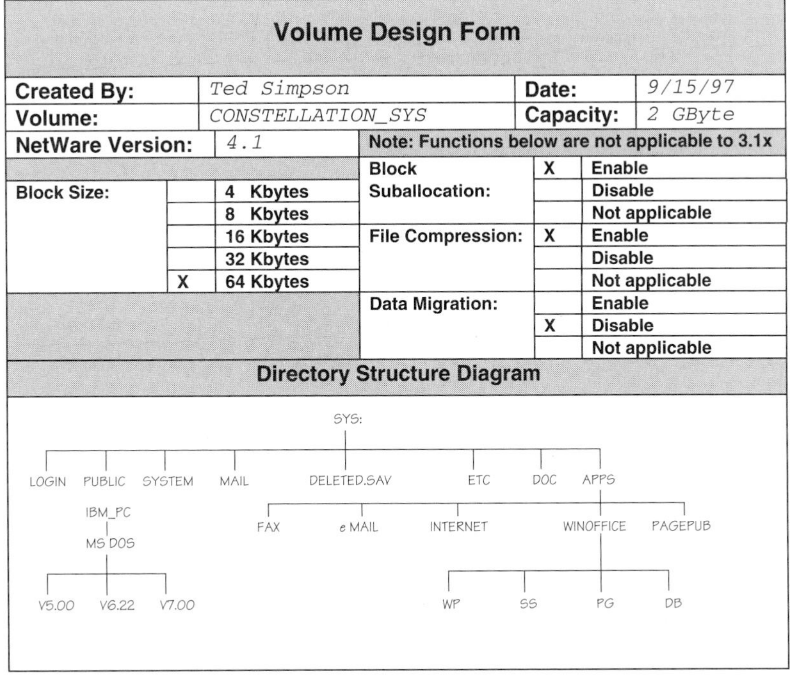

Volume Design Form			
Created By:	Ted Simpson	Date:	9/15/97
Volume:	CONSTELLATION_SYS	Capacity:	2 GByte
NetWare Version:	4.1	Note: Functions below are not applicable to 3.1x	

Block Size:				
	4 Kbytes	Block Suballocation:	X	Enable
	8 Kbytes			Disable
	16 Kbytes			Not applicable
	32 Kbytes	File Compression:	X	Enable
X	64 Kbytes			Disable
				Not applicable
		Data Migration:		Enable
			X	Disable
				Not applicable

Directory Structure Diagram

Figure 8-2 The CONSTELLATION_DATA: volume

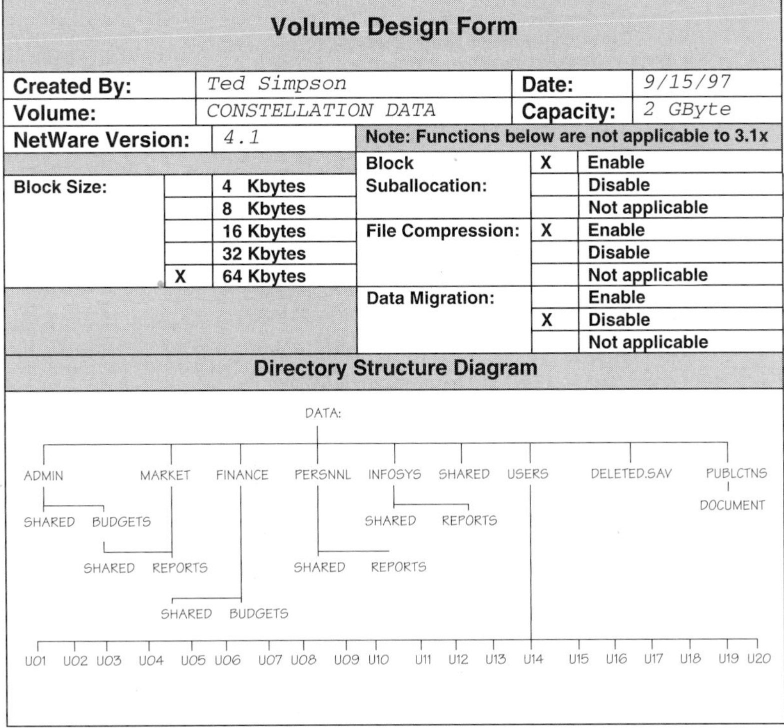

Volume Design Form			
Created By:	Ted Simpson	Date:	9/15/97
Volume:	CONSTELLATION DATA	Capacity:	2 GByte
NetWare Version:	4.1	Note: Functions below are not applicable to 3.1x	

Block Size:				
	4 Kbytes	Block Suballocation:	X	Enable
	8 Kbytes			Disable
	16 Kbytes			Not applicable
	32 Kbytes	File Compression:	X	Enable
X	64 Kbytes			Disable
				Not applicable
		Data Migration:		Enable
			X	Disable
				Not applicable

Directory Structure Diagram

DOS Commands

Many DOS commands you already use regularly can also be used to manipulate directories and files in NetWare volumes. DOS commands work with NetWare volumes through the drive letter that is assigned to that volume. When your workstation first loads the NetWare driver and client, for example, the requester provides DOS with a drive letter (drive G in this text, but other letters can be used and drive F is common) that is assigned to the SYS:LOGIN directory. This enables DOS to load and run the LOGIN.EXE program and provide you with access to the file server. Once you have logged into the network, the network drive letter is reassigned by default to the root of the SYS: volume. That is, most DOS commands treat network drives just like another local hard disk. DOS commands such as FORMAT, CHKDSK, and SCANDISK, however, do not work on a network drive letter because these commands are designed to access and control a local disk drive directly and have no direct control of a NetWare volume.

Although you can use the COPY, XCOPY, and DIR commands to copy and view file information, these commands do not work with complete NetWare paths because they do not recognize volume and file server names. In addition, these DOS commands yield less information and are less efficient than the corresponding NetWare command line utilities, which are designed to take advantage of enhanced NetWare capabilities. Use the NetWare command line utilities discussed in the next section rather than the standard DOS commands whenever you work with files stored in NetWare volumes.

The MD (Make Directory) Command

The DOS MD or Make Directory command, which can also be written as MKDIR, is used to create directories and subdirectories. You can use this command to create the necessary directory structure on a NetWare volume. For example, to create a directory named PROGRAMS, you would use the command

```
MD PROGRAMS
```

The RD command only deletes empty directories. You can use the DELTREE command to remove directories that are not empty.

The RD (Remove Directory) Command

The DOS RD or Remove Directory command, which can also be written as RMDIR, is used to delete directories and subdirectories. You can use this command when it necessary to remove a directory or subdirectory from a volume. For example, to delete the PROGRAMS subdirectory, you would use the command

```
RD PROGRAMS
```

The CD (Change Directory) Command

The DOS CD or Change Directory command is used to switch between directories and subdirectories. The CD command is enhanced by the NetWare shell, giving you more features when you access directories in NetWare volumes. With NetWare, for example, you can use the CD command to change to another volume or even switch your default path to another file server by entering the complete NetWare path. From your DOS experience you probably know how to use the CD command to move up one directory level on a local drive. When you use the CD command on a network drive letter, however, you can use multiple dots to move up more than one layer.

For example, the network administrator at CBE Labs needs to create the new NetWare directory structure on the CONSTELLATION_SYS volume, as shown in Figure 8-1. Figure 8-3 shows the use of the MD command to create the APPS directory and the use of the CD command to change to the APPS directory. In the APPS directory, the DOS DIR command is then used to list the files in the directory. Because this is a new directory, the output from the two commands shows no file, which is what you would expect to see.

Figure 8-3

The MD and CD commands

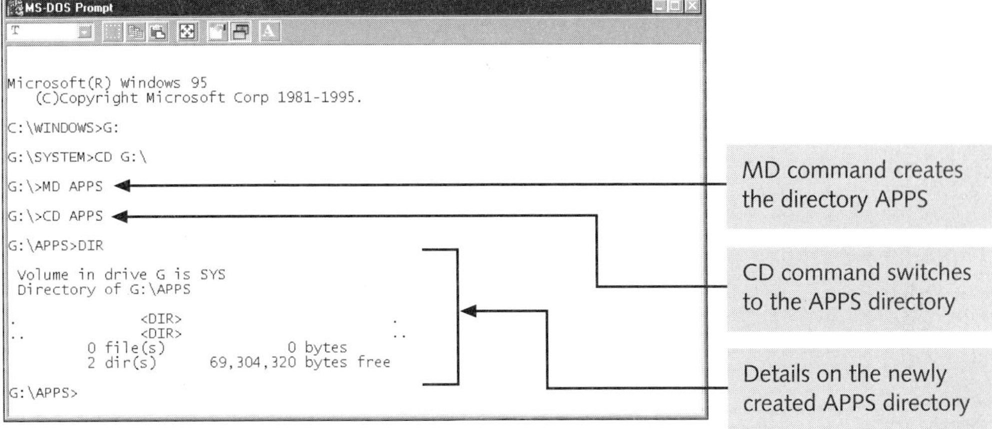

WINDOWS 95 COMMANDS

In Windows 95, directories and subdirectories are also called **folders**. Folders are created by using the File | New | Folder command.

For example, the CBE Labs network administrator needs to create the PAGEPUB subdirectory to the APPS directory.

To create the PAGEPUB subdirectory, follow these steps:

1. Click **Start | Programs | Windows Explorer** to launch Explorer. If necessary, click the **Maximize** button 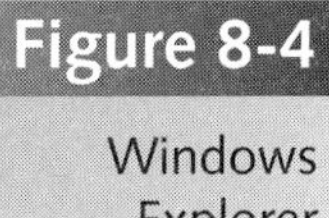 to expand the Explorer window to a full screen window. The Explorer screen appears as shown in Figure 8-4.

Figure 8-4

Windows Explorer

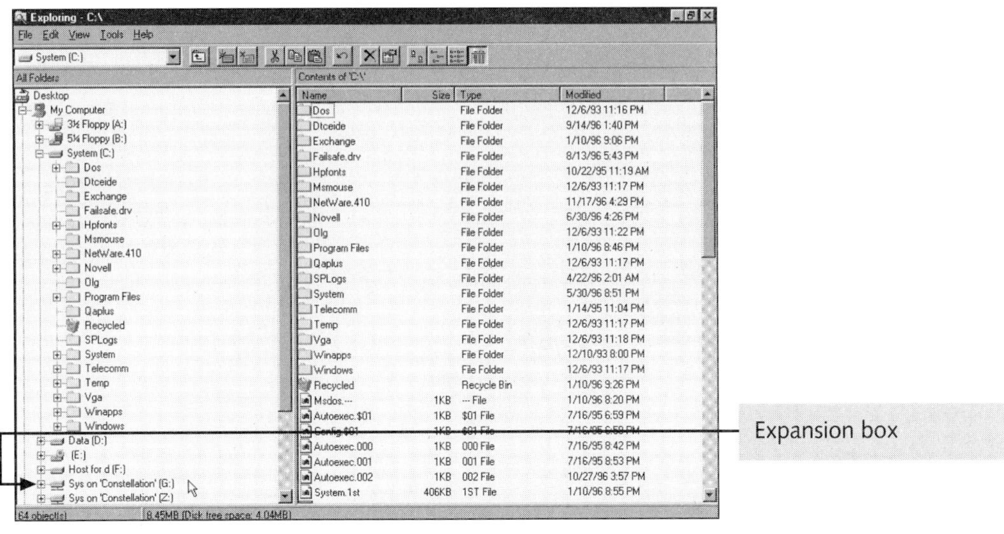

2. Click the **expansion** box in front of the Sys on Constellation (G) drive to view the subdirectories of the CONSTELLATION_SYS volume, then click **Sys on Constellation (G)** to display the contents of the CONSTELLATION_SYS volume.
3. Click the **Apps** folder to display the contents of the CONSTELLATION_SYS\APPS directory.
4. Click **File | New | Folder** to create a new folder (subdirectory) in the Apps folder, as shown in Figure 8-5.

Figure 8-5

The Explorer File | New | Folder command

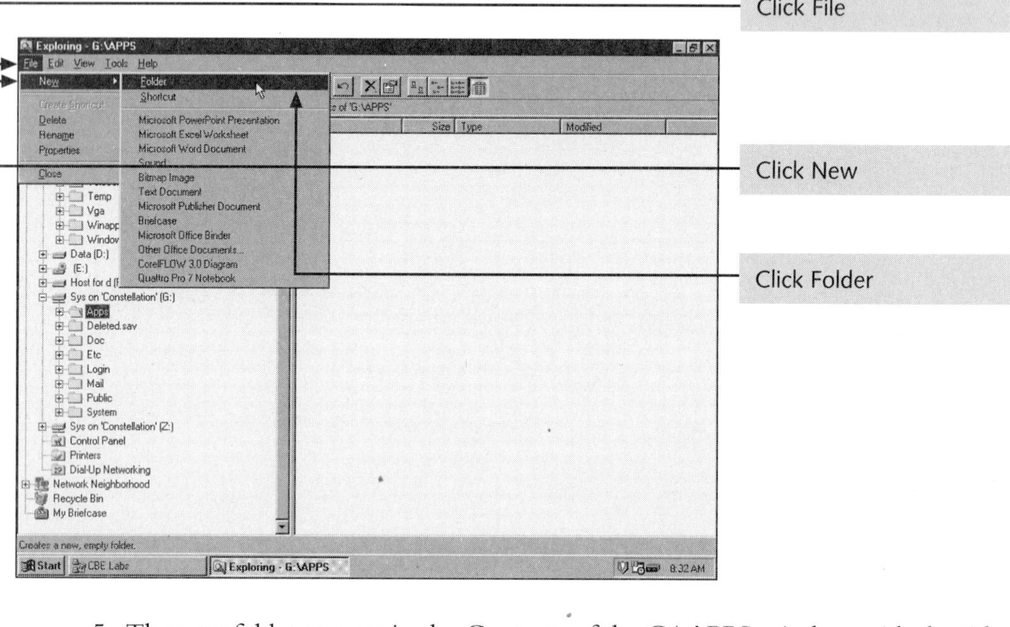

5. The new folder appears in the Contents of the G:\APPS window with the title Fldr in edit mode so that you can edit the folder name, as shown in Figure 8-6. The folder has a box around the folder name, and the folder name is highlighted indicating that the folder name can be edited.

Figure 8-6

Naming the new folder

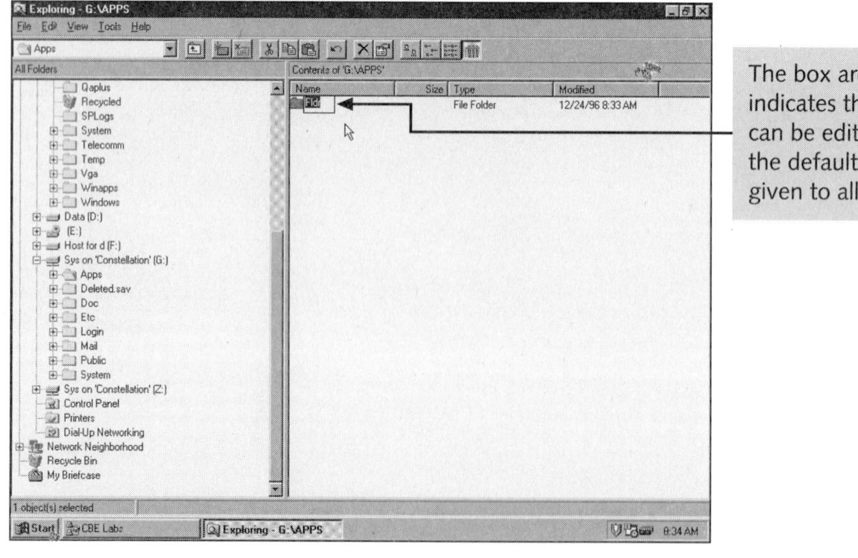

The box around "Fldr" indicates that the name can be edited; "Fldr" is the default name initially given to all new folders

6. Edit the folder name to read **PAGEPUB** and then press **[Enter]**. The new folder is named.
7. Click the **Close button** [X] to close Windows Explorer.

NetWare Administrator Commands

Directories and subdirectories can also be created by using the NetWare Administrator utility. Although not considered to be one of the NDS Directory tree objects, directories can be created for Volume objects and other directories.

To view the directory structure for a Volume object, you follow these steps:

- Double-click the Volume object icon when the directories are not displayed.

then

- Double-click each Directory icon to display the subdirectories (and files) in that directory. Repeat this step on each subdirectory until the entire directory tree is displayed.

To create a directory, you can follow these steps:

- Click the Volume or directory that will contain the directory; then press [Insert].

or

Click the Volume or directory that will contain the directory, click Object on the menu bar, and then click Create.

or

Right-click the Volume or directory that will contain the directory; then click Create on the QuickMenu.

then

- In the Create Directory dialog box, type the name of the directory; then click the Create button.

For example, the CBE Labs network administrator has created the first level of directories for the DATA volume and now needs to create the subdirectories for the FINANCE directory. The first subdirectory he will create is the SHARED subdirectory.

To create the SHARED subdirectory, follow these steps:

1. Launch the NetWare Administrator. If necessary, double-click each container object to display all leaf objects.
2. Double-click the **CONSTELLATION_DATA Volume** object to display the first level directory structure.
3. Click the **FINANCE directory** icon, click **Object**, and then click **Create**. The Create Directory dialog box is displayed, as shown in Figure 8-7.

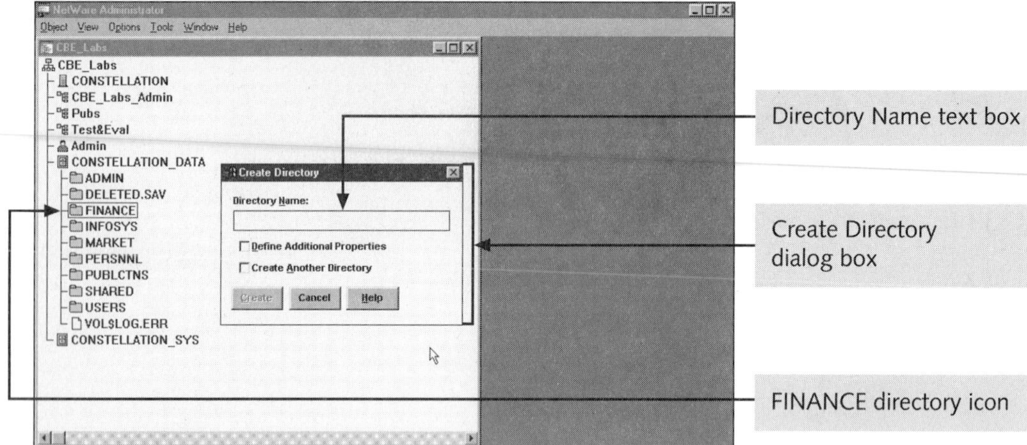

Figure 8-7 The Create Directory dialog box

4. Type **SHARED** in the Directory Name text box and then click the **Create** button. The SHARED subdirectory is created. If necessary, double-click the FINANCE directory icon to display the new directory.

CREATING THE DIRECTORY STRUCTURE

Using the commands discussed above, the CBE Labs network administrator can now create the rest of the directories and subdirectories needed in the directory structures on each volume. Note that even though Figure 8-2 shows subdirectories for each user, they are not created at this time. The user home directories are created when the User object is created for each user, which you will learn how to do in Chapter 9. Figure 8-8 shows the completed directory structure for the CONSTELLATION_SYS: volume in the Windows 95 Explorer program.

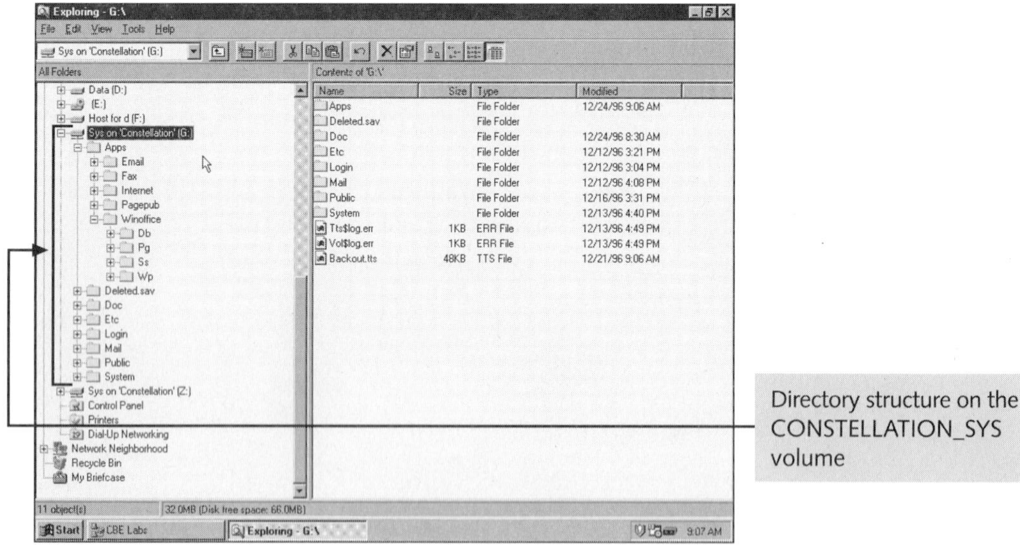

Figure 8-8 The CONSTELLATION_SYS directory structure

Figure 8-9 shows the completed directory structure for the CONSTELLATION_DATA: volume as displayed by NetWare Administrator graphics utility.

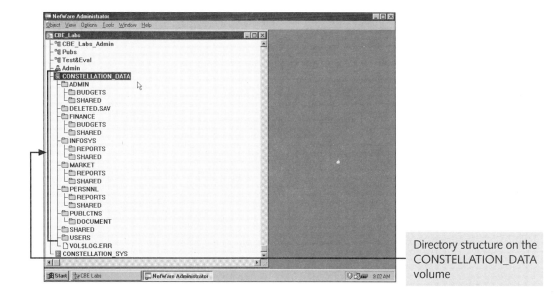

Figure 8-9 The CONSTELLATION_DATA directory structure

DRIVE POINTERS

In both NetWare and DOS environments, drive pointers play an important role in the accessing of files located on different devices and directories. A **drive pointer** is a letter of the alphabet that is used to reference storage areas in the file system. By default, DOS reserves the first five drive pointers (A–E) for storage devices on the local workstation. These letters are therefore often referred to as **local drive pointers**. Letters A and B are reserved for floppy disk drives, C and D are normally used for hard disks, and E is often reserved for a CD-ROM or other external storage device. When using a local drive pointer, you can use the DOS CD command to change the pointer to access any directory on that drive.

In a NetWare environment, the network administrator is responsible for establishing the drive pointers to reference software and data locations within the directory structure. These drive pointers must be assigned properly so that DOS and other non-NetWare applications can access network files and directories as if they were on a local hard disk. In this section you will learn about the various types of drive pointers and their use, along with how to assign drive pointers by using NetWare's MAP command line utility, the NETUSER menu utility, and the Windows 95 Explorer.

NETWORK DRIVE POINTERS

The NetWare Client 32 client software works with DOS to share drive pointers, eliminating the need to set aside separate drive pointers for NetWare uses. When the shell first starts, the drive pointer to be assigned to the SYS:LOGIN directory of the attached file server is specified in the FIRST NETWORK DRIVE parameter set in Client 32, as described in Chapter 6.

The NetWare DOS Requester client (VLMs) used with NetWare 3.1x and NetWare 4.x worked the same way but used the NET.CFG file to store the FIRST NETWORK DRIVE information. Additionally, in DOS and Windows 3.1x workstations, a LAST DRIVE = Z statement had to be added to the CONFIG.SYS file.

NetWare drive pointers can be one of three types: regular, root, or search. Regular and root drive pointers are usually assigned to directories containing data files; search drive pointers are assigned to network software directories.

Regular Drive Pointers

A **regular drive pointer** is assigned to a directory path and shows all directories and subdirectories leading to the storage area. A regular drive pointer should be assigned to each volume as well as to commonly used directories. This enables application software packages that cannot use NetWare complete paths to access the data in any volume.

Root Drive Pointers

A **root drive pointer** appears to the user or application as if the default path is at the root of the drive or volume. Figure 8-10 shows an example of two drive pointers, K and L. Notice that the K drive pointer is a regular pointer because it shows the entire path leading to the directory, whereas L is a root drive pointer that appears as if it were the first level in the directory structure. The advantage of the root drive pointer is that it prevents the mapping of the drive pointer from being changed by an application or DOS command to some other location in the directory structure. Root drive pointers are normally used to access user home directories along with shared data directories.

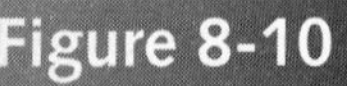

Regular and root drive pointers

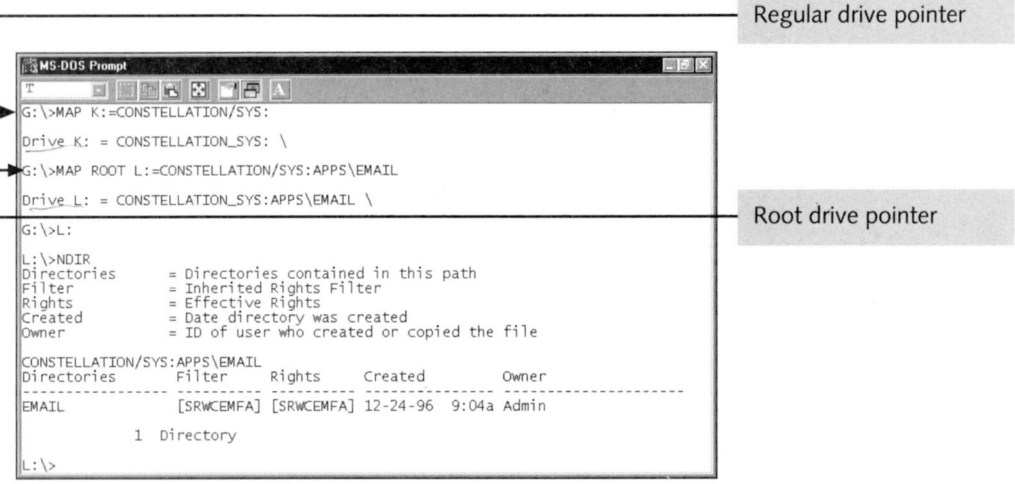

Search Drive Pointers

A **search drive pointer** is a regular or root drive pointer that has been added to the DOS path. The DOS path specifies a sequence of locations in which DOS and the NetWare shell will look for program files that are not in the current directory. Search drive pointers play a very important role in accessing the file system because they enable a network administrator to place data files in directories that are separate from the application software. This enables a user or application located in one directory path to access software and data located elsewhere in the directory structure. Search drive pointers should be assigned only to software directories that need to be accessed from other locations.

Windows 95 applications do not need to use search drives because the path to the windows application is provided in the application icon parameters. As a result, the more workstations that become Windows 95 environments, the less need there will be for NetWare search drives.

When you enter the command NDIR, for example, DOS first determines that the command is not one of its internal commands. DOS looks in the current directory for a program or batch file named NDIR. If none exists in the current directory, each search drive specified in the path will be searched, starting with S1, until either the NDIR program is found or the message "Bad command or filename" is displayed. You are able to run the NDIR command in addition to other NetWare commands from any directory in the file system because a search drive pointer is automatically assigned to the SYS:PUBLIC directory during the login process.

Search drives are assigned the letter S followed by a sequential number, from S1 to S16, and each search drive can point to only one directory location. Subdirectories of that directory location are not searched unless they are assigned to separate search drives. In addition to being assigned a sequence number, search drives are given a drive pointer; Z is assigned to S1, Y to S2, X to S3, and so on. Figure 8-11 illustrates one common division of drive pointers among local, regular, and search.

Figure 8-11

A drive pointer usage chart

Network and Search Drive Pointers

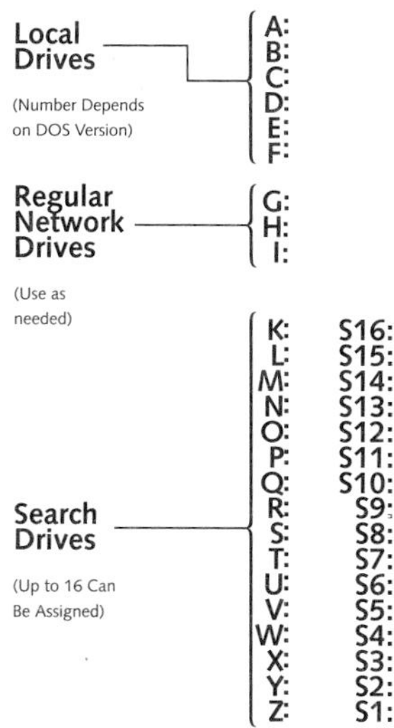

Using search drives is more efficient than using only the DOS path, because search drives enable the requester to work directly with the network, avoiding the need to go through DOS for each search. Search drives also make it easier for the network administrator to add, change, or remove directories from the search sequence by using the MAP, NETUSER, or Windows Explorer utilities rather than retyping the entire path statement as is necessary in the DOS environment.

Drive mappings are kept in a table stored in each workstation's RAM. Any changes made using the MAP or SESSION commands are effective only as long as the user is logged into the network. If you want certain drive pointers to be available each time you log in, you can place them in a login script command file. Because each workstation keeps track of its own drive pointers in memory, the same drive pointer can point to different directory locations in different workstations. For example, at CBE Labs one workstation can have the G drive pointer mapped to the SYS:PUBLIC directory and its S3 search drive mapped to SYS:APPS\WINOFFCE. Another workstation on the network might have the G drive pointer mapped to the DATA: volume and the S3 search drive mapped to the SYS:APPS\PAGEPUB directory.

The MAP command, NETUSER menu utility, and Windows Explorer with the NetWare Provider for Windows 95 extensions (included in NetWare Client 32) programs are the major tools used by a network administrator to establish and maintain drive pointers. MAP is a command line utility that can be used in login scripts as well as from the DOS prompt. NETUSER is a menu utility, which means it can easily manipulate drive pointer assignments. NetWare User Tools is a graphical utility that enables you to run it in the Windows environment. When used together with Client 32, the Windows 95 Explorer also enables you to create drive mappings. To become a network administrator, you need to know how to use these tools to maintain network drive pointers. Additionally, planning and implementing a proper set of network and search drive pointers are important steps in setting up a successful network environment. Later in this section you will read some tips and suggestions for organizing drive pointer usage for your file system.

THE MAP COMMAND

MAP is a versatile command line utility that is used by network administrators to create, modify, and delete both regular and search drive pointers. Although it is easier to manage a user's drive mappings by using the NetWare User Tool utility or the Windows 95 Explorer, the MAP command is used in login scripts to control a user's drive mappings at login. As you learned in Chapter 4, a login script is a file containing NetWare commands that the LOGIN.EXE program follows when a user successfully logs in to a file server. Because of the use of the MAP command in login scripts, you need to thoroughly understand this command. In this section you will learn the following required network administrator tasks by describing the purpose of each task, the syntax of the associated MAP command, and an example of its use.

- View current drive mappings
- Create regular drive pointers
- Create root drive pointers
- Change drive pointer mappings
- Create search drive pointers
- Remove a drive pointer
- Change a search drive path

The NetWare 4.1 MAP command is an enhancement of the command in NetWare 3.1x. If you are familiar with the NetWare 3.1x MAP command, you will already know most of this material.

The syntax of the MAP command is

```
MAP [P | NP] [option] drive:= [drive | path] [/?] [/VER]
```

Several parameters can be used with the MAP command. These are listed in Figure 8-12.

Figure 8-12

The MAP command parameters

Parameter	Use this parameter to
drive:	Specify the drive letter.
path	Specify the path to the directory being mapped. Include: NetWare server name Volume name Directory path on volume
/?	Access help about MAP. If this parameter is used, all others are ignored.
/VER	See the version number of the MAP command. If this parameter is used, all others are ignored.

As listed in Figure 8-13, several options can be used with MAP.

Figure 8-13

The MAP command options

Option	Use this option to
P	Map to a physical volume. This must be the first or second parameter listed.
NP	Not display a prompt before overwriting local or search drive mappings. This must be the first or second parameter listed.
C	Change the type of drive mapping from regular to search or search to regular.
DEL	Delete the drive mapping.
INS	Insert an additional search drive mapping. You can also use the word INSERT.
NEXT	Use the next available drive letter for the mapping. You can also use the letter N.
ROOT	Create a root drive mapping. You can also use just the letter R.
W	Keep the master environment the same.

Viewing Current Drive Mappings

Typing the MAP command without any parameters displays all drive pointers and their assigned directory locations. Viewing drive mappings enables you to determine the regular and search drive letters that a workstation is using on a network along with the directory paths each drive pointer is assigned to. If a user is unable to access a software application or data file, you should use this command to check that the user's drive pointers are mapped to the correct locations in the directory structure.

For example, the results of a MAP command are shown in Figure 8-14. Notice that the drive mappings shown in the figure are divided into regular drive mappings followed by search drive mappings. Root drive pointers are designated by a backslash following the drive pointer's path. From this information you can determine the following:

- Drive pointers A through F are assigned to local disks and controlled by DOS.
- Drive G is a regular drive pointer assigned to the root of the CONSTELLATION_SYS volume.
- Drive pointer Z is designated as SEARCH1 and is assigned to the CONSTELLATION_SYS:PUBLIC directory.
- Drive Y is designated SEARCH2 and is assigned to the CONSTELLATION_SYS directory.
- Additional search drive mappings are picked up from the DOS PATH statement.

Figure 8-14

Viewing drive mappings

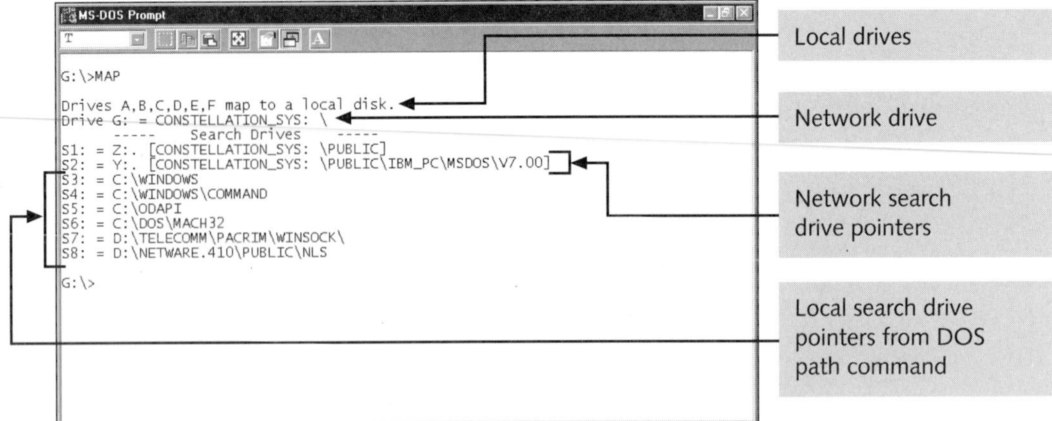

Drive pointer assignments are initially established for a user when the user logs in. The assignments are made with MAP commands contained in the login script files. You will learn about login scripts in Chapter 14. A default login script is used by the LOGIN program to establish the drive mappings if no other login scripts have been created.

Creating Regular Drive Pointers

You can use the MAP command to create regular drive pointers by assigning a NetWare path to a drive letter. Regular drive pointers are important for two reasons:

1. They make it easier to access data files because you do not need to supply a long path.
2. They enable applications and DOS commands that are not designed to work with complete NetWare paths to access files in multiple volumes or multiple file servers.

To use the map command to create a new drive letter, enter the command

```
MAP drive:=[path]
```

where *drive* can be any letter of alphabet (A–Z). You can replace the [path] with either a complete or partial NetWare path leading to the target directory. If you omit the path, the MAP command will assign the specified drive pointer to the current path. For example, if the CBE Labs network administrator wants to assign drive L to the DATA:MARKET directory on CONSTELLATION, he would use the following MAP command to specify a complete path:

```
G:\>MAP L:=CONSTELLATION/DATA:MARKET
```

If drive K is already assigned to the DATA: volume of CONSTELLATION, he can make K the active drive and then specify a partial path:

```
G:\>K:
K:\>MAP L:=\MARKET
```

You can also use an existing drive mapping as part of the path, as shown in the following command, which assigns the drive letter N to the DATA:MARKET\BUDGETS directory by using the L drive pointer, which is mapped to the DATA:MARKET directory as a starting point:

```
K:\>MAP N:=L:BUDGETS
```

Notice that there is no slash between the drive letter (L) and the path (BUDGETS). Placing a slash in the command would cause the system to search the root of the DATA: volume for the BUDGETS directory. Because no BUDGETS directory exists in the root of the DATA: volume, an error message indicating an invalid path would be displayed.

You can assign the current path to a different drive pointer by entering the MAP command without specifying a path following the equal sign. The following command makes K and O both point to the same location in the directory structure:

```
K:\MARKET\BUDGETS>MAP O:=
```

If you use a local drive pointer (A–F), the MAP command asks if you want to override the local pointer with a network path. If you answer yes, the local drive pointer will access the network path rather than the local drive. You can also use the NP parameter to override without the prompt appearing.

The command

```
MAP N [path]
```

can be used to assign the specified path to the next available drive letter, proceeding from F (or whatever drive is assigned using the FIRST NETWORK DRIVE parameter) through Z. You can also use the word NEXT instead of just N. This command is useful when you want to map an unused drive letter to a directory path and you do not care what letter is used. Suppose, for example, you want to map a drive to the SHARED subdirectory of the MARKET directory. The MAP NEXT command, as shown in the figure, maps the next available drive letter, in this case H, to the USER subdirectory.

Figure 8-15

Mapping regular drive mappings

```
MS-DOS Prompt
G:\>MAP NEXT CONSTELLATION/DATA:MARKET\SHARED
Drive H: = CONSTELLATION\DATA: \MARKET\SHARED
G:\>
```

H: is the next available drive

Creating Root Drive Pointers

A root drive pointer appears to the user or application program as if the drive pointer is at the beginning of a drive or volume. Root drive pointers are useful for two reasons:

1. Some applications access files only from the root of a directory path. This can be a problem for a network administrator, because users are not usually given rights to the root of a volume and also because you might want to keep the application contained in a certain directory in the structure. NetWare solves this problem by enabling the network administrator or users to map a drive to a "fake" root containing the application.
2. Root drive pointers make it more difficult for a user or application to change the drive pointer to another location inadvertently. For example, if a user's home directory is mapped to a regular drive pointer and the user issues a CD\ command, the mapping of the drive pointer is changed to the root of the current volume. Root drive mappings on the other hand appear to DOS as the beginning of a drive, causing CD\ to return to the directory to which the root drive is mapped to rather than going to the root of the volume.

The command syntax for mapping a root drive is the same as the syntax for creating a regular drive pointer except that the ROOT option precedes the drive letter:

```
MAP ROOT drive:=[path]
```

You can also use just the letter R instead of the word ROOT. Figure 8-16 shows an example of mapping L as a root drive to the DATA:MARKET and mapping K as a regular drive pointer to the DATA:MARKET\SHARED directory. When MAP is used to show the drive pointer assignments, the path for the root drive pointer L drive is followed by a backslash, whereas the path for regular drive pointer K does not have a backslash.

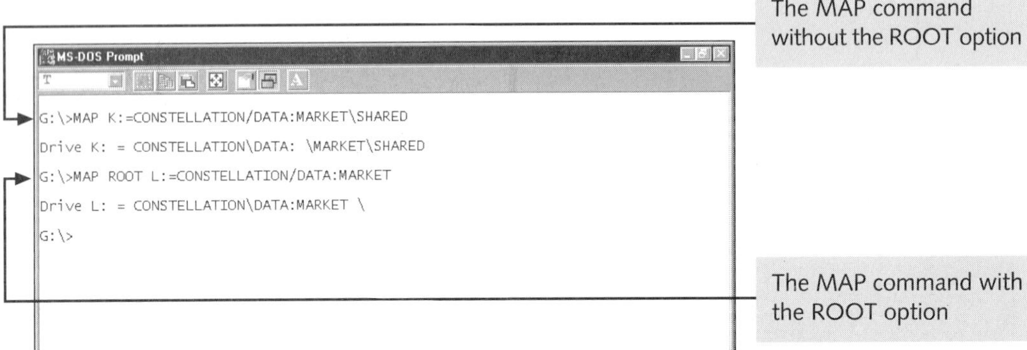

Figure 8-16 Mapping regular and root drive mappings

Changing Drive Pointer Mappings

When working with the file system, you will often want to change the path of a drive pointer to access another location. Sometimes you will also want to change a regular drive pointer into a root drive pointer and vice versa. You can change the path of a regular or root drive pointer by using either the DOS CD command or the MAP command.

Whenever you use the CD command to change to another directory, you are changing the current drive pointer mapping. Figure 8-17 demonstrates a CD [path] command used to change a drive mapping. The CD command can be used to change to a different volume as well as different directory.

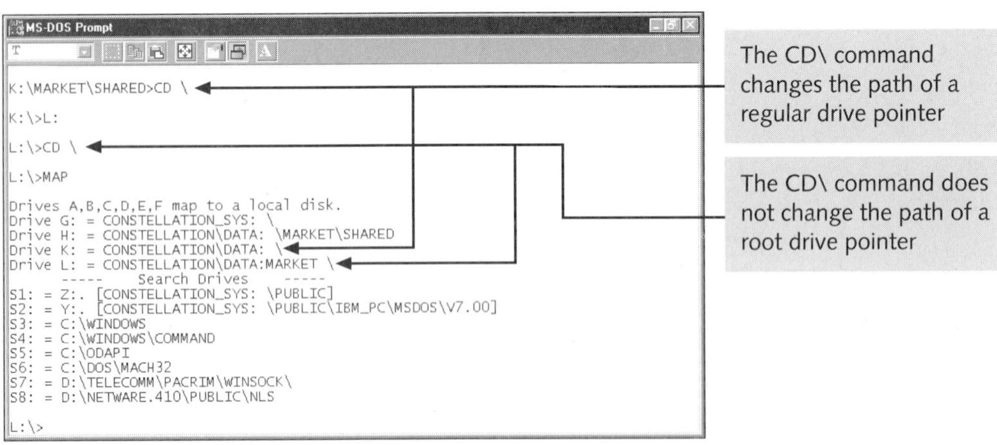

Figure 8-17 Changing mappings with the CD command

Although the CD\ command returns a regular drive mapping to the root of the volume, it returns a root drive pointer only to the directory path that was assigned to it. This makes root drive pointers a good choice when you do not want users to change their drive pointers to different locations of the directory structure accidentally.

The MAP ROOT *drive:*=[path] command can also be used to reassign a specified drive pointer to a new path. To change the mapping of the current drive pointer from the SYS:PUBLIC directory to the SYS:PUBLIC\IBM_PC\MSDOS\V7.00, you could use any of the following MAP commands. Notice that the first command contains a complete path, whereas the second command uses a partial path based on the location of the current drive. The third command is a shortcut that eliminates typing the drive letter if you are changing the path of the current drive.

```
G:\PUBLIC>MAP G:=SYS:PUBLIC\IBM_PC\MSDOS\V6.22
G:\PUBLIC>MAP G:=IBM_PC\MSDOS\V6.22
G:\PUBLIC>MAP IBM_PC\MSDOS\V6.22
```

To change the regular drive pointer K to a root drive, you can use the following command:

```
MAP ROOT K:=K:
```

To change the root drive pointer L to a regular drive pointer you can use the following command:

```
MAP L:=L:
```

Creating Search Drive Pointers

Search drives are drive pointers that are added to a workstation's DOS path in order to enable the workstation to access software that is stored in other directories. A maximum of 16 search drives can be assigned, starting with S1 and ending with S16. New search drives can be added to the list by using the MAP command either to assign the next available search drive number or to insert the search drive between two existing search drives. The syntax of the MAP command that adds new search drives is as follows:

```
MAP INS S#:=[path]
```

When you add a search drive to the end of the list, you do not include the INS option and you replace # with the next available search drive number from 1 through 16. If you skip search drive numbers, the MAP command will automatically assign the next available number. When you add a new search drive, NetWare automatically assigns the next available drive letter, starting with Z for S1 and ending with K for S16. For example, suppose you have the following search drives mapped:

```
S1:=Z:. [CONSTELLATION\SYS:\PUBLIC]
S2:=Y:. [CONSTELLATION\SYS:\PUBLIC\IBM_PC\MSDOS\V7.00]
S3:=C:\DOS
```

The next available search drive is Search4 (S4). To map search drive S4: to the SYS:APPS\WINOFFCE directory, you can use the following map command:

```
MAP S4:=SYS:APPS\WINOFFCE
```

When adding new search drives, you cannot skip search drive numbers. For example, if you attempt to map the preceding search drive to S5 before S4 is mapped, NetWare automatically uses the next sequential search drive number, in this case S4, as shown in Figure 8-18.

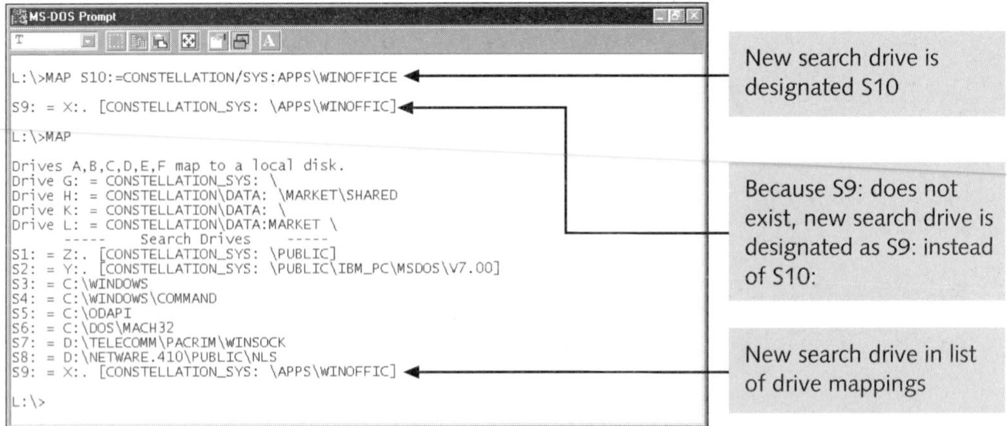

Figure 8-18 Adding a new search drive mapping

Because NetWare will not skip search drive numbers, you can use the command MAP S16:=[path] if you want to add a search drive to the end of the search list and cannot remember the number of the last search drive.

When inserting a search drive between two existing drives, include the INS option and replace # with the number of the search drive before which you want the new drive placed. When you set up search drives, assign the lower search drive numbers to the most commonly used paths. This makes the system more efficient by reducing the number of directories NetWare has to search through when it looks for a program file.

For example, assume you have the following search drives mapped:

```
S1:=Z:.[CONSTELLATION\SYS:PUBLIC]
S2:=Y:.[CONSTELLATION\SYS:PUBLIC\IBM_PC\MSDOS\V7.00]
S3:=X:.[CONSTELLATION\SYS:APPS\WINOFFCE]
```

Suppose that you want to use the word processing program located in the APPS\WINOFFICE\WP directory and still maintain the other search drive mappings. In order to make the word processing directory the first in the search order, you could use the MAP INS command shown in Figure 8-19 to create a new Search1 mapping. This will resequence the other search drives, as displayed by the MAP command.

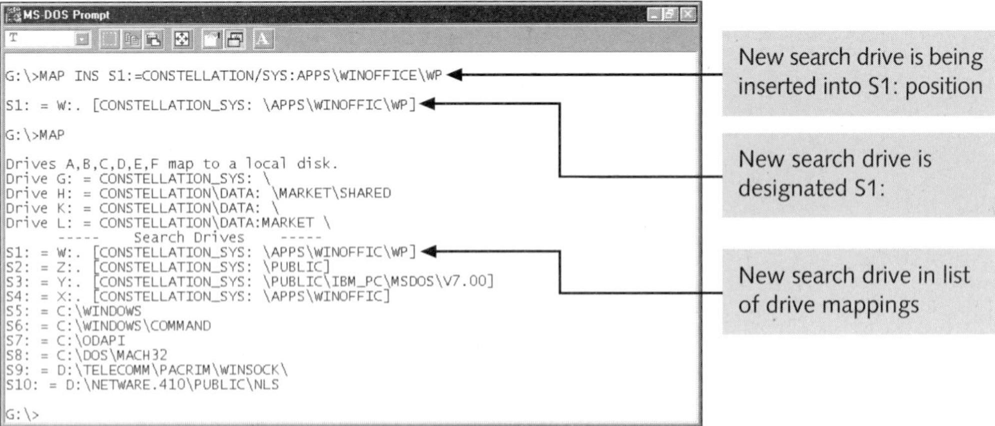

Figure 8-19 Inserting a search drive mapping

Notice that the drive letter W is assigned to the new search drive and that, although the other search drives are renumbered, they retain their drive letter assignments. The DOS MAP commands shown at the top and bottom of Figure 8-19 illustrate the way the search commands affect the DOS path. NetWare keeps track of search drive numbers by their sequence in the DOS path. Because drive W is now the first drive in the path, it becomes S1.

Removing a Drive Pointer

The advice "everything in moderation" certainly applies to drive pointers. Too many search drive pointers can slow down the workstation's performance and sometimes overlie existing regular and root drive pointers. Drive pointers also take up some of the file server's memory and can decrease its performance. (This is discussed further in Chapter 17.) In addition, trying to keep track of too many drive pointers can become confusing and counterproductive.

A network administrator can use the MAP DEL command to remove drive pointers that are no longer being used. The command

```
MAP DEL drive:
```

removes a regular, root, or search drive mapping when you replace *drive:* with the drive letter or search drive to be removed. When you remove a search drive mapping, the remaining search drive numbers are resequenced, as shown in Figure 8-20. The drive letter that was assigned to the deleted search drive is made available for the next search drive that you add.

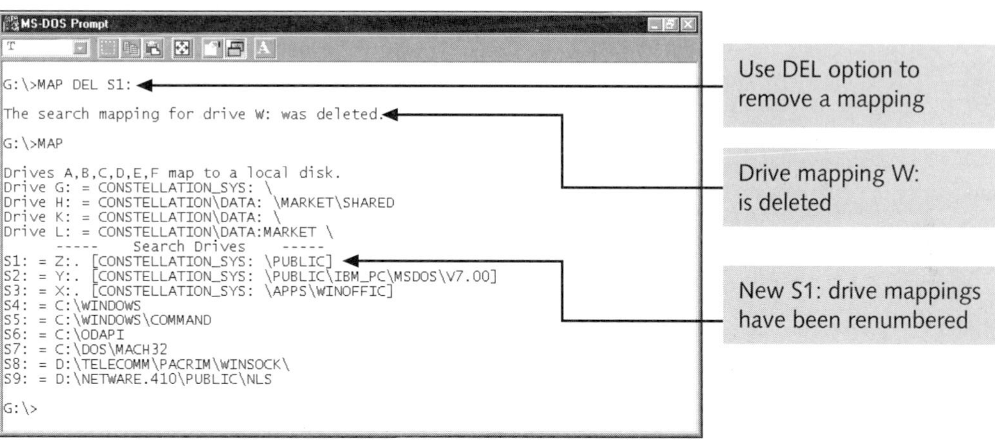

Figure 8-20 Removing a search drive mapping

Changing a Search Drive Path

Although most users will not need to change search drive paths after they are established, a network administrator sometimes needs to modify search drives when testing new software packages or reconfiguring a workstation for new applications. At other times, a network administrator might want to modify the search drive paths in a user's menu system rather than add a new search drive for each software package the user needs to access. This can keep the number of search drives from becoming excessive and slowing down system performance. In this section you will learn the different methods of modifying search drive paths.

There are three methods to change a search drive mapping to point to a different directory:

1. Remapping the existing search drive to the desired path
2. Deleting the original search drive and inserting a new search drive to the desired path
3. Using the CD command

The first method involves overwriting the search drive mapping with a new path. For example, assume you need to use the word processing program in the Windows Office software and have the following search drives mapped:

```
S1:=Z:. [CONSTELLATION\SYS: \PUBLIC]
S2:=Y:. [CONSTELLATION\SYS: \IBM_PC\MSDOS\V7.00]
S3:=X:. [CONSTELLATION\SYS: \APPS\PAGEPUB]
```

You replace the search drive mapping to the PAGEPUB directory with the WINOFFCE path by entering the following command:

```
MAP X:=SYS:APPS\WINOFFICE\WP
```

This command causes NetWare to remap the X drive to the WP directory, thereby changing search drive S3 to use the SYS:APPS\WINOFFICE\WP path.

The second method deletes the original search drive and then inserts a new search drive using the same search drive number, as follows:

```
MAP DEL S3:
MAP INS S3:=SYS:APPS\WINOFFICE\WP
```

The MAP DEL S3: command deletes the S3 drive mapping and resequences the search drive numbers. The second MAP command inserts a new search drive for S3, pointing to the WP directory. This method is often used in a batch file or in menus to enable a certain search drive number to be reused for several different applications. It keeps the number of search drives from becoming excessive in situations in which users need to access many different software packages.

Like regular drive pointers, search drive paths can be changed with the DOS CD command as well as with the NetWare MAP command. If a user is unable to run certain network applications, a network administrator should investigate for search drive paths that were inadvertently modified by a "power" user using the CD command. Figure 8-21 illustrates using the CD command to change a search drive mapping by first changing the default drive to the search drive to be modified and then using the CD command to change the path to another directory location. Notice that after the work drive is changed and the MAP command is invoked, the search path for S3 is changed to the path specified in the CD command.

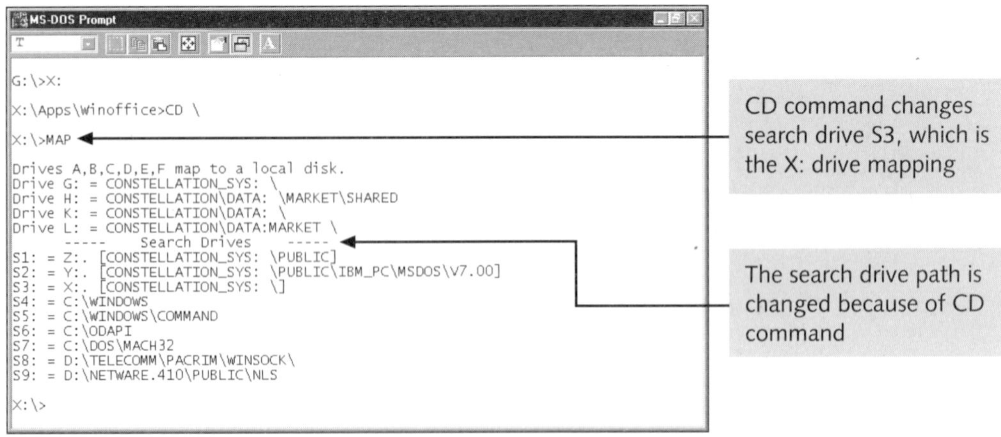

Figure 8-21 Using the CD command to change search drives

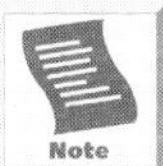

Changing the drive mapping of Search1 from the SYS:PUBLIC to some other directory will prevent a user from running NetWare utilities; the user will be unable to invoke the LOGOUT and MAP commands from outside the SYS:PUBLIC directory. If this happens, you can use the CD command to change to the SYS:PUBLIC directory in order to use LOGOUT or other NetWare utilities.

Changing a Search Drive Mapping to a Regular Drive Mapping

Usually there is no need to change the type of a drive mapping once it is created, but a network administrator may occasionally need to change the type of a drive mapping when troubleshooting workstation problems or in a menu system. The command you use is

```
MAP C drive:
```

If *drive:* is a search drive mapping, this command changes it to a regular drive mapping. If *drive:* is a regular drive mapping, this command changes it to a search drive mapping. For example, Figure 8-22 illustrates changing the search drive mapping S3: to a regular drive mapping.

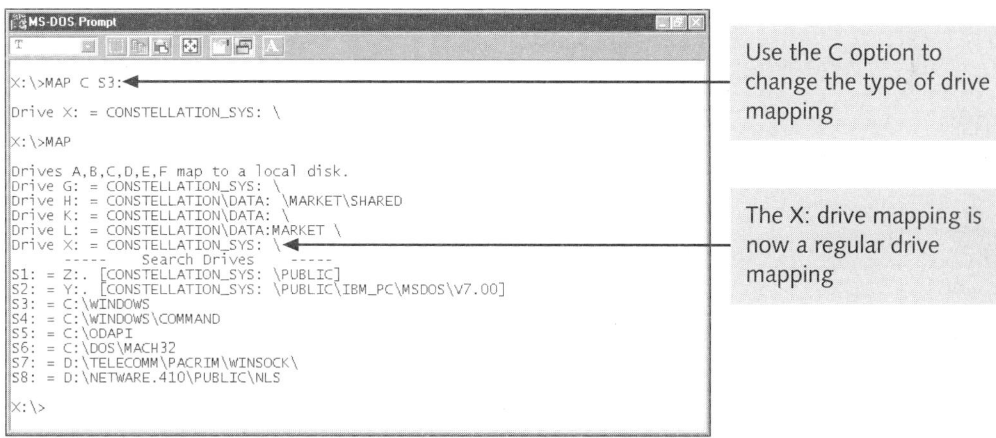

Figure 8-22
Changing the type of drive mapping

Directory Map Objects

A **Directory Map object** is a server-related leaf object that the network administrator can use in a MAP command to simplify administration of the drive mappings. The Directory Map object contains the path that you would normally use in a drive mapping. By using the Directory Map object in a MAP command, you are providing the drive mapping path as the path contained in the Directory Map object.

For example, the network administrator for CBE Labs wants to create a drive mapping to the files shared among all CBE Labs personnel. These reports are stored in the CONSTELLATION/DATA:SHARED directory. To create a regular drive mapping, the network administrator would use the following command:

```
MAP P:=CONSTELLATION/DATA:SHARED
```

To create a drive mapping by using a Directory Map object, the network administrator first creates the Directory Map object and enters the volume and path data that are needed for the drive mapping. For example, he could create a Directory Map object named SharedFiles in the CBE_Labs_Admin Organizational Unit of CBE_Labs. He would then use the following MAP command:

```
MAP P:=.SharedFiles.CBE_Labs_Admin.CBE_Labs
```

If the network administrator later wants to move these files to another location, he can change the drive mapping by simply changing the Volume and Path property values stored in the Directory Map object. This is easier than finding every use of the regular mapping in all the login scripts that use the drive mapping. For this reason, you will usually want to create Directory Map objects for use in drive mappings.

You can create Directory Map objects by using either the NETADMIN menu utility or the NetWare Administrator graphical utility. After they are created, you can use them in any MAP command. As usual, we'll work with NetWare Administrator in this chapter, and you'll have a chance to use NETADMIN in the exercises at the end of the chapter.

The CBE Labs network administrator wants to create a Directory Map object named SharedFiles in the CBE_Labs_Admin Organizational Unit container object. The Directory Map object will contain the path CONSTELLATION/DATA:SHARED.

To create the SharedFiles Directory Map object, follow these steps:

1. Launch the NetWare Administrator program.
2. Expand the Directory tree as necessary until you can see all Organization and Organizational Unit objects.
3. Click the **CBE_Labs_Admin** Organizational Unit object, click **Object** on the menu bar, and then click **Create**.
4. The New Object dialog box is displayed. Click **Directory Map** and then click **OK**. The Create Directory Map dialog box is displayed, as shown in Figure 8-23.

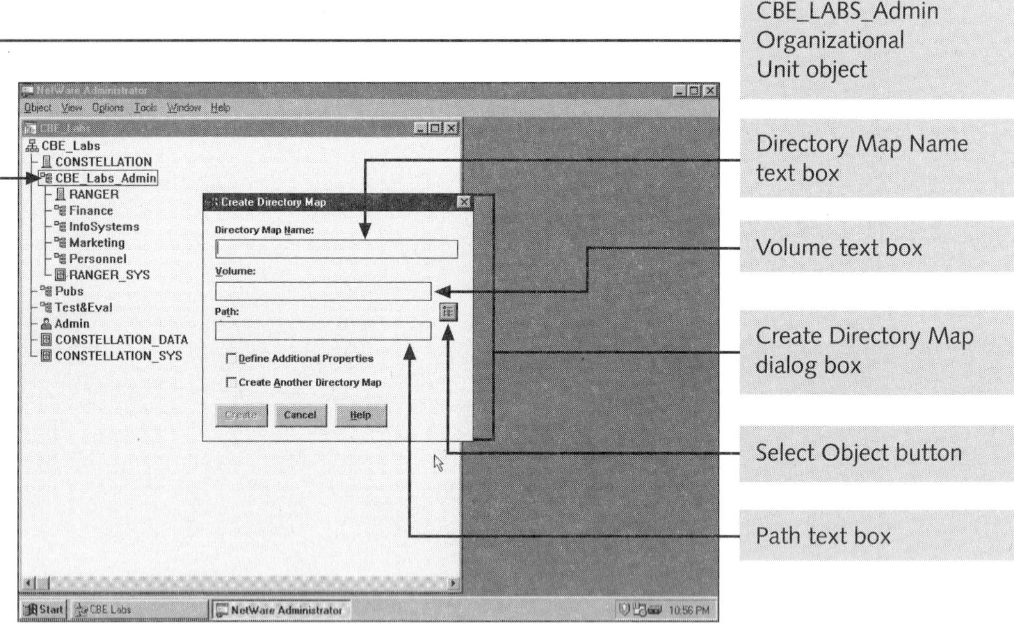

Figure 8-23 The Create Directory Map dialog box

5. Type **SharedFiles** in the Directory Map Name text box.
6. Click the **Volume** text box to activate it and then click the **Select Object** button [icon] to the right of the Volume text box. The Select Object dialog box is displayed.
7. The Select Object dialog box is used to browse the Directory tree context to find an object. In this case, the starting context is CBE_Labs. This is the correct context for the server CONSTELLATION that contains the DATA: volume, so

there is no need to browse the tree. In the Objects window, click the NetWare Volume object **CONSTELLATION_DATA**. The name of the selected object is displayed in the Selected Object text box.

8. Click **OK**. The volume name CONSTELLATION_DATA. CBE_Labs is displayed in the Volume text box of the Create Directory Map dialog box.
9. Click the **Path** text box to activate it and then click the **Select Object** button to the right of the Path text box. The Select Object dialog box is displayed.
10. In the Objects window, double-click the NetWare Volume object **CONSTELLATION_DATA** to view the directory structure. Click the **SHARED** directory folder to select it. The name of the selected object is displayed in the Selected Object text box. Click **OK**. The path SHARED is displayed in the Path text box of the Create Directory Map dialog box, as shown in Figure 8-24.

Figure 8-24

The completed Create Directory Map dialog box

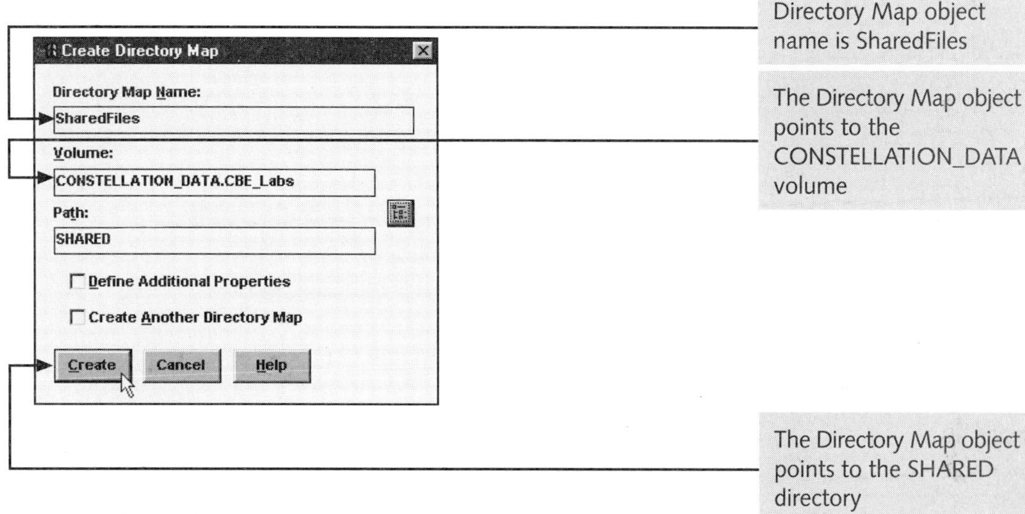

11. Click **Create**. The Directory Map object SharedFiles is created and added to the Directory tree, as shown in Figure 8-25.

Figure 8-25

The Directory tree with the SharedFiles directory map

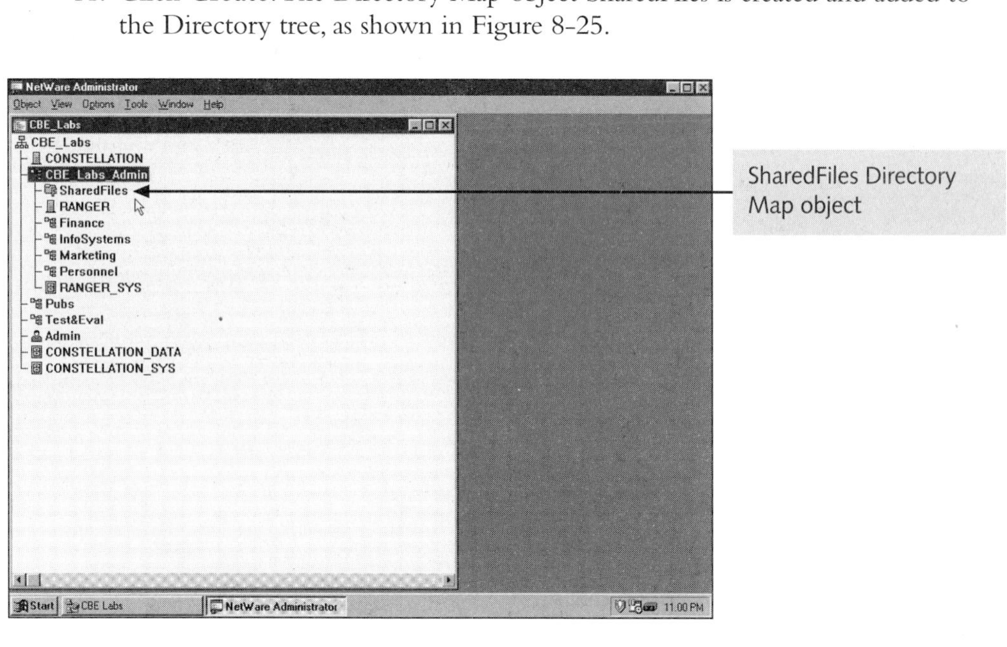

THE NETWARE MENU UTILITY NETUSER

A user can manage his or her drive mappings by using the NETUSER menu utility. The NETUSER utility is used to manage workstation NetWare tasks, such as network connections, drive mappings, messages, and network printing. NETUSER can also be used to change a user's context in the Directory tree.

The syntax of the command to start NETUSER utility is

```
NETUSER [/VER]
```

The /VER parameter is used to display the version number of the NETUSER utility and a file list of supporting files—the utility is not run if the parameter is used.

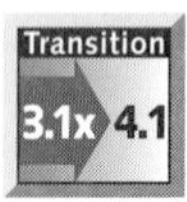

The NetWare 4.1 NETUSER menu utility replaces the NetWare 3.1x SESSION menu utility.

When NETUSER is started, a menu is displayed to enable the user to select a task. This is illustrated in Figure 8-26. Note that the user's context is displayed in the upper left of the screen.

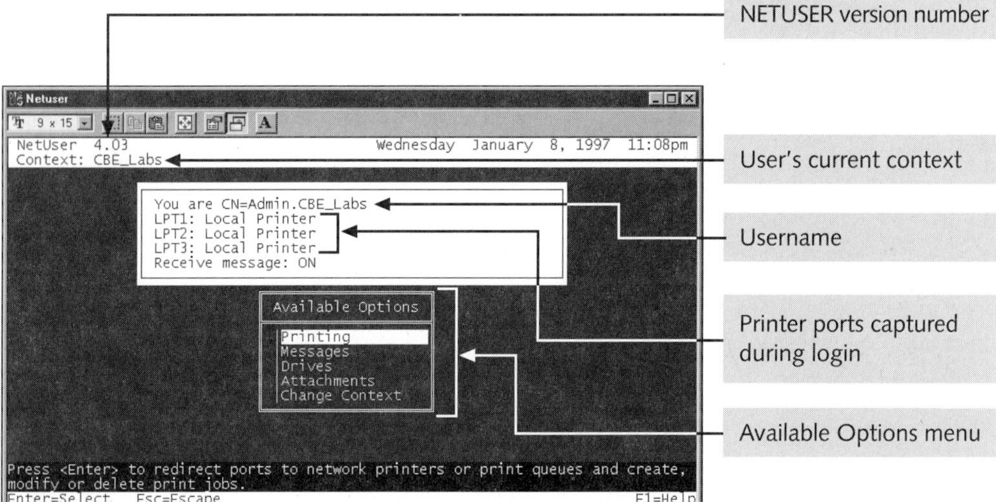
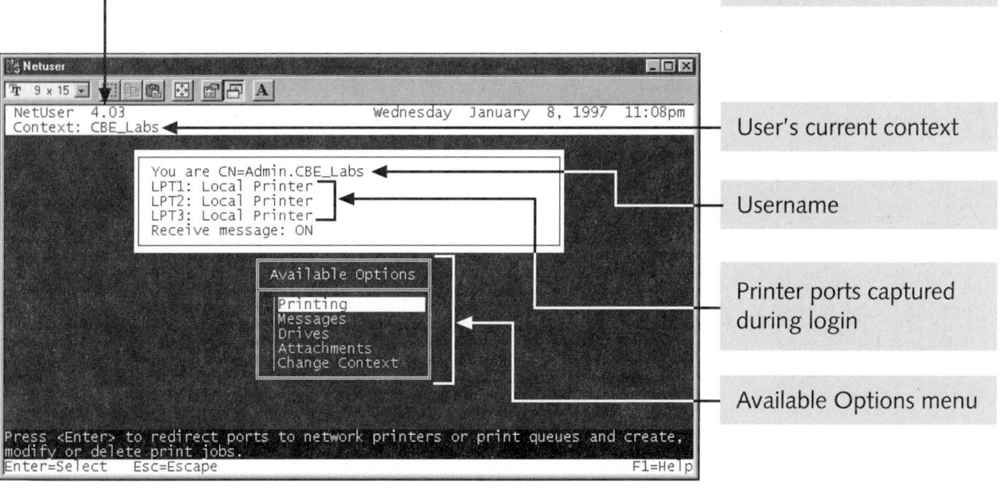

Figure 8-26 The NETUSER screen

To manage drive mappings, you select Drives from the menu. This displays a menu with the options of Drive Mappings and Search Mappings, as shown in Figure 8-27.

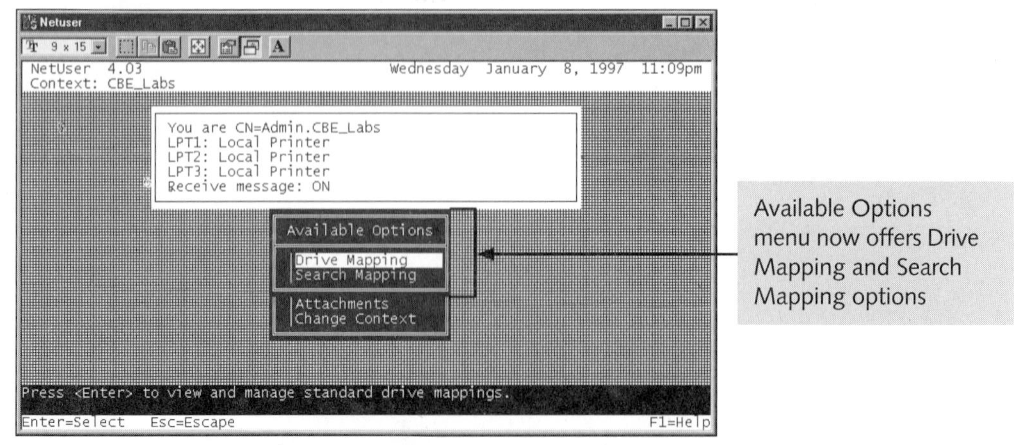

Figure 8-27 The NETUSER Drives screen

When you select Drive Mappings, it displays a list of current drive mappings; if you select Search Mappings, it displays a list of current search drive mappings. A list of drive mappings is shown in Figure 8-28.

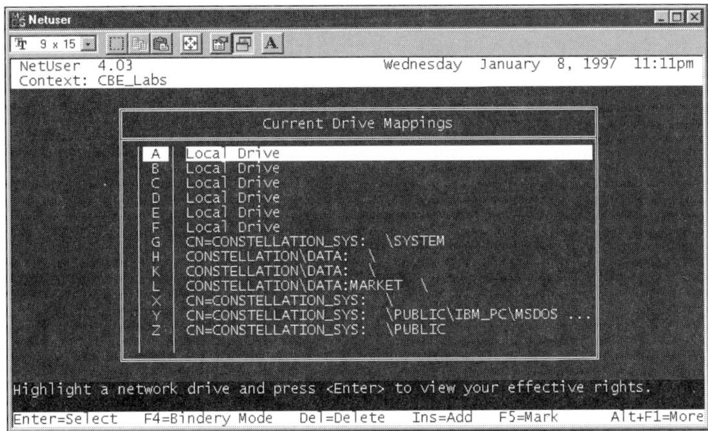

Figure 8-28 The NETUSER Current Drive Mappings screen

You can add a drive mapping by pressing [Ins], delete a drive mapping by pressing [Del], or change a drive mapping by pressing [F3]. In each case, NETUSER will prompt you for the necessary information to complete the action.

THE NETWARE PROVIDER FOR WINDOWS 95

When the NetWare DOS Requester was released, a graphical equivalent of the NETUSER menu utility called NetWare User Tools was included. The NetWare Client 32 software replaces this utility with extensions to Windows 95 called the **NetWare Provider for Windows 95** so that a separate utility is not needed because all the needed functionality is part of the Windows 95 utilities themselves. These extensions provide functions to Windows Explorer and Network Neighborhood that enable these utilities to display and use NDS and NetWare specific information. These include the following:

- Displaying NDS Directory tree structures
- Displaying NDS print and file objects
- Changing NDS context

The NetWare User Tools graphical utility is still available as part of the NetWare DOS Requester client, but it requires a special installation. Instructions for the installation are in the FAQ for NetWare Client 32 at the Novell Support Connection Web site.

Displaying NDS Directory Tree Structures

With the NetWare Provider for Windows 95, Network Neighborhood includes a NetWare Directory Services folder that displays all the NDS Directory trees on the network. Expanding a Directory tree shows the container objects in the tree. However, the container objects appear as Windows 95 documents rather than as Country, Organization, and Organizational Unit objects. This is shown in Figure 8-29.

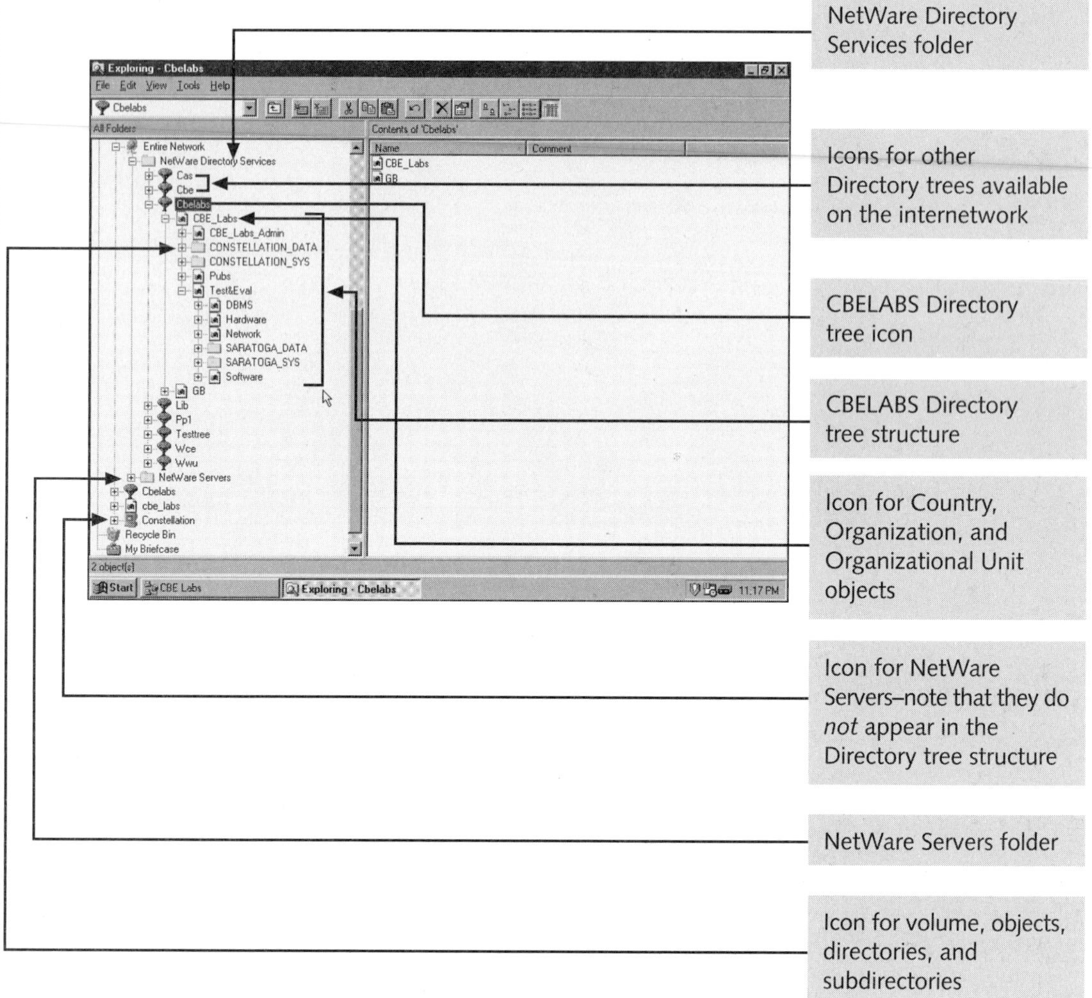

Figure 8-29 NDS Directory trees in Network Neighborhood

Displaying NDS Print and File System Objects

Some NDS file system objects are displayed. These are volumes, directories, and subdirectories. For example, in Figure 8-29 the CONSTELLATION_SYS volume is displayed. Print objects—printers, print servers, and print queues—are also displayed if they exist in the Directory tree.

Changing NDS Context

You can change context in a Directory tree by right-clicking on the tree and then clicking Change Context on the shortcut menu, as shown in Figure 8-30.

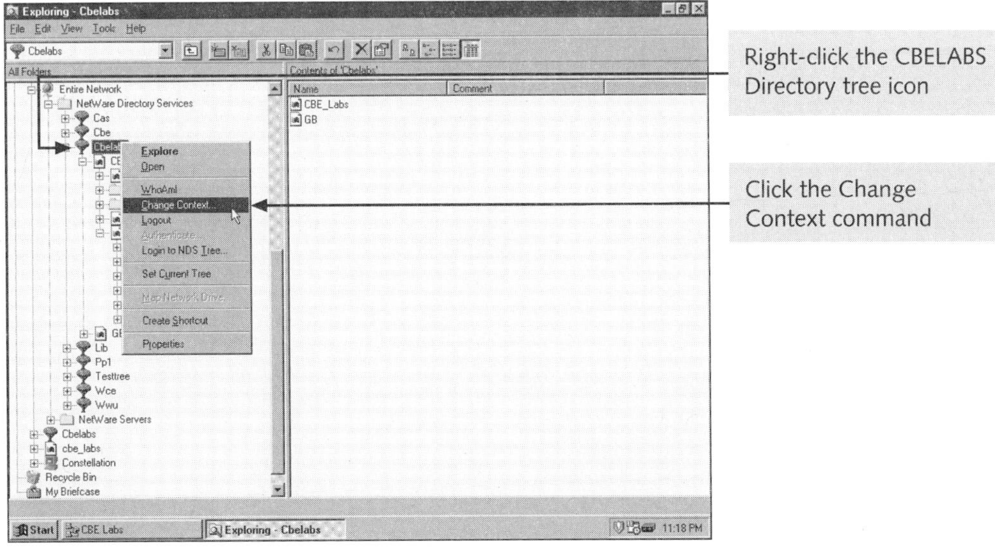

Figure 8-30 Changing context

This displays the Change NetWare Directory Services Context dialog box shown in Figure 8-31 (the name NetWare Directory Services as displayed shows that the software hasn't caught up with the name change to Novell Directory Services). You can change context by entering a new context in the Enter New Default Context text box.

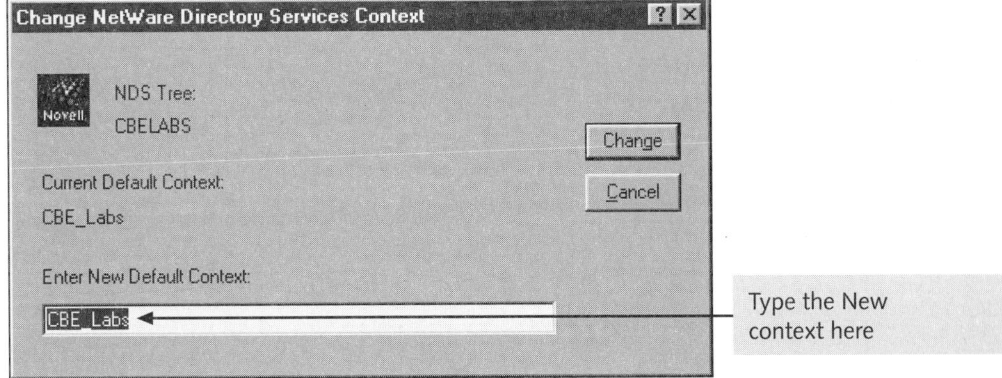

Figure 8-31 The Change NetWare Directory Services Context dialog box

MAPPING DRIVE POINTERS IN WINDOWS 95

You can create drive pointers in Windows 95 by using Windows Explorer. To create a drive pointer, you highlight the directory you want to map in the folders list and then use the Network Drive Mapping command in the File menu.

For example, the CBE Labs network administrator could have mapped the CONSTELLATION/SYS: root directory to the K: drive by using Windows Explorer.

To create the drive pointer by using Windows Explorer, follow these steps:

1. Click **Start | Programs | Windows Explorer** to launch Windows Explorer.
2. Click the **Network Neighborhood** display box to display all the available network connections. Click the expansion box in front of the icon for CONSTELLATION.
3. Right-click the folder icon for SYS to select it and display the shortcut menu.

4. Click **Map Network Drive** to display the Map Network Drive dialog box shown in Figure 8-32.

Figure 8-32

The Map Network Drive dialog box with mapping

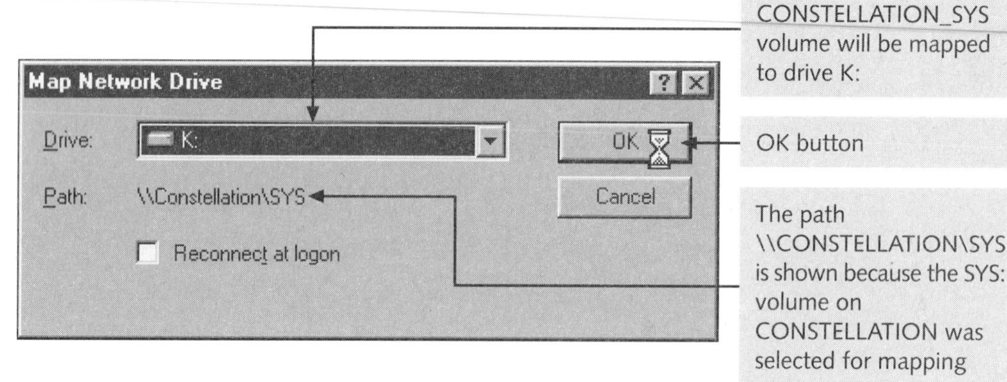

5. Click the **Drive** drop-down list button and then click **K:** to select the K: drive.
6. Click **OK** to create the drive mapping. The mapping appears in the list of drives under My Computer as shown in Figure 8-33.

Figure 8-33

The new drive mapping in My Computer

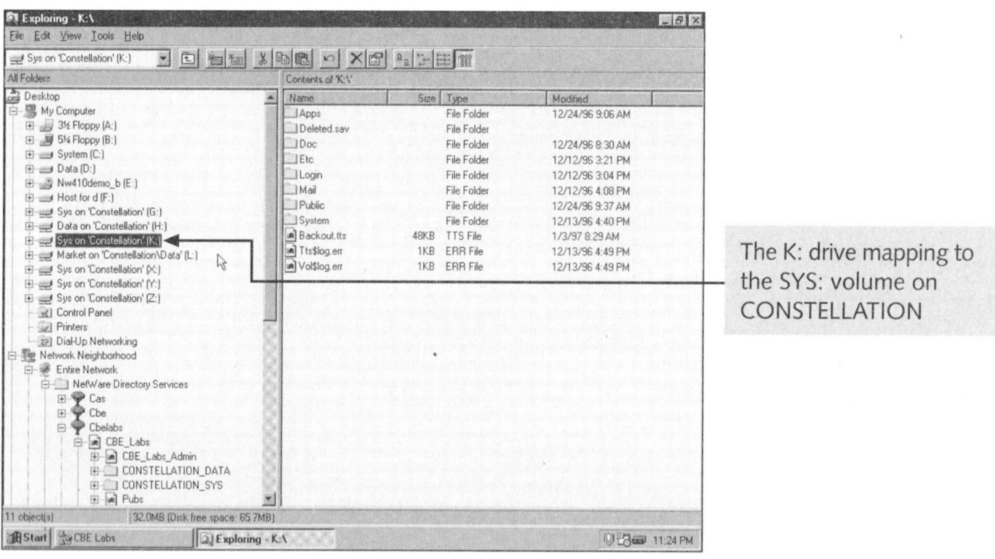

You can also create a drive mapping by clicking the Map Network Drive button in the Explorer Toolbar. As shown in Figure 8-34, this displays the Map Network Drive dialog box.

Figure 8-34

The Map Network Drive dialog box with typed mapping

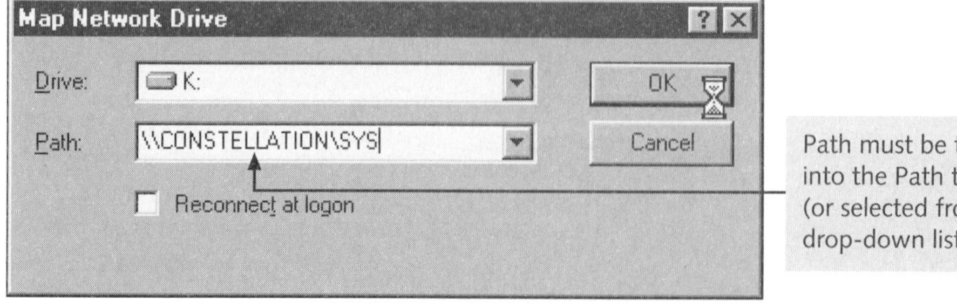

The drive to be mapped is selected from the Drive: drop-down list, and the mapping is selected from the Path: drop down list or typed into the Path: text box. When entering the mapping, you use **Universal Naming Convention (UNC)** paths. UNC paths include the server and volume name as part of the path by using double backward slashes in front of the NetWare server name, a single backward slash between the server and volume names, and a single backward slash between the volume name and the directory name (instead of a colon). The syntax looks like this:

```
\\ServerName\Volume\Directory\Subdirectory[\Subdirectory]
```

PLANNING YOUR DRIVE MAPPINGS

As a network administrator, you will have the important task of assigning the limited number of regular and search drive pointers so that users and applications can access information and software in your file system's directory structure. If each workstation had an unlimited number of drive pointers available to it, you could assign a regular or root drive pointer to each data directory to be accessed along with a search drive to each software package. Even if you had this luxury, however, not only would so many drive pointers be confusing to track, but too many search drives would slow the performance of the workstation because of the number of directories it would need to search through when it loads software. Because of this limitation, you need to plan a minimum set of standard drive pointers that will enable a workstation to run the necessary applications software and provide convenient access to the data with which the user needs to work.

When planning regular drive pointers, you should first determine what regular and root drive pointers are necessary to enable easy access to shared and private files using a drive letter rather than a long NetWare path. It is important to keep these drive pointers to a minimum, because most users cannot keep track of more than five different drive pointers. Typical drive pointers for each user should include the following:

- *A drive pointer to the root of each volume.* These drive pointers will enable all users to change to another volume quickly without using the CD volume name: command. They also provide a standard path for running applications because certain application packages require a drive letter and path to be assigned in order to reference configuration and data file locations. Having the same drive letter mapped to each volume for all users is necessary to run this software. When using a two-volume structure, many network administrators map one drive letter to the SYS: volume and then use another drive letter to access the DATA: volume.
- *A drive pointer to the shared work directories that are available to all users.* For example, if a shared work directory named WORK is created for all users on the root of the DATA: volume, any user can access files in this directory by using the mapping to the DATA volume. Similarly, if a shared word processing forms directory named FORMS is created on the root of the DATA: volume, then mapping a drive to the DATA volume will enable any user to access a common word processing form.
- *A root drive pointer mapped to the user's home directory.* This drive letter, usually H for "home" or U for "user," is the starting point for users' personal data storage. It will be a different path for each user. Making this a root drive is important because it prevents the user from accidentally changing the drive pointer to a different directory location. Users can create subdirectories within their home directories, for example, and then move around within those subdirectories using the CD\ command to bring them back to the beginning of their home directories rather than changing to the root of the volume.

- *A root drive pointer mapped to the user's workgroup directory.* This drive pointer enables users to access shared files within their workgroups. Users in the business department, for example, can have their L drive mapped to DATA:BUSINESS. The SALES department users can have their L drive mapped to the DATA:SALES directory. If a WORK directory is created for each department, every user in the system can get to his or her workgroup's shared work directory using the path L:\WORK.
- *Application drive pointers.* In addition to the standard drive pointers just described and depending on the installation instructions of some application packages, additional drive pointers might be necessary. When these drive pointers are planned, it is important that all users who will run the application can do so with the same drive pointer letter, because the software will often be installed using a specific drive letter for accessing its data and work files.

In addition to planning the regular drive pointers, the network administrator needs to plan the use of search drive pointers to enable users access to utilities and software packages that are frequently used. When planning search drive usage, it is important to keep the total number of search drives to fewer than eight in order to provide better performance and less chance of conflicts with regular drive pointers. Because most users will be running application packages from a menu or Windows environment, application search drive pointers can be temporarily mapped in the menu with the MAP INS command and then removed with the MAP DEL command after the application ends. Users running a Windows environment will not need search drives mapped to the Windows applications, because the path to these directories is stored in the properties of the Windows folders or icons. As a minimum, most network administrators establish the following search drive mappings:

- Search drive S1 to the SYS:PUBLIC directory
- Search drive S2 to the correct DOS version subdirectory
- Search drive S3 to the network WINDOWS directory if Windows 95 is being run from the network

A properly planned set of drive pointers includes the search drives needed to run DOS-based software packages and utilities along with a standard set of regular drive pointers that enable users easy access to data storage directories containing the files with which they need to work. The drive pointer planning form shown in Figure 8-35 shows an example that includes the following drive pointers for each user:

- The H drive pointer to the user's home directory enables each user to access his or her own private data easily.
- The J drive pointer mapped to each user's local department or workgroup enables users to access their department's shared work files by using the path J:\WORK.
- The G drive pointer to the SYS: volume gives each user access to software or utilities stored in the SYS: volume.
- The I drive pointer mapped to the root of the DATA: volume provides each user with access to the Global data structure for the organization. For example, a user can access the organization's global work directory with the path I:\WORK or access the organization's shared forms directory with the path I:\FORMS. If a department wants its own forms directory, it can be accessed with the path J:\FORMS.
- The K drive pointer mapped to each user's shared work group data.

Figure 8-35 Sample drive planning form

Drive Mapping Planning Form		
Organization:	**CBE Laboratories**	
Planned By:	**Ted Simpson**	
Date:	**9/15/97**	
GROUP:	**Everyone**	
Letter:	**Description of Use:**	**Path:**
S1:	NetWare Utilities	CONSTELLATION/SYS:PUBLIC
S2:		CONSTELLATION/SYS:
G:	Global SYS volume	CONSTELLATION/SYS:
I:	Global Data volume	CONSTELLATION/DATA:SHARED
GROUP:	**Marketing**	
Letter:	**Description of Use:**	**Path:**
H:	User data	CONSTELLATION/DATA:
		USERS/%Username
J:	Workgroup data	CONSTELLATION/DATA:MARKET
K:	Workgroup shared data	CONSTELLATION/DATA:
		MARKET/SHARED
GROUP:	**Finance**	
Letter:	**Description of Use:**	**Path:**
H:	User data	CONSTELLATION/DATA:
		USERS/%Username
J:	Workgroup data	CONSTELLATION/DATA:FINANCE
K:	Workgroup shared data	CONSTELLATION/DATA:
		FINANCE/SHARED
GROUP:		
Letter:	**Description of Use:**	**Path:**

Planning a good set of drive pointers will make it easier for you to establish login scripts, install software, and work with NetWare menus as well as provide a standard user environment that is convenient for your users to access and for you to troubleshoot and maintain.

FILE MANAGEMENT

After the network file system is in place and drive mappings have been created, the network administrator can install applications and users can put their data on the network. The directories and subdirectories of the network file system will be used for storing the application and data files. As a network administrator you will have to manage these files and their directories. In this section, you will study some tools that will help you accomplish this.

NetWare File Management Command Line Utilities

NetWare command line utilities are software tools specifically designed for the NetWare file system. This section contains a description and the syntax of each of these utilities and gives examples of applying them in a file system management situation. The NDIR, NCOPY, and RENDIR utilities were already described in Chapter 5 and need no additional explanation here.

The PURGE Command

The purge command is used to make deleted file space in the specified path immediately available to the NetWare operating system; it permanently deletes the erased files. One reason to use this command is to improve the file server's performance when the disk volume is almost full. It is faster for the operating system to reuse the space from purged files than to search for the oldest deleted file space. Another reason to use the PURGE command is to prevent sensitive information that has been deleted from being salvaged and used.

NetWare 4.1's block suballocation and file compression features will enable more efficient use of volume space, and you will probably find that you don't need to purge files as often for disk space reasons. Still, when you're finally low on disk space, you'll find PURGE to be a very useful utility.

The syntax of the PURGE command is

```
PURGE [filename | path] [/option] [/?] [/VER]
```

Several parameters can be used with PURGE. They are listed in Figure 8-36.

Figure 8-36 The PURGE command parameters

Parameter	Use this parameter to
filename	Specify the name(s) of the file(s) to be purged. You can use standard wildcard symbols to name groups of files.
path	Specify the directory path to the location of the file(s) you want to purge.
/?	Access help about PURGE. If this parameter is used, all others are ignored.
/VER	See the version number of the PURGE command. If this parameter is used, all others are ignored.

As shown in Figure 8-37, one option can be used with PURGE.

Figure 8-37 The PURGE command option

Option	Use this option to
/ALL	Purge all files in the specified directory and all subdirectories.

You can replace [path] with either a complete or partial NetWare directory path that contains the deleted files you want purged. If no path is specified, all deleted files in the current directory are purged. The /A option purges all files in the subdirectory structure within the path specified. To purge all files in the SYS:APPS\FAX, SYS:APPS\EMAIL, SYS:APPS\WINOFFCE, SYS:APPS\PAGEPUB, and SYS:APPS\INTERNET directories, for example, enter the following command:

```
PURGE SYS:APPS /ALL
```

NetWare File Management Menu Utilities

You learned about the NetWare menu utilities in Chapter 7 and have been introduced to several of them. Generally, however, if there is a graphical utility that performs the same functions as a menu utility, you will find it easier to use the graphical utility. For example, you will usually want to use the NetWare Administrator rather than NETADMIN, and NetWare User Tools rather than NETUSER. Sometimes, however, there is not a graphical version of the utility, or the menu utility is powerful enough that you will prefer using it. You will remember from Chapter 7 that the NetWare menu utilities often present information or menus in windows. Windows with double-lined borders enable you to add, change, or delete objects in the window. Windows with single-lined borders, however, enable you only to view the objects and information. You should also review the use of key functions in menu utilities shown in Figure 8-38.

Figure 8-38
NetWare menu utiltiy keys

Key	Function
[Enter]	Selects an option or item and moves to the next menu level.
[Esc]	Returns back one level in the menu; often used to save the entry you have just completed.
[Ins]	Adds a new entry to a list.
[Del]	Removes an item from a list.
[F1]	Provides additional help information. Pressing the F1 key twice provides a list of keys and their functions.
[F3]	Enables you to change the highlighted item. When using the FILER utility, for example, you can use the F3 key to highlight and then change the name of a directory or file. Used by most utilities.
[F5]	Highlights multiple items in a list. Pressing [F5] a second time removes an item from the highlighted list. In the FILER utility, the F5 key can be used to delete several files from a directory; you mark each file and then press Del to delete all files at one time.
[Alt][F10]	Directly exits a menu utility without returning to the opening menu.

The FILER NetWare Menu Utility

In the following sections you will learn about a menu utility that plays a major role in the NetWare file system: FILER. The FILER menu utility is the most complex of the file system utilities. It can perform many activities, including manipulating files and directories. It controls NetWare file system security by assigning trustee rights to users, sets attributes on files and directories, and enables you to recover deleted network files. This section will give you an overview of the available FILER menu options and then present examples to show you how to perform the functions. The FILER utility displays a warning if you attempt to perform a function that requires supervisor authority. This section identifies which functions require supervisor authorization.

The syntax of the command to start the FILER menu utility is

```
FILER [/VER]
```

The /VER parameter is used to display the version number of the FILER utility and a file list of supporting files—the utility is not run if the parameter is used.

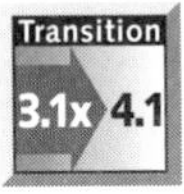

The NetWare 4.1 FILER menu utility significantly upgrades the NetWare 3.1x FILER menu utility. The new FILER includes the NetWare 3.1x FILER, SALVAGE, PURGE, and VOLINFO utilities.

To use the FILER utility, you first need to log into the network, preferably with supervisor rights, and then simply enter the command FILER. The directory path you start FILER from will become the current directory path displayed at the top of the FILER Available options screen, as shown in Figure 8-39. This screen contains the FILER main menu.

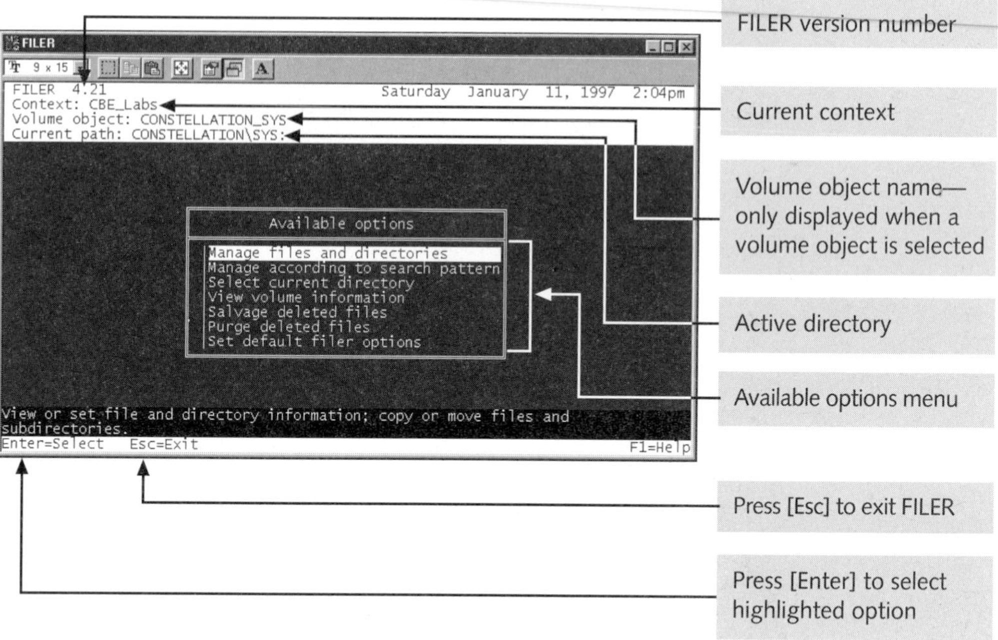

Figure 8-39 The FILER Available options screen

Manage Files and Directories

Selecting Manage files and directories from the Filer main menu enables you to work with directories, subdirectories, files, and trustee rights. When you select Manage files and directories, a directory browser screen is displayed, as shown in Figure 8-40.

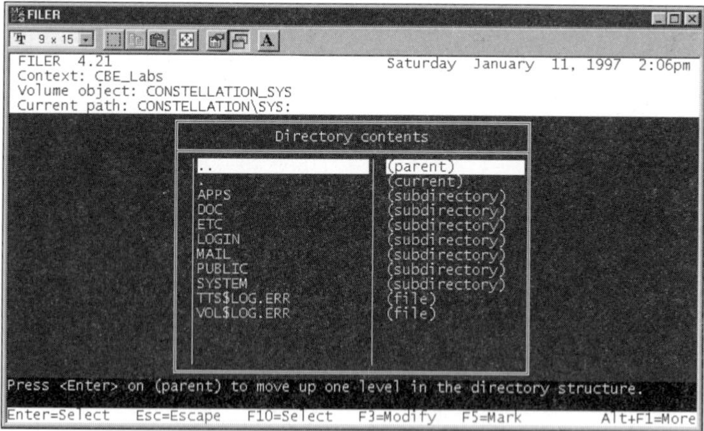

Figure 8-40 The FILER browser screen

Selecting (parent) and pressing [Enter] will move to the next directory toward the root of the directory tree. Selecting a subdirectory and pressing [Enter] will move to that subdirectory.

Using FILER to Manage the Current Directory

Selecting (current) and pressing [F10] will display the Subdirectory options menu, as shown in Figure 8-41.

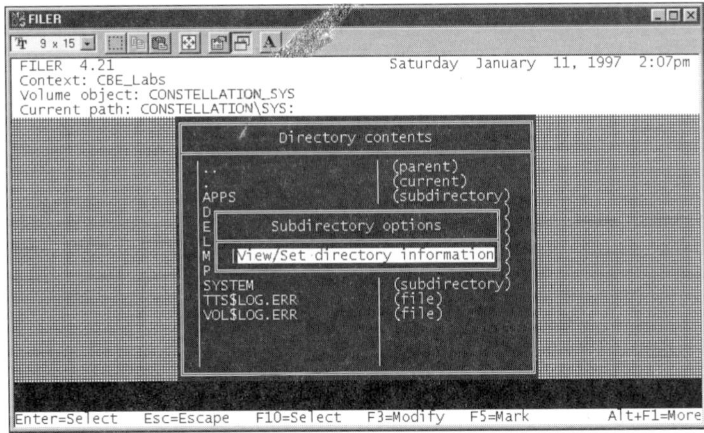

Figure 8-41 The Subdirectory options menu

This menu has the View/Set directory information option which is used to display the Directory Information screen for the selected subdirectory.

Selecting View/Set directory information from this menu will display information about the current directory and manage the directory. For example, the information about the CONSTELLATION/SYS: directory is shown in Figure 8-42.

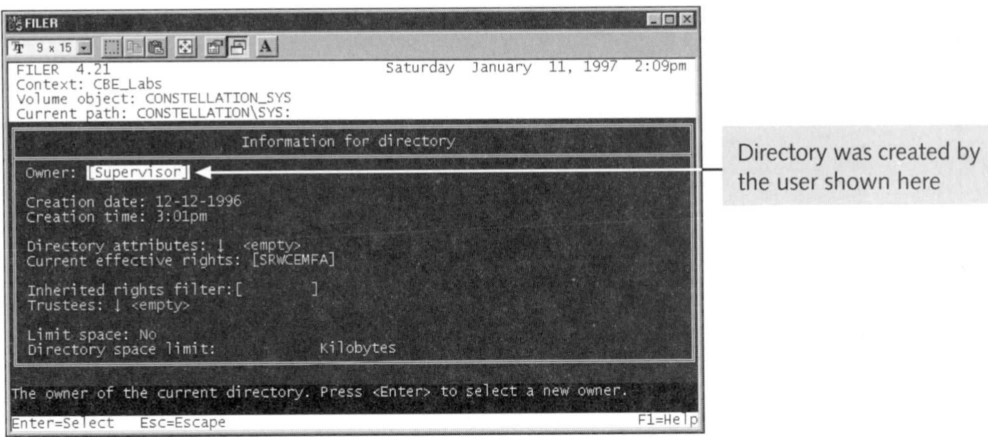

Figure 8-42 The CONSTELLATION /SYS: directory screen

Information about the directory, including the owner, attributes, a list of trustees with rights to the directory, and the effective rights of the current user are shown. Also shown are the creation date and time.

- The Owner field displays the name of the user who created the directory. Supervisor authority is required to change the information in this field.
- The Creation date and Creation time fields tell you when the directory was created and can be changed only if you are logged in with supervisor authority.
- The Directory attributes field contains a pop-up list of all attribute flags assigned to this directory. View the pop-up window by placing the cursor on the field and pressing [Enter]. You can then use the [Ins] and [Del] keys to add and remove attributes from the list.
- The Current effective rights field shows your effective access rights in this directory. You cannot directly change the information in this field because it is dependent on the privileges assigned to your username as well as any trustee assignments granted to you or a group you belong to. The information in this field will be described in more detail in Chapter 10.

- The Inherited rights filter field contains a list of access rights that the directory will allow to flow into it from its parent directories. The use of this field will be described in Chapter 10.
- The Trustees field contains a pop-up window that lists all users and groups who have been assigned rights to this directory. The [Ins] and [Del] keys can be used to add and delete users as trustees of this directory. Assigning trustees to a directory will be explained in more detail in Chapter 10.
- The Limit space field enables you to limit the number of kilobytes of disk space that this directory can use. If the size is limited, the remaining space is shown in the Directory space left field.

Using FILER to Copy or Move a Directory Structure

One of the powerful file management features of FILER is its ability to copy or move an entire directory structure easily from one location to another. No matter how good a job you do designing a directory structure, it is likely that at some point you will want to make modifications to the structure. This can entail moving a directory and all its files and trustee assignments from one location to another—a process you will need to know how to perform.

To copy or move a subdirectory structure, the Select current directory option is first used to select the current directory that contains the subdirectory you want to copy or move. After you select the subdirectory you want to move, select the Copy subdirectory's structure option or the Move subdirectory's structure option to copy or move the selected directory along with all its files and subdirectories to the location you specify in the target path. After you select the target path, FILER copies all the files and subdirectories from the source subdirectory into the target location you specified. If you select the move option, FILER deletes the source files and subdirectory structure after they are successfully copied to the new location.

Using FILER to Create a Directory Structure

FILER enables you to create new subdirectories. Use the browser to select the directory under which you want to make a new subdirectory. Highlight this directory in the list. To create a new subdirectory, simply press [Ins] and enter the subdirectory name.

Using FILER to Rename a Directory

There are times when the name of a directory no longer fits its use or when it conflicts with other directory and filenames. As a network administrator you might need to change the name of a user's home directory or the user's login name. You can easily change directory and filenames in FILER. Use the browser to select the directory you want to rename. To change the name of the directory (or file), simply highlight it and press [F3]. You can then use the Backspace key to erase the existing name and enter a new name. After you press [Enter], the new subdirectory or filename is displayed in the Directory contents window.

Using FILER to Delete a Directory Structure

When revising a directory structure or cleaning up a file server's volume, you sometimes need to delete an entire directory structure, including files and subdirectories. Before you do this, be absolutely certain that any files you or your users need have been backed up or moved to another directory. (Of course, it seems that whenever you throw something away you almost immediately find a use for it. If this happens with a file that you delete, you can use the SALVAGE utility described later in this section to recover it from the trash.)

To delete a directory structure, you must first change the current directory path to point to the directory or volume that contains the directory structure to be deleted. You can then highlight the target subdirectory and press [Del] or use the [F5] key to mark multiple subdirectories to be deleted and then press [Del]. FILER displays the Delete Subdirectory Options menu, giving you the option of deleting the entire subdirectory structure or deleting only the subdirectory's files. The Delete Subdirectory's Files Only option removes all files from the subdirectory but does not delete lower subdirectories or their files. To delete the entire subdirectory structure and all files, highlight the Delete Entire Subdirectory Structure option and press [Enter]. FILER then displays a confirmation box. To delete the entire subdirectory structure and all files, highlight Yes and press [Enter]. The entire subdirectory structure is removed from the volume.

Using FILER to Manage Files

The Manage files and directories options in the Filer main menu enables you to work with files. Selecting a filename and pressing [F10] will display the File options menu, as shown in Figure 8-43.

Figure 8-43

The File options menu

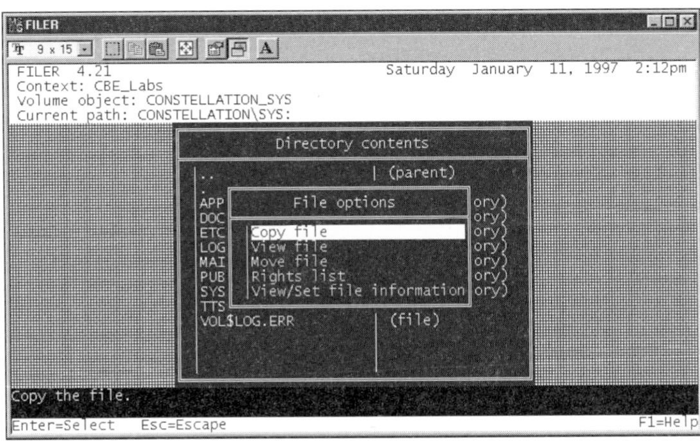

This menu has the following options:

- The Copy file option copies selected files to the path you specify.
- The View file option enables you to view the contents of the file.
- The Move file option enables you to move a file to a different location in the directory structure.
- The Rights list option is a supervisor-only option that displays a list of all users who have access rights to the selected directory. This option is useful when you want to verify that a directory is secured for use by only the designated users.
- The View/Set file information option is used to display the File Information screen for the selected file.

Selecting View/Set file information from this menu will display information about the file, as shown in Figure 8-44.

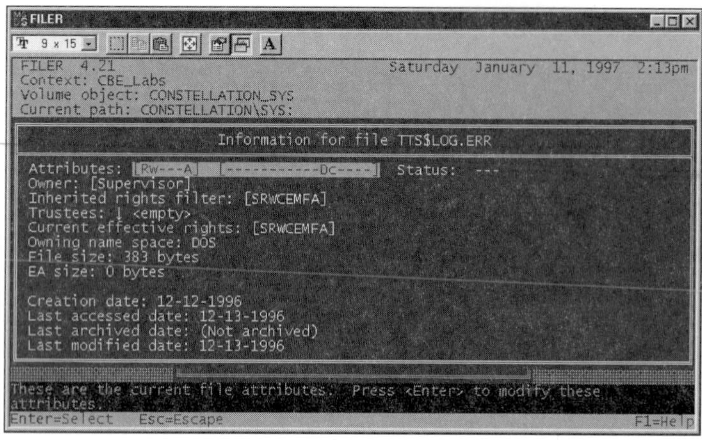

Figure 8-44 The Information for File TTS$LOG.ERR screen

The Information window contains the following fields:

- The Attributes field enables you to add or remove attribute flags by displaying a window of existing attributes when you highlight the field and press [F3] (modify). You can then use the [Ins] and [Del] keys to add or remove file attributes. The use of the NetWare file attributes will be described in Chapter 10.
- The Owner field identifies the user who originally created the file. Only a supervisor user can change the contents of the owner field. This is normally done if the name of the user who originally created the file is deleted from the system.
- The Inherited Rights filter and Trustees fields function the same way they do in the Directory Information window.
- The Current effective rights field is for information purposes only and cannot be changed, even by the supervisor.
- The Owning name space field shows whether the file is a DOS, 0S/2, or Macintosh file.
- The File size field shows the file size in bytes, whereas the EA (Extended Attributes) field shows the size in bytes of space used to store not-DOS file information.
- The Creation date, Last accessed date, Last modified date, and Last archived date fields are for informational purposes and can be changed only by the supervisor.

If you want to work with several files, use the [F5] key to highlight each file name and then press [Enter] to obtain the Multiple file operations window shown in Figure 8-45. This menu shows all options available to a supervisor, but if you do not have supervisor authority, your menu will not include the options to change owner or file date information.

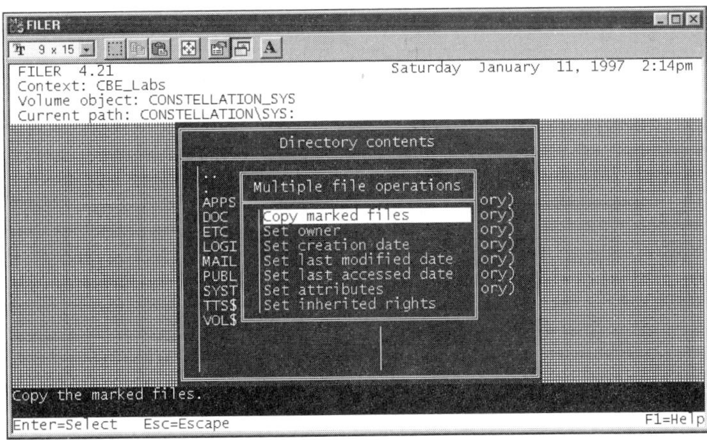

Figure 8-45 The Multiple File Operations menu

Using FILER to Copy Multiple Files

Although FILER is not the fastest or easiest way to copy files, it is often convenient for the network administrator to use it rather than exit the FILER program, perform the copy process, and then restart FILER to continue working with the file system. To copy files using FILER, first browse the directory containing the files you want to copy. Use the [F5] key to highlight each of the files you want to copy and press [Enter] to display the Multiple file operations menu, shown in Figure 8-45. Select the Copy marked files option and enter the target path to which you want the selected files to be copied. After a valid target path is entered, the selected files are copied into the specified directory.

Using FILER to Delete Files from a Directory

Deleting files from a directory is similar to copying files. You first change to the current directory containing the files to be deleted, mark the target files using the [F5] key, and then press [Del]. You can then select Yes in the Confirm File Deletion window to delete the marked files.

Manage According to Search Pattern

You can use the Manage according to search pattern option to control which directories and files are included or excluded from FILER operations. When you choose this option, the Set the search pattern and filter dialog box, shown in Figure 8-46, is displayed.

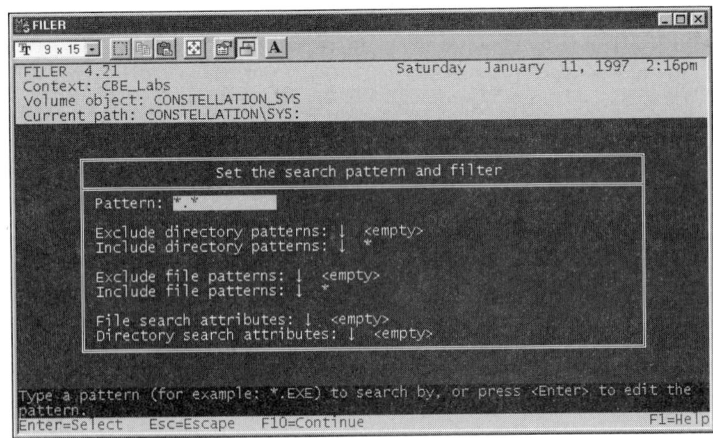

Figure 8-46 The Set the search pattern and filter dialog box

One of the most commonly used fields in the dialog box is the File search attributes field. Normally the Directory Contents window does not show hidden files or system files and directories. To access them, select the File search attributes field to display the Search file attributes window. To see hidden files and system files, add the Hidden and System attributes to the window by pressing [Ins]. This displays the Other attributes window. Use the [F5] key to highlight both the Hidden and System attributes. The selected attributes will be added to the Search file attributes window after you press [Enter]. You can then use the [Esc] key to return to the Set the search pattern and filter dialog box.

Select Current Directory

You can use the Select current directory option to change the current directory path shown at the top of the FILER screen. When FILER asks for the current directory path, you can either enter the complete path to the new location—server_name\volume:directory\subdirectory—or press [Ins] and then select each component of the directory path from a window, as shown in Figure 8-47. After all directories leading to the desired directory path have been selected, use the [Esc] key to exit the selection window and then press [Enter] to make the selected path your current work directory.

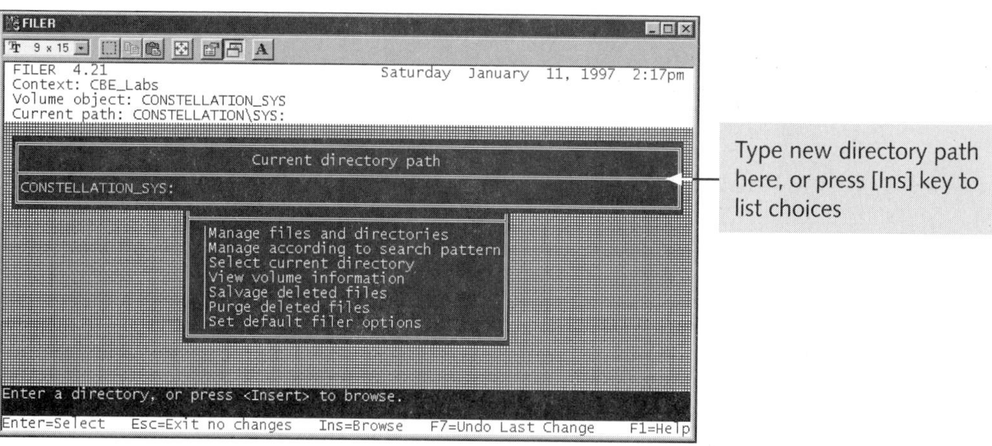

Figure 8-47 Selecting the Current Directory path

View Volume Information

The View volume information option enables you to view volume information in the current volume. When you select this option, a Volume menu is displayed with the following options:

- The Statistics option displays current space information about the volume.
- The Features option displays information about name spaces, compressions, and suballocation.
- The Dates and Times option displays dates and time associated with the volume.

Selecting the Statistics option displays the screen shown in Figure 8-48. The screen displayed by the Features option is shown in Figure 8-49, and the screen displayed by the Dates and Times option is shown in Figure 8-50.

Figure 8-48

Displaying volume statistics

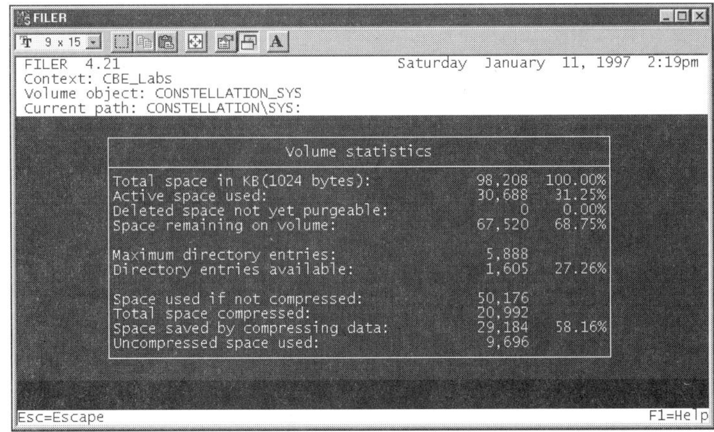

Figure 8-49

Displaying volume features information

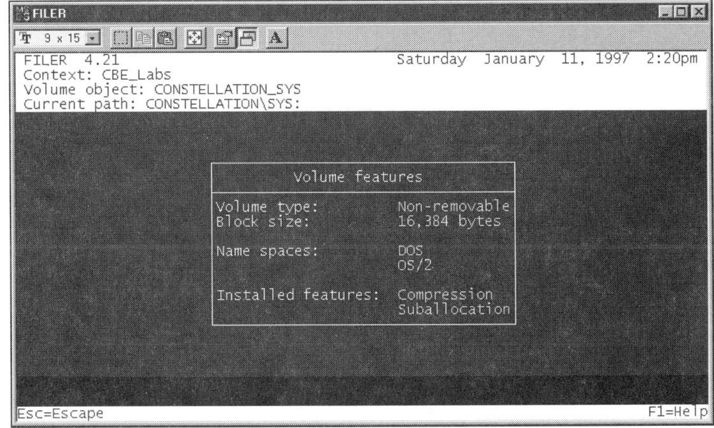

Figure 8-50

Displaying volume dates and times information

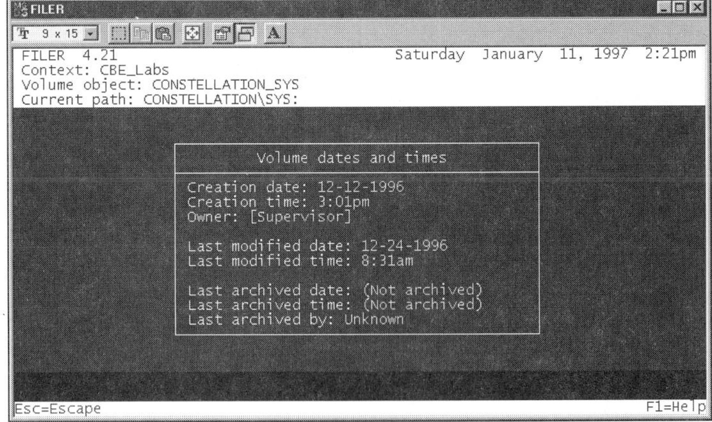

The NetWare 4.1 FILER option "View volume information" replaces the NetWare 3.1x VOLINFO utility.

Using FILER to Salvage Deleted Files

The purpose of the FILER Salvage deleted files option is to recover files that have been deleted from NetWare directories. This option will not, however, recover files deleted on local DOS drivers. As explained previously, unless a file is purged, the NetWare file server does not immediately use the space from the deleted file. Instead it tracks the deleted file information and uses a deleted file's space only after the space from all files that have been deleted previously has been reused. Knowing how to use the Salvage deleted files option is not only a requirement for being certified as a network administrator, but it can also make you a hero in the eyes of network users by "magically" recovering a valuable file.

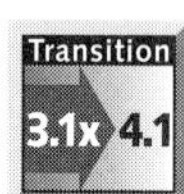

The NetWare 4.1 FILER option "Salvage deleted files" replaces the NetWare 3.1x SALVAGE utility. There is also a Salvage command in NetWare Administrator.

In this section you will learn how to use the Salvage deleted files option to recover files that have been deleted from an existing directory and even to recover files after their directory is removed. To recover deleted files, you need only the Create and File Scan access rights in the directory in which the deleted file was stored. (This means that a network administrator can train his or her users to salvage their own files.)

We'll start by salvaging only deleted files. The situation in which both files and the directories that contained them were deleted is discussed below. Before selecting the Salvage deleted files option, you need to use the Select current directory option to change directories to the directory that contains the deleted files. After this is done, choose the Salvage deleted files option. The Salvage menu is displayed, as shown in Figure 8-51.

The Salvage menu

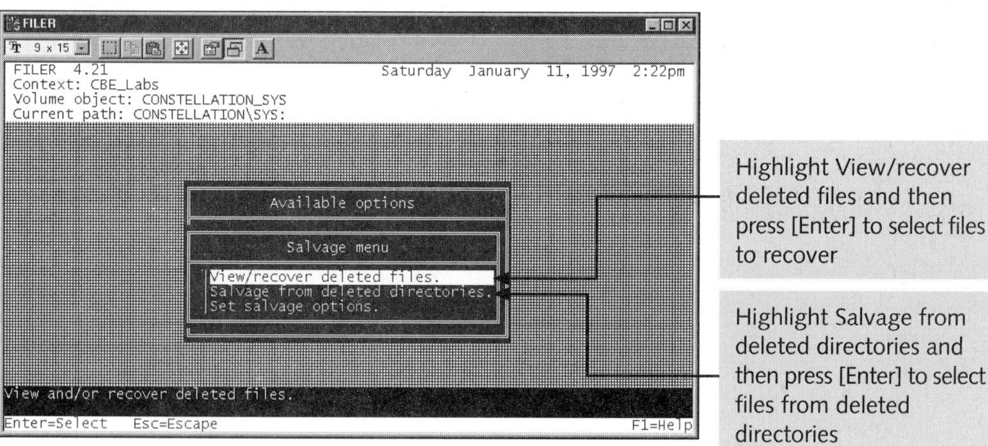

The View/recover deleted files option displays information about deleted files in the current directory path and enables you to recover any desired files.

The Salvage from deleted directories option is used to recover a file after the directory it was stored in is deleted. When directories are deleted, the files from these directories are stored in the DELETED.SAV directory on the volume the directory was on. DELETED.SAV is a hidden directory that exists on the root of each volume. Using this option enables you to search the DELETED.SAV directory for the file you want to recover. Files of the same name can exist in the DELETED.SAV directory, but because each file is stored with its deletion date and time, files with identical names can be differentiated with this information.

The Set salvage options option enables you to specify in what sequence you want to display the deleted files. Possible options include the following:

- By filename: This is the default sequence, and is suitable when you know the name of the file that you want to recover.
- By file size: This lists the largest deleted files first.
- By deletion date: This lists the most recently deleted files first and is handy when you are not sure of the name of the deleted file.
- By deleter: This sorts the list by the name of the user who deleted the file.

Salvaging a Deleted File from an Existing Directory

Select the View/recover deleted files option from the Salvage menu. The Erased file name pattern to Match dialog box is displayed. In this dialog box you can enter a search pattern, such as *.WK1, to view all deleted files with the .WK1 extension, or leave the default global name (an asterisk) to display all deleted files. When you have entered the pattern, press [Enter]. This displays the Salvageable files window, with a list of the deleted files in the directory, as shown in Figure 8-52. The files are listed in the sequence specified by the Salvage options selection in effect.

Figure 8-52 The Salvageable files window

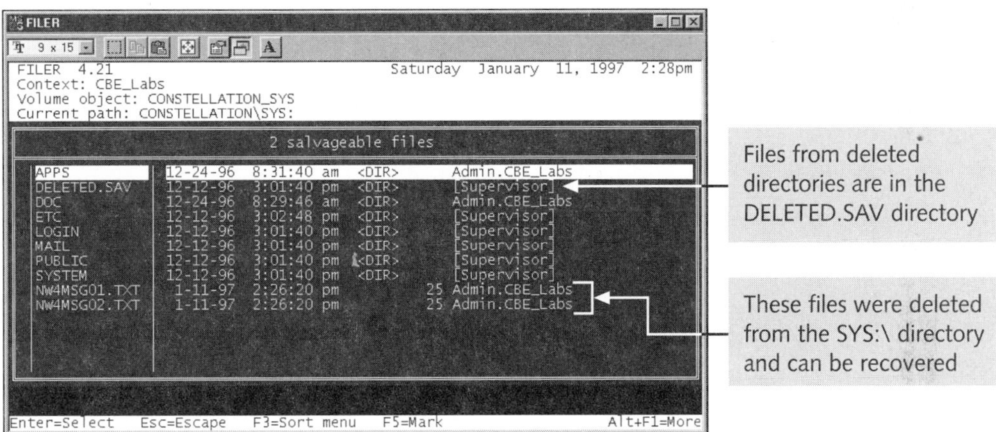

If you want to sort the files, you can press [F3]. This will display a menu that enables you to sort the files by filename, file size, deletion date, or deleter. To salvage a file, highlight the file in the list and press [Enter]. The screen shown in Figure 8-53 is displayed, followed by a dialog box with the prompt Recover this file. Select Yes and press [Enter] to salvage the file.

Figure 8-53 The Recover this file dialog box

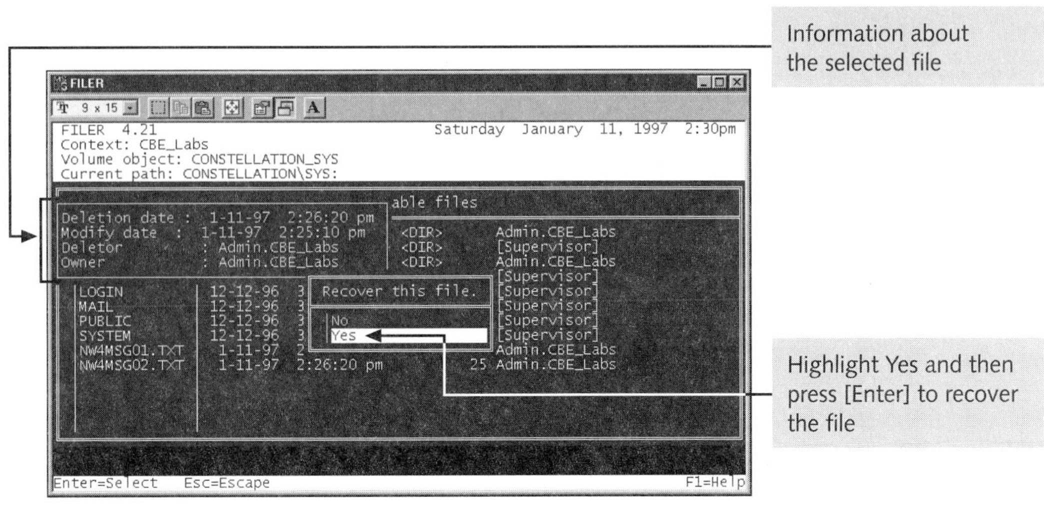

You can recover more than one file by using [F5] to mark the files you want to salvage. All the files you have marked will be returned to the current directory. If there is a file in the directory using the same name as the deleted file, you will be asked to specify a new name for the file that is being recovered.

Recovering Files from Deleted Directories

When a directory is removed, all files in the directory are moved to the DELETED.SAV directory on the root of the volume. Because DELETED.SAV is a hidden directory, you must have supervisor privileges to access this directory and recover its files.

When you are recovering a file from a directory that has been deleted, it helps if you first use the Set salvage options option to select the sort option that will make it easiest to spot the target files from the potentially large list of files from other deleted directories.

Select the Salvage from deleted directories option. SALVAGE displays a dialog box showing the names of all mounted volumes. Select the name of the volume that contained the files you want to recover and press [Enter] to display the Erased file name pattern to match dialog box. If you know the file's name or extension you can enter it at this time or press [Enter] to accept the global character and display all files from deleted directories. The Salvageable files window is displayed, listing all files in sequence by the salvage option you selected. You can recover a single file by highlighting the file's name and pressing [Enter], or you can use the [F5] key to mark multiple files to be recovered and press [Enter]. After salvaging, the recovered files are placed in the DELETED.SAV directory.

Returning to the FILER Menu

After you have recovered the files you wanted, press [Esc] twice to return to the FILER menu. If you recovered files in the DELETED. SAV directory, you can then use FILER to copy the recovered files from the DELETED.SAV directory to the directory path where they will be used.

Using FILER to Purge Deleted Files

The purpose of the FILER Purge deleted files option is the same as the PURGE command: to recover disk space from files that have been deleted but remain on the server for possible recovery. Purging immediately recovers the disk space used by deleted files. After a file has been purged, it cannot be recovered using FILER's Salvage deleted files option.

The NetWare 4.1 FILER Purge deleted files option incorporates the NetWare 3.1x PURGE command line utility but does not replace it. The PURGE command is still available.

When you select the Purge deleted files option, a File name pattern to purge dialog box is displayed. In this dialog box you can enter a search pattern, such as *.WK1, to purge only files with the .WK1 extension, or leave the default global name (an asterisk) to purge all deleted files. When you have entered the pattern, press [Enter]. The Purge options menu is displayed, as shown in Figure 8-54. You can choose to purge only the files in the current directory or all the files in the current directory and all its subdirectories.

Figure 8-54
The Purge options menu

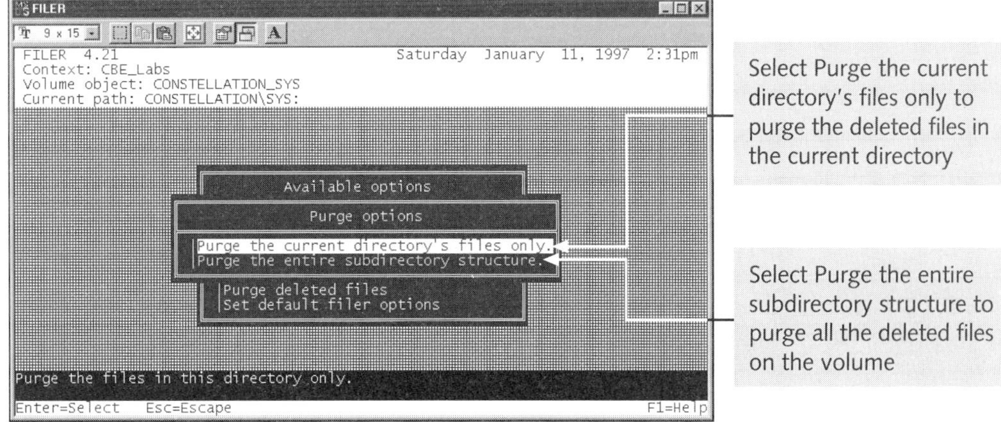

Set Default Filer Options

You can use the Set default filer settings option to change FILER settings that control confirmation messages, attributes to be copied, file and directory patterns you want to display, and search attributes. When you choose this option, the Filer settings dialog box, shown in Figure 8-55, is displayed.

Figure 8-55
The Filer settings dialog box

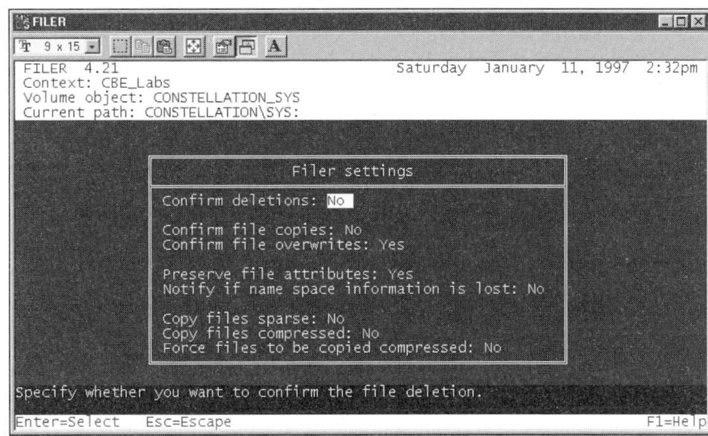

One of the most commonly used fields is the Confirm deletions option. By setting this option to "Yes," you can do a double check to make sure that you really want to delete the files.

NetWare File Management Graphical Utilities

The Windows 95 Windows Explorer can be used to copy, move, and delete files. You should already know how to use Windows Explorer to do these functions from your study of and knowledge of Windows 95. Windows Explorer, when used with the NetWare Client 32 client, can also be used to assign and control trustee rights, which will be discussed in Chapter 10.

In this section we'll discuss using NetWare Administrator to salvage and purge deleted files.

Using NetWare Administrator to Salvage and Purge Deleted Files

The same capability to salvage and purge deleted files that you used in the FILER utility is also available in the NetWare Administrator graphical utility. You select the directory you want to work with by selecting it in the NetWare Administrator browser window. You then select the Salvage command on the Tools menu to display the Salvage Files dialog box, as shown in Figure 8-56.

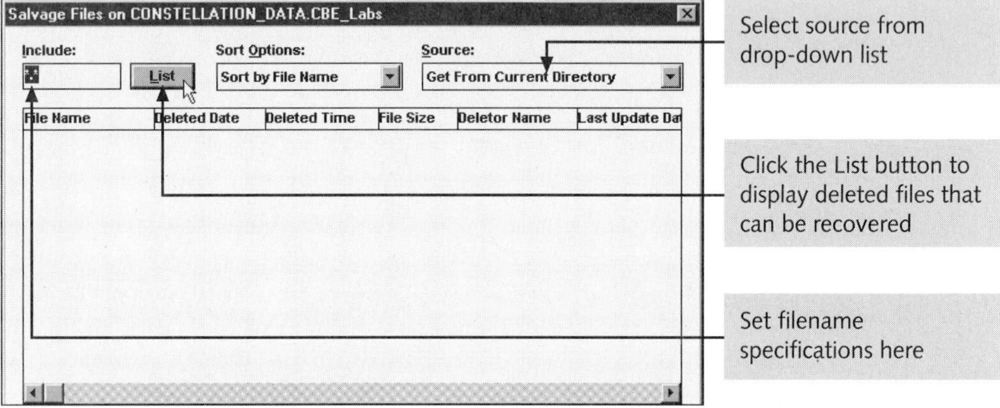

Figure 8-56 The Salvage Files dialog box

This dialog box has an Include text box in which you can specify a search pattern, such as *.WK1, to view all deleted files with the .WK1 extension, or leave the default global pattern (*.*) to display all deleted files. When you have edited the search pattern, you click the List button to display all deleted files matching the pattern. You can use the Sort Options drop-down list to control how the displayed files are sorted, and the Source drop-down list to display files from the current directory or from the DELETED.SAV directory. Files to be salvaged are selected by clicking the first filename and then holding down [Ctrl] while clicking on other filenames to add them to the selection. (Holding down [Shift] and clicking on a second filename will select *all* files between and including the first filename selected and the second filename.) Once the files are selected, you click the Salvage button to salvage the files. A dialog box is displayed to show where the restored files will be placed. Figure 8-57 shows a file selected for recovery.

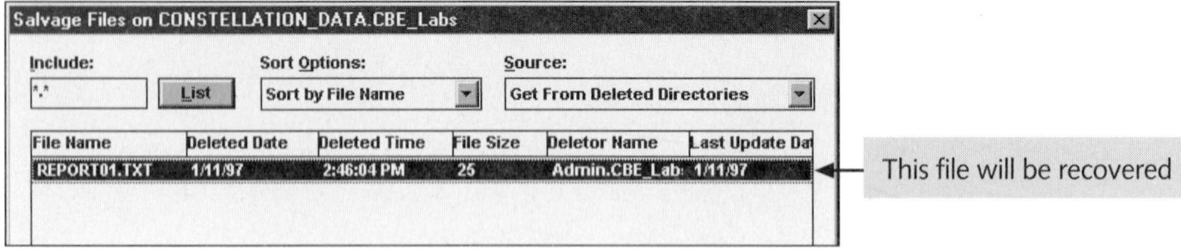

Figure 8-57 Selected files

Purging deleted files with NetWare Administrator works exactly like salvaging files, except after you have selected the files to be purged, you click the Purge button instead of the Salvage button. A dialog box will be displayed to confirm the purge.

CHAPTER SUMMARY

Directory management involves creating and removing directories and subdirectories on the various volumes in the network. This is known as creating and maintaining the directory structure for each volume. In Windows 95, directories are referred to as folders. Tools used to create directories and subdirectories include the DOS MD (Make Directory), RD (Remove Directory), and CD (Change Directory), commands, the Windows 95 File | New | Folder command, and the NetWare Administrator Create command.

Drive pointers are letters assigned to local drives and network directories for working with the file system and accessing software stored in other directories. The drive pointers A–G are normally reserved for DOS to use with local drives. Drive pointers H–Z are often used by NetWare to point to directory locations. Regular and root drive pointers are assigned to directories that contain data files; search drive pointers are assigned to software directories and work with the DOS path to enable a user to run programs that are not located in the current directory. Up to 16 search drives can be assigned, using letters Z for S1, Y for S2, and so on up to K for S16. Although letters R–K (S9–S16) are not normally assigned to search drives, using these pointers for regular drives risks conflicting with search paths. This leaves letters H–J always available for regular drive pointer assignments. Root drive pointers appear to DOS and applications as if the directory path were the beginning of a drive or volume. This enables the network administrator to make it more difficult for users or applications to move out of the assigned directory path. All drive pointer assignments are stored in the memory of the workstation until the user logs out. When a user logs in, drive pointers must be reset, either manually using the MAP and NetWare User Tools utilities or through the login script.

The MAP command is the utility used most frequently by network administrators to create and maintain drive pointers. As a network administrator, you should be able to use the MAP command to perform the following functions:

- View drive pointer assignments
- Create a regular drive pointer
- Create a root drive pointer
- Add a new search drive to the end of the current search drive list
- Insert a search drive within the existing search drives
- Remove a regular drive mapping
- Remove a search drive mapping

A Directory Map object is used in the NDS Directory tree to simplify mapping drive pointers in situations in which the mapped directory may change location in the file directory structure. By mapping a drive to the Directory Map object, the network administrator can change the drive pointer in just one place, the Directory Map object properties, when the directory location changes.

The Windows 95 Windows Explorer program and the NetWare menu utility NETUSER can be used by a user or the network administrator to change a user's drive pointer mappings. Because drive pointers play a major role in the way the NetWare file system is accessed by users, applications, and menus, it is important for a network administrator to establish standards for drive pointer usage in order to prevent conflicts and software configuration problems. As a general rule you should use a drive pointer planning form similar to one shown in Figure 8-35 to establish for each user a set of drive pointers that includes a regular drive pointer to the root of each volume, a root drive pointer to the user's home directory, and another root drive pointer to the shared work area for the user's workgroup. In addition to the required search drive to the SYS:PUBLIC directory, additional search drives need be allocated for each DOS-based software package and utility that is commonly used. Establishing a standard drive pointer usage plan will make accessing and maintaining the network file system much easier for both the users and the network administrator.

File management involves copying, moving, and deleting files in the various directories. Several NetWare utilities are useful in file management. The PURGE command line utility permanently erases deleted files and frees up disk space. Otherwise, NetWare maintains the deleted file on the volume until the disk is almost full and only then erases files to make room for new ones as necessary. When you are low on disk space, purging deleted files can often improve the NetWare server's performance.

The primary NetWare menu utility that is used with the file system is FILER. A network administrator needs to know what functions this utility performs and how to use it for the tasks described in this chapter. The FILER utility is one of the most sophisticated of the menu utilities and contains the following options: Manage files and directories, Manage according to search pattern, Select current directory, View volume information, Salvage deleted files, Purge deleted files, and Set default filer options. These options enable the network administrator to view and maintain current directory information, work with the file and subdirectory contained in the current directory, change the current directory path either by typing the path or by using the Ins key to select each component, select options such as what files to include or exclude, view information about the current volume, salvage deleted files, and purge deleted files. As a network administrator, you should know how to use FILER to complete the following:

- Change the current directory using the browser
- Change the current directory using the Ins key or typing the path
- Copy or move a directory structure
- Create directories
- Copy files
- Rename files and subdirectories
- Delete files and directory structures
- View volume information
- Salvage deleted files
- Purge deleted files

The FILER also enables network administrators to restrict disk space usage in each directory, and a network administrator needs to know how to restrict the amount of disk space available in the directory structure. The importance of the Salvage feature is its ability to recover files that have been deleted even when the directory structure in which the file was stored no longer exists. The Purge feature is identical to the PURGE command.

The NetWare Administrator graphical utility can also be used to salvage and purge deleted files, and a network administrator needs to know how to use it to do these tasks.

COMMAND SUMMARY

Command	Syntax	Definition
FILER	*FILER*	Menu utility that can be used to work with the file system. Menu options include: Manage files and directories Manage according to search pattern Select current directory View volume information Salvage deleted files Purge deleted files Set default filer options
MAP	*MAP d:=[path]*	Creates regular drive mappings.
	MAP N [path]	Creates a regular drive mapping using the next available drive letter.
	MAP ROOT d:= [path]	Creates root drive mappings.
	MAP S#:=[path]	Adds a search drive to the end of the search list.
	MAP INS S#:=[path]	Inserts a search drive before an existing drive number.
	MAP DEL d:	Removes either regular, root, or search drive pointers.
	MAP C drive	Changes a search drive mapping to a regular drive mapping and vice versa.
NETUSER	*NETUSER*	Menu utility that enables you to log into the network, change passwords, change the current context, work with drive and search mappings, control printing connections and jobs, send messages, and view information on effective rights on drives. Menu options include: Printing Messages Drives Attachments Change Context
PURGE	*PURGE [filename | path]* *[/option]* /? /VER	Erases deleted files. Filenames can be specified, or a path to a directory can be used. The only option is /A, which erases all deleted files in the specified directory and all its subdirectories.

KEY TERMS

Directory Map object
drive mapping
drive pointer
folder
local drive pointer
network drive pointer
regular drive pointer
root drive pointer
search drive pointer
Universal Naming Convention (UNC)

REVIEW QUESTIONS

1. Which of the following DOS commands will not work on a NetWare drive?

   XCOPY ____________________

   MD and CD ____________________

   CHKDSK ____________________

   FORMAT ____________________

   DIR ____________________

2. Describe how to create a new directory using DOS commands.

3. Describe how to create a new directory in Windows 95.

4. Describe how to create a new directory using NetWare Administrator.

5. Describe how to create a new directory using FILER.

6. _______________ drive pointers are used to reference data storage locations on the file server.

7. _______________ drive pointers are used to reference software storage directories on a file server.

8. Write a NetWare command to view all drive mappings.

   ____

9. Write a NetWare command to create a new root drive pointer H that will point to the SERVER01/DATA:USERS\JOHN directory.

   ____

10. Write a NetWare command to add a search drive pointer to the SERVER01/SYS:SOFTWARE\WP directory after the last search drive number when you don't know the number of the last search drive.

    ____

11. Write a NetWare command to insert a search drive into the SERVER01/SYS:SOFTWARE\SP directory between the existing S2 and S3 search drives.

    ____

12. Write commands to change the path of search drive S3 from the SYS:SOFTWARE\WP directory to the SYS:SOFTWARE\UTILITY directory without creating a regular drive pointer from the existing search drive.

    ____

Given the directory structure shown in Figure 8-58, write MAP commands to map drives to the marked areas.

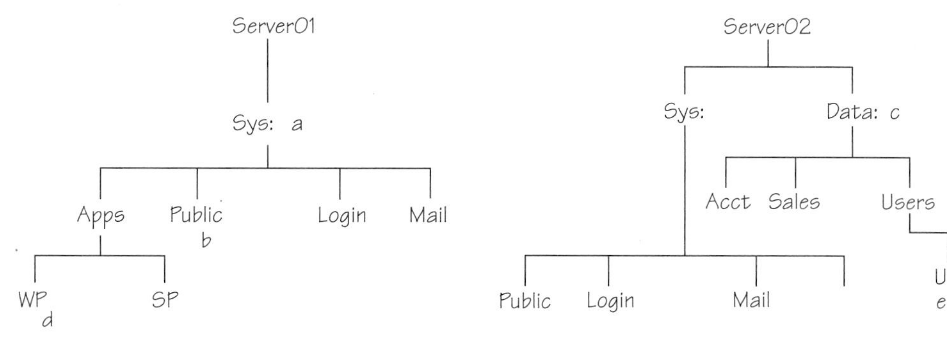

Figure 8-58 Sample directory structure

13. (a) ____

14. (b) ____

15. (c) ____

16. (d) ____

17. (e) ____

18. What is(are) the advantage(s) of using a Directory Map object instead of a direct drive pointer mapping?

19. Describe how you would use a Directory Map object to create a drive pointer to directory (c) in Figure 8-58.

20. Describe how you would use a Directory Map object to create a drive pointer to directory (d) in Figure 8-58.

21. A user or network administrator can map drive pointers on a user's PC using the ____________ menu utility or the ____________.

22. Describe how a user can create a drive pointer mapping using Windows 95.

23. Deleted files can be recovered using the ____________ command. This command is available in the ____________ menu utility and the ____________ graphical utility.

24. In order to permanently remove deleted files from a volume, you would use the ____________ command. This command is available in the ____________ command line utility, the ____________ menu utility, and the ____________ graphical utility.

25. When the FILER utility is used, the ____________ key can be used to mark several files for deletion.

26. The _______________ utility can be used to restrict the amount of space used by a subdirectory structure.

27. When using FILER to copy JAN95.WK1 from the SERVER01/DATA: BUSINESS\BUDGETS directory to the SERVER01/DATA:BUSINESS\WORK directory, you must first change to the _______________ directory.

Hands-On

EXERCISES

EXERCISE 8-1: USING FILER TO COPY A DIRECTORY STRUCTURE

In this exercise you practice using the FILER utility to copy a sample directory structure from the SYS: volume to a designated location in your home directory. The files and subdirectories in this structure will be used in subsequent hands-on exercises and case studies.

1. Log into the network using your student username.
2. Before using the NCOPY command to copy all files and subdirectories from the SERVER01/SYS:EXAMPLE directory to your home directory, you need to record the complete NetWare path to your directory. On the line below, record the complete path to your home directory including file server name, volume, and directory names.

   ____

3. Obtain a printout of the SYS:EXAMPLE directory structure showing all directories and subdirectories.
4. Use the CD command to change the default DOS prompt to point to your home directory. On the line below, record the CD command you use.

   ____

5. Use the MD command to create a directory for the sample structure at the beginning of your home directory, as shown below.

   VOLUME:
   ##ADMIN
   Sample

6. Use FILER to copy all files without attributes along with all the subdirectories from the SYS:EXAMPLE directory into the area you created in step 5. In the space below, record the steps you use in FILER.

   ____

   ____

   ____

   ____

   ____

7. Use the NDIR command with appropriate options to obtain a printout of your home directory and all subdirectories. Compare this directory listing with the one produced in step 3. Make sure all subdirectories are included. On the line below, record the NDIR command you use.

8. Use the NDIR command with the /R option to obtain a printout of all files and attributes in the SUPPORT\POLICY\SECTION3 subdirectory of your new sample directory structure. On the line below, record the command you use.

Exercise 8-2: Using FILER to Copy Files

In this exercise you practice using the FILER utility to copy files from one directory on the file server to another directory location.

1. Start FILER and use the "Select Current Directory" option to change to your ##ADMIN directory.

2. Copy all files that end with a number from the SOFTWARE.NTC\SP directory into the ADMIN\BUDGETS subdirectory of the sample directory structure. In the space below, record the FILER steps you use to do this.

Exercise 8-3: Using FILER to Rename Files and Directories

In this exercise you practice using the FILER utility to change the names of files and directories.

1. If you have not already done so, start FILER and use the "Select Current Directory" option to change to your ##NWTC directory.
2. In the SOFTWARE.NTC\SP directory, change the name of the worksheet file EARN01.WK1 by replacing the "01" in the filename with the current year (e.g., EARN1997). Change the name of the TAX02.WK1 file by replacing the "02" in the filename with last year (i.e. TAX1996).
3. Change the name of the FORMS directory located in your sample structure to CTIFORMS.
4. Exit FILER.
5. After completing the name changes, use NDIR to obtain a directory listing of the BUDGETS subdirectory. On the line below, record the NDIR command you use.

6. Use the NDIR command to obtain a printout showing the entire structure of your sample directory. On the line below, record the NDIR command you use.

Exercise 8-4: Deleting and Salvaging Files Using FILER

In this exercise you practice using FILER to delete files from the SUPPORT\POLICY \SECTION3 subdirectory of the sample structure and then the SALVAGE option to recover the deleted files.

1. Start FILER.
2. Use the Select Current Directory option and then use the Ins key to select the path leading to your SUPPORT\POLICY\SECTION3 subdirectory. On the line below, record the path you select.

   ____

3. Display all files in the SECTION3 directory using the Directory Information option.
4. Mark two files to be deleted. On the lines below, record the key you use along with the filenames.

   Key used to mark files: ______________________________

   Files marked: ______________________________

   ____

5. Delete the marked files.
6. Use the appropriate FILER option to determine the amount of space available from deleted files in this volume. On the line below, record the name of the option, the steps you use, and the amount of space available.

   OPTION: ______________________________

   STEPS: ______________________________

   ____

   ____

   ____

   ____

   ____

   SPACE: ______________________________

7. Start the SALVAGE option in FILER.
8. Change to the directory path you recorded in step 2.
9. Set the Salvage option to sort files by deletion time.
10. Use the appropriate option to display all deleted files.
11. Mark and salvage the files you deleted in step 5.
12. Exit the FILER utility.

Exercise 8-5: Salvaging Files Using NetWare Administrator

In this exercise you practice using the SALVAGE option of NetWare Administrator to recover deleted files. You delete the files from the SUPPORT\POLICY\SECTION3 subdirectory of the sample structure.

1. Launch Windows Explorer.
2. Select the SUPPORT\POLICY\SECTION3 subdirectory in your ##NWTC/SAMPLE directory. On the line below, record the path you select.

   ____

3. Select two files. On the lines below, record the filenames.

   Files marked: ______________________________

   ____

4. Delete the marked files.
5. Exit Windows Explorer.
6. Launch NetWare Administrator.
7. Use the appropriate NetWare Administrator option to determine the amount of space available from deleted files in this volume. On the line below, record the name of the option, the steps you use, and the amount of space available.

   OPTION: ______________________________

   STEPS: ______________________________

   ____

   ____

   ____

   ____

   ____

   SPACE: ______________________________

8. Start the SALVAGE option in NetWare Administrator.
9. Change to the directory path you recorded in step 2.
10. Set the Salvage option to sort files by deletion time.
11. Use the appropriate option to display all deleted files.
12. Mark and salvage the files you deleted in step 4.
13. Exit the NetWare Administrator utility.

Exercise 8-6: Restricting Disk Space Using NetWare Administrator

In this exercise you use the NetWare Administrator utility to restrict the disk space available to the SALES directory structure of your sample structure to 1 MB.

1. Launch the NetWare Administrator.
2. Select the directory that contains the SALES directory and expand the Directory tree until you can see that directory.
3. Select the SALES directory from your sample directory structure area. Display the properties for the directory and restrict the space available to 1 MB.
4. Exit the NetWare Administrator.

Exercise 8-7: Using the MAP Command

In this exercise you use the MAP command to create both regular and search drive mappings, display your drive mappings on the printer, and then test the search drive. After each of the map descriptions in step 1, record the MAP command you plan to use to create that drive mapping. Do not execute these map commands until step 3.

1. Write MAP commands for the following sample directory areas:

   A regular drive pointer to the sample directory in your student directory.

   ____

   A root drive pointer to Jon Ross's (JONROS) home directory, located in the USERS directory.

   ____

   A search drive pointer after the last existing search drive that points to the UTILITY subdirectory of the DATAPROC directory.

   ____

   Insert a search drive before the existing S1 that points to the SYS:SOFTWARE.NTC\SP directory.

   ____

2. The UTIL program is located in the DATAPROC\UTILITY directory of your sample structure. To illustrate the use of search drives, in this step you will try to run the UTIL program without a search drive and observe the error message. To try running the UTIL program from your current drive, launch a DOS window and then type the command UTIL and press [Enter]. In the space below, write the error message you receive and what this message means.
3. Use MAP commands to create the drive mappings you defined at the start of this exercise.
4. Use the command MAP > PRN to obtain a printout of the drive mapping you have created.
5. What letter is used by the S1 search drive mapping? ______________

6. To run the UTIL program, type the command UTIL and press [Enter].
   If your search drives are mapped correctly, you should receive a message screen. In the space below, record each directory that the computer needed to look in before finding the UTIL program:

7. Print the screen containing the results of your UTIL command.
8. Enter the command SP to test your S1 search drive mapping.
9. Delete the S1 search drive mapping. On the line below, record the command you use.

   ____

10. Use the MAP command to display the revised search drive list.

Exercise 8-8: Creating a Directory Map Object with NetWare Administrator

In this exercise you create a Directory Map object using NetWare Administrator.

1. Launch the NetWare Administrator.
2. Select the your ##NWTC Organizational Unit object.
3. Create a Directory Map object named Network Utilities that maps a drive pointer to the DATAPROC\UTILTY directory in your sample directory structure area.
4. Exit the NetWare Administrator.
5. Write a MAP command to use the Network Utilities Directory Map object in a search drive mapping. (If you did Exercise 8-7, use the same drive letter you used there). Record your command below:

   ____

6. Use MAP commands to create the drive mapping you defined.
7. Use the command MAP > PRN to obtain a printout of the drive mapping you have created.

Exercise 8-9: Creating a Directory Map Object with NETADMIN

In this exercise you create a Directory Map object using NETADMIN. NETADMIN is a NetWare Menu Utility that can perform many of the same functions as NetWare Administrator.

1. Launch a DOS session; then start NETADMIN.
2. Select the ##NWTC Organizational Unit object.
3. Create a Directory Map object named Network Utilities that maps a drive pointer to the SYS:SOFTWARE.NTC directory.
4. Exit NETADMIN.

5. Write a MAP command to use the Network Utilities Directory Map object in a search drive mapping. (If you did Exercise 8-7, use the same drive letter you used there). Record your command below:

____

6. Use MAP commands to create the drive mapping you defined.
7. Use the command MAP > PRN to obtain a printout of the drive mapping you have created.

Exercise 8-10: Using NETUSER

In this exercise you practice using the NETUSER menu utility instead of the MAP command to create the drive mappings defined in step 1 of Exercise 8-7.

1. Log out of the network in order to remove all existing drive pointers.
2. Log into the network again with same user name.
3. Launch a DOS session and display your drive mappings with the MAP command.
4. Use the NETUSER Tools utility to establish the drive mappings you identified in step 4 of Exercise 8-7.
5. Exit NETUSER.
6. Still in the DOS session, use the MAP command to verify the drive mappings.
7. At the DOS prompt, enter the command UTIL to test your search drive to the utility directory.
8. At the DOS prompt, enter the command SP to test your search drive to the spreadsheet software directory.
9. Exit the DOS session.

Exercises

Case 8-1: Setting Up a Drive Pointer Environment for the J. Q. Adams Corporation

The J. Q. Adams Corporation would like you to set up a drive pointer environment for the administrative users of its network. Each user needs a drive pointer to be able to access his or her home directory directly without accidentally changing to another location. In addition, all users in each department need to be able to access easily the shared work directory for their department as well as have access to the organization's work directory and word processing forms. The users in the sales department will need a special drive pointer to run the order entry system. All users in the company will need to be able to run either the word processing or spreadsheet application software stored in the SYS:SOFTWARE.NTC directory as well as be able to use NetWare and DOS commands.

1. Use the sample directory structure located in the SYS:EXAMPLE directory to complete a copy of the drive pointer planning form.
2. Use MAP commands to implement the drive pointers you recorded in step 1. Record the MAP commands you use in the space below, and use the MAP > PRN command to document the drive pointer assignments on the printer.

NORTHWESTERN TECHNICAL COLLEGE

PROJECT 8-1: CREATE THE NORTHWESTERN CAMPUS DIRECTORY STRUCTURE

Now that NetWare has been installed on the campus file servers and the user workstations are able to boot up and attach to the network, your next job is to create a directory structure that can support the processing needs of the organization. To perform this task, you recently had a meeting with Dave Johnson and together you have finalized the directory structure you were working on in Chapter 5. Although the final design shown in Figure 8-59 does not exactly match your original design, it has everyone's approval and will meet the processing needs of the campus. The design is departmentalized by computer lab, faculty, and administration. Each administrative unit and academic department has a work area, and home directories are planned for each user. Now Dave wants you to establish the framework for the directory structure by creating the major directories. The user home directories will not be created at this time but will be automatically created for you later when you use NetWare utilities to create the user accounts. Dave informed you that the software for administrative use has already been installed in the SOFTWARE.NTC directory of the NWTC_SERVER01_SYS volume and is ready for use. Similarly, the software for lab use has been installed in the SOFTWARE.NTC directory of the NWTC_SERVER02_SYS volume.

Figure 8-59 NWTC_Server 01_DATA directory structure

Volume Design Form

Created By:	Dave Johnson	Date:	9/15/97
Volume:	NWTC_Server01_DATA:	Capacity:	2 GByte
NetWare Version:	4.1	Note: Functions below are not applicable to 3.1x	

Block Size:					
Block Size:		4 Kbytes	Block Suballocation:	X	Enable
		8 Kbytes			Disable
		16 Kbytes			Not applicable
		32 Kbytes	File Compression:	X	Enable
	X	64 Kbytes			Disable
					Not applicable
			Data Migration:		Enable
				X	Disable
					Not applicable

Directory Structure Diagram

DATA:

ADMIN FORMS MENUS WORK BUSINESS INFOSYS STUDSERV SUPPORT FACULTY USERS

WORK BUDGETS ACCT PAYROLL

UTILITY WORK

WORK TESTING PLACEMNT

WORK POLICY SURVEY PUBLISH CATALOG

MGMT ACCT MRKT MIS

WORK WORK WORK WORK

U01 U02 U03 U04 U05 U06 U07 U08 U09 U10 U11 U12 U13 U14 U15 U16 U17 U18

Your task is to create the directory structure for only the SERVER01_DATA volume. The SERVER02_DATA volume directory structure has already been set up by your instructor.

1. Log into the network using your student username.
2. Launch NetWare Administrator.
3. Expand the SERVER01_DATA volume and select your home directory.
4. Use the NetWare Administrator utility to create the directory structure shown in Figure 8-59 for the SERVER01_DATA volume.
5. After creating the directory structure, print a copy of the Directory tree with the directory structure expanded.

Project 8-2: Plan Drive Pointer Usage

Now that the directory structure has been established, Dave would like you to develop a plan for how drive pointers will be defined for users and groups. Making a Drive Pointer Assignment form similar to the one shown in this chapter, fill out the form showing drive pointers that would be common to all users as well as drive pointer assignments for each department or workgroup and for the students in the lab. Dave explained, for example, that the computer lab users will need special search drives to the software packages in the lab, whereas faculty and office staff should have search drives for the software stored in the SERVER01/SYS:SOFTWARE.NTC directory. Faculty and office staff users should also have home directories along with drive pointers to their corresponding shared work areas and search drives to the SERVER01/SYS:SOFTWARE.NTC software directories. The student service staff will also need a way to access the placement and testing applications directories. You should fill out a drive pointer planning form for all users and another form for each workgroup that has separate drive mapping assignments.

Project 8-3: Installing and Testing Utility Programs

Suppose you have some handy utility programs located on your student work disk that you would like to copy onto the file server in the INFOSYS\UTILITY subdirectory of the Northwestern Technical College structure.

1. Use the NCOPY command to copy all files from the \UTILITY directory of your student work disk into the INFOSYS\UTILITY subdirectory. On the line below, record the command you use.

   ____

2. Use the NDIR command to obtain a printout of the files contained in the INFOSYS\UTILITY directory.
3. Establish a search drive mapping to your INFOSYS\UTILITY directory.
4. Use the CD SYS: command to change your default drive to the root of the SERVER01_SYS: volume.
5. Use the NDIR command to obtain a printout of the files contained in the SERVER01_SYS: directory.

CHAPTER NINE

MANAGING USERS, GROUPS, AND LOGIN SECURITY

Giving users convenient access to the file server and at the same time protecting sensitive or private information and services are the primary functions of a network security system. NetWare 4.1 provides the capabilities and tools the network administrator needs to establish a sophisticated security system that will meet these needs in a LAN environment. As a network administrator you will be expected to know how to use these capabilities and tools to perform the following security system functions:

- Create users and groups
- Determine what administrative functions can be delegated to user accounts and how to assign these privileges
- Protect user accounts from unauthorized use
- Use NetWare accounting to track system usage and charge users for network services
- Assign appropriate trustee rights to control access to NDS and the Directory tree

AFTER READING THIS CHAPTER AND COMPLETING THE EXERCISES YOU WILL BE ABLE TO:

- LIST THE THREE TYPES OF NETWARE SECURITY AND DESCRIBE HOW LOGIN SECURITY CAN BE USED TO RESTRICT ACCESS TO THE FILE SERVER.
- CREATE NEW USERS, GROUPS, ORGANIZATIONAL ROLES, AND PROFILES AND ASSIGN ACCESS RESTRICTIONS USING THE NETWARE ADMINISTRATOR, NETADMIN, AND UIMPORT UTILITIES.
- DESCRIBE HOW THE NETWARE ACCOUNTING SYSTEM CAN BE USED TO CHARGE FOR NETWORK SERVICES AND TO KEEP TRACK OF TOTAL SYSTEM USAGE AND GROWTH.
- USE THE DSREPAIR UTILITY TO CHECK FOR AND FIX POSSIBLE PROBLEMS IN THE NDS DATABASE.

- Assign appropriate trustee rights and file attributes to control access to the file system
- Secure the file server console from unauthorized access

To provide these functions, NetWare security can be described as having three levels: login security, trustee rights (NDS and file system) security, and console security. These are illustrated in Figure 9-1.

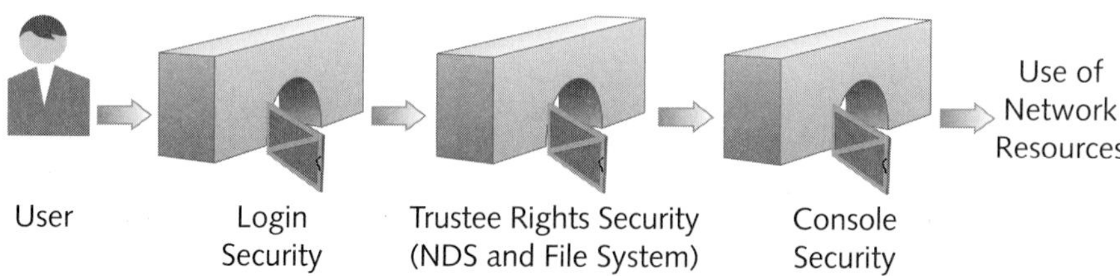

Figure 9-1 NetWare system security

You have already worked with login security, which controls initial access to the file server, when you had to enter a valid user name to log into a server and when you used the SETPASS utility to make your account more secure with an optional password. In this chapter, you will learn more about login security and how to use NetWare utilities such as NetWare Administrator, NETADMIN, and UIMPORT to create users and groups, assign privileges, and establish access restrictions. In Chapter 10 you will learn how Trustee rights (NDS and file system) security can provide users with the necessary access rights to perform their work without affecting other users and limit access to Directory tree objects, directories, and files that contain sensitive or secure information. Chapter 16 contains techniques and commands to make the file server console secure from unauthorized access.

LOGIN SECURITY

Login security is sometimes referred to as initial access security because it controls a user's ability to gain access to a file server. The login security system of NetWare 4.1 consists of five components that work together to provide users with the ability to access the file server and perform their assigned tasks:

1. User names
2. Passwords and password restrictions
3. Time restrictions
4. Station restrictions
5. Account restrictions

USER NAMES

When NetWare 4.1 is first installed and started, one user name and account, Admin, is automatically created, and the Admin User object is added to the Directory tree. The user Admin has access to all network services, the entire NDS Directory tree, and the entire file system.

As noted in Chapter 4, the network administrator account in NetWare 3.1x was named SUPERVISOR. Admin is the NetWare 4.1 equivalent of SUPERVISOR. NetWare 3.1x also created a user account for a user named GUEST, but the GUEST account is *not* created by the NetWare 4.1.

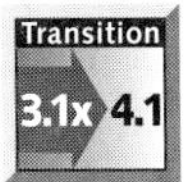

During the NetWare 3.1x installation process, a group named EVERYONE was created. Any user account that was created was automatically added to the EVERYONE group. The network administrator could easily handle assigning resources that needed to be shared by all users by assigning rights to the resource to the EVERYONE group. NetWare 4.1 does *not* create an EVERYONE group during installation. Instead, NetWare 4.1 uses the [Public] trustee to assign common rights to resources. The [Public] trustee is discussed briefly later in this chapter and in detail in Chapter 10.

Initially the network administrator logs in as Admin and then creates the NDS Directory tree, the directory structure, other users, groups, and access restrictions. In this section you will learn to assign user names and access privileges and properly construct the user environment.

After creating the NDS Directory tree and network file system, the network administrator next needs to create a User object in the Directory tree for each user. After the User object is created, access to network resources can be assigned to the user by granting access privileges to the User object.

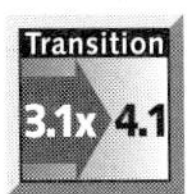

In NetWare 3.1x, if a user needed to access information and services on more than one file server, a user name had to be created on each server the user needed to access. In NetWare 4.1, all that is needed is one User object with appropriate access rights.

Although user names can be up to 64 characters in length, most network administrators try to limit user names to eight or fewer characters so they can create user's home directories with the same name as the login name. This makes it easier to map drives to user home directories automatically with login script files.

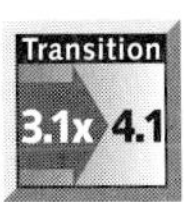

In NetWare 3.1x, user names were restricted to 47 characters in length.

One of the first considerations in creating user names is developing a consistent method of constructing a user name from each user's actual name. Two common methods are used to construct user names. One is to use the first letter of the user's first name followed by the first seven letters of his or her last name. For example, the user name for Mary Read is MREAD. The advantage of this method is that the user name is very similar to the user's actual name. The disadvantages are that most last names need to be truncated and frequent conflicts occur in which two or more users have the same first initial and last name. Such a case would be the user name for Michael Read, which is also MREAD.

The second common method for creating user names is to use the first three letters of the user's first name followed by the first three letters of the user's last name. In this method, for example, Mary Read's user name becomes MARREA. The advantages of this method are that the user names are almost uniformly of a consistent length and there is a smaller chance of duplicates. A disadvantage is that the user names are less recognizable. Whichever system you choose for creating user names, you must remember to be as consistent as possible.

NetWare 4.1 also enables a network administrator to assign special manager and operator privileges to user accounts so they can perform such basic network administrative functions as creating and maintaining user accounts and working with printers. This delegation of responsibility allows the network administrator to concentrate on more important network functions. Even if you do not want to delegate basic jobs to other users, you can use this capability to create user names that you use yourself to perform certain functions without having to log in as Admin. Logging in as Admin every time you need to do a network task that does not require supervisor privileges increases the risk of accidental damage to files or introduction of viruses into the network. (Because the Admin user name has all access rights to the entire network file system, if your workstation is infected by a computer virus, the virus software can copy itself into other network files and possibly erase network data.)

There is the case of a network administrator who logged in on a NetWare 3.1x server as SUPERVISOR and, while using the FILER utility to clean up the SYS: volume by removing unnecessary directories, accidentally marked and deleted the SYS:SYSTEM directory. This network administrator then had to restore the file server files from the NetWare installation disks.

The NetWare 3.1x special designations of workgroup manager, user account manager, and console operator don't exist in NetWare 4.1. Equivalents can be created by assigning appropriate Directory tree and network file system rights. The designations of print queue operator and print server operator still exist, and a user's privileges can still be made "SUPERVISOR equivalent" by setting the user's security equivalence to that of the Admin user.

One of the properties of the User object is Security Equivalence. Assigning a security equivalent to the Admin user privilege level gives a user the same privilege level and authority as the Admin user. Of course, this status should be limited to a small number of users. Most network administrators, however, establish at least one supervisor equivalent user to act as a backup, sometimes called a "back door," in case the Admin account is inadvertently disabled or deleted. Later in this chapter you will learn how the NETADMIN menu utility can be used to inform you which users on your file server have been granted supervisor equivalency.

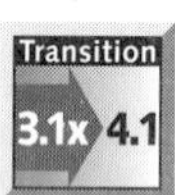

The NetWare 4.1 NETADMIN menu utility includes the functionality of the NetWare 3.1x SYSCON, DSPACE, and SECURITY utilities.

By granting appropriate privileges, you can create the equivalent of NetWare 3.1x **workgroup managers**, who can create and manage new users and groups without having access to the entire file server, and **user account managers**, who can modify but not create user accounts. The main purpose of creating users with these types of privileges is to enable the network administrator to delegate control of workgroups or departments to other capable users. In a large network, this reduces the amount of time the network administrator must spend performing these basic tasks.

NetWare 4.1 also enables you to designate users as **print queue operators**, so that specified users can control a print queue. A print queue is a directory on a file server that holds printed output until the designated printer is ready to receive it. The print queue allows multiple users to send output to a printer simultaneously. Print jobs need to be cleared from the print queue periodically due to incorrect printer selection. Print jobs can also be rearranged to allow more important output to be printed first.

You can also designate users as **print server operators**, which enables a user to control one or more printers. This privilege is usually assigned to users who have a printer attached to their workstations. Being a print server operator enables the user to perform such printer functions as changing forms, stopping the printer to clear paper jams, restarting the printer at a specific page number, and canceling a print job.

When a user logs in, the NetWare operating system checks his or her user account to see which level of privileges are assigned to that account.

PASSWORDS

Although user names and assigned privileges provide initial access to the server and delegate network management duties, they do little to prevent unauthorized access to restricted information or server functions. Networks need additional security to restrict who can use the file server in order to protect the information and the integrity of the file server environment. After user names, the first barrier in a security system is passwords on user accounts. The password for the Admin account is created during the installation process.

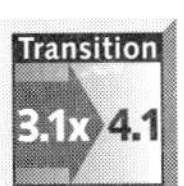

In NetWare 3.1x the password for the SUPERVISOR account was not set during installation. Until the network manager logged in as SUPERVISOR and created a password, anyone could log in as SUPERVISOR.

In NetWare 4.1, passwords can be up to 20 characters long; if you enable users to change their own passwords, you can increase password security by requiring some or all of the password restrictions described in the following paragraphs.

NetWare provides additional security against guessed user names and passwords by requiring a password whenever someone attempts to log in using a user name that does not exist. This feature makes it more difficult for people to guess user names because they can never be sure if they have entered a correct user name and wrong password or if they have entered an incorrect user name.

Set Minimum Password Length

To prevent the use of passwords that are short and easy to guess, most network administrators use Novell's recommendation of a five-character minimum for password length. In this chapter, you will learn how to change the minimum length of passwords assigned to existing or newly created users.

Force Periodic Password Changes

After a while, a user's password can become known to coworkers and no longer provides protection against unauthorized access to that user's account. Having users periodically change passwords lessens this problem. NetWare enables you to force selected user accounts to change passwords by establishing a limit on the time period a password remains valid. NetWare's default value of 40 days between password changes might be too frequent for most users. If the time period between password changes is too short, it is not uncommon for users to record their current password near their work areas where it can easily be found and used (under the keyboard and in a desk drawer are common hiding places). As network administrator, you can increase the time between password changes in order to improve file server security. In addition, you should encourage good password and login habits by periodically reminding users not to have their password information recorded near their workstations and to log out whenever they leave their workstations unattended.

Require Unique Passwords

Another way to increase password security is to require users to enter a different password each time they change their password. When you require unique passwords, the file server keeps track of the last 10 passwords that have been used by a user and rejects a new password that repeats one of the previous 10. NetWare's unique passwords option prevents users from alternating among a few favorite passwords, which therefore makes it more difficult for an intruder to log in using a known password. Network administrators often combine this option with forced periodic password changes in order to provide increased safety on security-sensitive user accounts such as the SUPERVISOR account or an account assigned to a payroll clerk.

Limit Login Grace Periods

When a password has been set to expire, the user is given a default of six **grace logins** to use the expired password. This six-login grace period prevents users from accidentally being locked out from the network after their passwords expire, and it also keeps users from using an expired password indefinitely. Each time a user logs in after password expiration, NetWare displays a reminder that the current password has expired and states the remaining number of grace logins. Six grace logins are adequate for most file server installations, but the network administrator or user account manager can change this number on an individual basis or change the default value that is assigned to all new user names when they are created.

Time Restrictions

Time restrictions enable the network administrator or user account manager to increase a user's account security by limiting the times during which the account can be used. This prevents someone who knows a user's password from logging in and accessing the network after business hours. Time restrictions can be set in half-hour increments. For example, a network administrator can establish time restrictions that allow a payroll clerk to use the file server only between 8:00 A.M. and 4:30 P.M. on weekdays. Time restrictions are important on high-security accounts, such as a payroll clerk's, because they prevent an intruder from accessing sensitive payroll information during nonbusiness hours.

Station Restrictions

Station restrictions can be used to limit the number of times a user account can be concurrently logged into the server and to specify from which workstations a user can log into the network. The NetWare default is that a user can log in from any workstation and be logged into the network at several workstations simultaneously. These defaults can be changed by the Admin user or other users with appropriate supervisor privileges.

Setting a user name to be valid for logging in from several workstations simultaneously enables a network administrator to create a general-purpose user name for multiple users. In most situations, however, limiting user accounts to one workstation at a time is important for the following reasons:

- Logging in from multiple workstations can cause software errors with some programs because certain control files are not sharable and therefore cannot be accessed simultaneously from more than one location by the same user.
- Restricting the user name to one workstation at a time helps users who move between multiple workstations remember not to leave a workstation unattended—and thus open to access by unauthorized users.
- Limiting a user account to access from a single workstation prevents an intruder who knows a user's name and password from logging in at an unattended workstation and gaining unauthorized access to the file server.

Restricting a user account to a specific network and workstation node address increases the security of highly sensitive information. A payroll clerk, for example, can be required to log in only on the workstation located in his or her office during normal office hours. In order for an intruder to access the payroll data, he or she would need to know the payroll clerk's user name and password, to enter the payroll clerk's office during normal business hours, and to log into the file server from the clerk's workstation. These limitations prevent all but a very bold intruder or a very well-trusted employee from making such an attempt, and his or her actions would likely be noticed by other employees.

Of course, if your Admin password is generally known to network users, all security efforts are in vain—anyone with the Admin password can log in from any workstation and have access to the entire network. To thwart this, you might want to enhance Admin account security by requiring any supervisor-equivalent user names to access the network from only two workstations that you can constantly monitor. Having your Admin account operate from two different workstations, or having a supervisor equivalent user name that operates on a separate workstation address, enables you to access the file server with supervisor privileges in the event that one of the workstations is out of order.

Account Restrictions

Account restrictions are conditions defined by the administrator to restrict user accounts. When an account is locked, no one can log in to the file server with that user name until the account is reactivated. A network administrator needs to know how account restrictions can be used and how to reactivate a user account after it has been locked through any of the following limitations:

- The user account expired.
- The number of grace logins is exceeded.
- The account's balance is depleted.
- The predetermined number of incorrect password attempts has been made.

Account Expiration Date

NetWare's account expiration date is used to set a date after which the user account becomes disabled. This is a good way to establish temporary user accounts that you do not want accessed after a certain date. Student user accounts, for example, can be set to expire at the end of a semester or school year. After the expiration date, if a user attempts to log in with an expired user name, NetWare requires a password and then displays a message that the account has been disabled. Figure 9-2 illustrates an example of a login attempt with an expired user name. Note that NetWare requires you to enter the password before issuing the error message.

NetWare's practice of requiring a user to enter a password prior to issuing any error messages makes it harder for an intruder to guess user names and passwords.

Figure 9-2 Expired username

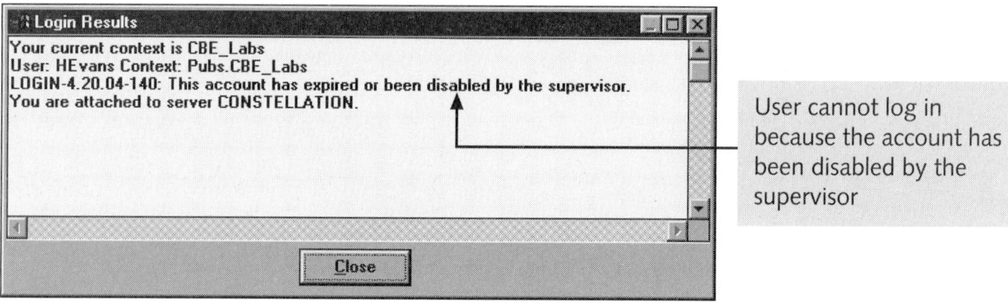

Number of Grace Logins Exceeded

Users who are forced to change their password after a specified number of days are granted a fixed number of logins with the old password after it has expired. Figure 9-3 shows the Change Password dialog box.

Figure 9-3 Change Password dialog box

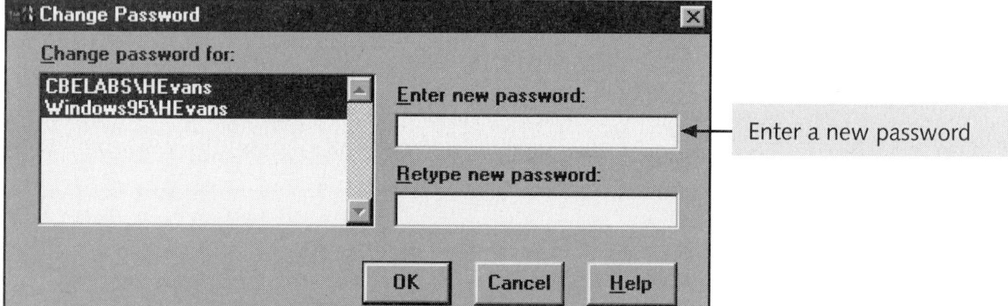

If a user fails to enter a new password within the granted number of grace logins, the account will be disabled until the SUPERVISOR or user account manager either assigns a new password or extends the number of grace logins. Figure 9-4 shows an example of a login attempt after a user's grace logins are used up

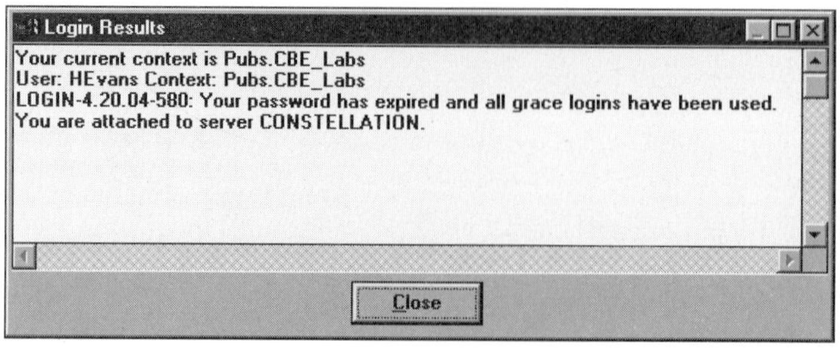

Figure 9-4 Grace logins expired

Login Results
Your current context is Pubs.CBE_Labs
User: HEvans Context: Pubs.CBE_Labs
LOGIN-4.20.04-580: Your password has expired and all grace logins have been used.
You are attached to server CONSTELLATION.
Close

Depleted Account Balance

If the accounting feature is enabled on a file server, records are kept of usage for such services as disk blocks read or written. Users can be "charged" for these services, and the charges are then deducted from the amount in the user's balance field. You can assign the following conditions:

- A balance to an individual user account that determines how much time the user can access the network
- A credit limit that allows the user to draw on an account balance up to the limit
- Unlimited credit to the user
- A default credit limit and account balance that is granted to each new user that is created

When the amount in a user's account balance falls below his or her credit limit, the user's account is disabled until a user with supervisor privileges increases the balance or provides more credit.

Intruder Detection

Unlike account restrictions that can be set individually for each user, NetWare's intruder detection is a feature that is turned on or off by the network administrator for all users in a container object. This means that intruder detection is configured individually for each Organization object or Organizational Unit object in a Directory tree.

In NetWare 3.1x intruder detection was controlled by the SUPERVISOR (or users with supervisor-equivalent security) for each NetWare server. If intruder detection was enabled, all users of that server were affected.

Intruder detection locks an account when a user fails to enter the correct password within the number of attempts specified by the supervisor. The purpose of intruder detection is to prevent someone who knows a user's name from trying to log into the user's network account by repeatedly entering likely password combinations. The intruder detection feature allows you to place a maximum on the number of times a user can attempt to enter his or her current password within a specified time period, and then set a length of time that the account will be locked when the specified number of attempts has been exceeded. Only a user with supervisor privileges for the container object can release a locked account before the specified time interval. Figure 9-5 shows an example of intruder detection locking up a user account after three login attempts.

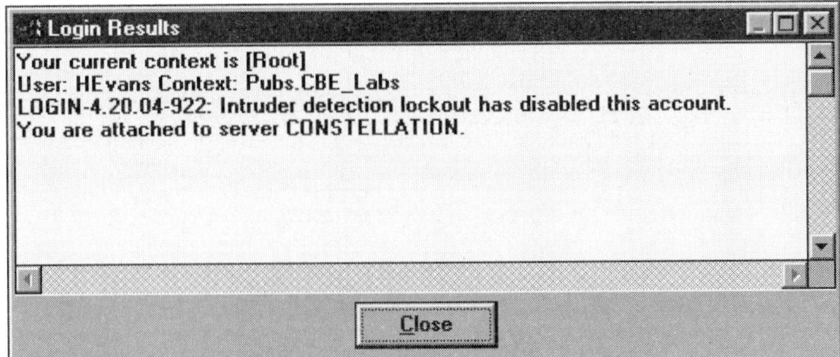

Figure 9-5 Intruder detection lockout

Managing Users and Groups

Now that you understand how login security works with user accounts to protect the NetWare environment, you are ready to create and manage users and groups. You will also learn about managing the network using user profiles and organizational roles.

User-Related Leaf Objects

As you learned in Chapter 4, User-related leaf objects have properties that enable you to manage the users on your network. User-related leaf objects include the User object, the Group object, the Organizational Role object, and the Profile object. These objects are summarized in Figure 9-6.

Figure 9-6

User-related leaf objects

Object Icon	Object	Purpose
	User	Represents a network user
	Group	Represents a group of users
	Organizational Role	Represents a position in an organization
	Profile	Provides information about groups of users that are not organized as a group

User-related objects, like other Directory tree objects, are created and managed using the NETADMIN menu utility or the NetWare Administrator graphical utility. You have already worked with both utilities in earlier chapters. In this chapter you will work with NetWare Administrator, and you will use NETADMIN in the exercises at the end of the chapter.

Users

Users, also called end users, are the individuals in the organization who use network resources such as computers and printers. The User object is used to represent and manage each network user and is represented in the Directory tree by the icon . Two properties, Login Name and Last Name, are mandatory and must be specified when you create each user. Login security is applied to each user through properties settings assigned to each User object.

The User object Admin and an associated user account are created during the installation of NetWare 4.1. The network administrator uses this user account to create other users. The User object for each user is created in the organizational unit of the Directory tree that represents the user's location in the organization.

To finish creating an object, you must supply the property values required in the Create *ObjectType* dialog box. In this dialog box, you are also given the options of (1) defining additional property values for the object you are creating, (2) immediately creating another object of the same type in the same container object, or (3) defining user defaults for the object.

For example, the CBE Labs network administrator needs to create user accounts for the network users at CBE Labs. The CBE Labs organizational chart, which is shown in Figure 1-9, shows the users who need accounts. The current Directory tree for CBE Labs is shown in Figure 9-7.

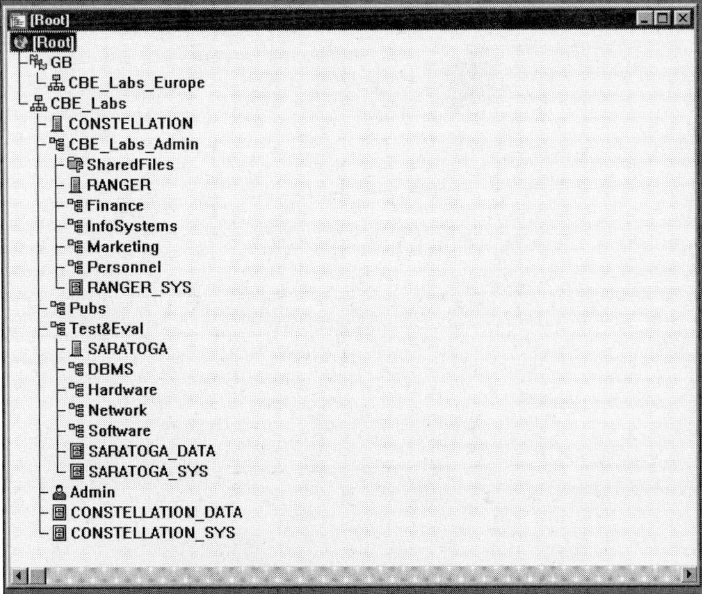

Figure 9-7 The current CBE Labs Directory tree

CBE Labs uses the user's first initial and full last name for login names. Although this creates user names longer than eight characters, CBE Labs management believes that it's easier for users to remember.

The User objects for President Joseph Cunningham and administrative assistant Steve Lopez will be created in the context CBE_Labs_Admin.CBE_Labs. User objects for all employees in Marketing, Finance, Personnel, and Information Systems will be created in their respective Organizational Unit container. User objects for Vice President Harold Evans and all employees in Publishing will be created in the Pubs Organizational Unit container. The User objects for Vice President Georgia Burns and administrative assistant Mike O'Donnell will be created in the context Test&Eval.CBE_Labs, with all employees in the Labs having their User object created in their respective workgroup.

Creating More Than One Object

When creating more than one of the same type of object, you can use the Create Another *ObjectType* option in the Create *ObjectType* dialog box to repeat the object creation process without having to start over in the browser window. In this case, the CBE Labs network administrator needs to create multiple users in each container object. By using the Create Another User option, he can create all the users in a container object without leaving the Create User dialog box.

Creating Home Directories

At CBE Labs, each user has his or her own home directory, a directory reserved for the user's personal files. Each user has home directory privileges in only his or her home directory. It is easiest to create home directories at the same time the user's User object is created. This is done by using the Create Home Directory option in the Create User dialog box.

The directory name for the user's home directory will be the first eight characters of the user's login name. If all user names are kept to eight characters or less, then the login name and the user directory name will be the same.

Creating User Objects

The CBE Labs network administrator is ready to create accounts for the CBE Labs users. He starts by creating the User objects for Joseph Cunningham and Steve Lopez.

To create the User objects for Cunningham and Lopez, follow these steps:

1. Launch NetWare Administrator.
2. Expand the Directory tree in the browser window so that you can see all the objects in the tree.
3. Click the **CBE_Labs_Admin Organizational Unit** object, click **Object** on the menu bar, and then click **Create**.
4. The New Object dialog box is displayed. Click **User**; then click **OK**. The Create User dialog box is displayed, as shown in Figure 9-8.

Figure 9-8 The Create User dialog box

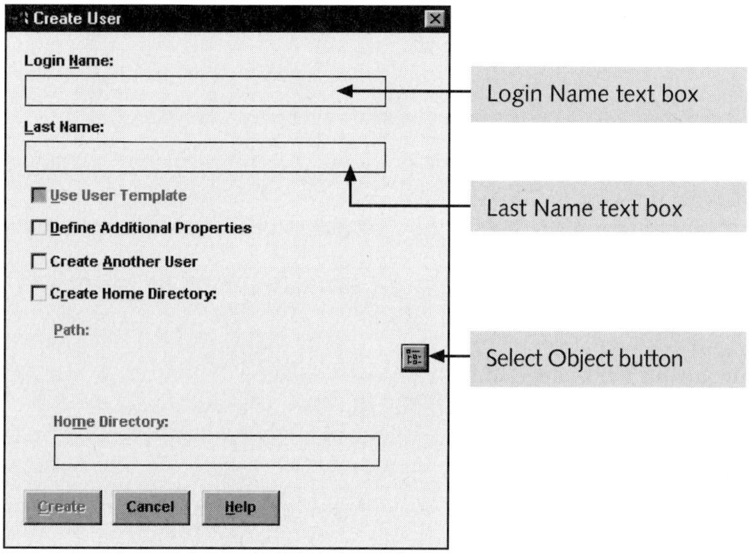

5. Because we want to create more than one user in this context, click the **Create Another User** check box.
6. Because each user will have a home directory, click the **Create Home Directory** check box.
7. Click the **Login Name** text box to activate it; then type **JCunningham**. The login name is required to create the User object.
8. Click the **Last Name** text box to activate it; then type **Cunningham**. The last name is required to create the User object.
9. The first eight characters of Joseph Cunningham's login name of JCunningham appear in the Home Directory text box as JCUNNING. This will be the directory name of his home directory. To specify the path for the home directory, click the **Select Object** button. The **Select Object** dialog box is displayed.
10. The Select Object dialog box is used to browse the Directory tree context to find an object. In this case, the starting context is CBE_Labs_Admin. The new context will be the Users directory on CONSTELLATION_DATA.CBE_Labs. Browse through the Directory tree until the Select Object dialog box appears as shown in Figure 9-9, with the context of CONSTELLATION_DATA.CBE_Labs, and the USERS directory as the selected object.

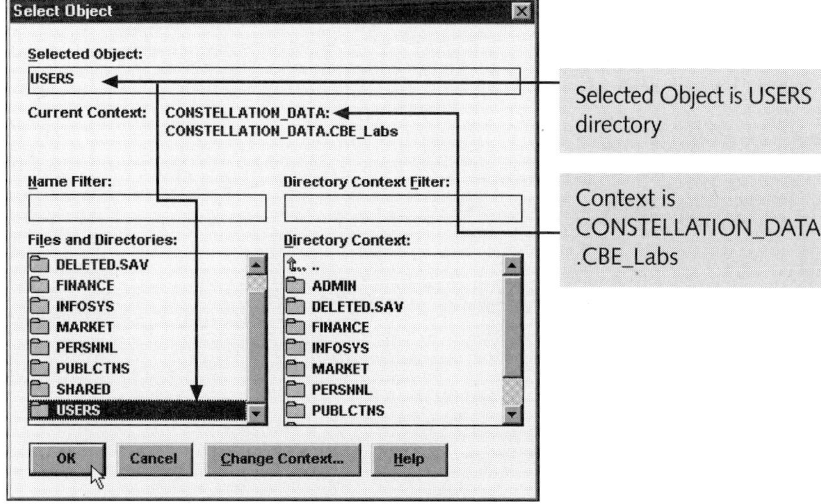

Figure 9-9

Specifying the path to the user's home directory

11. Click **OK**. The path to Joseph Cunningham's home directory appears in the Create User dialog box, as shown in Figure 9-10.

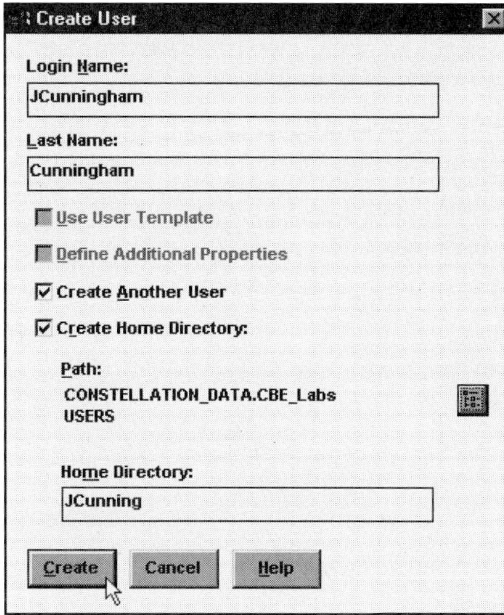

Figure 9-10

The completed Create User dialog box

12. Click the **Create** button. The JCunningham User object is created and added to the Directory tree, and the home directory is created on the CONSTELLATION_DATA volume.
13. Because the Create Another User option was selected, the Create User dialog box reappears. Repeat steps 7–12 using the login name SLopez and the last name of Lopez.
14. After the User object for Steve Lopez is created, the Create User dialog box appears again. Because there are no more users to be created in this context, click the **Cancel** button.
15. Close and redisplay the CBE_Labs_Admin branch of the Directory tree. The User objects now appear as shown in Figure 9-11.

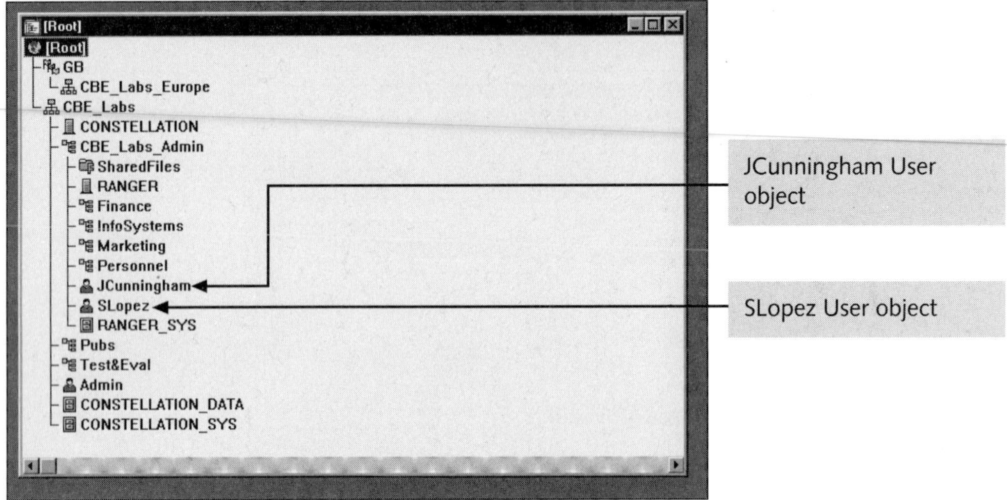

Figure 9-11 The CBE Labs Directory tree with the User objects

Managing User Object Property Values

Once a User object is created, you can set property values for the object to manage a user's access to network resources. You worked with object properties in Chapter 7, where you added postal office data for the CBE_Labs_Admin Organizational Unit. In this chapter you will work with the property values that specify a user's identity and control login security. In Chapter 10 you will work with user trustee right assignments to network resources through the Directory tree and the file directory structure.

Property values can be set for each User object as it is created if the Define Additional Properties check box is checked when the User object is created. Alternatively, as we are doing in this example, the network administrator can create the User objects and then set property values later.

To view a User object's properties you can follow these steps:

- Click the User object, and then press [Enter].

or

- Click the User object, click Object on the menu bar, and then click Details.

or

- Right-click the User object, and then click Details on the QuickMenu.

For example, the CBE Labs network administrator wants to enter some data for Joseph Cunningham to the property settings of the JCunningham User object.

To view the JCunningham User object properties, follow these steps:

1. Right-click the **JCunningham User** object, and then click Details. The User: JCunnigham object dialog box is displayed, as shown in Figure 9-12.

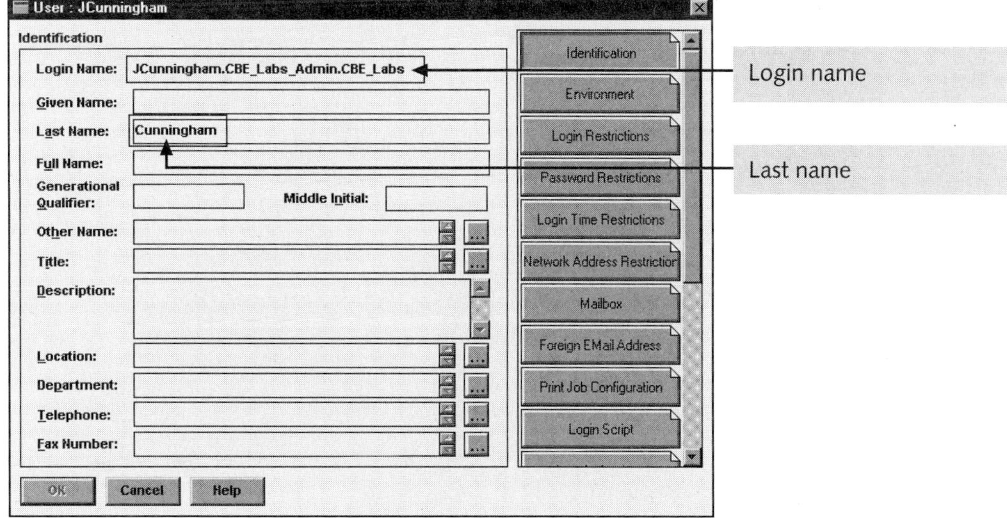

Figure 9-12 The User: JCunningham object dialog box

The object properties are grouped into pages that are identified by a screen name in the upper left corner of the screen and are accessed by clicking the associated button in the scrollable button bar on the right side of the dialog box. For example, as shown in Figure 9-12, the Identification page is displayed and the Identification button is shown as depressed (to indicate that it is selected) in the button bar. A group of Identification properties are shown on the Identification screen. You can change to another page by clicking the page's button. You can add, edit, or delete property values on a page by using the associated text box.

User Identification Page Properties

The properties on the Identification Page are shown in Figure 9-12. The Login Name and Last Name property are initially set when the User object is created. The Last Name property can be modified on this page, but to change the Login Name you must rename the User object. Additional information on this page includes more name data, organizational role data, and telephone numbers. The Full Name property is used by NetWare to display the user's name during login.

The CBE Labs network administrator needs to add additional identifying information about Joseph Cunningham.

To add Joseph Cunningham's identification information, follow these steps:

1. Click the **Given Name** text box; then type in the name **Joseph**. Do not press [Enter].
2. Click the **Full Name** text box; then type in the name **Joseph Cunningham**. Do not press [Enter].
3. Click the **Title** text box; then type in the title **President**. Do not press [Enter].
4. Click the **Department** text box; then type in the department name **Administration**. Do not press [Enter].
5. Click the **Telephone** text box; then type in the phone number **503-560-1540**. Do not press [Enter].
6. Click the **Fax Number** text box; then type in the phone number **503-560-1541**. Do not press [Enter] or click OK. The Identification page now appears as shown in Figure 9-13.

Figure 9-13 The completed Identification page

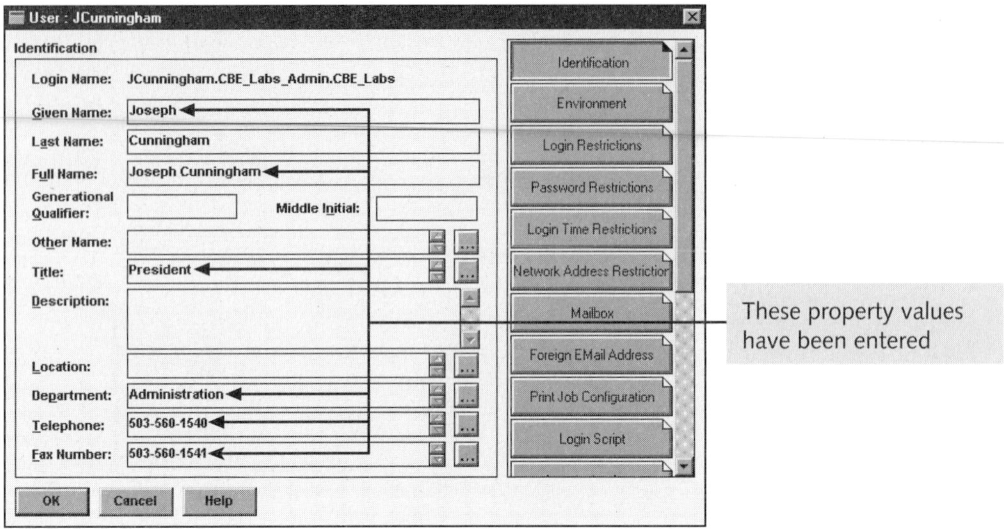

These property values have been entered

User Environment Page Properties

The second page in the User object properties is the Environment page. The Environment page properties include language, home directory, and default server data. If the user is logged in to the network, the user's network address is displayed. The Environment page is shown in Figure 9-14.

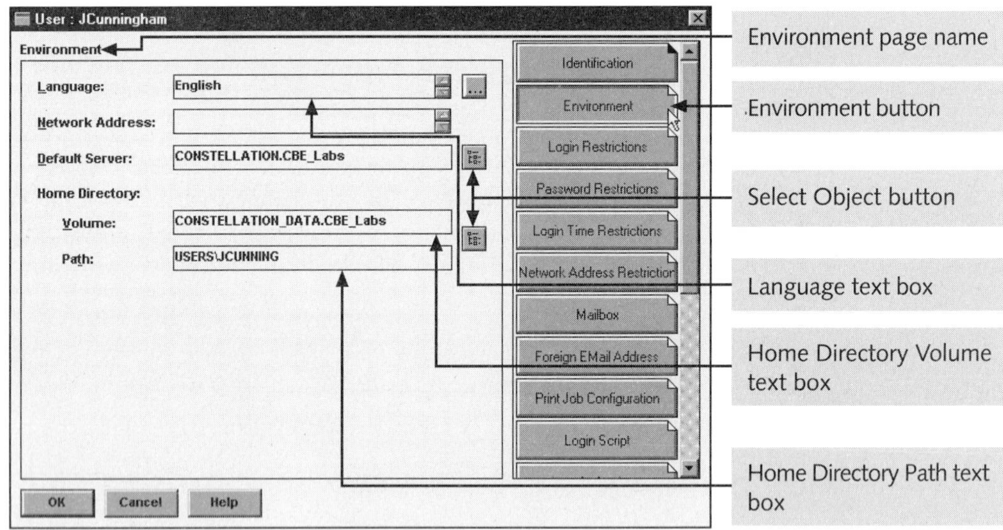

Figure 9-14 The Environment page

If your network supports multiple languages, the Language property allows you to specify which language the user sees displayed in NetWare dialog boxes, menus, and commands. The Home Directory Volume and Path properties enable you to create a home directory for the user or to modify the location of a previously created home directory. The Default Server property is used to specify which NetWare server receives messages for the user from other users.

User Postal Address Page Properties

The Postal Address page properties include street address, post office box, city, state, and ZIP code information along an area to create a mailing label. The Postal Address page is shown in Figure 9-15.

Figure 9-15

The Postal Address page

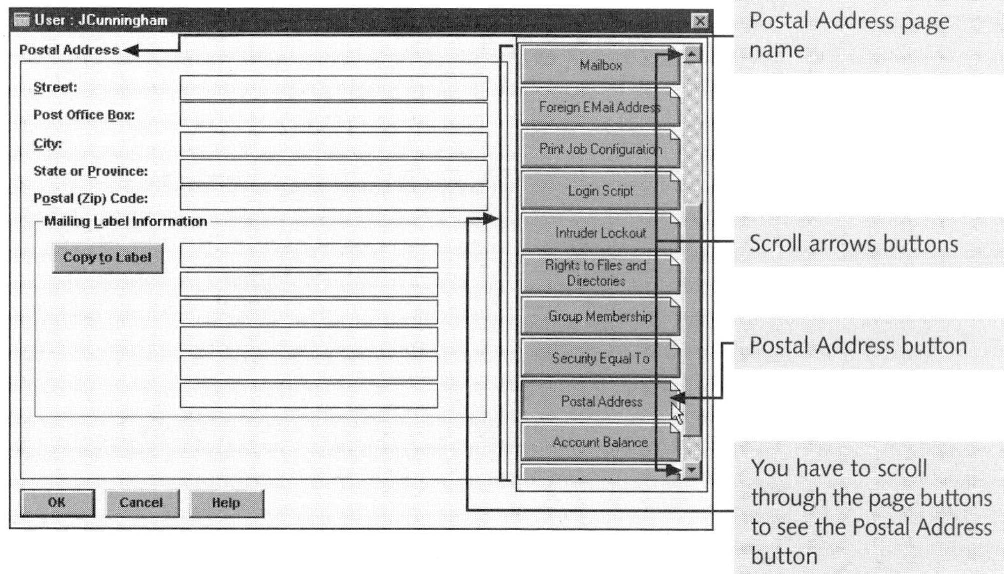

The CBE Labs network administrator needs to add the postal address for Joseph Cunningham.

To add Joseph Cunningham's postal address, follow these steps:

1. Use the down scroll arrow to scroll through the page buttons until the **Postal Address** button appears.
2. Click the **Postal Address** button in the button bar. The Postal Address page is displayed.
3. Click the **Street** text box; then type **539 Lincoln Avenue**. Do not press [Enter].
4. Click the **City** text box; then type **Portland**. Do not press [Enter].
5. Click the **State or Province** text box; then type **OR**. Do not press [Enter].
6. Click the **Postal (ZIP) Code** text box; then type **97205**. Do not press [Enter] or click OK. The Postal Address page now appears as shown in Figure 9-16.

Figure 9-16

The completed Postal Address page

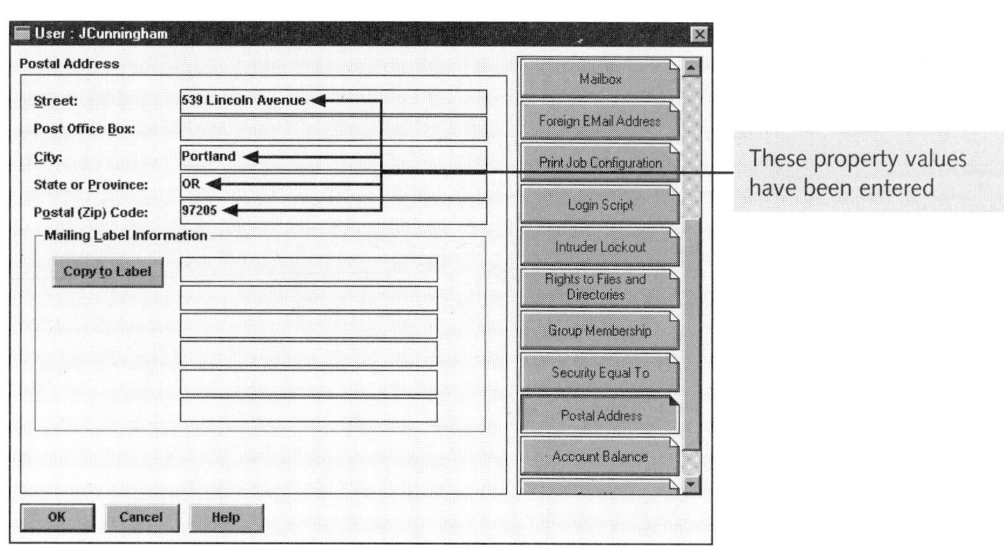

User Password Restrictions Properties

The first component of login security is creating a user name. This was done when the User object was created. The next component is creating a password and setting password restrictions. This is done on the Password Restrictions page, which is shown in Figure 9-17.

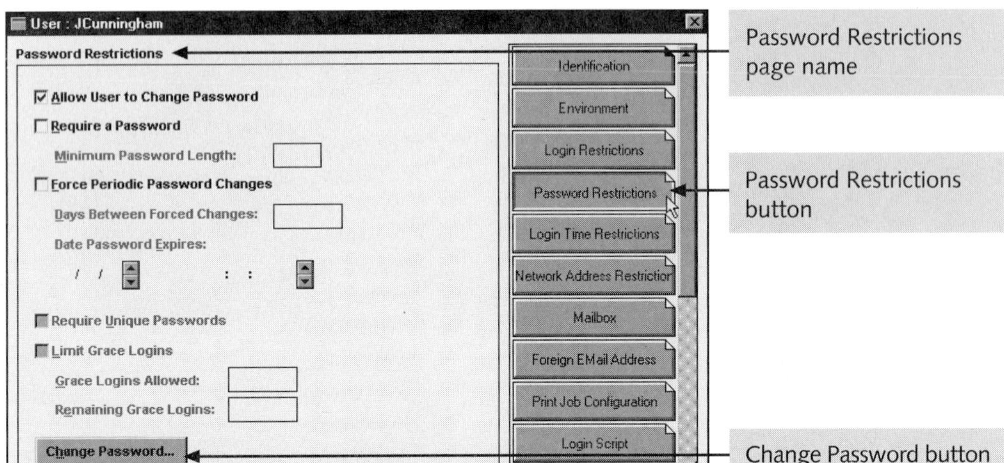

Figure 9-17 The Password Restrictions page

The Password Restrictions page enables the network administration to implement the steps of password security discussed earlier in this chapter. Check boxes and spin boxes can be used to require a password, set a minimum password length, force periodic password changes, require unique passwords, and limit the number of grace logins. This page also contains a Change Password button that is used to set a new password for a user.

A common practice is to create an initial password but set the password expiration date so that the password has already expired. This forces the user to change the password on one of their first logins, which lets users set their own passwords. Meanwhile, it keeps other users from logging in on an account without a password.

The CBE Labs network administrator needs to set password restrictions for Joseph Cunningham. In addition, he will set a password of CBELABS on the account to prevent anyone else from using the account.

To add Joseph Cunningham's password restrictions, follow these steps:

1. If necessary, use the scroll arrows to scroll through the page buttons until the Password Restrictions button appears.
2. Click the **Password Restrictions** button in the button bar. The Password Restrictions page is displayed.
3. Click the **Require a Password** text box. Do not press [Enter].
4. Click the **Minimum Password Length** text box. The NetWare default minimum password length 5 appears in the Minimum Password Length text box. Set the minimum length to **6**. Do not press [Enter].
5. Click the **Force Periodic Password Changes** check box. The NetWare default days between forced changes of 40 appears in the Days Between Forced Changes text box, and the current date and the time the User object was accessed appear in the Expiration Date and Time spin boxes. In the Days

Between Forced Changes text box, type **120**. Use the Expiration Date spin box arrows to set the date to **yesterday's date**. Use the Expiration Time spin box arrows to set the time to **11:59:59 PM**. Do not press [Enter].

6. Click the **Require Unique Passwords** check box. Do not press [Enter].
7. Click the **Limit Grace Logins** check box. The NetWare default grace logins of 6 appears in the Grace Logins Allowed text box and the Remaining Grace Logins text box. Set the Grace Logins Allowed and the Remaining Grace Logins to **3**. Do not press [Enter].
8. Click the **Change Password** button. The Change Password dialog box is displayed, as shown in Figure 9-18.

Figure 9-18

The Change Password dialog box

9. Click the **New Password** text box; then type **CBELABS**. Click the **Retype New Password** text box; then type **CBELABS**. Click **OK**.
10. The Password Restrictions page now appears as shown in Figure 9-19. Do not press [Enter] or click OK.

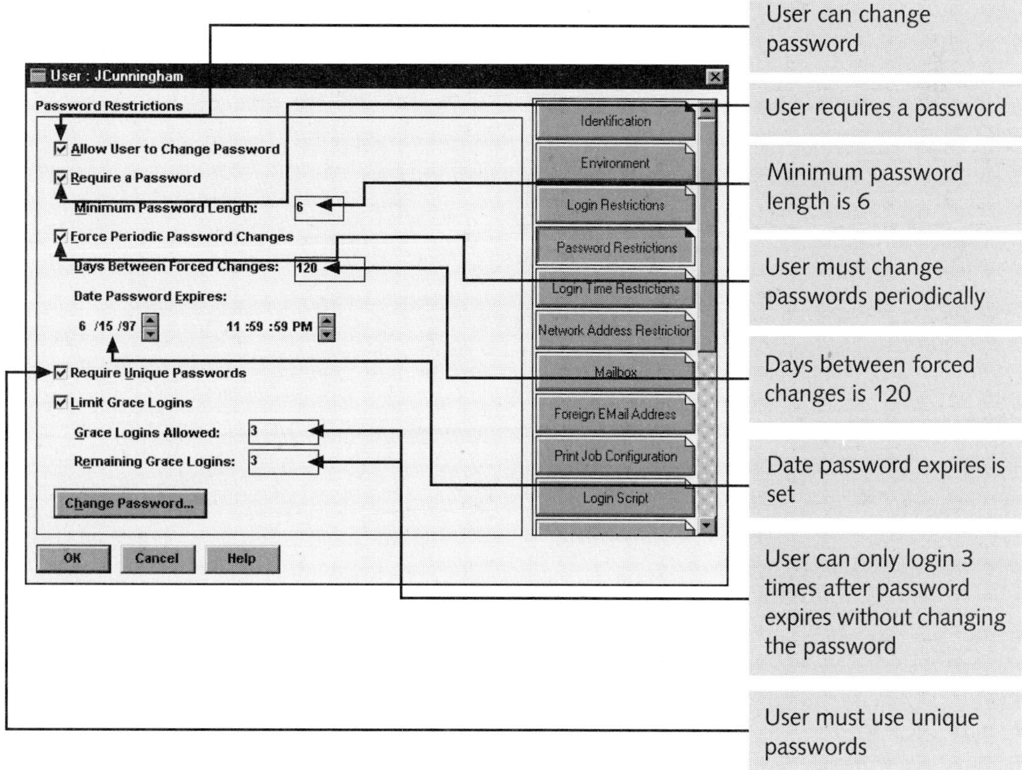

Figure 9-19

The completed Password Restrictions page

User Login Time Restrictions Properties

Time restrictions on user accounts are controlled on the Login Time Restrictions page, shown in Figure 9-20. The Login Time Restrictions page enables the network administration to specify which times a user can and cannot log in to the network.

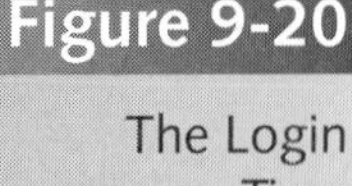

The Login Time Restrictions page

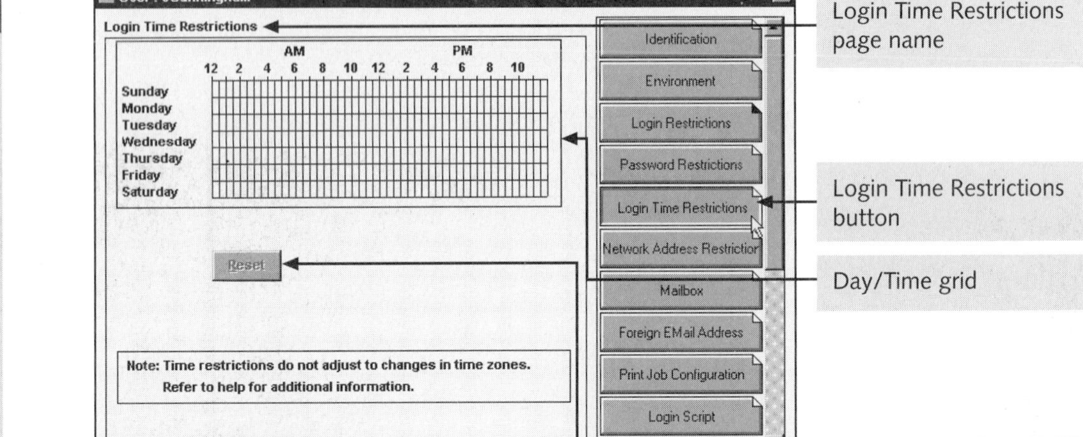

CBE Labs policy is that all users are restricted from logging in between midnight and 6:00 A.M. The CBE Labs network administrator needs to set these times for Joseph Cunningham.

To add Joseph Cunningham's login time restrictions, follow these steps:

1. If necessary, use the scroll arrows to scroll through the page buttons until the **Login Time Restrictions** button appears.
2. Click the **Login Time Restrictions** button in the button bar. The Login Time Restrictions page is displayed.
3. Click and drag the time block from **Sunday at 12:00 midnight** (in the upper left corner of the grid) to **Saturday at 6:00 A.M.** Do not press [Enter].
4. The Login Time Restrictions page now appears as shown in Figure 9-21. Do not press [Enter] or click OK.

Figure 9-21

The completed Login Time Restrictions page

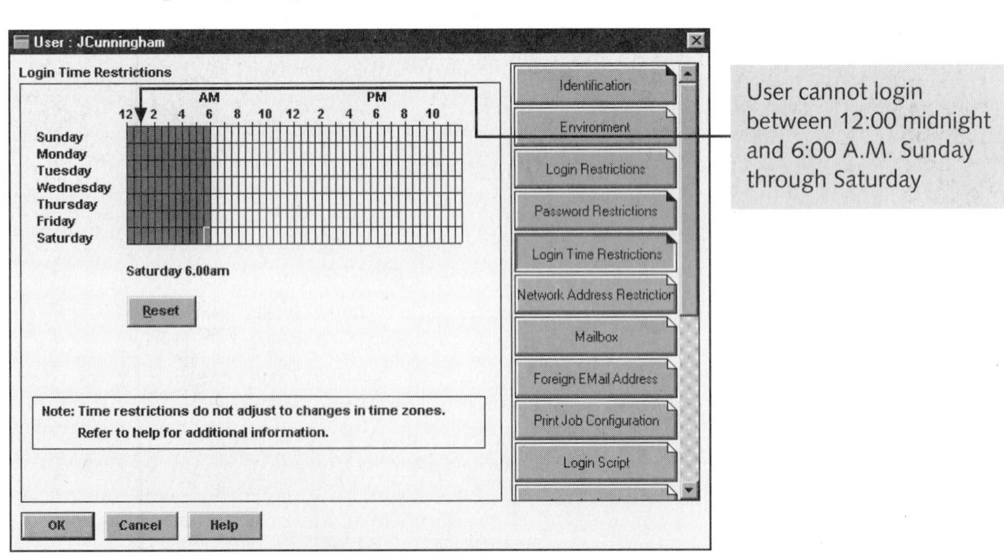

User Network Address Restrictions Properties

Network workstation restrictions are controlled on the Network Address Restriction page, shown in Figure 9-22.

Figure 9-22 The Network Address Restriction page

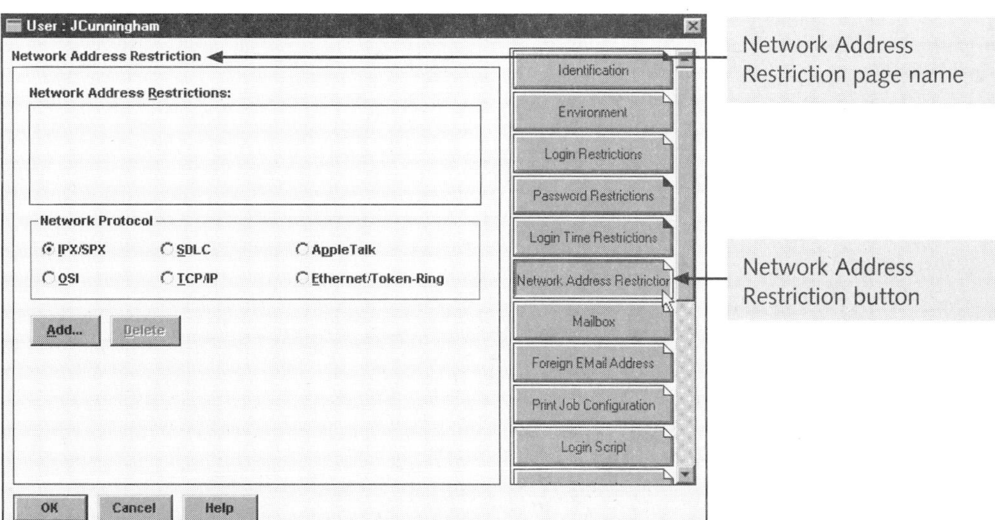

The Network Address Restriction page enables the network administration to specify which workstations a user must use in order to log in to the network, as well as the network protocol being used.

CBE Labs policy is that all users have unrestricted workstation address access. This allows them to check their e-mail from any workstation. There is no need for the CBE Labs network administrator to set a workstation address restriction for Joseph Cunningham.

User Login Restrictions Properties

The account restrictions are controlled on the Login Restrictions page, shown in Figure 9-23.

Figure 9-23 The Login Restrictions page

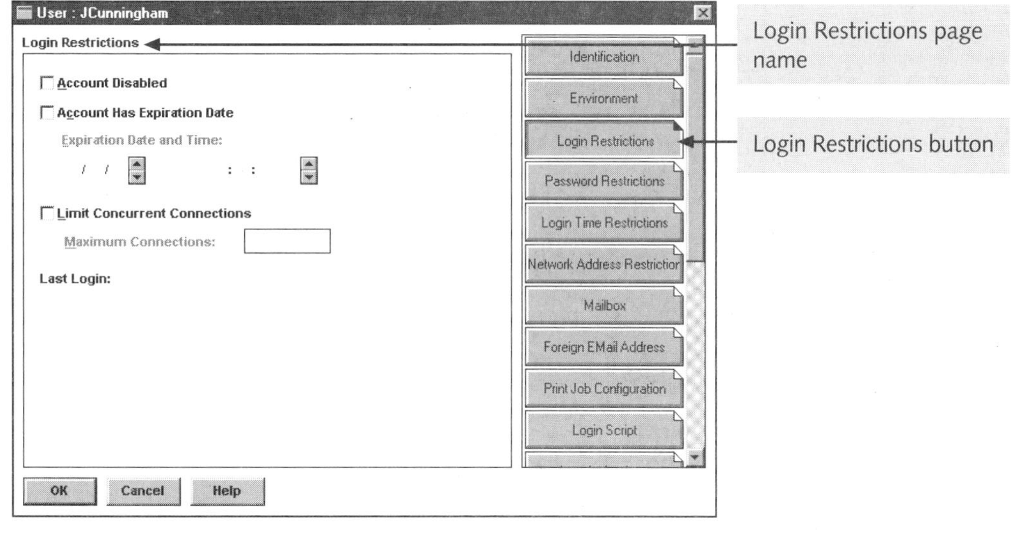

The Login Restrictions page enables the network administration to disable an account or set a date and time at which the account will expire and become disabled. The Network administrator can also limit the number of concurrent user connections to the network.

The CBE Labs network administrator needs to limit the number of concurrent connections for Joseph Cunningham to one.

To add Joseph Cunningham's account restrictions, follow these steps:

1. If necessary, use the scroll arrows to scroll through the page buttons until the **Login Restrictions** button appears.
2. Click the **Login Restrictions** button in the button bar. The Login Restrictions page is displayed.
3. Click the **Limit Concurrent Connections** check box. The NetWare default maximum connections of 1 appears in the Maximum Connections text box. Don't change this number. Do not press [Enter].
4. The Login Restrictions page now appears as shown in Figure 9-24. Do not press [Enter] or click OK.

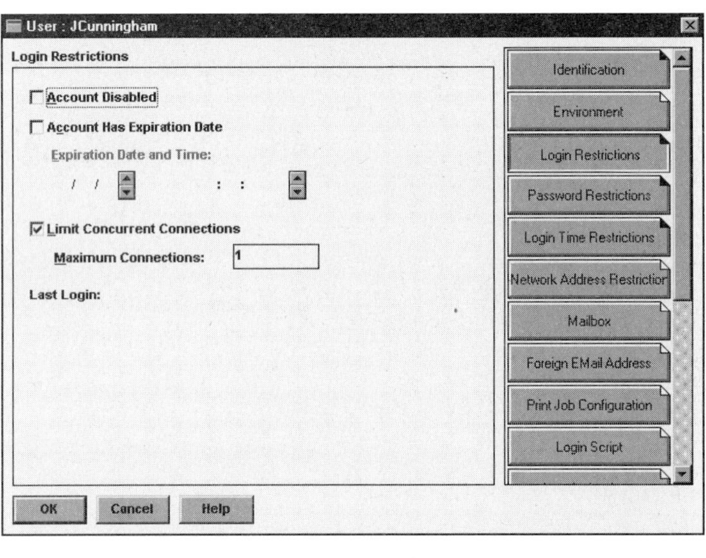

Figure 9-24 The completed Login Restrictions page

The network administrator has completed entering all the property settings necessary for Joseph Cunningham. Clicking the OK button at the bottom of the User:JCunningham object dialog box now will implement all the settings.

5. Click **OK**.

At this time the CBE Labs network administrator enters the same types of property values for Steve Lopez. The steps are the same as those used for Joseph Cunningham and will not be repeated here.

The NetWare Administrator utility included with NetWare 4.11 enables you to change multiple objects at the same time. For example, if all User objects included the same FAX phone number, you can change this for all User objects simultaneously. To do this, you select all User objects in the Directory tree, open a User dialog box (which will enable you to change only shared properties, not unique ones), and then change the FAX phone number. This is a much more efficient way to make changes to multiple objects.

Using USER_TEMPLATE Objects

Creating User objects one at a time can be a time-consuming task if there is a large number of users to be created. And often you will find yourself recreating the same property settings over and over again. This often happens, for example, with users in the same workgroup or in the same container object in a Directory tree. To simplify the User object creation process, NetWare 4.1 lets you create a set of default, or common, settings for all User objects in a container object by creating a **USER_TEMPLATE User object** for the container. There can be only one USER_TEMPLATE in a container, and the settings in the USER_TEMPLATE apply only to User objects created in that container *after* the USER_TEMPLATE object is created.

The NetWare 4.1 USER_TEMPLATE User object is similar to the user template created with the NetWare 3.1x USERDEF menu utility. The USERDEF menu utility is no longer available and has been integrated into the NetWare Administrator graphical utility and the NETADMIN menu utility.

The USER_TEMPLATE User object for a container object is created from the container object. When a new container object is being created, you are given a chance to create the USER_TEMPLATE at that time. This is done by checking the Define User Defaults check box in the Create Container ObjectName dialog box, as shown in Figure 9-25. When the container object is created, so is the USER_TEMPLATE User object.

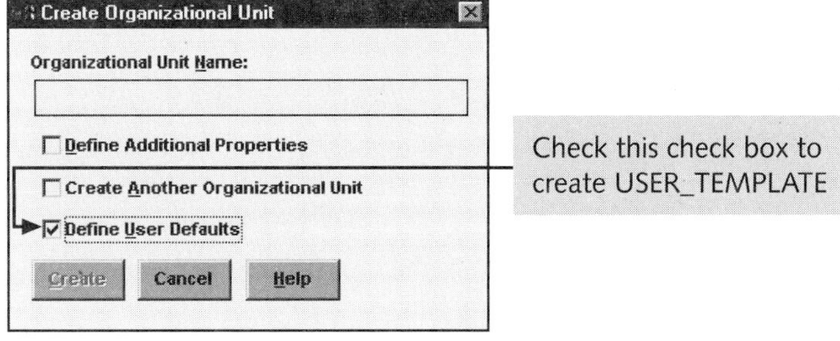

Figure 9-25 Creating the USER_TEMPLATE User object

If you didn't create the USER_TEMPLATE User object when the container object was created, you can create it later by using the User Template command on the Object menu.

To create a USER_TEMPLATE User object after the container object is created, follow these steps:

- Click the container object, click Object on the menu bar, and then click User Template.

For example, the CBE Labs network administrator needs to create user accounts for the CBE Labs personnel in the Finance Department. The User objects created will be contained in the Finance Organizational Unit object. Because all these accounts will share many property settings, the network administrator will create a USER_TEMPLATE User object first to define the common property settings. The individual User objects will be created based upon this template, so the property values will not have to be reentered for each User object. Of course, property values that are unique to each User object, such as Given Name, Full Name, and Title, will still have to be entered individually for each user.

The CBE Labs network administrator is ready to create the USER_TEMPLATE User object for the Finance Organizational Unit users.

To create the USER_TEMPLATE User object for the Finance Organizational Unit and enter the initial property settings, follow these steps:

1. If necessary, launch NetWare Administrator and expand the Directory tree in the browser window so that you can see all the objects in the tree.
2. Click the **Finance Organizational Unit** object to select it, click **Object** on the menu bar, and then click **User Template**. The USER_TEMPLATE User object is added to the Finance Organizational Unit object, and the User: USER_TEMPLATE object dialog box is displayed.
3. Click the **Department** text box; then type in the department name **Finance**. Do not press [Enter].
4. Click the **Telephone** text box; then type in the phone number **503-560-1544**. Do not press [Enter].
5. Click the **Fax Number** text box; then type in the phone number **503-560-1541**. Do not press [Enter] or click OK.
6. If necessary, use the down scroll arrow to scroll through the page buttons until the **Postal Address** button appears. Click the **Postal Address** button in the button bar. The Postal Address page is displayed.
7. Click the **Street** text box; then type **539 Lincoln Avenue**. Do not press [Enter].
8. Click the **City** text box; then type **Portland**. Do not press [Enter].
9. Click the **State or Province** text box; then type **OR**. Do not press [Enter].
10. Click the **Postal (ZIP) Code** text box; then type **97205**. Do not press [Enter] or click OK.

The CBE Labs network administrator now needs to set the Home directory location for the new users.

To create the Home directory path settings for the USER_TEMPLATE User object, follow these steps:

1. If necessary, use the down scroll arrow to scroll through the page buttons until the Environment button appears. Click the **Environment** button in the button bar. The Environment page is displayed.
2. To specify the path for the home directory, click the **Select Object** button to the right and below the Home Directory check box. The Select Object dialog box is displayed.
3. The Select Object dialog box is used to browse the Directory tree context to find an object. In this case, the starting context is Finance.CBE_Labs_Admin. The new context will be the USERS directory on CONSTELLATION_DATA.CBE_Labs. Browse through the Directory tree until the Select Object dialog box appears, as shown in Figure 9-26.

Figure 9-26
Specifying the path to the Finance user's home directory

4. Click **OK**. The path to Finance user's home directory appears on the Environment page, as shown in Figure 9-27.

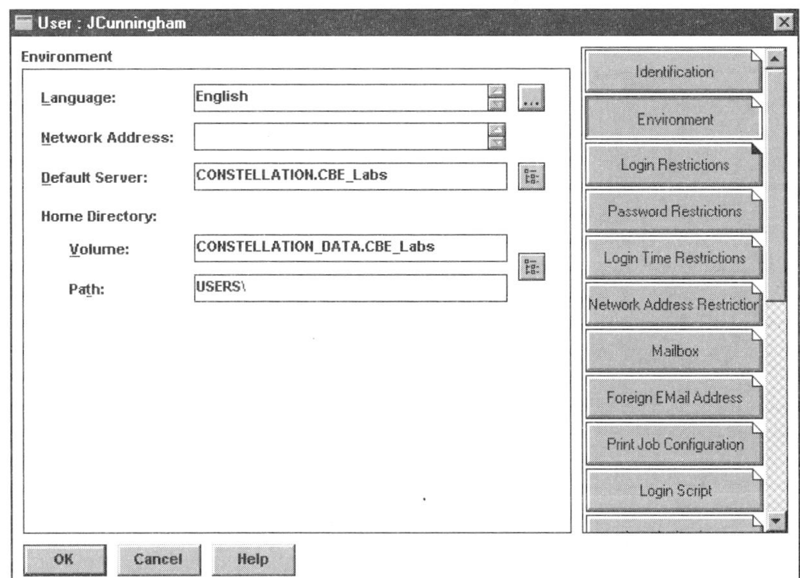

Figure 9-27
The Command Environment page

The CBE Labs network administrator is now ready to set the default or common login security property values for user accounts in the Finance Organizational Unit. These steps parallel the steps he took in setting up Joseph Cunningham's account, and you can refer to those steps if you have questions about the following steps.

To create login security initial property settings for the USER_TEMPLATE User object, follow these steps:

1. If necessary, use the scroll arrows to scroll through the page buttons until the **Password Restrictions** button appears. Click the **Password Restrictions** button in the button bar. The Password Restrictions page is displayed.
2. Click the **Require a Password** check box. Do not press [Enter].
3. Click the **Minimum Password Length** text box. Set the minimum length to **6**. Do not press [Enter].

4. Click the **Force Periodic Password Changes** check box. Set the Days Between Forced Changes to **120**. Use the Expiration Date spin box arrows to set the date to **yesterday's date**. Use the Expiration Time spin box arrows to set the time to **11:59:59 P.M.** Do not press [Enter].
5. Click the **Require Unique Passwords** check box. Do not press [Enter].
6. Click the **Limit Grace Logins** check box. Set the Grace Logins Allowed and the Remaining Grace Logins to **3**. Do not press [Enter].
7. Click the **Change Password** button to display the Password dialog box. Click the **New Password** text box; then type **CBELABS**. Click the **Retype New Password** text box; then type **CBELABS**. Click **OK**.
8. If necessary, use the scroll arrows to scroll through the page buttons until the **Login Time Restrictions** button appears. Click the **Login Time Restrictions** button in the button bar. The Login Time Restrictions page is displayed.
9. Click and drag the time block from **Sunday at 12:00 midnight** (in the upper-left corner of the grid) to **Saturday at 6:00 A.M.** Do not press [Enter].
10. If necessary, use the scroll arrows to scroll through the page buttons until the **Login Restrictions** button appears. Click the **Login Restrictions** button in the button bar. The Login Restrictions page is displayed.
11. Click the **Limit Concurrent Connections** check box. The NetWare default maximum connections of **1** appears in the Maximum Connections text box. Don't change this number. Do not press [Enter].
12. All default settings are now created for the USER_TEMPLATE User object in the Finance Organizational Unit container. Click **OK**.
13. Close and then re-expand the Finance Organizational Unit to update the display of the leaf objects in the container. The USER_TEMPLATE User object is now displayed, as shown in Figure 9-28.

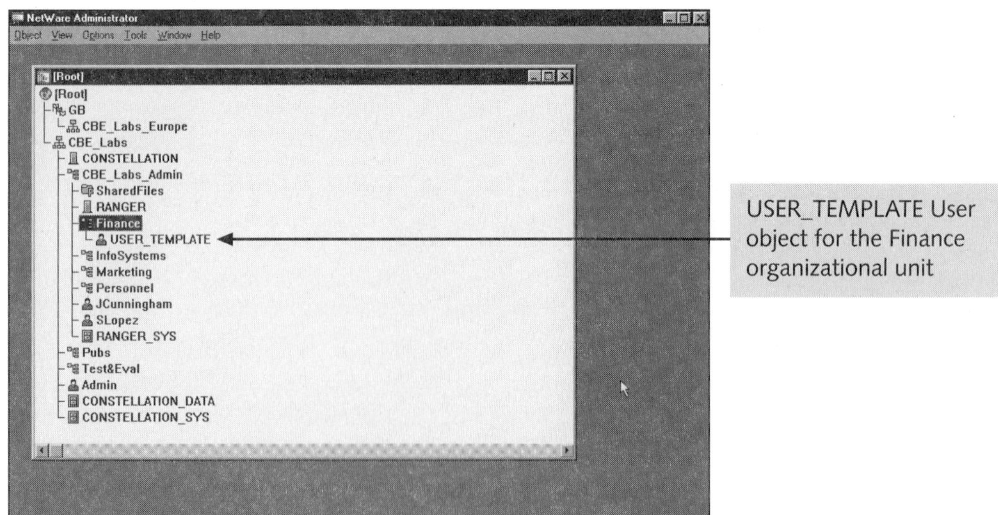

Figure 9-28 The USER_TEMPLATE User object

Creating User Objects Using the USER_TEMPLATE User Object

Once a USER_TEMPLATE User object is created, you can use it to create user accounts for users in the container object. For example, the CBE Labs network administrator needs to create accounts for Donna Kaneaka (Finance Director), Sarah Johnston (General

Ledger/Accounts Payable), and Thomas Meyer (Accounts Payable). Because all the common information is already in the USER_TEMPLATE User object, adding them requires only creating the unique information for each account.

To create the User objects for Kaneaka, Johnston, and Meyer, follow these steps:

1. If necessary, launch NetWare Administrator and expand the Directory tree in the browser window so that you can see all the objects in the tree.
2. Click the **Finance Organizational Unit** object to select it, click **Object** on the menu bar, and then click **Create**.
3. The New Object dialog box is displayed. Click **User**, and then click **OK**. The Create User dialog box is displayed with both the Use User Template check box and the Create Home Directory check box already checked.
4. Because we want to create more than one user in this context, click the **Create Another User** check box.
5. Click the **Login Name** text box to activate it; then type **DKaneaka**.
6. Click the **Last Name** text box to activate it; then type **Kaneaka**.
7. The first eight characters of Donna Kaneaka's login name of DKaneaka appear in the Home Directory text box as DKaneaka, and the Volume and Path are correctly specified.
8. Click the **Create** button. The DKaneaka User object is created and added to the Directory tree, and the home directory is created on the CONSTELLATION_DATA volume.
9. Because the Create Another User option was selected, the Create User dialog box reappears. Repeat steps 5–8 twice, the first time using the login name SJohnston and the last name of Johnston and the second time using the login name of TMeyer and the last name of Meyer.
10. After the User object for Thomas Meyer is created, the Create User dialog box reappears. Because there are no more users to be created in this context, click the **Cancel** button.
11. Close and redisplay the Finance branch of the Directory tree. The User objects now appear as shown in Figure 9-29.

Figure 9-29 The CBE Labs Directory tree with the Finance User objects

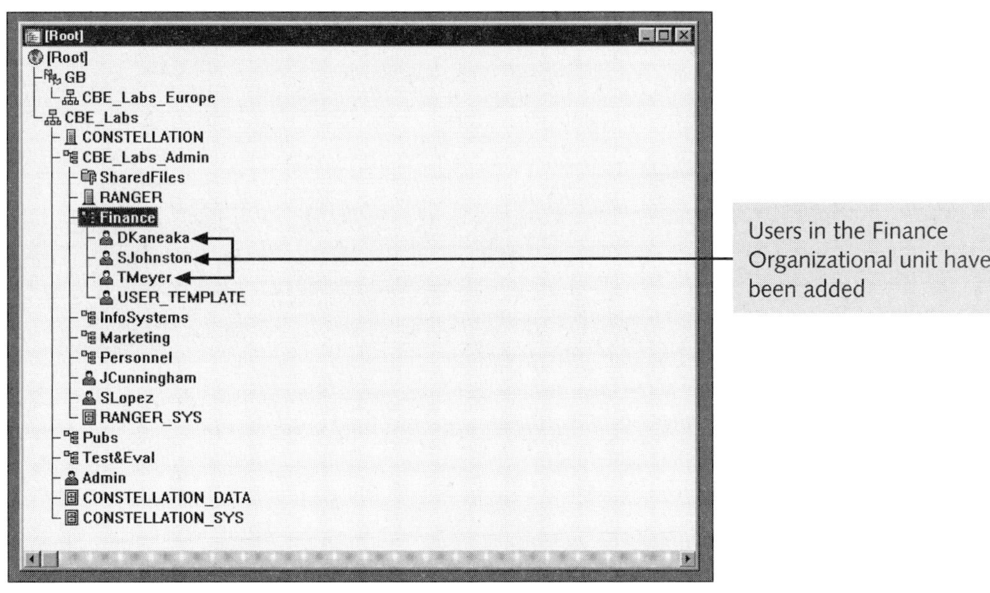

Of course, the unique property settings for each user still need to be added. The CBE network administrator now attends to these details.

To add Donna Kaneaka's unique information, follow these steps:

1. Right-click the **DKaneaka User** object; then click **Details**. The User: DKaneaka object dialog box is displayed, as shown in Figure 9-30. Note that the default Department, Telephone, and Fax Number are already entered and displayed.

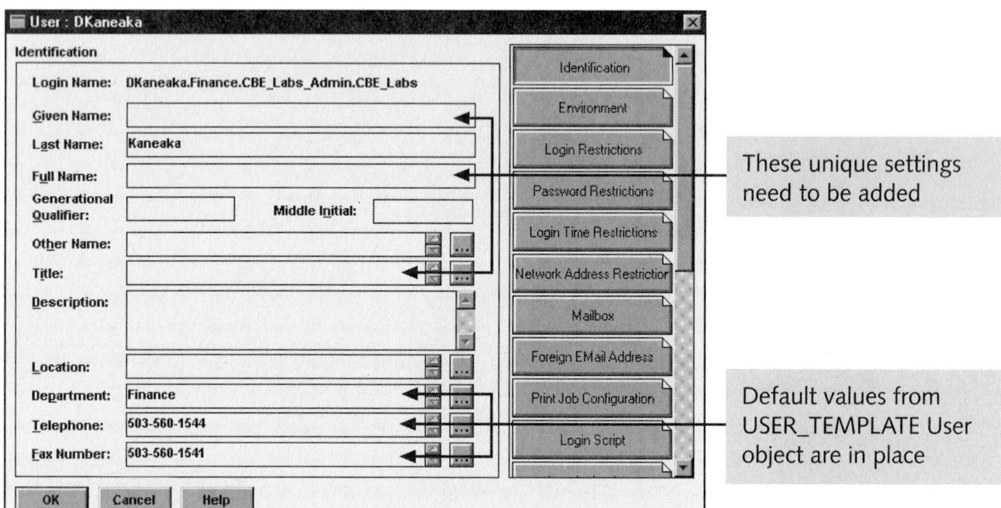

Figure 9-30 The User: DKaneaka object dialog box

2. Click the **Given Name** text box; then type in the name **Donna**. Do not press [Enter].
3. Click the **Full Name** text box; then type in the name **Donna Kaneaka**. Do not press [Enter].
4. Click the **Title** text box; then type in the title **Finance Director**. Do not press [Enter].
5. All unique property values for Donna Kaneaka are now entered. All other property values that needed to be set were set to the default values from the USER_TEMPLATE User object. Click **OK**.
6. Repeat steps 1–5 for Sarah Johnston and Thomas Meyer.

At this time the CBE Labs network administrator creates USER_TEMPLATE User objects for the other Organizational Unit objects in the CBE Labs Directory tree. Using these, the user accounts are created. A complete list of USER_TEMPLATE User objects and the User objects for CBE Labs, including the ones just created, are shown in Figure 9-31. In the following sections in this chapter, all objects shown in Figure 9-31 have been created.

Figure 9-31

USER_TEMPLATES and Users for CBE Labs

Organizational Unit	User Objects Created	Title
CBE_Labs_Admin	JCunningham	President
CBE_Labs_Admin	SLopez	Administrative Assistant
Finance	USER_TEMPLATE	
Finance	DKaneaka	Finance Director
Finance	SJohnston	
Finance	TMeyer	
Marketing	USER_TEMPLATE	
Marketing	SHayakawa	Marketing Director
Marketing	JJorgenson	
Marketing	SWells	
Personnel	USER_TEMPLATE	
Personnel	PRichardson	Personnel Director
InfoSystems	USER_TEMPLATE	
InfoSystems	TSimpson	Information Systems Manager
InfoSystems	DAuer	Network Administrator
InfoSystems	MCiampa	Network Administrator
Pubs	USER_TEMPLATE	
Pubs	HEvans	Vice President for Publishing
Pubs	RDeLucia	Administrative Assistant
Pubs	SMichelia	Editor
Pubs	GTennesson	
Pubs	CPatterson	
Test&Eval		USER_TEMPLATE
Test&Eval	GBurns	Vice President for Testing and Evaluation
Test&Eval	MODonnell	Administrative Assistant
Test&Eval	GLee	
Test&Eval	NNewman	
Test&Eval	TSkaggs	
Test&Eval	BFerguson	
Test&Eval	BSimpson	
Test&Eval	MThorndike	
Test&Eval	FNelson	
Test&Eval	SVanDorn	
Test&Eval	RPaulsen	
Test&Eval	WEllis	
Test&Eval	SGreene	
Test&Eval	NSingh	

Enabling Intruder Detection

In NetWare 4.1, intruder detection is enabled or disabled for each container object and applies only to User objects in that container. Intruder detection is started or stopped by using the Intruder Detection page in the Organization object or Organizational Unit object dialog box, as shown in Figure 9-32.

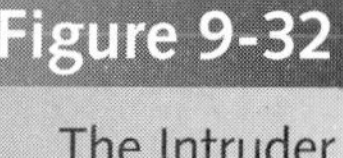

Figure 9-32

The Intruder Detection page

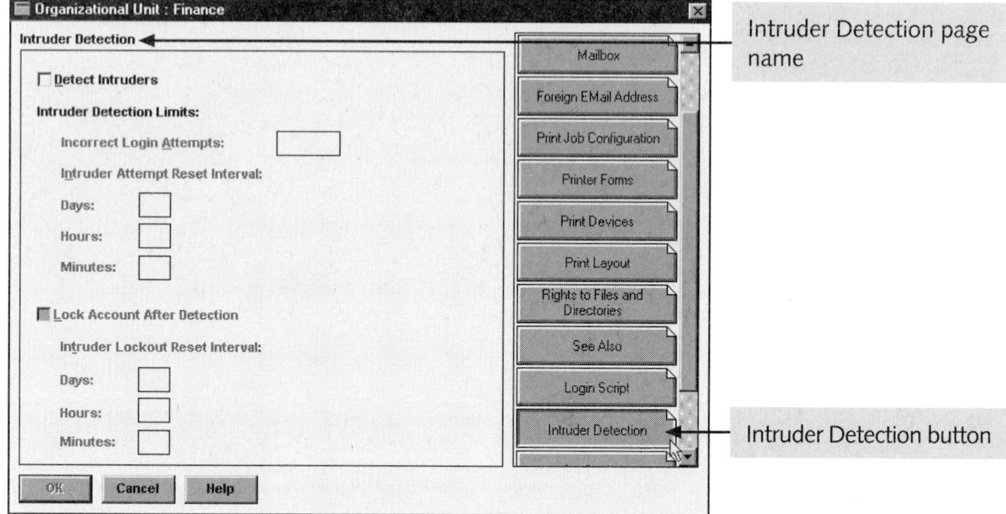

When intruder detection is enabled, the network administrator can set a limit on the number of times a user can try to log in within a certain time period before being labeled as an intruder, and how long the account will be locked if the intruder detection limit is passed.

For example, the CBE Labs network administrator wants to enable intruder detection for the user accounts for the CBE Labs personnel in the Finance Department.

To enable intruder detection for the Finance Organizational Unit, follow these steps:

1. Right-click the **Finance Organizational Unit** object, then click **Details**. The Organizational Unit: Finance object dialog box is displayed.
2. If necessary, use the scroll arrows to scroll through the page buttons until the **Intruder Detection** button appears. Click the **Intruder Detection** button in the button bar. The Intruder Detection page is displayed.
3. Click the **Detect Intruders** check box. Do not press [Enter].
4. Use the **Incorrect Login Attempts** text box arrows to set the number of allowed login attempts to **5**. Do not change the Intruder Attempt Reset Interval. Do not press [Enter].
5. Click the **Lock Account After Detection** check box. Do not change the Intruder Lockout Reset Interval. Do not press [Enter]. The completed Intruder Detection page appears as shown in Figure 9-33.

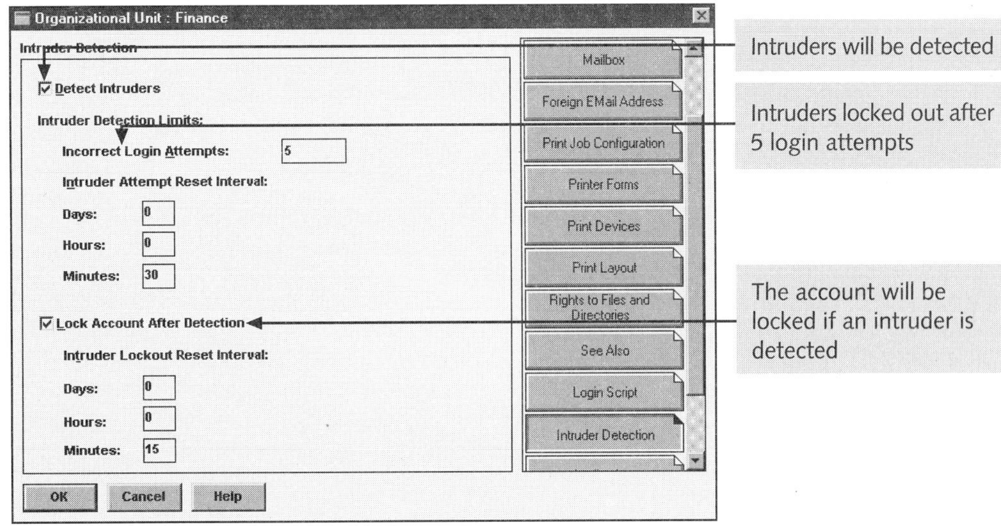

Figure 9-33 The Completed Intruder Detection page

6. Click **OK**.

Groups

The Group object is used to represent and manage groups of related users and is represented by the icon 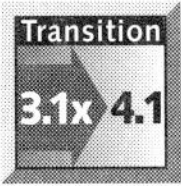. The Group Name must be specified when you create a group.

Groups are useful when you want to assign the use of some network resource to several users. For example, at CBE Labs, all users who work in the laboratories need access to the SARATOGA_SYS:APPS, SARATOGA_DATA:SHARED, and SARATOGA_DATA:REPORTS directories. These users also share access to a laser printer. Rather than assigning the access rights for these resources individually, the network administrator can create a group named Lab_Staff and assign the access rights to the group. By being a member of this group, a user is automatically given access to the resources.

Transition 3.1x 4.1

In NetWare 3.1x, a group named EVERYONE was automatically created during installation, and every user created was automatically assigned to this group. This group is not created in NetWare 4.1. If an EVERYONE group is desired, the network administrator must create it.

Groups can be created as needed in appropriate container objects. Users can be assigned to a group regardless of the Group object's context and the User object's context. Group membership can also be a property value in a USER_TEMPLATE User object. Access to network resources can be granted to all users by assigning the [Public] trustee to a resource; this is discussed in Chapter 10. In this chapter, we'll work with using groups to control network resource allocation.

For example, the CBE Labs network administrator is ready to create the Lab_Staff group and add users to it.

To create the Testing&Eval group, follow these steps:

1. If necessary, launch NetWare Administrator. Expand the Directory tree in the browser window so that you can see all the objects in the tree.
2. Click the **Test & Eval Organizational Unit** object, click **Object** on the menu bar, and then click **Create**.

3. The New Object dialog box is displayed. Click **Group**; then click **OK**. The Create Group dialog box is displayed, as shown in Figure 9-34.

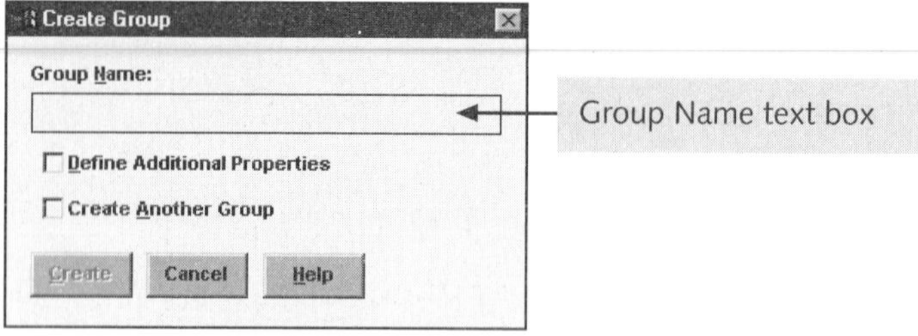

Figure 9-34 The Create Group dialog box

4. Click the **Group Name** text box to activate it; then type **Lab_Staff**.
5. Click the **Create** button. The Lab_Staff group is created.
6. Close and redisplay the Test&Eval branch of the Directory tree. The Group object now appears as shown in Figure 9-35.

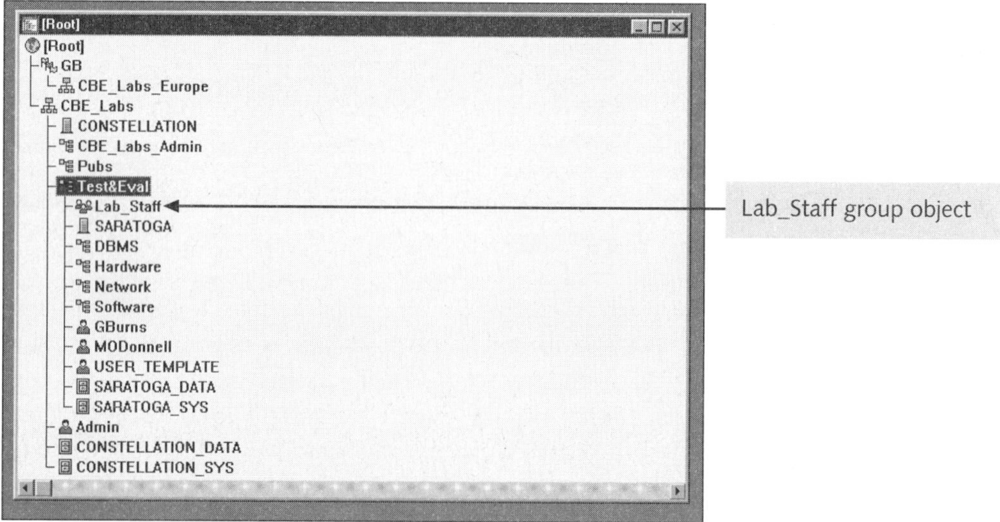

Figure 9-35 The CBE Labs Directory tree with the Group object

You can add users to a group in two ways:

- In the User: *UserName* object dialog box, you can add the user into a group on the Group Memberships page.
- In the Group: *GroupName* object dialog box, you can add members to the group on the User Members page.

For example, the CBE Labs network administrator needs to add Georgia Burns, CBE Labs's Vice President for Testing and Evaluation, and Mike O'Donnell into the Lab_Staff group. To illustrate the two ways of adding users to groups, we'll add Georgia from the User: *UserName* dialog box and Mike from the Group: *GroupName* dialog box.

To add Georgia Burns and Mike O'Donnell into the Lab_Staff group, follow these steps:

1. Double-click the **GBurns User** object. The User: GBurns object dialog box is displayed.
2. If necessary, use the scroll arrows to scroll through the page buttons until the **Group Membership** button appears. Click the **Group Membership** button in the button bar. The Group Membership page is displayed, as shown in Figure 9-36.

Figure 9-36

The Group Membership page

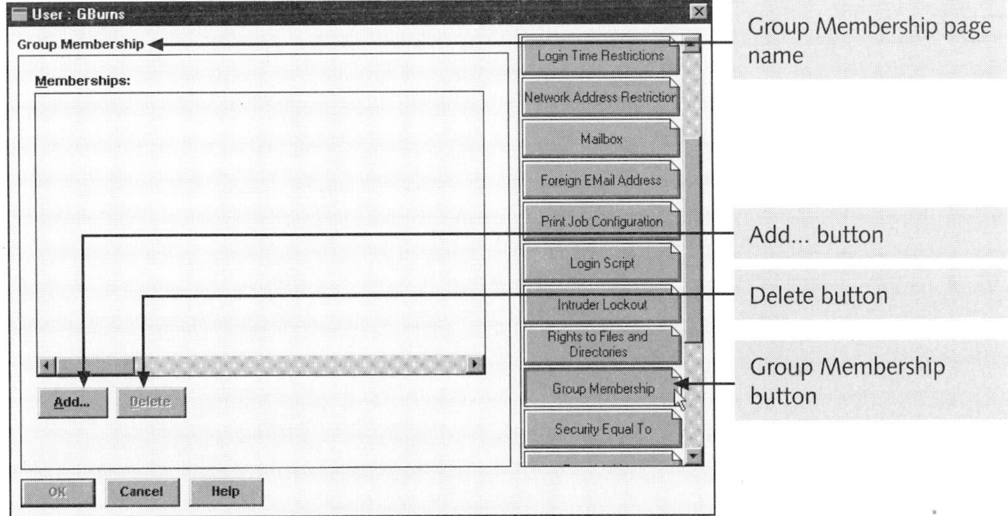

3. Click the **Add** button. The Select Object dialog box is displayed.
4. Click the **Lab_Staff Group** object in the Objects list to select it; then click **OK**. The group name Lab_Staff.Test&Eval.CBE_Labs appears in the Groups Memberships list.
5. Click **OK**.
6. Double-click the **Lab_Staff Group** object. The Group: Lab_Staff object dialog box is displayed.
7. Click the **Members** button in the button bar. The Members page is displayed, as shown in Figure 9-37. Notice that GBurns is listed as a member of the group.

Figure 9-37

The Members page

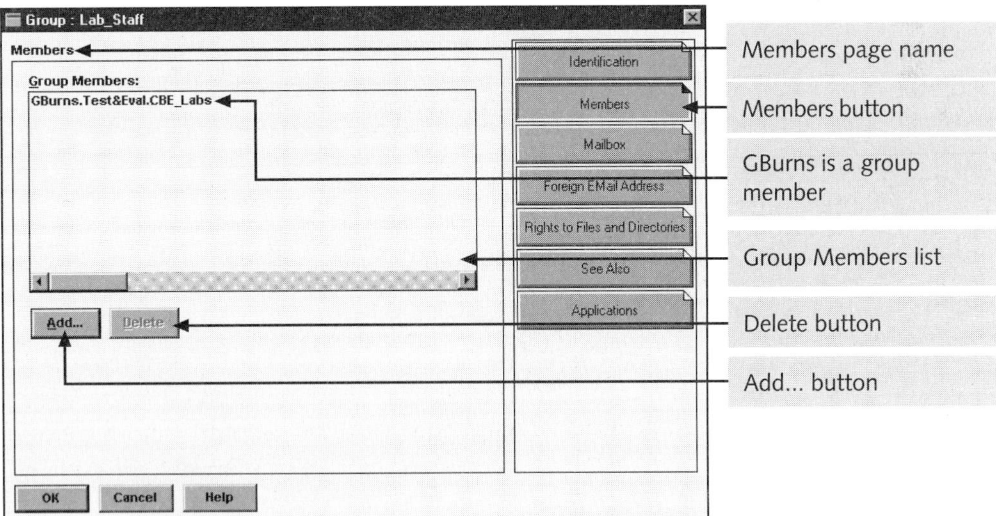

8. Click the **Add** button. The Select Object dialog box is displayed.
9. Click the **MODonnell User** object in the Objects list to select it; then click **OK**. The name MODonnell.Test&Eval.CBE_Labs appears in the Group Members list.
10. Click **OK**.

At this point, the CBE Labs network administrator adds all other members of Testing&Eval to the group. The easiest way to do this is to add members from the Members page in the Lab_Staff group object dialog box because all the members can be added from here without having to open the User object dialog box for each member. In the following sections in this chapter, all group members have been added.

In addition, the CBE Labs network administrator now creates the other groups needed in the CBE Labs Directory tree and adds the group members to each group. The Group objects and the members of each group are shown in Figure 9-38. In the following sections in this chapter, all objects shown and memberships shown in Figure 9-38 have been created.

Figure 9-38

Groups and group memberships for CBE Labs

Group	Context	Members
Executives	CBE_Labs_Admin.CBE_LABS	JCunningham, HEvans, GBurns
Admin_Assists	CBE_Labs_Admin.CBE_LABS	SLopez, RDeLucia, MODonnell
Admin_Staff	CBE_Labs_Admin.CBE_LABS	JCunningham, SLopez, SHayakawa, JJorgensen, SWells, DKaneaka, SJohnston, TMeyer, PRichardson, TSimpson, DAuer, MCiampa
Pub_Staff	Pubs.CBE_LABS	HEvans, RDeLucia, SMichelia, GTennesson, CPatterson
Lab_Staff	Test&Eval.CBE_LABS	GBurns, MODonnell, GLee, NNewman, TSkaggs, BFerguson, BSimpson, MThorndike, FNelson, SVanDorn, RPaulsen, WEllis, SGreene, NSigh
Hardware	Test&Eval.CBE_LABS	GLee, NNewman, TSkaggs
Software	Test&Eval.CBE_LABS	BFerguson, BSimpson, MThorndike
DBMS	Test&Eval.CBE_LABS	FNelson, SVanDorn, RPaulsen, GBurns
Network	Test&Eval.CBE_LABS	WEllis, SGreene, NSigh

Organizational Roles

The Organizational Role object is used to represent a position in an organization structure such as president, chief information officer (CIO), or production manager and is represented by the icon . The Organizational Role object is useful for recording and managing rights and resources assigned to an organizational role in the organization—whoever is assigned to that position is automatically assigned those rights and resources. The Organizational Role name must be specified when you create the Organizational Role object.

The power of the Organizational Role is found in the fact that although the individuals who fill organizational roles change, the responsibilities and rights associated with the role usually don't. By assigning access to network resources to an organizational role rather than to a user, it is easy to make sure that only the user or users in an organizational role have the appropriate rights for that position.

For example, at CBE Labs, Georgia Burns is Vice President for Testing and Evaluation. In this position, she should have access to all files in the SARATOGA_DATA:HARDWARE, SARATOGA_DATA:SOFTWARE, SARATOGA_DATA:DBMS, SARATOGA_DATA:NETWORK, SARATOGA_DATA:SHARED, and SARATOGA_DATA:REPORTS directories and all their subdirectories. Rather than assigning the access rights for these directories to her individually, the network administrator can create an organizational role named VP_Test&Eval and assign the access rights to the organizational role. By assigning GBurns to this role, she is automatically given access to the directories.

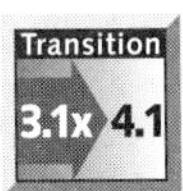

There was no equivalent to Organizational Roles in NetWare 3.1x.

Organizational Roles can be created as needed in appropriate container objects. Users can be assigned to an organizational role group regardless of the Organizational Roles object's context and the User object's context.

The CBE Labs network administrator is ready to create the VP_Testing&Evaluation organizational role and assign Georgia Burns to that role.

To create the VP_Testing&Evaluation organizational role, follow these steps:

1. If necessary, launch **NetWare Administrator**. Expand the Directory tree in the browser window so that you can see all the objects in the tree.
2. Click the **Test&Eval Organizational Unit** object, click **Object** on the menu bar, and then click **Create**.
3. The New Object dialog box is displayed. Click **Organizational Role**; then click **OK**. The Create Organizational Role dialog box is displayed.
4. Click the **Organizational Role Name** text box to activate it; then type **VP_Testing&Evaluation**.
5. Click the **Create** button. The VP_Testing&Evaluation organizational role is created. Close and redisplay the Test&Eval branch of the Directory tree. The Organizational Role object now appears as shown in Figure 9-39.

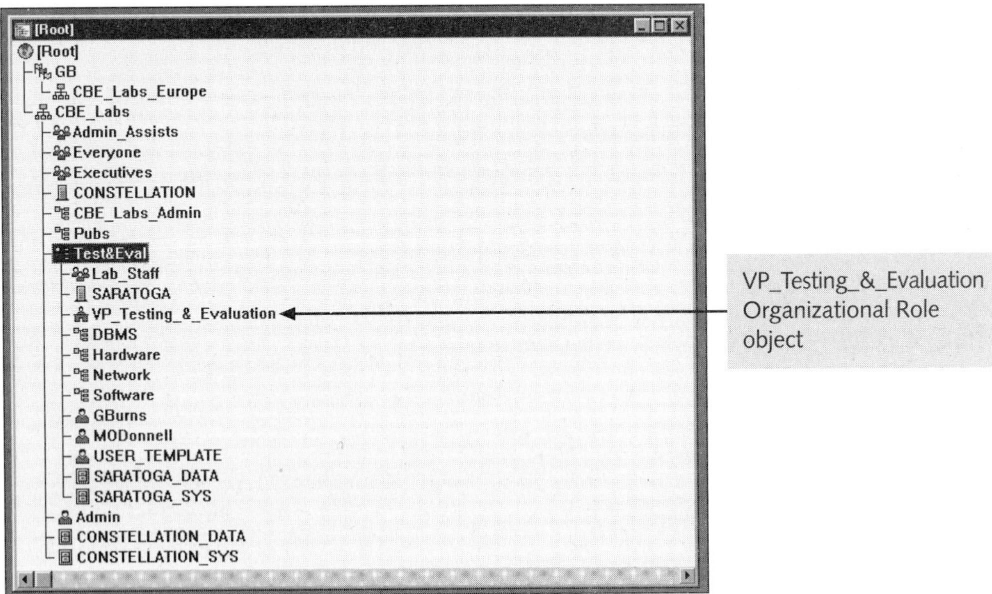

Figure 9-39 The CBE Labs Directory tree with the Organizational Role object

The CBE Labs network administrator now assigns Georgia Burns to the organizational role of VP_Testing&Evaluation. Once assigned, Georgia has all the rights associated with that organizational role.

To assign Georgia Burns to the organizational role of VP_Testing&Evaluation, follow these steps:

1. Double-click the **VP_Testing&Evaluation Organizational Role** object. The Organizational Role:VP_TESTING&EVALUATION object dialog box is displayed, as shown in Figure 9-40.

Figure 9-40

The Organizational Role: VP_TESTING& EVALUATION object dialog box

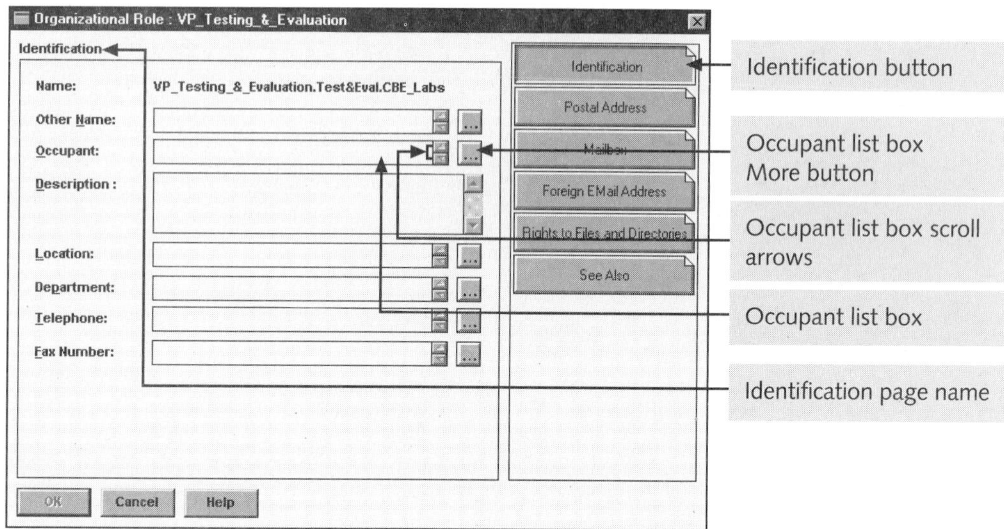

2. Click the **More** button to the right of the Occupant text box to display the Occupant dialog box.
3. Click the **Add** button. The Select Object dialog box is displayed.
4. The Select Object dialog box is used to browse the Directory tree context to find an object. In this case, the starting context is Labs. This is correct. Click the User object for GBurns in the Object list window; then click **OK**. Georgia Burns is added as the occupant of the VP_Testing&Evaluation position.
5. Click **OK** in the Occupant window.
6. Click **OK**.

At this point, the CBE Labs network Administrator adds all organizational roles to the NDS Directory tree. Figure 9-41 is a table of all organizational roles that will be used in the CBE Labs Directory tree, including Georgia Burns's role as VP_Testing&Evaluation. In the following sections in this chapter, all organizational roles have been created and occupants assigned.

Figure 9-41

Organizational Roles for CBE Labs

Organizational Role	Context	Occupant
President	CBE_Labs_Admin.CBE_LABS	JCunningham
AdminAssist	CBE_Labs_Admin.CBE_LABS	SLopez
VP_Publishing	Pubs.CBE_LABS	HEvans
AdminAssist	Pubs.CBE_LABS	RDeLucia
VP_Testing&Evaluation	Test&Eval.CBE_LABS	GBurns
AdminAssist	Test&Eval.CBE_LABS	MODonnell
Marketing_Director	CBE_Labs_Admin.CBE_LABS	SHayakawa
Finance_Director	CBE_Labs_Admin.CBE_LABS	DKaneaka
Personnel_Director	CBE_Labs_Admin.CBE_LABS	PRichardson
Information_Systems_Manager	CBE_Labs_Admin.CBE_LABS	TSimpson
Network_Administrator	CBE_Labs_Admin.CBE_LABS	DAuer, MCiampa
Editor	Pubs.CBE_LABS	SMichella

Profiles

The Profile object is used to run login scripts and assign resources to groups of users. Login scripts can be written for Organization objects, Organizational Unit objects, and User objects but not for a Group object. The Profile object provides the network administrator with a tool for creating login scripts for groups. The icon for the Profile object is . The Profile Name must be specified when you create a profile. The Profile objects also enables the network administrator to assign directory and file trustee rights to the profile, so that all users who share the profile will also share those access rights.

The Profile object is most useful when a container object login script cannot be easily applied to a set of users who need to share common network resources. This often happens when the set of users is a subset of those in the container or the set of users consists of users from two or more containers.

For example, in order to use Lab data for publications, some CBE Labs personnel in both the Pubs Organizational Unit and the Test&Eval Organizational Unit need access to the SARATOGA_DATA:SHARED and SARATOGA_DATA:REPORTS directories. These people include SMichella and GTennesson in Pubs and GLee, BFerguson, FNelson, and WEllis in Test&Eval. This set of users needs a Profile object so that a specialized login script can be created for them and specialized directory and file access can be set up if necessary.

The CBE Labs network administrator decides to create a Pubs&Labs_Profile Profile object.

To create the Pubs&Labs_Profile Profile object, follow these steps:

1. If necessary, launch **NetWare Administrator**. Expand the Directory tree in the browser window so that you can see all the objects in the tree.
2. Click the **CBE_Labs Organization** object, click **Object** on the menu bar, and then click **Create**.
3. The New Object dialog box is displayed. Click **Profile**; then click **OK**. The Create Profile dialog box is displayed.
4. Click the **Profile Name** text box to activate it; then type **Pubs&Labs_Profile**.
5. Click the **Create** button. The Pubs&Labs_Profile profile is created. Close and redisplay the CBE_Labs branch of the Directory tree. The Profile object now appears as shown in Figure 9-42.

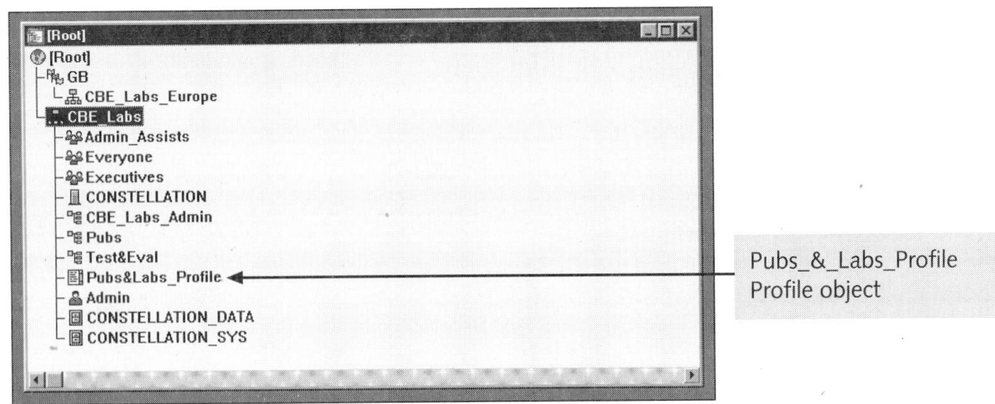

Figure 9-42 The CBE Labs Directory tree with the Profile object

The CBE Labs network administrator now assigns Susan Michella to the Pubs&Labs_Profile profile. Once assigned, Susan will use the profiles' login scripts and have all the rights associated with the profile.

To assign Susan Michella to the Pubs&Labs_Profile profile, follow these steps:

1. Double-click the **SMichella User** object. The User: SMICHELLA object dialog box is displayed.
2. If necessary, use the scroll arrows to scroll through the page buttons until the Login Script button appears. Click the **Login Script** button in the button bar. The Login Script page is displayed, as shown in Figure 9-43.

Figure 9-43 The Login Script page

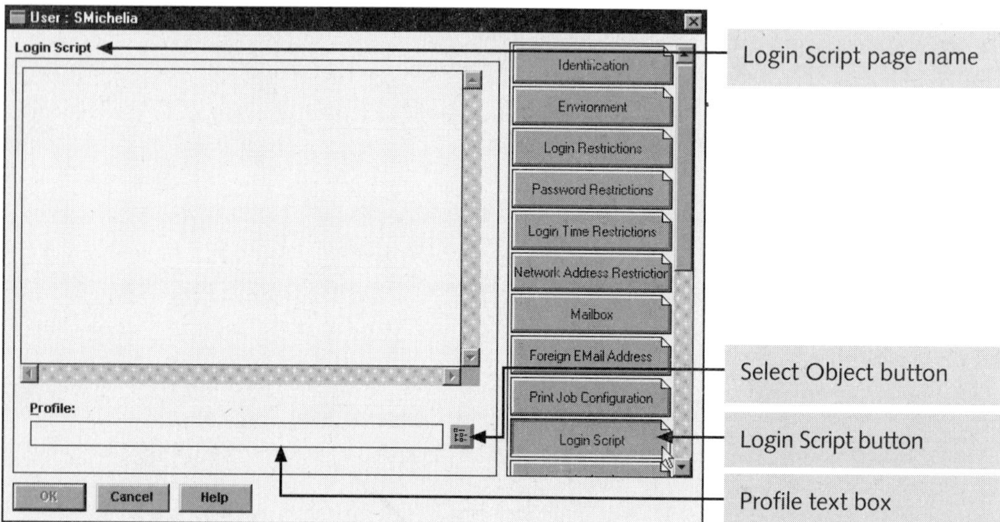

3. Click the **Select Object** button to the right of the Profile text box. The Select Object dialog box is displayed.
4. The Select Object dialog box is used to browse the Directory tree context to find an object. In this case, the starting context is Pubs. The context for the Pubs&Labs_Profile object, however, is .CBE_Labs. Browse until the context is .CBE_Labs and the Pubs&Labs_Profile object is displayed. Click the **Pubs&Labs_Profile** object in the Objects window; then click **OK**. The Pubs&Labs_Profile profile is displayed in the Profile text box, as shown in Figure 9-44.

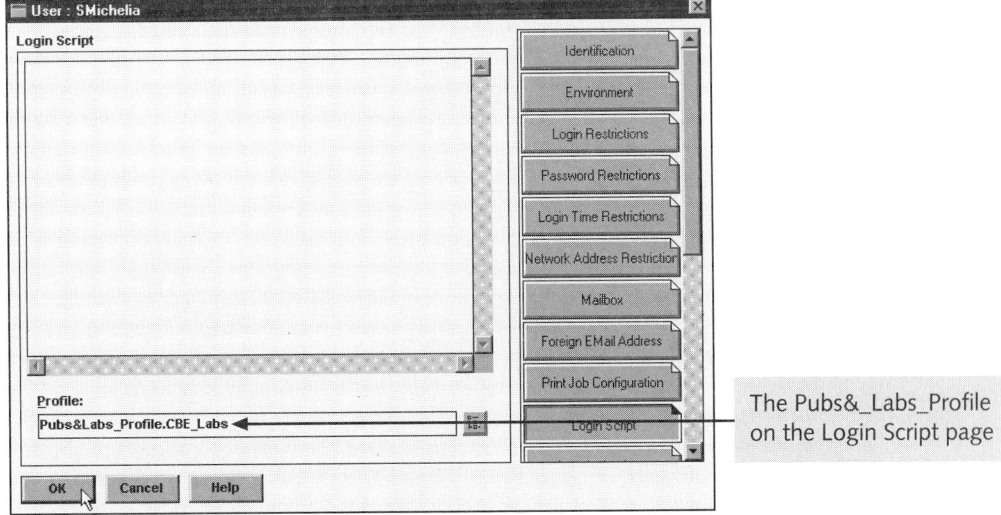

Figure 9-44 The completed Login Script page

5. Click **OK**.
6. A warning dialog box is displayed, as shown in Figure 9-45, stating that the user does not have needed rights to the Profile. These rights will be assigned in Chapter 10. Click the **Yes** button.

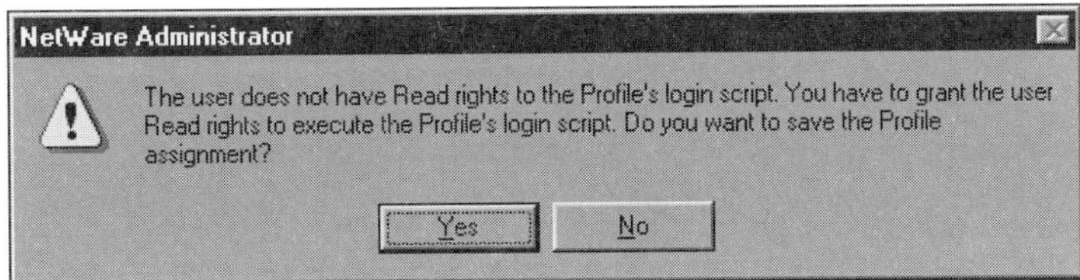

Figure 9-45 The Rights warning dialog box

At this point, the CBE Labs network Administrator adds the Pubs&Labs_Profile profile to the Login Script page property settings of all other users who need to share it. In the following sections in this chapter, this has been done. The Pubs&Labs Profile is the only profile that CBE Labs will use.

NETWARE ACCOUNTING

NetWare's accounting features enable the network administrator to track resources used on a network and charge users for their use. You can monitor user login and logout activity, charge customers for resource usage on the file server, or monitor file server usage in order to facilitate planning for file server expansion.

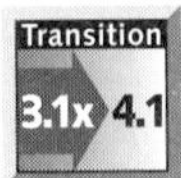

NetWare 4.1 separates the accounting and auditing tasks, which were combined in NetWare 3.1x. Auditing in NetWare 4.1 is handled by the AUDITCON utility, which replaces the NetWare 3.1x PAUDIT utility.

Data from the accounting functions is stored in the NET$ACCT.DAT file. The data in this file can be summarized and printed with NetWare's ATOTAL program, which shows the total usage by service for each week. Because the NET$ACCT.DAT file can become quite large over time, you should establish a schedule for printing reports, backing up the file before erasing it and starting the next reporting period. NetWare automatically recreates the file when the user next logs in.

CHARGING FOR FILE SERVER USAGE

NetWare's accounting functions can be used to record file server usage by the following categories:

- Disk activity
- Connect time
- Disk storage space consumed
- Service requests

Records of file server usage can be important tools in tracking the growth of a file server, enabling you to budget for future file server needs. Another use of the NetWare accounting feature is to charge users for services. This capability can be useful if your file server is shared by two or more profit centers. Each profit center can then be billed monthly based on its usage of the file server.

A teacher in a local school system used NetWare accounting to help motivate students to achieve better grades by rewarding good scores with additional credit on the file server. Having credit on the file server enabled students to run games and simulations from the server during their break time.

TYPES OF CHARGES

The disk activity charge includes the number of disk blocks read, the number of disk blocks written, or both. The amount to be charged for each block read can be specified in half-hour increments. This allows you to charge one rate during peak business hours—8:00 A.M. to 5:00 P.M.—and another rate for off-peak periods. The connect time figure enables you to charge for the number of minutes a user is logged in to the file server even if no services are accessed. Here, too, you can establish different charge rates for different time periods. The user will be charged the rate you establish for each minute of login time.

The disk storage figure enables you to charge for each block of disk space occupied by a file owned by a user. This charge is assigned once per day. The network administrator can select the time of day and charge rate to be used. At the specified time, the file server will scan its directories and compute the charges for each user's disk storage usage. The service requests figure enables you to charge for such file server activities as using directory services, accessing bindery files, and sending messages. You can establish different charge rates for different time periods based on half-hour increments. The specified charge rate is applied for each service request.

CHARGE RATE FORMULA

The amount a user is charged for accessing a service is automatically computed by NetWare according to a charge rate formula. The charge rate formula is based on a specific amount to be charged for each unit of service and is specified as a ratio consisting of a multiplier and divisor, as shown in the following example:

Blocks Read Charge Rate = 1/10

Based on this ratio, a user will be charged one unit for each 10 blocks of data read from the disk drive. Although the charge amount is arbitrary, Novell suggests that you begin by using one cent for each unit of service and then adjust this ratio as necessary for your network. Suppose, for example, your company maintains a database on a file server for which it needs to collect $150 per month for maintenance. You decide to base your charge for usage of the database on the number of blocks read from the disk. Assume that, after using the accounting feature to track network usage, you determine that an average of 10,000 blocks are read from the file server each week. In this case, the charge rate would be 15,000 cents ($150.00 × 100) divided by 40,000 blocks (10,000 × 4 weeks). This yields $0.375, which rounds off to $0.38 per block, giving a charge ratio of 38/1. With this charge ratio, users would be charged based on how much information they read from the database in any given month.

Before calculating the charge rate, you need to know how much money you want to obtain per month, what services you want to charge for, and the average usage of that service per month. The amount of money you need to make per month to cover network and administrative expenses is best arrived at by consulting your company accountant. It should be based on operational costs and how much of those costs should be paid by the consumer. Once you calculate the monthly charge figure, you need to determine what services you want to charge for. To keep things simple, you might choose to charge for only one service. If file server storage capacity is a concern for you, you might select the disk storage charge rate. If network utilization is high, you might want to charge for service requests. To prevent users from staying logged in when they are not working, you could charge for connect time.

Finally, to determine the average usage of the selected service, you need to track the total usage for the selected service over a minimum of two weeks. This can be done by performing the following steps:

1. Assign a 1/1 charge rate for the selected service.
2. Give all users unlimited credit. This is necessary to prevent user accounts from becoming disabled during the test period.
3. At the end of the test period, use NetWare's ATOTAL program to obtain the usage results. See the example shown in Figure 9-46. The totals can be entered in a spreadsheet to graph server usage.

Figure 9-46 Using ATOTAL to display usage totals

```
Finished - Atotal

Totals for week:
    Connect time:          93     Server requests:       6778
    Blocks read:          940     Blocks written:
    Blocks/day:

02/18/1997:
    Connect time:        5791     Server requests:      13279
    Blocks read:         1231     Blocks written:
    Blocks/day:

02/20/1997:
    Connect time:        2936     Server requests:      23398
    Blocks read:         1605     Blocks written:         630
    Blocks/day:

Totals for week:
    Connect time:        8727     Server requests:      36677
    Blocks read:         2836     Blocks written:         630
    Blocks/day:
```

After you have determined the charge rate, you can give your users a balance based on the amount paid for the month, remove the unlimited credit privilege, and optionally assign a credit limit. When a user's credit limit is exceeded, the file server displays a message indicating that the user's account balance has been exceeded and then grants the user several minutes to complete his or her work and log out. At this point, the user's account is disabled and the user cannot log in again until the balance field is updated or additional credit is assigned.

PLANNING FOR EXPANSION

One aspect of NetWare accounting that can be helpful for all network administrators is the ability to monitor file server usage and employ that information in planning for future server expansion. As the usage on your file server grows, you will eventually need to consider adding more disk storage, a faster disk system, more memory, or even a faster file server computer. If these needs are not anticipated and justified, you will probably have a hard time obtaining the budget for network improvements when you need them. With NetWare's accounting functions, the ATOTAL program can gather usage information and then use a spreadsheet program to graph the server usage information to illustrate disk access, storage capacity, and server requests for each week. By extrapolation, the graph you can then draw will project your server expansion needs for budgeting purposes.

IMPLEMENTING ACCOUNTING ON A SERVER

Because accounting tracks usage of resources on each NetWare server, it must be implemented on each NetWare server individually. This is done in the NetWare Server object dialog box. As shown in Figure 9-47, the NetWare Server object dialog box has an Accounting button at the bottom of the page. When you click this button, you are prompted to confirm the installation of accounting on the server, and upon confirmation accounting is installed.

Figure 9-47

Installing accounting on the NetWare server

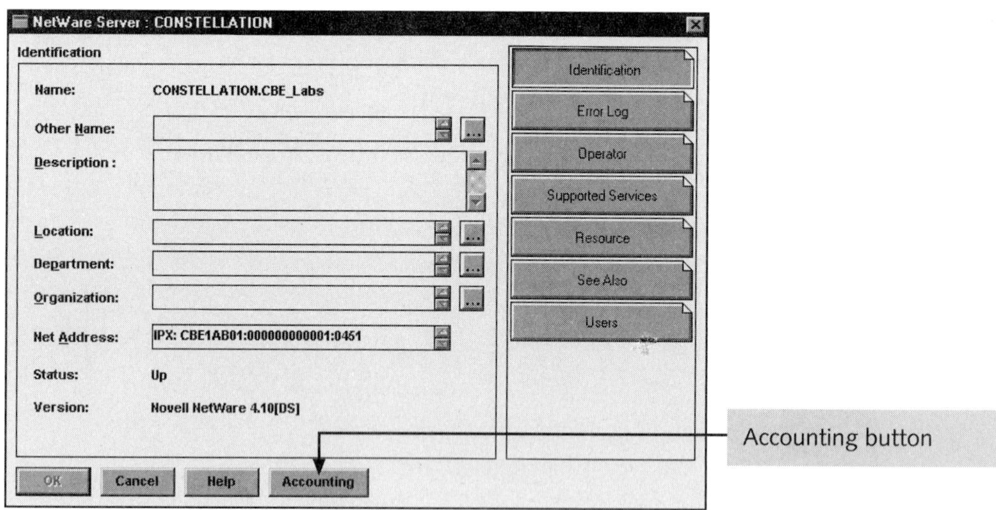

Once accounting is installed, five pages are added to the NetWare Server object dialog box and the corresponding page buttons are added to the page button list:

- Blocks Read
- Blocks Written
- Connect Time
- Disk Storage
- Service Requests

Charging for Blocks Read

The Blocks Read page enables you to enter the charge ratio you want to use for each block read for various specified time periods. Selecting this page displays the Blocks Read page shown in Figure 9-48.

Figure 9-48 The Blocks Read page

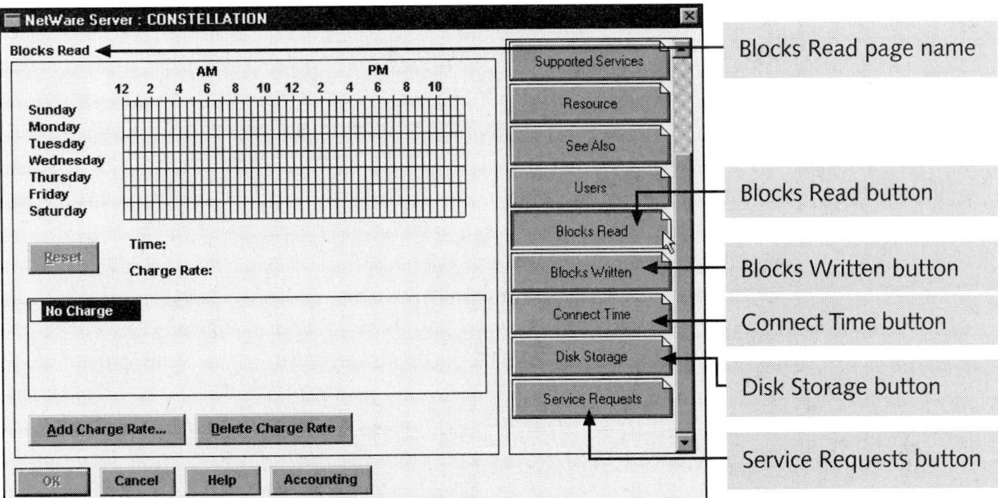

Notice that days and times are shown on a grid at the top of the page on the screen, and the existing charge rates are shown in the box at the bottom of the page. The initial assignment is no charge for all time periods. To set a charge rate, you first create the rate and then apply it to the time periods.

For example, the CBE Labs network administrator needs to set a charge ratio of 38 cents for each block read during CBE Labs normal business hours of Monday through Friday, 8:00 A.M. to 5:00 P.M. He starts with the NetWare server CONSTELLATION.

To add the block read charge to CONSTELLATION, follow these steps:

1. Right-click the **CONSTELLATION NetWare Server** object; then click **Details**. The NetWare Server: CONSTELLATION object dialog box is displayed.
2. Click the **Accounting** button to install accounting. When the Accounting dialog box is displayed to confirm the installation, click the **Yes** button. Five new pages and page buttons are added to the NetWare Server dialog box.
3. If necessary, use the scroll arrows to scroll through the page buttons until the **Blocks Read** button appears.
4. Click the **Blocks Read** button in the button bar. The Blocks Read page is displayed.
5. Click the **Add Charge Rate** button. The Add Charge Rate dialog box is displayed, as shown in Figure 9-49.

Figure 9-49 The Add Change Rate dialog box

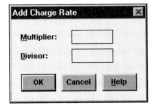

Add Charge Rate
Multiplier:
Divisor:
OK Cancel Help

6. Click the **Multiplier** text box to activate it; then type in the number **38**.
7. Click the **Divisor** text box to activate it; then type in the number **1**.
8. Click **OK**. The new rate is added to the list of rates.
9. Click the new rate in the list of rates to select it. Click (and keep the left mouse button down) the Monday at 8 cell in the day and time grid; then drag the highlight to cover from Monday at 8:00 A.M. through Friday at 5:00 P.M. The day and time grid now appears as shown in Figure 9-50.

Figure 9-50 The completed Blocks Read page

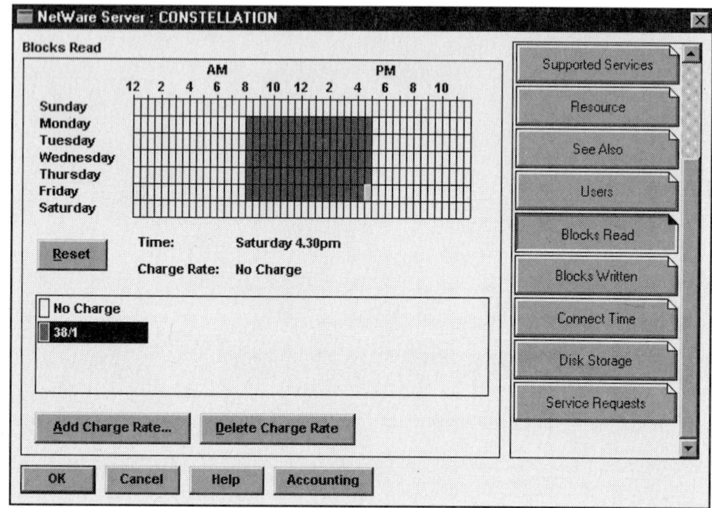

10. Click OK.

Charging for Blocks Written

The Blocks Written page enables you to enter the charge ratio you want to apply to each block written during the time period specified. The method of specifying charges is the same as for Blocks Read.

Charging for Connect Time

The Connect Time page enables you to enter the charge ratio you want to apply to each minute a user is connected to the file server during the time period specified. The method of specifying charges is the same as for Blocks Read.

Charging for Disk Storage

The Disk Storage Charge Rates option enables you to enter the charge ratio you want to apply to each block of disk space used per day. The method of specifying charges is the same as for Blocks Read.

Charging for Service Requests

The Service Requests page enables you to enter the charge ratio you want to apply to each server request made by a user during the time period specified. The method of specifying charges is the same as for Blocks Read.

Removing Accounting from a NetWare Server

To remove accounting from a file server, you use the same Accounting button you used to install it. When accounting is installed, however, clicking the Accounting button will remove the accounting feature (you are prompted to confirm removing accounting, just as you were prompted to confirm installing accounting).

Managing User Account Balances

When accounting is enabled on a NetWare server, user account balances are managed using the Account Balance page in the User object dialog box, as shown in Figure 9-51.

Figure 9-51
The Account Balance page

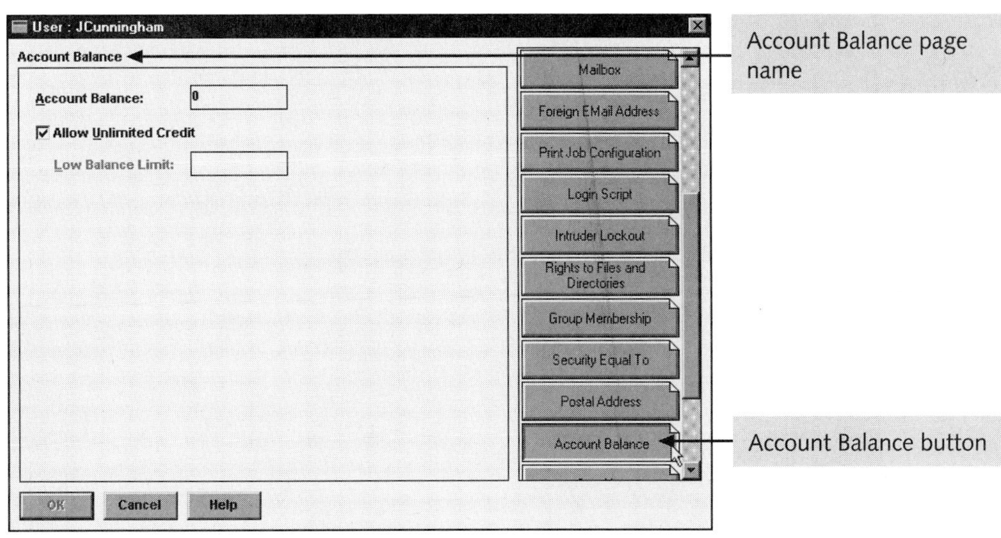

If a user has no restrictions on his or her usage of server resources controlled by NetWare accounting, the Allow Unlimited Credit check box is checked. This is the default for newly created User objects, but, of course, you can control this with the settings in a USER_PROFILE User object used to create new accounts. You can also control this for new user accounts created using the UIMPORT utility as discussed later in this chapter.

If a user does not have unlimited use of the resources, you uncheck the Allow Unlimited Credit check box and then set an initial Account Balance and a Low Balance Limit. The initial Account balance will be decreased as the user uses chargeable resources until the Low Balance Limit is reached. At that point, the user cannot use additional chargeable resources until his or her account balance is increased.

NetWare Utilities and Commands

The discussion of managing users and groups in this chapter used the Network Administrator graphical utility. As usual, the NETADMIN menu utility provides the network administrator with similar capabilities. You have already worked with NETADMIN in previous chapters, and you will use it to manage users and groups in the exercises at the end of this chapter.

NETADMIN is the NetWare 4.1 replacement of the NetWare 3.1x SYSCON menu utility. SYSCON was the network administrator's tool for creating and managing users and groups in NetWare 3.1x .

The ATOTAL Command Line Utility

As explained above, the ATOTAL utility provides usage summary information for chargeable network resources. The syntax of the ATOTAL command is

```
ATOTAL [destination path\filename] [/C] [/?] [/VER]
```

As shown in the syntax, the ATOTAL command has several parameters, as listed in Figure 9-52. Sample output from the ATOTAL utility is shown in Figure 9-46.

Figure 9-52 The ATOTAL command parameters

Parameter	Use this Parameter to
destination path\filename	Redirect the output to an ASCII file for viewing and printing.
/C	Scroll continuously through output instead of pausing after each page of output data.
/?	Access help about ATOTAL. If this parameter is used, all others are ignored.
/VER	See the version number of the ATOTAL command. If this parameter is used, all others are ignored.

The UIMPORT Command Line Utility

The **UIMPORT (user import) command line utility** is a batch-oriented utility, which means that it uses a command file, called the **import control file**, that contains statements. These statements are used to create specified user accounts from data contained in a **data file**. Both UIMPORT import control and data files are ASCII text files. The import control file consists of a list of statements containing keywords and parameters that are used by the UIMPORT program to determine how to create the specified user accounts. UIMPORT is a good way to create and delete users quickly when you are setting up a group consisting of many user accounts.

The syntax of the UIMPORT command is

```
UIMPORT [control file] [data file] [/C] [/?] [/VER]
```

As shown in the syntax, the UIMPORT command has several parameters that you can use with it. These are listed in Figure 9-53.

Figure 9-53

The UIMPORT command parameters

Parameter	Use this Parameter to
control file	Specify the name of the file containing information about loading the data in the data file.
data file	Specify the name of the file containing the data that will become the User object property values.
/C	Scroll continuously through output instead of pausing after each page of output data.
/?	Access help about UIMPORT. If this parameter is used, all others are ignored.
/VER	See the version number of the UIMPORT command. If this parameter is used, all others are ignored.

The UIMPORT Data Files

The data file supplies User object property values separated by commas and enclosed in quotation marks.

The UIMPORT Import Control File

The UIMPORT import control file is made up of two sections. The **import control section** contains **control parameters** that tell UIMPORT which options to use. The **fields section** tells UIMPORT which User object properties have values in the data file.

The import control section control parameters are shown in Figure 9-54.

Figure 9-54

UIMPORT control parameters

Parameter Values	Possible Value	Default	Comments
CREATE HOME DIRECTORY	Y, N	N	Y=Create a home directory N=Don't create a home directory
DELETE MAILBOX DIRS	Y, N	N	Used when moving a user's mailbox to a new messaging server, or when changing the user's mailbox ID. Y=Delete the mailbox directories N=Don't delete the directories
DELETE PROPERTY	Any ASCII character string		Used to delete property values from a User object. Including this character string in a data field will cause the current property value to be deleted. *Cannot* be used to delete: • Volume restrictions • Password • Home directory

Figure 9-54 (Continued)

Parameter Values	Possible Value	Default	Comments
HOME DIRECTORY PATH	Any path		Used to specify the path to the home directory. The path must be enclosed in quotes. *Must* be used together with HOME DIRECTORY VOLUME.
HOME DIRECTORY VOLUME	Any volume name		Used to specify the volume for the home directory. The volume must be enclosed in quotes. *Must* be used together with HOME DIRECTORY PATH.
IMPORT MODE	C, U, B, R	B	Used to control UIMPORTS actions. C = Create new objects only U = Update existing objects only B = Both C and U R = Remove objects
MAXIMUM DIRECTORY RETRIES	Any number	5	Used to specify how many attempts UIMPORT makes to get the object ID of a newly created user when creating home and mailbox directories. This is necessary when the User object is created on one server and the directory is located on another because the replica on the second server must contain the User object data. Since updating the replica takes some time, a number of retries may be necessary to allow the replica to be updated.
NAME CONTEXT	Any context	Current context	Used to specify the NDS context where the User objects will be located.
QUOTE	Any character	" (quotes)	Used to specify the character used to enclose data file values with spaces.
REPLACE VALUE	Y, N	N	Used to specify whether a data value should replace or be added to data values in a multivalued property setting. Y = Replace current value N = Insert as an additional value
SEPARATOR	Any character	, (comma)	Used to specify the character used to delineate data fields in the data file
USER TEMPLATE	Y, N	N	Used to specify whether or not to use the USER_TEMPLATE values when new User objects are created.

For example, the CBE Labs network administrator could have created the user accounts and User object for the employees in the Pubs Organizational Unit using UIMPORT. If he had done so, he could have used the following import control section:

```
IMPORT CONTROL

   CREATE HOME DIRECTORY = Y

   HOME DIRECTORY PATH = "USERS"

   HOME DIRECTORY VOLUME = "CONSTELLATION_DATA.CBE_Labs"

   NAME CONTEXT = ".PUBS.CBE_Labs"

   USER TEMPLATE = Y
```

The definitions of fields used in the fields section are shown in Figure 9-55. There is a field for most of the properties in the User object—the exceptions are login time restrictions and network station restrictions. The fields are arranged according to the page in the User object dialog box that they appear on: Identification page, Environment page, and so on. Single-value properties, for example *Last name*, can have only one setting value in the field. Multivalued properties, for example *Group membership*, can have more than one value in the field. Because the default value of the REPLACE VALUE control parameter is *N*, values will be *added* to multivalued fields unless you specify the REPLACE VALUE control parameter as *Y* in the import control section.

Figure 9-55

UIMPORT field definitions

User Object Dialog Box Page	Field (Property):	Single-Valued or Multivalued:	Comments
IDENTIFICATION	NAME	Single-valued	User's Login Name. An entry for this field is required.
IDENTIFICATION	LAST NAME	Single-valued	User's last name. An entry for this field is required.
IDENTIFICATION	GIVEN NAME	Single-valued	User's first or given name.
IDENTIFICATION	FULL NAME	Single-valued	User's full name.
IDENTIFICATION	GENERATIONAL QUALIFIER	Single-valued	User's generational qualifier such as Jr., III, etc.
IDENTIFICATION	INITIALS	Single-valued	The initial letter of the user's middle name.
IDENTIFICATION	OTHER NAME	Multivalued	Other names that are used to identify the user.
IDENTIFICATION	TITLE	Multivalued	Titles that are associated with the user.
IDENTIFICATION	DESCRIPTION	Single-valued	A description of any type about the user.
IDENTIFICATION	LOCATION	Multivalued	User's work locations.
IDENTIFICATION	DEPARTMENT	Multivalued	Departments the user works for.
IDENTIFICATION	TELEPHONE	Multivalued	User's phone numbers.
IDENTIFICATION	FAX NUMBER	Multivalued	User's fax telephone numbers.
ENVIRONMENT	LANGUAGE	Multivalued	Language directories used for utilities messages for the user.
ENVIRONMENT	DEFAULT SERVER	Single-valued	Server for user's NetWare network messages.

Figure 9-55
(Continued)

User Object Dialog Box Page	Field (Property):	Single-Valued or Multivalued:	Comments
ENVIRONMENT	HOME DIRECTORY	Single-valued	User's home directory location specified as *VolumeName:Path*. If used, this field value replaces any entry in the import control section.
LOGIN RESTRICTIONS	ACCOUNT DISABLED	Single-valued	If user's account is to be disabled, use Y in the field. The default is N.
LOGIN RESTRICTIONS	ACCOUNT HAS EXPIRATION DATE	Single-valued	Date user's account will expire. Use MM/DD/YY format.
LOGIN RESTRICTIONS	MAXIMUM CONNECTIONS	Single-valued	Number of simultaneous logins for user. Enter 0 for unlimited.
PASSWORD RESTRICTIONS	ALLOW USER TO CHANGE PASSWORD	Single-valued	If user can't change his or her pass word, use N in the field. The default is Y.
PASSWORD RESTRICTIONS	REQUIRE A PASSWORD	Single-valued	Y = a password *is* required. N = a password *isn't* required
PASSWORD RESTRICTIONS	MINIMUM PASSWORD LENGTH	Single-valued	The minimum number of characters in the user's password.
PASSWORD RESTRICTIONS	DAYS BETWEEN FORCED CHANGES	Single-valued	The maximum number of days the user can keep the same password.
PASSWORD RESTRICTIONS	DATE PASSWORD EXPIRES	Single-valued	Date password will expire. Use MM/DD/YY format.
PASSWORD RESTRICTIONS	REQUIRE UNIQUE PASSWORDS	Single-valued	Y = unique passwords *are* required. N = unique passwords *aren't* required.
PASSWORD RESTRICTIONS	GRACE LOGINS ALLOWED	Single-valued	Number of grace logins after password expires. 0 = no limit
PASSWORD RESTRICTIONS	REMAINING GRACE LOGINS	Single-valued	Used only with the MODIFY option, a number can be entered in the remaining grace logins is diferent than the normal number of grace logins allowed. Normally this num-ber is set equal to the number of grace logins allowed.
PASSWORD RESTRICTIONS	PASSWORD	Single-valued	The user's initial password.

Figure 9-55
(Continued)

User Object Dialog Box Page	Field (Property):	Single-Valued or Multivalued:	Comments
MAILBOX	MAILBOX LOCATION	Single-valued	The NDS Messaging Server object name with user's mailbox, using the complete name if the object is in a different context than where the user's User object will be created.
MAILBOX	MAILBOX ID	Single-valued	The directory name of the user's NetWare MHS directory. Generally, the same as the user's login name, shortened to 8 characters (without spaces or special characters) if necessary.
FOREIGN E-MAIL ADDRESS	FOREIGN E-MAIL ADDRESS	Single-valued	The user's e-mail address on a non MHS mail system. Format is Type:Value, where Type is the messaging protocol, and Value is the users e-mail address on the foreign system.
FOREIGN E-MAIL ADDRESS	FOREIGN E-MAIL ALIAS	Single-valued	The user's e-mail address in a non MHS mail format. Format is Type:Value, where Type is the messaging protocol, and Value is the users e-mail address on the foreign system.
LOGIN SCRIPT	LOGIN SCRIPT	Single-valued	Use the path (in DOS form) and filename of an ASCII text file containing the login script.
LOGIN SCRIPT	PROFILE	Single-valued	NDS Profile object name, using the complete name if the Profile object is in a different context than where the user's User object will be created.
GROUP MEMBERSHIPS	GROUP MEMBERSHIP	Multivalued	NDS Group object name of each group the user belongs to, using the complete name if the Group object is in a different context than where the user's User object will be created.
SECURITY EQUIVALENCES	SECURITY EQUAL TO	Multivalued	NDS object name of each object to which the user is equal in security access, using the complete name if the object is in a different context than where the user's User object will be created.
POSTAL ADDRESS	STREET ADDRESS	Single-valued	The user's street address.
POSTAL ADDRESS	POST OFFICE BOX	Single-valued	The user's post office box designation.

Figure 9-55
(Continued)

User Object Dialog Box Page	Field (Property):	Single-Valued or Multivalued:	Comments
POSTAL ADDRESS	CITY	Single-valued	The user's city.
POSTAL ADDRESS	STATE OR PROVINCE	Single-valued	The user's state or province.
POSTAL ADDRESS	POSTAL (ZIP) CODE	Single-valued	The user's ZIP code (five digit or five+four digit format) or Canadian postal code.
POSTAL ADDRESS	MAILING LABEL INFORMATION	Multivalued	Use this field once for each line of information in the mailing label. Maximum of 6 lines.
ACCOUNT BALANCE	ACCOUNT BALANCE	Single-valued	The user's beginning account balance
ACCOUNT BALANCE	ALLOW UNLIMITED CREDIT	Single-valued	If user has unlimited account credit, use Y in the field. The default is N.
ACCOUNT BALANCE	LOW BALANCE LIMIT	Single-valued	The minimum balance the user must have to use chargeable network resources.
SEE ALSO	SEE ALSO	Multivalued	NDS object name of any other object associated with the user, using the complete name if the object is in a different context than where the user's User object will be created.
	SKIP		A special field name that causes UIMPORT to ignore a data field in the data file.

For example, because the users in the Pubs Organizational Unit have a USER_TEMPLATE object that controls most of the property values, the CBE Labs network administrator would have needed to use only the following field definition section when he created the user accounts and User objects for the employees in the Pubs Organizational Unit using UIMPORT:

```
FIELDS
   NAME
   LAST NAME
   GIVEN NAME
```

The complete import control file would have been

```
IMPORT CONTROL
   CREATE HOME DIRECTORY = Y
   HOME DIRECTORY PATH = "USERS"
   HOME DIRECTORY VOLUME = "CONSTELLATION_DATA.CBE_Labs"
```

```
   NAME CONTEXT = ".PUBS.CBE_Labs"
   USER TEMPLATE = Y
FIELDS
   NAME
   LAST NAME
   GIVEN NAME
```

The data file would have been an ASCII text file containing the following lines:

"DKaneaka","Kaneaka","Donna"
"SJohnston","Johnston","Sarah"
"TMeyer","Thomas","Meyer"

The NetWare 4.1 UIMPORT command line utility replaces the NetWare 3.1x MAKEUSER menu utility.

THE DSREPAIR NLM UTILITY

DSREPAIR is a NetWare Loadable Module (NLM) that is used to check and, if necessary, repair the NDS database partition stored on a NetWare server. As with all NLMs, the DSREPAIR utility is loaded at the server console prompt with the load command. The syntax is

```
LOAD [path] DSREPAIR [-U]
```

The DSREPAIR utility options are shown in Figure 9-56.

Figure 9-56 The DSREPAIR options

Option	Use this Option to
path	Specify the path to DSREPAIR.NLM if needed.
-U	Run an unattended repair and then unload DSREPAIR automatically.

DSREPAIR works only with Directory Services database information on the NetWare server it is run on. When DSREPAIR is loaded, a menu of Available Options is displayed, as shown in Figure 9-57.

Figure 9-57 The DSREPAIR Available Options menu

```
NetWare 4.1 DS Repair  4.23a                         NetWare Loadable Module
Tree name: CBELAB
Server name: CONSTELLATION.CBE_LABS_Admin.CBE_LABS

                  Available Options
                  Unattended full repair
                  Time synchronization
                  Replica synchronization
                  View/Edit repair log file
                  Advanced options menu
                  Exit

Automated repair that performs all possible repair operations which do not
require operator assistance.  Records all actions in the log file.
Enter=Select menu action                                          Alt+F10=Exit
Esc=Exit                                                             F1=Help
```

The Menu options are these:

- *Unattended full repair.* DSREPAIR will do every operation it can that does not require input from the network administrator. This option checks the Directory Services database for problems and repairs any problems that it can.
- *Time synchronization.* All NetWare servers listed in the NDS database partition and replicas on the server are checked, and the NDS version and time synchronization status for each NetWare server are reported. When a replica of the [Root] partition is located on the NetWare server, every NetWare server in the Directory tree will be included in the report.
- *Replica synchronization.* All replicas in the Directory tree's replica table are checked, and the synchronization status of them is reported.
- *View/Edit repair log file.* A log of DSREPAIR actions is kept in a file. The default file for the log is named DSREPAIR.LOG and is stored in the SYS:SYSTEM directory.
- *Advanced options menu.* The repair operations that are run automatically under the menu choice Unattended Full Repair can be run individually using this option. Log file configuration information can also be entered here. See Figure 9-58.
- *Exit*

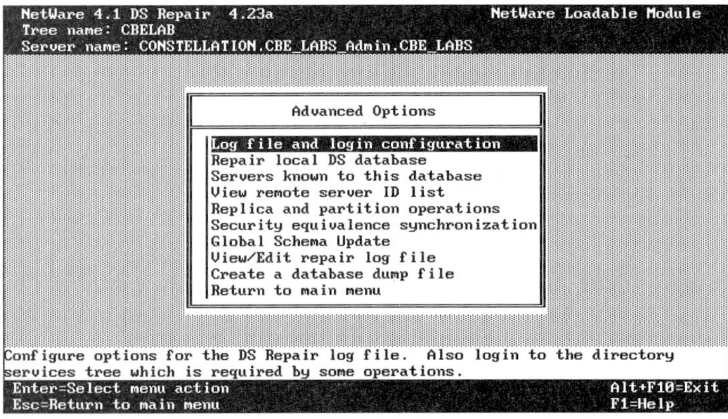

Figure 9-58

The DSREPAIR Advanced Options menu

The -U option enables the network administrator to run an unattended full repair without making menu choices. When the command LOAD DSREPAIR -U is entered at the console prompt, DSREPAIR is loaded, the unattended full repair is run, and DSREPAIR is unloaded without any further instructions from the network administrator.

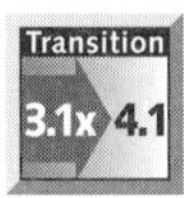

The NetWare 4.1 DSREPAIR NLM utility replaces the NetWare 3.1x BINDFIX and BINDREST menu utilities.

CHAPTER SUMMARY

The NetWare security system enables a network administrator to limit access to data and services on the file server in three different ways: login security, file system security, and console security. The login security system described in this chapter consists of user names, passwords, time restrictions, station restrictions, and account restrictions. User names can be a maximum of 47 characters and often consist of the user's first initial followed by the last name or of the first three letters of the first and last names, combined to make user names of six letters. User names can be given privileges to enable users to perform special administrative functions such as creating users or working with printers. Supervisor equivalent users have the same rights as the Admin account, and by granting rights you can create users that can manage workgroups and user accounts. A print queue operator or print server operator privilege provides users with control of the printing system.

NetWare provides additional security by enabling the network administrator to establish password requirements and access restrictions. Password requirements that can be placed on each user account include requiring passwords of a specified minimum length, forcing users to change passwords within a specified number of days, and requiring users to select a different or unique password rather than alternating among a few favorite passwords. Time restrictions enable a network administrator to increase the security on an account by specifying what times the user can be logged into the file server. Station restrictions provide further security by restricting a user account to one or more workstation addresses. Account restrictions, along with intruder detection, provide additional methods to disable a user's account when certain limits such as account expiration date or a maximum number of login attempts are reached.

The network administrator uses NetWare 4.1 NetWare Administrator or NETADMIN utilities to create and secure user and group accounts. User-related leaf objects include the User object, the Group object, the Organizational Role object, and the Profile object.

The User object represents a user of the network and contains property settings controlling login security for the user. These settings include home directory creation, password restrictions, login time restrictions, network address restrictions, and login restrictions. The network administrator can create a USER_TEMPLATE User object for each container object. The USER_TEMPLATE User object stores default property settings for all User objects created in that container. Intruder detection shuts a user out of the network after a specified number of failed login attempts. Intruder detection must be enabled for each individual container object.

The Group object represents a group of network users and contains property settings that assign appropriate network resources to members of the group. Assigning resources to the group instead of to each user enables the network administrator to more easily control who has certain system rights and privileges.

The Organizational Role object represents a position in an organization chart and contains property settings that give network privileges to any user assigned to the role. Because the privileges are associated with the position instead of the user, it is easy to reallocate them to a new user who takes over that role in the organization.

Like the Group object, the Profile Object enables network resources to be assigned to groups of users. The Profile Object, however, can have a login script associated with it, whereas the Group object can't.

NetWare accounting enables the network administrator to establish charge rates for such services as blocks read, blocks written, connection time, disk space used, and file server requests made. Using this feature, NetWare will deduct charges from the user account balances until the user account balance exceeds the credit limit, at which time the user account is disabled until the administrator assigns a new balance or increases the credit limit. The ATOTAL command line utility is used to prepare reports of the use of chargeable network resources.

The UIMPORT command line utility enables the network administrator to easily create large numbers of users from a text file, called the data file, that contains the data needed for User object property value settings. UIMPORT uses an import control file to specify parameters for the user account creation. This file consists of two sections: the import control section, which tells UIMPORT which control parameters to use, and the field section, which specifies which properties have setting values in the data file.

The DSREPAIR console utility is an NDS repair utility that is stored in the SYS:SYSTEM directory. It is used to fix problems with the NDS database, including replicas and replica synchronization.

COMMAND SUMMARY

Command	Syntax	Definition
ATOTAL	*ATOTAL [destination path\filename] [/C] [/?] [/VER]*	Command line utility used to summarize accounting charges for the chargeable resources on the NetWare servers.
DSREPAIR	*Load [path] DSREPAIR [-U]*	NLM utility that enables you to repair the NDS database. You can also check time synchronization and replica synchronization. The -U option unloads the NLM after an unattended full repair. Menu options include these: ■ Unattended full repair ■ Time synchronization ■ Replica synchronization ■ View/Edit repair log file ■ Advanced options menu ■ Exit
UIMPORT	*UIMPORT [control file] [data file] [/C] [/?] [/VER]*	Command line utility that enables you to create user accounts from data in an ASCII text data file. Import options and data field specifications are contained in the control file, which has two sections: import control and fields. Import control parameters and field definitions are too extensive to list here—see Figures 9-54 and 9-55.

Key Terms

blocks read charge
blocks written charge
connect time charge
data file
disk storage charge
fields section
grace login
home directory
import control section
import control file
intruder detection
print queue operator
print server operator
service requests charge
USER_TEMPLATE User object
user account manager
workgroup manager

Review Questions

1. Identify each of the following as being either a command line utility, menu utility, graphical utility, console command, or NetWare Loadable Module (NLM):

   ATOTAL ______________________
   UIMPORT ______________________
   DSREPAIR ______________________

2. List the three levels of NetWare security.

   ____
   ____
   ____

3. NetWare keeps track of user names, passwords, and other access restrictions in the ______________________.

4. List the five login security components that work together to provide you with the capability to access the network and perform your assigned tasks.

   ____
   ____
   ____
   ____
   ____

5. In the space below, list the users and groups that exist after NetWare is first installed on a file server.

6. A user name can be up to ______________ characters in length.

7. In the space below, briefly explain why many network administrators try to keep user names to eight or fewer characters.

8. List three restrictions you can assign to password security.

____

____

____

9. In the space below, give an example of how time restrictions can be used to help secure a payroll clerk's workstation.

10. In the space below, briefly describe two ways in which station restrictions can be used to provide better security.

11. List the four ways an account can be disabled.

____

____

____

____

12. List the four types of charges that can be tracked with NetWare's accounting functions (*Hint*: One type consists of two charges.)

____

____

____

____

13. The _______________ charge rate is most useful if you are charging customers for access to your database file.

14. The _______________ charge rate is most useful if you are charging customers for the amount of the server's processing time they use.

15. The _______________ charge rate can be used to prevent users from staying logged into the file server.

16. Which three utilities can be used to create users?

____

____

____

17. Which two utilities can be used to create groups?

____

____

18. The _______________ page of the User object dialog box is used to create or change a user's password.

19. The ____________________ page of the User object dialog box is used to set time restrictions on a user's account.

20. The ____________________ page of the User object dialog box is used to set the number of concurrent connections a user can have.

21. The ____________________ User object is used to specify default User object property settings within a container object.

22. Intruder detection is enabled using the ____________________.

23. List three ways to add users to groups:

    ____

    ____

    ____

24. In the space below, discuss why the Organizational Role object is useful.

25. In the space below, discuss why the Profile object is useful.

26. The ____________________ NetWare utility summarizes accounting charges.

27. The ____________________ NetWare utility can repair a damaged NDS database.

Hands-On

EXERCISES

EXERCISE 9-1: USING NETWARE ADMINISTRATOR TO CREATE USERS, GROUPS, ORGANIZATIONAL ROLES, AND PROFILES

In this exercise you use NetWare Administrator to create three users and two groups and then assign the users to groups. All user and group names you create need to be preceded by your student number in order to separate them from users and groups created by other students.

1. Log in using your assigned student user name (it must have workgroup manager privileges).
2. Launch NetWare Administrator.
3. On your assigned data volume, create a subdirectory named USERS in your ##ADMIN home directory.
4. In your ##PRACTICE container, create the three user accounts ##USER1, ##USER2, and ##USER3. Replace the number symbols with your assigned student number. A home directory should be created for each user in the ##ADMIN\USERS subdirectory you created previously.
5. Give ##USER1 your full name.

6. For all accounts, assign login restrictions so that a password is required to use each account. Use a common password of ##PASSWORD for all three accounts. Be sure to replace the number symbols with your assigned student number.
7. For all three accounts, set the accounts to expire on tomorrow's date.
8. In your ##PRACTICE container, create two groups called ##GROUP1 and ##GROUP2. Be sure to replace the number symbols with your assigned student number.
9. Use the ##USER1 object dialog box to add ##USER1 to ##GROUP1. Use the ##USER2 and ##USER3 object dialog boxes to add these users to ##GROUP1.
10. Using the ##GROUP2 object dialog box, add all three users to ##GROUP2.
11. In your ##ADMIN organizational unit, create an organizational role named ##ORGROLE1. Be sure to replace the number symbols with your assigned student number.
12. Assign ##USER1 to occupy ##ORGROLE1.
13. In your ##ADMIN organizational unit, create a profile named ##PROFILE1. Be sure to replace the number symbols with your assigned student number.
14. Assign ##USER2 and ##USER3 to ##PROFILE1.
15. Exit NetWare Administrator.
16. At the DOS prompt, change your default directory path to the ##ADMIN\USERS directory.
17. Use the NLIST command to obtain a list of trustee assignments for each of the user home directories; then rerun the command redirecting the output to a printer.
18. Log out.
19. Log in as ##USER1.
20. Launch NetWare Administrator and attempt to change User 2's first name. Record the result in the space below.
21. Exit NetWare Administrator.
22. Log out.
23. Log in using your assigned ##ADMIN user name.
24. Use NetWare Administrator to delete all the objects created in this exercise and the home directories created for ##USER1, ##USER2, and ##USER3.
25. Exit NetWare Administrator and log out.

Exercise 9-2: Using NETADMIN to Create Users, Groups, Organizational Roles, and Profiles

In this exercise you use the NETADMIN menu utility to create three users and two groups and then assign the users to groups. All user and group names you create need to be preceded by your student number in order to separate them from users and groups created by other students.

1. Log in using your assigned student user name (it must have workgroup manager privileges).
2. Start the NETADMIN menu utility.
3. If you haven't done so in Exercise 9-1, create a subdirectory named USERS in your ##ADMIN home directory on your assigned data volume.
4. In your ##PRACTICE container, create the three user accounts ##USER4, ##USER5, and ##USER6. Replace the number symbols with your assigned student number. A home directory should be created for each user in the ##ADMIN\USERS subdirectory you created previously.
5. Give ##USER4 your full name.
6. For all accounts, assign login restrictions so that a password is required to use each account. Use a common password of ##PASSWORD for all three accounts. Be sure to replace the number symbols with your assigned student number.
7. For all three accounts, set the accounts to expire on tomorrow's date.
8. In your ##PRACTICE container, create two groups called ##GROUP3 and ##GROUP4. Be sure to replace the number symbols with your assigned student number.
9. Use the ##USER4 object properties to add ##USER4 to ##GROUP3. Use the ##USER5 and ##USER6 object properties to add these users to ##GROUP3.
10. Using the ##GROUP4 object properties, add all three users to ##GROUP4.
11. In your ##PRACTICE container, create an organizational role named ##ORG-ROLE2. Be sure to replace the number symbols with your assigned student number.
12. Assign ##USER4 to occupy ##ORGROLE2.
13. In your ##PRACTICE container, create a profile named ##PROFILE2. Be sure to replace the number symbols with your assigned student number.
14. Assign ##USER5 and ## USER6 to ##PROFILE2.
15. Exit NETADMIN.
16. At the DOS prompt, change your default directory path to the ##ADMIN\USERS directory.
17. Use the NLIST command to obtain a list of trustee assignments for each of the user home directories; then rerun the command redirecting the output to a printer.
18. Log out.
19. Log in as ##USER4.

20. Run NETADMIN and attempt to change User 2's first name. Record the result in the space below.

21. Exit NETADMIN.
22. Log out.
23. Log in using your assigned ##ADMIN user name.
24. Use NETADMIN to delete all the objects created in this exercise.
25. Exit NETADMIN.
26. Use FILER to delete the home directories created for ##USER4, ##USER5, and ##USER6.
27. Exit FILER and log out.

Exercise 9-3: Setting Time and Station Restrictions

In this exercise you determine your current workstation's network and node address and then use SYSCON to create and restrict a user to logging in from only this station during a specified time period.

1. Log in using your ##ADMIN user name.
2. Launch NetWare Administrator.
3. Use the Environment page of the ##ADMIN User object dialog box to determine the network and node address of the workstation on which you are working. Record your workstation address information below.

   Network address: ____________ Node address: ____________
4. In your ##PRACTICE container, create user name ##BILL with a home directory in the ##ADMIN\USERS directory.
5. Do not require a password for ##BILL's account, but set login restrictions so that ##BILL can log in from two workstations at the same time.
6. Use the Network Address Restriction page to restrict ##BILL to the network and node address recorded in step 3.
7. Log out.
8. Log in as user ##BILL from your current workstation.
9. Go to another workstation and attempt to log in as ##BILL. In the space below, record any messages you see.

10. Return to your workstation and log out as ##BILL. Log in using your ##ADMIN user name.
11. For the ##BILL User object, use the Login Time Restrictions Page to prevent Bill from logging in during the current hour.

12. Exit NetWare Administrator.
13. Try logging in from your current workstation as ##BILL. In the space below, record the message you receive.
14. Log in with your ##ADMIN user name and delete the ##BILL user account and remove the ##BILL home directory.

Exercise 9-4: Enabling Intruder Detection

In this exercise you use NetWare Administrator to enable Intruder Detection for your ##ADMIN organizational unit. Because supervisor privileges are necessary to enable Intruder Detection, you will need to log into the file server with a user name that has supervisor equivalency to do this exercise. Your ##ADMIN account should already have the appropriate privileges. If not, your instructor will direct you regarding which user name to use.

1. Log in using the supervisor-equivalent user name.
2. Launch NetWare Administrator.
3. In your ##PRACTICE container, create a user named ##JOHN without a home directory. Set a password of PASSWORD on the ##JOHN account.
4. Open the ##ADMIN organizational unit object dialog box and use the Intruder Detection page to enable Intruder Detection. Record the settings below. Do not make any changes to these fields.

    Incorrect Login Attempts: ___

    Intruder Attempt Reset Interval: ____ Days ____ Hours ____ Minutes

    Intruder Lockout Reset Interval: ___ Days ____ Hours____ Minutes

5. Set the Incorrect Login Attempts to 3; then close the dialog box.
6. Log out.
7. Attempt to log in as ##JOHN using an incorrect password. Repeat this until you get a message that you are locked out of the system. Record the message below:

8. Log in as ##ADMIN and delete the ##JOHN account.

Exercises

Case 9-1: Using NetWare Accounting to Track Network Usage

Assume that you are working as a lab assistant for your college network administrator and that the administrator would like you to keep track of server usage in order to develop a budget for future file server needs. The previous network administrator had installed accounting and established a charge rate for blocks read. Your network administrator explains that a charge ratio is needed before NetWare will track server usage, but because the previous administrator did not want to have the users charged, he set up a charge at a time when no one should be using the server. Your network administrator wants you to document the charge ratio that was set up by the previous administrator for future reference. The network administrator also wants you to run the ATOTAL program each day and then use this information to create three separate graphs: one for blocks read, one for storage used, and one for the number of file server requests made.

To perform this activity, you first need to document the accounting charge rates and record the times there is a charge for the service along with the charge ratio used. Record the information in Figure 9-59.

Figure 9-59 Using NetWare Accounting Tables

Charge Ratio	Day	Times

To complete the assignment, you will need to run the ATOTAL program each day for the next three days and create graphs similar to the ones in Figure 9-60 showing NetWare server usage.

Figure 9-60 NetWare Server usage graphs

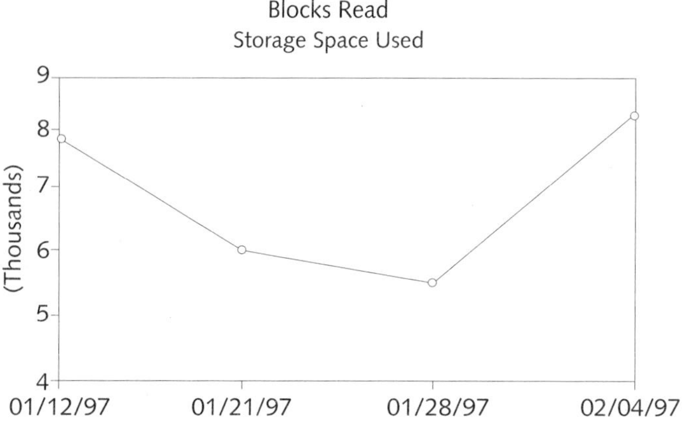

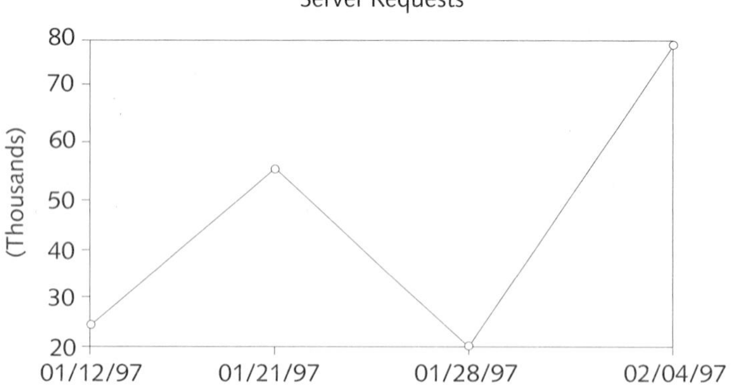

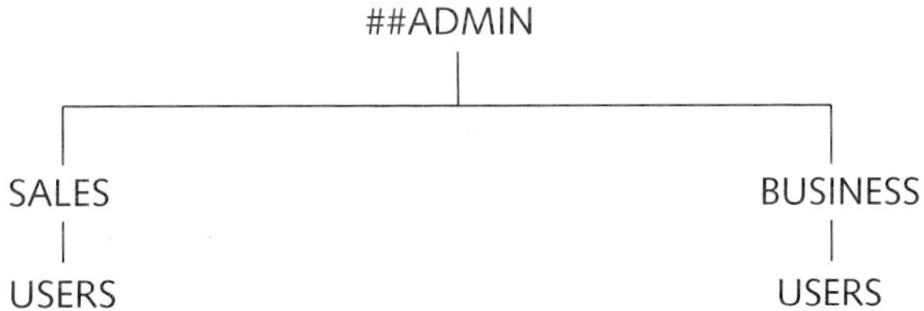

Figure 9-61
Creating Users with UIMPORT

CASE 9-2: CREATING USERS WITH UIMPORT

In this case study you create a USER_TEMPLATE to create templates and users for the J. Q. Adams company. Assume that you are the network administrator for the J. Q. Adams company and that you need to create users in the sales department. As a network administrator, you know that USER_TEMPLATE User objects can simplify the task of creating users by enabling the supervisor to define and use templates that contain account information common to all users in a department. In NetWare, only a supervisor-equivalent user can create USER_TEMPLATE objects. However, you can use DS Standard to create USER_TEMPLATE objects and to emulate the use of the UIMPORT utility. In all cases, substitute your assigned student number for the number symbols (##).

In order to perform this case project, you use the DS Standard Directory tree view J. Q. Adams @ Installation, which is shown in Figure 9-62.

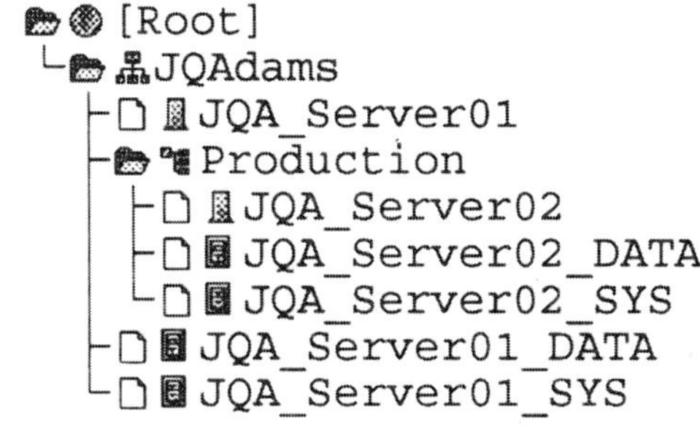

Figure 9-62
J.Q. Adams @ Installation

PART 1: CREATING USER_TEMPLATE OBJECTS

A USER_TEMPLATE object contains such information as home directory location, groups the users are to belong to, account balance information, and password requirements. You have decided to use a template to create the users for Team01 in the production department.

1. Launch DS Standard.
2. Create a Team01 Organizational Unit object in the Production container.
3. Create a Template object named USER_TEMPLATE in the Production container. Use the following settings:
   a. Set an initial Account Balance of 0. Leave the Limit Credit field set to No to provide unlimited credit.
   b. Require all users to have a password of at least five characters and force periodic password changes so that after 120 days the users have to invent a new password that is different from the previous 10 passwords the user has chosen. When a password expires, each user should be given 3 grace login times before his or her account is disabled.

4. Create a new user in the Team01 Organizational Unit using the USER_TEMPLATE and the following user name:

FULL NAME	USERNAME
Ben Avery	BAvery

After the User object is created, check to see how the defaults property settings have been created.

5. Exit DS Standard.

Part 2: Creating New Users with UIMPORT Files

Now that the Team01 template is created, you are ready to create the Team 01 users. Create the following users for the Team 01 by creating the appropriate UIMPORT files:

FULL NAME	USERNAME
Ned Lynch	NLynch
Ann Bonny	ABonny
George Moon	GMoon

1. Use the USER_TEMPLATE to establish the default property settings, and use the UIMPORT files to specify the Login Name, Last Name, Given Name, Full Name, and Department.
2. Use the DS Standard View | Object Import command to import the data from the UIMPORT files.

Write a memo to your instructor containing copies of the UMIPORT files you used in this exercise. Turn in this memo to your instructor accompanied by a copy of your DS Standard data disk.

NORTHWESTERN TECHNICAL COLLEGE

Dave Johnson was pleased with your work installing NetWare 4.1 and establishing a directory structure for the network in such a short time. However, the faculty and staff are eager to log into the file server and start using the network before school starts. As a result, your next assignment involves establishing user accounts and providing network security.

As before, because these exercises require a shared NetWare server or servers, the NWTC Directory tree that has been created differs from what you would expect to see in a standard network environment. Refer to previous chapters for details on the current NWTC Directory tree. Although the NetWare Server object names of Server41-1, Server41-2, and Server312 are used in these figures, your instructor may have different names for these servers. In that case, your instructor will tell you what server names you will see in your Directory tree.

If your computer lab setup is using only one NetWare 4.1 server, then all objects labeled as Server41-2 will appear in your tree as Alias objects, which are objects that appear as leaf objects in a container, but actually point to or reference a leaf object in another container. Similarly, the objects for the NetWare 3.12 server may appear as Alias objects in your Directory tree if your lab is not using a NetWare 3.12 server.

In the exercises that follow, you will add NDS objects only to your portion of the Directory tree.

PROJECT 9-1: CREATING NORTHWESTERN TECHNICAL COLLEGE CAMPUS USERS

You are ready to create the users accounts for NWTC. You have discussed the campus needs and the users with Dave Johnson, and he has given you the go-ahead to create the users shown in the following table.

Figure 9-63

NWTC users

ORGANIZATIONAL UNIT:	USER NAME:	LOGIN NAME:
NWTC_Admin.##NWTC	Roger McGregor	##RMcGregor
NWTC_Admin.##NWTC	Gale Chen	##GChen
NWTC_Admin.##NWTC	Lee Olsen	##LOlsen
NWTC_Admin.##NWTC	Lauri Hold	##LHolt
NWTC_Admin.##NWTC	Bert Richard	##BRichard
NWTC_Admin.##NWTC	Barbara Rau	##BRau
NWTC_Admin.##NWTC	USER_TEMPLATE	
StudentServ.##NWTC	Karl Dauer	##KDauer
Admissions.StudentServ.##NWTC	K Elliot	##KElliot
Counseling.StudentServ.##NWTC	S Chung	##SChung
Curriculum.StudentServ.##NWTC	G Gardini	##GGardini
MGMT.##NWTC	Rick Thompson	##RThompson
MGMT.##NWTC	USER_TEMPLATE	
ACCT&FIN.##NWTC	Maria Rodriguez	##MRodriguez
ACCT&FIN.##NWTC	USER_TEMPLATE	
MRKT.##NWTC	Neal Egan	##NEgan
MRKT.##NWTC	USER_TEMPLATE	
MIS.##NWTC	David Feinstein	##DFeinstein
MIS.##NWTC	USER_TEMPLATE	

Use the Network Administrator graphical utility to create these accounts. Dave would like you to place reasonable account restrictions on all user names, including limiting users to logging in from one workstation as well as requiring users to have passwords that expire within 120 days and be at least four characters in length. In addition, Barbara Rau should be limited to logging in only at her assigned workstation during the business hours of 8:00 A.M. through 5:00 P.M. Monday through Friday.

PROJECT 9-2: CREATING NORTHWESTERN TECHNICAL COLLEGE CAMPUS GROUPS

Having created the user accounts, create the following groups and assign the specified users to them as shown in the following table.

Figure 9-64

NWTC groups

CONTEXT	GROUP NAME:	MEMBERS:
NWTC_Admin.##NWTC	##NWTC_Admins	Roger McGregor, Gale Chen, Lee Olsen, Lauri Hold, Bert Richard, Barbara Rau, USER_TEMPLATE
StudentServ.##NWTC Gardini	##NWTC_StudentServ	Karl Dauer, K Elliot, S Chung, G
MGMT.##NWTC	##MGMT_Faculty	Rick Thompson, USER_TEMPLATE
ACCT&FIN.##NWTC	##ACCT&FIN_Faculty	Maria Rodriguez, USER_TEMPLATE
MRKT.##NWTC	##MRKT_Faculty	Neal Egan, USER_TEMPLATE
MIS.##NWTC	##MIS_Faculty	David Feinstein, USER_TEMPLATE
NWTC_CompLabs.##NWTC	##Students	

PROJECT 9-3: CREATING NORTHWESTERN TECHNICAL COLLEGE CAMPUS ORGANIZATIONAL ROLES

Create the following organizational roles and assign the specified users to them as shown in the following table.

Figure 9-65

NWTC organizational roles

CONTEXT:	ORGANIZATIONAL ROLE:	OCCUPIED BY:
NWTC_Admin.##NWTC	##Campus_Admin	Roger McGregor
NWTC_Admin.##NWTC	##AdminAssist	Gale Chen, Barbara Rau
NWTC_Admin.##NWTC	##BusManager	Lee Olsen
NWTC_Admin.##NWTC	##DeanInstruction	Karl Dauer
NWTC_Admin.##NWTC	##Director	Lauri Hold
NWTC_Admin.##NWTC	##DeanInstruction	Bert Richard
StudentServ.##NWTC	##StudentServ_Manager	Karl Dauer
Admissions.StudentServ.##NWTC	##Director	K Elliot
Counseling.StudentServ.##NWTC	##Counselor	S Chung
Curriculum.StudentServ.##NWTC	##Coordinator	G Gardini
MGMT.##NWTC	##Chair	Rick Thompson
ACCT&FIN.##NWTC	##Chair	Maria Rodriguez
MRKT.##NWTC	##Chair	Neal Egan
MIS.##NWTC	##Chair	David Feinstein

CHAPTER TEN

MANAGING TRUSTEE ASSIGNMENTS AND FILE ATTRIBUTES

After user accounts have been created and secured, the next level of NetWare security involves providing users with access to NDS and to the NetWare file system. This is the trustee assignments and file attributes security level. Initially, new users have rights only to work in their home directories and to run programs from the SYS:PUBLIC directory. An important responsibility of a network administrator is to provide users with the rights to access the network NDS objects, directories, and files they need and still protect sensitive network information.

Trustee assignments security controls who has rights to access network resources after the user has logged on to the network. Access rights are like a set of keys that are provided to a new employee. Just as keys allow access to rooms, access rights provide the new user with access to the directories that contain files they need to use.

Directories and files can also have additional protection in NetWare security. In addition to controlling access to them through trustee assignments, the network administrator can also assign directory and file attributes to a directory, file, or group of files. These attributes, described later in this chapter, can be attached as another means of limiting user access.

In this chapter, you will learn how to use access rights and attributes to provide users with the effective access to network resources that they need to perform their work.

AFTER READING THIS CHAPTER AND COMPLETING THE EXERCISES YOU WILL BE ABLE TO:

- IDENTIFY THE COMPONENTS OF NETWARE TRUSTEE RIGHTS (NDS AND FILE SYSTEM) SECURITY.
- DESCRIBE HOW EFFECTIVE RIGHTS ARE OBTAINED FROM A COMBINATION OF TRUSTEE ASSIGNMENTS, GROUP RIGHTS, AND INHERITED RIGHTS.
- DESCRIBE HOW THE INHERITED RIGHTS FILTER MODIFIES EFFECTIVE RIGHTS IN A DIRECTORY OR FILE.
- USE NETWARE UTILITIES TO GRANT TRUSTEE RIGHTS AND DETERMINE USER EFFECTIVE RIGHTS.
- WORK WITH NETWARE FILE AND DIRECTORY ATTRIBUTES.

Most software applications are being designed to take advantage of file sharing for workgroup computing. Because of this, the network administrator will need to balance file system security and integrity with providing shared access to directories that contain files used simultaneously by more than one workstation.

TRUSTEE ASSIGNMENTS

TRUSTEES, RIGHTS, AND ASSIGNMENTS

A **trustee** is a user who has been given access to NDS objects, directories, or files. The user is called a trustee because the user is responsible for the security of the objects, directories, or files to which he or she has access.

The term **rights** is used to describe the type of access the user has been given. For example, the file system *File Scan* right enables users to see directory and file listings, while the *Read* right enables users to see (but not change) the contents of a file. In NetWare 4.1 there are Object rights, Property rights, Directory rights, and File rights. These rights are summarized in Figure 10-1, and will be discussed in more detail later in this chapter.

Figure 10-1 Types of NetWare 4.1 trustee rights

Type of Rights	Trustee Access
Object rights	Trustee can work with an NDS Directory tree object as a whole but can't work with the properties of that object.
Property rights	Trustee can work with the properties of an NDS Directory tree object but must first be granted necessary Object rights to the object.
Directory rights	Trustee can work with a file system directory—and generally the files in that directory, although this can be blocked by assigned File rights and the file's Inherited Rights Filter (discussed later in this chapter).
File rights	Trustee can work with a file.

The terms **grant** and **assign** are used interchangeably to describe giving rights to a trustee. Therefore, you make the user JCunningham a *trustee* of the CBE Labs Directory tree by *granting* or *assigning* him specific NDS Object rights. The term **trustee assignment** refers to the rights given to the user. The *trustee assignments* given to JCunningham determine what access he has to the NDS Directory tree objects and the network file system directories and files.

A **trustee list** is the set of trustee assignments for an NDS object, directory, or file; it is used to determine who can access the object, directory, or file. The trustee list of an NDS object is stored in a property of the object, the **access control list (ACL)**.

As a network administrator, you will use trustee assignments to control which users have access to the network resources. By controlling access to those network resources by how you grant rights to trustees, you maintain network security by enabling only those users who need access to a resource to actually have that access. Trustee assignments are the network administrator's main tool for controlling network resources and maintaining system security after a user has logged on to the network.

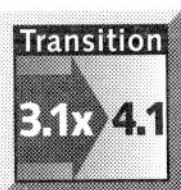

NetWare 3.1x had Directory rights and File rights only, and these stay the same in NetWare 4.1. When NDS was added to NetWare 4.x, Object rights and Property rights were added. The concept of trustee assignments is the same as in NetWare 3.1x.

Object Rights

Object rights give the user access to NDS objects. They do not, however, give access to the properties of the objects. Figure 10-2 summarizes the NetWare 4.1 Object rights.

Figure 10-2
NetWare 4.1 object rights

Right	Effect on Object
Supervisor [S]	Grants the user all rights to the object, and also grants the user all Property rights to the object.
Browse [B]	Enables the user to see the object in the Directory tree and to have the object's name show up in search results.
Create [C]	Applies only to container objects. Enables the user to create new objects in the container but not to create Property rights for the objects.
Delete [D]	Enables the user to delete the object from the Directory tree. If the object is a container object, it must be empty before it can be deleted.
Rename [R]	Enables the user to rename the object.

The **Browse right** enables users to see objects in the Directory tree. By not granting this right, the network administrator can control which parts of the Directory tree users can see. For example, consider the CBE Laboratories Directory tree shown in Figure 10-3.

Figure 10-3
CBE Labs Directory tree

```
[Root]
├─GB
└─CBE_Labs
  ├─Admin_Assists
  ├─Everyone
  ├─Executives
  ├─CONSTELLATION
  ├─CBE_Labs_Admin
  │ ├─SharedFiles
  │ ├─Admin_Staff
  │ ├─RANGER
  │ ├─Admin_Assist
  │ ├─President
  │ ├─Finance
  │ ├─InfoSystems
  │ ├─Marketing
  │ ├─Personnel
  │ ├─JCunningham
  │ ├─SLopez
  │ └─RANGER_SYS
  ├─Pubs
  ├─Test&Eval
  ├─Pubs&Labs_Profile
  ├─Admin
  ├─CONSTELLATION_DATA
  └─CONSTELLATION_SYS
```

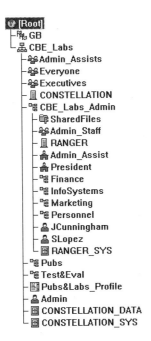

There may be no need for the users in the Test&Eval and Pubs organizational units to see some other sections of the Directory tree, such as the Finance, Marketing, and Personnel organizational units. By controlling the Browse right for users in Test&Eval and Pubs, the network administrator could make the three organizational units invisible to those users.

The **Create right**, which applies only to container objects, enables users to create objects in a container object. It does not, however, enable the user to set property values in the objects. The **Delete right** enables users to delete a Directory tree object. However, before a container object can be deleted, all objects in it must be deleted—you cannot delete a container object with objects in it. The **Rename right** enables users to change the name of an object, which changes the object's complete name.

The **Supervisor right** gives the user all the other Object rights. Additionally, it gives the user Supervisor rights to all properties of the object. This means that a user with Supervisor rights to an object can also change any property settings for that object.

Property Rights

Property rights enable the user to access the property settings of NDS objects. Before Property rights can be granted to a user, the user must, of course, have Object rights to the object. Figure 10-4 summarizes the NetWare 4.1 Property rights.

Figure 10-4

NetWare 4.1 Property rights

Right	Effect on Property
Supervisor [S]	Grants the user all rights to the property.
Compare [C]	Enables the user to compare a value to the value of the property, not to the value itself. Included in Read.
Read [R]	Enables the user to see the value of the property. Includes Compare.
Write [W]	Enables the user to change, add, or delete the value of the property. Includes Add or Delete Self.
Add or Delete Self [A]	Enables the user to add or delete himself or herself to or from the user list in objects that have user lists. The user can't change other property values. Included in Write.

The **Compare right** enables users to test the values of the property against a reference value, for example in a search, but the user cannot actually see the property value. When the user with Compare rights tests a property value, a True (equals test value) or False (doesn't equal test value) response can be returned, but the value stored in the property setting is never displayed. The **Read right** gives the user the ability to actually see the value of the property setting. The Compare right is included in the Read right, so that when the Read right is granted the user also has the ability to make comparisons.

Although the Read right enables the user to see the value of the property setting, it doesn't give the user the ability to change the value. To do this, the user must have the **Write right**. With the Write right, the user can add a value, modify a value, or delete a value. A special case of the Write right is the Add or Delete Self right. The **Add or Delete Self right** enables a user to add himself or herself to the ACL property if the object has one. An example of an object with an ACL property is a Group object; having the Add or Delete Self right to a Group object means that the user can add (or remove) himself or herself to (or from) the group. The Write right includes the Add or Delete Self right.

As usual, the **Supervisor right** gives the user all rights to the property. It is important to note that Property rights can be assigned for each object property individually, so that different users can have different access to an object's property values. In addition, granting the Supervisor Object rights to an object normally grants the Supervisor Property rights to all the object's properties (this can, however, be changed by using the Inherited Rights Filter discussed later in this chapter).

Directory and File Rights

Directory rights control access to the directories and subdirectories in the network file system, while **File rights** control user access to the files in these directories and subdirectories. The same eight rights are used for both Directory rights and File rights. It is important to note that the rights can be assigned to individual files as well as to directories. A user normally has the same access to files in a directory as to the directory itself. This can be modified using File rights on specific files or by using an Inherited Rights Filter on the file (discussed later in this chapter). Figure 10-5 summarizes the NetWare 4.1 Directory and File rights.

Figure 10-5 NetWare 4.1 Directory rights and File rights

Right	Effect on Directory	Effect on File
Supervisor [S]	Grants all rights to the specified directory and all subdirectories.	Grants all rights to the specified file.
Read [R]	Enables the user to read files or run programs in the directory.	Enables the user to read or run the specified file or program without having Read rights at the directory level.
Write [W]	Enables the user to change or add data to files in the specified directory.	Enables the user to change or add data to the specified file without having Write rights at the directory level.
Create [C]	Enables the user to create files and subdirectories.	Enables the user to salvage the specified file if it is deleted.
Erase [E]	Enables the user to delete files and remove subdirectories.	Enables the user to delete the specified file without having Erase rights at the directory level.
Modify [M]	Enables the user to change file and subdirectory names and use the FLAG and FLAGDIR commands to change the attribute settings on files or subdirectories.	Enables the user to change the name or attribute settings of the specified file without having Modify rights at the directory level.
File Scan [F]	Enables the user to obtain a directory of file and subdirectory names.	Enables the user to view the specified filename on a directory listing without having File Scan rights at the directory level.
Access Control [A]	Enables the user to grant access rights to other users for the specified directory.	Enables the user to grant access rights to the specified file without having Access Control rights at the directory level.

Being able to assign access rights to a specific file means that the network administrator can provide users with the ability to update a certain file or database within the directory while blocking rights to other files that exist in that storage area.

The **Read right** and **File Scan right** are often used together to enable users to access files or run programs in a specified directory. All users are given Read and File Scan rights to the SYS:PUBLIC directory. Having the **Create right** to a directory enables a user to create subdirectories as well as new files in the specified directory. The Create right enables a user to copy files into the directory as long as there is no other file in the directory with the same name. Granting the Create right to an existing file might seem meaningless, but it does enable the user to salvage the file if it is deleted.

You should be aware that assigning the **Erase right** to a directory enables a user not only to erase files but also to remove the entire directory and its subdirectories. There is an important difference between the Write right and the Modify right. The **Write right** enables the user to change or add data to an existing file; the **Modify right** enables a user to change a file's name or attributes only—it has nothing to do with changing the contents of the file. The **Access Control right** enables a user to determine which users can access the directory or file by granting access rights to other users. Because enabling users to grant rights to other users can make it difficult for the network administrator to keep track of file system security, the Access Control right should not normally be given to other users.

Having the **Supervisor right** is not quite the same as having all rights, because it applies to all subdirectories and cannot be changed at a lower directory. The Supervisor right is also different from the other rights in that it can be assigned only by the Admin user or by another user who has been granted Supervisor rights to the directory

Users who have the Access Control right in a directory but not the Supervisor right can accidentally restrict themselves from working in the directory by assigning themselves fewer rights to the directory or a subdirectory than they need. To avoid this, the Access Control right should be granted to a user only when it is absolutely necessary for the user to assign rights to other users.

You will understand better what access rights are necessary to perform functions in the network file system by looking at specific situations. Figure 10-6 lists typical operations that users need to perform on files and directories and the access rights required to perform the operations.

Figure 10-6 Rights required for common functions

Task	Typical Command or Program	Rights Required
Read a file	WORDPAD (Windows 95)	Read
Obtain a directory listing	NDIR command (NetWare)	File Scan
Change the contents of data in a file	WORDPAD (Windows 95)	Write
Write to a closed file using a text editor that creates a backup file	EDIT (DOS)	Write, Create, Erase, Modify (not always required)
Execute a program file	WORDPAD (Windows 95)	Read
Create and write to a new file	WORDPAD (Windows 95)	Create
Copy a file from a directory	NCOPY command (NetWare)	Read, File Scan
Copy a file into a directory	NCOPY command (NetWare)	Create
Copy multiple files to a directory with existing files	NCOPY command (NetWare)	Create, File Scan
Create a subdirectory	FILER utility (NetWare)	Create
Delete a file	FILER utility (NetWare)	Erase
Salvage deleted files	SALVAGE option in FILER (NetWare)	Read and File Scan on the file and Create in the directory or on filename
Change attributes	FILER utility (NetWare)	Modify
Rename a file or subdirectory	RENDIR command (NetWare)	Rename
Change the Inherited Rights Filter	FILER utility (NetWare)	Access Control
Make or change a trustee assignment	NETADMIN utility (NetWare)	Access Control

Directory trustee assignments are kept track of in the **directory entry table (DET)** of each volume. A DET for a file or directory can hold up to six trustee assignments. If more than six trustees are assigned to a directory, an additional entry in the DET is made for that directory name. It is a good idea, however, to keep trustee assignments to six or fewer for each directory. You can usually do this by assigning a group as a trustee and then making users who need access to that directory a member of the group. File trustee assignments are also tracked in the DET. If more than six trustees are assigned to a file, an additional entry in the DET is needed for that filename.

Assigned Rights, Inherited Rights, and Effective Rights

We can refer to those rights granted directly to a user or another NDS object as **assigned rights**. It is always a user who can actually use and exercise trustee rights. However, a user can gain access to trustee rights in six ways:

1. A trustee assignment is made to the *user.*
2. The user is a member of a *group,* and the group has trustee assignments.
3. The user occupies an *organizational role,* and the organizational role has trustee assignments.
4. The user's User object is located in a *container object* that has trustee assignments.
5. The user has been given a *security equivalence* to another user who has trustee assignments.
6. The user's trustee assignments granted in a parent container object or directory are *inherited by* (passed down to) subordinate container objects and directories. This applies, however, only if there are no rights specifically assigned for that object or directory. This is discussed in more detail below.

The rights that a user actually has to an object, an object's properties, a directory, or a file are called **effective rights**. Effective rights refer to the functions a user can perform on an object or property, or in a specific directory or file. In many cases, a user's effective rights are the same as his or her trustee assignments. However, a user's effective rights are a combination of the rights gained through the six methods listed above, modified by the network administrator's ability to restrict rights that a user otherwise would have. We'll discuss how effective rights are restricted later in this chapter.

Now you will look at the ways of gaining effective rights. Although the techniques for managing all trustee assignments are similar, it's easier to understand trustee assignment management by discussing Object and Property rights separately from Directory and File rights. We'll start with Object and Property rights management, and then discuss managing Directory and File rights.

Managing Object Rights and Property Rights

When you are assigning Object rights and Property rights, the assignment is made using either the object to which access is being granted or the object which is getting access to the object. This means, for example, that if you want a user to have rights in a container object, the trustee assignment can be granted to the user either in the container object's object dialog box or in the user's object dialog box.

Rights Assigned to the User

The simplest and most straightforward way for a user to gain effective rights is to be granted a trustee assignment. You will look at a simple example and then see how trustee assignments are actually made using the CBE Laboratories example.

EXAMPLE 10-1: Assigning user Trustee rights at F. D. Roosevelt Investments Inc.

F. D. Roosevelt Investments Inc., or FDR as it commonly referred to, is a small investment brokerage house that manages a variety of mutual funds. Investors can invest in the mutual funds through any of several investment options offered by the company.

FDR is organized into three business units: Administration, Sales, and Investments. The FDR organizational chart is shown in Figure 10-7, and the NDS Directory tree for FDR is shown in Figure 10-8.

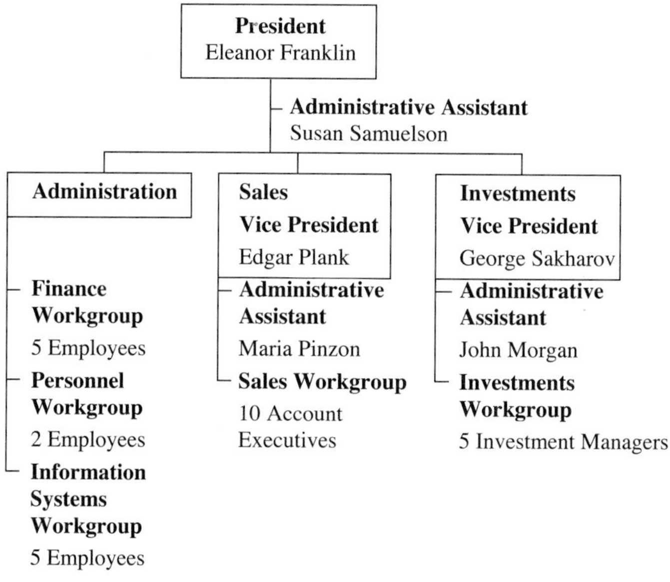

Figure 10-7 F. D. Roosevelt Investments Inc. organizational chart

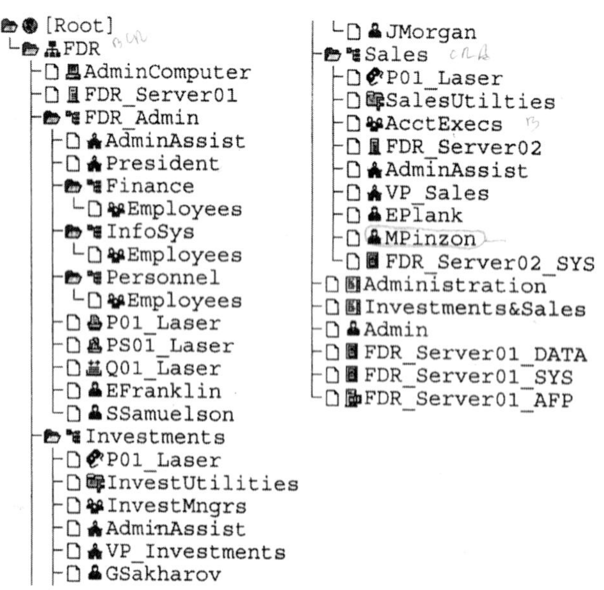

Figure 10-8 FDR Directory Tree

Paul Drake, the lead account executive at FDR, needs the ability to manage NDS objects in the Sales organizational unit. He will be granted the Supervisor object right to the Sales Organizational Unit object. When the Supervisor object right is granted, it gives the trustee the Supervisor right to all properties of that object, as shown in Figure 10-9.

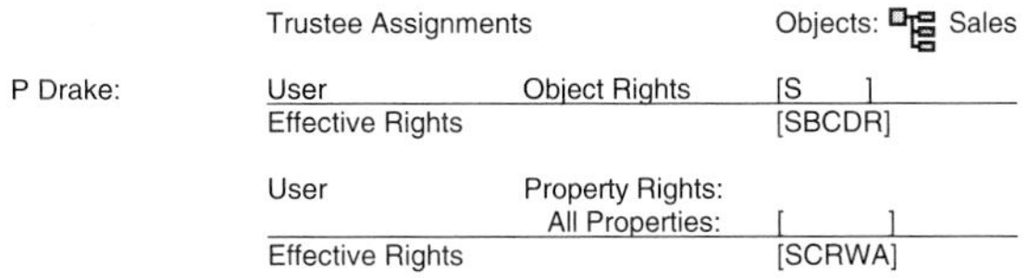

Trustee Assignments
Objects: Sales
P Drake:
User
Object Rights
[S]
Effective Rights
[SBCDR]
User
Property Rights:
All Properties:
[ ]
Effective Rights
[SCRWA]

Figure 10-9 Paul's Object rights

Now you will consider another example: the implementation of Object and Property rights at CBE Laboratories. Georgia Burns, the CBE Labs Vice President for Testing and Evaluation, is very knowledgeable about network administration. In order to expedite administration of the Test&Eval branch of the CBE Labs Directory tree, it has been agreed that she will be given the rights to administer the Test&Eval branch. This means that she must be given the Supervisor right to the Test&Eval Organizational Unit object. The Test&Eval branch of the CBE Labs Directory tree is shown in Figure 10-10.

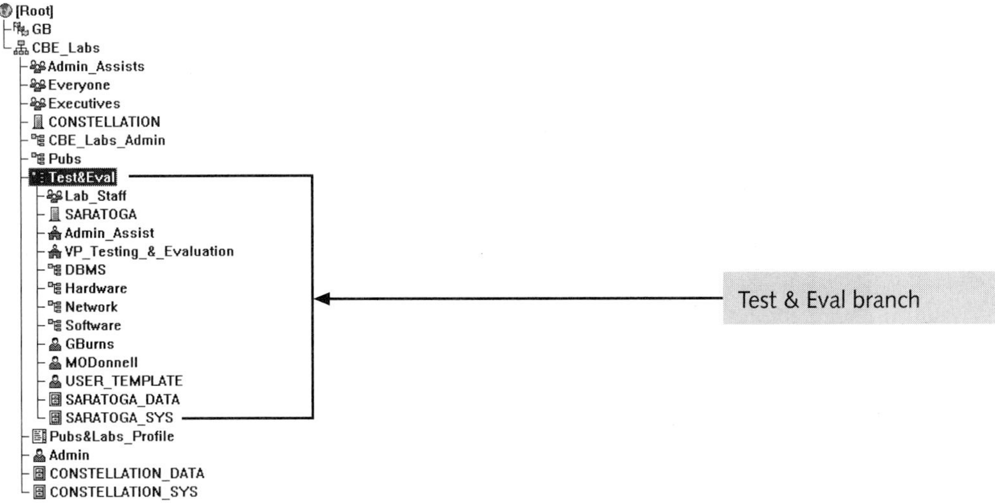

Figure 10-10 The Test&Eval branch of the CBE Labs Directory tree

Assigning trustee rights to an object from the object itself. When you assign trustee rights from an object, you select the object and then open a dialog box that displays the trustees of the object.

To grant property and object trustee rights to an object from the object itself, you follow these steps:

- Click the object name or icon to select it. Then click Object on the menu bar, and click Trustees of this Object to display the Trustee of Object dialog box.

  or

- Right-click the object name or icon to select it and display the shortcut menu. Then click Trustees of this Object to display the Trustee of Object dialog box.

  then

- Use the settings controls in the Trustee of Object dialog box to manage trustees and trustee rights assignments.

You will use this method to give Georgia Burns her trustee assignment to the Test&Eval Organizational Unit object.

To grant Georgia Burns Trustee rights to the Test&Eval Organizational Unit object from the Test&Eval Organizational Unit object, follow these steps:

1. If NetWare Administrator is not open, launch it.
2. Click the **Test&Eval Organizational Unit** object to select it; then click **Object** in the menu bar. The Object menu appears, as shown in Figure 10-11.

Figure 10-11 The Trustees of this Object command on the Object menu

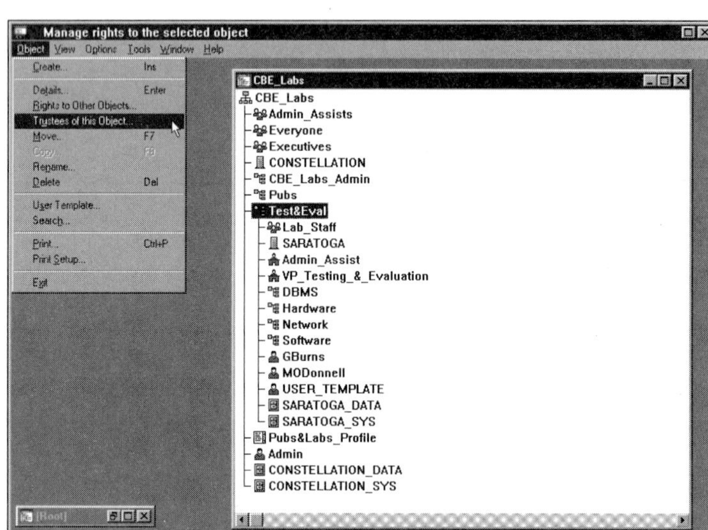

3. Click **Trustees of this Object** on the Object menu. The Trustees of Test&Eval dialog box is displayed, as shown in Figure 10-12.

Figure 10-12 The Trustees of Test&Eval dialog box

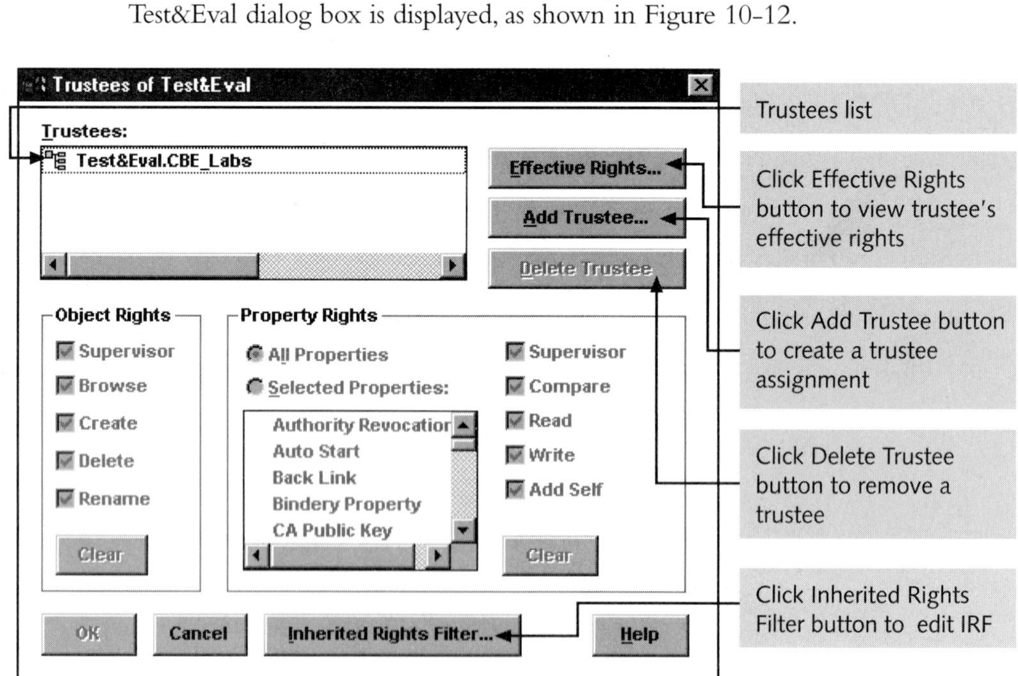

The object is a trustee of itself. Checked check boxes indicate that the right is granted; empty check boxes indicate that it is not. Grayed-out check boxes indicate that the right is not applicable to the selected object—this usually occurs when no objects have been selected.

4. Click the **Add Trustees** button to display the Select Object dialog box.
5. Select the **GBurns User object**; then click **OK**. GBurns is made a trustee of the Test&Eval Organizational Unit object, as shown in Figure 10-13. *Do not close the Trustees of Test&Eval dialog box at this time.*

Figure 10-13

Trustees of Test&Eval dialog box

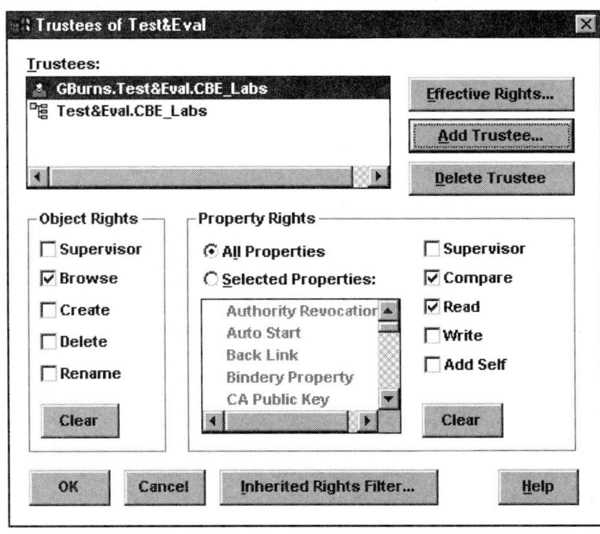

Now that Georgia Burns is a trustee of the Test&Eval Organizational Unit, her specific rights can be assigned. Note that in Figure 10-13 the default rights granted are the Browse Object right `[ B ]` and the Compare and Read Property rights `[ CR ]` to all properties. These rights would enable her to see the object in the Directory tree and to see all the values of the property settings for the object. Remember that the Compare right is included in the Read right, so nothing is gained by assigning the Compare right in addition to the Read right.

Also notice in Figure 10-13 that Property rights can be assigned for each property individually by using the selected property radio button. This affords the network administrator total control of exactly what each trustee can do with the properties of the object.

Georgia Burns needs to be given the Supervisor Object right. This includes the Supervisor Property right to all properties, but it's a good idea to explicitly grant the Supervisor Property right to all properties in the dialog box as well—this serves as a visual reminder of the rights that have been granted to the trustee.

To grant Georgia Burns Object rights and Property rights to the Test&Eval Organizational Unit object, follow these steps:

1. Make sure that the GBurns.Test&Eval.CBE_Labs trustee is selected in the Trustees list. If it isn't, click it to select it.

2. In the Object Rights box, click the **Supervisor** check box to select it, and click the **Browse** check box to unselect it (although it isn't necessary to unselect the Browse right, doing so presents a clearer picture of the trustee's rights).
3. In the Property Rights box, make sure that the All Properties radio button is selected. If it isn't, click it to select it.
4. In the Property Rights box, click the **Supervisor** check box to select it, and click the **Compare** check box and **Read** check box to unselect them (although it isn't necessary to unselect the Compare and Read rights, doing so presents a clearer picture of the trustee's rights). The Trustees of Test&Eval dialog box now appears as shown in Figure 10-14. *Do not close the Trustees of Test&Eval dialog box at this time.*

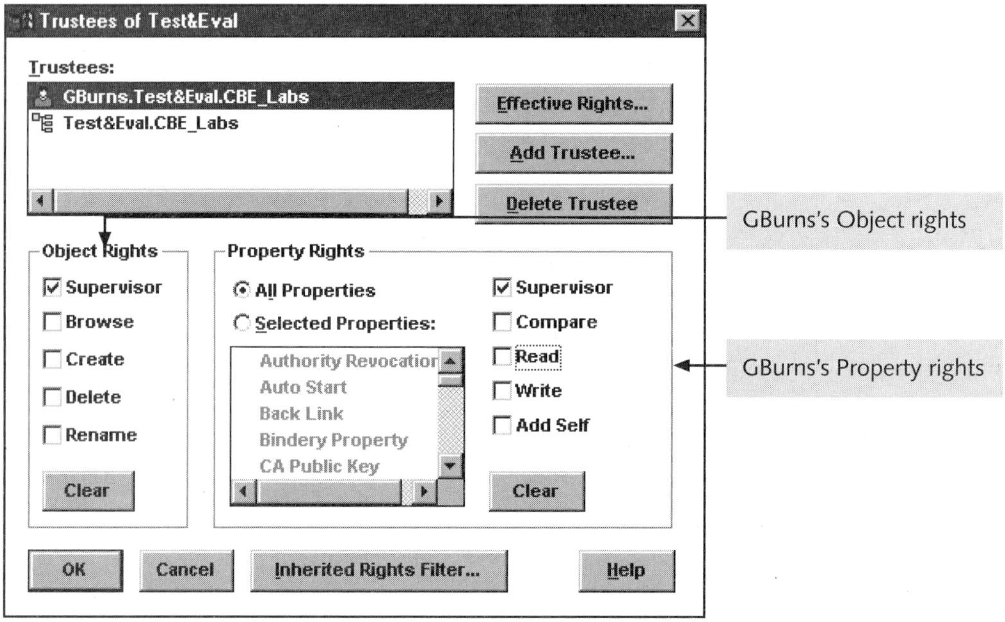

Figure 10-14
GBurns's Object and Property rights to Test&Eval

GBurns's Object rights

GBurns's Property rights

The Trustees of *ObjectName* dialog box gives the network administrator a quick way to check a trustee's effective rights to an object. To check the effective rights, select the trustee in the Trustees list, and then click the Effective Rights button.

To view Georgia Burns's effective Object rights and Property rights to the Test&Eval Organizational Unit object, follow these steps:

1. Make sure that the GBurns.Test&Eval.CBE_Labs trustee is selected in the Trustees list. If it isn't, click it to select it.
2. Click the **Effective Rights** button to display the Effective Rights dialog box, as shown in Figure 10-15.

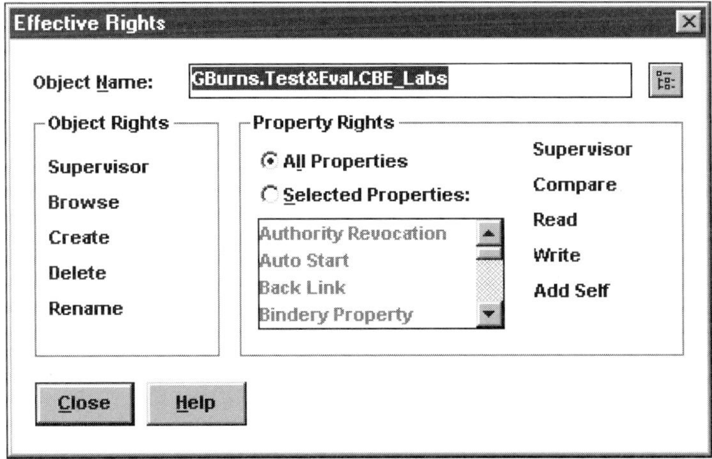

Figure 10-15 The Effective Rights dialog box

Notice that the effective Object and Property rights are displayed in boldface type. In this case, all rights are in bold, indicating that Georgia Burns has all Object and Property rights to the Test&Eval Organizational Unit object. Rights not assigned would be shown in a lighter line weight instead of bold.

Also notice the Select Object button. You can use this button to check the effective rights of other objects in the Directory tree to the current object.

3. Click the **Close** button to close the Effective Rights dialog box. The Trustees of Test&Eval dialog box is displayed.
4. Click **OK** to close the Trustees of Test&Eval dialog box.

Assigning Trustee rights to an object from a Trustee object. Alternatively, you can assign trustee rights from the object that is being granted the trustee assignment. To do this, you select the Trustee object and then open a dialog box that displays the trustees assignments of the Trustee object.

To grant property and object Trustee rights to an object from a Trustee object itself, you follow these steps:

- Click the object name or icon to select it. Then click Object on the menu bar, and click Rights to Other Objects to display the Search Context dialog box.

  or

- Right-click the object name or icon to select it and display the shortcut menu. Then click Rights to Other Objects to display the Search Context dialog box.

  then

- Use the Search Context dialog box to set the search context for the search for the trustee's rights to other objects in the Directory tree and to search for the trustee rights.

  then

- Use the settings controls in the Rights to Other Objects dialog box to manage trustees and trustee rights assignments.

When the trustee assignment is made from the User object (or other Trustee object), NetWare first searches the Directory tree to find and list the objects for which the user has rights assigned. The context for this search—all of the tree or a branch of it—is specified as part of the search. Searching the Directory tree takes time, so it is faster to limit the area of the tree that needs to be evaluated. Normally, you should limit the search context to only the part of the Directory tree that includes the objects for which you are granting trustee rights to the user.

Let's see how this method could be used to give Georgia Burns her trustee assignment to the Test&Eval Organizational Unit object. We will start at the point at which she doesn't have the trustee assignment yet.

To grant Georgia Burns Trustee rights to the Test&Eval Organizational Unit object from the GBurns User object, follow these steps:

1. If NetWare Administrator is not open, launch it.
2. Click the **GBurns User object** to select it; then click **Object** in the menu bar. The Object menu appears, as shown in Figure 10-16.

Figure 10-16

The Rights to Other Objects command on the Object menu

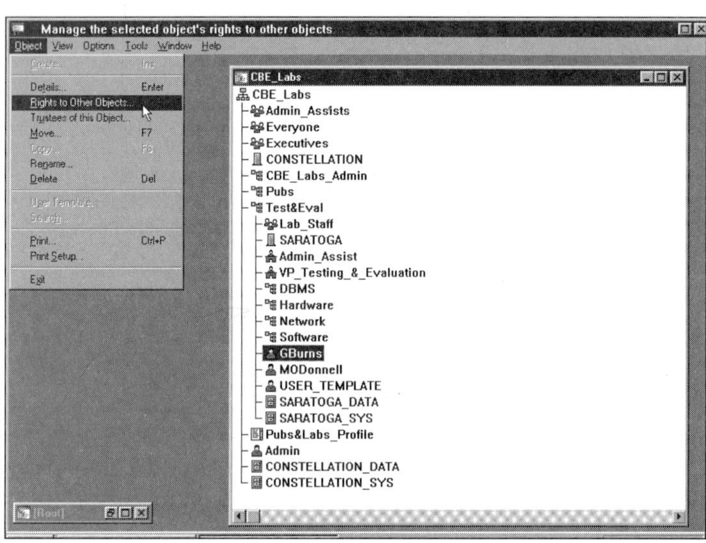

3. Click **Rights to Other Objects** on the Object menu. The Search Context dialog box is displayed, as shown in Figure 10-17.

Figure 10-17

The Search Context dialog box

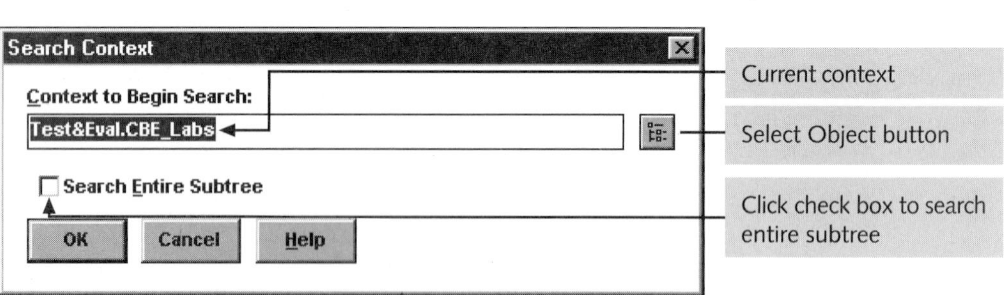

4. Click the **Select Object** button to display the Select Object dialog box. In the Select Object dialog box, select the **CBE_Labs Organization object**; then click **OK**.
5. The Search Context dialog box is displayed with CBE_Labs in the Context to Begin Search text box. Click the **Search Entire Subtree** check box to select it; then click **OK**. A search is done for object trustee assignments for Georgia

Burns, and then the Rights to Other Objects dialog box is displayed for User: GBurns, as shown in Figure 10-18. Note that there are no Assigned Objects because we are illustrating the initial assignment of Trustee rights to the Test&Eval Organizational Unit object to Georgia Burns.

Figure 10-18

The Rights to Other Objects—User: GBurns dialog box

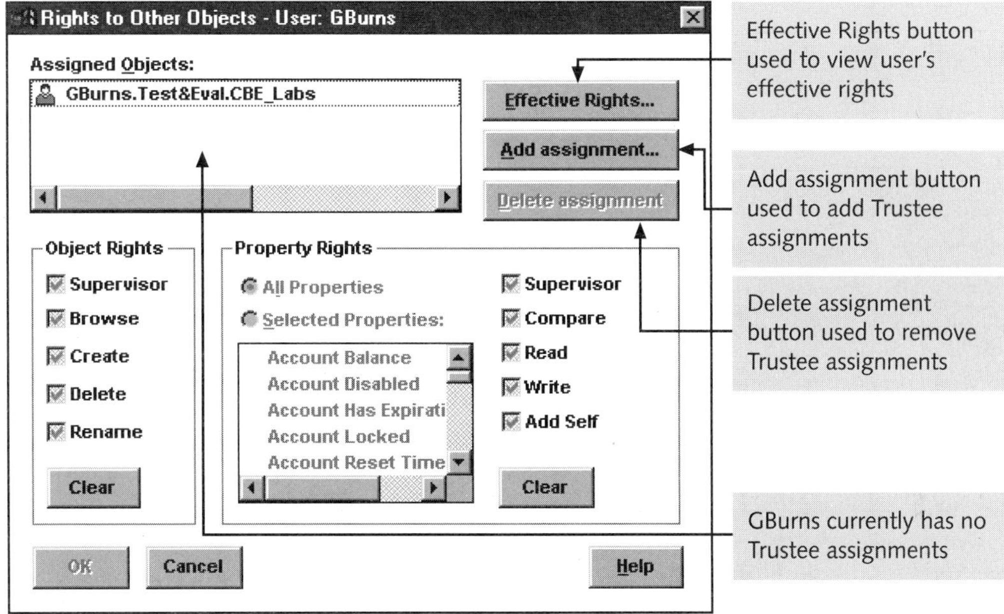

6. Click the **Add assignment** button to display the Select Object dialog box.
7. Select the **Test&Eval Organizational Unit** object; then click **OK**. GBurns is assigned Trustee rights to the Test&Eval Organizational Unit object, as shown in Figure 10-19. Do not close the Rights to Other Objects dialog box at this time.

Figure 10-19

GBurns assigned a trustee of the Test&Eval.CBE_Labs Organizational Unit object

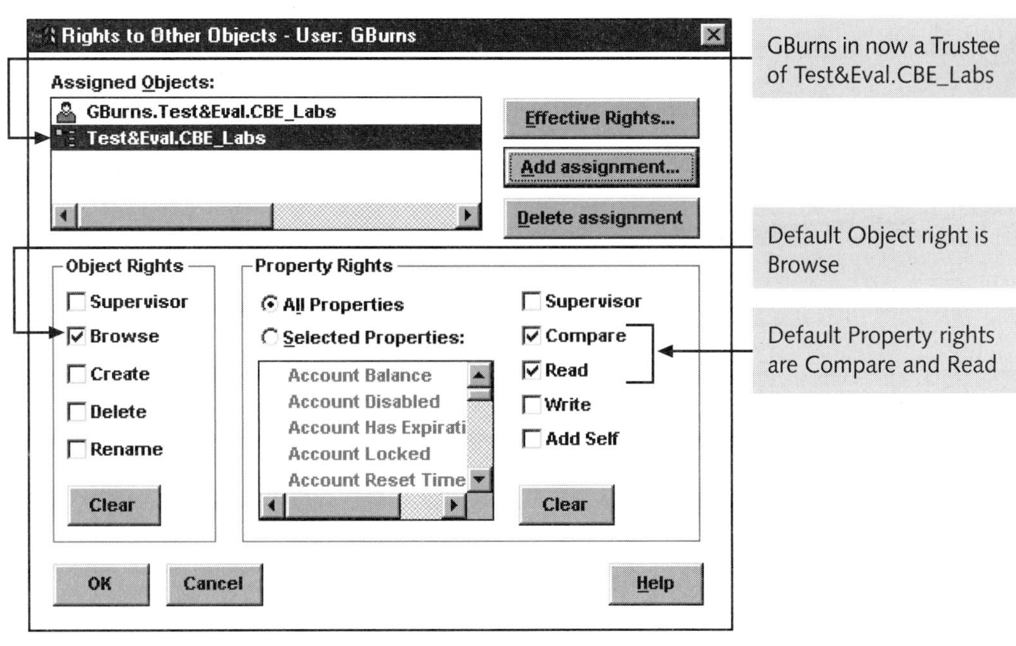

Georgia Burns's specific Object and Property rights could also be assigned from the Rights to Other Objects dialog box. The Rights to Other Objects dialog box uses exactly the same methods of granting specific Object rights and Property rights to trustees that are used in the Trustees of *ObjectName* dialog box. Note that in Figure 10-19 the Rights to Other Objects dialog box shows that the same default Object rights of Browse Object [B] and the same default Property rights of Compare and Read property [CR] to all properties are granted. The specific steps for granting Georgia Burns Object and Property rights would be exactly the same as those already shown above, so there is no need to repeat them again.

Also similar to the Trustees of *ObjectName* dialog box is the ability to use the Rights to Other Objects dialog box to check a trustee's effective rights to an object. To check the effective rights, select the object in the Assigned Objects list, and then click the Effective Rights button.

Rights Assigned to a Group

Groups are composed of users who have common network requirements. Grouping users can simplify making trustee assignments. When a group is made a trustee of an object, all members of that group are also considered trustees of the object and thus have the same rights as the group. A user's effective rights in a directory are then a combination of his or her trustee assignment plus any rights he or she obtains from being a member of a group.

A special case of a group is **[Public]**. When [Public] is made a trustee of an object, *every* object in the NDS Directory tree—users, groups, organizational units, and so on—inherits the same [Public] rights to the object. Additionally, [Public] rights are available to users who have loaded the NetWare client software but haven't logged into the network yet. When you install NetWare 4.1, the [Public] is made a trustee of the [Root] object and given the Browse Object right [B]. This means that, by default, anyone with access to your network can see your whole Directory tree *before* logging into the network!

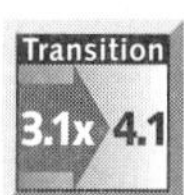

The NetWare 4.1 [Public] trustee replaces and extends the EVERYONE group in NetWare 3.1x. By default, [Public] enables users who aren't logged into the network to Browse the Directory tree before logging in. EVERYONE was a group created during NetWare 3.1x installation to which every user was added as the user account was created. If you want to use an EVERYONE group in NetWare 4.1, you must create one yourself.

If you don't want all users, logged in or not, to view your Directory tree, you must delete [Public] as a trustee to the [Root] of the Directory tree.

Novell recommends making a container object an object trustee instead of [Public]. This grants rights only to the users, groups, and other objects in that container, and the user must be logged in to have those rights.

Now you will look at a couple of examples of using groups to assign Trustee rights.

EXAMPLE 10-2: Assigning group Trustee rights at F. D. Roosevelt Investments Inc.

FDR has removed the [Public] trustee assignment from the [Root] of the Directory tree and has granted the AcctExecs group the Browse Object right [B] and Compare and Read Property rights [CR] for the Sales Organizational Unit. This enables the group to see all objects in their branch of the Directory tree and read the object property values.

In addition, the AcctExecs Group is being given the right to enable group members to add themselves to Access Control Lists (ACLs) for objects in the Sales Organizational Unit object. This will be especially useful for printing problems, because all members of the group will then have more control of the printing process using the workgroup's laser printer.

What effective rights does Maria Pinzon, the Administrative Assistant for Sales, have to the Sales Organizational Unit object? As shown in Figure 10-20, because Maria doesn't have any trustee assignments as a user, her effective rights are determined by her group membership.

Figure 10-20

Maria's Object rights

	Trustee Assignments		Object: Sales
MPinzon:	User	Object Rights	[ ]
	Group AcctExecs	Object Rights	[B]
	Effective Rights		[B]
	User	Property Rights: All Properties	[ ]
	Group AcctExecs	Property Rights: All Properties	[CR A]
	Effective Rights	All Properties:	[CR A]

What effective rights does Paul Drake have to the Sales Organizational Unit object? As shown in Figure 10-21, Paul's Supervisor object right `[S]` and Supervisor Property right `[S]` still give Paul rights to the object and its properties.

Figure 10-21

Paul's Object rights

	Trustee Assignments		Object: Sales
PDrake:	User	Object Rights	[S]
	Group AcctExecs	Object Rights	[B]
	Effective Rights		[SBCDR]
	User	Property Rights: All Properties	[S]
	Group AcctExecs	Property Rights: All Properties	[CR A]
	Effective Rights	All Properties:	[SCRWA]

For another example, let's return to CBE Labs. The Testing & Evaluation Staff workgroup of CBE Labs has asked permission to link some of the servers it tests into the CBE Labs network. After much consideration, permission has been granted. In order to facilitate management of the servers and their associated volumes in the CBE Labs Directory tree, the NetWare servers and their associated volumes will be placed in the Network Organizational Unit object.

The members of the Lab_Staff group will have Supervisor rights to the Network object. This will enable them to create and manage objects as necessary in this section of the Directory tree.

The process for assigning rights to groups is the same as for assigning rights to individual users. Just as with individual users, Object rights and Property rights are granted using either the object to which access is being granted or the object that is receiving the trustee assignment. The same steps detailed above for granting Georgia Burns Trustee rights to the Test&Eval Organizational Unit object are used to grant the Lab_Staff group a trustee assignment to the Network Organizational Unit. We'll use the method of granting the trustee assignment from the object that the rights will access, and we'll also use the shortcut menu to open the Trustees of *ObjectName* dialog box.

To grant the Lab_Staff group trustee rights to the Network Organizational Unit object from the Network Organizational Unit object, follow these steps:

1. If NetWare Administrator is not open, launch it.
2. Right-click the **Network Organizational Unit** object to select it. The object shortcut menu appears, as shown in Figure 10-22.

Figure 10-22

The object shortcut menu

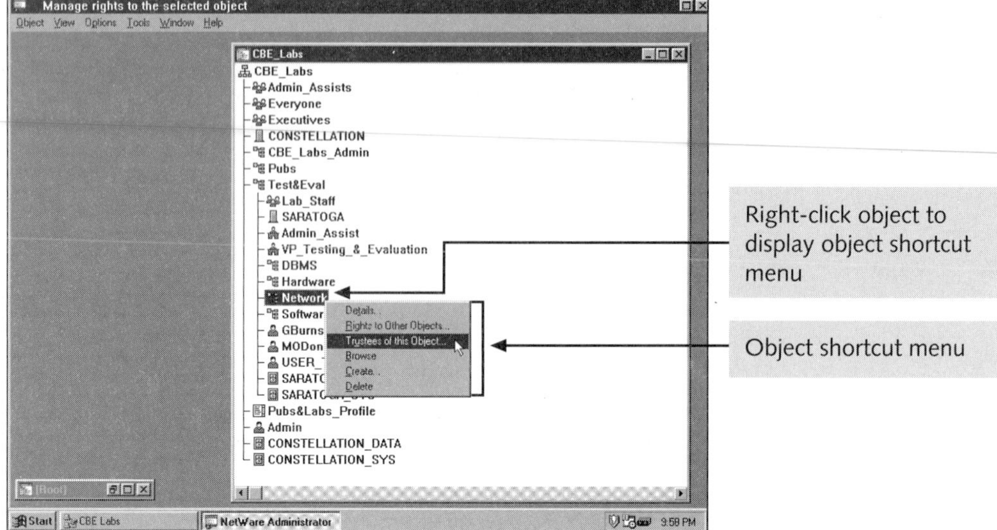

Notice that the object shortcut menu includes both the Rights to Other Objects command and the Trustees of this Object command. You can use the object shortcut menu to display either the Rights to Other Objects dialog box or the Trustees of *ObjectName* dialog box.

3. Click the **Trustees of this Object** command on the object shortcut menu. The Trustees of Network dialog box is displayed.
4. Click the **Add Trustee** button to display the Select Object dialog box.
5. Select the **Lab_Staff Group** object; then click **OK**. The Lab_Staff group is made a trustee of the Network Organizational Unit object, as shown in Figure 10-23. Do not close the Trustees of Network dialog box at this time.

Figure 10-23

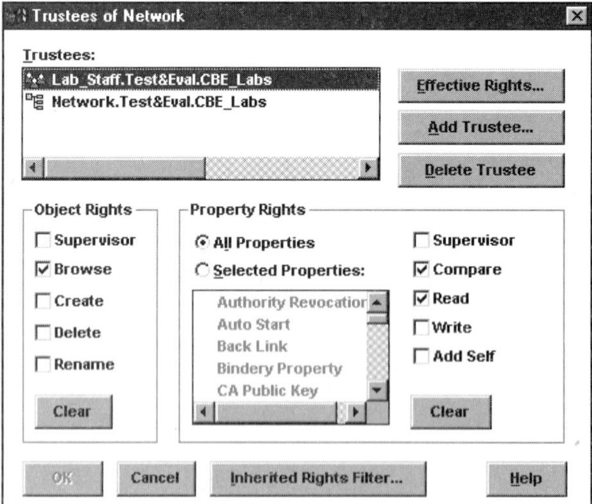

The steps for granting the Lab_Staff group specific Object rights and Property rights are identical to those that were used for granting specific rights to Georgia Burns.

To grant the Lab_Staff group Object rights and Property rights to the Test&Eval Organizational Unit object, follow these steps:

1. Make sure that the Lab_Staff.Test&Eval.CBE_Labs trustee is selected in the Trustees list. If it isn't, click it to select it.

2. In the Object Rights box, click the **Supervisor** check box to select it; then click the **Browse** check box to unselect it.
3. In the Property Rights box, make sure that the All Properties radio button is selected. If it isn't, click it to select it.
4. In the Property Rights box, click the **Supervisor** check box to select it; then click the **Compare** check box and **Read** check box to unselect them. The Trustees of Network dialog box now appears as shown in Figure 10-24.

Figure 10-24

The Network group's Object and Property rights to Network

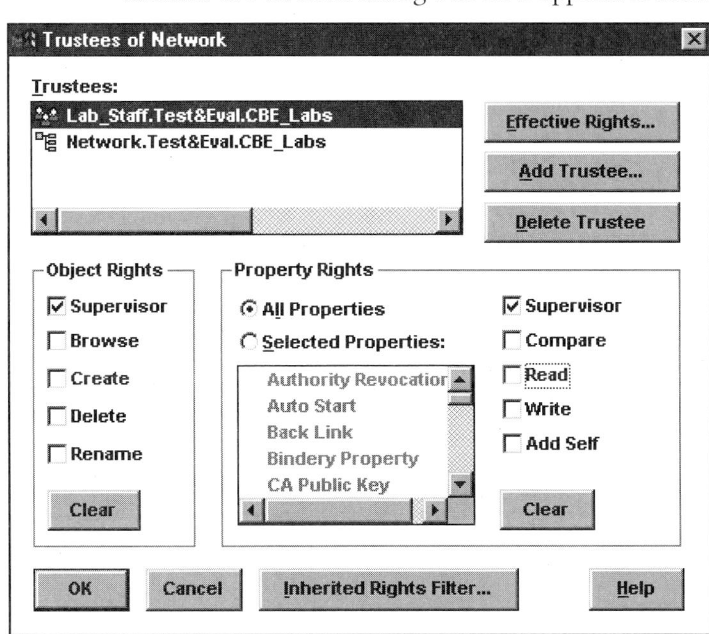

5. Click **OK** to close the Trustees of Network dialog box.

Rights Assigned to an Organizational Role

You can also create assigned rights by granting trustee assignments to an Organizational Role object. These rights will be available to any user who occupies this organizational role. The advantage of this method is that when a new person takes over a job, you don't have to take away trustee assignments from one user and create them for another—you simply change the occupant of the position. Because the trustee assignments belong to the position, they are available only to the person(s) occupying the position.

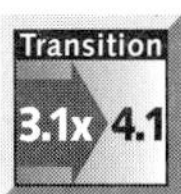

There was no NetWare 3.1x equivalent of organizational roles or of trustee assignments to organizational roles. This is a powerful new feature of NetWare 4.1.

The user's effective rights are the combination of his or her (1) user trustee assignments, (2) group memberships, and (3) organizational roles occupied.

You will start by looking at the FDR example; and then you will look at CBE Labs.

EXAMPLE 10-3: Assigning organizational role Trustee rights at F. D. Roosevelt Investments, Inc.

Edgar Plank is the FDR Vice President for Sales and as such is the occupant of the VP_Sales organizational role in the FDR Directory tree. He is also a member of the AcctExecs group, which has the Browse Object right [B] and Compare and Read Property rights [CR] for the Sales Organizational Unit. Edgar has no trustee assignments granted directly to him.

The VP_Sales Organizational Role object is granted the create, delete, and rename Object rights `[   CDR]` and the Supervisor Property right to all properties `[SCRWA]`.

What effective rights does Edgar Plank have to the Sales Organizational Unit object? As shown in Figure 10-25, because Edgar doesn't have any trustee assignments as a user, his effective rights are determined by his group membership and the organizational role he occupies.

Figure 10-25

Edgar's Object rights

```
               Trustee Assignments                  Object:      Sales

EPlank:        User                Object Rights    [      ]
               Group AcctExecs     Object Rights    [ B    ]
               OrgRole VP_Sales    Object Rights    [  CDR ]
               ------------------------------------------------
               Effective RIghts                     [ BCDR ]

               User                Property Rights:
                                     All Properties [      ]
               Group AcctExecs     Property Rights:
                                     All Properties [CR   A]
               OrgRole: VP_Sales   Property Rights:
                                     All Properties [S     ]
               ------------------------------------------------
               Effective Rights      All Properties: [SCRWA]
```

Paul Drake does not occupy any organizational role defined in the Directory tree.

What effective rights does Paul Drake have to the Sales Organizational Unit object? As shown in Figure 10-26, Paul's Supervisor Object right `[S]` and Supervisor Property right `[S]` still give Paul rights to the object and its properties.

Figure 10-26

Paul's Object rights

```
               Trustee Assignments                  Object:      Sales

PDrake:        User                Object Rights    [S      ]
               Group AcctExecs     Object Rights    [ B     ]
               OrgRole None        Object Rights    [       ]
               Effective RIghts                     [SBCDR  ]

               User                Property Rights:
                                     All Properties [S      ]
               GroupAcctExecs      Property Rights:
                                     All Properties [ CR   A]
               OrgRole: None       Property Rights:
                                     All Properties [       ]
               Effective Rights      All Properties: [SCRWA]
```

For another example, you will consider the trustee assignments made at CBE Labs. Georgia Burns, the Vice President for Testing and Evaluation, has been granted Supervisor Object and Property rights to the Test&Eval branch of the CBE Labs Directory tree because of her acknowledged skill as a network administrator. At CBE Labs, however, network administration skills are a requirement for this position. This means that whomever occupies the position of Vice President for Testing and Evaluation can administer the Test&Eval branch of the Directory tree. Therefore, it makes sense to the make the supervisor Object and Property rights trustee assignment for that branch to the VP_Testing&_Evaluation Organizational Role object. Then, whomever occupies that organizational role will automatically have the needed rights. Furthermore, the network administrator won't have to delete the trustee assignment for one User object and assign it to another.

The CBE Labs network administrator has not removed the [Public] trustee assignment to the [Root] object. Taking this into account, Georgia's effective rights to the Test&Eval organizational Unit object after the trustee assignment has been shifted are shown in Figure 10-27.

Figure 10-27 Georgia's Object rights

	Trustee Assignments	Object: Test&Eval	
GBurns:	User	Object Rights	[ ]
	[Public] trustee	Object Rights	[B]
	Group: LabStaff	Object Rights	[ ]
	OrgRole: VP_Testing_&_Evaluation	Object Rights	[S]
	Effective Rights		[SBCDR]
	User	Property Rights: All Properties	[ ]
	[Public] Trustee	Property Rights: All Properties	[ ]
	Group: LabStaff	Property Rights All Properties	[ ]
	OrgRole: VP_Testing_&_Evaluation	Property Rights: All Properties	[S]
	Effective Rights	All Properties:	[SCRWA]

The CBE Labs network administrator needs to delete the trustee assignment for the GBurns User object to the Test&Eval Organizational Unit object and then add the VP_Testing&_Evaluation Organizational Role object as a trustee. Because the GBurns User object occupies the VP_Testing&_Evaluation organizational role, Georgia Burns will still have the same access to network resources as before.

Trustee assignments for organizational roles are made in exactly the same way as for users and groups, using either the Trustees of *ObjectName* dialog box or the Rights to Other Objects dialog box. Trustee assignments can also be deleted using either the Delete Trustee button in the Trustees of *ObjectName* dialog box or the Delete assignment button in the Rights to Other Objects dialog box.

To delete property and object trustee rights to an object from the object itself, you follow these steps:

- Click the object name or icon to select it. Then click Object on the menu bar and click Trustees of this Object to display the Trustee of Object dialog box.

  or

- Right-click the object name or icon to select it and display the shortcut menu. Then click Trustees of this Object to display the Trustee of Object dialog box.

  then

- Click the trustee in the Trustee list to select it; then click the Delete Trustee button.

To delete property and object trustee rights to an object from a Trustee object itself, you follow these steps:

- Click the object name or icon to select it. Then click Object on the menu bar and click Rights to Other Objects to display the Search Context dialog box.

  or

- Right-click the object name or icon to select it and display the shortcut menu. Then click Rights to Other Objects to display the Search Context dialog box.

then

- Use the Search Context dialog box to set the search context for the search for the trustee's rights to other objects in the Directory tree and to search for these trustee rights.

then

- Click the object in the Assigned Objects list to select it; then click the Delete assignment button.

To delete the trustee assignment to Georgia Burns and grant the VP_Testing_&_Evaluation organizational role trustee rights to the Test&Eval Organizational Unit object from the Test&Eval Organizational Unit object, follow these steps:

1. If NetWare Administrator is not open, launch it.
2. Click the **Test&Eval Organizational Unit** object to select it, click **Object** in the menu bar, and then click the **Trustees of this Object** command on the Object menu. The Trustees of Test&Eval dialog box is displayed.
3. Click the trustee **GBurns.Test&Eval.CBE_Labs** in the Trustees list, as shown in Figure 10-28.

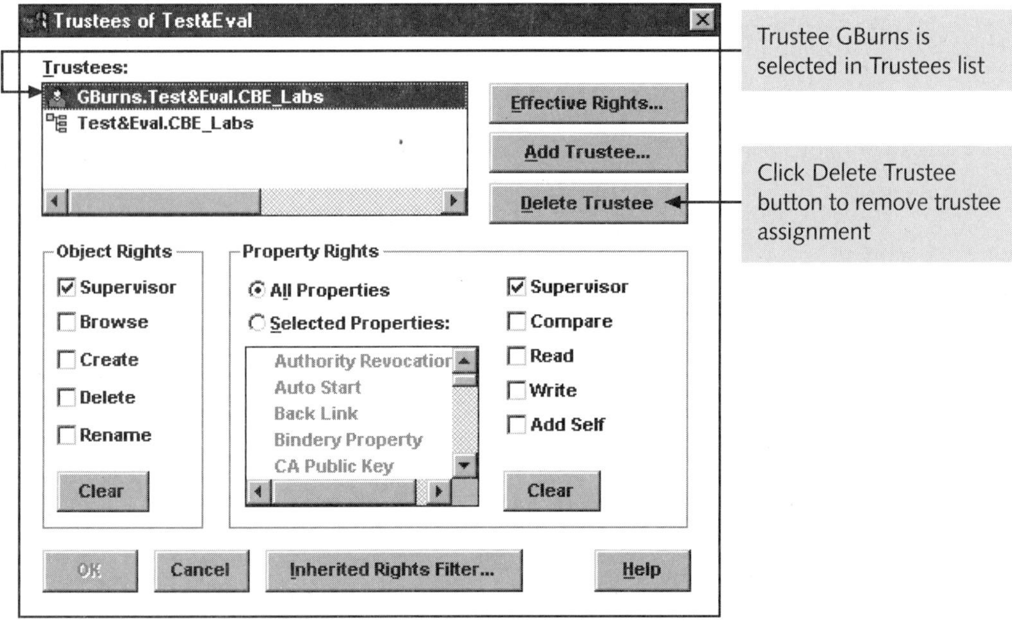

Figure 10-28 GBurns selected in the Trustees of Test&Eval dialog box

4. Click the **Delete Trustee** button to delete the trustee GBurns.Test&Eval.CBE_Labs from the Trustees list.
5. Click the **Add Trustee** button to display the Select Object dialog box.
6. Select the **VP_Test&Eval Organizational Role** object, then click **OK**. The VP_Testing&_Evaluation Organizational Role object is made a trustee of the Test&Eval Organizational Unit object.
7. In the Object Rights box, click the **Supervisor** check box to select it; then click the **Browse** check box to unselect it.
8. In the Property Rights box, make sure that the **All Properties** radio button is selected. If it isn't, click it to select it.

9. In the Property Rights box, click the **Supervisor** check box to select it; then click the **Compare** check box and **Read** check box to unselect them. The Trustees of Test&Eval dialog box now appears as shown in Figure 10-29.

Figure 10-29 The VP_Testing_& _Evaluation Organizational Role object's Object and Property rights to Test&Eval

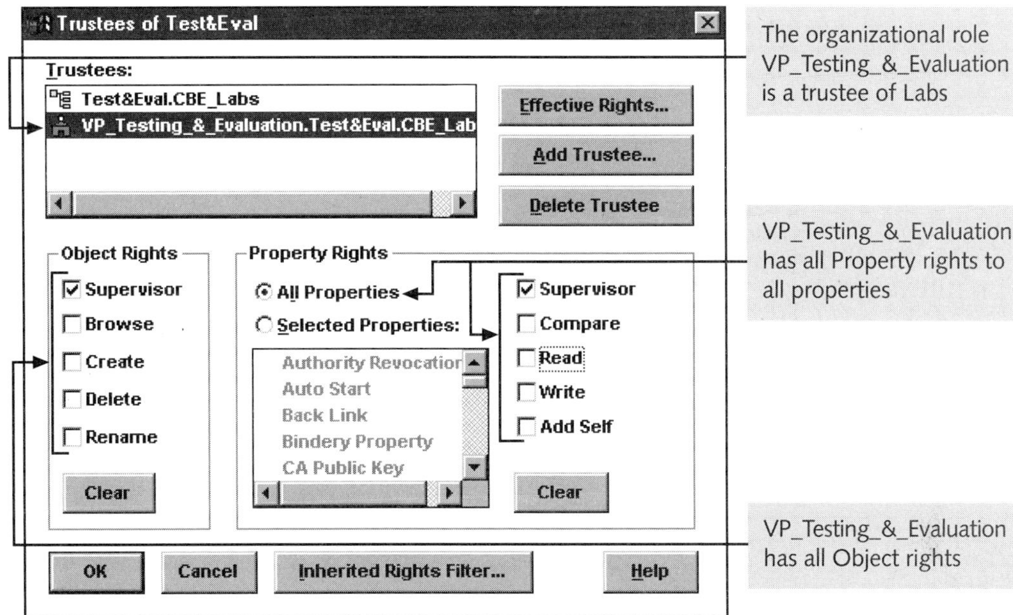

10. Click **OK** to close the Trustees of Test&Eval dialog box.

Security Equivalence and Rights Assigned to a Container Object

Container objects—The [Root] object, Country objects, Organization objects, and Organizational Unit objects—can be granted Trustee rights. These rights will be directly available to any user, group, or organizational role that is in the container object, because each object in a container object is **security equivalent** to the container object. When Object A is security equivalent to Object B, Object A is granted all the rights that Object B has been granted. This means that because the User object GBurns is located in the Test&Eval Organizational Unit container, GBurns is security equivalent to Test&Eval.CBE_Labs and automatically has all the rights that have been granted to Test&Eval.CBE_Labs.

Actually, it's little more complex than this. An object in a container is security equivalent to all the container objects in the object's complete name. This means that GBurns is also security equivalent of CBE_Labs. This is shown in Figure 10-30.

Figure 10-30 Security equivalence and container objects

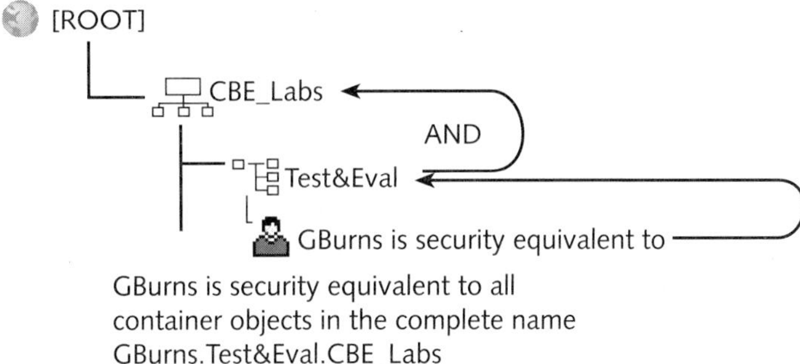

Assigning rights to container objects is a powerful tool for controlling trustee assignments. Every object in the container object, or in child container objects in the Directory tree, has the access rights of the trustee assignments granted to the container. This means that all users, groups, and organizational roles, for example, in a container have the same access to network resources created by the trustee assignments to the container.

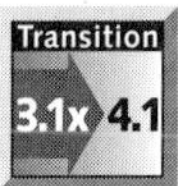

There was no NetWare 3.1x equivalent of container object or trustee assignments to container objects. Like organizational role, this is a powerful new feature of NetWare 4.1.

As usual, we'll start by looking at the FDR example; then we'll look at CBE Labs.

EXAMPLE 10-4: Assigning container object Trustee rights at F. D. Roosevelt Investments Inc.

Although the network administrator for FDR has removed the [Public] trustee from the [Root] of the Directory tree, he still wants to let the users Browse the tree. To do this, he has assigned the Browse Object right [B] to the FDR Organization object. He has also assigned the Compare and Read Property rights [CR] to all properties to the FDR Organization object, so that users can see the setting values for the objects in the Directory tree.

Edgar Plank, the FDR Vice President for Sales, occupies the VP_Sales organizational role in the FDR Directory tree and is a member of the AcctExecs group. Edgar has no trustee assignments granted directly to him.

What effective rights does Edgar Plank have to the FDR Organization object? Edgar doesn't have any trustee assignments as a user, and the rights he has because of his group membership and organizational role occupancy are only for the Sales Organizational Unit. As shown in Figure 10-31, his effective rights are determined by the rights granted to the FDR Organization object and his security equivalence to this object because it is part of his complete name—EPlank.Sales.FDR.

Figure 10-31 Edgar's Object rights

	Trustee Assignments	Object: FDR	
EPlank:	User	Object Rights	[ ]
	Group AcctExecs	Object Rights	[ ]
	OrgRole VP_Sales	Object Rights	[ ]
	Container: FDR		[B]
	Effective RIghts		[B]
	User	Property Rights: All Properties	[ ]
	Group AcctExecs	Property Rights: All Properties	[ ]
	OrgRole: VP_Sales	Property Rights: All Properties	[ ]
	Container: FDR	Property Rights: All Properties	[CR]
	Effective Rights	All Properties:	[CR]

For another example, you return to CBE Labs. In order to enable all the CBE Labs employees in the Test&Eval to see the objects in the Test&Eval Organizational Unit, the trustee assignment needs to be made only to the Test&Eval Organizational Unit object itself. However, it turns out that NetWare automatically makes a container object a trustee of itself, but leaves the Object and Property rights undefined. Undefined rights are indicated by grayed boxes next to the Object and Property rights lists, as shown in Figure 10-32.

This means that any rights the network administrator wants to grant to objects in the container, typically the Browse Object right [B] and the Compare and Read Property rights [CR] must be assigned by the network administrator. To change the trustee rights for a contain object, we would use the process for assigning rights already discussed.

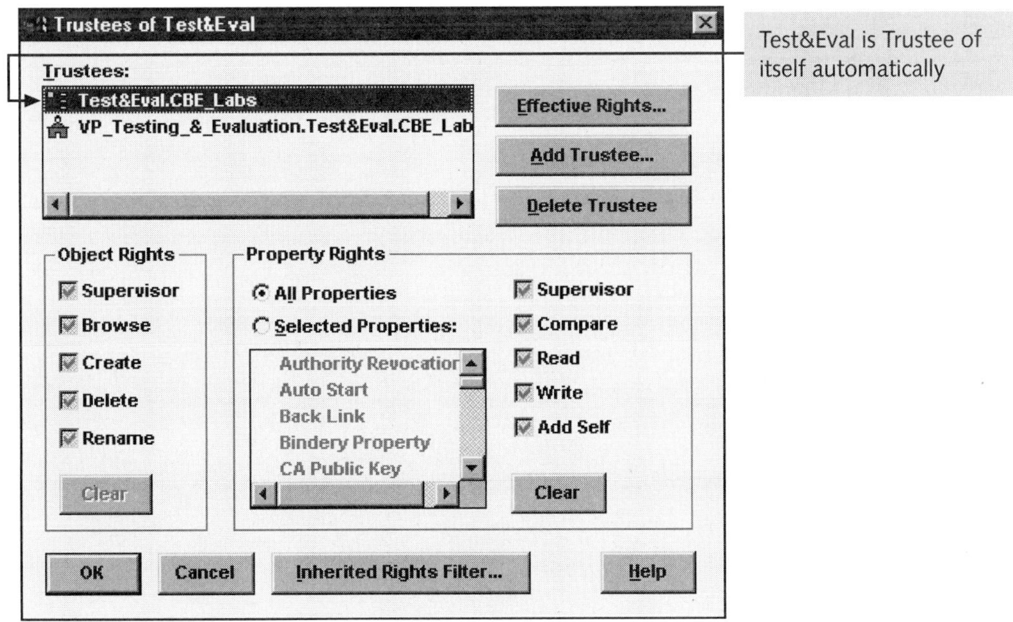

Figure 10-32 The Test&Eval Organizational Unit object as a trustee of itself

Rights Assigned Directly by Security Equivalence

Any object in a container object is automatically security equivalent to the container object because of its context in that container. However, you can also create security equivalence by directly assigning it on an object's Security Equal To page in the object's Object dialog box. Granting access rights using the Security Equal To page is similar to granting access rights by making a user a member of a group. It is also important to note that security equivalence of Object A to Object B grants Object A only the rights *specifically granted* to Object B, not to any rights that Object B has because of security equivalence. That is, if Object B is security equivalent to Object C, Object A does *not* have the rights that Object B obtains by being security equivalent to Object C.

A common use of security equivalence is granting select users supervisor privileges on the network by making them security equivalent to the Admin user.

Although an object is security equivalent to all container objects in the object's complete name, the container objects are not listed in the Security Equal To list on the Security Equal To page.

EXAMPLE 10-5: Assigning security equivalence at F. D. Roosevelt Investments Inc.

Eleanor Franklin is the President of FDR. She has asked the network administrator for FDR to grant her supervisor privileges on the network so that she can check whatever she needs to whenever she needs to. To do this, the network administrator has made her security equivalent to the Admin object. Regardless of whatever other rights Eleanor has assigned to her, her security equivalence to Admin grants her full supervisory rights throughout the network.

Edgar Plank, the FDR Vice President for Sales, has also been made security equivalent to the Admin user. Although he occupies he VP_Sales organizational role in the FDR Directory tree and is a member of the AcctExecs group, Edgar has no trustee assignments granted directly to him.

What effective rights does Edgar Plank have to the Investments Organizational Unit object? Edgar doesn't have any trustee assignments as a user, and the rights he has because of his group membership and organizational role occupancy are only for the Sales Organizational Unit. However, as shown in Figure 10-33, his security equivalence to Admin grants him full access to the Investments object.

Figure 10-33 Edgar's Object rights

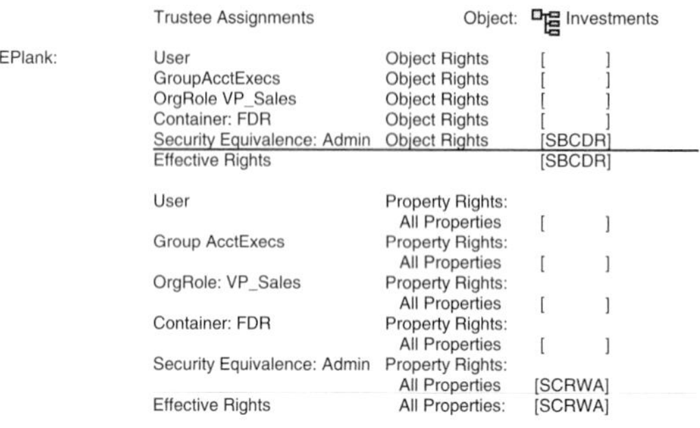

	Trustee Assignments	Object: Investments	
EPlank:	User	Object Rights	[ ]
	GroupAcctExecs	Object Rights	[ ]
	OrgRole VP_Sales	Object Rights	[ ]
	Container: FDR	Object Rights	[ ]
	Security Equivalence: Admin	Object Rights	[SBCDR]
	Effective Rights		[SBCDR]
	User	Property Rights: All Properties	[ ]
	Group AcctExecs	Property Rights: All Properties	[ ]
	OrgRole: VP_Sales	Property Rights: All Properties	[ ]
	Container: FDR	Property Rights: All Properties	[ ]
	Security Equivalence: Admin	Property Rights: All Properties	[SCRWA]
	Effective Rights	All Properties:	[SCRWA]

Now you will look at an example at CBE Labs. Ted Simpson is the Information Systems Manager for CBE Labs, and as such he needs to have the security equivalence of the Admin user.

To make Ted Simpson security equivalent of the Admin user, follow these steps:

1. If NetWare Administrator is not open, launch it.
2. Double-click the **TSimpson User** object in InfoSystems.CBE_Labs_Admin.CBE_Labs to display the User:TSimpson object dialog box.
3. If necessary, use the scroll arrows to scroll through the page buttons until the Security Equal To button appears.
4. Click the **Security Equal To** button in the button bar. The Security Equal To page is displayed, as shown in Figure 10-34.

Figure 10-34 The Security Equal To page

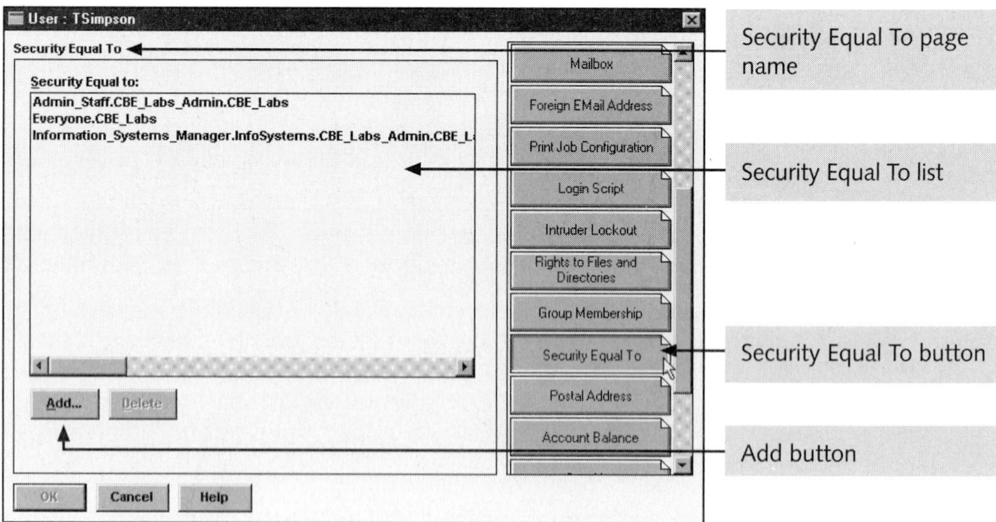

Notice that although Ted Simpson has security equivalence to the container objects InfoSystems, CBE_Labs_Admin, and CBE_Labs, none of these is listed in the Security Equal To list. The security equivalence to container objects is not displayed in this list.

Group memberships, however, also give a member a security equivalence to the group, and that security equivalence does appear in the Security Equal to list.

5. Click the **Add** button to display the Select Object dialog box. Select the Admin.CBE_Labs object, as shown in Figure 10-35.

Figure 10-35 Selecting the Admin object

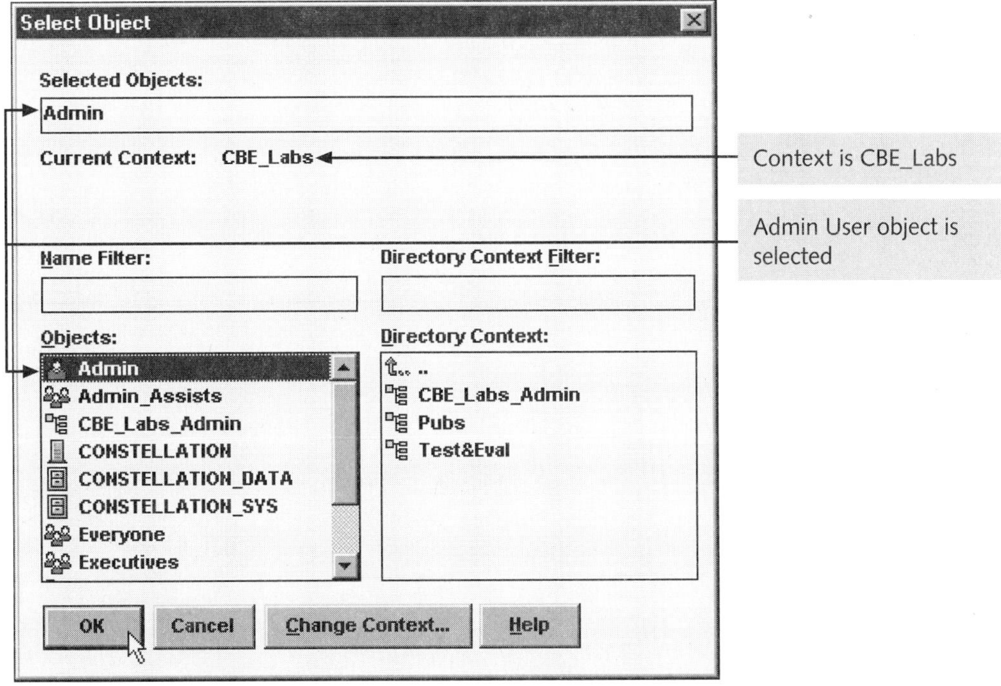

6. Click **OK**. The Admin.CBE_Labs object is added to the Security Equal To list, as shown in Figure 10-36.

Figure 10-36 The completed Security Equal To page

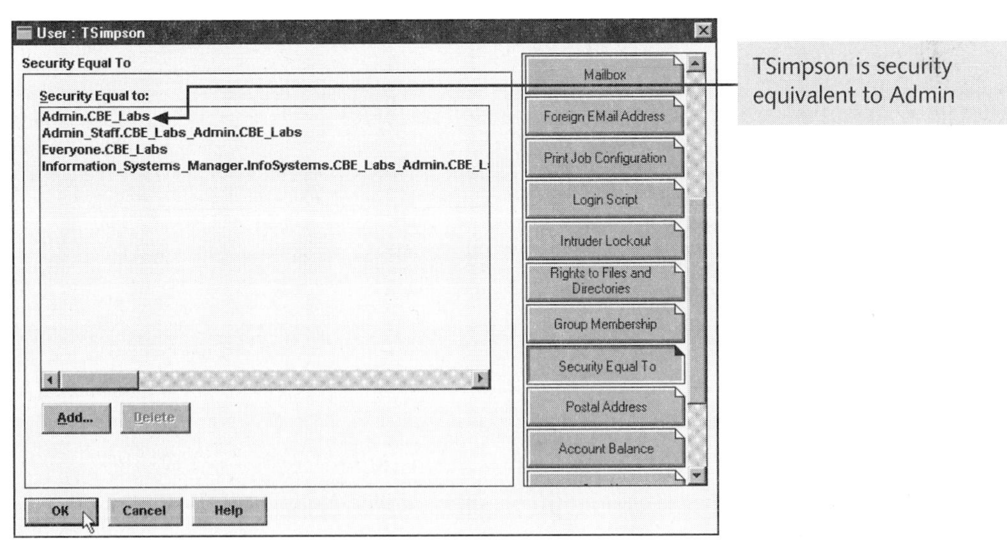

7. Click **OK** to close the User:TSimpson Object dialog box.

Users should not have the ability to add themselves to their own Security Equal To list. If they do, they could assign themselves security equivalence of the Admin user or another network administrator.

Inherited Rights

So far we've discussed trustee assignments made directly to the user, or to a group or organizational role that is associated with the user. We've also discussed trustee assignments made to the [Public] trustee and object security equivalence to container objects and leaf objects as a way to gain access to network resources.

Generally, the user's effective rights are the sum of all these rights. However, calculating a user's effective rights is actually a little more complex than this because of inherited rights.

Inherited rights in a Directory tree are rights available in one container that were actually granted to a container higher in the Directory tree. These rights will be available to any object in the lower container object. This is illustrated in Figure 10-37.

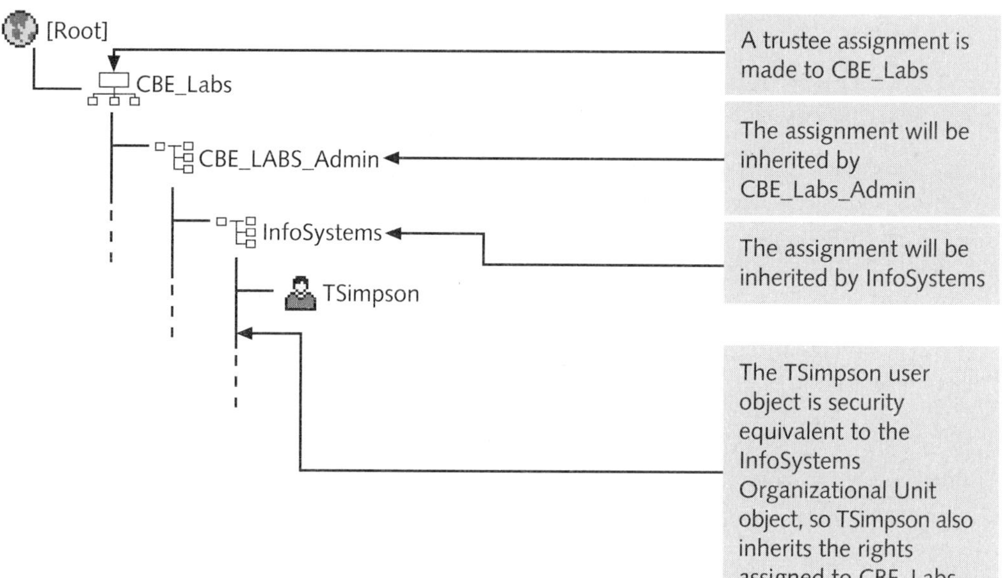

Figure 10-37 Inherited rights and container objects

Inherited rights are available in the Directory tree because an object is security equivalent to each container in its complete name. However, inherited rights differs from security equivalence because inheritance works only if no direct trustee assignments are made to an object.

EXAMPLE 10-6: Inherited rights at F. D. Roosevelt Investments Inc.

Maria Pinzon, the Administrative Assistant for Sales, is a member of the AcctExecs group but has no trustee assignments granted directly to her. AcctExecs has the Browse Object right `[ B ]` and the Compare, Read, and Add Self Property rights `[ CR A]` for all properties to the Sales Organizational Unit. There are no rights granted to the [Public] trustee.

The FDR network manager has just granted the Browse Object right `[ B ]` and the Compare and Read Property rights `[ CR ]` for all properties to the FDR Organization object.

What effective rights does Maria have to the Sales Organizational Unit object? Because Maria has specific trustee assignments for the AcctExecs group, the rights granted to the FDR Organization object have no effect on her rights in the Sales Organizational Unit, as shown in Figure 10-38.

Figure 10-38 Maria's effective rights in Sales

	Trustee Assignments	Object: Sales	
MPinzon:	User	Object Rights	[ ]
	Group AcctExecs	Object Rights	[B]
	[Public] trustee	Object Rights	[ ]
	Container: Sales	Object Rights	[ ]
	Container: FDR	Object Rights	NO EFFECT
	Effective Rights		[B]
	User	Property Rights: All Properties	[ ]
	Group AcctExecs	Property Rights: All Properties	[CR A]
	[Public] Trustee	Property Rights: All Properties	[ ]
	Container: Sales	Property Rights: All Properties	[ ]
	Container: FDR	Property Rights: All Properties	NO EFFECT
	Effective Rights	All Properties:	[CR A]

What effective rights does Maria have to the Investments Organizational Unit object? Maria's group membership has no specific rights granted here. Therefore, her rights are those inherited from the trustee assignments granted to the FDR Organization object, as shown in Figure 10-39.

Figure 10-39 Maria's effective rights in Investments

	Trustee Assignments	Object: Investments	
MPinzon:	User	Object Rights	[ ]
	Group AcctExecs	Object Rights	[ ]
	[Public] trustee	Object Rights	[ ]
	Container: Sales	Object Rights	[ ]
	Container: FDR	Object Rights	[B]
	Effective Rights		[B]
	User	Property Rights: All Properties	[ ]
	Group AcctExecs	Property Rights: All Properties	[ ]
	[Public] Trustee	Property Rights: All Properties	[ ]
	Container: Sales	Property Rights: All Properties	[ ]
	Container: FDR	Property Rights: All Properties	[CR]
	Effective Rights	All Properties:	[CR]

In the FDR example above, Maria inherited the Property rights from the FDR container object. However, Property rights are inherited only if they are granted to all properties of the object. For example, if the FDR Organization object had been granted only the Compare and Read Property rights [CR] to object names instead of to all properties, these rights would not be inherited by containers lower in the Directory tree.

Thus, if no trustee assignment is made for a user or group in a container, the user or group will inherit the rights from the parent container(s). A user's effective rights in a container can be modified by making a new trustee assignment to either the user or to a group to which the user belongs. The rights specified in the new trustee assignment will override the inherited rights for that group or user name in the specified container, as in Maria's rights to the Sales Organizational Unit.

The Inherited Rights Filter

As we discussed above, when you make a specific trustee assignment in a container, this assignment overrides any rights that would be inherited from a parent container. You can also block rights from being inherited even if there is no specific trustee assignment made. When you do not want trustee assignments to be inherited into a lower container, NetWare enables you to prevent rights from being inherited by providing each container object and directory with what is called an **Inherited Rights Filter (IRF)**. The IRF blocks selected rights from passing into the lower container object structure. When you first create a container, the IRF enables all rights to be inherited. Thereafter, removing rights from the IRF prevents the container or directory from inheriting those rights that are no longer specified in the IRF.

The IRF filters rights that are inherited from a higher container object, but it does not affect a trustee assignment made in the current container object.

The Inherited Rights Filter (IRF) was called the Inherited Rights Mask (IRM) in NetWare 3.1x and applied only to directories and files (because there was no NDS). NetWare 4.1 extends inheritance and the IRF to the NDS Directory tree.

An IRF is created for every object (and, as you will learn below, for every directory and file) and is used to determine which rights a trustee inherits. You can picture the IRF as a series of gates—one for each right. This is illustrated in Figure 10-40.

Figure 10-40 The inherited Rights Filter for Object rights and Property rights

Object Rights IRF:

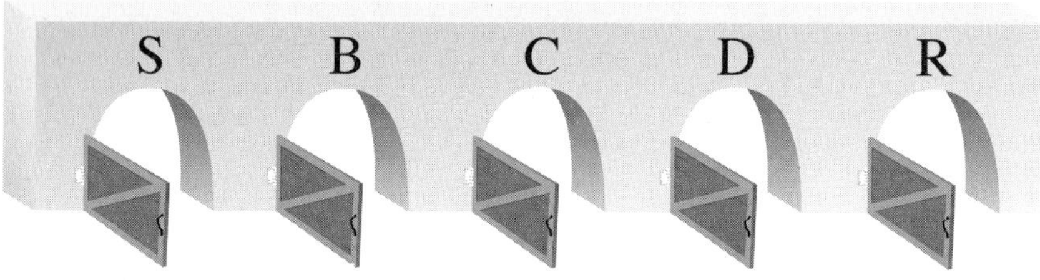

Property Rights IRF:

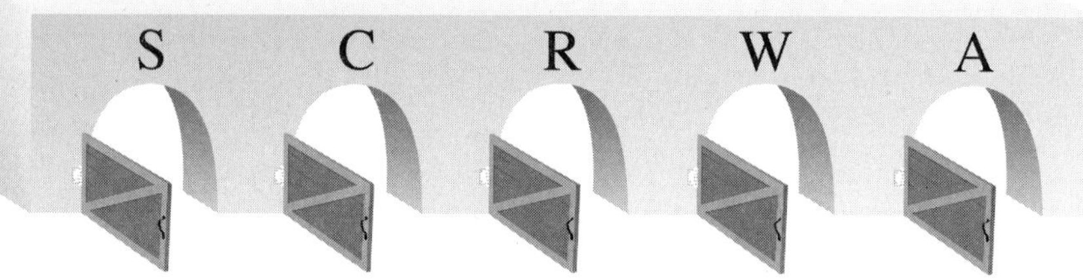

Initially, as shown in Figure 10-40, the IRF enables all rights to be inherited—all the gates are open. This can also be seen in the Inherited Rights Filter dialog box used in NetWare Administrator, which is shown in Figure 10-41.

Figure 10-41 The Inherited Rights Filter dialog box in NetWare Administrator

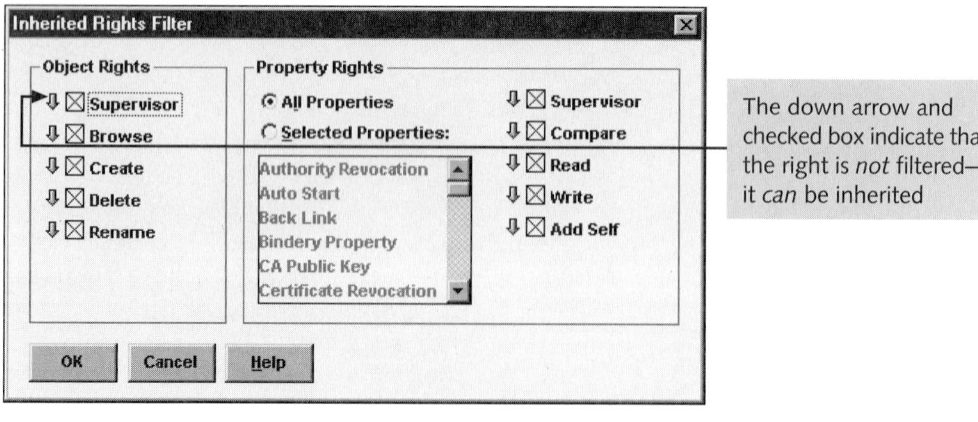

In the Inherited Rights Filter dialog box in Figure 10-41, all the check boxes are checked and a downward pointing arrow is displayed next to each check box. A checked check box with a downward pointing arrow indicates that the right is not being filtered. That is, the gate is open and the right can be inherited.

To filter a right—to prevent it from being inherited—you uncheck the appropriate check box in the Inherited Rights Filter dialog box for the object. This "closes the gate" and stops inherited rights from getting through.

For example, the Lab_Staff group at CBE Labs now has supervisory rights to the Network Organizational Unit object. The group does not want other users to be able to modify this object or its properties. Therefore, they will use the IRF for the Network object to block the Create, Delete, and Rename Object rights `[ CDR]` and the Supervisor, Write, and Add Self Property rights `[SWA]` from being inherited. When this has been done, the "gates" to NetLab will appear as shown in Figure 10-42.

Figure 10-42

The Inherited Rights Filter for Object rights and Property rights for Network

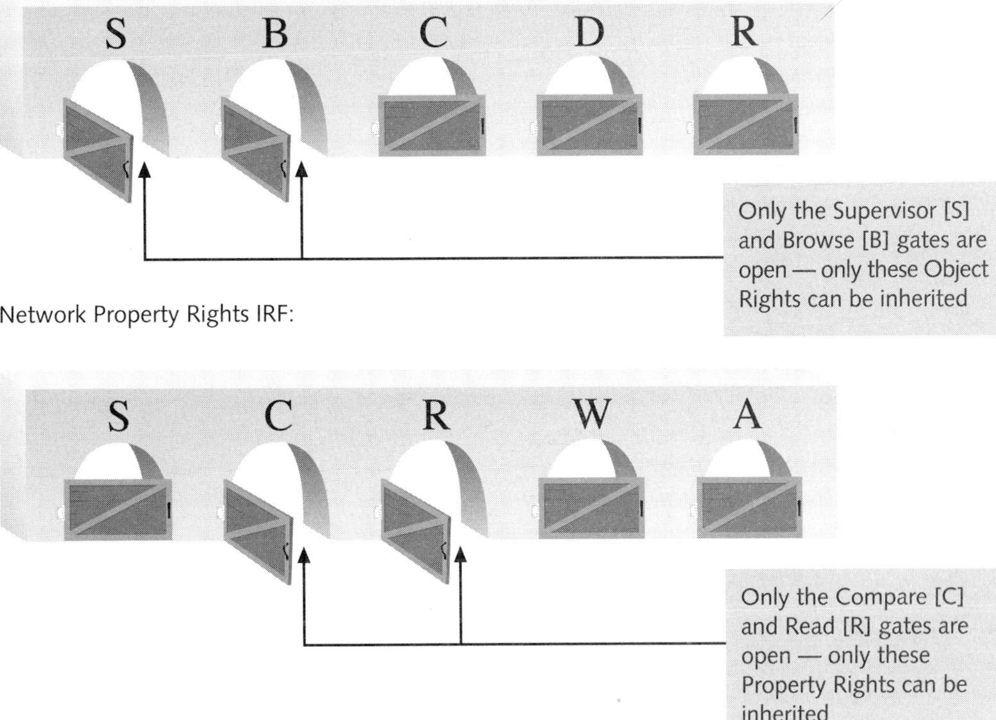
NetLab Object Rights IRF:
S
B
C
D
R
Only the Supervisor [S] and Browse [B] gates are open — only these Object Rights can be inherited
Network Property Rights IRF:
S
C
R
W
A
Only the Compare [C] and Read [R] gates are open — only these Property Rights can be inherited

The IRF for an object is accessed through the Trustees of *ObjectName* dialog box.

To modify the Inherited Rights Filter for Object and Property trustee rights of an object, you follow these steps:

- Click the object name or icon to select it. Then click Object on the menu bar, and click Trustees of this Object to display the Trustee of Object dialog box.

  or

- Right-click the object name or icon to select it and display the shortcut menu. Then click Trustees of this Object to display the Trustee of Object dialog box.

then

- Click the Inherited Rights Filter button.

then

- Use the settings controls in the Inherited Rights Filter dialog box to manage inherited Object and Property rights.

To set the Inherited Rights Filter for the Network Organizational Unit object, follow these steps:

1. If NetWare Administrator is not open, launch it.
2. Click the **Network Organizational Unit** object to select it; then click **Object** in the menu bar.
3. Click **Trustees of this Object** on the Object menu. The Trustees of Network dialog box is displayed, as shown in Figure 10-43.

Figure 10-43 Trustees of Network dialog box

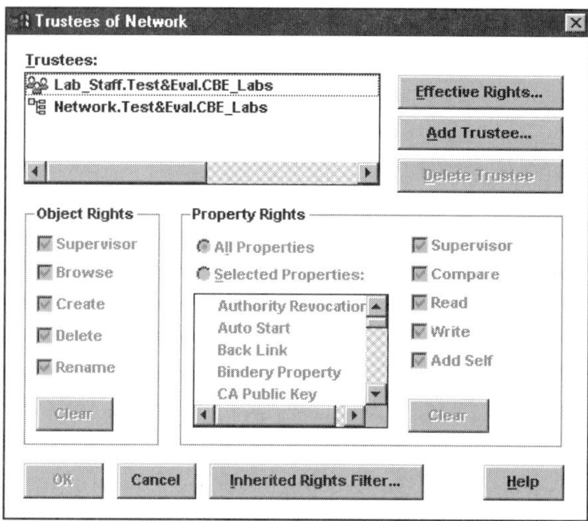
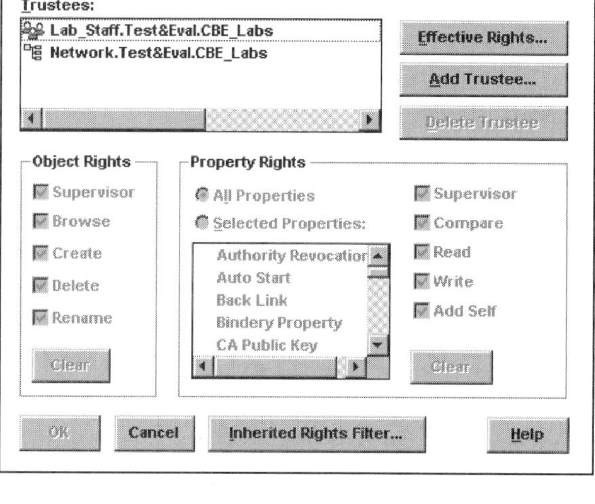

4. Click the **Inherited Rights Filter** button to display the Inherited Rights Filter dialog box.
5. In the Inherited Rights Filter dialog box, click the **Create [C]**, **Delete [D]**, **and Rename [R] Object rights** check boxes to deselect them. Then click the **Supervisor [S]**, **Write [W]**, and **Add Self [A] Property rights** check boxes to deselect them. The Inherited Rights Filter dialog box now appears as shown in Figure 10-44.

Figure 10-44 The completed Inherited Rights Filter dialog box for NetLab

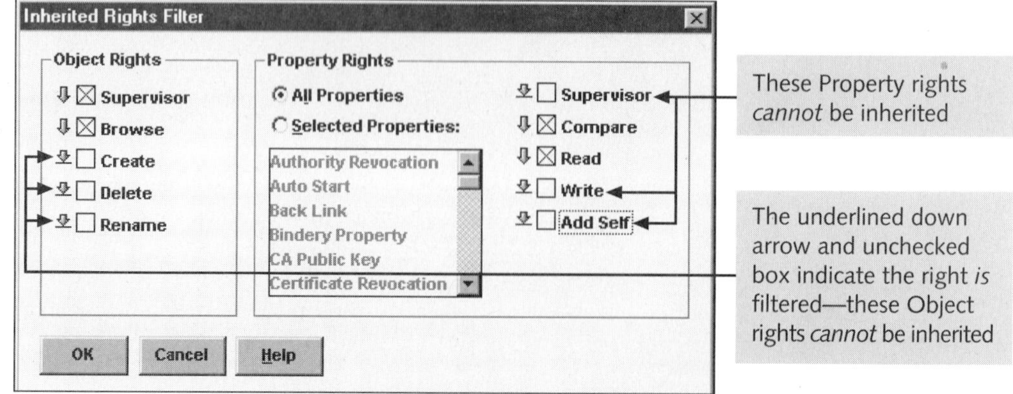

Notice in Figure 10-44 that each downward pointing arrow has been replaced with an arrow with a line under it for all rights that are being filtered. This symbol and the unchecked check box indicate a filtered or blocked ability to inherit a trustee right.

6. Click **OK** to return to the Trustees of Network dialog box.
7. Click **OK**.

The Inherited Rights Filter only reduces rights and never adds to them.

When you are calculating a trustee's effective rights for an object, you must subtract any Inherited Rights Filtered by the object's IRF. Remember, however, that the IRF blocks only inherited rights, not what rights can be directly granted to an object. Moreover, remember that if trustee rights are directly granted to an object, this grant itself stops all inherited rights so that the IRF has no effect in this case. The IRF blocks only inherited rights when such rights can, in fact, be inherited.

Now you will consider an example at FDR Investments.

EXAMPLE 10-7: Inherited rights at F. D. Roosevelt Investments Inc.

Maria Pinzon, the Administrative Assistant for Sales, is a member of the AcctExecs group but has no trustee assignments granted directly to her. AcctExecs has the Browse Object right [B] and the Compare, Read, and Add Self Property rights [CR A] for all properties to the Sales Organizational Unit only, not to other branches of the Directory tree. There are no rights granted to the [Public] trustee.

The FDR network manager has granted the Browse Object right [B] and the Compare and Read Property rights [CR] for all properties to the FDR Organization object. However, because the Investments group has decided that it doesn't want users reading property values for objects in the Investments organizational unit, the network manager has also implemented an IRF for the Investment Organizational Unit object that blocks all Property rights except Supervisor [CRWA].

What effective rights does Maria have to the Investments Organizational Unit object? Maria's group membership has no specific rights granted here. Therefore, her rights are those inherited from the trustee assignments granted to the FDR Organization object, less those blocked by the IRF, as shown in Figure 10-45.

	Trustee Assignments	Object:	Investments
MPinzon:	User	Object Rights	[ ]
	Group AcctExecs	Object Rights	[ ]
	[Public] trustee	Object Rights	[ ]
	Container: Investments	Object Rights	[ ]
	Container: FDR	Object Rights	[B]
LESS	IRF: Investments	Object Rights	[ ]
	Effective RIghts		[B]
	User	Property Rights: All Properties	[ ]
	Group AcctExecs	Property Rights: All Properties	[ ]
	[Public] Trustee	Property Rights: All Properties	[ ]
	Container: Investments	Property Rights: All Properties	[ ]
	Container: FDR	Property Rights: All Properties	[CR]
LESS	IRF: Investments	Property Rights: All Properties	[CRWA]
	Effective Rights	All Properties:	[ ]

Figure 10-45

Maria's effective rights in Investments

In the FDR example above, Maria inherited the Compare and Read Property rights [CR] to Investments from the FDR container object. However, the IRF blocks these Property rights, so Maria has no Property rights to Investments.

The Supervisor right needs to be handled carefully in IRFs. Although the Supervisor right cannot be removed from an IRF for a directory or file (as you'll learn below), it can be removed from an IRF for an object. This makes it possible to split administrative duties throughout the Directory tree. For example, the CBE Labs organization in Great Britain could be managed by a different person than the CBE Labs organization in the United States. Blocking the Supervisor right appropriately using IRFs would ensure that each of the two network administrators would have control of only his or her portion of the CBE Labs Directory tree.

There is a potential problem here, however. If no trustee was assigned Supervisor rights to an object and then the object's IRF blocked inherited Supervisor rights, then the object would be cut off from anyone's control. To help prevent this, Novell has designed the NetWare 4.1 utilities so that you cannot block the Supervisor Object right unless some object has been granted specific Supervisor rights to the object.

Unfortunately, the Supervisor right can be assigned to any object, including the object that will have the IRF set. For example, you could assign the Supervisor Object right to the Test&Eval Organizational Unit object in the CBE Labs Directory tree and then block the Supervisor right in the Test&Eval Organizational Unit object's IRF. Because the Supervisor object right had been assigned, this would be permitted. But doing this would cut off the Test&Eval branch of the tree because there is no way for a user to access the granted Supervisor right—you can't log in as an Organizational Unit, only as a User. Thus you must be very careful to assign an object's Supervisor Object right to a user before using the object IRF.

In general, IRFs should be used only when absolutely necessary, and a network administrator can usually control access to network resources through direct assignments of trustee rights without using IRFs.

Managing Directory Rights and File Rights

Directory rights and File rights control access to the network file system resources. The same concepts and techniques that you learned for trustee assignments of Object rights and files can be applied to Directory rights and File rights. In fact many of these concepts and techniques, such as trustee assignments, inherited rights, effective rights, and blocking inherited rights were originally written for Directory and File rights in earlier versions of NetWare. With the introduction of NDS in NetWare 4.0, it became necessary to extend these ideas to the Directory tree and its objects.

Trustee assignments for directories and files can be made to the same objects that can have trustee assignments for objects and properties. When you are assigning Directory and File rights, the assignment is made using either the user's User object or the directory or file object dialog box. You can also use the NetWare Client 32 extensions to the Windows 95 Explorer to manage Directory and File rights.

Granting trustee rights to a directory automatically grants the same rights to all files in that directory. To change the trustee rights for a file within that directory, you must change the rights assigned for that specific file.

Although granting the Supervisor Directory or File right [S] automatically grants all Directory and File rights, many network administrators also specifically grant all the other rights as well when granting the Supervisor right [S].

Rights Assigned to the User

Just as with Object and Property rights, the simplest and most straightforward way for a user to gain effective rights is to be granted a trustee assignment as a user. A simple example follows; then you'll see how trustee assignments are actually made using the CBE Laboratories example.

EXAMPLE 10-8: Assigning user directory and file Trustee rights at F. D. Roosevelt Investments Inc.

The Volume Directory Structure Design Form for the FDR_SERVER01_DATA volume is shown in Figure 10-46.

Figure 10-46 The FDR_SERVER01_DATA: volume

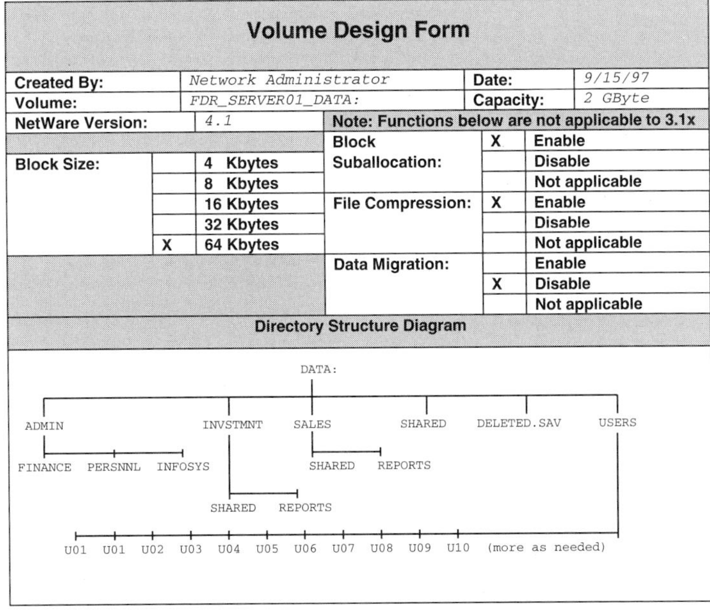

Volume Design Form

Created By:	Network Administrator	Date:	9/15/97
Volume:	FDR_SERVER01_DATA:	Capacity:	2 GByte
NetWare Version:	4.1	Note: Functions below are not applicable to 3.1x	

Block Size:					
			Block Suballocation:	X	Enable
Block Size:		4 Kbytes			Disable
		8 Kbytes			Not applicable
		16 Kbytes	File Compression:	X	Enable
		32 Kbytes			Disable
	X	64 Kbytes			Not applicable
			Data Migration:		Enable
				X	Disable
					Not applicable

Directory Structure Diagram

Paul Drake, the lead account executive at FDR, needs the ability to manage the SALES directory and its subdirectories on the FDR_SERVER01_DATA volume. He will be granted all rights—including the Supervisor right—to the SALES directory. When the Supervisor right is granted in the directory, it gives Paul the Supervisor right to all files in that directory, as shown in Figure 10-47.

Figure 10-47 Paul's effective rights in SALES

	Trustee Assignments		Object: SALES
PDrake:	User	Directory Rights	[S]
	Effective Rights		[SRWCEMFA]
	User	File Rights:	[S] [may be modified for each file as needed]
	Effective Rights		[SRWCEMFA]

Now you'll consider another example: the implementation of Directory and File rights at CBE Laboratories. Georgia Burns will also be given all rights (Supervisor `[S]` and all others) so that she can administer the SARATOGA_SYS and SARATOGA_DATA volumes. For reference, the directory structure of SARATOGA_SYS is shown in Figure 10-48, and the directory structure of SARATOGA_DATA is shown in Figure 10-49.

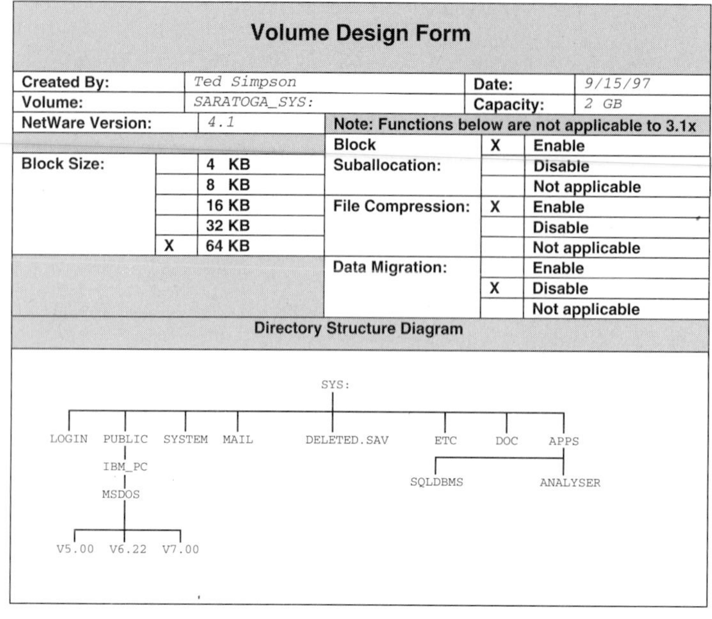

Volume Design Form

Created By:	Ted Simpson	Date:	9/15/97
Volume:	SARATOGA_SYS:	Capacity:	2 GB
NetWare Version:	4.1	Note: Functions below are not applicable to 3.1x	

Block Size:					
		4 KB	Block Suballocation:	X	Enable
		8 KB			Disable
		16 KB			Not applicable
		32 KB	File Compression:	X	Enable
	X	64 KB			Disable
					Not applicable
			Data Migration:		Enable
				X	Disable
					Not applicable

Directory Structure Diagram

Figure 10-48 Volume Directory Structure Design Form for the SARATOGA_SYS volume

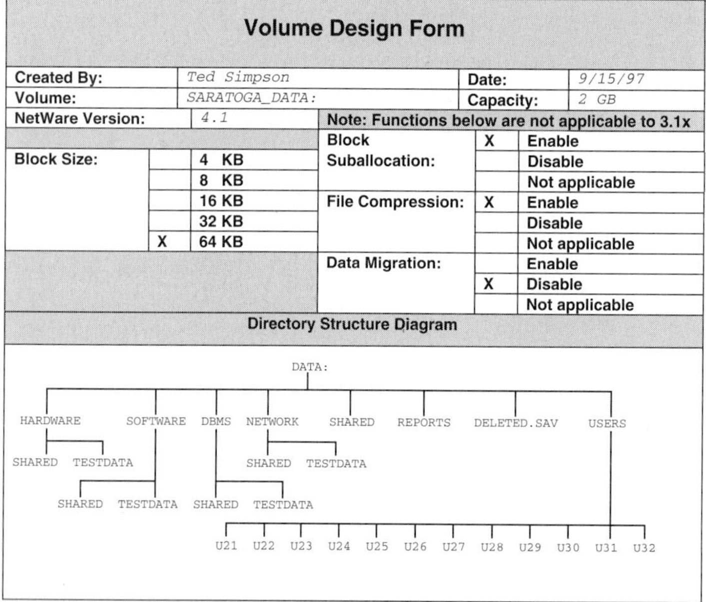

Volume Design Form

Created By:	Ted Simpson	Date:	9/15/97
Volume:	SARATOGA_DATA:	Capacity:	2 GB
NetWare Version:	4.1	Note: Functions below are not applicable to 3.1x	

Block Size:					
		4 KB	Block Suballocation:	X	Enable
		8 KB			Disable
		16 KB			Not applicable
		32 KB	File Compression:	X	Enable
	X	64 KB			Disable
					Not applicable
			Data Migration:		Enable
				X	Disable
					Not applicable

Directory Structure Diagram

Figure 10-49 Volume Directory Structure Design Form for the SARAGTOGA_DATA volume

Assigning Trustee rights to a directory or file from a Trustee object. You begin by making the trustee assignment to Georgia Burns. As with Object rights, you're assigning trustee rights from the object that is being granted the trustee assignment. This varies from the previous procedure, however, because you do this from the object's object dialog box.

To grant directory and file trustee rights to an object from a Trustee object itself, you follow these steps:

- Click the User object; then press [Enter].

  or

  Click the User object, click Object on the menu bar, and then click Details.

  or

  Right-click the User object; then click Details on the QuickMenu.

then

- Switch to the Rights to Files and Directories page.
- Click the Find button to open the Search Context dialog box and search the Directory tree for existing trustee assignments in the desired context.
- Click the Add button and use the Select Object dialog box to select the directory or file for which the trustee rights are being granted.
- Click the appropriate check boxes in the Rights section to select or deselect the rights to be granted.
- Click OK.

When the trustee assignment is made from the User object (or other Trustee object), NetWare can first search the Directory tree to find and list the directories and files for which the user has rights assigned. The context for this search—all of the tree or a branch of it—is specified as part of the search. Searching the Directory tree takes time, so it is faster to limit the area of the tree that needs to be evaluated. Normally, you should limit the search context to only the part of the Directory tree that includes the objects for which you are granting trustee rights to the user. This step is not required for adding a new trustee assignment, but it is helpful to see what assignments have already been made so that you aren't inadvertently duplicating a previous assignment.

Now you will see how this method could be used to give Georgia Burns her trustee assignment to the root of the SARATOGA_DATA volume, SARATOGA_DATA:\.

To grant Georgia Burns Trustee rights to the SARATOGA_DATA:\ directory, follow these steps:

1. If NetWare Administrator is not open, launch it.
2. Right-click the **GBurns User** object, then click **Details**. The User: GBurns object dialog box is displayed.
3. Use the down scroll arrow to scroll through the page buttons until the **Rights to Files and Directories** button appears.
4. Click the **Rights to Files and Directories** button in the button bar. The Rights to Files and Directories page is displayed, as shown in Figure 10-50.

Figure 10-50 Rights to Files and Directories page

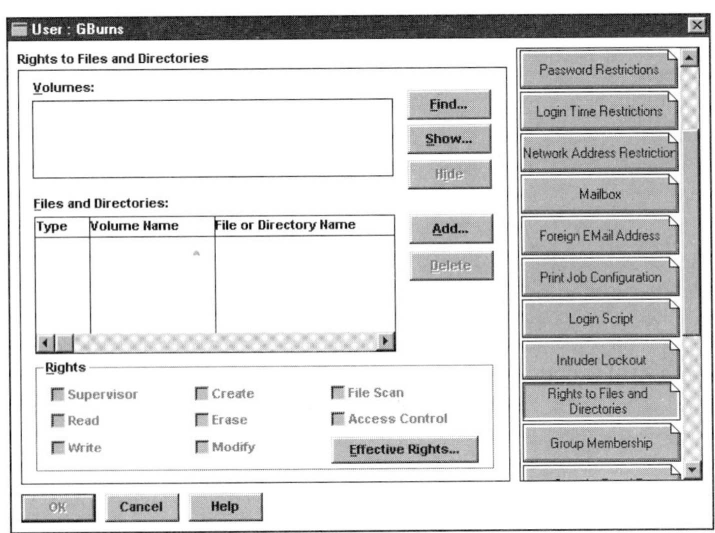

5. Click the **Find** button. The Search Context dialog box appears. Click the **Select Object** button to display the Select Object dialog box. In the Select Object dialog box, select the **Test&Eval Organizational Unit** object; then click **OK**.
6. The Search Context dialog box is displayed with Test&Eval.CBE_Labs in the Context to Begin Search text box. Click the **Search Entire Subtree** check box to select it, then click **OK**. A search is done for directory and file trustee assignments for Georgia Burns, and these are then displayed in the Volumes list and Files and Directories list. As shown in Figure 10-51, the only existing trustee assignment for GBurns is to her home directory on the SARATOGA_DATA volume.

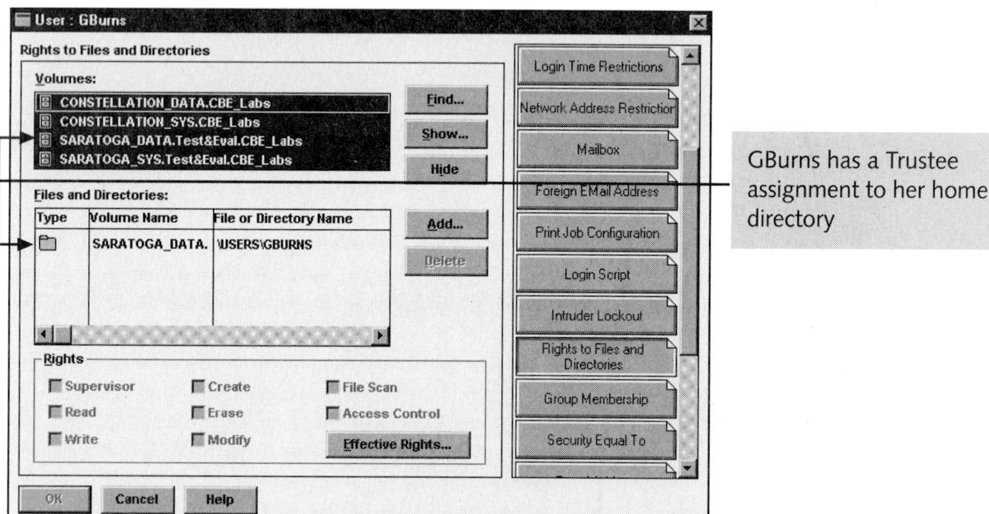

Figure 10-51 User:GBurns dialog box showing current directory and File Trustee rights

7. Click the **Add** button to display the Select Object dialog box.
8. Select the **SARATOGA_DATA Volume** object; then click **OK**. GBurns is assigned default trustee rights of Read `[R]` and File Scan `[F]` to the root of the SARATOGA_DATA:\ directory.
9. Click all the unchecked check boxes in the Rights section to assign GBurns all Trustee rights to this directory. The User:GBurns object dialog box appears as shown in Figure 10-52.

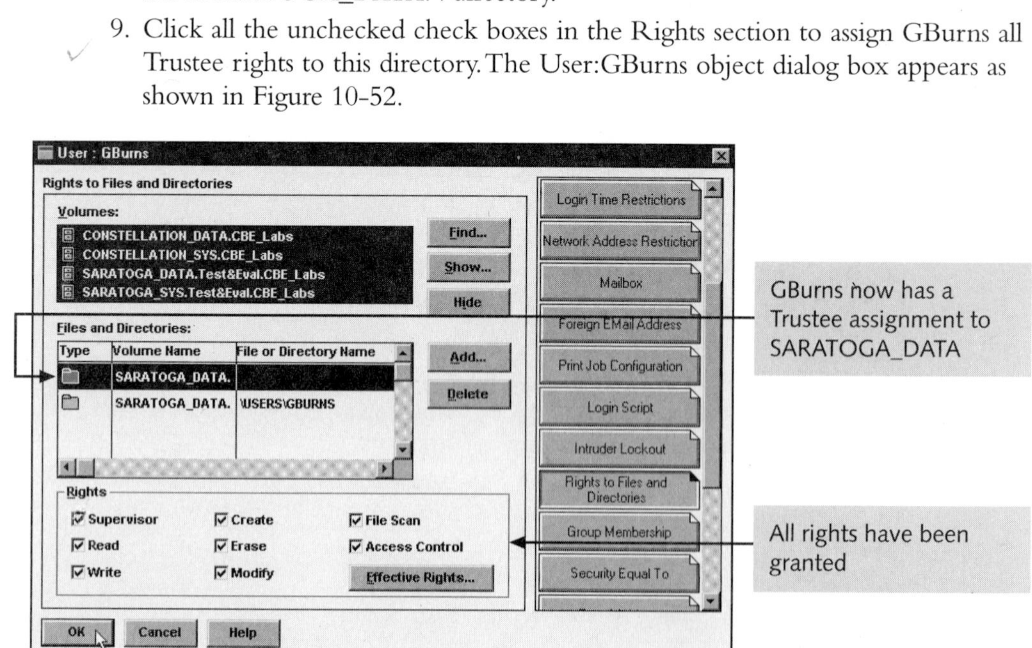

Figure 10-52 GBurns assigned all Trustee rights to the SARATOGA_DATA:\ directory

10. Click **OK**.

Assigning trustee rights to a directory or file from Windows 95 Explorer. Novell's Client 32 network client software includes extensions to the Windows 95 Explorer program that enable you to manage most Directory and File rights from Explorer. There is, however, one important exception to this capability: you cannot assign the Supervisor right [S] to a directory or file through Explorer.

To grant directory and file trustee rights to an object from Windows 95 Explorer, you follow these steps:

- Launch Explorer.
- If necessary, create a drive mapping to the volume that contains the directory or file.
- Expand the branch of the Explorer tree that contains the drive mapping until the directory or file is displayed.
- Click the directory or file to select it, click File, and then click Properties to display the *ObjectName* Properties dialog box.
- Click the NetWare Rights tab to display the NetWare rights page.
- Expand the displayed NDS Directory tree until the object for which the trustee assignment is to be made is displayed.
- Click the Add button.
- In the Trustees list, click the object name to select it.
- Click the check boxes to assign the appropriate rights.
- Click OK.

The Client 32 extensions to Explorer enable the NDS directory tree to be fully displayed with all the proper icons. Being able to Browse the Directory tree easily in Explorer makes this method quickly accessible when you're using Explorer to check directory structure and contents. The inability to assign the Supervisor right [S], however, somewhat limits the usefulness of this method—you can use it effectively only when you're not concerned about granting the Supervisor right [S].

You will look at one example: you'll again show how Georgia Burns would have her rights to the SARATOGA_DATA:\ directory assigned. This is exactly the same assignment you've already made—we're simply illustrating a third way to do it.

To grant Georgia Burns Trustee rights to the SARATOGA_DATA:\ directory, follow these steps:

1. Launch Explorer.
2. Expand the Network Neighborhood branch of the Cbelabs tree until the SARATOGA_DATA volume is visible. Click the **SARATOGA_DATA** icon to select it, click **File**, and then click **Properties**, as shown in Figure 10-53.

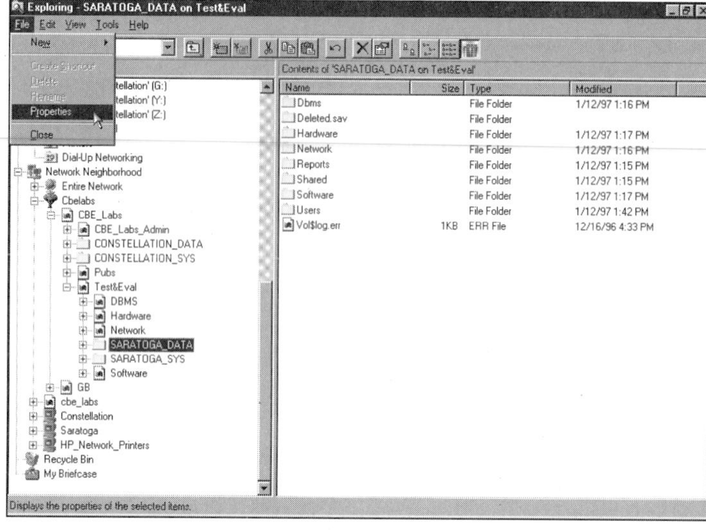

Figure 10-53 The File\Properties command

The SARATOGA_DATA on Test&Eval Properties dialog box is displayed, as shown in Figure 10-54.

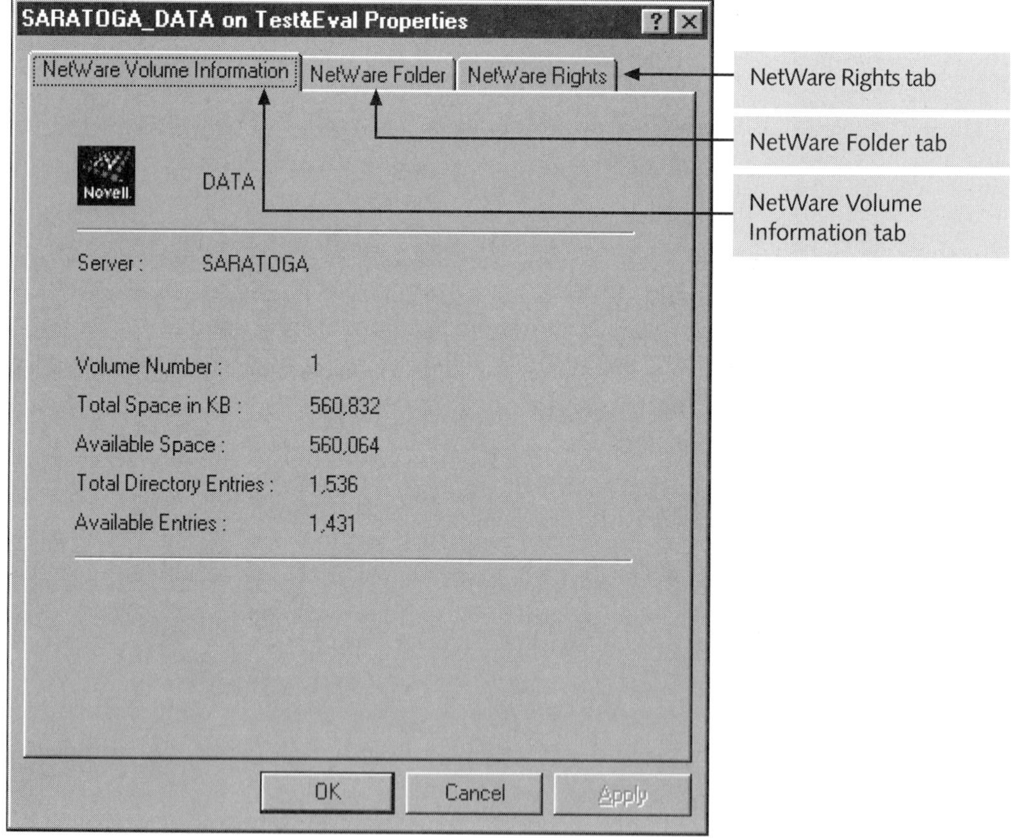

Figure 10-54 The SARATOGA_DATA on Test&Eval Properties dialog box

Notice that the NetWare Volume Information page is initially displayed, showing volume statistics such as Total Space and Available Space on the volume.

3. Click the **NetWare Rights** tab. The NetWare Rights page is displayed as shown in Figure 10-55.

Figure 10-55

The NetWare Rights page

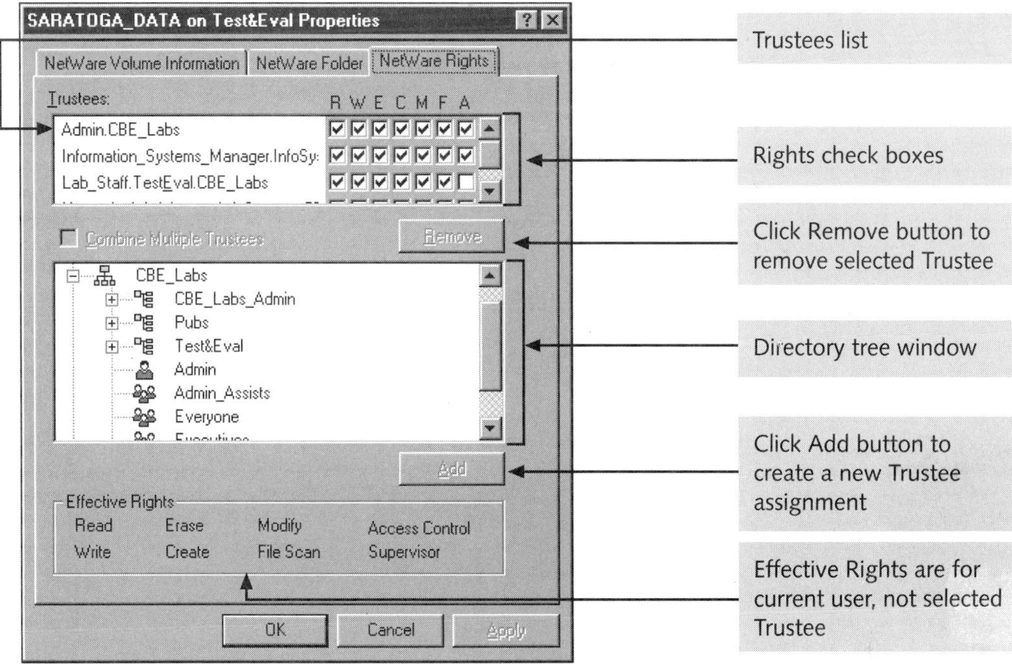

This page includes a Trustees list, a window displaying the Directory tree, and a list of the effective rights of the current user. Note that the effective rights are for the current user, not for a trustee. In this case, the current user is DAuer, the CBE Labs network administrator; because he has security equivalent to the Admin user, he has all rights including supervisor.

4. In the Directory tree window, expand the Directory tree until the GBurns User object is visible, then click the **GBurns User** object to select it, as shown in Figure 10-56.

Figure 10-56

Selecting the GBurns User object

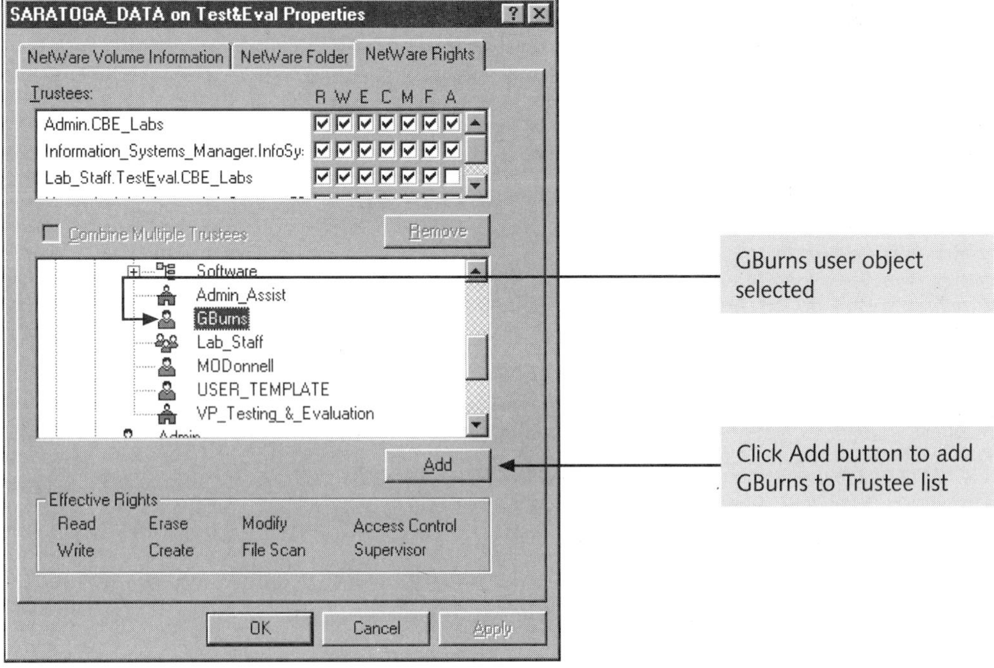

5. Click the **Add** button. GBurns.Test&Eval.CBE_Labs is added to the Trustees list, with default rights of Read `[R]` and File Scan `[F]`.

6. Click **GBurns.Test&Eval.CBE_LABS** in the trustees list to select GBurns. Click the check boxes for all the unselected rights to grant them to GBurns. Note that there is no check box for the Supervisor right `[S]`, which means that the Supervisor right `[S]` cannot be granted using this method. The dialog box now appears as shown in Figure 10-57.
7. Click **OK**.

Rights Assigned to Groups, Profiles, and Organizational Roles

Directory and file fights can also be assigned to groups and organizational roles, just as Object and Property rights were assigned. Additionally, you can grant trustee rights to Profile objects. You have already learned that the Profile object is similar to the Group object, with the particular advantage of being able to have its own login script. The ability to also assign Directory and File rights to a Profile object gives the network administrator a convenient method of assigning Directory and File rights to those who use the Profile objects login script.

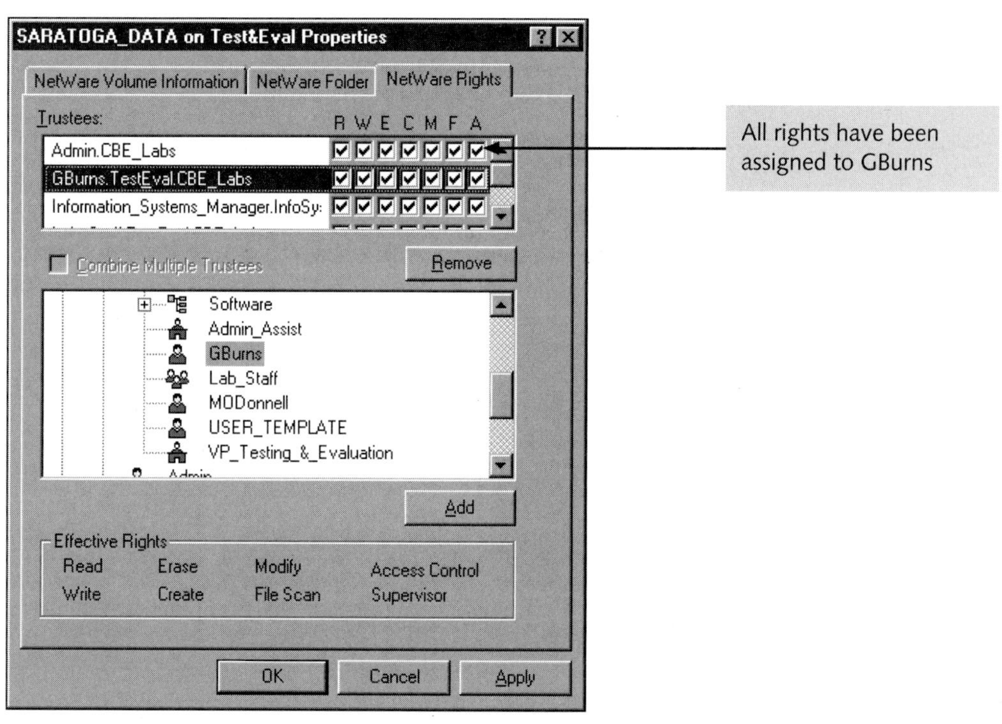

Figure 10-57 Granting Trustee rights to GBurns

The same methods of assigning Directory and File rights to users discussed above are used for granting rights to groups and organizational roles. When you decide whether to assign rights to an organizational role, a group, or individual users, the same advantages still apply: it is easier to administer rights to organizational roles and groups. By granting rights to organizational roles and groups, users automatically get appropriate rights if they need them, and removing a user from a group or organizational role effectively removes the user's rights.

For example, Georgia Burns has decided to give the Lab_Staff group Read and File Scan rights `[ R F ]` to the SARATOGA_DATA volume. This is the volume where the Lab staff keeps its data, and these rights will enable everyone to see what files exist and to open and read them. However, it will not let the files be changed, deleted, or renamed, so these additional rights will have to be granted to the appropriate users. One case is the

Lab_Staff group, which also needs such rights to the NETWORK directory (and its subdirectories). The Lab_Staff group will therefore be granted Write, Create, Erase, and Modify rights [WCEM] to the NETWORK directory. Because trustee assignments made in one directory are inherited by (flow down to) subdirectories, the Network group will inherit the same rights in the NETWORK\SHARED, NETWORK\TESTDATA, and NETWORK\REPORTS subdirectories.

Rights Assigned to Container Objects and Security Equivalence

You can assign Directory and File rights to container objects just as you assigned Object and Property rights. Again, the same methods that were used for assigning Directory and File rights to individual users are used for granting rights to container objects.

Security equivalencies also work the same. If Object A is security equivalent to Object B, Object A is granted all the Directory and File rights that Object B has been granted. For example, because the CBE Labs Information Systems Manager Ted Simpson is security equivalent to the Admin user, Ted Simpson effectively has the same Directory and File rights as the Admin user. This gives Ted all rights including the Supervisor right [S] to all directories and files on all volumes of all CBE Labs servers.

Inherited Rights and the Inherited Rights Filter

Inherited rights work almost the same for Directory and File rights as they do for Object and Property rights, but with one important exception: the IRF cannot block the Supervisor right [S] for Directory and File rights. The IRFs for Directory and File rights can be visualized as shown in Figure 10-58.

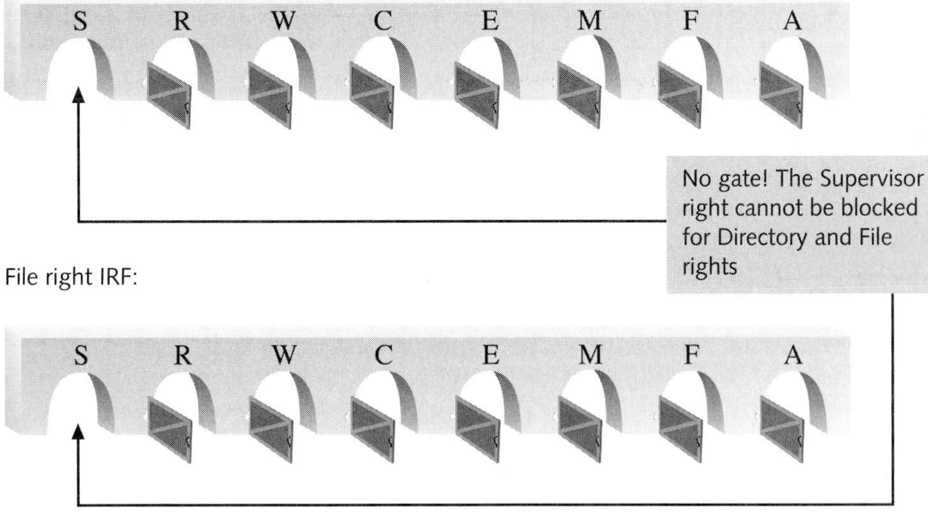

Figure 10-58 The Inherited Rights Filter for Directory rights and File rights

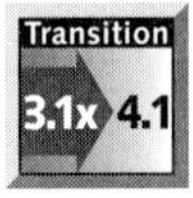

The Inherited Rights Filter (IRF) for directories and files in NetWare 4.1 works exactly the same as the Inherited Rights Mask (IRM) in NetWare 3.1x. The inability to block the Supervisor Directory and File right [S] is carried over from NetWare 3.1x.

The IRF for a directory or file is accessed through the *ObjectName* object dialog box.

To use NetWare Administrator modify the Inherited Rights Filter for Directory or File trustee rights of a directory or file, you follow these steps:

- Click the directory or filename or icon to select it. Then click Object on the menu bar, and click Details to display the *ObjectName* object dialog box.

  or

- Double-click the directory or filename or icon to select it and display the *ObjectName* object dialog box.

  or

- Right-click the object name or icon to select it and display the shortcut menu, then click Details to display the *ObjectName* object dialog box.

  then

- Click the Trustees of this Directory or Trustees of this File button.
- On the Trustees of this Directory or Trustees of this File page, use check boxes in the Inheritance Filter area to set the IRF. A checked box enables the right to be inherited; an unchecked box blocks inheritance.
- Click OK.

Notice that the method of setting the IRF for directories and files is the same as the method of setting the IRF for objects and properties. The IRF default is all check boxes checked, which enables all rights to be inherited, and you must uncheck a check box to block the inheritance of the right. The only difference is the directory and file Supervisor right `[S]`, which cannot be blocked.

For example, the Lab_Staff group at CBE Labs wants only those users who have specifically been granted rights to the SARATOGA_DATA:NETWORK directory to be able to use that directory. You will create the necessary IRF to do this.

To set the Inherited Rights Filter for the SARATOGA_DATA:NETWORK directory, follow these steps:

1. If NetWare Administrator is not open, launch it.
2. Expand the Directory tree until the directories on the SARATOGA_DATA volume are visible. Click the **NETWORK Directory** object to select it; then click **Object** in the menu bar, then click **Details**.
3. Click the **Trustees of this Directory** button. The Trustees of this Directory page is displayed, as shown in Figure 10-59.

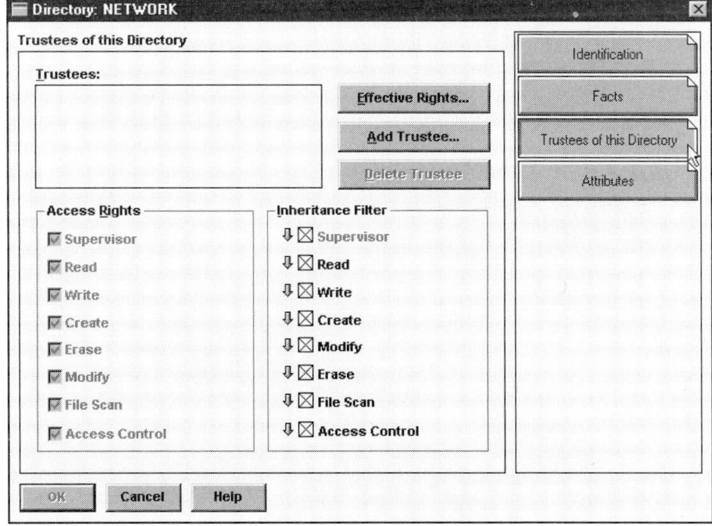

Figure 10-59

The Trustees of this Directory page

4. Looking at the Inheritance Filter area, notice that all the check boxes are checked. The Supervisor right [S] check box is checked and grayed-out, indicating that you cannot change the setting for this right.
5. Click each of the other check boxes to block those rights from being inherited, as shown in Figure 10-60.

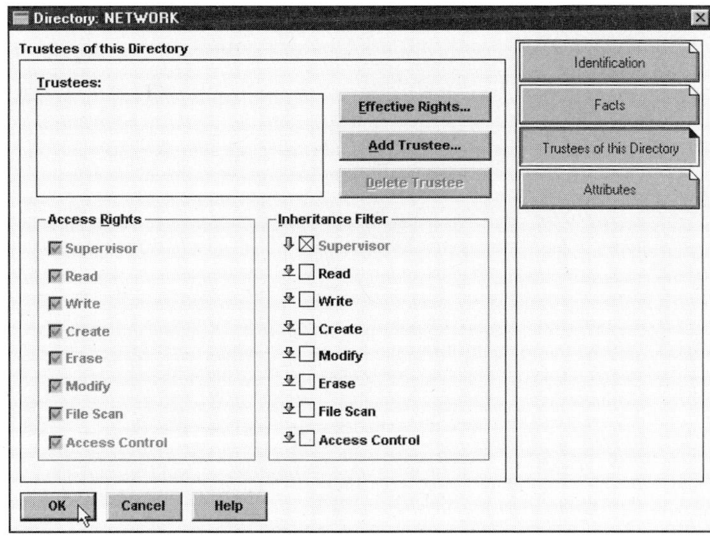

Figure 10-60

The completed Trustees of this Directory page

Notice that in Figure 10-60 each downward pointing arrow has been replaced with an arrow with a line under it for all rights that are being filtered. This symbol and the unchecked check box indicate a filtered or blocked ability to inherit a trustee right.

6. Click **OK**.

Just as with Object and Property rights, a user's effective rights are a combination of his or her assigned rights and inherited rights. Again, it is always a *user* who actually uses trustee rights. You can calculate a user's effective Directory or File rights to a particular directory or file as follows:

1. Combine the assigned rights from trustee assignments made to:
   - The *user*

- The user as a member of a *group*
- The user as a member of a *profile*
- The user as an occupant of an *organizational role*
- The user as an occupant of a *container object*
- The user as security equivalent to other objects

If the user has assigned rights granted to the directory or file, the assigned rights take precedence over inherited rights, inherited rights do not apply, and the IRF has no effect. This combination of rights is the user's effective rights.

2. If the user has no assigned rights granted, the user's trustee assignments granted in a parent container object or directory are inherited. The inherited rights must be checked against the IRF for the directory or file. The inherited rights not blocked by the IRF are the user's effective rights.

EXAMPLE 10-9: Inherited Directory Rights at F. D. Roosevelt Investments Inc.

Maria Pinzon, the Administrative Assistant for Sales, is a member of the AcctExecs group, but has no trustee assignments granted directly to her. AcctExecs has the Read, Write, Create, Erase, Modify, and File Scan Directory rights `[ RWCEMF ]` to the FDR_SERVER01/DATA:SALES directory. There is an EVERYONE group at FDR, and Maria, along with everyone else, is a member. The EVERYONE group has Read and File Scan rights `[ R    F ]` to the FDR_SERVER01/DATA:\ (the [Root] directory on the DATA volume). There are no directory or File rights granted to the [Public] trustee. There are no other trustee assignments that affect Maria directly, but IRFs may limit her inherited rights.

What effective rights does Maria have to the FDR_SERVER01/DATA:SALES directory? Because Maria has specific trustee assignments to SALES from the AcctExecs group, the rights granted to the EVERYONE group to the [Root] directory have no effect on her rights in the SALES directory, as shown in Figure 10-61.

Figure 10-61 Maria's effective rights in SALES

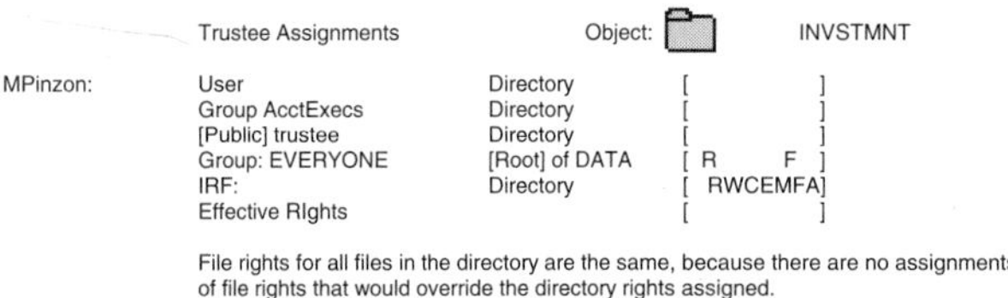

What effective rights does Maria have to the FDR_SERVER01/DATA:ADMIN directory? Because Maria has no specific trustee assignments to ADMIN from the AcctExecs group, the rights granted to the EVERYONE group to the [Root] directory will be inherited subject to an IRF. There is no IRF for ADMIN. Maria's rights in the ADMIN directory are shown in Figure 10-62.

Figure 10-62 Maria's effective rights in ADMIN

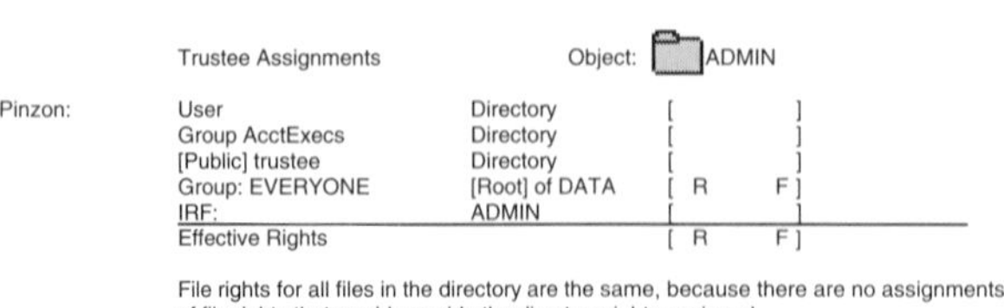

What effective rights does Maria have to the FDR_SERVER01/DATA:INVSTMNT directory? Because Maria has no specific trustee assignments to INVSTMNT from the AcctExecs group, the rights granted to the EVERYONE group to the [Root] directory will again be inherited subject to an IRF. INVSTMNT does have an IRF, which blocks the Read, Write, Create, Erase, Modify, File Scan, and Access Control Directory rights `[RWCEMFA]`. Maria's rights in the INVSTMNT directory are shown in Figure 10-63.

Figure 10-63 Maria's effective rights in INVSTMNT

	Trustee Assignments		Object: INVSTMNT
MPinzon:	User	Directory	[ ]
	Group AcctExecs	Directory	[ ]
	[Public] trustee	Directory	[ ]
	Group: EVERYONE	[Root] of DATA	[R F]
	IRF:	Directory	[RWCEMFA]
	Effective RIghts		[ ]

File rights for all files in the directory are the same, because there are no assignments of file rights that would override the directory rights assigned.

In this case, the IRF completely blocks any rights Maria would have had in the INVSTMNT directory. She cannot see or use this directory, any of its subdirectories, or any of the files in any of those directories.

PLANNING DIRECTORY TREE AND FILE SYSTEM SECURITY

Computing effective rights can be a complex task when multiple container, profile group, and user trustee assignments are involved. Good strategies in planning Directory tree and file system security include using as few trustee assignments as possible and keeping the use of IRFs to a minimum. If you need to use an IRF, it might indicate that you should rethink your assignment of rights, the organization of your Directory tree, or the directories in your file system. Imagine, for example, that you are a network administrator for a company and that your predecessor created a directory structure in which word processing document files were stored in subdirectories of the SOFTWARE\WP directory, as shown in Figure 10-64.

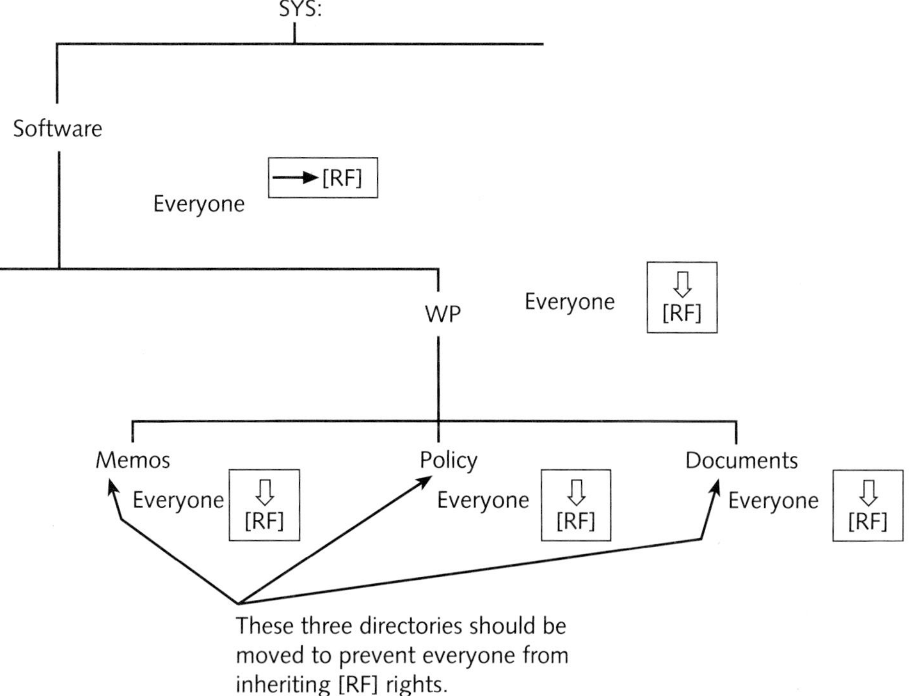

Figure 10-64 The directory structure

Your predecessor also created a Group object named EVERYONE (all users are added to the group) and made the EVERYONE group a trustee of SOFTWARE with `[ R F ]` rights. This means that all users inherit `[ R F ]` rights to the document subdirectories. This creates a security problem because all users have the ability to read any document. To eliminate this problem, you set the IRFs of the document subdirectories to block the inherited rights and then grant appropriate users the necessary trustee assignments to these subdirectories. Although this solution will work, it does not address the real problem: Data directories and software directories should be in separate locations. The best solution in this example is to move the document subdirectories to another location in the file system.

To help keep the trustee assignment security as simple and effective as possible, a network administrator should follow two simple strategies when planning trustee assignment security:

1. Plan rights from the top down.
2. Plan trustee assignments in this order: groups, profiles, organizational roles, and container objects.

Remember that rights are inherited from parent container objects into subordinate container objects and from parent directories into subordinate subdirectories and files.

Planning the NDS Directory tree and the network directory structure from the top down takes advantage of this principle. The following guidelines can help you implement a top-down strategy:

- Place at the top of your directory structure directories that are least frequently accessed. Place the most frequently accessed directories at the bottom.
- Start planning rights at the department or highest level directory and work down to the subdirectories and files within it.
- Grant only the rights needed based on the needs of the user or group at any given level of the Directory tree or the file system.
- Use the inheritance principle. Use IRFs to protect objects and directories against trustees inheriting unwanted rights, but keep IRFs to an absolute minimum.
- Create and use an EVERYONE group.

When planning trustee assignments, start by assigning rights to the groups and profiles that have the most users. It is often helpful to create an EVERYONE group and assign common trustee rights for all users to this group. Next assign rights to other groups and profiles. It helps to think of profiles as simply another type of group—a group created specifically to enable assignment of resources on login via the login script. This means that profiles often group together exactly those users who can benefit from common directory and file trustee assignments. Organizational roles can also be thought of as a type of group, albeit often a group that has only one member. Use organizational roles for the allocation of specialized resources needed by the occupants of that role. Container objects provide the basis for yet another type of group: those people who share a common location in the organizational schema. Their common resource needs can provide the basis for trustee assignments.

Finally, make individual user trustee assignments. This keeps user trustee assignments to a minimum. You will usually find some group or organizational role that it is more appropriate to assign the trustee rights to. Some network administrators go to the extreme of never making trustee assignments to users; they make the trustee assignment to a group name instead and then make the user who needs the access rights a member of that group.

When assigning trustee rights to groups and users, follow the same pattern as when you planned the rights assignments:

1. Assign rights to groups, starting with the group EVERYONE.
2. Assign rights to profiles.
3. Assign rights to organizational roles.
4. Assign rights to container objects.
5. Assign rights to individual users.

NETWARE UTILITIES AND COMMANDS FOR MANAGING TRUSTEE ASSIGNMENTS

Command Line Utilities

NetWare includes command line utilities that enable a network administrator to grant Trustee rights and to obtain information about a user's effective rights in a directory. The following paragraphs describe these command line utilities, showing their command syntax and illustrating their use with examples.

The RIGHTS command

You use the RIGHTS command to view or modify the volume, directory, or File rights of a user or group. You can also use the RIGHTS command to determine the effective rights of the currently logged in user name in the specified directory path. If no path is specified, the RIGHTS command displays the user's rights in the current directory path.

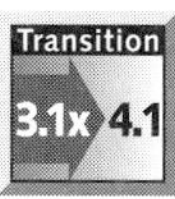

The NetWare 4.1 RIGHTS command incorporates the NetWare 3.1x commands ALLOW, GRANT, REMOVE, REVOKE, RIGHTS, and TLIST.

The syntax of the RIGHTS command is

```
RIGHTS path [[ + | - ] rights] [/option] [/?] [/VER]
```

There are several parameters that can be used with RIGHTS. These are listed in Figure 10-65.

Figure 10-65 The RIGHTS command parameters

Parameter	Use this parameter to
path	Specify the directory path to the volume, directory, or file you want to work with. This parameter is mandatory.
+l-	Add rights (+) or delete rights (-).
rights	Specify one or more Directory or File rights.
/?	Access help about RIGHTS. If this parameter is used, all others are ignored.
/VER	See the version number of the RIGHTS command. If this parameter is used, all others are ignored.

There are also several options that can be used with RIGHTS. These are listed in Figure 10-66.

Figure 10-66

The RIGHTS command options

Option	Use this option to
/C	Let the output scroll continuously.
/F	View the IRF.
/I	View inherited rights information. Using this option shows the source of the inherited rights.
/NAME=username	View or change the rights for a user or group.
/S	View or change subdirectories below the current level.
/T	View the trustee assignments in a directory.

The set of rights symbols that can be used with the RIGHTS command is an augmented set of the Directory and File rights shown in Figure 10-5 and is shown in Figure 10-69.

Figure 10-67

Directory and File rights symbols used with the RIGHTS COMMAND

Right Symbol	Effect on Directory	Effect on File
S [Supervisor]	Grants all rights to the specified directory and all subdirectories.	Grants all rights to the specified file.
R [Read]	Enables the user to read files or run programs in the directory.	Enables the user to read or run the specified file or program without having Read rights at the directory level.
W [Write]	Enables the user to change or add data to files in the specified directory.	Enables the user to change or add data to the specified file without having Write rights at the directory level.
C [Create]	Enables the user to create files and subdirectories.	Enables the user to salvage the specified file if it is deleted.
E [Erase]	Enables the user to delete files and remove subdirectories.	Enables the user to delete the specified file without having Erase rights at the directory level.
M [Modify]	Enables the user to change file and subdirectory names and use the FLAG and FLAGDIR commands to change the attribute settings on files or subdirectories.	Enables the user to change the name or attribute settings of the specified file without having Modify rights at the directory level.
F [File scan]	Enables the user to obtain a directory of file and subdirectory names.	Enables the user to view the specified filename on a directory listing without having File Scan rights at the directory level.
A [Access control]	Enables the user to grant access rights to other users for this specified directory.	Enables the user to grant access rights to the specified file without having Access Control rights at the directory level.
N [No rights]	Removes all the user's rights to this directory.	Removes all the user's rights to the file.
REM	Removes the user as a trustee of this directory.	Removes the user as a trustee of this file.
ALL	Gives the user all rights to the directory except Supervisor.	Gives the user all rights to the file except Supervisor.

Using the RIGHTS command with just a path will show you your effective rights for that directory. For example, Figure 10-70 shows the effective rights for the CBE Labs network administrator DAuer in the CONSTELLATION/SYS:PUBLIC directory.

Figure 10-68

DAuer's effective rights in the CONSTELLATION/SYS:PUBLIC directory

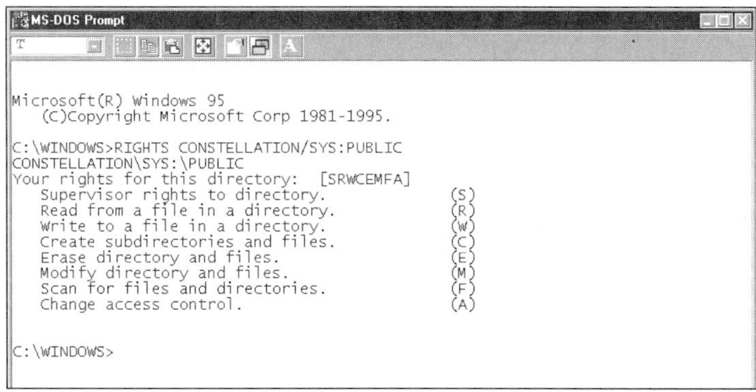

MS-DOS Prompt
Microsoft(R) Windows 95
(C)Copyright Microsoft Corp 1981-1995.
C:\WINDOWS>RIGHTS CONSTELLATION/SYS:PUBLIC
CONSTELLATION\SYS:\PUBLIC
Your rights for this directory: [SRWCEMFA]
Supervisor rights to directory. (S)
Read from a file in a directory. (R)
Write to a file in a directory. (W)
Create subdirectories and files. (C)
Erase directory and files. (E)
Modify directory and files. (M)
Scan for files and directories. (F)
Change access control. (A)
C:\WINDOWS>

You can also use the NDIR command with the /R parameter to view rights and file attributes. Attributes are discussed later in this chapter.

In NetWare 3.1x , you could use the WHOAMI /R command to obtain a list of the trustee assignments in the entire file system that have been granted to a currently logged in user or to a group of which the user is a member. In NetWare 4.1, this command may still be used, but only with NetWare 3.1x bindery servers.

To see the trustees of a directory, you use the RIGHTS command with the /T parameter. Figure 10-69 shows the trustees of the CBE Labs CONSTELLATION\SYS:\ directory.

Figure 10-69

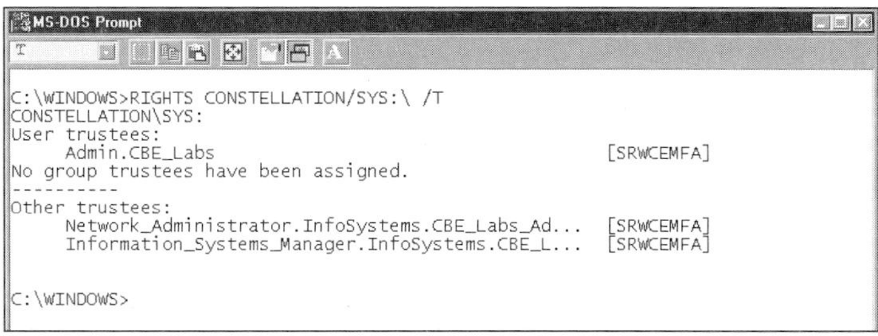

This use of the RIGHTS command is the equivalent of the NetWare 3.1x TLIST command.

If you wanted to grant Write, Create, Erase, and Modify rights `[ WCEM ]` in the CONSTELLATION/SYS:PUBLIC to the user SLopez, you would use the following command:

```
F:\>RIGHTS CONSTELLATION/SYS:PUBLIC +WCEM /NAME=SLopez
```

You can separate the abbreviations by spaces, but do not place them in brackets. Use the word *ALL* to specify all rights or the letter *N* to specify no rights for the user or group in the specified directory. Use a complete or partial path leading to the directory in which you want to make the trustee assignment. If you are not an Admin equivalent user, you will need to have the Supervisor right `[S]` or Access Control right `[A]` to the directory path specified. If no path is specified, the assignment will be made to the current directory.

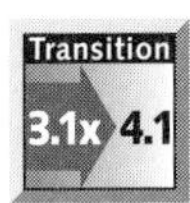

This use of the RIGHTS command is the equivalent of the NetWare 3.1x GRANT command.

When you use the RIGHTS command with the – (minus sign), you remove access rights from an existing trustee assignment made to a user or group in the specified directory path. You can use the word *all* to specify all rights are to be removed, providing the user or group with no rights to the specified directory.

If you wanted to remove the Write, Create, Erase, and Modify rights `[ WCEM ]` in the CONSTELLATION/SYS:PUBLIC from the user SLopez, you would use the following command:

```
F:\>RIGHTS CONSTELLATION/SYS:PUBLIC -WCEM /NAME=SLopez
```

This use of the RIGHTS command the equivalent of the NetWare 3.1x REVOKE command.

When you use the RIGHTS command with the REM attribute, you remove the user's or group's trustee assignment itself, not just particular access rights from an existing trustee assignment made to a user or group in the specified directory path.

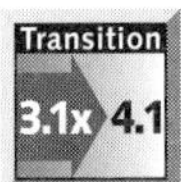

This use of the RIGHTS command is the equivalent of the NetWare 3.1x REMOVE command.

In some situations, removing a trustee assignment for a user or group from a subdirectory can actually increase that user's or group's effective rights by enabling the subdirectory to inherit rights from the parent directory.

You can use the RIGHTS command with the /F parameter to view or modify the IRF. If you wanted to grant Write, Create, Erase, and Modify rights `[ WCEM ]` in the IRF for the CONSTELLATION/SYS:PUBLIC directory, you would use the following command:

```
F:\>RIGHTS CONSTELLATION/SYS:PUBLIC +WCEM /F
```

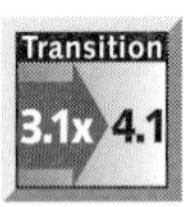

This use of the RIGHTS command is the equivalent of the NetWare 3.1x ALLOW command.

Menu Utilities

The NetWare command line utilities can be used efficiently to grant or view trustee assignments from the DOS prompt. They have two drawbacks, however. They entail many keystrokes, especially if you need to make several entries, which of course increases the chance for errors. They also require exact syntax to work correctly. You can, however, use Novell menu utilities for assigning trustees and managing effective rights. Both the NETADMIN and FILER utilities contain menu options that enable you to assign trustee rights to users and groups. NETADMIN works with both the NDS directory tree and the network file structure, whereas FILER works with only the directories and files of the network file structure.

Using NETADMIN to Manage Trustee Assignments

As usual, the NETADMIN menu utility can do most of the same work you can do in the NetWare Administrator graphical utility. You can use NETADMIN with Object and Property rights and with Directory and File rights. You can grant and revoke trustee assignments, as well as manage specific rights assignments. The IRF can also be viewed and modified. You will have a chance to work with NETADMIN in the end of chapter exercises.

Using FILER

The FILER menu utility was discussed in detail in Chapter 8. FILER is a very useful program for managing directories and files but cannot be used for managing the objects in the NDS Directory tree. As you might expect, FILER can also be used to manage trustee assignments.

Using FILER to manage trustee assignments. To add or delete a trustee for a directory or file, you use the Manage files and directories option. Browsing the directory structure, you select the desired directory. When the desired directory is the current directory, you highlight the single dot that represents the current directory and press [Enter] to select it. The Information for directory screen appears, as shown in Figure 10-70.

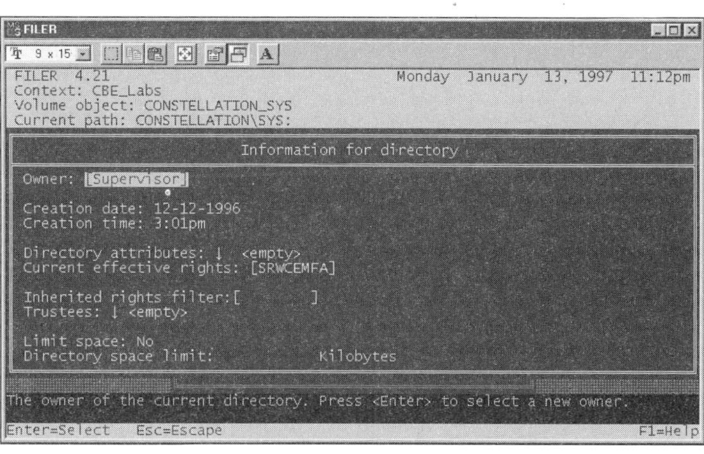

Figure 10-70 The Information for directory screen

Your current effective rights, the IRF, and a list of Trustees can all be viewed and modified in this screen. To work with trustee assignments, simply select the Trustees field. Pressing [Enter] displays a window containing a list of any existing trustees.

To add new trustees to this list, press [Ins] and then use [F5] to highlight the names of the users you want to add from the Others windows and press [Enter]. The users or groups you have marked will now appear in the trustee window with the default rights of `[ R    F ]`. To add additional rights to one of the users or groups, use the arrow keys to select the user or group and press [Enter]. The Trustee Rights window, listing the existing rights, will be displayed. To add rights to the Trustee Rights window, press [Ins] to display the Other Rights window.

Now use [F5] to mark the rights you want to add to this user's or group's trustee assignment and then press [Enter] to have the selected rights added to the Trustee Rights window. To save the updated Trustee rights, press [Esc]. The user name appears with its assigned rights in the trustee list.

To revoke one or more rights from a trustee assignment, you first select the user or group name from the trustee window and then press [Enter] to display the Trustee Rights window. Use F5 to mark the rights you want to remove and press [Del]. FILER will ask you to confirm the deletion. After you confirm the deletion, FILER removes the rights from the Trustee Rights window. Pressing [Esc] returns you to the trustee window, which shows the remaining rights for the selected user or group.

To remove a trustee of the directory, simply use the arrow keys in the trustee window to select the user or group name and then press [Del]. After you confirm the deletion, the user or group is removed from the trustee window. With FILER, multiple trustees can be removed from the directory. Use [F5] to mark all the trustees you want to remove and then press [Del].

Using FILER to view effective rights. As shown in Figure 10-70, the user's effective rights are displayed in the Information for directory screen.

Using FILER to change the Inherited Rights Filter. The FILER Information for directory screen makes it easy to view or change the IRF for a directory. The IRF is displayed in the screen. To work with the IRF for this directory, highlight the Inherited Rights Filter field. Pressing [Enter] displays a window containing a list of all rights that this directory can inherit. Use the arrow keys along with [F5] to highlight any right (except the Supervisor right) you want to remove. Pressing [Del] removes the selected rights. If you need to add rights back to the IRF, press [Ins] and then use [F5] to mark the desired rights in the "Other Rights" window. Pressing [Enter] includes the selected rights in the IRF. Now press [Esc] to save the new inherited rights and return to the directory information screen.

Using FILER to manage rights for files. The above sections dealt with directories, but FILER can also work with files. Simply choose the file from the files listed in the directory instead of the single dot that represents the current directory. Other actions are the same.

DIRECTORY AND FILE ATTRIBUTES

Attributes are flags or codes that can be associated with files and directories. They indicate to the NetWare operating system what type of processing can be performed on the associated file and directory.

Attributes apply only to file system components (directories and files). They do not apply to NDS objects.

Attributes are often placed on directories and files by the network administrator in order to provide additional protection against accidental change or deletion. Attributes are also used to specify special processing such as making a file sharable or purging all files that are deleted from a specific directory. Attributes override user effective rights in a directory or file. If a file is flagged with the Read Only attribute, the only operations you can perform on the file—no matter what your effective rights are—are Read and File Scan. Assume, for example, a user has the Supervisor Trustee right `[S]` to the SALES directory and therefore would inherit all access rights to the files and subdirectories in the SALES structure. If a file named ZIPCODE.DAT is stored in the SALES directory and is flagged with the Read Only attribute, this user has only read access to the ZIPCODE.DAT file. Because this user has a Supervisor `[S]` trustee assignment to the SALES directory, however, he or she can use the Modify right to remove the Read Only attribute and then change or even delete the ZIPCODE.DAT file.

ATTRIBUTES

Figure 10-71 contains a list of all attributes used by NetWare 4.1, along with their corresponding abbreviations and whether they can be applied to directories, files, or both. Figure 10-71 also indicates whether the attribute was used in NetWare 3.1x or is new to NetWare 4.1.

Figure 10-71

NetWare 4.1 directory and file attributes

Attribute	NetWare 3.1x	Applies To	Abbreviation
Archive Needed	Yes	File	A
Can't Compress	No	File	Cc
Compressed	No	File	Co
Copy Inhibit	Yes	File	Ci
Delete Inhibit	Yes	File, Directory	Di
Don't Compress	No	File, Directory	Dc
Don't Migrate	No	File, Directory	Dm
Don't Suballocate	No	File	Ds
Execute Only	Yes	File	X
Hidden	Yes	File, Directory	H
Immediate Compress	No	File, Directory	Ic
Migrated	No	File	M
Normal	No	File, Directory	N
Purge Immediate	Yes	File, Directory	P
Read Only	Yes	File	Ro
Read Write	Yes	File	Rw
Rename Inhibit	Yes	File, Directory	Ri
Sharable	Yes	File	Sh
System	Yes	File, Directory	Sy
Transactional	Yes	File	T

Of these twenty attributes, four are from DOS: Archive Needed [A], Hidden [H], Read Only [Ro in NetWare, just R in DOS], and System [Sy in NetWare, just S in DOS]. NetWare supports the four DOS attributes and adds sixteen additional attributes.

NetWare 3.1x also used the Indexed [I] attribute, which was automatically assigned by the NetWare 3.1x operating system to files that need more than 64 blocks of disk storage. It indicated that the file is indexed for fast access. It was listed on screen for information only, however, because its setting could not be changed by the network administrator or user. The Novell documentation for NetWare 4.1 is inconsistent about whether this attribute still exists.

NetWare 3.1x through NetWare 4.1 also enables the Read Audit and Write Audit attributes, but they are not used by NetWare 3.1x through NetWare 4.1. Although these attributes can be assigned to files, their use has not yet been defined by Novell. As a result, these attributes are not used by network administrators.

Archive Needed

The **Archive Needed [A]** attribute is assigned automatically to files when the contents of a file are modified and is one of the four DOS attributes supported by NetWare. Copy or backup utilities can remove this attribute after the file is copied to another storage location. This attribute is important in controlling what files are copied to a backup disk. It is possible to back up only the files that have been changed since the last backup.

Can't Compress

The **Can't Compress [Cc]** attribute is a status flag that shows that the file can't be compressed using NetWare's file compression because the compression wouldn't save a significant amount of disk space. Although displayed on attribute lists, the Cc attribute can't be set by a user—NetWare automatically sets it.

Compressed

Like Can't Compress, the **Compressed [Co]** attribute is also a status flag that is displayed in attribute lists but can't be set by the user. The Co attribute shows that the file is compressed using NetWare's file compression.

Copy Inhibit

The **Copy Inhibit [Ci]** attribute is used to protect specified files from being copied by Macintosh users. Setting this attribute prevents Macintosh computers running the Apple Filing Protocol v2.0 and above from copying the file. The Copy Inhibit attribute could be used on PC-specific files such as software programs to prevent them from being accidentally copied to a Macintosh computer.

Delete Inhibit

The **Delete Inhibit [Di]** attribute prevents a file or directory from being deleted. If assigned to a file, the file's contents can be changed or the file renamed, but the file cannot be deleted unless a user who has been granted the Modify right `[M]` first removes the Delete Inhibit attribute. The Delete Inhibit attribute is often useful to protect an important data file from accidentally being deleted yet still enables its contents to be changed. You should consider setting the Delete Inhibit attribute on many of your organization's permanent files, such as customer, payroll, inventory, and accounting files. Setting the Delete Inhibit attribute on a directory prevents the directory's name from being removed but will not prevent the contents of the directory or its files and subdirectories from being deleted. You might want to protect the fixed parts of your organization's directory structure from being modified by flagging all main directories with the Delete Inhibit attribute.

Don't Compress

The **Don't Compress [Dc]** attribute is used to keep files or directories from being compressed by NetWare's file compression system. The Dc attribute can be set by the user.

Don't Migrate

Migration is used to move files that haven't been used for a long period of time to secondary storage mediums such as DAT tape or optical disks. NetWare 4.1 has two attributes that work with migration systems. The first is **Don't Migrate [Dm]**, which is set by the user to keep a file from being Migrated regardless of how long it has been on a volume without being used. For example, you don't want NetWare system files Migrated even if you haven't used them. The Dm attribute can be set for directories as well as files. When the attribute is set for a directory, none of the files in that directory will be Migrated. For example, by setting the *ServerName*/SYS:SYSTEM directory Dm attribute, you don't have to set the Dm attribute for every file in SYSTEM.

Don't Suballocate

NetWare's block suballocation scheme is used to save disk space, and normally you should use block suballocation. If there are certain files that shouldn't be stored using block suballocation, you use the **Don't Suballocate [Ds]** attribute to prevent the use of block suballocation when storing those files.

Execute Only

Whereas the Copy Inhibit attribute keeps Macintosh files from being copied, the **Execute Only [X]** attribute is used to protect software files from being illegally copied. The Execute Only attribute can be set only on .EXE and .COM files by a supervisor-equivalent user. Once set, Execute Only cannot be removed, even by the supervisor. As a result, do not assign Execute Only to files unless backup copies of the files exist. Certain program files will not run when they are flagged Execute Only, because these programs need to copy information from their program files into the workstation's memory—the Execute Only attribute prevents this. Because the Execute Only attribute cannot be removed, to get rid of it you need to delete the file and reinstall it from another disk.

Hidden

The **Hidden [H]** attribute is a DOS attribute used to hide files and directories from DOS utilities and certain software applications. However, the NDIR and NCOPY commands will display hidden files and directories—and show the H attribute, when it is enabled. One simple way to help protect software from illegal copying is to use the Hidden attribute to make the software directories and files hidden from normal DOS utilities. If you move the NCOPY and NDIR commands from the SYS:PUBLIC directory to the SYS:SYSTEM directory or some other location, standard users will not have access to them.

Another way to protect the NCOPY and NDIR commands from unauthorized use is to place an IRF on the files in question to prevent users from inheriting the `[ R F ]` rights to these files and then make a specific trustee assignment to a special group. Only members of the special group can then use the NCOPY and NDIR commands.

The Hidden attribute can be especially useful when you have workstations using the Microsoft Windows environment. With Windows it is very easy for users to explore the directory structure using the File Manager. By hiding directories and files, you can make the file structure much less accessible.

Immediate Compress

The **Immediate Compress [Ic]** attribute is set for files and directories that you want to be compressed as soon as possible. Normally NetWare 4.1 will wait until the file has not been used for a specific period of time before compressing the file.

Migrated

The second of the two NetWare 4.1 attributes that work with migration systems, the **Migrated [M]** attribute is a status flag set by NetWare after a file has been Migrated. A file that appears in a listing with the M attribute has actually been moved to another storage medium and is no longer physically on the volume. When you try to work with such a file, it must first be retrieved from the other storage medium and recopied to the volume. If the other storage medium is easily accessible, such as a DAT tape already in the DAT tape drive, the retrieval can be fairly quick. However, if the file is stored on a medium that is not easily accessible, such as a DAT tape stored in a different building, you will have to retrieve the storage medium yourself first and place it in the appropriate drive before it can be recopied to the volume.

Normal

If none of the attributes are set, the file is considered to be **Normal [N]**.

Purge Immediate

As described in Chapter 8, NetWare enables deleted files to be retrieved with the Salvage command in NetWare Administrator until either the deleted file's space is reused by the file server, or the directory is purged using the Purge command in NetWare Administrator, or the PURGE command line utility. Space from files that have been purged is no longer available to the operating system, preventing the file from being recovered with the SALVAGE utility. The **Purge Immediate [P]** attribute can be assigned to either a file or a directory if you want the NetWare file server to immediately reuse the space from deleted files. When assigned to a file, the Purge Immediate attribute causes the file to be purged as soon as it is deleted, thereby making its space immediately available to the system for reuse. When Purge Immediate is assigned to a directory, any file that is deleted from the directory is automatically purged and its space reused. The Purge Immediate attribute is often assigned to directories that contain temporary files in order to reuse the temporary file space as soon as the file is deleted. The Purge Immediate attribute can also be assigned, for security reasons, to files that contain sensitive data, thereby preventing an intruder from salvaging and then accessing information from these files after they have been deleted.

Read Only

The **Read Only [Ro]** attribute applies only to files. It protects the contents of a file from being modified. The Read Only attribute performs a function similar to opening the write-protect tab on a disk. Files containing data that is not normally changed—such as a ZIP code file or a program file—are usually flagged Read Only. When you first set the Read Only attribute, the Rename Inhibit and Delete Inhibit attributes are also set by default. If for some reason you want to enable the file to be renamed or deleted but do not want its contents changed, you can remove the Rename Inhibit and Delete Inhibit attributes.

Read Write

The **Read Write [Rw]** attribute applies only to files. It is the opposite of Read Only, and indicates that the contents of the file can be added to or changed. When files are created, the Read Write attribute is automatically set, enabling the contents of the file to be added to or changed. When file attributes are listed, either Rw or Ro will be listed.

Rename Inhibit

The **Rename Inhibit [Ri]** attribute can be assigned to either files or directories. When assigned to a file, it protects the filename from being changed. During installation, many software packages create data and configuration files that might need to be updated and changed, but those filenames must remain constant in order for the software package to operate properly. After installing a software package that requests certain file or directory names, it is a good idea to use the Rename Inhibit attribute on these files and directories to prevent someone from changing the file or directory name and causing an error or crash in the application. Using the Rename Inhibit attribute on a directory prevents that directory's name from being changed while still enabling files and subdirectories contained within that directory to be renamed.

Sharable

When files are created, they are available to only one user at a time. Suppose, for example, you create a spreadsheet file called BUDGET95.WK1 on the file server and a coworker opens up this file with a spreadsheet program. If you attempt to access the BUDGET95.WK1 file, you will receive an error message that the file is in use or not accessible. With spreadsheet files and word processing documents, if more than one user can access the file at one time, any changes made by one user can be overwritten by another user. Program files and certain database files, however, should be made available to multiple users at the same time. For example, you would want as many users as have licenses to be able to run the word processing software you just installed, or perhaps have access to a common database of customers. To enable a file to be opened by more than one user at a time, the **Sharable [Sh]** attribute for that file must be enabled. Normally you need to flag all program files Sharable after performing an installation.

In addition to Sharable, most program files are also flagged as Read Only to prevent users from deleting or making changes to the software. Most document and data files are not flagged as sharable in order to prevent multiple users from making changes to the file at the same time.

System

The **System [Sy]** attribute is a DOS attribute that is also often assigned to files and directories that are part of the NetWare operating system. Print queues are actually subdirectories in the SYS:SYSTEM directory and are flagged with the System attribute. Like the Hidden attribute, the System attribute hides files from the DOS utilities and application software packages but also marks the file or directory as being for operating system use only. NetWare utilities display directories and files with the System and Hidden attributes set if the user has the File Scan right.

Transactional

The **Transactional [T]** attribute can be assigned only to files and is used to indicate that the file will be protected by the **Transaction Tracking System (TTS)**. The TTS ensures that when changes or transactions are applied to a file, either all transactions are completed or the file is left in its original state. The TTS is particularly important for database files—when a workstation is in the process of updating a record and crashes before the update is complete, the integrity of the file is protected. Assume, for example, that a NetWare file server is used to maintain an on-line order-entry system containing customer and inventory files. When an order is entered, at least two transactions are necessary: one to update the customer's account balance and the other to record the inventory item to be shipped. Suppose that while you are entering the order, the workstation you are using crashes after it updates the customer balance and therefore fails to record the item on the shipping list. In this case, TTS cancels the transaction and restores the customer's balance to its original amount, enabling you to reenter the complete order. Because TTS is a feature used by application software, using the Transactional attribute does not implement TTS protection—you also need to have the proper system design and application software.

SETTING ATTRIBUTES FOR A DIRECTORY OR FILE FROM THE DIRECTORY OR FILE "OBJECT" ITSELF

You've already read about how to use NetWare Administrator to grant trustee assignment and rights to directories and files. You can also use NetWare Administrator to set directory and file attributes. You do this by selecting the directory or file object in the NDS Directory tree and then opening the *ObjectName* object dialog box. The *ObjectName* object dialog box for a directory or file contains an Attributes page, with a set of check boxes to set attributes. For files, NetWare also displays another set of check boxes (which cannot be changed by the user) that show whether a file can or can't be compressed (Cc attribute), is or isn't compressed (Co attribute), and is or isn't Migrated (M attribute).

To set directory and file attributes from the directory or file object itself, you follow these steps:

- Click the Directory or File object; then press [Enter].

  or

  Click the Directory or File object, click Object on the menu bar, and then click Details.

  or

  Right-click the Directory or File object; then click Details on the QuickMenu.

  then

- Switch to the Attributes page.
- Click the appropriate check boxes in the Directory Attributes or File Attributes section for the attributes to be set.
- Click OK.

For example, the network administrator at CBE Labs has decided to protect the files in the CONSTELLATION/SYS:PUBLIC directory from accidental erasure and renaming by using Delete Inhibit (Di) and Rename Inhibit (Ri). Setting these attributes means that users cannot delete or rename the files in the PUBLIC directory. CBE Labs does not migrate files. If migration were used, the Don't Migrate (Dm) attribute would also have to be set for this directory—otherwise rarely used but still needed NetWare system files would be removed from the volume.

To set directory attributes for the CONSTELLATION_SYS:PUBLIC directory from the CONSTELLATION_SYS:PUBLIC directory object, follow these steps:

1. If NetWare Administrator is not open, launch it. Expand the tree until the directories of the CONSTELLATION_SYS volume are visible.
2. Double-click the **CONSTELLATION_SYS:PUBLIC Directory** object to select it and display the Directory: PUBLIC object dialog box.
3. Click the **Attributes** button in the button bar. The Attributes page is displayed, as shown in Figure 10-72.

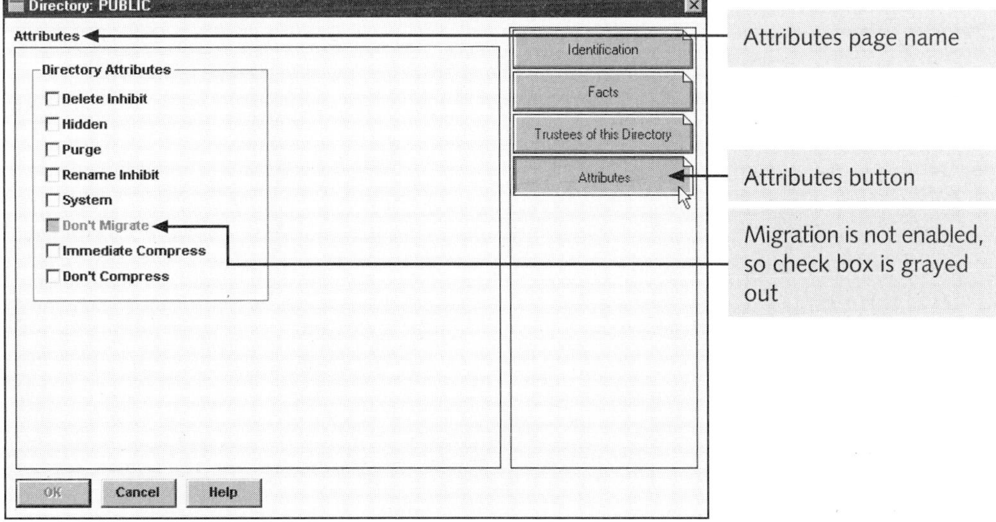

Figure 10-72 The PUBLIC Attributes page

4. Click the **Delete Inhibit** and **Rename Inhibit** check boxes in the Attributes section to set the Delete Inhibit (Di) and Rename Inhibit (Ri) attributes. The Directory: PUBLIC object dialog box appears as shown in Figure 10-73.

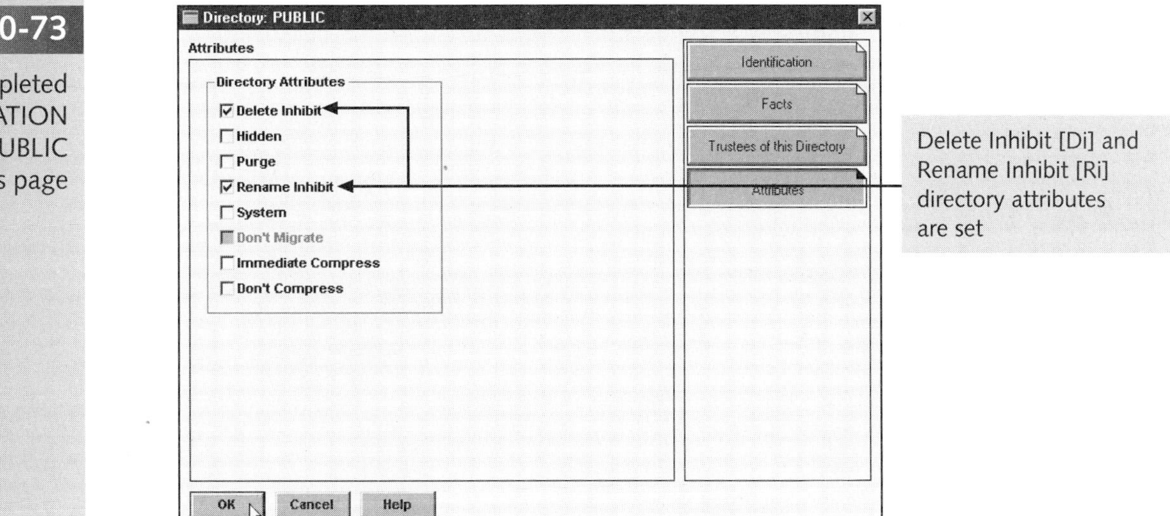

Figure 10-73 The completed CONSTELLATION _SYS:PUBLIC Attributes page

5. Click **OK**. *Do not close NetWare Administrator.*

The NDIR.EXE file in the CONSTELLATION/SYS:PUBLIC directory is a frequently used file. However, the file is subject to compression if it isn't used for seven days. Although NetWare's compression and decompression utilities are fast enough that the user wouldn't notice much delay in starting the file, the CBE network administrator has decided to set the Don't Compress attribute on the file. This will keep the file uncompressed and ready to use.

To set file attributes for the NDIR.EXE file in the CONSTELLATION_SYS:PUBLIC directory from the NDIR.EXE file object, follow these steps:

1. Expand the Directory tree until the files in the CONSTELLATION_SYS:PUBLIC directory are visible.
2. Double-click the **NDIR.EXE File** object to select it and display the CONSTELLATION/SYS:\PUBLIC\NDIR.EXE object dialog box.

3. Click the **Attributes** button in the button bar. The Attributes page is displayed, as shown in Figure 10-74.

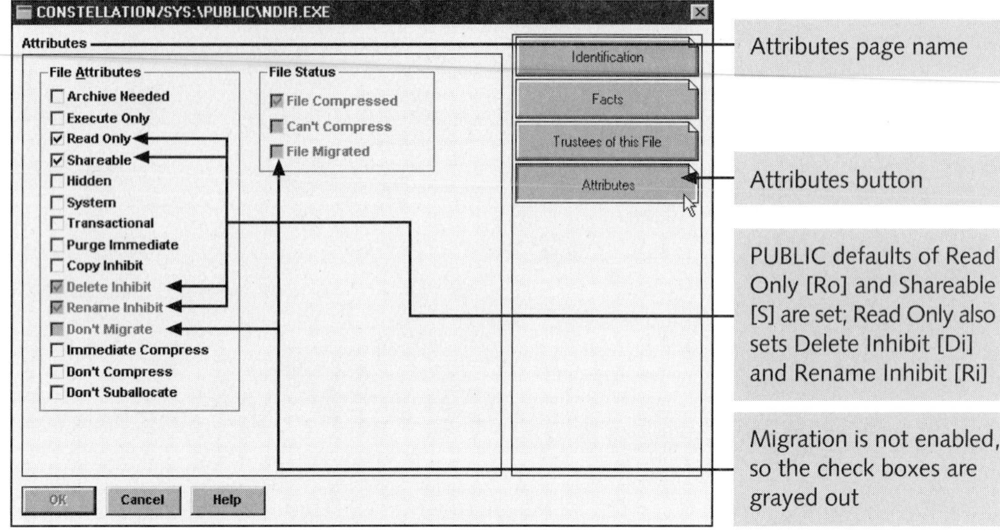

Figure 10-74
CONSTELLATION/SYS:\PUBLIC\NDIR.EXE Attributes page

Note that by default the files in the Public directory are set as Read Only (Ro), which automatically also sets them as Delete Inhibit (Di) and Rename Inhibit (Ri). By default, the files are also set as Sharable (Sh).

4. Click the check box in the Attributes section to set the Don't Compress (Dc) attribute. The Directory: CONSTELLATION_SYS:\PUBLIC\NDIR.EXE object dialog box appears as shown in Figure 10-75.

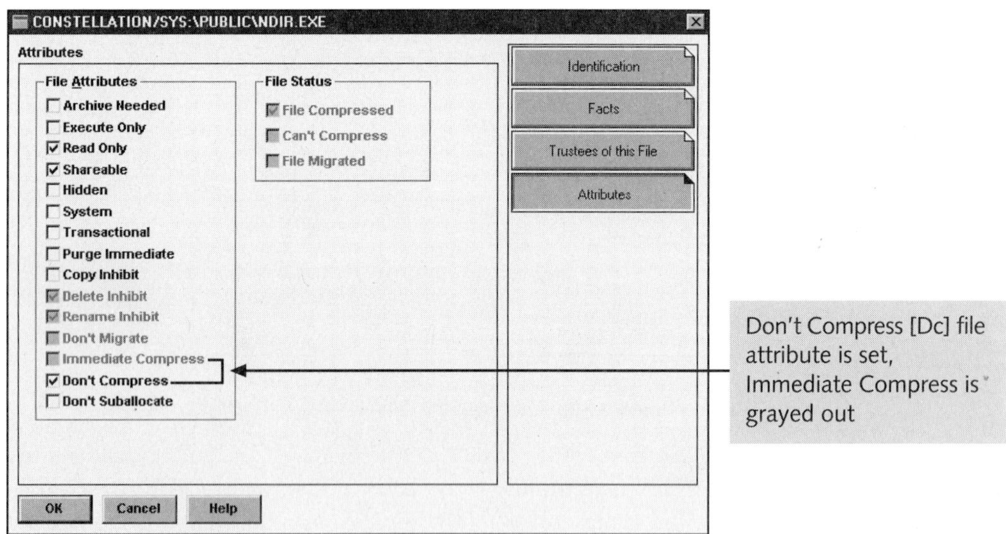

Figure 10-75
The completed CONSTELLATION/SYS:\PUBLIC\NDIR.EXE Attributes page

5. Click **OK**.

Setting Attributes for a Directory or File from Windows 95 Explorer

Just as Novell's Client 32 extensions to the Windows 95 Explorer program enable you to manage most Directory and File rights from Explorer, you can also manage most directory and file attributes. This is an effective way of setting many attributes without launching

NetWare Administrator. Figure 10-76 shows which directory and file attributes can be set in Explorer.

Figure 10-76

NetWare 4.1 directory and file attributes in Explorer

Attribute	Applies To	Set Directory (Folder) Attribute in Explorer	Set File Attribute in Explorer
Archive Needed [A]	File	YES for files in it	YES
Canít Compress [Cc]	File		
Compressed [Co]	File		
Copy Inhibit [Ci]	File		YES
Delete Inhibit [Di]	File, Directory	YES	YES
Don't Compress [Dc]	File, Directory	YES	
Don't Migrate [Dm]	File, Directory		
Don't Suballocate [Ds]	File		
Execute Only [E]	File		
Hidden [H]	File, Directory	YES	YES
Immediate Compress [Ic]	File, Directory	YES	
Migrated [M]	File		
Normal [N]	File, Directory		
Purge Immediate [P]	File, Directory	YES	YES
Read Only [Ro]	File	YES for files in it	YES
Read Write [Rw]	File	YES = No Ro	YES = No Ro
Rename Inhibit [Ri]	File, Directory	YES	YES
Sharable [Sh]	File		YES
System [Sy]	File, Directory		
Transactional [T]	File		YES

To set directory and file attributes to a directory or file from Windows 95 Explorer you follow these steps:

- Launch Explorer.
- Expand the Network Neighborhood branch of the Explorer tree until the directory or file is displayed.
- Click the directory or file to select it.
- Click File; then click Properties to display the *ObjectName* Properties dialog box.

  or

  Click the Properties button on the toolbar.
- Click the NetWare Folder or NetWare file tab to display the NetWare Folder or NetWare file page.
- Click the check boxes to set the appropriate attributes.
- Click OK.

The CBE Labs Network Administrator needs to set the same directory attributes for the SARATOGA/SYS:PUBLIC directory that he set for the CONSTELLATION/SYS:-PUBLIC directory. He also needs to set the attributes for the NDIR.EXE file in the SARATOGA/SYS:PUBLIC directory. You will use Explorer to set these attributes.

To set directory attributes for the SARATOGA/SYS:PUBLIC directory from Explorer, follow these steps:

1. Launch Explorer.
2. Expand the Network Neighborhood branch of the Cbelabs tree until the SARATOGA_SYS volume is visible. Click the **SARATOGA_SYS** icon to select it; then click the **Properties** button.
3. Click the **NetWare Folder** tab. The NetWare Folder page is displayed as shown in Figure 10-77.

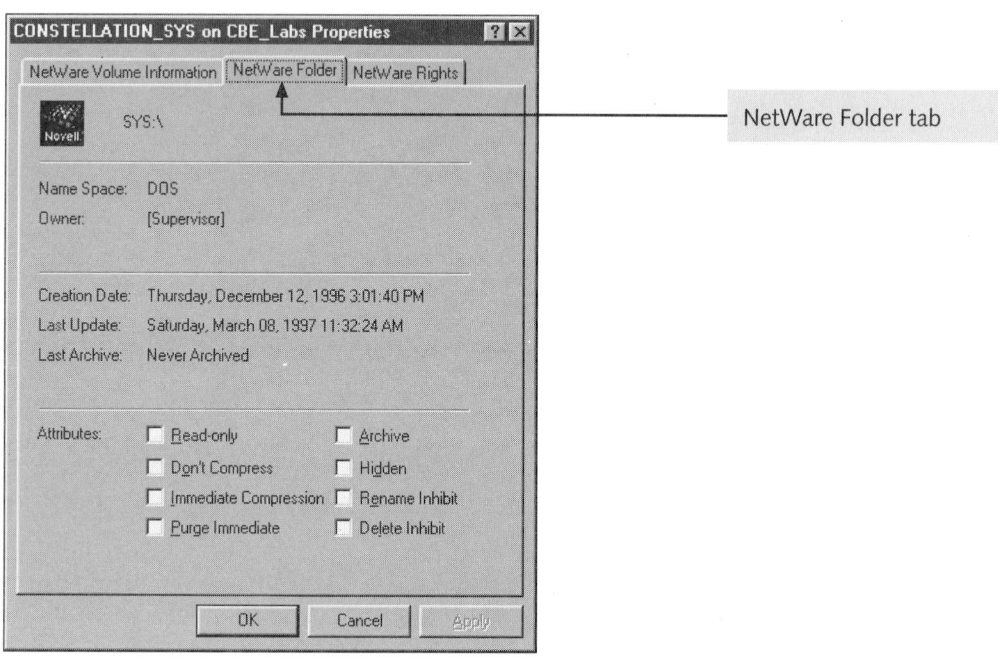

Figure 10-77 The NetWare Folder page

This page shows the name space, owner, and date information about the directory (folder).

4. Click the **Delete Inhibit** and **Rename Inhibit** check boxes in the Attributes section to set the Delete Inhibit (Di) and Rename Inhibit (Ri) attributes. The NetWare Folder page appears as shown in Figure 10-78.

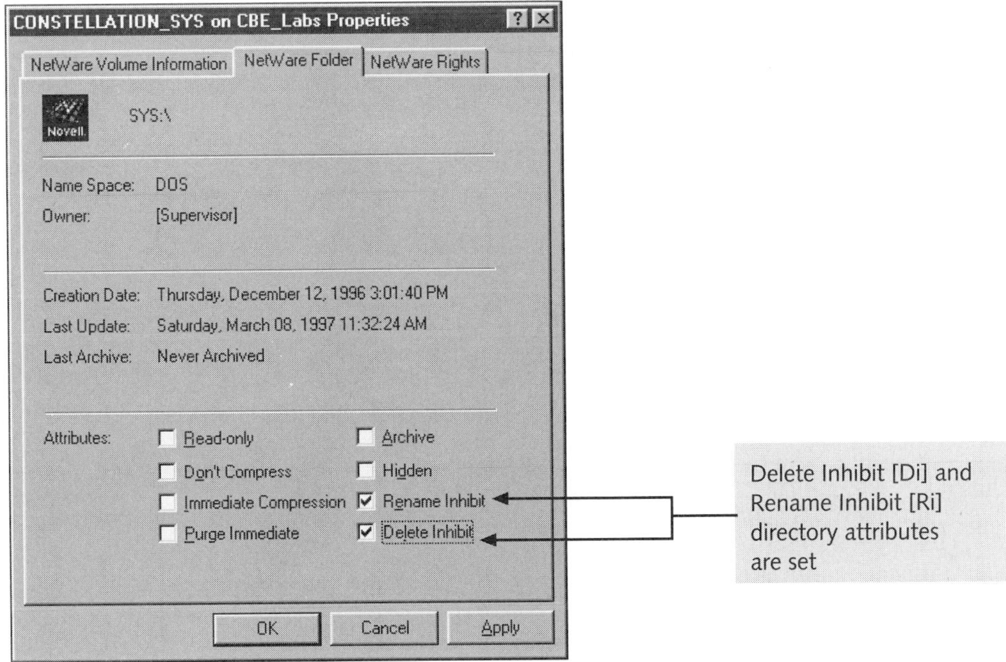

Figure 10-78 The completed NetWare Folder page

5. Click **OK**. Don't close Explorer at this time.

Now let's set the file attributes for NDIR.EXE.

To set file attributes for the NDIR.EXE file in the SARATOGA/SYS:PUBLIC directory from Explorer, follow these steps:

1. Expand the Network Neighborhood branch of the Cbelabs tree until the NDIR.EXE file on the SARATOGA_SYS volume is visible in the PUBLIC directory. Click the **NDIR.EXE** icon to select it, click **File**, and then click **Properties**.

2. Click the **NetWare File** tab. The NetWare File page is displayed, as shown in Figure 10-79.

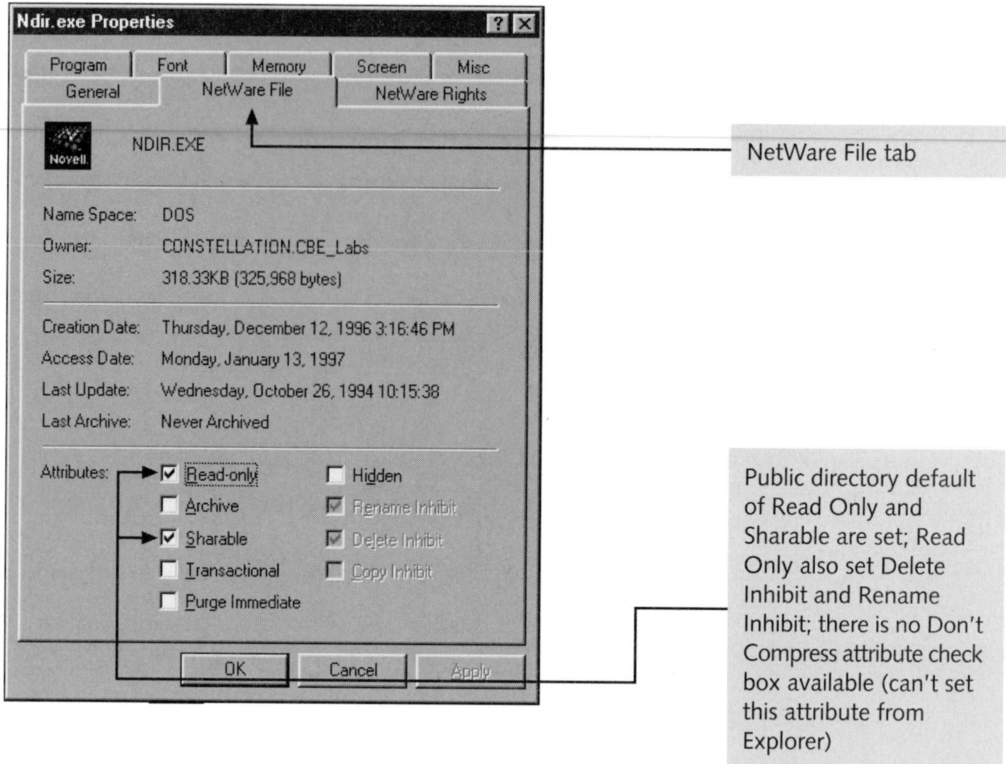

Figure 10-79 The NetWare File page

This page shows the name space, owner, and date information about the file. Notice that the default Read Only (Ro) setting shows up, with the associated Rename Inhibit (Ri) and Delete Inhibit (Di) check boxes checked and grayed-out. Also notice that there is no check box for the Don't Compress (Dc) attribute. The NetWare File page does not contain as comprehensive a set of settings as the File object Attributes page in NetWare Administrator.

3. Click **OK**.

NetWare Utilities and Commands for Managing Attributes

The FLAG Command

The command line utility used with attributes is FLAG.

The NetWare 4.1 FLAG command incorporates the NetWare 3.1x commands FLAG and FLAGDIR.

The syntax of the FLAG command is

```
FLAG path [[ + | - ] attribute] [/option] [/?] [/VER]
```

There are several parameters that can be used with FLAG. These are listed in Figure 10-80.

Figure 10-80

The FLAG command parameters

Parameter	Use this parameter to
path	Specify the directory path to the directory or file you want to work with. This parameter is mandatory.
+ | -	Add attributes (+) or delete attributes (-). You can add and delete attributes in the same command.
attribute	Specify one or more directory or file attributes.
/?	Access help about FLAG. If this parameter is used, all others are ignored.
/VER	See the version number of the FLAG command. If this parameter is used, all others are ignored.

There are also several options that can be used with FLAG. These are listed in Figure 10-81.

Figure 10-81

The FLAG command options

Option	Use this option to
/C	Let the output scroll continuously.
/D	View details for a directory or file.
/DO	View or change directories only.
/FO	View or change files only.
/NAME | GROUP=*name*	Change the directory or file owner.
/M=*mode*	Modify the search mode used by executable files.
/S	Search the specified directory and all subdirectories below it.

The set of *attribute* symbols that can be used with the FLAG command and is shown in Figure 10-82.

Figure 10-82

NetWare 4.1 directory and file attributes used with the FLAG command

Attribute	Used with Directories	Used with Files
ALL	YES - Includes Di, H, Ic, P, Ri and Sy for directories	YES - Includes A, Ci: (Macintosh files), Di, Dc
[A] Archive Needed		YES
[Ci] Copy Inhibit		YES - Macintosh files only
[Di] Delete Inhibit	YES	YES
[Dc] Don't Compress	YES	YES
[Dm] Don't Migrate	YES	YES
[Ds] Don't Suballocate		YES
[H] Hidden	YES	YES
[Ic] Immediate Compress	YES	YES
[N] Normal	YES	
[P] Purge Immediate	YES	YES
[Ro] Read Only		YES - Includes Di and Ri
[Rw] Read Write		YES
[Ri] Rename Inhibit	YES	YES
[Sh] Sharable		YES
[Sy] System	YES	YES
[T] Transactional		YES
[X] Execute Only		YES

Certain attribute symbols that you learned about earlier show up as file status flags in the output of the FLAG command. These are shown in Figure 10-83. You cannot set these attributes, but you should be able to recognize them in the output.

Figure 10-83

NetWare 4.1 file attributes used as status flags

Attribute
[Cc] Can't Compress
[Co] Compressed
[M] Migrated

The /M=Mode option is a rarely used option that sets a search mode for executable files. It will not be covered in this chapter.

If you use the FLAG command by itself with no parameter, a list of all files in the current directory and their attribute status is displayed.

You use the FLAG command to view or change the attributes of files in the specified directory. You can replace the path with either a complete or partial path leading to the desired file or files. If you specify no path, you access files in the current directory. The filename in the path can be replaced with the name of the file you want to access, or you can use global (*) and wildcard (?) characters to access several files. If no filename is specified, the FLAG command will affect all files in the specified path. To see a list of the attributes on all files in the current directory, simply type FLAG and press [Enter]. Replace the flag list field with the letters, separated by spaces, of the attributes you want to set.

Using FILER to Set Directory and File Attributes

The FILER utility can be used to modify the attribute flags for files and directories, just as you can set rights. Because FILER is a menu utility, it requires less typing and enables you to select attributes and filenames interactively without having to enter the complete syntax or exact filenames required by FLAG. FILER also enables you to set attributes on multiple files. Suppose, for example, you want to set the Read Only attribute on all the previous year's budget files in order to protect them from being changed, deleted, or renamed. You could use the FLAG command to do this, but it would require that you know the name of each of the files and would involve entering the command several times. Instead, you can use the FILER utility to perform this function.

CHAPTER SUMMARY

Just as a physical building, such as a warehouse, needs to be secured with locks and keys, the NetWare NDS and file systems must also be secured. Trustee assignments provide access rights that, like keys, give users entry to the Directory tree and file server storage areas they need to access. Four types of rights can be assigned: Object rights, Property rights, Directory rights, and File rights. Object rights are rights to the objects in the NDS Directory tree, and Property rights are rights to the properties of those objects. Directory rights are rights to the directories and subdirectories in the NetWare file system, and File rights are rights to the files in those directories.

Object rights provide access to objects in the NDS Directory tree. There are five Object rights: Supervisor, Browse, Create, Delete, and Rename. The Supervisor right grants all the other Object rights to the trustee and also grants all Property rights for the object. The Browse right enables the user to see the object in the Directory tree. The Create right applies only to container objects and enables the user to create new objects in that container. It does not, however, enable the user to create Property rights for those objects. The Delete right enables the user to delete the object from the Directory tree, and the Rename right enables the user to rename the object.

Property rights provide access to the property settings of an object in the Directory tree. There are five Property rights: Supervisor, Compare, Read, Write, and Add or Delete Self. The rights may be granted for all properties of an object, or for selected properties. One user may have varying rights to different properties of an object. The Supervisor right grants the user all rights to the property. The Compare right enables the user to compare a value to the property setting but not to actually see the property setting. The Read right enables the user to see the property setting and includes the Compare right. The Write right enables the user to change the values of the property setting and includes the Add or Delete Self right, which enables the users to add or delete themselves from a user list if the object has a user list property.

Directory and File rights provide access to the file system directories and files, respectively. There are eight access rights for directories and files: Supervisor, Read, Write, Create, Erase, Modify, File Scan, and Access control. The Supervisor right can be assigned only by a supervisor-equivalent user and provides a user with all rights to the directory and all subdirectories, including the right to assign the Supervisor right to other users. In addition, because the Supervisor right cannot be revoked or blocked at any lower level, assigning the Supervisor right is a good way to make a user act as a supervisor of a portion of the directory structure. The File Scan right enables users to see the directory or file in the file system, whereas the Read right enables users to actually read or use a file. The Write right enables users to change the contents of a file, the Create right enables users to create new files or salvage deleted ones, and the Modify right enables users to change attributes or rename a file or subdirectory. The Access Control right enables a user to assign other rights, except Supervisor, to other users.

Rights are granted to users by trustee assignments. Trustee assignments can be made to User objects, Group objects, Profile objects, Organizational Role objects, and Container objects. Effective rights for a user are a combination of rights given to a user's name combined with the rights given to any other object with which the user is associated. Granted Trustee rights are then inherited by (1) all container objects in the Directory tree subordinate to the container to which the trustee assignment was made or (2) the subdirectories and files within the directory for which the trustee assignment was made. As a result, a user's effective rights often consist of inherited rights that have flowed down to a container object, directory or file from a trustee assignment made in a higher-level container object or directory.

An Inherited Rights Filter (IRF) exists for each object, directory, and file to control what rights the object, directory, or file inherits from higher-level objects and directories. When an object, directory, or file is first created, the IRF enables all rights to be inherited. Later you can remove rights from the IRF to block those rights from being inherited.

Several utilities are used to set and view trustee assignments and the IRFs. The main graphics utility is the NetWare Administrator. The Client 32 extensions to the Windows 95 Explorer can also be used to manage trustee assignments. The NETADMIN menu utility duplicates most of the functionality of the NetWare Administrator, and you can use NETADMIN to manage trustee assignments. The FILER menu utility also has features for managing trustee assignments. Additionally, the RIGHTS command line utility provides a comprehensive tool for managing trustee assignments from the DOS prompt.

Attributes play an important role in file system security because they enable you to protect directories and files from such operations as deletion, renaming, and copying. Attributes can also be used to control file sharing, suballocation, compressing, purging, and migrating. Directory attributes include Delete Inhibit, Don't Compress, Don't Migrate, Hidden, Immediate Compress, Normal, Purge Immediate, Rename Inhibit, and System. File attributes include Archive Needed, Copy Inhibit, Delete Inhibit, Don't Compress, Don't Migrate, Don't Suballocate, Execute Only, Hidden, Immediate

Compress, Purge Immediate, Read Only, Read Write, Rename Inhibit, Sharable, System, and Transactional. File status flags, which are displayed but which you cannot set, are Can't Compress, Compress, and Migrated.

The same graphic and menu utilities (NetWare Administrator, NETADMIN, and FILER) that are used to set and view trustee assignments are used to set and view attributes. The Client 32 extensions to the Windows 95 Explorer again enable Explorer to be used to manage some attributes. The FLAG command line utility provides a comprehensive tool for managing directory and file attributes from the DOS prompt.

COMMAND SUMMARY

Command	Syntax	Definition
FLAG	*FLAG path [[+ | -] attribute] [/option] [/?][/VER]*	When used without any options, the FLAG command will display the attribute settings of all files in the current directory. To set attributes on one or more files, replace the path with the path and name of a file or use global file identifiers such as * and replace attributes with one or more of the following attribute flags separated by spaces (those attributes marked [Dir] work with directories as well as files): ALL Set all attributes [Dir] A Archive needed Ci Copy Inhibit Di Delete Inhibit [Dir] Dc Don't Compress [Dir] Dm Don't Migrate [Dir] Ds Don't Suballocate H Hidden [Dir] Ic Immediate Compress [Dir] N Normal [Dir] P Purge Immediate [Dir] Ri Rename Inhibit [Dir] Ro Read Only Rw Read Write Sh Sharable Sy System [Dir] T Transactional X Execute Only Options that can be used include: /C Continuous output /D View details /DO Directories only /FO Files only /NAME | GROUP = name Change the owner /S Include subdirectories

FILER	*FILER*	In addition to creating directories and copying files, the FILER utility enables a user to grant trustee assignments, set the IRF, and view or set file and directory attributes.
NETADMIN	*NETADMIN*	NETADMIN enables a user to manage object and Property rights for the NDS Directory tree, as well as manage directory and file trustee assignments.
RIGHTS	*RIGHTS path [[+ | -] rights] [/option] [/?][/VER]*	When used without any options, RIGHTS lists the current user's effective rights in the current directory. Using a path enables the effective rights to be viewed for any directory. To add or delete rights, specify the path and replace rights with one or more of the following rights symbols: ALL — All rights except Supervisor N — No rights—removes all rights REM — Remove the trustee assignment S — Supervisor R — Read W — Write C — Create E — Erase M — Modify F — File Scan A — Access Control Options that can be used include: /C — Continuous output /F — View the IRF /I — View inherited rights information /NAME = user name — View or change the right for a trustee /S — Include subdirectories /T — View trustee assignments

KEY TERMS

Access Control right (A)
access control list (ACL)
Add or Delete Self right (A)
Archive Needed (A)
assign
assigned rights
attribute
Browse right (B)
Can't Compress (Cc)
Compare right (C)
Compressed (Co)
Copy Inhibit (Ci)
Create right (C)
Delete right (D)
Delete Inhibit (Di)
directory entry table (DET)
Directory rights
Don't Compress (Dc)
Don't Migrate (Dm)
Don't Suballocate (Ds)
effective rights
Erase right (E)
Execute Only (X)
File rights
File Scan right (F)
grant
Hidden (H)
Immediate Compress (Ic)
inherited rights
Inherited Rights Filter (IRF)
Migrated (M)
Modify right (M)
Normal (N)
Object rights
Property rights
[Public]
Purge Immediate (P)
Read Only (Ro)
Read right (R)
Read Write (Rw)
Rename Inhibit (Ri)
Rename right
rights
security equivalence
Sharable
Supervisor right (S)
System (Sy)
transaction tracking system (TTS)
Transactional (T)
trustee
trustee assignment
trustee list
Write right (W)

Review Questions

1. Identify each of the following as being either a command line utility, menu utility, graphical utility, console command, or NetWare Loadable Module (NLM):

   FLAG ______________________________

   FILER ______________________________

   NETADMIN ______________________________

   NetWare Administrator ______________________________

   RIGHTS ______________________________

2. ______________ define a user's access to NDS and the NetWare file system.
3. List the four types of rights:

   ____

   ____

   ____

   ____

4. What is the purpose of Object rights? ______________________________
5. The ______________ right enables a user to see an object in the NDS Directory tree.
6. The ______________ right enables a user to create NDS objects in a container object.
7. What is the purpose of Property rights? ______________________________
8. The ______________ right enables a user to compare a value to a property setting but not to see the value itself.
9. The ______________ right enables users to add themselves to a user list if the object has one.
10. What is the purpose of Directory rights? ______________________________
11. The ______________ Directory right enables a user to see file and subdirectory names.
12. The ______________ Directory right enables a user to rename the directory.
13. The ______________ Directory right enables a user to assign rights to other users.
14. What is the purpose of File rights? ______________________________
15. The ______________ File right enables a user to salvage a file if it is deleted.
16. The ______________ File right enables users to read a file if they do not have the necessary Directory rights.
17. The ______________ File right enables a user to change data within an existing file.
18. The ______________ Directory right cannot be revoked or blocked within the directory structure in which it is defined.
19. ______________________________ consists of a subset of the access rights and controls what functions a user can perform in a directory or file.

Figure 10-84 shows the NDS Directory tree for FDR Investments. Use this Directory tree as the basis for answering questions 20-25. [Public] has no rights in the tree.

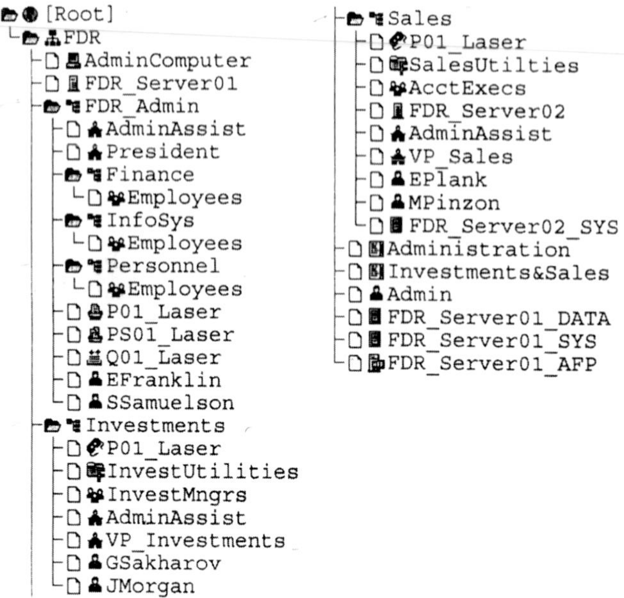

Figure 10-84 FDR Directory Tree

20. You work in administration and have been given the `[ BCD ]` rights to the FDR Organization object and the `[SBCDR]` rights to the FDR_Admin organizational unit. What are your effective rights in the Finance.FDR_Admin.FDR organizational unit? Why do you have these rights?

21. You work in administration and have been given the `[ BCD ]` rights to the FDR Organization object and the `[SBCDR]` rights to the FDR_Admin organizational unit. What are your effective rights in the Sales.FDR organizational unit? Why do you have these rights?

22. You work in sales and are a member of AcctExecs. You have been given the `[ B ]` right to the FDR Organization object and the `[BCDR]` rights to the Sales.FDR organizational unit. In addition, AcctExecs has the `[S]` right to Sales.FDR. What are your effective rights in the Sales.FDR organizational object? Why do you have these rights?

23. You are the new VP for Investments and are a member of InvestManagers. You have been given the `[ B ]` right to the FDR Organization object and the `[ B ]` right to the Investments.FDR organizational unit. In addition, InvestManagers has the `[ CD ]` rights to Investments.FDR. As VP for Investments you have the `[ R ]` right for Investments.FDR. What are your effective rights in the Investments.FDR organizational object? Why do you have these rights?

24. Given that you are a member of the AcctExecs group that has been granted the `[ RW F ]` rights to a directory called BUSINESS and have a trustee assignment of `[ R C F ]` to the BUSINESS directory, what are your effective rights in the BUSINESS directory?

25. Assume you have been given a trustee assignment of `[ R C F ]` to the BUSINESS directory and a trustee assignment of Erase and Write to the BUSINESS\ SPDATA\BUDGETS subdirectory. What are your effective rights in the BUSINESS\SPDATA subdirectory?

For questions 26–28, use the following rights assignment information: You have a trustee assignment of [WCE] to the BUSINESS directory and a trustee assignment of [E W] to the BUSINESS\SPDATA\BUDGETS subdirectory. In addition, you belong to a group that was granted the [R F] rights to the BUSINESS directory.

26. What are your effective rights in the BUSINESS\SPDATA\BUDGETS subdirectory?

27. Assume all rights except [R] and [F] are removed from the IRF of the BUSINESS\SPDATA subdirectory. What are your rights in the BUSINESS\SPDATA subdirectory?

28. What are your rights in the BUSINESS\SPDATA\BUDGETS subdirectory?

Questions 29–37 all deal with Taft Distribution, Inc. and its personnel. Rights granted in one question are assumed to still be granted in following questions, and rights deleted in one question are assumed to still be deleted in following questions.

29. On the lines below, write the RIGHTS commands to give the user JMann the [WCEM A] rights to the SERVER01/DATA:BUSINESS\BUDGETS directory and the ADMIN group the [RW F] rights to the SERVER01/DATA:BUSINESS directory.

____

____

30. Write the RIGHTS command to remove the Modify and Access Control rights from the trustee assignment made for the user JMann in the DATA:BUSINESS\BUDGETS directory.

____

31. Write a RIGHTS command to display all the trustee assignments in the DATA:BUSINESS directory.

____

32. Write a RIGHTS command to determine your effective rights in the BUSINESS\SPDATA directory.

____

33. Write a RIGHTS command that would prevent users and groups from inheriting rights in the BUSINESS\USER subdirectory.

____

34. Write a RIGHTS command to assign the user JMann the [E] and [M] rights in the BUSINESS\SPDATA subdirectory.

____

35. Write a RIGHTS command to delete the trustee assignment made to the user JMan in the BUSINESS\SPDATA\BUDGETS subdirectory.

____

36. Assume the user JMan was given a trustee assignment of [RWCEMF] to the BUSINESS\SPDATA directory and initially had a trustee assignment of [RWC F] in the BUSINESS\SPDATA\BUDGETS subdirectory. What are JMan's effective rights in the BUSINESS\SPDATA\BUDGETS subdirectory after his trustee assignment to BUDGETS was deleted in Question 35?

37. In the space below, state whether the user JMann gained or lost rights in the BUDGETS directory and explain why.

38. When you set the Read Only attribute, what other attributes are also set by default?

39. Which of the following attributes are used with directories?

Archive needed	______________
Copy inhibit	______________
Delete inhibit	______________
Don't compress	______________
Don't migrate	______________
Don't suballocate	______________
Execute only	______________
Hidden	______________
Immediate compress	______________
Purge immediate	______________
Read only	______________
Read write	______________
Rename inhibit	______________
Sharable	______________
System	______________
Transactional	______________

40. Write a FLAG command setting the attributes to enable software files in a SYS:SOFTWARE\WP directory to be used by more than one user at a time and also prevent the files from being deleted or changed.

    ____

41. Write a FLAG command setting the directory attribute that will prevent deleted files in the SYS:SOFTWARE\TEMP directory from being salvaged.

    ____

42. In the space below, explain the advantages to be gained from setting the Purge Immediate attribute on a directory.

EXERCISES

EXERCISE 10-1: WORKING WITH ACCESS RIGHTS

The objective of this exercise is to provide you with practice assigning access rights to a directory and then attempting to perform several disk operations in that directory to see how the access rights affect use of the file system. In the following steps, make sure to substitute your assigned student number for the number symbols (##).

1. Log in using your assigned student user name and change to your ##ADMIN directory.
2. Create a directory called CHAP10 within your ##ADMIN directory.
3. Use the NCOPY command to copy all files with the *.WK1 extension from the SYS:SOFTWARE.NTC\SP subdirectory into the CHAP10 subdirectory.
4. Use NETADMIN to create a user named ##USER10 and a group called ##GROUP10.

5. Use NETADMIN to assign ##USER10 the Access Control right to CHAP10 and Read and File Scan rights to SYS:SOFTWARE.NTC.
6. Log out.
7. Log in as ##USER10 and change to the ##ADMIN\CHAP10 directory.
8. Use the DIR command to view the files. Record your results below.

9. Use NETADMIN to grant ##USER10 File Scan rights to CHAP10.
10. Repeat step 8 and record your observations in the space below.

11. Try to read the contents of a file by using the TYPE filename command. Record the results in the space below.

12. Use NETADMIN to give ##GROUP10 the Read right to the CHAP10 directory.
13. Repeat step 11 and record your observations in the space below.

14. Try creating a subdirectory called PRACTICE. Record your observations in the space below.

15. Use NETADMIN to give ##USER10 only the Create and Access Control rights to the CHAP10 directory.
16. Repeat step 14 and record the results below.

17. What two ways could you use to make the directories visible?

    ____

    ____

18. Try using the COPY command to copy the SP.BAT file from SYS:SOFTWARE.NTC\SP to the CHAP10 directory. Record your results in the space below.

19. Try using the COPY command to copy all files from the SYS:SOFTWARE.NTC\DB subdirectory in the CHAP10 directory. Record your results in the space below.

20. Add the File Scan right to ##GROUP10 so that you have effective rights of `[ R C   FA]` in the CHAP10 directory and then repeat step 19. Record your observations in the space below.
21. Log out.
22. Log in using your assigned ##ADMIN user name and delete any users and groups you created in this exercise.

Exercise 10-2: Using the Inherited Rights Filter

In this exercise you create a directory structure and two users and then use NetWare command line utilities to grant trustee assignments and set up an IRF in order to observe how effective rights are inherited.

Part 1: Create Directory Structure and Users

1. Log in using your assigned student user name and change to your ##ADMIN directory.
2. If you have not already done so, create a directory in your ##ADMIN work area named CHAP10.
3. Create two directories in the CHAP10 directory named ORDERS and USERS.
4. Create two users called ##CLERK1 and ##CLERK2. Create home directories for these users in the CHAP10\USERS directory.
5. Create a group named ##CLERKS.
6. Give the group ##CLERKS Read and File Scan rights to the CHAP10 directory.
7. Make ##CLERK1 a manager of the CHAP10 directory structure by granting the user name the Supervisor right.
8. Make ##CLERK2 a trustee of the CHAP10 directory with the `[   WCEM   ]` rights.
9. Log out.

Part 2: Check Effective Rights

1. Log in as ##CLERK2.
2. Use the RIGHTS command to record your effective rights in the directories listed in the following table.

Directory Path	Effective Rights
CHAP10	
CHAP10\ORDERS	
CHAP10\USERS	

3. Log out.

Part 3: Modify Trustee Assignments

In this part of the exercise you observe how making a new trustee assignment to the group of which a user is a member will change the effective rights inherited by the user to a subdirectory.

1. Log in using your assigned student user name and change to your ##ADMIN directory.
2. Use FILER to assign the ##CLERKS group no rights to the CHAP10\ORDERS subdirectory.
3. Log out.
4. Log in as ##CLERK2
5. On the line below, record your effective rights in the CHAP10 directory.

   ____

6. On the line below, record your effective rights in the CHAP10\ORDERS subdirectory.

   ____

7. Why didn't your effective rights in the CHAP10 directory flow down to the CHAP10\ORDERS directory? Explain in the space below.
8. Log out.

Part 4: Using IRFs to Change Effective Rights

1. Log in using your assigned ##ADMIN user name.
2. Use NETADMIN or FILER to remove all rights except File Scan and Supervisor from the IRF of the CHAP10\USERS directory.
3. Use NETADMIN or FILER to enable the CHAP10\ORDERS directory to inherit only Read and File Scan rights.
4. Log out.
5. Log in as ##CLERK2.
6. Use the RIGHTS command to record your effective rights in the subdirectories shown in the following table.

Directory Path	Effective Rights
CHAP10	
CHAP10\ORDERS	
CHAP10\USERS	

7. Log out.
8. Log in as ##CLERK1.

9. Use the RIGHTS command to record your effective rights in the subdirectories shown in the following table.

Directory Path	Effective Rights
CHAP10	
CHAP10\ORDERS	
CHAP10\USERS	

Exercise 10-3: Using FILER to Work with Directory Attributes

The objective of this exercise is to provide you with experience using the FILER utility and to set directory attributes.

1. Log in using your assigned ##ADMIN user name.
2. Start FILER.
3. Change the directory path to your ##ADMIN directory.
4. Create a new directory named MENUS.
5. Add the Don't Compress attribute to the MENUS subdirectory.
6. Exit FILER.
7. Use a FLAG command to display the directory attributes. You should see the Don't Compress attribute.
8. Use FILER to remove the MENUS directory.
9. Log out.

Exercises

Case 10-1: J. Q. Adams Company Security

Assume that you are the network administrator for J. Q. Adams. Lois, John, and Ann are employees of J. Q. Adams who all work in the business department. The business department's directory structure is shown in Figure 10-85.

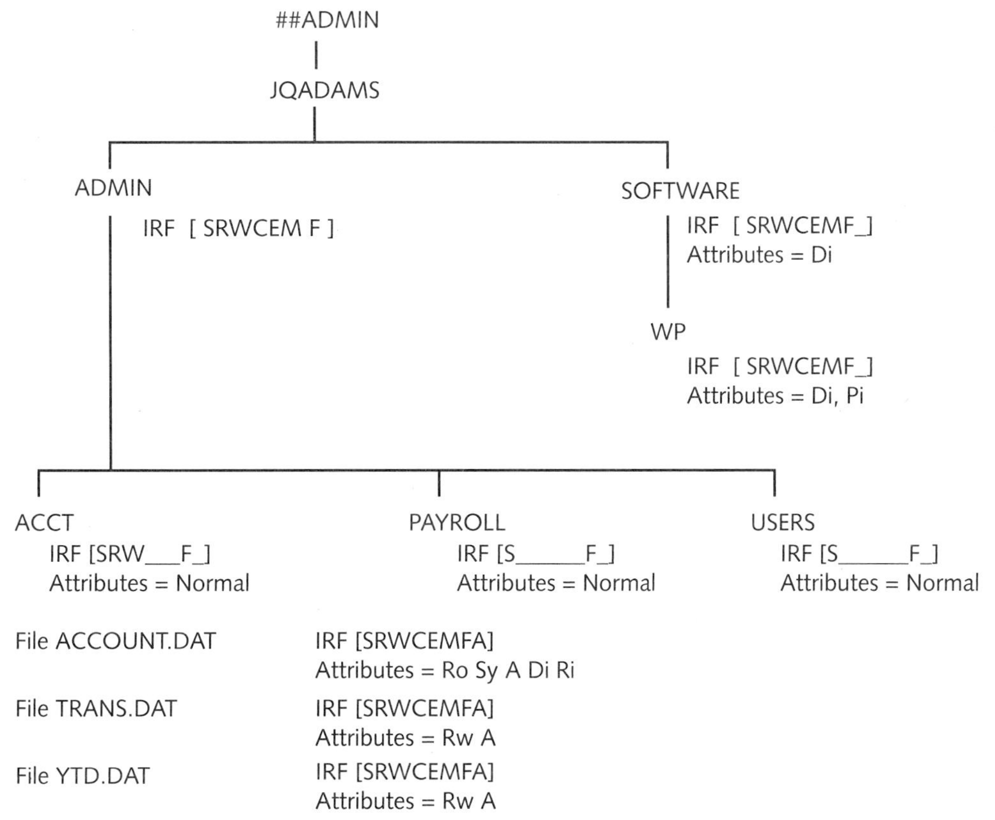

Figure 10-85 J. Q. Adams business department directory structure

Step 1: Creating a Structure

In order to perform this exercise and answer the questions, you first need to create the directory structure for J. Q. ADAMS in your ##ADMIN student work area by performing the following steps:

1. Log in using your assigned student user name.
2. Using NetWare Administrator, create the directory structure shown in Figure 10-85.
3. Set the IRFs for each of the directories as indicated in Figure 10-85.
4. Set the Delete Inhibit attribute on each of the directories in the JQADAMS structure.
5. Obtain a hard copy of your JQ ADAMS directory structure including the IRFs for each directory.
6. Use the FLAG command to display the attributes for each of your JQADAMS directories and subdirectories.
7. Use the Print Scrn key to print the screen showing your directory attributes.

Step 2: Working with Files

In this case study exercise you need to create the general ledger files for the ACCT directory and use FLAG commands to set attributes necessary to meet the requirements specified in the problem.

1. Use the MAP command to create a root drive mapping (L:) to the JQADAMS directory.
2. Change your default DOS prompt to the L:\JQADAMS\ACCT directory.

3. Use the following COPY command to create the ACCOUNT.DAT file in the ACCT directory.

   COPY CON ACCOUNT.DAT

   This is the Accounts Database. [press Enter]

   General ledger accounts and their descriptions are stored here. [press Enter]

   [press F6] [press Enter]

4. Use a text editor to create the TRANS and YTD files shown in Figure 10-86.

   TRANS.DAT:

   This is the Accounts Transaction file.

   Debit and Credit entries are stored here.

   YDT.DAT

   This is the year-to-date summary file.

   End of year totals are stored here.

Figure 10-86

Directory/File	Attribute Requirements
ACCOUNT.DAT	Protect the file from being changed and enable shared access.
TRANS.DAT	Protect the file from being erased or renamed, but allow changes to the contents.
YTD.DAT	Protect the file from being erased or renamed, but allow changes to the contents.
SOFTWARE:	Hide this directory.
SOFTWARE\WP:	Immediately purge any deleted files.

5. Use the appropriate command or utility to set the file and directory attributes as described in Figure 10-86. On the lines below, record each command or utility you used.

   ACCOUNT.DAT file: ______________________________

   TRANS.DAT file: ______________________________

   YTD.DAT file: ______________________________

   SOFTWARE:______________________________

   SOFTWARE\WP: ______________________________

6. Use the NDIR command to obtain a hardcopy of all files in the ACCT directory.
7. Use FLAG commands to obtain a hard copy of all directory attributes. This can be done by adding ">PRN" to the end of the FLAG commands you enter.

Step 3: Creating Users and Groups

In this exercise you will create the users and groups needed for the J. Q. Adams business department. Be sure to replace the number symbols (##) in each user name with your assigned student number.

1. Create the group ##ADMIN and assign the group [R F] rights to the JQADAMS directory.
2. Create the following user accounts having home directories in the JQADAMS\USERS subdirectory. Make all users members of the ADMIN group.

Figure 10-87

J. Q. Adams user accounts

User	User and Home Directory Name
John Combs	##JCcombs
Lois Kent	##LKent
Ann Bonny	##ABonny

Step 4: Assigning Trustee Rights

In this case study exercise you use NetWare Administrator to grant trustee assignments for the JQADAMS directory structure to the business department users you created.

1. Launch NetWare Administrator.
2. Because John is the supervisor of the business department, grant him the Supervisor right in the JQADAMS directory structure.
3. Make Ann a trustee of the payroll directory by giving her all rights to the PAYROLL subdirectory.
4. Make Lois a trustee with `[ RWFC E ]` rights to the ACCT directory.
5. Grant the ##ADMIN group `[ R    F ]` rights to the JQADAMS directory.
6. Obtain a hard copy of the trustee assignments for each of the JQADAMS directories.

Step 5: Determining Effective Rights

In this case study exercise you use the appropriate NetWare commands to answer questions regarding the user's effective rights to the directory structure. Following each question are lines for you to record what command you used to determine the rights and who you were logged in as when you used the command. In addition, explain why the user or group has these rights and how the rights were obtained.

1. What are John's rights in PAYROLL? ____________________

   Command used: ____________________

   Logged in as: ____________________

   In the space below, explain how John got these rights.

   ____

   ____

2. In the space below, explain what you would do if you no longer wanted John to have all rights to the PAYROLL subdirectory but still have Supervisor rights in the other subdirectories of the JQADAMS structure.

   ____

   ____

3. What are Ann's rights in the ACCT directory? ____________________

   Command used: ____________________

   Logged in as: ____________________

   In the space below, explain how Ann got these rights.

   ____

   ____

4. What are Ann's rights in the PAYROLL directory? ________________

   Command used: ________________

   Logged in as: ________________

   In the space below, explain how Ann got these rights.

5. What are Lois's rights in the ACCT directory? ________________

   Command used: ________________

   Logged in as: ________________

   In the space below, explain how Lois got these rights.

6. Are Lois's rights in the ACCT subdirectory sufficient for her to keep the files updated? ________________

   If not, explain why:

   If not, provide her with the necessary rights. Record below how you did it:

7. Log in as John and determine what his effective rights are to the ACCOUNT.DAT file.

   Command used: ________________

   Logged in as: ________________

8. Try to use the DOS EDIT command to change the contents of the ACCOUNT.DAT file. Record your results in the space below.

9. Explain briefly what John must do if he needs to add information accounts to the ACCOUNTS.DAT file.

10. Use the appropriate command line utility to implement the solution you defined in step 9. Record the option you used below.

11. Ann needs to be able to post payroll transactions to the TRANS file. Briefly explain what steps you should follow to enable Ann to post to the TRANS file but not give her access to the other files in the ACCT directory.

NORTHWESTERN TECHNICAL COLLEGE

Dave Johnson is pleased with your progress in setting up the NDS Directory tree and file system structure, and creating user accounts for Northwestern Technical College. He feels the system is starting to come together nicely and is sending you a memo that will help you continue by assigning users the necessary rights to the file system. In the following problems, you will be implementing the trustee assignments defined by Dave along with setting up the necessary file and directory attributes.

For your next task, Dave Johnson would like you to document the trustee assignments for the Northwestern Technical College campus that are necessary to provide the users with the effective rights they will need in the NDS Directory tree and directories and files, while at the same time protecting the NDS Directory tree and the file system from accidental erasure and preventing unauthorized access by student users who will be sharing the same NetWare server. To do this, Dave has provided you with processing requirements for each department.

All users Except Students

1. Directory tree: All campus users need to be able to Browse the entire Directory tree. The ability to view properties, however, should be reserved for particular groups.
2. File System: All campus users will need rights to find and read files in the FORMS directory and have all rights to the campus shared work directory. In addition, they will need the necessary rights to run all software stored in the SYS:SOFTWARE.NTC directory.

Student Services Department

1. Directory tree: All members have rights to read object properties. The Student Services Manager has all Object and Property rights including Supervisor.
2. File System: All the users in the student services department need rights in the department's shared work directory to do everything except assign rights to other users.

Support Personnel

1. Directory tree: All members have rights to read object properties. The Support Staff Manger has Write Property rights to all properties.
2. File System: Mimi Ito does work for the faculty and will need rights to Create, Erase, and Maintain files in departmental work directories. Laurie Holt is responsible for working with the policies, surveys, etc., so she needs access to all subdirectories of the SUPPORT directory. Both Mimi and Laurie need rights to work with files in the shared work directory, but only Mimi should have the ability to clean up the directory by deleting files. Laurie will be given the responsibility of maintaining files in the FORMS directory.

InfoSys

1. Directory tree: Supervisor rights to all objects and all properties throughout the tree.
2. File System: Supervisor rights throughout the file structure.

Faculty

1. Directory tree: Faculty can read properties on all objects. Department chairs have Write Property rights to the faculty User objects in their department.
2. File System: In addition to all rights to their home directories, faculty members need all rights except Access Control and Supervisor to the faculty shared work directory, and all rights except Access Control and Supervisor in their departmental work directories. They should also have rights to Create, Read, and Find files in the Support WORK directory. This will enable the faculty members to place files in the directory for Mimi Ito to work on and then read the file after she has finished. Mimi will be the only user responsible for changing and deleting the files after they have been placed in the directory.

Computer Lab

1. Directory tree: Students can Browse only the Lab portion of the tree and can read properties on other students. They cannot read properties for faculty or staff.
2. File System: Other than for their home directories, where they have all rights, except Access Control and Supervisor, the computer workstation users should have only the rights to run programs in the computer lab software directory and Read and Find files in the CLASSES directory.

Project 10-1: Make Trustee Assignments

In this Northwestern Technical College problem you need to define and make the NDS Directory tree and file system trustee assignments discussed above. First, define the trustee assignments that you are going to make. You should write this assignment in memo form for collection by your instructor. Second, implement the trustee assignments you've planned in your portion of the NDS tree.

Project 10-2: File and Directory Attributes

Dave Johnson would like to see all files in the FORMS directory protected from accidental deletion while still enabling them to be changed. In addition, he would like you to create two TEMP directories: one for the computer lab and one for administration and faculty users. Because the TEMP directories will be used to store work files that are erased after use, both directories should be flagged with the appropriate attribute to prevent these files from being saved for salvaging. Furthermore, the MENUS directory in the computer lab should be Hidden to discourage students from browsing through the menus. Finally, you should protect each of the directories in your structure from being accidentally erased.

1. Protect all files in the FORMS directory from accidental deletion.
2. Set the appropriate attributes on the TEMP and MENU directories along with protecting the directory structure.
3. Use the NDIR command to obtain a hard copy listing all files in the FORMS directory along with their attributes.

4. Use the FLAG command to print out the attributes on the following directories:

   FORMS

   MENUS

   All subdirectories of the ADMIN directory

   All subdirectories of the LAB directory

5. After your directory structure has been protected, test your system by logging in as one of the users and attempting to access files and delete parts of the directory structure.

CHAPTER ELEVEN

INSTALLING APPLICATIONS

Your responsibilities as a network administrator will include the installation, configuration, and testing of application software. Before adding any software on the file server, you need to be sure you do not violate the terms of the software license agreement. Read the software license agreement to determine if it is legal to run the software from a file server and be sure you have the correct number of licenses to cover the number of users who will be accessing the application at one time. As the network administrator, you will be held responsible if the organization you work for is found to be in violation of the software license, so you need to make certain that the software you install on the server does not violate copyrights.

AFTER READING THIS CHAPTER AND COMPLETING THE EXERCISES YOU WILL BE ABLE TO:

- LIST AND DEFINE THE THREE LEVELS OF NETWARE COMPATIBILITY.
- DESCRIBE THE THREE TYPES OF NETWORK-COMPATIBLE PROGRAMS.
- CREATE THE FILE STRUCTURE NECESSARY FOR INSTALLING NETWORK APPLICATIONS.
- USE NETWARE COMMANDS TO INSTALL SOFTWARE AND GRANT USERS THE RIGHTS THEY NEED TO RUN SOFTWARE.
- INSTALL AND TEST SIMULATED APPLICATIONS.
- USE THE NETWARE APPLICATION LAUNCHER.

Because software packages have such a wide variety of specialized installation programs and procedures, it is not feasible to provide a detailed set of rules and techniques that will work for installing all applications. Refer to the installation instructions that come with each application to work out the details of installing that product on the file server. There are, however, several general steps that should be followed for most software installations. This chapter describes the following eight steps of software installation:

1. Determine NetWare compatibility.
2. Determine single-user or multiuser capability.
3. Determine the appropriate directory structure.
4. Perform the application installation procedure.
5. Set appropriate directory and file attributes.
6. Provide user access rights.
7. Modify configuration files.
8. Test the software.

Determining NetWare Compatibility

When you install an application on a NetWare server, it is important to first determine the application's level of NetWare compatibility. Most new applications are designed and written for use on networks and can be installed by following the network installation instructions that are included with the software package. Because NetWare is very compatible with DOS, most older applications will also run flawlessly from the server even though they were originally written for a stand-alone computer. Certain programs, however, cannot be installed on a NetWare drive, and others will not run properly after installation. In this section, you will learn about the three basic levels of NetWare compatibility and how they affect the installation procedure: NetWare incompatible, NetWare compatible, and NetWare aware.

NetWare Incompatible

Certain applications are designed to work only from a local workstation's hard drive. This is often the case with older applications—especially those that have copy protection systems built into the software or installation program. Some of these copy protection systems require a special disk containing the software license number to be in the disk drive of the machine running the program. Sometimes these applications will run when installed on a file server; the workstation running the software, however, will need to have the original disk. Other software installation procedures involve writing information, such as the software license, directly to the hard drive of the computer in which the software is installed. Because these installation programs write directly to the DOS partition of the local computer's hard drive, they cannot be used to install the software onto the file server. As a result, these software packages will either fail to be installed into the NetWare file system or not run properly if copied into a NetWare directory.

Today almost all commercially available software packages are designed to run from either a network file server or a workstation's local hard drive. Some software companies, however, have designed their programs to run from a file server only when you purchase the network version of the application. When you attempt to copy the workstation version of one of these programs to the file server and then run the program from an attached workstation, an error message informs you that the application cannot be run from a network drive. This problem is easily solved by purchasing a network upgrade for the software package, which allows the number of workstations specified in your license to access the software from the server at the same time.

NetWare Compatible

Thousands of software applications are certified by Novell as being NetWare compatible. **NetWare compatible** means that the software can be installed in the NetWare file system and will then run properly from any workstation just as if it were running from that workstation's local disk drive. Although many programs are not specifically designed for NetWare, the NetWare DOS requester or NetWare Client 32 makes the NetWare file system appear as a local drive. Most applications, therefore, are not aware of the fact that they are being run from a file server rather than the local hard disk. To deal with these programs, the network administrator usually uses NetWare drive mappings to establish regular or search drives in order to install and run these programs from the file server. To determine if a software package you are considering is NetWare compatible, refer to one of the following sources:

- Novell's Internet site
- A regional Novell sales office
- The supplier of the application

NetWare Aware

Many software applications today are designed to take advantage of the features found in LAN operating systems. They therefore often include special NetWare installation options such as setting up network printing or creating separate work and configuration files for each user. These software packages are referred to as being **NetWare aware**.

Microsoft Windows applications can automatically take advantage of many network functions when Windows is installed on networked workstations. A user running the Microsoft Word application on a networked workstation, for example, can choose to send output directly to a NetWare printer or access a document file using a drive pointer that has been previously mapped to the NetWare file system.

When purchasing an application that is NetWare aware, check with the supplier regarding software license requirements. Some NetWare-aware software products have built-in limitations on the number of users that can access the application at one time, based on your license agreement. You need to obtain additional license disks that you then install on the server in order to increase the number of users who can run the software applications with these built-in limitations. For software packages that do not have built-in software license counters, the purchaser is expected to obtain licenses to accommodate the number of users who need to run the software concurrently. It is the network administrator's responsibility to see that this is done.

Network metering software is available to allow a network administrator to place a limit on the number of users who can run a specified program at the same time. Installing this type of license-counting software can greatly assist you in enforcing software license agreements on your network.

Determining Single-User or Multiuser Capability

After you determine that a software package is compatible with your NetWare file server, the next step toward installation is to determine the capability of the application in terms of the number of users it supports. There are three types of network compatible programs: single-user, multiple-user, and multiuser. This section describes the three capabilities and explains how they relate to installing and using the application on your network.

Single-User Capability

Many NetWare-compatible software packages are designed to operate from the workstation's local disk drive and are therefore limited to being run by only one user at a time. These are called **single-user applications**. This limitation can be imposed by a software license or by the way the application is designed. Many software programs use temporary files to store the system information the program needs to operate. Because single-user software applications are designed to be used by only one user at a time, when two users attempt to access the application simultaneously, the information written to the temporary file for the second user can overwrite control information needed by the first user. This causes the software application to issue error messages or to crash.

Figure 11-1 illustrates the attempt by two users at CBE Labs, Jon Jorgenson and Shelly Wells, to run a single-user spreadsheet program. Jon starts the program first and opens a file named BUDGET.XLS on a network disk drive. Information about the file, including the file's name, is then written to the temporary file in the spreadsheet software directory. Shelly then starts the spreadsheet program and opens a file called SALES.XLS on a workstation's local hard drive. The spreadsheet program next writes control information from the SALES files to the same temporary file used to store the control information for the BUDGET file. The result is that the control information for Jon is erased, causing his spreadsheet program to crash or produce an error message when the file information is needed.

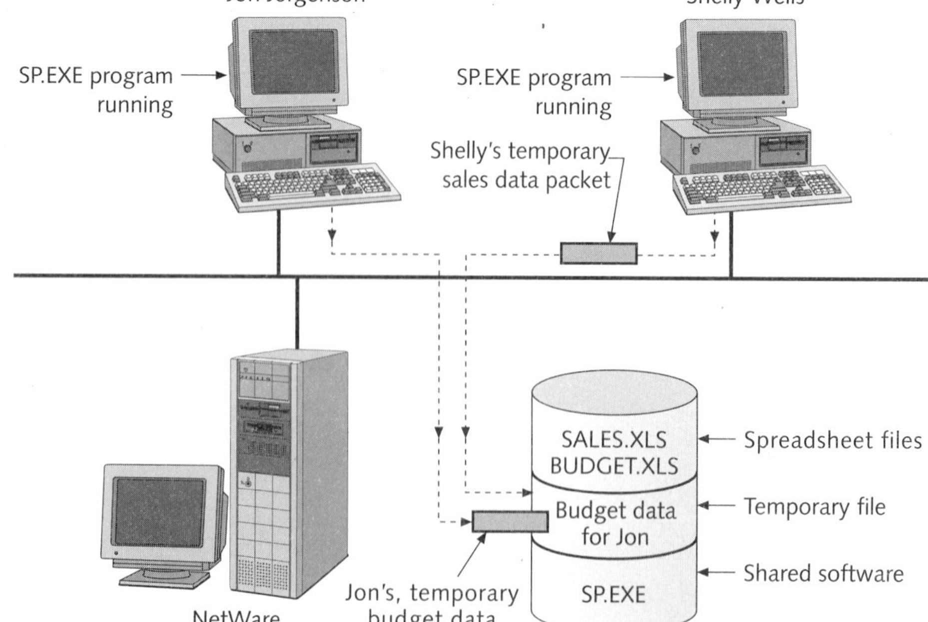

Figure 11-1 Single-user software application

Even if a software application supports only one user at a time, there are still advantages to placing it on a file server rather than on a local workstation. One advantage is that it can be used by more than one user, as long as it is not done simultaneously. Another advantage is that it prevents users from modifying the configuration files or illegally copying the software to another machine. When a software program is installed on a NetWare file server, you can use access rights and file attributes to prevent files from being changed or copied. A disadvantage of running certain applications from a file server can be the additional load placed on the network cable system, causing the speed of the network to suffer. Running Aldus PageMaker over a network can significantly slow down other network operations because of the large amount of software and other data loaded during normal program operation. The best way to determine where to place applications to maximize their performance is to load the application on both a server and a workstation and compare its speed during normal operation.

The first step in deciding to place a single-user software package on the server is to consult the license agreement to be sure it is legal for you to run the program from a file server. Even though a single-user application can be run by only one user at a time, some software companies consider placement of their applications on a server a violation of the copyright agreement and might require you to obtain a network license in order to use the program legally.

MULTIPLE-USER CAPABILITY

A **multiple-user application** is either NetWare aware—and therefore designed to support multiple users—or is designed with enough flexibility so that the application can be set up to keep each user's work files separated. Figure 11-2 illustrates a multiple-user application. Both Thomas Myer and Sarah Johnston of CBE Labs are running a multiple-user word processing application and are working with document files on their local hard drives. Because the word processing software is designed for multiple users, Thomas's control information for the LETTER1 document file is kept in a temporary file that is separate from the control information for Sarah's MEMO2 document file. Keeping each user's temporary and configuration data in separate files is one way multiple-user software applications support simultaneous use of a program.

Figure 11-2 Multiple-user software application

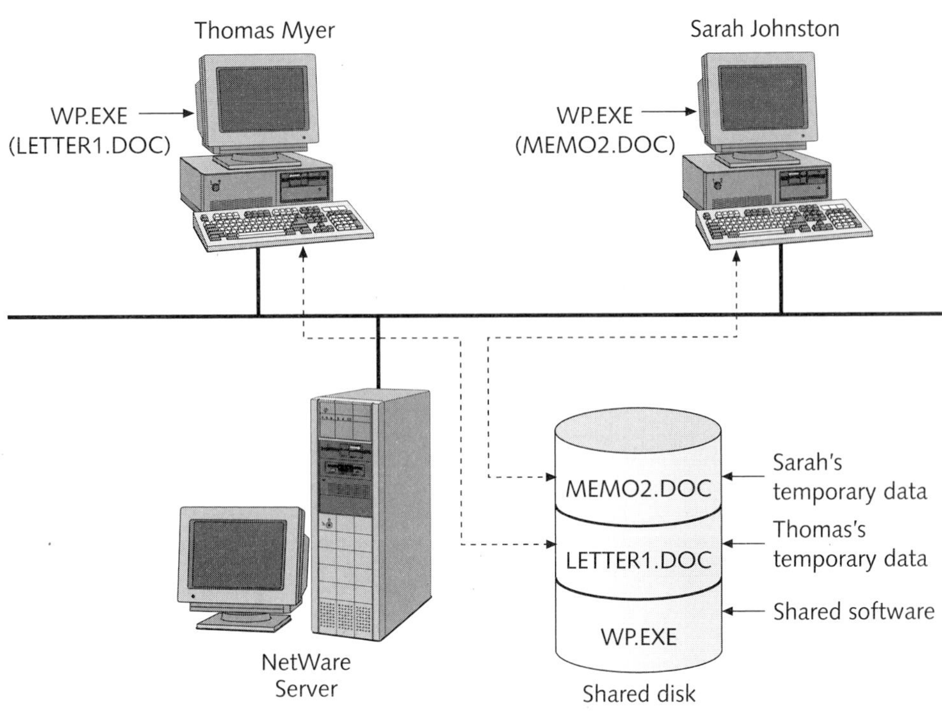

Some applications that are designed for use by a single user on a local workstation can be adapted to support multiple users on a network. This is done by setting up a search drive to the software directory, flagging the program files as sharable, and then providing separate work directories for each user's configuration files. This is a complicated procedure that can be a difficult experience if you are not very familiar with the workings of the program or don't have the advice of someone who has reconfigured an application in this way.

Most network system software (such as Microsoft Windows), and general-purpose software applications (such as word processors, desktop publishing, spreadsheets, and database management software) are accessed simultaneously by many users. This means that the network administrator needs to maintain only one copy of the applications on the file server rather than keep track of multiple copies installed on separate workstations. NetWare-aware programs are designed to support multiple users simultaneously and, provided you obtain the correct number of licenses for the number of users, can be installed by following the instructions for your network system. Multiple-user applications enable users to manage data and document files located anywhere in the network file system. A user in the finance department, for example, can access a spreadsheet program to create a graph showing projected sales for the quarter while a user in the accounting department runs the same spreadsheet software to do a cash flow analysis report.

Although a multiple-user application enables more than one user to run the program at the same time to work on separate files, it does not enable two or more users to access the same file simultaneously. Two users can, for example, use the same word processing program, but they cannot access the same document file and make changes to it simultaneously. The first user must finish his or her changes and close the file before the next user can access the document to view or change it.

MULTIUSER CAPABILITY

A **multiuser application** is a special type of multiple-user software that enables more than one user to access the same file simultaneously. Multiuser applications are often required in a database system when more than one user needs to access data. This situation occurs, for example, in an order-entry system—like the one shown in Figure 11-3—when two or more records in the Orders database need to be updated by clerks processing orders at the same time. In this illustration, Sarah Johnston and Thomas Myer from CBE Labs receive calls at the same time from different customers placing orders. Customer 4 orders 10 subscriptions; Customer 2 orders 3. Because the ORDERS program is designed to enable more than one user to access the Orders database, Sarah can be writing Customer 4's order to disk at the same time Thomas is updating Customer 2's order information, which is stored in a separate database record.

Application systems with multiuser programs—such as order-entry systems or airline reservation systems—often use programs that include special features to prevent one user's changes from overwriting changes made by another user. **Record locking** is one of the features included with most multiuser applications to protect the database records from corruption in the event that two users access the same record simultaneously. Record locking enables a multiuser program to prevent users on the network from editing a specific record in a file while it is being updated. While a sales clerk is working with Customer 4, for example, no other user on the network can edit Customer 4's order information.

Figure 11-3

Multiuser software application

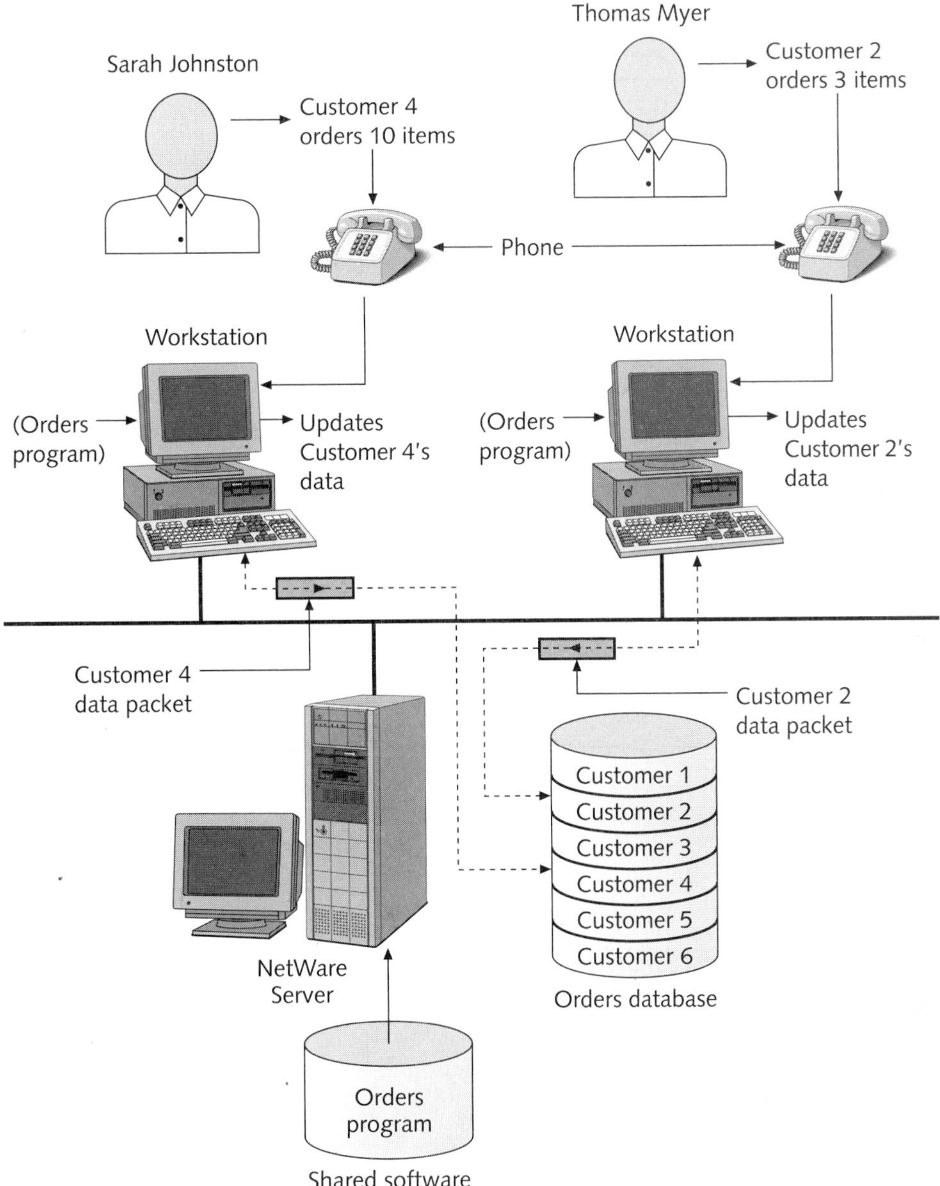

In addition to record locking, NetWare includes a feature called the **Transaction Tracking System (TTS)**. The TTS, working with record locking, enables software packages to recover data in the event that a workstation crashes in the middle of processing a transaction. Assume, for example, that Thomas Myer's computer crashes after Customer 4's order has been written to disk but before the customer's accounts receivable data is updated. Transaction tracking enables Thomas to return the customer order information to its preorder status and then re-enter Customer 4's order. Without transaction tracking, Customer 4's order could accidentally be placed twice while the account balance is updated only once. Both record locking and transaction tracking require that the application software be written to make use of special multiuser instructions in order to enable the application to implement the record locking and transaction tracking features of NetWare.

Integrated network applications such as Microsoft Office make use of a process in Microsoft Windows called dynamic linking. This process enables a master document file to consist of multiple object documents. Each object document can then be accessed by a different user, enabling the master document to be updated automatically with any changes that are made to the object documents.

Determining the Appropriate Directory Structure

After you determine the NetWare compatibility level of the application with which you are working, the next step is to decide where the application belongs in the organization's directory structure. Where you place an application's directory in the file system is determined to a large extent by your directory structure design and by what type of application you are installing. This section provides suggestions for placement of an application's directory, based on whether the application is single-user, multiple-user, or multiuser.

Single-User Application

Because single-user applications will be used by only one user at a time, access to them is usually restricted to just a few users in an organization. Because of this, a single-user application is best stored in a location of the directory structure that is closest to the users who will be running the application. A single-user payroll application for CBE Labs, for example, is normally used by one or two users in the Finance department. The logical location for the directory containing the payroll software and data is therefore within the Finance department's shared directory structure, as shown in Figure 11-4.

CONSTELLATION
CONSTELLATION_SYS:
CONSTELLATION_DATA:
FINANCE
SHARED
BUDGETS

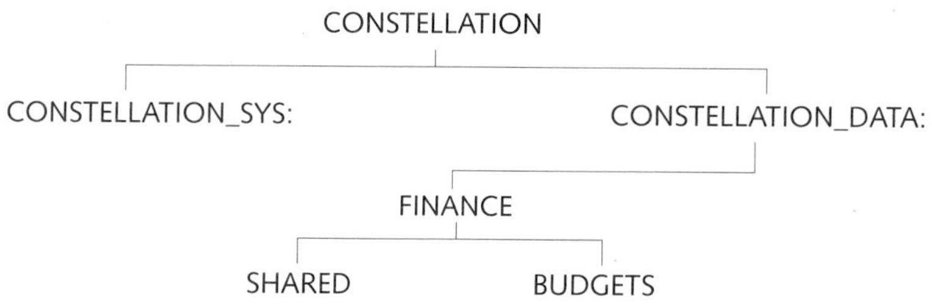

Figure 11-4 Single-user application directory structure

Multiple-User Applications

General-purpose multiple-user applications such as word processors, spreadsheets, graphics, or database software applications that are accessed by many users in an organization to maintain their own separate files are often placed in a common directory in the SYS: volume, as shown in Figure 11-5. This directory structure enables the network administrator to use the inherited rights principle (described in Chapter 10) to easily provide read and file scan rights to the general-purpose applications for all users to the APPS directory.

CONSTELLATION
CONSTELLATION_SYS:
CONSTELLATION_DATA:
APPS
WINOFFICE
PAGEPUB

Figure 11-5 Multiple-user application directory structure

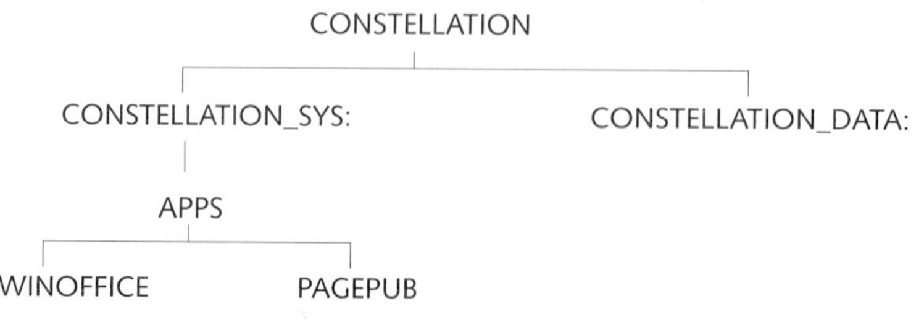

When Microsoft Windows 3.x is installed on a network, a Windows directory is usually created in the NetWare file system to contain the shared Windows program files. The files in this directory can then be shared by all users after all files are copied into the shared Windows directory with the SETUP/A installation command. This use of shared program files saves much installation time and disk space that would otherwise be required for multiple installations of the same files.

MULTIUSER APPLICATIONS

As described earlier in this chapter, multiuser applications need to be specially written to take advantage of such network features as record locking and transaction tracking. As a result, multiuser applications are usually designed for specific database-oriented applications that handle such tasks as order entry, reservations, or inventory control. Because of the specialized nature of multiuser applications, their location can often be based on the users of each application. CBE Labs, for example, may locate programs that the entire Marketing group needs in the SHARED directory, as shown in Figure 11-6. On the other hand, employee review, which is accessed only by users of the Personnel department, can be located within the PERSNNL directory structure, as shown in Figure 11-6.

Figure 11-6 Multiuser application directory structure

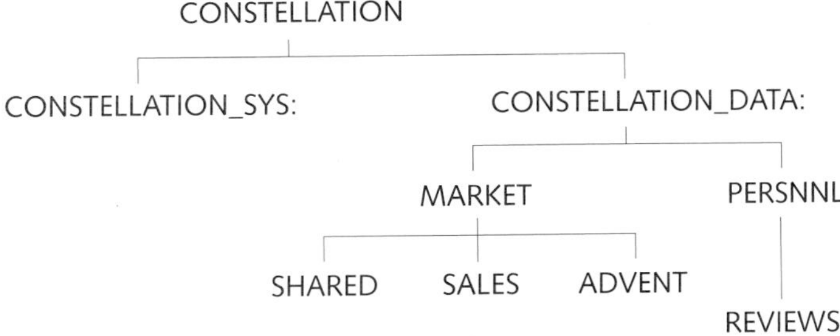

TEMPORARY AND CONFIGURATION FILES

Many NetWare-aware software programs need to store configuration information and temporary files for each user. Before you install an application, therefore, it is important to study the installation instructions to determine what options you have for placement of temporary and user configuration files. Temporary files are usually created when a user starts the application and are deleted when the application program is terminated. Configuration files, on the other hand, are permanent files that are normally used to store software settings such as printer type and default data storage path for each user. With separate configuration files, each user can customize the application to accommodate his or her normal usage. Most NetWare-aware software installation programs enable the network administrator to specify where the user's temporary and configuration files will be stored. You need to decide where these files will be stored before installing software applications. One option is to store these files on the workstation's local hard disk drive. Using the local hard disk has the advantages of keeping user files separate and reducing demands on the network. A disadvantage, however, is that the user must run the software from his or her assigned workstation to use the customized settings.

A user's Windows 3.x environment is created by using the Windows SETUP/N command to copy selected files to the specified directory for that user. This directory can be located on either a local hard disk or within a user home directory on the file server and enables each user to customize his or her Windows environment by storing configuration and temporary files separately for each user.

Because temporary files involve much more disk activity than configuration files, a good compromise, when possible, is to store configuration files on the network and have the temporary files kept on the local hard disk. When configuration files are stored on the file server, they can be placed in each user's home directory, or all user configuration files for the software package can be placed in a common configuration directory.

The Microsoft Windows 3.x operating system uses temporary files, called swap files, to extend the workstation RAM when multiple applications are run. When you install Microsoft Windows 3.x on a network, it is important to place these temporary or permanent swap files on the local hard disk of each workstation rather than on the file server. This prevents serious network performance degradation that results from Windows' need for heavy access to the swap file.

Performing the Application Installation Procedure

The installation procedure for applications generally involves running a SETUP or INSTALL program that will ask you for several items of information, including the location of the software disk, the drive or directory path into which you want to install, the location of work and configuration files, printer types, and specialized software configuration parameters. Although software configuration parameters depend on the application being installed, the network administrator needs to provide the installation program with a path to the appropriate directory locations and select the proper printers and ports that will work on the network. This section describes some of the installation considerations you need to be aware of when selecting directories and printers.

Planning Drive Pointer Usage

Prior to running the installation program for a software product, you must define any drive pointers that will be needed to install the application. Application installation programs need to know the path to the directory that will contain the application program files as well as the location of the user configuration and temporary files. Because each user who runs this application will need to have access to the application and configuration files, you should plan to use a drive pointer that will be mapped to the same volume for all users. This is important because if the drive letter you select is mapped to a different volume for some users, the directory path will not be found on the specified drive letter when these users attempt to run the application and the application will terminate. Suppose, for example, that you plan to place configuration files in the SYS:SOFTWARE\WP\SETUP directory, and during installation you specify the path to the configuration files as G:\SOFTWARE\WP\SETUP because drive G is currently mapped to the SYS: volume. Assume that after you install the application, a user, who has drive G mapped to the DATA: volume, attempts to run the application. Because the DATA: volume does not contain the \SOFTWARE\WP\SETUP directory, the application program will terminate because it cannot locate the user configuration files. In order for users to be able to run the application package, therefore, it is imperative that the paths specified for software configuration and temporary files use a drive letter that will be mapped to the same path for all users. You can do this by setting up standard drive mappings in the container login script file, as described in Chapter 14.

When installing software that is not NetWare aware, you might need to use the MAP ROOT command for the drive letter you plan to use to contain the application directory. Mapping a root drive is necessary with installation programs that are not NetWare aware because some installation programs have been known to create their own directory structure at the root of the drive letter you specify. Mapping a root drive will cause these installation programs to create the application directory within the directory structure to which you have mapped the root drive rather than at the root of the NetWare volume. If you wanted, for example, to install a payroll application that is not NetWare aware in the FINANCE directory shown in Figure 11-4, you would first select a drive letter, such as P, to be used for the payroll application and then root map the drive P pointer to the FINANCE directory using the following command:

```
MAP ROOT P:=DATA:FINANCE
```

Now when the installation program attempts to create a payroll directory in path P:\, it will actually be making the directory in the BUSINESS directory structure.

SPECIFYING THE DIRECTORY PATH

Your first step prior to running an installation program is to be sure that the drive mappings you plan to use for the application and configuration files have been established. Immediately after starting, most software installation programs will ask you to specify the path to the directory in which the application program files are to be installed. Later during the installation process, you might also have options to enter paths for both temporary and configuration files. When entering the paths, be sure to specify the drive pointers you defined when planning your directory structure.

Figure 11-7 shows a screen that appears during installation of the WordPerfect application, which includes the paths for installing the application on a network drive. Notice that the F network drive letter is being used for installation of the software along with the dictionary and other files used by the WordPerfect program. Suppose that the SOFTWARE\WP61 directory of the volume is mapped to drive F and the default directory for user document files is located on drive H. This means that, in order to use the application, each user will need to have his or her drive F letter mapped to the volume that contains the WP61 directory along with a drive H pointer mapped to the default document directory.

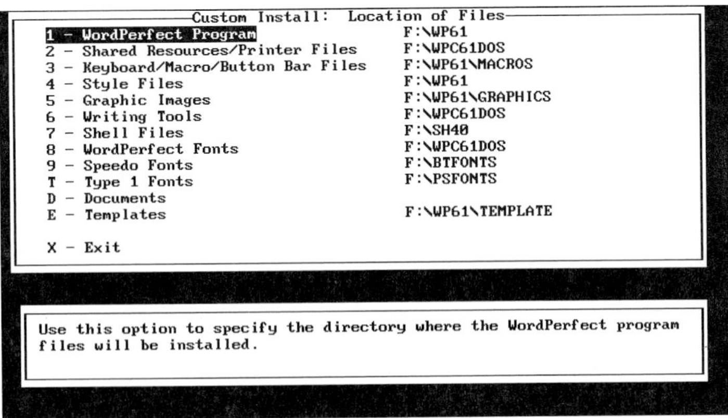

Figure 11-7 WordPerfect installation screen

SPECIFYING PRINTER TYPES AND PORTS

Most applications enable you to select one or more printer types along with the port used to obtain hard copy output. Multiple-user applications that include word processors and spreadsheets enable the installer to select many printer types for the user to choose. In these cases, you select the printer types that will be available on the user's workstations or can be shared on the network. If the application is NetWare aware, you should be able either to select a printer port, such as LPT1: through LPT3:, or enter the name of a print queue, as described in Chapter 12.

Installation programs for single-user applications might limit you to only one printer type during installation. To enable multiple users to run a software package that is installed for only one type of printer, you might want to place the selected printer on the network. Placing a printer on the network will enable all users to access the same printer type. The best solution is to select the best printer type you can afford for this application and then place that printer on the network, as described in Chapter 12. The printed output from the program can then be redirected to the network printer so that the output will be directed to the correct printer type no matter which user is operating the program.

SETTING APPROPRIATE DIRECTORY AND FILE ATTRIBUTES

After you run the software installation program, you need to be sure the application directory and files are secure. If the software is designed for multiple users, you need to provide for its shared use. If the installation program is NetWare aware, it might set the necessary file and directory attributes for you. You might, however, want to add attributes to increase file security or provide extra functions such as transaction tracking. This section discusses which attributes are appropriate for what applications. Figure 11-8 summarizes the attribute settings for each application type.

Figure 11-8

Attribute settings

Application Type	Data Files	Application Program Files
Single-user Example: Payroll	Read Write nonsharable	Read Only nonsharable (some software programs might enable multiple users to access them even if flagged nonsharable)
Multiple-User Example: word processor	Read Write nonsharable	Read Only Sharable
Multiuser Example: database system	Read Write Transactional Sharable (requires the program to provide record locking and transaction tracking)	Read Only Sharable

The function of the sharable attribute on a document file can be used to enable multiple users to access that file at the same time, as described in Chapter 10. It is usually set on record-locking database files.

SINGLE-USER APPLICATIONS

Because a single-user application can be used by only one user at a time, both data files and executable program files require no special attributes—except possibly the Read Only attribute to protect them from accidental erasure or modification by either a user or a software virus. The Read Only attribute is important for applications in which users need to be granted Erase, Modify, or Write access rights in order to work with data or temporary files that are stored in the application's directory. Setting the Read Only attribute, however, can sometimes cause application errors for certain software products that store configuration information in the program files. Make sure to test the application after setting any Read Only attributes to be sure users can perform their necessary functions. An alternative to using the Read Only attribute to protect application files from being renamed or erased and still enable changes to be made is to use the Delete Inhibit and Rename Inhibit attributes. Setting Delete Inhibit and Rename Inhibit on a file enables the contents of the file to be changed but prevents the file from being renamed or deleted.

Even though program files in a single-user application are not flagged Sharable, in some applications it is possible for two or more users to run the application at the same time, causing program problems or corrupt data files. Test a newly installed application by running it from two different workstations to determine if more than one user can access the programs simultaneously. If more than one user can run the programs at the same time, you need to develop a procedure to prevent multiple access, or else install the application in a separate directory for each user. If multiple users need access to the same data files, replace the single-user application with a NetWare-aware application that is designed to accommodate multiple users.

MULTIPLE-USER APPLICATIONS

The major difference in attribute settings between a multiple-user application and a single-user application is that the files that run the multiple-user application should be flagged Sharable to enable more than one user to access the software simultaneously. Because most multiple-user applications are NetWare aware, they are designed for shared access, and the installation process might not require you to use the FLAG command to set the Sharable attribute. You should check with the installation instructions, however, to determine if it is necessary to set any additional attributes after installation. Like those for single-user applications, data files for multiple-user applications need to be left nonsharable and Read Write in order to prevent multiple users from overwriting each other's changes. Leaving the data files nonsharable will enable only one user at a time to access and modify information in a specific file.

When some applications, such as Microsoft Word, are used on a network, a document file can be opened by two users at the same time even when it is not flagged Sharable. However, only the first user to open the document can save changes to the document under its original name. Changes made by the second user can be saved to a different filename. If the second user attempts to save the file using its original name, an "Access denied" error message is displayed.

MULTIUSER APPLICATIONS

As already stated, a multiuser application is a special form of a multiple-user application that enables more than one user to update the same data file simultaneously. The major difference in attribute settings between multiple-user and multiuser applications is that the data files to be shared should have the Sharable attribute set for multiuser applications in order to enable multiple users to access and update the database records simultaneously. In addition, in order that TTS is enabled on a shared database system, the database files need to be flagged with the Transactional attribute in addition to being made sharable. This is illustrated in a sample order entry system, shown in Figure 11-9.

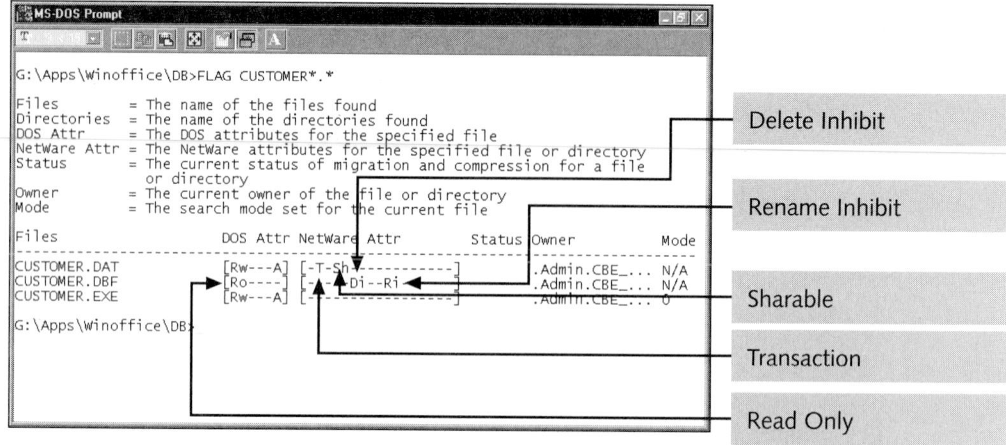

Figure 11-9 Setting multiuser file attributes

Notice that in addition to the Transactional attribute (T), the CUSTOMER database files are also flagged Delete Inhibit (DI) and Rename Inhibit (RI). These additional attributes prevent the files from being accidentally deleted or renamed by users who have been given Erase or Modify access rights. Flagging the *.EXE program files Read Only will prevent them from being changed or deleted by a user or a software virus.

ALL APPLICATIONS

In addition to the attributes already described, you might want to use NetWare's Hidden attribute to make it more difficult for users to copy program files illegally onto a local disk. To prevent an executable file from being copied, you can use the FLAG command to place the Execute Only attribute on the file. This prevents the program file from being copied while still enabling it to be run. The disadvantage of the Execute Only attribute is that once it is set on a file it cannot be removed, even by the administrator. Because of this, make sure to have original installation disks or a working backup of the application file before setting the Execute Only attribute. Certain software applications—those that open their executable program files in the read mode in order to access messages and other information—will not run correctly when the Execute Only attribute is set. Because the Execute Only attribute enables the program files to be opened only in run mode, these programs crash when they attempt to read from their program files. Make sure to test the application after you set the Execute Only attribute. Figure 11-10 shows a FLAG command that sets the Execute Only attribute and then an attempt to copy the protected file.

```
MS-DOS Prompt

G:\Apps\Winoffice\DB>FLAG *.EXE

Files        = The name of the files found
Directories  = The name of the directories found
DOS Attr     = The DOS attributes for the specified file
NetWare Attr = The NetWare attributes for the specified file or directory
Status       = The current status of migration and compression for a file
               or directory
Owner        = The current owner of the file or directory
Mode         = The search mode set for the current file

Files                 DOS Attr NetWare Attr        Status Owner          Mode
-------------------------------------------------------------------------------
CUSTOMER.EXE          [Rw---A] [----------------]         .Admin.CBE_... 0
UPDATE.EXE            [Rw---A] [X---------------]         .Admin.CBE_... 0

G:\Apps\Winoffice\DB>COPY UPDATE.EXE G:\APPS\WINOFFICE\WP
File not found - UPDATE.EXE
        0 file(s) copied

G:\Apps\Winoffice\DB>
```

Figure 11-10 Using the Execute Only attribute

Another directory attribute to consider in this context is Purge. Flagging directories that contain temporary files with the Purge attribute will cause the space used by a temporary file to be immediately reclaimed by the NetWare operating system when the temporary file is deleted. Because it is unlikely you would ever want to salvage a temporary file, flagging temporary file directories with the Purge attribute can help improve system performance and provide more time before NetWare will need to reuse space occupied by other deleted data files—ones that might be more in need of salvaging.

PROVIDING USER ACCESS RIGHTS

In order to use a newly installed application, users need access rights to the software directory along with appropriate drive mappings. As a network administrator, you need to determine the minimum set of access rights that will enable users to work with the application software and still prevent them from changing or deleting programs or files that must remain unaltered. In order to separate application software from the data, the network administrator must also define regular and search drives that will enable users to run application software from the directory containing data files. This section discusses several considerations and techniques that will help you plan and provide user access.

ACCESS RIGHTS

At a minimum, all users will need Read and File scan rights to the directory containing an application. Whenever possible, assign trustee rights to groups rather than to individual users—this makes it easier to add or change access rights later. In addition to providing these rights, you might need to assign additional rights for either of the following two conditions:

- If you are storing temporary files in the application software directory, you will need to provide users with at least the Create and Erase rights to this directory. In addition, if the software application needs to rename temporary files, you must assign the Modify right. This creates a security problem, however, in that users with the Modify right can change the attributes on program files. You can prevent this either by placing temporary files in a different directory (if possible) or by using the Inherited Rights Filter (IRF) on each of the program files, enabling them to inherit only Read and File scan rights.
- If the user configuration files are stored in the software directory and you want users to be able to customize their configuration settings, you will need to provide them with at least the Write right. If you place user configuration files in a separate directory, then assign the users Read, File Scan, Write, Create, Erase, and Modify rights to the directory that contains the configuration files.

To run a word processing application on your network, Novell suggests that you create a group of word processing users and then grant this group the following access rights:

Executable Files: Read, File Scan
Setup and Temporary Files: All except Supervisor and Access Control
Backup, Macros, Keyboard, etc: All except Supervisor and Access Control
Printer Files: Read, File Scan

DRIVE MAPPINGS

In order for users to run application software and access data files, you need to establish both search and regular drive pointers. (These drive mappings will need to be included in the login script files, as described in Chapter 14.) Regular drive pointers should provide users easy access to the directory location containing their data, with a maximum of three directory layers. The regular drive pointers consist of a drive pointer to the root of the volume, a drive pointer to the user's workgroup, and a drive pointer to the user's home directory. These drive pointers should be sufficient to access most application data files. If a data directory is accessed by users in multiple departments, however, a special drive mapping to that directory should be established for all users who need to use the data.

Search drive mappings should be established for all general-purpose software directories. When planning search drive mappings, try to keep the total number of search drives for any user to eight or fewer. This can be done by providing a menu system that will insert a search drive mapping for the application being run and then deleting that search drive mapping when the program terminates.

MODIFYING CONFIGURATION FILES

The final step of installing an application involves modifying the CONFIG.SYS files on all workstations running DOS or Windows 3.x that will be running an application. As a network administrator you need to know the statements that might need to be added to the CONFIG.SYS file of each workstation on the network. Installation programs often modify the CONFIG.SYS of the workstation in which you install the software, but the other workstations that will run this application from the network will also need to have their CONFIG.SYS files modified in order to use the application.

Figure 11-11 shows three common CONFIG.SYS statements with examples. The FILES statement increases the number of file handles available to DOS. A file handle contains information on each file that is currently open. Most network software will require at least 25 file handles. The BUFFERS statement increases the number of disk blocks that DOS will keep in memory. When NetWare drives are accessed, this number can be kept quite low, because most information comes from the network and each block takes up to 532 KB of RAM on the workstation. Between 12 and 15 blocks will be sufficient for most network workstations. The SHELL statement increases the environment space available to hold the DOS paths and search drives. In addition, certain software variables and directory locations are stored here. Because of this, it is often necessary to increase the space to at least 1024 bytes for most network workstations. If you receive the message "Out of Environment Space," you should increase the environment space by an additional 256 bytes.

Figure 11-11 Common CONFIG.SYS Statements

Statement	Example
FILES=n	FILES=25
BUFFERS=n	BUFFERS=15
SHELL=[path]COMMAND.COM/P/E:n	SHELL=COMMAND.COM/P/E:1024 The /E:1024 parameter defines 1024 bytes of environment space.

TESTING THE SOFTWARE

After all steps in the installation process have been completed, the network administrator needs to test the installation by running the application software. First test the application while logged in with Supervisor rights. Use the MAP command to establish the drive mappings you defined for the application software, change to the data directory, and issue the necessary commands to start the application. Test as many functions of the application as possible, including data entry, file access, and printing.

When you are confident that the application is installed correctly and the correct drive mappings have been defined, log out and then log back in with a username that will run the application. Repeat the tests you ran as supervisor to make sure users have been granted the rights necessary to work with the application. After you have determined that the software will run from your workstation when you log in as a user, proceed to each user's workstation and test the application to be sure the workstation configurations support the application properly. Finally, check the user's effective rights in each of the directories and program files to make sure the users cannot erase or change critical files.

NETWARE APPLICATION LAUNCHER

A new feature of the NetWare Client 32 software is the **NetWare Application Launcher (NAL)**. The NAL assists network administrators in configuring and managing applications. Once configured, users can simply choose the NAL object from the NDS tree and launch the application by clicking on it. This relieves the users from needing to know which server, volume, and directory an application is installed upon, and it also relieves the network administrator from much of the detail of managing applications on the network.

The NAL is included with both the NetWare Client 32 for Windows 95 and the NetWare Client 32 for DOS and Windows 3.x.

NAL is incorporated fully into NetWare 4.11.

To use the NAL to define an application object:

1. Launch the NetWare Administrator program.
2. Select the Organization or Organizational Unit container in which to locate the Application object.
3. Right-click the container object and select **Create** to display the available objects as shown in Figure 11-12. Note that there are four application objects, one for DOS applications, one for Windows 3.x applications, one for Windows 95 applications, and one for Windows NT applications.

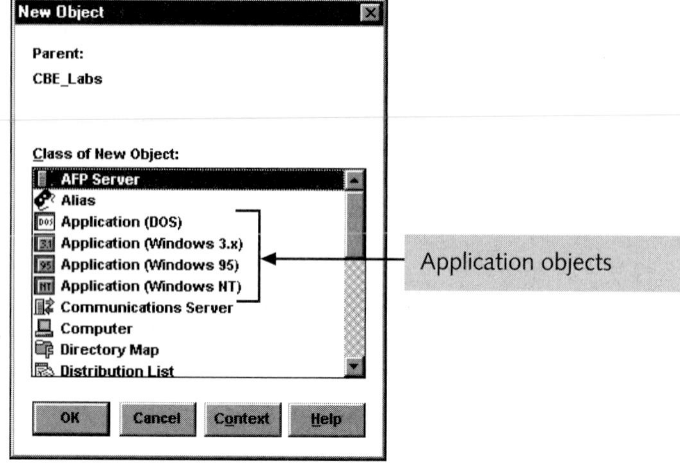

Figure 11-12 Application object

4. Click **Application (Windows 95)** and then click **OK** to display the Create Application window, as shown in Figure 11-13.

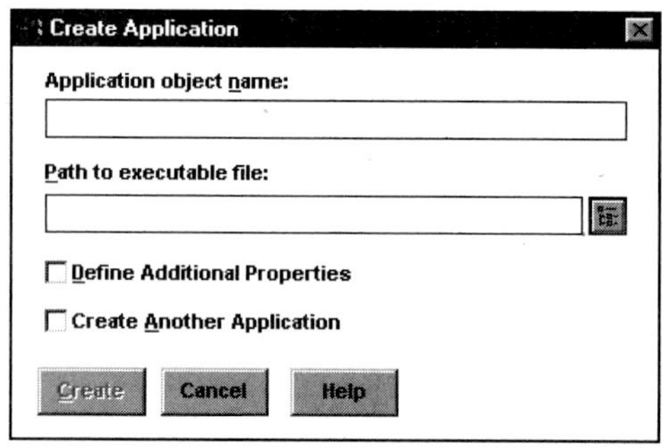

Figure 11-13 Create Application window

5. Type the name of the application as you want it to appear on the NDS tree in the Application object name text box, in this case **WinOffice Word Processor**.
6. Type the location of the file to be executed in the Path to executable file text box, in this case **\\CONSTELLATION\SYS\APPS\WINOFFICE\WP\WINWP.EXE**.
7. Click the **Define additional properties** check box to display the Application window as shown in Figure 11-14.
8. Click **Create**.

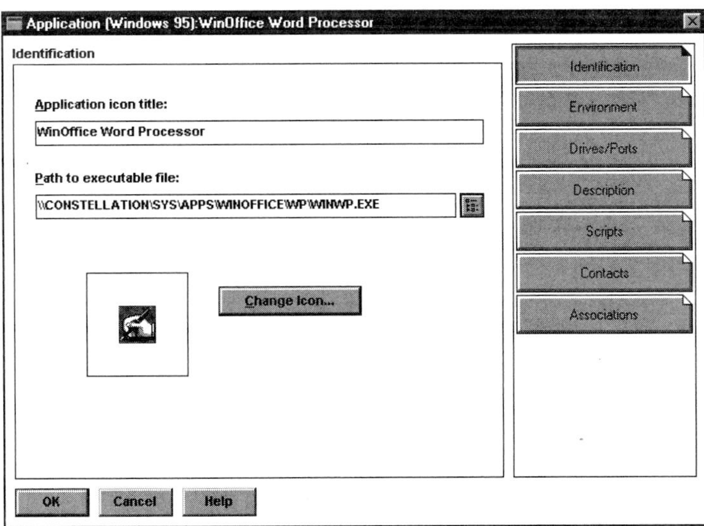

Figure 11-14 Application window

The application can be configured by selecting one of the pages from this window:

- Identification—This page permits you to change the application's icon, the title of the icon, and the path to the executable files.
- Environment—You can enter any command-line parameters that the application needs on this page.
- Drives/Ports—This page enables you to specify extra drive mappings that users may need to access the application and related data.
- Description—You can write a description of the application for users who may be unfamiliar with it. Users can then refer to this page for any information they might need.
- Scripts—You can specify login script commands that are executed either before or after the application executes.
- Contacts—This page permits you to specify whom users should contact if they encounter problems with the application.
- Associations—You can identify the User, Group, Profile, or container objects that can access the Application object.

If you right-click an NAL icon, a Quick Menu with two commands will appear: Open and Properties. The Open command will start the application; the Properties command will display the description information about the application.

9. Click **OK** and the Application object will be added to the tree, as shown in Figure 11-15.

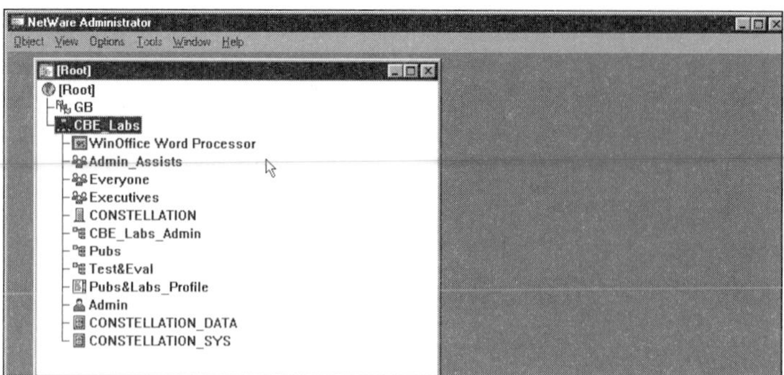

Figure 11-15 WinOffice Word Processor application object in the CBE_Labs directory tree

CHAPTER SUMMARY

Installing application software can generally be divided into eight steps. The first step is determining the application's level of NetWare compatibility. Some software is not compatible with networks and will run properly only if installed on the local hard drive of a workstation. Because NetWare is designed to work closely with DOS, most DOS applications will run from a NetWare file server without any special features or modifications. Today many software companies design their products to be aware of network features and take advantage of running from a file server.

After you determine that an application will run on a NetWare file server, the second installation step is to determine whether the application has single-user, multiple-user, or multiuser capability. A single-user application enables only one user at a time to operate the software and access the data. A multiple-user application, such as a word processor or spreadsheet program, supports multiple users running the software but enables only one user to access a specific file at a time. A multiuser application—usually a database system that tracks such information as order entry or inventory—will support multiple users accessing the same file simultaneously.

The third step in the installation process involves determining the application software directory. Shared multiple-user applications, such as word processors and spreadsheets, are usually stored in a general-purpose software directory located in the SYS: volume. In a departmentalized directory structure, single-user applications and special-purpose multiuser applications are often stored in a subdirectory of a department's workgroup directory structure.

After you decide on the location of the application's directory, the fourth step is to run the installation program and copy the application files into the selected directory path. This process usually involves entering such information as the source and target drives, the path in which to store temporary and configuration files, the type of printer and port, and special settings needed by the particular application.

Once an application's files have been copied, the fifth step is to set file and directory attributes in order to secure the files and enable shared access to multiple-user applications. Files can be protected from illegal copying by flagging them with the Hidden or Execute Only attribute. The directory structure can also be protected by flagging directories Delete Inhibit and Rename Inhibit. To improve performance, you can flag directories that contain temporary files with the Purge attribute. This recovers the file space immediately after file deletion rather than making temporary files available for salvaging.

After the file and directory attributes have been set, the sixth step involves granting trustee assignments to enable users to run the applications. To enable all users to run the general-purpose application software, you can create a group named EVERYONE and include all users in the group. Then assign the group the Read and File Scan rights to the SYS:SOFTWARE directory. In single-user and special-purpose multiuser application directories, it is sometimes also necessary to provide users with Write, Create, Erase, and Modify rights to enable them to work with configuration and data files that are stored in the same directory in which the application is stored. Whenever possible, configuration and data files should be kept in a separate directory. This avoids the necessity of assigning extra rights to the software directories.

After the software installation is complete, you need to test the installation. First run the programs while logged in with Supervisor rights. After you are confident the software has been installed correctly, log in as one of the users of the application and test each of the tasks the users will be expected to perform. The final test of the application is to run the software from each workstation in order to make sure the configuration files are correct. After all testing has been completed, you will be ready to proceed to automating the user environment with login scripts and menus as described in Chapters 14 and 15.

A new feature of the NetWare Client 32 software is the NetWare Application Launcher (NAL). The NAL enables users to choose the NAL object from the NDS tree and launch a software application by clicking on it. This relieves the users from needing to know which server, volume, and directory an application is installed upon, and it also relieves the network administrator from much of the detail of managing applications on the network.

KEY TERMS

Multiple-user application
multiuser application
NetWare Application Launcher (NAL)
NetWare aware
NetWare compatible
record locking
single-user application
transaction tracking system (TTS)

REVIEW QUESTIONS

1. What is the first step a network administrator needs to complete before installing an application?

 ____

2. After the application files have been copied into the NetWare directory by the installation program, what is the next step to be performed?

 ____

3. If you see the message "Out of Environment Space" when running a DOS or Windows 3.x application, you need to place the ______________ statement in the ______________ file.

4. List the three levels of NetWare compatibility.

 ____

 ____

 ____

5. A(n) ______________ application type enables multiple users to run the software, but only one user at a time can access a specific data file.

6. A(n) ______________ application type enables multiple users to access the same file simultaneously.

7. Which of the following would be acceptable locations in which to install a spreadsheet application that will be used by several users in a company? For each unacceptable location, briefly explain why that directory path would not make a good location.

   a. SYS:SYSTEM\SS

   b. SYS:PUBLIC

   c. SYS:APPS\SS

   d. DATA:BUSINESS\SS

   e. SYS:SS

8. What are two important directory locations that the network administrator usually needs to provide during an installation procedure?

   ____

9. The __________ attribute should generally be set on all program files.

10. The __________ attribute should also be set on multiple-user program files.

11. The __________ attribute can be set on .EXE and .COM files to prevent them from being copied.

12. What directory attribute might you consider setting on the software directories in order to secure them from curious users browsing the network?

    ____

13. At a minimum, users will need the __________ and __________ access rights to run the application software.

14. In the space below, briefly explain why it is important that the drive letter you specify in the directory path for the application's work files be one that is mapped to the same location for all users.

15. In the space below, briefly explain why it is important first to test an application logged in with supervisor rights and then test it again while logged in as a user.

16. Assume you install a database application that is designed to be used on a standalone PC on the file server. In the space below, give one reason why you should not make the database file sharable.

17. When would you not want to make program files sharable?

    ____

EXERCISES

Exercise 11-1: Testing a Single-User DOS Application

In this exercise you experiment with creating and sharing a DOS-based application program that is intended for use by a single user. The objective of this exercise is to demonstrate that a single-user application can often be accessed by more than one user at the same time despite the fact that the files are not flagged Sharable. To complete this exercise you will need to coordinate your activity with one or more students or have access to two different workstations from which you can log in and test the application. Your instructor will provide you with information regarding dividing the class into teams.

1. Identify the other student(s) with whom you are to work with and exchange usernames.
2. In his or her ##ADMIN work area, one team member should create a SOFTWARE directory that contains subdirectories for word processing (WP) and spreadsheet (SS) applications.
3. Copy the following programs from your local computer to the WP directory:

   `EDIT.HLP`

   `EDIT.COM`

   If your computer is running Windows 3.x or DOS, the files will be found in the DOS subdirectory; if your computer is running Windows 95, the files are found in the WINDOWS\COMMAND subdirectory.
4. Grant [RFWCEM] rights for this directory to all team members.
5. Each team member should log in and map a drive to the shared WP software directory.
6. From one team member's workstation, run the EDIT program and create a document file that contains a list of five movies you have seen during the last year.
7. Save the document with the name MOVIES.TXT.
8. Use the FLAG command to record the attributes set on each of the three files in the following list. Record the FLAG command you use on the lines below:

Filename	Attribute(s)
`EDIT.HLP`	____________
`EDIT.COM`	____________
`MOVIES.TXT`	____________

9. Each team member should now change to the WP drive and use the EDIT program to access the MOVIES document. Do you think EDIT will enable multiple users to open the same document without the Sharable attribute?

   ____

   Does EDIT enable all team members to access the MOVIES document file?

   ____

10. An important reason for making document files nonsharable is to protect changes made by one user from being overwritten by another user. In this step, each team member should use the EDIT program to call up the MOVIES document and then place his or her name at the top of the document.

11. One user should save his or her document. Then another user should save his or her changes. Does EDIT enable each user to save his or her changes?

    ____

    What is the name of the user who saved his or her document first?

    ____

    What is the name of the user who saved his or her document last?

    ____

12. Access the MOVIES document. In the space below, record which user's changes were saved.

    ____

13. If both users were able to save their documents, record the name of the user whose changes now appear in the document.

    ____

14. Based on this test, how should the EDIT program be used on the network? In the space below, record the recommendations you would make.

    ____

EXERCISES

Case 11-1: Creating an Application Object for the Jefferson County Courthouse

In this exercise you use the NetWare Application Launcher (NAL) to define an application object using DS Standard for the Jefferson County Courthouse Directory tree.

1. If necessary, boot the PC workstation, launch Windows 95, and start DS Standard.
2. Click Start.
3. Click Programs to display the Programs menu, click DS Standard NDS Manager v3 to display the DS Standard NDS Manager 3.0 menu, and then click DS Standard NDS Manager to open the DS Standard NDS manager.
4. Click File, click Open View, and then click Jefferson County Courthouse to display the NDS tree.
5. Select the container object in which to locate the Application object. What object will that be? ______________
6. Right-click the object and select Add Object to see a display of the available objects. Note that the last object listed is Application Object.
7. Click Application Object to see the types of application objects and select Application (Windows 95) to see the Create Application Window.
8. Key in Microsoft Excel in the "Application Icon Title" line and the path to the file. It will be located on the JCCH_Server01_SYS volume.
9. Configure the application by using the pages from the Properties Window. All users will have access to this application.

Turn in a copy of your data disk to your instructor.

Case 11-2: OfficePro

The OfficePro company specializes in providing word processing services for other businesses. Currently it employs five word processing staff members, each of whom has his or her own personal computer. Recently OfficePro installed a NetWare network to enable its employees to share laser printers and to have access to common documents. In addition, OfficePro obtained a NetWare-aware version of its word processing software, which will enable all users to share the same software package and provide them with special network capabilities. Rita Dunn, manager of OfficePro, has recently asked you to install the new word processing program on OfficePro's file server and has provided you with the installation notes for the software package (shown in Figure 11-16). Rita Dunn also gave you a copy of OfficePro's current file server directory structure (shown in Figure 11-17). Your job is to add the necessary directories to support the word processing application software, install the package, and provide the necessary rights for the users.

Figure 11-16

Word processing installation notes

The LetterPerfect word processing software can either be installed on a local hard disk or a Novell NetWare file server. When using the network installation option, you will need to provide the install program with the type of network to install onto in addition to the location of software, temporary, and configuration files. Follow the instructions below when installing the LetterPerfect software on your network system.

Software Files:

The installation program will ask for the drive and directory to contain the LetterPerfect software package program and work files. Users will need to have a search drive mapped to this directory in order to run the package from any drive or directory in the network file system. All users will need a minimum of Read and File scan rights to this directory unless you plan to keep configuration files in this directory, in which case refer to the following configuration file instructions.

Configuration Files:

Each user must be supplied with a three-letter username that allows the software to separate user configuration files by naming the file LPxxx.CFG where "xxx" is the three -letter username. By default each user configuration file will be stored in the directory from which the LetterPerfect software is started. However, if a user enters a different three-letter username or starts the LetterPerfect software from a different directory, a new LPxxx.CFG file will be created with default configuration information. If you wish to place configuration files in a separate directory, you will need to supply the installation program with the drive and path to the directory that is to contain the user configuration files. In this case, the user LPxxx.CFG configuration files will be stored in that directory rather than the default directory. All users will need to have a minimum of Read, Write, File scan, and Create rights to this directory. Be sure the drive letter you use when entering the location for user configuration files is available when the user runs the LetterPerfect software.

Temporary Files:

Temporary files are used to contain control information such as current filename and location information while the user is running the LetterPerfect software. By default temporary files will be stored in the directory from which the user starts the LetterPerfect software and will be erased when the application is terminated. If you wish you can choose to have temporary files stored in an alternate directory on either the file server or local computer hard disk. Because temporary filenames include the user's three-letter username, multiple user temporary files can be placed in the same directory. Users will need a minimum of Read, File scan, Write, Create, and Erase rights in the directory used to store temporary files. Be sure the drive letter you use when entering the location for user temporary files is available when the user runs the LetterPerfect software.

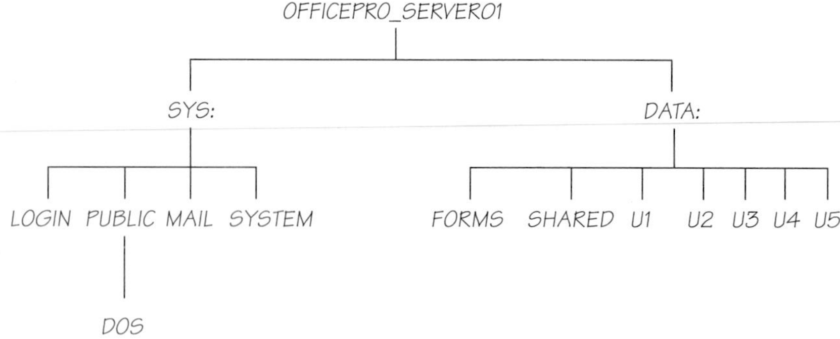

Figure 11-17
OfficePro directory structure

1. Use a copy of the volume design form to design a directory structure that will support the network word processing application.
2. Record any necessary drive mappings below.

   Drive Path

   ____________ ________________________

   ____________ ________________________

   ____________ ________________________

3. Document the trustee rights for each directory you defined in Step 1.
4. On the lines below, record any FLAG or FLAGDIR commands you need to use to establish special file or directory attribute settings.

   ____

NORTHWESTERN TECHNICAL COLLEGE

As a result of your work, the users at Northwestern Technical College now have the access rights they need to store and access files in the file system you created. It is now necessary to install the applications.

Northwestern Technical College recently acquired a network version of the Windows 95 graphics software package (GRAPHPRO) that the support staff and faculty will use for campus promotional materials and for classroom training. Dave Johnson has informed you that the application license will support any number of users on one NetWare server. A separate license is required for each server on which the package is to be installed. NWTC has acquired one license. Your job is to install the package on the NetWare server and make it available both to students in the computer lab and to support staff.

Your instructor will tell you the path to the GRAPHPRO executable file. Record the path on the line below:

____

Using the NAL objects in NetWare Administrator, create an Application object (Windows 95) named GRAPHPRO for the GRAPHPRO application in the NWTC Organization object.

CHAPTER TWELVE

INSTALLING NETWARE PRINTING

Printer sharing is an important benefit of a local area network. Among its advantages are cost savings, increased work space, flexible printer selection, and printer fault tolerance. To become a network administrator, you need to know the NetWare printing system and the NetWare printing utilities that let you set up, customize, and maintain the printing environment on your network. This chapter provides the NetWare printing concepts and skills you will need to understand the NetWare printing components and to implement a sophisticated network printing environment for your organization using NetWare utilities. Chapter 13 provides additional information about managing and customizing network printing to meet special printing needs and properly maintain network printing environments.

AFTER READING THIS CHAPTER AND COMPLETING THE EXERCISES YOU WILL BE ABLE TO:

- IDENTIFY AND DESCRIBE THE NETWARE PRINTING COMPONENTS AND THEIR RELATIONSHIPS TO EACH OTHER.
- USE THE NETWARE ADMINISTRATOR UTILITY TO CREATE, CONFIGURE, AND WORK WITH PRINT QUEUES AND PRINT SERVERS.
- LOAD A PRINT SERVER.
- USE THE NETWARE COMMANDS TO DIRECT OUTPUT FROM A WORKSTATION TO A PRINT QUEUE.

NetWare Printing Components

Before you can implement a network printing environment, you need to understand the basic network printing components and how they work together. In this section, you will learn about each of the following four network components and how they are implemented in a NetWare printing environment:

- Print queues
- Print servers
- Printers
- Workstations

Print Queues

A **print queue** is a network holding area that stores output from workstations in a form that is ready to be sent directly to a printer. A print queue enables multiple workstations on a network to use the same printer by storing the printer output from each workstation as separate print jobs. In NetWare, a **print job** is a file that contains output formatted for a specific printer. After being stored in the print queue, print jobs are then printed one at a time as the printer becomes available. Figure 12-1 illustrates the principle of print queue use.

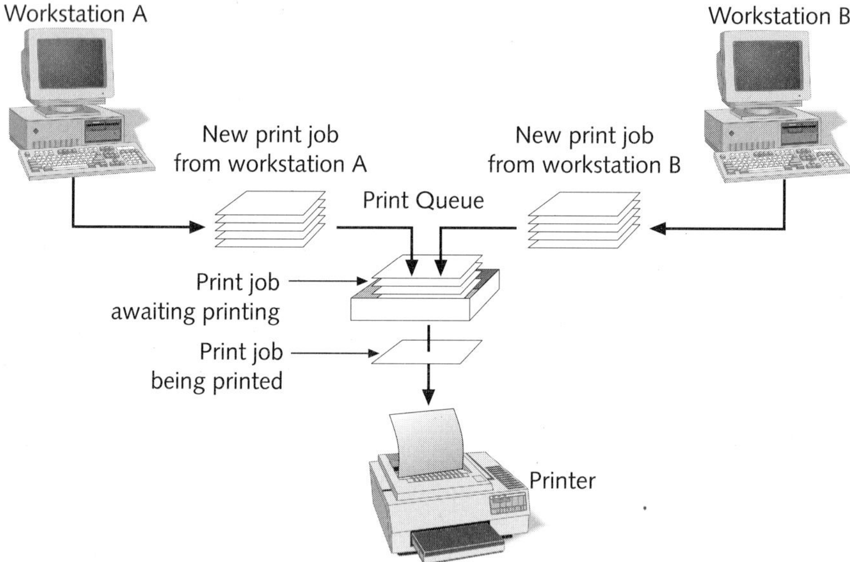

Figure 12-1 Print queues

In many ways, having a workstation send output to a print queue is very similar to storing files on a server. When a file is saved on the server, the data is transferred from the workstation to the server and then stored in a file located in the specified directory. A similar thing happens when printing using the network. Instead of sending the data directly to a printer attached to the computer, the data is sent to the server, which temporarily stores it as a file and then prints it. Thus, placing a job in a print queue involves redirecting the printer data from the application to a file, called a **print job**, that is located in the specified print queue. Print queues are actually directories on the NetWare file server, as illustrated in Figure 12-2.

Figure 12-2

NetWare print queue

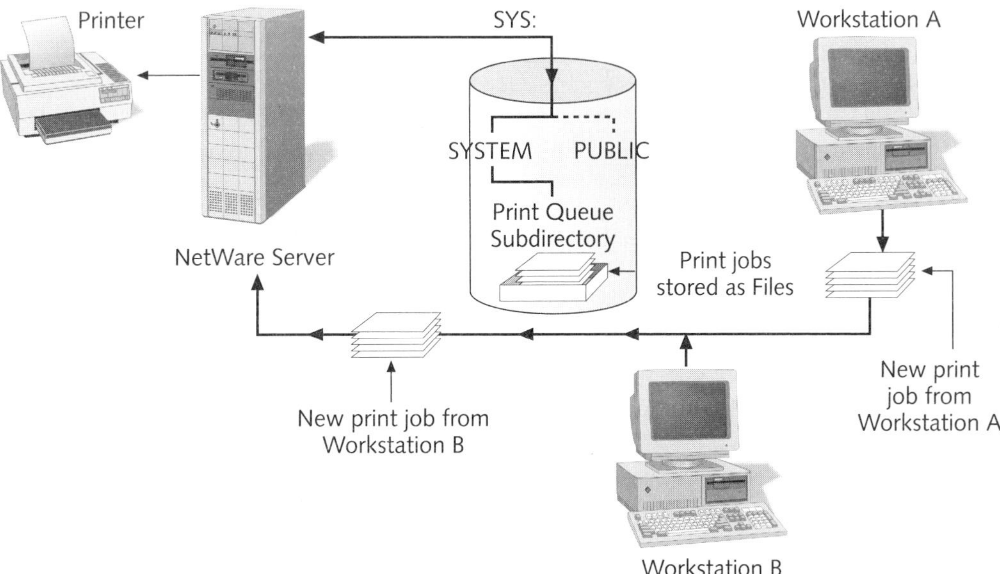

Print queues are created with the NetWare Administrator or PCONSOLE utility, which will be described later in this chapter. When you set up a NetWare printing environment, you create at least one print queue for each networked printer. Output from workstations that needs to be sent to a specific printer can be directed to the print queue associated with that printer by using the NetWare CAPTURE command. Once print jobs have been stored in the print queue, they are processed by the printer assigned to the print queue in the sequence in which they were received. After a job has been printed, it is automatically deleted from the print queue.

A network user who has been designated as a print queue operator is able to rearrange the sequence of print jobs, remove a print job, or place a print job on hold.

If a printer cannot keep up with the number of print jobs that are being generated, you might want to assign two or more printers to that print queue, as illustrated in Figure 12-3. In this example, printer 1 can print output from print job A while printer 2 prints the output from print job B. Whichever printer finishes first will then begin printing job C.

Figure 12-3

Multiple printers per print queue

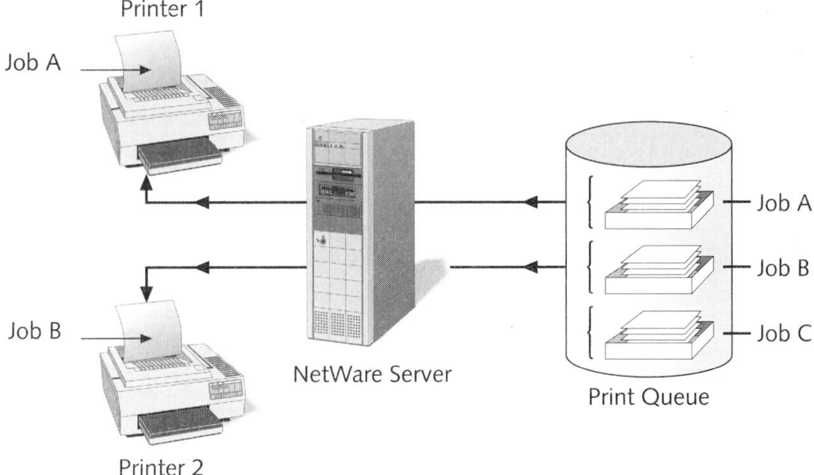

When you want to print high-priority jobs before other jobs that are currently in the print queue, you can either manually rearrange the jobs in the print queue or you can establish multiple print queues for the same printer. When two print queues are assigned to the same printer, one print queue can be given a higher priority, as shown in Figure 12-4. Print queue A has a higher priority than print queue B. Normal print jobs are placed in print queue B, which prints each job in the order in which it is received. However, if a print job is sent to print queue A, that job will be printed next, while the jobs in print queue B are temporarily suspended. Once the job in print queue A is completed, print queue B can resume its work. Using two print queues for one printer enables you to print high-priority jobs out of sequence by placing them in the high-priority print queue. This can be important if a network uses a printer almost constantly yet has occasional rush jobs.

Figure 12-4

Multiple print queues per printer

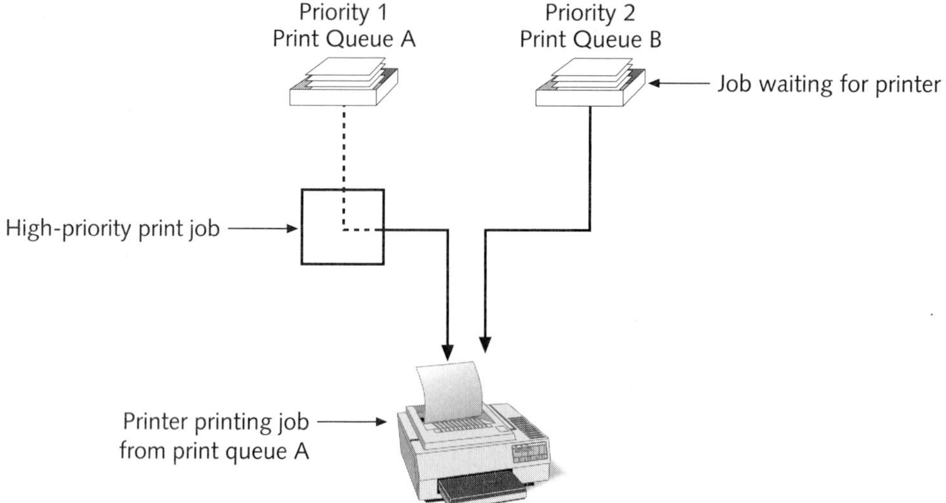

PRINT SERVERS

A **print server** is software that actually controls printing by taking print jobs from a print queue and sending them to the assigned printer, as shown in Figure 12-5. Print servers are also responsible for sending control commands to printers and reporting printer status to the print server operator.

NetWare 4.1 permits each print server to control 256 printers, whereas NetWare 3.11 allows a print server to control a maximum of only 16 printers.

Figure 12-5

NetWare print server

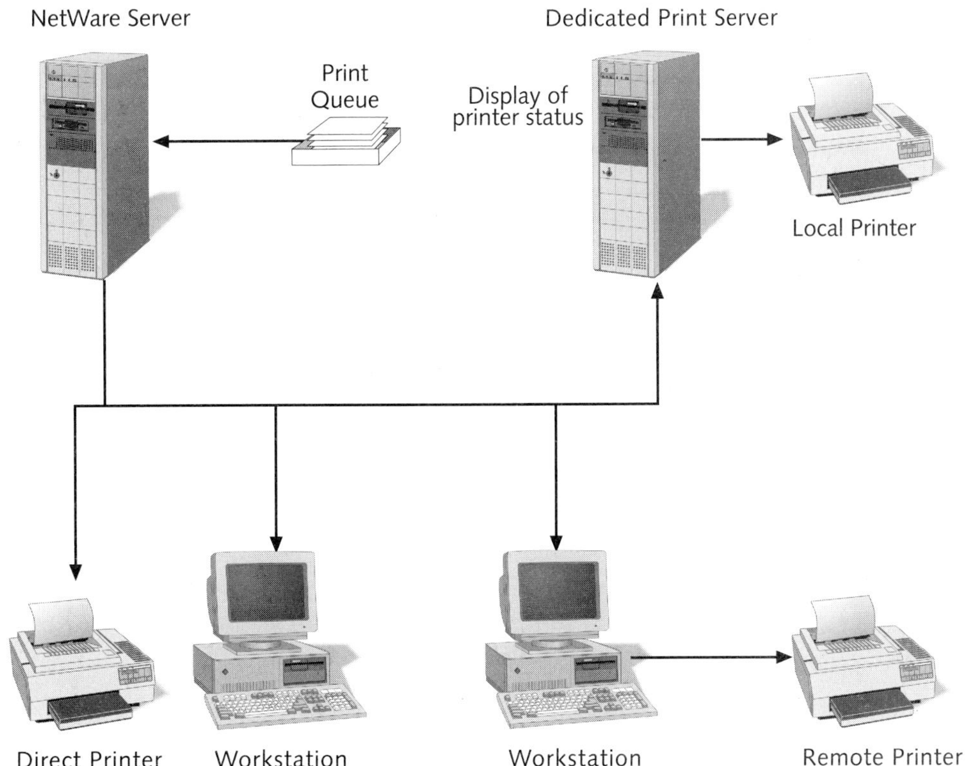

Print queues and print servers can be created with the NetWare Administrator or PCONSOLE utility. After the print queues and the print server are defined, the NetWare print server software can be loaded and run.

With NetWare 3.11 it was possible to create a print server on a network client. However, this is no longer available in NetWare 4.1.

PRINTERS

Although there is an almost unlimited number of different printer models and configurations, most printers commonly found on microcomputer systems can be grouped into three general types: dot matrix, laser, and ink jet. Each of these printer types requires different print job formats. As a network administrator, you will need to know the types and models of printers used on your network so that you can correctly configure network printing. This will ensure that the correct output is sent to the appropriate printer. A workstation's word processing program, for example, can support both dot matrix and laser printers. If a user selects a laser printer and prints a document, the network printing configuration must ensure that the job is sent to the laser printer that the job has been formatted to use.

Up to five of the printers controlled by a print server program can be attached directly to the computer running the program and are called **local printers**. Of the remaining printers, any number can be attached to other networked workstations and are referred to as **remote printers**. A **direct printer** is attached directly to the network cable using its own network interface card and software.

You must consider the printer attachment method when you configure the network printing environment. Each attachment method has advantages and will affect the way printers are distributed on the network. Many network administrators use a combination of printer attachments based on the type of printer and its expected usage. In this section, you will learn about each of the printer attachment options and how they affect network printing.

Local Attachment

Local printers are attached directly to one of the printer ports of the NetWare server that is running the print server program. Output is sent directly from the print server to the local printers through the local printer ports of the print server computer. Local printers can be attached to the parallel (LPT) or serial (COM) ports of the file server that is running the print server software. The advantages of a local printer attached directly to the print server include printing performance that is faster than that of remote printers and a reduction in network traffic. Figure 12-6 illustrates two local printers attached to the print server.

Figure 12-6 Local printer attachment

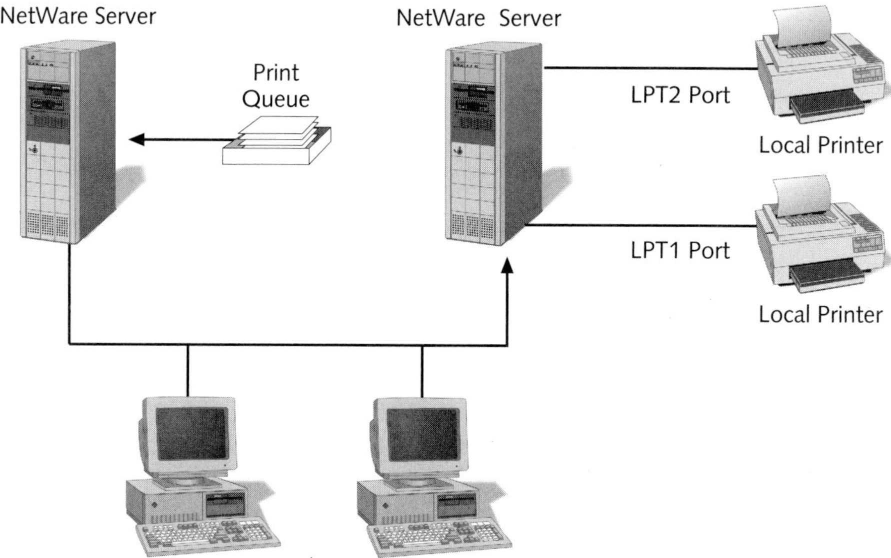

Remote Attachment

Remote printers are attached to other workstations on the network, as shown in Figure 12-7. Output is sent from the print server to the workstation that has a remote printer attached via the network cable in packets of printed data. For Windows 95 you must install and configure the Microsoft Print Services for NetWare utility. The name of the program is MSPSRV.EXE. The disadvantages of remote printing include increased network traffic and the need to run the MSPSRV.EXE program on each workstation that supports a shared network printer. Another disadvantage to using a remote printer means that both the printer and the work-station must be turned on and attached to the network in order for users to print their output.

When using DOS or Windows 3.11, a DOS terminate-and-stay resident (TSR) program has to be loaded on a workstation that has attached to it a printer you want to share. The TSR program receives the packets of printer output from the print server and prints them on the attached printer without interrupting any software applications being used on that workstation. Problems with running a TSR program on a workstation often involved the compatibility of the TSR program with other application or system software that might be running on the workstation. Finally, in some cases, workstation software conflicts can cause the remote printer to scramble or lose data and, in extreme cases, cause the workstation computer to crash.

Figure 12-7

Remote printer attachment

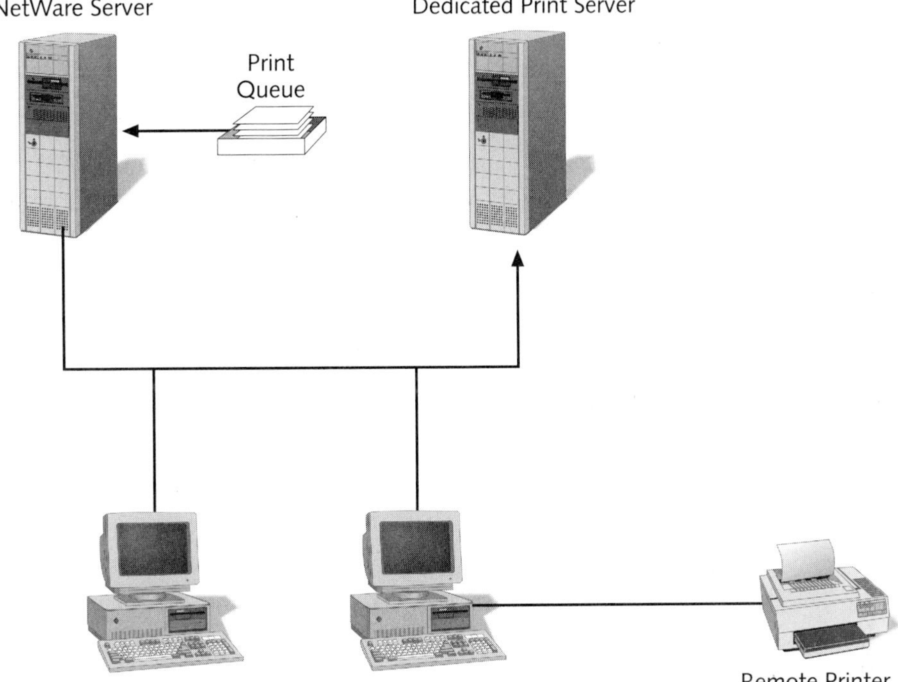

Direct Attachment

You can attach a printer directly to the network cable by obtaining a special network card option for the printer. Many printer manufacturers offer optional network cards that can be installed in their printers to enable the printer to be attached directly to the network cable, as shown in Figure 12-8.

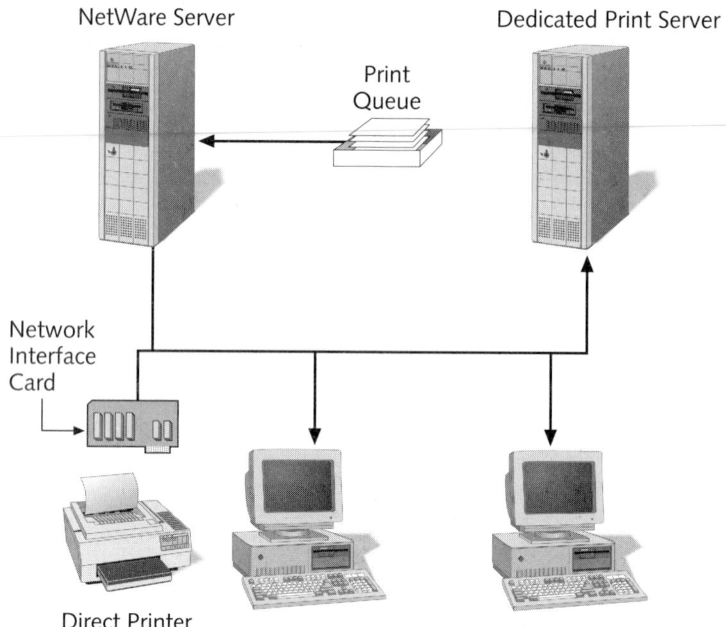

Figure 12-8
Direct printer attachment

With the direct attachment option, the printer actually becomes its own print server and is able to print jobs directly from a NetWare print queue. The disadvantages of direct printer attachment are the extra cost of the network attachment option needed for each printer. In addition, making each printer a separate print server can use up network connections to your file server and potentially cause your file server to reach the maximum limit of your NetWare license.

Many network laser printers today are installed with a direct printer attachment option that enables the printer to act as either an independent print server or a remote printer attached to an existing print server.

WORKSTATIONS

The last component of network printing is the user workstation that sends its output to a shared printer. Most software is designed to recognize the existence of network printing. However, some older DOS software applications are designed to send output directly to one of the LPT ports on the local workstation and do not recognize print queues or print servers. Because of this, it is sometimes necessary to redirect the output of these applications to a print queue and store it as a print job without the application needing to be aware of the network. NetWare includes command utilities that enable the output from a workstation to be directed, with a number of customized options, to a specific print queue. As a network administrator you need to know how to use these workstation utilities to establish and maintain a network printing environment that is easy for your users and transparent to your applications.

Defining a Printing Environment

The first task a network administrator needs to perform when establishing a network printing environment is to define the printing needs supported by the network. Defining the printing environment involves the following steps:

1. Define the printing requirements of each user's applications.
2. Determine printer locations and types of attachment.
3. Define names for all printers and print queues.

In this section, you will learn about each of these steps and how to apply them to defining a network printer environment for your organization by filling out a print server definition form.

Defining Printer Requirements

The first step in defining a printing environment is to identify the number and types of network printers and print servers that will be needed. You start by analyzing the requirements of each user's application software and printing needs. Because a print server can support up to 256 printers, one print server is usually sufficient for most organizations. A sample print server definition form is shown in Figure 12-9. Using the printer definition form will help you define your printer needs by documenting each printer attached to a single print server. A separate print server definition form should be filled out for each print server. In the top part of the form, enter the name of the print server and the file servers that will contain the print queues. Identify the print server as dedicated or nondedicated and enter the name of the file server where a nondedicated print server will be located.

Try to keep the printing system as simple as possible by standardizing the make and model of printer to be used for dot matrix, laser, and ink jet printer types. The print server definition form includes columns in which you identify the model and type along with the users and applications for each network printer that will be attached to a print server.

Figure 12-9 Sample print server definition form

PRINT SERVER DEFINITION FORM

Prepared by: TED SIMPSON   Date: 9/15/97

Organization: CBE Labs

Print Server Name: CBELABS-PSERVER   File Server Name: CONSTELLATION

Printer Name	Printer type	Make/Model	Attachment Type	Location	Users/Applications	Print Queue Name
0	Laser	HP Laserjet iiiSi			finance documents	
1	Dot Matrix	Epson LQ-570+			finance accounting	
2	Color ink-jet	Tektronix 140			all presentations	
3	Laser	HP Laserjet iiiSi			marketing documents	
4	Dot Matrix	Epson LQ-570+			marketing invoice	
5	Dot Matrix	Epson LQ-570+			marketing reports	

Let's look at an example of a print server definition for the marketing and finance departments of CBE Labs. The finance department uses a spreadsheet program to manage budget data along with a payroll and general ledger accounting system. The administration department needs a dot matrix printer for local printing of spreadsheet data and a high-speed dot matrix printer to print accounting reports and payroll checks. The administration users need access to a laser printer for output of graphs and word processing documents for presentation purposes. Each member of the marketing department uses a personal computer to enter orders and produce price quotations. Price quotations need to be printed on company stationery. What is needed is a laser printer with stationery in tray 1 and standard paper in tray 2. Invoices are printed on one dot matrix printer that has invoice forms always mounted, and sales reports are printed on a second dot matrix printer that has standard tractor-feed paper. The marketing department has new presentation software that enables users to produce attractive handouts for sales presentations. For these they need access to a color printer.

From the preceding information, a print server definition form can be filled in, as shown in Figure 12-9. It defines one print server, named CBELABS-PSERVER, that controls six printers. As you can see on the form, the finance department needs two printers on the network, a dot matrix printer for accounting and spreadsheet applications and a laser printer for word processing documents and graphs. Three printers have been defined to meet the printing needs of the marketing department: a laser printer for printing price quotations and two dot matrix printers for invoices and sales reports. With two dot matrix printers, users won't need to change back and forth between invoice forms and standard paper for reports. In addition, users in both the marketing and finance departments need to send presentation output and graphs to a color ink-jet printer.

PRINTER LOCATION AND ATTACHMENT

Once printer requirements are defined, the next consideration is the location of each printer—including how it will be attached to the network. Use the following guidelines when planning locations and attachment methods for printers:

- Determine whether the printer is to be locally attached to the print server, remotely attached to a workstation, or directly attached to the network.
- Place the printer close to the user who is responsible for it.
- Identify the printer port where each printer will be attached.
- Avoid attaching remote printers to workstations running applications that might conflict with the remote printer software. Use a direct attachment option if necessary.

Figure 12-10 Sample printer attachments

PRINT SERVER DEFINITION FORM

Prepared by: TED SIMPSON Date: 9/15/97

Organization: CBE Labs

Print Server Name: CBELABS-PSERVER File Server Name: CONSTELLATION

	Printer Name	Printer type	Make/Model	Attachment Type	Location	Users/Applications	Print Queue Name
0		Laser	HPLaserjet iiiSi	remote LPT1	finance dept	finance documents	
1		Dot Matrix	Epson LQ-570+	remote LPT1	finance dept payroll	finance accounting	
2		Color ink-jet	Tektronix 140	local LPT1	information systems	all presentations	
3		Laser	HP Laserjet iiiSi	remote LPT1	marketing dept office area	marketing documents	
4		Dot Matrix	Epson LQ-5704	remote LPT1	marketing dept office area	marketing invoice	
5		Dot Matrix	Epson LQ-5704	remote LPT1	marketing dept office area	marketing reports	

Notice in Figure 12-10 that in addition to the attachment type, the printer port used to connect the printer is also identified. You will need to know the printer port, the printer number, and attachment information when you use a NetWare utility to define the printer definitions, described later in this chapter. Notice that the color ink-jet printer (the Tektronix Phaser 140) is locally attached to the LPT1 port of the print server. Depending on the location of the print server computer, this can provide access to the printer to both marketing and finance department users. A local attachment also reduces network traffic and provides faster and more reliable access for graphics-oriented applications.

Naming Printers and Print Queues

To keep your printing system as simple as possible, select printer and print queue names that enable you to identify the following printer information:

- Location
- Printer model
- Attachment method
- Printer number

NetWare 4.1 allows printer names up to a maximum of 47 characters that can contain any number of ASCII characters including spaces and special characters. One way to create meaningful printer names is to define one- to three-character codes for each of the printer information fields. Each printer name could consist of the combined codes for the four listed items separated by dashes (-) or underscores (_). The printer name FIN_EPS_570_R0, for example, identifies the Epson 570 dot matrix printer that is located in the finance department attached as remote printer number 0. However, Windows 95 has trouble handling "special characters," which means that you should only use letters and numbers in names, not dashes, underscores, and so on. Therefore, the printer name becomes FINEPS570R0.

Location

The printer location can be a three- to four-character field that identifies the name of the department or place where the printer is located. FIN, for example, can be used to identify a printer located in the finance department; a room number, such as 209A, can be used to identify a printer located in a specific room or office. If a printer is moved, its name can be changed to identify its new location. Avoid using a user's name or workstation model to identify a printer. These labels often change and can leave the printer with a name that no longer identifies its location.

Printer Model

A three- to five-character code representing the make or use of the printer can be included in its name to help you remember what type of printer output can be sent to this printer. INV, for example, can be used to represent the dot matrix printer to which invoices are sent; EPS570 can be used to represent an Epson LQ-570 dot matrix printer that is available for general use.

Attachment and Number

Include an attachment code—L for local, R for remote, or D for direct—along with the port and the number of the printer. The printer number value ranges from 0 to 255 and corresponds to the printer number assigned during configuration of the print server. The code L1, for example, identifies printer 1 as locally attached to the printer server; R2 identifies printer 2 as remotely attached to a port on a networked workstation.

Naming Print Queues

Print queue names should be the same as the printer name with the addition of the letter Q followed by the priority of the print queue. This enables two or more print queues to be assigned to the same printer. Q1 indicates the highest priority, Q2 the next priority, and so on.

Figure 12-11 shows the sample print server definition form complete with printer names written according to these guidelines. Notice that the color ink-jet printer has been assigned two print queues, which will enable high-priority jobs to be printed while normal jobs wait in the lower priority queue. If two printers use the same print queue, you can omit the printer number from the print queue name. If the finance department, for example, has two laser printers, FINHP3R0 and FINHP3R6, assigned to the same print queue, the name of the print queue could be FINHP3Q1.

Figure 12-11 Sample printer and queue names

PRINT SERVER DEFINITION FORM

Prepared by: TED SIMPSON   Date: 9/15/97

Organization: CBE Labs

Print Server Name: CBELABS-PSERVER   File Server Name: CONSTELLATION

	Printer Name	Printer type	Make/Model	Attachment Type	Location	Users/Applications	Print Queue Name
0	FINHP3RO	Laser	HP Laserjet iiiSi	remote LPT1	finance dept	finance documents	FINHP3ROQ1
1	FINEPS570R1	Dot Matrix	Epson LQ-570+	remote LPT1	finance dept	finance accounting	FINEPS570R1Q1
2	CBETEK140R2	Color ink-jet	Tektronix 140	local LPT1	information□ systems	all presentations	CBETEK140L2Q1/ CBETEK140R2Q2
3	MKTHP3R3	Laser	HP Laserjet iiiSi	remote LPT1	marketing□ dept office□ area	marketing documents	MKTHP3R3Q1
4	MKTEPS570R4	Dot Matrix	Epson LQ-5704	remote COM	marketing dept office area	marketing invoice	MKTEPS570
5	MKTEPS570R5	Dot Matrix	Epson LQ-5704	remote LPT1	marketing dept office area	marketing reports	MKTEPS570R5Q1

Print queue names can be a maximum of 47 characters. Unlike printer names, print queue names cannot include spaces, commas, slashes, colons, semicolons, question marks, plus signs, equal signs, greater- or less-than symbols, or square brackets.

After you define printer names when creating print queues and the print server, it is a good idea to label each physical printer with its assigned name. This will make it easier for both the network administrator and users to identify them.

SETTING UP THE PRINTING ENVIRONMENT

There are two basic steps to set up the printing environment in NetWare 4. First, the three printing components must be created: the queue, the printer, and the print server. Next, links must be established among these three objects.

NetWare provides two different methods for the network administrator to set up the printing environment. PCONSOLE is the main NetWare menu utility used by network administrators, operators, and users to manage the network printing environment. The network administrator uses PCONSOLE to establish and maintain the network printing environment. Print queue operators and print server operators use it to work with their assigned print queues and servers. Users can also utilize PCONSOLE to view, modify, or remove jobs they have placed in a print queue and determine the length of time before a job will print by viewing its sequence number in the print queue. An alternative method is to use NetWare Administrator to create the objects and establish the links.

In this section, you will learn how to use the PCONSOLE utility and NetWare Administrator to perform the following tasks:

- Create print queues.
- Define print queue users and operators.
- Create the print server.

- Define and configure the printers.
- Assign print queues to each printer.
- Identify print server operators.

The NetWare PCONSOLE utility permits the network administrator to create the necessary print objects and establish the links in two ways, by Quick Setup or by a standard setup.

PCONSOLE Quick Setup

The PCONSOLE Quick Setup is the fastest method to set up printing in NetWare 4.1. In one screen a network administrator may define all three printing objects and establish the links between them. This is ideal if you have only a few printers that you need to set up quickly.

To use PCONSOLE, first log into the network as a user with the necessary rights to create objects under the desired container. Run the program PCONSOLE.EXE, and the PCONSOLE opening screen will appear, as shown in Figure 12-12.

Figure 12-12

PCONSOLE Available Options menu

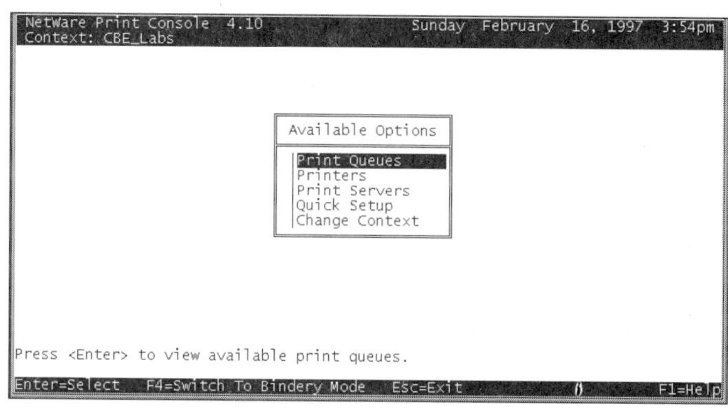

Select Change Context if necessary to change to the correct container. Then choose Quick Setup, and the Print Services Quick Setup menu will appear, as shown in Figure 12-13.

Figure 12-13

Print Services Quick Setup menu

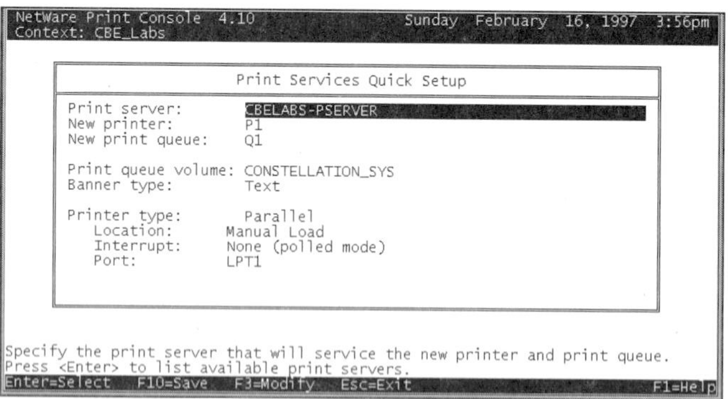

From here you may accept NetWare's defaults, which are based on your current context and printer configuration, or enter the basic information for the three printing objects that you want to create. The values to enter are as follows:

- *Print Server:* This is the name of the Print Server object. The default is *PS-container*, where *container* is the name of the current context container.
- *New Printer:* This is the name of the new printer which you are adding. The default is *Pn*, with *n* being a number starting with 1.
- *New Print Queue:* This is the name of the new print queue that you are adding. The default is *Qn*, with *n* being a number starting with 1.
- *Print Queue Volume:* This is the name of the NetWare volume that will temporarily contain the print jobs until they are printed.
- *Banner Type:* Either *Text* or *Postscript* can be entered here, depending on the type of printing that will be done on this printer.
- *Printer Type:* Depending on the type of printer, the options available are *Parallel* (connected to any standard parallel port), *Serial* (connected to a serial port), *Unix* (attached to a Unix workstation), *AppleTalk Printer* (using AppleTalk protocols), or *Other*. The most common type is *Parallel*.

The remaining entries depend upon which printer type is selected. If you choose the typical *Parallel*, then the values are as follows:

- Location: *Auto Load (Local)*, the default, means that the printer is attached to a file server that is running the print server software. The other option is *Manual Load*, which means you must load the software.
- Interrupt: *None (polled mode)* makes use of the computer's own CPU. As an alternative you could enter any of the available interrupts (*2-15*).
- Port: The choices are *LPT1*, *LPT2*, and *LPT3*.

Press [F10] when finished. This information will be entered into the NetWare Directory Services tree, and the necessary links among print queue, printer, and print server will be established.

PCONSOLE STANDARD SETUP

Creating Print Queues

In addition to the Quick Setup, you can also create Print Server, Print Queue, and Printer objects separately in PCONSOLE. To use PCONSOLE, first log into the network as a user with the necessary rights to create objects under the desired container. Run PCONSOLE.EXE, and the PCONSOLE opening screen will appear. Select Change Context if necessary to change to the correct container. Then choose Print Queues. This displays a window showing all existing print queues, as shown in Figure 12-14.

Figure 12-14

Available print queues

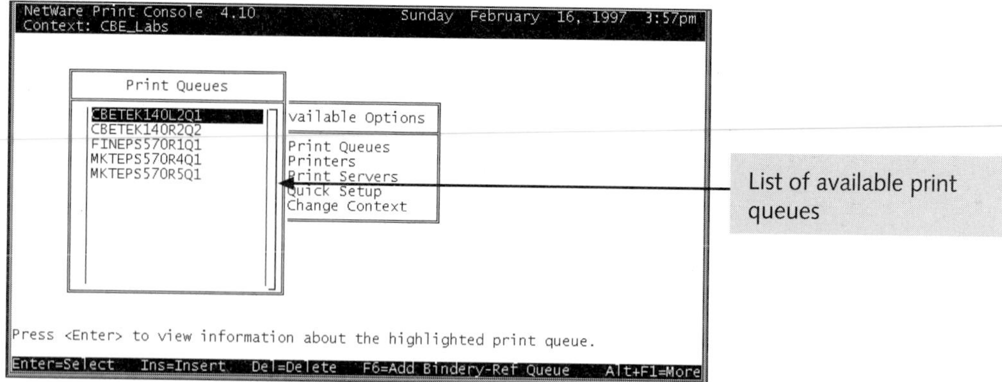

To create a new print queue, press [Ins] and enter the name of the print queue. PCONSOLE will also ask for the print queue's volume name. You may specify it by typing the directory or by pressing [Ins] and selecting a volume. After you press [Enter], the new print queue name will appear in the Print Queues window. To change the name of an existing print queue, highlight the print queue name and press [Enter]. You can then use [Backspace][/] to erase the existing name and type the new name. Finally, to delete an existing print queue, highlight its name and press [Del]. The print queue will be deleted after you press [Enter] and respond with a Yes to the delete print queue confirmation window.

Defining Print Queue Users and Operators

By default, the Admin user is the only print queue user and operator. To make another user a print queue operator of a print queue, highlight the name of the print queue and press [Enter] to display the Print Queue Information menu shown in Figure 12-15. Use the Print Jobs option to display and manage jobs that are currently in the selected print queue. The Status option enables the print queue operator to take the print queue off line, which will prevent users or print servers from accessing it. The Information option can be used to display the name of the SYS:SYSTEM subdirectory that is used to store print jobs for this print queue.

To make a user an operator of the selected print queue, highlight the Operators option and press [Enter] to display a window listing existing queue operators. (Initially Admin will be the only operator of a new print queue.) To add a user to the print queue operator window, press [Ins] and highlight the username from the "Object, Class" window. When you press [Enter], the selected username will be added to the Queue Operators window. Pressing [Esc] will then return you to the Print Queue Information menu.

Figure 12-15

Print Queue Information menu

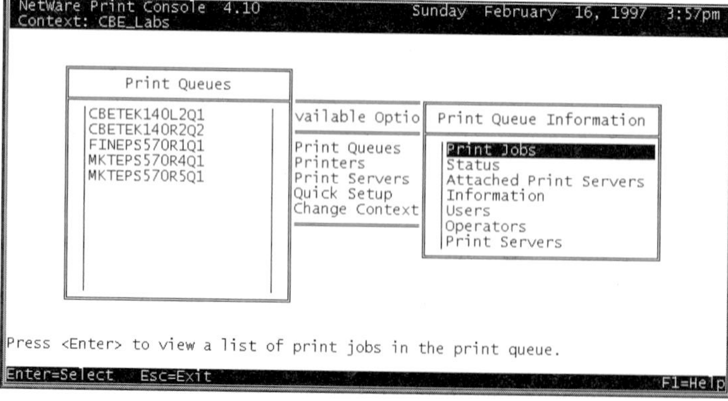

By default, all users can place jobs in newly created print queues. In certain cases, however, you might want to restrict printer access to a certain user or group of users. The Users option enables the network administrator to limit which users can place jobs in a specified print queue. To restrict the selected print queue, first select the Users option to display a window showing all existing print queue users. Initially this window will show the user Admin as the current user of the print queue. To enable specified users and groups to place jobs in the print queue, press [Ins] to display the "Object, Class" window and then use [F5] to mark the names of the users and groups you want added as users of the selected print queue. When you press [Enter], any selected groups and usernames will be included in the Users window. You can now use [Esc] to return to the Print Queue Information window.

Creating the Print Server Definition

Before you can run the print server software, you need to use PCONSOLE to create a configuration file that will define each printer's name, location, port, and associated print queues. To create a print server definition, select the Print Servers option from the PCONSOLE Available Options menu and press [Enter]. The Print Servers window, showing any existing print servers, will be displayed. To create a new print server definition, simply press [Ins] and type the name for the new print server definition file.

Print server definition filenames can be a maximum of 47 characters and cannot include spaces, commas, slashes, colons, semicolons, question marks, plus signs, equal signs, greater- or less-than symbols, or square brackets.

If you want to change the name of an existing print server definition, highlight the current name and press [F3]. You can then use [Backspace] to erase the existing name and then retype the new name. To delete a print server definition, highlight the name of the print server to be deleted and press [Del].

Defining and Configuring the Printers

After the print server definition has been created, the network administrator configures the printers by providing the name, location, and port for each printer that will be controlled by the print server. To use PCONSOLE to configure the printers, first highlight the print server in the Print Servers window and press [Enter] to display the Print Server Information menu shown in Figure 12-16.

Figure 12-16 Print Server Information menu

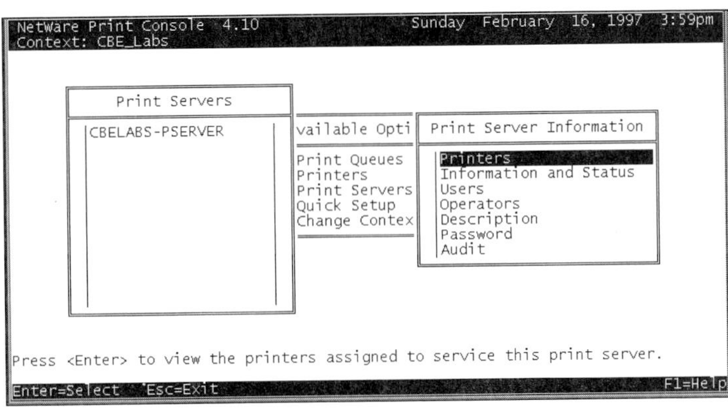

Each print server can be assigned a password and full name. The password prevents an unauthorized operator from loading the print server on a computer. Use the Information and Status option to assign a longer name to the print server for documentation purposes. Use the Operators and Users options to assign operators and users control of the printer attached to the print server. Users who will need to control printers and respond to problems should be made print server operators.

To configure printers, select the Printers option and press [Enter] to display the Serviced Printers menu shown in Figure 12-17.

Figure 12-17

Serviced Printers menu

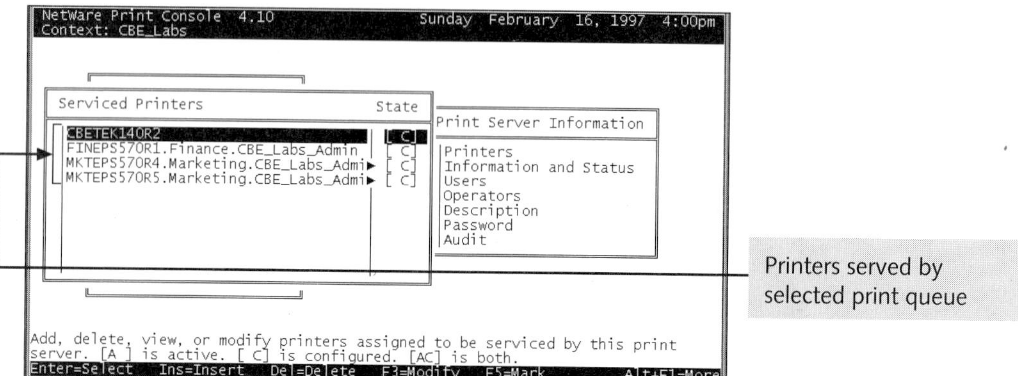

To define the configuration for each network printer, select the desired printer and press [Enter] to display the Printer Configuration window shown in Figure 12-18.

Figure 12-18

Printer Configuration window

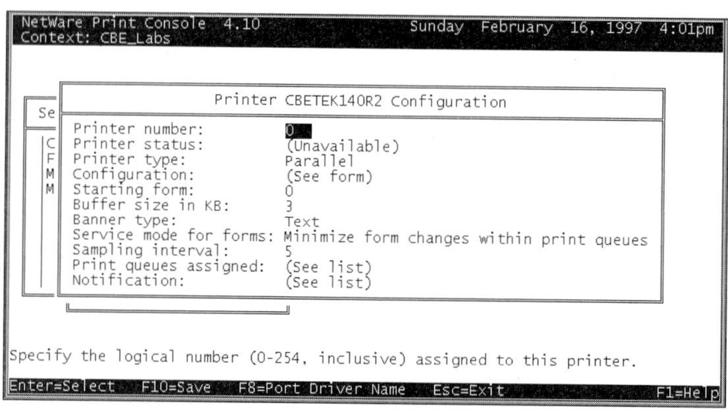

Advance to the Printer Type field and press [Enter] to display the Printer Type window shown in Figure 12-19.

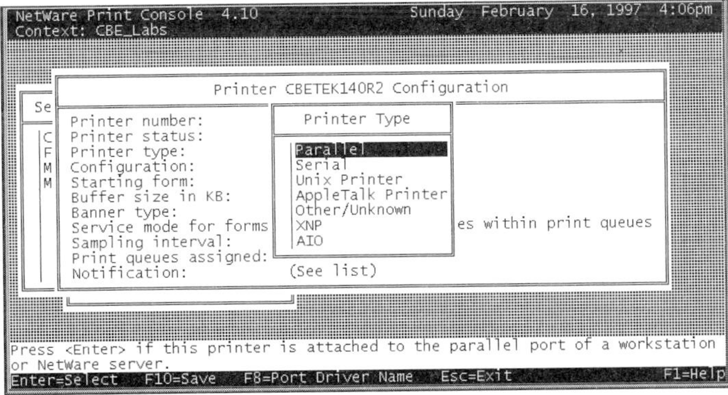

Figure 12-19 Printer Type window

To configure a local printer attached to the LPT port of the print server computer, select the Parallel option from the "Printer Types" window and press [Enter]. After selecting the printer type, select Configuration and press [Enter]. PCONSOLE will display the printer specifics window shown in Figure 12-20. When all printers have been defined, you can use [Esc] to return to the Printer Configuration window and continue with the print server configuration.

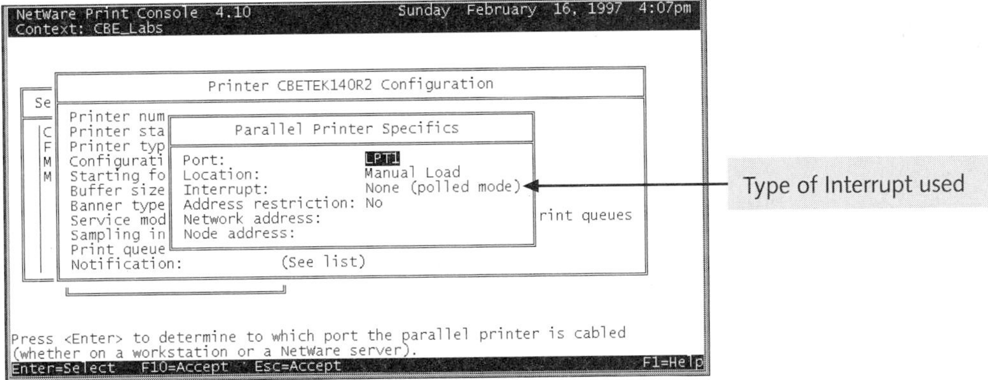

Figure 12-20 Printer Specifics window

The "Interrupt" field identifies the interrupt that will be used by the printer. As described in Chapter 2, interrupts are used to notify the computer's processor that a device or port needs attention. You can enter any of the available interrupts (2–15) or you may select "None (polled mode)," which makes use of the computers' own CPU. Polled mode permits other software packages, like Microsoft Windows, to run along with NPRINTER. You can use [Esc] to return to the Printer Configuration window and continue with the print server configuration.

The "Buffer size in KB" field may be used to change the amount of memory used to store output to the selected printer. Although the default of 3KB is sufficient for most printers, some network administrators increase this value to 5KB on printers that will be used to print large print jobs. In addition to the interrupt and buffer settings, the "Service mode for forms" field can be used to select the way print jobs with different form types are printed. If you will be using different form types in this printer, highlight this field and press [Enter] to display the possible queue service modes shown in Figure 12-21. The option to "Minimize form changes within print queues will reduce the number of times you will have to change paper in the printer by causing the print server to print all forms of the same type no matter what sequence has been placed in the print queue.

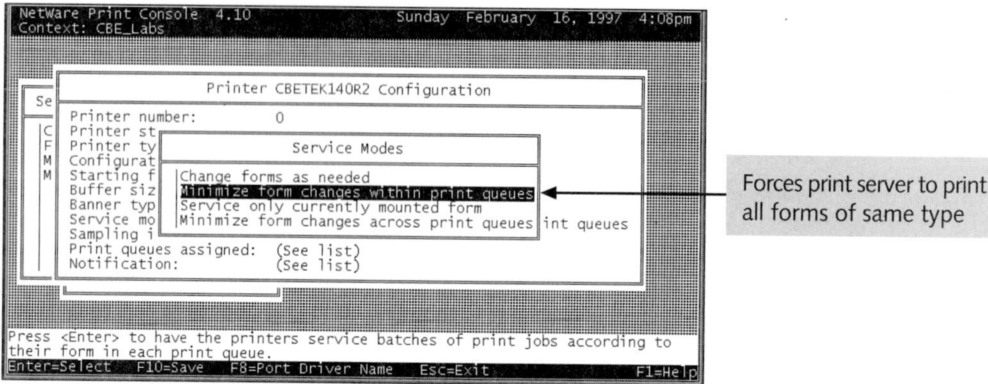

Figure 12-21 Service Modes menu

It is important to designate a user as a print server operator. This person will be responsible for receiving messages from printers in his or her work area and can respond to such problems as a printer that is jammed or out of paper. To have a user notified when there is a printer problem, you need to add that user to the notification list for each of the printers in his or her charge.

To add a user to the notification list for a printer, select the Notification option. A window is displayed, which lists the users who will be notified about printer problems. Press [Ins] to display the "Object, Class" window, which lists all available users and groups on the system. You can then use [F5] to highlight the names of users you want notified and press [Enter] to display the Notify Intervals window shown in Figure 12-22. To accept the default values of 1 minute until the first message is issued and then 1 minute between messages, press [Esc] and then press [Enter] to save the changes. The selected usernames will now be added to the notify list for this printer. After updating the notify list for any additional printers, press [Esc] to return to the Printer Configuration menu.

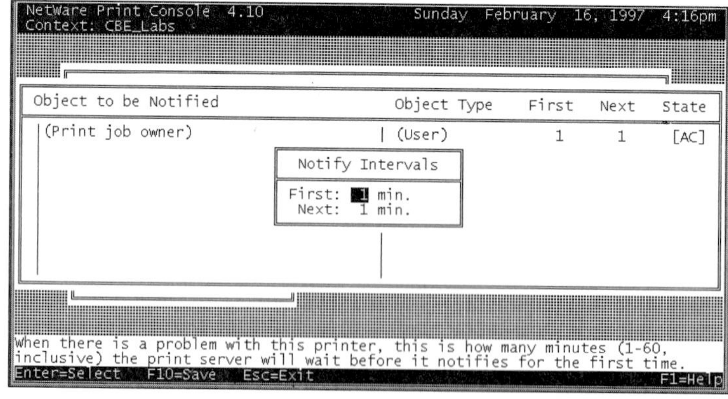

Figure 12-22 Notify Intervals window

Assigning Print Queues

Assigning print queues to the printers you have defined is one of the most important steps in configuring your print server because it ties each printer to its corresponding print queue or queues. A common error made by many network administrators hurrying to complete the setup of the printing environment is forgetting to perform this step. To configure a printer to service a print queue, select the Print Queues Assigned option from the Printer Configuration menu to display a list of all existing print queues that have been assigned to this printer. To add a print queue to be serviced by this printer, press [Ins] to display the "Object, Class" window, highlight the name of the print queue to be serviced, and press [Enter]. PCONSOLE will then request the print queue priority, as shown in Figure 12-23. Enter priority 1 for your first print queue. This designates the highest level priority. Additional print queues assigned to this printer can be given lower priority settings from 2 on. After you assign a print queue to each printer, your basic print server configuration is complete and you can press [Esc] until you return to the Print Server Information window.

Figure 12-23
Print Queue priority

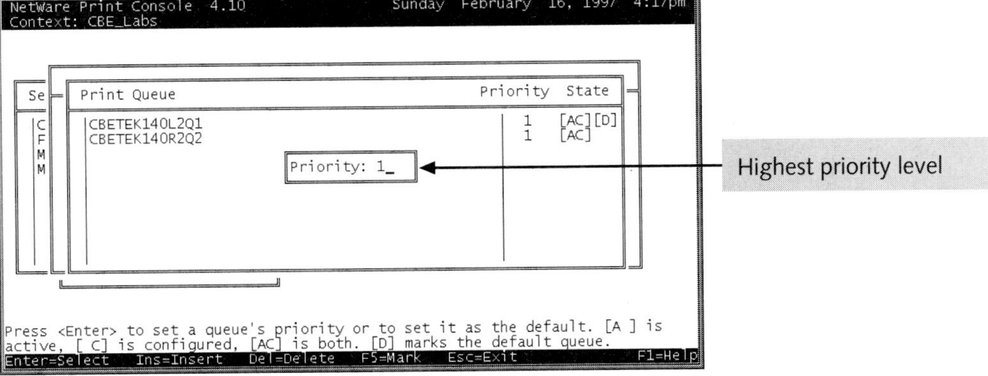

Identifying Print Server Operators

The last step in completing a basic print server configuration is assigning print server operators and users. The default print server operator is the Admin user. If you add other users to the notification list for printers, however, they should be assigned as print server operators. Print server operators can stop and restart printers in the event of a paper jam or other printing problem. To assign additional print server operators, select the Operators option from the Print Server Information menu to display a list of the existing print server operators. Initially only the ADMIN user will appear as a print server operator. To add more users, simply press [Ins] to display the Print Server Operator Candidates window. You can then use [F5] to highlight the names of any users you want to make print server operators and press [Enter] to add the selected users to the Print Server Operators window. After all print server operators are defined, press [Esc] to return to the Print Server Information menu. The printer environment should now be ready for testing. Use the [Alt][F10] key combination to exit the PCONSOLE utility.

USING NETWARE ADMINISTRATOR

Printing objects can also be set up by using the NetWare Administrator utility. The same steps still apply with this program as with PCONSOLE: the three printing components (the queue, the printer, and the print server) must be created, and then links must be established among these three objects. Let's use NetWare Administrator to create the laser printer in the finance department of CBE Labs.

Creating Print Queue Objects

First log into the network as a user with the necessary rights to create objects under the desired container. From Windows 95, Launch NetWare Administrator. Click on the container object in which you want to create the print objects. In this example we will select the Finance icon from the NDS tree. Then select Create from the Object menu, and the New Object dialog box will appear. Select Print Queue from this list, and the Create Print Queue dialog box will appear, as shown in Figure 12-24.

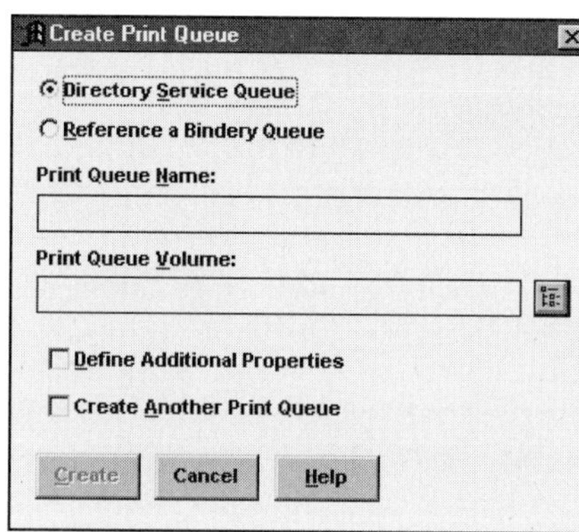

Figure 12-24 Create Print Queue dialog box

Type the name of the printer queue, FINHP3R0Q1, use the Object Select button to select the Print Queue Volume CONSTELLATION_SYS, and click Create. The print queue object now appears in the NDS tree, as shown in Figure 12-25.

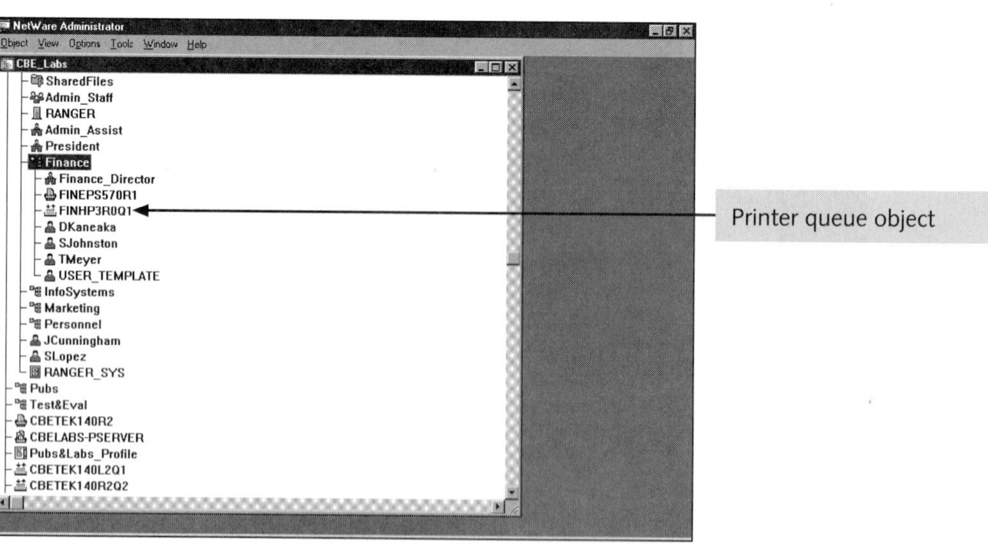

Figure 12-25 Printer Queue object

Defining Print Queue Users and Operators

The container in which the print queue was created becomes a print queue user, which means that all objects below this container now have access to this print queue. There may be occasions in which you want to restrict users from accessing this queue. In order to do so, click the print queue in the NDS tree and select Details from the Object menu. The Print Queue dialog box will appear, as shown in Figure 12-26.

Figure 12-26

Print Queue dialog box

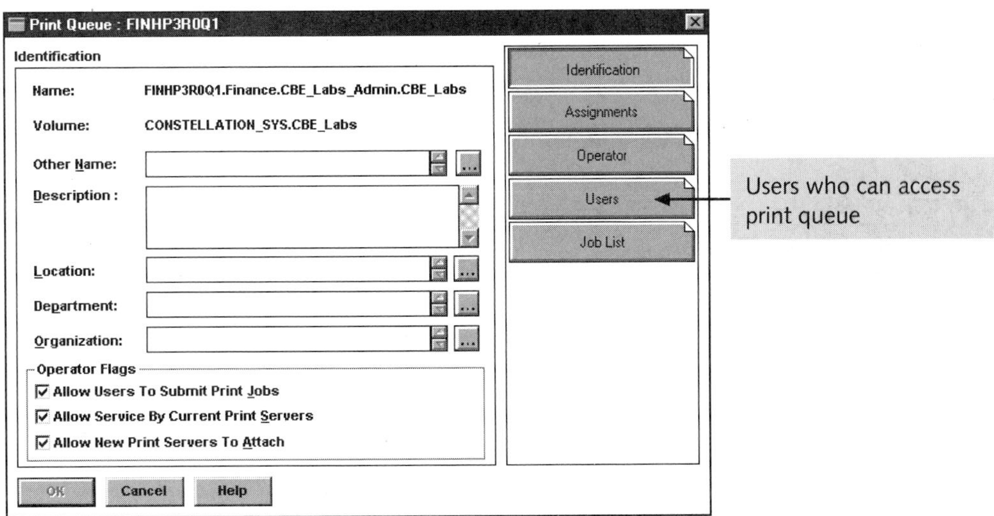

Click Users to see the objects that have access to this print queue. From here you may remove those user objects that you do not want to have access or select Add to add additional user objects.

In this example, add user TSimpson as a user who can access this print queue.

1. Select the object **FINHP3R0Q1** from the CBE Labs NDS tree.
2. Click the **Object** menu and select **Details**.
3. Click the **Users** button.
4. Click the **Add** button.
5. Click the **Browse** button and then select user **TSimpson**.
6. Click **OK**.

In order to assign or remove operators, click the Operators button and follow the same steps.

Creating Print Server Objects

To create a Print Server object, click the container object in which you want to create the Print Server object. Then select Create from the Object menu, and the New Object dialog box will appear. Select Print Server from this list, and the Create Print Server dialog box will appear, as shown in Figure 12-27.

Figure 12-27

Create Print Server dialog box

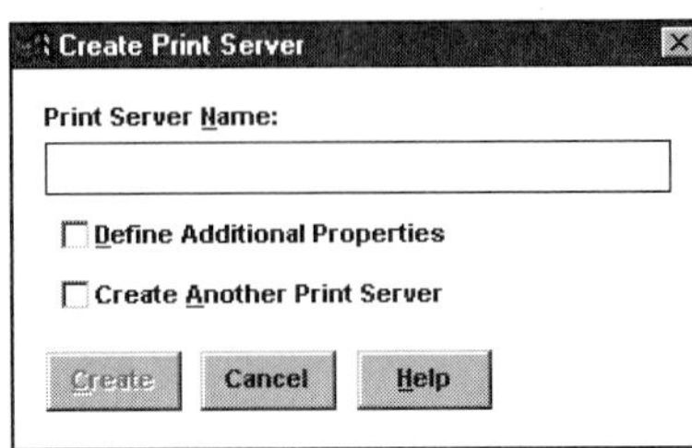

Key in the name of the print server and click OK. This print server object now appears in the NDS tree.

To create the print server for CBE Labs:

1. Select the object **CBE_Labs**.
2. Select the menu **Object**.
3. Select the menu option **Create**.
4. Click **Print Server**.
5. Type **CBELABS_PSERVER** as the print server name.
6. Click **Create**.

If you wish to change any of the settings (such as restrict users to this Print Server), click on the print server icon in the NDS tree and select Details from the Object menu. The Print Server dialog box will appear, from which you can make the necessary changes.

Defining and Configuring the Printers

Creating a printer object is done in the same manner as creating a print queue and print server. Click on the container object in which you want to create the Printer object. Then select Create from the Object menu, and the New Object dialog box will appear. Select Printer from this list, and the Create Printer dialog box will appear, as shown in Figure 12-28.

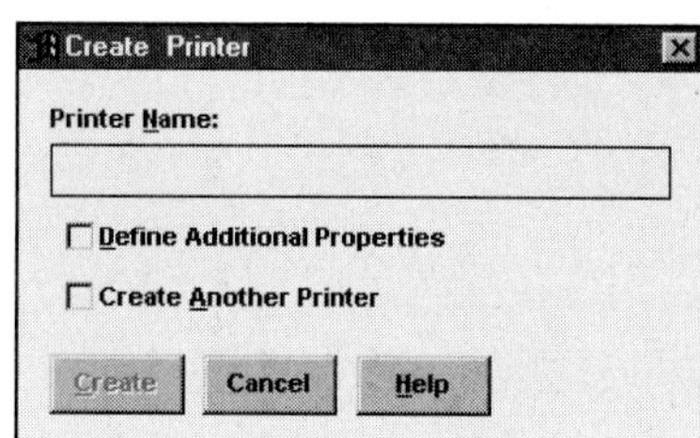

Figure 12-28 Create Printer dialog box

Type the name of the printer and click OK. This printer object now appears in the NDS tree.

To create a printer for the finance department of CBE Labs:

1. Select the object **Finance**.
2. Select the menu **Object**.
3. Select the menu option **Create**.
4. Click **Printer**.
5. Type **FINHP3R0** as the printer name.
6. Click **Create**.

To configure this printer, click the printer icon and select Details from the Object menu to display the Printer dialog box. Select Configuration to display the printer configuration options, as shown in Figure 12-29.

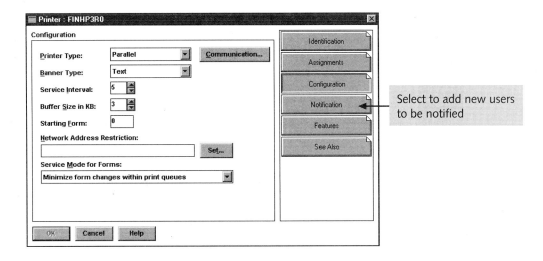

Figure 12-29
Printer Configuration dialog box

Select to add new users to be notified

The options are the same as with PCONSOLE.

To add a user to the notification list, click the Notification button from the Printer dialog box. The print job owner by default will be notified if a printing problem develops. To notify a print server operator, click Add and select that user's icon from the NDS tree.

Assigning Print Queues

In order to associate a print queue with a printer, click the printer object and select Details from the Object menu. The Printer dialog box will appear. Click the Assignments button to display the Assignments dialog box, as shown in Figure 12-30.

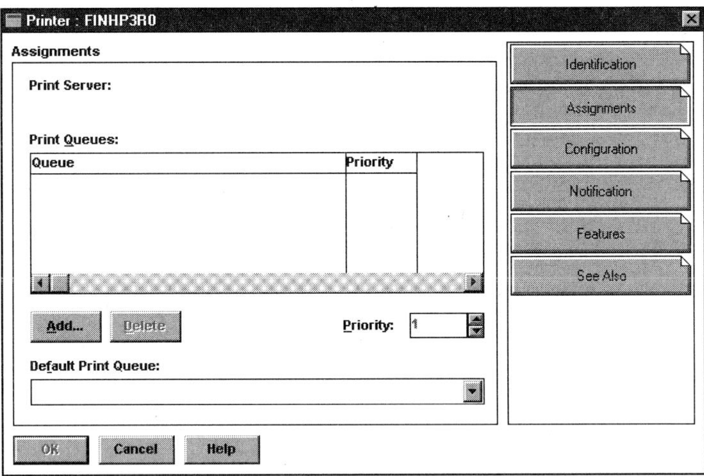

Figure 12-30
Printer Assignments dialog box

Click the Add button and select the desired print queue. That queue is now associated with that printer.

To assign the printer FINHP3R0 to the print queue FINHP3R0Q1:

1. Select the printer object **FINHP3R0**.
2. Click the **Object** menu.
3. Click **Details**.
4. Click the **Assignments** button.

5. Click the **Add** button.
6. Type **FINHP3R0Q1**.
7. Click **OK**.

The final step is to associate the printer with the print server. Click the print server object in the NDS tree and select Details from the Object menu to display the Print Server dialog box. Click the Assignments button to see the Assignments dialog box, as shown in Figure 12-31.

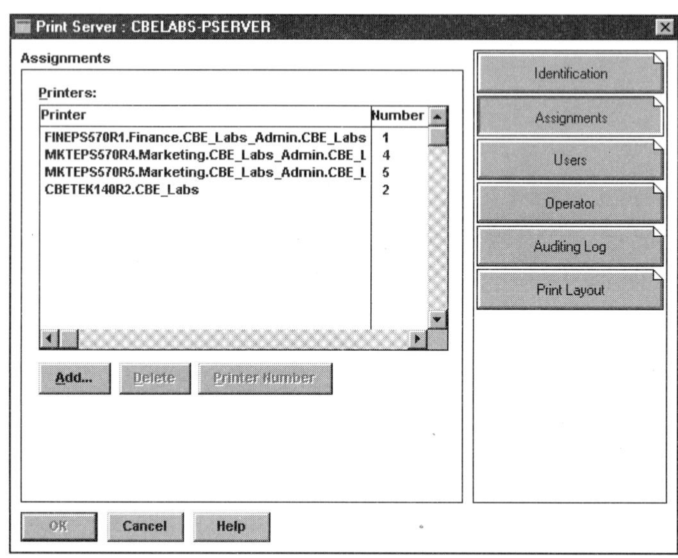

Figure 12-31 Print Server Assignments dialog box

To assign the printer FINHP3R0 to the print server CBELABS-PSERVER:

1. Select the print server object **CBELABS-PSERVER**.
2. Click the **Object** menu.
3. Click **Details**.
4. Click the **Assignment** button.
5. Click the **Add** button.
6. Type **FINHP3R0**.
7. Click **OK**.

CONFIGURING WINDOWS 95 CLIENTS

In order to print on the network using a Windows 95 client, it is necessary to configure Windows 95 for network printing. The easiest method is to use the Network Neighborhood, which permits you to quickly enable and disable printing to a specific port. The Network Neighborhood permits you to associate a specific port (LPT1, LPT2, LPT3, etc.) to a NetWare print queue.

Network Neighborhood is only one of several ways to configure Windows 95 for network printing. You may also configure it by using the Printer Settings window, the NWUSER.EXE program, or the CAPTURE.EXE command, which is explained below.

To configure Windows 95 using the Network Neighborhood, follow these steps:

1. Select the **Network Neighborhood** icon from the Windows 95 desktop. The Network Neighborhood window will appear, as shown in Figure 12-32.

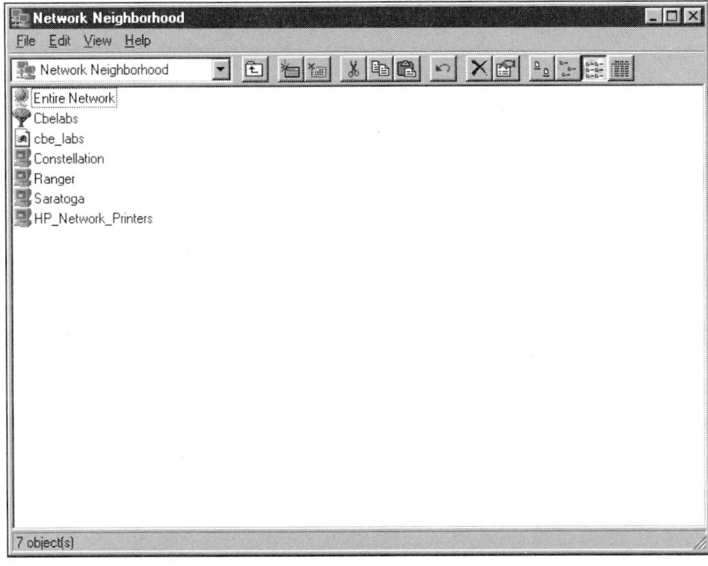

Figure 12-32 Network Neighborhood window

2. Select the server that contains the print queue. For example, to configure a Windows 95 client for the print queue FINHP3R0Q1, select the server Constellation.
3. Choose the appropriate print queue from the list.
4. Select **Capture Printer Port** from the File menu to display the Capture Printer Port window. You may select the port to be used for network printing by selecting the drop-down list box under Device. You can choose from the list of available printer ports (LPT1, LPT2, LPT3, etc.). Also, place a checkmark in the Reconnect at Logon box if you want to reestablish this printing whenever you start up the computer.
5. Click **OK**.

Using Windows 95 Network Neighborhood to look for print queues cancels the benefits of NDS, because you must know which server the print queue is located upon.

TESTING THE PRINTING ENVIRONMENT

After the printing environment has been established, it is important to test each remote and local printer by placing a job in the appropriate print queue and verifying that it is printed correctly. Testing can be completed by following these four steps:

1. Load the print server.
2. Load the remote printing software on each workstation that controls a network printer.
3. Place a test job in each print queue.
4. Monitor printing results.

LOADING THE PRINT SERVER

The print server software is run from the file server by loading PSERVER.NLM on the file server console. The SYS:SYSTEM directory contains PSERVER.NLM, a NetWare Loadable Module (NLM) version of the print server software. To load and run this NLM on your server computer, you will first need to have the exact name and password of the print server you want to load. Next, go to the file server console and, if necessary, use the [Alt] and [Esc] keys to switch to the console screen. From the colon (:) console prompt, enter the command LOAD PSERVER *name*, replacing *name* with the exact name of the print server definition file you created with the PCONSOLE utility. If you cannot remember the exact name of the print server, you can retrieve it by returning to your workstation and using the PCONSOLE utility to view the print server. If you make a typing error or do not enter the exact name, NetWare will ask you to enter a password for the print server. As with usernames, this is intended to make it more difficult to guess a password or print server name.

After loading several support modules, NetWare will start the print server program and display the print server information screen for up to eight printers at a time, as shown in Figure 12-33. You can press the spacebar to view the status of the next eight printers.

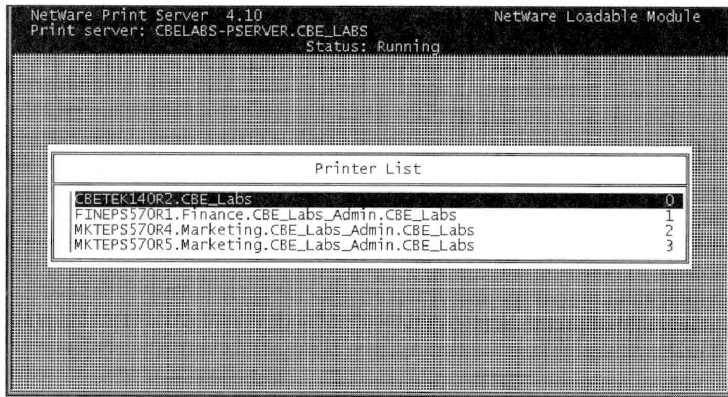

Figure 12-33 Print Server information screen

LOADING REMOTE PRINTING SOFTWARE

The second step in implementing network printing is to configure the Windows 95 client to service a remote printer. This is done by installing and configuring the Microsoft Print Services for NetWare utility. However, for a Windows 95 workstation to handle remote print jobs, the Microsoft documentation states that the remote print jobs must be configured with the Microsoft Client for NetWare Networks and that the print server must be bindery based.

To install this software on a Windows 95 client, follow these steps:

1. Select **Control Panel** from the Windows 95 desktop.
2. Double-click the **Network** icon and the Network window appears.
3. Click the **Add** button to display the Select Network Component Type window.
4. Select **Service** from the list of components.

5. Click the **Add** button to display the Select Network Service window.
6. Insert the Windows 95 installation CD into your CD-ROM drive.
7. Click the **Have Disk** button. You'll be asked to enter the path to the Windows 95 installation disk. Type ***drive*:\Admin\Nettools\Prtagent** (where *drive* is the letter of your CD-ROM drive).
8. When Windows 95 has read the installation data, the Select Network Services window will again appear with Microsoft Print Agent for NetWare Networks indicated. Choose **OK**.
9. You'll now be returned to the Network window. Make sure that the Microsoft Print Agent for NetWare Networks appears on the list of network components; then click **OK**.

You must now reboot your Windows 95 computer. Once it restarts, you can configure this computer to support a remote printer by following these steps.

1. From the Printers window, select the local printer that you want to make available as a remote NetWare printer.
2. Select **Properties** from the File menu.
3. Select the **Print Server** page.
4. Select **Enable Microsoft Print Server for NetWare**.
5. Specify the NetWare Server and Print Server.

PLACING JOBS IN PRINT QUEUES

Once all the printing components are connected, the next task is to test the printing system by placing jobs in each of the print queues and verifying that they are properly printed. There are several ways in which jobs can be placed in a print queue for printing:

- Use a software application to print directly to the network printer port.
- Use the CAPTURE command to redirect application output to the print queue.
- Use the NPRINT command to transfer an ASCII text file directly to a print queue.

Use a Software Application to Print Directly to the Network Printer Port

Earlier we assigned a specific printer port (LPT1, LPT2, LPT3, etc.) to a network print queue. That means that now any software that prints to that port will automatically print to the network printer associated with that queue. With Windows-aware software, it will automatically recognize that association from within the application, and when you select a printer for your output, it will associate that printer with a port and the print queue. With some older DOS-based software, you may have to tell the application to print to a certain port. For example, if LPT2 was the port you had associated with the print queue, you may have to tell this older software to print using LPT2 in order to have the output sent to the network printer.

Using CAPTURE to Redirect Application Output to a Print Queue

If you are working with an application that does not know about NetWare print queues and you want its output to be printed on a network printer, you need to use the CAPTURE command to redirect the output from the application directly to the print queue. An important part of using the CAPTURE command is determining when the application has finished its output so the print job can be made available to the print server for printing. There are three ways in which you can have the CAPTURE command determine when a print job is complete and is ready for printing:

1. Timeout
2. End the application
3. End the capture

The timeout method involves establishing a time value that tells the CAPTURE command how many seconds of inactivity to allow before the application is assumed to be finished printing. If you set a timeout value of 7 sec., for example, and then use the spreadsheet program to print a balance sheet, 7 seconds after the spreadsheet program has finished printing, the print job will be closed and made available to the print server. The problem with the timeout system is that some applications pause the printing for more than several seconds while they perform calculations or graphics manipulation. When this happens, the output can be separated into two different print jobs, resulting in a broken printout. If you find that your print jobs are broken up on separate pages, increase the number of seconds in the timeout factor.

Another method of ending a print job is to wait for the application to exit before releasing the print job to the print server. In this method, if you use the spreadsheet software to print both a balance sheet and budget reports, for example, you would not receive any printouts until after you exit the spreadsheet program. When the spreadsheet program ends, the print job containing both reports is sent to the print server and printed. This method is referred to as AUTOENDCAP.

The third method of ending a print job is to end the capture function by using the CAPTURE/EC (EC stands for "end capture") or logging out of the file server. This method is referred to as NOAUTOENDCAP and is useful if you want to hold output from all applications until the user issues the ENDCAP command or logs out of the file server. The CAPTURE command syntax is CAPTURE [options]. If no options are specified, the CAPTURE command attempts to send output to the default print queue using the default parameters. You can replace options with one or more of the parameters listed in Figure 12-34. For example, here is the CAPTURE command needed to redirect output from the LPT2 port to a laser printer print queue using a timeout of 5 seconds, printing a banner page containing the name FINANCE on the upper half and FIN_REPORT on the lower half, in byte stream format, with an automatic form feed at the end of the printout, and also notify the user upon completion of the print job:

```
CAPTURE Q=FINHP3R0Q1 TI=5 NAM=FINANCE B=FIN_REPORT NT FF NOTI
```

Figure 12-34
CAPTURE command options

Parameter	Description
SH (show)	Displays the current capture status of the printer ports.
TI=*n* (timeout)	Determines when the application is done processing a print job based on no printed output being sent in the specified time period. For example, TI=5 tells the system that the print job is complete if no output is received in a 5-sec. period.
A (autoendcap)	By default, if no timeout is specified, the job will be ready for printing when the application ends. For example, you might print three spreadsheets and not receive any output until you exit the spreadsheet program, at which time all three printouts will be generated.
NA (no autoendcap)	Specifies that no output will be released for printing until the user either logs out or issues the ENDCAP command to end the capture settings.
L=*n* (local)	Specifies the number of the LPT port to be re-routed to the print queue. By default, LPT1 is redirected.
CR=*path* (create)	Creates a file in the specified path that will contain the output in printer format. You can then later use the NPRINT command to print the file, or you might want to include it with a document for documentation or training purposes.
K (keep)	Specifies that the job should be kept on the print queue in the event the workstation crashes before the output is complete. If you do not include the Keep parameter and the workstation "crashes" during the capture process, the file server will discard the data it has received.

Using CAPTURE/EC

The CAPTURE/EC command is used to return an output port back to the local printer. Its syntax is CAPTURE/EC [L=*n*] [ALL]. Replace *n* with the number of the printer port you want to return to local control. Use the ALL option to return all LPT ports to local control. If you issue this command with no parameters, the default is L=1. Suppose, for example, you issue a CAPTURE command to redirect output from your workstation's LPT1 port to a laser printer. After sending the print job, you want to continue working with the dot-matrix printer attached to the LPT1 port of your workstation. To end the capture of the LPT printer output to the laser printer and return to using your local dot-matrix printer, issue the CAPTURE/EC L=1 command. You can also issue CAPTURE/EC with no parameters to get the same result.

Using NPRINT to Transfer an ASCII File Directly to a Print Queue

The NPRINT utility can be used to place ASCII text files in a print queue. This can be useful if you need to print the contents of an ASCII documentation file, such as a README file on a disk.

Because NPRINT does not perform any file translation, the file you print must be in ASCII text format so that it can be displayed on the screen using the TYPE filename command.

The syntax of the NPRINT command is

NPRINT *path\filename [options]*

Replace *path\filename* with the directory path leading to the specified filename to be printed. Replace *options* with one or more of the parameters shown in Figure 12-35. If, for example, you want to print the README file from the A: disk drive to the FINHP3SIR0 printer with no banner, with a form feed, in byte stream format, and then be notified when the printing is complete, you could enter a command similar to the following:

```
NPRINT A:README Q=FINHP3R0Q1 NB FF NT NOTI
```

Parameter	Description
NOTI (notify)	Causes a message to be sent notifying the user who submitted the print job when the job has been printed. By default, the sending user will not be notified.
PS=*printserver*	Normally not needed when the print queue name and file server names are specified.
S=*fileserver*	Names the file server that contains the specified print queue. By default, the current file server's name is used.
Q=*queuename*	The name of the print queue in which you want the output placed.
J=*job configuration*	Specifying a specific PRINTCON job will cause the NPRINT command to get all unspecified parameters from the given print configuration job name.
F=*form* or ##	Specifies the type of form to be used. The default form type is 0. Form types 0–9 may be specified. It is the network administrator's responsibility to identify the type of paper to be used with each form type.
C=*n* (copies)	Specifies the number of copies of the job to be placed in the print queue.
T(tabs)	Specifies the number of spaces to leave for each tab code encountered. The default is eight spaces per tab code.
NT (no tabs)	Specifies that "Byte stream" output format is to be used with no tab codes expanded.
NB (no banner)	Specifies that no banner page is to be printed. By default a banner page will be printed.
NAM=*name*	Specifies the name to appear in the upper part of the banner page. The default is the username.
B=*bannername*	Specifies the name to appear in the bottom part of the banner page. By default the file name is used.
FF (form feed)	By default, this option is enabled. Causes the printer to eject a page after printing the file listing.
NFF (no form feed)	Disables the form feed after the file has printed. Output from the next print job will then start printing on the same page.
D (delete)	Causes the original file to be deleted after it has been printed. By default, the original text file is not deleted after printing.

Figure 12-35 NPRINT command options

CHAPTER SUMMARY

An important task of the network administrator is establishing and maintaining a network printing environment that will provide users with access to a variety of printers. As a Network Administrator, you will be expected to know the printing concepts and utilities described in this chapter and be able to implement and maintain a NetWare printing environment consisting of print queues, a print server, printers, and workstations. A print queue is a subdirectory that is used to hold print jobs until the printer is ready to print them. A print server is the software component that controls printing by taking print jobs from the queues and sending them to network printers. The NetWare print server consists of a configuration file that defines the print server's printing environment along with the print server program PSERVER.NLM, which runs on the file server computer and enables you to use that computer as both a file server and print server. A NetWare 4.1 print server can control up to 256 printers, of which five can be locally attached to the computer running the print server software. The other printers are defined as remote printers. For Windows 95, you must install and configure MSPSRV.EXE, the Microsoft Print Services for NetWare utility.

The first task in establishing the printer environment is defining the printing requirements for each user's applications, determining the types and number of printers necessary to meet these requirements, and determining the location of the printers on the network and whether they will be locally attached to the print server or remotely attached to printer ports on the workstations. The next step in defining the printer environment is developing a naming system for printers and print queues that will make it easy for you to identify the printer location, type of printer, and method of attachment.

After you have defined the printing environment, you must install the printing system. The NWADMIN or PCONSOLE menu utility performs most of the work involved with setting up and maintaining the NetWare printing system. To install the printing system initially, you need to create print queues, assign print queue users and operators, create the print server, define up to a maximum of 256 network printers that will be controlled by the print server, and then assign one or more print queues to each of the printers.

The final task in setting up the printing system is loading the PSERVER software on the file server as a NetWare Loadable Module. Once the network printing system is operational, ASCII files that are in a printable format can be placed directly in a print queue using the NPRINT command. The CAPTURE command is commonly used to redirect the output of application programs from local LPT printer ports to specified print queues. Parameters added to the CAPTURE and NPRINT commands enable the user to specify such options as the name of the print queue, form feeds, an optional banner page, number of copies, and a timeout value for the CAPTURE command to determine when an application has completed printing. Output can be directed to a network printer through the Network Neighborhood.

COMMAND SUMMARY

Command	Syntax	Definition
CAPTURE	*CAPTURE [options]*	Redirects output from an LPT printer port to the specified print queue. In addition, the CAPTURE command contains options to determine when printing is complete. Use either the timeout factor or the AUTOENDCAP to release the print job when the application program ends.
NPRINT	*NPRINT path\filename [options]*	Sends an existing ASCII text file directly to the specified print queue. Often used to print documentation and batch files, NPRINT uses many of the same options as the CAPTURE command.
PCONSOLE	*PCONSOLE*	A menu utility for establishing, maintaining, and controlling the network printing environment.
PSERVER	*PSERVER name*	Takes jobs from print queues and sends them to the network printers. The PSERVER.EXE can be run on a dedicated workstation, whereas PSERVER.NLM is to be run on the file server.

NPRINTER	*NPRINTER*	A TSR program loaded into the memory of a workstation that has a remote printer attached to it. The NPRINTER program stays in memory and transfers print data from the print server to the attached network printer.

KEY TERMS

direct printer
local printer
print job
print queue
print server
remote printer

REVIEW QUESTIONS

1. The ________________ is the network printing component that holds printed output until the printer is ready to print.

2. A(n) ________________ is software that actually makes network printing happen.

3. Up to ________________ local printers can be attached to a print server.

4. Print queues and print servers can be created with either the ________________ or ________________ utility.

5. A network printer attached to a workstation is called a(n) ____________ printer.

6. A print server can control a maximum of ________________ printers.

7. A NetWare 4.1 print queue is a subdirectory that can be placed in which directory?

8. On the lines below, list three ways of attaching a printer to the network.

   ____

   ____

   ____

9. On the lines below, list the four items of information that should be included in a printer's name.

   ____

   ____

   ____

   ____

10. On the lines below, list in sequence the five steps required to set up a networked printing environment.

____

____

____

____

11. The ______________ utility contains a Quick Setup feature that can be used to quickly perform the steps necessary to set up the network printing environment.

12. By default, ______________ can send jobs to a newly created print queue.

13. What option on the Print Server Information menu defines new printers on the print server?

14. After information in the print server definition is changed, what must be done in order for the changes to be implemented?

15. To create a print server definition, select the ______________ option from the PCONSOLE Available Options menu.

16. To print using Windows 95, the ______________ permits you to enable and disable printing to a specific port.

17. On the lines below, list three ways jobs can be placed in a print queue.

____

____

____

____

18. You can use the ______________ command line utility to print a file called README from drive A to the BUS-EPS70-R1-Q1 print queue.

19. On the line below, write the command that will print the README file in question 18 with no banner, a form feed, and eight spaces per tab code and will notify you when printing is complete.

____

20. On the line below, write a command to direct output from a spreadsheet program to the BUS-EPS70-R1-Q1 print queue with a banner containing your username on the top of the banner page and the message "BUDGET_REPORT" on the bottom. Include a form feed, no tabs, a timeout of 10 sec., and notification when printing is complete.

____

21. On the line below, write a command to return all printer ports to the local workstation's printer.

____

EXERCISES

EXERCISE 12-1: CREATING PRINT QUEUES

In this exercise, you need to log in with a username that has ADMIN equivalency in order to establish print queues and print queue operators. If you do not have access to a supervisor equivalent name on your file server, your instructor will need to create the print queues for you.

1. Use PCONSOLE or NetWare Administrator to create the following print queues. (Replace ## with your assigned student number.)

   `##REMOTE`

   `##LOCAL`

2. Make your student username an operator of each of the print queues.
3. Log out.
4. Log in using your assigned student username.
5. Enter a CAPTURE command to send output from your computer's LPT2 port to the ##REMOTE print queue using a timeout of 5 sec.
6. Enter a CAPTURE command to send output from your computer's LPT3 port to the ##LOCAL print queue using a timeout of 10 sec.
7. Enter the CAPTURE SH command to display the capture status of your computer. Record the capture status of each port on the lines below.

   LPT1: ____________________

   LPT2: ____________________

   LPT3: ____________________

8. Enter the CAPTURE/EC command and then use the CAPTURE SH command to view your results. Record the capture status of each port on the lines below.

   LPT1: ____________________

   LPT2: ____________________

   LPT3: ____________________

9. Enter a command to return all ports to the local workstation. On the line below, record the command you use.

   ____

EXERCISE 12-2: PLACING JOBS IN PRINT QUEUES

In this exercise you use the NPRINT and PCONSOLE utilities to place jobs in the specified print queues. This exercise assumes that you have two print queues named ##REMOTE and ##LOCAL that were created either by your instructor or by you in exercise 1.These print queues will need to be created before you can complete this exercise.

1. Log in using your assigned student username.
2. Use PCONSOLE to verify the existence of the required print queues. (If the ##REMOTE and ##LOCAL print queues do not exist, complete exercise 1 or contact your instructor.)
3. Create the following document with either Notepad, Windows Write, or DOS Edit and title it PRINTJOB:

There are three ways in which jobs can be placed in a print queue for printing:

- Use a software application to print directly to the network printer port.
- The CAPTURE command will redirect application output to the print queue.
- The NPRINT command will transfer an ASCII text file directly to a print queue.

4. Use the NPRINT command to print two copies of the PRINTJOB document. Place the job in your ##REMOTE print queue with a banner page containing your name on the top half and the filename on the lower half. Include a form feed and no tabs and have the print server notify you when the job is printed. What NPRINT command did you use? ______________________________

5. Use the NPRINT command to place a copy of your workstation's AUTOEXEC.BAT file in your ##LOCAL print queue with no banner, no tabs, no form feed, and forms type 2. What NPRINT command did you use?

 ____

6. Use the PCONSOLE utility to place a copy of the PRINTJOB document into your ##LOCAL print queue using the PCONSOLE default settings.

7. Use PCONSOLE to display all print jobs in the ##LOCAL print queue. Record those jobs below:

 ____

 ____

 ____

8. Exit PCONSOLE.

9. Log out.

Exercise 12-3: Redirecting Printer Output

In this exercise you use the CAPTURE command to redirect printer output from your workstation to a NetWare print queue. This exercise assumes that you or your instructor created two print queues, ##REMOTE and ##LOCAL, for your use. If these print queues do not exist, notify your instructor or complete exercise 1 in order to create the required print queues.

1. Log in using your assigned student username.

2. Use PCONSOLE to verify the existence of the required print queues. (If the ##REMOTE and ##LOCAL print queues do not exist, perform exercise 1 or contact your instructor.)

3. Open a DOS prompt in Windows.

4. Enter a CAPTURE to redirect the output sent to the LPT2 port to print queue ##LOCAL using the correct parameter to cause the print job not to be available for printing until after the application program exits. The print job should contain no banner and no tabs and should be kept in the print queue in the event the application program aborts prior to completion. Record the CAPTURE command you use on the line below.

 ____

5. Use the appropriate parameter of the CAPTURE command to display the capture status of all printer ports. On the line below, record the command you use.

 ____

6. Use the following command to type a copy of the document PRINTJOB to the LPT2 printer port:

```
TYPE PRINTJOB > LPT2
```

Exercise 12-4: Using a NetWare Print Queue from Windows 95

In the following exercise you learn how to configure and redirect output from Windows 95 to the ##REMOTE and ##LOCAL print queues. This exercise assumes that Windows 95 has been properly installed to work with your network and that the ##REMOTE and ##LOCAL print queues have already been created by either you or your instructor.

1. Log in using your assigned student username.
2. Open a DOS prompt. Use the CAPTURE SH command to view the capture status of your workstation. On the lines below, record the capture status.

   LPT1: ______________________________

   LPT2: ______________________________

   LPT3: ______________________________
3. Close the DOS prompt.
4. Select the Network Neighborhood icon from the Windows 95 desktop.
5. Select the server that contains the print queue.
6. Choose the ##REMOTE print queue from the list.
7. Select Capture Printer Port from the File menu to display the Capture Printer Port window.
8. Select the port to be used for network printing by selecting the drop-down list box under Device and choose LPT3.
9. Click OK.
10. Use Notepad to create a short document—maybe describing your plans for this coming weekend.
11. Use the Print option of Notepad to send output to the network print queue.
12. Open a DOS prompt.
13. Enter the CAPTURE SH command and record your capture settings below.

    LPT1: ______________________________

    LPT2: ______________________________

    LPT3: ______________________________

Exercises

Case 12-1: Creating a Printing Environment for the Jefferson County Courthouse

In this exercise you create a printing environment by using DS Standard for the Jefferson County Courthouse Directory tree created in Case 7-1. Refer back to that exercise if necessary.

Part 1: Create and configure the print queue

1. If necessary, boot the PC workstation, launch Windows 95.
2. Click the Start button.
3. Click Programs to display the Programs menu, click DS Standard NDS Manager v3 to display the DS Standard NDS Manager 3.0 menu, and then click DS Standard NDS Manager to open the DS Standard NDS manager.
4. Click File, click Open View, and then click Jefferson County Courthouse to display the NDS tree.
5. Select the container object SOCSERVICES to locate the print queue object.
6. Click Edit on the menu bar and click Add Object to see a display of the available objects.
7. Click Print Queue.
8. Type SSHP5Q1 as the name of the print queue.

Part 2: Create and configure the print server

1. Select the container object SOCSERVICES to locate the print server object.
2. Click Edit the menu bar and click Add Object to see a display of the available objects.
3. Click Print Server.
4. Type PS1 as the name of the print server.

Part 3: Create and configure the printer

1. Select the container object SOCSERVICES in which to locate the printer object.
2. Click Edit on the menu bar and click Add Object to see a display of the available objects.
3. Click Printer.
4. Type SSHP5R0 as the name of the printer.

Part 4: Assign the print queues

1. Select the printer object SSHP5R0 by double-clicking on it.
2. Click the Assignments button.
3. Click the Add button.
4. Type SSHP5Q1 as the name of your print queue.

Turn in a copy of your data disk to your instructor.

Case 12-2: Creating a Printing Environment for the J. Q. Adams Company

In this exercise you create a printing environment by using DS Standard for the J. Q. Adams Company Directory tree created in Case 7-2. Refer back to that exercise if necessary.

Part 1: Create and confirm the print queue

1. If necessary, boot the PC workstation, launch Windows 95.
2. Click the Start button.

3. Click Programs to display the Programs menu, click DS Standard NDS Manager v3 to display the DS Standard NDS Manager 3.0 menu, and then click DS Standard NDS Manager to open the DS Standard NDS manager.
4. Click File, click Open View, and then click J. Q. Adams Company to display the NDS tree.
5. Select the container object SALES&MRKTING to locate the print queue object.
6. Click Edit on the menu bar and click Add Object to see a display of the available objects.
7. Click Print Queue.
8. Type SMHP5Q1 as the name of the print queue.

Part 2: Create and configure the print server

1. Select the container objects SALES&MRKTING to locate the print server object.
2. Click Edit on the menu bar and click Add Object to see a display of the available objects.
3. Click Print Server.
4. Type PS1 as the name of the print server.

Part 3: Create and configure the printer

1. Select the container object SALES&MRKTING to locate the printer object.
2. Click Edit on the menu bar and click Add Object to see a display of the available objects.
3. Click Printer.
4. Type SSMHP5R0 as the name of the printer.

Part 4: Assign the print queues

1. Select the printer object SSMHP5R0.
2. Click the Assignments button.
3. Click the Add button.
4. Type SMHP5Q1 as the name of the print queue.

Turn in a copy of your data disk to your instructor.

Northwestern Technical College

A new color laser printer has been delivered to the Administration building at Northwestern Technical College (NWTC). This laser can be used by any administrative user. In addition, the students who have received special permission may also have access to the printer. However, because of the expense of the consumable supplies (toner, special paper, etc.), any student use will be closely monitored. Your job is to install the printer and make it available to the users.

PROJECT 12-1: INSTALLING THE PRINTER

Lee Olsen, Manager of the Business group, has sent a memo requesting that the new color laser printer be connected to the computer in his office. Lee states that he knows that network printers can be connected in this manner and that it would be the cheapest solution. In addition, he maintains that he can monitor its usage to ensure that it is not abused. However, there are no other printers in the area connected to a user's workstation, and several employees have already indicated their displeasure at this proposed configuration.

Write a memo to Lee outlining the different ways in which a printer can be connected to a network. Because Lee does not have a strong network background, be sure not to make the memo too technical. Discuss the advantages and disadvantages of each type of arrangement. Emphasize the problems that could be encountered if the printer is located in his office (e.g., how to retrieve the printouts when his office is locked, constant traffic in and out of his office, etc.). Research the cost of a network print box and include that figure in your memo. Finally, give your input regarding where you think the printer should be physically located.

Turn in a copy of your memo to your instructor.

PROJECT 12-2: CREATING PRINT QUEUES, PRINT SERVERS, AND PRINTERS

Assuming that your memo persuades Lee to change his mind, it is decided that the color laser printer will be a direct attachment to the network. Once the printer is installed, you must now configure NetWare in order that the users in Administration can access it.

Create the necessary print queue, print server, and printer object so that all Administrative users can access the printer. Remember that a few selected students may likewise have the rights to use the printer. Keep that in mind as you place these objects in the Directory tree.

CHAPTER THIRTEEN

CUSTOMIZING NETWARE PRINTING

Once the network printing environment has been installed, an ongoing responsibility of the network administrator is managing and customizing the printing environment to meet the ever-changing needs of users and applications. Managing network printing involves such operational tasks as working with print jobs and controlling the print server. And in order to reduce the amount of time you spend working with print jobs and controlling printers, you will want to train other users to be print queue and print server operators.

Customizing printing to accommodate different types of paper and to provide printer setup features for applications that require special printing is another important part of maintaining a network printing environment. In this chapter you will learn how to use the PRINTDEF utility to help you manage multiple print forms and create printer setup sequences that take advantage of features found in many printers. You will see how the PRINTCON utility can be used to create and maintain customized print jobs. You will also learn how to configure your print server to access and print jobs from print queues located on other file servers.

AFTER READING THIS CHAPTER AND COMPLETING THE EXERCISES YOU WILL BE ABLE TO:

- MANAGE JOBS IN A PRINT QUEUE WITH PCONSOLE AND WINDOWS 95.
- USE PCONSOLE AND PSC TO CONTROL THE PRINT SERVER.
- CUSTOMIZE THE PRINTING ENVIRONMENT WITH THE PRINTDEF AND PRINTCON UTILITIES.

MANAGING THE PRINTING ENVIRONMENT

After you install the network printing system, one of the first tasks you will face is manipulating print jobs and controlling network printers. The PCONSOLE utility is used to manage print queue jobs as well as view and change the status of a print queue in order to make the print queue temporarily inaccessible to users or print servers. Another useful feature of NetWare printing enables you to hold a print job for printing at a later time. This can be helpful if you need to print a job that will take a long time; rather than tie up the printer during the day when it is needed by other users, you can print such a job during off hours.

Another important part of managing the printing environment is being able to control networked printers in order to cancel jobs, change paper, clear paper jams, and properly unload the print server. In this section you will learn how you can perform these duties. Finally, customizing NetWare printing to the environment in which you work is also discussed.

MANAGING PRINT JOBS WITH PCONSOLE

Once jobs are placed in a print queue, it is sometimes necessary to rearrange the sequence, to defer printing until a later time, or to change such print job parameters as the banner, the number of copies, or the file contents. Managing print jobs can be performed by using the PCONSOLE utility or in a limited fashion through Windows 95. As a network administrator you will be required to know how to use PCONSOLE to perform the functions described in this section.

Rearranging Print Jobs

It is sometimes necessary for a print queue operator to rearrange the sequence of jobs in a print queue. This enables a high-priority job to be printed ahead of other jobs placed in the print queue before it. For example, suppose the marketing director of CBE Labs, Stephen Hayakawa, needs a certain print job printed immediately to use as part of a presentation being made to stockholders. If the presentation print job is located after several other large print jobs in the laser print queue, the print queue operator will need to change the sequence number of the presentation print job to cause it to print next.

To change the sequence of the jobs in a print queue, follow these steps:

1. Start PCONSOLE and select the **Print Queues** option, which displays a list of existing print queues.
2. Highlight the name of the print queue containing the jobs to be resequenced and press **[Enter]** to obtain the Print Queue Information menu.
3. Highlight the first option, **Print Jobs**. Press **[Enter]** to display the current print job entries window, which shows all jobs in the print queue along with their status and job number, as shown in Figure 13-1.

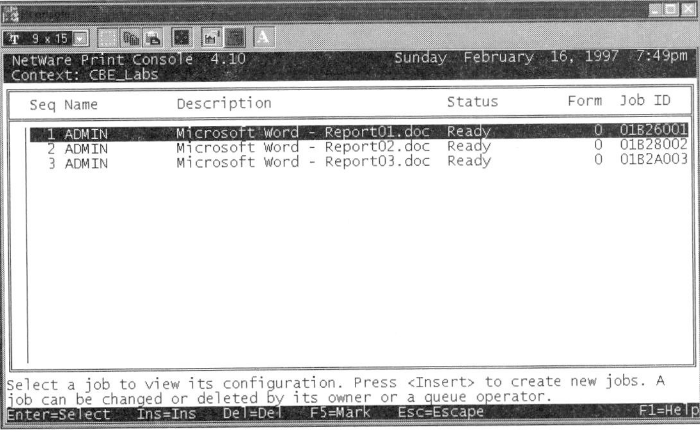

Figure 13-1 Current print job entries

4. The status field indicates the status of the current job entry. A "Ready" status indicates that the print job is available for printing by the print server. A status of "Adding" indicates that a workstation is still placing information in the print job, and the "Active" status indicates that the print job is currently being printed. The "Seq" column indicates the order in which the job will be printed.

5. To change the sequence number of a print job, highlight the job you want to change. Press **[Enter]** to display the Print Job Information window shown in Figure 13-2.

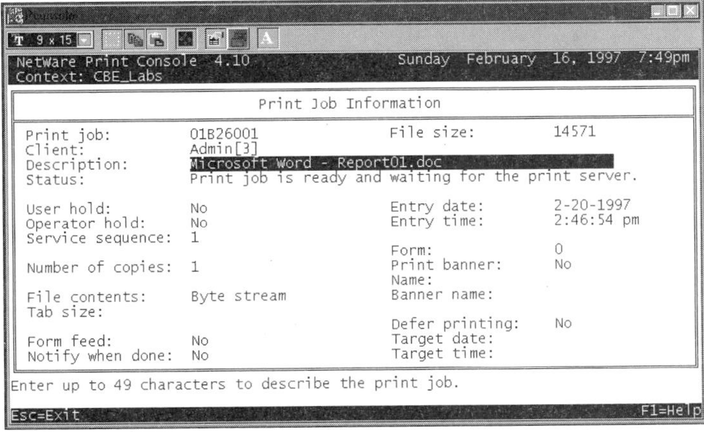

Figure 13-2 Print Job Information window

6. Highlight the "**Service sequence**" field and change the existing sequence number to reflect the new position of the job in the print queue. In Figure 13-2, for example, changing the sequence number to a 1 would make this job the next one to be printed.

7. Press **[Esc]** to save the change and return to the window showing the revised sequence numbers of all jobs in the selected print queue.

Changing Print Queue Status

To prevent the print jobs from starting to print while you are resequencing a print queue, you need to take the queue off line temporarily. A print queue operator for a print queue can use PCONSOLE to take the print queue off line by selecting it from the Print

Queue window and then using the Status option to display the Print Queue Status window, as shown in Figure 13-3. To take the print queue off line, highlight the "Allow service by current print servers" field and change the Yes to a No. The queue will now enable users to place jobs in it, but no jobs will be printed until the status is changed back to Yes. Press [Esc] to save the status change and return to the Print Queue Information menu.

Figure 13-3

Print Queue Status window

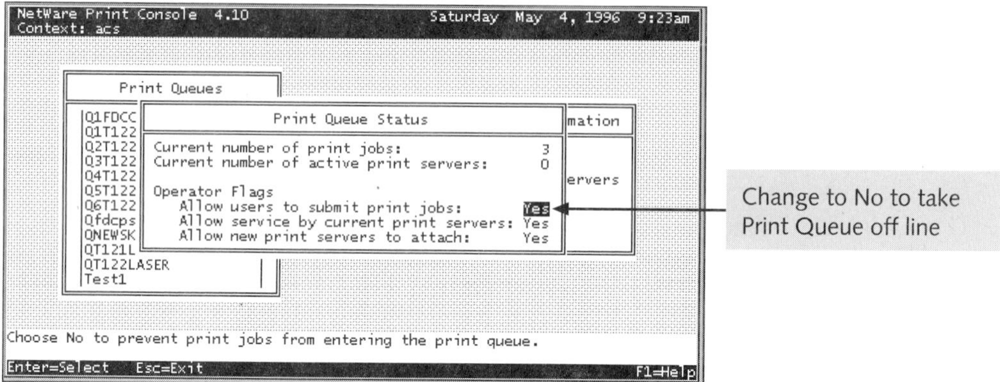

Delaying a Print Job

You can start printing a long print job late at night and avoid tying up the printer during office hours. This is especially useful with desktop publishing jobs, which typically take a long time to print because of their high-resolution graphics. Let's send a job to a finance print queue and then delay it to print later. To delay a print job, follow these steps:

1. Change the status of the print queue FINHP3SIR0Q1 to halt printing temporarily.
2. Place a job in the print queue using an application or the CAPTURE command.
3. Run the PCONSOLE utility and select the print queue **FINHP3R0Q1**.
4. Use the Print Jobs option to display the jobs.
5. Highlight the print job you just sent to the queue and then press **[Enter]** to display the Print Jobs Information window. It will be similar to the one shown in Figure 13-2.
6. To schedule the job to print at a different time, highlight the "**Defer printing**" option and change No to **Yes**.
7. By default, the job will be set to start printing at 11:59:59 P.M. the following day, as shown in Figure 13-4. Change the print date to today's date and the time to 15 minutes from now. After you defer the printing of a print job, the status column for that job will change from Ready to Waiting. The Waiting status means the job is set for deferred printing.

Figure 13-4

Changing the Defer printing field

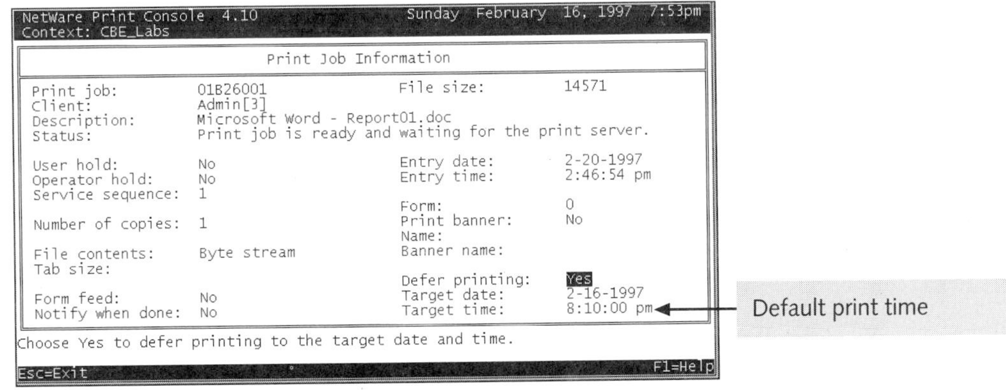

8. Exit the PCONSOLE utility. The job will be printed at the specified time if the print server computer is running and the printer is ready.

Managing Print Jobs with Windows 95

Microsoft Windows 95 also provides users with a limited ability to manage print jobs. The advantage of using Windows over PCONSOLE is that users will already be familiar with the Windows environment and will not have to learn new commands in PCONSOLE. In addition, some of these commands can be executed from within Windows without the need to run another program.

Managing Print Jobs from the Windows 95 Desktop

Windows 95 also enables you to control print jobs from the desktop. From the Start icon, select Settings and then choose the Printers icon. Select the printer icon that represents the printer to which the output is being sent. Double-click this icon and you will see the Windows 95 Printer Control window, as shown in Figure 13-5.

Figure 13-5

Windows 95 Printer Control window

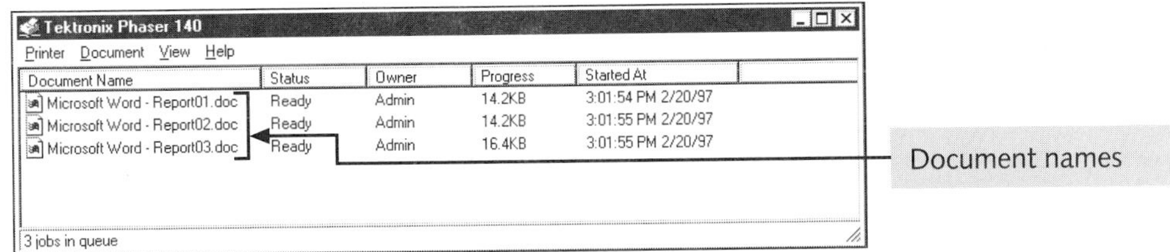

The fields for this window indicate the name of the document, its printing status (*Spooling,* which means it is being added to the print queue, *Paused, Printing, Deleting,* and *Out of Paper* are the five status indicators), the person who started the print job, how much has been printed, and the date and time it was placed in the queue.

Both users and queue operators can manage print jobs from Windows 95. Whereas users can change the status only of their own print jobs, queue operators can change the status of any jobs that are in the queue.

The actions that may be performed are as follows:

- To place a hold on a print job, select that document from the Printer Control window and select Pause Printing from the Document menu (Users or Queue Operators).
- To place a hold on all print jobs, select Pause Printing from the Printer menu (Queue Operators).
- To remove a document from the print queue, select Cancel Printing from the Document menu (Users or Queue Operators).
- To remove all documents from the print queue, select Purge Print Jobs from the Printer menu (Queue Operators).
- To change the order of a print job, select that document and then drag and drop it to its new position (Users or Queue Operators).

CONTROLLING THE PRINT SERVER

Network printers running on a print server often require the operator to perform certain control functions, such as changing print forms, pausing a printer, canceling a print job, or checking printer status. It is sometimes necessary to attach a print queue temporarily to a different printer or to send printer notification messages to another user if the print server operator is not available. All these functions can be accessed via the Print Server option of the PCONSOLE utility.

In addition to the PCONSOLE menu utility, NetWare also provides a printer control command line utility, called PSC, that can be used to control or view the status of any printers on the network. In this section you will learn about managing printers using either the PSC command or the PCONSOLE utility.

Using PCONSOLE to Control Printers

A print server operator might at times need to change print forms in a printer. There are special paper forms, such as labels or invoices, which are used as well as standard paper for printing reports. The print server operator is notified when a printer requires a print form change. The operator responds by manually changing the paper type in the printer and also by changing the form specification in the Printer Status window. You use the PCONSOLE utility to perform this task by selecting the Print Servers option and selecting the print server that is currently running. The Print Server Information menu shown in Figure 13-6 contains the Printers option.

Figure 13-6 Print Server Information window

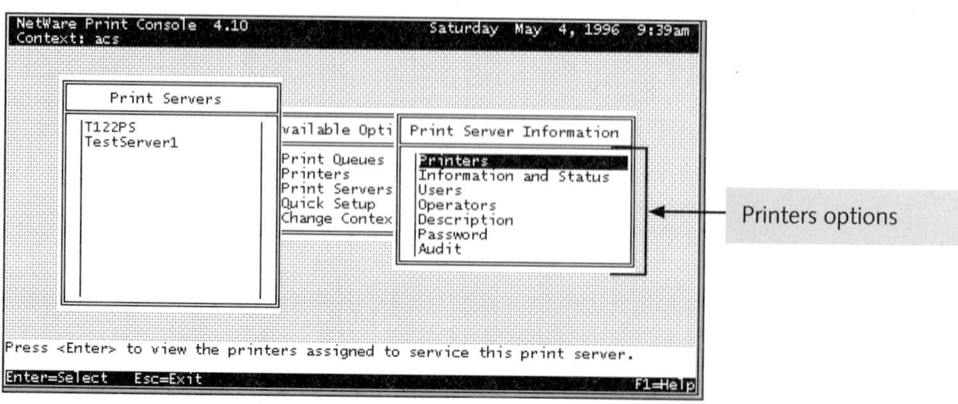

At this point you would mount new forms in the printer. Then select the Printers option and the printer in which the new forms have been mounted from the Serviced Printers window. PCONSOLE displays the configuration window for the selected printer, as shown in Figure 13-7. The window in Figure 13-7 shows that the currently mounted form, called the Starting form, is form 0 (zero), which is the default form number. To change to a different form number, highlight the "Mounted form" field and change the form number to the number appropriate for the job you want to print. Later in this chapter you will learn how to use the PRINTDEF utility and the CAPTURE command to assign a form number and name to a print job.

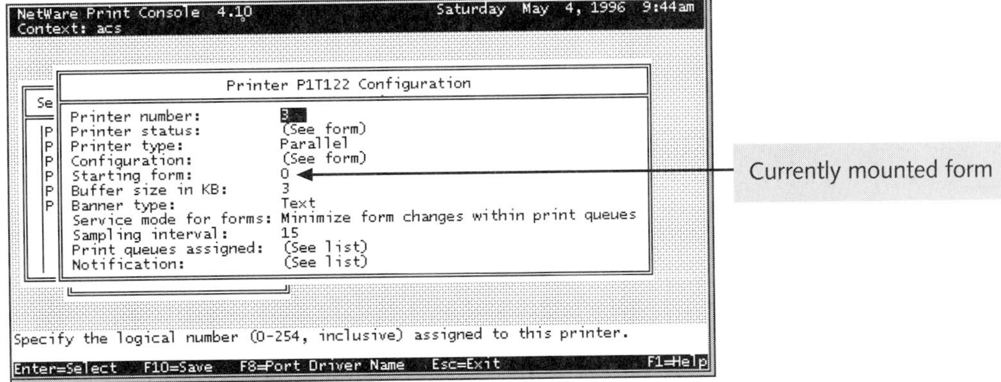

Figure 13-7 Printer Configuration window

Once the form number is changed, the printer will immediately start printing the job. As a result, prior to changing the form number you need to be sure the new forms have been properly mounted so that the information is printed in the correct location on the form. One way to do this is to print a test line on the form. From the server console, view the Printer Server and select Printer Status from the Available Options. Pick the printer you want to view from the Printer List, highlight the Printer Control option in the printer status window, and press [Enter] to display the printer control options shown in Figure 13-8. You can then use the "Mark top of form" option to print a line across the top of the print forms. When you are confident that the forms are loaded correctly, you can use the [Esc] key to return to the "Status" window and then change the form number to begin printing on the new forms. After all print jobs requiring the new form have been printed, the print server will display a message. The printer operator can now mount the next form required by the printer and repeat this process to start the printer again.

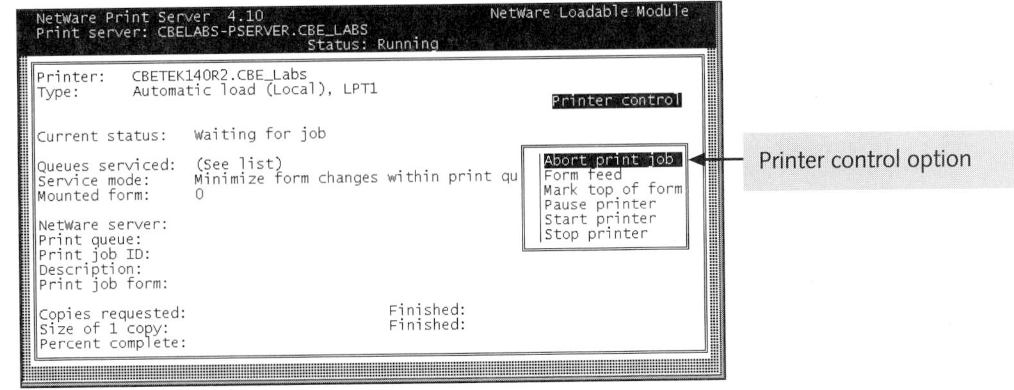

Figure 13-8 Printer control options

Using PCONSOLE to Attach a Temporary Print Queue

If a printer needs to be taken off line for repairs or servicing, you can enable the printing to continue by sending print jobs to another similar printer attached to the network. This can be done by attaching the print queue temporarily to another printer. Suppose, for example, the CBE Labs' finance department's laser printer stopped printing. You have scheduled a service call for tomorrow morning. Yet to enable the department users to continue printing for the remainder of the day, you can use the PCONSOLE utility to attach the finance laser print queue to the marketing department's laser printer temporarily. Because both of these printers use the same printer language, you will be able to send the finance department's output to the marketing department's laser printer without modifying the applications or user procedures.

To use PCONSOLE to attach a print queue to a printer without restarting the print server, follow these steps:

1. Start PCONSOLE.
2. Select the **Print Servers** option and select the currently running print server, **CBELABS-PSERVER**.
3. Select the **Printers** option.
4. Select **Printer** from the Print Server Information option and pick the appropriate printer, **MKTHP3R3**.
5. Choose **Print Queues Assigned** from the Printer Configuration menu. PCONSOLE displays a window showing all print queues currently attached to the selected printer.
6. To add another print queue to this printer temporarily, press **[Ins]** and select the print queue you want to attach—in this example it's the finance department's print queue, FINHP3ROQ1. The selected print queue will now be added to the list of queues serviced by the marketing laser printer. Press **[Esc]** to save this change and return to the main PCONSOLE menu.

Note that this change is not permanent; the print queue will not be included in this printer's service list when the print server is restarted.

Using PCONSOLE to Change a Printer's Notification List

Jon Jorgenson serves as the print server operator of the marketing staff at CBE Labs. However, Jon is scheduled to go on vacation for two weeks, and Shelly Wells will serve temporarily as the print server operator during that time. Shelly will need to have printer notification messages sent to her by users during this period. In order to enable another user to receive messages from a printer, you temporarily add the user to the notification list for that printer. Using PCONSOLE, select the Printer from the Print Server Information option and pick the appropriate printer, MKTHP3R3. Press [Enter] on the Notification field. This displays a window showing all users who will currently be sent any printer messages affecting this printer. To add another user like Shelly, simply press [Ins] and then select the user's name. When you press [Enter], PCONSOLE displays the Notify Intervals window. The default interval is 1, which means that the first message is sent 1 minute after a problem occurs; repeat messages are sent every minute until the situation is corrected. You can change the default settings or press [Esc] to save the settings. The selected user will now be temporarily added to the notification list for this printer. Press [Esc] to return to the PCONSOLE menu or use the [Alt][F10] key combination to exit the PCONSOLE utility. Because this is a temporary change, the user will not be included in the list when the print server is restarted.

Using PSC to Manage Printers

The PSC (Printer Server Control) utility can be used to control the printer directly from a menu, a batch file, or even the DOS prompt. This enables the network administrator to simplify printer control by setting up the PSC command for each of the print server operators. As a Network Administrator you will be required to know the syntax of the PSC command and how to use it to view printer status, cancel, or stop and restart a network printer. The syntax of the PSC command is

```
PSC [PS=printservername] [P=printernumber] action
```

Replace the *printservername* parameter with the name of the print server that contains the printer to which you want to send the control command. Use the *printernumber* parameter to identify the number of the printer to which you want to send the control command. Printer numbers ranging from to 0 to 255 are defined in PCONSOLE when you set up the configuration. Replace *action* with one of the options shown in Figure 13-9.

Figure 13-9

PSC command option

Parameter	Description
STAT (status)	Displays one of the following status messages for the selected printer: Waiting for job Ready to go down In private mode Mounted form *n* Stopped Offline Printing job Not connected Out of paper Paused Not installed *Example: PSC PS=CBELABS-PSERVER P=1 STAT*
PAU (pause)	Temporarily stops printer output until the start command is received. *Example: PSC PS=CBELABS-PSERVER P=1 PAU*
AB (abort)	Stops printing the current job. The job is deleted from the queue and the printer continues with the next job in the queue. *Example: PSC PS=CBELABS-PSERVER P=1 AB*
STO [K] (stop [keep])	Stops the printer and deletes the current print job unless the keep option is specified. *Example: PSC PS=CBELABS-PSERVER P=1 STO K*
STAR (start)	Restarts the printer after you have stopped or paused it. *Example: PSC PS=CBELABS-PSERVER P=1 STAR*
M [character] (mark)	Prints a line of whatever character you select. Used for determining where the printer will start printing the page. *Example: PSC PS=CBELABS-PSERVER P=1 M**
FF (form feed)	Advances the paper to the top of the next page. *Example: PSC PS=CBELABS-PSERVER P=1 FF*
MO F=n	Informs the print server that you have mounted a new form of the indicated number on the selected printer. *Example: PSC PS=CBELABS-PSERVER P=1 MO F=2*

Figure 13-9

PSC command option (continued)

PRI (private)	Used from a workstation that is running NPRINTER to reserve the printer for local use only. It should be issued if an application will be printing directly to the local printer in order to prevent output from the local application from being mixed with output from the print server. *Example: PSC PS=CBELABS-PSERVER P=1 PRI*
SHA (shared)	Changes a workstation that has been placed in private mode back to allowing the print server to send output to the printer attached to its local port. *Example: PSC PS=CBELABS-PSERVER P=1 SHA*
CD (cancel down)	Cancels the PCONSOLE command to down the print server after all jobs have been printed. *Example: PSC PS=CBELABS-PSERVER P=1 CD*
L (list)	Shows the relationships between printing objects managed by this print server. *Example: PSC PS=CBELABS-PSERVER P=1 L*

Adding the status option to the PSC command displays one of the messages indicated for the printer you have selected. This is useful if a user needs to check on the status of a printer prior to sending a print job. The pause option temporarily stops the printer. Use it if you want to verify that a job is printing correctly. The start option restarts the printer from the point at which it was stopped when the pause command was issued. The abort option is useful if a job is printing on the wrong printer, on the wrong paper type, or if for some other reason it needs to be stopped and deleted. Note that the abort option deletes the job from the print queue. If you want to stop printing a job but still keep it in the current print queue, use the stop keep option. The form feed option automatically advances the printer to the next page. This is for jobs that leave the last page in the printer. Using the form feed option means you don't need to use the buttons on the printer's control panel to advance the paper. The mount form option specifies printer forms. Assume, for example, a print server operator has been notified that a new form is required in printer number 0 for print server CBELABS-PSERVER. The operator would first mount the new paper type in the printer. Next the operator would issue the following PSC command from his or her workstation:

```
PSC PS=CBELABS-PSERVER P=0 MO F=1
```

The private option is especially useful for workstations that have remote printers attached to them. The private option takes the remote printer off line and enables the workstation to send a job directly to its locally attached printer rather than routing it through the print queue.

CUSTOMIZING NETWORK PRINTING

After the network printing system is operational, the next task is to customize the printing environment. This will make it easier to use, and it will meet any special printing needs of user applications. Factors that make network printing easier to use include defining a form number for each paper type and automating printing configurations for each user. In this section you will learn about form definitions and how to use the PRINTDEF utility and NetWare Administrator to assign names to form numbers. You will also learn about defining printer setup sequences that can be used to change printer modes and functions. These changes are needed by some applications whose output requires the printer to be configured in a special manner. You use the PRINTDEF utility to manage this task as well as for form definitions. With PRINTDEF you can maintain a database of printer modes and functions that can be used to configure a network printer for these print jobs.

MANAGING FORMS

Unless you have a printer designated for and preloaded with each type of paper you use in your organization, it will periodically be necessary to change the paper type in the printers attached to the network. Changing the paper type can cause problems, however, when another user decides to send regular output to the printer containing the special forms. Assume, for example, that Thomas Meyer in Finance has just placed payroll checks in the dot matrix printer and is getting ready to run a check-printing program just as another user sends a report from a workstation to the same dot matrix printer. Printing the report on the payroll check forms is definitely not what either user wants.

To prevent this kind of mistake, Novell included with NetWare a system for defining and controlling print forms. The default form number, used for standard paper, is predefined as form 0. It is up to the network administrator, however, to establish a set of form numbers that represents the other paper types and printing formats that are going to be used on network printers. Because form number 0 is the default form number used by the CAPTURE and NPRINT commands, the standard paper you use for printing should be defined as form 0. Figure 13-10 contains an example of form numbers defined for some typical paper types.

Figure 13-10 Sample printer forms

Form Number	Description
0	standard 8½"×11" paper
1	company letterhead
2	legal 8½"×14" paper
3	payroll checks
4	invoice forms
5	labels

Mounting Forms

The process of informing NetWare which form is in the printer is known as "mounting" forms. There are several ways to mount a form. First, forms can be mounted through NetWare Administrator. Select the desired printer icon from the NDS tree and then select Details from the Object menu. Click the Configuration button and you will see the NetWare Administrator Printer Configuration window, as shown in Figure 13-11. The Starting Form option enables you to select the form number that you wish to use.

Figure 13-11 NetWare Administrator Printer Configuration window

Starting Form option

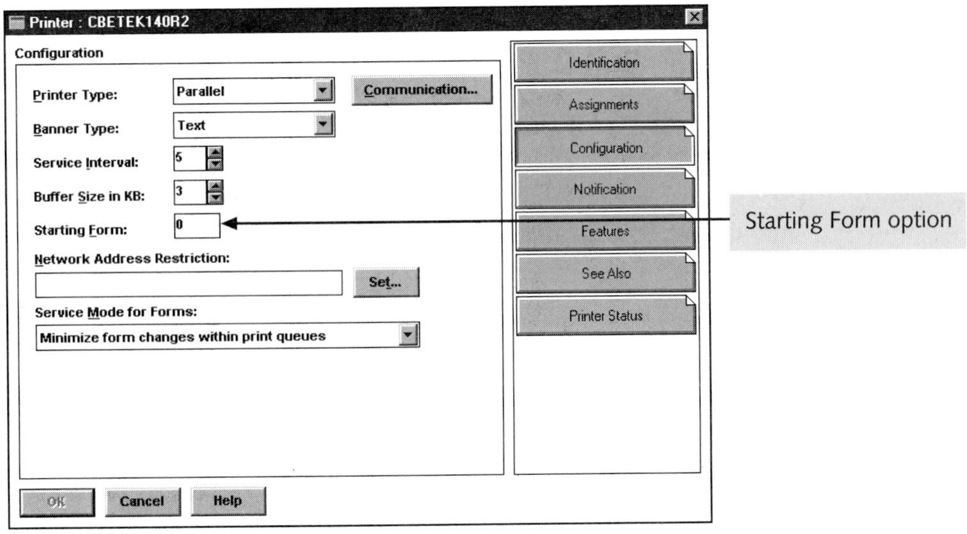

Forms can also be mounted from Windows 95 directly. Click the Windows 95 Start button, then click Settings, and then click Printers. Select the printer icon that represents the printer to which the output is being sent. Double-click this icon and you will see the Windows 95 Printer Control window. Select Properties from the Printer menu and then choose Printer Settings, as shown in Figure 13-12.

Figure 13-12

Windows 95 Printer Properties Printer Settings

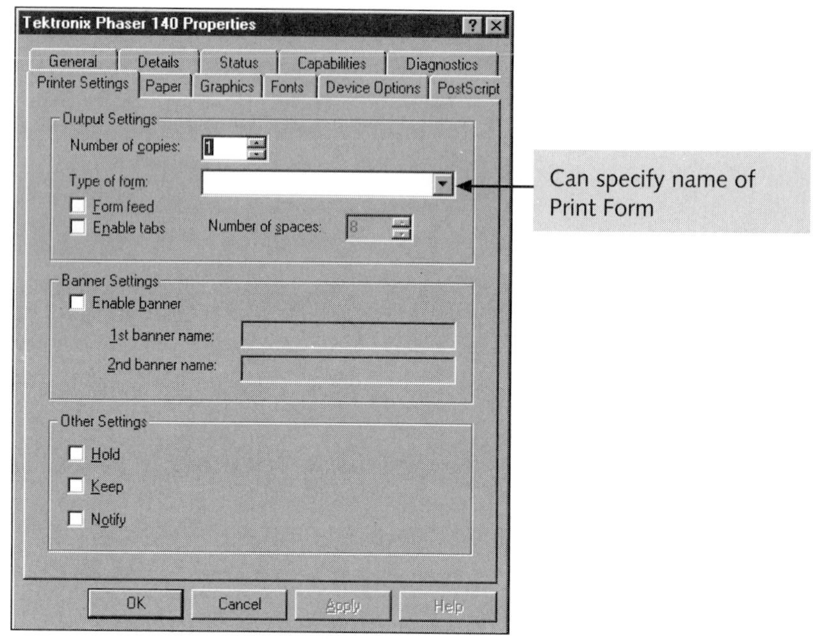

The Type of Form enables you to specify the name of the print form.

Finally, if you are creating a menu (which will be discussed in Chapter 15), you could place the following CAPTURE command in a batch file that starts the payroll check-printing program:

```
CAPTURE Q=FINEPS570R1Q1 TI=10 NB NT NFF F=3
```

This CAPTURE command includes the F=3 parameter to indicate that the output requires form type 3 to be mounted in the printer. The print server keeps track of what form number was used on the most recent print job. When it encounters the command containing the form 3 parameter, it will stop and display a message asking for form 3 to be mounted (unless form 3 was the paper type for the previous job as well). Once the form 3 job is completed, the printer will stop again and request the next form needed.

Changing the Print Queue Service Mode

The process of starting and stopping the print server can be a problem if users' print jobs often require different forms. Suppose, for example, you have a laser printer that is used for both legal and standard paper. Thomas Meyers and Sarah Johnston, both in the Finance Department, send jobs to this print queue. However, Thomas's jobs require legal forms and Sarah's jobs require standard forms. The print server operator will spend a lot of time changing paper in the printer. This situation also slows down printer output because of the frequent stops. You can reduce this problem by having the print server print all jobs in the queue that use the same form—regardless of sequence—before asking for the next form to be mounted. This can greatly reduce the number of times the print server operator will need to change paper in a printer.

To change a printer so that it prints all jobs with the same form number before asking for another form to be mounted, follow these steps:

1. Start PCONSOLE.
2. Select the **Print Servers** option from the Available Options menu.
3. Select the print server definition you want to change, **CBELABS_PSERVER**, and then select **Printers** from the Print Server Information menu, which lists all printers controlled by the print server.
4. Highlight the printer with which you want to work, **FINHP3R0Q1**, and press **[Enter]** to display the window that shows that printer's configuration.
5. To change the way forms are serviced, select the **queue service mode** field to display the Print Queue Service Modes window, as shown in Figure 13-13. To reduce the number of form changes that need to be made for this printer, select "**Minimize form changes within Print queues**" and press **[Enter]**. When there are multiple jobs in the print queue with different form types, the print server will scan the print queue for all jobs that have the current form type and print them before requesting the next form type.

Figure 13-13

Print Queue Service Modes window

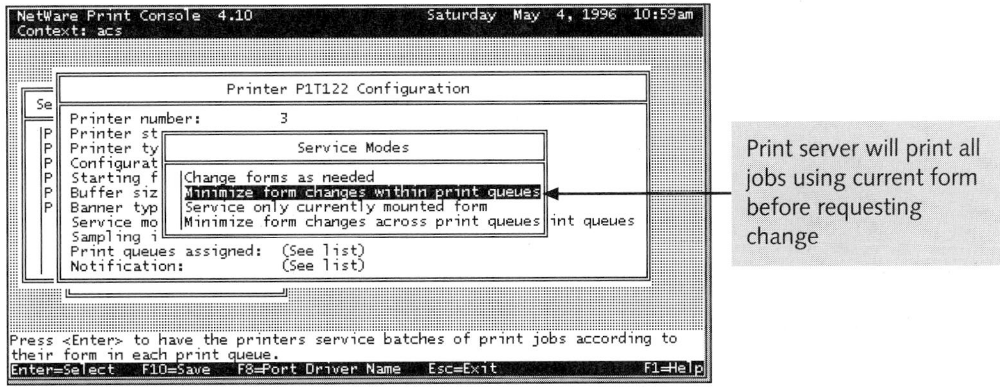

6. Save your changes and return to the Configured Printers window, press **[Esc]**, and then press **[Enter]**. You can now configure another printer or press [Esc] to return to the Print Server Configuration menu and exit the PCONSOLE utility.

Before the changes you make to the print server configuration become effective, you will need to down the print server and restart it. The best way to down the print server is to use the PCONSOLE utility as described previously in this chapter. Remember that unloading the PSERVER.NLM from the file server can cause print jobs that are in progress to be lost.

CUSTOMIZING PRINTER OUTPUT WITH PRINTDEF

With the PRINTDEF utility, network administrators can customize their printing environments by assigning names to form types and establishing special printer control modes and functions. As a network administrator, you will need to know how to use the PRINTDEF utility to assign form names and establish printer control sequences as described in this section.

Assigning Names to Forms

Assigning names to different form types can make it easier for users and print server operators to work with forms and perform operational tasks such as mounting the correct forms in the printer. For example, if the name PAYCHECK is assigned to form type 3, it will be easier for the print server operator to respond to the message "Mount Forms PAYCHECK" rather than the less transparent "Mount Forms 3." You can use the PRINTDEF utility to assign names to your form types by logging in with the necessary privileges and running the PRINTDEF utility, which displays the PRINTDEF Options menu shown in Figure 13-14.

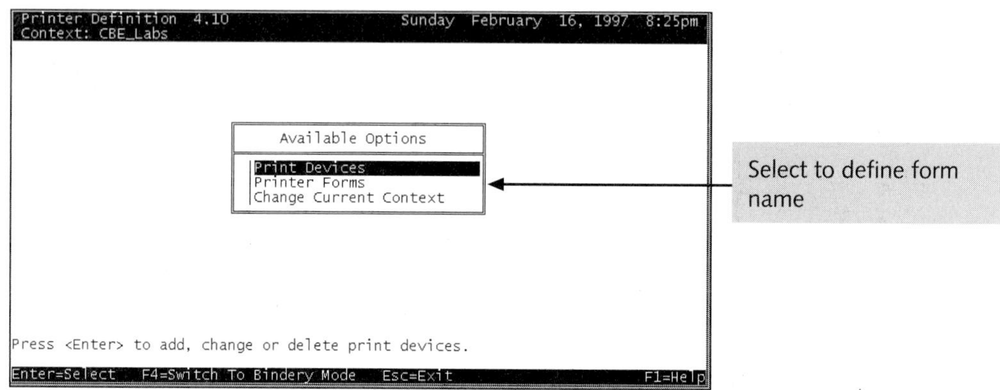

Figure 13-14 PRINTDEF Options menu

To define form names, select the Printer Forms option. This displays a window showing all existing form definitions in the NET$PRN.DAT database. To add a new form type, press [Ins] to display the Form Definition window shown in Figure 13-15.

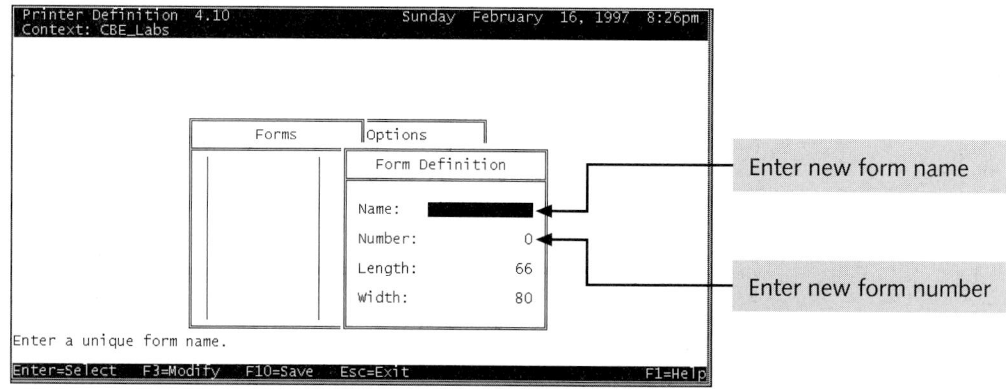

Figure 13-15 Printer Form Definition window

Remember, form 0 is the default form type. As a result, you should define form type 0 for standard paper before defining additional form types. To define a form type, first enter the name to be used for the form in the "Name" field, followed by the form number in the "Number" field. Although values must be placed in the "Length" and the "Width" fields, they are for documentation purposes only and are not used by the print server.

Working with Printer Functions and Modes

There are still many applications in use that are not network aware. Such applications are not able to take advantage of special printer functions such as changing character sizes, paper trays, or paper orientation. Some non-network-aware software packages do enable users to select special printing modes, such as condensed print and landscape printing, but they can also leave the printer in that mode and cause the next user's output to be printed incorrectly.

There are two paper orientations. Landscape printing is a function of laser printers in which they print a maximum line width of 11". Portrait printing is more commonly used and has a maximum line width of 8.5".

PRINTDEF enables the network administrator to manage form types and establish special printer functions and modes. A **printer function** is a specific printer escape code sequence that causes the printer to perform one operation, such as changing to landscape mode, selecting a paper tray, changing the character size, or setting page length. A **printer mode** consists of one or more functions that set up the printer for the desired configuration. The legal-landscape mode, for example, might contain functions to change to legal size paper, use landscape format, and then select the lower paper tray in which the legal paper is stored.

Novell has provided printer definition files (in the SYS:PUBLIC directory) that contain functions and modes for many popular printers. You can use PRINTDEF to merge one or more of the printer definition files into your printer database and then modify them, or you can create new printer definitions by entering your own escape code sequences. Entering your own escape code sequences, however, is slow and prone to error. You will therefore want to use the escape code sequences and modes included in the printer definition files as much as possible.

Merging a Printer Definition File into Your Printer Database

Before you can use the predefined printer functions and modes, you need to merge the printer definition file (PDF) into your printer database. To merge a printer definition file into your network printer database, select the Print Devices option from the PRINTDEF Options menu. This displays the Print Device Options menu shown in Figure 13-16.

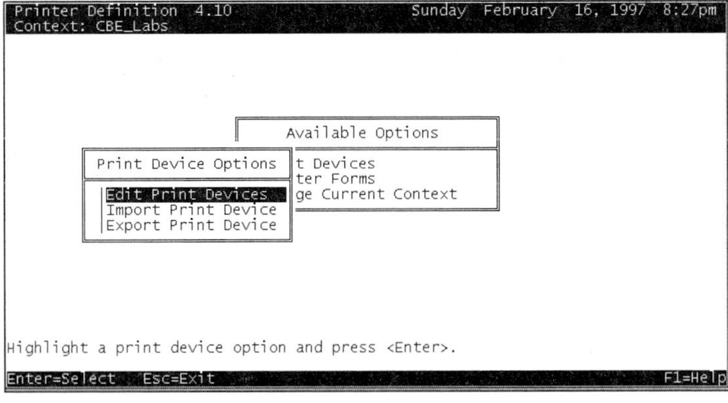

Figure 13-16
Print Device Options menu

To display a list of all available devices, select the Edit Print Devices option. If you have already defined modes and functions for a printer device in your database and want to create a new printer definition file that can be imported to other servers, use the Export Print Device option to select the printer definition and then enter a name for the Printer Definition File (PDF) you want to create. To add another printer definition file to your database, select Import Print Device and press [Enter]. This displays the Source Directory window, which shows your current directory as the default location for the printer definition files. Because the Novell-supplied PDF files are located in the SYS:PUBLIC directory, you will need to enter SYS:PUBLIC to access the standard printer definition files. If you want to load a PDF from another source—a floppy disk drive, for example—you can enter the path to that location.

After you press [Enter] to accept the source directory path, PRINTDEF displays the Available .PDFs window shown in Figure 13-17. This window lists all printer definition files in the specified directory. To work with a laser printer that uses the standard HP LaserJet III Printer Control language, for example, highlight HP3SIPCL.PDF and press [Enter]. The print device HP LaserJet IIISi-PCL will then be added to the Defined Print Devices window. You can now press [Esc] until you return to the PRINTDEF Options menu.

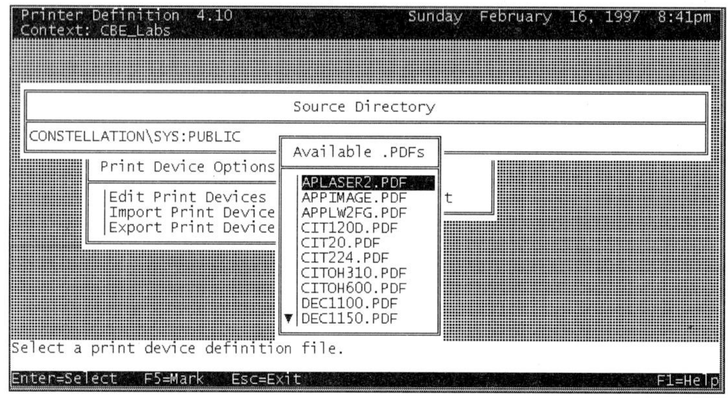

Available .PDFs window

Notice that the printer definition files have abbreviated names to represent the printer make and model. As a result, it is sometimes difficult to determine which printer definition file is the correct one for your printer model. To obtain the correct printer definition file for your printer, select a filename that appears similar to your printer model. After a printer definition file is placed in your printer database, the description of the printer will appear in the Defined Print Devices window. If you have selected the wrong definition file, you can then use the [Del] key to remove the printer definition from your database and try selecting another.

If you try to define a print device that already exists in the database, an error message informs you that you cannot have two devices with the same name. After you press [Esc], PRINTDEF enables you to change the printer name and create a new device in the database.

Editing Print Devices

You can use the PRINTDEF utility to create, modify, or view printer modes and functions by selecting the Edit Print Devices option on the Print Device Options menu. To create a new print device, press [Ins] and enter the new device name. To change the name of an existing print device, highlight the name of the device you want to change and press [F3]. You can then use [Backspace] to erase the existing name and enter the revised name. To delete an existing print device, highlight the name of the device you want to delete, press [Del], and then press [Enter] to confirm the deletion of the device.

To view or work with the functions and modes of an existing printer, first select the Print Devices option from the PrintDef Options menu to display the Print Device Options menu. Next, select the Edit Print Devices option. This displays the Defined Print Devices window, which lists all printers that exist in the NET$PRN.DAT database. To change the modes and functions of an existing printer, highlight the name of the printer and press [Enter]. This displays the Device Options menu, which contains options for device modes and device functions. (Remember, modes consist of one or more functions and are used to establish a printer setup.) To view or modify the existing modes for the selected printer, highlight Device Modes and press [Enter]. This displays a list of modes. Figure 13-18 shows the list of modes for an HP LaserJet printer.

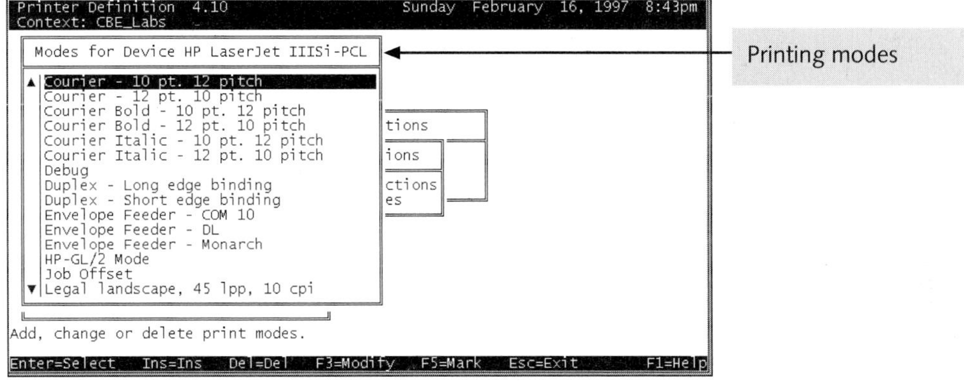

Figure 13-18 HP LaserJet IIISi printing modes

Use the up and down arrow keys to view all modes defined for the selected printer. Notice that the first mode is <Re-initialize>. This is a required mode for all print devices and consists of the functions necessary to reset the printer to the power-on defaults. The mode is used by the print server at the end of each print job to put the printer back in standard mode for the next print job. To view the functions that make up the re-initialize mode of the LaserJet printer, highlight it and press [Enter]. The <Re-initialize> Functions window, showing the Printer Reset function, is displayed, as shown in Figure 13-19.

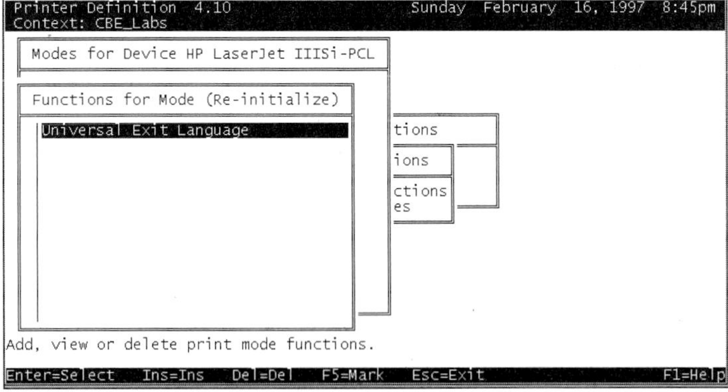

Figure 13-19 HP LaserJet IIISi re-initialize functions

To view the escape code sequence that makes up a reset function, highlight Printer Reset and press [Enter]. The Control Sequence of Function Printer Reset window showing the escape code sequence is displayed, as shown in Figure 13-20.

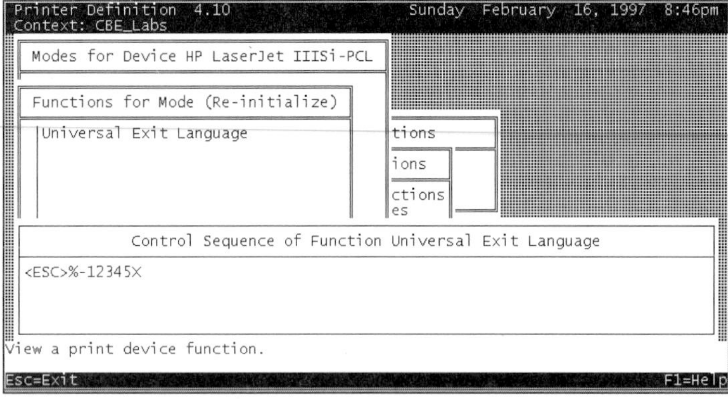

Figure 13-20
HP LaserJet IIISi printer reset functions

You can view functions only when you use the Modes option of the Device Options menu. To add or change printer functions, you need to use the Functions option.

Many modes consist of multiple functions. The "Letter landscape, 60 lpp, 10cpi" mode shown in Figure 13-21, for example, consists of five functions. The first function is the printer reset function, which ensures that the printer is returned to its basic settings, even if some other misbehaved application did not reset the printer upon exiting. The other functions include escape sequences to select paper type, paper orientation, and character style and size. You can highlight any function and press [Enter] to view its escape code sequence, as described previously for the Printer Reset function.

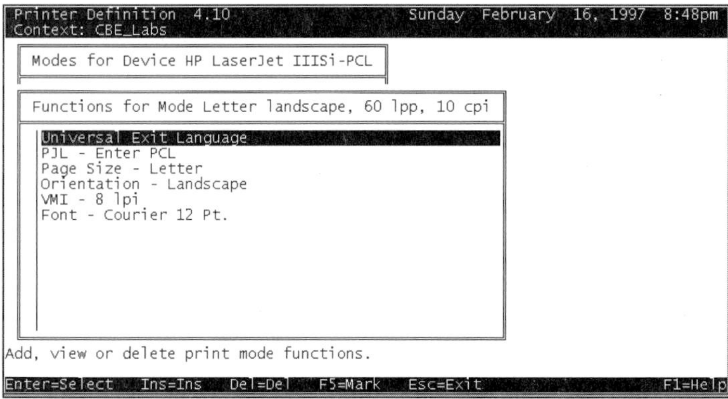

Figure 13-21
Viewing a print mode's function

Adding a New Function to a Mode

Sometimes you will need to add a function to an existing mode in order to meet your printing needs. Suppose, for example, you need to use the lower paper tray of an HP LaserJet III laser printer to store standard paper and the top tray to store CBE Labs company letterhead. To be sure that landscape output is printed on standard paper, not on letterhead, you could add the "Paper source - Lower tray" function to the landscape printer mode.

1. Use the Edit Print Devices option to select the laser printer **FINHP3R0Q1**.
2. Select the **Device Modes** option to display all the existing printer setup modes.
3. To add another function to the landscape mode, use the arrow keys to scroll the modes window until you find the desired "Letter landscape" mode and then press **[Enter]** to display the "Letter landscape" functions window.
4. Press **[Ins]** to display the Available Functions for Device HP LaserJet IIISi window and then use the arrow keys to highlight the "Paper Source - Lower Paper Tray" function, as shown in Figure 13-22. Press **[Enter]**. The Lower Paper Tray function will now be added to the end of the functions list.
5. Press **[Esc]** to return to the HP LaserJet IIISi Modes window.

Figure 13-22

Adding a new function to a mode

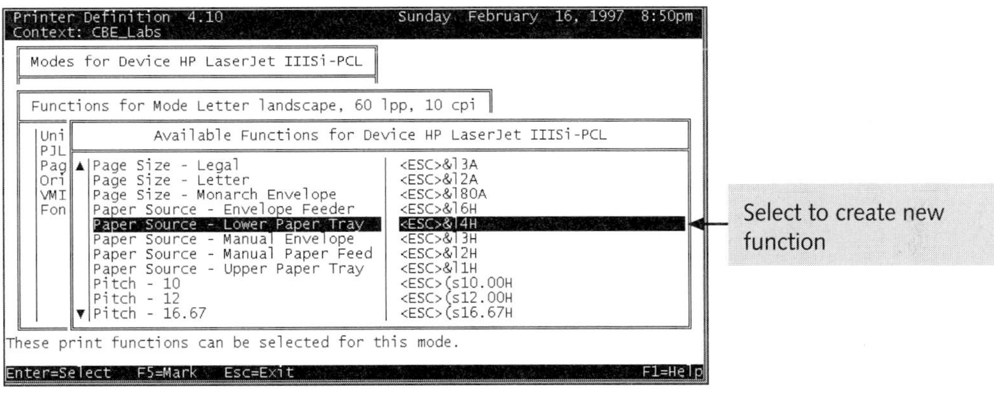

Adding a New Mode

If CBE Labs has a special printing need that has not been defined as one of the standard printing modes, you will need to create a new mode to meet that need. Suppose, for example, you need a printer mode that will enable you to print on smaller, executive-size paper located in the upper tray of an HP LaserJet IIISi printer. Because this is not one of the standard modes included in the PDF file, you can add your own mode for executive-size paper.

1. Use the Edit Print Device option to select the appropriate printer, **FINHP3R0Q1**.
2. Select the **Device Modes** option.
3. Press **[Ins]** from the HP LaserJet IIISi Modes window to display a blank New Mode Name window.
4. Enter a name that describes the new print mode, such as "Executive Paper," and press **[Enter]**. The mode Executive Paper now appears in the list.
5. Highlight this new mode and press **[Enter]**, and a blank Executive Paper Functions window is displayed.
6. Press **[Ins]** and select **Printer Reset** as the first function. It is important to include Printer Reset as the first function; it ensures that the printer will be set to its defaults before it receives other setup commands.
7. Continue to use **[Ins]** to select the other functions you want to include in this printer mode. In the Executive Paper mode, for example, you would need to include the Page Size - Executive and Paper Source - Upper Tray functions, as shown in Figure 13-23.

8. After all functions have been selected, press **[Esc]** to add the new mode to your printer modes window.
9. Press **[Esc]** to exit the modes window and return to the Device Option menu.

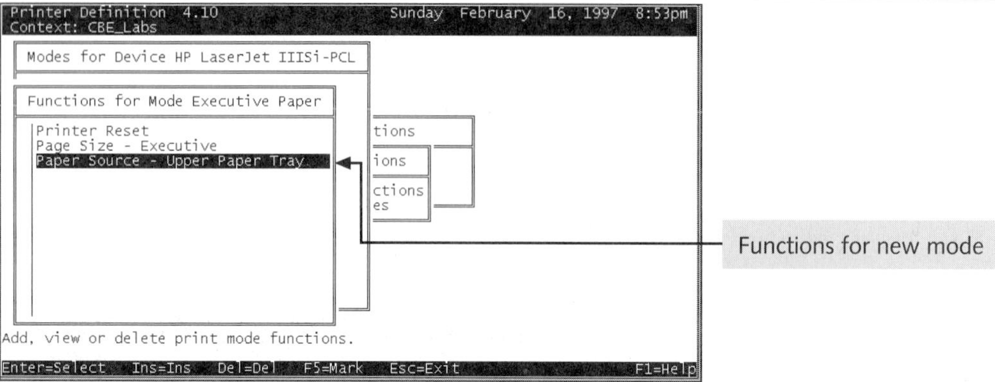

Figure 13-23 Creating a new mode

Adding a New Function

One of the more complex tasks that uses the PRINTDEF utility is adding new printer functions. A function consists of an escape code sequence that causes the printer to perform some specific operation, such as setting the character size or paper orientation. You can find the escape code sequence for each function the printer can perform in the printer's operation manual. Assume, for example, you need to set the page orientation for an HP LaserJet IIISi laser printer when it prints. First, refer to the printer's manual and find the escape code sequence that will set the printer to do the desired page orientation. For an HP LaserJet III/Si printer, the code sequence is [ESC]&L10. [ESC] represents the escape key, which has a decimal value of 27.

To add this code sequence to your printer database, select the Edit Print Devices option and then select the HP LaserJet IIISi-PCL defined print device. Select the Device Functions option to display the HP LaserJet IIISi-PCL Functions window, which shows all the predefined functions for the HP LaserJet IIISi printer. To add a new function, press [Ins] to display the Function Definition window. Enter a name for the new function, as shown in Figure 13-24. You can enter a descriptive name of up to 32 characters for the new function. The name "Landscape Orientation" would be appropriate for this example. After entering the function name, press [Enter] to advance the cursor to the Control Sequence field. Each character of the Control Sequence field must be entered using one of the following three formats. NetWare will then automatically convert the character into its corresponding binary value. You may enter the values in one of three ways:

- The exact ASCII character
- The binary value of the byte expressed as a decimal number enclosed in angle brackets (< >)
- The name of an ASCII control character enclosed in angle brackets (< >). A window of ASCII control characters, as shown in Figure 13-25, may be displayed by first highlighting a function, pressing [F1], and then using the Page Down key.

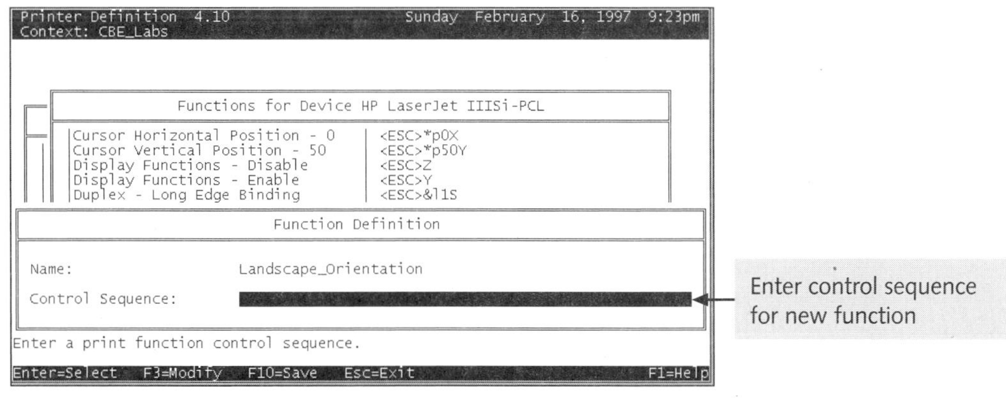

Figure 13-24 Creating a new function

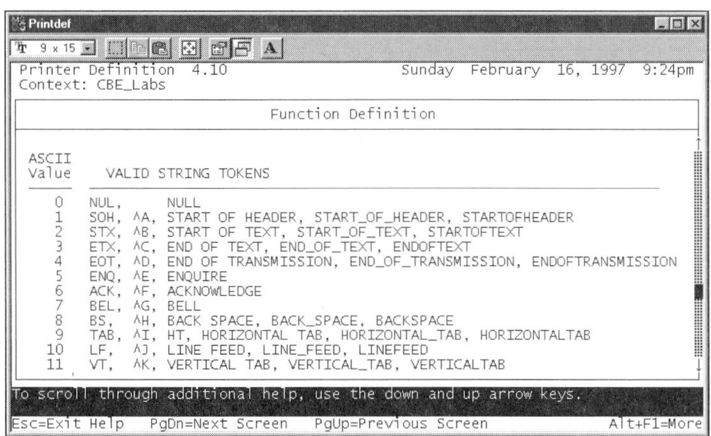

Figure 13-25 Help screen showing ASCII control characters

For the example under discussion, the escape sequence can be entered as <ESC>&L10, as shown in Figure 13-26. Once the Function Definition window is completed, use [Esc] and [Enter] to save the new function and return to the functions window. When you have no more new functions to add, use [Esc] until you return to the PrintDef Options main menu.

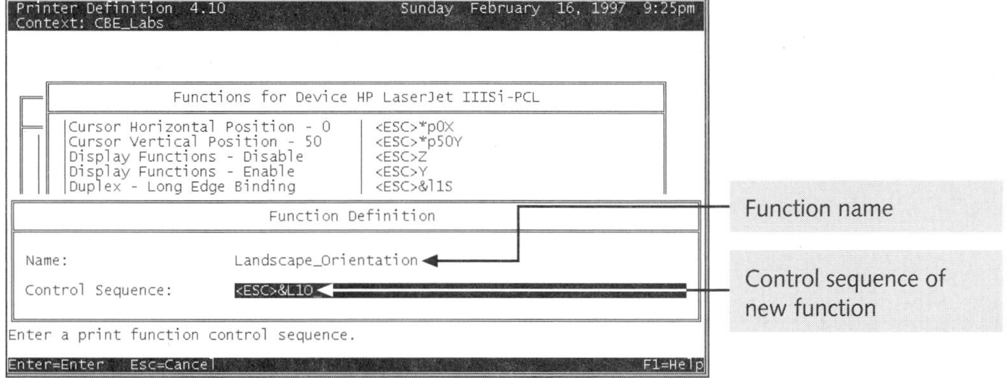

Figure 13-26 Entering a control code sequence

Creating a New Print Device

If you have a new printer that does not yet have a printer definition file, you might need to create a special printer device in your NET$PRN.DAT database. Suppose, for example, CBE Labs has purchased a new color bubble-jet printer and you cannot locate a .PDF file for this printer model. To create this printer definition in the database, you first need to locate the required escape code sequences in the printer documentation and then define what functions and modes your users will need. Regardless of what modes and functions you use, make sure to identify and enter the functions that will reset the printer back to its startup mode. The print server needs these functions when it uses the re-initialize mode to reset the printer upon completing a print job.

After identifying the printer modes you will need and the corresponding functions, use the PRINTDEF utility to create the print device and define the modes and functions. First select Print Devices from the PrintDef Options menu. Use the Edit Print Devices option to display the print devices currently available. To create the new print device, press [Ins] and enter a descriptive name for the new printer. Pressing [Enter] adds the new print device to the Print Devices window.

To add device functions and modes for the new printer, select the new device and press [Enter] to display the Device Options menu. The first step in setting up the new print device is entering the functions. Select the Device Functions option and use [Ins] to enter the functions, as described previously. Next, define the new printer modes. Select the Device Modes option and use [Ins] to enter the modes, as described previously. After you have entered the printer modes, press [Esc] until you return to the PRINTDEF Options menu. The new printer definition is ready for testing as soon as you exit the PRINTDEF utility and save the changes you have made to your printer database.

Working with Print Job Configurations

The network administrator can establish individual printer configurations for each user. The configuration can include special printer modes and functions as well as standard command parameters, such as timeout and banner information. Each set of print job configurations is stored as an object in the NDS tree. The first print configuration created in a user's PRINTCON database becomes the default print configuration for print jobs created by that user. If a CAPTURE or NPRINT command is issued by that user with no parameters, the print queue, timeout, banner, notify option, and other parameters will be obtained from the default print job configuration. This means that the first configuration you create in a user's PRINTCON database should be the one the user will access most frequently. PRINTCON enables you to change the default print configuration or assign a different print configuration to be the default. Although PRINTCON enables you to create, change, and delete print configurations, it does not enable you to delete a user's print configuration database.

Using PRINTCON to Manage Print Configurations

To use PRINTCON to work with print configurations, first log in as the user whose print configurations you want to access. Then start the PRINTCON utility from any network directory to display the Available Options menu shown in Figure 13-27. To access the current user's print configurations, select the Edit Print Job Configurations option. This displays the Print Job Configurations window, showing any existing print configurations.

Figure 13-27

PRINTCON's Available Options menu

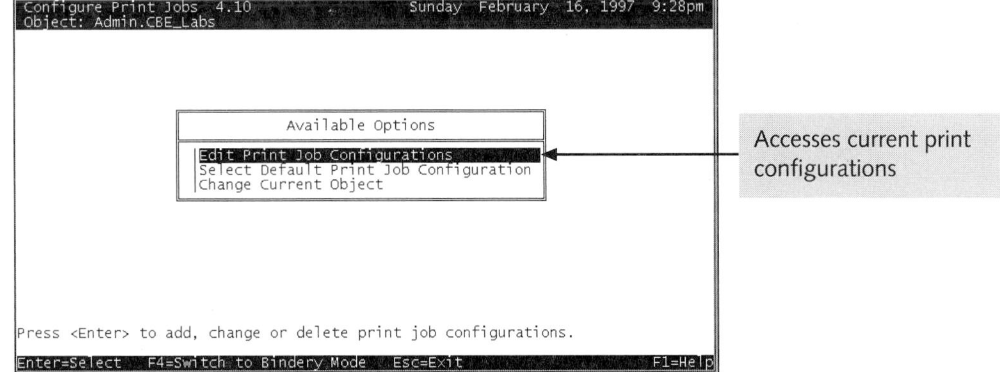

To create a new print job configuration, press [Ins] and enter a name for it. The name should identify the print job configuration clearly, but should also be as brief as possible to make it easier to remember. After the name has been entered for the new print job configuration, PRINTCON displays it in the Print Job Configuration window. Press [Enter] to see the Edit Print Job Configuration window, as shown in Figure 13-28. Notice that most of the fields correspond to CAPTURE command parameters. The "File contents" field corresponds to the T (tab) and NT (no tab) options on the CAPTURE or NPRINT command and consists of either byte stream or text options. (Byte stream corresponds to the no tab parameter, and text corresponds to the tab parameter.) You should use the byte stream rather than the text option when sending output to sophisticated printers, such as lasers, because the text option will attempt to expand tab codes into several spaces. This can cause incorrect output results on laser printers because the tab codes might actually be part of a special printer setup mode.

Figure 13-28

Edit Print Job Configuration window

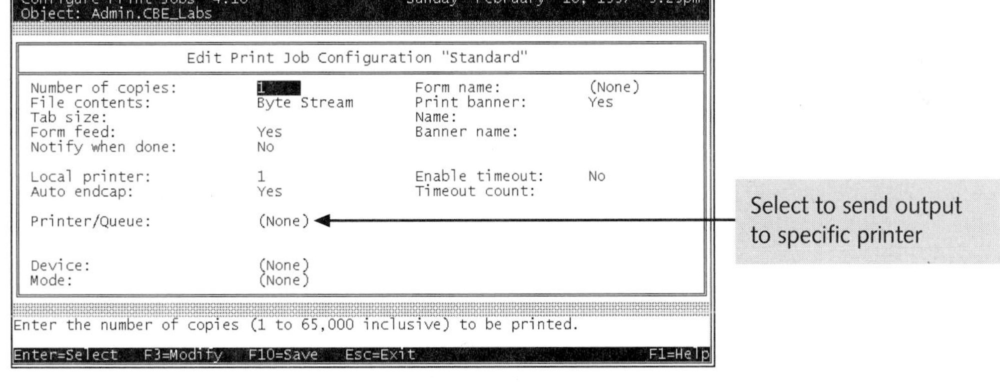

To send output to a specific printer, select the Printer/Queue field and then press [Enter] to display a list of print queues on the default file server. You can then highlight the print queue for the desired printer and press [Enter]. To use one of the print modes defined for a printer, highlight the Device field. Pressing [Enter] displays a window showing all print devices available. Highlight the correct printer for the specified print queue and press [Enter] to select that printer. After the correct print device has been selected, highlight the Mode field and press [Enter]. This displays a window showing all modes defined for the printer selected in the Device field. You can now select the desired printer setup mode and press [Enter] to attach that mode to this print job. To prevent printing a banner before each print job, select the "Print banner" field and change the Yes to No. To enable a timeout for the CAPTURE command, select the "Enable timeout" field and change the No to Yes. The default timeout,

5 seconds, appears in the "Timeout count" field. You can change the default from 5 seconds up to a maximum of 1000 seconds by highlighting the field and pressing [Enter]. Use [Backspace] to erase the existing time and enter a new number of seconds.

Placing too small a value in the "Timeout count" field can cause printer output to be separated and printed as two different print jobs.

Once the fields on the Edit Print Job Configuration window are changed to your satisfaction, press [Esc] to save the print job and return to the Print Job Configurations window. Notice that the first print job configuration is automatically defined as the default for this user account.

To change an existing print job configuration, highlight the print job configuration you want to change and press [Enter]. The Edit Print Job Configuration window containing the options shown in Figure 13-28 is displayed. Make any necessary changes and press [Esc] to save the modified print configuration. To delete a print configuration, simply highlight the configuration you want to delete and press [Del]. After the deletion is confirmed, the print configuration is removed from the print configuration database for that user. You cannot delete the default print configuration, however. If you want to remove all print configurations for a user, you need to delete the item from the NDS tree.

Using NetWare Administrator to Manage Print Configurations

NetWare Administrator can likewise be used to manage print configurations. Each user can have his or her own configurations that govern how a print job comes out. To manage print configurations using NetWare Administrator, follow these steps:

1. Launch NetWare Administrator.
2. Select the **user** icon.
3. Select **Details** from the Object menu.
4. Select the **Print Job Configuration** button to display the Print Job Configuration Window, as shown in Figure 13-29. A list of the print job configurations will be displayed.

Figure 13-29

Print Job Configuration window

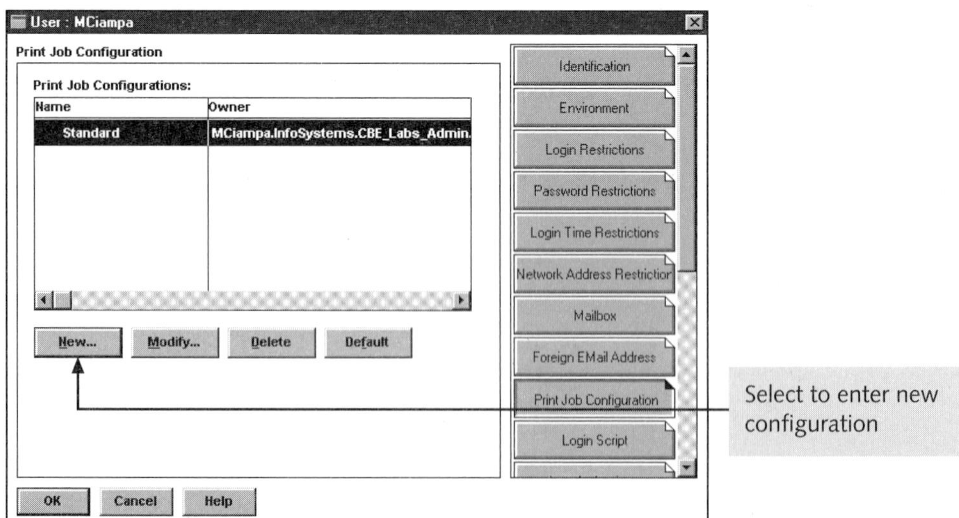

5. To enter a new configuration, select the **New** button to display the New Print Job Configuration window, as shown in Figure 13-30.

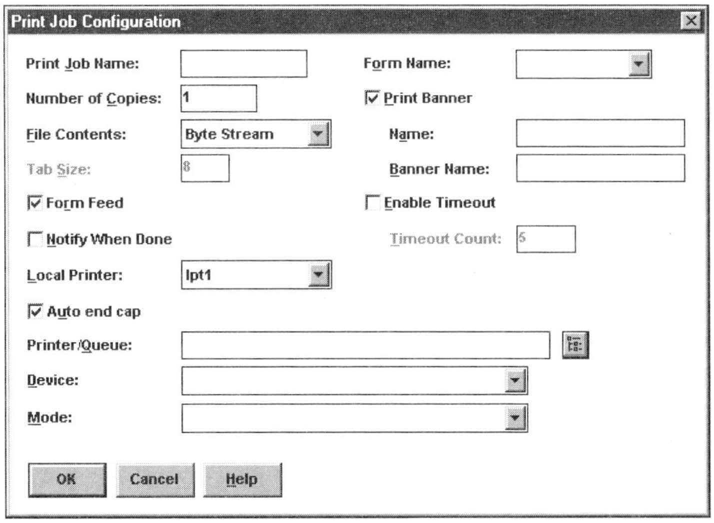

Figure 13-30 New Print Job Configuration window

6. Enter the appropriate configurations and select **OK** when finished.

CHAPTER SUMMARY

After installing the network printing environment, network administrators need to focus attention on the customization and day-to-day management of network printing. Managing network printing involves monitoring network printer status, controlling printers, and working with print queues. The PCONSOLE utility maintains print queues and print server configurations and can also be used by print server operators to provide such printer controls as mounting new forms, stopping and starting printers, and marking the top of the form. The print server operator can also use PCONSOLE to make temporary changes to a running print server, such as adding a print queue to a printer or including another user in a printer's notification list. As an alternative, the PSC command can be used to issue control commands to network printers directly from a menu or the DOS prompt, and Windows 95 users can perform management functions by using the Windows 95 desktop.

Customizing network printing involves establishing form numbers for different sizes of paper and defining special printer setup sequences, called modes. When a paper change is needed, the network printer pauses. A message is issued to the operator asking for the new form. After changing the paper, the printer operator can use the PCONSOLE or PSC command to restart the printer.

The PRINTDEF utility is used to customize the printing environment. It maintains an object in the NDS tree that consists of special modes and functions for print devices along with print form definitions. You can use the PRINTDEF utility to import printer definition files (PDFs). The PDFs contain printer setup modes that consist of one or more printer functions. Each printer function defines a printer escape code sequence that directs the printer to perform a specific function. The PRINTCON utility enables each user to have a customized set of print configurations that simplify access to printers and allow for special printer setup modes.

Command Summary

Command	Syntax	Definition
PCONSOLE	*PCONSOLE*	Creates, deletes, and manages print queues and print servers. Also controls and monitors printers and manages and resequences jobs stored in print queues.
PRINTCON	*PRINTCON*	Creates, maintains, and copies print job configurations and can be used to establish defaults and standard printing configurations used by the CAPTURE, NPRINT, and PCONSOLE commands when jobs are placed in a print queue.
PRINTDEF	*PRINTDEF*	Maintains the information on print devices and print forms.
PSC	*PSC [PS=printserver] [P=printserver]Action*	Sends control commands directly from the DOS prompt or batch file to the specified printer. Replace *printservername* with the name of the print server that controls the printer. Replace *printnumber* with the number of the printer to which you want to send the control command. Command options include mark, status, pause, start, abort, stop, keep, form feed, mount form, and cancel down.

Key Terms

printer function

printer mode

Review Questions

1. Rearranging print jobs in a print queue can be accomplished by using ________________, or ________________.
2. Give the definition of the following status indicators when using PCONSOLE to rearrange print jobs:

   READY ________________________________

   ADDING ________________________________

   ACTIVE ________________________________
3. To rearrange a print job in a print queue so that it prints first, the __________ field must be changed to a 1.
4. To take the print queue off line, highlight the ____________________ field and change the Yes to a No.
5. When deferring a print job so that it prints at a later time, the new printing time will default to ____________________.

6. Although both users and queue operators can manage print jobs from Windows 95, only _______________ can change the status of any jobs that are in the queue.
7. To remove all documents from the print queue in Windows 95, select _______________ from the Printer menu.
8. The _______________ utility is used to change the form specification.
9. As an alternative to PCONSOLE, the _______________ command can be used to issue control commands to network printers directly from a menu or the DOS prompt.
10. The standard form number in NetWare is _______________.
11. The process of informing NetWare which form is in the printer is called _______________.
12. List the four ways in which forms can be mounted:

    ____

    ____

    ____

    ____

13. The _______________ will enable you to change a printer so that all jobs with the same form number will print before another form must be mounted.
14. Assigning names to different forms can be performed by using the _______________ utility.
15. What is a printer function?
16. What is a printer mode?
17. Before you can use the predefined printer functions and modes, you need to merge the _______________ into your printer database.
18. Novell-supplied Printer Definition Files are located in which directory?
19. The utility _______________ can be used to create, modify, or view printer modes and functions.
20. A function consists of _______________ sequences that cause the printer to perform specific operations.
21. List the three ways in which values can be entered to create new printer functions:

    ____

    ____

    ____

22. The utility _______________ enables you to change the default print configuration or assign a different print configuration.

EXERCISES

EXERCISE 13-1: REARRANGING PRINT JOBS

In this exercise you use the PCONSOLE utility to change print job parameters and rearrange the sequence of jobs in print queues. To perform this exercise, you need to have a print queue named ##LOCAL that has your student username defined as a print queue operator. If this print queue does not currently exist, you will need to log in using the necessary privileges and use PCONSOLE to create a print queue named ##LOCAL, and then make your username the print queue operator. If you are not able to access a supervisor-equivalent username, your instructor will create this print queue for you.

For the second part of this exercise, your instructor will need to have the classroom print server running, and your username must be an operator of the classroom print server in order to enable you to add your print queue to the classroom printer.

1. Log in using your assigned student username.
2. Create the following document with either Notepad, Windows Write, or DOS Edit and entitle it PJOB1:

   To prevent the print jobs from starting to print while you are resequencing a print queue, you need to take the queue off line temporarily. A print queue operator for a print queue can use PCONSOLE to take the print queue off line by selecting it from the Print Queue window and then using the Status option to display the Print Queue Status window.
3. Create the following document with either Notepad, Windows Write, or DOS Edit and entitle it PJOB2:

   It is sometimes necessary for a print queue operator to rearrange the sequence of jobs in a print queue. This enables a high–priority job to be printed ahead of other jobs placed in the print queue before it.
4. Use PCONSOLE to change the status of the ##LOCAL print queue to prevent print servers from printing jobs.
5. Place the two documents in the print queue to be printed. Be sure that PJOB1 is entered first and then PJOB2. Use either CAPTURE or NPRINT. Record the command that you used on the line below.

   ____
6. Use the PCONSOLE utility to rearrange the sequence of print jobs in the ##LOCAL print queue so that PJOB2 appears before PJOB1.
7. Change the PJOB2 print job to print 20 minutes from now.
8. Exit the PCONSOLE utility.
9. Return all printer ports to local mode. On the line below, record the command you use.
10. Use the appropriate option of the CAPTURE command to verify that all ports are in local mode.

Exercise 13-2: Adding a Print Queue

In this exercise you use the PCONSOLE utility to add your print queue to a printer running on the classroom print server and change the print queue status to enable the classroom print server to get jobs from your print queue.

1. Start PCONSOLE.
2. Use the Printers option to select your ##LOCAL print queue.
3. Select the option that will make your print jobs available to the print server. On the line below, record the option you use.

   ____

4. Use the Print Servers option to select the classroom print server.
5. Select the Printers option to display the Printer Configuration Menu.
6. Select the option that will enable you to add a print queue to an existing printer. On the line below, record the name of the option.

___

7. Select printer number 0, which is a local printer attached to the print server. On the line below, record the name of the printer you plan to use.

___

8. Add your print queue to the printer with a priority of 2.
9. Add your name to the notification list of the printer selected in step 7.
10. Select the option that will enable you to monitor and control the printer that will be printing your print jobs. On the line below, record the option you select.

___

11. Submit a print job.
12. Wait for the printer to ask for form 2 to be mounted.
13. Change the form number to 2. Record the results below.

___

14. When the printer asks for form number 0, cancel the print job. On the line below, record the name of the print job that was canceled.

___

15. Print the remaining job using form number 0.
16. Use the Print Jobs option to remove your print queue from the printer's queue list and your name from the printer notification list.
17. Use [Alt][F10] to exit.
18. Log out.
19. Have your instructor check your printed output.

EXERCISES

CASE 13-1: MANAGING PRINT CONFIGURATIONS AT J.Q. ADAMS

In this exercise you change print configurations using DS Standard for the J. Q. Adams Directory tree.

Part 1: Create and Configure the Print Queue

1. If necessary, boot the PC workstation, launch Windows 95, and start DS Standard.
2. Click the Start button.
3. Click Programs to display the Programs menu, click DS Standard NDS Manager v3 to display the DS Standard NDS Manager 3.0 menu, and then click DS Standard NDS Manager to open the DS Standard NDS manager.
4. Click File, click Open View, and then click J. Q. Adams to display the NDS tree.

5. Select the container object PRODUCTION in which to locate the print queue object.
6. Click Edit on the menu bar and then click Add Object to see a display of the available objects.
7. Click Print Queue.
8. Type PRHP5Q1 as the name of the print queue.

Part 2: Create and Configure the Print Server

1. Select the container object PRODUCTION in which to locate the print server object.
2. Click Edit on the menu bar and then click Add Object to see a display of the available objects.
3. Click Print Server.
4. Type PS2 as the name of the print server.

Part 3: Create and Configure the Printers

1. Select the container object PRODUCTION in which to locate the printer object.
2. Click Edit on the menu bar and then click Add Object to see a display of the available objects.
3. Click Printers.
4. Type PROHP5RO as the name of the printer.

Part 4: Assign the Print Queues

1. Select the printer object PROHP5RO by double-clicking it.
2. Click the Assignment button.
3. Click the Add button.
4. Type PS2 as the name of the printer server.

Part 5: Change Print Configurations

1. Double-click the user Bavery.
2. Click the Print Job Configuration button.
3. Type the printer name PROHP5RO in the Printer/Queue field.
4. Make the following changes:
   a. The Mode should be Executive Paper.
   b. The File Contents should be Text.
   c. The Banner Name should be Avery.
   d. Timeout should be set to 60 seconds.

Turn in a copy of your data disk to your instructor.

CASE 13-2: BAYVIEW WINDOW & DOOR

The Bayview Window & Door company sells and installs customized windows and doors to construction companies in a three-state region. It currently uses a Novell network to support PC applications in its sales department. The sales department uses an HP LaserJet III–compatible printer that is used for printing on company letterhead. The letterhead paper is located in the top tray of the printer; standard forms are located in the lower tray. Occasionally the department needs to print on legal forms and has a special legal-size paper tray that can be loaded in the lower paper drawer of the printer. Lately the department has needed to print landscape output on both legal and standard paper, but members have been unable to set the printer up properly for landscape mode with their current application software. They have called on you to help them customize their printing environment so they can print landscape output on both standard and legal paper as well as prevent output that was intended for legal forms from being printed on standard paper. Sales department staff occasionally need to print labels on special label forms. Because the labels are fairly expensive, it's important not to print other jobs on them by mistake.

The work for Bayview Window & Door involves the following tasks:

1. Document the form types and associated form numbers in the following table.

Form Number	Form Name	Description
F##		
F##		
F##		

2. Log in with the necessary rights.
3. Use PRINTDEF to define the form types you documented in step 1. Be sure to include "F##" at the beginning of each form number to separate it from forms created by other students.
4. Use PRINTDEF to import the HP LaserJet III printer definition file; then change the printer device name to ##HPIII.
5. Use PRINTDEF to remove all printer modes except the following:

   Letter Landscape, 45 lpp, 10 cpi

   Legal Landscape, 45 lpp, 10 cpi

   Letter Portrait, 60 lpp, 10 cpi

   Legal Portrait, 78 lpp, 10 cpi
6. Add the lower paper tray function to the printer modes listed in step 5.
7. Create a new printer mode called Letterhead. Include all the functions from the Letter Portrait mode, replacing the lower paper tray with the upper paper tray.
8. Exit PRINTDEF and save the printer database changes.
9. Create a user named ##SALES1.
10. Use PCONSOLE to create a ##LOCAL print queue if you do not already have one.
11. Log out.
12. Log in as user ##SALES1.
13. Use PRINTCON to set up the following standard print configurations for the ##SALES1 user.

```
PRINT JOB CONFIGURATION NAME  PRINT JOB DESCRIPTION
Standard (default print job)  Q=##LOCAL
                              no banner
                              timeout of 10 seconds
                              print mode = Letter Portrait
                              form type = standard paper
```

Legal	Q=##LOCAL no banner timeout of 10 seconds print mode = Legal Portrait form type = legal paper
Standard Landscape	Q=##LOCAL no banner timeout of 10 seconds print mode = Letter Landscape form type = standard paper
Legal Landscape	Q=##LOCAL no banner timeout of 10 seconds print mode = Legal Landscape form type = legal paper
Letterhead	Q=##LOCAL no banner timeout of 10 seconds print mode = Letterhead form type = standard paper

14. Issue a CAPTURE command to use the default print configuration. On the line below, record the command.

    ____

15. Place PJOB1 in the ##LOCAL print queue.
16. Issue a CAPTURE command to use the letterhead print mode. On the line below, record the command.

    ____

17. Place PJOB2 in the ##LOCAL print queue.
18. Use PCONSOLE to view the jobs in your print queue.
19. Have your instructor check your print queue jobs and PRINTCON configuration and sign below when they are satisfactory.

    Instructor signature: ______________________________
20. Log in with the necessary rights.
21. Use PRINTDEF to remove your form definitions and the ##HPIII print device.
22. Log out.

Northwestern Technical College

Now that the college's network printing environment has been installed and tested, you are to customize the printing with form names and special printer modes.

Project 13-1: Customizing the Printer Configuration

Stephen Rodriguiz, John Rose, and Doris McCabe in Finance will be sharing an HP LaserJet IV–SI laser printer with letterhead paper in the upper tray and standard forms in the lower tray to perform most of their network printing. Periodically Doris needs to print labels from the upper paper tray and wants a way to prevent other users from printing from the upper tray when labels are loaded. John occasionally needs to print output from a database file using landscape orientation in order to get all the fields to fit across the page. He would like to have the option of printing in landscape mode on the laser printer.

The student services department has both laser and dot-matrix printers. Staff members would like to have reports generated by both the graduate system and the testing system sent to the dot-matrix printer. Word processing documents should be printed on the laser printer. Letterhead stationery is normally kept in the upper tray of the laser printer and plain paper in the lower tray. Occasionally staff members need to print on legal-size forms. They would like to have a way to stop the printer and enable the legal forms tray to be loaded in the lower paper drawer before printing is resumed.

Develop a set of printer configurations for both the support staff and the student services staff and then document these print modes in a memo.

Project 13-2: Setting Up Forms

After the print configurations and forms are defined to meet the customized printing needs of the departments, your next task is to use the PRINTDEF utility to add the form definitions to the printer device database. If you do not have access to the classroom server as a supervisor equivalent user, your instructor will provide you with a list of forms that have been established for you to use.

Start PRINTDEF and use the Forms option to define the print forms you documented in Project 13-1. Precede each form name with F##n, where ## represents your assigned student number and n represents the form number. Because other students will be setting up forms on the classroom file server, the actual form number you use will be based on the existing form definitions. Record the actual form number and your form name below.

Form Number:

____

Form Name:

____

Project 13-3: Defining Printer Modes

After all form numbers have been defined, the next task is to import the HP LaserJet IV– SI printer definition file and establish the necessary printer modes. If you do not have access to the classroom server as a supervisor-equivalent user, your instructor will load the HP LaserJet IV–SI printer definition file with the necessary print modes. You can use PRINTDEF to verify and document the printer modes and functions with which you will be working.

1. Use PRINTDEF to import the HP LaserJet IV–SI printer definition file and then change the printer device name to ##HPIII.
2. Modify the letter landscape and letter portrait modes to use the lower paper tray function.
3. Create a new mode, called Letterhead, that contains functions to reset the printer, select portrait orientation, and use the upper paper tray.
4. Document the functions contained in each of the printer modes you documented in Project 13-1.

PROJECT 13-4: PRINTING PRINT JOBS

Once the print forms and modes have been defined, the final task in customizing the printer environment is creating the print job configurations you documented in Project 13-1 for the Finance and Student Services departments.

Test your print jobs by using the CAPTURE command to select each print job and then send sample output to the print queue. You can then use PCONSOLE to view the print job parameters and compare them to your printer configuration.

After you have completed testing the print configurations for each user, have your instructor check your printing environment and sign on the line below.

Instructor signature: ____

CHAPTER FOURTEEN

LOGIN SCRIPTS

Once the network directory structure has been established and secured, the user accounts created, the applications installed, and the network printing environment configured, the next challenge for the network administrator is to make this complex system easy to access and use. Workstations using Microsoft Windows 95 can have the workstation drive mappings and printer setup configured in the local workstation's environment. However, for DOS-based workstations and certain applications, making the network system easy to use requires creating login scripts and menus. Login scripts make it possible for users to log into a file server and access network services by establishing drive mappings, providing informational messages, redirecting printer output to default printers, and executing special programs.

Establishing the user environment is an important part in the job of a network administrator. In this chapter, you will learn about login scripts and how to establish the necessary login scripts for your network system. Chapter 15 will cover the NetWare 4.1 menu system and show you how to create menus.

AFTER READING THIS CHAPTER AND COMPLETING THE EXERCISES YOU WILL BE ABLE TO:

- IDENTIFY THE FOUR CATEGORIES OF LOGIN SCRIPT FILES AND HOW THEY ARE USED.
- IDENTIFY THE PURPOSE AND CORRECT SYNTAX OF LOGIN SCRIPT COMMANDS.
- WRITE CONTAINER LOGIN SCRIPTS TO MEET THE NEEDS OF A TYPICAL NETWORK ORGANIZATION.
- WRITE USER AND PROFILE LOGIN SCRIPTS TO MEET THE PERSONAL PROCESSING NEEDS OF USERS.

Workstations logging in using Apple Macintosh computers, like Windows 95, do not need a login script to be executed because they can have the workstation drive mappings and printer setup configured in the local workstations' environment.

NETWARE LOGIN SCRIPTS

As you learned in previous chapters, any drive mapping or printer capture commands you establish while you are logged into a file server are effective only until you log out. The next time you log in, you must again map each drive pointer you want to use and issue CAPTURE commands to redirect printer output to the appropriate print queues. Requiring users to reestablish their drive pointers and print queues not only means they must have much technical knowledge about the system, but also takes time away from productive work. To remedy this problem, NetWare enables you to configure the workstation environment for each user automatically. Each time a user logs into a file server, NetWare executes a set of commands contained in login script files.

A NetWare **login script** is a file that contains a set of valid NetWare login command statements, as illustrated in Figure 14-1.

Figure 14-1

Login script

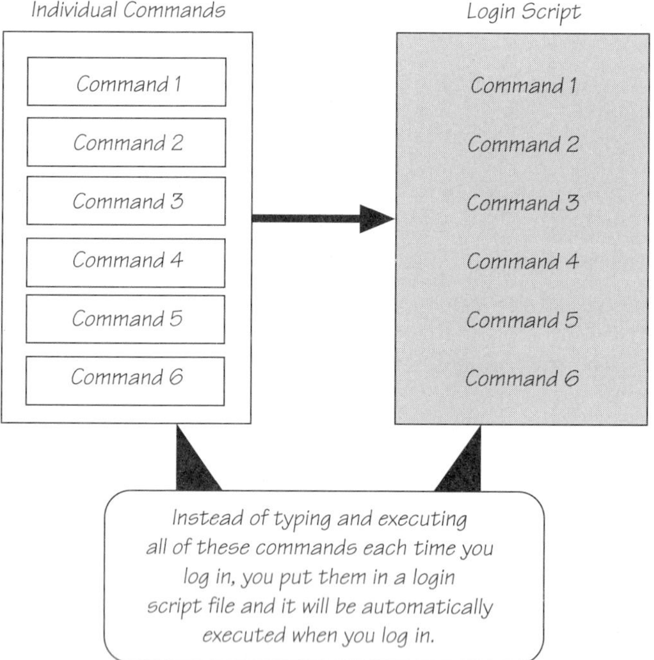

Each login script command statement must contain a valid login script or NetWare command. The command statements in a login script file form a program that is processed by the LOGIN.EXE program after a user has logged in. Figure 14-2 contains a simple system login script command file that contains statements to map drive pointers for all users and displays a message that greets users when they log in.

Figure 14-2

Sample Login script

```
MAP DISPLAY OFF
DISPLAY "Welcome to the CBE Labs Network"
MAP ROOT H:=CONSTELLATION/DATA:USERS\%LOGIN_NAME
MAP ROOT I:=CONSTELLATION/SYS:\PUBLIC
MAP J:= CONSTELLATION/SYS:APPS\EMAIL
DRIVE H:
```

A limited number of commands can be used in login script programs. You need to understand the individual statements before you can design and write login script programs. The following sections present valid login script command statements and how they are used.

Some login script command statements, such as MAP and ATTACH, have corresponding NetWare command line utilities. Although the syntax and purpose of these commands are very similar to those of the command line utilities, the login script commands include special options or variables that are not available with the corresponding command line utility.

LOGIN SCRIPT VARIABLES

Many login script commands enable the use of variables as part of the command line. A **login script variable** contains a value which will vary with each user's login. One common use of a login script variable, for example, is to map a drive letter to each user's home directory. If each user's home directory has the same name as his or her username, the following login script command, included in the system login script, will map the drive letter H to the home directory of each user when he or she logs in:

```
MAP ROOT H:=CONSTELLATION/DATA:USERS\%LOGIN_NAME
```

Notice that the variable, %LOGIN_NAME, is preceded by a percent sign (%). This identifies LOGIN_NAME as a variable rather than the name of a directory. The LOGIN.EXE program will substitute the name of the user who is currently logging in for the %LOGIN_NAME variable in the MAP command statement. It will then map the H drive letter to the user's specified home directory. Assume, for example, a user logs in with the username GBurns. The login program will substitute the name GBurns for the variable %LOGIN_NAME, creating the statement MAP ROOT H:=CONSTELLATION/DATA:USERS\GBURNS.

Login script variables can be divided into several types, based on their usage. The **date variables** contain information about the current month, day, and year in a variety of formats, as shown in Figure 14-3. Date variables are useful for displaying current date information. The login script can also check for a specific day in order to perform special setup instructions. By including a DAY_OF_WEEK variable, you can write a login script command that sends a message reminding users of a weekly 2:30 P.M. meeting when they login each Tuesday. The value of a date variable is stored as an ASCII string of a fixed length. The DAY variable represents the day number of the current month and might contain only the values 01 to 31. The NDAY_OF_WEEK variable represents the day number of the week with Sunday being day number 1 and Saturday being day number 7.

When using the DAY variable in an IF statement, it is important to include the leading 0 in front of day numbers 01 through 09 and then enclose the day numbers in quotation marks (e.g., IF DAY>"09"THEN. . .).

Figure 14-3
Date variables

VARIABLE	DESCRIPTION
DAY	Day number of the current month (possible values 01–31)
DAY_OF_WEEK	Name of the current day of the week
MONTH	Number of the current month (possible values 01–12)
MONTH_NAME	Name of the current month
NDAY_OF_WEEK	Current weekday number (possible values 01–07)
SHORT_YEAR	Last two digits of the current year (1997 would be 97)
YEAR	Full four-digit year

The **network variables** shown in Figure 14-4 can be used to display or check the network address and name of the current file server of the user who is currently logging in. The **time variables** shown in Figure 14-5 provide a variety of methods to view or check the login time. The GREETING_TIME variable is most often used to display welcome messages. The difference between the HOUR24 variable and the HOUR variable is that the HOUR variable requires inclusion of the am_pm variable to specify if the time is before or after noon. The HOUR24 variable is based on a 24-hour system, in which 12 represents noon and 13 represents 1:00 P.M. If you want to specify a time in the login script, the HOUR24 variable is often easier to use. If you want all users who log in before 3:00 P.M. to be notified of a special meeting, for example, you could write login script commands that use the HOUR24 variable to compare the current login hour to 15. If HOUR24 is less than 15, the login script commands could then display a notice of the meeting.

Figure 14-4
Network variables

VARIABLE	DESCRIPTION
NETWORK_ADDRESS	Network address of the cabling system to which the user's workstation is attached (expressed as an eight-digit hexadecimal number)
FILE_SERVER	Name of the current file server

Figure 14-5
Time variables

VARIABLE	DESCRIPTION
AM_PM	Day or night (A.M. or P.M.)
GREETING_TIME	Time of day (possible values: Morning, Afternoon, or Evening.) Most commonly used in welcome message.
HOUR	Current hour of day or night (possible values 01–12).
HOUR24	Current hour in 24-hour mode (possible values 01 for 1:00 A.M. through 24 for midnight)
MINUTE	Current minute (possible values 00–59).
SECOND	Current second (possible values 00–59).

The **user variables** (see Figure 14-6) enable you to view or check the user's login name, full name, last name, or the hexadecimal ID given to the user. As described previously, the LOGIN_NAME variable is commonly used to map a drive letter to a user's home directory, provided the name of the user's home directory is the same as the user's login name. The FULL_NAME variable can be used to personalize greeting messages by including the user's name as part of the message.

Figure 14-6

User variables

VARIABLE	DESCRIPTION
FULL_NAME	User's full name
LOGIN_NAME	User's unique login name
USER_ID	Hexadecimal number assigned by NetWare for the user login name
LAST_NAME	User's last name

The **workstation variables** MACHINE, OS, and OS_VERSION, shown in Figure 14-7, are most commonly used in the system login script when a search drive is mapped to the correct DOS version used on the workstation. The STATION variable contains the connection number assigned to the user's workstation. It can be used by some software packages to separate user temporary files when the station number is included as part of the temporary filename. You can use the STATION variable to separate temporary files when you create menus. The P_STATION variable contains the actual node address of the workstation that is logging in and can be used in login script files to cause certain processing to be performed on specific workstations. Suppose, for example, the workstation address 0800DC03D7D27 is used to run CAD software. You could include in the login script commands that use the P_STATION variable to check for station address 0800DC03D7D27, establish the necessary drive mappings, and then start the CAD software.

Figure 14-7

Workstation variables

VARIABLE	DESCRIPTION
OS	Workstation's operating system (default value MSDOS)
OS_VERSION	Workstation's operating system version (example: v6.20)
MACHINE	Long machine name that can be assigned in the NET.CFG file (example: IBMPC)
P_STATION	12-digit hexadecimal node address of the network card in the workstation
SMACHINE	Long machine name that can be assigned in the NET.CFG file (example: IBM)
STATION NETWARE_REQUESTER NETWORK_ADDRESS	Connection number of the current station Version of the VLM requester 12-digit hexadecimal network number of the cabling system
SHELL_TYPE	Workstation's shell version number

Login Script Commands

In many ways, creating login scripts is very similar to writing a computer program. Like any programming language, NetWare login scripts include commands that cause the computer to perform certain processing tasks. Also like any programming language, login script commands are written according to rules that must be followed in order for the commands to be processed. These rules are commonly referred to as the **syntax** of the programming language. This section will show you the valid syntax of each NetWare login script command and provide examples of how to use it to perform common login functions. Before you turn to the individual login script commands, you should be aware of the following general rules that apply to all login script commands:

- Only valid login script command statements and comments can be placed in a login script file.

- Login script command lines can contain a maximum of 150 characters.
- Long commands can be allowed to "wrap" to the next line if there is not enough room on one line.
- The LOGIN.EXE program reads the login script commands one line at a time, and only one command is allowed on any command line.
- Commands can be entered in either uppercase or lowercase letters. Variables that are enclosed in quotation marks, however, must be preceded by a percent sign (%) and typed in uppercase letters.
- Comments are entered by preceding the text either with the REM command or with one of two symbols, an asterisk (*) or a semicolon (;).

MAP

The MAP command is the most important login script command. It is used to establish automatically the regular and search drive mappings a user needs to work with the NetWare environment. The syntax and use of the MAP login script command are very similar to the MAP command line utility described earlier. In the login script version, however, you can use identifier variables and relative drive letters as part of the MAP command syntax, as follows:

```
MAP [option] [drive:=path;drive:=path] [variable]
```

You can replace *option* in the MAP command with one of the parameters that are shown in Figure 14-8.

Figure 14-8 Map command parameters

OPTIONAL PARAMETER	DESCRIPTION
ROOT	Makes a drive appear as the root of a volume to DOS and the application programs
INS	Used with search drives to insert a new search drive at the sequence number you specify and then renumber any existing search drives
DISPLAY ON/OFF	Turns on or off the results of the map statements on the screen
ERRORS ON/OFF	Turns on or off any MAP error messages that may be displayed on the screen
C	Changes a search drive mapping to a regular drive mapping
P	Maps a drive to the physical volume of a server instead of to the volume object's name
N	Maps the next available drive
DEL	Removes the specified drive mapping

You can replace *drive* with any valid network, local, or search drive. In addition to specifying a drive letter, you can use a relative drive specification, such as *1, to indicate the first network drive, *2 the second network drive, and so on. If the workstation's first network drive letter is G, *1 will be replaced with G and *2 will be replaced with H. If, on the other hand, a workstation's first network drive is L, *1 will be replaced with L and *2 will be replaced with M. Replace *path* with a full directory path beginning with a DOS drive letter or NetWare volume name.

With the login script version of the MAP command, additional drive mappings can be placed on the same line by separating them with semicolons. If you want to map the G drive to the SYS: volume and the K drive to the DATA: volume, for example, you can issue the following MAP command statement:

```
MAP G:=SYS:; K:=DATA:
```

As mentioned earlier, login script variables can be included in the MAP statement. Commonly used variables include %LOGIN_NAME, %OS, %OS_VERSION, and %MACHINE. The %OS, %OS_VERSION, and %MACHINE variables are often used to map a search drive to a specific DOS directory based on the version of DOS being used on the workstation logging in. For example, Figure 14-9 displays the CBE directory structure which stores three different versions of DOS. You can use the following MAP command statement in a login script file to map the second search drive to the appropriate DOS version for the workstation currently logging in:

```
MAP S2:=CONSTELLATION/SYS:PUBLIC\%MACHINE\%OS\%OS_VERSION
```

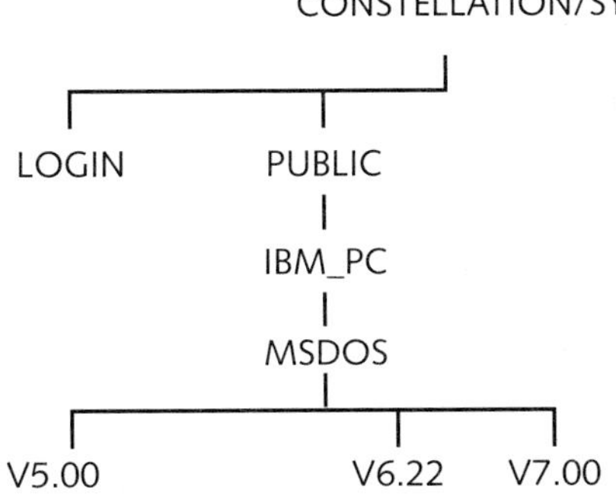

Figure 14-9 Constellation directory structure

Other special MAP command statements include MAP DISPLAY OFF or MAP DISPLAY ON and MAP ERRORS OFF or MAP ERRORS ON. By default, MAP DISPLAY is set ON displaying the results of each MAP command in the login script. The MAP DISPLAY OFF command prevents the map commands from being displayed on the user workstation while they are executed. This MAP command is often included at the beginning of a login script command to reduce the amount of information that is displayed on the user workstations. The MAP ERRORS OFF command can be used to prevent the display on a user's workstation of error messages generated by MAP commands that specify invalid paths. This command is useful if you include drive mapping commands in a login script that you know will not be valid for all users. Rather than have a user be confused by error messages that do not affect him or her, include the MAP ERRORS OFF command before the MAP commands that contain the invalid drive paths.

COMSPEC

When DOS is booted from a local workstation, it stores the location of the COMMAND.COM file in the DOS environment space variable COMSPEC. Thereafter, anytime a program exits and COMMAND.COM has to be reloaded, DOS will check the environment space to determine the location of the command processor program. If workstations on your network do not have hard disk drives, it is important that you identify a location on the file server from which DOS can reload the COMMAND.COM program. The COMSPEC command enables the network administrator to set a location for loading

COMMAND.COM in the DOS environment space.The proper syntax of the COMSPEC command is as follows:

```
COMSPEC = [path]COMMAND.COM
```

You can replace the optional *path* parameter with the location at which DOS can find the proper version of the COMMAND.COM program. Because there can be more than one version of DOS running on the workstations attached to the network, it is necessary to specify a path that will point to the correct COMMAND.COM for the DOS version that the workstation is running. To do this, most network administrators place the COMSPEC command after the MAP command that maps a search drive to the DOS external command directory. For example, at CBE Labs a login script would look like this:

```
MAP S2:=CONSTELLATION/SYS:PUBLIC\%MACHINE\%OS\%OS_VERSION
COMSPEC=S2:COMMAND.COM
```

Notice that there is no forward slash (/) between S2: and COMMAND.COM. A forward slash in this position would indicate that the COMMAND.COM file is located on the root of the CONSTELLATION_SYS: volume.

WRITE

The WRITE command is used to place simple messages enclosed in quotation marks (" ") on the screen of the workstation. In addition to text, messages can contain identifier variables and special control strings, as shown in the following WRITE command syntax:

```
WRITE "text [control string] [%variable]"
```

In addition to replacing the *text* parameter with any message you want displayed when the user logs in, you can add the control characters shown in Figure 14-10 anywhere in the text string. Notice that all options must be preceded by a backslash (\). Any options preceded with a forward slash (/) will be ignored and treated as normal text that appears on the screen.

Figure 14-10

Control characters for WRITE

VARIABLE	DEFAULT VALUE
\r	Inserts a return and line feed
\n	Inserts a blank line
\"	Inserts an embedded quotation mark within the text
\7	Inserts a beep sound on the speaker

Login script variables can also be placed into the text by capitalizing all characters of the variable name and preceding them with a percent sign (%). As it does with the MAP command, the login script processor will substitute the value of the variable into the text string before displaying it on the workstation. Login script variables that are often used with the WRITE statement include %GREETING_TIME and %FULL_NAME. The %GREETING_TIME variable contains the current time expressed as either Morning, Afternoon, or Evening. For example, the CBE network administrator may include a welcome message at the beginning of their login scripts similar to the following:

```
WRITE "Good %GREETING_TIME %FULL_NAME \n Welcome to the CBE
Labs network"
```

You can make sure that all users see and acknowledge important messages by including the following PAUSE statement in your login script:

```
WRITE "File server will be coming down today, March 1, at
5:00pm for a maintenance call." PAUSE
```

When the PAUSE command is executed, NetWare stops the login script processing and displays the message "strike any key when ready. . ." on the screen.

DISPLAY and FDISPLAY

The DISPLAY and FDISPLAY commands show the contents of an ASCII text file on the screen during the execution of the login script. The proper syntax of either command is

```
[F]DISPLAY [directory path] filename
```

If the filename specified is in the current directory, or if a search drive has been established to the directory containing the filename, the directory path is not needed. To show the WELCOME.MSG file stored on the CONSTELLATION_DATA: volume in the PUBLCNTS\DOCUMENT directory at CBE Labs, for example, you can place the following FDISPLAY command in your system login script:

```
MAP INS S1:=CONSTELLATION/DATA:
FDISPLAY S1:\PUBLCNTS\DOCUMENT\WELCOME.MSG
PAUSE
```

It is important to follow the DISPLAY command with a PAUSE statement. This gives the user time to read the message file. The difference between DISPLAY and FDISPLAY is that the FDISPLAY command filters and formats the contents of the specified filename so that only the ASCII text itself is displayed. FDISPLAY will not display tabs. The DISPLAY command, on the other hand, displays the exact characters contained in the file, including "garbage" characters such as printer or word processing edit codes. It is usually more appropriate to use FDISPLAY for displaying files that have been created with word processing packages. If you use a word processing package, however, make sure to save the file in ASCII text format or it's possible that even if FDISPLAY is used, it will not be readable.

Suppose the CBE network administrator wants to display a schedule of events for each day of the week. At the beginning of the week he would receive the schedule for the following days. He can use the FDISPLAY command to display the appropriate day's menu by creating files named after weekdays. For example, MONDAY.MSG would contain Monday's schedule, and so on. He can then use the following DAY_OF_WEEK login script variable to display the appropriate day's schedule:

```
FDISPLAY S1:\PUBLCTNS\DOCUMENT\%DAY_OF_WEEK.MSG
```

(Execute a DOS Program)

The external program execution command, #, can load and run an .EXE or .COM program without exiting the LOGIN script processor. When the program is complete, the next login script command line is executed. The syntax of the # command is as follows:

```
# [path] filename [parameter]
```

You can optionally replace the path parameter with a full directory path, using either a drive letter or NetWare volume name, that points to the directory containing the program to be run. If no path is specified, the program must exist in either the current directory or be located in one of the paths specified by previous search drive mappings. Replace filename with the name of the .COM or .EXE program you want executed. The filename extension is not needed. Depending on the program you are running, you can replace *parameter* with any parameters that are to be passed to the specified program. The format of the entries you place in the parameter string is dependent upon the command being run.

The external program execution character, #, is important because it lets you run other command line utilities or DOS commands from inside the login script. Suppose, for example, you want to establish a default network printer for user output. Because CAPTURE is not a login script command, you can use the # command to run the CAPTURE command with the appropriate parameters.

Do not use the # command to load terminate-and-stay resident programs (TSR) into a workstation. Because the LOGIN program is kept in memory during the execution of the TSR program, the TSR program will be loaded after the LOGIN program, causing the memory from the LOGIN program to be unavailable to the workstation after the LOGIN.EXE program exits.

When application programs are run from a login script, you might encounter an "Out of memory" message indicating that there is not enough room in the DOS 640-KB memory space for both the LOGIN.EXE program and the application to be loaded. When this happens, use the EXIT filename command statement to end the login script and then pass control to the application software specified by the filename parameter after LOGIN.EXE has exited.

To provide more memory for application software, do not use the # command to run a menu system. The LOGIN.EXE program will take up memory from the menu and any application software that is run from the menu.

IF . . . THEN . . . ELSE

The IF login statement is used to customize a login script for specific users or groups, as well as to perform special processing when a condition—such as a specific day, time, or station—exists. The syntax of a simple IF statement is as follows:

```
IF condition THEN command
```

The *condition* parameter is replaced with a conditional statement that has a value of either true or false. Conditional statements usually consist of an identifier variable and a value enclosed in quotation marks. Figure 14-11 shows examples of several commonly used conditional statements.

Figure 14-11 Sample conditional statements

CONDITION	DESCRIPTION
MEMBER OF "group"	This statement is true if the user is a member of the specified group.
DAY_OF_WEEK = "Monday"	This statement is true if the name of the day is Monday. Either uppercase or lowercase letters may be used.
DAY = "05"	This statement is true on the fifth day of the month. Valid day values range from 01 to 31. It is necessary to include the leading zero for day numbers less than 10.
MONTH = "June"	This statement is true for the month of June. Either uppercase or lowercase letters may be used.
NDAY_OF_WEEK = "1"	This statement is true on Sunday, which is a 1. Valid numbers range from 1 to 7.

The *command* parameter can be replaced with any valid login script command statement. The following is an example of a simple IF statement with a single condition:

```
IF DAY_OF_WEEK = "FRIDAY" THEN WRITE "Hurrah, it's Friday!"
```

More complex IF statements can consist of multiple commands followed by the END statement. The syntax of a multiple-command IF statement is as follows:

```
IF condition THEN
      command 1
      command 2
      command n
END
```

In a multiple-command IF statement, all commands between the IF statement and the END statement are performed when the condition is true. If you want to map certain drive pointers for the marketing department users of CBE Labs, for example, you can use an IF statement similar to the one shown in Figure 14-12.

Figure 14-12 Multiple-command IF statement

```
IF MEMBER OF "MARKETEING" THEN
   MAP ROOT H:CONSTELLATION/DATA:USERS\%LOGIN_NAME
   MAP ROOT L:CONSTELLATION/DATA:MARKET
   MAP INS S1:CONSTELLATION/SYS:APPS\SP
END
```

Sometimes it is desirable to combine multiple conditions using AND or OR. When using OR to connect two conditions, the login command statements will be performed if either condition is true. If you want all members of either the marketing or finance groups to be informed of a weekly meeting, for example, you can use the following condition:

```
IF MEMBER OF "MARKETING" OR MEMBER OF "FINANCE"
```

Use the word AND when you want both statements to be true before the commands are processed. Suppose, for example, you want to remind all finance users of a meeting on Monday morning. Before displaying the reminder, you want to make sure the user is a member of the finance department, the day is Monday, and the login time is before noon. To do this you can use AND to connect these three conditions, as shown in Figure 14-13.

Figure 14-13 Using AND in an IF statement

```
IF MEMBER OF "FINANCE" AND DAY_OF_WEEK = "MONDAY" AND HOUR24 < "10" THEN
 WRITE "Remember the meeting at 10 AM"
 PAUSE
END
```

The optional word ELSE is an important feature of the IF statement because it enables you to perform either one set of commands or another based on the condition. An example of an IF. . . THEN. . . ELSE command is shown in Figure 14-14. All members of the finance department will have their drive pointers mapped to the *FINANCE* directory of the CONSTELLATION/DATA VOLUME. All other users will have their drive pointers mapped to the SHARED Directory of the CONSTELLATION/DATA VOLUME.

Figure 14-14 Sample IF... THEN...ELSE statement

```
IF MEMBER OF "FINANCE" THEN
     MAP ROOT K:=CONSTELLATION/DATA:FINANCE
ELSE
     MAP ROOT K:=CONSTELLATION/DATA:SHARED
END
```

Some IF commands can become quite complex, consisting of IF commands within IF commands. The process of placing one IF command within another IF command is called **nesting**. NetWare allows as many as 10 levels of IF statements to be nested. When nesting IF statements, make sure each IF statement has a corresponding END statement, as shown in Figure 14-15. Indenting of IF statements makes this job much easier as well as more accurate.

Figure 14-15

Nested IF command

```
IF MEMBER OF "FINANCE" THEN
      MAP ROOT K:=CONSTELLATION/DATA:FINANCE

      IF LOGIN_NAME = "DKaneaka" THEN

            MAP I: = CONSTELLATION/DATA:ADMIN

      END

ELSE

      MAP ROOT K:=CONSTELLATION/DATA:SHARED

END
```

The first nested IF statement shown checks to see whether the user is a member of the finance department. If the user is a member of that group, the login script next checks to see if the login name is DKaneaka. If it is, an I: drive is mapped. However, if the user was not a member of the finance department then a K: drive is mapped to CONSTELLATION /DATA:SHARED. Although indenting is not necessary for the IF statement to work, lining up the IF and associated ELSE and END statements and then indenting the commands to be performed is a standard programming practice that makes it much easier to read and maintain complex IF statements.

DRIVE

The DRIVE command is used to set the default drive for DOS to use after the LOGIN.EXE program is executed. The syntax for the DRIVE command is as follows:

DRIVE drive

Replace the *drive* parameter with a network drive letter. Be sure the drive letter has been mapped to a directory path in which the user has the necessary access rights. Most network administrators use the drive near the end of the login script to place the user in either his or her home directory drive or a drive location from which the menu system is run.

EXIT

The EXIT command stops execution of the login script and exits the LOGIN.EXE program. Because the EXIT command ends the LOGIN.EXE program and returns control to DOS, no additional login script commands will be processed after the EXIT command is executed. In addition to ending the login script processing, the EXIT command can also be used to pass a command to DOS by using the following syntax:

EXIT ["command-line"]

Replace the *command-line* parameter with any statement, up to a maximum of 15 characters enclosed in quotation marks, that you want passed to the DOS command prompt.

INCLUDE

The INCLUDE command enables you to process login script commands that are stored in another file and then return to the login script statement following the INCLUDE command. It is similar to the CALL statement in DOS. The filename specified in the INCLUDE command must contain valid login script commands stored in standard ASCII text format. The proper syntax of the INCLUDE command is as follows:

`INCLUDE [path] filename [nds object]`

If the filename parameter containing the login script commands is not located in the SYS:LOGIN or SYS:PUBLIC directory, you will need to replace the path with the complete directory path leading to the specified filename.

The INCLUDE command can be used to make your primary login script file shorter and easier to understand by including other login script files as modules or subroutines that are called from the primary script. Suppose, for example, CBE Labs wants to establish a special login script process for all finance users. Rather than placing many commands in the system login script or having to maintain a complex login script for each finance user, a file named FINANCE.LOG, containing all finance login script commands, can be created in the CONSTELLATION/DATA:FINANCE directory. After you create the FINANCE.LOG file, you can use an INCLUDE command in the NetWare system login script, as shown in Figure 14-16, to call the FINANCE.LOG file whenever a user logs in.

Figure 14-16 Sample INCLUDE command

```
IF MEMBER = "FINANCE" THEN
 INCLUDE FINANCE.LOG
END
```

GOTO

The GOTO statement enables you to skip login script statements and continue processing at the specified label. The proper syntax for the GOTO command is as follows:

`GOTO label`

A label is a single word that identifies a specific location in the login script. You enter labels into the login script by specifying the label name as a single word ending with a colon (:) and aligned on the left margin. If, for example, you want to continue the system login script at a specific location rather than continuing with the login script after executing a set of commands, you can use commands as shown in Figure 14-17.

Figure 14-17 Sample GOTO command

```
IF MEMBER OF "FINANCE" THEN
      MAP ROOT K:=CONSTELLATION/DATA:FINANCE

      MAP I: = CONSTELLATION/DATA:ADMIN

      GOTO CONTINUE:

END

(Additional login statements)

CONTINUE:

(Final login statements)
```

The GOTO statement can easily be used incorrectly and create a login script that is difficult to follow. GOTO should be used only to advance in the script and never to go backward.

FIRE PHASERS

The purpose of the FIRE PHASERS command is to make a noise with the PC speaker to alert the operator of a message or condition encountered in the login process:

```
FIRE [PHASERS] n [TIMES]
```

Replace *n* with a number from 1 to 9 representing how many successive times the phaser sound will be made. The words PHASERS and TIMES are optional and can be omitted from the FIRE login script command. The FIRE PHASERS command is often used in conjunction with the IF statement to notify the user of a certain condition.

REM

Comment lines can be placed in the login script. The LOGIN.EXE program will skip any line that begins with REM, REMARK, an asterisk (*), or a semicolon (;). Using comments in your login script can make the script much easier for you or another administrator to read and understand. If you place a comment on the same line as other login script commands, however, you will cause errors when the script is interpreted. It is a good idea to precede each section of your login script with a comment identifying the function of that section. Figure 14-18 shows an example.

Figure 14-18

Sample REMARK commands

```
REM Login Script
REM Written by Ted Simpson
;
* Preliminary Commands
MAP DISPLAY OFF
;
* Map Statements
```

DOS SET

The DOS SET command can be used to place values in the DOS environment space for later use by menu programs or batch files. Each value placed in the DOS environment space can be assigned to a variable name, as shown in the following syntax:

```
[Temp] [DOS] SET variable="value"
```

The *variable* parameter must be replaced with a unique and meaningful name that represents the data to be stored. The variable name must consist of a single word with eight or fewer characters. Replace "*value*" with any character string or with a login script variable preceded by a percent sign (%). (Include the quotation marks.) The word DOS is optional and can be omitted from the SET login script command. The word Temp signifies that the variable is set only during the login script and doesn't affect the DOS environment.

The most common use of the DOS SET command is to set the DOS prompt and store certain identifier variables for later use. To set the DOS prompt to display the current directory path and store the user's login name and workstation node address in the DOS environment space, include the following commands in the login script:

```
DOS SET PROMPT="$p$g"
DOS SET USERNAME="%LOGIN_NAME"
DOS SET NODE="%P_STATION"
```

BREAK ON/OFF

The BREAK ON command enables the user to stop execution of the login script by using the [Ctrl][Break] key combination. BREAK OFF is assumed by default, so if you want to enable users to be able to break out of the login script, you will need to include the BREAK ON command after the necessary login script commands. The BREAK OFF command instructs the login script processor to ignore the use of the [Ctrl][Break] key combination. Because BREAK OFF is the default condition, the BREAK OFF command is not usually needed unless you have used the BREAK ON command previously. One example of the BREAK ON command would be providing a "window" in the login script in which a user could use the [Ctrl][Break] key combination to exit the login script.

NO_DEFAULT

The NO_DEFAULT command prevents LOGIN.EXE from executing the default login script. It can be placed in either the container or profile login script. The syntax is:

```
NO_DEFAULT
```

IMPLEMENTING LOGIN SCRIPTS

Once you understand the syntax and function of the login script commands, you can learn how to apply login scripts to establish a network environment for each user's workstation when he or she logs in. Before you implement a login script system, you need to understand how NetWare stores and processes login scripts. This will help you determine the best way to design and implement your login scripts.

TYPES OF LOGIN SCRIPTS

The NetWare login script system consists of four types of login script files: container, profile, user, and default. The four types of login script files enable the network administrator to provide a standard environment for all users and still provide flexibility so the network administrator can meet individual user needs. The **container login script** file enables the network administrator to establish a standard configuration for each user that logs into that container. The commands it contains are executed for all users of that container when they first log in. **Profile login scripts** execute for all members of a group, not just those in one container. You can set up a group and then assign any users to it. Individual user requirements can then be met with **user login script** files. Each user has his or her own personal login script file, which contains additional statements that are executed for that user after the system login script commands are executed. The **default login script** is a set of commands that establishes a default working environment for each user who does not have a container, profile, or user login script. To become a CNA, you need to know how these login script files work. This will enable you to configure a reliable and efficient login script system for your network. Figure 14-19 contains a flowchart that illustrates the relationships among the login script files.

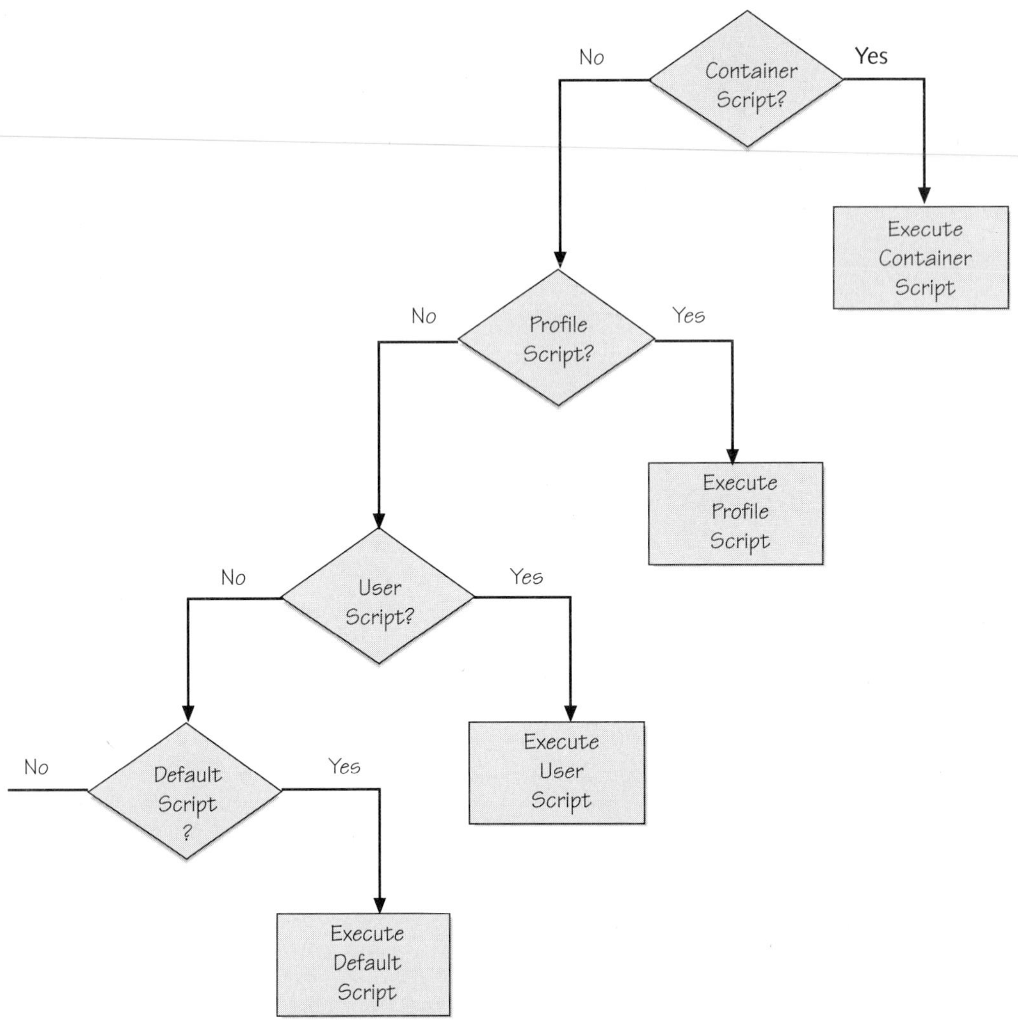

Figure 14-19 Login script files

Notice that once the login script for a container is created, its commands are performed for all users in that container when they log in. Once all commands in the container login script have been executed, NetWare will determine whether the user is assigned to a profile object. If the user object has a profile script defined, NetWare will execute the login script commands included in that profile script. Finally, NetWare will execute commands in either the user login script or the default login script.

To prevent default login script commands from being executed, you must either create a personal login script for each user that contains the EXIT command or include the NO_DEFAULT command in the container login script.

Container Login Scripts

As stated earlier, the container login script file applies to each user who is a member of that container. That is, the login script of a particular parent container will be executed whenever any User object "beneath" that container connects to the network. For example, in Figure 14-20, a container login script for the object CBE_LABS_Admin would apply whenever the User objects JCunningham or SLopez logged into the network.

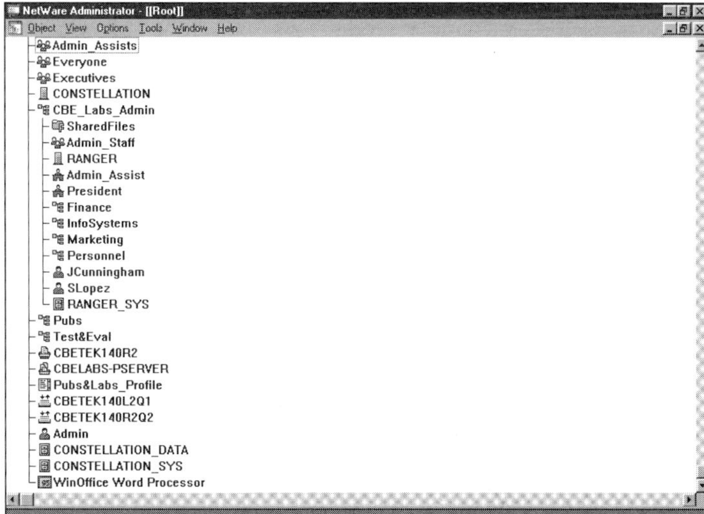

Figure 14-20 CBE Labs NDS tree

Note that a container login script applies only when that container is a direct parent of a User object. Again in Figure 14-20, a container login script in CBE_LABS would not apply to the User objects JCunningham or SLopez; only the container login script found in the direct parent of these users (in CBE_LABS_Admin) would be executed when they log in.

Although container login scripts are properties of container objects, the script itself is stored in the NDS.

The container login script should include all the necessary commands to set up a standard working environment for all the users in that container. It may include drive mappings, setting DOS environment variables, and any other commands that would apply to all users of the container.

Container login scripts in NetWare 4.1 replace System Login scripts found in the previous versions of NetWare.

Profile Login Scripts

Profile login scripts apply to a "group" of selected users. That is, a profile login script will enable you to create a set of login commands that will be executed only by certain selected users. Thus a profile login script lies between a container script (which applies to all users in a container) and a user login script (which applies to only one user).

The users who make up a "group" do not have to be part of a specific container or be located in a particular part of the NDS tree. Instead, a Profile object is created, and a login script for that Profile object is then entered. Then, the Profile Login Script is assigned to that user. Any user who is to be added to this "group" would simply be given Read property rights to the Profile object's Login Script property. Anytime they logged in, the Profile login script would then be executed.

Profile login scripts are intended for multiple users who are not all part of the same container object. In Figure 14-21, suppose that users DAuer, TSimpson, and MCiampa needed the same login script but SJohnson and SLopez needed a different login script. A Profile object can be created, and all users who need to have the same login script could be given Read Property rights to that object and have the Profile Login Script assigned to them. Then, anytime they logged in, the Profile's login script would be executed.

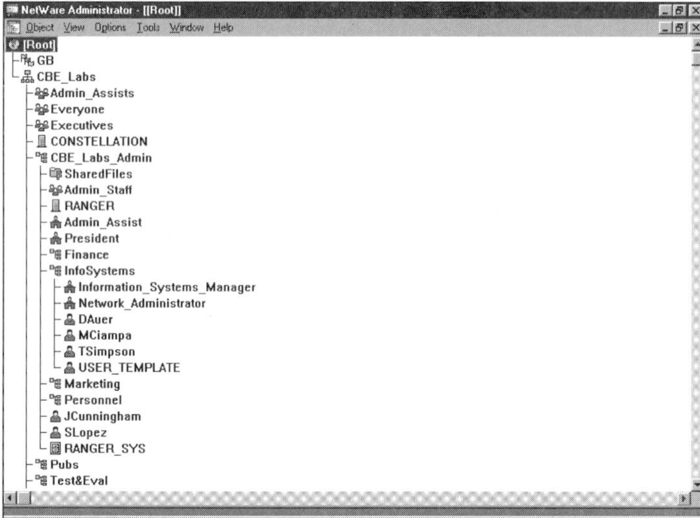

Figure 14-21 Profile login script users

User Login Script

User login scripts are for commands that apply to individual users. These scripts are located in the Login Script property of each User object. They contain such commands as special drive mappings or unique environment variables for a specific program that only that user would run.

However, user login scripts are strongly discouraged and are often used only as a last resort. They can become very difficult to maintain. Many network managers have spent untold hours trying to track down a network problem only to later discover that a user changed his or her login script, which created the problem. In addition, if a change takes place that affects all users, it is a very tedious task to individually change each user's login script.

To prevent users from modifying their own login scripts, remove the Write property right from the user's Login Script property.

Default Login Scripts

The final type of login script is the default login script. These commands, contained in the LOGIN.EXE program, are executed only if there is no container, profile, or user login script. The purpose of the default login script is to provide the user with the basic drive mappings.

Because the default login script is contained in LOGIN.EXE, it cannot be modified.

The commands that make up the default login script are as follows:

```
WRITE "Good %GREETING_TIME, %LOGIN_NAME"
MAP DISPLAY OFF
MAP ERRORS OFF
MAP *1:=SYS:
MAP INS S1:=SYS:PUBLIC
MAP INS S2:=S1:IBM_PC\MSDOS\%OS_VERSION
MAP DISPLAY ON
MAP
```

Once the network administrator has established a container login script that contains the basic drive mapping for the network, it is important to prevent the default login script from being executed. Failure to do this will cause drive mappings made in the system login script to be either overwritten or duplicated. There are three ways to stop the default login script from being executed:

1. Put the NO_DEFAULT statement in the container or profile login script.
2. Create a user login script that contains only the command EXIT.
3. Put the EXIT statement in the container login script. This will cause the LOGIN.EXE program to terminate and prevent the execution of a profile, user, or default script. However, this method has the drawback of preventing any profile login scripts from executing.

If you plan to implement user login scripts, remember that you must include a login script for each user, even if it contains only the EXIT command. Otherwise, the default login script will execute.

Planning Login Scripts

To design a login script system, you start by identifying a standard set of regular and search drive mappings that will be needed by all users to run software and access data in the network file system. Next, identify any special setup needs for each workgroup in the organization. Finally, identify any special setups that are unique for individual users.

If most of the user workstation setup needs are the same for groups of users (and they generally are), these can be met through the container and profile commands. If your network has many special or individualized setup requirements, you might try to determine if you want to create a container or profile login script that contains only the essential commands, such as mapping a search drive to SYS:PUBLIC. You would then implement user login scripts to handle the workstation setup for each individual user.

Just as network administrators differ in the ways they design a directory structure, they also implement login script systems differently, depending on their preferences and experience. The important thing is to develop a workable strategy that meets both the needs of your organization and your personal preferences.

WRITING A LOGIN SCRIPT

After you identify your login script needs and strategy, the next step is to write the necessary login script commands. You might find it helpful to use a login script worksheet, such as the one shown in Figure 14-22. The worksheet is divided into sections by REM statements that define the start of each section. The first part contains sections that are executed by all users. The Preliminary Commands section can contain any initializing commands. The command MAP DISPLAY OFF, for example, will prevent MAP commands from displaying results on the workstation and will clear the screen. The Preliminary Commands section can also be used to clear the screen and display a message greeting the user. The #C:COMMAND /C CLS command used in the example will clear the screen by running the CLS command from the DOS COMMAND.COM program located in the root of the local workstation's C drive. The #C: preceding the statement causes the login program to go to the root of the C drive to run the COMMAND.COM program. This means that the #C:COMMAND.COM /C CLS command will not work if the workstation does not boot off its local hard disk. If your network contains workstations that do not have hard drives, you will need to place the #COMMAND /C CLS command in the DOS Setup section of the script after a search drive to the correct DOS directory is mapped, as described below.

The DOS Setup section is used if you are planning to map a search drive to a network DOS directory and then set the workstation COMSPEC to that DOS directory. In addition, the DOS Setup section can contain the #COMMAND.COM /C CLS command as shown, along with any SET commands needed to store information in the workstation DOS environment space. In the example, SET commands are included to store such workstation information as username, and station address.

The Common Application Search Drive Mappings section contains the search drive mappings to DOS-based application packages that are to be accessed by all users. In the example login script in Figure 14-22, all CBE Lab users will be able to run the microcomputer applications.

Figure 14-22

Sample login script worksheet

```
REM Preliminary Commands
MAP DISPLAY OFF
#C:\COMMAND /C CLS
WRITE "Good %GREETING_TIME, %FULL_NAME"

REM DOS Setup
MAP INS S2:=SYS:PUBLIC\%MACHINE\%OS\%OS_VERSION
COMSPEC=S2:COMMAND.COM
DOS SET USERNAME = "%LOGIN_NAME"
DOS SET NODE="%P_STATION"

REM Common Application Search Drive Mappings
MAP INS S3:=CONSTELLATION/SYS:APPS\WINOFFICE
MAP INS S4:=CONSTELLATION/SYS:APPS\PAGEPUB

REM Common Regular Drive Mappings
MAP H:=CONSTELLATION/DATA:USERS\%LOGIN_NAME
MAP K:=CONSTELLATION/:DATA:SHARED

REM Mapping for Workgroup
IF MEMBER OF "MARKETING" THEN
      MAP ROOT L:=CONSTELLATION/DATA:MARKET
      #CAPTURE Q=MAREPS570R1Q1 TI=10 NB NT NFF F=3
END

IF MEMBER OF "FINANCE" THEN
      MAP ROOT L:=CONSTELLATION/DATA:FINANCE
      IF DAY_OF_WEEK = "Tuesday" AND HOUR24 < "09" THEN
            WRITE "Remember training at 8:30 AM"
            PAUSE
      END
END

REM End of Login Script Commands
DRIVE H:
MAP DISPLAY ON
EXIT
```

The second part of the login script worksheet contains sections for individual workgroups. These contain login script commands that are executed only for users who are members of the specified workgroup. The Common Regular Drive Mappings section contains drive pointers that will be available for all users. On many networks, for example, a drive pointer would be mapped to each NetWare volume as well as a possible drive mapping to the directory containing user menus. The Mapping for Workgroup section contains commands based on the workgroup of which the user is a member. In the example, the user who is a member of the marketing workgroup will have his or her home drive mapped to the directory and a CAPTURE command has been included to send printer output to the default marketing laser printer. Notice the # at the beginning of the CAPTURE command; it will cause the CAPTURE.EXE program to be run as an external command. A user who is a member of the finance workgroup will receive a drive pointer to the FINANCE directory.

The End of Login Script Commands section can contain any commands that all users will perform before they exit the login script. In the example, the DRIVE H: command will place all users in their home directory before turning the MAP display on and exiting from the system login script. Because the EXIT command was not included in the sample system login script, NetWare will next execute either the user or the default login script commands.

Entering Login Scripts

After you write and check the login script, the next step is to enter and test it. As a network administrator you will need to know how to use NetWare Administrator to create and maintain the three types of login scripts—container, profile, and user—over which you create the user's work environment (naturally you will not work with default login scripts).

Entering Container Login Scripts

To enter a container login script, follow these steps:

1. Launch NetWare Administrator.
2. Select the container for which you want to create the login script. In this example, you'll create a container login script for the CBE_LABS_Admin container, as shown in Figure 14-21.
3. Use the right mouse button to click **CBE_LABS_Admin** and select **Details** to display the Identification window, as shown in Figure 14-23.

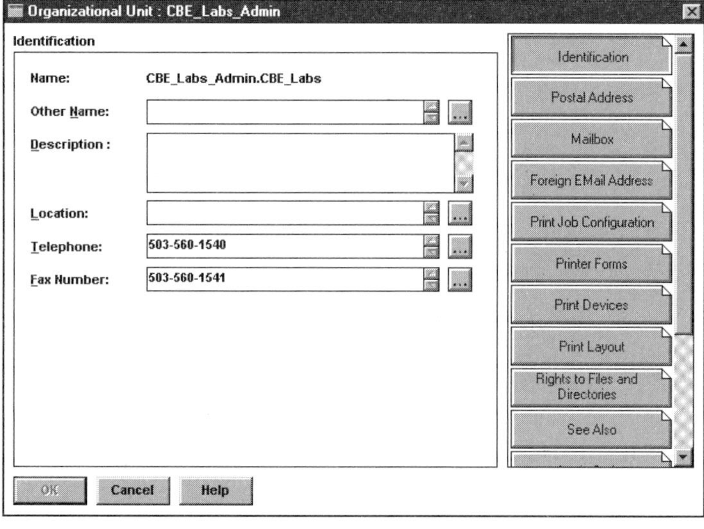

Figure 14-23 Identification window

4. Click **Login Script** to go to the Login Script window, as shown in Figure 14-24.

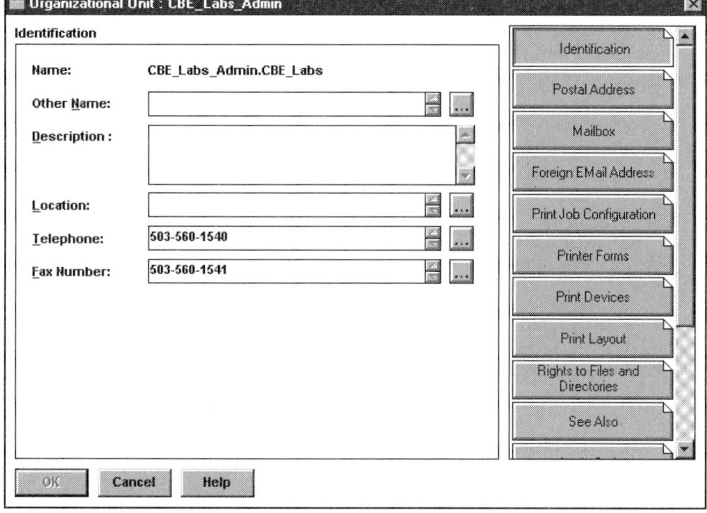

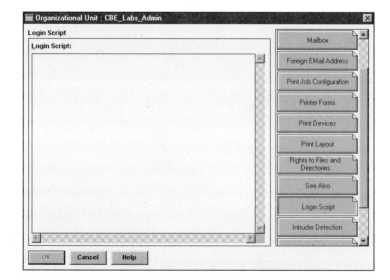

Figure 14-24 Login Script window

5. Type in your login script.
6. Click **OK** when finished to save the script and return to the browser window.

Entering Profile Login Scripts

Entering a profile login script first requires that you create a Profile object and then assign the users Read Property rights to the login script property. In this example you will create a profile that will contain the users SLopez and SJohnson.

1. Launch NetWare Administrator.
2. Locate the container under which you want to create the Profile object. In this example you'll create it under CBE_LABS_Admin.
3. Select **Create** from the Object menu, and the New Object list appears.
4. Select **Profile** from the New Object list. Click **OK**.
5. Enter the name of the Profile to be created. You'll use Group_1. Click **Create**.
6. Select **Details** from the Object menu to see the Profile window, as shown in Figure 14-25.
7. Select **Login Script** to see the Profile login script window.
8. Type in your profile login script and click **OK** to save the script and return to the browser window.
9. From the NDS tree, select the User object to which you want to assign the Profile script.
10. Select **Details** from the Object menu.
11. Select **Login Script**.
12. Enter the name of the Profile object in the Profile field.
13. Click **OK**.

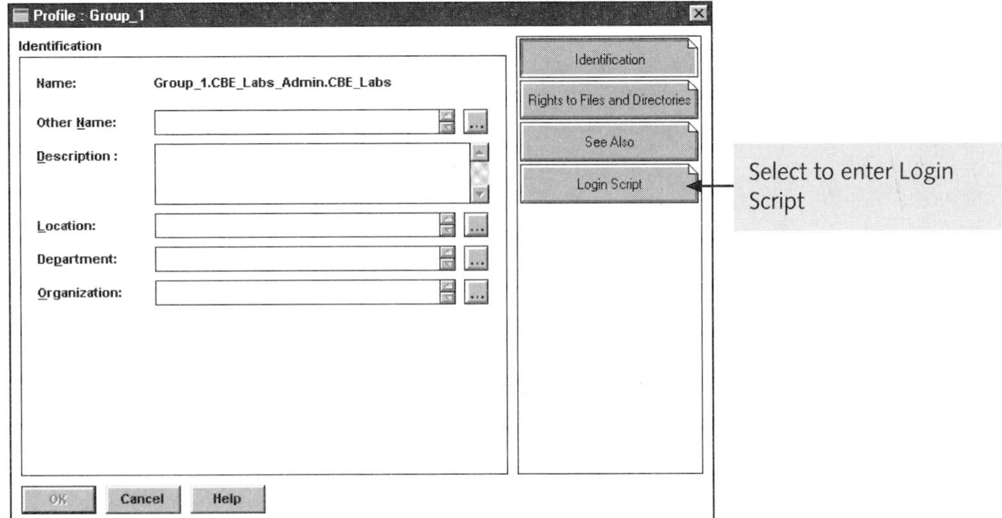

Figure 14-25 Profile window

Once the Profile object has been created and the login script entered, you assign the user to the profile script.

1. Locate the User object you want to assign to this Profile login script. In this example, you'll select SLopez.
2. Select **Details** from the Object menu.
3. Click **Login Script**, and the Login Script window appears, as shown in Figure 14-26.
4. Notice the Profile line beneath the area to key in the Login Script. Type in Group_1 (or click on the browse button and select the profile Group_1 from the tree).

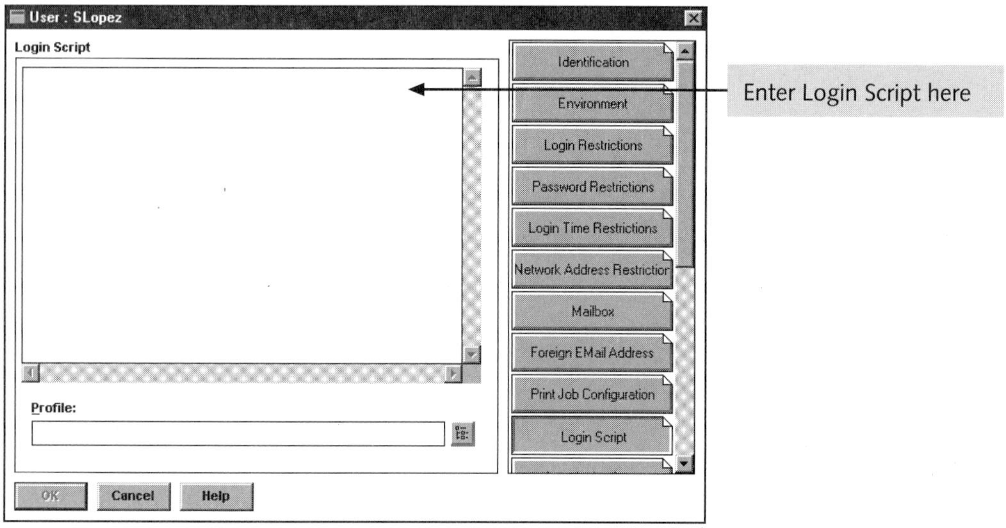

Figure 14-26 User Login Script window

The last step is to grant the user (SLopez) Read rights to the Profile object (Group_1).

1. Select the Profile object **Group_1.**
2. Select **Trustees** from the Object menu.
3. Click **Add Trustee** and indicate the user to add (SLopez).
4. Click **Selected Properties** and then select **Login Script**. Place a checkmark next to the Read property. Click **OK**.

Entering User Login Scripts

Entering a user login script requires only that you select that User object and type in the script.

1. Launch NetWare Administrator.
2. Select the user for whom you want to create the login script. In this example, you'll create a user login script for JCunningham.
3. Use the right mouse button to click **JCunningham** and select **Details** to display the Identification window.
4. Click **Login Script** to go to the Login Script window.
5. Type in your login script.
6. Click **OK** when finished to save the script and return to the browser window.

TESTING AND DEBUGGING LOGIN SCRIPTS

After the login scripts have been entered, you should test the login script system for at least one user in each workgroup by logging in with that user's name and checking to be sure that all commands are executed properly. If your system login script does not use the EXIT command, it is important to prevent the default login script commands from being executed before you test the login script files. This is done, as described previously, by placing the EXIT statement in each user's login script.

To test login scripts, you will need to log in with a username from each workgroup you have defined. After logging in, determine whether all commands are being executed properly by first looking for any error messages on the screen. Next, use the MAP command to determine whether all drives have been properly mapped for this user. If your login script sets a default print queue, display and check the status of the capture command to be sure it is directed to the correct print queue.

If you should get a "Bad Command or File Name" message and you cannot execute the MAP commands, then either the user does not have a drive mapping to SYS:PUBLIC or else the user does not have rights to the SYS:PUBLIC directory. To determine which of these problems exists, first try changing to the PUBLIC directory by entering the command **CD SYS:PUBLIC**. After changing to the PUBLIC directory, you can use the MAP command to determine what drives are currently mapped. You will often be able to determine from the drive mapping information whether the user login script or AUTOEXEC.BAT file has overwritten the mapping to the SYS:PUBLIC directory. If the search mapping for the PUBLIC directory has been overwritten, the drive letter, usually Z, will appear with the regular drive mappings. Search drives can be overwritten by the user login script containing MAP S#:=[path] commands or by a DOS PATH statement in an AUTOEXEC.BAT file following the LOGIN command.

If no drive mapping to the SYS:PUBLIC directory exists, you need to determine whether the user has rights to the SYS:PUBLIC directory by using the **CD SYS:PUBLIC** command to change the default path to the PUBLIC directory. If you cannot change to the PUBLIC directory, then the user must not have Read and File Scan rights to SYS:PUBLIC. The most common reason for a user not having access rights to SYS:PUBLIC is that the default server the user is attached to does not exist in their container. You can correct this problem by using NetWare Administrator to make the user's parent container a trustee of SYS:PUBLIC.

If the MAP command contains duplicated drive mappings to the SYS:PUBLIC directory, the most likely problem is that the default login script is causing a second drive mapping to be made. You can correct this problem by adding NO_DEFAULT to the user's container login script.

When all login scripts have been debugged, you should document drive mappings and other special setup commands that are performed for each workgroup or user. Because users will need to know certain drive mappings in order to access data and applications through the network file system effectively, it is also important that you provide users with the necessary documentation or training they will need to use the workstation environment provided by the login script. The time spent in documenting and training users in the use of the system will pay off later in fewer problems and support calls.

After you have determined that all users can log in successfully and have their necessary workstation environments established, you are ready to proceed with the final step of automating the user environment—establishing menus, as described in Chapter 15.

CHAPTER SUMMARY

Establishing a workstation environment that makes the network easy to use is an important responsibility of the network administrator. NetWare provides a powerful way to automate workstation activities through login scripts. NetWare login script files contain commands that provide drive mappings and other workstation setup functions that are executed during the login process. The login script commands provided by Novell can be used to map drive letters, set the DOS environment of a workstation, display messages and files, execute other programs, and execute certain commands based on whether a given condition is true or false. Using login script variables with commands enables you to create general-purpose login scripts that work for multiple users. Login script variables can be divided into several types, including date variables such as DAY_OF_WEEK, time variables such as HOUR24, user variables such as LOGIN_NAME, and workstation variables such as OS and OS_VERSION. An example of a login script command with a variable mapping a drive pointer to the home directory of each user is MAP ROOT H:=DATA:USERS\%LOGIN_NAME. The percent sign in front of a variable name tells NetWare to substitute the value of the variable into the login script command when it is executed.

Four types of NetWare login script files can be executed by the LOGIN.EXE program: the container login script, the profile login script, the user login script, and the default login script. The container login script is executed for all users of that container when they first log in. After the container login script is executed, the login script processor will look for a profile login script. A profile login script enables users scattered across the tree to be considered as one group. If no profile login script exists, LOGIN.EXE looks for the existence of a user login script. If no user login script file exists, the login script processor will execute the default login script commands stored in the LOGIN.EXE program. Most login script commands should be stored, whenever possible, in the container login script. By including the EXIT command in the container login script, you can prevent NetWare from executing the user or default login script statements. If you do not place an EXIT command at the end of the container login script, it is very important to create a user login script for each user, even if it contains only an EXIT statement. Creating a login script for each user prevents the default login script from being run and provides additional security.

NetWare Administrator is used to create and maintain the three types of login scripts—container, profile, and user—over which you create the user's work environment (naturally you will not work with default login scripts).

COMMAND SUMMARY

Command	Syntax	Definition
#	*#[path]filename[parameter]*	Executes the specified DOS program and returns control back to the login script program. The LOGIN.EXE program remains in memory while the requested program is being run.

BREAK	*BREAK ON/OFF*	The BREAK ON command enables the user to use the [Ctrl][Break] key combination to terminate processing of the login script commands. By default, BREAK OFF prevents the user from halting the login script process.
COMSPEC	*COMSPEC [path] filename*	Specifies the directory path and filename DOS uses to reload the command processor.
DISPLAY	*DISPLAY [path] filename*	Types the contents of the specified [path] filename to the screen. If the filename specified is not in the current directory or search drive, include the full NetWare path to the specified filename. The DISPLAY command shows all characters in the file, including tabs and other printer control characters. (See FDISPLAY.)
DOS SET	*DOS SET variable="value"*	Enables you to place a value in the DOS environment space using the specified variable name.
DRIVE	*DRIVE [drive:]*	Sets the specified drive letter as the default DOS drive. Unless you specify this command, the default drive will be set to the first network drive letter, usually F.
EXIT	*EXIT "command-line"*	Ends the login script processing and exits.
FDISPLAY	*FDISPLAY [path] filename*	Like the DISPLAY command, except that the FDISPLAY command filters out any tab or printer control characters, making files that contain these control characters more readable.
FIRE	*FIRE FIRE [PHASERS] n [TIMES]*	Produces a phaser sound on the PC speaker the number of times specified, up to nine.
GOTO	*GOTO label*	Transfers control to the specified label. A label is a single left-aligned word ending in a colon.
IF...THEN	*IF condition(s) THEN command*	The IF statement enables you to specify commands to be executed only when the specified condition is true. Commands following the ELSE statement will be executed if the condition is false. Each IF statement must conclude with an END statement and can contain up to 10 additional nested IF statements.

INCLUDE	*INCLUDE [path] filename*	Causes the login processor to obtain commands from the file specified. If the file is not in the current directory or search drive, you need to specify the complete NetWare path leading to the desired file.
MAP	*MAP [option] [drive:=path]*	Creates both regular and search drive mappings from the login script. The path statement can contain identifier variables preceded by percent signs, e.g., %MACHINE, %OS, %OS_VERSION, %LOGIN_NAME. Special MAP commands include MAP DISPLAY OFF/ON, and MAP ERRORS OFF/ON.
PAUSE	*PAUSE*	Suspends login script processing.
REM	*REM[ARK] [text]*	Enables comments to be placed in login script files.
WRITE	*WRITE "text"*	Displays the message string enclosed in quotation marks on the console. Special control codes, such as /r for a new line, along with identifier variables preceded by percent signs, can be included within the quotation marks.

KEY TERMS

container login script
date variables
default login script
login script
login script variable
nesting
network variables
profile login script
syntax
time variables
user login script
user variables
workstation variables

REVIEW QUESTIONS

1. In the space below, briefly describe the importance of login scripts to a DOS-based workstation.

2. The COMSPEC command would most likely be found in the _______________ login script file.

3. The _______________ command is used to write the contents of an ASCII text file to the display screen.

4. The ________________ command enables you to execute login script statements contained in a specified ASCII text file.

5. The ________________ command is used to display a brief message on the screen.

6. The ________________ login script is executed before the profile login script.

7. The default login script is executed if ________________________________.

8. Suppose you notice that a user has two drive mappings to the SYS:PUBLIC directory. In the space below, explain the most likely reason for this problem.

9. On the lines below, list two ways you can prevent the default login script commands from being executed.

____

____

10. The ________________ utility is used to create and maintain the login scripts.

11. The ________________ command is most often found in user login scripts because it can be used to link the user to his or her menu.

12. Suppose the first network drive on your workstation is L. What drive letter would the login script command MAP *3:=DATA: use to access the DATA: volume?

13. On the line below, write a login script command that will display a welcome message containing today's date, including the name of the day, the month, the day, and the year.

____

14. On the line below, write a condition that can be used to determine if a user is logging in on the third day of the week.

____

15. On the line below, write a MAP command that uses identifier variables to map H as a root drive pointer to the user's home directory located in the DATA:USERS directory path.

____

16. On the line below, write a search mapping to the SYS:PUBLIC directory and appropriate DOS version assuming the directory structure shown below:

____

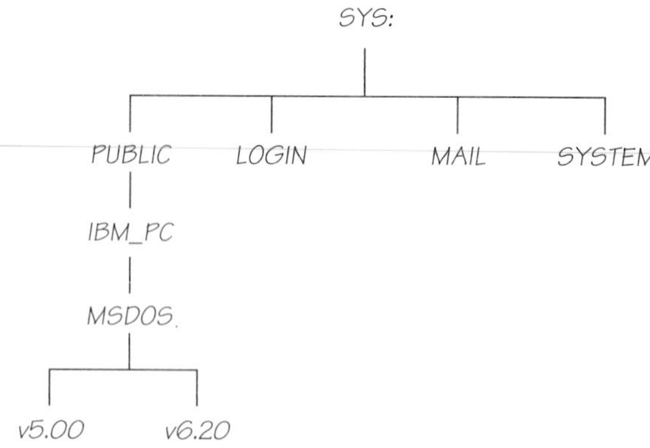

17. On the line below, write a login script command to redirect output from the LPT1 printer port to the SAL_HP3_R3_Q1 print queue with a timeout of 5 seconds, no banner, no tabs, and no form feed.

____

18. The ______________ login script command can be used to change to the user's home directory on drive H.

19. Will executing the EXIT command from the container login script prevent the default login script commands from being executed when a user has no user login script file?

20. Assume the home directories for the sales department are stored in the DATA:SALES\USERS directory. On the line below, write an IF statement for the container login script that will map H as a root drive to the correct home directory path for each sales department user.

____

Identify and correct any errors in each of the following login script commands:

21. TURN MAP DISPLAY OFF

____

22. MAP S2=SYS\PUBLIC\%MACHINE\%OS\%OSVERSION

____

23. COMSPEC=S2:\COMMAND.COM

____

24. CAPTURE Q=FINHP3SIR0Q1 TI=5 NT NB NFF

____

25. WRITE "Good %Greeting_Time," %Login_name

____

EXERCISES

EXERCISE 14-1: DOCUMENTING THE CONTAINER LOGIN SCRIPT ON YOUR FILE SERVER

In this exercise you demonstrate your knowledge of login script commands by examining the container login script on your file server and explaining the purpose of each of its commands.

1. Log into the file server using your assigned student username.
2. View the container, profile, and user login scripts with NetWare Administrator and record the scripts.
3. Next to each login script command, briefly describe the command's function in the login script.

EXERCISE 14-2: PRACTICING WITH LOGIN SCRIPT COMMANDS

In this exercise you practice writing and testing several login script commands by creating a practice user and then providing that user with a user login script.

1. Log in using your assigned student username.
2. Open a DOS session window.
3. Use the LISTDIR /S command to document the DOS directory structure on your assigned file server.
4. Create a new user named ##USER, where ## represents your assigned student number.
5. Change to your ##ADMIN directory and create a subdirectory called WORK. Grant the new user Read, File Scan, Write, Create, and Delete rights to your ##ADMIN\WORK directory.
6. Enter all the required drive mappings along with the COMSPEC statement that will enable this user to execute NetWare utilities and DOS external commands.
7. Log out and test the login script you have created by logging in as ##USER.
8. Log in using your assigned student username and add the following login commands to the user login script for ##USER:

   Write the necessary command to display the daily message file based on the day of the week. For example, on Monday the login script should display a message called MONDAY.MSG, on Tuesday display TUESDAY.MSG, and so on. Record the command on the line below.

   ____

   Write a command to redirect printer output from LPT1 to any print queue on the file server with a timeout of 7 seconds, a banner containing your name, no tabs, and a form feed. Your instructor will provide you with the names of print queues on the file server that you can access. Record the command on the line below.

   ____

Assume the user's birthday is today and include an IF statement that will display a short "Happy Birthday" message along with phaser fire on today's date. Record the IF command on the lines below.

Write a command to map a root drive to your \##ADMIN\WORK directory. Record the command on the line below.

At the end of the user login script, write an EXIT command to run the SESSION program. Record the EXIT command on the line below.

---

9. Test the login script you have created by logging in as ##USER.
10. Enter the MAP command to check the drive mappings.
11. Enter the CAPTURE command to check your default capture status.
12. Print a hard copy of the login script to be checked by your instructor.

EXERCISES

CASE 14-1: DESIGNING A CONTAINER LOGIN SCRIPT FOR J.Q. ADAMS

In this exercise you will write a container login script for the J. Q. Adams Corporation. Because you don't have the J. Q. Adams network available, you'll use DS Standard to create the scripts.

Create a container login script to perform the following functions:

- Create a drive mapping to each volume on the JQA_Server01 NetWare server.
- Include a search drive mapping to the WP and SS subdirectories of WinOffice for all users.
- Production department users should have a drive mapped to the InvTrack Itdata subdirectory and a root drive mapping to InvTrack subdirectory.
- All in Sales and Marketing should have access to the SMHP5Q1 print queue.
- Save the user's login name in the DOS environment for later use of the menu system.
- Before noon on Mondays, a message should be displayed for all Production department users reminding them of the weekly meeting in conference room 210A.

Turn in a copy of your data disk to your instructor.

NORTHWESTERN TECHNICAL COLLEGE

Now that the network printing environment has been established and the software packages are installed, the Northwestern Technical College staff is eager to begin using the network. Before the users can begin to take advantage of the network's capability, however, it is necessary for you to automate the network login process by planning and implementing a login script system that will provide easy and standardized access to network resources.

PROJECT 14-1: DEFINING THE CONTAINER LOGIN SCRIPT

You will write login scripts for three of the four major groups: support services, student services, and faculty. In this problem you will write the container login script along with any user login script commands. Dave Johnson would like to avoid user login script commands, if possible. He would rather place most or all of the login script processing in the container login script.

Support Services

The support staff will have the following login script requirements:

- Search drives to all the NWTC_SERVER02_SYS:APPS.NTC software subdirectories.
- A root drive pointer to the users' home directories.
- A root drive pointer to the shared work area that enables users to access the MENUS and CLASSES directories easily.
- Drive pointers and SET commands to run the database software in the SQLDBMS directory. (The database software requires each user to have a separate configuration file stored in the directory path specified during software installation. To create a unique file for each user, Dave Johnson recommends that you use a SET command to store the contents of the LOGIN_NAME variable in the DOS environment space using the variable name specified in the software documentation.)
- By default, support services' printer output sent to the LPT1 port should be redirected to the laser print queue.
- A message that is displayed when support services staff log in during the first week of a month. The message is a reminder that there is a meeting agenda due by the end of that week.

Student Services

Users in the student services department have the following login script requirements:

- Search drives to all the NWTC_SERVER02_SYS:APPS.NTC software subdirectories
- A root drive pointer to users' home directories.
- A root drive pointer to the student services shared work area.
- Default printer redirection to the student services laser printer.

Faculty

In addition to needing search drives to run the application software, faculty users will need the following drive mappings and special commands:

- A root drive mapping to users' home directories.
- A root drive mapping to the shared faculty work area.
- A root drive mapping to the support services faculty work area.
- Default printer redirection to the support services laser printer.
- A reminder message that there is a faculty meeting at 11:30 A.M. on the first Thursday of each month.

Project 14-2: Testing and Documenting Your System

1. Test the container login script by logging in as one user from each of the groups and use the MAP command to check the users' drive mappings.
2. Print the screen that shows the drive mappings of each of the following groups:
   - Student services
   - Support services
   - Faculty

Once the login scripts have been tested, Dave Johnson would like you to prepare instructions for each user informing them how to use the drive pointers you have established for their departments. These instructions should take the form of a memo. The memo should also request the scheduling of a meeting in which you will provide staff training after the menus have been implemented. Use a word processing package to develop and print the memo.

CHAPTER FIFTEEN

THE MENU SYSTEM

Graphical user interfaces, such as Microsoft Windows 95 or IBM OS/2, are rapidly becoming the standard user environment. However, there are still many DOS-based applications and workstations. These systems can benefit from a menu system that enables the users to select the commands that they want to perform from of a list of choices, called a **menu**, instead of keying in lengthy statements. The menu system provides an easy environment in which users can easily access their applications.

AFTER READING THIS CHAPTER AND COMPLETING THE EXERCISES YOU WILL BE ABLE TO:

- IDENTIFY THE COMPONENTS OF THE NETWARE MENU SYSTEM.
- DESIGN AND CREATE MENUS AND SUBMENUS.
- DESCRIBE TWO ALTERNATE METHODS TO RUN THE MENU SYSTEM.
- ASSIGN THE ACCESS RIGHTS NECESSARY FOR MULTIPLE USERS TO RUN NETWARE MENUS.
- DESIGN AND IMPLEMENT A NETWARE MENU SYSTEM FOR AN ORGANIZATION.

A menu system is one popular kind of user interface that works well with DOS-based applications. It provides users with option lists arranged in main menus and optional submenus, as shown in Figure 15-1.

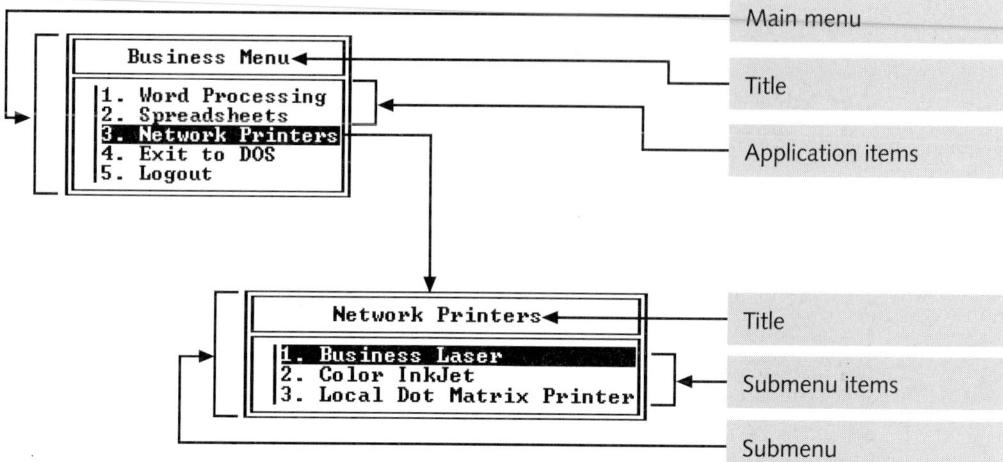

Figure 15-1 Sample menu system

The main menu, called "Business Menu," contains the major options to which the user needs quick access. To run the word processing software, for example, the user simply selects option number 1. This can be done by either pressing [1] or by using the arrow keys to highlight the choice and then pressing [Enter]. Selecting an option in the main menu may invoke submenus that contain additional options. In this example, when the Network Printers option is selected, it calls up the Network Printers submenu, which in turn offers three choices.

Prior to NetWare 3.12, Novell had developed its own menu system. The Novell menu system, while simple to use, lacked some of the features found in other popular DOS-based menu systems. With the introduction of NetWare 3.12, however, a new menu system based on the Saber menu system, a popular third-party DOS-based menu system used on many computer systems, was introduced.

Figure 15-2 shows the menu command statements that produce the menu shown in Figure 15-1. Each menu starts with a MENU statement, indicating its title and the number that is used to access it. In this example the MENU statement defines the menu number as 01 and names it "Business Menu." This name will be the title of the menu. An ITEM statement defines the text that will be displayed for each menu option. "ITEM ^1Word Processing" will cause "Word Processing" to be displayed as the first choice. The ITEM statement, which can include an optional caret symbol (^) followed by a digit or letter, causes the menu system to display that character prior to the menu option. The "^1" preceding the "Word Processing" option, for example, will cause a 1 to appear before the option name.

Figure 15-2

Sample menu command statements

```
MENU 01, Business Menu
ITEM  ^1Word Processing {chdir}
       EXEC WP
ITEM ^2Spreadsheets
       EXEC SP
ITEM ^3Network Printers
       SHOW 02
ITEM ^4Exit to DOS
       EXEC EXIT
ITEM ^5Logout
       EXEC LOGOUT
MENU 02, Network Printers
ITEM ^1Business Laser
       EXEC CAPTURE Q=BUS_HP3_RO TI=5 NB NT NFF
       PAUSE
ITEM ^2Color InkJet
       EXEC CAPTURE Q=SERV_BJ200_L1 TI=10 NB NT NFF
       PAUSE
ITEM ^3Local Dot Matrix Printer
       EXEC CAPTURE/EC
       PAUSE
```

The EXEC statements contain DOS-executable commands that will be processed when a user selects an option. Inclusion of the CHDIR parameter enclosed in braces {} tells the menu system to return to the directory from which it was launched after completion of the option. Thus, when the word processing program ends, the menu system automatically returns to the default menu directory.

Because there are multiple printer selection possibilities, option 3, Network Printers, contains the SHOW command, which then displays menu 02, Network Printers. The Logout option enables the user to log out from the network and end the menu program. The Exit to DOS option enables users to quit the menu system and return to the DOS prompt. If you want to prevent users from exiting the menu system, you can omit the Exit to DOS option.

The second MENU statement in Figure 15-2 defines menu number 02 as the Network Printers menu. Each ITEM statement of menu 02 invokes a CAPTURE command to redirect printer output to the desired print queue. Notice the use of the PAUSE parameter following the ITEM statements. The PAUSE option causes the menu system to pause after it executes the CAPTURE command and ask the user to press any key to continue. This provides the user with an opportunity to view the results of the command and report any problems. Pressing [Esc] will exit the Network Printers menu and return to the Business Menu.

The NetWare menu system's menus have the look and feel of a NetWare menu utility, like PCONSOLE, which links them smoothly to the NetWare menu utilities. As a network adnimistrator you will be required to know how to use NetWare's menu system to create, maintain, and debug network menus. In this chapter you will learn about the NetWare menu system and how to create and maintain NetWare menus.

MENU SYSTEM COMPONENTS

In order to develop and implement the NetWare menu system on your network, you first need to be familiar with the components of the menu system and how they work together. Figure 15-3 illustrates the NetWare menu system.

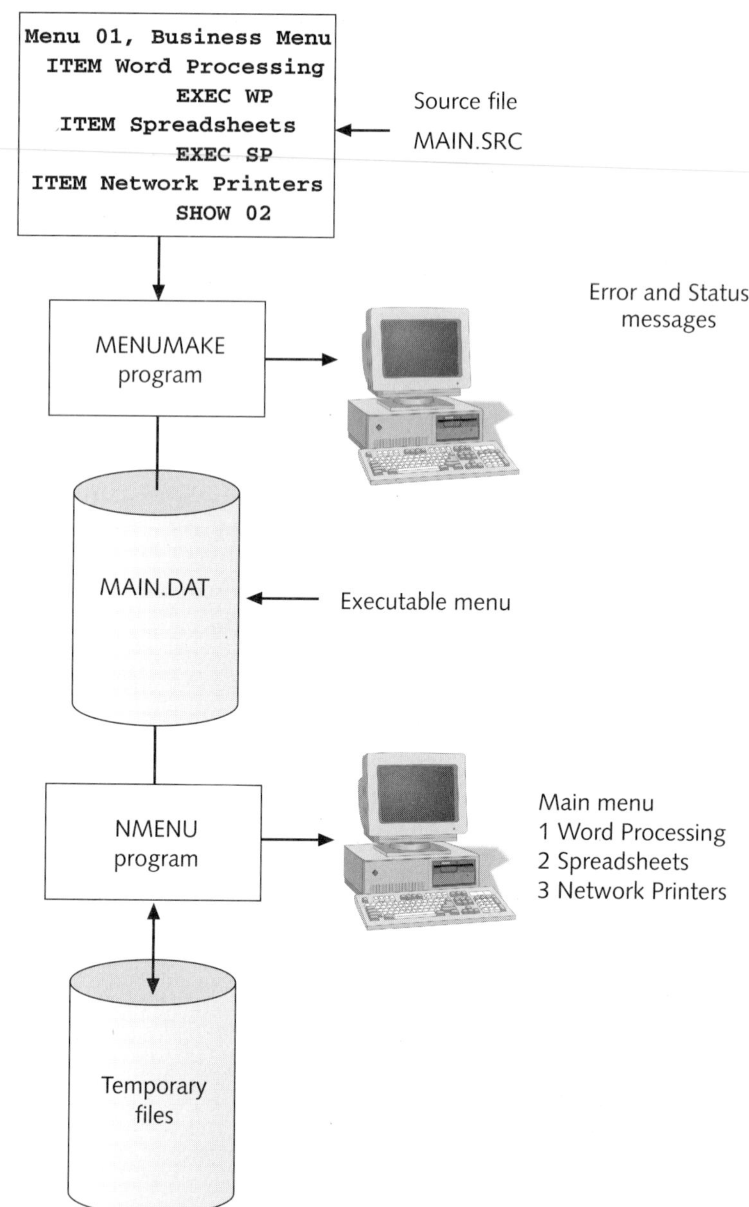

Figure 15-3 NetWare menu system components

The source file contains valid menu command statements, such as the MENU, ITEM, and EXEC statements mentioned earlier. Because this file is in ASCII format, a standard text editor program can be used to create and edit the contents of the source file. The MENUMAKE program translates the source statements into an executable menu file. As it creates the executable file, the MENUMAKE program checks each command for any syntax errors. If errors are discovered, the executable file will not be created, and a list of invalid menu command statements will be displayed. When no errors are detected, the MENUMAKE program creates a new executable menu file, with the extension .DAT, that contains the executable menu. Because this file is in a non-ASCII format, its contents cannot be viewed or changed with a text editor program. After the executable menu file is created, the NMENU program runs the executable file and displays the menu options on the user's workstation.

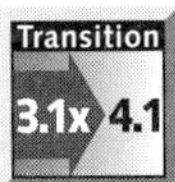

The MENUCNVT program can be used to convert a menu file created with the older NetWare menu system to be used with NetWare v4.1. The command is MENUCNVT *oldmenu*. The MENUCNVT program reads the old menu file and creates a file containing the new menu commands. The MENUMAKE command then must be used to compile the converted menu to an executable menu file.

CREATING A MENU SYSTEM

A good menu system should be secure and easy to understand and should provide users with the options they need to do their jobs. In order to meet these requirements, a network administrator needs to take care in planning what menus need to be created and how the menu system will be run. Only then can the network administrator proceed to create and test the menu command files. In this section you will learn how to plan a complete menu system. You will follow the creation of a sample menu system for CBE Labs. The process entails the following five steps:

1. Design the menu files.
2. Write, compile, and test the menu.
3. Plan the location of the menu files.
4. Provide access rights to users.
5. Modify the login scripts as necessary.

DESIGNING THE MENU FILES

The first step in designing and writing the menu command files is determining what applications and system functions need to be included on each user or workgroup menu and what commands are necessary to start and run each of the menu items. In most cases, a common menu can be designed for all workgroups or departments, even though some items on the menu might not be applicable to all users. Another option is having a separate menu for each user, which, of course, makes maintaining the menu system much more difficult because changing an item common to all menus means changing and compiling several menu command files.

A technique that saves time in writing and maintaining the menu system is identifying functions that are common to all menus and placing them in separate submenu files. By placing common commands in separate submenus, you can easily include these commands in each department's main menu simply by including an option that uses the SHOW command to access the desired submenu. For example, assume that users in CBE Labs' finance department need to run common applications (word processing, spreadsheet, payroll, and accounting applications) as well as send output to the laser, color ink jet, or dot-matrix printer attached to their local workstations. Finance department users, like all users in the company, need to be able to perform certain network functions such as changing their passwords, working with drive mappings, and sending messages.

Figure 15-4 illustrates the use of the menu design form to define the menus and submenus that will meet the needs of CBE Labs' finance department. The Network Functions submenu contains options, such as changing password and drive mappings, that can be used by all departments. Placing these functions in a menu file and making a separate executable menu allows access to these functions from any department menu, as described later in this section.

Figure 15-4

CBE Labs' finance department menu design

Main Menu

Title: Finance Menu

Number: 01

Option	Description	Command
1	Word Processing	WP
2	Spreadsheet	SP
3	Accounting	L: CD\ACCT GL
4	Payroll	L: CD\Payroll Pay
5	Network Printers	Submenu
6	Network Functions	Submenu
X	Exit to DOS	Exit DOS
L	Logout	Logout

Submenu Name: Network Printers
Submenu Number: 02

Option	Description	Command
1	Finance Laser	Capture Q=FINHP3RO
2	Color Ink-Jet	Capture Q=CBETEK140R2Q2
3	Local Printer	Capture/EC

Submenu Name: Network Functions
Submenu Number: 03

Option	Description	Command
1	Change Password	SETPASS
2	Drive Mappings	SESSION
3	Send Message	SEND
4	Work with Print Jobs	PCONSOLE

In the example shown in Figure 15-4, the payroll application option will appear on the menu for all the finance department users. Only specified users, however, will be assigned the rights necessary to run the payroll application. If the user does not have these rights and selects the payroll option, NetWare displays an error message indicating that access is denied. At CBE Labs, all accounting applications are stored on the NetWare server RANGER.

To restrict all other users besides the finance department from accessing the payroll application and data, the Admin user can create a Payroll group and grant it administrative rights to the NetWare server object RANGER and the volume RANGER_SYS. Then the workgroup can create an Inherited Rights Filter (IRF) that blocks all other objects that are higher in the tree—including the Admin user—from inheriting access to these objects.

WRITING MENUS

After you have determined what options you will need for each menu and submenu, the next step is to write the commands necessary to produce each department's menu and then use a text editor that creates an ASCII document to enter them into the appropriate source files. **Source menu files** consist of a combination of organizational and control commands. **Organizational commands** establish the content and organization of the menus the user sees on the screen; **control commands** tell the NMENU program how to perform an action, such as running a DOS command, starting an application, or linking to a submenu.

Figure 15-5 provides an overview of both organizational and control commands. As a network administrator, you need to be familiar with these commands. Keep the following guidelines in mind when you create the source command files:

- The maximum number of menu levels is 11: one main menu followed by 10 submenu levels.
- The maximum number of menu screens is 255.
- The maximum length of a menu name is 40 characters.
- The maximum width of an ITEM line is 40 characters.
- The maximum text file width is 80 characters. If a command wraps to another line, place a plus sign (+) at the end of the line and continue the command on the next line.
- The main menu must be at the beginning of the source file. The main menu then calls up any submenus by menu number.

Figure 15-5

Netware menu command table

Command	Command Type	Description
MENU	Organizational	Marks the beginning of a new menu or submenu screen.
ITEM	Organizational	Identifies a menu option to be included in the menu defined by the preceeding MENU statement.
EXEC	Control	Instructs DOS to execute the command following the EXEC statement.
LOAD	Control	Displays a separate executable menu file as a submenu.
SHOW	Control	Displays a submenu included in the current menu file.
GETO	Control	Requests optional input from the user prior to executing the next statement in ITEM.
GETR	Control	Requests required input from the user prior to executing the next statement in ITEM.
GETP	Control	Requests input from the user and then stores the input in parameter variables. The first input is stored in parameter %1, the next in %2, etc.

The MENU Statement

A title and number must be assigned to each menu and submenu that is identified on the menu design form. Use the MENU *number, title* statement to define each menu and submenu. The menu number can be any unique number ranging from 1 to 255 that does not already exist in this menu file. The *number* is used with the SHOW command to call up a submenu. Menu numbers do not need to be in sequence. The first menu in the source file becomes the main menu regardless of its menu number. The *title* is the title of the menu that will be displayed above the menu box. The menu title (up to 40 characters) should describe the menu. Figure 15-6 shows the menu statements that correspond to the menu plan shown in Figure 15-4.

Figure 15-6

Sample MENU statements

```
MENU 01,Finance Menu

MENU 02,Network Printers

MENU 03,Network Functions
```

The ITEM Statement

Every MENU statement must be followed by two or more ITEM statements to define each option that will be displayed in that menu. The ITEM *name [{option}]* statement defines each option that will be a part of the menu defined by the preceding MENU statement. The *name* parameter contains the descriptive name for the menu item that you want displayed in the menu box. A name can consist of up to 40 characters and should identify the option's function to the user. Menu items are displayed on the menu in the order in which you enter them in the source file. The NMENU program automatically places a letter, starting with A, before each item name in a menu. If you want to use your own number or character to mark an item, include in the *name* parameter a caret symbol (^) and the number or letter you want to use. If you do assign an item letter or number, you must do so to the rest of the items on the same menu. If you do not, NetWare will assign its default letter sequence, which might duplicate a letter you have chosen. The following ITEM command, for example, marks the menu's exit option with the letter X:

```
ITEM ^XExit the Menu
```

The ITEM command not only identifies a menu option but can include the options CHDIR, BATCH, PAUSE, or SHOW. These options must be enclosed in braces. The {CHDIR} option, for example, changes the drive and directory back to the path that was in use before the commands contained in the associated ITEM statement were executed. Without this option, the most recent drive and directory used by the application will remain in effect, possibly causing errors in the menu program. It is generally a good practice to include a {CHDIR} option with each menu item that will run an application program. The {CHDIR} option ensures that the menu system will return to the starting directory prior to ending the menu item.

The {BATCH} option removes the menu program from memory before the commands contained in the option are executed. Without this option, a portion of memory is reserved for the menu software (approximately 32 KB), which reduces the amount of memory available to the application software. Because the BATCH option automatically includes the CHDIR option, it is unnecessary to place both BATCH and CHDIR in the same ITEM statement.

The {PAUSE} option causes the menu program to stop and display the message "Press any key to continue" after the commands in this item are executed. Use this option to give the user time to view the message or results displayed by the commands in the menu item. The following example shows a {PAUSE} option used after a menu item to display the list of files:

```
ITEM Display Files {PAUSE}

EXEC NDIR
```

The {SHOW} option displays each EXEC command performed in ITEM. The {SHOW} option is useful during testing of the menu. Two or more options can be combined in one ITEM statement by placing both options inside the braces separated by spaces. If you want to include both the SHOW and CHDIR options with the word processing option, you could use the following sample ITEM statement:

```
ITEM Word Processing {CHDIR SHOW}
```

The EXEC Statement

EXEC statements must follow an ITEM statement. They start applications or execute DOS NetWare commands and can also perform special menu functions. Figure 15-7 lists the EXEC commands.

Figure 15-7

Special EXEC commands

Command	Description
EXEC EXIT	Exits the menu program and returns to the DOS prompt. Users cannot exit the menu system and return to the DOS prompt unless this command is included in one of the menu items. EXIT must be typed in uppercase letters.
EXEC CALL *batch_file*	Runs a batch file from the menu program and returns control to the following statement upon completion of the DOS batch file.
EXEC DOS	Runs the DOS command processor (COMMAND.COM) providing the user with a DOS prompt. The menu user can type EXIT at the DOS prompt to return to the menu system. DOS must be in uppercase.
EXEC LOGOUT	Ends a session by logging out of all file servers and exiting the menu system.

The SHOW Statement

The SHOW statement is used to access a submenu located in the current menu file using the number parameter defined in the MENU command of the desired submenu. Notice that the SHOW command requires the use of the menu's assigned number, not the menu's title.

Figure 15-8 illustrates the ITEM, EXEC, and SHOW commands that will perform the processing required by the options in the CBE Labs finance department main menu. Notice the use of the multiple EXEC statements following the accounting and payroll applications. The first EXEC statement changes the default drive to drive letter L; the second EXEC statement changes to the directory containing the appropriate business application. This requires that the users in the business department have a drive letter L mapped as a root drive to the business directory structure, which contains the general ledger and payroll software directories. The Exit to DOS option has been included to enable more convenient testing and debugging of the business menu. After the menu is operational, this option will be removed to prevent users from accidentally exiting the menu system.

Figure 15-8

Sample finance menu statements

```
MENU 01,Finance Menu
ITEM ^1Word Processing {BATCH}
     EXEC WP
ITEM ^2Spreadsheet   {CHDIR}
     EXEC SP
ITEM ^3Accounting    {CHDIR}
     EXEC L:
     EXEC CD \ACCT
     EXEC GL
ITEM ^4Payroll   {CHDIR}
     EXEC L:
     EXEC CD \PAYROLL
     EXEC PAY
ITEM ^5Network Printers
     SHOW 02
ITEM ^6Network Functions
     SHOW 03
ITEM ^XExit to DOS
     EXEC EXIT
ITEM ^LLog Out
     EXEC LOGOUT
```

The LOAD Statement

The LOAD statement can be used to include other menu files in the main menu. This enables you to keep a complex menu system easier to work with by breaking it into small separate submenu files. The menu files being accessed from a LOAD command must first be translated into executable files by the MENUMAKE program. After the executable submenu files have been created, they can be accessed from the main menu by using the LOAD *filename* statement, where *filename* is replaced with the name of the executable menu file containing the .DAT extension.

Suppose, for example, that multiple workgroup menus need to include the network functions found in the Network Functions menu defined previously in the sample menu design form in Figure 15-4. Rather than including the Network Function submenu statements in the source menu file for each workgroup, you can create and compile a separate NETWORK.SRC file containing the network function menu statements. In the main menu for each workgroup you then include the network functions by placing the following menu commands in the main menu:

```
ITEM ^NNetwork Functions
LOAD NETWORK.DAT
```

Obtaining User Input

It is often necessary to obtain information from the user before a command statement can be executed. In order to use the Send Message option under Network Functions, for example, you must obtain the message to be sent and the name of the user to whom the message is to be sent. The Novell menu system handles user input with the following GET statements:

- The GETO command is used when the user's input is optional, such as when asking for optional command parameters. A GETO command might be used, for example, to ask for a volume name to be used with the NDIR command. If no volume name is specified, the current volume information will be displayed.
- The GETR command is used when the user's input is required—for example, when user input is needed for the SEND command.
- The GETP command is used when user input needs to be stored. The first input is stored in the variable %1, the second in variable %2, and so on, up to %9.

The syntax of all the GET statements is as follows:

```
GETx prompt {prepend} length,prefill, {append}
```

The *prompt* field contains text you want to be displayed when the user is asked to enter a value. It can contain up to 40 characters. The *prepend* field, which must be enclosed in braces, contains characters to be added to the beginning of the user's entry. The *length* field is used to set the characters to be added to the beginning of the user's entry and to set the maximum number of characters for the user input field. The *length* parameter is required but can be a zero if the user is only required to press [Enter] in order to confirm an action. The *prefill* field is used to provide a default response that will be displayed with the prompt. When using the GETO command, the user can accept the default, change the response by typing over the characters, or cancel the selection of the item. The *prefill* field is optional and can be omitted by typing a second comma after the comma that follows the length field (see the example below). The *append* field must be enclosed in braces {} and is used to contain characters you want added after the user's response. If you want to make sure a colon is placed after the drive letter entered by the user, for example, you could use the *append* field as shown in the following GETR statement:

```
GETR Enter destination drive { } 1,, {:}
```

This command will force the user to enter a single-character drive letter and then place a colon after the drive letter specified. If you want a default value of drive C to be placed in the destination drive field, place the letter C in the *prefill* field of the GETR command, as follows:

```
GETR Enter destination drive { } 1,C, {:}
```

When you use the GETO and GETR commands, you must include a space in the *prepend* field in order to separate the user's input from the command line. With the GETO and GETR statements, the user's input is automatically placed after the EXEC statement in the associated ITEM statement. If, for example, you want a menu item that enables a user to list information of any volume, you can use the GETO statement shown in Figure 15-9. The user input is placed immediately following the EXEC NDIR statement. Note the space included in the *prepend* field. If no space is left in the *prepend* field, the volume name the user enters will be placed immediately following the word NDIR, causing an error to be displayed. If the user enters the volume name DATA:, for example, the EXEC command becomes EXEC NDIRDATA:.

Figure 15-9

Sample GETO statement

```
ITEM List Volume Information {PAUSE}
   GETO Enter volume name: { } 8,,{}
   EXEC NDIR
```

Figure 15-10 illustrates the use of the GETR command to obtain user input for the Send Messages option in the Network Functions menu defined in the sample menu design form in Figure 15-4. Notice that the sequence of the GETR statements must match the syntax of the SEND statements, requiring the user to enter the message followed by the name of the user to whom the message will be sent. In addition, a double quotation mark (") must be included in the *prepend* and *append* fields of the first GETR statement. This supplies the quotation marks required by the syntax of the SEND statement. Remember to include a space in the *prepend* field of the second GETR statement to separate the message from the username in the final SEND command.

Figure 15-10

Sample Network Functions submenu

```
MENU 03,Network Functions
ITEM ^1Change Password
       EXEC SETPASS
ITEM ^2Drive Mappings
       EXEC SESSION
ITEM ^3Send a Message {PAUSE}
       GETR Enter message line {  "} 60,,{"}
       GETR Enter username {  } 12,,{}
       EXEC SEND
ITEM ^4Work with Print Jobs
       EXEC PCONSOLE
```

The GETP statement enables you to control exactly where the user input will be placed. The variables %1, %2, . . . %9 are specified in the GETP statement. Figure 15-11 shows an example of the GETP command with the ITEM for the Send Message statement. Notice that with the GETP statement, the sequence of the user input does not determine the use of the input in the EXEC statement because the %1 and %2 variables can be placed in any sequence. In addition, when the GETP statement is used, no *prepend* or *append* parameters are necessary; the spaces and quotation marks can be placed directly in the EXEC command.

Figure 15-11

Sample GETP statements

```
ITEM ^3Send a Message {PAUSE}
     GETP Enter username to send message to {} 12,,{}
     GETP Enter message line {} 60,,{}
     EXEC SEND "%2"  %1
```

COMPILING AND TESTING THE MENUS

After you write the menu statements, your next task is to use a text editor to create and save a menu source file with the filename extension .SRC. At this time, it is wise to place an Exit to DOS option in the main menu to enable you to return to the DOS prompt easily. This will enable you to make any necessary corrections to the menu file or drive mappings when a menu item does not work properly. If the main menu does not contain an Exit to DOS option, you will need to use the logout option to end the menu program and then log in again in order to make corrections to the menu items. After the menu is working properly, you can remove the Exit to DOS option and recompile the menu in order to prevent users from exiting to the DOS prompt.

After the source file has been created, you use the MENUMAKE program to translate the source file into an executable menu file with the .DAT extension. Figure 15-12 illustrates the use of the MENUMAKE command to translate the finance menu source file, named FINAMENU.SRC, into an executable menu file. Notice the error messages generated as a result of syntax errors in some of the menu command statements. The errors must be corrected in the menu source file (FINAMENU.SRC) with a text editor program.

Figure 15-12

Unsuccessful MENUMAKE compile

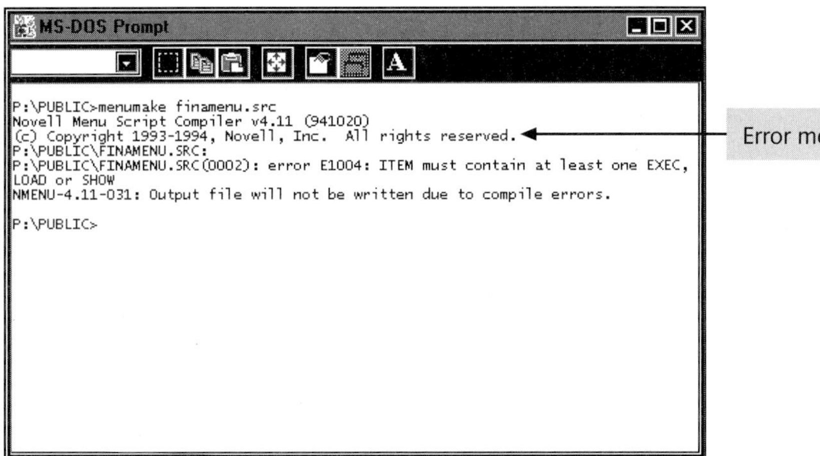

Once the errors have been corrected, the MENUMAKE command again can be used to re-create the executable menu file successfully. An .SRC file with no errors will compile and produce the message indicating its success, as shown in Figure 15-13.

Figure 15-13

Successful MENUMAKE compile

```
MS-DOS Prompt
P:\PUBLIC>menumake finamenu.src
Novell Menu Script Compiler v4.11 (941020)
(c) Copyright 1993-1994, Novell, Inc.  All rights reserved.
P:\PUBLIC\FINAMENU.SRC:
P:\PUBLIC\FINAMENU.DAT written.

P:\PUBLIC>
```

To test the menu file, first you need to establish any necessary search and regular drive pointer mappings that are used by the menu items. After all necessary drive mappings have been established, you can run the menu by using the command NMENU FINAMENU. Figure 15-14 shows an example of running the finance menu, selecting the Network Functions option, and using the Send a Message option. Notice the User Input Requested window generated by the GETR statements (see Figure 15-10). After entering information in each input field, the user must press [F10] to continue and send the message.

Figure 15-14

Running the Finance Menu

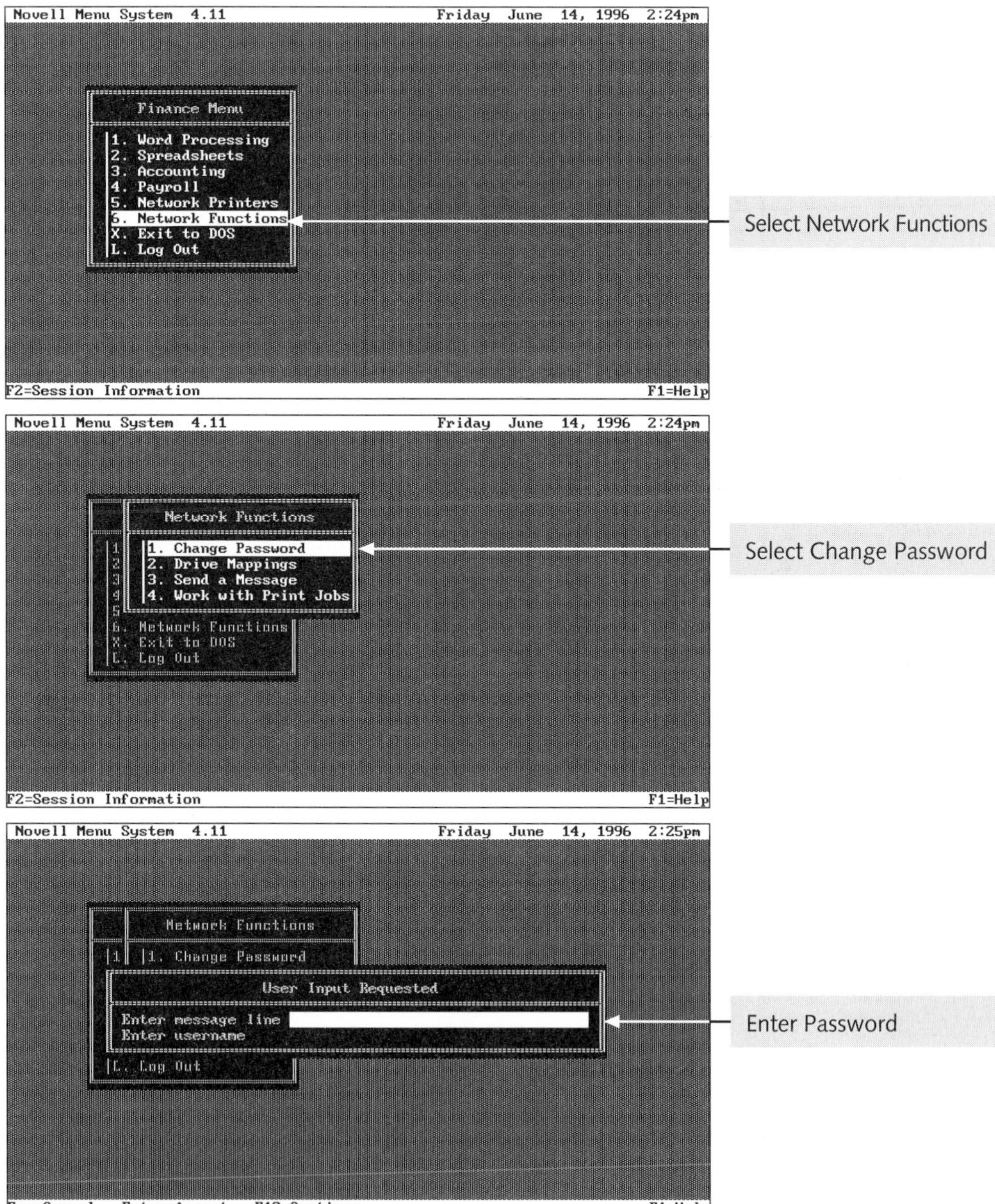

After compiling your menu system, you should test each option. Make notes on any drive mappings or other DOS environment settings you need to run each application. You will use this information to create the environment that users will need to run the menu items.

To create a menu, follow these steps:

1. Key in the menu using an ASCII text editor and save it with a .SRC file extension.

2. Compile the menu with MENUMAKE *filename*.SRC.
3. Run the menu with NMENU *filename*.DAT.

PLANNING THE MENU DIRECTORY STRUCTURE

Many of the network administrator's activities require decisions and compromises. Planning the menu system directory structure is such a situation. Before setting up the menu system for your users, you first need to determine what menu directories you need and where they should be placed in your file system. In order to make these decisions, you need to decide what directory the users will access to run their menus.

The two most popular alternatives used by many network administrators are to have users run the menu system from either the menu directory or from their own home directories. The advantages of having users run the menu system from their home directories are that the users have all rights in their home directories for creating and erasing temporary files and that they have access to files and data stored in their home directories without changing to another drive. The major disadvantage of running the menu system from the users' home directories is that you will need to map a search drive to the menu executable directory in order for the users to access the menu command files. Although this is normally not a problem, it does reduce the number of search drives available to your system and can slow down the system somewhat when it searches for programs and files. An alternative to using a search drive is to specify a drive letter ahead of the menu name when the menu is executed. For example, to execute a menu file called FINAMENU located in a directory mapped to the M drive letter, you could use the NMENU M:FINAMENU command from the user's home directory. Although this method does not require a search drive to the MENUS directory, the drive letter must be used each time any reference to a menu file is made.

The second alternative is to run the menus directly from the directory containing the menu executable files. The advantages to this method are that you will not need to use a search drive or include the drive letter to find the menu files.

After you decide where users will run their menu files, your next decision is what directory or directories will be used to store the menu source and executable files. One option is to store all the menu files in the SYS:PUBLIC directory rather than creating a separate MENU directory. In the CBE Labs example, the finance department's menus would be stored in CONSTELLATION/SYS:PUBLIC subdirectory. This not only avoids having to create a separate directory, it also means that all users have a search drive along with Read and File Scan rights to the SYS:PUBLIC directory. If you use this method, however, the finance users will need to run menus from their home directories in order to create and delete the temporary files. Another disadvantage to storing menu files in SYS:PUBLIC is that they will be combined with the NetWare utilities and command files, increasing the chances that they will be inadvertently erased or lost when NetWare server upgrades are performed. Yet another disadvantage of storing the source menu files in SYS:PUBLIC is that it enables users to display the contents of the source files and other menu options.

Because of the disadvantages associated with storing menus in the SYS:PUBLIC directory, most network administrators create a separate directory for their menu files. For CBE Labs, CONSTALLATION_ DATA:SHARED could be used to store the menu files for the finance department. It would also be good to have the source files separated from the menu executable files by creating a subdirectory called SOURCE, as shown in Figure 15-15. All rights can then be removed from the Inherited Rights Filter on the SOURCE subdirectory to prevent users from inheriting rights into this subdirectory.

Figure 15-15

Suggested menu directory structure

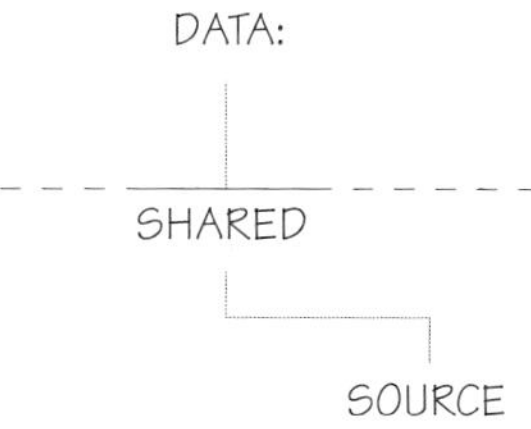

The last decision you need to make is where to store the temporary files. If users are running the menus from their home directories, you can default to having the temporary files stored in the current directory. However, if users will be accessing the menus from the MENU directory where they have only Read and File Scan rights, you will need to create a directory for the temporary files, as shown in Figure 15-16, and then give the users Read, File Scan, Create, and Erase rights to the temporary file directory. In addition, you can set the Purge attribute on the TEMP directory in order to make the space used by the temporary files immediately available to the system after the files are deleted. This will make other files available for salvaging for a longer time and provide a slight increase in system performance.

Figure 15-16

Menu temporary file structure

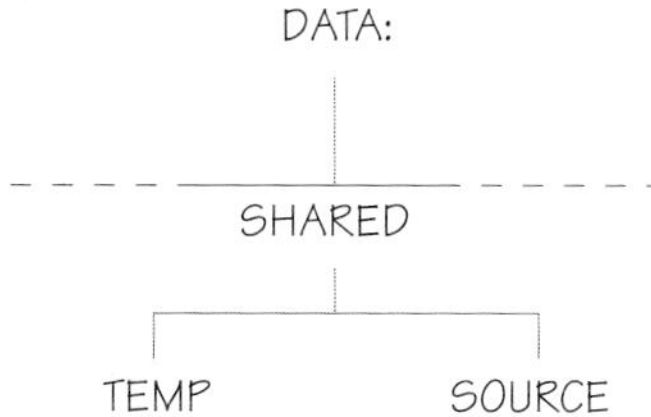

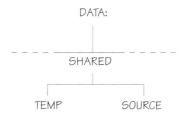

If you plan to use a separate directory to hold temporary files, it is necessary to tell the menu system the name of the path to the temporary directory along with the user's connection number. Because multiple users will be storing their temporary files in the same directory, the user's connection numbers are needed to keep each user's temporary files separate. The connection number is included as part of the temporary filenames.

The DOS SET command can be used to identify the path to the temporary directory as well as the user's connection number. Include the following commands in the login script after the MAP command to create the M drive printer to the DATA:SHARED directory:

```
DOS SET S_FILEDIR="M:TEMP"
DOS SET S_FILE="%STATION"
```

PROVIDING USER ACCESS RIGHTS

To run the menu system, the CBE Labs finance department users will need a minimum of Read and File Scan rights in the directory containing the menu executable files, along with Read, File Scan, Create, and Erase rights in the directory containing the temporary files. If users will be running the menus from their home directories, you will need to provide Read and File Scan rights to the menu executable directory only, because by default, temporary files will be created and erased from the user's home directory.

When the menus are executed from the directory containing the executable files, you need to either assign Read, File Scan, Create, and Erase rights to the executable file directory or separate the temporary files into a different directory. Then assign Read and File Scan rights to the executable directory and Read, File Scan, Create, and Erase rights to the temporary directory.

MODIFYING THE LOGIN SCRIPTS

Once the menus are tested and ready to run, the last step is to automate the menu system by placing the necessary commands in the container and user login scripts. The login script commands to run most menu systems consist of commands to map a drive to the menu directory, optional DOS SET commands, and an EXIT command to link the user to the correct menu.

In most cases, you will want to use the container login script to map at least one drive to the directory structure containing the menu system. If users are running the menus from their home directories, you might want to make this a search drive. This will ensure that the menu executable files can be found without inclusion of the drive or path when a menu command file is referenced. If users will be running the menus from the directory containing the executable files, you should map a root drive pointer, such as M, to the menu directory. Using a root drive helps ensure that the path to the drive containing the menu files will not accidentally be changed from an application program or DOS command.

If you plan to store user temporary files in a separate directory, you will need to include DOS SET commands in the container login script. These commands tell the menu program the path to the temporary directory and the user's connection number. Finally, each user must be linked to his or her appropriate menu. This can be done by including EXIT NMENU *menuname* as the last or only command in each user's personal login script. If you do not plan to use personal login scripts in your system, you will need to include the EXIT command as the last command executed for each workgroup.

In addition to the EXIT command, you need to be sure the user's default drive points to the directory from which you want the menu system to be run. Use the DRIVE drive: login script command in either the container or user login script. If you want users to run the menu system from their home directories, for example, include the commands shown in Figure 15-17 in the container and user login scripts. If you want users to run the menu system from the SHARED directory and store temporary files in the SHARED\TEMP directory, include the commands shown in Figure 15-18 in the container and user login scripts.

Figure 15-17 Login script with menu run from user home directory

```
Containter Login Script
MAP INS S4:=CONSTELLATION_DATA:SHARED
IF MEMBER OF "FINANCE" THEN
   MAP ROOT H:=CONSTELLATION_DATA:USERS\%LOGIN_NAME
END

User Login Script
DRIVE H:
EXIT "NMENU FINAMENU"
```

Figure 15-18 Login script with menu run from SHARED directory

```
Container Login Script
MAP ROOT M:=CONSTELLATION_DATA:SHARED
DOS SET S_FILEDIR="M:\TEMP"
DOS SET S_FILE="%STATION"
IF MEMBER OF "FINANCE" THEN
   MAP ROOT H:=CONSTELLATION_DATA:USERS\%LOGIN_NAME
END

User Login Script
DRIVE M:
EXIT "NMENU FINAMENU"
```

TRAINING USERS

The final step in implementing a successful menu system is providing training so users understand and can operate the menu system you have designed. This is best done by working with each department separately. First show the users how to move between the menus and submenus with the [Esc] key. Make sure to stress the importance of logging out prior to leaving the workstation and then show them how they can use the LOGIN command to log back in and redisplay their menu.

Next, explain any special menu options, such as working with drive pointers and selecting network printers. Be sure that each user feels comfortable using the menu system to access application software and to send output to the correct network printer. Show users how to change their passwords and explain any password restrictions, such as minimum password length and frequency between password changes. Making sure all users know how to use the menu properly to access network resources will increase their efficiency and decrease the problems and frustrations caused by their unfamiliarity with the system.

CHAPTER SUMMARY

A good menu system is necessary for users of DOS-based computers to access the network and perform their jobs easily. The overall impression your users have of the network system is often determined by how well the menu system works. A network administrator needs to be able to establish and maintain a menu system that will meet the needs of users and provide secure access to the network resources.

The NetWare menu system uses less memory and includes features found in more powerful menu systems. Among the features are creating executable menu files, linking menus, and preventing users from accidentally exiting the menu system. In addition, the menu system contains control functions, such as the ability to place temporary files in a separate directory, to return to the original menu directory automatically, and to remove the menu program from memory during the execution of a menu item.

The NMENU system consists of several components: the source menu files, which have the extension .SRC; the MENUMAKE program, which compiles source menu statements and creates executable menu files with the extension .DAT; the NMENU program, which runs the executable menu files; temporary files created by the NMENU program, which contain the batch commands being executed for a menu item; and the MENUCNVT program, which is used to convert NetWare 3.x menu files with the extension .MNU to files containing the new menu commands with the extension .SRC.

Creating menus involves planning the contents of each workgroup or user menu and defining common needs and submenus. Commands in the NMENU system can be divided into two classifications. The organizational commands consist of such statements as the MENU statement, which defines a menu's title and number; the ITEM statement, which identifies each item to be displayed in a menu; and control options such as BATCH, PAUSE, CHDIR, and SHOW. The control commands consist of such statements as EXEC, LOAD, and SHOW. The EXEC statement causes DOS to execute the specified command or application or perform a special function. Some special function statements are EXEC EXIT to exit the menu system, EXEC CALL to call a DOS batch program, EXEC DOS to display a DOS prompt, and EXEC LOGOUT to end the user's session on the network. The LOAD statement enables you to pass control to another executable menu file; the SHOW statement executes a submenu within the current menu file by using the menu's number.

After writing the menu files, you need to enter, compile, and test each menu. A standard text editor program can be used to enter the menu source file and save it with the extension .SRC. Next, you use the MENUMAKE program to translate, or compile, the source menu into an executable menu file. If errors are listed by the MENUMAKE program, you will need to use the text editor to correct the errors and then use the MENUMAKE command again to create an executable menu file. After the executable file has been successfully created, you can proceed to test each menu option. This often involves setting up the necessary drive mappings or copying files to the executable directory and logging in as individual users.

To implement the menu system, first you need to decide on the location from which users will run the menu system, and the location of the menu files. One alternative is to have users run the menus from their home directories. This allows temporary files to be stored in a user's home directory, but requires a separate search drive to the menu directory as well as requiring all users, including temporary workers, to have a home directory. An alternative is to have users run the menu system directly from the menu executable directory. Although this reduces the number of search drives needed and enables any user to run the menu system, it has the disadvantage of requiring the network administrator to establish a location for the temporary files.

Many network administrators create separate directories for the source and executable menu files, enabling users to run menus without being able to display the contents of the source file. In addition, another directory is often created for temporary files, which enables users to run the menu system from the menu directory without needing access rights to create and erase files. In this setup, the network administrator needs to assign users Read and File Scan rights to the menu directory only. Once the directories are created, you assign users Read and File Scan rights in the directory containing the executable files, and Create and Erase rights in the directory that will contain the temporary files.

The final step in implementing the menu system is modifying the container and user login script files. The system login script needs to contain a drive mapping to the menu directory along with optional DOS SET statements to set the S_FILEDIR and S_FILE environment variables to contain the path to the temporary directory and the user's connection number. If user login scripts are used, each user's login script needs to be modified to contain the DRIVE drive: command in order to place the user in the correct directory to run the menus, and the EXEC NMENU *menuname* command to link the login script automatically to the correct menu file. You then need to log in as each user and verify that the login script and menu system work together to provide the user with an environment that makes the network transparent and easy to use.

COMMAND SUMMARY

Command	Syntax	Definition
EXEC	*EXEC command*	Control command used to start applications or run commands within an ITEM statement. Special commands include EXEC LOGOUT, EXEC DOS, and EXEC EXIT.

GETO	*GETO prompt {prepend} length, prefill, {append}*	Control command used to obtain optional input from the user. The *prompt* parameter contains the message to be displayed. The *prepend* field contains a space followed by any characters you want placed ahead of the user's input. The *prefill* parameter places a default value in the input field. The *append* parameter specifies any characters you want added after the user's input.
GETP	*GETP prompt {prepend} length, prefill, {append}*	Control command used to store input from the user in labeled variables. The first user input is stored in variable %1, the second in %2, and so on. The *prompt* parameter contains the message to be displayed. The *prepend* field contains a space followed by any characters you want placed ahead of the user's input. The *prefill* parameter places a default value in the input field. The *append* parameter specifies any characters you want added after the user's input.
GETR	*GETR prompt {prepend} length, prefill, {append}*	Control command used to obtain required input from users. The *prompt* parameter contains the message to be displayed. The *prepend* field contains a space followed by any characters you want placed ahead of the user's input. The *prefill* parameter places a default value in the input field. The *append* parameter specifies any characters you want added after the user's input.
ITEM	*ITEM name [{option}]*	Organizational command used to define each option in a menu. Options include CHDIR, PAUSE, BATCH, and SHOW.
LOAD	*LOAD filename*	Control command used to access another menu contained in a separate executable menu file identified by the *filename* parameter.
MENU	*MENU number, title*	Organizational command used in a menu source file to define the title and number of a menu or submenu.
MENUCNVT	*MENUCNVT filename*	Converts early NetWare menu files, creating source files with the extension .SRC, which contains the new menu statements that will implement the original menu in the new menu system.
MENUMAKE	*MENUMAKE filename .SRC*	Compiles a source menu file with the extension .SRC, creating an executable menu file with the extension .DAT, which can be run with the NMENU command.
NMENU	*NMENU filename.DAT*	Executes compiled menu files with the extension .DAT.
SHOW	*SHOW number*	Control command used to display the submenu identified by the menu number following the command. The submenu must be contained in the menu file.

Key Terms

control commands
menu
organizational commands
source menu files

Review Questions

1. The ________________ NetWare menu command is used to access a submenu.
2. List two command categories used in NetWare menus.

   ____

   ____

3. List three components of the NetWare menu system.

   ____

   ____

   ____

4. List the two commands needed to run the MAIN.SRC menu file.

   ____

   ____

5. Menu executable files have the default filename extension of ________________.
6. Write the two DOS SET login script commands that will store all temporary files in the DATA:MENUS\TEMP directory when drive letter G is mapped to the DATA: volume.

   ____

   ____

7. Write the three commands that will run an original NetWare 3.x menu file named MYMENU.MNU using the NetWare menu system.

   ____

   ____

   ____

8. Write a menu command that will cause the menu system to display the option "Database system" and contain options to remove the menu program from memory during the execution of this application and return to the menu default directory.

   ____

9. Write the menu command lines that will provide a menu option to display a directory of the current path, pausing after the last screen is displayed.

   ____

   ____

10. Modify the menu item in question 9 to add a GETx statement that will ask the operator to enter the path for the directory listing. Record all menu statements.

    ____

    ____

    ____

11. Write the menu command to display a DOS prompt and then return to the menu system when the user enters the command EXIT at the DOS prompt.

    ____

12. Write a menu item that passes control to another menu file named DOS.DAT.

    ____

13. Write a menu item that passes control to a submenu. The submenu is located in a menu control file that starts with the command MENU 04,Network Control.

    ____

14. On the lines below, list the three steps involved in creating the menu system.

    ____

    ____

    ____

15. Indicate the access rights a user needs to the directories that contain the following files:

    The directory containing the temporary files: ______________

    The directory containing the menu executable files: ______________

    The directory containing the source menu files: ______________

16. List below at least one advantage and one disadvantage of running the menu system from a user's home directory.

    Advantage: ______________

    Disadvantage: ______________

17. The ______________ command is used when user input is required.

18. Complete the following statements to create a menu item that uses the GETO statement to ask the user to enter a directory path and then executes the NetWare command necessary to list all filenames in the directory path specified by the user.

    ITEM Directory Listing ______________

    GETO ______________

    EXEC ______________

19. Write the GETP and EXEC statements that will obtain input to grant rights to a specified user in the given directory path.

    ____

    ____

20. List two advantages of using the GETP statement as compared to using GETO.

    ____

    ____

EXERCISES

EXERCISE 15-1: ENTERING AND RUNNING A MENU

In this exercise you create a simple menu and then use the NetWare menu system to compile and run the menu.

1. Change to your ##ADMIN directory.
2. Create a subdirectory called PRACTICE.
3. Change to the PRACTICE directory.
4. Use a text editor to enter the sample menu shown in Figure 15-2. Change the title of the menu to contain your name.
5. Use the appropriate menu commands to compile and run the sample menu.

Exercise 15-2: Practicing with Menus

In the following exercise you learn more about how temporary files are used by developing menu items and viewing the names and contents of the temporary files created by the menu system. In this exercise you need to create a special menu that can be used to find and view the location of the temporary files.

1. Change to your ##ADMIN directory.
2. Create a subdirectory called MENUS.
3. Make a subdirectory of your ##ADMIN\MENUS directory and name it TEMP.
4. Change to the MENUS directory created in step 2.
5. Use your text editor program to enter the source file shown in Figure 15-19.

Figure 15-19

Sample menu source file

```
MENU 1,TEST MENU
ITEM View temporary filenames [PAUSE]
        EXEC DIR/P
        EXEC DIR\##ADMIN\MENUS\TEMP
        EXEC DIR\##ADMIN\MENUS
ITEM View temporary file contents [PAUSE]
        GETP Enter tempory filename:[]11,,[]
        GETP Enter directory path:[]20,,[]
        EXEC DIR %2
        EXEC TYPE %2\%1
ITEM Display DOS prompt
        EXEC DOS
ITEM Exit to DOS
        EXEC EXIT
```

6. Compile the menu.
7. Run the menu and use the first option to determine the location of the temporary files. Record the location of the temporary files and their filenames in the space below.

8. Exit to the DOS prompt.

Exercise 15-3: Running a Menu from Another Directory

In this exercise you create a search drive and run a menu from a directory that does not contain the menu executable file.

1. Change to your ##ADMIN directory.
2. Create a subdirectory called PRACTICE.
3. Change to the PRACTICE directory.

4. Use a text editor to enter the sample menu shown in Figure 15-2. Change the title of the menu to contain your name and add an option to enable you to exit to the DOS prompt.
5. Use the MENUMAKE command to create an executable menu file.
6. Change your default path to the ##ADMIN directory.
7. Use the MAP command to create a search drive mapping to your PRACTICE directory.
8. Execute the menu created in step 5.
9. Exit to the DOS prompt.

Exercise 15-4: Multiple Users

One problem associated with a common temporary directory is the possibility of one user's temporary files overwriting another user's temporary files if they both run their menus at the same time. In this exercise you will see how the S_FILE environment variable can be used to separate temporary files by user connection.

1. Determine your connection number by using the USERLIST command.
2. Use the appropriate SET command to set the S_FILE environment variable to your connection number.
3. Run the TEST menu system and determine the name and location of the menu temporary files.
4. Record the temporary filenames in the space below.

   ____

   ____

   ____

5. Display the DOS prompt and see if you can change to the temporary directory and display the contents of the temporary file. Record your observations in the space below.

   ____

   ____

   ____

6. Return to the menu system.
7. Exit to the DOS prompt.

Exercises

Case 15-1: The Equity Coop

The Equity Coop is a local cooperative store that uses its network to perform word processing and spreadsheet functions and to maintain an inventory of feeds. The store has a dot-matrix printer for printing output from spreadsheets and inventory reports and a laser printer for word processing and for generating letter-quality documents. Currently the only way staff can use the system and control the printers is from the DOS prompt. They have asked you to set up a NetWare menu system that will contain options to run each of the company's application packages and provide them with an easy way to redirect printer output and perform such printer control functions as stopping and starting the printer and changing forms.

Users at Equity first need to change to the SYS:SOFTWARE.STC\WP directory and enter the command WP to run the word processing software. To run the spreadsheet software, they change to the SYS:SOFTWARE.STC\SP directory and enter the command SP. In order to run inventory software they must first change to the SYS:SOFTWARE.STC\DB directory and then enter the command DB. To send output to the dot-matrix printer, they need to issue the command CAPTURE Q=queuename NB NT TI=5 before starting the application software. The command to access the laser print queue is CAPTURE Q=queuename NB NT TI=10 NFF. It must be entered before the WP software is started.

Design a menu system for Equity Coop that will automate the process of running applications and accessing the network print queues. In addition, create a printer control submenu that uses the PSC commands to enable print server operators to start, stop, and change forms in the dot-matrix printer. The form change menu option should ask the user to enter the new form number before the appropriate PSC command is executed. Your instructor will provide you with the following printer information, which you need to create and test the printer menu items:

Laser print queue name: ______________________

Dot matrix print queue name: ______________________

Print server name: ______________________

Dot matrix printer number: ______________________

1. Change to your ##ADMIN directory and create a subdirectory named COOP MENU.
2. Change to the COOPMENU directory and use a text editor to create a source menu file for the Equity Coop store.
3. Compile and test the menu.
4. Obtain a hard copy listing of your source menu file.
5. Use the NDIR command to obtain a listing of the COOPMENU directory.
6. Use [Print Scrn] to print the screen showing the COOPMENU menu.
7. Have the instructor check your Equity Coop menu and sign on the line below.
   Instructor signature: ______________________

Northwestern Technical College

Now that you have established container and user login script files for the staff at Northwestern Technical College, the next step in automating the user environment is creating menus for each workgroup and then combining them with the college login scripts. Because school will be starting soon, Dave Johnson is eager to have the menu system up and running so you can spend some time training users in the use of the menus and network environment.

PROJECT 15-1: DESIGNING A MENU SYSTEM

Design menus for both the support staff and student services personnel based on the following requirements:

- Support staff need to be able to run the word processing and spreadsheet software.
- Student services department users need to access the word processing and database software.
- Users in all departments need to be able to select any printer on the network and send output to it.
- Both the support and the student services staff need a submenu to control their network printers and enable them to stop the printer, start the printer, cancel a print job, view printer status, and mount a new form number in the printer.
- All staff need a submenu containing network options to send messages, change passwords, and run the PCONSOLE utilities.

PROJECT 15-2: WRITING AND TESTING WORKGROUP MENUS

In this project you write the menu command statements for each of the menus you defined in Project 15-1, and then use a text editor program to enter and save each of the workgroup menus as separate source files in your ##NWTC\MENUS directory. Include an option in each menu that will enable you to exit to the DOS prompt while testing the menu options. Be sure to use the extension .SRC for each menu source file. After a menu file has been entered, use the MENUMAKE program to compile the menu file and correct any syntax errors. Obtain a printout of each successfully compiled menu.

After the menus have been compiled, test each menu by making the necessary drive mappings to run the menu applications and then test each menu option to be sure it works correctly. Record the drive mappings you require for each workgroup menu in the following table:

STUDENT SERVICES

Drive Letter ____________ Path ____

Drive Letter ____________ Path ____

Drive Letter ____________ Path ____

Drive Letter ____________ Path ____

Drive Letter ____________ Path ____

SUPPORT STAFF

Drive Letter ____________ Path ____

Drive Letter ____________ Path ____

Drive Letter ____________ Path ____

Drive Letter ____________ Path ____

Drive Letter ____________ Path ____

Certain application software, as well as the menu system, might require DOS environment variables to be set in the workstation. In the following table, document any DOS environment variables that you need to set:

Environment Variable ________ Value ________ Description ________ Purpose ________

Environment Variable ________ Value ________ Description ________ Purpose ________

Environment Variable ________ Value ________ Description ________ Purpose ________
Environment Variable ________ Value ________ Description ________ Purpose ________
Environment Variable ________ Value ________ Description ________ Purpose ________
Environment Variable ________ Value ________ Description ________ Purpose ________

Project 15-3: Providing User Access

After you have tested the menus to be sure all options work with the correct drive mappings and environment setups, you need to implement the menu system in your directory structure by providing for user access.

1. In the spaces provided, document the locations from which you want administrative users to run their menu systems.

Staff Menu System	Path	Access Rights
Directory to run menu system:	________	________
Directory for temporary files:	________	________
Location of executable files:	________	________
Location of source files:	________	________

2. Create the directories listed in step 1 and provide your users with the access rights you have defined.
3. Use the FLAG command to document the rights you have assigned to each menu directory defined in step 1.
4. Create a container login script so that it provides drive mappings or DOS environment variables necessary to run the menu system and application software.
5. Obtain a printout of your container login script after making any corrections needed to run your menu options. If your system executes everything from the container login script and does not use user login scripts, modify the container login script to exit to the appropriate workgroup menu. Highlight each statement you added or changed to facilitate the menu system.
6. If your system uses user login scripts, modify the user login scripts for all users in the support staff and student services workgroups to run their appropriate network menus.

Project 15-4: Testing the Menu System

Test your menu system by logging in and testing the menu options. When you believe your menu system is operational, have your instructor check it and sign on the line below.

Instructor signature: ________________________________

Project 15-5: Training Users

Develop and document a training procedure to educate the staff at Northwestern Technical College in the use of the network menu system. Your plan should include the following:

- Determine the time to spend with each department.
- Develop a brief outline of the information you plan to cover in the training session.

Write a brief memo to each department head regarding your training plan and the time period in which you want to implement the network for the department. Attach a copy of the training outline to the memo.

Turn in your outline and memos to your instructor.

CHAPTER SIXTEEN

MANAGING THE NETWORK

In the previous chapters of this book you learned how to install and configure a NetWare network. However, once a network is up and running, the work has just begun. Managing the network is a daily task, while many of these activities take place at the workstation, there are, however, times when it is necessary to access the file server console to perform various commands and load modules, such as during installation of NetWare and the Message Handling System. It becomes even more important for the network administrator to know how to use the file server console to perform a variety of tasks. In this chapter you will learn additional commands and options that are important for monitoring, backing up, and securing the file server. You will also learn how to access the file server console from another workstation attached either to the LAN or via a modem. Finally, the tasks involved in synchronizing the network will be studied.

AFTER READING THIS CHAPTER AND COMPLETING THE EXERCISES YOU WILL BE ABLE TO:

- Use NetWare console commands to perform file server commands.
- Perform remote console management to access the file server console from a workstation attached to the network.
- Fix volume problems with the VREPAIR NetWare Loadable Module.
- Fix NDS problems with the DSREPAIR NetWare Loadable Module.
- Use NetWare's Storage Management System to back up network data.

CONSOLE OPERATIONS

File server operation entails using commands that can be divided into two major categories: console commands and NetWare Loadable Modules (NLMs). **Console commands** are similar to the DOS internal commands on a workstation in that they are built into the core file server operating system program (SERVER.EXE). **NetWare Loadable Modules** are external programs that are loaded into the memory of the file server computer and add functionality to the NetWare core operating system. In this section you will learn about the console commands and several of the most common NLMs.

CONSOLE COMMANDS

In order to operate a file server console effectively, you need to know how to use the basic console commands that are built into the NetWare operating system. Because there are many different console commands, the console commands described in this section have been divided into separate functional categories: installation commands, configuration commands, maintenance commands, and security commands.

Installation Commands

The commands shown in Figure 16-1 are included in the installation category because they are most frequently used when you first install NetWare on the file server, when you expand the system, or when you install a separate application, such as MHS.

The ADD NAME SPACE command is used to enable non-DOS filenames, such as those used with Macintosh or UNIX, to be used in a NetWare volume. The ADD NAME SPACE command will modify the directory entry table (DET) in the specified volume to allow for the storage of non-DOS filenames. This command needs to be executed only once for each volume in which the non-DOS files are going to be stored. Replace the *name* parameter with the name of the name space module you loaded. Common names are OS/2 and MAC. Replace the *volume_name* parameter with the name of the volume to which you want the specified name space to be added.

In order use long file names for a Windows 95 client on a Novell NetWare network, load the OS/2 name space module. This module works because OS/2, like Windows 95, permits filenames up to 256 characters in length.

The LOAD command reads an NLM into memory and executes it. By default, the LOAD command searches for the requested module in the SYS:SYSTEM directory unless a different path is specified. Valid paths can include NetWare volume names as well as local drive letters. When a module is loaded into memory, it remains there until the console operator ends the program or uses the UNLOAD command to remove the software from memory. Optional parameters can be placed after the LOAD command depending on the needs of the module being loaded.

Figure 16-1
Installation commands

Command Syntax	Description
ADD NAME SPACE *name* [TO VOLUME] *volume_name*	Adds space to a volume's directory entry table in order to support other operating system file naming conventions. Replace *name* with MAC or OS/2. Replace *volume_name* with the volume to which the specified name space is to be added.

Figure 16-1

Installation commands (continued)

Command Syntax	Description
BIND *protocol* TO *driver|board_name* [*driver_parameters*]	Attaches a *protocol* to a LAN card. Replace *protocol* with protocol name (e.g., IPX or IP). Replace *driver|board_name* with either the name of the card drive program or an optional name assigned to the network board. Optionally replace *driver_parameters* with the hardware settings that identify the network interface card (e.g., I/O port and interrupt).
LOAD [*path*]*module_name* [*parameters*]	Loads an NLM in the file server's RAM. Optionally replace *path* with the DOS or NetWare path leading to the directory containing the module to be loaded. Replace *module_name* with the name of the NLM you want to load. Optional *parameters* can be entered, depending on the module being loaded.
REGISTER MEMORY *start length*	Allows servers using an ISA bus to access memory above 16 MB.
SEARCH [ADD *path*] SEARCH [DEL *number*]	Adds or removes a directory path from the search path used by the LOAD command when NLMs are being loaded. When no parameters are specified, the current server search paths are displayed. To add a search path, replace *path* with the DOS or NetWare path leading to the directory from which you want to load NLMs. To delete an existing search path, replace *number* with the number of the search path to be deleted.

When a LAN driver is loaded, for example, the *I/O port* and *option name* parameters can be included in the LOAD command. For example, to access an E100S Ethernet LAN driver for a card that is in system board slot 2 and will assign it the name E100S_1_8022, the network administrator would use the following LOAD command:

```
LOAD E100S SLOT=2 NAME=E100S_1_8022
```

The name E100S_1_8022 can later be used to reference this card driver, as described under the BIND command. Several popular NLMs and their associated parameters are described in more detail in the section on NLMs.

The BIND command attaches a protocol stack to a network card and is necessary to enable workstations using that protocol to communicate with the file server. Replace the *protocol* parameter with the name of the protocol stack you want to attach to the network card. The IPX protocol is built into the core operating system and can be bound to a network card simply by using the BIND command. Replace *driver|board_name* with either the name of the card driver loaded previously with the LOAD command or the name you assigned to the card driver when it was loaded. If you have loaded the driver program more than once on different cards or with different frame types, you can replace *driver_parameters* with a combination of any of the parameters shown in Figure 16-2 that uniquely identify the driver program to which you want to bind the specified protocol.

Figure 16-2

BIND driver parameters

Parameter Syntax	Description
DMA=*number*	Identifies the DMA channel the LAN driver is using. Use the same DMA channel that you used when you loaded the driver for the board.
FRAME=*name*	Identifies the frame type used when the driver program was loaded.

Figure 16-2

BIND driver parameters (continued)

Parameter Syntax	Description
INT=*number*	Identifies the interrupt the driver is using for the network board. Bind the protocol with the same interrupt that you used when you loaded the LAN driver.
NET=*network_address*	Assigns a network address consisting of one to eight hexidecimal digits to the LAN card.
MEM=*number*	Identifies the memory address used when the driver was loaded.
PORT=*number*	Identifies the I/O port number the driver is using for the network board.
SLOT=*number*	On a microchannel computer, the slot identifies the network board used when the LAN driver was loaded.

Use the driver—parameters item to specify options unique to the protocol being loaded. When using the IPX protocol, you are required to specify a network address for use with the cable system to which the card is attached. For example, when the network administrator for CBE Labs needed to use the BIND command to attach the IPX protocol stack with a network address of 00019200 to an E100S driver assigned to an Ethernet card in the system board slot 2, he used the following statement:

```
BIND IPX TO E100S SLOT=2 NET=19200
```

If the E100S network driver assigned to the Ethernet card had been assigned a name when it was loaded with the LOAD command, the BIND command could use the name assigned to the driver to specify uniquely the correct card. (See the LOAD command for an example of naming a network card driver.) To bind IPX to a card driver named E100S_1_E8022 he would enter the following command:

```
BIND IPX TO E100S_1_E8022 NET=19200
```

The REGISTER MEMORY command is used to permit a certain type of file server to recognize additional RAM memory. NetWare will recognize all the RAM memory present in EISA and MCA bus computers and up to 64 MB in PCI bus computers. However, NetWare running on a file server with an ISA bus does not recognize installed memory above 16 MB. To access the memory above 16 MB in an ISA bus file server, replace the *start* parameter with the starting hexadecimal address at which the memory beyond 16 MB begins (the starting address will be 1000000) and replace *length* with a hexadecimal number that corresponds to the amount of memory installed above 16 MB. For example, of the three NetWare servers in the CBE Labs network, one of those servers, RANGER, is a file server with an ISA bus that has 24 MB of RAM. The network administrator would use the following REGISTER MEMORY command to enable the file server to "see" the additional memory:

```
REGISTER MEMORY 1000000 800000
```

Use REGISTER MEMORY only for the actual RAM memory that is installed in the file server. Do not use it with shadow RAM, because this might be mapped to lower memory regions.

The SEARCH ADD statement tells NetWare where to look for files. Unless a specific path is used, the NetWare server operating system normally checks for modules and files in the SYS:SYSTEM directory. However, just as the MAP INS S1:=path statement enables you to add another directory to the search path of a workstation, the SEARCH ADD statement can be used to specify an additional directory path that contains files or programs to be used by the file server. Using the SEARCH ADD statement to add directory paths for the file server does not affect the search drive mappings of the workstations.

As shown in Figure 16-3, you can enter the SEARCH command by itself to display a list of all active search paths and their corresponding numbers. The SEARCH DEL number command shown in Figure 16-3 deletes an existing search drive by specifying the number of the search drive to be deleted. When a file server is restarted, all current search paths are removed, making it necessary to include SEARCH ADD statements for all necessary directories in the AUTOEXEC.NCF startup file.

Figure 16-3

Sample SEARCH commands

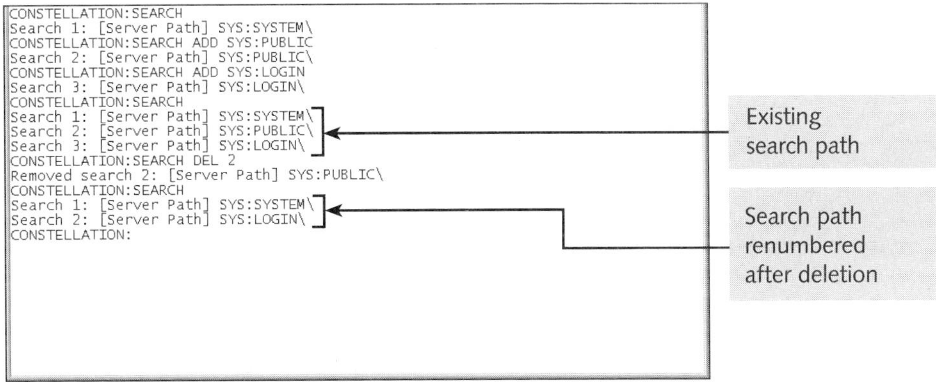

Configuration Commands

The configuration console commands shown in Figure 16-4 are used to view the configuration of the file server and associated network cards. The information obtained by using these commands helps the network administrator identify the configuration of LAN cards and protocols, view other servers and networks, change the server date and time, and expand the network.

Figure 16-4

Configuration commands

Command Syntax	Description
CONFIG	Displays configuration information about each network card, including hardware settings, network address, protocol, and frame type.
DISPLAY NETWORKS	Shows all networks to which the file server has access, including the number of routers (hops) and the time in ticks ($\frac{1}{18}$ sec.) it takes to reach each network.
DISPLAY SERVERS	Shows all servers in the file server's router table, including the number of routers (hops) to get to each server.
LIST DEVICES	Indicates all devices currently registered with the NetWare operating system.
MEMORY	Displays the total amount of memory available to the file server computer.
NAME	Displays the name of the file server.
PROTOCOL	Displays all protocols that are currently in use.
SET	Allows you to view or change current file server environment settings.
SET TIME [*month/day/year*] [*hour:minute:second*]	Allows you to change the file server's current system date and time.

The CONFIG command displays information about the file server and network card configuration, as shown in Figure 16-5. Notice that in addition to displaying the file server's name and internal network address, the CONFIG command displays the following information about each network adapter in the file server:

- Name of the LAN driver

- Current hardware settings, including interrupt, I/O port, memory address, and Direct Memory Access (DMA) channel
- Node (station) address assigned to the network adapter
- Frame type assigned to the network adapter
- Board name assigned when the LAN driver was loaded
- Protocol stack that was bound to the network adapter
- Network address of the cabling scheme for the network adapter

Figure 16-5 Sample CONFIG command

```
IPX internal network number: CBE1AB01
     Node address: 000000000001
     Frame type: VIRTUAL_LAN
     LAN protocol: IPX network CBE1AB01
Server Up Time:  2 Hours 43 Minutes 32 Seconds

Intel EtherExpress(tm) PRO LAN Adapter
     Version 1.48    September 16, 1994
     Hardware setting: I/O ports 300h to 30Fh, Interrupt Bh
     Node address: 00AA005F0E36
     Frame type: ETHERNET_802.2
     Board name: EPRO_E8022
     LAN protocol: IPX network 00019200

Intel EtherExpress(tm) PRO LAN Adapter
     Version 1.48    September 16, 1994
     Hardware setting: I/O ports 300h to 30Fh, Interrupt Bh
     Node address: 00AA005F0E36
     Frame type: ETHERNET_802.3
     Board name: EPRO_E8023
     LAN protocol: IPX network 00019300

Tree Name: CBELABS
Bindery Context(s):
<Press ESC to terminate or any other key to continue>
```

Use the CONFIG command before installing memory boards or network adapters in the file server so that you have a current list of all hardware settings on the existing boards. This will help you select unique interrupt and I/O address settings for the new cards. The CONFIG command can also be used to determine the network address of a cable system before you add another file server to the network. If you accidentally bring up another file server using a different network address for the same cable system, router configuration errors between the file servers will interfere with network communications.

The DISPLAY NETWORKS command lists all network addresses and internal network numbers in use on the network system, as shown in Figure 16-6. In addition to showing the address of each network, the DISPLAY NETWORKS command shows the amount of time required to access the network, measured by the number of hops and ticks required to reach each network from the current server. Each hop is a router that must be crossed in order to reach the given network. Each tick is a time interval of one-eighteenth of a second.

Figure 16-6 Sample DISPLAY NETWORKS command

```
CONSTELLATION:DISPLAY NETWORKS
   00000001  1/1      000000F1  2/3      000000F5  2/3      00000666  3/4
   00000D17  4/6      00001001  2/3      00001002  2/3      00001003  2/3
   00001100  1/1      00003001  2/3      00003002  2/3      00003100  1/1
   00004100  2/3      00005001  2/3      00006100  2/3      00008001  2/3
   00008002  2/3      00008003  2/3      00008004  2/3      00008005  2/3
   00008006  2/3      00008100  1/1      00009999  3/3      0000A100  1/1
   0000B100  1/1      0000BAD1  2/3      0000BAD2  2/3      0000C100  2/2
   0000D001  3/4      0000D002  3/4      0000D100  2/2      0000D300  3/4
   0000F001  3/4      0000F002  3/4      0000F300  2/2      0000FFFA  3/4
   0000FFFB  2/3      00012001  2/3      00012100  1/1      00013100  2/3
   00014100  2/3      00015100  1/1      00016100  2/2      00017001  2/3
   00017002  2/3      00018100  2/3      00019100  1/1      00019200  0/1
   00019300  0/1      00020001  2/3      00020100  2/3      00024001  2/3
   00025200  1/1      00026006  2/3      00026300  1/1      00028100  2/2
   00029001  2/3      00029002  2/3      00029100  1/1      00031001  2/3
   00031002  2/3      00031003  2/3      00032100  2/2      00033100  3/9
   00034100  1/1      00035100  2/3      00037001  4/5      00037002  4/5
   00037300  3/3      00C00009  2/3      00C0000A  2/3      00C0000B  2/3
   8CA08C00  2/3      8CA08CDA  2/3      8CA08CDE  3/4      CBE00001  1/2
   CBE00002  1/2      CBE00003  1/2      CBE1AB01  0/1      CBE1AB02  1/2
   DEED0000  3/12     DEED0001  3/20
There are 82 known networks
CONSTELLATION:
```

Ticks

Hops

The DISPLAY SERVERS command is useful to determine if the file server is properly attached to a multiserver network. When a file server is first attached to a network, it sends a broadcast to all machines on the network advertising its presence. From these broadcasts, the file servers and workstations on the network build router tables that include the names of all servers and routers on the network. The DISPLAY SERVERS command lists all servers that have been inserted into the router table.

For example, when the network administrator for CBE Labs, attempted to add the server RANGER to the network, he encountered some difficulties. First, RANGER did not appear in other servers' (CONSTELLATION and SARATOGA) router tables and RANGER did does not "see" the other servers on the network. He determined that this was because the IPX protocol had not been bound to the network card. Another frequent cause of this trouble is that the network card driver is using a frame type that is different from that of other servers. After making this correction, RANGER then showed up on other file servers, but CONSTELLATION and SARATOGA did not appear on RANGER. By using the CONFIG command to check for an overlapping interrupt or memory address, he found that the network card in RANGER had a conflicting interrupt and was not able to receive network packets from other servers. A conflicting memory address is also a frequent cause of this problem.

The LIST DEVICES command lists information about all storage device drivers attached to the file server, including disk drives, tape drives, and CD-ROMs. Information includes device number, description, and the NetWare assigned device ID, as shown in Figure 16-7, and can be useful when you are checking to see if all devices are loaded.

```
CONSTELLATION:DISPLAY NETWORKS
   00000001  1/1      000000F1  2/3      000000F5  2/3      00000666  3/4
   00000D17  4/6      00001001  2/3      00001002  2/3      00001003  2/3
   00001100  1/1      00003001  2/3      00003002  2/3      00003100  1/1
   00004100  2/3      00005001  2/3      00006100  2/3      00008001  2/3
   00008002  2/3      00008003  2/3      00008004  2/3      00008005  2/3
   00008006  2/3      00008100  1/1      00009999  3/3      0000A100  1/1
   0000B100  1/1      0000BAD1  2/3      0000BAD2  2/3      0000C100  2/2
   0000D001  3/4      0000D002  3/4      0000D100  2/2      0000D300  3/4
   0000F001  3/4      0000F002  3/4      0000F300  2/2      0000FFFA  3/4
   0000FFFB  2/3      00012001  2/3      00012100  1/1      00013100  2/3
   00014100  2/3      00015100  1/1      00016100  2/2      00017001  2/3
   00017002  2/3      00018100  2/3      00019100  1/1      00019200  0/1
   00019300  0/1      00020001  2/3      00020100  2/3      00024001  2/3
   00025200  1/1      00026006  2/3      00026300  1/1      00028100  2/2
   00029001  2/3      00029002  2/3      00029100  1/1      00031001  2/3
   00031002  2/3      00031003  2/3      00032100  2/2      00033100  3/9
   00034100  1/1      00035100  2/3      00037001  4/5      00037002  4/5
   00037300  3/3      00C00009  2/3      00C0000A  2/3      00C0000B  2/3
   8CA08C00  2/3      8CA08CDA  2/3      8CA08CDE  3/4      CBE00001  1/2
   CBE00002  1/2      CBE00003  1/2      CBE1AB01  0/1      CBE1AB02  1/2
   DEED0000  3/12     DEED0001  3/20
There are 82 known networks
CONSTELLATION:
```

Figure 16-7

Sample LIST DEVICES command

The MEMORY command enables you to determine the total amount of memory available to the file server. If you have more than 16 MB of RAM memory installed and the MEMORY command displays only 16 MB or less, you might need to use the REGISTER MEMORY command to enable use of the additional memory. If you have less than 16 MB and the memory displayed is smaller than the total memory in the file server computer, check to be sure that the computer is not loading HIMEM.SYS when DOS is booted. Loading HIMEM.SYS can take up part of the extended memory available to the NetWare operating system.

The NAME command simply displays the name of the file server on the console. By default, the NetWare 4.1 operating systems display the server name as part of the console prompt, so the NAME command is not needed to identify these file server consoles. With NetWare 3.11 or earlier, however, the file server name does not appear as part of the console prompt. You might find the NAME command useful when you are working in an environment with several older file servers. You can confirm the name of the file server console on which you are working.

As shown in Figure 16-8, the PROTOCOL command displays all protocols that are registered with the file server along with the network frame types associated with the protocol. Initially, only the IPX protocol is registered with the NetWare operating system. Other popular protocols, like TCP/IP, need to be loaded and registered before they can be used.

Figure 16-8

Sample PROTOCOL command

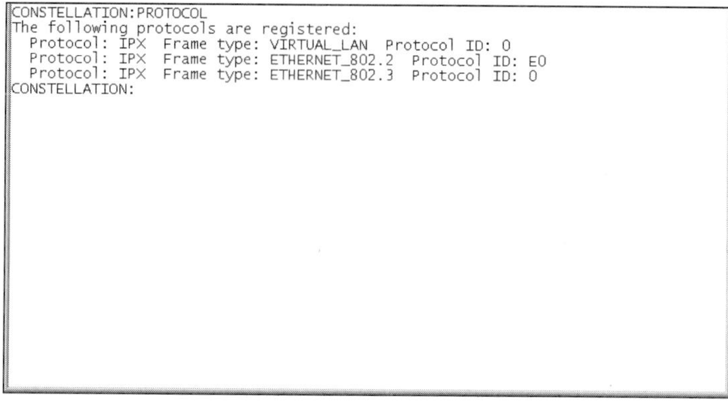

```
CONSTELLATION:PROTOCOL
The following protocols are registered:
  Protocol: IPX  Frame type: VIRTUAL_LAN  Protocol ID: 0
  Protocol: IPX  Frame type: ETHERNET_802.2  Protocol ID: E0
  Protocol: IPX  Frame type: ETHERNET_802.3  Protocol ID: 0
CONSTELLATION:
```

The PROTOCOL command can also be used to register additional protocols and frame types. The syntax for adding the new types is PROTOCOL *protocol frame id#* REGISTER, where *protocol* is the name of the protocol, *frame* is the name of the frame type to be bound, and *id#* is a special protocol identification number (PID), that identifies data coming from a network board through a designated communications protocol like IPX. REGISTER is used only when you are using a new media.

Use the SET command to view or change settings for the configuration categories shown in Figure 16-9.

Figure 16-9

SET configuration options

```
CONSTELLATION:SET
Settable configuration parameter categories
  1. Communications
  2. Memory
  3. File caching
  4. Directory caching
  5. File system
  6. Locks
  7. Transaction tracking
  8. Disk
  9. Time
  10. NCP
  11. Miscellaneous
  12. Error Handling
  13. Directory Services
Which category do you want to view:
```

Use the SET TIME command to change the current server time or date. The following commands show three variations of using SET TIME to change the NetWare server's current date and time to 3:00 P.M., October 30, 1999 (the third variation uses two SET TIME commands):

```
SET TIME 10/30/99 3:00p.m.
SET TIME October 30, 1999 3:00p.m.
SET TIME October 30, 1999
SET TIME 3:00p.m.
```

Maintenance Commands

The maintenance commands shown in Figure 16-10 are the console commands commonly used by the network administrator to control access to the file server and volumes, to broadcast messages, to look for network problems, and to shut down the file server for upgrades or maintenance.

Use the SEND command to send a message to all users who are currently logged into the file server. The message will appear on the user's workstation unless the user has issued the SEND /A=N command to prevent all messages from being displayed. The SEND /A=C command allows messages from the server to be displayed and ignores messages from other workstations. Users should be discouraged from using SEND /A=N command because it can result in the loss of data if the server is brought down without their knowledge.

Use the CLEAR STATION command to terminate a workstation's connection to the file server. A connection to a file server is made when the workstation runs the Client 32 requester. The connection continues to be active, whether or not a user is logged in to the file server, until the workstation is rebooted or turned off. If a user is logged in when the connection is cleared, data can be lost due to incomplete updating of files that are open at the time the station's connection to the file server is terminated.

Each NetWare operating system is designed to support a maximum number of connections depending on the license purchased. If your maximum number of connections is reached and if you have workstations not currently being used, you can use the CLEAR STATION command to terminate unused connections, making room for other workstations to be attached to the file server. You can use the MONITOR utility, described later in this chapter, to determine which connections are not currently being used.

The CLS and OFF commands can be used to clear the file server console screen, enabling you to see new console messages more easily. A common practice is to use the CLS or OFF command prior to loading new modules or recording error messages.

Another use for the CLEAR STATION command is to force workstations to log off the file server prior to downing the server or performing a backup. For example, the Network Administrator for CBE Labs, comes into work on a holiday and, after completing his work, decides to do a backup of the system. However, before terminating a connection, he uses MONITOR to determine if any data files are open and also uses the SEND command to send a message to the user of that station to close the open files and log out.

The DISABLE LOGIN command prevents new users from logging in to the file server. Prior to downing the file server, he issues the DISABLE LOGIN message to prevent any additional CBE Labs users from logging in. He then uses the SEND command to send a message to all connected users telling them that the server will be downed after the specified time period and that they should close all files and log out of the server. If the DISABLE LOGIN command is not issued, new CBE Labs users can log in to the server after the message is broadcast, unaware that the server is about to be downed.

Figure 16-10

Maintenance commands

Command Syntax	Description
SEND *message*	Sends the specified *message* to all currently logged in users.
CLEAR STATION *number*	Terminates the specified workstation connection number in the command.
CLS/OFF	Clears the file server console screen.
DISABLE/ENABLE LOGIN	Prevents or enables new user logins.
DOWN	Closes all files and volumes, disconnects all users, and takes the file server off line.
EXIT	Returns the server to the DOS prompt. If DOS is not loaded, the server computer will reboot.
MODULES	Lists all currently loaded modules starting with the last module loaded.
MOUNT *volume_name* [ALL] DISMOUNT *volume_name* [ALL]	Places a volume on or off line. Replace *volume_name* with the name of the volume you want mounted or use ALL to mount all NetWare volumes.
RESET ROUTER	Rebuilds the file server's router table, including any new servers and removing any servers that do not respond.
SCAN FOR NEW DEVICES	Registers new devices that have been switched on since the server was booted.
SEND "*message*" [TO] *username|connection_number*	Sends a message to a specified user. Replace *message* with a message (enclosed in quotes) you want sent. Replace *username|connection_number* with either the name of the currently logged in user or the connection number assigned to the user. The *connection_number* can be obtained from the Connection option of the MONITOR NLM.
TRACK ON/TRACK OFF	Displays service advertising packets that are sent or received.
UNBIND *protocol* [FROM] *driver|board_name*	Removes a protocol from a LAN card. Replace *protocol* with the name of the protocol stack (e.g., IPX) you want to remove from the card. Replace *driver|board_name* with either the name of the driver program that has been loaded for the network card or the name assigned to the network card by the LOAD command.
UNLOAD *module_name*	Removes a NetWare Loadable Module from memory and returns the memory space to the operating system. Replace *module_name* with the name of the currently loaded module, as stated in the MODULES command.

The DOWN command deactivates the NetWare server operating system and removes all workstation connections. Before issuing the DOWN command, you should disable new logins and broadcast a message to all users. You can then use the MONITOR command to be sure all connections are logged out prior to entering the DOWN command. The command sequence is shown in Figure 16-11.

Figure 16-11

Command sequence for downing a server

```
CONSTELLATION:DISABLE LOGIN
 3-08-97  12:43:57 pm:     SERVER-4.10-2488
     Login is now disabled

CONSTELLATION:SEND "CONSTELLATION IS GOING OFF LINE.  PLEASE LOG OUT"
CONSTELLATION:DOWN
File TCLASS31.DLL in use by user ADMIN on station 5
File NWMOD01.DLL in use by user ADMIN on station 5
File NWVIS01.DLL in use by user ADMIN on station 5
File NWVCTRLS.DLL in use by user ADMIN on station 5
File NWMOD00.DLL in use by user ADMIN on station 5
File NWCNTRLS.DLL in use by user ADMIN on station 5
File NWCODS.DLL in use by user ADMIN on station 5
File NWBRWS.DLL in use by user ADMIN on station 5
File NWADMINR.DLL in use by user ADMIN on station 5
File NWPARR.DLL in use by user ADMIN on station 5
File NWPAR.DLL in use by user ADMIN on station 5
File RCONSOLE.HEP in use by user ADMIN on station 5
File TEXTUTIL.IDX in use by user ADMIN on station 5
File TEXTUTIL.MSG in use by user ADMIN on station 5
File RCONSOLE.MSG in use by user ADMIN on station 5
*** WARNING *** There are active files open.
Down server? n
```

Active users

If active sessions exist, the NetWare operating system will issue a warning message asking you if you want to terminate active sessions. If you see this message, you should cancel the DOWN command and use the MONITOR utility to determine which connections have open files. Then send messages to those users to log out. If no one is at the workstation and data files have been left open, you will need to go to the station yourself to close the open files and log out for the user. Remind users that their workstations should not be left unattended while data files are open.

The EXIT command terminates the NetWare operating system and attempts to return the computer to the DOS prompt. If DOS has been removed from the file server computer with the REMOVE DOS command, NetWare will reboot the file server computer when the EXIT command is executed.

As mentioned above, NLMs are external programs that are loaded into the memory of the file server computer to add functionality to the NetWare core operating system. The MODULES command lists all the currently loaded modules with their names, version numbers, and release dates. The modules are listed in sequence, starting with the last module loaded and ending with the first module loaded. In addition to showing what modules have been loaded, the MODULES command also lets you quickly check the version number and date of a module. You need this information to determine NetWare compatibility or to look for network problems that are known to be caused by defective versions of certain modules.

The CompuServe Novell NetWare forum, along with the Novell Internet home page, are good places to check for information regarding problems with NLMs. They also provide information on obtaining corrected versions of the defective modules.

Mounting a volume is the process of loading information from the volume's directory entry table (DET) into the file server's RAM. This makes the volume available for access by users and the file server's operating system. The MOUNT command is needed to mount a volume that did not mount correctly when the file server was booted or has been taken off line with the DISMOUNT command. Normally the MOUNT ALL command is inserted into the file server's AUTOEXEC.NCF startup file during installation; it attempts to mount all volumes when the file server is brought up. Yet in some cases, such as after a file server crash, some volumes might not mount due to errors in their file allocation tables (FATs) or DETs. When this happens, it is necessary the correct the problem and then use the MOUNT command to bring the repaired volume on line.

When a new file server is first brought onto a network, it sends out **service advertising packets (SAPs)** to inform all other machines of its name and network address. Other machines on the network then add the new server to their router tables, enabling them to pass packets to any of the servers. The DISPLAY SERVERS command enables you to view all machines currently in a server's router table. Servers continue to send out SAPs periodically to notify other servers that they are still available as well as to notify new servers of existing server name and address information. When a server is taken off the network, it can take a few minutes for all machines to become aware that the server is no longer sending advertising packets. There is thus a time delay before the inactive server is removed from the router tables. This means that servers can appear in the DISPLAY SERVERS list after they have been taken off the network. The RESET ROUTER command causes a server to rebuild its router table by sending out a broadcast packet asking all servers to identify themselves with their SAPs.

You should normally use the RESET ROUTER and DISPLAY SERVERS commands on a new server to confirm that the new server can communicate with other servers on the network. On a large internetwork it can take several minutes for a downed server to be removed from all server router tables. Because of this, it is a good idea to issue the RESET ROUTER command prior to the DISPLAY SERVERS command, when you want to view the active server list. Then you can be sure that all servers listed are currently on the network.

The DISPLAY SERVERS command will show all servers that are sending SAP packets. These include servers that are providing NetWare Directory Services (NDS), Storage Management Services (SMS), and Structured Query Language (SQL) services.

The SCAN FOR NEW DEVICES command causes the NetWare operating system to check for any new devices that have been brought on line since the file server was booted. The most common use for this command is if you have external tape and CD-ROM devices attached to the SCSI interface. If a tape drive or CD-ROM device is not turned on when the file server is booted, it will not be available for use unless you issue the SCAN FOR NEW DEVICES command. The SCAN FOR NEW DEVICES command enables the NetWare operating system to register new devices without having to be restarted.

The SEND command on the file server console is used to transmit a message to a workstation on the network. The most common use of the SEND command is to request a user to log out prior to downing the file server. Messages can be sent either to a user's login name or to a connection number by enclosing the message in quotation marks and following it with the connection number or username.

The TRACK ON command can be used to view SAPs and router information packets that are either received by or sent from your file server, as shown in Figure 16-12. All servers, including a print server or MHS messaging server, periodically send out SAPs to inform other machines of their presence. In addition to SAPs, file servers periodically (approximately once each minute) send out special packets called router information packets (RIPs). The RIP contains a list of all network addresses and the number of ticks and hops required to reach each network from the sending server.

Figure 16-12

Sample TRACK ON command

```
         0000BAD2  2/3      0000BAD1  2/3      00017001  2/3      00037300  3/3
         00037002  4/5      00037001  4/5      00017002  2/3      8CA08CDA  2/3
         8CA08CDE  3/4      00018100  2/3      00008001  2/3      00008100  1/1
IN     [00019300:00000C0E24AE] 12:47:13 pm     00008001  2/3      00008100  1/1
         00008002  2/3      00008003  2/3      CBE1AB02  2/3      00028100  2/2
         00008004  2/3      00008005  2/3      00008006  2/3      00029002  2/3
         00019100  1/1      00029001  2/3      00029100  1/1      00019200  1/1
         8CA08C00  2/3      0000A100  1/1      0000B100  1/1      0000C100  2/2
         00C00009  2/3      00C0000A  2/3      00C0000B  2/3      0000D001  3/4
         0000D100  2/2      0000D002  3/4      0000D300  3/4      000000F1  2/3
         0000F001  3/4      0000F002  3/4      0000F300  2/2      000000F5  2/3
IN     [00019200:08000913A49D] 12:47:13 pm     08000913A49D  1
IN     [00019200:00000C0E24AE] 12:47:13 pm     00008002  2/3      00008003  2/3
         00028100  2/2      00008004  2/3      00008005  2/3      00008006  2/3
         00029002  2/3      00019100  1/1      00019300  1/1      00029001  2/3
         00029100  1/1      8CA08C00  2/3      0000A100  1/1      0000B100  1/1
         0000C100  2/2      00C00009  2/3      00C0000A  2/3      00C0000B  2/3
         0000D001  3/4      0000D100  2/2      0000D002  3/4      0000D300  3/4
         000000F1  2/3      0000F001  3/4      0000F002  3/4      0000F300  2/2
         000000F5  2/3
IN     [00019300:08000913A49D] 12:47:14 pm     08000913A49D  1
IN     [CBE1AB01:000000000001] 12:47:14 pm     CBELABS_____  1
IN     [00019300:0800098A025F] 12:47:16 pm     0800098A025F  1
<Use ALT-ESC or CTRL-ESC to switch screens, or any other key to pause>
```

This router information is used by other servers on the network to maintain their local router tables. Use the TRACK ON command to display any SAPs and RIPs with the name and network address of the sender. This information can help you determine what is happening on the network and whether the server in question is functioning properly. If, for example, a server is sending but not receiving any packets, it means the server is using the wrong frame type, other servers on the network are not functioning, or there is a problem with the network cable system.

After the TRACK ON command is issued, the console screen displays all SAPs that are being sent or received. You can use the [Alt][Esc] key combination to change back to the console prompt or to any other module. To end the TRACK ON command, use [Alt][Esc] or [Ctrl][Esc] to return to the console prompt. Then enter the TRACK OFF command.

The network administrator at CBE Labs is having a problem on the network. The NetWare server CONSTELLATION is on but does not show up in response to the DISPLAY SERVERS command. He then uses the TRACK ON command along with the RESET ROUTER command to determine whether the server is sending out SAPs. If the NetWare server CONSTELLATION is sending out SAPs but the SAPs are not being received, it can indicate an error in the network card or cable system. If SAPs are not being sent out from the NetWare server CONSTELLATION, it can mean that the server is down or has crashed. He would then need to reload the server in order to bring it back on line.

Use the UNBIND command to unload a protocol stack from a LAN driver. This will cause the server to stop communicating with other machines using that protocol. The most common use of the UNBIND command is to take a defective server off the network. Assume, for example, that the network administrator had bound the IPX protocol to a LAN driver yet used the wrong network number for the cable system. Almost immediately, the servers on the network will begin to signal that the router is calling the network a different name. To stop this problem, Dave uses the UNBIND command to remove the protocol from the network card and then reissues the BIND command using the correct network address, as shown in Figure 16-13.

Figure 16-13

Sample UNBIND command

```
CONSTELLATION:BIND IPX TO EPRO_EII NET=10BA5E
IPX LAN protocol bound to Intel EtherExpress(tm) PRO LAN Adapter

 3-08-97   1:54:20 pm:     SERVER-4.10-1365
     Router configuration error detected
     Node 00000C0E24AE claims network 0010BA5E should be 00019100


 3-08-97   1:54:30 pm:     SERVER-4.10-19
     Router configuration error detected
     Node 08000913A49D () claims network 0010BA5E should be 00019100

CONSTELLATION:UNBIND IPX FROM EPRO_EII

 3-08-97   1:54:42 pm:     SERVER-4.10-2134
     IPX local network 0010BA5E removed because of unbind request

IPX LAN protocol unbound from Intel EtherExpress(tm) PRO LAN Adapter
CONSTELLATION:BIND IPX TO EPRO_EII NET=19100
```

The UNLOAD command terminates an NLM and removes it from the file server's memory. If your file server has a marginal amount of memory, it might be necessary to remove modules in order to make space for file caching. Another common use for the UNLOAD command is to disconnect the server from a network card so that you can test or fix a problem without downing the server and affecting users on different networks.

Assume, for example, that the CBE Labs server has both token ring and Ethernet cards in it, and the network administrator for CBE Labs, needs to down the token ring network for maintenance. If he disconnects the server computer from the token ring cable, a string of error messages from the LAN driver indicating that the card is not connected will tie up his server console. To prevent this from happening, he instead uses the UNLOAD TOKEN command to remove the TOKEN LAN driver prior to disconnecting the cable from the file server. Although the users on the Ethernet network will not be affected, he is sure to notify all users on the token ring network that they need to log out before he unloads the

TOKEN LAN driver and disconnects the server, or else valuable data might be lost. After performing the necessary work on the token ring network, he re-establishes communications with the token ring users by using the LOAD command to load the TOKEN LAN driver module and then using the BIND command to bind IPX to the token driver. The users on the token ring network can then log back in and resume using the server.

Security Commands

Securing the NetWare server console is necessary to prevent unauthorized users from entering console commands or loading NLMs. Depending on your organization, the need for NetWare server console security can range from keeping the server in a separate room to providing maximum security from intruders who are attempting to gain access to your network. Locking the server room is one of the first measures of NetWare server security that can be put in place. The security console commands shown in Figure 16-14 enable you to provide extra protection from unauthorized use of console commands.

Figure 16-14

Security Console commands

Command Syntax	Description
REMOVE DOS	Removes DOS from the file server's memory, preventing operators from loading modules from the DOS local drives. Causes the server to reboot when the EXIT command is used.
SECURE CONSOLE	Removes DOS and prevents NLMs from being loaded from any other directory except SYS:SYSTEM.

The REMOVE DOS command can provide both extra memory as well as extra security for the NetWare server. The network administrator at CBE Labs uses the REMOVE DOS command on the NetWare server CONSTELLATION for several reasons. First, by removing DOS from the NetWare server's RAM, it will free up additional memory. Second, REMOVE DOS will prevent access to any DOS devices on the NetWare server. This would prevent someone from loading an NLM from the server's DOS drives. And because REMOVE DOS will cause the NetWare server computer to reboot when the operator enters the EXIT command, this further increases the security of the NetWare server. If he can combine this action with removing the floppy disk drive, using a computer with a power-on password, and creating an AUTOEXEC.BAT file that contains only the commands necessary to start SERVER, he can prevent anyone from booting the computer as a DOS machine and running programs that can change information in the NetWare partition.

The SECURE CONSOLE command automatically performs the following security functions intended to prevent several types of breaches in security:

- Removes DOS
- Prevents NLMs from being loaded from any directory other than the SYS:SYSTEM directory
- Prevents keyboard entry into the operating system debugger
- Prevents the use of the SET TIME command to change date and time from the console (a console operator or supervisor can still change the date and time by using the FCONSOLE utility from a workstation)
- Prevents a module from being loaded from a DOS partition, diskette drive, or NetWare volume

One way an intruder could access or alter information in the NetWare server CONSTELLATION at CBE Labs would be to load a special NLM from the console that directly accesses data files. Because the SECURE CONSOLE command enables NLMs to be loaded only from the SYS:SYSTEM directory, an intruder will not be able to load the offending module from a DOS drive or some other directory on the server in which he or she has rights. The only way an intruder can load a module after the SECURE CONSOLE command has been issued is to have necessary rights to copy the module into the SYS:SYSTEM directory. Of course, for this part of the SECURE CONSOLE command to be effective in preventing unwanted loading of NLMs, you must be sure that no one has rights to SYS:SYSTEM and that your accounts are secure.

Some security and accounting features depend on date and time for their enforcement. Suppose, for example, Thomas Meyers in Finance at CBE Labs has his username secured both by a password and by a restriction on when and from what workstation he can log in. An intruder learns Thomas's password and gains access to the workstation on a weekend. Because the intruder has the equivalent of a master key, he or she gains access to the NetWare server console and uses the SET TIME command to change the date and time to a normal weekday. The intruder can then access or change the payroll data files. The SECURE CONSOLE command would prevent this by disabling the SET TIME command.

NetWare Loadable Modules

One of the major strengths of NetWare is its use of NetWare Loadable Modules (NLMs) to add functionality to the operating system. As discussed previously, the SERVER.EXE program provides the core NetWare services and acts like a software bus, enabling NLMs to be added to support hardware devices and software functions such as print servers and electronic messaging. Because NLMs play such an important role in the tailoring of the NetWare network, it is important that a CNA be familiar with the standard NLMs that are included with the NetWare operating system.

As shown in Figure 16-15, NLMs can be classified into four general categories based on their function. Each category has its own extension. In this section you will learn what you need to know about each of these NLMs in order, to manage your file server environments effectively.

Figure 16-15

NLM categories

Category	Extension	Description
Disk drivers	.DSK	Control access to the NetWare disk partitions.
LAN drivers	.LAN	Each network card must be controlled by a compatible LAN driver.
Name space modules	.NAM	Contain logic to support other workstation naming conventions, such as those found on Apple Macintosh computers or OS/2- and Unix-based computers.
General-purpose modules	.NLM	Add additional services and functions to the file server's operating system.

Disk Drivers

When you first start the NetWare operating system by running the SERVER.EXE program, it does not have a way of directly controlling the disk drives on the file server computer until a disk driver module is loaded. Accessing the DOS partition of the hard disk and floppy disk drives does not require the disk driver. The DOS partition is available through the local DOS operating system until it is removed from the computer by either the REMOVE DOS or SECURE CONSOLE command. As described previously, when NetWare is installed on the file server computer, disk driver modules with the extension .DSK are copied into the DOS partition. The command to load the appropriate disk driver module for your computer is later placed in the STARTUP.NCF file so that when the SERVER.EXE program starts, it will load the correct disk drive in order to access the NetWare volumes.

LAN Drivers

Before a file server can access the network cable, a LAN driver for the network controller card must be loaded and a protocol bound to that LAN driver. Standard network drivers all have the extension .LAN and can be found in the SYS:SYSTEM directory after you have installed the NetWare operating system files. If your network card does not use one of the standard drivers, the correct driver software should be included on a disk that comes with the network card.

Name Space Modules

As mentioned above, name space modules add logic to the NetWare operating system that enables it to support non-DOS filenames. By default, NetWare supports standard DOS file specifications consisting of eight-letter filenames and three-letter extensions. However, other operating systems, like UNIX and Macintosh, enable users to create filenames that can contain up to 255 characters including spaces, special symbols, and graphic icon attributes. NetWare includes special NLMs, called name modules, that can interpret these filenames on a NetWare server. Figure 16-16 shows two name modules that are included with NetWare and can be found in the SYS:SYSTEM directory with the .NAM extension. When you use name space support, you need to load the appropriate .NAM modules after the disk driver in the STARTUP.NCF file. Later in this chapter you will learn how to add and remove name space support from a volume.

Figure 16-16

NetWare name space modules

Name Space Module	Description
MAC.NAM	Supports Apple Macintosh file naming conventions.
OS2.NAM	Supports IBM OS/2 workstation filenames.

General-Purpose Modules

In addition to special modules for controlling disk and network cards, a number of general-purpose NLMs are included in NetWare's SYS:SYSTEM directory. They have the extension .NLM and provide a wide range of capabilities, as described in Figure 16-17. The rest of this section describes the modules a CNA will use to manage network file servers.

Figure 16-17

General-purpose NLMs

Module	Description
CDROM.NLM	Provides support for CD-ROM commands.
INSTALL.NLM	Used to work with NetWare partitions, volumes, and system files.
MONITOR.NLM	Used to monitor file server performance, hardware status, and memory usage.
DSREPAIR.NLM	Corrects problem in NDS tree.
REMOTE.NLM	Provides the ability to view and operate the NetWare server console from a remote workstation. Requires a password.
RSPX.NLM	Enables the REMOTE module to send and receive console screens and commands over the local network cable.
RS232.NLM	Enables the REMOTE module to send and receive console screens and commands over the asynchronous port.
UPS.NLM	Provides the ability to monitor the status of the UPS and down the server prior to depleting the battery.
VREPAIR.NLM	Checks the specified volume for errors and enables the operator to write corrections to the disk.

CDROM

The CDROM module enables a file server to use a CD-ROM device attached to a device driver as a read-only volume. In order to attach a CD-ROM device to your file server, you will need both the CD-ROM device plus the necessary drivers for use with your NetWare file server. Most CD-ROM devices attached to NetWare servers today use a SCSI controller card along with associated SCSI disk driver software. You may need to load additional support modules.

Sharing CD-ROMs that contain desktop publishing clip art, sound files, and video for multimedia applications is an important function of the NetWare server in most organizations.

After loading the CDROM module, use the console commands shown in Figure 16-18 to manage the attached CD-ROM devices. Use the CD DEVICE LIST command to obtain a list of volume names and device numbers.

Figure 16-18
CD-ROM commands

CD Command	Description
CD HELP	Displays a list of CD-ROM commands and options.
CD DEVICE LIST	Lists all CD-ROM devices that the NetWare operating system can access. Information about the CD-ROM devices includes device number, name, volume name, and whether the CD-ROM volume is mounted.
CD VOLUME LIST	Displays a list of all CD-ROM volumes that are currently mounted.
CD MOUNT [*volume_name*] [*device_number*]	Mounts the volume specified by either the volume name or device number.
CD DISMOUNT [*volume_name*] [*device_number*]	Dismounts the specified volume, freeing up all system resources used by the volume.
CD CHANGE [*volume_name*] [*device_number*]	Enables you to change the CD-ROM mounted in the specified device. The volume specified will be dismounted and you will be prompted for the new volume. The new medium will be automatically mounted as a NetWare volume.
CD DIR [*volume_name*] [*device_number*]	Enables you to view the contents of the root directory of the specified CD-ROM volume. A volume does not need to be mounted for you to use the CD DIR command.

The network administrator wants to make a CD-ROM available to users on the NetWare server SARATOGA at CBE Labs. He will use the CD MOUNT command to mount a CD-ROM as a NetWare read-only volume. Each user workstation can map a drive letter to the CD-ROM volume and access files. Because of the amount of information on CD-ROMs and their relatively slow access times as compared to fixed disk drives, it can often take several minutes to mount a CD-ROM volume.

When working with several CD-ROMs that have large directories, decrease the amount of time required to remount a volume by including the /R option with the CD MOUNT command. The /R option tells NetWare to reuse existing data files instead of rebuilding or recreating them.

Install

You have already learned how to use the INSTALL module to perform such installation tasks as creating NetWare partitions and volumes on existing hard drives, copying all system and public files in the SYS: volume, and creating the STARTUP.NCF and AUTOEXEC.NCF files. After NetWare is installed, the INSTALL module can be used to add new disk space to an existing volume, maintain the STARTUP and AUTOEXEC files, and install new products such as the Message Handling System.

Suppose the NetWare server CONSTELLATION at CBE Labs is filling up and the network administrator needs to add disk space to an existing volume. Naturally, he must first have additional disk space available in the current NetWare partitions of existing disk drives or he would have to add a new hard drive to the file server's computer. Adding disk space from another disk partition to your volume is called *spanning* the volume. One of the biggest problems of spanning a volume across multiple partitions is the increased probability that a failure of any of the drives the volume occupies will bring down the entire volume. Therefore, if he plans to span a volume onto a new drive, the preferred method is to add two drives of the same capacity and then use the mirroring feature to synchronize the drives. This way, if one of the drives used by the volume fails, the mirrored drive will still allow access to the volume and its data.

Monitor

The MONITOR utility module is one of the most powerful NLMs supplied with the NetWare operating system. It can be used to lock the file server console as well as view file server performance, connection information, and disk and network statistics.

After the MONITOR utility is loaded, the General Information screen shown is displayed. If you leave MONITOR running with no keyboard activity for 10 seconds, the General Information screen expands, as shown in Figure 16-19 (the [Tab] key toggles between normal and expanded screens). This screen displays information regarding the file server's available memory and performance. Server up time measures the length of time the server has been running since it was last booted. The Utilization field shows the percentage of time the processor is busy. In most cases, utilization should be less than 70%. The Original cache buffers field contains the number of buffers (in blocks of 4 KB) that were available when the server was first booted. The Total cache buffers field contains the number of buffers currently available for file caching.

If the number of total cache buffers is less than one third of the original cache buffers, the server is running low on memory and you should either unload modules or add more RAM as soon as possible.

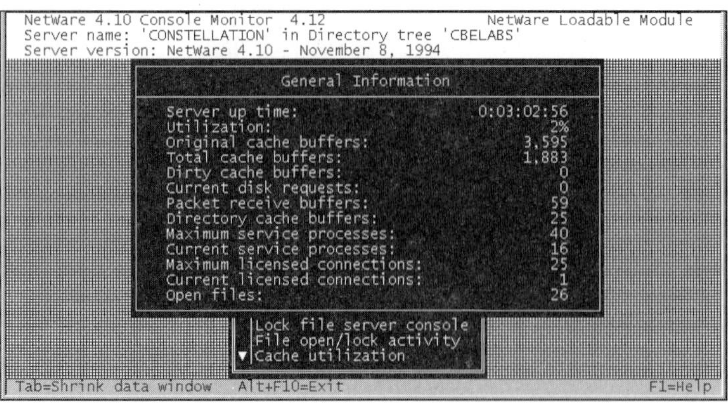

Figure 16-19
Monitor screen

The Dirty cache buffers field contains a count of the number of buffers that have had modifications made but are waiting to be written to disk. A large number of dirty cache buffers indicates that the disk system is bogging down and a faster disk or an additional disk controller card might be necessary. The Current disk requests field shows how many requests for disk access are currently waiting to be processed. Like the dirty cache buffers, this number can be used to determine whether disk performance is slowing down the network.

The value in the Packet receive buffers field indicates the number of buffers that have been established to process packets that have been received by the server and are waiting to be serviced. The Directory cache buffers value indicates the number of buffers that have been reserved for disk directory blocks. Increasing the initial number of directory cache buffers available when the server first starts can sometimes improve the performance of the server when it is first booted. The Maximum service processes value indicates the number of task handlers that have been allocated for station requests, and the Current service processes represents the number of task handlers currently activated. The Maximum licensed connections indicates the number of connections that are allowed by the version of NetWare; the Current licensed connections is the number of connections currently in use. You can use the Open files field to determine whether any files are currently open prior to downing the server.

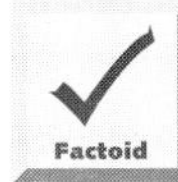

The file server Utilization, Total cache buffers, and Dirty cache buffers statistics together can give you a quick picture of your file server's health. The utilization should be under 70%, the total cache buffers figure should be at least 50% of the original cache buffers figure, and the dirty cache buffers figure should be less than 30% of the total cache buffers figure.

In addition to the General Information window, the MONITOR utility has several options that you can use to view information about the performance and operation of your file server. Selecting the Connection information option displays a window that shows all active connections and the usernames currently logged in. If no user is logged in to a given connection number, the message "NOT-LOGGED-IN" will appear next to the connection number. To view information about any connection, select the connection number and press [Enter]. A window showing connection information for the user logged in to that connection will be displayed. Also displayed are the names of any currently open files, as shown in Figure 16-20. Notice that the window shows the network address, the number of requests, kilobytes read and written, and currently open files for the selected username.

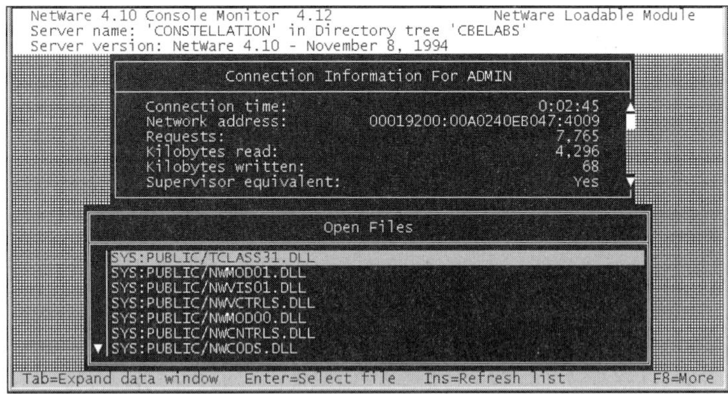

Figure 16-20 Connection Information window

Use the Disk information option to check the status of a disk drive. The size of the disk drive, the disk driver, the number of partitions, mirroring, and hot fix status are indicated. A piece of information in the Disk Information screen that is important to monitor is the number of blocks that appear in the Redirected blocks field. This number tells you how many times a block of the disk failed to work properly, causing data to be redirected to the redirection area of the disk partition. When the number of redirected blocks starts to grow, it is a sign that the disk drive is wearing out. You will want to make plans to replace it before all the redirection blocks are used up, at which point you will start losing data as a result of disk write errors.

Selecting the LAN/WAN information option displays a window showing all LAN drivers currently loaded on the file server. If you are experiencing sluggish network performance and the file server utilization is low, you should use the LAN information option to view the error summary for the network card. In addition to recording the total packets sent and received, the LAN information option keeps track of a number of error statistics.

RS232

The RS232 NLM is part of the remote console management system that enables the file server to be attached to a modem on COM1 or COM2. When used in combination with the REMOTE module, this module enables the network administrator to dial into the server from a remote computer and gain access to the file server's console screen. More information regarding the use of the RS232 and REMOTE modules is provided later in this chapter.

RSPX

The RSPX NLM enables the remote console management system to communicate with workstations attached to the LAN cable. When used with the REMOTE module, RSPX enables the network administrator to use the RCONSOLE program from any workstation attached to the network and gain access to the file server's console screen. RSPX provides SPX driver support and also advertises the file server's ability across the network to any connected workstations running the RCONSOLE utility.

Remote

The REMOTE NLM is the component of the remote console management system that communicates with a workstation running RCONSOLE. It is responsible for sending console screens and receiving input from the remote workstation. REMOTE works with the RS232 module to communicate with remote workstations over a dial-up phone line or with the RSPX module to communicate with local workstations.

When you load the REMOTE module, you will be prompted to enter a password. This helps prevent unauthorized access to the console from a remote workstation. The password can be included when you load the REMOTE module by specifying it after the REMOTE command. This is often done when the REMOTE command is inserted in the AUTOEXEC.NCF file in order to load it when the file server is booted (described in the next section). Whenever a workstation running RCONSOLE attempts to access the server, the user will be prompted to enter this password before being granted access to the console screen. To provide additional security, the date, time, and node address of any workstation that accesses the console through REMOTE is logged to the console screen and file server log file.

UPS

The UPS module enables your file server to monitor the status of the uninterruptible power system, enabling the file server to down itself in the event of an extended power outage. The UPS can be connected to the file server in a number of different ways in order for the server to "know" when the UPS is supplying the power. The syntax for loading the UPS module is

```
UPS [type port discharge recharge wait]
```

When you load the UPS module, replace the type field with one of the connector types shown in Figure 16-21.

Figure 16-21
UPS Connection Types

Connection Type	Description
DCB	Disk controller board
EDCB	Enhanced disk controller board
STANDALONE	Novell stand-alone UPS card
KEYCARD	Novell keycard with UPS connection
MOUSE	Mouse port
OTHER	Vendor's interface card

In addition to supplying the type and port fields, you need to replace the discharge field with the number of minutes the network file server can operate on UPS battery power before it depletes the battery. Refer to the UPS battery documentation for these time estimates based on the number of amps required by the equipment attached to the UPS. Next, consult the UPS owner's manual to determine how much time is required for the battery to be recharged after the UPS has been operating on battery power. The recharge field can then be used to provide an estimate of the number of minutes the battery will need to recharge after the server has been on battery power. As the battery ages, you should increase the time in the recharge field to allow the battery to recharge fully.

Newer models of UPSs provide extensive features and may come with their own server interface card as well as their own NLM.

VREPAIR

The VREPAIR module can often be used to repair the FAT of a volume that cannot be mounted. If your file server crashes due to a hardware problem, power failure, or software bug, the file server might not restart because of errors in the FAT of the SYS: volume. In this situation, you can often use the VREPAIR utility to fix the problems in the FAT in order to mount the SYS: volume and get the server up and running again. Because of the importance of VREPAIR for fixing volume errors and checking for volume problems, a CNA needs to be familiar with the VREPAIR utility. VREPAIR can be used to perform other tasks, such as removing name space support from a volume (described later in this chapter).

The VREPAIR utility is located in the SYS:SYSTEM directory. However, if the volume that contains VREPAIR cannot be mounted, then you won't be able to run that program. It's a good idea to keep a copy of VREPAIR on the DOS partition of the server's drive or on a diskette. The purpose of having a copy in the DOS directory is to enable you to run VREPAIR from the C drive in the event the SYS: volume cannot be mounted due to a FAT or directory error.

VREPAIR can be used only on volumes that are not currently mounted on the server. If you want to use VREPAIR to check an existing volume, you first need to use the DISMOUNT command to close the volume and unload it from the NetWare operating system. When more than one volume is dismounted, VREPAIR displays a window asking you to select the volume to be serviced. If only one volume is dismounted, VREPAIR assumes that volume is to be repaired and starts checking it immediately after you select the Repair a Volume option from the VREPAIR menu.

If a volume cannot be mounted, VREPAIR automatically loads.

After checking a volume, VREPAIR enables you to choose whether you want to save the repairs. If you save the repairs to disk, you should then run VREPAIR again to confirm that the volume has been fixed. It sometimes happens that when repairs are written to disk, other volume errors are generated. Running VREPAIR a second time enables you to check and fix any new volume errors that were not detected in the previous run. Once VREPAIR runs with no errors, you can mount the volume.

Another problem that sometimes occurs when VREPAIR runs is that valuable data files are corrupted when VREPAIR writes its fixes to the disk. Any time FAT entries are modified, there is a risk that data in the files being fixed can actually be lost due to incorrect reconnection of FAT chains. In a worst-case scenario, lost or corrupted records in an important database file might not be discovered until several weeks or months have elapsed, causing lost time and money for a company. To help prevent this problem, VREPAIR reports each file in which it finds FAT or directory problems. You can make a note of each file and then thoroughly test or restore the data from any important database or document files.

To use the VREPAIR command to check or fix problems on an existing volume, follow these steps:

- Enter the command LOAD VREPAIR. If you are using VREPAIR to fix problems on the SYS: volume that prevent it from being mounted, you will need to load the VREPAIR program from the DOS partition by using the command LOAD C:VREPAIR. This displays the Volume Repair Utility menu shown in Figure 16-22.
then
- Select option 2 in order to view and set the VREPAIR options shown in Figure 16-23. Notice that the currently active settings are displayed at the top of the screen. Additional options, preceded by numbers, are listed on the lower half of the screen. Generally it is best to use the Keep changes in memory for later update item. This gives you the option of writing the changes to disk after you have noted all files that are being fixed. Use option 5 to return to the VREPAIR main menu after you have finished setting options on the VREPAIR configuration screen.
then
- Select the 1. Repair A Volume item from the main menu to start the volume repairs. If more than one volume is currently dismounted, VREPAIR enables you to select the volume to be repaired. If only one volume is currently dismounted, VREPAIR immediately begins scanning that volume. If no volumes have been dismounted, the error message "There are no unmounted volumes" will be displayed.
then
- During the repair process, VREPAIR will stop whenever it encounters a FAT or directory error and report the error message along with the filename. In order to verify that the files are correctly restored by VREPAIR, you should record the error messages and filename. You can then have the appropriate users check the status of the corrected files to determine whether they were restored correctly.
then
- To record filenames and error messages automatically in a text file for later analysis, press [F1] to display the additional VREPAIR options. Use option 2, Log errors to a file, to write each message to the text file you specify. Use option 1, Do not pause after errors, to prevent VREPAIR from pausing after each error message. Option 0 enables you to continue with volume repair process.
then
- After the volume has been restored, VREPAIR pauses and asks whether you want to write the repairs to disk. Normally you should enter Y and press [Enter] to write the new FAT and directory table to the disk. If you have written any changes to disk, you should run the VREPAIR program again to scan the

volume and check for any additional volume problems. In some cases, it will take several passes to fix all problems.

then

- When you receive a clean report showing that there are no corrections to write to disk, you can exit the VREPAIR program and mount the volume.

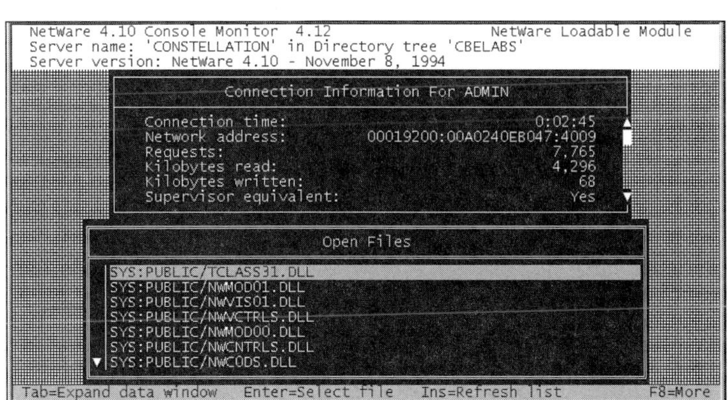

Figure 16-22

VREPAIR main menu

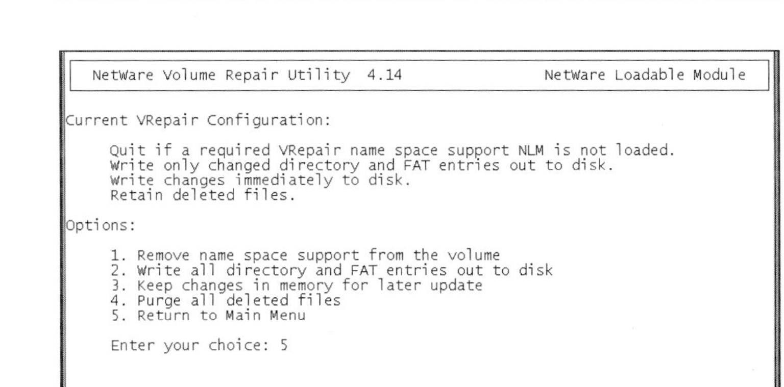

NetWare Volume Repair Utility 4.14 NetWare Loadable Module
Current VRepair Configuration:
Quit if a required VRepair name space support NLM is not loaded.
Write only changed directory and FAT entries out to disk.
Write changes immediately to disk.
Retain deleted files.
Options:
1. Remove name space support from the volume
2. Write all directory and FAT entries out to disk
3. Keep changes in memory for later update
4. Purge all deleted files
5. Return to Main Menu
Enter your choice: 5

Figure 16-23

VREPAIR options

DSREPAIR. As stated earlier, the NDS directory tree is a distributed and replicated database which is stored on several different servers. Because of this distribution, the NDS directory tree can occasionally develop problems with consistency between the servers. The NLM module DSREPAIR allows you to correct those problems. To run the program, enter the command LOAD DSREPAIR. The main menu has the following options:

- Unattended Full Repair—This option performs a comprehensive check of the tree for any inconsistencies and repairs any problems which it finds.
- Time Synchronization—This option checks and then displays the version of NDS and the status of time synchronization of each server.
- Replica Synchronization—DSREPAIR synchronizes all partitions on every server that contains a replica of the partition.
- View/Edit Repair Log File—DSREPAIR keeps a log file (SYS:SYSTEM\DSREPAIR_LOG) of all actions which are taken. This option allows you to view that file.
- Advanced Options File—This option displays a submenu of options that allow you to perform individual repair tasks.

Remote Console Management

There are times when it is difficult or time consuming to go to the file server console to check server status, make changes, or fix problems with the NetWare operating system. Sometimes it means spending valuable time driving to the file server's location just to spend a few minutes at the console. To get around this problem, NetWare makes it possible to perform console operations from a workstation computer located on the local network or attached through a wide area network via telephone.

Beginning with NetWare 3.11, Novell developed the Remote Management Facility (**RMF**) to enable a network administrator to manage all file servers from a remote location. RMF actually brings the file server's console screen to the remote workstation, enabling the network administrator to work with the server as if he or she were actually at the file server computer.

Understanding Remote Management

RMF works by using software and hardware to establish with a file server a communication link that enables a workstation to act as the console's keyboard and display screen. Using RMF to control a console over the communication link does not disable actual console operation, but provides for concurrent operation of the file server console from both the file server computer and the remote workstation. This capability means that a network administrator can perform certain console operations from a location other than at the file server. Three kinds of RMF communication links can be established: a direct link, an asynchronous link, and a redundant link.

In a direct link, as illustrated in Figure 16-24, the workstation and file server are attached to the same network system, enabling packets to be sent directly from the workstation's network card to the file server. The advantages of a direct link include high speed, reliability, and the ability to copy files from the workstation directly to the file server.

Figure 16-24

RMF direct communication link

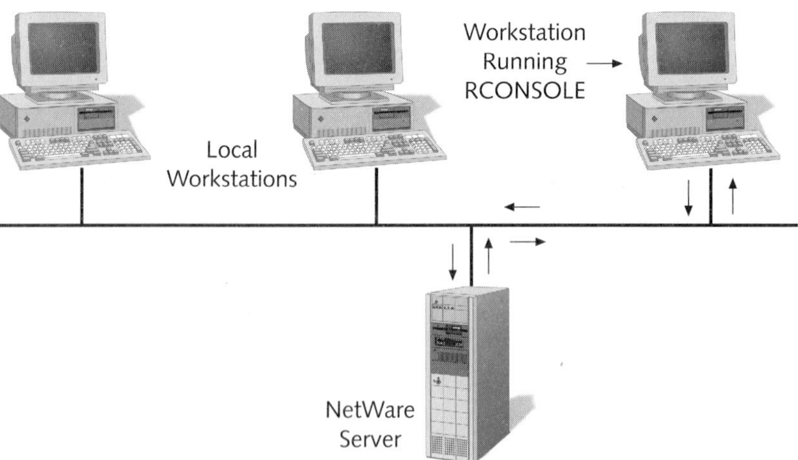

In an asynchronous link, as illustrated in Figure 16-25, the workstation and file server are connected by modems using a dial-up telephone line. The asynchronous link provides the ability to support a file server from any PC within reach of a telephone. It also means that you can access the server if the network system is down. The major disadvantages of this system are its relatively slow speed and the possibility of communication errors, both of which slow down operations and prevent reliable transfer of large files from the workstation to the file server.

The term *asynchronous link* describes the way data is sent between the file server and the remote workstation. In asynchronous communication, each byte of data is sent separately, encapsulated with a start and stop bit. Asynchronous communication enables the use of lower-cost modems and is very effective for handling keyboard input between a terminal and host computer.

Figure 16-25

RMF asynchronous link

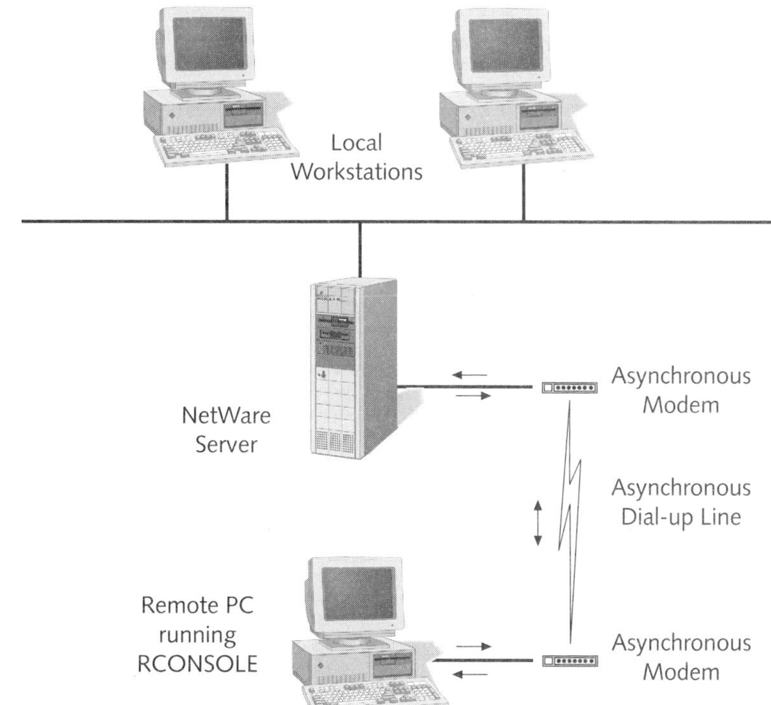

A redundant link, as shown in Figure 16-26, enables you to combine the speed advantage of a direct link with the fail-safe ability of an asynchronous link to access the file server console if the network system fails or if the network driver needs to be unloaded so that a problem can be fixed or the driver software can be updated.

Figure 16-26

RMF redundant link

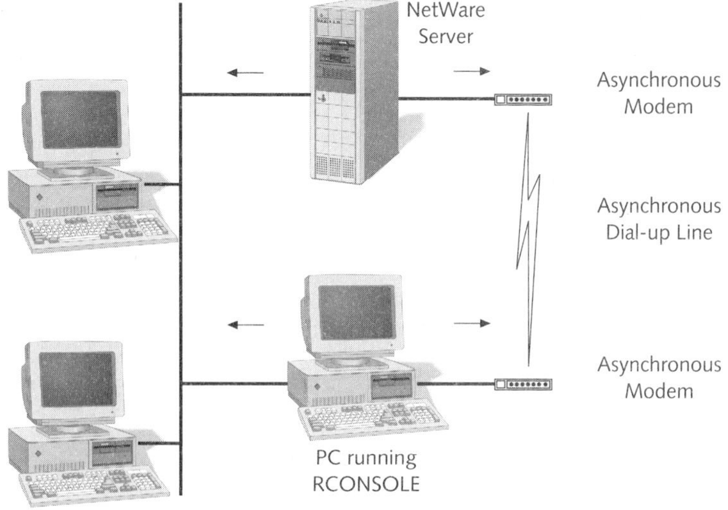

Factoid

The advantage of a redundant link is the ability to access the server console in more than one way. This enables you to use the faster direct link for normal file server commands and to switch to the asynchronous link if the network fails or you need to unload the LAN driver software.

Before you establish the remote management feature on your network, you need to understand the hardware and software component requirements of both the file server and workstation for supporting communication links. These are illustrated in Figure 16-27.

Figure 16-27

RMF components

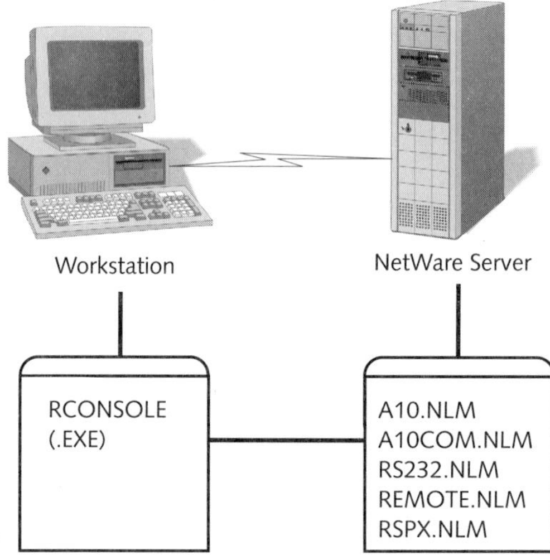

Setting Up Remote Management

Setting up an RMF connection on a file server involves loading the appropriate NLMs for the connection type to be used. Placing commands for the desired connection type in the AUTOEXEC.NCF file will cause the server to load remote console management automatically each time the server is booted.

For a direct link connection, place the LOAD REMOTE and LOAD RSPX commands in the AUTOEXEC.NCF file. It is important to place the LOAD REMOTE command first because RSPX requires the REMOTE module in order to run. When loading REMOTE, you should follow the REMOTE command with the password. If no password is specified, the commands following the LOAD REMOTE command will not be executed until the operator enters the password. Placing a password after the LOAD REMOTE command enables the server to load the remote software automatically and continue without waiting for operator input.

To support an asynchronous link, you must next load three additional NLMs besides REMOTE and RSPX: AIO.NLM, AIOCOMX.NLM, and RS232.NLM. AIO.NLM is the Asynchronous I/O Services interface module, and AIOCOMX.NLM is the communications port driver for the file server. The last NLM, RS232.NLM, has the following parameters:

```
LOAD RS232 [port number] [modem speed] [n] [c]
```

The port number is either 1 or 2 depending on the communication port to which the modem is attached. Modem speed is from 2400 to 38,400 bps, depending on the speed of the modem. If you do not enter a communication port or modem speed, the RS232 module will prompt you to select the communication port number and modem speed. The "n" enables you to use a null modem cable as your connection type, and the "c" enables you to use the call-back feature. Placing these values after the command enables the file server to start the remote console without operator intervention.

The callback feature in RS232.NLM provides an extra layer of protection from unwanted intruders. It enables you to create a list of telephone numbers from which someone may dial into the file server. When the file server receives an attempt from a user to make a remote dial-up connection, it determines the telephone number from which the call came and then immediately disconnects the line. If the phone number is located in the callback list, the file server will dial back the number and reestablish the connection; if the number is not in the list, the file server does not return the call.

For a redundant link, include both the LOAD RSPX and LOAD RS232 statements in the AUTOEXEC.NCF file.

Creating a Remote Console Operator

A remote console operator is a user who has been granted the rights necessary to run the RCONSOLE software and who also knows the password assigned to the REMOTE module. Suppose, for example, the network administrator at CBE Labs, wants to make a user a remote console operator so that the user can view and respond to any file server error messages when the administrator is unavailable. He must give that user at least Read file trustee rights to RCONSOLE.EXE and its supporting files. After the necessary rights are granted, the user must be trained to run the RCONSOLE program and given the password needed to access the file server's console.

Starting RCONSOLE

Once the RMF software to support a direct link has been loaded on the file server, you can go to a workstation and use the RCONSOLE utility to gain access to the console of the file server. To use RCONSOLE, follow these steps:

- First log in as the Administrator or remote console operator, change to the SYS:SYSTEM directory, and type RCONSOLE to display the Available Servers window.
- You will be asked if you want to establish an asynchronous or direct (SPX) connection.
- All servers on the network that are running the REMOTE and RSPX modules will appear in this window. Select the file server console you want to access and press [Enter].
- The RCONSOLE program prompts you to enter the password for that file server. You can type either the remote operator password supplied when the REMOTE module is loaded or the Administrator password and press [Enter].
- The console of the selected file server is displayed; it shows whatever screen was last displayed on the server console. (If the MONITOR utility was used to lock the console, you will need to enter the correct password to unlock MONITOR before being granted access to the file server's console.)
- Now enter any console commands just as if you were operating on the actual file server computer.

The RCONSOLE Menu

The RCONSOLE program provides a number of additional functions through the Available Options menu, shown in Figure 16-28. This menu is available by pressing [ALT] + [F1].

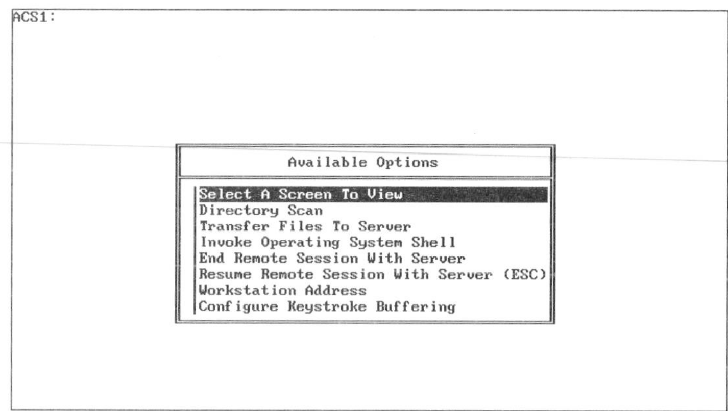

Figure 16-28 Available Options menu

The Select A Screen To View option displays a window containing all tasks currently running on the file server that have a display screen available. You can then change the console to any of the screens simply by entering the number of the screen you want to view and pressing [Enter]. The Directory Scan option enables you to search any directory on the file server by specifying the drive letter or volume name, followed by the directory path. You can also include a global file specification to search for specific filenames. The Transfer Files To Server option can be used to copy files from the local workstation to any directory on the file server. The Invoke Operating System Shell option may be used to access the DOS prompt on your workstation. This is handy because it saves you from having to exit the RCONSOLE utility in order to perform a DOS command. After completing the DOS function, you can use the EXIT command to return to the RCONSOLE menu. Use the End Remote Session With Server option to exit the current remote console session and return to the Available Servers window. The Resume Remote Session With Server option simply closes the Available Options menu and returns the remote workstation to the console screen. The Workstation Address option gives you the workstation network and node address. Configure Keystroke Buffering enables you to control when your keystrokes appear on the server console screen. This is helpful when there is a process running on the server or a series of error messages that might prevent you from seeing your keystrokes displayed.

PROTECTING NETWORK DATA

An organization's data plays a critical role in today's highly competitive and rapidly changing world of business and industry. A company robbed of its information would certainly suffer major losses and could even be forced out of business. As a network administrator in an organization that relies on the network for data storage and retrieval, therefore, you become the "keeper of the flame." You are responsible for many, if not all, of your organization's critical data files. Management counts on your knowledge to provide a reliable storage system that is secure from unauthorized access and protected from accidental loss due to equipment failure, operator error, or natural disaster.

In previous chapters you learned how the NetWare network can be used to establish a secure directory structure that protects the organization's data from unauthorized access. Now we will look at how NetWare can provide a centralized backup-and-restore procedure that can protect valuable data from being lost due to equipment or operator error. With NetWare, you can also implement a disaster recovery procedure that can enable your organization to continue to operate despite the loss of the file server or even an entire building.

THE STORAGE MANAGEMENT SYSTEM

Backing up data on a network is far more complex than backing up on a single PC. A network may contain client workstations that are running different operating systems—such as Windows 95, UNIX, OS/2, and DOS—that each contain different file types. In addition, these files have special attributes (like compression and migration) and rights information that must be retained. And network users will need the data stored both on the file server as well as their local computer backed up on a regular basis.

To tackle these complex backup issues, Novell developed the **Storage Management System (SMS).** SMS enables you to back up even complex networks consisting of data that resides on multiple file servers as well as data on workstations running different operating systems. The file server that runs the backup program and has the tape or other backup medium attached to it is referred to as the **host** server. The file servers and client workstations that are being backed up are referred to as **target** machines. A **Target Service Agent (TSA)** is a program that helps handle data transfers between the host and target. SMS uses NLMs on the host server to communicate with modules on target devices, reading the information from the target devices and sending it to the backup medium, as illustrated in Figure 16-29.

Figure 16-29

SMS Backup Process

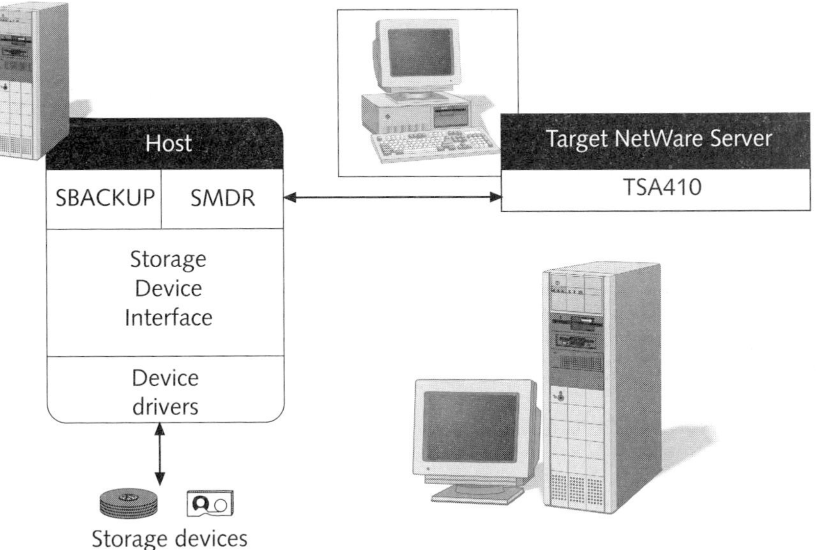

SMS can work with an entire range of archiving hardware, from single tape backup systems to optical jukeboxes that hold gigabytes of data.

The NetWare SMS consists of the following software components. They can be run on NetWare file servers as well as on client workstations.

- Storage device drivers that are loaded on the host server. They control the mechanical operation of various storage devices and media, such as tape drives.
- TSAs that are loaded on the target servers. The purpose of TSAs is to get information from the target server's volumes and send it to the SBACKUP program running on the host server. A server can act as both host and target by running both the backup and TSA software.
- The store management data requester (SMDR), which passes commands and information between the backup program and the storage devices and media.

- Workstation TSAs that are run on the local clients. They back up data located on the local drives across the network through the SMDR.
- The backup software, SBACKUP. This NLM provided with NetWare is the principal module that works with the SMS architecture to control the backup process on the host server. It makes requests for data to the SMDR device and then routes the returned data to the storage device.

ESTABLISHING A BACKUP SYSTEM

The first step in establishing a backup system for your network is calculating how much data needs to be copied to the backup tape on a daily basis. First, determine what volumes and directories you plan to back up. If possible, you should then try to obtain an SMS-compatible tape backup system that has capacity sufficient to store one day's records on one tape cartridge. In a single-file-server environment, the file server acts as both the host and target devices, requiring you to load both the SBACKUP and TSA modules on the same server. An advantage of one file server functioning as both host and target device is that a file server backing up its own data runs almost four times faster than a host file server backing up data across the network from a target file server. When you implement SMS in a multiple-file-server environment, you should plan on making the file server that has the largest amount of data be the host system.

Installing SMS on the File Server

In order to back up data, you need to install a backup tape device along with its software drivers on the host file server. The host file server will need to have 3 MB of RAM above the minimum required to run NetWare and at least 2 MB of free disk space on the SYS: volume for temporary file storage. In addition to storing temporary files on the host server, the SMS also stores temporary files on the target servers. It is important to monitor the size of these files regularly (using the command NDIR SYS:SYSTEM\TSA$TMP.*) because they can become quite large. Erase them as necessary.

To load the SMS modules and run SBACKUP, follow these steps:

- Load the device drivers for the backup device. For example, to load Novell's generic driver, you would key LOAD TAPEDAI.DSK.
- Register the storage device with the operating system by keying SCAN FOR NEW DEVICES.
- Load the appropriate TSA modules for the type of backup. For example, to backup a NetWare 4.1 host server, you would key LOAD TSA410.
- Load the SBACKUP utility by keying LOAD SBACKUP.
- If you want to backup workstations, go to those clients and load the TSA software. For example, on a DOS workstation, key TSADOS.

Running SBACKUP

When you load the SBACKUP utility at the server, you will see the main menu as displayed in Figure 16-30. To backup a target device, follow these steps:

- Highlight the Backup option and press [Enter].
- Select the target whose data you want to backup.
- Choose the TSA you want to use.

- Key the username and password for the target you want to backup.
- Select the device to which you want to backup.
- Specify a location for the session log and error files.
- Choose the type of backup you want to perform.
- Specify the date and time you want the backup to begin.

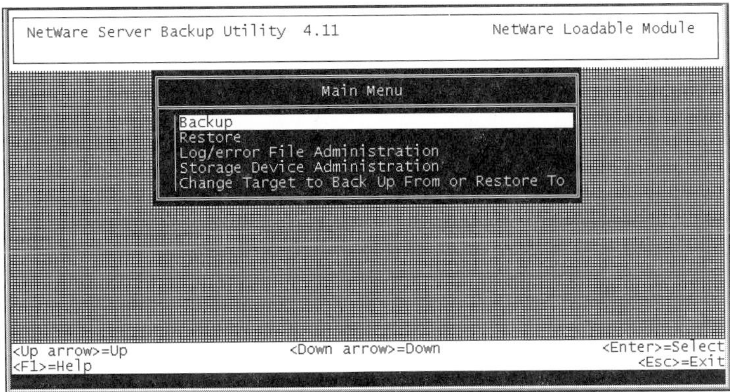

Figure 16-30

SBACKUP main menu

The Archive Needed [A] attribute is set to Y by the system when a file has been changed. When you perform a backup, this bit is changed back to N until the file is modified again.

After a backup has been successfully completed, try testing your backup system by restoring selected files from the backup medium. Doing a complete restore is often not feasible due to time constraints as well as to the possible loss of data should the restore process fail. To restore selected files, select the Restore option from the main SBACKUP menu. Enter the path to the working directory you used when the backup tape was created. Next, select the option to "Restore session" files and select the session you named previously when the backup was created. Now fill in the restore screen by entering the names of the files or directories you want to be copied from the backup tape to the server. After the restore screen is filled in, press [Esc] and select the option to start the restore process. The selected files should be copied back to their appropriate directories. When the restore process is complete, log in from a user workstation and verify that the files have been correctly restored.

Developing a Backup Procedure

Once the backup system has been tested, you need to implement a reliable disaster recovery plan. This entails developing a tape rotation procedure and backup schedule. A procedure that rotates multiple tapes means that backups can be saved for long time periods. This is an important part of a disaster recovery plan because it provides a way to restore an earlier backup. It also provides a means of storing backup tapes in a separate building in order to protect them in case of catastrophic damage at your location. It is sometimes important to be able to recover a file from an earlier backup if that file should become corrupted by a software virus, operator error, or software bug and the damage to the file is not discovered for several days or weeks. If you were rotating your backups on a limited number of tapes, by the time such an error is discovered, the original backup containing the valid file might have been overwritten by a backup copy of the corrupted file. To help prevent this scenario, a good tape rotation system should consist of 19 tapes, as illustrated in Figure 16-31.

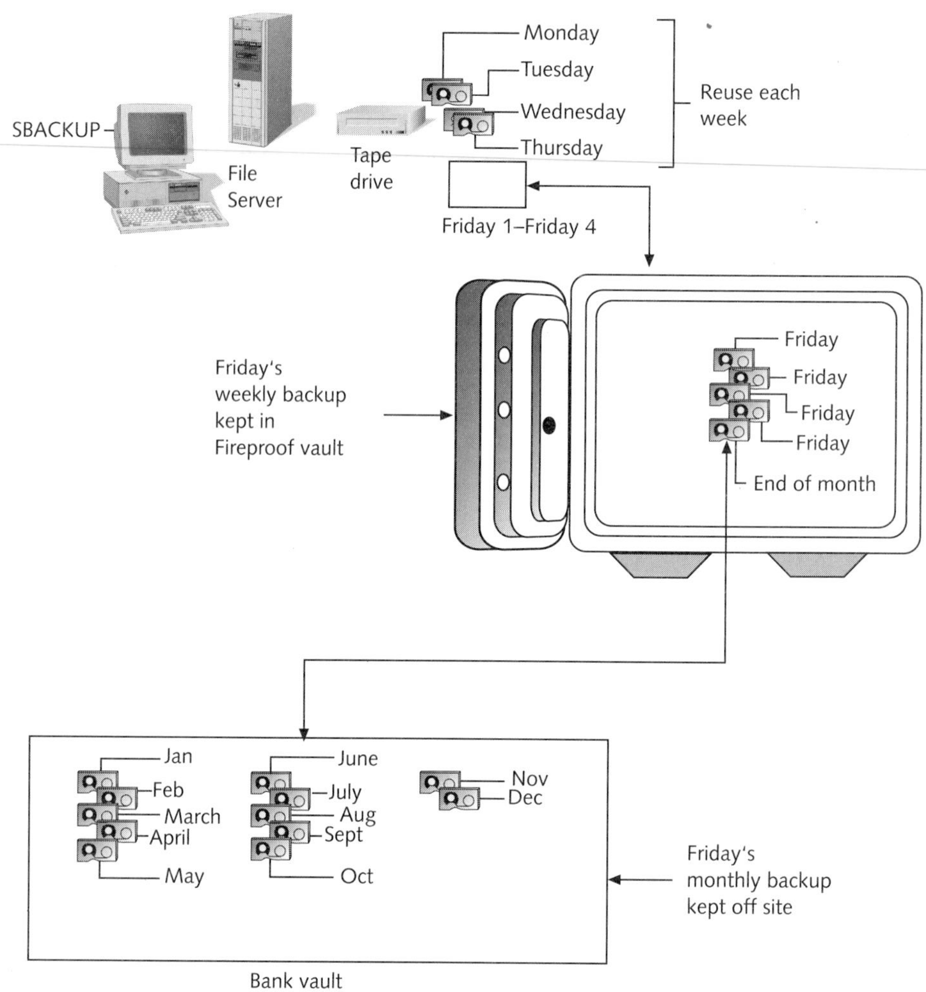

Figure 16-31

Tape rotation procedure

Four tapes are labeled Monday through Thursday and are rotated each week. Four tapes are labeled Friday 1 through Friday 4. Friday 1 is used on the first Friday of the month, Friday 2 on the second, Friday 3 on the third, and Friday 4 on the fourth. In addition, 12 tapes are labeled January through December. These tapes are rotated each year and can be used on the last Friday of each month by replacing the Friday # tape with the appropriate monthly backup. Another alternative, if someone is available to change the tape, is to make the monthly backup on the last Saturday of each month. The storage of the backup tapes is also important in the event of a fire or damage to the building. As a result, many administrators store weekly backups in an onsite fireproof vault and keep monthly backup tapes offsite in a secure location, such as a bank safety deposit vault.

The final step in implementing the backup system is to establish a time for the backup to be performed and to ensure that no users are logged in during the backup process. To prevent interference with user work schedules, many network administrators start the backup each night at about midnight. To restrict night owls from working late and to prevent users from leaving their workstations logged in during the backup, all user accounts, except the username used to back up the system, should have a time restriction to prevent users from accessing the network between midnight and 5:00 A.M. This provides a 5-hour time interval that should be sufficient to create the backup. If extra time is needed, the backup can be set to begin at 11:00 P.M. and/or extend to 6:00 A.M., provided user time restrictions are also set for the longer backup period.

You need to develop a procedure to deal with the files in the working directory, because the size of these files continues to grow with each backup that is made. The session files in the working directory play an important role in the restore process by enabling you to select quickly the files and directories you want to restore. One way to deal with the restore files is to copy them to a floppy disk each day and store the floppy disk with the corresponding backup tape. If you need to restore a backup tape, you can then copy the corresponding floppy disk into the working directory prior to restoring the files with the SBACKUP program. Using this procedure, each morning you can first check the status of the backup to be sure all files were successfully copied. Next, copy the files from the working directory specified in the SBACKUP program to a floppy disk and delete the session files in the working directory. Finally, store the backup tape and corresponding disk in a secure location. Once the disaster recovery procedure is in place and operating, you can rest easier knowing that you have done all you can to provide a secure environment for your organization's precious data and software.

SYNCHRONIZING THE NETWORK

The dictionary defines the word *synchronize* as: "Cause to operate at the same time; harmonize." Imagine the havoc that would take place if all the various components of the network did not function together as one system. Nothing could ever be done on the network. NetWare provides two tools to assist the CNA in ensuring that the network will function in harmony: WSUPDATE and NETSYNC.

WSUPDATE

Keeping the latest version of the NetWare driver and requester software on each of the networked workstations is an ongoing task for all network administrators. Updated versions of software components can be downloaded regularly from Novell's Internet site and then must be copied onto each workstation. In large networks consisting of 100 or more workstations, carrying a floppy disk to each workstation in order to update the software drivers would be a waste of a network administrator's time. To help automate this job and save time for the administrator, Novell supplies a program called WSUPDATE. This program checks the date of the current programs on each workstation and then automatically updates a program having a date prior to the version stored on the server.

The WSUPDATE command can be used from either the DOS prompt or the container login script. It updates files on the client workstation by checking the dates of the specified files and then copying files with more recent dates from the server to a directory on the client workstation. The syntax for the WSUPDATE command is as follows:

```
WSUPDATE [source_path\filename] [target_path\filename]
[/options]
```

Replace *source_path\filename* with the full NetWare directory path, including filename. Replace *target_path\filename* with the local drive letter and filename to be updated. If the filename parameter is not included in the *target_path\filename* field, WSUPDATE will use the filename specified by the source_path as the destination file's name.

The WSUPDATE command includes a number of additional parameters that can be used to accomplish the tasks described in Figure 16-32. When WSUPDATE finds an older version of the specified file, by default it prompts the user to copy over the old file, rename the old file, or ignore the update and leave the file unchanged. Using the /C parameter will automatically replace the old file with the newer one. When a workstation's system files are flagged Read Only (to prevent accidental erasure), you can include the /O option to overwrite them.

Figure 16-32

WSUPDATE command parameters

Option	Description
/F=*[path]filename*	Add this option if the commands are contained in a separate file specified by the given path and filename.
/C	Include this option to overwrite the old version of the file automatically without pausing.
/R	Include this option to rename the old version of the file automatically with the .OLD extension prior to copying the new version to the workstation.
/O	Include this option to overwrite read-only files automatically.
/S	Include this option to search for older versions of the specified file in all subdirectories of the target drive.
/L=*[path]filename*	Include this option, with the path and filename, when you want a log of all workstations that have been updated. The log file includes the username, date, and network address of each workstation that has been updated.
/N	Add this option when you want to create the file and path on the target drive if they do not already exist. Do not use this option with /S or /ALL.
/ALL	Searches all drive letters.
/LOCAL	Searches all local drive letters.

By default the WSUPDATE searches only the path you specify in the *target_path\filename* field. If you include the /S parameter, WSUPDATE will search the directory tree that starts with that directory. If you want to search all drives on the workstation (including network drives), replace *target_path\filename* with the keyword /ALL. If you want to search only the drives on that workstation and exclude any network drives, use the keyword /LOCAL instead.

Another important parameter is /F=filename. When you have several new files to update, the /F option enables you to specify the name of a file that contains a list of new files to be updated. When you have several files that you want to update, using the /F=filename parameter is more efficient than running several WSUPDATE commands. This is because each WSUPDATE command placed in the system login script requires the workstation to load and run the WSUPDATE.EXE program. When using the /F=filename parameter, you need to use a text editor program to create an ASCII file specified by the filename parameter. Enter separate command lines for each new file you want to update.

For example, the network administrator of CBE Labs needs to update the VLM.EXE and IPXODI.COM files on the CBE Labs workstations. He first creates a file with an ASCII text editor entitled 11_25_UP that contains the following lines:

```
WSUPDATE CONSTALLATION_SYS:PUBLIC\VLM.EXE C:\NWCLIENT\
VLM.EXE /C

WSUPDATE CONSTALLATION_SYS:PUBLIC\IPXODI.COM /LOCAL /S /C
```

The first line will cause WSUPDATE to copy the VLM.EXE file from the server onto the local hard drive of the workstation if the date of the server file is newer than that on the local hard drive. The /C option tells WSUPDATE to automatically copy the file, if the date is newer, without prompting the user. The second line will cause WSUPDATE to search all the drives on the local workstation for the file and then automatically make the change. He would then executes this file with the command line:

```
WSUPDATE /F=11_25_UP
```

A common use of the WSUPDATE program to replace old versions of Novell driver files with new versions is to include the #WSUPDATE commands in the container login script.

NETSYNC

As discussed in previous chapters, the problem with managing networks that contain NetWare 3.x servers is that each server is independent of all other servers on the network. If you needed to make a change to a NetWare 3.x network, you are forced to log into each server and make that change. There was no facility to make a change in one place and have it duplicated automatically on each server. However, NetWare 4.1 introduced a new feature entitled NetSync. NetSync can be used to synchronize bindery information between the NDS and the bindery files of a NetWare 3.x server. With NetSync you can integrate the bindery files of NetWare 3.x servers into your NDS tree.

In order to take advantage of NetSync on a network running both 3.x and 4.1 servers, you must purchase the upgrade to NetWare 4.1 for all your 3.x servers.

NetSync functions through a series of NLMs that run on both the 3.x and 4.1 servers. On the NetWare 4.1 servers, the NLMs are NETSYNC4.NLM and REMAPID.NLM. NETSYNC4 maintains the NetWare 3.x servers, and REMAPID maintains the password synchronization for users between the servers. On the NetWare 3.x servers, NETSYNC3.NLM runs and both reports to NETSYNC4 and receives from it changes to the bindery.

NetSync supports up to 12 NetWare 3.x servers per NetWare 4.1 server.

Once NetSync is functioning, the bindery information for all 3.x servers can be managed through NETADMIN or NWADMIN. Any updates to the bindery files of all 3.x servers are automatically replicated to each server. In addition, printer servers from the 3.x servers are merged into a single print server running on the 4.1 server. Although the 3.x print queues still appear the same to users, this provides 4.1 users with easy access to printing resources. Thus the management functions of a network running NetWare 3.x and 4.1 servers are much easier.

However, not all items can be synchronized by NetSync. Figure 16-33 lists the items that are and are not available.

Figure 16-33

NetSync Items Synchronized

Item	Synchronized
Users	Yes
Passwords	Yes
Login Scripts	Yes
Group EVERYONE	Yes
Account Balances	Yes
PRINTCON database	Yes
PRINTDEF database	Yes
SUPERVISOR	Yes
Accounting	No
File System Trustee Rights	No
Home Directories	No

CHAPTER SUMMARY

Managing a network involves mastering the NetWare console commands and using several NetWare Loadable Modules (NLMs) to perform various tasks on the server computer. Console commands are built into the NetWare operating system and can be divided into four categories based on their use: installation commands, configuration commands, maintenance commands, and security commands. NLMs are external programs that are loaded into the file server to control devices and add more functionality to the server. NLMs can also be divided into four categories based on their three-letter filename extensions. Disk drivers have the filename extension .DSK and enable NetWare to control the attached hard disk drives. LAN drivers have the extension .LAN and are used to attach the file server to a network topology. Name space modules have the extension .NAM and provide NetWare with the additional logic needed to translate file naming conventions from other workstation operating systems to NetWare's directory system. General-purpose modules have the extension .NLM and provide services to the network such as the MONITOR utility, which enables you to view file server performance and status; the INSTALL module, which is used for installation; and the PSERVER module, which enables a file server to function as a print server.

It is often more convenient for a network administrator to operate the file server console from a workstation in his or her office than to go to the file server computer. The Remote Management System (RMS) enables the file server's console to be accessed from other locations on the network. This is done by loading the REMOTE and RSPX NLMs on the servers to be managed and then running the RCONSOLE program from the remote workstation. This is referred to as a direct link: The network cards in the file server and workstation provide direct, high-speed communication to the file server console. By attaching a modem to a file server and loading the RS232 NLM, you can access the server's console over a dial-up telephone line. This connection is referred to as an asynchronous link and provides a method of accessing the server from a distant site in addition to providing access to the console in the event of a network failure.

Protecting critical network data is one of the most important functions of a network administrator. Novell provides the Storage Management System (SMS) for this purpose. It enables the network administrator to establish a backup-and-restore system that is capable of backing up all file servers as well as data contained on local drives of the client workstations running a variety of operating systems.

The importance of synchronizing the pieces of the network can never be overlooked. Novell provides two important tools to assist in maintaining this harmony. WSUPDATE checks the date of the current programs on each workstation and then automatically updates a program having a date prior to the version stored on the server. NetSync is used to synchronize bindery information between the NDS and the bindery files of a NetWare 3.x server, thus permitting improved management on networks that run both 3.x and 4.1 servers.

COMMAND SUMMARY

Command	Syntax	Definition
ADD NAME SPACE	*ADD NAME SPACE NAME [TO VOLUME] volume-name*	Adds space to a volume's *d*irectory entry table in order tosupport other operating system file naming conventions. Replace *name* with MAC or OS/2. Replace *volume_name* with the volume to which the specified name space is to be added.

BIND	*BIND protocol TO driver | board_name [driver_parameters]*	Attaches a protocol to a LAN card. Replace [*driver_parameters*] with protocol name (e.g., IPX or IP). Replace *driver | board_name* with either the name of the card drive program or an optional name assigned to the network board. You can optionally replace *driver_parameters* with the hardware settings that identify the network interface card (e.g., I/O port and interrupt).
LOAD	*LOAD [path] module_name [parameters]*	Loads an NLM in the file server's RAM. An optional path can be entered, depending on the module being loaded. [parameters] Optionally replace path with the DOS or NetWare path leading to the directory containing the module to be loaded. Replace module_name with the name of the NLM you want to load. Optional parameters can be entered, depending on the module being loaded.
REGISTER MEMORY	*REGISTER MEMORY start length*	Enables servers using an ISA bus to access memory above 16 MB.
SEARCH	*SEARCH [ADD path] [DEL number]*	Adds or removes a directory path from the search path used by the LOAD command when NLMs are being loaded. When no parameters are specified, the current server search paths are displayed. To add a search path, replace *path* with the DOS or NetWare path leading to the directory from which you want to load NLMs. To delete an existing search path, replace number with the *number* of the search path to be deleted.
CONFIG	*CONFIG*	Displays the current file server's internal network number and information about each network card.
DISPLAY NETWORKS	*DISPLAY NETWORKS*	Displays all network addresses and internal network numbers currently in the server's router table.
DISPLAY SERVERS	*DISPLAY SERVERS*	Displays the name of each network server currently in the file server's router table.
LIST DEVICES	*LIST DEVICES*	Displays a list containing information about all device drivers attached to the network file server.
MEMORY	*MEMORY*	Displays the total amount of memory in the file server computer.

NAME	*NAME*	Displays on the console the name of the file server computer.
PROTOCOL	*PROTOCOL*	Displays all protocols currently in use.
SET	*SET*	Displays a menu of options that enable you to view or change network configuration parameters in the file server.
SET TIME	*SET TIME [month/day/year] [hour:minute:second]*	Used by itself to display the current server time. Used with the date and time settings to change the server date and time.
DSREPAIR	*DSREPAIR*	Allows you to repair the NDS directory tree.
CLEAR STATION	*CLEAR STATION number*	Terminates the specified connection number.
CLS/OFF	*CLS/OFF*	Clears the file server console screen.
DISABLE LOGIN	*DISABLE LOGIN*	Prevents additional users from logging on.
DOWN	*DOWN*	Removes all attachments to the file server, dismounts the volumes, and takes the file server off line.
EXIT	*EXIT*	Terminates the NetWare operating system and attempts to return the computer to the DOS prompt. If DOS has been removed from the file server computer with the REMOVE DOS command, NetWare will reboot the file server computer when the EXIT command is executed.
MOUNT	*MOUNT volume_name [ALL]*	Opens a volume for use on the network.
DISMOUNT	*DISMOUNT volume_name [ALL]*	Closes a volume and removes it from the network.
MODULES	*MODULES*	Lists all currently loaded modules.
RESET ROUTER	*RESET ROUTER*	Causes the file server to send out a packet on the network asking all servers to identify their addresses and names.
SCAN FOR NEW DEVICES	*SCAN FOR NEW DEVICES*	Causes the server to search for any additional devices that have been activated since the server was booted.
SEND	*SEND 'message' TO username/ connection_number*	Transmits a message to a specific user or connection number.
TRACK	*TRACK ON/OFF*	Enables you to view all service advertising packets that are sent or received by the file server.
UNBIND	*UNBIND protocol FROM LAN_driver/ board_name*	Removes a protocol stack from a network card.

UNLOAD	*UNLOAD module_name*	Removes a NetWare Loadable Module from memory.
REMOVE DOS	*REMOVE DOS*	Removes the DOS operating system from memory.
SECURE CONSOLE	*SECURE CONSOLE*	Increases the file server's console security.
WSUPDATE	*WSUPDATE [source_path\filename] [target_drive\filename] [/options]*	Compares the file date of the source_path file with the target_path file and copies the newer source to the target if the source has a more recent date.

Key Terms

console commands

host

Remote Management Facility (RMF)

service advertising packet (SAP)

Storage Management System (SMS)

target

Target Service Agent (TSA)

Review Questions

1. The ____________ are external programs that are loaded into the memory of the file server computer to add functionality to the NetWare operating system.
2. Console commands are build into the core file server operating system program ____________.
3. The ____________ command is used to provide space on a volume for non-DOS filenames such as Macintosh or OS/2.
4. The ____________ command assigns a network address to a LAN driver.
5. To read an NLM into memory and execute it is accomplished by using the ____________ command.
6. The ____________ command shows total file memory available on the file server computer.
7. Assume the command in question 6 shows that your ISA file server has 16 MB of RAM rather than the 20 MB of RAM you have installed. The ____________ command can be used to cause the server to recognize the additional 4 MB of RAM.
8. The ____________ command will cause the file server to load NLMs from the SYS:SYSTEM\NLM directory when it does not find the requested module in the SYS:SYSTEM directory.
9. The ____________ console command displays the network addresses assigned to each LAN in the file server.
10. The ____________ console command lets you know whether your newly installed file server can "see" other file servers on the network.

11. Suppose your file server is up and running and you have just switched on an external CD-ROM drive but it does not show up in the CD-ROM device list. What would you do next?
12. On the line below, write a console command that changes the file server's clock to 11:59 P.M. on December 31, 1999.

    ____

13. In the space below, write the sequence of commands a network administrator should enter before turning off the file server computer in the middle of the day.
14. After booting the file server, you notice that the TEXT: volume did not mount because of errors in the file allocation table. In the space below, identify which NLM can be used to fix the volume and then the command necessary to bring the TEXT: volume back online.
15. After you load the NE2000 Ethernet card driver and bind the IPX protocol with the network address 1EEE8023, your file server begins reporting router configuration errors that indicate that other servers on the network are using the network address 10BA5E2 for the Ethernet LAN. In the space below, write the commands you can use to correct the problem.
16. The ______________ console command prevents NetWare from loading NLMs from the SYS:PUBLIC\NLM directory.
17. The ______________ console command causes the file server to reboot when you enter the EXIT command.
18. NetWare disk drivers all have ______________ for a file extension.
19. If the number in the Total cache buffers field on the MONITOR screen is less than ______________ of the amount in the Original cache buffers field, you need to add more memory to your file server.
20. Your file server has just crashed and now the SYS: volume will not load. The ______________ utility can be used to repair that volume.
21. In the space below, enter in the correct sequence of commands to provide a redundant remote console link on your file server.
22. In the space below, list the software modules that must be installed on the host file server so that the SMS backup facility can be used.
23. The ______________ program checks the date of the current programs on each workstation and then automatically updates a program having a date prior to the version stored on the server.
24. ______________ can be used to synchronize bindery information between the NDS and the bindery files of a NetWare 3.x server.

Hands-On

EXERCISES

Exercise 16-1: Downing the Server

In this exercise, you use NetWare console commands to perform the specified console operations and obtain requested information. So that you can perform this exercise, your instructor will provide you with access to a specified NetWare server console.

1. Use the CONFIG command to obtain the following information about a network board:

   Driver: ______________________________

   I/O port: ______________________________

   Network address: ______________________________

   Frame type: ______________________________

   Protocol: ______________________________

2. Use the DISPLAY NETWORKS command to document two different networks currently in use at your location. On the lines below, identify each network address along with the number of hops and ticks required to reach that network.

Network Address	Number of Hops	Number of Ticks

3. Use the DISPLAY SERVERS command to identify up to three servers available from your network. On the lines below, identify each server's name along with the number of hops needed to reach that server.

NetWare Server Name	Number of Hops

4. Set the date and time on the file server to 8:30 A.M. on December 28, 1999. On the line below, record the command you use.

   ____

5. Down the server by performing the following procedures. In the spaces provided, record each command you use.

   Load MONITOR to determine the number of connections.

   ____

   Prevent any new logins.

   ____

   Send a message to all users that the server is going down.

   ____

   Take the SYS: volume off line.

   ____

Use the VREPAIR utility from the DOS partition of your file server (drive C) and check the volume for any errors.

Use the DSREPAIR utility to check directory services for errors.

Bring the volume back on line.

Remove DOS.

Try to load the VREPAIR utility from the C disk drive and record the message below.

Clear any existing connections.

Down the server.

Exit to DOS.

Because DOS has been removed from the server, exiting the server should cause the file server computer to reboot. In the space below, record what happened on your file server computer when you exited to the DOS prompt.

Now let's bring the server back on line.

6. Use the TRACK ON command to view the router tracking screen. Record an OUT packet message on the line below and identify it as either a SAP or RIP packet.

   Type of packet (SAP or RIP):

   ---

7. Change from the TRACK screen to the console prompt using the [Control] and [Esc] keys.
8. Enter the RESET ROUTER command to rebuild the router table. Then use the [Alt] and [Esc] keys to rotate to the TRACK screen. In the space below, record any observations regarding the effect of the RESET ROUTER command on the TRACK screen.

   ---

9. Use the TRACK OFF command to exit the tracking function.
10. Use the UNBIND and BIND commands to change the network address assigned to the network card from its current address to BEEBEE. In the space below, record the command you use.

    ---

11. Change the address back to its original number. In the space below, record the command you use.

    ---

12. Enter the SECURE CONSOLE command. Attempt to change the date back one year. Record the results on the line below.

____

13. In the space below, record the modules that are currently loaded in the server.

Exercise 16-2: Working with NLMs

In this exercise, you will use NLMs to obtain information but you do not modify the existing file server environment. It can therefore be done on any file server to which the instructor has provided you access.

1. Use the MONITOR NLM to obtain the following information about your file server:

   Version and release date of server:

   ____

   Original cache buffers:

   ____

   Total cache buffers:

   ____

   Packet receive buffers:

   ____

   Number of connections:

   ____

   Number of redirection blocks:

   ____

   Number of redirected blocks:

   ____

   Total packets received:

   ____

   Number of packets received that were too large:

   ____

2. Use MONITOR to lock the console with a password obtained from your instructor.
3. Load the CD-ROM module.
4. Use the CD HELP command to obtain information on CD-ROM commands.
5. Use the appropriate command to list any existing devices. In the space below, record the fields of information available in the CD DEVICE LIST window.

6. Use the INSTALL module to determine the following:

   The size of the SYS: volume in blocks:

   ____

   Whether any free blocks are available to be assigned to an existing volume:

   Record the number of free blocks:

   ____

The size of the DOS and NetWare partitions:

DOS:

____

NetWare:

____

Exercise 16-3: Managing a Remote Console

In this exercise you load RMF on the file server designated by your instructor and perform the following procedure from the server:

1. Load support for remote console management on the designated server. Modify the startup files to load this support automatically each time the server is booted. In the space below, record the commands you place in the startup file.

   Name of startup file containing remote console commands:

   ____

   Commands included:

   ____

2. Create a remote console operator. If you do not have supervisory rights on the server, your instructor will provide you with rights to the RCONSOLE programs.
3. Log in as a remote console operator from a workstation.
4. Access the file server console. On the line space below, record the console message received as a result of accessing the remote console.

   ____

5. Scan the files in the server's DOS drive.
6. Copy a file from the workstation to the C drive of the server.
7. Print the screen and highlight the new file.

EXERCISES

Case 16-1: Rebooting a Remote Server

Nashville Net and Twine (NN&T), a leading distributor of commercial and recreational nets and accessories, has a long history of working with local area schools in a co-op program. One area in which NN&T has just started using students is in their Information Systems support group. You have been asked to participate in the co-op and help NN&T with networking. First, you are asked to help them develop the steps to reboot a remote server located at their warehouse. These steps will be in the form of a document that will be available for the third-shift Information Systems employees who only occasionally may need to perform this function yet need written documentation to help remind them of the steps.

To perform this exercise you need to have access to a file server that is not currently being used by other students. Your instructor will provide you with a time when—or a NetWare server on which—this exercise can be performed.

For each step below record the actions that you took.

1. Disable new logins.

 ____

2. Broadcast a message indicating that employees of NN&T cannot log in until further notice.

 ____

3. Use the LOAD EDIT C:\AUTOEXEC.BAT command to be sure the server will automatically load when the computer is rebooted.

 ____

4. Use the EDIT command to create an NCF file using your name and the extension .NCF. In the NCF file, include the commands necessary to reboot the file server. Record the commands in the space below.

5. Execute the NCF file to reboot the server.

 ____

6. Wait for the server to come back on line and then attempt to access it through the RCONSOLE utility. If necessary, reboot your workstation and log back in. In the space below, record what actions you need to take in order to re-attach to the server once it is back on line.

 ____

Create a document that outlines the steps listed above.

Case 16-2: Backing Up the NetWare Server

Nashville Net and Twine (NN&T) has now requested that you document for them the steps involved in backing up the server. Although they have an employee who performs this function each evening, they still want to have this document on file in the event she is out sick or on vacation. In this exercise you use the SBACKUP program along with the device driver provided by your instructor to back up the SYS:PUBLIC directory on the "installation" file server.

Create a document that outlines the steps to back up the server.

Case 16-3: Updating Workstation Software

In the process of helping NN&T, you have become aware that their NetWare Client 32 software is not the most recent version available from Novell. Some of the minor problems that they have been having may be due to these outdated files. You have taken it upon yourself to update NetWare Client 32.

Through the Internet, access a NetWare site and find the latest Client 32 versions. Download these files and place them on the file server. Using WSUPDATE and the /F command parameter, write a file to update Client 32 and place the procedure in the profile login script.

Northwestern Technical College

Project 16-1: Implementing Name Space Support

Dave Johnson purchased two Macintosh computers to be attached to the campus network for the purpose of creating and maintaining an in-house system of program flyers. In the past, the campus has always gone to an outside printing company to design and print the program flyers. Dave claims that the number of changes to the existing programs on an annual basis will justify the purchase of the Macintosh computers for use in creating the flyers in-house.

Dave has contracted with a local Apple vendor to install the Macintosh computers and train the users, but now he wants you to add name space support for the Macs to the NWTC_Server01_DATA: volume. This will enable the new Macs to store and share files with each other and with other Windows-type applications currently in use. Dave asks you to document this procedure for future reference.

In this project you need to use a designated NetWare server to add name space support to the NWTC_Server: volume by following the process defined in this chapter. Document each step of the procedure you perform. Write a memo to your instructor containing your documentation.

Project 16-2: Removing Name Space Support

Despite your concerns, the Macintosh computers work out well and save money. However, the Macintosh computers have used up most of the space on your NWTC_Server01_DATA: volume, requiring you to obtain and install an additional disk drive just for the Mac flyer files. Now that the NWTC_Server01_MAC: volume is online, you want to remove the Macintosh name space support from the NWTC_Server01_DATA: volume.

To do this exercise, you need to have access to the same NetWare server used in Project 16-1. Go through the steps described in this chapter to remove name space support from a volume. Document each step of the procedure. Write a memo to your instructor containing your documentation.

GLOSSARY

[Public] A special trustee, [Public] is similar to a group. When [Public] is made a trustee of an object, every object in the NDS Directory tree inherits the [Public] rights. In addition, [Public] rights are available to users who are not even logged into the Directory tree, as long as they have a NetWare client running on their computer.

[Root] The starting point of an hierarchical structure, such as a tree, that starts at one point (the [Root]) and branches out from the starting point. When referring to NDS, [Root] is the [Root] object.

[Root] object When referring to NDS, the starting point of the Directory tree.

[Root] partition When referring to NDS, the partition of the Directory tree that contains the [Root] object.

10BASE2 A 10 Mbps linear-bus implementation of CSMA/CD Ethernet using coaxial cable with T-connectors to attach networked computers. A terminator is used at each of the coaxial cable wire segment.

10BASET A 10 Mbps star implementation of CSMA/CD Ethernet using twisted-pair wires to connect all stations to a central concentrator.

100BASEFX A 100 Mbps star implementation of CSMA/CD Ethernet using fiber optic cables to connect all stations to a central concentrator.

100BASETX A 100 Mbps star implementation of CSMA/CD Ethernet using twisted-pair wires to connect all stations to a central concentrator.

100VG-AnyLAN A 100 MHz demand priority network system developed by Hewlett-Packard, AT&T Microelectronics and IBM which allows upgrades from either Ethernet or Token Ring network systems.

A

absolute directory path Another name for a complete directory path, which identifies the location of a file or directory by specifying the path: NetWare Server/Volume:Directory\Subdirectory[\Subdirectory]

access arm A device used on disk drives to position the recording heads over the desired disk track.

Access Control right (A) A NetWare trustee right that allows a user to assign rights to other users.

Access Control List (ACL) A property of an NDS object that stores the trustee list for that object.

access rights When referring to NDS, access rights control which NDS objects and properties a user can work with. Object access rights, also referred to as Object rights, include: Supervisor, Browse, Create, Delete, and Rename. Property access rights, also referred to as Property rights, include: Supervisor, Compare, Read, Write, and Add or Delete Self. When referring to the network file system, access rights control what disk functions a user can perform in a directory or on a file. Directory and file access rights, also referred to as Directory rights and File rights include: Read, File Scan, Write, Create, Erase, Modify, Access Control, and Supervisor.

access time The time required for a storage device to locate and transfer a block of data into RAM.

active hub A central hub device used on ARCnet networks to regenerate signals and send them up to 2,000 feet to another hub or computer.

adapter When referring to Windows 95, an adapter is the term used for a network interface card (NIC).

ADD NAME SPACE utility The NetWare utility that must be run on a volume to add name space support for Macintosh, OS/2 and Windows 95 long file names.

Add or Delete Self right (A) An NDS Property right that enables a user to add himself to or remove himself from the object's Access Control List (ACL).

address When referring to a workstation's memory, a number used to identify the location of data within the computer system. When referring to NetWare's MHS and FirstMail e-mail program, an address on a foreign e-mail system which allows FirstMail to route the message to the user's local mailbox.

address bus The number of bits that are sent from the CPU to the memory indicating the memory byte to be accessed. The size of the address bus determines the amount of memory that can be directly accessed. The 20-bit address bus used on the 8088 computer limited it to 1 MB. The 24-bit address bus used on 80286 and 80386SX computers provides for up to 16 Mbytes. The 32-bit address bus used on 80386DX and above computers can access up to 2 GB of memory.

AFP Server object An NDS informational leaf object that represents a network AppleTalk File Protocol server in the Directory tree.

agent When referring to Windows 95, an agent is the term used for client software that allows the workstation to use network resources provided by server software on an applications server.

Alias object An NDS miscellaneous leaf object that represents an NDS leaf object located in another part of the Directory tree.

American National Standards Institute (ANSI) The United States organization that creates standards for telecommunications, networking, and programming languages. It also represents the U.S. in the International Standardization Organization (ISO).

American Standard Code for Information Interchange (ASCII) An American National Standards Institute (ANSI) standard which has a separate 7 bit code for all characters on the keyboard. This defines 128 characters with binary values between 0 and 127 (since a byte has 8 bits, this leaves an additional 128 characters that may be defined by manufacturers).

analog signals The signals carried by a broadband system such as radio or television.

AppleTalk File Protocol (AFP) server A NetWare 4.1 server running NetWare's AppleTalk File Protocol (AFP) so that Apple workstations can connect to the network.

Apple Address Resolution Protocol (AARP) One component of the AppleTalk protocol, the AARP works at the physical and data link layers.

AppleTalk Apple's network protocol developed to enable Macintosh computers to work in peer-to-peer networks.

application layer The top software layer of the OSI model that interacts with the user in order to perform a communication process on a network.

application server A network server that stores software applications for use by network users.

application-oriented structure A directory structure that groups directories and subdirectories according to application or use rather than by department or owner.

Archive Needed A file attribute set by the computer whenever the contents of a file have changed.

ARCnet A star-bus network topology that uses a special packet called a token that is passed from computer to computer allowing only one computer to transmit at any one time.

assign The act of giving rights to a trustee (*see* grant).

assigned rights The set of rights granted or assigned to a trustee.

asynchronous communication A form of communication where each byte is encapsulated with start and stop bits and then sent separately across the transmission media.

Attribute A flag that is used by NetWare to determine the type of processing which can be performed on files and directories. Directory attributes include: Delete inhibit, Don't Compress, Don't Migrate, Hidden, Immediate Compress, Normal, Purge, Rename inhibit, and System. File attributes include: Archive Needed, Can't Compress, Compressed, Copy inhibit, Delete inhibit, Don't Compress, Execute Only, Hidden, Immediate Compress, Migrated, Normal, Purge, Read Only, Read Write, Rename inhibit, Sharable, System, and Transactional.

authenticating The process of sending a username and password to the NDS Directory or a NetWare server and having them checked and validated.

AUTOEXEC.NCF A NetWare Command File (NCF) that is run when the server is booting up after SERVER.EXE is started.

B

backbone network A network cable system that is used to connect network servers and host computer systems. Each network server or host may then contain a separate network card that attaches it to client computers.

bandwidth A measurement of the range of signals that can be sent across a communications system.

baseband A digital signaling system that consists of only two signals representing one and zero.

baud rate A measurement of the number of signal changes per second.

binary A number system with only two digits—0 and 1 (mathematicians call this Base 2).

binary digit One of the two digits in the binary number system—0 or 1. Commonly called a bit.

bindery The NetWare 3.1x files that contain security information such as usernames, passwords, and account restrictions. The bindery files are stored on NetWare 3.1x servers in the SYS:SYSTEM directory and consist of NET$OBJ.SYS, NET$PROP.SYS, and NET$VAL.SYS.

bindery context The set of Directory tree contexts that have data represented as part of the mimicked NetWare 3.1x bindery in bindery emulation mode.

bindery emulation mode A mode of operation on a NetWare 4.1 server that mimics the NetWare 3.1x bindery for devices that can't work with NDS.

Bindery object An NDS miscellaneous leaf object that represents NetWare 3.1x bindery data in the Directory tree.

Bindery Queue object An NDS miscellaneous leaf object that represents a NetWare 3.1x bindery queue in the Directory tree.

bindery services The NetWare 3.1x bindery services provided by NetWare 4.1's bindery emulation mode.

binding The process of attaching a network protocol stack—such as IPX—to a network card.

bit A shortened form of the term binary digit.

blind carbon copy When referring to NetWare's MHS and FirstMail e-mail system, a carbon copy that does not require that any recipient of the original e-mail be notified that a copy has been sent to the recipient of the blind carbon copy.

block When referring to a database, a collection of data records that can be read or written from the computer RAM to a storage device at one time. When referring to a hard disk, a storage location on the physical disk volume consisting of 4 KB, 8 KB, 16 KB, 32 KB, or 64 KB.

block suballocation A method that allows data from more than one file to be placed in a single data block.

blocks read charge In NetWare accounting, a charge to a user account for reading data from disk drives.

blocks written charge In NetWare accounting, a charge to a user account for writing data to disk drives.

bounded media Media that confines a signal within a cable.

bridge A device used to connect networks of similar topology. Operates at the data link layer.

broadband A signaling system that uses analog signals to carry data across the media.

Browse right (B) An NDS Object right that enables a trustee to see the object in the Directory tree and have the object's name appear in search results.

browsing When referring to NetWare's MHS and FirstMail e-mail system, organizing and working with messages that have already been sent or received.

buffer A storage location in memory used to hold blocks of data from disk in order to reduce the number of disk accesses needed to process a request.

bundled pair Fifty or more pairs of twisted wire put together in one large cable.

bus An electronic pathway that connects computer components.

bus mastering A technique used by certain high-speed adapter cards to transfer data directly into a computer's RAM.

byte A group of eight bits.

C

cable system The physical wire system used to connect computers in a local area network.

cache memory The memory area used to temporarily hold data from lower-speed storage devices in order to provide better access time.

Can't Compress (Cc) A NetWare file attribute used to flag files that can't be compressed.

carbon copy When referring to NetWare's MHS and FirstMail e-mail system, a copy of an e-mail message which is sent to other users on the network. This function is useful when you want other users to be informed of the contents of a message without expecting them to respond.

carrier sense multiple access with collision detection (CSMA/CD) A channel access control method used on Ethernet networks where a computer waits for the media to have an open carrier signal before attempting to transmit. Collisions occur when two or more devices sense an open carrier and attempt to transmit at the same instant.

central processing unit (CPU) The "brain" of the computer that controls operations and does the computations.

centralized processing A processing method where program execution takes place on a central host computer rather than at a user workstation.

Certified Novell Administrator (CNA) A network administrator who has taken and passed the Novell CNA exam.

Certified Novell Engineer (CNE) A network administrator who has taken and passed the Novell CNE exam.

channel access method A method of controlling when a device can transmit data over a local area network. Common access methods include token-ring and CSMA/CD.

child partition When referring to NDS, a partition that is below (farther away from the [Root]) a parent partition, in the Directory tree structure. The child partition is subordinate to the parent partition.

children When referring to NDS, container levels that are subordinate (farther away from the [Root]) to another container. The superior (closer to the [Root]) container level is called the parent.

client When referring to Windows 95, a client is the software that provides network connectivity for the workstation, which is called a Network Interface Card (NIC) driver in NetWare.

client-server *See* client-server network operating system.

client-server applications A type of application where part of the application runs on the network server and part of the application runs on the client workstations.

client-server network operating system A type of network operating system where certain computers are dedicated to performing server functions while other computers called clients run application software for users.

client workstation A networked computer that runs user application software and is able to request data from a file server.

clock A device in the system unit of a computer that sends out a fixed number of pulses or signals per second. The clock pulses are used to synchronize actions in the system unit. The clock speed is measured in millions of cycles per second called megahertz or MHz. The faster the clock speed, the more work a given system unit can do per second.

coaxial cable A thick plastic cable containing a center conductor and shield.

Color Graphics Adapter (CGA) A graphics card used on early PC-based computers that allowed up to four colors to be displayed using a resolution of 320 × 200 pixels.

collision An event that occurs when two or more nodes attempt to transmit on the network at the same time. After the collision, the nodes wait a random time interval before retrying.

common name (CN) The name type associated with an NDS leaf object.

command line utility (CLU) A NetWare utility that performs a specific function from the DOS prompt given specific command line parameters. Examples are NDIR, NCOPY, and MAP.

command queuing A method of storing commands for future processing.

compact disk read-only memory (CD-ROM) A data storage device that uses the compact disk format and can store about 680 MB of data. The data is recorded by the manufacturer and cannot be altered by the user.

Compare right (C) An NDS Property right that enables a trustee to compare a value to the value of the property, but not to see the value itself (the Read (R) right is needed to see the value).

compiler A program that converts source commands to a form that is executable by the computer system.

complementary metal oxide semiconductor (CMOS) memory A type of memory that is capable of holding data with very little power requirements. This type of memory is used to store configuration data that is backed up by a battery on the motherboard. The battery prevents CMOS from being erased when power is turned off.

complete directory path Identifies the location of a file or directory by specifying the path: NetWare Server/Volume:Directory\Subdirectory[\Subdirectory].

complex instruction set computer (CISC) A computer with a microprocessor that uses instructions in a wide range of formats that can require more that one clock cycle to complete.

composite monochrome monitor A monochrome monitor that has the same resolution (320 × 200 pixels) as a CGA monitor.

Compressed (Co) A NetWare file attribute used to flag files that are compressed.

computer aided design (CAD) A software application that uses computers to perform complex drafting and design applications.

computer network Two or more computers connected so that they can communicate with each other.

Computer object An NDS informational leaf object that represents a user's workstation in the Directory tree.

concentrator A central hub device used to connect 10BASET computers together to form a network.

conditional variables Login script variables that have a value of "True" or "False."

connect time charge In NetWare accounting, a charge to a user account for the length of time a user workstation has been logged in to a NetWare server.

console command A command that affects the NetWare server and is issued from the NetWare server console. Examples include CONFIG, LOAD, and DOWN.

consistent The same throughout. When referring to NDS, the all replicas of a partition need to be updated so that they are consistent. Since the updating process takes time, the Directory database is said to be loosely consistent at any moment in time.

Console operator A username that has been assigned the privilege of running the FCONSOLE program. Console operators are assigned using the Supervisor Options of SYSCON.

Container object An NDS object that contains other NDS objects. The NDS container objects are the [Root], Country, Organization, and Organizational Unit objects.

container login script A login script stored in a container object, and which is used by all users within the container unless the user is assigned a profile login script or has a user login script.

contention access method A channel access method where computer nodes are allowed to talk whenever they detect that the channel is not in use. This often results in collisions between packets. In Ethernet, this becomes the carrier sense multiple access with collision detection (CSMA/CD) method.

context The location of an NDS object in the Directory tree

control commands Used to tell the NetWare NMENU program how to perform actions such as running a DOS command or starting an application.

controller card An adapter card used to control storage devices such as disk drives.

conventional memory The first 640K of memory used by DOS to run application programs.

Copy inhibit (Ci) A NetWare file attribute that prevents Macintosh computers from accessing certain PC file types.

Country object An NDS container object that represents a country in the Directory tree.

Create right (C) When referring to NDS Object rights, enables a user to create new objects in a container (applies to container objects only). When referring to the network file system, a NetWare Directory right and File right that allows a user to create new files and subdirectories.

current context The user's current location in the NDS Directory tree

custom device module (CDM) One of the components of the Novell Peripheral Architecture (NPA) introduced in NetWare 4.1. Using NPA, drivers are broken into two parts—the host adapter module (HAM) and the custom device module (CDM).

cycle The time it takes a signal to return to its starting state.

cyclic redundancy check (CRC) An error checking system that allows a receiving computer to determine if a block of data was received correctly by applying a formula to the data and checking the results against the value supplied by the sending computer.

cylinder The number of disk tracks that can be accessed without moving the access arm of the hard drive mechanism.

CX command A NetWare command line utility, the CX (Change Context) command is used to change the user's context in the Directory tree and to display the Directory tree.

D

data bus The "highway" that leads from a device to the CPU. Computers based on 80286 and 80386SX have 16-bit data bus architecture compared to 32 bits on the 80386DX and 80486 computer models and 64 bits on Pentium-based computers.

data communications equipment (DCE) The type of a connector used on a computer that connects to the computer-modem cable.

data compression algorithm The algorithm used by NetWare's file compression system to compress the file size.

data file Used with the NetWare UIMPORT command line utility, the data file contains the specific data for each user account to be created.

data frame packet The packet created at the data link layer based on the datagram received from the network layer.

data link layer The OSI software layer that controls access to the network card.

data migration A NetWare feature that moves files that have not been used for a long time to another type of storage medium such as an optical disk. The filename is retained on the volume, and if the file is needed, it is retrieved.

data terminal equipment (DTE) The type of a connector used on a modem that connects to the computer-modem cable.

Datagram Delivery Protocol (DDP) One component of the AppleTalk protocol, the DDP works at the network layer.

datagram packet The name of an information packet at the network layer.

dataflow analysis One of three processing techniques used by the Pentium Pro CPU's Dynamic Execution feature. Dataflow analysis creates an optimized schedule for the execution of program instructions. The other two Dynamic Execution techniques are multiple branch prediction and speculative execution.

date variables Login script variables that contain date information such as month, name, day of week, and year.

dedicated A network server is a dedicated server if it cannot also be used as a client workstation.

default directory The directory from which data will be accessed when no path is supplied.

default drive The drive from which data will be accessed when no path is supplied.

default login script The default login script is the login script which is used if no other login script exists for a user.

default volume name The name automatically assigned to a volume by NetWare if no other name is specified. The first volume is named SYS, the next is named VOL1, the next is named VOL2 and so on.

Delete right (D) An NDS Object right that enables users to delete the object from the Directory tree.

Delete Inhibit (Di) A NetWare attribute that prevents a file or directory from being removed.

demand priority The channel access method used by 100VG-AnyLAN, which allows only one computer to broadcast at a time based on a priority system.

departmental structure A directory structure that groups directories and subdirectories according to the workgroup or department that uses or controls them.

depth When referring to the NDS Directory tree, the number of levels in the tree (*see* width). A Directory tree should be planned with only as much depth as necessary because each level adds another term to the distinguished name of objects at that level.

device driver A software program that controls physical access to an external device such as a network card or storage drive.

Digital signals Signals that can have only a value of zero or one.

direct memory access (DMA) channel A direct memory access (DMA) channel is a device used to transfer data between RAM and an external device without taking time from the processor.

direct printer A printer that is connected to the network by its own network interface card.

directly attached printer A printer that is connected to the network by its own network interface card.

directory When referring to the network file system, a logical storage unit on a volume. Called a folder in Windows 95

directory caching A method of improving hard disk access time by keeping the directory entry table (DET) and file allocation table (FAT) in memory.

Directory database The NetWare database that stores NDS data.

directory entry table (DET) A table on a storage device that contains the names and locations of all files.

directory hashing A method of improving access time by indexing entries in the directory entry table.

Directory Map object An NDS server-related leaf object that is used in the Directory tree to reference a drive mapping

directory path A list of network file system component, such as the names of directories and subdirectories, identifying the location of data on a storage device.

Directory rights The set of rights to directories in the network file system that can be granted to a trustee. Directory rights also generally apply to files in the directory, although they can be blocked with individual File rights. Directory rights include Supervisor (S), Read (R), Write (W), Create (C), Erase (E), Modify (M), File Scan (F) and Access Control (A).

Directory tree The hierarchical tree structure created to visualize the organization of the NDS Directory database.

Directory tree name The name of the NDS Directory tree.

disk duplexing A method of synchronizing data on storage devices attached to different controller cards.

disk storage charge In NetWare accounting, a charge to a user account for storing data on a disk.

dismounting a volume A method of taking a disk volume off line in order to perform system functions.

distinguished name When referring to an NDS object, an object's distinguished name is it's complete name, which is the object's common name plus the object's context. A distinguished name always shows the path to the object from the [Root] An example of a distinguished name is *.EFranklin.FDR_Admin.FDR.*

distributed database A database that is split into parts, with each part residing on a different server.

distributed processing A processing method where application software is executed on the client workstations.

distribution list When referring to NetWare's MHS and FirstMail e-mail system, a named group of e-mail users that allows a message to be automatically sent to all users included in the specified distribution list without naming each individual user.

Don't Compress (Dc) A NetWare file attribute used to flag files that you do not want compressed.

Don't Migrate (Dm) A NetWare file attribute used to flag files that you do not want migrated.

Don't Suballocate (Ds) A NetWare file attribute used to flag files that you do not want suballocated.

dot pitch A measurement of the spacing between color spots on video monitors. A smaller dot pitch provides sharper images.

DOWN command The console command used to take a NetWare server off line.

drive mapping The assignment of a drive pointer to a storage area on a hard disk.

drive pointer A drive pointer is a letter of the alphabet that is used to reference storage areas in the file system.

driver software When referring to a Network Interface Card (NIC), the software needed to control the NIC and interface between the data link layer and the network layer software.

DSMERGE.NLM A NetWare NLM that allows you to merge to Directory trees.

Dynamic Execution A feature of the Intel Pentium Pro CPU. It consists of three processing techniques: multiple branch prediction, dataflow analysis, and speculative execution.

dynamic RAM (DRAM) A common form of dynamic memory chip, used in computer RAM, that requires a refresh cycle to retain data contents.

E

e-mail address When referring to NetWare's MHS and FirstMail e-mail system, each user of the MHS system must have a unique address composed of the user's name and workgroup. For example, Mary Read's user address could be "MREAD@PCSOLUTION" where MREAD is Mary's username and "PCSOLUTION" is the organization's workgroup name.

effective rights A subset of the access rights that control which disk processing a user can perform on a specific directory or file. Effective rights consist of a combination of rights the user has as a user and as a member of groups, container objects, and so on.

Enhanced Graphics Adapter (EGA) A graphics adapter that provides up to 16 colors and a 640 × 480 pixel resolution.

electronic mail (e-mail) applications Software applications that allow network users to send messages to each other.

electromagnetic interference (EMI) An undesirable electronic noise created on a wire cable when it runs close to a strong power source or magnetic field.

elevator seeking A technique used in NetWare file servers to increase disk access performance by smoothly moving an access arm across a hard disk surface to read and write the requested data blocks in the sequence they are encountered rather than in the sequence received.

end user The person who uses the computer to directly accomplish his or her job tasks.

enhanced IDE A disk drive system that improves on the standard IDE system by supporting up to four disk drives with higher-drive capacities (above the 528 megabyte limitation of IDE), and faster performance.

entry-level PC The PC configuration typically purchased by a company as it's standard configuration.

Erase right (E) When referring to network file system, a NetWare Directory and File right that allows the user to delete files and remove subdirectories when assigned to a directory.

error checking and correcting (ECC) memory A type of RAM that can automatically recognize and correct memory errors.

Ethernet A network system that uses the Carrier Sense Multiple Access with Collision Detection (CSMA/CD) access method to connect networked computers. Originally, the term also meant only the 10BASE2 system, but now refers to the entire Ethernet family, also including 10BASET, 100BASETX, and 100BASEFX.

Execute Only (X) A NetWare file attribute that may be used with executable (.COM and .EXE) program files to prevent the files from being copied while still allowing users to run them.

expanded memory Memory located on a separate expansion card that is accessed by dividing it into pages and then swapping the pages in and out of page frames located within the upper-memory area.

expanded memory system Software that supports the use of expanded memory.

expansion bus The system board bus that allows expansion cards plugged into expansion slots on a computer's system board that connects the adapter cards to the rest of the computer.

expansion card A circuit board that plugs into an expansion slot and extends the computers capabilities, such as a network interface card or modem.

expansion slot An electrical connection on the system board that expansion cards plug into.

extended data out (EDO) ram A faster version of RAM now standard in Pentium, Pentium MMX, and Pentium Pro computers.

extended industry standard architecture (EISA) bus A system board expansion bus that supports both ISA cards along with high-speed 32-bit cards for increased performance.

extended memory Memory above one Megabyte. This memory requires special software to access it.

F

fault tolerance A measurement of how well a system can continue to operate despite the failure of certain hardware components.

fetching The process of loading instructions into the CPU from RAM.

fiber optic cable A cable made of light conducting glass fibers which allows high-speed communications.

Fields section Used with the NetWare UIMPORT command line utility, the fields section of the import control file contains a list of the NDS object fields that correspond to the data contained in the data file.

file allocation table (FAT) A table stored on a disk that is used to link together the storage blocks belonging to each file.

file attribute A flag used by NetWare to determine what type of processing can be performed on the file.

file caching A method used by a NetWare file server to increase performance by storing the most frequently accessed file blocks in RAM.

file compression A method of coding the data in a file to reduce the file size.

File rights The set of rights to files in the network file system that can be granted to a trustee. File rights include Supervisor (S), Read (R), Write (W), Create (C), Erase (E), Modify (M), File Scan (F) and Access Control (A).

File Scan right (F) When referring to the network file system, a NetWare Directory and File right that allows the user to view file and directory names.

file server A network server used to store files (software applications and data) for network users.

file system security A security system that prevents unauthorized users from accessing or modifying file data.

file trustee A user or group that has been granted access rights to a file.

FirstMail An e-mail program included with NetWare 4.1.

folder When referring to NetWare's MHS and FirstMail e-mail system, the directories in which FirstMail stores e-mail messages. When referring to the network file system or a user's workstation, the Windows 95 term for a directory or subdirectory.

foreign e-mail address When referring to NetWare's MHS and FirstMail e-mail system, a foreign e-mail address is used when a user already has another e-mail address on a foreign e-mail system. This allows FirstMail to route the message to the user's local mailbox. A foreign e-mail alias is used when a user does not have an additional e-mail address on the foreign e-mail system, but only has one local e-mail address (this permits the external mail systems to "see" the user's local mailbox).

foreign e-mail alias When referring to NetWare's MHS and FirstMail e-mail system, a foreign e-mail alias is used when a user does not have an additional e-mail address on a foreign mail system, but only has one local e-mail address. This permits the external mail systems to "see" the user's local mailbox.

frame The name of an information packet at the data link layer.

G

general-purpose application An application package such as a word processor or s spreadsheet that is used to perform many different functions.

global shared directory A directory in which all users in an organization may store and retrieve files.

grace login An extra login given to a user after the user's password has expired to allow the user a chance to change his or her password.

grant To give to someone. When referring to NetWare trustee rights, to assign rights to a user, group or other NDS object (*see* assign).

graphical utility A NetWare utility run on a workstation that uses a graphical user interface such as Windows 95 or OS/2. An example is NetWare Administrator.

graphics accelerator A video adapter with a microprocessor preprogrammed to speed up graphics operations.

Group object An NDS user-related leaf object that is used in the Directory tree to manage groups of users.

H

Hidden (H) A NetWare file or directory attribute used to prevent a file or directory from appearing on directory listings.

hierarchical structure An logical organizational structure that starts at one point, called the [Root], and branches out from the starting point. Points in the structure are logically above or below other points on the same branch.

home directory A private directory where a user typically stores personal files and works on projects that are not shared with other users.

host adapter module (HAM) One of the components of the Novell Peripheral Architecture (NPA) introduced in NetWare 4.1. Using NPA, drivers are broken into two parts—the host adapter module (HAM) and the custom device module (CDM).

host server When using SMS, the host file server is the server that contains the backup tape drive and backs up data from other computers called "target" devices.

hot fix A NetWare feature whereby data on bad and unreliable disk storage sectors is copied to a reserved redirection area located in a different area on the hard disk.

hot-swapping A fault tolerant system that allows a disk drive to be replaced without shutting down the computer system.

hub A central connection device in which each cable of a star topology network is connected together.

I

Identifier variables Login script variables that may be used in login script commands to represent such information as the user login name, date, time, and DOS version.

Immediate Compress (Ic) A NetWare file attribute used to flag files that should be compressed immediately instead of waiting for the standard waiting period to elapse.

import control section Used with the NetWare UIMPORT command line utility, the import control section of the import control file contains control parameters that specify UIMPORT options.

import control file Used with the NetWare UIMPORT command line utility, the import control file controls the creation of user accounts by specifying general information that applies to all user accounts being created. It has two sections: the import control section and the fields section

industry standard architecture (ISA) bus A system board bus structure that supports 16-bit data and 24-bit address buses at 8 Mhz clock speed. This bus was developed for the IBM AT computer in 1984, and is still popular. However, when using it with high-speed processors, it greatly reduces the performance of expansion cards.

infrared An unbounded media system that uses infrared light to transmit information. Commonly used on television remote control devices and small wireless LANs.

Informational leaf objects A group of NDS objects, including the Computer object and the AFP Server object, that store data that would otherwise be unrepresented in the NDS Directory tree.

inherited rights Inherited rights are rights that flow down into a container object, directory, or file from a higher level. For example, if a user is granted the R F W rights to the DATA:SALES directory, they will also inherit the R F W rights into the DATA:SALES\ORDERS and DATA:SALES\USERS subdirectories.

inherited rights filter (IRF) Each container object, directory, and file contains an Inherited Rights Filter that controls what access rights can flow down to the container object, directory, or file from a higher-level.

input/output (I/O) port An interface used to transfer data and commands to and from external devices.

Institute of Electrical and Electronic Engineers (IEEE) An organization that has established standards for LAN topologies.

instruction set The set of binary command codes a CPU chip can recognize and execute.

Institute of Electrical and Electronic Engineers (IEEE) A United States professional organization that works on network standards.

integrate drive electronics (IDE) A type of hard disk controller that can control up to two hard drives with capacities up to 528 megabytes.

internal network number A network address used internally by NetWare to communicate with its software components.

International Standards Organization (ISO) The group responsible for administering the OSI model.

internet An information highway that is not controlled by any single organization and is used worldwide to connect business, government, education, and private users.

internetwork One or more network cable systems connected together by bridges or routers.

internetwork packet exchange (IPX) The NetWare protocol that manages packet routing and formatting at the network layer.

interoperability The ability of computers on different networks to communicate.

interrupt request (IRQ) A signal that is sent from an external device to notify the CPU that it needs attention.

K

KB Kilobyte or 1024 bytes.

L

leading period When referring to an NDS object, a period that appears at the beginning of the object's context or the object's common name in it's distinguished name. The leading period indicates the path to the object is beginning at the [Root]. In the context *.Admin_FDR.FDR*, the period before Admin_FDR is the leading period.

leaf object An NDS Directory tree object that cannot contain other objects. Leaf objects are used to store data about network resources, such as NetWare servers, volumes, users, groups, and printers.

linear bus topology A LAN topology that consists of a coaxial cable segment that connects computers by running from one machine to the next with a terminating resistor on each end of the cable segment.

link support layer (LSL) A software component of Novell's ODI specification, it connects the data link layer of the protocol stack and the network interface card (NIC) driver.

local area network (LAN) A high-speed, limited distance communication system designed to support distributed processing.

local bus A term that refers to the internal address, data and instruction buses of the system board, often used to refer to a high-speed expansion bus structure that allows adapter cards to operate close to the speed of the internal system board.

local drive pointer A drive pointer (normally A: through F:) that is used to reference a local device on the workstation such as a floppy or hard disk drive.

local printer When used in context to network printing, a local printer is used to refer to a network printer that is attached directly to a port of the print server computer. When used in context of a workstation, a local printer is the printer attached directly to a port on the workstation.

local shared directory A directory in which all users of a department or workgroup may store and retrieve files.

logical block address (LBA) A feature of the enhanced integrated drive electronics (EIDE) interface that allows EIDE drives to provide up to 8.4 gigabytes of storage.

logical entity When referring to NDS, a network resource that exists as a logical or mental creation, such as an organizational entity that models the structure of an organization (*see* physical entity).

logical link control (LLC) layer A sublayer of the data link layer of the OSI model, in interfaces with the physical layer.

login name The name a user enters at the login prompt or in the NetWare Client 32 Login dialog box when logging into the network. The login name is also the name displayed for the users' User object in the NDS Directory tree

login script A set of NetWare commands that are performed each time a user logs into the file server.

login script variable A reserved word that may be used to substitute values into login script statements in order to modify processing.

login security A security system that employs usernames, passwords, and account restrictions to prevent unauthorized users from accessing the network.

loosely consistent The same throughout, more or less. When referring to NDS, the all replicas of a partition need to be updated so that they are consistent. Since the updating process takes time, the Directory database is said to be loosely consistent at any moment in time.

M

machine language A program consisting of binary codes that the CPU can directly interpret and execute.

mainframe computer A term used to refer to large computers where the processing power is in the computer and users access it via terminals.

master replica When referring to NDS, the main copy of a partition. There is only one master replica for each partition. A master replica that can be read from and written to, and can be used for login purposes.

math coprocessor An extension of the CPU that allows it to directly perform mathematical functions and floating point arithmetic.

media The device or material used to record and retrieve data.

media access control (MAC) layer A sublayer of the data link layer of the OSI model, in interfaces with the network layer.

megahertz (MHz) A million cycles per second.

memory buffers Computer memory used to temporarily store data being transferred to and from external devices.

menu utility An interactive NetWare utility that uses menus and windows to prompt users for input and display messages. Examples include FILER, SALVAGE, and SESSION.

Message Handling Service (MHS) Novell's standard message delivery system which allows MHS-compatible applications to send messages between users. MHS provides the back-end services which are needed to implement such applications as electronic mail, electronic data interchange (EDI), workgroup scheduling, and other collaborative workflow applications. MHS is sometimes called a "message transport engine." Which means that it provides all the necessary services to store and forward messages on a LAN or to transport messages to other LANs which have their own engines.

message packet A packet containing data that is being sent via the network from one user to another.

Messaging-related leaf objects An group of NDS Directory tree objects, including the Messaging Server object, the Distribution List object, the Message Routing Group object, and the External Entity object, that are used to managed the NetWare Message Handling Service (MHS) and the FirstMail e-mail program.

Micro Channel bus A system board design patented by IBM that allows for 32-bit expansion cards along with automatic card configuration.

microcomputer A term used to refer to small-sized computers, including personal computers (PCs) where the processing power is in the computer and users access it directly.

microprocessor The Central Processing Unit of a microcomputer system.

Migrated (M) A NetWare file attribute used to flag files that have been migrated.

millions of instructions per second (MIPS) A measure of speed for computer CPUs.

minicomputer A term used to refer to medium-sized computers where the processing power is in the minicomputer and users access it via terminals.

minimum compression percentage gain The minimum file size reduction that must be possible before NetWare will compress the file. The default is 2%.

mirroring A disk fault tolerance system that synchronizes data on two drives that are attached to a single controller card.

Miscellaneous leaf objects An group of NDS Directory tree objects, including the Alias object, the Bindery object, the Bindery Queue object and the Unknown object, that are not classified as other types of leaf objects.

mission-critical application An application that is necessary to perform the day-to-day operations of a business or an organization.

Modify right (M) When referring to the network file system, a NetWare Directory and File right that allows a user to change file and directory attributes as well as rename files and subdirectories.

MONITOR utility A NetWare console utility that displays essential information about NetWare server performance.

monochrome monitor A monitor that displays only one color, typically green, amber, or white against a black background.

motherboard Another name for the system board, the main circuit board in a computer that ties together the CPU, memory, and expansion slots.

mounting a volume The process of loading the File Allocation Table and Directory Entry Table of a volume into memory. A volume must be mounted before it can be accessed on a network.

multiple branch prediction One of three processing techniques used by the Pentium Pro CPU's Dynamic Execution feature. Multiple branch prediction looks several steps ahead in a program to predict which steps will be processed next. The other two Dynamic Execution techniques are dataflow analysis and speculative execution.

multiple NetWare server network A network with more than one NetWare server attached.

multiple link interface driver (MLID) The term used by Novell's ODI specification for a network interface card (NIC) driver.

multiple station access unit (MSAU) A central hub device used to connect IBM token ring network systems.

multiplexing Placing multiple message packets into one segment.

multiple-user application An application which is either NetWare aware (and designed to support multiple users) or is designed with enough flexibility so that the application can be set up to keep each user's work files separated.

multiuser application A special type of multiple-user application that allows more than one user to access the same file simultaneously.

N

name context When referring to NetWare Client 32, the context of the user's User object.

name space A NetWare module that provides support for Macintosh, OS/2, or Windows 95 long file names.

name type A NetWare NDS descriptor of object types. There are four name types: Country name type (abbreviated as C), Organization name type (abbreviated as O), Organizational Unit name type (abbreviated as OU), and common name type (which refers to all leaf objects and is abbreviated as CN). There is no name type for the [Root] object.

NCP Server object Another name for the NetWare Server object, which is an NDS Server-related leaf object used in the Directory tree to manage NetWare servers. NCP is an abbreviation for NetWare Core Protocol.

NDS Directory tree A visual structure used to organize NDS objects.

NDS security A security system that prevents unauthorized users from accessing or modifying the NDS database and the NDS Directory tree.

nesting A programming technique involving placing one IF statement inside another so that the second IF statement is executed only when the first IF statement is true.

NET.CFG The network shell configuration file used with the NETX shell and the NetWare DOS Requester shell.

NETADMIN utility A NetWare menu utility used to manage NDS objects.

NetBEUI Microsoft's network protocol stack, integrated into Windows for Workgroups, Windows 95, and Windows NT. It consists of NETBIOS and service message blocks (SMBs) at the session layer and NetBIOS frames (NBF) at the transport layer. NBF can be replaced with NETBIOS over TCP/IP (NBT) for direct communication over TCP/IP-based networks

NETBIOS The Network Basic Input/Output System (NETBIOS) was developed by IBM and is now used in Microsoft's NetBEUI protocol.

NETBIOS frames (NBF) One component of Microsoft's NetBEUI protocol.

NETBIOS over TCP/IP (NBT) An alternate component of Microsoft's NetBEUI protocol that enables its use with TCP/IP networks.

NetWare Administrator utility A NetWare graphical utility used to manage NDS objects.

NetWare Application Launcher (NAL) A NetWare feature that assists network administrators configure and manage applications from within the NDS Directory tree. The NAL software resides on the user's workstation, while NetWare Application Manager (NAM) software resides on the NetWare server.

NetWare Application Manager (NAM) A NetWare feature that assists network administrators configure and manage applications from within the NDS Directory tree. The NAM software resides on the NetWare server, while NetWare Application Launcher (NAL) software resides on the user's workstation.

NetWare Application Manager-related objects An group of NDS Directory tree objects, including the DOS Application object, the Windows 3.x Application object, the Windows 95 Application object and the Windows NT Application object, that are used to manage applications as part of the NetWare Applications Manager and NetWare Applications Launcher software.

NetWare aware Software designed to take advantage of the features found in NetWare, such as printing or separate work and configuration files for each user. The NETX redirector and the NetWare DOS Requester shells used 16-bit code.

NetWare Client 32 Novell's current network shell, the NetWare Client 32 software is written as a requester and uses 32-bit code to speed up its performance.

NetWare compatible Software that can be installed in the NetWare file system and will run properly from any workstation.

NetWare Command File (NCF) A NetWare Command File is similar to a DOS batch file in that it contains console commands and program startup commands that will be executed by the operating system. Examples are STARTUP.NCF and AUTOEXEC.NCF

NetWare Core Protocol (NCP) The NetWare protocol that provides session and presentation layer services.

NetWare DOS Requester A requester type of network shell for workstations. It was introduced after NETX, and before NetWare Client 32. The NetWare DOS requester is based on Virtual Loadable Modules (VLMs).

NetWare file server A term used to refer to network servers in a NetWare LAN for NetWare versions 3.1x and earlier. For NetWare 4.x, the term NetWare server is used.

NetWare Loadable Module (NLM) A program that may be loaded and run on the NetWare server. There are four types of NetWare Loadable Modules identified by their three letter extension. The filename extension NLM is used for general purpose programs, DSK for disk drivers, LAN for network card drivers, and NAM for name space support modules.

NetWare Provider for Windows 95 A component of the NetWare Client 32 network shell that extends the capabilities of Windows 95 programs (such as Explorer) to provide access to NetWare features.

NetWare server A term used to refer to network servers in a NetWare LAN for NetWare version 4.x.

NetWare server name The name that a NetWare server broadcasts over the network. When referring to NDS, the name of the NetWare Server object.

NetWare Server object An NDS Server-related leaf object used in the Directory tree to manage NetWare servers.

network address An address used by the network layer to identify computers on the network.

network administrator The network user in charge of the network and all its resources, and responsible for the maintenance, allocation, and protection of the network.

network-centric A network where a user logs in only once to the network itself, and not to each network server, as is done in a server-centric network.

network drive pointer A network drive pointer is a letter that is assigned to a location on a NetWare server and controlled by NetWare, normally G: through Z:.

Network Driver Interface Specifications (NDIS) A set of standard specifications developed by Microsoft to allow network card suppliers to interface their network cards with the Microsoft Windows operating system.

network file system The logical organizational structure of file storage on network volumes

network interface card (NIC) An adapter card that attaches a computer system to the physical network cable system.

network interface card (NIC) driver The software that controls a network interface card (NIC) and access to the network.

network layer An OSI software layer that is responsible for routing packets between different networks.

network layout The physical topology of the network cable system.

network media The method used to carry electronic signals from one computer to another.

network operating system (NOS) The software used to provide services to client workstations.

network shell The workstation software component that carries out session and presentation layer functions on the workstation.

network standards Agreements about how to operate the network.

network topology The physical geometry or layout of the network cable system. Common topologies include ring, bus, and star.

network variables Login script variables that contain the workstation's network and node address information.

NETX An early redirector type of network shell for workstations.

non-dedicated A computer that can be used for multiple purposes. A non-dedicated file server can also be used as a client workstation.

Normal (N) A NetWare file attribute used to identify files that have no attributes set.

Novell Directory Services (NDS) The main administrative tool for NetWare 4.x, NDS is a database to store information about network resources combined with tools to use the data. The database is referred to as the Directory database or just the Directory. NDS was formerly called NetWare Directory Services, but the name was changed to reflect a use of NDS on systems besides NetWare.

Novel Peripheral Architecture (NPA) A new driver architecture introduced in NetWare 4.1. Using NPA, drivers are broken into two parts—the host adapter module (HAM) and the custom device module (CDM).

NuBus An expansion slot used on Macintosh computers to allow adapter cards to be plugged into the system board.

null modem cable A special type of RS232 cable used to connect two DTE computers without the use of a modem.

nybble Half of a byte or four bits.

O

object When referring to NDS, a representation of a network resource in the Directory database which appears as an icon in the Directory tree. NDS objects can be associated with physical entities and logical entities.

object dependencies When referring to the DS Standard NDS Manager, a reference between objects. For example, Group objects have member lists that refer to User objects.

object dialog box A dialog box that displays data about an NDS object, and allows you to manage that data.

Object rights The set of rights to NDS objects that can be granted to a trustee. Object rights include Supervisor (S), Browse (B), Create (C), Delete (D) and Rename (R).

open data interface (ODI) A set of standard specifications developed by Novell to allow network card suppliers to interface their network cards with multiple protocols including the IPX protocol used with the NetWare operating system.

open systems interconnect (OSI) model A model for developing network systems consisting of the following seven layers: Application, Presentation, Session, Transport, Network, Data link, and Physical.

optical disk A type of high capacity storage medium used for long term storage in data migration systems.

Organization object An NDS container object used to organize the structure of the Directory tree, the Organization object can contain Organizational Unit objects and leaf objects.

organizational entity When referring to NDS, a logical entity that models the structure of an organization.

organizational commands Used in the NetWare NMENU system to establish the content and organization of the menus the user sees on the screen.

Organizational Unit object An NDS container object used to organize the structure of the Directory tree, the Organizational Unit object can contain other Organizational Unit objects and leaf objects.

Organizational Role object An NDS User-related leaf object used in the Directory tree to manage users' privileges by associating them with specific positions, such as President, Vice President, and so on, in an organizational structure. The privileges are assigned to the Organizational Role object, and the users assigned to that role inherit those privileges.

P

packet A group of consecutive bits sent from one computer to another over a network.

packet burst mode A packet transmission technique used by NetWare workstation clients to provide faster communication by acknowledging a group of packets from the server rather than acknowledging each packet separately.

packet signature A security technique used by NetWare workstation clients that places a unique packet signature on each packet, making it possible for NetWare to be sure the packet came from an authorized workstation.

page One screen in an object dialog box that displays data about an NDS object.

parallel port A communications interface that transfers eight or more bits of information at one time.

parent When referring to NDS, a designated container level that has other container levels which are subordinate to it (farther away from the [Root]). The subordinate container levels are called the children. When referring to the network file system, a data set such as a directory or subdirectory.

parent partition When referring to NDS, a partition that is above (closest to the [Root]) another partition called a child partition, in the Directory tree structure.

parity bit A ninth bit added to a byte for error checking purposes.

partial directory path Identifies the location of a file or directory by specifying all directories and sub-directories starting from the user's current default directory location. Also called a relative directory path.

partition When referring to NDS, a logical division of the Directory database based on the Directory tree structure.

partitioning When referring to hard drives in NetWare server or user workstation, a method of allocating storage space on a disk drive to an operating system.

PARTMGR A NetWare graphical utility that allows you to manage NDS partitions.

passive hub A signal splitting device that is used to connect up to four (4) nodes together. The nodes may be workstations or active hubs. The maximum distance between a passive hub and a node is 100 feet.

patch A supplementary NetWare NOS program written to correct a problem discovered in NetWare.

patch cable A cable segment used to connect a network card to the main cable system.

patch panel A panel that consists of a connector for each cable segment that is used to connect the desired cable segments together using a central hub.

PC workstation A personal computer (PC) used by an end user

PCI bus A high-speed expansion bus developed by Intel for use in Pentium-based computer systems.

peer-to-peer A network system in which each computer can act as both a server and client.

peripheral component interconnect (PCI) bus The current expansion bus design by Intel that is used in older 80486, Pentium, Pentium MMX, and Pentium Pro computers. It is a local bus design that moves data at 60 to 66 MHz.

Peripherals External devices such as printers, monitors, and disk drives.

personal computer (PC) A term used to refer to small-sized computers, also called microcomputers, where the processing power is in the computer and users access it directly.

physical address An unique hexadecimal network interface card (NIC) address coded into the NICs electronics. This first part of the address identifies the manufacturer, while the second part is a unique number for that manufacturer.

physical entity When referring to NDS, a network resource that has a physical existence, such as a NetWare server (*see* logical entity).

physical layer The lowest layer of the OSI model consisting of the cable system and connectors.

pixel A picture element, the smallest point on a monitor screen that can be addressed individually for color changes, etc.

presentation layer The OSI layer that is responsible for the translation and encoding of data to be transferred over a network system.

PowerPC processor A microprocessor build by Motorola, IBM, and Apple for use in Apple and other vendors PCs as an alternative to Intel microprocessors.

primary time server (PTS) When designated a primary time server (PTS), a NetWare server synchronizes the official network time by working with all other primary time servers and any reference time server (RTS) on the network.

print data The material to be printed.

print job Print jobs are items in a print queue just as files are items in a directory. Print jobs contain data and printing parameters in a format that can be sent by a print server to a printer.

print queue A holding area where print jobs are kept until the printer is available to print them. In NetWare a print queue is a subdirectory on an assigned volume.

Print Queue object An NDS Printer-related leaf object used in the Directory tree to manage print queues.

print queue operator A user account that has been assigned the privilege of managing print jobs in one or more print queues.

print server The software component of the network printing environment that makes printing happen by taking jobs from a print queue and sending them to a printer. In NetWare a print server can support up to 16 printers.

Print Server object An NDS Printer-related leaf object used in the Directory tree to manage print servers.

print server operator A user account that has been assigned the privilege of managing one or more network printers.

printer function A specific escape code sequence that causes the printer to perform one specific operation such as setting landscape mode.

printer mode A printer mode is a configuration setting for a printer that consists of one or more functions.

Printer object An NDS Printer-related leaf object used in the Directory tree to manage printers.

Printer-related leaf objects An group of NDS Directory tree objects, including the Printer object, the Print Queue object and the Print Server object, that are used to managed the NetWare print services.

profile login script A login script stored in a Profile object, and used by all users assigned that script.

Profile object An NDS User-related leaf object used in the Directory tree to manage users' login scripts. The login script is stored in the Profile object, and the users assigned to that Profile use the login script.

property When referring to NDS, an aspect of an NDS object, such as the user's last name for the User object. An actual user's last name, for example Burns, is the property value.

Property rights The set of rights to the properties of an NDS object that can be granted to a trustee. Object rights include Supervisor (S), Compare (C), Read (R), Write (W) and Add or Delete Self (A).

property value When referring to NDS, an actual value of an NDS object property. For example, the user's last name is a property of the User object, and an actual user's last name, for example Burns, is the property value.

protected mode The mode used by 80286 and above processor chips that allows access to up to 16 Mbytes of memory and the ability to run multiple programs in memory without one program conflicting with another.

protocol stack The software used to send and receive packets among networked computers.

Purge Immediate (P) A NetWare file or directory attribute that specifies the storage space of a file that is to be immediately made available for reuse by the server.

R

RAM shadowing A method of increasing computer system performance by copying instructions from slower ROM to high speed RAM.

random-access memory (RAM) The main work memory of the computer that is used to store program instructions and data currently being processed. The contents of RAM are erased when a computer's power is interrupted or switched off.

Read right (R) When referring to NDS, the Property right that enables a trustee to see the property values of an object. When referring to the network file system, a Directory and File right that allows a user to open and read data from a file or run programs.

Read Only (Ro) A NetWare file attribute that prevents data in a file from being erased or changed.

read-only memory (ROM) Memory that is set at a computer's factory and cannot be erased. ROM is used to store startup and hardware control instructions for your computer.

read-only replica When referring to NDS, a copy of the master replica that can only be read from, not written to, and cannot be used for login purposes.

Read Write (Rw) A NetWare file attribute that allows data in a file to be modified or appended to.

read/write replica When referring to NDS, a copy of the master replica that can only be read from and written to, and can be used for login purposes.

Real mode The processing mode used by 8088 computers.

record locking A NetWare feature that allows a multiuser application program to prevent network users from accessing a specific database record in a file while it is being updated.

recording tracks the concentric circular areas on a disk where data is stored.

redirector A type of network shell that checks workstation operations to see if the operation requires workstation or network resources. *See* requester.

reduced instruction set computer (RISC) A computer with a microprocessor that uses instructions in a uniform format that require only one clock cycle to complete. A RISC workstation provides high performance for CAD workstations and scientific applications by using a simplified and highly efficient set of instructions that lends itself to parallel processing.

redundant array of inexpensive disks (RAID) A method of writing data across several disks that provides fault tolerance.

reference time server (RTS) A NetWare server that is connected to an "official" time source, such as an atomic clock. Reference time servers synchronize with every primary time server (PTS), but don't change their time which forces the PTSs to change theirs.

register A storage location inside the microprocessor unit.

requester A type of **network shell** that is called by the workstation's operating systems when network resources are needed. *See* redirector.

regular drive pointer A network drive pointer that is normally assigned to a file storage directory on the NetWare server.

relative directory path Identifies the location of a file or directory by specifying all directories and sub-directories starting from the user's current default directory location. Also called a partial directory path.

relative distinguished name When referring to an NDS object, an object's distinguished name is it's complete name, which is the object's common name plus the object's context. A distinguished name always shows the path to the object from the [Root]. An example of a distinguished name is *.EFranklin.FDR_Admin.FDR.* An object's relative distinguished name specifies the path to the object from an object other than the [Root]. An example of a relative distinguished name is *EFranklin.FDR_Admin.* Note that there is no leading period, since the path is not from the [Root].

Remote Management Facility (RMF) Enables access to NetWare server consoles from either a workstation attached to the LAN or through an asynchronous communication link.

remote printer A printer attached to a port of a networked workstation and controlled by the print server. In NetWare, remote printing is done by running the RPRINTER software on each workstation that supports a network printer.

Rename right (R) When referring to NDS, the Object right that enables a user to change the object's name.

Rename Inhibit (Ri) A NetWare file or directory attribute that prevents changing the name of the file or directory.

repeater A network device that allows multiple network cable segments to be connected.

replica When referring to NDS, a copy of a partition. There are four types of replicas: master, read/write, read-only and subordinate reference.

replica synchronization When referring to NDS, the process of updating all replicas of a partition so that they are consistent.

resolution A measurement of the number of bits on a display screen. Higher resolution provides better screen images.

rights When referring to NDS or the network file system, the type of access that has been granted or assigned to a user, who is called a trustee. In NDS there are Object rights and Property rights, while the network file system has Directory rights and File rights.

ring topology A topology where the cable runs to each computer and then back to the first, forming a circle.

root drive pointer A regular drive pointer that appears to DOS and application software as if it were the beginning or "root" of a drive or volume.

rotational delay The time required for a disk sector to make a complete circle and arrive at the disk drive's read/write head.

router A device used to connect more complex networks consisting of different topologies. Router's operate at the Network layer.

RS232 A serial communication standard developed by the Electronics Industry Association that specifies which voltage levels and functions are to be used with the 24-pin interface.

S

scaleability The capability to work with systems of different sizes.

scheduling applications Software applications used to create and maintain personal and workgroup time schedules.

SCSI-2 An advanced version of the SCSI controller specification that allows for higher speed and more device types.

secondary time server (STS) A NetWare server that gets network time from other time servers, and then sends the time to workstations.

search drive pointer A network drive pointer that has been added to the DOS path. Search drives are usually assigned to directories containing software to make the software available to run from any other location..

sector A physical recording area on a disk recording track. Each recording track is divided into multiple recording sectors in order to provide direct access to data blocks.

security equivalence An NDS object assignment that grants one object the same set of rights as another object.

seek time A measurement of the amount of time required to move the recording head to the specified disk track or cylinder.

Segment When referring to packets on a network, the name of an information packet at the Transport layer. When referring to the physical network structure, a single cable run.

sequenced packet exchange (SPX) The NetWare protocol that operates at the transport layer.

serial port A communication port that sends one bit of data per time interval.

server A network computer used for a special purpose such as storing files, controlling printing, or running network application software.

server-centric A network where a user logs into each network server in the network that he or she needs access to, rather than logging in only once to the network itself in a network-centric network.

server duplexing A fault tolerance technique that uses two identical servers so that if one goes down the other is still available.

Server-related leaf objects A group of NDS Directory tree objects, including the NetWare Server object, the Volume object and the Directory Map object, that are used to managed NetWare servers, the network file system and drive mappings.

SERVER.EXE The core of the NetWare network operating system. When SERVER.EXE is started, the NetWare NOS replaces DOS as the NetWare server's operating system.

service advertising packet (SAP) SAPs are broadcast from each NetWare server on the network and identify the server's name and network location. SAPs are used to create and maintain entries in the router tables.

service message block (SMB) One component of Microsoft's NetBEUI protocol.

service request charge In NetWare accounting, a charge to a user account for using NetWare server services.

session layer The OSI software layer that establishes and maintains a communication session with the host computer.

SET commands NetWare console commands used to control NetWare performance parameters

Sharable (S) A NetWare file attribute that allows multiple users to access or update data in a file at the same time.

shielded twisted-pair (STP) cable A type of twisted-pair cable that has electromagnetic shielding, and is thus less susceptible to external electrical interference.

single in-line memory module (SIMM) A memory circuit that consists of multiple chips and provides the system board with memory expansion capabilities.

single reference time server (SRTS) A NetWare server that provides the only time source on the network. The time on a SRTS is set by the network administrator.

single-user application A software package which is designed to operate from the user's workstation, and is limited to being used by only one user at a time.

small computer system interface (SCSI) A general purpose controller card bus that can be used to attach disk drives, CD-ROMs, tape drives, and other external devices to a computer system.

speculative execution One of three processing techniques used by the Pentium Pro CPU's Dynamic Execution feature. The other two Dynamic Execution techniques are multiple branch prediction and dataflow analysis. Speculative execution performs the steps scheduled by dataflow analysis.

source menu file A NetWare NMENU component that contains the menu commands in ASCII text format. A source menu file must be compiled before it can be used by the NMENU software.

source tree When two Directory trees are being merged, the source tree is the tree that is merged into the combined Directory tree, and thus loses its original name.

spanning A technique available with NetWare that allows a volume to be expanded by adding space from up to 32 disk drives.

Static RAM (SRAM) Static RAM provides high-speed memory that can operate at CPU speeds without the use of wait states. SRAM chips are often used on high-speed computers in order to increase system performance by storing the most frequently used memory bytes.

star topology A cable system where the cables radiate out from central hubs.

STARTUP.NCF A NetWare Command File (NCF) that is run when the server is booting up but before SERVER.EXE is started. It is limited to commands that can be run with the resources on the DOS partition of the NetWare server.

Storage Management System (SMS) The SMS consists of several NLMs along with workstation software that enables the host computer to backup data from one or more target devices by using the SBACKUP NLM.

subdirectory When referring to the network file system, a division of a directory.

subnetwork A separate logical network based on a specific frame type. For example, if the network is using both the 802.3 and 802.3 frame types, there are two subnetworks.

subordinate Below or under. When referring to NDS, a child partition is a partition that is below (farther away from the [Root]) another partition, called a parent partition, in the Directory tree structure. The child partition is subordinate to the parent partition.

subordinate reference replica When referring to NDS, a copy of the master replica that is automatically generated by NetWare 4.1 to make sure that a child partition has a replica on a NetWare server that has a replica of the child's parent partition. The subordinate reference replica is non-modifiable. Subordinate reference replicas are used to ensure that there are sufficient replicas of all partitions.

subtree An NDS container object that contains leaf objects.

supervisor utility A command line or menu utility that is normally stored in the SYS:SYSTEM directory and requires supervisor privileges to run.

Supervisor right (S) A NetWare access right that provides a user with all rights to an NDS object and its properties and the entire directory structure. Once assigned, the supervisory right cannot be restricted on the network file systems (Directory and File rights), but it can be restricted for NDS rights (Object and Property rights).

Super VGA (SVGA) Video systems that provide higher resolutions (800 × 600 pixels and greater) and additional color combinations (up to 16.7 million colors) than the VGA systems.

switching power supply A power supply used with most computers that will cut off power in the event of an electrical problem.

synchronous communication A serial communication system that sends data in blocks or packets where each packet includes necessary control and error checking bits.

syntax The rules of a programming language and of NetWare login scripts.

System (S) A NetWare file attribute used to flag system files.

system board The main circuit board of a computer system that contains the CPU, memory, and expansion bus (also called the motherboard).

system console The monitor and keyboard on a network server.

system console security A security system that prevents unauthorized users from accessing the system console.

T

target A workstation or NetWare server that has data which is being backed up by a host server.

Target Service Agent (TSA) NetWare software that helps handle data transfers between a target and host server during backups.

target tree When two Directory trees are being merged, the target tree is the tree that maintains its identity in the combined Directory tree, and thus keeps its original name.

terminals User workstations that connect to a mainframe computer or minicomputer, without a CPU of their own so that the mainframe computer or minicomputer must do all processing.

ThinNet A Ethernet network system that uses T-connectors to attach networked computers to the RG-58 coaxial cable system.

tick A time measurement representing 1–18 of a second.

time variables Login script variables that contain system time information such as hour, minute, and a.m./p.m.

token A special packet that is sent from one computer to the next in order to control which computer can transmit when using a token passing channel access method.

token passing method A channel access method that requires a computer to obtain the token packet before transmitting data on the network cable system.

topology The geometry of a network cable system.

tracks Circular recording areas on a disk surface.

trailing period When referring to an NDS object, a period that appears after an object's common name or other object name in the object's distinguished name or context. The trailing period indicates a shift up one level in the Directory tree. In the context *.Admin_FDR.FDR*, the period after Admin_FDR is a trailing period.

Glossary/3208 Page 849 3/25/97

Transmission Control Protocol/Internet Protocol (TCP/IP) TCP/IP is the most common communication protocol used to connect heterogeneous computers over both local and wide area networks. In addition to being used on the Internet, the Unix operating system uses TCP/IP to communicate between host computers and file servers.

Transaction Tracking System (TTS) A NetWare fault tolerance system that returns database records to their original value if a client computer system fails while processing a transaction.

Transactional (T) A NetWare file attribute that enables Transaction Tracking on a database file.

transfer time The time required to transfer a block of data to or from a disk sector.

transport layer The OSI layer responsible for reliable delivery of a packet to the receiving computer by requiring some sort of acknowledgment.

tree metric When referring to the DS Standard NDS Manager, a parameter used to control tree variables such as maximum common name length and maximum number of levels in the Directory tree.

trustee A user given access to NDS object and network file system directories and file. Access is given when rights are assigned or granted to the user or another NDS object that the user is associated with.

trustee assignments The set of NDS or file system rights granted to user.

trustee list The set of trustee assignments for an NDS object or network file system directory or file.

trustee rights The set of NDS or file system privileges that can be assigned to users.

Transistor-to-Transistor Logic (TTL) monitor A monochrome video monitor using the 5-volt TTL system for high-speed transfer of ones and zeros between devices on the computer's system board.

twisted-pair wire Cable consisting of pairs of wires twisted together to reduce errors.

typeful name When referring to an NDS object, when an object's distinguished name is written with name type abbreviations, it's referred to as a typeful name An example of a typeful name is .CN=*EFranklin.OU*=*FDR_Admin.O*=*FDR*.

typeless name When referring to an NDS object, when an object's distinguished name is written without name type abbreviations, it's referred to as a typeless name An example of a typeless name is *.EFranklin.FDR_Admin.FDR*.

U

unbounded media Signals that are sent through the air or space.

uninterruptible power system (UPS) A battery backup power system that can continue to supply power to a computer for a limited time in the event of a commercial power failure.

Unknown object An NDS Miscellaneous object used in the Directory tree to identify corrupted objects that cannot be recognized by NDS.

Universal Naming Convention (UNC) A systematic specification of a location in the file system in the form \\ServerName\Volume\Directory\Subdirectory[\Subdirectory].

unshielded twisted-pair (UTP) cable A type of twisted-pair cable that has no electromagnetic shielding, and is thus susceptible to external electrical interference.

upper memory The memory above 640K used by controller cards as well as by DOS when loading device drivers into high memory.

USER_TEMPLATE User object An NDS object that allows you to specify property values that will be used whenever an User object is created.

user account manager A user account name that has been assigned one or more user account or group to manage.

user login script A login script stored in a User object, and are executed for only a single user.

User object An NDS User-related leaf object used in the Directory tree to manage network users.

User-related leaf objects A group of NDS Directory tree objects, including the User object, the Group object, the Organizational Role object, and the Profile object, that are used to manage network users.

user variables Login script variables that contain information about the currently logged in user, such as the user's login name, full name, or the hexadecimal ID given to the user.

users The people who use PC workstations to do their jobs.

V

VESA bus A fast local bus expansion bus designed by the Video Electronics Standards Association.

vertical application A software application that is designed for a specific type of processing. Vertical applications are often unique to a certain type of business such as a dental billing system or an auto parts inventory system.

video graphics array (VGA) The video graphics array is a standard video circuit used in many conventional PCs that provides up to 640 x 320 resolution and up to 256 different colors.

virtual file allocation table (VFAT) A 32-bit extension to the standard FAT introduced in Windows 95 and MS-DOS 7.0.

virtual loadable module (VLM) A NetWare software component used in the NetWare DOS Requester network shell. VLMs can be loaded as necessary to provide exactly the needed network capabilities for each workstation.

virtual memory Allows the computer system to use its disk drive as if it were RAM by swapping between disk and memory.

virtual real mode An instruction mode available in 80386 and above microprocessors that allows access to 2 GB of memory and concurrent DOS programs running at the same time.

volume The major division of the NetWare file system consisting of the physical storage space on one or more hard drives or CD-ROMs of a file server. A volume can span up to 32 disk segments with a maximum capacity of 32 terabytes. Up to 64 volumes can exist on a file server.

Volume object An NDS Server-related leaf object used in the Directory tree to manage volumes on NetWare servers.

W

wait state A clock cycle in which the CPU does no processing. This allows the slower DRAM memory chips to respond to requests from the CPU.

wide area network (WAN) Two or more local area networks in geographically separated locations connected by telephone line connections.

width When referring to the NDS Directory tree, the number of branches at any level of the tree—particularly the first (*see* depth).

word size The number of bits in the microprocessor's registers.

workgroup manager A user account that has the privilege to create new users and groups and to be an account manager to the users created.

workstation Generally used as a term for PC workstation; also refers to RISC workstations that run the UNIX operating system and are sold for graphics-intensive uses such as CAD.

workstation variables Login script variables that contain information about the workstation's environment such as machine type, operating system, operating system version, and station node address.

Write right (W) When referring to NDS, a Property right that enables a trustee to change, add or delete the value of the property. When referring to the network file system, the NetWare Directory, or File right that allows a user to change or add data to a file.

INDEX

E

F

M

O

P

T

U

V

W

X